√ Ch. 1   3, 11, 21, 24, 26, 28, 30
√ Ch. 2   2, 7, 8, 10, 13, 20, 23, 24, 25 Ice
          27, 29, 32, 33.   Thurs

√ Ch. 3   21, 22, 23, 26, 27, 28, 31 Read 52. → TYPO
√ Ch. 4   19, 22, 25, 28, 31
√ Ch. 5   5, 21, 22, 25, 29, 30
√ Ch. 6   New Book. 15, 16, 20, 21, 23, 25, 31, 35.
√ Ch. 7   New 10, 28, 29, 30, 31
          Old — 26 — 28 —
√ Ch. 8   10, 27, 29, 32, 33

    Test. Feb. 11. 97. In class 80% of 20 pure marks. = 16 + 20 = 36 ↓16.8
                                                                    = 52.8
                                                                    = 53
√ Ch. 9
√ Ch. 10 6, 9, 20, 24, 29, 33
√ Ch. 11 11, 5, 19, 27, 28, 29, 31
√ Ch. 12 12, 20, 30, 31, 32, 34
√ Ch. 13 10, 13, 22, 24, 25, 27, 30
√ Ch. 14 2, 8, 27, 31, 34.

! √ Ch. 15 4, 5, 14, 33, 34, 38. 548 #33. ③ Identify one, not two.

√ Ch. 22 4, 7, 9, 23, 25, 33, 34
  Ch. 23 2, 3, 12, 26, 28   7, 14, 24, 25, 32
      631 P.85   study study. study.

      Test Final. April 25. 97.   % of 40 pure marks =

      Project. Due April 3 97   84% of 20 pure marks = 16.8

Auditing
An Integrated Approach

Auditing
An Integrated Approach

W. Morley Lemon
University of Waterloo

Alvin A. Arens
Michigan State University

James K. Loebbecke
University of Utah

Canadian Fifth Edition

Prentice Hall Canada Series in Accounting

Prentice Hall Canada Inc., Scarborough, Ontario

Canadian Cataloguing in Publication Data

Lemon, W. Morley, 1939–
    Auditing: an integrated approach

Canadian 5th ed.
ISBN 0–13–052036–5

1. Auditing. I. Arens, Alvin A. II. Loebbecke, James K. III. Title.

HF5667.L45 1993   657'.45   C92–094404–3

Prentice-Hall, Inc., Englewood Cliffs, New Jersey
Prentice-Hall International, Inc., London
Prentice-Hall of Australia, Pty., Ltd., Sydney
Prentice-Hall of India Pvt., Ltd., New Delhi
Prentice-Hall of Japan, Inc., Tokyo
Prentice-Hall of Southeast Asia (Pte.) Ltd., Singapore
Editora Prentice-Hall do Brasil Ltda., Rio de Janeiro
Prentice-Hall Hispanoamericana, S.A., Mexico

ISBN 0–13–052036–5

Acquisitions Editor: Yolanda de Rooy
Developmental Editor: David Jolliffe
Copy Editor: Deborah Burrett
Production Editor: Dick Hemingway
Production Coordinator: Florence Rousseau
Cover Design: Pronk & Associates
Typesetting: Colborne, Cox & Burns Inc.
Technical Illustration: Phillip Allen

Original English language edition published by Prentice-Hall, Inc.,
Englewood Cliffs, New Jersey
Copyright © 1991, 1988, 1984, 1980, 1976.

    3 4 5   97 96 95 94 93

Printed and bound in U.S.A.

TABLE OF CONTENTS

PART 2   THE AUDITING PROCESS

20 Audit of the Capital Acquisition and Repayment Cycle 679

21 Audit of Cash Balances 699

PART 6 COMPLETING THE AUDIT AND OFFERING OTHER SERVICES

22 Completing the Audit 728

23 Other Engagements, Services and Reports 763

24   Operational and Comprehensive Auditing   804

PREFACE

Objectives

The Canadian Fifth Edition of *Auditing: An Integrated Approach* contains numerous changes and revisions, but the objectives and emphasis remain essentially the same.

The book is an introduction to auditing for students who have not had significant experience in auditing. It is intended for a one-semester course at the undergraduate or graduate level. The book is also appropriate for introductory professional development courses for public accounting firms, internal auditors, and government auditors.

The primary emphasis in this text is on the auditor's decision-making process. We believe the most fundamental concepts in auditing concern determining the nature and amount of evidence the auditor should accumulate after considering the unique circumstances of each engagement. If a student of auditing understands the objectives to be accomplished in a given audit area, the circumstances of the engagement, and the decisions to be made, he or she should be able to determine the appropriate evidence to gather and how to evaluate the evidence obtained.

As the title of the book reflects, our purpose is to integrate the most important concepts of auditing as well as certain practical aspects in a logical manner to assist students in understanding audit decision making and evidence accumulation. For example, internal control is integrated into each of the chapters dealing with a particular functional area and is related to tests of controls; tests of controls are, in turn, related to the tests of details of financial statement balances for the area; and statistical sampling is applied to the accumulation of audit evidence rather than treated as a separate topic.

Major Changes in the Fifth Edition

There were many changes made in this edition. The following are the most important ones.

Assumption of computerized accounting systems rather than manual ones In the Fifth Edition, all concepts, examples, and problem materials assume the client's accounting system is computerized. There are now very few manual accounting systems used in business and government. The authors concluded that it is unrealistic to discuss and illustrate manual systems and assume their use. Computerized accounting systems in practice vary from simple or noncomplex to highly complex. Noncomplex systems are assumed throughout the text, except in Chapter 15, to provide students a realistic but easy way to understand systems' environments. Chapter 15 discusses the effect of complex computerized accounting systems on auditing.

Addition of a section in Chapter Three that deals with business and professional ethical responsibilities and conflicts Business schools and departments of accounting are increasingly emphasizing business and professional men's and women's ethical responsibilities, as distinguished from formal codes of professional conduct. Chapter Three on professional conduct now includes a section dealing with the meaning of ethical conduct in business and professions, the types of ethical dilemmas professional accountants are likely to encounter, and ways to resolve these ethical dilemmas. The chapter also discusses ethics in the public accounting profession focussing on certain of the more important rules that govern the professional lives of public accountants.

Updated legal liability chapter and review by a professor of business law As authors, we believe that the increased exposure of public accounting firms to legal liability makes it essential that Chapter Four on legal liability be especially current and relevant. After revising the chapter for changes in legal liability concepts applicable to public accounting firms, we had the chapter reviewed by a professor of business law who has an interest in and expertise concerning the law as it pertains to accountants. Her comments and suggestions have been incorporated into the revision.

Updated information Since the last revision, there have been significant changes in the *CICA Handbook* and the professional literature. These changes including the most recent releases by the CICA have been incorporated into the Fifth Edition.

Additional emphasis on integrating concepts As authors, we have always believed that the title, *Auditing: An Integrated Approach*, reflects the importance of integrating auditing concepts throughout the book. Several figures have been added, especially at the end of chapters, to improve the integration. The discussions in the text and examples also do the same thing. Problem materials have also been changed to assist students in being able to integrate concepts.

Addition of learning objectives The most important points of learning have been added to the beginning of each chapter. These learning objectives are also shown in the margin of each chapter section where discussion of the point of learning occurs.

Glossary Students often need quick clarification or reinforcement of the meaning of a term. We have included an end-of-book glossary that defines the most important text terminology and provides page references.

Organization
The text is divided into six parts.

Part 1, The Auditing Profession (Chapters 1-4) The book begins with a description of the nature of auditing and auditing firms, public accounting and the accounting bodies in Canada and the CICA. In Chapter 2, there is a detailed discussion of auditor's reports. It emphasizes the conditions that affect the type of report the auditor must issue and the type of auditor's report applicable to each condition under varying levels of materiality. Chapter 3 explains ethical dilemmas, professional ethics, and the rules of conduct governing the professional activities of public accountants in Canada. Chapter 4 ends this part with an investigation of auditors' legal liability.

Part 2, The Auditing Process (Chapters 5-10) The first two of these chapters discuss auditors' and management's responsibilities, audit objectives, and general concepts of evidence accumulation. The remaining chapters deal with planning the engagement and the decision process the auditor goes through. Chapter 7 emphasizes analytical procedures as an audit tool. Chapter 8 introduces materiality and risk, and shows their effect on the audit. Understanding internal control and assessing control risk are discussed in Chapter 9; the chapter emphasizes a proper methodology for understanding the two elements of internal control. Chapter 10 summarizes Chapters 5 through 9 and integrates them with the remainder of the text.

Part 3, Application of the Auditing Process to the Sales and Collection Cycle (Chapters 11-14) These chapters apply the concepts from Part 2 to the audit of sales, cash receipts, and the related income statement and balance sheet accounts. The appropriate audit procedures for sales and cash receipts are related to internal control and audit objectives for tests of controls and tests of details of balances. Students learn to apply attributes statistical sampling to the audit of sales and cash receipts, and dollar unit sampling and variables sampling to the audit of accounts receivable.

Part 4, Auditing Complex EDP Systems (Chapter 15) This chapter is concerned with understanding internal control and assessing control risk for more complex EDP systems, the audit of systems that include significant EDP applications, and auditing with the use of the computer. The emphasis in this chapter is on the effect of complex EDP on the way an audit is conducted.

Part 5, Application of the Auditing Process to Other Cycles (Chapters 16-21) Each of these chapters deals with a specific transaction cycle or part of a transaction cycle in much the same manner as Chapters 11 through 14 deal with the sales and collection cycle. Each chapter in Part 5 is meant to demonstrate the relationship of internal control and tests of controls for each broad category of transactions to the related balance sheet and income statement accounts. Cash in the bank is studied late in the text to demonstrate how the audit of cash balances is related to most other audit areas.

Part 6, Completing the Audit and Offering Other Services (Chapters 22-24) This set of chapters begins by summarizing all audit tests, reviewing working papers and other aspects of completing the audit. The remaining two chapters examine various types of engagements and reports, other than the audit of financial statements using generally accepted accounting principles. Chapter 23 discusses special engagements, reviews and compilations, the auditor's involvement with prospectuses, reports on the application of accounting principles, examinations of future-oriented financial information, the auditor's involvement with pensions, and attestation standards. Chapter 24 examines operatonal auditing and comprehensive auditing.

Supplements
Several supplements are available for faculty and, in some cases, students' use.

Solutions Manual Solutions to all end-of-chapter review questions, multiple choice questions, problems, and cases.

Instructor's Resource Manual Items to assist the instructor in teaching the course:
Suggestions by the authors of effective ways to use each chapter.
Instructions for assignments and use of software templates.
Transparency masters for each chapter.

Software Templates Problem materials from text converted to a computerized format. Faculty members can assign identified problems for students to solve using their computer and the software templates.

Practice Set Lakeside Company: Thirteen Mini-Cases in the Life Cycle of an Audit Prepared by Joseph Hoyle, Richard Scott, and Melanie Russell, the cases provide actual practice in conducting an audit in Canada. The practice set includes microcompuer assignments, but can be used with or without computers. A Solutions Manual is available to instructors.

Acknowledgments for the U.S. Fifth Edition

We acknowledge the American Institute of Certified Public Accountants for permission to quote extensively from statements on auditing standards, the *Code of Professional Conduct*, Accounting Principles Board Opinions, Uniform CPA Examinations, and other publications. The willingness of this major accounting organization to permit the use of its materials is a significant contribution to the book.

The continuing generous support of the Price Waterhouse Foundation is acknowledged, particularly in regard to the word processing, editing, and moral support for this text.

We also gratefully acknowledge the contributions of the following reviewers for their suggestions and support: Sherri Anderson, Sonoma State University; Dale E. Armstrong, Oklahoma State University; Stephen K. Asare, University of Florida; William L. Felix, University of Arizona; Gary L. Holstrum, University of South Florida; C. Randy Howard, Eastern Montana College; James Jiambalvo, University of Washington; David S. Kerr, Texas A & M University; Dennis Lee Kimmell, University of Akron; William R. Kinney, Jr., University of Texas; W. Robert Knechel, University of Florida; Heidi H. Meier, Cleveland State University; Tad Miller, California Polytechnic State University; Lawrence C. Mohrweis, Indiana University; Frederick L. Neumann, University of Illinois; Bradley J. Schwieger, St. Cloud State University; Robert R. Tucker, University of Wisconsin; D. Dewey Ward, Michigan State University.

A special note of thanks is extended to Mary Jo Mercer for word processing and to Janice L. Bukovac and Kathleen M. Mazzeo for their editorial efforts.

We also express appreciation for assistance by Robert D. Allen, Kevin T. Kohlmeier, and Paul G. Gaskin.

Finally, the encouragement and support of our families are acknowledged.

Acknowledgements for the Canadian Fifth Edition

I would like to thank the Canadian Institute of Chartered Accountants for permission to quote from its various publications, in particular the *CICA Handbook*. Every effort has been made to ensure that the material used from these sources was accurate and current. I would also like to thank the Canadian Comprehensive Auditing Foundation, J. Efrim Boritz, and J.M. Schneider Inc. for granting permission to use material prepared or published by them.

Thanks go the following for their reviews and contributions: Stephen J. Aldersley, Ernst & Young; J. Efrim Boritz and Sally P. Gunz, School of Accountancy, University of Waterloo; James C. Gaa, McMaster University; and Melanie E. Russell, Toronto-Dominion Bank, Toronto.

I would like to acknowledge the editorial work and support of David Jolliffe and Marta Tomins, the copy editing of Deborah Burrett and the support of Yolanda de Rooy of Prentice Hall Canada. Thanks also to Lynn Miske for her assistance.

This book is dedicated to Margie whose life and spirit have been my inspiration.

1

AN OVERVIEW OF AUDITING

LEARNING OBJECTIVES — THOROUGH STUDY OF THIS CHAPTER WILL ENABLE YOU TO:

1. Define and explain auditing

2. Distinguish between auditing and accounting

3. Describe the relationships among the various types of audits and auditors

4. Discuss why reducing information risk is the prime economic reason behind the demand for audits

5. Describe the nature of accounting firms and public accounting

6. Describe the functions performed by the CICA

7. Use generally accepted auditing standards as a basis for further study

8. Discuss Auditing Recommendations and their role in the work of the auditor

9. Identify quality control standards and practices within the accounting profession

☐ This chapter presents background information about the nature of auditing and the major influences affecting auditing activities. The first part of the chapter is a discussion of the professional accounting/auditing organizations in Canada. This is followed by a discussion of auditing in a broad sense. The discussion considers what auditing is, why it is needed, the various types of auditors and the economics of auditing. This is followed by a discussion of the influence of the Canadian Institute of Chartered Accountants (CICA) and the nature of generally accepted auditing standards and Auditing Recommendations. Considered finally is quality control.

Professional Accounting/ Auditing Organizations

Before beginning a discussion of auditing, it is appropriate to disclose who performs the auditing function – external and internal – in Canada. There are four major organizations in Canada that provide a professional designation relating to accounting/auditing. The organizations, the designation awarded and the manner of qualifying for the designation are discussed below.

The senior body is the Canadian Institute of Chartered Accountants whose members are chartered accountants or CAs. The use of the title "chartered accountant" (CA) is regulated by provincial law. The experience requirements and educational requirements for becoming a CA vary among provinces. All provinces, however, require that an individual, to qualify as a CA, have a university degree and pass a national uniform examination administered by the CICA.

The use of the title "certified general accountant" (CGA), awarded by the Certified General Accountants Association of Canada (CGAAC), is also regulated by provincial law. The experience and educational requirements for becoming a CGA vary from province to province but in all provinces the individual must either pass national examinations administered by the CGAAC in the various subject areas or gain exemption by taking specified university courses. Certain subjects may only be passed by national examination.

The Society of Management Accountants of Canada (SMAC) administers the Certified Management Accountant (CMA) program, leading to the CMA designation. The use of the term CMA is restricted by provincial law to those persons earning the right to use it. A university degree is required to become a CMA. Students must also pass exams in required subject areas as well as uniform national exams administered by the SMAC at the end of the course. It is possible to gain exemption from subject area exams by taking appropriate university courses. Students, furthermore, must meet experience requirements.

Internal auditors have a professional organization, the Institute of Internal Auditors (IIA), and a professional designation, Certified Internal Auditor (CIA). The designation is earned by passing a set of exams that are administered worldwide by the IIA and by meeting experience requirements. A university degree is required to write the exams. Unlike the other professional organizations discussed above, the IIA membership includes persons not having a CIA.

Nature of Auditing

> Auditing is the process by which a competent, independent person accumulates and evaluates evidence about quantifiable information related to a specific economic entity for the purpose of determining and reporting on the degree of correspondence between the quantifiable information and established criteria.

OBJECTIVE 1

Define and explain auditing.

This definition includes several key words and phrases. Each is discussed in this section and analyzed more extensively in later chapters. For ease of understanding, the terms are discussed in a different order than they occur in the definition.

Quantifiable Information and Established Criteria

To do an audit, there must be information in a *verifiable form* and some standards (*criteria*) by which the auditor can evaluate the information.

Quantifiable information can and does take many forms. It is possible to audit such things as a company's financial statements, the amount of time it takes an employee to complete an assigned task, the total cost of a government construction contract, and an individual's tax return.

The criteria for evaluating quantitative information also vary. For example, in the audit of historical financial statements of public accounting firms, the criteria are generally accepted accounting principles. To illustrate, this means that in the audit of John Labatt Limited's financial statements Ernst & Young, the CA firm, determines whether John Labatt's financial statements have been prepared in accordance with generally accepted accounting principles. For the audit of tax returns by Revenue Canada, the criteria are the provisions of the *Income Tax Act*. In the audit of John Labatt's corporate tax return by Revenue Canada, the *Income Tax Act*, rather than generally accepted accounting principles, would provide the criteria for correctness.

Economic Entity

Whenever an audit is conducted, the scope of the auditor's responsibility must be made clear. The primary method involves defining the *economic entity* and the *time period*. In most instances the economic entity is also a legal entity, such as a corporation, unit of government, partnership, or proprietorship. In some cases, however, the entity is defined as a division, a department, or even an individual. The time period for conducting an audit is typically one year, but there are also audits for a month, a quarter, several years, and in some cases the lifetime of an entity.

Accumulating and Evaluating Evidence

Evidence is defined as any information used by the auditor to determine whether the quantifiable information being audited is stated in accordance with the established criteria. Evidence takes many different forms, including oral testimony of the auditee (client), written communication with outsiders, and observations by the auditor. It is important to obtain a sufficient quality and volume of evidence to satisfy the audit objectives. The process of determining the amount of evidence necessary and evaluating whether the quantifiable information corresponds to the established criteria is a critical part of every audit. It is the primary subject of this book.

Competent, Independent Person

The auditor must be *qualified* to understand the criteria used and *competent* to know the types and amount of evidence to accumulate to reach the proper conclusion after the evidence has been examined. The auditor also must have an *independent mental attitude*. It does little good to have a competent person who is biased performing the evidence accumulation when unbiased information and objective thinking are needed for the judgments and decisions to be made.

Independence cannot be absolute by any means, but it must be a goal that is worked toward, and it can be achieved to a certain degree. For example, even though an auditor is paid a fee by a company, he or she may still be sufficiently independent to conduct audits that can be relied upon by users. Auditors may not be sufficiently independent if they are also company employees.

Reporting

The final stage in the audit process is the *audit report* – the communication of the findings to users. Reports differ in nature, but in all cases they must inform readers of the degree of correspondence between quantifiable information and established criteria. Reports also differ in form and can vary from the highly technical types usually associated with financial statements to a simple oral report in the case of an audit conducted for a particular individual.

Figure 1–1 summarizes the important ideas in the definition of auditing by illustrating an audit of an individual's tax return by a Revenue Canada auditor.

FIGURE 1–1   Audit of a Tax Return

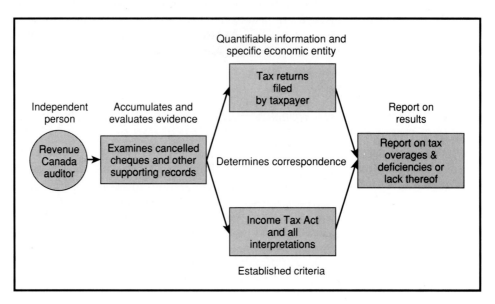

The auditor examines supporting records provided by the taxpayer and from other sources, such as the taxpayer's employer. The objective is to determine whether the tax return was prepared in a manner consistent with the requirements of the *Income Tax Act*. After completing the audit, the Revenue Canada auditor will issue a report to the taxpayer assessing additional taxes, advising that a refund is due, or stating that there is no change in the status of his or her return.

Distinction Between Auditing and Accounting

Many financial statement users and members of the general public confuse *auditing* and *accounting*. The confusion results because most auditing is concerned with accounting information, and many auditors have considerable expertise in accounting matters. The confusion is increased by giving the title "public accountant" to individuals performing a major portion of the audit function. The term "public accountant" is discussed on page 9.

    Accounting is the process of recording, classifying, and summarizing economic events in a logical manner for the purpose of providing financial information for decision making. The function of accounting, to an entity and to society as a whole, is to provide certain types of quantitative information that management and others can use to make decisions. To provide relevant information, accountants must have a thorough understanding of the principles and rules that provide the basis for preparing the accounting information. In addition, accountants must develop a system to make sure that the entity's economic events are properly recorded on a timely basis and at a reasonable cost.

    In *auditing* accounting data, the concern is with determining whether recorded information properly reflects the economic events that occurred during the accounting period. Since the accounting rules are the criteria for evaluating whether the accounting information is properly recorded, any auditor involved with these data must also thoroughly understand the rules. In the context of the audit of financial statements, these are generally accepted accounting principles. Throughout this text the assumption is made that the reader has already studied generally accepted accounting principles.

OBJECTIVE 2

Distinguish between auditing and accounting.

1-3 ℗ In addition to understanding accounting, the auditor must also possess expertise in the accumulation and interpretation of audit evidence. It is this expertise that distinguishes auditors from accountants. Determining the proper audit procedures, sample size, particular items to examine, timing of the tests, and evaluating the results are problems unique to the auditor.

Types of Audits

Four types of audits are discussed in this section: operational audits, compliance audits, audits of financial statements, and comprehensive audits.

Operational Audits

An *operational audit* is a review of any part of an organization's operating procedures and methods for the purpose of evaluating *efficiency and effectiveness*. At the completion of an operational audit, recommendations to management for improving operations are normally expected.

> ### OBJECTIVE 3
> Describe the relationships among the various types of audits and auditors.

Because of the many different areas in which operational effectiveness can be evaluated, it is impossible to characterize the conduct of a typical operational audit. In one organization, the auditor might evaluate the relevancy and sufficiency of the information used by management in making decisions to acquire new fixed assets, while in a different organization the auditor might evaluate the efficiency of the paper flow in processing sales. In operational auditing, the reviews are not limited to accounting. They can include the evaluation of organization structure, computer operations, production methods, marketing, and any other area in which the auditor is qualified.

The conduct of an operational audit and the reported results are less easily defined than either of the other two types of audits. Efficiency and effectiveness of operations are far more difficult to evaluate objectively than compliance or the presentation of financial statements in accordance with generally accepted accounting principles; and establishing criteria for evaluating the quantifiable information in an operational audit is an extremely subjective matter. In this sense, operational auditing is more similar to management consulting than to what is generally regarded as auditing. Operational auditing has increased in importance in the past decade. It is studied in greater depth in Chapter 24.

Compliance Audits

The purpose of a *compliance audit* is to determine whether the auditee is following specific procedures or rules set down by some higher authority. A compliance audit for a private business could include determining whether accounting personnel are following the procedures prescribed by the company controller, reviewing wage rates for compliance with minimum wage laws, or examining contractual agreements with bankers and other lenders to be sure the company is complying with legal requirements. In the audit of governmental units such as school boards, there is increased compliance auditing due to extensive regulation by higher government authorities. In virtually every private and not-for-profit organization, there are prescribed policies, contractual agreements, and legal requirements that may call for compliance auditing.

Results of compliance audits are generally reported to someone within the organizational unit being audited rather than to a broad spectrum of users. Management, as opposed to outside users, is the primary group concerned with the extent of compliance with certain prescribed procedures and regulations. Hence, a significant portion of work of this type is done by auditors employed by the organizational units themselves. There are exceptions. When an organization wants to determine whether individuals or organizations that are obliged to follow its requirements are actually complying, the auditor is employed by the organization issuing the requirements. An example is the auditing of taxpayers for compliance with the *Income Tax Act* – the auditor is employed by the government to audit the taxpayers' tax returns.

Audit of Financial Statements

An *audit of financial statements* is conducted to determine whether the *overall* financial statements – the quantifiable information being verified – are stated in accordance with specified criteria. Normally, the criteria are generally accepted accounting principles, although it is also common to conduct audits of financial statements prepared using the cash basis or some other basis of accounting appropriate for the organization. The financial statements most commonly included are the statement of financial position, income statement, and statement of changes in financial position, including accompanying footnotes.

The assumption underlying an audit of financial statements is that they will be used by different groups for different purposes. Therefore, it is more efficient to have one auditor perform an audit and draw conclusions that can be relied upon by all users than to have each user perform his or her own audit. If a user believes that the general audit does not provide sufficient information for his or her purposes, the user has the option of obtaining more data. For example, a general audit of a business may provide sufficient financial information for a banker considering a loan to the company, but a corporation considering a merger with that business may also wish to know the replacement cost of fixed assets and other information relevant to the decision. The corporation may use its own auditors to get the additional information.

Comprehensive Audits

The term *comprehensive audit* was coined by James J. Macdonnell, a former Auditor General of Canada, to describe the auditing process carried out by his office. A comprehensive audit has three components:

1. A financial statement audit,
2. A compliance audit, and
3. A value-for-money audit which is a form of operational audit. A value-for-money audit considers economy, efficiency, and effectiveness.

Comprehensive audits will be considered further in the following discussion of government auditors and in Chapter 24.

Types of Auditors

In this section, the four most widely known types of auditors are discussed briefly. They are government auditors, Revenue Canada auditors, internal auditors, and public accountants.

Government Auditors

The Government of Canada and the various provincial governments have Auditor Generals who are responsible for auditing the ministries, departments, and agencies who report to that government. These government auditors may be appointed by a bi-partisan committee or by the government or party in power in that jurisdiction. They report to their respective legislatures and are responsible to the body appointing them. The primary responsibility of the government audit staff is to perform the audit function for government. The extent and scope of the audits performed are determined by legislation in the various jurisdictions. For example, in 1977, the federal parliament made a revision to existing legislation in passing the *Auditor General Act* that required the Auditor General to report to the House of Commons on the *efficiency* and *economy* of expenditures or whether *value-for-money* had been received.

In 1984, the House of Commons passed *Bill C-24* which amended the *Financial Administration Act* with respect to Crown corporations.[1] The implications are significant for auditors in public practice and in the government. Included among its stipulations are the following:

1. Internal audits that look at financial matters or compliance with regulations, and audits that look at whether or not the operations are conducted in an efficient, effective, and economic manner would be required.
2. External audits of the financial statements would be required.
3. Special examinations of efficiency, effectiveness, and economy be carried out every five years.

The audit responsibilities of these government auditors are much like those of a public accounting firm. Much of the financial information prepared by various government agencies and, in some cases, by Crown corporations is audited by these government auditors before the information is submitted to the various legislatures. Since the authority for expenditures and receipts of governmental agencies is defined by law, there is considerable emphasis on compliance in these audits.

James J. Macdonnell defined comprehensive auditing as being

> broader than the traditional financial audit. It assesses the adequacy of management control systems to ensure due regard to economy and efficiency, as well as the procedures employed to measure and report on the effectiveness of the programs on which the funds are spent. It calls for a combination of audit concepts and methods and integrates a variety of disciplines ranging well beyond the traditional financial accounting orientation. Comprehensive auditing at the federal level in Canada has introduced a new dimension of public disclosure: whether public funds have been providing value for money. This new dimension is . . . one of the key elements of comprehensive auditing.[2]

He was instrumental in organizing the Canadian Comprehensive Auditing Foundation in 1980. The Foundation is made up of governmental auditors from the federal and provincial governments, accountants from the private sector, including public accounting firms, and academics. The goal of the Foundation is to develop comprehensive auditing techniques to improve the work of the public sector auditor.

---

1 The interested reader is referred to *A Director's Introduction to the Audit and Special Examination Provisions of the Financial Administration Act (as amended by Bill C-24)* published by the Canadian Comprehensive Auditing Foundation from which this material is taken.

2 From an unpublished speech given by James J. Macdonnell on May 14, 1980, to the second seminar of Senior Government Audit Institutions in Mexico City.

The Canadian Comprehensive Auditing Foundation defines a comprehensive audit as follows:

> An examination that provides an objective and constructive assessment of the extent to which:
>
> ■ financial, human and physical resources are managed with regard to economy, efficiency and effectiveness; and
>
> ■ accountability relationships are reasonably served.
>
> The comprehensive audit examines both financial and management controls, including information systems and reporting practices, and recommends improvements where appropriate.[3]

An example of the audit work in the public sector is the evaluation of the computer operations of a particular governmental unit. The auditor can review and evaluate any aspect of the computer system, but he or she is likely to emphasize the adequacy of the equipment, the efficiency of the operations, the adequacy and usefulness of the output, and similar matters, with the objective of identifying means of providing the same services for less cost.

In many provinces, experience as a government auditor fulfills the experience requirement for becoming a CA, CGA, CMA or CIA. In those provinces, if an individual passes the CA, CGA, CMA or CIA examination and fulfills the experience stipulations of the particular professional organization, he or she may then obtain a CA, CGA, CMA or CIA certificate respectively.

As a result of their great responsibility for auditing the expenditures of the various governments, their use of advanced auditing concepts, their eligibility to be professional accountants, and their opportunities for performing comprehensive audits, government auditors are highly regarded in the auditing profession.

Revenue Canada Auditors

Revenue Canada Taxation, under the direction of the Minister of National Revenue, has as its responsibility the enforcement of the federal tax laws as they have been defined by Parliament and interpreted by the courts. A major responsibility of Revenue Canada is to audit the returns of taxpayers to determine whether they have complied with the tax laws. The auditors, who perform these examinations, are referred to as Revenue Canada auditors. These audits can be regarded as solely compliance audits.

It might seem that the audit of returns for compliance with the federal tax laws would be a simple and straightforward problem, but nothing could be further from the truth. The tax laws are highly complicated, and there are hundreds of volumes of court interpretations. The tax returns being audited vary from the simple returns of individuals who work for only one employer and take the standard tax deductions to the highly complex returns of multinational corporations. There are taxation problems involving individual taxpayers, sales taxes, corporate taxes, trusts, and so forth. An auditor involved in any of these areas must have considerable knowledge to conduct an audit.

Internal Auditors

Internal auditors, many of whom are members of the IIA, are employed by individual companies to audit for management, much as the Auditor General does for Parliament. The internal audit group in some large firms can include over a

---

3 The interested reader is referred to *Comprehensive Auditing: Concepts, Components and Characteristics* published by the Canadian Comprehensive Auditing Foundation from which this material is taken.

hundred persons and typically reports directly to the president, another high executive officer, or even the audit committee of the board of directors.

Internal auditors' responsibilities vary considerably, depending upon the employer. Some internal audit staffs consist of only one or two employees who may spend most of their time doing routine compliance auditing. Other internal audit staffs consist of numerous employees who have diverse responsibilities, including many outside the accounting area. In recent years, many internal auditors have become involved in operational auditing or have developed expertise in evaluating computer systems.

To operate effectively, an internal auditor must be independent of the line functions in an organization, but will not be independent of the entity as long as an employer-employee relationship exists. Internal auditors provide management with valuable information for making decisions concerning the efficient and effective operation of its business. Users from outside the entity, however, are unlikely to want to rely on information verified by internal auditors because of their lack of independence. This lack of independence is the major difference between internal auditors and public accounting firms.

Public Accountants   Public accounting firms have as their primary responsibility the performance of the audit function on published financial statements of all publicly traded companies and most other reasonably large companies. Such an audit is known as an *attest* audit because the auditor attests to the fair presentation in the financial statements. Because of the widespread use of audited financial statements in the Canadian economy, as well as businesses' and other users' familiarity with these statements, it is common to use the terms *auditor* and *public accounting firm* synonymously even though there are several types of auditors. Another term frequently used to describe a public accounting firm is *independent auditor*.

A number of Canadian provinces restrict the audit attest function to chartered accountants licenced in that province. Other provinces also licence certified general accountants to perform the full audit attest function while still other provinces do not require a licence to perform an attest audit. The two bodies whose members perform most of the attest audits in Canada are the Canadian Institute of Chartered Accountants (CICA) and the Certified General Accountants Association of Canada (CGAAC). The term *public accountant* is used frequently throughout this book to describe an individual who is licenced to perform the audit attest function.

Most young professionals who want to become public accountants start their careers working for a public accounting firm. After they become public accountants many leave the firm to work in industry, government, or education. These people may continue to be members of a professional body (e.g., CAs) but ordinarily lose their right to practice as independent auditors. CAs must meet licensing requirements to maintain their right to practice in most provinces. It is common, therefore, to find people who are CAs but who have not practiced as independent auditors for a time.

Summary   The major emphasis in this book is the audit of financial statements by public accounting firms. There are three reasons for this: A larger percentage of students who become auditors initially work for a public accounting firm than for any other type of audit organizations; public accounting firms have more clearly defined audit responsibilities than the other major audit organizations; and there are more

TABLE 1–1

Types of Audits and
Auditors

AUDIT	USUAL AUDITOR	EXAMPLE
Operational audit	Auditor General Internal auditor	Evaluate whether the EDP department is operating as efficiently as practical.
Compliance audit	Auditor General Revenue Canada Internal auditor Public accounting firm	Determine if the minimum current ratio requirement of 2:1 in a loan agreement has been met.
Audit of financial statements	Public accounting firm	Annual audit of Noranda Mines Ltd. financial statements.
Comprehensive audit	Auditor General Public accounting firm	Audit of Canada Post.

professional and auditing requirements for public accounting firms than for the other organizations because external users need to rely on the financial statements.

Table 1–1 summarizes the types of audits and auditors discussed in this section. Notice that it would be far more difficult to establish criteria for the example of an operational audit than for either the financial statement or compliance audit.

Economics of Auditing

Auditing services are used extensively by business, government, and other not-for-profit organizations. A brief study of the economic reasons for auditing is useful for understanding why auditing is so necessary, as well as some of the legal problems auditors face. To keep the discussion simple, only the audit of historical financial statements by public accounting firms will be considered.

To illustrate the need for auditing, consider the decision of a bank manager in making a loan to a business. That decision will be based on such factors as previous financial relations with the business and the financial condition of the business as reflected by its financial statements. Assuming the bank makes the loan, it will charge a rate of interest determined primarily by three factors:

> **OBJECTIVE 4**
>
> Discuss why reducing information risk is the prime economic reason behind the demand for audits.

1. *Risk-free interest rate.* This is approximately the rate the bank could earn by investing in Canada Treasury Bills for the same length of time as the business loan.
2. *Business risk for the customer.* This risk reflects the possibility that the business will not be able to repay its loan because of economic or business conditions such as a recession, poor management decisions, or unexpected competition in the industry.
3. *Information risk.* This risk reflects the possibility that the information upon which the business risk decision was made was inaccurate. A likely cause of the information risk is the possibility of inaccurate financial statements.

Auditing has no effect on either the risk-free interest rate or business risk. It can have a significant effect on information risk. If the bank manager is satisfied that there is no information risk, the risk is eliminated and the overall interest rate to the borrower can be reduced. Even if information risk cannot be totally eliminated, its reduction can have a significant effect on the borrower's ability to obtain capital and succeed in business.

Causes of Information Risk

As society becomes more complex, there is an increased likelihood that unreliable information will be provided to decision makers. There are several reasons for

this: remoteness of information, bias and motives of provider, voluminous data, and the existence of complex exchange transactions.

Remoteness of information   In the modern world, it is virtually impossible for a decision maker to have much firsthand knowledge about the organization with which he or she does business. Information provided by others must be relied upon. Whenever information is obtained from others, the likelihood of it being intentionally or unintentionally misstated is increased.

Bias and motives of provider   If information is provided by someone whose goals are inconsistent with those of the decision maker, the information may be *biased* in favor of the provider. The reason could be an honest optimism about future events or an intentional emphasis designed to influence users in a certain manner. In either case, the result is a misstatement of information. For example, in a lending decision in which the borrower provides financial statements to the lender, there is considerable likelihood that the statements will be biased in favor of the borrower to enhance the chance of obtaining a loan. The misstatement could be in the form of outright incorrect dollar amounts or inadequate or incomplete disclosures of information.

Voluminous data   As organizations become larger, so does the volume of their exchange transactions. This increases the likelihood that improperly recorded information will be included in the records – perhaps buried in a large amount of other information. For example, if a cheque issued by a large government agency in payment of a vendor's invoice is overstated by $200, there is a fairly good chance it will not be uncovered unless the agency has instituted reasonably complex procedures to find this type of error. If large numbers of minor errors remain undiscovered, the combined total could be significant.

Complex exchange transactions   In the past few decades, exchange transactions between organizations have become increasingly complex and hence more difficult to record properly. For example, the correct accounting treatment of pension costs and obligations or the proper way to account for foreign operations pose relatively difficult and important problems. The proper combining and disclosing of the results of operations of subsidiaries in different industries or calculating lease liabilities are other difficult accounting problems management faces.

Reducing Information Risk   Managements of businesses and the users of their financial statements may conclude that the best way to deal with information risk is simply to have it remain reasonably high. A small company may find it less expensive to pay higher interest costs than to increase the costs of reducing information risk. For larger businesses, however, it is usually practical to incur such costs. There are three main ways to reduce information risk:

User verifies information   The user may go to the business premises to examine records and obtain information about the reliability of the statements. Normally, that is impractical because of costs. In addition, it would be economically inefficient for all users to verify the information individually. Nevertheless, some users perform their own verification. For example, Revenue Canada does considerable verification of businesses and individuals to determine whether tax returns filed reflect the actual tax due the government.

User shares information risk with management There is considerable legal precedent indicating that management is responsible for providing reliable information to users. If users rely on inaccurate financial statements and as a result incur a financial loss, there is a basis for a lawsuit against management.

A difficulty with sharing information risk with management is that users may not be able to collect on losses. If a company is unable to repay a loan because of bankruptcy, it is unlikely that management will have sufficient funds to repay users. Nevertheless, users do evaluate the likelihood of being able to share their information risk loss with management.

Audited financial statements are provided A common way to obtain reliable information is to have an independent audit performed. The audited information is then used in the decision-making process on the assumption that it is reasonably complete, accurate, and unbiased.

Whenever more than one decision maker uses a particular type of information, it is usually less expensive to have someone perform the audit for all the users than to have each user verify the information individually. Since the financial statements of most companies have many users, there is considerable demand for auditing.

Typically, management engages the auditor to provide assurances to users that the financial statements are reliable. If the financial statements are ultimately determined to be incorrect, the auditor can be sued by both the users and management. Users sue on the basis that the auditor had a professional responsibility to make sure the financial information was reliable. Users are also likely to sue management. Management sues the auditor as an agent who had a responsibility to management to make sure the information was reliable. Auditors obviously have considerable legal responsibility for their work.

Summary In business practice, all three methods are used to reduce information risk. As society becomes more complex, reliance on auditors to reduce information risk increases. In many cases, federal or provincial regulations have been passed requiring an annual audit by a public accounting firm. For example, all companies filing annually with the various provincial securities commissions, such as the Alberta Securities Commission, are required to have an annual audit. Similarly, governmental units such as Crown corporations and municipalities must be periodically audited. Although not required by specific regulations, many lenders such as banks require annual audits for companies having loans over a certain amount outstanding to their bank.

Public Accounting Firms There are currently more than a thousand public accounting firms in Canada. These firms range in size from a sole practitioner to the more than 6,000 professional and support staff employed by Canada's largest CA firm, Peat Marwick Thorne. Four size categories can be used to describe public accounting firms: Big Six international firms, national firms, large local and regional firms, and small local firms.

*International
Firms*

The six largest accounting firms in the world are referred to as international public accounting firms. In Canada, these firms are the first five (Peat Marwick Thorne, Deloitte & Touche, Ernst & Young, Price Waterhouse) and eighth (Arthur Andersen) largest firms in the country.[4] Between them, they audit more than 90 percent of the 1,000 largest companies in Canada.[5] Their gross revenues ranged from $121 million to $534 million for 1990; international revenues are more than $5 billion for the largest of these firms. These firms range in size from a staff of several hundred professionals in Toronto to smaller offices with fewer than twenty people.

> **OBJECTIVE 5**
>
> Describe the nature of accounting firms and public accounting.

Prior to 1989, there were eight large public accounting firms, and they were referred to as the Big Eight. In 1989, two mergers of two firms resulted in the Big Six. There was no single reason for these mergers, but a major factor is the need for international public accounting firms able to serve all major international cities as the globalization of businesses increases. For example, if a Canadian company has branches in the United States, Brazil, and Spain, the public accounting firm doing their audit needs auditors in each of those countries. Each of the Big Six now has the capability to serve all major international markets.

National Firms

In addition to the Big Six, several other firms in Canada are referred to as national firms because they have offices in most major cities. These firms perform the same services as Big Six firms and compete directly with them for clients. In addition, each is affiliated with firms in other countries and therefore has an international capability.

*Large Local and
Regional Firms*

There are less than a hundred public accounting firms with professional staffs of more than fifty people. Some have only one office and serve clients primarily within commuting distance. Others have several offices in a province or region and service a larger radius of clients. These firms compete with other public accounting firms, including the Big Six, for clients. Many of them become affiliated with associations of public accounting firms to share resources for such matters as technical information and continuing education.

Small Local Firms

Most public accounting firms have fewer than twenty-five professionals in their single-office firm. They perform audits and related services primarily for smaller businesses and not-for-profit entities, although some do have one or two clients with public ownership.

**Activities of
Public
Accounting Firms**

Public accounting firms perform seven broad categories of services: audits, reviews, compilations, special reports, tax services, management advisory services, and accounting and bookkeeping services.

Audits

Audits of historical cost financial statements are the predominate type of service provided by many of the larger public accounting firms. In the audit of financial statements, the responsible other party is the client who is making various assertions in the form of its published financial statements. The auditor's report

---

4 *The Financial Post 500* (Summer, 1991). The data provided are as at December 31, 1990.

5 *The Bottom Line* (April, 1991).

expresses an opinion on whether those financial statements are in conformity with generally accepted accounting principles. External users of financial statements look to the auditor's report as an indication of the reliability of the statements for their decision-making purposes.

Reviews

Many smaller non-public companies wish to issue financial statements to various users, but do not wish to incur the cost of an auditor's report to accompany them. A review, which provides a much lower degree of assurance than an audit, is usually provided to the company in such a situation. The amount of work done by the public accountant is considerably less than in an audit and so the cost to the client is much less.

Compilations

A compilation involves the preparation by the public accountant of financial statements from the client's records or from information provided to the public accountant. The work done by the public accountant is much less extensive than in a review and the cost is correspondingly much less. No assurance is provided by a compilation.

Special Reports

Public accountants may also prepare special reports for clients where the public accountant audits and provides an opinion on financial information other than financial statements or on compliance with an agreement or regulations, or where the public accountant performs specified audit procedures on financial information other than financial statements. For example, an auditor might provide an opinion on the sales at a Shopper's Drug Mart in a Saskatoon shopping mall because the store's rent is based on sales and the owner of the mall requires an audit opinion. (Reviews, compilations, and special reports are discussed in Chapter 23.)

Tax Services

Public accounting firms prepare corporate and individual tax returns for both audit and nonaudit clients. In addition, sales tax, tax planning, and other aspects of tax services are provided by most firms. Tax services are now performed by almost every public accounting firm, and for many small firms such services are far more important to their practice than auditing.

Management Advisory Services

Most public accounting firms provide certain services that enable their clients to operate their businesses more effectively. These range from simple suggestions for improving the client's accounting system to aids in marketing strategies, computer installations, and actuarial benefit consulting. Many large firms now have departments involved exclusively in management advisory services with little interaction with the audit or tax staff.

Accounting and Bookkeeping Services

Some small clients lack the personnel or expertise to prepare even their own journals and ledgers. Many small public accounting firms spend much of their time performing this type of work, termed *write-up* work. In recent years, many firms have used electronic data-processing systems to provide bookkeeping services to clients. In some instances, the public accounting firm also conducts a review or even an audit after the bookkeeping services have been provided; in other instances, financial statements are compiled by the public accounting firm.

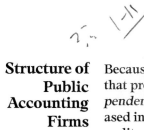

Structure of Public Accounting Firms

Because of their responsibility for the audit of financial statements, it is essential that professionals working for public accounting firms have a high level of *independence* and *competence*. Independence permits the auditors to remain unbiased in drawing conclusions about the financial statements. Competence permits auditors to conduct the audit efficiently and effectively. Confidence in an auditor's independence and competence enables users to rely upon the statements. The large number of public accounting firms in Canada makes it impossible for users to evaluate the independence and competence of individual firms. Consequently, an organizational structure for public accounting firms has emerged that encourages, but certainly does not guarantee, these qualities.

The organizational form used by public accounting firms is that of a *sole proprietorship* or a *partnership*. In a typical firm, several CAs or CGAs join together to practice as partners, offering auditing and other services to interested parties. The partners normally hire professional staff to assist them in their work. These assistants are, or aspire to become, CAs or CGAs.

The existence of a separate entity to perform audits encourages independence by avoiding an employee-employer relationship between public accounting firms and their clients. A separate entity also enables a public accounting firm to become sufficiently large to prevent any one client from representing a significant portion of a partner's total income and thereby endangering the firm's independence. Competence is encouraged by having a larger number of professionals with related interests associated in one firm, which facilitates a professional attitude and makes continuing professional education more meaningful.

The organizational hierarchy in a typical public accounting firm includes partners, managers, supervisors, seniors or in-charge auditors, and assistants, with a new employee usually starting as an assistant and spending two or three years in each classification before achieving partner status. The titles of the position vary from firm to firm, but the structure is basically the same in all. When we refer in this text to the *auditor*, we mean the particular person performing some aspect of an audit. It is common to have one or more auditors from each level on larger engagements.

CICA

The CICA serves two main functions: 1) it is the umbrella organization to which all CAs belong by virtue of their membership in a provincial institute or the Quebec *ordre*; and 2) it has been given the authority by the *Canada Business Corporations Act* and the various provincial incorporating acts to set accounting and auditing standards which must be followed by public accountants doing audits of companies chartered under one of those acts. In addition, the Canadian Securities Administrators, a body made up of the heads of the various provincial securities commissions, in National Policy Statement 27 deemed the *CICA Handbook* to be the source of generally accepted accounting principles (GAAP) and generally accepted auditing standards (GAAS) for companies listed on the various stock exchanges.

> **OBJECTIVE 6**
>
> Describe the functions performed by the CICA.

Research and Publications

In its role as representative of the CAs in Canada, the CICA publishes a wide range of materials. These include the monthly *CAmagazine*, accounting and auditing research studies, and the bi-annual *Financial Reporting in Canada*. It coordinates the Uniform Final [CA] Exam and publishes the Board of Examiner's Report on each year's exam. It also coordinates the common activities of the provincial institutes and *ordre*.

Continuing Education

The CICA is very active in continuing professional education, sponsoring seminars and enveloping and providing material to the provincial institutes and *ordre* for use by their membership.

The Certified General Accountants Association of Canada plays a similar role in the professional lives of CGAs, as does the Society of Management Accountants of Canada in the lives of CMAs and the Institute of Internal Auditors in the lives of CIAs. For example, CGAAC publishers *CGA Magazine* and SMAC publishes *CMA*. In addition, CGAAC and SMAC administer exams, provide professional guidance and continuing professional education. They also conduct research and publish materials of interest to their members and students.

Establishing Standards and Rules

In its role as standard setter, the CICA supports research by its own research staff and, through grants, by others. It also sets the standards, which are called "Recommendations" and are codified in the *CICA Handbook*, and proposes guidelines and rules for members and other public accountants to follow.

You learned in an earlier accounting course about the accounting standards or Recommendations (Sections 1000 to 4999 of the *CICA Handbook*) issued by the Accounting Standards Board and about the Accounting Guidelines also issued by the Accounting Standards Board of the CICA. This text will focus on the auditing standards, or Recommendations, in Sections 5000 to 9200 and on the Auditing Guidelines.

Auditing Recommendations are issued by the Auditing Standards Board and are the rules underlying the audits and related services activities carried on by the public accountants. Auditing Recommendations are the italicized portions of Sections 5000 to 9200 of the *CICA Handbook*. These are considered to be authoritative rules.

Auditing Guidelines also are issued by the Auditing Standards Board. They do not have the authority of Auditing Recommendations and are either interpretations of existing Recommendations or the views of the Steering Committee on a particular matter of concern. An example of the latter is the Auditing Guideline issued in October 1990 entitled "Auditor's report on comparative financial statements."

In 1981, the Public Sector Accounting and Auditing Committee was established by the CICA. Its purpose is to issue standards and encourage research in both accounting and auditing in the public sector area.[6] To date, four Auditing Statements have been issued: (1) "Auditing in the Public Sector," (2) "Audit of Financial Statements in the Public Sector," (3) "Auditing for Compliance with Legislative and Related Authorities," (4) "Value-for-Money Auditing Standards." In addition, three Public Sector Auditing Guidelines have been issued: (1) "Planning for Value-for-Money Audits," (2) "Knowledge of the Audit Entity in Planning Value-for-Money Audits," (3) "Engaging and Using Specialists in Value-for-Money Audits." Public Sector auditing will be discussed further in Chapter 24.

---

6 The introduction to the Public Sector Accounting and Auditing Recommendations defines "public sector" as "federal, provincial, territorial and local governments and government entities such as government funds, agencies and corporations." (1986; p. 1)

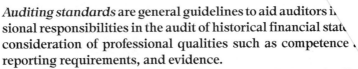

Generally Accepted Auditing Standards

OBJECTIVE 7

Use generally accepted auditing standards as a basis for further study.

Auditing standards are general guidelines to aid auditors i~~n~~ sional responsibilities in the audit of historical financial stat~~e~~ consideration of professional qualities such as competence reporting requirements, and evidence.

The broadest guidelines available are the eight *generally ac~~cepted~~ standards (GAAS)*. Developed by the CICA in 1975, they, with the e~~xception of~~ reporting standards which were substantially changed in 1990, hav~~e~~ changed since their conception. These standards are not sufficiently ~~specifi~~c to provide any meaningful guide to practitioners, but they do represent a framework upon which the CICA can provide Recommendations. These eight standards, summarized in Figure 1–2, are stated in their entirety as follows:

GENERAL STANDARD

The examination should be performed and the report prepared by a person or persons having adequate technical training and proficiency in auditing, with due care and with an objective state of mind.

EXAMINATION STANDARDS

(i) The work should be adequately planned and properly executed. If assistants are employed they should be properly supervised.

(ii) A sufficient understanding of internal control should be obtained to plan the audit. When control risk is assessed below maximum, sufficient appropriate audit evidence should be obtained through tests of controls to support the assessment.

(iii) Sufficient appropriate audit evidence should be obtained, by such means as inspection, observation, enquiry, confirmation, computation, and analysis, to afford a reasonable basis to support the content of the report.

REPORTING STANDARDS

(i) The report should identify the financial statements and distinguish between the responsibilities of management and of the auditor.

(ii) The report should describe the scope of the auditor's examination.

(iii) The report should contain either an expression of opinion on the financial statements or an assertion that an opinion cannot be expressed. In the latter case, the reasons therefore should be stated.

(iv) Where an opinion is expressed, it should indicate whether the financial statements present fairly, in all material respects, the financial position, results of operations and changes in financial position in accordance with an appropriate disclosed basis of accounting, which except in special circumstances should be generally accepted accounting principles. The report should provide adequate explanation with respect to any reservation contained in such opinion.

Auditing Recommendations

OBJECTIVE 8

Discuss Auditing Recommendations and their role in the work of the auditor.

As was previously indicated, the Recommendations in the *CICA Handbook* are the most authoritative references available to public accountants performing audits of the financial statements of companies incorporated under the various federal or provincial incorporating acts or listed on one of the Canadian stock exchanges. In addition, CAs are required by their rules of professional conduct to follow the Recommendations of the *CICA Handbook*. The Recommendations are a framework for the auditor to use to assist him or her in the conduct of the audit engagement. The framework is built upon the eight generally accepted auditing standards. Frequently these Recommendations are referred to as auditing standards or GAAS, even though they are not one of the eight generally accepted auditing standards.

Auditing standards in the United States are issued by the American Institute

FIGURE 1–2

Summary of 10
Generally Accepted
Auditing Standards

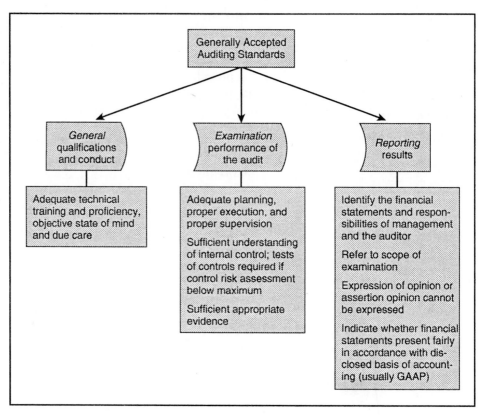

of Certified Public Accountants (AICPA). They are called Statements on Auditing Standards (SASs) and are numbered 1 to 64 (at time of writing). In certain areas the CICA will not have issued a Recommendation; for example, omitted procedures. In those instances, reference will be made to the American standard, if one exists, which in this example would be SAS 46 entitled "Consideration of Omitted Procedures After the Report Date."

The Auditing Recommendations are classified as

5000	General Auditing
6000	Specific Items-Auditing
7000	Specialized Areas-Auditing
8000	Related Services

New Recommendations are assigned a number within an appropriate series. For example, "Audit of Accounting Estimates" was assigned Section 5305 when it was issued in 1988.

Although GAAS and the Auditing Recommendations are the authoritative auditing guidelines for members of the profession, they provide less direction to auditors than might be assumed. There are almost no specific audit procedures required by the standards; and there are no specific requirements for auditors' decisions, such as determining sample size, selecting sample items from the population for testing, or evaluating results. Some practitioners believe the standards should provide more clearly defined guidelines for determining the extent of evidence to be accumulated. Such specificity would eliminate some difficult audit decisions and provide a line of defense for a public accounting firm charged with conducting an inadequate audit. However, highly specific requirements could turn auditing into mechanistic evidence gathering, devoid of professional judgment. From the point of view of both the profession and the users of auditing services, there is probably greater harm in defining authoritative guidelines too specifically than too broadly.

GAAS and the Auditing Recommendations should be looked upon by practitioners as _minimum standards_ of performance, rather than as maximum standards or ideals. Any professional auditor constantly seeking means of reducing the scope of the audit by relying only on the standards, rather than evaluating the substance of the situation, fails to satisfy the spirit of the standards. At the same time, the existence of auditing standards does not mean the auditor must always follow them blindly. If the requirement of a Recommendation is impossible to perform, the auditor might adopt some other course of action that allows adherence to the spirit of the Recommendation. Similarly, if the amount involved is not material, it is also unnecessary to follow the standard. It is important to note, however, that the burden of justifying departures from the standards falls upon the practitioner.

When auditors desire more specific guidelines, they must turn to less authoritative sources. These include the SASs issued by the AICPA, textbooks, journals, and technical publications. Materials published by the CICA, mentioned earlier in the chapter, such as _CAmagazine_ and audit technique studies, are particularly useful in furnishing assistance on specific questions.

The CICA, the CGAAC and the SMAC are members of the International Federation of Accountants (IFAC), a body that seeks to harmonize auditing standards on a world-wide basis. IFAC, through the International Auditing Practices Committee (IAPC) issues International Auditing Guidelines (IAGs) to member countries.

Section 5101 of the _CICA Handbook_ is entitled "International Auditing Guidelines." It describes Canada's role in the IFAC and lists the 26 IAGs with which the AuSC has dealt. The AuSC carefully considers each IAG in the context of the _Handbook_. If the two are in agreement on a particular issue, for example, IAG 18 and Section 5360, "Using an Expert or Specialist," Section 5101 indicates the agreement. If the two are not in agreement, for example, IAG 21 and Section 5405, "Date of the Auditor's Report," Section 5101 explains the differences. The _Handbook_ takes precedence over the IAGs with respect to audits in Canada.

In the remainder of this section, GAAS are discussed briefly. There is further study of the standards and frequent reference to Auditing Recommendations throughout the text.

Adequate
Technical Training
and Proficiency

The _general standard_ stresses the important qualities the auditor should possess. The general standard is normally interpreted as requiring the auditor to have formal education in auditing and accounting, adequate practical experience for the work being performed, and continuing professional education. Recent court cases in the United States clearly demonstrate that the auditor must be technically qualified and experienced in those industries in which the auditor has clients.

In any case in which the public accountant or the accountant's assistants are not qualified to perform the work, a professional obligation exists to acquire the requisite knowledge and skills, suggest someone else who is qualified to perform the work, or decline the engagement.

Objective State of Mind

The importance of an objective state of mind or independence was stressed earlier in the definition of auditing. The *Rules of Professional Conduct* of the various provincial institutes of CAs and the *ordre* as well as the GAAS in the *CICA Handbook* stress the need for independence. The rules of conduct of CGAAC also stress the need for independence for CGAs engaged in public accounting. The *Canada Business Corporations Act*, which is similar to several of the provincial incorporating acts, also requires the auditor to be independent. Public accounting firms are required to follow several practices to increase the likelihood of independence of all personnel. For example, there are established procedures for larger audits that usually utilize an audit committee whenever there is a dispute between management and the auditors.[7] Specific methods to ensure that auditors maintain their independence are studied in Chapter 3.

Due Care

The general standard involves *due care* in the performance of all aspects of auditing. Simply stated, this means that the auditor is a professional responsible for fulfilling his or her duties diligently and carefully. As an illustration, due care includes consideration of the completeness of the working papers, the sufficiency of the audit evidence, and the appropriateness of the audit report. As a professional, the auditor must avoid negligence and bad faith, but he or she is not expected to make perfect judgments in every instance.

Adequate Planning, Proper Execution, and Proper Supervision

The *examination standards* concern evidence accumulation and other activities during the actual conduct of the audit in the field. The first standard deals with ascertaining that the engagement is sufficiently well planned and executed to ensure an adequate audit and that there is proper supervision of assistants. Supervision is essential in auditing because a considerable portion of the field work or examination is done by inexperienced staff members.

Appropriate Study and Evaluation of Internal Control

One of the most widely accepted points in the theory and practice of auditing is the importance of the client's accounting systems and whether internal controls are sufficient to generate reliable financial information. If the auditor is convinced the client has an excellent system, one that includes controls for providing reliable data and for safeguarding assets and records, the amount of audit evidence to be accumulated can be significantly less than for a system that is not adequate. In some instances the controls may be so inadequate as to preclude reliance.

Sufficient Appropriate Evidence

The decision as to how much evidence to accumulate for a given set of circumstances is one requiring professional judgment. A major portion of this book is concerned with the study of evidence accumulation and the circumstances affecting the amount needed.

Four Reporting Standards

The four reporting standards require the auditor to prepare a report on the financial statements identifying the financial statements and the responsibilities of management and the auditors and indicating the scope of the auditor's examination. The report must contain either an expression of opinion or explain why no

---

7 An audit committee is a subcommittee of the board of directors of a company. The majority of the audit committee members should be composed of directors not belonging to management. The internal and external auditors usually report to the audit committee.

opinion can be expressed. The opinion should indicate whether or not the statements are in accordance with an appropriate disclosed basis of accounting (usually GAAP). Section 5400 of the *CICA Handbook*, which deals more specifically with the auditor's report, is discussed in Chapter 2.

Quality Control

For a public accounting firm, quality control comprises the methods used to make sure that the firm meets its professional responsibilities to clients. These methods include the organizational structure of the public accounting firm and the procedures the firm sets up. For example, a public accounting firm might have an organizational structure that assures the technical review of every engagement by a partner who has expertise in the client's industry.

Quality control is closely related to, but distinct from, GAAS. A public accounting firm must make sure that generally accepted auditing standards are followed on every audit. Quality controls are the methods used by the firm that help it meet those standards consistently on every engagement. Quality controls are therefore established for the entire public accounting firm and all the activities in which the firm is involved; GAAS, on the other hand, are applied to each engagement on an individual basis.

While Canada does not have explicit quality control standards, in the United States SAS 25 requires a CPA firm to establish quality control policies and procedures. The standard recognizes that a quality control system can only provide reasonable assurance, rather than a guarantee, that GAAS are followed.

OBJECTIVE 9

Identify quality control standards and practices within the accounting profession.

Elements of Quality Control

Neither CICA nor the AICPA has set out specific quality control procedures for public accounting firms. Procedures depend on the size of the firm, the number of practice offices, and the nature of the practice. The quality control procedures of a 150-office international firm with many complex multinational clients would vary considerably from those of a five-person firm specializing in small audits in one or two industries.

The Quality Control Standards Committee of the AICPA has identified nine basic elements of quality control that firms should consider in setting up their own policies and procedures. They are listed in Table 1–2 with a brief description of the requirement for each element and an example of a quality control procedure a firm might use to satisfy the requirement.

One of the ways in which the CA profession in Canada has dealt with quality control is through the establishment of *practice inspection* by most of the provincial institutes and *ordre*. Practice inspection is administered by the provincial institute or *ordre* and is usually mandatory for CAs in public practice. A practice inspection of each practice unit (usually an office but it could be each partner in the office) is normally completed every four years but could be yearly if the practice unit is not found to be maintaining the level of practice standards set forth by the provincial practice inspection committee.

In essence, practice inspection involves a review, by full-time or part-time practice inspectors hired by the provincial practice inspection committee, of the practice unit's quality control procedures over its auditing and accounting engagements and the unit's compliance with the *CICA Handbook*. Practice inspection in Ontario is representative of that carried out by other provincial institutes and is used to illustrate practice inspection generally. The practice

TABLE 1–2
Nine Elements of
Quality Control

ELEMENT	SUMMARY OF REQUIREMENTS	EXAMPLE OF A PROCEDURE
Independence	All personnel on engagements should meet the independence requirements of the AICPA *Code of Professional Conduct.*	Each partner and employee must answer an "independence questionnaire" annually, dealing with such things as stock ownership and membership on boards of directors.
Assigning personnel to engagements	All personnel on engagements should have an adequate degree of technical training and proficiency.	Assignment of all personnel is made by one partner who knows the firm's clients and assigns personnel at least two months in advance.
Consultation	When staff or partners have technical problems, procedures should ensure that they seek guidance from qualified personnel.	The firm's director of accounting and auditing is available for consultation and must approve all engagements before their completion.
Supervision	Policies to assure proper supervision of work at all levels should exist on every engagement.	Review and approval of audit programs by an audit partner is required before detailed testing takes place.
Hiring	All new personnel should be qualified to perform their work competently.	All personnel being considered for employment must be interviewed and approved by the personnel partner and a partner in the technical areas in which the person will work.
Professional development	All personnel should receive sufficient professional development to enable them to perform their work competently.	Each professional must receive forty hours of continuing education annually plus additional hours as recommended by the personnel partner.
Advancement	Promotion policies should be established to ensure that promoted personnel are qualified for their new responsibilities.	Each professional must be evaluated on every engagement using the firm's individual engagement evaluation report.
Acceptance and continuation of clients	All potential and existing clients should be evaluated to minimize the chance of associating with management lacking integrity.	A client evaluation form, dealing with such matters as predecessor auditor comments and evaluation of management, must be prepared for every new client before acceptance.
Inspection	Policies and procedures should exist to make sure the procedures to meet the other eight quality control elements are being consistently followed.	The quality control partner must test the quality control procedures at least annually to make sure the firm is in compliance.

procedures to be reviewed have been determined by the Institute of Chartered Accountants of Ontario to include

- File and statement preparation including the use of appropriate forms, documentation, and second-person review
- Objectivity
- Maintenance of professional skills and standards through professional development, review of periodicals, self-study, and other aids

- Staff recruiting, advancement, and supervision including planning and budgeting of time, assigning of personnel, on-the-job training, and staff progress reviews
- Outside consultation as necessary including the use of practice advisers, the CICA technical advisory bureau, other practitioners, and non-CA specialists
- Office administration in relation to supervision of internal quality control, liability insurance, file retention, professional conduct, and acceptance and continuation of engagements

The amount of work done by the practice inspector depends on the degree of documentation the practice unit has on its quality control procedures. If the controls are well documented and the practice inspector finds that the controls are being complied with, the inspection will be much briefer than if there is no documentation or if the controls are not being complied with.

While the purpose of practice inspection in Ontario is educational, the Practice Inspection Committee does have sanctions it can impose. These range from re-inspection the following year and referral to the Professional Conduct Committee, whose powers include the power to require the member to take courses, the power to remove the practice unit's right to train students, and the power to expel the member from the Institute and forfeit the member's right to use the appellation Chartered Accountant.

Practice inspection can be beneficial to the profession and individual firms. The profession gains if reviews result in practitioners doing higher quality audits. A firm can also gain if the practice inspection improves the firm's practices and thereby enhances its reputation and effectiveness and reduces the likelihood of lawsuits. Of course, practice inspection is costly. There is always a trade-off between cost and benefit.

Another form of quality control is continuing professional education or professional development. As mentioned earlier, each provincial institute or *ordre* has a professional development program created to assist its members in maintaining their professional skills. It behooves the member, whether in practice or in industry, government, or education to avail himself or herself of professional development opportunities.

Provincial Securities Commissions

Securities regulation in Canada is a provincial matter; therefore companies that issue securities in Canada must abide by rules promulgated by the provincial securities commission. There is an umbrella organization, the Canadian Securities Administrators, made up of members of the securities commission of British Columbia, Alberta, Saskatchewan, Manitoba, Ontario and Quebec, which sets policies to which the member commissions agree to adhere. For example, *National Policy Statement No. 27*, issued in 1972, established the *CICA Handbook* as GAAP for securities issued under the authority of the members of the Canadian Securities Administrators.

The provincial securities commissions are responsible for administering the purchase and sale of securities within their jurisdictions. For example, the British Columbia Securities Commission includes the Vancouver Stock Exchange in its jurisdiction. While the *CICA Handbook* sets GAAP for prospectuses in Section 7100, the securities commissions must approve each actual prospectus. Prospectuses are discussed further in Chapter 23.

Securities and Exchange Commission

Many Canadian companies sell their stocks and borrow money in the United States and must therefore meet the requirements of the Securities and Exchange Commission (SEC). It is therefore appropriate to review the functions and operations of that body.

The overall purpose of the Securities and Exchange Commission (SEC), an agency of the federal government, is to assist in providing investors with reliable information upon which to make investment decisions. To this end, the Securities Act of 1933 requires most companies planning to issue *new securities* to the public to submit a registration statement to the SEC for approval. The Securities Act of 1934 provides additional protection by requiring the same companies and others to file detailed annual reports with the commission. The commission examines these statements for completeness and adequacy before permitting the company to sell its securities through the securities exchanges.

Although the SEC requires considerable information that is not of direct interest to CPAs, the securities acts of 1933 and 1934 require financial statements, accompanied by the opinion of an independent certified public accountant, as part of a registration statement and subsequent reports.

Of special interest to auditors are several specific reports that are subject to the reporting provisions of the securities acts. The most important of these are:

- *Forms S-1 to S-16.* These forms must be completed and registered with the SEC whenever a company plans to issue new securities to the public. The S-1 form is the general form when there is no specifically prescribed form. The others are specialized forms. For example, S-10 is for restrictions of landholders' royalty interests in gas and oil. All S forms apply to the Securities Act of 1933.
- *Form 8-K.* This report is filed at the end of any month in which significant events have occurred that are of interest to public investors. Such events include the acquisition or sale of a subsidiary, a change in officers or directors, an addition of a new product line, or a change in auditors.
- *Form 10-K.* This report must be filed annually within ninety days after the close of each fiscal year. Extensive detailed financial information is contained in this report, including audited financial statements.
- *Form 10-Q.* This report must be filed quarterly for all publicly held companies. It contains certain financial information and requires audit involvement whenever there is a change in accounting principles.

Since large CPA firms usually have clients that must file one or more of these reports each year, and the rules and regulations affecting filings with the SEC are extremely complex, most CPA firms have specialists who spend a large portion of their time making sure their clients satisfy all SEC requirements.

The SEC has considerable influence in setting generally accepted accounting principles and disclosure requirements for financial statements as a result of its authority for specifying reporting requirements considered necessary for fair disclosure to investors. The Accounting Principles Board followed the practice of working closely with the SEC, and the Financial Accounting Standards Board (FASB) has continued that tradition. In addition, the SEC has power to establish rules for any CPA associated with audited financial statements submitted to the commission. Even though the commission has taken the position that accounting principles and auditing standards should be set by the profession, the SEC's attitude is generally considered in any major change proposed by the FASB or the Auditing Standards Board.

The SEC requirements of greatest interest to CPAs are set forth in the commission's Regulation S-X and Accounting Series Releases. These publications constitute important basic regulations, as well as decisions and opinions on accounting and auditing issues affecting any CPA dealing with publicly held companies.

REVIEW QUESTIONS

1–1 Explain what is meant by determining the degree of correspondence between quantifiable information and established criteria. What are the quantifiable information and established criteria for the audit of Jones Ltd.'s tax return by a Revenue Canada auditor? What are they for the audit of Jones Ltd.'s financial statements by a public accounting firm?

1–2 Describe the nature of evidence the Revenue Canada auditor will use in the audit of Jones Ltd.'s tax return.

1–3 In the conduct of audits of financial statements it would be a serious breach of responsibility if the auditor did not thoroughly understand accounting. However, many competent accountants do not have an understanding of the auditing process. What causes this difference?

1–4 What are the differences between and similarities among audits of financial statements, compliance audits, and operational audits?

1–5 List five examples of specific operational audits that could be conducted by an internal auditor in a manufacturing company.

1–6 What are the major differences in the scope of the audit responsibilities for public accountants, auditors from the Auditor General's office, Revenue Canada auditors, and internal auditors?

1–7 Discuss the major factors in today's society that have made the need for independent audits much greater than it was fifty years ago.

1–8 Distinguish the following three risks: risk-free interest rate, business risk, and information risk. Which one or ones does the auditor reduce by performing an audit?

1–9 Identify the major causes of information risk and identify the three main ways information risk can be reduced. What are the advantages and disadvantages of each?

1–10 State the seven functions public accountants perform and explain each.

1–11 What major characteristics of the organization and conduct of public accounting firms permit them to fulfill their social function competently and independently?

1–12 What roles are played by the CICA, the CGAAC, and the SMAC for their members? What role does the *CICA Handbook* have in the professional activities of public accountants in Canada?

1–13 Distinguish between generally accepted auditing standards and generally accepted accounting principles, and give two examples of each.

1–14 The first examination standard requires the performance of the examination by a person or persons having adequate technical training and proficiency as an auditor. What are the various ways auditors can fulfill the requirement of the standard?

1–15 Generally accepted auditing standards have been criticized by different sources for failing to provide useful guidelines for conducting an audit. The critics believe the standards should be more specific to enable practitioners to improve the quality of their performance; as the standards are now stated they provide little more than an excuse to conduct inadequate audits. Evaluate this criticism of the eight generally accepted auditing standards.

1–16 What is meant by the term "quality control" as it relates to a public accounting firm?

1–17 The following is an example of a public accounting firm's quality control procedure requirement: "Any person being considered for employment by the firm must have completed a basic auditing course and have been interviewed and approved by an audit partner of the firm before he or she can be hired as a full-time member of the audit staff." Which element of quality control does this procedure affect, and what is the purpose of the requirement?

1–18 State what is meant by the term "practice inspection"? What are the implications of the term for the CA profession?

1–19 What is comprehensive auditing? Describe the role of the Auditor General of Canada.

1–20 Briefly describe the four accounting organizations that exist in Canada.

MULTIPLE CHOICE QUESTIONS

1–21 The following questions deal with audits by public accounting firms. Select the best response for each question.

a. Which of the following *best* describes why an independent auditor is asked to express an opinion on the fair presentation of financial statements?

(1) It is difficult to prepare financial statements that fairly present a company's financial position and changes in financial position and operations without the expertise of an independent auditor.

(2) It is management's responsibility to seek available independent aid in the appraisal of the financial information shown in its financial statements.

(3) The opinion of an independent party is needed because a company may *not* be objective with respect to its own financial statements.

(4) It is a customary courtesy for all shareholders of a company to receive an independent report on management's stewardship of the affairs of the business.

b. Independent auditing can *best* be described as

(1) a branch of accounting.

(2) a discipline that attests to the results of accounting and other functional operations and data.

(3) a professional activity that measures and communicates financial and business data.

(4) a regulatory function that prevents the issuance of improper financial information.

c. The policies of Rogers & Co., public accountants, require that all members of the audit staff submit weekly time reports to the audit manager, who then prepares a weekly summary report for Rogers' review on any variance from the budget. This practice is evidence of Rogers & Co.'s professional concern about compliance with which of the following generally accepted auditing standards?

(1) Quality control.

(2) Due professional care.

(3) Adequate review.

(4) Adequate planning.

(AICPA adapted)

1–22 The following questions deal with operational audits and governmental audits. Select the best response for each question.

a. Operational audits generally have been conducted by internal auditors and governmental audit agencies but may be performed by public accountants. A primary purpose of an operational audit is to provide

(1) a means of assurance that internal accounting controls are functioning as planned.

(2) a measure of management performance in meeting organizational goals.

(3) the results of internal examinations of financial and accounting matters to a company's top-level management.

(4) aid to the independent auditor, who is conducting the examination of the financial statements.

b. In comparison to the external auditor, an internal auditor is more likely to be concerned with

(1) internal administrative control.

(2) cost accounting procedures.

(3) operational auditing.

(4) internal accounting control.

c. Which of the following *best* describes the operational audit?

(1) It requires the constant review by internal auditors of the administrative controls as they relate to the operations of the company.

(2) It concentrates on implementing financial and accounting control in a newly organized company.

(3) It attempts and is designed to verify the fair presentation of the results of a company's operations.

(4) It concentrates on seeking aspects of the operations in which waste could be reduced by the introduction of controls.

d. Comprehensive auditing extends beyond examinations leading to the expression of opinion on the fairness of financial presentation and includes audits of efficiency, economy, effectiveness, as well as

(1) accuracy.

(2) evaluation.

(3) compliance.

(4) internal control.   (AICPA adapted)

1–23 The following questions deal with generally accepted auditing standards (GAAS). Select the one response that is best for each question.

a. The general standard, which states in part that the examination is to be performed by a person or persons having adequate technical training, requires that an auditor have

(1) education and experience in the field of auditing.

(2) ability in planning and supervision of the audit work.

(3) proficiency in business and financial matters.

(4) knowledge in the areas of financial accounting.

b. Which of the following *best* describes what is meant by generally accepted auditing standards?

(1) Acts to be performed by the auditor.

(2) Measures of the quality of the auditor's performance.

(3) Procedures to be used to gather evidence to support financial statements.

(4) Audit objectives generally determined on audit engagements.

c. The general standard of the generally accepted auditing standards includes a requirement that

(1) field work be adequately planned and supervised.

(2) the auditor's report state whether or not the financial statements conform to generally accepted accounting principles.

(3) due professional care be exercised by the auditor.

(4) informative disclosures in the financial statements be reasonably adequate.

d. What is the common concern or character of the three generally accepted auditing standards classified as examination standards?

(1) The competence, independence, and professional care of persons performing the audit.

(2) Criteria for the content of the auditor's report on financial statements and related footnote disclosures.

(3) The criteria of audit planning and evidence gathering.

(4) The need to maintain an independence in mental attitude in all matters relating to the audit.   (AICPA adapted)

DISCUSSION QUESTIONS AND PROBLEMS

1–24 Daniel Charon is the loan officer of the Georgian Bay Bank. Georgian has a loan of $260,000 outstanding from Regional Delivery Service Ltd., a company specializing in the delivery of products of all types on behalf of smaller companies. Georgian Bay's collateral on the loan consists of thirty-five small delivery trucks with an average original cost of $11,000.

Charon is concerned about the collectibility of the outstanding loan and whether the trucks still exist. He therefore engages Susan Virms, public accountant, to count the trucks, using registration information held by Charon. She is engaged because she spends most of her time auditing used automobile and truck dealerships and has extensive specialized knowledge about used trucks. Charon requests that Virms issue a report stating

1. which of the thirty-five trucks is parked in Regional's parking lot on the night of 6/30/X8.

2. the condition of each truck, using the categories of poor, good, and excellent.

3. the fair market value of each truck using the current "blue book" for trucks, which states the approximate wholesale prices of all used truck models, and the conditions of the trucks using the poor, good, and excellent categories.

Required:

a. Identify which aspects of this narrative fit each of the following parts of the definition of auditing:

(1) competent independent person.

(2) accumulates and evaluates evidence.

(3) specific economic entity.

(4) quantifiable information.

(5) established criteria.

(6) report of results.

b. Identify the greatest difficulties Virms is likely to have doing this audit.

1–25 Four undergraduates with majors in accounting are discussing alternative career plans. The first student plans to become a Revenue Canada auditor because his primary interest is income taxes. He believes a background in tax auditing will provide him with a better exposure to income taxes than will any other available career choice. The second undergraduate has decided to go to work for a public accounting firm for at least five years, possibly as a permanent career. She feels a wide variety of experience in auditing and related fields offers a better alternative than any other option. The third student has decided upon a career in internal auditing with a large industrial company because of the many different aspects of the organization with which internal auditors become involved. A fourth student plans to pursue some aspect of auditing as a career but has not decided upon the particular type of organization to enter. He is especially interested in an opportunity to continue to grow professionally, but meaningful and interesting employment is also an important consideration.

Required:

a. What are the major advantages and disadvantages of each of the three types of auditing careers?

b. What other types of auditing careers are available to those who are qualified?

1–26 In the normal course of performing their responsibilities, auditors frequently conduct examinations or reviews of the following:

1. Federal income tax returns of an officer of the corporation to determine whether she has included all taxable income in her return.

2. Disbursements of a branch of the Canadian government for a special research project to determine whether it would have been feasible to accomplish the same research results at a lower cost to the taxpayers.

3. Computer operations of a corporation to evaluate whether the computer center is being operated as efficiently as possible.

4. Annual statements for the use of management.

5. Operations of Revenue Canada to determine whether Revenue Canada auditors are using their time efficiently in conducting audits.

6. Statements for bankers and other creditors when the client is too small to have an audit staff.

7. Financial statements of a branch of the Canadian government to make sure the statements present fairly the actual disbursements made during a certain period.

8. Federal income tax returns of a corporation to determine whether the tax laws have been followed.

9. Financial statements for the use of shareholders when there is an internal audit staff.

10. A bond indenture agreement to make sure a company is following all requirements of the contract.

11. The computer operations of a large corporation to evaluate whether the internal controls are likely to prevent errors in accounting and operating data.

12. Disbursements of a branch of the Canadian government for a special research project to determine whether the expenditures were consistent with the legislative bill that authorized the project.

Required:

For each of the examples above, state the type of auditor (public accountant, Auditor General, Revenue Canada, or internal) that would most likely be used and the type of audit (audit of financial statements, compliance audit, operational audit or comprehensive audit) that would take place.

1–27 A large conglomerate is considering acquiring a medium-sized manufacturing company in a closely related industry. A major consideration for the management of the conglomerate in deciding whether to pursue the merger is the operational efficiency of the company. Management has decided to obtain a detailed report, based on an intensive investigation, of the operational efficiency of the sales, production, and research and development departments.

Required:

a. Whom should the conglomerate engage to conduct the operational audit?

b. What major problems are the auditors likely to encounter in conducting the investigation and writing the report?

1–28 The Consumers' Union is a nonprofit organization that provides information and counsel on consumer goods and services. A major part of its function is testing different brands of consumer products that are bought on the open market and reporting the results of the tests in *Consumer Canada*, a monthly publication. Examples of the types of products it tests are middle-sized automobiles, residential dehumidifiers, canned tuna, and children's jeans.

Required:

a. Compare the concept of information risk introduced in this chapter with the information risk problem faced by a buyer of an automobile.

b. Compare the four causes of information risk faced by users of financial statements that were discussed in the chapter with those faced by a buyer of an automobile.

c. Compare the three ways users of financial statements can reduce information risk with those available to a buyer of an automobile.

d. In what ways is the service provided by Consumers' Union similar to audit services, and in what ways does it differ? *No Regulating Body, In Severance?*

1–29 The following comments summarize the beliefs of some practitioners about quality control and practice inspection.

Quality control and practice inspection are quasi-governmental methods of regulating the profession. There are two effects of such regulation. First, it gives a competitive advantage to national CA firms because they already need formal structures to administer the complex organizations. Quality control requirements do not significantly affect their structure. Smaller firms now need a more costly organizational structure, which has proven unnecessary because of existing partner involvement on engagements. The major advantage smaller CA firms have traditionally had is a simple and efficient organizational structure. Now that advantage has been eliminated because of quality control requirements. Second, quality control and practice inspection are not needed to regulate the profession. The first eight elements of quality control have always existed, at least informally, for quality firms. Three things already provide sufficient assurance that informal quality control elements are followed without practice inspection. They are competitive pressures to do quality work, legal liability for inadequate performance, and a code of professional ethics requiring that CAs follow generally accepted auditing standards.

Required:

a. State the pros and cons of these comments.

b. Evaluate whether control requirements and practice inspection are worth their cost.

1–30 For each of the following quality control procedures taken from the quality control manual of a medium-sized regional public accounting firm, identify the applicable element of quality control from Table 1–2.

a. Appropriate accounting and auditing research requires adequate technical reference library facilities. Each practice office must maintain minimal facilities including a list of individuals within the firm who have specialized knowledge of various industries to help ensure an awareness of problems unique to specific industries. In addition, an extensive library of industry auditing material is maintained in the office of the director of accounting and auditing.

b. Each audit engagement of the firm is directed by a partner and, in most instances, a manager of the firm. On every engagement, an attempt is made to maintain a continuity of personnel on a year-to-year basis.

c. When prospective employees are interviewed by campus recruiters and are deemed to possess the potential for employment, they will be further screened by a practice office interview pursuant to the firm procedure for practice office visitation. Practice office partners make the final hiring decisions pursuant to the guidelines established by the director of personnel.

d. At all stages of any engagement, effort is made to involve professional staff at appropriate levels in the accounting and auditing decisions. Various approvals of the manager or senior accountant are obtained throughout the audit.

e. No employee will have any direct or indirect financial interest, association, or relationship (for example, a close relative serving a client in a decision-making capacity) not disclosed that might be adverse to the firm's best interest.

f. Each office of the firm shall be visited on at least an annual basis by review persons selected by the director of accounting and auditing. The procedures to be undertaken by the reviewers are illustrated in the office review program.

g. A closing conference including all staff will be held and those in attendance shall sign the checklist indicating they have reviewed certain points with the director of accounting and auditing.

h. Existing clients of the firm are reviewed on a continuing basis by the engagement partner. Termination may result if circumstances indicate there is a reason to question the integrity of management or our independence, or if accounting and auditing differences of opinion cannot be reconciled. Doubts concerning whether the client-auditor relationship should be continued must be promptly discussed with the director of accounting and auditing.

i. Individual partners submit the nominations of those persons whom they wish to be considered for partners. To become a partner, an individual must have exhibited a high degree of technical competence, possess integrity, motivation, judgment, and a desire to help the firm progress through the efficient dispatch of the job responsibilities to which he or she is assigned.

j. Through our continuing employee evaluation and counselling program, and through the quality control review procedures as established by the firm, educational needs are reviewed and formal staff training programs modified to accommodate changing needs. At the conclusion of practice office reviews, apparent accounting and auditing deficiencies are summarized and reported to the firm's director of personnel.

1–31 Harley Brown, a junior in a public accounting firm, isn't sure if there is a difference between Auditing Recommendations and Auditing Guidelines. He thinks the CICA is responsible for the issue of both and that both have equal force. Mary Jones, the manager of your staff has asked you to explain recommendations and guidelines to Harley and other new juniors and also to tell them who is responsible for issuing each.

Required: Prepare notes for your discussion of the issues raised by Harley's questions.

CASE

1–32 Raymonde, the owner of a small company, asked Holmes, public accountant, to conduct an audit of the company's records. Raymonde told Holmes that an audit is to be completed in time to submit audited financial statements to a bank as part of a loan application. Holmes immediately accepted the engagement and agreed to provide an auditor's report within three weeks. Raymonde agreed to pay Holmes a fixed fee plus a bonus if the loan was granted.

Holmes hired two accounting students to conduct the audit and spent several hours telling them exactly what to do. Holmes told the students not to spend time reviewing the controls but instead to concentrate on proving the mathematical accuracy of the ledger accounts, and summarizing the data in the accounting records that support Raymonde's financial statements. The students followed Holmes' instruction and after two weeks gave Holmes the financial statements, which did not include footnotes. Holmes reviewed the statements and prepared an unqualified auditor's report. The report did not refer to generally accepted accounting principles.

Required:
Briefly describe each of the generally accepted auditing standards and indicate how the actions of Holmes resulted in a failure to comply with each standard.
Organize your answer as follows:

Brief Description of GAAS	Holmes' Actions Resulting in Failure to Comply with GAAS

(AICPA adapted)

2

THE AUDITOR'S REPORT

LEARNING OBJECTIVES

THOROUGH STUDY OF THIS CHAPTER WILL ENABLE YOU TO:

1. Describe the nature of and need for the auditor's report

2. Specify the conditions that justify issuing the standard unqualified auditor's report, and describe the report

3. List the two conditions requiring a departure from an unqualified auditor's report

4. Identify the three types of auditor's reports that can be issued when an unqualified opinion is not justified

5. Explain how materiality affects audit reporting decisions

6. Draft appropriately modified auditor's reports under a variety of circumstances

7. Describe the circumstances when an unqualified report with an explanatory paragraph or modified wording is appropriate

---

OBJECTIVE 1

Describe the nature of and need for the auditor's report.

☐ The definition of auditing in Chapter 1 includes reporting the auditor's findings to users. Reporting is essential to the audit process because it explains what the auditor did and the conclusions reached. Frequently, it is the only part of the audit users see. Therefore, from the users' point of view, the report is the product of an audit.

Section 5020.10 of the *CICA Handbook* requires that a public accountant who "associates himself or herself with information by performing services in respect of that information [communicate] the nature and extent of his or her involvement with the information ...." *Association* arises when the public accountant performs services with respect to the information or permits his or her name to be used in connection with the information. The term "services" includes audits, review engagements, and compilations. An example of an auditor "consenting to the use of his or her name" would be when the client prepares condensed financial information from the audited financial statements and indicates that the information came from financial statements audited and reported on by the public accountant.

Section 5220 refers to "information" and is not limited to financial statements. You will learn in Chapter 23 that the public accountant performs a range of services for clients of which audits are only a part; the communication provided by the public accountant ranges from an auditor's report in the case of an audit engagement to a notice to reader in the case of a compilation engagement. An auditor's report is the appropriate and required communication only when an audit is conducted.

As indicated in Chapter 1, the focus of this text will be on the audit of financial statements and thus on the auditor's report; the other form of communication, however, will be discussed in Chapter 23.

The basic requirements for issuing auditor's reports are derived from the four generally accepted auditing standards of reporting, included on page 17. The first standard requires the identification of the financial statements included and a clear differentiation between the responsibilities of management and those of the auditor. The second standard requires a clear-cut statement from the auditor on the nature of his or her examination. The third standard is especially important because it requires an expression of opinion about the overall financial statements or an explicit statement that an opinion is not possible, along with the reasons it is not possible. The fourth standard states that when an opinion is expressed by the auditor, "it should indicate whether the financial statements present fairly, in all material respects, the financial position, results of operations, and changes in financial position in accordance with an appropriate disclosed basis of accounting." The appropriate disclosed basis normally would be GAAP; however, in some situations, it might not be. Section 5100.05 suggests financial statements prepared in accordance with regulatory legislation as an example of a situation in which financial statements would not be prepared according to GAAP.

A significant portion of the Auditing Recommendations in the *Handbook* concern reporting requirements. Given the importance of auditors' reports as a communication device, that is not surprising.

The accounting profession recognizes the need for uniformity in reporting as a means of avoiding confusion. Users would have considerable difficulty interpreting the meaning of an auditor's report if each were an original creation. The professional standards, therefore, have defined and enumerated the types of auditor's report that should be included with financial statements. The wording of auditor's reports is reasonably uniform, but different audit reports are appropriate for different circumstances. The auditor must use judgment to determine what report and, thus, what wording, is appropriate.

The auditor's report is the final step in the entire audit process. The reason for studying it now, rather than later, is to permit reference to different auditor's reports as evidence accumulation is studied throughout the text. Once the form and content of the final product of the audit is understood, evidence accumulation concepts become more meaningful.

Standard (Unqualified) Auditor's Report

The most common type of audit report is the *standard unqualified auditor's report*. It is also often referred to as the *auditor's standard report*. It is used when the following conditions have been met:

Conditions for Standard Unqualified Report

1. An audit engagement has been undertaken.
2. The general standard has been followed by the auditor in all respects on the engagement.
3. Sufficient appropriate evidence has been accumulated, and the auditor has conducted the engagement in a manner that allows him or her to conclude that the three examination standards have been met.
4. The financial statements, which include the balance sheet, the income statement, the statement of retained earnings, the statement of changes in financial position, and the notes to the financial statements are fairly presented in accordance with an appropriate disclosed basis of accounting, which usually is generally accepted accounting principles.
5. There are no circumstances which, in the opinion of the auditor, would require him or her to modify the wording of the report or to add an additional explanatory paragraph.

> **OBJECTIVE 2**
>
> Specify the conditions that justify issuing the standard unqualified auditor's report, and describe the report.

When these conditions are met, the standard unqualified auditor's report on the financial statements, as shown in Figure 2–1, is issued. Different auditors may vary the wording slightly in the standard report, but the meaning will be the same.

Parts of Standard Unqualified Auditor's Report

Each standard unqualified auditor's report includes eight distinct parts. These parts are labelled in bold letters in Figure 2–1.

1. *Report Title.* Section 5400.07 states that the auditor's report should be titled.
2. *Addressee.* Section 5400.31 requires that the addressee of the auditor's report be disclosed. In most cases the addressees are the shareholders since it is usually they who appoint the auditor. If the auditor is appointed by some other person or group, the report should be addressed to that body.
3. *Introductory Paragraph.* The first paragraph of the auditor's report does three things. First, it makes the simple statement that the public accounting firm has done an *audit*. The scope paragraph clarifies what is meant by an audit.

   Second, it lists the financial statements that were audited, including the balance sheet date and the accounting periods for the income statement, the statement of retained earnings and the statement of changes in financial position. While the notes to the financial statements are not mentioned specifically, they are an integral part of the financial statements and their inclusion is implicit. The terms used to describe the financial statements in the auditor's report should be identical to those used by management on the financial statements.

   Third, the introductory paragraph states that the financial statements are the responsibility of management and that the auditor's responsibility is to express an opinion on the financial statements. In this way, the introductory paragraph (a) communicates that management is responsible for selecting the appropriate generally accepted accounting principles and for making the measurement decisions and disclosures in applying those principles, and (b) clarifies the respective roles of management and the auditor.
4. *Scope Paragraph.* The scope paragraph is a factual statement about what the auditor did in the audit. This paragraph first states that the auditor followed generally accepted auditing standards. The remainder briefly describes important aspects of an audit.

FIGURE 2–1 The Standard Auditor's Report

REPORT TITLE	AUDITOR'S REPORT
ADDRESSEE	To the Shareholders of Far West Industries Ltd.
INTRODUCTORY PARAGRAPH (factual statement)	We have audited the balance sheet of Far West Industries Ltd. as at June 30, 19X2, and the statements of income, retained earnings, and changes in financial position for the year then ended. These financial statements are the responsibility of the company's management. Our responsibility is to express an opinion on these financial statements based on our audit.
SCOPE PARAGRAPH (factual statement)	We conducted our audit in accordance with generally accepted auditing standards. Those standards require that we plan and perform an audit to obtain reasonable assurance whether the financial statements are free of material misstatement. An audit includes examining, on a test basis, evidence supporting the amounts and disclosures in the financial statements. An audit also includes assessing the accounting principles used and significant estimates made by management, as well as evaluating the overall financial statement presentation.
OPINION PARAGRAPH (conclusions)	In our opinion, these financial statements present fairly, in all material respects, the financial position of the company as at June 30, 19X2 and the results of its operations and the changes in its financial position for the year then ended in accordance with generally accepted accounting principles.
NAME OF PUBLIC ACCOUNTING FIRM	*Zackery White* Chartered Accountants
PLACE OF ISSUE	Red Deer
AUDIT REPORT DATE	October 15, 19X2

The scope paragraph states that the audit is designed to obtain *reasonable assurance* about whether the statements are free of *material* misstatement. The inclusion of the word "material" conveys that auditors are responsible only to search for significant misstatements, not minor errors that do not affect users' decisions. The use of the term "reasonable assurance" is intended to indicate that an audit cannot be expected to eliminate completely the possibility that a material error or irregularity will exist in the financial statements. In other words, an audit provides a high level of assurance, but it is not a guarantee.

The remainder of the scope paragraph discusses the audit evidence accumulated and states that the auditor believes the evidence accumulated was appropriate for the circumstances to express the opinion presented. The words "test basis" indicate that sampling was used rather than an audit of every transaction and amount on the statements. Whereas the introductory paragraph of the report states that management is responsible for the preparation and content of the financial statements, the scope paragraph states that the auditor evaluates the appropriateness of those accounting principles, estimates, and financial statement disclosures and presentations given.

5. *Opinion Paragraph*. The third paragraph in the standard auditor's report states the auditor's conclusions based on the results of the audit evidence. This auditor's part of the report is so important that frequently the entire auditor's report is referred to simply as the *auditor's opinion*. The opinion paragraph is stated as an opinion rather than as a statement of absolute fact or a guarantee. The intent is to indicate that the conclusions are based on professional judgment. Using the terminology of Chapter 1, the phrase "in our opinion" indicates that there may be some information risk associated with the financial statements, even though the statements have been audited.

    The opinion paragraph is directly related to the four generally accepted auditing reporting standards listed on page 17. The auditor is required to state an opinion about the financial statements taken as whole, including a conclusion about whether the company followed an appropriate disclosed basis of accounting, usually generally accepted accounting principles.

    One of the most controversial parts of the auditor's report is the meaning of the term *presents fairly*. The auditor means that the financial statements are presented in accordance with generally accepted accounting principles or GAAP. A lay person may mistake it to mean that the values in the financial statements represent the realizable values of the assets. It is important that lay people be educated to understand the auditor's meaning.

    GAAP normally results in the most appropriate disclosure; if GAAP does not provide the most appropriate disclosure, the auditor will utilize another form of disclosure that does provide the most appropriate disclosure. The presumption is that GAAP *will* result in the most appropriate disclosure; the auditor who deviates from GAAP must be able to explain the deviation if called upon to do so. Occasionally the courts have concluded that auditors are responsible to look beyond generally accepted accounting principles to determine whether users might be mislead if those principles are followed. It is also necessary to examine the substance of transactions and balances for possible misinformation. For example, the rules of professional conduct promulgated by the professional accounting bodies in Canada state that a member of that body shall not be associated with financial information that is false or misleading or fail to reveal any material fact or misstatement of which the member is aware that makes the financial statement false or misleading.

    The auditor's report was, at one time, known as a "two-part" opinion. The opinion paragraph stated that the financial statements ". . . present(ed) fairly . . ." and ". . . (were) in accordance with generally accepted accounting principles." The implication then was that the two criteria were separate. In 1977, the auditor's report was changed to the present "one-part" opinion; now the financial statements "present fairly in accordance with generally accepted accounting principles." The implication now is that fair presentation results from adherence to GAAP. There may be exceptions, but they are infrequent.

    In 1985, Section 5400.14 was italicized and the auditor's reporting responsibilities were modified to require the auditor to

    > . . . exercise professional judgment as to the appropriateness of the selection and application of principles to the particular circumstances of an entity and as to the overall effect on financial statements of separate decisions made in their preparation.

6. *Name of Public Accounting Firm*. The name identifies the public accounting firm or practitioner that has performed the audit. Typically, the firm's name is used, since the entire firm has the legal and professional responsibility to make certain the quality of the audit meets professional standards.

7. *Place of Issue*. Section 5400.32 suggests that the place of issue may be identified in the letterhead on which the auditor's report is printed or at the foot of the report as is illustrated in Figure 2–1.

8. *Auditor's Report Date*. The appropriate date for the report is the one on which the auditor has completed the most important auditing procedures in the field. Section 5405 refers to " . . . substantial completion of examination . . . ." This date is important to users because it indicates the last day of the auditor's responsibility for the review of significant events that occurred after the date of the financial statements. For example, if the balance sheet is dated December 31, 19X7, and the audit report is dated March 6, 19X8, the implication is that the auditor has searched for material, unrecorded transactions and events that occurred up to March 6, 19X8.

   Section 5405 discusses, among other things, double dating of the auditor's report. Double dating is done when an event occurs after the completion of field work and thus after the date of the auditor's report and before the date the report is issued. If the event is material, the auditor will review the amended financial statements for the inclusion of a note about the event and any additional disclosures that are required. The auditor will then double date the report as follows:

> March 6, 19X8
> except for Note
> 17 which is
> as of April 2, 19X8

If the event was so material as to change the financial statements significantly, the auditor would probably extend the audit for the financial statements as a whole and date the report with the revised date for completion of field work. In the example provided, the new date of the auditor's report might be April 2, 19X8.

Conditions Requiring a Departure

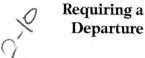

It is essential that auditors and readers of auditor's reports understand the circumstances when a standard unqualified report is not appropriate and the type of auditor's report issued in each circumstance. In the study of auditor's reports that depart from an unqualified report, there are three closely related topics that must be understood: the conditions requiring a departure from an unqualified opinion, the types of opinions other than unqualified, and materiality.

First, the two conditions requiring a departure are briefly summarized. Each is discussed in greater depth later in the chapter.

> **OBJECTIVE 3**
>
> List the two conditions requiring a departure from an unqualified auditor's report.

CONDITION 1. The Scope of the Auditor's Examination has been Restricted When the auditor has not accumulated sufficient evidence to determine if financial statements are stated in accordance with GAAP, a scope restriction exists. There are two major causes of scope restrictions: restrictions imposed by the client and those caused by circumstances beyond either the client's or auditor's control. An example of a client restriction is management's refusal to permit the auditor to confirm material receivables or to physically examine inventory. An example of a restriction caused by circumstances is when the engagement is not agreed upon until after the client's year end. It may not be possible to physically observe inventories, confirm receivables, or perform other important procedures after the balance sheet date.

CONDITION 2. The Financial Statements have not been Prepared in Accordance with Generally Accepted Accounting Principles Section 5510.06 lists three examples of departures from generally accepted accounting principles:

1. An inappropriate accounting treatment; for example, failure to capitalize a capital lease.
2. An inappropriate valuation of an item in the financial statements; for example, failure to provide an adequate allowance for doubtful accounts.
3. A failure to disclose essential information in an informative manner; for example, failure to adequately disclose a going concern situation.

Auditor's Reports Other than Unqualified

Whenever any of the three conditions requiring a departure from an unqualified report exists and is material, a report other than an unqualified report must be issued. Three main types of auditor's reports are issued under these conditions: *adverse opinion*, *denial of opinion*, and *qualified opinion*.

Review Engagement Report and *Notice to Reader* are the forms of communication on unaudited and compiled financial statements respectively. They are not, as their name implies, auditor's reports. Several types of *special reports* are issued by public accounting firms for audits of financial information other than financial statements, for reporting the results of applying specified auditing procedures to financial information other than financial statements and for audits of compliance with contractual agreements. Unaudited statements and special reports are considered in Chapter 23.

OBJECTIVE 4

Identify the three types of auditor's reports that can be issued when an unqualified opinion is not justified.

Adverse Opinion

An adverse opinion is used only when the auditor believes the overall financial statements are so *materially misstated or misleading* that they do not present fairly the financial position or results of operations and changes in financial position in conformity with generally accepted accounting principles (condition 2). The adverse opinion report can arise only when the auditor has knowledge, after an adequate investigation, of the absence of conformity. This is not a common occurrence and thus the adverse opinion is rarely employed.

Denial of Opinion

A denial is issued whenever the auditor has been *unable to satisfy himself or herself* that the overall financial statements are fairly presented. The necessity for denying an opinion may arise because of a *severe limitation on the scope* of the audit examination (condition 1) which would prevent the auditor from expressing an opinion on the financial statements as a whole.

The denial is distinguished from an adverse opinion in that it can arise only from a *lack of knowledge* by the auditor, whereas to express an adverse opinion the auditor must have knowledge that the financial statements are not fairly stated. Both denials and adverse opinions are used only when the condition is highly material.

Qualified Opinion

A qualified opinion can result from a limitation on the scope of the audit (condition 1) or failure to follow generally accepted accounting principles (condition 2).

A qualified opinion *can be used only when the auditor believes that the overall financial statements and the auditor's report result in fair presentation*. A denial or an adverse opinion must be used if the auditor believes the condition being reported upon is extremely material. For this reason, the qualified opinion is considered a less severe type of report for disclosing departures from an unqualified opinion.

A qualified opinion can take the form of a *qualification of both the scope and the opinion or of the opinion alone*. It is possible to have more than one qualification in the same report. A scope and opinion qualification can be issued only when the auditor has not been able to accumulate all the evidence required by generally accepted standards. Therefore, this type of qualification is used when the auditor's scope has been restricted by the client or when circumstances exist that prevent the auditor from conducting a complete audit (condition 1). The use of a qualification of the opinion alone is normally restricted to those situations in which condition 2 exists.

Whenever an auditor issues a qualified opinion, he or she must use either the term *except for* or, less frequently, *except that* and *except as* in the opinion paragraph. The implication is that the auditor is satisfied that the overall financial statements are correctly stated "except for" a particular part. Examples of qualifications are given later in the chapter. It is unacceptable to use these phrases with any type of audit opinion other than a qualified one.

The conditions requiring a departure from an unqualified report are summarized in Table 2–1.

It is worth noting that qualified opinions are fairly rare in practice. The provincial securities commissions will accept qualified statements from a public company only in rare circumstances. Lenders or creditors may not accept qualified statements from private companies.

Materiality

Materiality is an essential consideration in determining the appropriate type of report for a given set of circumstances. For example, if a misstatement is immaterial relative to the financial statements of the entity for the current period and is not expected to have a material effect in future periods, it is appropriate to issue an unqualified report. A common instance is the immediate expensing of office supplies rather than carrying the unused portion in inventory because the amount is insignificant.

OBJECTIVE 5

Explain how materiality affects audit reporting decisions.

The situation is totally different when the amounts are of such significance that the financial statements are materially affected as a whole. In these circumstances it is necessary to issue a *denial of opinion* or an *adverse opinion*, depending on the nature of the misstatement. In other situations, of lesser materiality, a qualified opinion is appropriate.

Definition

The common definition of materiality as it applies to accounting and, therefore, to audit reporting is

> A misstatement in the financial statements can be considered material if knowledge of the misstatement would affect a decision of a reasonable user of the statements.

In applying this definition, three graduations of materiality are used for determining the type of opinion to issue.

Amounts are immaterial When a misstatement in the financial statements exists, due to one of the two conditions identified in Table 2–1, but is unlikely to affect the decisions of a reasonable user, it is considered to be immaterial.

TABLE 2–1

Conditions Requiring
a Qualified Report

CONDITIONS	NATURE OF THE QUALIFICATION
1. Scope restricted by client or by circumstances	Scope and opinion (*except for*)
2. Statements are not in accordance with GAAP	Opinion only (*except for*)

Note: A qualified opinion is appropriate when the auditor is satisfied that the overall financial statements are fairly stated, but there is a material exception.

An unqualified opinion is therefore appropriate. For example, assume management recorded unexpired insurance as an asset in the previous year and decides to expense it in the current year to reduce record-keeping costs. Management has failed to follow GAAP (condition 2) but if the amounts are small, the misstatement would be immaterial, and a standard unqualified audit report would be appropriate.

Amounts are material but do not overshadow the financial statements as a whole The second level of materiality exists when a misstatement in the financial statements would affect a user's decision, but the overall statements are still fairly stated, and therefore useful. For example, knowledge of a large misstatement in permanent assets might affect a user's willingness to loan money to a company if the assets were the collateral. A misstatement of inventory does not mean that cash, accounts receivable, and other elements of the financial statements, or the financial statements as a whole, are materially incorrect.

To make materiality decisions when a condition requiring a departure from an unqualified report exists, the auditor must evaluate all effects on the financial statements. Assume the auditor is unable to satisfy himself or herself whether inventory is fairly stated (condition 1) in deciding on the appropriate type of opinion. Because of the effect of a misstatement in inventory on other accounts and on totals in the statements, the auditor needs to consider the materiality of the combined effect on inventory, total current assets, total working capital, total assets, income taxes, income taxes payable, total current liabilities, cost of goods sold, net income before taxes, and net income after taxes.

When the auditor concludes that a misstatement is material but does not overshadow the financial statements as a whole, a qualified opinion (using "except for") is appropriate.

Amounts are so material or so pervasive that overall fairness of statements is in question The highest level of materiality exists when users are likely to make incorrect decisions if they rely on the overall financial statements. To return to the previous example, if inventory is the largest balance on the financial statements, a large misstatement would probably be so material that the auditor's report should indicate the financial statements taken as a whole cannot be considered fairly stated. When the highest level of materiality exists, the auditor must issue either a denial of opinion or an adverse opinion depending on which conditions exist.

When determining whether an exception is highly material, the extent to which the exception affects different parts of the financial statements must be considered. This is referred to as *pervasiveness*. A misclassification between cash and accounts receivable affects only those two accounts and is therefore not pervasive. On the other hand, failure to record a material sale is highly pervasive in that it affects sales, accounts receivable, income tax expense, accrued income taxes, and retained earnings, which in turn affect current assets, total assets, current liabilities, total liabilities, owners' equity, gross margin, and operating income.

As errors become more pervasive, the likelihood of issuing an adverse opinion rather than a qualified opinion is increased. For example, suppose the auditor decides a misclassification between cash and accounts receivable should result in a qualified opinion because it is material; the failure to record a sale of the same dollar amount may result in an adverse opinion because of pervasiveness.

Materiality Decisions In concept, the effect of materiality on the type of opinion to issue is straightforward. In application, deciding upon actual materiality in a given situation is a difficult judgment. There are no simple, well-defined guidelines that enable auditors to decide when something is immaterial, material, or highly material.

Materiality decisions – non-GAAP condition There are differences in applying materiality to the conditions requiring a departure from an unqualified opinion. To illustrate the difficulties, discussion follows of the considerations affecting the materiality decision for the type of opinion to issue when the client has failed to correctly apply GAAP (unqualified, qualified, or adverse). Several aspects of materiality must be considered.

Dollar Amounts Compared with a Base The primary concern in measuring materiality when a client has failed to follow GAAP is usually the total dollar error in the accounts involved, compared with some base. A $10,000 misstatement might be material for a small company, but not for a larger one. Errors must, therefore, be compared with some measurement base before a decision can be made about the materiality of the failure to follow GAAP. Common bases include net income before taxes, revenue, gross profit, total assets, and equity.

For example, assume the auditor believes there is a $100,000 overstatement error in inventory because of the client's failure to follow GAAP. Also assume recorded inventory of $1,000,000, revenue of $10,000,000, and net income before taxes of $2,000,000. In this case, the auditor must evaluate the materiality of a misstatement of inventory of 10 percent, revenue of 1 percent, and net income before taxes of 5 percent.

To evaluate overall materiality, the auditor must also combine all unadjusted errors and judge whether there may be individually immaterial errors that, when combined, significantly affect the statements. In the inventory example above, assume the auditor believes there is also an overstatement error of $150,000 in accounts receivable. The total effect on revenue is now 2.5 percent ($250,000 divided by $10,000,000) and on net income before taxes is 12.5 percent ($250,000 divided by $2,000,000).

When comparing potential errors with a base, the auditor must carefully consider all accounts affected by a misstatement (pervasiveness). It is, for example, important not to overlook the effect of an understatement of inventory on income tax expense and accrued income taxes payable.

Measurability The dollar error of some misstatements cannot be accurately measured. For example, a client's unwillingness to disclose an existing lawsuit or the acquisition of a new company subsequent to the balance sheet date is difficult, if

3 things. Au considered when Deciding materiality
1: Amount.
2. Amount - Aggregate.
3. Pervasive.

CHAPTER 2   THE AUDITOR'S REPORT   **43**

TABLE 2–2

Relationship of Materiality to Type of Opinion

3 - Levels

MATERIALITY LEVEL	SIGNIFICANCE IN TERMS OF REASONABLE USER'S DECISIONS	TYPE OF OPINION
Immaterial	Decisions are unlikely to be affected.	Unqualified
Material	Decisions are likely to be affected only if the information in question is important to the specific decisions being made. The overall financial statements are considered fairly stated.	Qualified
Highly Material	Most or all decisions based on the financial statements are likely to be significantly affected.	Denial or Adverse

not impossible, to measure in terms of dollar errors. The materiality question the auditor must evaluate in such a situation is the effect on statement users of the failure to make the disclosure.

Nature of the Item   The decision of a user may also be affected by the kind of error in the statement. The following may affect the user's decision and, therefore, the auditor's opinion in a different way than most errors.

1. Transactions are illegal or fraudulent.
2. An item may materially affect some future period even though it is immaterial when only the current period is considered.
3. An item has a "psychic" effect (for example, small profit versus small loss or cash balance versus overdraft).
4. An item may be important in terms of possible consequences arising from contractual obligations (for example, the effect of failure to comply with a debt restriction may result in a material loan being called).

Materiality decisions – scope limitations condition   The size of *potential* errors, where there are scope limitations, is important in determining whether an unqualified report, a qualified report, or a denial of opinion is appropriate. For example, if recorded accounts payable of $400,000 was not audited, the auditor must evaluate the potential misstatement in accounts payable and decide how materially the financial statements could be affected. The pervasiveness of these potential misstatements must also be considered.

It is typically more difficult to evaluate the materiality of potential errors resulting from scope limitations than for failure to follow GAAP. Errors resulting from failure to follow GAAP are known. Those resulting from scope limitations must usually be subjectively measured in terms of potential or likely errors. For example, the recorded accounts payable of $400,000 might be understated by more than a million dollars, which may affect several totals including gross margin, net earnings, and total liabilities.

Discussion of Conditions Requiring a Departure

You should now understand the relationship among the conditions requiring a departure from an unqualified report, the major types of reports other than unqualified, and the three levels of materiality. This part of the chapter examines the conditions requiring a departure from an unqualified report in greater detail and shows examples of reports.

Auditor's Scope Has Been Restricted

There are two major categories of scope restrictions: those caused by a client and those caused by conditions beyond the control of either the client or the auditor. The effect on the auditor's report is the same for either, but the interpretation of materiality is likely to be different. Whenever there is a scope restriction, the appropriate response is to issue an unqualified report, a qualification of scope and opinion, or a denial of opinion, depending on materiality.

> **OBJECTIVE 6**
>
> Draft appropriately modified auditor's reports under a variety of circumstances.

For client-imposed restrictions, the auditor should be concerned about the possibility that management is trying to prevent discovery of misstated information. In such cases, it would probably be appropriate to issue a denial of opinion whenever materiality is in question. When restrictions are due to conditions beyond the client's control, a qualification of scope and opinion is more likely.

Two restrictions occasionally imposed by clients on the auditor's scope relate to the observation of physical inventory and the confirmation of accounts receivable, but other restrictions may also occur. Reasons for client-imposed scope restrictions may be a desire to save audit fees and, in the case of confirming receivables, to prevent possible conflicts between the client and customer when amounts differ. A qualified report or denial of opinion resulting from a client restriction requires a reservation paragraph to describe the restriction; the reservation paragraph is located between the scope and opinion paragraph. In addition, the opinion paragraph must be modified.

The most common case in which conditions beyond the client's and auditor's control cause a scope restriction is an engagement agreed upon after the client's balance sheet date. The confirmation of accounts receivable, physical examination of inventory, and other important procedures may not be possible under those circumstances. When the auditor cannot perform procedures he or she considers desirable but can be satisfied with alternative procedures that the information being verified is fairly stated, an unqualified report is appropriate. If alternative procedures cannot be performed, a scope qualification and, depending on the materiality, either an opinion qualification or a denial of opinion is necessary. A reservation paragraph would describe the restriction.

For example, the report in Figure 2–2 would be appropriate for an audit in which the amounts were material but not pervasive, and the auditor had not been on hand to observe inventory and could not satisfy himself or herself by alternative procedures. The first paragraph is omitted because it contains standard wording.

When the amounts are so material that a denial of opinion is required, the introductory, scope, and middle paragraphs could remain the same, but the opinion paragraph might be as shown in Figure 2–3.

Statements Are Not in Conformity with GAAP

When the auditor knows that the financial statements may be misleading because they were not prepared in conformity with generally accepted accounting principles, he or she must issue a qualified or an adverse opinion, depending on the materiality of the item in question. The opinion must clearly state the nature of the deviation from accepted principles and the amount of the misstatement, if it is known. Figure 2–4 shows an example of a qualified opinion when a client did not capitalize leases as required by GAAP. The first and second paragraphs are omitted because they include standard wording.

When the amounts are so material or pervasive that an adverse opinion is required, the scope would still be unqualified, the reservation paragraph could remain the same, but the opinion paragraph might be as shown in Figure 2–5.

FIGURE 2–2   Qualified Scope and Opinion Report due to Scope Restriction

---

AUDITOR'S REPORT

INTRODUCTORY PARAGRAPH	(Same introductory paragraph as standard report)
SCOPE PARAGRAPH – QUALIFIED	Except as explained in the following paragraph, we conducted our audit . . . (remainder is the same as the scope paragraph in the standard report).
THIRD PARAGRAPH – ADDED	We were unable to obtain audited financial statements supporting the Company's investment in a foreign affiliate stated at $475,000, or its equity in earnings of that affiliate of $365,000, which is included in net income, as described in Note X to the financial statements. Because of the nature of the Company's records, we were unable to satisfy ourselves as to the carrying value of the investment or the equity in its earnings by means of other auditing procedures.
OPINION PARAGRAPH – QUALIFIED	In our opinion, except for the effects of such adjustments, if any, as might have been determined to be necessary had we been able to examine evidence regarding the foreign affiliate investment and earnings, these financial statements present fairly, in all material respects, the financial position of Laughlin Corporation as of December 31, 19X5, and the results of its operations and the changes in its financial position for the year then ended in accordance with generally accepted accounting principles.

When the client fails to include information that is necessary for the fair presentation of financial statements in the body of the statements or in the related footnotes, it is the responsibility of the auditor to present the information in the audit report and to issue a qualified or an adverse opinion. It is common to put this type of qualification in an added paragraph (the scope paragraph will remain unqualified) and to refer to the added paragraph in the opinion paragraph. Figure

FIGURE 2–3   Denial of Opinion due to Scope Restriction

AUDITOR'S REPORT

INTRODUCTORY PARAGRAPH	(Same introductory paragraph as standard report)
SCOPE PARAGRAPH – QUALIFIED	(Same scope paragraph as Figure 2–2)
THIRD PARAGRAPH – ADDED	(Same third paragraph as Figure 2–2)
OPINION PARAGRAPH – DENIAL	In view of the possible material effects on the financial statements of the matters described in the preceding paragraph, we are unable to express an opinion as to whether these financial statements are presented fairly in accordance with generally accepted accounting principles.

FIGURE 2–4 Qualified Opinion Report due to Non-GAAP

AUDITOR'S REPORT

INTRODUCTORY AND SCOPE PARAGRAPHS

(Same introductory and scope paragraphs as standard report)

THIRD PARAGRAPH – ADDED

The Company has excluded from property and debt in the accompanying balance sheet certain lease obligations that, in our opinion, should be capitalized in order to conform with generally accepted accounting principles. If these lease obligations were capitalized, property would be increased by $4,600,000, long-term debt by $4,200,000, and retained earnings by $400,000 as of December 31, 19X5, and net income and earnings per share would be increased by $400,000 and $1.75, respectively, for the year then ended.

OPINION PARAGRAPH – QUALIFIED

In our opinion, except for the effects of not capitalizing lease obligations, as discussed in the preceding paragraph, these financial statements present fairly, in all material respects, the financial position of Ajax, Inc., as of December 31, 19X5, and the results of its operations and the changes in its financial position for the year then ended in accordance with generally accepted accounting principles.

2–6 shows an example of an audit report in which the auditor considered the financial statement disclosure inadequate.

Existence of More Than One Condition Requiring a Qualification

Auditors may encounter situations involving more than one of the conditions requiring modification of the unqualified report. In these circumstances, the auditor should qualify his or her opinion for each condition. Section 5510.33 states that "[it] is essential that all reservations be disclosed because the reader of an auditor's report should be able to assume that the financial statements, except with respect to matters on which the auditor has expressed a reservation of opinion, are presented fairly in accordance with generally accepted accounting principles." An example is presented in Figure 2–7.

FIGURE 2–5 Adverse Opinion due to Non-GAAP

AUDITOR'S REPORT

INTRODUCTORY AND SCOPE PARAGRAPHS

(Same introductory and scope paragraphs as standard report)

THIRD PARAGRAPH – ADDED

(Same third paragraph as that used for the third paragraph in Figure 2–4)

OPINION PARAGRAPH – ADVERSE

In our opinion, because of the effects of the matters discussed in the preceding paragraph, these financial statements do not present fairly, in accordance with generally accepted accounting principles, the financial position of Ajax, Inc. as of December 31, 19X5, or the results of its operations and the changes in its financial position for the year then ended.

FIGURE 2–6   Qualified Opinion due to Inadequate Disclosure

AUDITOR'S REPORT

INTRODUCTORY AND
SCOPE PARAGRAPHS

(Same introductory and scope paragraphs as standard report)

THIRD PARAGRAPH –
ADDED

On January 15, 19X8 the company issued debentures in the amount of $3,600,000 for the purpose of financing plant expansion. The debenture agreement restricts the payment of future cash dividends to earnings after December 31, 19X7. In our opinion, disclosure of this information is required to conform with generally accepted accounting principles.

OPINION
PARAGRAPH –
QUALIFIED

In our opinion, except for the omission of the information discussed in the preceding paragraph, these financial statements present fairly . . . (remainder is the same as the opinion in the standard report).

FIGURE 2–7   Qualified Opinion (Departure from GAAP and a Scope Limitation)

AUDITOR'S REPORT

INTRODUCTORY
PARAGRAPH

(Same introductory paragraph as standard report)

SCOPE PARAGRAPH –
MODIFIED WORDING

Except as explained in the following paragraph, we conducted our audit . . . (remainder is the same as the scope paragraph in the standard report).

THIRD PARAGRAPH –
ADDED

Management has advised us that the company may become liable with respect to guarantees given for a indebtedness of a subsidiary located in another country. However, management has declined to provide us with further information and will not permit us to contact the subsidiary as management believes disclosure is not in the company's best interests. As a result, we have been unable to obtain sufficient audit evidence to form an opinion with respect to the possible liability. Furthermore, the matter has not been disclosed in the notes to the financial statements. In our opinion, such disclosure is required under generally accepted accounting principles.

OPINION
PARAGRAPH –
MODIFIED WORDING

In our opinion, except that disclosure has not been made with respect to the contingent liability referred to in the preceding paragraph and except for the effect of adjustments, if any, which we may have determined to be necessary had we been able to obtain sufficient information regarding this matter, these financial statements present fairly, in all material respects, . . . (remainder is the same as the opinion in the standard report).

Reports Involving Reliance on Another Auditor or a Specialist

In Canada, although the main or primary auditor may rely on another auditor or a specialist in determining the appropriate opinion to issue on the financial statements, the primary auditor takes responsibility for that opinion, and only the name of the primary auditor appears on the auditor's report. *CICA Handbook* Sections 6930 and 5360 deal with the (primary) auditor's reliance on another auditor and on a specialist respectively.

The auditor may rely on another auditor because the client's business is either too complex or widespread and the primary auditor either does not have the personnel or the proximity to all the client locations to do the audits with his or her own personnel. For example, the primary auditor, a public accounting firm located in Halifax, may rely on another public accounting firm located in Regina as the secondary auditor to audit the Halifax client's subsidiary located in Regina.

Section 6930 requires the primary auditor to assess the secondary auditor's professional qualifications, competence and integrity in determining whether or not to rely on the secondary auditor. As you will discover in Chapter 4, the primary auditor who does rely on a secondary auditor is responsible for any deficiencies in the secondary auditor's work. The decision on whether or not to rely is based on the primary auditor's judgment.

As was mentioned above, if the primary auditor decides that an unqualified opinion is appropriate, the name of the secondary auditor is not mentioned. If however, the primary auditor decides that a qualified or denial of opinion is appropriate *and the qualification arises because of inability to rely on the work of the secondary auditor*, the explanation of the qualification in the third paragraph would mention the name of the secondary auditor in explaining the reason for the qualification.

The auditor may have to rely on a specialist, such as an actuary, in completing the audit. Normally the auditor would not mention the specialist nor reliance on the specialist. However, if the auditor believes that a qualified or denial of opinion is appropriate *and the qualification arises because of inability to rely on the work of the specialist*, the explanation of the qualification in the third paragraph would mention the name of the specialist in explaining the reason for the qualification.

Unqualified Auditor's Report with Explanatory Paragraph or Modified Wording

In certain situations, an unqualified auditor's report is issued, but the wording deviates from the standard unqualified report. It is important to distinguish between these reports and the qualified, adverse and denial reports already discussed. The *unqualified report with explanatory paragraph or modified wording* meets the criteria of a complete audit with satisfactory results and financial statements that are fairly presented, but the auditor believes it is important, or is required, to provide additional information. In a *qualified, adverse or denial report*, the auditor either has not performed a satisfactory audit or is not satisfied that the financial statements are fairly presented.

There are several reasons for the addition of an explanatory paragraph or a modification in the wording of the unqualified standard report:

- The appropriate disclosed basis of accounting is not generally accepted accounting principles
- The auditor wishes to provide additional explanatory information

Both of these situations are discussed in turn below.

> **OBJECTIVE 7**
>
> Describe the circumstances when an unqualified report with an explanatory paragraph or modified wording is appropriate.

Unqualified Auditor's Report When the Appropriate Disclosed Basis of Accounting Is Not Generally Accepted Accounting Principles

In certain situations an unqualified auditor's report is issued when the disclosed basis of accounting is not generally accepted accounting principles.

Section 5400.22 permits a departure from the *CICA Handbook* Recommendations when "the auditor concludes that following the Recommendations would result in misleading financial statements." An unqualified opinion is appropriate if the auditor is satisfied that the disclosure related to the departure is adequate.

Reporting standard (iv) requires the auditor's report to state "whether the financial statements present fairly, in all material respects, the financial position, results of operations and changes in financial position in accordance with an appropriate disclosed basis of accounting, which except in special circumstances should be generally accepted accounting principles." Section 5100.05 suggests that such situations might include financial statements prepared in accordance with regulatory legislation or with contractual requirements. In such circumstances the auditor would express the opinion that the financial statements presented fairly the financial position, results of operations, and changes in financial position in accordance with the disclosed basis of accounting.

Modifications in the Standard Unqualified Auditor's Report

The auditor may be reporting under the requirements of a statute that requires the auditor to include information in addition to that provided in the auditor's report. Normally, such explanatory information, if it is lengthy, should be included in a separate paragraph after the opinion paragraph. In addition, Section 5701.05 suggests that if the auditor wishes to expand his or her report to include other information and explanations, such information should also be included in a paragraph following the opinion paragraph. For example, when comparative financial statements are presented that were not audited or were audited by another auditor, that information would be disclosed in a paragraph following the opinion paragraph.

Changes in Generally Accepted Accounting Principles or the Application Thereof

Section 5400.17 requires the auditor to evaluate a change in accounting principle or in the application of an accounting principle in the financial statements being reported on and to assess whether or not the new principle, or the application, is in accordance with generally accepted accounting principles. In addition, the auditor must assess whether the method of accounting for the change, which may be retroactive or prospective, and the disclosure of the change are also in accordance with GAAP.

If the change, its application, and its disclosure are in accordance with GAAP, the auditor should express an unqualified opinion. On the other hand, if the change or its application or its disclosure in the financial statements are not in accordance with GAAP, the auditor should issue a qualified or adverse opinion.

Recall that the financial statements must be in accordance with generally accepted accounting principles or an appropriate disclosed basis of accounting. Accordingly, Section 5400.17 applies also in the case of a change when the basis of accounting is an appropriate disclosed basis and not GAAP.

Certain changes in the financial statements may not be changes in principle or in their application. Examples of such changes include:

1. Changes in an estimate, such as a decrease in the life of an asset for depreciation purposes.
2. Error corrections not involving principles, such as a previous year's mathematical error.
3. Variations in format and presentation of financial information.

4. Changes because of substantially different transactions or events, such as new endeavors in research and development or the sale of a subsidiary.

A change in estimate need not be disclosed in the notes although disclosure may be desirable. An error correction, on the other hand, must be fully disclosed.

Unusual Uncertainties Affecting the Financial Statements

A number of estimates are customarily made by management in the preparation of financial statements, including the useful lives of depreciable assets, the collectibility of receivables, and the realizability of inventory and other assets. There is usually enough evidence to permit reasonable estimation of these items. Sometimes, however, the auditor encounters a situation in which the outcome of a matter cannot be reasonably estimated at the time the statements are being issued. These matters are defined as contingencies. Examples include threats of the expropriation of assets, income tax or litigation contingencies (collectible or payable) and guarantees of the indebtedness of others.

There are also less specific situations in which the ability of the company to continue to operate as a going concern is open to question.[1] Section 5510.51-.53 of the *CICA Handbook* addresses this problem. For instance, the existence of one or more of the following factors causes uncertainty about the ability of a company to continue to operate:

- Recurring operating losses
- Serious deficiencies in working capital
- An inability to obtain financing sufficient for continued operations
- An inability to comply with terms of existing loan agreements
- The possibility of an adverse outcome of one or more contingencies
- Insufficient funds to meet liabilities
- A plan to significantly curtail or liquidate operations
- External factors that could force an otherwise solvent enterprise to cease operations

The auditor's concern in such situations is the possibility that recorded assets will not be recoverable at their recorded value. For example, fixed assets recorded at cost may be worth far less if the company is forced to liquidate because of bankruptcy.

The appropriate type of opinion to issue when either specific or general uncertainties exist depends on the materiality of the items in question and on the disclosure of the items by management in the notes. An unqualified opinion is appropriate if the uncertainty is not disclosed but is immaterial. If the amount involved is material but the accounting treatment, disclosure, and presentation of either a contingency or going concern problem are in accordance with GAAP, the auditor would not refer to the uncertainty in the auditor's report. The auditor must be very sure that the disclosure is such that it draws attention to the uncertainty.

Canadian practice prior to August 1980, and present American practice, required the auditor to draw the reader's attention to material contingencies or going concern problems by mention in the auditor's report. The topic was well researched by the Auditing Standards Committee of the CICA and that body concluded that disclosure of contingencies and going concern problems was management's responsibility. Therefore, if the contingency is accounted for and

---

1   For a thorough and interesting discussion of this topic see Boritz, J.E., *The "Going Concern" Assumption: Accounting and Auditing Implications*, Toronto: CICA, 1991.

disclosed in accordance with GAAP or if the going concern problem is adequately disclosed the auditor makes no mention of either in the auditor's report.

Negative Assurance

It is inappropriate to include in the auditor's report any additional comments that counterbalance the auditor's opinion. For example, the use of such terminology as "However, nothing came to our attention that would lead us to question the fairness of the presentations" as a part of a denial of opinion is inappropriate and a violation of the standards of reporting. A statement of this kind, which is referred to as negative assurance, tends to confuse readers about the nature of the auditor's examination and the degree of responsibility he or she is assuming.

The use of negative assurance is considered appropriate only in the case of review engagements (Section 8000) and prospectuses (Section 7000). These are considered in Chapter 23.

Summary

A summary of the types of audit reports and their use with the two conditions requiring a departure from an unqualified report is shown in Table 2–3.

The use of an additional paragraph to modify audit reports was discussed throughout this chapter. Ordinarily, an additional or third paragraph is not used, so users of audited financial statements often look to the presence of that paragraph as an important signal that something unusual exists regarding the financial statements that requires their attention.

TABLE 2–3

Auditor's Report for Each Condition Requiring a Departure from a Standard Unqualified Report at Different Levels of Materiality

CONDITIONS REQUIRING A DEPARTURE	LEVEL OF MATERIALITY		
	Immaterial	*Material, But Do Not Overshadow Financial Statements As A Whole*	*So Material That Overall Fairness is in Question*
Auditing Related Scope restricted by client or conditions	Unqualified report	Qualified scope, additional paragraph, and qualified opinion (*except for*)	Denial of opinion
Accounting Related Financial statements not prepared in accordance with GAAP*	Unqualified report	Additional paragraph and qualified opinion (*except for*)	Adverse opinion

* Or an appropriate disclosed basis of accounting.

REVIEW QUESTIONS

2–1 Explain why auditors' reports are important to users of financial statements.

2–2 What five circumstances are required for a standard unqualified report to be issued?

2–3 List the eight parts of an unqualified audit report and explain the meaning of each part. How do the parts compare with those found in a qualified report?

2–4 What are the purposes of the introductory paragraph in the auditor's report? Identify the most important information included in the introductory paragraph.

2–5 What are the purposes of the scope paragraph in the auditor's report? Identify the most important information included in the scope paragraph.

2–6 What are the purposes of the opinion paragraph in the auditor's report? Identify the most important information included in the opinion paragraph.

2–7 What is meant by the term "appropriate disclosed basis of accounting"? How does such a basis differ from GAAP? When is such a basis acceptable?

2–8 At times, for a variety of reasons, an auditor must rely on another firm of auditors to perform part of the audit. What reference does the primary auditor make to the secondary auditor in the auditor's report?

2–9 On February 17, 1989, a public accountant completed the examination on the financial statements for the Buckheizer Corporation for the year ended December 31, 19X8. The audit is satisfactory in all respects. On February 26 the auditor completed the tax return and the pencil draft of the financial statement. The final auditor's report was completed, attached to the financial statements, and delivered to the client on March 7. What is the appropriate date on the auditor's report?

2–10 List the conditions requiring a departure from an unqualified opinion, and give one specific example of each of those conditions.

2–11 Distinguish between a qualified opinion, an adverse opinion, and a denial of opinion, and explain the circumstances under which each is appropriate.

2–12 Define materiality as it is used in audit reporting. What conditions will affect the auditor's determination of materiality?

2–13 What is the difference between a scope limitation caused by client restrictions and a limitation resulting from conditions beyond the client's control? What is the effect of each on the auditor's work?

2–14 Identify the three alternative opinions that may be appropriate when the client's financial statements are not in accordance with GAAP. Under what circumstance is each appropriate?

2–15 Identify two different situations that may cause the client's financial statements to be not in accordance with GAAP. Briefly describe how the auditor's report would be different in each situation.

2–16 What type of opinion should an auditor issue when the financial statements are not in accordance with generally accepted accounting principles because the client obtained a court order permitting the non-adherence?

2–17 The client has restated the prior year statements to accord with a change from the use of accelerated to straight-line depreciation. How should this alteration be reflected in the auditor's report?

2–18 The client proposes not to treat the change in method of depreciation from straight-line to units-of-production retroactively because she cannot estimate the effect of the change on prior periods. How should this change be reflected in the auditor's report?

2–19 Explain what is meant by "contingencies." Give an example of a contingency and discuss its appropriate disclosure in the financial statements.

2–20 What is meant by "going concern" consideration? Provide an example of such a condition and disclose how it might be appropriately disclosed in the financial statements.

2–21 Discuss why the CICA requires "an objective state of mind" of the auditor.

2–22 When an auditor discovers more than one condition that requires modification of the unqualified report, what should the auditor's report include?

MULTIPLE CHOICE QUESTIONS

2-23 The following questions concern unqualified auditor's reports. Choose the best response.

a. An auditor's unqualified standard report

   (1) implies only that items disclosed in the financial statements and footnotes are properly presented and takes no position on the adequacy of disclosure.

   (2) implies that disclosure is adequate in the financial statements and footnotes.

   (3) explicitly states that disclosure is adequate in the financial statements and footnotes.

   (4) explicitly states that all material items have been disclosed in conformity with generally accepted accounting principles.

b. The date of a public accountant's opinion on the financial statements of a client should be the date of the

   (1) closing of the client's books.

   (2) receipt of the client's letter of representation.

   (3) completion of all important audit procedures.

   (4) submission of the report to the client.

c. A primary auditor would refer in the auditor's report to the examination of another auditor, because

   (1) the other auditor is not the primary auditor's agent.

   (2) the principle auditor was unable to express an opinion without reservation because of an inability to rely on the other auditor.

   (3) the work of the other auditor was material in relation to the primary auditor's work.

   (4) the primary auditor had doubts as to the competence of the secondary auditor. (AICPA adapted)

2-24 The following questions concern auditor's reports other than unqualified reports. Choose the best response.

a. If an auditor issues a non-GAAP auditor's report when there is a contingency, the reader of the auditor's report should conclude that

   (1) the auditor was not able to form an opinion on the financial statements taken as a whole.

   (2) the auditor became aware of the contingency after the balance sheet date but prior to the audit report date.

   (3) there were no audit procedures available to the auditor by which he or she could obtain satisfaction concerning the outcome of uncertainty.

   (4) the company will be unable to continue as a going concern.

b. A public accountant will issue an adverse auditor's opinion if

   (1) the scope of his or her examination is limited by the client.

   (2) his or her exception to the fairness of presentation is so material that an "except for" opinion is not justified.

   (3) he or she did not perform sufficient auditing procedures to form an opinion on the financial statements taken as a whole.

   (4) major uncertainties exist concerning the company's future such that an "except for" opinion is not justified.

c. An auditor will express an "except for" opinion if

   (1) the client refuses to provide for a probable income tax deficiency that is highly material.

(2) there is a high degree of uncertainty associated with the client company's future. *(handwritten: Lw Br Probably Disclose:)*

(3) he or she did not perform procedures sufficient to form an opinion on the consistency of application of generally accepted accounting principles.

(4) he or she is basing his or her opinion in part upon work done by another auditor.

d. Under which of the following set of circumstances should an auditor issue a qualified opinion?

(1) The financial statements contain a departure from generally accepted accounting principles, the effect of which is material.

(handwritten: Quality Scope.)
(2) The primary auditor decides to make reference to the report of another auditor who audited a subsidiary.

(handwritten: No consistent Applied Cons)
(3) There has been a material change between periods in the method of the application of accounting principles.

(4) Note disclosure describing significant uncertainties affecting the financial statements is not adequate. *(handwritten: Departure from Gaap.)*   (AICPA adapted)

DISCUSSION QUESTIONS AND PROBLEMS

2–25 A careful reading of a standard unqualified auditor's report indicates several important phrases. Explain why each of the following phrases or clauses is used rather than the alternative provided.

a. "In our opinion, these financial statements present fairly" rather than "These financial statements present fairly."

b. "We conducted our audit in accordance with generally accepted auditing standards" rather than "Our audit was performed to detect material errors in the financial statements."

c. "These financial statements present fairly, in all material respects, the financial position" rather than "These financial statements are correctly stated."

d. "In accordance with generally accepted accounting principles" rather than "are properly stated to represent the true economic conditions."

e. "Brown & Phillips, CAs (firm name)," rather than "James E. Brown, CA (individual partner's name)."

2–26 Roscoe, public accountant, has completed the examination of the financial statements of Excelsior Corporation as of and for the year ended December 31, 19X5. Roscoe also examined and reported on the Excelsior financial statements for the prior year. Roscoe drafted the following report for 19X5.

We have audited the balance sheet and statements of income and retained earnings of Excelsior Corporation as of December 31, 19X5. We conducted our audit in accordance with generally accepted accounting standards. Those standards require that we plan and perform the audit to obtain reasonable assurance about whether the financial statements are free of misstatement.

We believe that our audits provide a reasonable basis for our opinion.

In our opinion, the financial statements referred to above present fairly the financial position of Excelsior Corporation as of December 31, 19X5, and the results of its operations for the year then ended in conformity with generally accepted auditing standards, applied on a basis consistent with those of the preceding year.

Roscoe, Public Accountant
(Signed)

OTHER INFORMATION:

- Excelsior is presenting comparative financial statements.
- Excelsior does not wish to present a statement of cash flows for either year.
- During 19X5 Excelsior changed its method of accounting for long-term construction contracts and properly reflected the effect of the change in the current year's financial statements and restated the prior year's statements. Roscoe is satisfied with Excelsior's justification for making the change. The change is discussed in footnote 12.
- Roscoe was unable to perform normal accounts receivable confirmation procedures, but alternate procedures were used to satisfy Roscoe as to the validity of the receivables.
- Excelsior Corporation is the defendant in a litigation, the outcome of which is highly uncertain. If the case is settled in favor of the plaintiff, Excelsior will be required to pay a substantial amount of cash which might require the sale of certain fixed assets. The litigation and the possible effects have been properly disclosed in footnote 11.
- Excelsior issued debentures on January 31, 19X4, in the amount of $10,000,000. The funds obtained from the issuance were used to finance the expansion of plant facilities. The debenture agreement restricts the payment of future cash dividends to earnings after December 31, 19X9. Excelsior declined to disclose this essential data in the footnotes to the financial statements.

Required:
a. Identify and explain any items included in "Other Information" that need not be part of the auditor's report.
b. Explain the deficiencies in Roscoe's auditor's report as drafted.

(AICPA adapted)

2–27 For the following independent situations, assume you are the audit partner on the engagement:

1. During your examination of Debold Batteries Ltd., you conclude there is a possibility that inventory is materially overstated. The client refuses to allow you to expand the scope of your examination sufficiently to verify whether the balance is actually misstated.

2. You are auditing Woodcolt Linen Services, Inc., for the first time. Woodcolt has been in business for several years but has never had an audit before. After the audit is completed, you conclude that the current year balance sheet is stated correctly in accordance with GAAP. The client did not authorize you to do test work for any of the previous years.

3. You were engaged to examine the Cutter Steel Corp.'s financial statements after the close of the corporation's fiscal year. Because you were not engaged until after the balance sheet date, you were not able to physically observe inventory, which is highly material. On the completion of your audit, you are satisfied that Cutter's financial statements are presented fairly, including inventory about which you were able to satisfy yourself by the use of alternative audit procedures.

4. Four weeks after the year-end date, a major customer of Prince Construction Ltd. declared bankruptcy. Because the customer had confirmed the balance due to Prince at the balance sheet date, management refuses to charge off the account or otherwise disclose the information. The receivable represents approximately 10 percent of accounts receivable and 20 percent of net earnings before taxes.

5. You complete the audit of Johnson Department Store Ltd., and, in your opinion, the financial statements are fairly presented. On the last day of the examination,

you discover that one of your supervisors assigned to the audit had a material investment in Johnson.

6. Auto Delivery Company Ltd. has a fleet of several delivery trucks. In the past, Auto Delivery had followed the policy of purchasing all equipment. In the current year they decided to lease the trucks. The method of accounting for the trucks is therefore changed to lease capitalization. This change in policy is fully disclosed in footnotes.

Required:

For each situation, state the type of auditor's report that should be issued. If your decision depends on additional information, state the alternative reports you are considering and the additional information you need to make the decision.

2–28 For the following independent situations, assume you are the audit partner on the engagement:

1. Kieko Corporation has prepared financial statements but has decided to exclude the statement of changes in financial position. Management explains to you that the users of their financial statements find that particular statement confusing and prefer not to have it included.

2. Jet Stream Airlines, Inc., has been audited by your firm for ten years. In the past three years their financial condition has steadily declined. In the current year, for the first time, the current ratio is below 2:1, which is the minimum requirement specified in Jet Stream's major loan agreement. You now have reservations about the ability of Jet Stream to continue in operation for the next year.

3. Approximately 20 percent of the audit for Fur Farms, Inc., was performed by a different public accounting firm, selected by you. You have reviewed their working papers and believe they did an excellent job on their portion of the audit. Nevertheless, you are unwilling to take complete responsibility for their work.

4. The controller of Fair City Hotels Co. Ltd. will not allow you to confirm the receivable balance from two of its major customers. The amount of the receivable is material in relation to Fair City's financial statements. You are unable to satisfy yourself as to the receivable balance by alternative procedures.

5. In the last three months of the current year, Oil Refining Corp. decided to change direction and go significantly into the oil drilling business. Management recognizes that this business is exceptionally risky and could jeopardize the success of its existing refining business, but there are significant potential rewards. During the short period of operation in drilling, the company has had three dry wells and no successes. The facts are adequately disclosed in footnotes.

6. Your client, Auto Rental Corporation, has changed from straight-line to accelerated depreciation. The effect on this year's income is immaterial, but the effect in future years is likely to be material. The facts are adequately disclosed in footnotes.

Required:

State the appropriate auditor's report from the following choices:

a. Unqualified – standard wording

b. Qualified opinion only – except for

c. Scope and opinion qualified

d. Denial

e. Adverse

2–29 The following are independent situations for which you will recommend an appropriate auditor's report:

1. Subsequent to the date of the financial statements as part of the postbalance sheet date audit procedures, a public accountant learned of heavy damage to one of a client's two plants due to a recent fire; the loss will not be reimbursed by insurance. The newspapers described the event in detail. The financial state-

ments and appended notes as prepared by the client did not disclose the loss caused by the fire.

2. A public accountant is engaged in the examination of the financial statements of a large manufacturing company with branch offices in many widely separate cities. The public accountant was not able to count the substantial undeposited cash receipts at the close of business on the last day of the fiscal year at all branch offices.

    As an alternative to this auditing procedure used to verify the accurate cutoff of cash receipts, the public accountant observed that deposits in transit as shown on the year-end bank reconciliation appeared as credits on the bank statement on the first business day of the new year. The public accountant was satisfied as to the cutoff of cash receipts by the use of the alternative procedure.

3. On January 2, 19X7, the Retail Auto Parts Company Limited received a notice from its primary supplier that, effective immediately, all wholesale prices would be increased 10 percent. On the basis of the notice, Retail Auto Parts revalued its December 31, 19X6, inventory to reflect the higher costs. The inventory constituted a material proportion of total assets; however, the effect of the revaluation was material to current assets but not to total assets or net income. The increase in valuation is adequately disclosed in the footnotes.

4. During 19X7, the research staff of Scientific Research Corporation devoted its entire efforts toward developing a new pollution-control device. All costs that could be attributed directly to the project were accounted for as deferred charges and classified on the balance sheet at December 31, 19X7, as a noncurrent asset. In the course of her audit of the corporation's 19X7 financial statements, Marika, public accountant, found persuasive evidence that the research conducted to date would probably result in a marketable product. The deferred research charges are significantly material in relation to both income and total assets.

5. For the past five years a public accountant has audited the financial statements of a manufacturing company. During this period, the examination scope was limited by the client as to the observation of the annual physical inventory. Since the public accountant considered the inventories to be of material amount and he was not able to satisfy himself by other auditing procedures, he was not able to express an unqualified opinion on the financial statements in each of the five years.

    The public accountant was allowed to observe physical inventories for the current year ended December 31, 19X7, because the client's banker would no longer accept the auditor's reports. In the interest of economy, the client requested the public accountant not to extend his audit procedures to the inventory as of January 1, 19X7.

6. During the course of the examination of the financial statements of a corporation for the purpose of expressing an opinion on the statements, a public accountant is refused permission to inspect the minute books. The corporation secretary instead offers to give the public accountant a certified copy of all resolutions and actions relating to accounting matters.

7. A public accountant has completed her examination of the financial statements of a bus company for the year ended December 31, 19X7. Prior to 19X7, the company had been depreciating its buses over a ten-year period. During 19X7, the company determined that a more realistic estimated life for its buses was 12 years and computed the 19X7 depreciation on the basis of the revised estimate. The public accountant has satisfied herself that the 12-year life is reasonable.

    The company has adequately disclosed the change in estimated useful lives of its buses and the effect of the change on 19X7 income in a note to the financial statements.

Required:

a. For each situation, identify the reason the auditor would qualify the auditor's report where qualification is warranted.

b. State the appropriate auditor's report from the following alternatives:
   (1) Unqualified – standard wording
   (2) Qualified opinion only – except for
   (3) Qualified scope and opinion
   (4) Denial
   (5) Adverse

(AICPA adapted)

2–30 GAAP (*CICA Handbook*, Section 1000.23) suggests that accounting principles need to be consistently applied if the financial statements of an entity are to be comparable over time. Users of audited financial statements are entitled to assume therefore that accounting principles have been consistently applied unless the footnotes and/or the auditor's report provide information to the contrary.

Assume that the following list describes changes that have a material effect on a client's financial statements for the current year.

1. A change from the FIFO method of inventory pricing to the LIFO method of inventory pricing.
2. A change from the completed-contract method to the percentage-of-completion method of accounting for long-term construction contracts.
3. A change in the estimated useful life of previously recorded fixed assets based on newly acquired information.
4. Correction of a mathematical error in inventory pricing made in a prior period.
5. A change from direct costing to full absorption costing for inventory valuation.
6. A change from presentation of statements of individual companies to presentation of consolidated statements.
7. A change from deferring and amortizing preproduction costs to recording such costs as an expense when incurred because future benefits of the costs have become doubtful. The new accounting method was adopted in recognition of the change in estimated future benefits.
8. A change in the percentages applied to aged accounts receivable in determining the appropriate allowance for doubtful accounts. The new percentages are based on a change in the company's credit policy.

Required:

Identify the type of change described in each item above, and indicate how the change would be disclosed to users of the financial statements. Organize your answer sheet as shown below. For example, the change from the FIFO method of inventory pricing to the LIFO method of inventory pricing described in (1) above would appear as shown.

Assume that each item is material.

ITEM NO.	TYPE OF CHANGE	DESCRIPTION OF DISCLOSURE
1.	A change from one generally accepted method of cost determination of inventory for another generally accepted method of cost determination of inventory.	The change should be applied retroactively with restatement of all prior periods presented. The notes to the financial statements should describe the change and the effect of the change as well as the fact that the change was applied retroactively.

(AICPA adapted)

2–31 You are the senior on the audit of Kootenay Real Estate Holdings Ltd., a company listed on the Vancouver Stock Exchange whose year-end is December 31. As you complete your audit and prepare your auditor's report you learn that a U.S.

subsidiary, Kootenay (U.S.), Inc., whose year-end is September 30, has been subjected to a series of foreclosures over the past four months on properties located in Texas. Although you are concerned that the continued viability of Kootenay (U.S.) may be threatened, the management of the Canadian parent does not want to delay the issue of the consolidated financial statements. Management will not permit you to request the auditors of the U.S. firm to follow up on your discovery.

Required: Draft the auditor's report you deem to be appropriate for the year ended December 31, 19X7. Consider Kootenay (U.S.), Inc., to be material to the Canadian parent. The audit was completed March 9, 19X8.

2–32 You are the in-charge on the audit of Saskatoon Building Products Limited (SBP), a company listed on the Alberta Stock Exchange. In the course of your audit for the year ended March 31, 19X2, you discover that SBP's working capital ratio is below 2:1 and that therefore the company is in default on a substantial loan from Prairie Bank. Management announces to you its intention to sell a large block of provincial bonds that were included in long-term investments, and some land that had been purchased for expansion that was included in fixed assets and proposes including the bonds and land as current assets pending disposition. Such inclusion would increase the current ratio to 2.2:1.

Prairie Bank and your client have not enjoyed cordial relations of late, and you have been advised by Avril Chui, the manager of the Saskatoon branch, that they "are looking forward to receiving the audited statements because they are concerned that SBP has been having problems."

Required: (a) Draft the memo to your partner outlining the problem.

(b) Draft the auditor's report.

2–33 The following are two unrelated situations:

1. You are the auditor of Xact Ltd., a company which at December 31, 19X7, had working capital of $200,000, total assets of $2,500,000, and total liabilities of $2,200,000. During the three years ended December 31, 19X7, the company has sustained operating losses totalling $700,000.

Management has been informed that Butler Inc. will not renew a debenture they hold issued by Xact in the amount of $500,000 and maturing September 30, 19X8. The debenture is presently classed as a long-term liability. Although preliminary discussions have already been held with various commercial lenders, it presently appears uncertain as to whether Xact will be able to refinance this debt. In addition, it appears doubtful that Xact will be able to obtain short-term borrowing to finance the debt.

2. Your client, Bat Ltd., owns 15 percent of the shares of Bird Ltd. The 19X7 pre-tax net income of Bat is $1,000,000 and its shareholder's equity is $3,000,000.

The investment in Bird is carried on Bat's balance sheet (as of December 31, 19X7) at $250,000, which represents original cost. Bird has incurred significant losses in the past few years. A current appraisal by a qualified business valuator indicates that the current market value of 100 percent of the issued and outstanding shares of Bird is $1,000,000. You are also aware that an investor who held 20 percent of the shares of Bird recently sold those shares for $180,000.

Your client, Bat Ltd., insists that the shares be shown at their original cost of $250,000 but is willing to expand note disclosure.

Required: (a) Outline with reasons possible deviations (if any) from a standard auditor's report that may be necessary. State your assumptions.

(b) Outline the minimum note disclosure you would consider adequate in the circumstances. What additional disclosure would be desirable?

(CICA adapted)

2–34   The following is an auditor's report, except for the opinion paragraph, of Tri-Nation Corp.

AUDITOR'S REPORT

To the Shareholders of Tri-Nation Corp.

We have audited the accompanying consolidated balance sheet of Tri-Nation Coin Investments and subsidiaries as of July 31, 19X6, and the related statements of income, shareholders' equity, and changes in financial position for the year then ended. These financial statements are the responsibility of the company's management. Our responsibility is to express an opinion on these financial statements based on our audit.

Except as explained in the following paragraph, we conducted our audit in accordance with generally accepted auditing standards. Those standards require that we plan and perform an audit to obtain reasonable assurance whether the financial statements are free of material misstatement. An audit includes examining, on a test basis, evidence supporting the amounts and disclosures in the financial statements. An audit also includes assessing the accounting principles used and significant estimates made by management, as well as evaluating the overall financial statement presentation.

The company had significant deficiencies in internal control including the lack of detailed records and certain supporting data which were not available for our examination. Therefore, we were not able to obtain sufficient evidence in order to form an opinion on the accompanying financial statements including whether the inventory at July 31, 19X6 ($670,490) was stated at lower of cost or market, or whether the deferred subscription revenue ($90,260) is an adequate estimate for the applicable liability, as discussed in notes 5 and 12, respectively.

Required: Write the opinion paragraph for this auditor's report. State any assumptions you have made.

2–35   The following tentative auditor's report was drafted by a staff accountant and submitted to a partner in the public accounting firm of Better & Best.

AUDITOR'S REPORT

To the Audit Committee of Athabaska Widgets, Inc.

We have examined the consolidated balance sheet of Athabaska Widgets, Inc., and subsidiaries as of December 31, 19X4, and the related consolidated statement of income, retained earnings, and changes in financial position for the year then ended. These financial statements are the responsibility of the company's management. Our responsibility is to express an opinion on these financial statements based on our audit.

Our examinations were made in accordance with generally accepted auditing standards as we considered necessary in the circumstances. Other auditors examined the financial statements of certain subsidiaries and have furnished us with reports thereon containing no exceptions. Our opinion expressed herein, insofar as it relates to the amounts included for those subsidiaries, is based solely upon the reports of the other auditors.

As discussed in note 4 to the financial statements, on January 8, 19X5, the company halted the production of certain medical equipment as a result of inquiries by the Alberta Medical Association, which raised questions as to the adequacy of some of the company's sterilization equipment and related procedures. Management is not in a position to evaluate the effect of this production halt and the ensuing litigation, which may have an adverse effect on the financial position of Athabaska Widgets, Inc.

As fully discussed in note 7 to the financial statements, in 19X4 the company extended the use of the average cost method of accounting to include all inventories. In examining inventories, we engaged Dr. Irwin Same (Nobel Prize winner 19X2) to test check the technical requirements and specifications of certain items of equipment manufactured by the company.

In our opinion, except for the effects, if any, on the financial statements of the ultimate resolution of the matter discussed in the second preceding paragraph, the financial statements referred to above present fairly the financial position of Athabaska Widgets, Inc., as of December 31, 19X4, the results of operations for the year then ended, in conformity with generally accepted accounting principles.

To be signed by
Better & Best

March 1, 19X5, except for note 4
as to which the date is January 8, 19X5

Required: Identify deficiencies in the staff accountant's tentative report that constitute departures from the generally accepted standards of reporting.   (AICPA adapted)

CASE

2–36 Following are the complete financial statements of the Young Manufacturing Corporation and the auditor's report of their examination for the year ended January 31, 19X7. The examination was conducted by John Smith, an individual practitioner who has examined the corporation's financial statements and has reported on them for many years.

YOUNG MANUFACTURING CORPORATION
Statements of Condition January 31, 19X7 and 19X6

	19X7	19X6
Assets		
Current assets:		
Cash	$ 43,822	$ 51,862
Accounts receivable, pledged – less allowances for doubtful accounts of $3,800 in 19X7 and $3,000 in 19X6 (see note)	65,298	46,922
Inventories, pledged – at average cost, not in excess of replacement cost	148,910	118,264
Other current assets	6,280	5,192
Total current assets	$264,310	$222,240

Fixed assets:		
Land – at cost	38,900	62,300
Buildings – at cost, less accumulated depreciation of $50,800 in 19X7 and $53,400 in 19X6	174,400	150,200
Machinery and equipment – at cost, less accumulated depreciation of $30,500 in 19X7 and $25,640 in 19X6	98,540	78,560
Total fixed assets	$311,840	$291,060
Total assets	$576,150	$513,300

Liabilities and Shareholders' Equity

Current liabilities:		
Accounts payable	$ 27,926	$ 48,161
Other liabilities	68,743	64,513
Current portion of long-term mortgage payable	3,600	3,600
Income taxes payable	46,840	30,866
Total current liabilities	$147,109	$147,140

	19X7	19X6
Long-term liabilities:		
Mortgage payable	90,400	94,000
Total liabilities	$237,509	$241,140
Shareholders' equity:		
Capital stock, no par value, 1,000 shares authorized, issued and outstanding	$100,000	$100,000
Retained earnings	238,641	172,160
Total shareholders' equity	$338,641	$272,160
Total liabilities and shareholders' equity	$576,150	$513,300

YOUNG MANUFACTURING CORPORATION
Income Statements for the Year Ended January 31, 19X7 and 19X6

	19X7	19X6
Income:		
Sales	$884,932	$682,131
Other income	3,872	2,851
Total	$888,804	$684,982
Costs and expenses:		
Costs of goods sold	$463,570	$353,842
Selling expenses	241,698	201,986
Administrative expenses	72,154	66,582
Provision for income taxes	45,876	19,940
Other expenses	12,582	13,649
Total	$835,880	$655,999
Net income	$ 52,924	$ 28,983

To: Mr. Paul Young, President   January 31, 19X7
     Young Manufacturing Corporation

I have examined the balance sheet of the Young Manufacturing Corporation and the related statements of income and retained earnings.

These statements present fairly the financial position and results of operations in conformity with generally accepted principles of accounting applied on a consistent basis. My examination was made in accordance with generally accepted auditing standards and, accordingly, included such tests of the accounting records and such other auditing procedures as I considered necessary in the circumstances.

(Signed) John Smith

Required:

List and discuss the deficiencies of the auditor's report prepared by John Smith. Your discussion should include justifications that the matters you cited are deficiencies. (Do not check the additions in the statements. Assume that the additions are correct.)   (AICPA adapted)

3

PROFESSIONAL ETHICS

LEARNING OBJECTIVES

THOROUGH STUDY OF THIS CHAPTER WILL ENABLE YOU TO:

1. Distinguish ethical behavior from unethical behavior in personal, professional, and business contexts

2. Identify ethical dilemmas and describe how they can be addressed

3. Describe the ethical concerns specific to the accounting profession

4. Explain the purpose and general content of a typical professional accounting code of ethics

5. Discuss independence as it applies to a public accountant

6. Discuss confidentiality as it applies to a public accountant

7. Discuss the standard of behavior required of a public accountant

8. Discuss integrity and due care as they apply to a public accountant

9. Discuss the responsibility of a public accountant to maintain professional competence

10. Discuss the responsibility of a public accountant neither to associate himself or herself with false or misleading information nor to fail to reveal material omissions from the financial statements but rather to comply with the standards of practice incorporated in the Recommendations of the *CICA Handbook*

11. Discuss advertising and solicitation from the perspective of a public accountant

12. Discuss other rules of conduct, including those dealing with contingent fees and with reporting breaches of the rules

☐ Ethics is a topic that is receiving a great deal of attention throughout our society today. This attention is an indication of both the importance of ethical behavior to maintaining a civil society, and a significant number of notable instances of unethical behavior. The authors believe that ethical behavior is the backbone of the practice of public accounting and deserving of serious study by all accounting students. This chapter is intended to motivate such study. It begins with a definition and discussion of ethics at a general level, continues with a consideration of ethical dilemmas and how they can be approached, and ends with a discussion of ethics in the accounting profession focused on certain of the more important rules of conduct of Chartered Accountants and Certified General Accountants, who make up the bulk of practicing public accountants in Canada. Certified Management Accountants and Certified Internal Auditors also have rules of conduct promulgated by their respective organizations, but their rules tend to focus more on their dealings with their employers than on their relationship with the public.

While certain of the rules to be discussed, such as integrity and due care, are common to CAs, CGAs, CMAs, and CIAs, others, such as independence, relate more to public accountants performing the attest function and engaged in internal auditing. The focus of this chapter will be on, primarily, those rules of conduct which apply to public accounting; many of those rules also apply to internal auditing. The references to public accountants or professional public accountants in this chapter are to CAs, CGAs or CMAs who serve the public in a variety of ways through the firms to which they belong; the references are not to firms made up of individuals who may also provide services to the public but who do not have a professional designation.

What Are Ethics?

Ethics can be defined broadly as a set of moral principles or values. Each of us has such a set of values, although we may or may not have considered them explicitly. Philosophers, religious organizations, and other groups have defined in various ways ideal sets of moral principles or values. Examples of prescribed sets of moral principles or values at the implementation level include laws and regulations, church doctrine, codes of business ethics for professional groups such as CAs, CGAs, CMAs, CIAs and codes of conduct within individual organizations.

An example of a prescribed set of principles that was developed by the Josephson Institute for the Advancement of Ethics is included in Figure 3–1. The Josephson Institute was established as a not-for-profit foundation to encourage ethical conduct of professionals in the fields of government, law, medicine, business, accounting, and journalism.

OBJECTIVE 1

Distinguish ethical behavior from unethical behavior in personal, professional, and business contexts.

FIGURE 3–1
Illustrative Prescribed Ethical Principles

The following list of ethical principles incorporates the characteristics and values that most people associate with ethical behavior.

Honesty Be *truthful, sincere, forthright, straightforward, frank, candid*; do not *cheat, steal, lie, deceive,* or act *deviously*.

Integrity Be *principled, honorable, upright, courageous,* and *act on convictions*; do not be *two-faced,* or *unscrupulous,* or adopt an *end-justifies-the-means* philosophy that ignores principle.

Promise Keeping Be *worthy of trust, keep promises, fulfill commitments, abide by the spirit as well as the letter of an agreement*; do not interpret agreements in an *unreasonably technical or legalistic manner* in order to rationalize noncompliance or create excuses and justifications for breaking commitments.

Loyalty (Fidelity) Be *faithful* and *loyal* to family, friends, employers, clients, and country; do not *use or disclose information learned in confidence*; in a professional context, *safeguard the ability to make independent professional judgments* by scrupulously *avoiding undue influences and conflicts of interest.*

Fairness Be *fair* and *open-minded,* be willing to admit error and, where appropriate, change positions and beliefs, demonstrate a commitment to *justice,* the *equal treatment* of individuals, *tolerance for and acceptance of diversity,* do not *overreach* or *take undue advantage of another's mistakes or adversities.*

Caring for Others Be *caring, kind,* and *compassionate; share,* be *giving,* be of *service to others; help those in need* and *avoid harming others.*

Respect for Others Demonstrate *respect for human dignity, privacy,* and *the right to self-determination* of all people; be *courteous, prompt,* and *decent; provide others with the information they need to make informed decisions about their own lives;* do not *patronize, embarrass,* or *demean.*

Responsible Citizenship *Obey just laws;* if a law is unjust, openly protest it; *exercise all democratic rights and privileges responsibly* by *participation* (voting and expressing informed views), *social consciousness* and *public service;* when in a position of leadership or authority, *openly respect* and *honor democratic processes of decision making, avoid unnecessary secrecy* or *concealment of information,* and *assure that others have all the information they need to make intelligent choices and exercise their rights.*

Pursuit of Excellence *Pursue excellence* in all matters; in meeting your personal and professional responsibilities, be *diligent, reliable, industrious,* and *committed;* perform all tasks to the *best of your ability,* develop and maintain a *high degree of competence,* be *well informed* and *well prepared;* do not be *content with mediocrity;* do not *"win at any cost."*

Accountability Be *accountable, accept responsibility for decisions,* for the *foreseeable consequences of actions and inactions,* and for *setting an example for others.* Parents, teachers, employers, many professionals, and public officials have a special obligation to *lead by example,* to *safeguard and advance the integrity and reputation of their families, companies, professions and the government itself;* an ethically sensitive individual *avoids even the appearance of impropriety,* and *takes whatever actions are necessary to correct or prevent inappropriate conduct of others.*

It is common for people to differ in their moral principles or values. For example, a person might examine the Josephson Institute's ethical principles and conclude that several principles should not be included. Even if two people agree on the ethical principles that determine ethical behavior, it is unlikely that they will agree on the relative importance of each principle. These differences result from all of our life experiences. Parents, teachers, friends, and employers are known to influence our values, but so do television, team sports, life successes and failures, and thousands of other experiences.

Need for Ethics Ethical behavior is necessary for a society to function in an orderly manner. It can be argued that ethics is the glue that holds a society together. Imagine, for example, what would happen if we couldn't depend on the people we deal with to be honest. If parents, teachers, employers, siblings, coworkers, and friends all consistently lied, it would be almost impossible for effective communication to occur.

The need for ethics in society is sufficiently important that many commonly held ethical values are incorporated into laws. For example, laws dealing with driving while intoxicated and selling drugs concern responsible citizenship and respect for others. Similarly, if a company sells a defective product it can be held accountable if harmed parties choose to sue through the legal system.

A considerable portion of the ethical values of a society cannot be incorporated into law, because of the judgmental nature of certain values. Looking again at Figure 3–1 at the honesty principle, it is practical to have laws that deal with cheating, stealing, lying, or deceiving others. It is far more difficult to establish meaningful laws that deal with many aspects of principles such as integrity, loyalty, and pursuit of excellence. That does not imply that these principles are less important for an orderly society.

Why People Act Unethically Most people define unethical behavior as conduct which differs from what they believe would have been appropriate given the circumstances. Each of us decides for ourselves what we consider unethical behavior, both for ourselves and others. It is important to understand what causes people to act in a manner that we decide is unethical.

There are two primary reasons why people act unethically: the person's ethical standards are different than those of society as a whole, or the person chooses to act selfishly. In many instances, both reasons exist.

Person's ethical standards differ from general society Extreme examples of people whose behavior violates almost everyone's ethical standards are drug dealers, bank robbers, and larcenists. Most people who commit such acts feel no remorse when they are apprehended because their ethical standards differ from those of society as a whole.

There are also many far less extreme examples where others violate our ethical values. When people cheat on their tax returns, treat other people with hostility, lie on employment applications, or perform below their competence level as employees, most of us regard that as unethical behavior. If the other person has decided that this behavior is ethical and acceptable, there is a conflict of ethical values that is unlikely to be resolved.

The person chooses to act selfishly The difference between ethical standards that differ from general society's and acting selfishly is illustrated in the following example. Person A finds a briefcase in an airport containing important papers and $1,000. He tosses the briefcase and keeps the money. He brags to his family and friends about his good fortune. Person A's values probably differ from most of society's. Person B faces the same situation but responds differently. He keeps the money but leaves the briefcase in a conspicuous place. He tells nobody and spends the money on a new wardrobe. It is likely that Person B has violated his own ethical standards, but he decided that the money was too important to pass up. He has chosen to act selfishly.

A considerable portion of unethical behavior results from selfish behavior. Watergate and other political scandals resulted from the desire for political power; cheating on tax returns and expense reports is motivated by financial greed; performing below one's competence and cheating on tests are typically due to laziness. In each case, the person knows that the behavior is inappropriate, but chooses to do it anyway because of the personal sacrifice needed to act ethically.

Ethics in Business

There have been many well-publicized cases of failures by businesspersons to conduct their affairs consistently with society's ethical values. For example, recently a well-known food manufacturer admitted to intentionally mislabeling a food product for the purpose of reducing product costs. Similarly, management of several financial institutions over the past decade have been charged with misusing company assets for personal gain and in some cases converting company assets to personal use.There are several potential effects of these types of cases and the frequent criticisms of business in movies, television, and other media. One is to create the impression that unethical business behavior is normal behavior. Another is to conclude that management cannot conduct itself ethically and also have its business succeed financially. Finally and perhaps most important is to conclude that actions must be extreme to constitute unethical behavior. There is considerable evidence that none of these conclusions about business ethics is correct. A large number of highly successful businesses follow ethical business practices because management believes that it has a social responsibility to conduct itself ethically, but also because it is good business to do so. For example, it is socially responsible to treat employees, customers, and vendors honestly and fairly, but in the long run such actions also result in business success.

The decision of management to operate its business ethically is not a new business philosophy. For example, in the 1930s, Rotary International developed its code of ethics that is still used extensively by millions of businesspeople. It uses four questions that are called the *Four Way Test* of ethical behavior for any ethical issue a business faces:

- Is it the truth?
- Is it fair to all concerned?
- Will it build goodwill and better friendships?
- Will it be beneficial to all concerned?

Many companies have established their own formal ethical codes of conduct for management and employees. These codes are intended to encourage all personnel to act ethically and to provide guidance as to what constitutes ethical behavior. For example, the last paragraph of the Report of Management from the Schneider Corporation annual report (Figure 5-4 on page 136) discusses management's responsibility for the ethical conduct of the company and its employees and states that the company has adopted a code of conduct to govern management conduct.

Ethical Dilemmas

An ethical dilemma is a situation a person faces in which a decision must be made about the appropriate behavior. A simple example of an ethical dilemma is finding a diamond ring which necessitates deciding whether to attempt to find the owner or to keep it. A far more difficult ethical dilemma to resolve is the following one; it is the type of case that might be used in an ethics course:

OBJECTIVE 2

Identify ethical dilemmas and describe how they can be addressed.

- Qin Zhang is the in-charge on the September 30, 19X3, audit of Paquette Forest Products Inc., a forest products company that produces lumber and paper products in northern Manitoba. The company employs 375 people and is the main employer in the remote town of Duck Lake, Manitoba; the other businesses in Duck Lake provide goods and services to Paquette Forest Products and its employees.

    In the course of the audit, Qin discovers that the company has had a number of failures of the equipment that removes the sulphuric acid from the paper production process and as a result thousands of gallons of untreated water have been dumped into the Loon River and Duck Lake. Qin learns that the cost of replacing the equipment so that no further spills are likely is much more than the company can afford and that if ordered to replace the equipment by the environment ministry, the company would be forced to cease operations. What should Qin do?

Auditors, accountants, and other business people face many ethical dilemmas in their business careers. Dealing with a client who threatens to seek a new auditor unless an unqualified opinion is issued presents a serious ethical dilemma if an unqualified opinion is inappropriate. Deciding whether to confront a supervisor who has materially overstated departmental revenues as a means of receiving a larger bonus is a difficult ethical dilemma. Continuing to be a part of the management of a company that harasses and mistreats employees or treats customers dishonestly is a moral dilemma, especially if the person has a family to support and the job market is tight.

Resolving Ethical Dilemmas

There are alternative ways to resolve ethical dilemmas, but care must be taken to avoid methods that are rationalizations of unethical behavior. The following are rationalization methods commonly employed that can easily result in unethical conduct:

Everybody does it The argument that it is acceptable behavior to falsify tax returns, cheat on exams, or sell defective products is commonly based on the rationalization that everyone else is doing it and therefore it is acceptable.

If it's legal, it's ethical Using the argument that all legal behavior is ethical relies heavily on the perfection of laws. Under this philosophy, one would have no obligation to return a lost object unless the other person could prove that it was his or hers.

Likelihood of discovery and consequences This philosophy relies on evaluating the likelihood that someone else will discover the behavior. Typically, the person also assesses the severity of the penalty (consequences) if there is a discovery. An example is deciding whether to correct an unintentional overbilling to a customer where the customer has already paid the full billing. If the seller believes the customer will detect the error and respond by not buying in the future, the seller will inform the customer now, otherwise the seller will wait to see if the customer complains.

In recent years, formal frameworks have been developed to help people resolve ethical dilemmas. The purpose of such a framework is in identifying the ethical issues and deciding an appropriate course of action using the person's own values. The six-step approach that follows is intended to be a relatively simple approach to resolving ethical dilemmas:

1. Obtain the relevant facts.
2. Identify the ethical issues from the facts.
3. Determine who is affected by the outcome of the dilemma and how each person or group is affected.
4. Identify the alternatives available to the person who must resolve the dilemma.
5. Identify the likely consequence of each alternative.
6. Decide the appropriate action.

An illustration is used to demonstrate how a person might use this six-step approach to resolve an ethical dilemma.

Ethical Dilemma   Bryan Longview has been working six months as a staff assistant for De Souza & Shah, public accountants. Currently he is assigned to the audit of Reyon Manufacturing Corp. under the supervision of Karen Van Staveren, an experienced audit senior. There are three auditors assigned to the audit, including Karen, Bryan, and a more experienced assistant, Martha Mills. During lunch on the first day, Karen says, "It will be necessary for us to work a few extra hours on our own time to make sure we come in on budget. This audit isn't very profitable anyway, and we don't want to hurt our firm by going over budget. We can accomplish this easily by coming in a half hour early, taking a short lunch break, and working an hour or so after normal quitting time. We just won't write that time down on our time report." Bryan recalls reading in the firm's policy manual that working hours and not charging for them on the time report is a violation of De Souza & Shah's employment policy. He also knows that seniors are paid bonuses, instead of overtime, whereas staff are paid for overtime but get no bonuses. Later, when discussing the issue with Martha, she says, "Karen does this on all of her jobs. She is likely to be our firm's next audit manager. The partners think she's great because her jobs always come in under budget. She rewards us by giving us good engagement evaluations, especially under the cooperative attitude category. Several of the other audit seniors follow the same practice."

Resolving the
Ethical Dilemma
Using the Six-Step
Approach

Relevant facts   There are three key facts in this situation that deal with the ethical issue and how the issue will likely be resolved:

- The staff person has been informed he will work hours without recording them as hours worked.
- Firm policy prohibits this practice.
- Another staff person has stated that this is common practice in the firm.

Ethical issue   The ethical issue in this situation is not difficult to identify. Is it ethical for Bryan to work hours and not record them as hours worked in this situation?

Who is affected and how is each affected   There are typically more people affected in situations where ethical dilemmas occur than would normally be expected. The following are the key persons involved in this situation:

WHO	HOW AFFECTED
Bryan	Being asked to violate firm policy.
	Hours of work will be affected.
	Pay will be affected.
	Performance evaluations may be affected.
	Attitude about firm may be affected.
Martha	Same as Bryan.
Karen	Success on engagement and in firm may be affected.
	Hours of work will be affected.
De Souza & Shah	Stated firm policy is being violated.
	May result in under billing clients in the current and future engagements.
	May affect firm's ability to realistically budget engagements and bill clients.
	May affect the firm's ability to motivate and retain employees

| Staff assigned to Reyon Manufacturing in the future | May result in unrealistic time budgets. May result in unfavorable time performance evaluations. May result in pressures to continue practice of not charging for hours worked. |
| Other staff in firm | Following the practice on this engagement may motivate others to follow the same practice on other engagements. |

Bryan's available alternatives

- Refuse to work the additional hours.
- Perform in the manner requested.
- Inform Karen that he will not work the additional hours or will charge the additional hours to the engagement.
- Talk to a manager or partner about Karen's request.
- Refuse to work on the engagement.
- Quit working for the firm.

Each of these options includes a potential consequence, the worst likely one being termination by the firm.

Consequences of each alternative In deciding the consequences of each alternative, it is essential to evaluate both the short- and long-term effects. There is a natural tendency to emphasize the short term because those consequences will occur quickly, even when the long-term consequences may be more important. For example, consider the potential consequences if Bryan decides to work the additional hours and not report them. In the short term, he will likely get good evaluations for cooperation and perhaps a salary increase. In the longer term, what will be the effect of not reporting the hours this time when other ethical conflicts arise? Consider the following similar ethical dilemmas Bryan might face in his career as he advances:

- A supervisor asks Bryan to work 3 unreported hours daily and 15 each weekend.
- A supervisor asks Bryan to initial certain audit procedures as having been performed when they were not.
- Bryan concludes that he cannot be promoted to manager unless he persuades assistants to work hours that they do not record.
- Management informs Bryan, who is now a partner, that either the company gets an unqualified opinion for a $40,000 audit fee or the company will change auditors.
- Management informs Bryan that the audit fee will be increased $25,000 if Bryan can find a plausible way to increase earnings by $1 million.

Notice how each dilemma is more serious than the one preceeding it; the penalty that Bryan would face if he were to be caught grows more severe as the dilemma grows more serious. In short, if Bryan agrees to work the additional hours and not report them, he has put himself on a slippery slope that grows ever steeper.

Appropriate action Only Bryan can decide the appropriate option to select in the circumstances after considering his ethical values and the likely consequences of each option. At one extreme Bryan could decide that the only relevant consequence is the potential impact on his career. Most of us would conclude that Bryan is an unethical person if he follows that course. At the other extreme, Bryan can decide to refuse to work for a firm that permits even one supervisor to violate firm policies. Many people would consider such an extreme reaction naive.

Special Need for Ethical Conduct in Professions

Our society has attached a special meaning to the term professional. A professional is expected to conduct him- or herself at a higher level than most other members of society. For example, when the press reports that a physician, clergyperson, member of Parliament, or CA, CGA, or CMA has been indicted for a crime, most people feel more disappointment than when the same thing happens to people who are not labeled as professionals.

The term professional means a responsibility for conduct that extends beyond satisfying the person's responsibilities to him-or herself and beyond the requirements of our society's laws and regulations. A CA, CGA, or CMA in public practice, as a professional, recognizes a responsibility to the public, to the client, and to fellow practitioners, including honorable behavior, even if that means personal sacrifice.

The underlying reason for a high level of professional conduct by any profession is the need for *public confidence* in the quality of service by the profession, regardless of the individual providing it. For the professional public accountant, it is essential that the client and external financial statement users have confidence in the quality of audits and other services. If users of services do not have confidence in physicians, judges, or public accountants, the ability of those professionals to serve clients and the public effectively is diminished.

It is not practical for users to evaluate the performance of professional services because of their *complexity*. A patient cannot be expected to evaluate whether an operation was properly performed. A financial statement user cannot be expected to evaluate audit performance. Most users have neither the competence nor the time for such an evaluation. Public confidence in the quality of professional services is enhanced when the profession encourages high standards of performance and conduct on the part of all practitioners.

In recent years increased competition has made it more difficult for professional public accountants and many other professionals to conduct themselves in a professional manner. Increased competition sometimes has the effect of making public accounting firms more concerned about keeping clients and maintaining a reasonable profit. Because of the increased competition, many public accounting firms have implemented philosophies and practices that are frequently referred to as *improved business practices*. These include such things as improved recruiting and personnel practices, better office management, and more effective advertising and other promotional methods. Public accounting firms are also attempting to become more efficient in doing audits in a variety of ways. For example, they are obtaining efficiency through the use of microcomputers, effective audit planning, and careful assignment of staff.

Most people, including the authors, believe these changes are desirable for our society's benefit as long as they do not interfere with the conduct of CAs, CGAs, or CMAs as professionals. A public accounting firm can implement effective business practices and still conduct itself in a highly professional manner.

OBJECTIVE 3
Describe the ethical concerns specific to the accounting profession.

FIGURE 3–2

Ways the Profession
and Society Encourage
Public Accountants to
Conduct Themselves at
a High Level

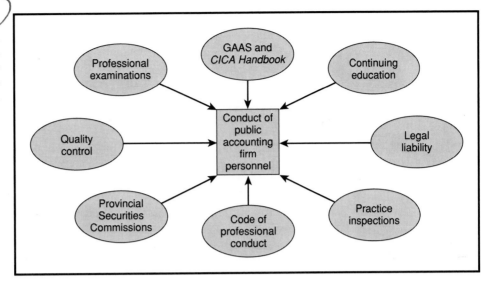

*Difference Between
Public Accounting
Firms and Other
Professionals*

Public accounting firms who provide attestation services have a different relationship with users of financial statements than most other professionals have with the users of their services. Lawyers, for example, are typically engaged and paid by a client and have primary responsibility to be an advocate for that client. Public accounting firms providing attestation services are engaged and paid by the company issuing the financial statements, but the primary beneficiaries of the audit are statement users. Frequently the auditor doesn't know or have contact with the statement users, but has frequent meetings and ongoing relationships with client personnel.

It is essential that users regard such public accounting firms as competent and unbiased. If users were to believe that such public accounting firms do not perform a valuable service (reduce information risk), the value of those firms' audit and other attestation reports would be reduced, and the demand for audits would thereby also be reduced. There is, therefore, considerable incentive for such public accounting firms to conduct themselves at a high professional level.

**Ways
Professional
Accountants in
Public Practice
Are Encouraged
to Conduct
Themselves
Professionally**

There are several ways in which society and the accounting bodies whose respective members are in public practice conducting audits (for example CAs and CGAs) encourage those in public practice to conduct themselves appropriately and to do high-quality audits and related services. Figure 3–2 shows the most important ways. Several of these were discussed in Chapter 1 including GAAS requirements and the Recommendations of the *CICA Handbook*, professional examinations, quality control, the provincial securities commissions, practice inspection, and continuing education. The ability of individuals to sue public accounting firms also exerts considerable influence on the way practitioners conduct themselves and audits. Legal liability is studied in Chapter 4. The *code of professional conduct* of the public accountant's respective accounting body also has a significant influence on the practitioner. It is meant to provide a standard of conduct for members of that body. These codes, some of their more important tenets and related issues of professional conduct are the content of the remainder of this chapter.

Code of Professional Conduct

OBJECTIVE 4

Explain the purpose and content of a *code of professional conduct*.

A code of conduct can consist of *general statements* of ideal conduct or *specific rules* that define unacceptable behavior. The advantage of general statements is the emphasis on positive activities that encourage a high level of performance. The disadvantage is the difficulty of enforcing general ideals because there are no minimum standards of behavior. The advantage of carefully defined specific rules is the enforceability of minimum behavior and performance standards. The disadvantage is the tendency of some practitioners to define the rules as maximum rather than minimum standards.

A code of conduct serves both the members of the body promulgating the code and the public. It serves members by setting standards the members must meet and providing a benchmark against which the members will be measured by their peers. The public is served because the code provides it with a list of the standards to which the members of the body adhere and helps the public determine their expectations of members' behavior.

The provincial institutes and Quebec *ordre* of chartered accountants determine the rules of professional conduct for members and students of that provincial institute or *ordre*. At the present time there is a move underway to harmonize the rules across Canada so that all chartered accountants will be bound by the same rules. Certain of the rules (for example, confidentiality, which is discussed below) apply to students as well as to members. All of the rules apply to members in public practice, while a smaller number of them also apply to members who are not engaged in the practice of public accounting. A recent development is to apply the rules of conduct to public accounting firms as well as to individual members; previously, only individual members of a firm could face charges before the Discipline Committee. This change had been suggested by the Commission to Study the Public's Expectation of Audits[1] as well as by members of the chartered accountancy profession over the past several years.

The rules of conduct for certified general accountants are determined by the CGAAC and apply to all CGAs in Canada; the provincial associations are charged with administering the code and have the power to amend and add to this national code of conduct. The rules do not apply to students. While all the rules apply to members in public practice, certain of the rules apply also to "accountants in employment"; that is, members not in public practice.

The rules of conduct for certified management accountants are a provincial matter. They do not apply to students who are aspiring to become members. The provincial societies do not differentiate between members in public practice and other members, although certain rules do apply to members in public practice.

Generally the codes of conduct of the three professional accounting bodies, the CICA, the CGAAC and the SMAC, have attempted to accomplish both the objectives of general statements of ideal conduct and of specific rules. For example, there are three parts to the *Rules of Professional Conduct* of the Institute of Chartered Accountants of Ontario: principles which are stated in broad terms, the rules themselves, and interpretations of the rules. Figure 3–3 is illustrative. The parts are listed in order of increasing specificity: the principles provide ideal standards of conduct, whereas ethical rulings are more specific, and the interpretations are very specific.

1 See Recommendation 26, "50 Ways to Change Our Ways," *CA Magazine* (July 1988), pp. 37 and 44.

FIGURE 3–3

Code of Professional
Conduct

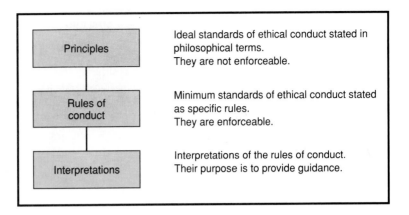

Principles	Ideal standards of ethical conduct stated in philosophical terms. They are not enforceable.
Rules of conduct	Minimum standards of ethical conduct stated as specific rules. They are enforceable.
Interpretations	Interpretations of the rules of conduct. Their purpose is to provide guidance.

Principles of Professional Conduct

The principles generally are characteristics that the professional body deems desirable in its members. An organization is judged by the behavior of its members; therefore, one principle would be that members behave in a way that enhances and does not detract from the reputation of all the members. Members should act ethically and act in a way that will serve the public interest. When a member of a profession is disciplined by the courts, the profession's reputation suffers along with that of the member. It is a mistake to think that only the member loses reputation in such a situation.

Other common principles are that members act with integrity and due care in the performance of their professional activities, that they maintain (that is, keep current) their professional competence, that they do not undertake work for which they lack the necessary competence, and that they behave in a professional way towards colleagues. The accountant must keep confidential the affairs and business of the client. There is one principle that relates more specifically to public accountants: the accountant should ensure that he or she maintains an independent or objective state of mind when providing attestation services (for example, audits or reviews) for clients.

A careful examination of these principles will likely lead us to conclude that most are applicable to any professional, not just professional accountants. For example, physicians should behave in a way that is not discreditable to their profession, they should act ethically and in a way that serves the public interest, and they should exercise integrity and due care. Physicians should maintain their professional competence and behave in a professional way towards their colleagues. They should not breach their clients' confidentiality. One difference between auditors and other professionals, as discussed earlier, is that most professionals need not be concerned about remaining independent.

These principles will be explored more fully in the balance of this chapter.

Rules of Conduct

The discussion that follows will consider some of the more important rules of conduct followed by public accountants in Canada. A student interested in obtaining a particular professional designation (e.g., CA, CGA, CMA, or CIA) should refer to the specific rules of conduct of the body to which he or she seeks admission.

As was mentioned previously, while all the rules discussed below apply to members of the professional accounting bodies in public practice, some of the rules discussed do not apply to members who are not engaged in the practice of public accounting. The difference will be apparent in the ensuing discussion.

Figure 3–3 indicated that while principles are not enforceable, the rules of conduct are. For that reason, the rules of conduct of the accounting bodies are stated in more precise language than the principles can be. Because of their enforceability, the rules are often called *Rules or Code of Professional Conduct*.

The difference between the standards of conduct set by the *principles* and those set by the *rules of conduct* is shown in Figure 3–4. When practitioners conduct themselves at the minimum level in Figure 3–4, that does not imply unsatisfactory conduct. The profession has presumably set the standards sufficiently high to make the minimum conduct satisfactory.

At what level do practitioners conduct themselves in practice? As in any profession, the level varies among practitioners. Some operate at high levels, whereas others operate as close to the minimum level as possible. Unfortunately, some also conduct themselves below the minimum level set by the profession. It is hoped that there are few of those.

Interpretations of Rules of Conduct

The need for published interpretations of the rules of conduct arises when there are frequent questions from practitioners about a particular rule. The various institutes and *ordre* of chartered accountants issue interpretations of certain rules of conduct together with the rules themselves. Interpretations are not officially enforceable, but a departure from the interpretations would be difficult, if not impossible, for a practitioner to justify in a disciplinary hearing.

Applicability of the Rules of Conduct

As was mentioned previously, the rules of conduct for CAs and CGAs specifically state that the rules apply to *all* members except that certain rules may not apply to members who are not in public practice.

It would be a violation of the rules if someone did something on behalf of a member that would have been a violation if the member had done it. An example is a banker who states in a newsletter that Johnson and Able, public accountants, have the best tax department in the province and consistently get large refunds for their tax clients. That is likely to create false or unjustified expectations and is a violation of both the CA and CGA rules of conduct.

A member is also responsible for compliance with the rules by employees and partners.

Definitions

A few definitions must be understood to minimize misinterpretation of the rules to be discussed below.

Client The person(s) or entity which retains a member or his or her firm, engaged in the practice of public accounting, for the performance of professional services.

Firm A proprietorship or partnership engaged in the practice of public accounting, including individual partners thereof.

Member A member of the Canadian Institute of Chartered Accountants (and a provincial institute or *ordre*) or of the Certified General Accountants Association of Canada (and a provincial association).

FIGURE 3–4
Standards of Conduct

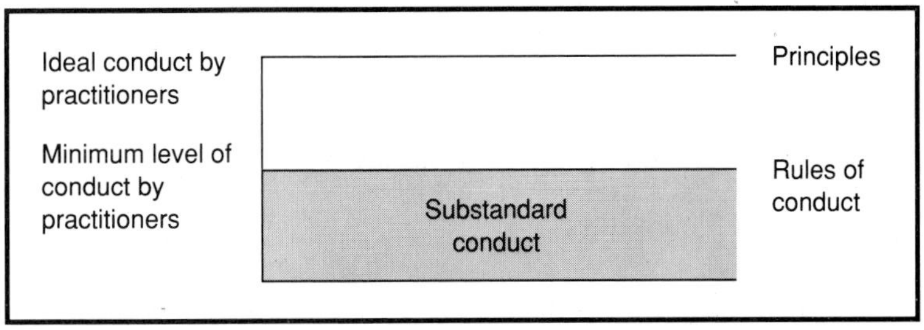

The intent of this section is to discuss several rules of conduct that are fundamental to the practice of public accounting. As such, they are found in differing forms and to differing degrees in the rules of professional conduct of CAs, CGAs, CMAs and CIAs. It must be pointed out that the rules of conduct governing the behavior of these four groups of professionals are much more extensive and detailed than the ensuing discussion; a student wishing to become a CA, a CGA, a CMA or a CIA should become familiar with the rules of professional conduct for the accounting body who issues those designations.

Practice of public accounting Holding out to be a public accountant and at the same time performing for a client one or more types of services rendered by public accountants.

Summary of the Basic Components of a Code of Conduct

Independence

OBJECTIVE 5

Discuss independence as it applies to a public accountant.

Cause +
Appearance.

Generally, the rules of conduct promulgated by the accounting bodies require their members who are engaged in the practice of public accounting to be independent when they perform certain functions. For example, the rules require that auditors of historical financial statements be independent. Independence may also be required for other types of attestation engagements such as review engagements. However the rules usually permit a public accounting firm to do tax returns and provide management services without being independent.

As you learned in Chapter 1, independence is also very important for internal auditors if they are to properly carry out their jobs. *Standards for the Professional Practice of Internal Auditing* published by the Institute of Internal Auditors provides guidance to persons engaged in internal auditing, not just to members of the IIA. The first standard in the publication states that "Internal auditors should be independent of the activities they audit." It is possible for internal auditors to be independent even though they are employees of their client; this can be accomplished through the internal auditor's organizational status and by the internal auditor having an independent mental attitude. The ensuing discussion will focus on attest audits but applies equally to internal audits.

Independence is one of the most important rules of conduct and it tends to be thoroughly discussed. This is as it should be. Without independence the attest function has no relevance in society.

Independence in auditing means taking an *unbiased viewpoint* in the performance of audit tests, the evaluation of the results, and the issuance of the auditor's report. If the auditor is an advocate for the client, a particular banker, or anyone else, he or she cannot be considered independent. Independence must certainly be regarded as the auditor's most critical characteristic. The reason that many diverse users are willing to rely upon the professional public accountant's reports as to the fairness of financial statements is their expectation of an unbiased viewpoint.

Not only is it essential that professional public accountants maintain an independent attitude in fulfilling their responsibilities, but it is also important that the users of financial statements have confidence in that independence. These two objectives are frequently identified as *independence in fact* and *independence in appearance*. Independence in fact exists when the auditor is actually able to maintain an unbiased attitude throughout the audit, whereas independence in appearance is the result of others' interpretations of this independence. If auditors are independent in fact but users believe them to be advocates for the client, most of the benefit of the audit function will be lost.

Although it is possible to take the extreme position that anything affecting either independence in fact or in appearance must be eliminated to ensure a high level of respect in the community, it is doubtful whether this would solve as many problems as it would create. The difficulty with this position is that it is likely to restrict significantly the services offered to clients, the freedom of public accountants to practice in the traditional manner, and the ability of public accounting firms to hire competent staff. At this point it will be helpful to examine some conflicts of independence that have arisen, evaluate their significance, and determine how the profession has resolved them.

Four Facets of Independence

Independence may be broadly thought of as having four facets

- financial independence
- independence of mental attitude
- investigative independence
- reporting independence

The four facets essential to independence are discussed in turn below.

Financial independence   Financial independence relates to having a financial interest in the client and may be manifested by:

- owning stock in the client
- owing money to or being owed money by a client (considerations such as banking at a client bank or being owed an audit fee by the client would be excluded)
- having a single client whose fee(s) represents a major portion of the public accountant's total revenue
- being engaged and paid by management. In some audit situations, while the shareholders appoint the auditors at their annual meeting, in fact the shareholders are voting on a firm suggested by management, the very people whose work the auditor will be reviewing. One way to improve the situation is to have the audit committee of the board of directors nominate the auditors. Independence is also enhanced if the audit committee, which is discussed in more detail below, sets the audit fee and determines the scope of the audit in consultation with the auditors.
- performing management advisory services for the client. This point has been contentious for a number of years. One group believes that an auditor can become so beholden to a client that the auditor will fail to have the appropriate scepticism; for example, the consultancy fee may exceed the audit fee. Another group believes that the public accountants's professionalism will result in a proper audit and that there are synergistic effects for both the audit and the management advi-

sory services flowing from the same firm doing both. The issue is not resolved; there are no specific bars to performing management consulting for an audit client in the various rules of professional conduct.

Rules of conduct of the CAs, CGAs, and CMAs deal with financial independence because lack of independence is likely to affect the users' perceptions of the auditors' independence. It is the authors' experience that individual public accounting firms often have rules that are more stringent than those of the professional association. This is especially true with respect to independence. Some public accounting firms do not permit any ownership by staff of client's stock regardless of which office serves the client. These firms have decided to have higher requirements than the minimums set by the rules of conduct of the various professional associations.

Independence of mental attitude An independent mental attitude is essential to achieving independence in fact. Section 5000.04 of the *CICA Handbook* states that "The auditor performs the audit with an attitude of professional scepticism" while assuming management's good faith. Section 5000.04 captures the spirit of independence of mental attitude. The auditor should not allow long association or friendship to colour his or her evaluation, nor should the auditor approach an audit with the view that management and the employees are dishonest.

An auditor's professionalism dictates that the auditor be unbiased; however, there is no yardstick, as there is with financial independence, to measure whether or not the auditor has an independent mental attitude. This is an issue which the auditor must decide for him- or herself.

Investigative independence Investigative independence means that the auditor has the time and resources (that is, the fee is adequate for the job and staffing is appropriate for the job) to obtain sufficient appropriate evidence and that the auditor has access to all evidence needed to reach the proper opinion as to the fairness of the financial statements. Investigative independence would be impaired if there was a deadline so that the job was rushed, if the fee was too low so that the auditor cut back on testing, or if the auditor was denied access to evidence (for example, if the auditor were not permitted to count inventory).

Reporting independence Reporting independence means reporting at a sufficiently high level that the report will be acted on. For example, an auditor who reported to management, when the auditor believed management to be guilty of fraud, would not have reporting independence. On the other hand, if the auditor reported to an audit committee (discussed below) made up of independent (i.e., non-management) members of the board of directors, the auditor would have reporting independence.

Summary Independence is broader than not owning shares in a client. The four facets of independence discussed above take the broadest view of independence; all four must be present if the auditor is to be truly independent.

Audit Committee An audit committee is a selected number of members of a company's board of directors who provide a forum that is independent of management for both the external and internal auditors. Most audit committees are made up of three to five or sometimes as many as seven directors; the majority of the committee must be outside directors (i.e., not part of company management).

A typical audit committee decides such things as which public accounting firm to retain and the scope of services the public accounting firm is to perform. The audit committee also meets with the public accounting firm to discuss the progress and findings of the audit and helps resolve conflicts between the public accounting firm and management. Many of the same comments could be made about the audit committee and the internal auditors. While audit committees are looked upon with favor by most auditors, users, and management, they exist mainly on the boards of directors of larger companies.

Section 165(1) of the *Canada Business Corporations Act* states that an audit committee is required for all companies incorporated under the Act that distribute their securities to the public. Section 165(2) permits the Director who administrates the *Canada Business Corporations Act* to waive this requirement if he or she thinks such a waiver is appropriate. The sole duty required of a member of the audit committee by the Act is in Section 165(3) and is to review the financial statements before they are issued. Other incorporating acts also require corporations to have audit committees; the responsibilities assigned to the committee vary.

The auditor has the right to attend meetings of the audit committee and to call meetings if he or she feels they are necessary. Directors who become aware of *any* misstatements in issued financial statements must notify the auditor and the audit committee of the misstatements.

The audit committee may do the minimum required by statute or may be more active. Among other activities, some audit committees

- Review the entire annual report
- Review the scope and cost of the audit with the external auditors
- Act as a liaison between the external auditors and management
- Adjudicate disputes between the external auditors and management
- Act as a liaison between the internal auditors and management
- Adjudicate disputes between the internal auditors and management.

Needless to say, the audit committee can add significantly to the external auditor's independence.

Bookkeeping Services and Audits for the Same Client

If a public accountant records transactions in the journals for the client, posts monthly totals to the general ledger, makes adjusting entries, and subsequently does an audit, there is some question as to whether the public accountant can be independent in his or her audit role. Generally, the rules of conduct permit a public accounting firm to do both bookkeeping and auditing for the same client. This conclusion is presumably based on a comparison of the effect on independence of having both bookkeeping and auditing services performed by the same public accounting firm with the additional cost of having a different public accounting firm do the audit. There are three important requirements that the auditor should satisfy before it is acceptable to do bookkeeping and auditing for the client:

1. The client must accept full responsibility for the financial statements. The client must be sufficiently knowledgeable about the enterprise's activities and financial condition and the applicable accounting principles so that the client can reasonably accept such responsibility, including the fairness of valuation and presentation and the adequacy of disclosure. When necessary, the public accountant

should discuss accounting matters with the client to be sure that the client has the required degree of understanding.

2. The public accountant must not assume the role of employee or of management conducting the operations of an enterprise. For example, the public accountant should not consummate transactions, have custody of assets, or exercise authority on behalf of the client. The client must prepare the source documents on all transactions in sufficient detail to identify clearly the nature and amount of such transactions and maintain accounting control over data processed by the public accountant, such as control totals and document counts.

3. The public accountant, in making an examination of financial statements prepared from books and records that the public accountant has maintained completely or in part, must conform to generally accepted auditing standards. The fact that the public accountant has processed or maintained certain records does not eliminate the need to make sufficient audit tests.

The first two requirements are often difficult to satisfy for smaller clients where the owner may have little knowledge of or interest in accounting or processing transactions.

Aids to Maintaining Independence

The profession and society, especially in the past decade, have been concerned about ensuring that (1) auditors maintain an unbiased attitude in performing their work (independence in fact) and (2) users perceive auditors as being independent (independence in appearance). Many of the elements shown in Figure 3–2 and other requirements or inducements encourage public accountants to maintain independence in fact and appearance. These are now briefly summarized. The most important have already been discussed in Chapter 1 and early in Chapter 2.

Legal liability The penalty involved when a court concludes that a practitioner is not independent can be severe, including criminal action. The courts have certainly provided major incentives for auditors to remain independent. Legal liability is studied in the next chapter.

Rules of professional conduct The existing rules of conduct restrict public accountants in their financial and business relationships with clients. They are a considerable aid in maintaining independence.

Generally accepted auditing standards The general standard requires the auditor to maintain an objective state of mind in all matters related to the assignment.

Public accounting firm quality control standards Most public accounting firms establish policies and procedures to provide reasonable assurance that all personnel are independent.

Audit committee An audit committee, as was discussed above, can help auditors remain independent of management.

Shopping for accounting principles Management may consult with other accountants on the application of accounting principles. Although consultation with other accountants is an appropriate practice, it can lead to a loss of independence in certain circumstances. For example, suppose one public accounting firm replaces the existing auditors on the strength of accounting advice offered but later finds facts and circumstances that require the public accounting firm to change its stance. It may be difficult for the new public accounting firm to remain independent in such a situation. The Auditing Standards Board issued Section 7600 setting out requirements that must be met when a public accounting firm is requested to provide a written opinion on the application of accounting principles or auditing standards by a party other than the client. Such an opinion would be issued for specific circumstances or transactions relating to an audit, review or compilation client of another public accounting firm. It applies if the public accountant is asked to provide a generic or hypothetical opinion on the application of accounting principles or auditing standards.

The purpose of the Auditing Standards Board's requirements is to minimize the likelihood of management following the practice commonly called "opinion shopping" and the potential threat to independence of the kind described above. Primary among the requirements is that the consulted or "reporting" accounting firm should communicate with the entity's incumbent accountant to ascertain all the available facts relevant to forming a professional judgment on the matters the firm has been requested to report on.

Approval of auditor by shareholders   The *Canada Business Corporations Act* and other incorporating acts require shareholders to approve the selection of a new auditor or continuation of the existing one. Shareholders are usually a more objective group than management. It is questionable, however, whether they are in a position to evaluate the performance of previous or potential auditors.

Conclusion   Regardless of the rules set forth by the rules of conduct of the various accounting bodies, it is essential that the public accountant maintain an unbiased relationship with management and all other parties affected by the performance of the public accountant's responsibilities. In every engagement, including those involving management advisory and tax services, the public accountant must not subordinate his or her professional judgment to that of others. Even though pressures on the public accountant's objectivity and integrity are frequent, the long-run standing of the profession in the financial community demands resisting those pressures. If the conflicts are sufficiently great to compromise the public accountant's objectivity, it may be necessary for the public accounting firm to resign from the engagement.

Confidentiality

OBJECTIVE 6

Discuss confidentiality as it applies to a public accountant.

The rules of conduct for CAs, CGAs, and CMAs state that members shall not disclose any confidential client or employer information without the specific consent of the client or employer. In general, the rules also prohibit using confidential or inside information to earn profits or benefits.

The rule against disclosure does not apply if the member is called upon to disclose the information by the courts. Communication between an auditor and client is not privileged as it is between lawyer and client; a court can require a public accountant to produce all files and documents held by the public accountant including confidential advice provided to the client by the public accountant. For this reason, the auditor must be careful what information is put into the file, recognizing that the file could appear as a court document. The rule against disclosure also does not apply if the member's professional body requires the confidentiality rule to be waived in connection with the body's exercise of its duties (for example, when an auditor is called upon to produce working papers in connection with the disciplinary process, or when an auditor is required to produce files as part of practice inspection).

Need for Confidentiality

During an audit or other type of engagement, practitioners obtain a considerable amount of information of a confidential nature, including officers' salaries, product pricing and advertising plans, and product cost data. If auditors divulged this information to outsiders or to client employees who have been denied access to the information, their relationship with management would be seriously strained and, in extreme cases, would cause the client harm. The confidentiality requirement applies to all services provided by public accounting firms, including tax and management services.

Ordinarily, the public accounting firm's working papers can be provided to someone else only with the express permission of the client. This is the case even if a public accountant sells his or her practice to another public accounting firm or is willing to permit a successor auditor to examine the working papers prepared for a former client. Permission is not required from the client, however, if the working papers are subpoenaed by a court or are used as part of practice inspection. If the working papers are subpoenaed, the client should be informed immediately. The client and its lawyer may wish to challenge the subpoena.

Maintenance of the Reputation of the Profession

OBJECTIVE 7

Discuss the standard of behavior required of a public accountant

The rules of all three accounting bodies in Canada require their members to behave in the best interest of their profession and the public. This means accountants should not take advantage of the trust placed in them by their profession and by the public. It means that an accountant should not be publicly critical of a colleague (that is, by making a complaint about the colleague's behavior to their professional body or by being critical, as a successor auditor, to the new client) without giving the colleague a chance to explain his or her actions first.

Actions by a member of a professional body – in law, medicine, or any other profession – reflect on the member but also on the body itself. For example, a lawyer who steals trust monies sullies not only his or her own reputation but also that of the law profession; the theft brings all lawyers into disrepute. Therefore, it is essential that an accountant behave in an exemplary manner as a member of the professional body.

Integrity and Due Care

OBJECTIVE 8

Discuss integrity and due care as they apply to a public accountant.

The rules of conduct for CAs, CGAs and CMAs require their members to act with integrity and due care. Integrity is one of the hallmarks of the profession. One of a professional accountant's most important assets is his or her reputation for honesty and fair dealing; if users of financial statements audited by or prepared by an accountant do not believe in the practitioner's honesty or fairness, the value of the financial statements or the audit is diminished. The professional accountant's behavior with clients, colleagues and employers and employees must be above reproach.

Due care in the performance of his or her duties is also a hallmark of a professional. The public accountant has a legal duty of care to certain users of financial statements, as will be seen in Chapter 4. Due care means the application by a professional of a level of care and skill in accordance with what would reasonably be expected of a person of his or her rank and training. Note that due care is mentioned in the general standard of GAAS in Section 5100 of the *CICA Handbook*.

Competence

As a professional, a CA, CGA or CMA has a responsibility to maintain his or her professional competence. The rules of conduct of the three professional bodies require practitioners to maintain competence; similarly the GAAS state the necessity of "adequate technical training and proficiency." The public expects that all professionals will strive to keep abreast of the latest techniques and methodologies.

The accounting associations offer continuing professional education courses in a variety of subject areas to assist their members in maintaining their competence. In addition, there are a number of other organizations which provide courses.

Members are encouraged to keep current in a variety of ways. The various institutes and the *ordre* of chartered accountants have practice inspections (discussed in Chapter 1) over a four-year period of all public practice units. Certified general accountants are required to attend a certain number of continuing professional education courses a year. Primarily, however, it is a professional accountant's professionalism that dictates that he or she keep current.

Adherence to GAAP and GAAS

All three professional accounting bodies require their members in practice as public accountants and working in industry not to associate themselves with false or misleading information nor to fail to reveal material omissions from financial statements. Users of financial statements prepared by or audited by professional accountants are entitled to believe that the financial statements are complete and fairly present the financial position of the company. They are entitled to believe that the financial statements are not false and misleading. They are entitled to rely on the integrity of the accountants involved.

Given that public trust of professional accountants does exist, if an accountant were to betray this trust and provide a clean opinion on financial statements he or she knows to be misleading, users would accept the statements as correct and would suffer a loss. Objective 8 above discusses integrity and its importance to a public accountant; discovery that the public accountant was associated with false and misleading financial information or failed to reveal a material fact would destroy the accountant's reputation for integrity.

CAs, CGAs and CMAs are required to comply with professional standards when preparing and auditing financial statements. These standards would include the standards of the professional body but, more importantly, GAAP and GAAS as set out in the *CICA Handbook*. As you learned in Chapter 1, the *Canada Business Corporations Act* and the incorporating acts of many of the provinces require financial statements to be prepared according to GAAP as specified by the *CICA Handbook* and also require the auditor's report to be in accordance with the standards of the *Handbook*. Recall also that the Canadian Securities Administrators who set policy for the securities commissions and stock exchanges in Canada also specify the *Handbook* as the source of GAAP.

Advertising and Solicitation

A profession's reputation is not enhanced if the members openly solicit each others' clients or engage in advertising that is overly aggressive, self-laudatory, critical of other members of the profession or that makes claims that cannot be

OBJECTIVE 11

Discuss advertising and solicitation from the perspective of a public accountant.

substantiated. As a consequence, the three professional accounting bodies in Canada either explicitly or implicitly prohibit solicitation of another public accountant's client and advertising which is not in keeping with the profession's high standards.

Responding to a request for information from a client of another public accounting firm is not solicitation, nor is responding to an invitation to tender from another firm's client. Rather, solicitation is approaching the client of another public accounting firm to convince them to switch to one's own firm.

Advertising that is in good taste is acceptable. It may include complimentary material about the accounting firm but should not claim any superior skills or make promises that can't be kept (for example, a promise that certain favorable results will be achieved).

There has been a gradual change over the past few years as the rules regarding solicitation and advertising have been made less stringent. As a consequence, the public accounting firms are competing much more strenuously than before. Advertising in the various media is much more common. There is an increased emphasis on marketing and more competitive pricing of services. Many public accounting firms have developed sophisticated advertising for national journals read by business people and for local newspapers. It is common for public accounting firms to make formal and informal presentations at the request of management in order to convince them to change public accounting firms. Price bidding for audits and other services is now common and often highly competitive. As a result of these changes, some companies now change auditors more often than previously to reduce audit cost. Most practitioners believe audits are less profitable than previously.

Has the quality of audits become endangered by these changes? The existing legal exposure of public accountants, the disciplinary processes of the professional accounting bodies, practice inspection requirements, and the potential for interference by the securities commissions and government has kept audit quality high. In the opinion of the authors, the changes in the rules have caused greater competition in the profession, but not so much that high-quality, efficiently run public accounting firms have been significantly harmed. However, for this to continue to be so, public accounting firms need to be on guard so that increasing competitive pressures do not cause auditors to reduce quality below an acceptable level.

Other rules

Breaches of the rules The rules of conduct of the professional accounting bodies require members who are aware of a breach of the rules by another member to report that member to the profession's discipline committee after first advising the member of the intent to make a report. The three bodies are self-regulating and therefore must police themselves. It is important that the member be notified of the intent to report the breach in case there are mitigating circumstances of which the reporting member is not aware.

OBJECTIVE 12

Discuss other rules of conduct including those dealing with contingent fees and with reporting breaches of the rules.

Contingent fees The charging of a fee based on the outcome of an audit, such as the granting of a loan by a bank, could easily impair the auditor's independence. Contingent fees are therefore prohibited.

Communication with predecessor auditor The rules of conduct of the CAs and CGAs and incorporating acts such as the *Canada Business Corporations Act* require a (potential) successor auditor, prior to accepting an appointment as auditor, to communicate with the incumbent auditor to inquire if there are any circumstances of which the incumbent is aware that might preclude the successor from accepting the appointment. The successor would ask the potential client to authorize the incumbent to provide the information requested. If the client refuses to do so, the successor should be reluctant to accept the appointment because it is likely that the client is hiding something.

Professionalism dictates that the incumbent *should* respond to the successor's request and be candid in responding. However, the incumbent may not respond or may not be as frank as he or she could be.

The communication between the incumbent and the successor is important because it prevents a successor from unknowingly accepting an appointment that might, if all the facts were known, be rejected. For example, if the incumbent resigned after finding that management of the client was dishonest and was engaged in fraud, it is unlikely any public accounting firm would accept the client if the incumbent had passed on that knowledge. In short, the required communication protects prospective successors, and thus the profession, from getting involved with undesirable clients. The client acceptance decision is discussed in Chapter 7.

Other rules The rules of conduct of the professional accounting bodies include many more rules than have been described here; an aspiring professional accountant should make him- or herself aware of the rules of conduct of the professional body to which membership is sought. The rules not covered, and those described above, may be categorized as general rules, rules which deal with protection of the public, rules which deal with relations with other accountants, and rules which relate to the conduct of a professional practice.

Enforcement

The rules of conduct for chartered accountants are established and administered provincially. The rules of conduct for certified general accountants are promulgated by CGA-Canada. The provincial CGA associations have the power to add rules and have the responsibility for enforcing the rules. The rules of conduct for certified management accountants are promulgated and administered by the provincial societies.

The various professional bodies have the power to impose penalties ranging from public censure in the body's newsletter, or requiring courses to be taken to upgrade skills, through to levying fines, and even expulsion. As pointed out above, the three professional accounting bodies are self-regulating; that is, they have the responsibility for developing their own rules of conduct and for disciplining members who violate the rules. There is a danger that the public will perceive that the disciplinary process is not as stringent as it should be and that there is a reluctance to punish members who break the rules. One way this issue is being dealt with is by including lay-persons on the disciplinary committees. A second approach is to make information available to the public about findings of the discipline committees and punishments meted out by them.

REVIEW QUESTIONS

3–1 Explain the need for a code of professional ethics for public accountants. In which ways should the public accountants' code of ethics be similar to and different from that of other professional groups, such as lawyers or dentists?

3–2 List the three parts which normally comprise a code of professional conduct, and state the purpose of each.

3–3 Distinguish between independence in fact and independence in appearance. State three activities that may not affect independence in fact but are likely to affect independence in appearance.

3–4 Why is an auditor's independence so essential?

3–5 What are the four facets of independence discussed in the chapter. Explain why each is a necessary component of a public accountant's independence.

3–6 Some observers object to public accounting firms providing management advisory services for an audit client. Why do they object? Are they correct in objecting?

3–7 Many people believe that a public accountant cannot be truly independent when payment of fees is dependent on the management of the client. Explain a way of reducing this appearance of lack of independence.

3–8 After accepting an engagement, a public accountant discovers that the client's industry is more technical than at first realized and that he or she (i.e., the accountant) is not competent in certain areas of the operation. What should the public accountant do in this situation?

3–9 What is meant by the statement, "The rules of professional conduct of a professional accounting organization should be regarded as a minimum standard"?

3–10 Assume an auditor makes an agreement with a client that the audit fee will be contingent upon the number of days required to complete the engagement. Is this likely to be a violation of the auditor's rules of conduct? What is the essence of the rule of professional ethics dealing with contingent fees, and what are the reasons for the rule?

3–11 The auditor's working papers usually can be provided to someone else only with the permission of the client. What is the rationale for such a rule?

3–12 Define what is meant by solicitation, and explain why you think the accounting professions have rules against solicitation.

3–13 Identify and explain factors that should keep the quality of audits high even though advertising and tendering are allowed.

3–14 What do you think are the reasons that the rules of conduct of the professional accounting bodies contain restrictions on advertising by public accounting firms?

3–15 Why do you think the rules of conduct of the professional accounting bodies which pertain to public accounting ban contingent fees?

3–16 Why is it so important that a successor auditor communicate with the incumbent before accepting appointment as auditor? What should the successor do if the incumbent doesn't reply?

3–17 Why do the rules of conduct of CAs and CGAs contain a restriction on what names a public accounting firm might use?

3–18 Why do the rules of conduct of CAs, CGAs and CMAs require them to report a breach of the rules of conduct by a member to their profession's disciplinary body? What should they do before making such a report?

MULTIPLE CHOICE QUESTIONS

3–19 The following questions concern independence and the rules of professional conduct or GAAS. Choose the best response.

Without Bias.

a. What is the meaning of the generally accepted auditing standard that requires the auditor to be independent?

    (1) The auditor must be without bias with respect to the client under audit.
    (2) The auditor must adopt a critical attitude during the audit.
    (3) The auditor's sole obligation is to third parties.
    (4) The auditor may have a direct ownership interest in his or her client's business if it is not material.

b. The independent audit is important to readers of financial statements because it

    (1) determines the future stewardship of the management of the company whose financial statements are audited.
    (2) measures and communicates financial and business data included in financial statements.
    (3) involves the objective examination of and reporting on management-prepared statements.
    (4) reports on the accuracy of all information in the financial statements.

                                                      (AICPA adapted)

3–20 The following questions concern possible violations of the rules of conduct discussed in the chapter. Choose the best response.

a. In which one of the following situations would a public accountant be in violation of the rules of conduct in determining his or her audit fee?

    (1) A fee based on whether the public accountant's report on the client's financial statements results in the approval of a bank loan.
    (2) A fee equal to last year's fee plus 10 percent.
    (3) A fee based on the nature of the service rendered and the public accountant's particular expertise instead of the actual time spent on the engagement.
    (4) A fee based on the fee charged by the prior auditor.

b. The rules of conduct state that a public accountant shall not disclose any confidential information obtained in the course of a professional engagement except with the consent of his or her client. In which one of the situations given below would disclosure by a public accountant be in violation of the rules?

    (1) Disclosing confidential information in order to properly discharge the public accountant's responsibilities in accordance with his or her profession's standards.
    (2) Disclosing confidential information in compliance with a subpoena issued by a court.
    (3) Disclosing confidential information to another accountant interested in purchasing the public accountant's practice.
    (4) Disclosing confidential information in connection with a disciplinary hearing by the public accountant's professional conduct committee.

                                                      (AICPA adapted)

DISCUSSION QUESTIONS AND PROBLEMS

3–21 Mary Frost, an audit senior in your office, states that members of her public accounting firm should not have any social interaction with a client's staff because such interaction threatens independence. Norman Amey, another senior, disagrees, saying social interaction makes for a smoother audit.

Required: What do you think is the correct view and why?

3–22 Trish Mulcahy, a new junior in your office, says that she can't see why she can't work on the audit of a company which is a client of your firm but which is owned by her uncle. Trish says she knows she must have an independent attitude and she will; her relationship to the owner is not important.

Required: What will you say in answer to her question? Will you let her work on the audit?

3–23 The following each involves a possible violation of the rules of conduct discussed in the chapter. Indicate whether each is a violation and explain why if you think it is.

    a. John Brown is a public accountant, but not a partner, with three years of professional experience with Lyle and Lyle, Public Accountants, a one-office public accounting firm. He owns 25 shares of stock in an audit client of the firm, but he does not take part in the audit of the client and the amount of stock is not material in relation to his total wealth.

    b. In preparing the personal tax returns for a client, Phyllis Allen, public accountant, observed that the deductions for contributions and interest were unusually large. When she asked the client for backup information to support the deductions, she was told, "Ask me no questions, and I will tell you no lies." Allen completed the return on the basis of the information acquired from the client.

    c. A client requests assistance of Kim Tanabe, public accountant, in the installation of a computer system for maintaining production records. Tanabe had no experience in this type of work and no knowledge of the client's production records, so he obtained assistance from a computer consultant. The consultant is not in the practice of public accounting, but Tanabe is confident of her professional skills. Because of the highly technical nature of the work, Tanabe is not able to review the consultant's work.

    d. Five small Moncton public accounting firms have become involved in an information project by taking part in an interfirm working paper review program. Under the program, each firm designates two partners to review the working papers, including the tax returns and the financial statements of another public accounting firm taking part in the program. At the end of each review, the auditors who prepared the working papers and the reviewers have a conference to discuss the strengths and weaknesses of the audit. They do not obtain the authorization from the audit client before the review takes place.

    e. James Thurgood, public accountant, stayed longer than he should have at the annual Christmas party of Thurgood and Thurgood, Public Accountants. On his way home he drove through a red light and was stopped by a policeman, who observed that he was intoxicated. In a jury trial, Thurgood was found guilty of driving under the influence of alcohol. Since this was not his first offense, he was sentenced to 30 days in jail and his driver's license was revoked for 1 year.

    f. Bill Wendal, public accountant, set up a casualty and fire insurance agency to complement his auditing and tax services. He does not use his own name on anything pertaining to the insurance agency and has a highly competent manager, Renate Jones, who runs it. Wendal frequently requests Jones to review with the management of an audit client the adequacy of the client's insurance if it seems underinsured. He feels that he provides a valuable service to clients by informing them when they are underinsured.

    g. Michelle Rankin, public accountant, provides tax services, management advisory services, and bookkeeping services and conducts audits for the same client. Since the firm is small, the same person frequently provides all the services.

3–24 The following each involve possible violations of the rules of conduct that apply to professional accountants in Canada that are discussed in the chapter. For each situation, state whether it is a violation of the rules as described. In those cases in which it is a violation, explain the nature of the violation and the rationale for the existing rule.

a. Mario Danielli is the partner on the audit of a nonprofit charitable organization. He is also a member of the board of directors, but this position is honorary and does not involve performing a management function.

b. Fenn and Company, Public Accountants, has time available on a computer that it uses primarily for its own record keeping. Aware that the computer facilities of Delta Equipment Corp., one of Fenn's audit clients, are inadequate for company needs, Fenn maintains on its computer certain routine accounting records for Delta.

c. Marie Godette, public accountant, has a law practice. Godette has recommended one of her clients to Sean O'Doyle, public accountant. O'Doyle has agreed to pay Godette 10 percent of the fee for services rendered by O'Doyle to Godette's client.

d. Theresa Barnes, CA, has an audit client, De Souza, Inc., which uses another public accounting firm for management services work. Barnes sends her firm's literature covering its management services capabilities to De Souza on a monthly basis, unsolicited.

e. A bank issued a notice to its depositors that it was being audited and requested them to comply with the public accounting firm's effort to obtain a confirmation on the deposit balances. The bank printed the name and address of the public accounting firm in the notice. The public accounting firm has knowledge of the notice.

f. Wally Gutowski, a practicing public accountant, has written a tax article that is being published in a professional publication. The publication wishes to inform its readers about Gutowski's background. The information, which Gutowski has approved, includes his academic degrees, other articles he has had published in professional journals, and a statement that he is a tax expert.

g. Marcel Poust, public accountant, has sold his public accounting practice, which includes bookkeeping, tax services, and auditing, to Sheila Lyons, public accountant. Poust obtained permission from all audit clients for audit-related working papers before making them available to Lyons. He did not get permission before releasing tax- and management services-related working papers.

h. Murphy and Company, Public Accountants, is the principal auditor of the consolidated financial statements of Cranbrook, Inc., and subsidiaries. Cranbrook accounts for approximately 98 percent of consolidated assets and consolidated net income. The two subsidiaries are audited by Trotman and Company, Public Accountants, a firm with an excellent professional reputation. Murphy insists on auditing the two subsidiaries because he deems this necessary to warrant the expression of an opinion.

3–25 The *Canada Business Corporations Act* requires all companies incorporated under it to have audit committees.

Required:
a. Describe an audit committee.
b. What are the typical functions performed by an audit committee?
c. Explain how an audit committee can help an auditor be more independent.
d. The mother of a friend of yours who is chair of an audit committee of a large publicly traded company knows that you are studying auditing and has asked you for advice on how she can make the audit committee she chairs more effective. Your response should consider both sides of each recommendation you make.

3–26 Diane Harris, public accountant, is the auditor of Fine Deal Furniture, Inc. In the course of her audit for the year ended December 31, 19X8, she discovered that Fine Deal had serious going concern problems. Henri Fine, the owner of Fine Deal, asked Harris to delay completing her audit.

Harris is also the auditor of Master Furniture Builders Ltd., whose year end is January 31. The largest receivable on Master Furniture's list of receivables is Fine Deal Furniture; the amount owing represents about 45 percent of Master Furniture's total receivables, which in turn are 60 percent of Master Furniture's net assets. The management of Master Furniture is not aware of Fine Deal's problems and is certain the amount will be collected in full.

Master Furniture is in a hurry to get the January 31, 19X9 audit finished because the company has made an application for a sizable loan from their bank to expand their operations. The bank has informally agreed to advance the funds based on draft financial statements submitted by Master Furniture just after the year end.

Required: What action should Harris take and why?

3–27 The following relate to auditors' independence:

Required:
a. Why is independence so essential for auditors?
b. Compare the importance of independence of professional public accountants with that of other professionals, such as lawyers.
c. Explain the difference between independence in appearance and in fact.
d. Describe the four facets of independence. Can any one of the four be ignored?
e. Discuss how each of the following could affect independence in fact and independence in appearance, and evaluate the social consequence of prohibiting auditors from doing each one.
   (1) Ownership of stock in a client company.
   (2) Having bookkeeping services for an audit client performed by the same person who does the audit.
   (3) Recommending adjusting entries to the client's financial statements and preparing financial statements, including footnotes, for the client.
   (4) Having management services for an audit client performed by individuals in a department that is separate from the audit department.
   (5) Having the annual audit performed by the same audit team, except for assistants, for five years in a row.
   (6) Having the annual audit performed by the same public accounting firm for 10 years in a row.
   (7) Having management select the public accounting firm.

3–28 Marie Janes encounters the following situations in doing the audit of a large auto dealership. Janes is not a partner.

1. The sales manager tells her that there is a sale on new cars (at a substantial discount) that is limited to long-established customers of the dealership. Because her firm has been doing the audit for several years, the sales manager has decided Janes should also be eligible for the discount.
2. The auto dealership has an executive lunchroom that is available free to employees above a certain level. The controller informs Janes that she can also eat there any time.
3. Janes is invited to and attends the company's annual Christmas party. When presents are handed out, she is surprised to find her name included. The present has a value of approximately $200.

Required:
a. Assuming Janes accepts the offer or gift in each situation, has she violated the rules of conduct?
b. Discuss what Janes should do in each situation.

CASES

3–29 The following are situations that may violate the general rules of conduct of professional accountants discussed in the chapter. Assume in each case, that the public accountant is a partner.

1. Simone Able, public accountant, owns a substantial limited partnership interest in an apartment building. Juan Rodriquez is a 100 percent owner in Rodriquez Marine Ltd. Rodriquez also owns a substantial interest in the same limited partnership as Able. Able does the audit of Rodriquez Marine Ltd.

2. Sarah Baker, public accountant, approaches a new audit client and tells the president that she has an idea that could result in a substantial tax refund in the prior year's tax return by application of a technical provision in the tax law that the client had overlooked. Baker adds that the fee will be 50 percent of the tax refund after it has been resolved by Revenue Canada. The client agrees to the proposal.

3. Chantal Contel, public accountant, advertises in the local paper that her firm does the audit of 14 of the 36 largest drug stores in the city. The advertisement also states that the average audit fee, as a percentage of total assets for the drug stores she audits, is lower than any other public accounting firm's in the city.

4. Olaf Gustafson, public accountant, sets up a small loan company specializing in loans to business executives and small companies. Gustafson does not spend much time in the business because he spends full time with his public accounting practice. No employees of Gustafson's public accounting firm are involved in the small loan company.

5. Louise Elbert, public accountant, owns a material amount of stock in a mutual fund investment company, which in turn owns stock in Elbert's largest audit client. Reading the investment company's most recent financial report, Elbert is surprised to learn that the company's ownership in her client has increased dramatically.

6. Kerry Finigan, public accountant, does the audit, tax return, bookkeeping, and management services work for Gilligan Construction Company Limited. Before she makes any major business decision, Mildred Gilligan follows the practice of calling Finigan to determine the effect on her company's taxes and the financial statements. Finigan attends continuing education courses in the construction industry to make sure she is technically competent and knowledgeable about the industry. Finigan normally attends board of director meetings and accompanies Gilligan when she is seeking loans. Mildred Gilligan often jokingly introduces Finigan with this statement, "I have my three business partners – my banker, the government, and my public accountant, but Finny's the only one that is on my side."

Required: Discuss whether the facts in any of the situations indicate violations of the rules of conduct for professional accountants discussed in the chapter. If so, identify the nature of the violation(s).

3–30 Gilbert and Bradley formed a corporation called Financial Services, Inc., each man taking 50 percent of the authorized common stock. Gilbert is a public accountant and a member of one of the professional accounting bodies in Canada. Bradley is a CPCU (Chartered Property Casualty Underwriter). The corporation performs auditing and tax services under Gilbert's direction and insurance services under Bradley's supervision. The opening of the corporation's office was announced by a three-inch, two-column "card" in the local newspaper.

One of the corporation's first audit clients was the Grandtime Corp. Grandtime had total assets of $600,000 and total liabilities of $270,000. In the course of his examination, Gilbert found that Grandtime's building, with a book value of

$240,000, was pledged as security for a 10-year term note in the amount of $200,000. The client's statements did not mention that the building was pledged as security for the note. However, as the failure to disclose the lien did not affect either the value of the assets or the amount of the liabilities and his examination was satisfactory in all other respects, Gilbert rendered an unqualified opinion on Grandtime's financial statements. About two months after the date of his opinion, Gilbert learned that an insurance company was planning to loan Grandtime $150,000 in the form of a first mortgage note on the building. Realizing that the insurance company was unaware of the existing lien on the building, Gilbert had Bradley notify the insurance company of the fact that Grandtime's building was pledged as security for the term note.

Shortly after the events just described, Gilbert was charged with a violation of professional ethics.

Required: Identify and discuss the ethical implications of those acts by Gilbert that were in violation of the rules of conduct discussed in the chapter.

3–31 Barbara Whitley had great expectations about her future as she sat in her graduation ceremony in May 19X1. She was about to receive her Masters of Accountancy degree, and next week she would begin her career on the audit staff of Green, Thresher & Co., a public accounting firm. Things looked a little different to Barbara in February 19X2. She was working on the audit of Delancey Fabrics Ltd., a textile manufacturer with a calendar year-end. The pressure was enormous. Everyone on the audit team was putting in 70-hour weeks and it still looked as if the audit wouldn't be done on time. Barbara was doing work in the property area, vouching additions for the year. The audit program indicated that a sample of all items over $10,000 should be selected, plus a judgmental sample of smaller items. When Barbara went to take the sample, Jack Bean, the senior, had left the client's office and couldn't answer her questions about the appropriate size of the judgmental sample. Barbara forged ahead with her own judgment and selected 50 smaller items. Her basis for doing this was that there were about 250 such items, so 50 was a reasonably good proportion of such additions.

Barbara audited the additions with the following results: the items over $10,000 contained no errors; however, the 50 small items contained a large number of errors. In fact, when Barbara projected them to all such additions, the amount seemed quite significant.

A couple of days later, Jack Bean returned to the client's office. Barbara brought her work to Jack in order to apprise him of the problems she found, and got the following response:

- My God Barbara, why did you do this? You were only supposed to look at the items over $10,000 plus 5 or 10 little ones. You've wasted a whole day on that work, and we can't afford to spend any more time on it. I want you to throw the schedules where you tested the last 40 small items away and forget you ever did them.

When Barbara asked about the possible audit adjustment regarding the small items, none of which arose from the first 10 items, Jack responded, "Don't worry, it's not material anyway. You just forget it, it's my concern, not yours."

Required:
a. In what way is this an ethical dilemma for Barbara?
b. Use the six-step approach discussed in the book to resolve the ethical dilemma.

3–32 In 1989, Giles Nadeau was a bright, upcoming audit manager in the Winnipeg office of a national public accounting firm. He was an excellent technician and a good "people person." Giles also was able to bring new business into the firm as the result of his contacts in the francophone business community.

Giles was assigned a new client in 1990, XYZ Securities, Inc., a privately held broker-dealer in the secondary market for Canadian government securities. Neither

Giles, nor anyone else in the Winnipeg office, had broker-dealer audit experience. However, Giles was able to obtain audit aids for the industry from his firm's national office, which he used to get started.

Giles was promoted to partner in 1990. Although this was a great step forward for him (he was a new staff assistant in 1981), Giles was also under a great deal of pressure. Upon making partner, he was required to contribute capital to the firm. He also felt he must maintain a special image with his firm, his clients, and within the francophone community. To accomplish this, Giles maintained an impressive wardrobe, bought a Cadillac Seville and a small speedboat, and traded up to a nicer house. He also entertained freely. Giles financed much of this higher living with credit cards. He had six American Express, en Route and Visa cards and ran up a balance of about $40,000.

After the audit was completed and before the 1991 audit was to begin, Giles contacted Lynda Oakes, the CFO of XYZ Securities, with a question. Giles had noticed an anomaly in the financial statements that he couldn't understand and asked Oakes for an explanation. Lynda's reply was as follows:

- Giles, the 1990 financial statements were materially misstated and you guys just blew it. I thought you might realize this and call me, so here's my advice to you. Keep your mouth shut. We'll make up this year the loss we covered up last year, and nobody will ever know the difference. If you blow the whistle on us, your firm will know you screwed up and your career as the star in the office will be down the tubes.

Giles said he'd think about this and get back to Lynda the next day. When Giles called Lynda, he had decided to go along with her. After all, it would only be a "shift" of a loss between two adjacent years. XYZ is a private company and no one would be hurt or know the difference. In reality, he was the only person exposed to any harm in this situation, and he had to protect himself, didn't he?

When Giles went to XYZ to plan for the 1991 audit, he asked Lynda how things were going and she assured him they were fine. He then said to Oakes,

- Lynda you guys are in the money business, maybe you can give me some advice. I've run up some debts and I need to refinance them. How should I go about it?

After some discussions, Lynda volunteered a "plan." She would give Giles a cheque for $15,000. XYZ would request its bank to put $60,000 in an account in Giles' name and guarantee the loan security on it. Giles would pay back the $15,000 and have $45,000 of refinancing. Giles thought the plan was great and obtained Lynda's cheque for $15,000.

During 1991 through 1993, three things happened. First, Giles incurred more debts, and went back to the well at XYZ. By the end of 1993, he had "borrowed" a total of $125,000. Second, the company continued to lose money in various "off-the-books" investment schemes. These losses were covered up by falsifying the results of normal operations. Third, the audit team, under Giles' leadership, "failed to find" the frauds and issued unqualified opinions.

In 1992, Lynda had a tax audit of her personal 1991 return. She asked Giles' firm to handle it, and the job was assigned to Bob Smith, a tax manager. In reviewing Lynda's records, Smith found a $15,000 cheque payable from Oakes to Nadeau. Smith asked to see Nadeau and inquired about the cheque. Giles somewhat broke down and confided in Smith about his problems. Smith responded by saying, "Don't worry Giles, I understand. And believe me, I'll never tell a soul."

In 1994, XYZ's continuing losses caused it to be unable to deliver nonexistent securities when requested by a customer. This led to an investigation and bankruptcy by XYZ. Losses totaled in the millions. Giles' firm was held liable, and Giles was found guilty of conspiracy to defraud. He is still in prison today.

Required:

1. Try and put yourself in Giles' shoes. What would you have done (be honest with yourself) when told of the material misstatement in mid-1991?
2. What do you think of Bob Smith's actions to help Giles?
3. Where does one draw the line between ethical and unethical behavior in the situations described in this case study?

3–33 Frank Dorrance, a senior audit manager for Bright and Lorren, a public accounting firm, has recently been informed that the firm plans to promote him to partner within the next year or two if he continues to perform at the same high-quality level as in the past. Frank excels at dealing effectively with all people, including client personnel, professional staff, partners and potential clients. He has recently built a bigger home for entertaining and has joined the city's most prestigious golf and tennis club. He is excited about his future with the firm.

Frank has recently been assigned to the audit of Machine International Corp., a large wholesale company that ships goods throughout the world. It is one of Bright and Lorren's most prestigious clients. During the audit, Frank determines that Machine International uses a method of revenue recognition called "bill and hold" that has recently been questioned by the Ontario Securities Commission (OSC). After considerable research, Frank concludes that the method of revenue recognition is not appropriate for Machine International. In a discussion of the matter with the engagement partner, Maria da Silva, she concludes that the accounting method has been used for more than 10 years by the client and is appropriate, especially considering that the client does not file with the OSC. Da Silva is certain the firm would lose the client if the revenue recognition method is found inappropriate. Frank argues that the revenue recognition method was appropriate in prior years, but the OSC ruling makes it inappropriate in the current year. Frank recognizes the partners' responsibility to make the final decision but he feels strongly enough to state that he plans to follow the requirements of SAS 22 and include a statement in the working papers that he disagrees with the partners' decision. Da Silva informs Frank that she is unwilling to permit such a statement because of the potential legal implications. She is willing, however, to write a letter to Frank stating that she takes full responsibility for making the final decision if a legal dispute ever arises. She concludes by saying, "Frank, partners must act like partners, not like loose cannons trying to make life difficult for their partners. You have some growing up to do before I would feel comfortable with you as a partner."

Required:

Use the six-step approach discussed in the book to resolve the ethical dilemma.

4

LEGAL LIABILITY

LEARNING OBJECTIVES

THOROUGH STUDY OF THIS CHAPTER WILL ENABLE YOU TO:

1. Appreciate the litigious environment in which public accountants practice

2. Explain why the failure of financial statement users to differentiate among business failure, audit failure, and audit risk has led to lawsuits against auditors

3. Define the primary legal concepts and terms concerning accountant's liability

4. Describe accountant's liability to clients, the related defenses, and some significant legal cases

5. Describe accountant's liability to third parties under common law, the related defenses, and some significant legal cases

6. Specify what constitutes criminal liability for accountants, and describe an important U.S. legal case

7. Discuss the auditor's legal responsibilities for client confidentiality

8. Describe what the profession and the individual public accountant can do to reduce the threat of litigation

☐ This chapter discusses the nature of legal liability of public accountants. First, the reasons for increased litigation against public accountants are discussed. This is followed by a detailed examination of the nature of the lawsuits and the sources of potential liability. Significant lawsuits involving public accountants that relate to the various issues are presented in summary form. You will note that the cases discussed come from the United States, the United Kingdom and Canada; the

This chapter was reviewed by Professor Sally Gunz who teaches commercial law at the University of Waterloo. The authors gratefully acknowledge her thoughtful insights and suggestions.

legal systems in all three countries (except in Quebec, whose private laws are based on French civil law[1]) are based on English common law; as a consequence, when judges in all three countries hand down decisions, while they have no obligation to follow decisions in the other countries, they will often refer to those decisions in the course of giving their own judgment. The chapter ends with a discussion of the options available to the profession and individual practitioners to minimize liability while meeting society's needs.

Changed Legal Environment

> **OBJECTIVE 1**
>
> Appreciate the litigious environment in which public accountants practice.

Professionals have always had a duty to provide a reasonable level of care while performing work for those they serve. Audit professionals have a responsibility under common law to fulfill implied or expressed contracts with clients. They are liable to their clients for negligence and/or breach of contract should they fail to provide the services or should they fail to exercise due care in their performance. Auditors may also be held liable under the tort of negligence to parties other than their clients in certain circumstances. Although the precise legal definition of the auditor's *third party* (people who do not have a contract with the auditor) liability is still evolving, the position of the Supreme Court of Canada, at this time, remains that the auditor owes a duty of care to third parties who are part of a limited group of persons whom the auditor actually knew would use and rely on the audit. Note the use of the term "evolving" here; in Canada, as in other countries, lower courts are presenting other definitions. You will see further discussion of this below. Finally, in rare cases auditors have also been held liable for criminal acts. A criminal conviction against an auditor can result only when it is demonstrated that the auditor intended to deceive or harm others and typically relates to acts of fraud.

The four sources of auditor's legal liability identified in the previous paragraph are the main focus of this chapter. They are summarized in Figure 4–1, with an example of a potential claim from each source.

In recent years, both the number of lawsuits and size of awards to plaintiffs have significantly increased in both Canada and the United States, although the increase in the United States has been more significant because of a number of factors, including the more litigious climate in that country. Many of the lawsuits brought against auditors are brought by third parties. There are no simple reasons for this increase, but the following are major factors:

- The growing awareness of the responsibilities of public accountants by users of financial statements.
- An increased consciousness on the part of the provincial securities commissions regarding their responsibility for protecting investors' interests.
- The greater complexity of auditing and accounting due to such factors as the increasing size of business, the existence of the computer, and the intricacies of business operations.
- Society's increasing acceptance of lawsuits by injured parties against anyone who might be able to provide compensation, and who appears to be at least partially responsible for the loss. This is frequently called the "deep-pocket" concept of liability.
- The willingness of public accounting firms to settle their legal problems out of

1 Smyth, J.E., Soberman, D.A., and Easson, A.J., *The Law and Business Administration in Canada*, Sixth Edition, Scarborough, Ontario: Prentice-Hall Canada Inc., 1991.

FIGURE 4–1

Four Major Sources of
Auditor's Legal
Liability

SOURCE OF LIABILITY	EXAMPLE OF POTENTIAL CLAIM
Client – common law	Client sues auditor for not discovering a defalcation during the audit.
Third party – common law	Bank sues auditor for not discovering materially misstated financial statements.
Provincial securities acts	A purchaser of stock issued by a company sues the auditor for not discovering materially misstated financial statements in a prospectus.
Criminal	Court prosecutes auditor under the *Criminal Code of Canada* for knowingly issuing an incorrect auditor's report.

court in an attempt to avoid costly legal fees and adverse publicity rather than resolving them through the judicial process.

- The many alternative accounting principles from which clients can elect to present their financial statements, and the lack of clear-cut criteria for the auditor to evaluate whether the proper alternative was selected.

Distinction Among Business Failure, Audit Failure, and Audit Risk

Many accounting and legal professionals believe that a major cause of lawsuits against public accounting firms is the lack of understanding by financial statement users of the difference between a *business* failure and an *audit* failure and between an *audit failure* and *audit risk*. These terms are first defined, then followed by a discussion of how misunderstanding the differences between the terms often results in lawsuits against auditors.

Business failure This occurs when a business is unable to repay its lenders, or meet the expectations of its investors, because of economic or business conditions such as a recession, poor management decisions, or unexpected competition in the industry. The extreme case of business failure is filing for bankruptcy. As stated in Chapter 1, there is always some risk that a business will fail.

Audit failure This occurs when the auditor issues an erroneous audit opinion as the result of an underlying failure to comply with the requirements of generally accepted auditing standards. For example, the auditor may have assigned unqualified assistants to perform audit tasks, and, because of their lack of competence, they failed to find material misstatements that qualified auditors would have discovered.

Audit risk This is the risk that the auditor will conclude that the financial statements are fairly stated and an unqualified opinion can therefore be issued when, in fact, they are materially misstated. As will be shown in subsequent chapters, auditing cannot be expected to uncover all material financial statement misstatements. Auditing is limited to sampling, and certain errors and well-concealed frauds are extremely difficult to detect; therefore, there is always some risk that the audit will not uncover a material financial statement misstatement.

Most accounting professionals agree that when an audit has failed to uncover material misstatements, and the wrong type of audit opinion is therefore issued, the public accounting firm should be asked to defend the quality of the audit. If the auditor failed to use due care – in other words, was negligent – in the conduct of the audit then there is an audit failure, and the public accounting firm

> OBJECTIVE 2
>
> Explain why the failure of financial statement users to differentiate among business failure, audit failure, and audit risk has led to lawsuits against auditors.

Must be able to defend
Quality of Audit.

and its insurance company should be expected to compensate those parties to whom the auditor owed a duty of care for losses. It is difficult in practice to determine when the auditor has failed to use due care because of the complexity of auditing. It is also not always clear who has a right to expect the benefits of an audit because of the evolving nature of the law. Nevertheless, an auditor's failure to follow due care can be expected to result in a claim of negligence and, where appropriate, damages against the public accounting firm.

The difficulty arises when there has been a business failure, but not an audit failure. For example, when a company goes bankrupt or cannot pay its debts, it is common for statement users to claim there was an audit failure, particularly when the most recently issued auditor's opinion indicates the financial statements were fairly stated. This conflict between statement users and auditors often arises because of what is referred to as the *expectation gap between users and auditors.*[2] Most auditors believe the conduct of the audit in accordance with generally accepted auditing standards is all that can be expected of auditors. Many users believe auditors guarantee the accuracy of financial statements and some users even believe the auditor guarantees the financial viability of the business. While courts continue to support the auditor's view, the expectation gap often results in unwarranted lawsuits. Perhaps the profession has a responsibility to educate statement users about the role of auditors and the difference between business risk, audit failure, and audit risk. Realistically, however, auditors must recognize that, in part, the claims of audit failure may also result from the hope of those who suffer a business loss to recover from any source, regardless of who is at fault.

Legal Concepts Affecting Liability

The public accountant is responsible for every aspect of his or her public accounting work, including auditing, taxes, management advisory services, and accounting and bookkeeping services. For example, if a public accountant negligently failed to prepare and file a client's tax return properly, the public accountant can be held liable for any penalties and interest the client was required to pay plus the tax preparation fee charged. It is possible the court could also assess punitive damages where the accountant was exceptionally careless.

Most of the major lawsuits against public accounting firms have dealt with audited or unaudited financial statements. The discussion in this chapter is restricted primarily to those two aspects of public accounting. The areas of liability in auditing can be classified as (1) liability to clients, (2) liability to third parties under common law and statute law, and (3) criminal liability. Several legal concepts apply to all these types of lawsuits against public accountants. These are the *reasonable person concept, liability for the acts of others,* and the *lack of privileged communication.*

> **OBJECTIVE 3**
>
> Define the primary legal concepts and terms concerning accountant's liability.

Reasonable Person Concept

There is agreement within the profession and the courts that the auditor is not a guarantor or insurer of financial statements. The auditor is only expected to

---

2 In 1988, the report of a committee, formed by the Canadian Institute of Chartered Accountants to study the "expectations gap" and chaired by William A. Macdonald, a partner in a Toronto law firm, was published by the CICA. The *Report of the Commission to Study the Public's Expectation of Audits* was a comprehensive examination of the expectations gap and provides some thoughtful ways of reducing the gap. The interested reader is directed to the report itself; also, the July, 1988, issue of *CA Magazine* includes commentary on the report and lists the fifty recommendations made by the Macdonald Commission.

conduct the audit with due care. Even then, the auditor cannot be expected to be perfect.

The standard of due care to which the auditor is expected to be held is often referred to as the *reasonable person concept*. It is expressed in *Cooley on Torts* as follows:

> Every man who offers his service to another and is employed assumes the duty to exercise in the employment such skill as he possesses with reasonable care and diligence. In all these employments where peculiar skill is prerequisite, if one offers his service, he is understood as holding himself out to the public as possessing the degree of skill commonly possessed by others in the same employment, and, if his pretentions are unfounded, he commits a species of fraud upon every man who employs him in reliance on his public profession. But no man, whether skilled or unskilled, undertakes that the task he assumes shall be performed successfully, and without fault or error. *He undertakes for good faith and integrity, but not for infallibility*, and he is liable to his employer for negligence, bad faith, or dishonesty, but not for losses consequent upon pure errors of judgment.

Liability for Acts of Others

The partners of a public accounting firm may have *joint and several liability* if a suit for tort or negligence is brought against the partnership. In other words, each partner may be held liable in a civil action for the tort or negligent actions of each of the other partners in the partnership.

The partners may also be liable for the work of others on whom they rely under the laws of agency. The three groups an auditor is most likely to rely on are *employees*, other *public accounting firms* engaged to do part of the work, and *specialists* called upon to provide technical information. For example, if an employee performs improperly in doing an audit, the partners can be held liable for the employee's performance.

Lack of Privileged Communication

Public accountants do not have the right under common law to withhold information from the courts on the grounds that the information is privileged. As stated in Chapter 3, information in an auditor's working papers can be subpoenaed by a court. Confidential discussions between the client and auditor cannot be withheld from the courts.

Definitions of Legal Terms

The material in the rest of the chapter can be covered more effectively if the most common legal terms affecting public accountant's liability are understood.

Negligence and Fraud

The first four terms deal with the degree to which the auditor is negligent or fraudulent. The distinctions are useful for discussing the application of the law to various types of lawsuits against auditors because they affect the outcome of many suits.

Negligence   Absence of reasonable care that can be expected of a person in a set of circumstances. When negligence of an auditor is being evaluated, it is in terms of what other competent auditors would have done in the same situation. A plaintiff, in a tort action (that is, a case brought by a plaintiff for an alleged wrong suffered at the hands of the defendant) for negligence against a public accountant must prove all of the following to succeed:

1. The accountant (defendant) must owe a duty of care to the plaintiff.
2. The defendant must have been negligent in the performance of that duty (that is, did not act in accordance with the reasonable person concept).
3. The plaintiff must have suffered a loss.
4. There must be a connection between the defendant's negligence and the plaintiff's loss. For example, the plaintiff relied on financial statements audited by the defendant, who was negligent in the performance of the audit, and the plaintiff suffered a loss because of that reliance.

[handwritten: Knowingly]

Fraud A false assertion that has been made knowingly, or without belief in its truth, or recklessly without caring whether it is true or not. The plaintiff must also be able to prove that the accountant intended the plaintiff to act on the assertion, that the plaintiff did act on it, and that as a consequence the plaintiff suffered a loss. An example is an auditor giving a standard (unqualified) opinion on financial statements that will be used to obtain a loan when the auditor *knows* the financial statements contain a material misstatement(s).

[handwritten: So Reckless]

Constructive fraud Existence of such recklessness that even though there was no actual intent to defraud, a court will impute or construe fraud to the action. For example, if a public accountant failed to follow most of the generally accepted auditing standards, he or she may be found to have committed constructive fraud even though no intent to deceive statement users has been proved.

[handwritten: Did not follow & Rules or conduct not followed]

Tort action for negligence Failure of a party to meet its social or professional obligations, contractual or otherwise, thereby causing injury to another party to whom a duty was owed. A typical negligence action against a public accountant is a bank's claim that an auditor had a duty to uncover material errors in financial statements that had been relied on in making a loan.

Contract Law

[handwritten: Failure to Perform]

Breach of contract Failure of one or both parties in a contract to fulfill the requirements of the contract. An example is the failure of a public accounting firm to deliver a tax return on the agreed-upon date. Parties who have a relationship that is established by a contract are said to have *privity of contract*.

[handwritten: "Sign An Agreement letter"]

Typically, public accounting firms and clients sign an *engagement letter* to formalize their agreement about the services to be provided, fees, and timing. There can be privity of contract without a written agreement, but an engagement letter defines the contract more clearly.

Third-party beneficiary A third party who does not have privity of contract but is known to the contracting parties and is intended to have certain rights and benefits under the contract. A common example is a bank that has a large loan outstanding at the balance sheet date and requires an audit as a part of its loan agreement. The naming of a third party in an engagement letter often establishes that party as a third-party beneficiary.

Common and Statutory Law

Common law, judge-made law, or case law Laws that have been developed through court decisions rather than through government statutes. The bulk of the law of negligence has been created in this fashion. An example is an auditor's liability to a bank related to the auditor's failure to discover material misstatements in financial statements that were relied on in issuing a loan. This law is continually evolving as new decisions are handed down by the courts; what might be used as a successful defense by an auditor today may not be successful tomorrow, while a defense that was not successful in the past now might be successful. The thing to remember is that common law is always evolving.

Statutory law   Laws and regulations that have been passed by a Canadian governmental body, either federal or provincial. The *Canada Business Corporations Act* is an important statutory law affecting auditors of companies incorporated under its jurisdiction.

Other Terms   **Civil action**   An action between individuals such as those that may be brought for breach of contract or tort.

Criminal action   An action brought under a provision of criminal statute law, for example, the *Criminal Code of Canada*.

Contributory negligence   When a person injured by a public accountant's negligence has also been negligent and this negligence has also caused or contributed to the person's loss or injuries is called contributory negligence. A common example of such negligence is failure to give a public accountant information requested during the preparation of a tax return. The client later sues the accountant for improper preparation of the return. The court may hold that there was contributory negligence by the client and any damages that the client is awarded would be reduced in proportion to the amount that the client's own negligence was responsible for the loss.

Liability to Clients

OBJECTIVE 4

Describe accountant's liability to clients, the related defenses, and some significant legal cases.

The term *client* refers to the entity being audited and not to its owners or shareholders. Although the shareholders vote to appoint the auditors, the contract is between the enterprise and the auditors. In effect, shareholders are therefore third parties. Since shareholders are not in privity, it is not clear from present common law whether or not a shareholder would succeed in an action against a public accounting firm for negligence. It has been argued that financial statements are prepared for shareholders to assist them in making resource allocation or investment decisions. If that argument is accepted, shareholders could succeed. If, on the other hand, the argument that financial statements are prepared for shareholders to evaluate management's stewardship and not to make investment decisions is accepted, then shareholders might not be successful in a suit for negligence on the grounds that they were not in privity.

The most frequent source of lawsuits against public accountants is from clients. The suits vary widely, including such claims as failure to complete an unaudited engagement on the agreed upon date, inappropriate withdrawal from an audit, failure to discover a defalcation, and breach of the confidentiality requirements of public accountants. Typically, the amount of these lawsuits is relatively small, and they do not receive the publicity often given to other types of suits. The *Fund of Funds* case discussed in Figure 4–13 below is an American case but does illustrate the issue; the case is also a notable exception because the court awarded the company $80 million in a suit against a public accounting firm for breach of confidentiality requirements.

A typical lawsuit involves a claim that the auditor did not discover an employee defalcation (theft of assets) as a result of negligence in the conduct of the audit. The lawsuit can be for breach of contract, a tort action for negligence, or both. Tort actions can be based on ordinary negligence or fraud. Note that, while it might sound odd for plaintiffs to claim under both negligence and tort, the way each is proven and the amount of damages available under each might be different. By claiming under both, the plaintiff is thus covering all bases. The plaintiff cannot, however, be awarded damages twice for one event or loss.

The principal issue in cases involving alleged negligence is usually the level of care required. Although it is generally agreed that nobody is perfect, not even a professional, in most instances any significant misstatement will create at least a presumption of negligence that the professional will have to rebut. In the auditing environment, failure to meet generally accepted auditing standards is often strong evidence of negligence. An example of an audit case raising the question of negligent performance by a public accounting firm is the case of *Haig* v. *Bamford* (see Figure 4–8). The reader should remember from the study of generally accepted auditing standards in Chapter 1 that determining due care and the amount and type of evidence to be obtained on an audit are subjective decisions. In a suit where negligence by an auditor was alleged, the court would hear evidence from one or more expert (auditing) witnesses as to the decision they would have reached in similar circumstances. From this evidence, a judge or jury would decide what the average public accountant would do and, therefore, what the accountant being sued should have done. In this way, negligence is determined.

The question of level of care becomes more difficult in the environment of unaudited financial statements (that is, a review or compilation) in which there are few accepted standards to evaluate performance. An example of a lawsuit dealing with the failure to uncover fraud in unaudited financial statements is the U.S. *1136 Tenants* case, summarized in Figure 4–2.

Auditor's Defenses Against Client Suits for Negligence

The public accounting firm normally uses one or a combination of four defenses when there are legal claims of negligence by clients: lack of duty to perform the service, nonnegligent performance, contributory negligence, and absence of causal connection.

Lack of duty   The lack of duty to perform the service means that the public accounting firm claims there was no duty owed to the client to perform the task that is now said to have been negligently performed. For example, the public accounting firm might claim that errors were not uncovered because the firm did a review engagement, not an audit. A common way for a public accounting firm to demonstrate a lack of duty to perform is by use of an *engagement letter*.[3] Many litigation experts believe well-written engagement letters are one of the most important ways public accounting firms can reduce the likelihood of adverse legal actions.

Harry Kuziw et al v. *James W. Abbott* et al. (Figure 4–3) illustrates reliance and a lack of duty.

---

3 Two types of letters that are commonly used by auditors to reduce potential liability to clients: an engagement letter and a representation letter. An engagement letter is a signed agreement between the public accounting firm and the client identifying such items as whether an audit is to be done, other services to be provided, the date the work is to be completed by, and the fees. The representation letter documents oral communication between auditors and management, and states management's responsibilities for fair presentation in the financial statements.

week to v, 103.

FIGURE 4–2

1136 TENANTS V. MAX ROTHENBERG AND COMPANY (1967)

The *1136 Tenants* case was a civil case concerning a CPA's failure to uncover fraud as a part of unaudited financial statements. The tenants recovered approximately $235,000.

A CPA firm was engaged by a real estate managing agent for $600 per year to prepare financial statements, a tax return, and a schedule showing the apportionment of real estate taxes for the 1136 Tenants Corporation, a cooperative apartment house. The statements were sent periodically to the tenants. The statements included the words "unaudited" and there was a cover letter stating that "The statement was prepared from the books and records of the corporation and no independent verifications were taken thereon."

During the period of the engagement, from 1963 to 1965, the manager of the management firm embezzled significant funds from the tenants of the cooperative. The tenants sued the CPA firm for negligence and breach of contract for failure to find the fraud.There were two central issues in the case. Was the CPA firm engaged to do an audit instead of only write-up work, and was there negligence on the part of the CPA firm? The court answered yes on both counts. The reasoning for the court's conclusion that an audit had taken place was the performance of "some audit procedures" by the CPA firm, including the preparation of a worksheet entitled "missing invoices." Had the CPA followed up on these, the fraud would likely have been uncovered. Most important, the court concluded that even if the engagement had not been considered an audit, the CPA had a duty to follow up on any potential significant exceptions uncovered during an engagement.

The case has two implications for public accountants:

1. Engagement letters that detail what the client and auditor expect to be done are very important so that both know exactly what is to be done.

2. All unexplained and unusual items should be followed to their conclusion unless they are not material. However the public accountant should be very careful to ensure that the item that is not material is not part of a larger material item or a symptom of a serious (and possibly material) problem.

Nonnegligent performance Evidence to refute a claim would be that the audit was performed in accordance with generally accepted auditing standards. Even if there were undiscovered mistakes (errors) or intentional misstatements or misrepresentations (fraud and other irregularities), the auditors will argue that they are not responsible if the audit was properly conducted. The public accounting firm is not expected to be infallible. Similarly, Sections 5000 and 5135 of the *CICA Handbook* make it clear that an audit in accordance with GAAS is subject to limitations and cannot be relied upon for complete assurance that all errors and fraud and other irregularities will be found.

Section 5000 states, in part:

The objective of an audit of financial statements is to express an opinion whether the financial statements present fairly. . . . Such an opinion is not an assurance as to the future viability of the enterprise nor an opinion as to the effectiveness with which its operations, including internal control, have been conducted.

The operations of an enterprise are under the control of management, which has the responsibility for the accurate recording of transactions and the preparation of

FIGURE 4–3

KUZIW ET AL. V. *ABBOTT* ET AL. (1984)

Abbott *et al.* provided accounting services to Graf-Tech Publication Services Ltd. for several years. William J. Hemenway, a member of the firm of Abbott *et al.*, who had done work for Harry Kuziw in connection with other investments that Kuziw had made, introduced Kuziw to Graf-Tech in early 1980 in response to Kuziw's request for information about "business opportunities."

Graf-Tech was suffering from cash shortages and was being pressed by Revenue Canada for overdue payroll deductions. It was also suffering from managerial weaknesses. Hemenway explained both the positive and negative aspects of Graf-Tech to Kuziw and provided him with statements with "Accountant's Comments" dated June 30, 1979 and with statements for January and February 1980, that had each been prepared with a "Notice to Reader." Kuziw knew that no audit had been done and appeared to understand the implications of work done under Section 8100 of the *CICA Handbook*. The Court found that Kuziw had conducted an extensive investigation on his own including discussions with the senior management of Graf-Tech and with the manager of the bank where Graf-Tech banked. Kuziw's lawyer suggested outside accounting advice but Kuziw demurred.

Kuziw made two investments and gave guarantees totalling $235,000 over the next several months. In addition, he became active in Graf-Tech's management. Despite this assistance, the company went into receivership in late 1980. Among the reasons for the receivership was the fact that Graf-Tech's principle contract was much less profitable than had been believed and than had been indicated by the financial statements prepared by Hemenway's firm some months earlier.

The Court of the Queen's Bench of Manitoba, upheld on appeal by the Court of Appeal of Manitoba, found that while Hemenway had known that Kuziw planned to rely on the financial statements he had prepared, Kuziw had not relied to any significant degree on the information. Accordingly, Kuziw could not succeed. The Court went on to state that it believed that Hemenway had "discharged his professional responsibility."

This case is of interest, in addition to its finding, because the judgment discusses at some length the difference between an audit and work done under Section 8100 as well as the responsibility of the accountant under the latter.

---

financial statements. . . . The financial statements [are] the representations of management.[4]

The section goes on to explain that "The auditor . . . seeks reasonable assurance whether the financial statements are free of material misstatement [that is, material error or fraud]." It also states that "absolute assurance in auditing is not attainable" and lists the reasons. These include the need for judgment, the use of testing (that is, sampling rather than examining the entire population), the inherent limitations of internal control, and the fact that the evidence an auditor examines is persuasive, not conclusive. These factors should be remembered when reading about risk in Chapter 8.

Section 5135.15 states, in part:

In an audit conducted in accordance with generally accepted auditing standards, the auditor's professional responsibility is fulfilled by complying with those standards. . . . An audit does not guarantee all material misstatements will be detected. . . . A

---

4 The judge, in the 1933 decision by the Manitoba Court of Appeal in the case of *International Laboratories Limited* v. *Dewar* et al., put the onus on management for the detection of fraud.

material misstatement may subsequently be discovered in the financial statements even though the auditor has adhered to generally accepted auditing standards. . . .

It is likely that the courts will accept the *CICA Handbook* as evidence of appropriate standards of behavior for the auditor; but it is possible that the courts could decide that an auditor who complied with the *Handbook* had been negligent. Such circumstances would be rare, but could occur if the court thought the auditor had complied with the letter and not the spirit of the rules.

The courts recognize that it is possible to make a valid exercise of judgment that, nonetheless, has an unfavorable outcome. In that case, the auditor would not be found negligent. The auditor would want expert testimony that he or she had made a valid exercise of judgment. For example, the auditor might have selected a sample from a population for testing that was not representative of that population and, hence, had not found a material misstatement that was present in the population. The courts would likely determine that the auditor had not been negligent since the auditor had made a valid exercise in judgment in selecting the sample.

Requiring auditors to discover all material errors and fraud would, in essence, make them insurers or guarantors of the accuracy of the financial statements. The courts do not require that. *Cameron* v. *Piers, Conrod & Allen* (Figure 4–4) is an example of a case where the public accountant was not negligent; the court ruled that the auditor had satisfied the reasonable person concept.

Contributory negligence A defense of contributory negligence by the client means that the public accounting firm claims that part or all of the loss arose because of the claimant's own negligence. For example, suppose the client is the claimant and argues that the public accounting firm was negligent in not uncovering an employee theft of cash. A likely contributory negligence defense is the auditor's claim that the public accounting firm informed management of a weakness in the system of internal control that enhanced the likelihood of the fraud, but management did not correct it. Management often does not correct internal control weaknesses because of cost considerations, attitudes about employee honesty, or procrastination. In the event of a lawsuit of the nature described, the auditor is unlikely to lose the suit, assuming a strong contributory negligence defense, if the client was informed in writing of the internal control weaknesses. An example of contributory negligence as a partial defense is the case of *H.E. Kane Agencies Ltd.* v. *Coopers & Lybrand* summarized in Figure 4–5.

Absence of causal connection To succeed in an action against the auditor, the client must be able to show that there is a close causal connection between the auditor's breach of the standard of due care and the damages suffered by the client. For example, assume an auditor failed to complete an audit on the agreed-upon date. The client alleges that this caused a bank not to renew an outstanding loan, which caused damages. A potential auditor defense is that the bank refused to renew the loan for other reasons, such as the weakening financial condition of the client. The case of *Toromont Industrial Holdings* v. *Thorne* et al., discussed in Figure 4–9 on page 111, illustrates absence of causal connection; the court ruled that the purchaser, Toromont, did not rely on an incorrect auditor's report but rather had decided to purchase Cimco Ltd. prior to receiving the audited financial statements.[5]

---

5 Smyth, J.E., Soberman, D.A., and Easson, A.J., *The Law and Business Administration in Canada*, Sixth Edition, Scarborough, Ontario: Prentice-Hall Canada Inc., 1991, pp. 123-124.

FIGURE 4–4

Proper Sample
But error
not in
sample

(Took issue
in the col
Sample)

CAMERON V. PIERS, CONROD & ALLEN (1985)[6]

Piers, Conrod & Allen (PCA) were the auditors for Cameron Limited and its subsidiary, Kentville Publishing Company Limited. The year end of the latter company was October 31, while that of the former company was December 31. Kentville was run by a competent accountant who was in frequent contact with and highly regarded by the owner of Cameron Limited.

PCA normally began the audit of Kentville early in the new year but were unable to gain access to the books for the year ended October 31, 1979 at that time. Kentville's manager continued to delay the Kentville audit through March and April 1980. In the meantime PCA had begun the audit of Cameron and in that connection needed to verify the valuation of Kentville on the Cameron books.

The auditor from PCA received reassurances from the Kentville manager that the owner of Cameron Limited was being kept abreast of the situation at Kentville. In addition, the auditor had talked to the owner's son, who was himself an accountant, and had made him aware of the delay.

The auditor from PCA and his staff went to the offices of Kentville and did what work was considered necessary to complete the audit of Cameron. At that time, there was no indication of any serious problems at Kentville. The Cameron December 31, 1979 financial statements were issued with an unqualified opinion. The notes to the financial statements indicated that the accounts of Kentville and other subsidiaries were not consolidated but were carried at cost.

Subsequently, the manager of Kentville was hospitalized. The records and financial affairs of Kentville were found to be in disarray. PCA was hired to go in to Kentville and straighten the records out. It was discovered that the reports that the manager had been giving to the owner of Cameron and to the auditor were not accurate.

Cameron Limited sued PCA on the grounds that PCA had been negligent in evaluating Cameron's investment in Kentville as at December 31, 1979. The court found (sustained on appeal) that the auditor had not been negligent in that he had exercised reasonable care and skill in attempting to evaluate Cameron's investment in Kentville. It was not inappropriate for the auditor to rely on the manager of Kentville, a trusted employee of the owner of Cameron; the auditor did his best to ascertain the facts.

Liability to Third Parties Under Common Law

A public accounting firm may be potentially liable to third parties if a loss was incurred by the claimant due to reliance on misleading financial statements. Third parties are any people with whom the auditor did *not* enter into a contract and include actual and potential shareholders, vendors, bankers and other creditors or investors, employees, and customers. A typical suit might occur when a bank is unable to collect a major loan from an insolvent customer. The bank will claim that misleading audited financial statements were relied upon in making the loan, and that the public accounting firm should be held responsible because it failed to perform the audit with due care. Understanding when the auditor will be held liable calls for an understanding of the continuing evolution of this area of the law. What the final resolution will be remains unclear.

Evolution of Liability

The leading precedent-setting auditing case in third party liability was a 1931 United States case, *Ultramares Corporation v. Touche*. It established the tradi-

---

6 Rowan, Hugh, Q.C., "Stymied by Management: A Case of Negligence?" *CA Magazine* (April 1986), pp.80-87.

FIGURE 4–5

H.E. KANE AGENCIES LTD. V. COOPERS & LYBRAND (1983)[7]

Coopers & Lybrand had been the auditors of H.E. Kane Agencies Ltd. for a number of years. The president of Kane Agencies was Harold Kane, and he ran the operation; his son Charles was an employee. In 1967 Charles persuaded his father to expand into the travel business, and Kane Agencies became an agent for Air Canada.

An invoice was prepared whenever an airline ticket was sold, but the sale was not recorded until payment was received from the customer. Kane Senior did not like credit and so very little credit was extended. Reports were submitted twice monthly to Air Canada indicating ticket sales with the net cost of the tickets enclosed. Initially, sales were for a relatively small amount to a wide variety of customers.

In 1974 Kane Agencies changed the thrust of its travel business when it started doing business with Trade Resources (International) Limited. Now Kane Agencies did have a dominant customer. The accounting for ticket sales was changed for this new customer; an invoice was prepared when payment was received and not, as previously, when the ticket was sold. As a result, Charles Kane knew about the size of the outstanding receivable from Trade Resources, but his father did not. Charles would report the sale to Air Canada at the time the ticket was paid for and not when it was issued, so that there was a delay in recording the liability.

Trade Resources went bankrupt in 1976 owing Kane Agencies in excess of $250,000. Kane sued Coopers & Lybrand claiming that the accounting firm had been negligent in not discovering the deception that Charles was perpetrating on his father and Air Canada. Coopers & Lybrand claimed that Harold Kane had not supervised the travel division and that Charles Kane had wilfully concealed the unreported ticket sales from them.

The judge assessed Kane Agencies damages at $87,599 but found that the company had contributed to the loss through the conduct of Harold in not supervising the travel business and not noticing the Trade Resources receivable and the conduct of Charles in setting up the arrangement that caused the loss. Accordingly, the damages payable by Coopers & Lybrand to Kane Agencies were reduced by 50 percent.

OBJECTIVE 5

Describe accountant's liability to third parties under common law, the related defenses, and some significant legal cases.

tional common law approach known as the *Ultramares* doctrine. The case has been cited many times in England and Canada. It is summarized in Figure 4–6.

The key aspect of the *Ultramares* doctrine is that ordinary negligence is insufficient for liability to third parties, because of the lack of privity of contract between the third party and the auditor. In addition, *Ultramares* also held that if there had been fraud or constructive fraud, the auditor could be held liable to more general third parties.

Traditionally, third parties in Canada were in a similar position to those in the United States: they were effectively prevented from suing successfully for negligent misstatements if they had no contract with the auditor. The situation began to change in 1963 with an English case, *Hedley Byrne & Co. Ltd.* v. *Heller & Partners Ltd.* (Figure 4–7). This case too was a landmark case. Although the case was British, not Canadian, and did not deal specifically with accountants, it contained very real implications for them. In the United Kingdom it was viewed as the long-awaited statement about the law of negligent misstatement and it came from the most senior court of that country, the House of Lords. All common law countries were naturally interested in its outcome. The defense of lack of privity enunciated in *Ultramares* was said by the House of Lords to no longer be relevant.

---

7 See Rowan, Hugh, Q.C., "Giving Credit where Credit's Not Due, Part 1," *CA Magazine* (June 1983), pp. 69-71; Rowan, "Giving Credit where Credit's Not Due, Part 2," *CA Magazine* (August 1983), pp. 97-102; and Rowan, "When Fault is Divided," *CA Magazine* (August 1986), pp.84-87.

FIGURE 4–6

ULTRAMARES CORPORATION v. *TOUCHE* (1931)

The creditors of an insolvent corporation (Ultramares) relied on the audited financials and subsequently sued the accountants, alleging that they were guilty of negligence and fraudulent misrepresentation. The accounts receivable had been falsified by adding to approximately $650,000 in accounts receivable another item of over $700,000. The creditors alleged that careful investigation would have shown the $700,000 to be fraudulent. The accounts payable contained similar discrepancies.The court held that the accountants had been negligent but ruled that accountants would not be liable to third parties for honest blunders beyond the bounds of the original contract unless they were third-party beneficiaries. The court held that only one who enters into a contract with an accountant for services can sue if those services are rendered negligently.

The court went on, however, to order a new trial on the issue of fraudulent misstatement. The form of certificate then used said, "We further certify that subject to provisions for federal taxes on income the said statement in our opinion presents a true and correct view of the financial condition." The court pointed out that to make such a representation if one did not have an honest belief in its truth would be fraudulent misrepresentation.

The various opinions of the Law Lords on the case did not make it clear to whom those providing opinions on statements would owe a duty of care. The notion of foreseeable third parties was introduced as a possible test of the extent of duty. The case then said those uttering negligent misstatements may be liable to third parties but did not make it clear precisely under what circumstances. Courts in a number of countries have been grappling with the issue ever since.

The next case of importance on this issue was decided by the Supreme Court of Canada in 1976. The case was *Gordon T. Haig* v. *Ralph L. Bamford* et al.; see Figure 4–8.

This case confirms in Canada the finding in *Hedley Byrne* v. *Heller* insofar as lack of privity being a defense is concerned. However, the Supreme Court decided it should not consider the foreseeability test (that is, test 1) as it was not relevant to the particular circumstances. Instead, the narrower test of actual knowledge of the limited class was deemed to be appropriate; that is, in Canada, persons making negligent misstatements (in this case, auditors) are potentially

FIGURE 4–7

HEDLEY BYRNE v. *HELLER & PARTNERS* (1963)

Hedley Byrne was an advertising agency that was about to incur a liability for advertising for a client. They asked their bankers to find out from the client's bankers, Heller & Partners, if the client was credit-worthy. Heller replied in the affirmative to the banker, who passed the information on to Hedley Byrne and so Hedley Byrne, a third party, incurred the liability. Subsequently the client was unable to pay its accounts, and Hedley Byrne sued Heller for negligence.

Heller & Partners had issued a disclaimer together with their opinion and thus the House of Lords ruled in their favor. However, with respect to the lack of privity, the Lords found that not to be a bar to success by the plaintiff, Hedley Byrne. Some of the Law Lords argued that despite the lack or privity, Heller owed a duty of care to Hedley Byrne and that Heller should have foreseen that Hedley Byrne would rely on their statement about the client.

Refer to P.s 103

FIGURE 4–8

HAIG V. *BAMFORD* ET AL. (1976)

Scholler Furniture & Fixtures Ltd. needed additional working capital and approached Saskatchewan Economic Development Corporation (SEDCO) for further advances. SEDCO agreed to grant the advances providing Scholler would produce satisfactory audited financial statements for the fiscal period ended March 31, 1965 and gain the infusion of additional equity capital in the amount of $20,000.

Scholler told his accountants, Bamford *et al.* that he needed audited financial statements for SEDCO, his bank and a potential but then unknown investor. The statements were prepared, with an auditor's report appended and shown to Haig who invested the required $20,000.

Subsequently, the company again foundered and investigation revealed that the financial statements included $28,000 of revenue received in advance as earned revenue; the corrected statements showed that the company had lost money and not earned a sizable profit as shown by the earlier statements. Subsequently it was discovered that Bamford *et al.*, although they were told an audit was required and although they appended an auditor's report, had not done an audit.

Later Haig advanced additional funds but the company went into receivership. Haig sued the accountants for negligence and sought to recover both his original investment and later advance.

The Supreme Court, in their decision, concurred with lower courts that Bamford *et al.* had been negligent. Insofar as the extent of the duty of care on the part of the accountants to third parties, the court said there were three possible tests:

1. Foreseeability of the use of audited financial statements by the plaintiff.
2. Actual knowledge of the limited class who will rely on the audited statements.
3. Actual knowledge of the person who will rely on the audited statements.

The appropriate test was deemed to be 2. The court decided that Haig was entitled to recover his original investment from the auditors because he had relied on the financial statement that had been negligently prepared. He was not entitled to recover subsequent investments because he made them based on his own information.

liable to all those third parties who were members of a limited group of whom the auditors had knowledge at the time the audit was performed and the audited financial statements were issued. For example, the test of actual knowledge would apply if an auditor was asked to give an opinion on financial statements to be shown to several local banks for purposes of obtaining a loan.

At about the same time, another case of interest was unfolding; it was *Toromont Industrial Holdings Limited v. Thorne, Gunn, Helliwell & Christenson.* This case, summarized in Figure 4–9, reached its final resolution in the High Court of Justice in Ontario.

The *Toromont* case raises several interesting issues. The judgment, which referred both to *Hedley Byrne* and a lower court decision on *Haig v. Bamford*,[8] confirmed the broadening of an auditor's liability to third parties known to be using the audited financial statements. In the case of *Toromont v. Thorne*, Toromont was able to prove that Thorne *et al.* owed a duty of care to Toromont and that

---

8 The *Haig* v. *Bamford* case first decided in a lower court in 1972 for the plaintiff. That decision was appealed and reversed by the Saskatchewan Court of Appeal in 1974. Haig appealed that decision and was successful in the Supreme Court of Canada in 1976.

Refer to Pg 106

FIGURE 4–9

TOROMONT V. *THORNE* ET AL. (1975)

Toromont proposed to acquire all of the shares of Cimco Ltd. for cash and Toromont shares. The purchase price was based on Cimco's assets, liabilities and financial position at that date. Prior to purchase, a partner from the accounting firm that did Toromont's audit talked to a partner of Thorne, Cimco's auditors, about the work the latter had done with regard to the December 31, 1968 financial statements. Cimco's financial statements at this point were in draft form. In other words, Thorne *et al.* were aware of Toromont's interest in the financial statements prior to their being issued.

The court decided that the financial statements did present fairly the financial position at December 31, 1968, but that the auditors, Thorne *et al.*, had been negligent in their performance of the 1968 audit. The reasons given were as follows:

1. They did not obtain sufficient evidence about certain contracts.
2. They relied too heavily on oral evidence from management.
3. They did not adequately check the system of internal control in force although they relied on it.
4. The accounts included goodwill with respect to a company sold two years previously.

In addition a senior partner of Thorne, although not connected with the audit, was very involved with Cimco's senior management.

The court concluded that Thorne *et al.* had been negligent and that Toromont did have a right of action as Thorne knew Toromont would be relying on the financial statements. The court, however, also concluded that Toromont did not suffer any loss from the negligence, and so the case was dismissed.

Thorne *et al.* had been negligent in the performance of that duty, but Toromont was not able to prove that it suffered a loss; as a consequence, Toromont did not succeed.

Another case that is often cited in Canada is *Albert Dupuis* v. *Pan American Mines* et al. It is interesting because it is concerned with the auditor's liability on a prospectus. The case is shown in Figure 4–10.

Although this case appears to widen the auditor's liability to third parties *who had relied on the financial statements in a prospectus to make a decision* (this point is important when considering the following discussion), some care should be taken in interpreting its significance. It was not a case heard before the Supreme Court of Canada, nor did it refer to the *Haig* v. *Bamford* decision. At this time, it is best considered as evidence of the uncertain status of the auditor's liability. Further, it should be noted that other investors in Pan American who were unable to prove that they had relied on the prospectus were not successful. As will be discussed later, proving both negligence and reliance remain important components of a successful action.

The next discussion flows from two English decisions made in 1989: *Caparo Industries PLC* v. *Dickmans* and *Al Saudi Banque* et al. v. *Clark Pixley*. Prior to the decision in these cases, the consensus among commentators was that the duty of care expected of auditors was expanding. These cases, therefore, came as something of a surprise as they appear to restrict the auditor's liability.

FIGURE 4–10

DUPUIS V. *PAN AMERICAN MINES* ET AL. (1979)[9]

Thorne *et al.* were auditors of Pan American Mines Ltd. while Seidman & Seidman were the auditors of a wholly-owned subsidiary, Central Mining Corporation, located in the United States. Both accounting firms were members of an international group of firms known then as Binder-Seidman-Thorne International Group.

Thorne, as primary auditor, expressed a clean opinion on the financial statements of Pan American, and its consolidated subsidiary, Central Mining, that were included in a prospectus, filed in connection with a new share offering with the Quebec Securities Commission in early 1971. Later in that same year the Pan American Stock was delisted.

Albert Dupuis bought stock in Pan American when it was first issued and, after it was delisted, brought suit against the auditors, among others, for losses suffered. This action was based on alleged inaccuracies in the financial information included in the prospectus.

The judge decided that Seidman & Seidman, and by extension Thorne through their role as primary auditor, were negligent in not confirming a substantial financial commitment to Central Mining and, in fact, whether or not the company making the commitment could honour it. The judge concluded that there was further negligence in that the auditors did not check the title to mining claims described in the notes to the financial statements.

Dupuis was able to satisfy the court that he had relied on the audited financial statements, that he had suffered a loss and that the loss flowed from the reliance. The court decided that the auditors had been negligent and that they had owed a duty of care to prospective investors who relied on a prospectus including financial statements audited by them.

In *Caparo*,[10] the Law Lords determined that an auditor would not be liable to investors who made a decision to invest in a company after the audited financial statements had been published nor to shareholders at the time the audit was conducted who made an investment decision (for example, to hold or sell shares already owned or to buy additional shares) after the statements had been published. The Court held that the persons uttering the statements should only be liable if the third parties used them for the purpose for which they were prepared. In this case, the Law Lords held that the audit was provided to evaluate management and to give investment information. In *Al Saudi Banque*, the courts found that auditors were not liable to creditors who relied on financial statements on which the auditors had opined.

In November, 1989, the B.C. Supreme Court, in the case of *Dixon* v. *Deacon, Morgan, McEwan, Easson* et al., handed down a decision in which they agreed that, while it was foreseeable that Dixon would rely on the audited financial statements, the requirement of proximity was lacking. In addition, the court decided after weighing "the relationship of the parties, the nature of the risk and the public interest in the proposed solution"[11] that it would not be fair to impose a

---

9 Rowan, Hugh, "Third Party Liability Extended?" *CA Magazine* (August 1979), pp. 78-82.

10 The ensuing material comes from Rowan, Hugh, "A Fair Share of Care," *CA Magazine* (December 1989), pp. 63-68; Paskell-Mede, Mindy, "Duty's not in the Eye of the Beholder," *CA Magazine* (April 1990), pp. 29-31; Pound, Richard W., "Duty in Question," *CGA Magazine* (August 1990), pp. 14-15; DuPlessis, Dorothy, and Trenholm, Barbara, "Limiting Auditor Liability," *CGA Magazine*, (November 1991), pp. 30-35.

11 Pound, Richard W., "Duty in Question," *CGA Magazine* (August 1990), p. 14.

duty of care on the auditors because it would give Dixon a cause of action which was not included in securities acts.

The answer to the question of where the duty of care presently stands in Canada is far from clear. *Caparo* is obviously not a binding case in Canada; however, coming from such a senior court as the House of Lords, it is influential. There are recent cases in the United Kingdom which suggest courts are broadening the duty of care again by giving a generous definition of "purpose." In Canada there have been contradictory B.C. and Ontario cases which leave the present position unclear. It will only be resolved when the Supreme Court of Canada decides a case that requires it to resolve the issue it left unstated in *Haig* v. *Bamford*; specifically, does the *Haig* v. *Bamford* test apply or is the correct test the broader one of foreseeability?

Auditor Defenses Against Third Party Suits

The defenses available to auditors in suits by clients are also available in third-party lawsuits.

The previous section outlined the lack of duty of care defense. As the preceding discussion has suggested, the court, in *Ultramares*, limited the auditor's liability for negligence to parties being in privity with the auditor. *Hedley Byrne* introduced the notion of the auditor having a duty of care to foreseeable third parties; *Haig* v. *Bamford* narrowed the responsibility for due care by the auditor to the limited class whom the auditor actually knew would use and rely on the financial statements. The more recent cases in both the United Kingdom and Canada suggest the final decision is still not available to us.

The second defense in third-party suits is nonnegligent performance. If the auditor conducted the audit in accordance with GAAS, there is a strong inference of no negligence. Recognize, however, that nonnegligent performance is difficult to demonstrate to a court, especially if it is a jury trial and the jury is made up of lay people.

Absence of causal connection in third-party suits usually means nonreliance on the financial statements by the user. For example, assume the auditor can demonstrate that a lender relied upon an ongoing banking relationship with a customer, rather than the financial statements, in making a loan. The fact that the auditor was negligent in the conduct of the audit would not be relevant in that situation.

Finally, it is possible to find contributory negligence if it could be said the claimants were themselves negligent, say, by ignoring other relevant information. It would be more common however for the auditor to defend on one of the other bases outlined above.

Criminal Liability

Fraud by anyone can be a criminal act and the perpetrator can be subject to criminal prosecution.[12] The criminal action would be brought by the Attorney-General; conviction of a professional accountant would result in a charge of criminal misconduct by the professional accountant's institute (or *ordre*) in the case of CAs, his or her association in the case of CGAs, or society in the case of CMAs. In addition, a civil action for damages could be brought by the person(s) suffering a loss from the fraudulent act.

Fraud may include an auditor's association with financial statements he or

---

12 Section 338 of the *Criminal Code of Canada*.

OBJECTIVE 6

Specify what constitutes criminal liability for accountants, and describe an important U.S. legal case.

she knows are materially misstated or false. For example, if the auditor of a company gave an unqualified auditor's report on the company's financial statement knowing that inventory was grossly overvalued, it is possible the auditor would be found guilty of criminal fraud and could be sued in a civil action.

A defense that the auditor in the situation just described might use is that the financial statements were in accordance with generally accepted accounting principles. Yet let us suppose in this case that inventory was valued at the lower of cost or market but the auditor knew that a new untested invention by the company could make the inventory obsolete when the invention was revealed. Failure to reflect all the information in her possession in the financial statements would make them misleading *despite their being in accordance with GAAP*. The auditor could be judged guilty of fraud.

While there are almost no Canadian cases involving fraud in this area, there have been several U.S. cases. Although these are not great in absolute number, they have the effect of damaging the integrity of the profession, and reducing the profession's ability to attract and retain outstanding people. On the positive side, criminal actions encourage practitioners to use extreme care and exercise good faith in their activities.

The leading case of criminal action against CPAs is *United States* v. *Simon*, which occurred in 1969. That case is summarized in Figure 4–11. Simon has been followed by three additional major criminal cases. In *United States* v. *Natelli* (1975), two auditors were convicted of criminal liability for certifying financial statements of *National Student Marketing Corporation* that contained inadequate disclosures pertaining to accounts receivable.

In *United States* v. *Weiner* (1975), three auditors were convicted of securities fraud in connection with their audit of *Equity Funding Corporation of America*. Equity Funding was a financial conglomerate whose financial statements had been overstated through a massive fraud by management. The fraud was so extensive and the audit work so poor, that the court concluded the auditors must have been aware of the fraud and were therefore guilty of complicity.

In *ESM Government Securities* v. *Alexander Grant & Co.* (1986), it was revealed by management to the partner in charge of the audit of ESM that the previous year's audited financial statements contained a material misstatement. Rather than complying with professional and firm standards in such circumstances, the partner agreed to say nothing in the hope that management would work its way out of the problem during the current year. Instead, the situation worsened, eventually to the point where losses exceeded $300 million. The partner was convicted of criminal charges for his role in sustaining the fraud and is now serving a 12-year prison term.

Several critical lessons can be learned from these four cases:

- An investigation of the integrity of management is an important part of deciding on the acceptability of clients and the extent of work to perform.
- The auditor can be found criminally guilty in the conduct of an audit even if the person's background indicates integrity in his or her personal and professional life. The criminal liability can extend to partners and staff.
- Independence in appearance and fact by all individuals on the engagement is essential, especially in a defense involving criminal actions.
- Transactions with related parties require special scrutiny because of the potential for misstatement.
- Generally accepted accounting principles cannot be relied upon exclusively in

deciding whether financial statements are fairly presented. The substance of the statements, considering all facts, is required.

■ Good documentation may be just as important in the auditor's defense of criminal charges as in a civil suit.

■ The potential consequences of the auditor knowingly committing a wrongful act are so severe that it is unlikely that the potential benefits could ever justify the actions.

Responsibilities for Confidentiality

There is an issue that arose in the 1980s in the United States that is of interest to public accountants in Canada, although there have been no Canadian cases at the time of writing. At issue is whether a public accountant has greater responsibility for the rule of professional conduct regarding confidentiality or for the rule regarding association with false and misleading financial information.

Consider the following scenario which could easily occur in a smaller public accounting firm. PA & Co., public accountants, are the auditor for both BG Construction Inc. (BG) and Carter Building Supplies Ltd.(CBS). BG, whose year end is January 31, 19X2, owes a large amount of money to CBS, whose year end is February 28, 19X2. Suppose an audit of BG is completed but the statements have not been issued; as BG's auditor you are concerned about whether the company will be able to continue to operate or will become insolvent.

As auditor of BG, you are aware during your audit of CBS that a material asset of CBS (the receivable from BG) may be worthless. How do you ensure that CBS's February 28, 19X2 financial statements are not misleading? There is the conflict between the confidentiality due BG and the association with CBS's financial statements (potentially false and misleading if the receivable from BG is not reserved) if you provide a clean opinion. If the auditor cannot persuade BG to disclose the problem to CBS either directly or through the issue of BG's financial statements, the auditor should probably resign from the CBS audit. The BG confidentiality issue is a common problem because a public accounting firm often has clients who transact business with each other.

Two U.S. cases in the early 1980s addressed the question of public accounting firms' responsibility to inform users when they have information normally considered confidential under the public accounting profession's rules of conduct. They are *Consolidata Services, Inc.* and *Fund of Funds*. Both are included as illustrative cases in Figures 4–12 and 4–13, respectively.

In both cases the information had or would have had a significant effect on the plaintiff client or other clients of the same CPA firm. In the *Consolidata Services* case, the CPA firm informed other clients of confidential information that was obtained during a conference with Consolidata Services. The CPA firm did so on the advice of legal counsel and contended it had a professional duty to inform other clients and help them avoid losses. In the *Fund of Funds* case, the CPA firm obtained confidential information during the course of another audit that would have been beneficial to Fund of Funds. On the advice of legal counsel, the CPA firm did not use the confidential information to help Fund of Funds avoid losses. In both cases, the CPA firm lost the court case to the client. These cases are apparently contradictory but, as in every case, the facts are not identical. This points to a dilemma facing public accounting firms in both Canada and the U.S. It is difficult to do the "right thing" even when there are good intentions. Cases such as these make public accounting firms critical of the legal system. These last two cases also point out the need for the auditing profession to examine the rules of

OBJECTIVE 7

Discuss the auditor's legal responsibilities for client confidentiality.

FIGURE 4-11

UNITED STATES V. SIMON (1969)

The case was a criminal one concerning three auditors prosecuted for filing false statements with a government agency and violation of the 1934 *Securities Exchange Act*. The CPA firm had already settled out of court for civil liability issues for over $2 million after the audit client, Continental Vending Corporation, filed for bankruptcy.

The main issue of the trial was the reporting of transactions between Continental and its affiliate, Valley Commercial Corporation. Before the audit was complete, the auditors had learned that Valley was not in a position to repay its debt, and it was accordingly arranged that collateral would be posted. The president of Continental Vending, Roth, and members of his family transferred their equity in certain securities to Continental's counsel, as trustee to secure Roth's debt to Valley and Valley's debt to Continental. Note 2 included with the financial statements read as follows:

- The amount receivable from Valley Commercial Corp. (an affiliated company of which Mr. Harold Roth is an officer, director, and stockholder) bears interest at 12 percent a year. Such amount, less the balance of the notes payable to that company, is secured by the assignment to the Company of Valley's equity in certain marketable securities. As of February 15, 1963, the amount of such equity at current market quotations exceeded the net amount receivable.

The government contended that this note was inadequate and should have disclosed that the amount receivable from Valley was uncollectable at September 30, 1962, since Valley had loaned approximately the same amount to Roth, who was unable to pay. The note should also have stated that approximately 80 percent of the securities Roth had pledged was stock and convertible debentures of Continental Vending. The defendants called eight expert independent accountants as witnesses. They testified generally that, except for the error with respect to netting, the treatment of the Valley receivable in note 2 was in no way inconsistent with generally accepted accounting principles or generally accepted auditing standards. Specifically, they testified that neither generally accepted accounting principles nor generally accepted auditing standards required disclosure of the makeup of the collateral or of the increase in the receivables after the closing date of the balance sheet, although three of the eight stated that in light of hindsight they would have preferred that the makeup of the collateral be disclosed. The witnesses also testified that the disclosure of the Roth borrowings from Valley was not required, and seven of the eight were of the opinion that such disclosure would be inappropriate.

The defendants asked for two instructions which, in substance, would have told the jury that a defendant could be found guilty only if, according to generally accepted accounting principles, the statements as a whole did not fairly present the financial condition of Continental at September 30, 1962, and then only if this departure from accepted standards was due to willful disregard of those standards with knowledge of the falsity of the statements and an intent to deceive.

The judge declined to give those instructions and instead said that the critical test was whether the *statements were fairly presented and, if not, whether the defendants had acted in good faith*. Proof of compliance with generally accepted standards was "evidence which may be very persuasive but not necessarily conclusive that he acted in good faith, and that the facts as certified were not materially false or misleading."

The appeals court upheld the earlier conviction of the three auditors with the comment that even without satisfactory showing of motive, "the government produced sufficient evidence of criminal intent. Its burden was not to show that the defendants were wicked men . . . but rather that they had certified a statement knowing it to be false."

The effect on the three men was significant. The total fine was $17,000, but far more important, they lost their CPA certificates and were forced to leave the profession. They were ultimately pardoned by President Nixon.

FIGURE 4–12

CONSOLIDATA SERVICES, INC. V. ALEXANDER GRANT & COMPANY (1981)

Consolidata Services Inc. was a payroll services company that prepared payroll cheques and disbursed payroll monies to clients, employees, and taxing authorities. The CPA firm's relationship with Consolidata involved tax work rather than auditing or accounting services. In addition, the CPA firm recommended the payroll services to existing clients, and Consolidata, in return, recommended the CPA firm to its clients.

In a meeting between representatives of the CPA firm and Consolidata, it was determined that Consolidata was insolvent. After discussion with its legal counsel, the CPA firm requested that Consolidata notify its customers about the insolvency, but management refused to do so. The president then informed the CPA firm that he had resigned. The CPA firm informed management of its intent to inform its customers of Consolidata's insolvency. Consolidata requested the CPA firm to wait ten days to enable them to borrow money to correct their solvency problems.

The CPA firm partners decided to call all twelve of its clients that used Consolidata's payroll services to advise them not to send in any more money. No one informed Consolidata's other 24 customers.

The client sued for negligence and breach of contract for breaking an obligation of confidentiality. The court found in favor of Consolidata Services, Inc., in the amount of $1.3 million.

FIGURE 4–13

THE FUND OF FUNDS LIMITED V. ARTHUR ANDERSEN & CO. (1982)

Fund of Funds was a mutual investment company specializing in buying other mutual funds. In the late 1970s, management decided to diversify by making large investments in oil and gas properties. Approximately $90 million was paid for more than 400 natural resource properties under an agreement with King Resources Company. An agreement was signed between Fund of Funds and King Resources that all properties were to be sold on an arm's-length basis at prices no less favorable to Fund of Funds than King Resources ordinarily received. An important fact in the case was that the CPA firm audited both Fund of Funds and King Resources and the same key audit personnel were involved in both audits under separate contracts. During the audit of King Resources, it came to the CPA firm's attention that profits on oil and gas property sales to Fund of Funds were actually much higher than comparable sales to other customers of King Resources. The CPA firm did not report that information to Fund of Funds' management and Fund of Funds' management did not determine the facts until considerably later. Fund of Funds' management contended that the CPA firm had a duty either to inform them of the violation of the agreement or resign from one of the audits. The CPA firm contended it had a responsibility under the rules of conduct of the *AICPA Code of Professional Ethics* to keep the information confidential.

The court awarded damages to Fund of Funds' shareholders in the amount of $80 million, the largest judgment ever made against a CPA firm at that time.

conduct for confidentiality and attempt to clarify the requirements consistent with common law.

Although there have not been cases like *Consolidata Services* and *Fund of Funds* in Canada, the cases are interesting because they illustrate a conflict Canadian public accountants may face.

The Profession's Response to Legal Liability

There are a number of things the CICA, the CGAAC and the SMAC and the public accounting profession as a whole can do to reduce the practitioner's exposure to lawsuits. The instituting of practice inspection of members in public practice (discussed in Chapter 1) is one positive step in recognizing additional responsibility that the public demands of professionals. Some of the others are discussed briefly.

OBJECTIVE 8

Describe what the profession and the individual public accountant can do to reduce the threat of litigation.

---

1. *Research in auditing.* Continued research is important in finding better ways to do such things as uncover unintentional material misstatements or management and employee fraud, communicate audit results to statement users, and make sure that auditors are independent. Significant research already takes place through the CICA, CGAAC, SMAC, public accounting firms, and universities. For example, one public accounting firm has funded auditing symposia at the University of Waterloo at which auditing research and problems are discussed by an audience of academics and practitioners.

2. *Standard and rule setting.* The CICA must constantly set standards and revise them to meet the changing needs of auditing. New auditing Recommendations and Guidelines, revisions of the rules of conduct of the various professional accounting bodies, and other pronouncements must be issued as society's needs change and as new technology arises from experience and research.

3. *Set requirements to protect auditors.* The CICA can help protect public accountants by setting certain requirements that better practitioners already follow. Naturally, these requirements should not be in conflict with meeting users' needs. An example of a practice that presently does not exist as a standard, but that many auditors follow is procuring a written letter of representation from management in all audits.

4. *Establish practice inspection requirements.* The periodic examination of a firm's practices and procedures is a way to educate practitioners and identify firms not meeting the standards of the profession.

5. *Defend unjustified lawsuits.* It is important that public accounting firms continue to oppose unwarranted lawsuits even if, in the short run, the costs of winning are greater than the costs of settling.

6. *Educate users.* It is important to educate investors and others who read financial statements as to the meaning of the auditor's opinion and the extent and nature of the auditor's work. Users must be educated to understand that auditors do not test 100 percent of all records and do not guarantee the accuracy of the financial records or the future prosperity of the company. It is also important to educate users to understand that accounting and auditing are arts, not sciences, and that perfection and precision are unachievable. The new auditor's report is much more informative to users than the previous report.

7. *Sanction members for improper conduct and performance.* One characteristic of a profession is its responsibility for policing its own membership. The three professional accounting bodies have disciplinary procedures that are

designed to deal with the problems of inadequate performance by members in public practice, but more rigorous review of alleged failures is still needed.

8. *Lobby for changes in laws.* If the risk exposure of auditors to legal liability becomes too high, insurance will either be prohibitively expensive or unobtainable, and self-insurance is not an option. If the risk exposure does start to approach an unacceptable level, governments should be lobbied at least to ensure viable insurance coverage exists.

The Individual Professional Accountant's Response to Legal Liability

Practising auditors may also take specific action to minimize their liability. Most of this book deals with that subject. A summary of several of these practices is included at this point.

1. *Deal only with clients possessing integrity.* There is an increased likelihood of having legal problems when a client lacks integrity in dealing with customers, employees, units of government, and others. A public accounting firm needs procedures to evaluate the integrity of clients and should dissociate itself from clients found lacking.

2. *Hire qualified personnel and train and supervise them properly.* A considerable portion of most audits is done by young professionals with relatively little experience. Given the high degree of risk public accounting firms have in doing audits, it is important that these young professionals be qualified and well trained. Supervision of their work by experienced and qualified professionals is also essential.

3. *Follow the standards of the profession.* A firm must implement procedures to make sure that all firm members understand and follow the Recommendations of the *CICA Handbook* and other authoritative sources of GAAP and GAAS, their profession's rules of conduct, and other professional guidelines.

4. *Maintain independence.* Independence is more than merely financial. Independence, in fact, requires an attitude of responsibility separate from the client's interest. Much litigation has arisen from a too willing acceptance by an auditor of a client's representation or of a client's pressures. The auditor must maintain an attitude of *healthy skepticism.*

5. *Understand the client's business.* The lack of knowledge of industry practices and client operations has been a major factor in auditors failing to uncover errors in several cases. It is important that the audit team be educated in these areas.

6. *Perform quality audits.* Quality audits require that appropriate evidence be obtained and appropriate judgments be made about the evidence. It is essential, for example, that proper internal control evaluation be made and the evidence be properly modified to reflect the findings. Improved auditing reduces the likelihood of misstatements and the likelihood of lawsuits.

7. *Document the work properly.* The preparation of good working papers helps in organizing and performing quality audits. Quality working papers are essential if an auditor has to defend an audit in court.

8. *Obtain an engagement letter and a representation letter.* These two letters are essential in defining the respective obligations of client and auditor. They are helpful especially in lawsuits between the client and auditor, but also in third-party lawsuits.

9. *Maintain confidential relations.* Auditors are under an ethical and sometimes legal obligation not to disclose client matters to outsiders.

10. *Carry adequate insurance.* It is essential for a public accounting firm to have adequate insurance protection in the event of a lawsuit. Although insurance rates have risen considerably in the past few years as a result of increasing litigation, professional liability insurance is still available for all public accountants.

11. *Seek legal counsel.* Whenever serious problems occur during an audit, a public accountant would be wise to consult experienced counsel. In the event of a potential or actual lawsuit, the auditor should immediately seek an experienced lawyer.

Conclusion

The auditing profession has been under a great deal of attack in recent years not only in court but also by politicians and the media. Demands for increased regulation and increased legal liability are heard frequently. The profession is struggling to respond constructively to these pressures.

The determination of the extent to which auditors should be legally responsible for the reliability of financial statements is relevant to both the profession and society. Clearly, the existence of legal responsibility is an important deterrent to the inadequate and even dishonest activities of some auditors.

No reasonable public accountant would want the profession's legal responsibility for fraudulent or incompetent performance eliminated. It is certainly in the profession's self-interest to maintain public trust in the competent performance of the auditing function.

However, it is unreasonable for auditors to be held legally responsible for every misstatement in financial statements. The auditor cannot serve as the insurer or guarantor of financial statement accuracy or business health. The audit costs to society that would be required to achieve such high levels of assurance would exceed the benefits. Moreover, even with increased audit costs, well-planned frauds would not necessarily be discovered, nor errors of judgment eliminated.

It is necessary for the profession and society to determine a reasonable trade-off between the degree of responsibility the auditor should take for fair presentation and the audit cost to society. Public accountants, the various provincial securities commissions and the courts will all have a major influence in shaping the final solution.

APPENDIX A United States Laws

In Chapter 1 it was pointed out that a number of Canadian companies were listed on American stock exchanges or sold securities in the United States or both, and that these companies were therefore subject to the requirements of the *Securities Act of 1933* and the *Securities Exchange Act of 1934*. The following discussion pertains to the civil liability of accountants under the two acts.

Civil Liability Under the Federal Securities Laws

The Securities Act of 1933   This act deals with the information in registration statements and prospectuses. It concerns only the reporting requirements for companies issuing new securities. The only parties that can recover from auditors under the 1933 act are original purchasers of securities. The amount of the potential recovery is the original purchase price less the value of the securities at the time of the suit. If the securities have been sold, users can recover the amount of the loss incurred.

The *Securities Act of 1933* imposes an unusual burden on the auditor. Section 11 of the 1933 act defines the rights of third parties and auditors. These are summarized as follows:

■ Any third party who purchased securities described in the registration statement may sue the auditor for material misrepresentations or omissions in audited financial statements included in the registration statement.

■ The third-party user does not have the burden of proof that he or she relied on the financial statements or that the auditor was negligent or fraudulent in doing the audit. The user must only prove that the audited financial statements contained a material misrepresentation or omission.

■ The auditor has the burden of demonstrating as a defense that (1) an adequate audit was conducted in the circumstances or (2) that all or a portion of the plaintiff's loss was caused by factors other than the misleading financial statements. The 1933 act is the only common or statutory law where the burden of proof is on the defendant.

■ The auditor has responsibility for making sure the financial statements were fairly stated beyond the date of issuance, up to the date the registration statement became effective, which could be several months later. For example, assume the audit report date for December 31, 1991 financial statements is February 10, 1992, but the registration statement is dated November 1, 1992. In a typical audit, the auditor must review transactions through the audit report date, February 10, 1992. In statements filed under the 1933 act, the auditor is responsible to review transactions through the registration statement date, November 1, 1992.

Although the burden may appear harsh to auditors, there have been few cases tried under the 1933 act.

Securities Exchange Act of 1934 The liability of auditors under the Securities Exchange Act of 1934 frequently centers on the audited financial statements issued to the public in annual reports or submitted to the SEC as a part of annual 10-K reports.

Every company with securities traded on national and over-the-counter exchanges is required to submit audited statements annually. There are obviously a much larger number of statements falling under the 1934 act than under the 1933 act.

In addition to annual audited financial statements, there is potential legal exposure to auditors for quarterly (10-Q), monthly (8-K), or other reporting information. The auditor is frequently involved in reviewing the information in these other reports; therefore, there may be legal responsibility. However, few cases have involved auditors for reports other than auditor's reports.

SEC Sanctions Closely related to auditor's liability is the SEC's authority to sanction. The SEC has the power in certain circumstances to sanction or suspend practitioners from doing audits for SEC companies. Rule 2(e) of the SEC's *Rules of Practice* says:

> The commission may deny, temporarily or permanently, the privilege of appearing or practicing before it in any way to any person who is found by the commission . . . (1) not to possess the requisite qualifications to represent others, or (2) to be lacking in character or integrity or to have engaged in unethical or improper professional conduct.

The SEC has temporarily suspended a number of individual CPAs from doing any audits of SEC clients in recent years. It has similarly prohibited a number of CPA firms from accepting any new SEC clients for a period, such as six months. At times, the SEC has required an extensive review of a major CPA firm's practices by another CPA firm. In some cases, individual CPAs and their firms have been required to participate in continuing education programs and to make changes in their practice. Sanctions such as these are published by the SEC and are often reported in the business press, making them a significant embarrassment to those involved.

Foreign Corrupt Practices Act of 1977   Another significant congressional action affecting both CPA firms and their clients was the passage of the *Foreign Corrupt Practices Act of 1977*. The act makes it illegal to offer a bribe to an official of a foreign country for the purpose of exerting influence and obtaining or retaining business. The prohibition against payments to foreign officials is applicable to all U.S. domestic firms, regardless of whether they are publicly or privately held, and to foreign companies filing with the SEC.

Apart from the bribery provisions that affect all companies, the law also requires SEC registrants under the *Securities Exchange Act of 1934* to meet additional requirements. These include the maintenance of reasonably complete and accurate records and an adequate system of internal control. The law significantly affects all SEC companies, but the unanswered question to the profession at this time is how it affects auditors.

The act may affect auditors through their responsibility to review and evaluate systems of internal control as a part of doing the audit. Most auditors believe that they are not currently required to do a review of internal control thorough enough to judge whether their clients meet the requirements of the *Foreign Corrupt Practices Act.* To date, there have been no legal cases affecting auditors' legal responsibilities under the *Foreign Corrupt Practices Act*. But there is considerable disagreement about auditors' responsibilities under the law. There is likely to be ongoing discussion and litigation to resolve the issue.

REVIEW QUESTIONS

4–1   The legal environment in which a public accountant in Canada operates is changing. Discuss some of the reasons for the changes.

4–2   What effect do you think litigation against a public accountant has on other public accountants and on society as a whole?

4–3   Distinguish between business risk and audit risk. Why is business risk a concern to auditors?

4–4   How does the *reasonable person concept* affect the liability of the auditor?

4–5   A partner in a public accounting firm may be held liable for errors in the work of others. Identify at least two groups of such others and explain why the partner might be liable.

4–6   Differentiate between a "criminal action" and a "civil action."

4–7   A common type of lawsuit against public accountants is for the failure to detect a defalcation. State the auditor's responsibility for such discovery. Give authoritative support for your answer.

4–8 What is meant by "contributory negligence"? Under what conditions will this likely be a successful defense?

4–9 What are the purposes of a letter of representation and an engagement letter?

4–10 Discuss auditor's liability to third party user in common law, describing how it has changed over time.

4–11 Is the auditor's liability affected if the third party was unknown rather than known? Explain.

4–12 The *Caparo* case decision in England was enthusiastically received by auditors in Canada. What effect did it have on Canadian common law. Will *Caparo* "solve" the auditor-third party liability problem? If not, why not?

4–13 Distinguish between the auditor's potential liability to the client, liability to third parties under common law, and criminal liability. Describe one situation for each type of liability in which the auditor could be held legally responsible.

4–14 In what ways can the profession positively respond and reduce liability in auditing?

4–15 In what ways can an individual public accountant positively respond and reduce liability in auditing?

MULTIPLE CHOICE QUESTIONS

4–16 The following questions concern public accounting firms' liability under common law. Choose the best response.

a. Natasha Sharp, a public accountant, was engaged by Peters & Sons, a partnership, to give an opinion on the financial statements that were to be submitted to several prospective partners as part of a planned expansion of the firm. Sharp's fee was fixed on a *per diem* basis. After a period of intensive work, Sharp completed about half of the necessary field work. Then, due to unanticipated demands upon her time by other clients, Sharp was forced to abandon the work. The planned expansion of the firm failed to materialize because the prospective partners lost interest when the auditor's report was not promptly available. Sharp offered to complete the task at a later date. This offer was refused. Peters & Sons suffered damages of $4,000 as a result. Under the circumstances, what is the probable outcome of a lawsuit between Sharp and Peters & Sons?

(1) Sharp will be compensated for the reasonable value of the services actually performed.

(2) Peters & Sons will recover damages for breach of contract.

(3) Peters & Sons will recover both punitive damages and damages for breach of contract.

(4) Neither Sharp nor Peters & Sons will recover against the other.

b. Magnus Enterprises Inc. engaged a public accounting firm to perform the annual examination of its financial statements. Which of the following is a correct statement with respect to the public accounting firm's liability to Magnus for negligence?

(1) Such liability cannot be varied by agreement of the parties.

(2) The public accounting firm will be liable for any fraudulent scheme it does not detect.

(3) The public accounting firm will not be liable if it can show that it exercised the ordinary care and skill of a reasonable person in the conduct of its own affairs.

(4) The public accounting firm must not only exercise reasonable care in what

it does, but also must possess at least that degree of accounting knowledge and skill expected of a public accountant.

c. Wilhelm Corporation orally engaged Humm & Dawson to audit its year-end financial statements. The engagement was to be completed within two months after the close of Martin's fiscal year for a fixed fee of $22,500. Under these circumstances what obligation is assumed by Humm & Dawson?

   (1) None, because the contract is unenforceable since it is not in writing.
   (2) An implied promise to exercise reasonable standards of competence and care.
   (3) An implied obligation to take extraordinary steps to discover all defalcations.
   (4) The obligation of an insurer of its work, which is liable without fault.

d. If a public accounting firm is being sued for civil fraud by a third party based upon materially false financial statements, which of the following is the best defense the accountants could assert?

   (1) Lack of privity.
   (2) Lack of reliance.
   (3) A disclaimer contained in the engagement letter.
   (4) Contributory negligence on the part of the client.   (AICPA adapted)

4–17 The following questions deal with important cases in accountants' liability. Choose the best response.

a. The most significant aspect of the *Haig v. Bamford* case was that it
   (1) created a more general awareness of the auditor's responsibility for discovering errors.
   (2) defined the auditor's responsibilities in tort law to third parties.
   (3) extended the auditor's responsibility for events after the end of the audit period.
   (4) defined foreseeable third parties.

b. The *Pan American* v. *Dupuis* case is important because it
   (1) appeared to define the liability of the primary auditor.
   (2) appeared to define the liability of the secondary auditor.
   (3) appeared to define the responsibility of an auditor who prepares financial statements for a prospectus.
   (4) appeared to define the responsibility of an auditor to all third parties.

DISCUSSION QUESTIONS AND PROBLEMS

4–18 Helmut & Co., a public accounting firm, were the new auditors of Mountain Ltd., a private company in the farm equipment and supply business. The previous auditors, Lopez and Williams, had been Mountain's auditor for the previous ten years ending with the December 31, 19X1 statements.

In early February, 19X3, Helmut & Co. began the audit for the year ended December 31, 19X2. The audit was to be run by Frost, a senior who had just joined Helmut from another firm. Frost was to be assisted by two juniors.

Harold Mountain, the President of Mountain Ltd., approached Frost and said that the Bank of Trail was prepared to increase their loan to Mountain upon receipt of the 19X2 financial statements so there was some urgency in finishing the audit.

The juniors were assigned the accounts receivable and inventory sections, both of which were significant in relation to total assets, while Frost concentrated on the income statement and the remaining balance sheet accounts. The audit was finished quickly, and after a cursory review of the file and statements by Martin Helmut, senior partner of Helmut & Co., the signed auditor's report was appended to the financial statements, which were delivered to Mountain who in turn sent them to the bank.

The bank increased the bank loan significantly based principally on the very successful year the company had enjoyed, especially because the farm supply business was depressed. Several months later, Mountain Ltd. made an assignment in bankruptcy. The trustee found that many accounts receivable were still outstanding from the balance sheet date and that inventory on hand included substantial quantities of obsolete and damaged goods that had been included in the year end inventory at cost. In addition, the year end inventory amount included inventory that had been sold prior to the year end.

Trail Bank sued Helmut & Co. for negligence. Helmut's lawyers argued they were not in privity and had not been negligent in any event.

Required:

Discuss Helmut & Co.'s defense: Is lack of privity a defense in this case? Was Helmut & Co. negligent? Explain your answer fully.

4–19 Verna Cosden & Co., a medium-sized public accounting firm, was engaged to audit Joslin Supply Inc. Several staff were involved in the audit, all of whom had attended the firm's in-house training program in effective auditing methods. Throughout the audit, Cosden spent most of her time in the field planning the audit, supervising the staff, and reviewing their work.

A significant part of the audit entailed verifying the physical count, cost, and summarization of inventory. Inventory was highly significant to the financial statements and Cosden knew that the inventory was pledged as collateral for a large loan to Maritimes Eastern Bank. In reviewing Joslin's inventory count procedures, Cosden told the president that she believed the method of counting inventory at different locations on different days was highly undesirable. The president stated that it was impractical to count all inventory on the same day because of personnel shortages and customer preference. After considerable discussion, Cosden agreed to permit the practice if the president would sign a statement that no other method was practical. The public accounting firm had at least one person at each site to audit the inventory count procedures and actual count. There were more than forty locations.

Eighteen months later Cosden found out that the worst had happened. Management below the president's level had conspired to materially overstate inventory, as a means of covering up obsolete inventory and inventory losses due to mismanagement. The misstatement had occurred by physically transporting inventory at night to other locations after it had been counted in a given location. The accounting records were inadequate to uncover these illegal transfers.

Both Joslin Supply Inc. and Maritimes Eastern Bank sued Verna Cosden & Co.

Required:

Answer the following questions, setting forth reasons for any conclusions stated:

a. What defense should Cosden & Co. use in the suit by Joslin?

b. What defense should Cosden & Co. use in the suit by Maritimes Eastern Bank?

c. Is Cosden likely to be successful in her defenses?

d. Would the issues or outcome be significantly different if Joslin Supply Inc. was a public company?

4–20 The public accounting firm of André, Mathieu & Paquette (AMP) was expanding very rapidly. Consequently, it hired several junior accountants, including a man named Small. The partners of the firm eventually became dissatisfied with Small's production and warned him that they would be forced to discharge him unless his output increased significantly.

At that time, Small was engaged in audits of several clients. He decided that to avoid being fired, he would reduce or omit entirely some of the standard auditing procedures listed in audit programs prepared by the partners. One of the public accounting firm's clients, Newell Corporation, was in serious financial difficulty and had adjusted several of the accounts being examined by Small to appear financially sound. Small prepared fictitious working papers in his home at night to support purported completion of auditing procedures assigned to him, although he in fact did not examine the adjusting entries. The public accounting firm rendered an unqualified opinion on Newell's financial statements, which were grossly misstated. Several creditors, relying on the audited financial statements, subsequently extended large sums of money to Newell Corporation.

Required: Would the public accounting firm be liable to the creditors who extended the money because of their reliance on the erroneous financial statements if Newell Corporation should fail to pay them? Explain.   (AICPA adapted)

4–21 Watts and Williams, a firm of public accountants, audited the accounts of Sampson Skins, Inc., a corporation that imports and deals in fine furs. Upon completion of the examination, the auditors supplied Sampson Skins with 20 copies of the audited financial statements. The firm knew in a general way that Sampson Skins wanted that number of copies of the auditor's report to furnish to banks and other potential lenders.

The balance sheet was in error by approximately $800,000. Instead of having a $600,000 net worth, the corporation was insolvent. The management of Sampson Skins had doctored the books to avoid bankruptcy. The assets had been overstated by $500,000 of fictitious and nonexisting accounts receivable and $300,000 of nonexisting skins listed as inventory, when in fact Sampson Skins had only empty boxes. The audit failed to detect these fraudulent entries. Martinson, relying on the audited financial statements, loaned Sampson Skins $200,000. He seeks to recover his loss from Watts and Williams.

Required: State whether each of the following is true or false and give your reasons:

a. If Martinson alleges and proves negligence on the part of Watts and Williams, he will be able to recover his loss.

b. If Martinson alleges and proves fraud on the part of Watts and Williams, he will be able to recover his loss.

c. Martinson does not have a contract with Watts and Williams.

d. Martinson is a third-party beneficiary of the contract Watts and Williams made with Sampson Skins.   (AICPA adapted)

4–22 Donald Sharpe recently joined the public accounting firm of Spark, Watts, and Wilcox. He quickly established a reputation for thoroughness and a steadfast dedication to following prescribed auditing procedures to the letter. On his third audit for the firm, Sharpe examined the underlying documentation of 200 disbursements as a test of purchasing, receiving, vouchers payable, and cash disbursement procedures. In the process he found 12 disbursements for the purchase of materials with no receiving reports in the documentation. He noted the exceptions in his working papers and called them to the attention of the in-charge accountant. Relying on prior experience with the client, the in-charge accountant disregarded Sharpe's comments, and nothing further was done about the exceptions.

Subsequently, it was learned that one of the client's purchasing agents and a member of its accounting department were engaged in a fraudulent scheme whereby they diverted the receipt of materials to a public warehouse while sending the invoices to the client. When the client discovered the fraud, the conspirators had obtained approximately $70,000, $50,000 of which was recovered after the completion of the audit.

Required: Discuss the legal implications and liabilities to Spark, Watts, and Wilcox as a result of the facts just described.   (AICPA adapted)

4–23 In confirming accounts receivable on December 31, 19X7, the auditor found 15 discrepancies between the customer's records and the recorded amounts in the subsidiary ledger. A copy of all confirmations that had exceptions was turned over to the company controller to investigate the reason for the difference. He, in turn, had the bookkeeper perform the analysis. The bookkeeper analyzed each exception, determined its cause, and prepared an elaborate working paper explaining each difference. Most of the differences in the bookkeeper's report indicated that the errors were caused by timing differences in the client's and customer's records. The auditor reviewed the working paper and concluded that there were no material exceptions in accounts receivable.

Two years subsequent to the audit, it was determined that the bookkeeper had stolen thousands of dollars in the past three years by taking cash and overstating accounts receivable. In a lawsuit by the client against the public accountant, an examination of the auditor's December 31, 19X7 accounts receivable working papers, which were subpoenaed by the court, indicated that one of the explanations in the bookkeeper's analysis of the exceptions was fictitious. The analysis stated the error was caused by a sales allowance granted to the customer for defective merchandise the day before the end of the year. The difference was actually caused by the bookkeeper's theft.

Required:
a. What are the legal issues involved in this situation? What should the auditor use as a defense in the event that she is sued?
b. What was the public accountant's deficiency in conducting the audit of accounts receivable?

4–24 Ann Abbass, a public accountant, is the auditor for Juniper Manufacturing Corporation, a privately owned company that has a June 30 fiscal year. Juniper arranged for a substantial bank loan that was dependent on the bank receiving, by September 30, audited financial statements which showed a current ratio of at least 2 to 1. On September 25, just before the audit report was to be issued, Abbass received an anonymous letter on Juniper's stationery indicating that a five-year lease by Juniper, as lessee, of a factory building accounted for in the financial statements as an operating lease was, in fact, a capital lease. The letter stated that there was a secret written agreement with the lessor modifying the lease and creating a capital lease.

Abbass confronted the president of Juniper, who admitted that a secret agreement existed but said it was necessary to treat the lease as an operating lease to meet the current ratio requirement of the pending loan and that nobody would ever discover the secret agreement with the lessor. The president said that if Abbass did not issue her report by September 30, Juniper would sue Abbass for substantial damages that would result from not getting the loan. Under this pressure and because the working papers contained a copy of the five-year lease agreement that supported the operating lease treatment, Abbass issued her report with an unqualified opinion on September 29.

In spite of the fact that the loan was received, Juniper went bankrupt within two years. The bank is suing Abbass to recover its losses on the loan and the lessor is suing Abbass to recover uncollected rents.

Required: Answer the following questions, setting forth reasons for any conclusions stated:
a. Is Abbass liable to the bank?
b. Is Abbass liable to the lessor?
c. Is there potential for criminal action against Abbass?   (AICPA adapted)

4–25 Shen & Vetzel, a public accounting firm, were the auditors of South-Western Development, Inc., a real estate company that owned several shopping centers in southwestern Ontario. It was South-Western's practice to let each shopping center manager negotiate that center's leases; they felt that such an arrangement resulted in much better leases because a local person did the negotiating.

Two of the center managers were killed in a plane accident returning home from a company meeting at the head office in Windsor. In both cases, the new managers appointed to take their places discovered kickback schemes in operation; the manager had negotiated lower rents than normal in return for kickbacks from the tenants.

South-Western brought in a new public accounting firm, Jasper & Co., to investigate the extent of the fraud at those two locations and the possibility of similar frauds at other centers. Jasper & Co. completed their investigation and found that four locations were involved quite independently of each other and that the total loss over five years was over $1,000,000.

South-Western sued Shen & Vetzel for negligence for $1,000,000 plus interest.

Required:

What defense would Shen & Vetzel use? What would they have to prove?

4–26 Gordon & Groton, a public accounting firm, were the auditors of Georgian Securities Ltd., a brokerage firm and member of the Alberta Stock Exchange. Gordon & Groton examined and reported on the financial statements of Georgian Securities, which were filed with the Alberta Securities Commission.

Several of Georgian's customers were swindled by a fraudulent scheme perpetrated by Georgian's president, who owned 90 percent of the voting stock of the company. The facts establish that Gordon & Groton were negligent in the conduct of the audit, but neither participated in the fraudulent scheme or knew of its existence.

The customers are suing Gordon & Groton for aiding and abetting the fraudulent scheme of the president. The customers' suit, a tort action for negligence, is predicated exclusively on the failure of the auditors to conduct a proper audit, thereby failing to discover the fraudulent scheme.

Required:

Answer the following questions, setting forth reasons for any conclusions stated:

a. What is the probable outcome of the lawsuit?

b. What defense might the auditors have used that could reduce their liability?

(AICPA adapted)

4–27 Marino Rossi, a public accountant, audited the financial statements of Newfoundland Rugs Ltd. Cooke, the President of Newfoundland Rugs, told Rossi that the company was planning a private placement of company bonds to raise $500,000 of needed capital. The audit proceeded smoothly, and the audited financial statements were issued.

Unbeknownst to Rossi, several significant receivables represented consignment accounts and not receivables, but Cooke had persuaded the companies involved to sign the receivable confirmations Rossi had sent out, indicating they agreed that they owed the balances reported at the balance sheet date. In addition, a large number of rolls of low quality interior carpeting had been classed as first quality. The effect of these two fraudulent acts resulted in a profit of $150,000 instead of a loss of $480,000 and a positive net worth (instead of a negative net worth).

Newfoundland Rugs borrowed the money on the private placement and then went bankrupt several months later.

Required:

(a) Could the lenders on the private placement succeed in a suit against Rossi? If so, what must they prove?

(b) What defense would Rossi use?

4–28 Sarah Robertson, a public accountant, was the auditor of Majestic Ltd. and had been for several years. As she and her staff prepared for the audit for the year ended December 31, 19X3, Herb Majestic told her that he needed a large bank loan to "tide him over" until sales picked up as expected in late 19X4.

In the course of the audit Robertson discovered that the financial situation at Majestic was worse than Majestic had revealed and that the company was technically bankrupt. She discussed the situation with Majestic, who pointed out that the bank loan would "be his solution" – he was sure he would get it as long as the financial statements didn't look too bad.

Robertson stated that she believed the statements would have to include a going concern note. Majestic said that such a note really wasn't needed because the bank loan was so certain and that inclusion of such a note would certainly cause the management of the bank to change its mind about the loan.

Robertson finally acquiesced and the audited statements were issued without the note. The company received the loan but things didn't improve as Majestic thought they would and the company filed for bankruptcy in August 19X4.

The bank sued Sarah Robertson for fraud.

Required: Indicate whether or not you think the bank would succeed. Support your answer.

4–29 A fundamental purpose of the external audit is to allow users to place reliance on the financial statements to which the auditor's report is attached. As a result, the auditor may be responsible to a variety of users of financial statements.

Required: Discuss the external auditor's potential liability to third parties for negligence and the effect this potential liability has on the conduct of the audit.   (CICA adapted)

4–30 A partner in your public accounting firm has asked you to explain to a group of juniors the importance of engagement letters and the importance of following up unusual or unexplained items discovered during the audit or review.

Required: Provide the discussion your partner has requested using material from the chapter.

CASE

4–31 Pelham & Kamanga, a public accounting firm, were retained for a review engagement by Tom Stone, sole proprietor of Stone Housebuilders. Stone advised Pelham & Kamanga that the financial statements would be used in connection with a possible incorporation of the business and sale of stock to friends.

Mary Weston, the senior from Pelham & Kamanga who was to undertake the review engagement, found the books and records in total disarray when she arrived at Stone Housebuilders. In particular, invoices and statements from suppliers were scattered all over the office; many of the latter had stickers attached indicating the account was overdue.

Mary Weston and the staff from Pelham & Kamanga proceeded with the engagement, applying all applicable procedures for a review engagement. They failed, however, to detect and disclose in the financial statements Stone's liability for certain unpaid bills. Documentation concerning those bills was available for the staff from Pelham & Kamanga's inspection had they looked. This omission led to a material understatement of trade accounts payable and overstatement of income of $60,000.

Pelham & Kamanga delivered the financial statements to Tom Stone with their review engagement report which indicated that while Pelham & Kamanga were not expressing an opinion on the financial statements of Stone Housebuilders, "nothing had come to [their] attention that caused [them] to believe that [the] financial statements are not, in all material respects, in accordance with generally accepted accounting principles." Tom Stone met with Pelham and Kamanga and two prospective investors, Dickerson and Nicholls. At the meeting Pelham stated that she was confident that the trade accounts payable balance was accurate to within $8,000.

Stone Housebuilders was incorporated as Stone Homes Ltd. Dickerson and Nicholls, relying on the financial statements, became shareholders along with Tom Stone. Shortly thereafter, the understatement of trade accounts payable was detected. As a result, Dickerson and Nicholls discovered they had paid substantially more for the stock than it was worth at the time of purchase.

Required:

Will Pelham & Kamanga be liable to Dickerson and Nicholls in an action for damages? Explain fully why you reached the conclusions you did reach.

5

AUDIT OBJECTIVES

LEARNING OBJECTIVES

THOROUGH STUDY OF THIS CHAPTER WILL ENABLE YOU TO:

1. Know the objective of conducting an audit of financial statements

2. Describe the role of management in preparing financial statements

3. Describe the auditor's role in verifying financial statements and the auditor's responsibility to discover misstatements (errors or fraud and other irregularities)

4. Describe the financial-statement-cycles approach to segmenting the audit, and use this approach as a basis for further study

5. Discuss the five categories of management assertions about financial information

6. Describe how the auditor develops general and specific audit objectives from management's assertions

7. Describe the process by which audit objectives are met, and use it as a basis for further study

☐ With this chapter the study of evidence accumulation begins. It is necessary first to understand the objectives of an audit and the way the auditor approaches accumulating evidence. Those are the most important topics covered in this chapter. Figure 5–1 summarizes the five topics that provide keys to understanding evidence accumulation; these are the steps used to develop audit objectives.

Figure 5–2 presents the December 31, 19X8 financial statements of Hillsburg Hardware Ltd. which is incorporated under the *Canada Business Corporations Act*. The adjusted trial balance from which the financial statements were prepared is included in Figure 5–3. These financial statements will be used as a frame of reference for subsequent discussion. Footnotes and the statement of changes in financial position have been excluded to keep the discussion as simple

FIGURE 5–1

Steps to Develop Audit
Objectives

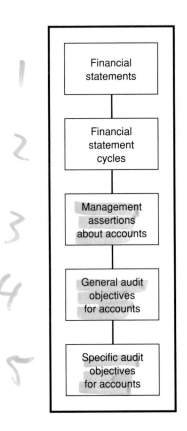

as practical. Assume Ross and Co., CAs, audited the December 31, 19X7 financial statements and are also doing the 19X8 audit.

Overall Objective

Section 5000.01 of the *CICA Handbook* states (in part):

> The objective of an audit of financial statements is to express an opinion whether the financial statements present fairly, in all material respects, the financial position, results of operations and changes in financial position in accordance with generally accepted accounting principles. . . .

Section 5000.01 appropriately emphasizes the expression of an opinion on *financial statements*. The only reason auditors accumulate evidence is to enable them to reach conclusions about whether financial statements are fairly stated and to issue an appropriate auditor's report.

When, on the basis of adequate evidence, the auditor concludes that the financial statements are unlikely to mislead a prudent user, the auditor gives an audit opinion on their fair presentation and associates his or her name with the statements. If facts or evidence discovered subsequent to their issuance indicate that the statements were actually not fairly presented, the auditor is likely to have to demonstrate to the courts or regulatory agencies that he or she conducted the audit in a proper manner and drew reasonable conclusions. Although not an insurer or a guarantor of the fairness of the presentations in the statements, the auditor has considerable responsibility for notifying users as to whether or not the statements are properly stated. If the auditor believes the statements are not fairly

---

OBJECTIVE 1

Know the objective of conducting an audit of financial statements.

FIGURE 5–2 Hillsburg Hardware Ltd. Financial Statements

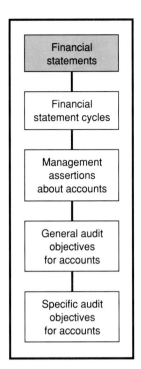

HILLSBURG HARDWARE LTD.
BALANCE SHEET
December 31, 19X8
(in thousands)

Assets

Current assets

Cash	$ 41	
Trade accounts receivable (net)	948	
Other accounts receivable	47	
Inventories	1,493	
Prepaid expenses	21	
Total current assets		$2,550

Property, plant, and equipment

Land	$ 173	
Buildings	1,625	
Delivery equipment	188	
Furniture and fixtures	127	
Less: Accumulated depreciation	(1,596)	
Net book value of property, plant, and equipment		517
Total assets		$3,067

Liabilities and Shareholders' Equity

Current liabilities

Trade accounts payable	$ 236	
Notes payable	167	
Accrued payroll	67	
Accrued payroll benefits	6	
Accrued interest and dividends payable	102	
Estimated income tax	39	
Goods and services tax payable	42	
Total current liabilities		$ 659

Long-term liabilities

Notes payable	$1,206	
Deferred tax	37	
Other accrued payables	41	
Total long-term liabilities		1,284

Shareholders' equity

Capital stock	$ 250	
Retained earnings	874	
Total shareholders' equity		1,124
Total liabilities and shareholders' equity		$3,067

HILLSBURG HARDWARE LTD.
COMBINED STATEMENT OF
INCOME AND RETAINED EARNINGS
for Year Ending December 31, 19X8
(in thousands)

Sales		$7,721
Less: Goods and services tax		505
Returns and allowances		62
Net sales		$7,154
Cost of goods sold		5,162
Gross profit		$1,992

Selling expense

Salaries and commissions	$ 387	
Sales payroll benefits	71	
Travel and entertainment	56	
Advertising	131	
Sales and promotional literature	16	
Sales meetings and training	46	
Miscellaneous sales expense	34	
Total selling expense		$ 741

Sidebar flowchart:

- Financial statements
- Financial statement cycles
- Management assertions about accounts
- General audit objectives for accounts
- Specific audit objectives for accounts

FIGURE 5–2   (Continued)

Administrative expense			
Executive and office salaries	$ 276		
Administrative payroll benefits	34		
Travel and entertainment	28		
Stationery and supplies	38		
Postage	12		
Telephone and telegraph	36		
Dues and memberships	3		
Rent	16		
Legal fees and retainers	14		
Auditing	12		
Depreciation – office building and equipment	73		
Bad debt expense	166		
Insurance	44		
Office repairs and maintenance	57		
Miscellaneous office expense	47		
Miscellaneous general expense	26		
Total administrative expense		882	
Total selling and administrative expense			1,623
Earnings from operations		369	
Other income and expense			
Interest expense	$ 120		
Gain on sale of assets	(36)		84
Earnings before income taxes			$ 285
Income taxes			87
Net income			$ 198
Retained earnings at January 1, 19X8			771
			$ 969
Dividends			(95)
Retained earnings at December 31, 19X8			$ 874

presented or is unable to reach a conclusion because of insufficient evidence or prevailing conditions, the auditor has the responsibility for notifying the users through the auditor's report.

Management's Responsibility

OBJECTIVE 2

Describe the role of management in preparing financial statements.

The professional literature makes it clear that the responsibility for adopting sound accounting policies, maintaining an adequate internal control structure, and making fair representations in the financial statements *rests with management* rather than with the auditor.

In recent years, the annual reports of many public companies have included a statement about management's responsibilities and relationship with the public accounting firm. Figure 5–4 presents a report of management's responsibility by the management of Schneider Corporation, one of Canada's largest producers of food products. It is taken from Schneider Corporation's 1990 annual report. The first paragraph states management's responsibilities for the fair presentation of the financial statements. The second paragraph discusses management's responsibilities with respect to internal control, while the third paragraph comments on the Audit Committee. The last paragraph indicates that management recognizes its own responsibility for ethical conduct.

Management's responsibility for the fairness of the representations (assertions) in the financial statements carries with it the privilege of determining which disclosures it considers necessary. Although management has the responsibility

FIGURE 5–3

Hillsburg Hardware Ltd. Adjusted Trial Balance

HILLSBURG HARDWARE LTD.
TRIAL BALANCE
December 31, 19X8

TRANSACTION CYCLE		DEBIT	CREDIT
S,A,P,C	Cash in bank	$ 41,378	
S	Trade accounts receivable	1,009,800	
S	Allowance for uncollectible accounts		$ 62,000
S	Other accounts receivable	47,251	
A,I	Inventories	1,493,231	
A	Prepaid expenses	21,578	
A	Land	172,821	
A	Buildings	1,625,200	
A	Delivery equipment	187,917	
A	Furniture and fixtures	127,321	
A	Accumulated depreciation		1,596,006
A	Trade accounts payable		235,999
C	Notes payable		166,700
P	Accrued payroll		67,489
P	Accrued payroll benefits		5,983
C	Accrued interest		7,478
C	Dividends payable		95,000
A	Income tax payable		39,772
A	Goods and services tax payable		42,281
C	Long-term notes payable		1,206,000
A	Deferred taxes		36,912
A	Other accrued payables		41,499
C	Capital stock		250,000
C	Retained earnings		771,354
S	Sales		7,721,389
A	Goods and services tax	505,000	
S	Sales returns and allowances	62,083	
I	Cost of goods sold	5,162,038	
P	Salaries and commissions	386,900	
P	Sales payroll benefits	71,100	
A	Travel and entertainment – selling	55,517	
A	Advertising	130,563	
A	Sales and promotional literature	16,081	
A	Sales meetings and training	46,224	
A	Miscellaneous sales expense	34,052	
P	Executive and office salaries	276,198	
P	Administrative payroll benefits	34,115	
A	Travel and entertainment – administrative	28,080	
A	Stationery and supplies	38,128	
A	Postage	12,221	
A	Telephone and telegraph	36,115	
A	Dues and memberships	3,013	
A	Rent	15,607	
A	Legal fees and retainers	14,153	
A	Auditing	12,142	
A	Depreciation – office building and equipment	72,604	
S	Bad debt expense	166,154	
A	Insurance	44,134	
A	Office repairs and maintenance	57,196	
A	Miscellaneous office expense	47,180	
A	Miscellaneous general expense	26,192	
A	Gain on sale of assets		35,987
A	Income taxes	87,330	
C	Interest expense	120,432	
C	Dividends	95,000	
		$12,381,849	$12,381,849

Note: Letters in the lefthand column refer to the following transaction cycles, which are discussed later.
S = Sales and collection   I = Inventory and warehousing
A = Acquisition and payment   C = Capital acquisition and repayment
P = Payroll and personnel

FIGURE 5–4

Management's Report

Fin State. 1

Internal cntrol. 2

Audit comite 3

ethical 4

MANAGEMENT'S REPORT

Management of Schneider Corporation and its subsidiary company is responsible for the integrity and objectivity of the financial statements and all other information contained in the Annual Report. The financial statements have been prepared in accordance with generally accepted accounting principles and are based on management's best information and judgments.

In fulfilling its responsibilities, management has developed internal control systems and procedures designed to provide reasonable assurance that company assets are safeguarded, that transactions are executed in accordance with appropriate authorization and that accounting records may be relied upon to properly reflect the company's business transactions. To augment the internal control systems, the company maintains an internal audit department which evaluates company operations and formally reports on the adequacy and effectiveness of the controls and procedures to the Audit Committee of the Board of Directors.

The Audit Committee of the Board of Directors is composed of a majority of outside directors. The committee meets periodically and independently with management, the internal auditors and the shareholders' auditors to discuss the company's financial reporting and internal controls. Both the internal auditors and the independent external auditors have unrestricted access to the Audit Committee.

Management recognizes its responsibility for conducting the company's affairs in the best interests of its shareholders. The responsibility is characterized in the Code of Conduct signed by each management employee which provides for compliance with laws of each jurisdiction in which the company operates and for observance of rules of ethical business conduct.

Douglas W. Dodds
President and
Chief Executive Officer

Gerald A. Hooper
Vice-President and
Chief Financial Officer

for the preparation of the financial statements and the accompanying footnotes, it is acceptable for an auditor to prepare a draft for the client or to offer suggestions for clarification. In the event that management insists on financial statement disclosure that the auditor finds unacceptable, the auditor can either issue an adverse or qualified opinion or, as a last resort, withdraw from the engagement.

Auditor's Responsibility

OBJECTIVE 3

Describe the auditor's role in verifying financial statements and the auditor's responsibility to discover misstatements (errors or fraud and other irregularities).

Section 5100.04 of the *CICA Handbook* states that "The auditor performs the audit with an attitude of professional scepticism, and seeks reasonable assurance whether the financial statements are free of material misstatement." The Section goes on to suggest that the auditor should assume good faith on the part of management in conducting the audit.

The requirement for an attitude of scepticism does not mean that the auditor should conduct the audit with an attitude of disbelief or of distrust in management. Rather, it means that the auditor should not be blind to evidence that suggests that documents or books or records have been altered or are incorrect. The auditor should not assume that management is dishonest, but the possibility of dishonesty must be considered.

The concept of reasonable assurance indicates that the auditor is not an insurer or guarantor of the correctness of the financial statements. If the auditor were responsible for making certain that all the assertions in the statements were correct, evidence requirements and the resulting cost of the audit function would be increased to such an extent that audits would not be economically feasible. The auditor's best defense when material misstatements are not uncovered in the audit is that the audit was conducted in accordance with generally accepted auditing standards.

Section 5100.05 points out that "The assumption of management's good faith is a fundamental auditing postulate." If the auditor were to assume the contrary, he or she could not accept evidence supplied by management since the auditor would believe that evidence to be false. Instead, the auditor accepts evidence believing it to be true unless his or her testing of the evidence indicates otherwise.

The professional literature in Section 5135 of the *CICA Handbook* distinguishes between two types of misstatements, *errors* and *fraud and other irregularities*. An error is an *unintentional* misstatement of the financial statements, whereas fraud or other irregularities are *intentional*. Two examples of errors are a mistake in extending price times quantity on a sales invoice and overlooking older raw materials in determining lower of cost or market for inventory.

For fraud or other irregularities, a distinction can be drawn between *theft of assets*, often called defalcation or employee fraud, and *fraudulent financial reporting*, often called management fraud. Another way of characterizing the difference is that employee fraud is perpetrated against the company while management fraud is perpetrated for the company (that is, for the company's benefit). An example of theft of assets is a clerk taking cash at the time a sale is made and not entering the sale in the cash register. An example of fraudulent financial reporting is the intentional overstatement of sales near the balance sheet date to increase reported earnings. In the case of the former, the company loses the money stolen; in the case of the latter, the company appears more profitable and, presumably, its stock rises in price.

It is usually more difficult for auditors to uncover fraud than errors. This is because of the intended deception associated with fraud. The auditor's responsibility for uncovering fraud deserves special mention.

Management fraud Management fraud is inherently difficult to uncover because it is possible for one or more members of management to override internal controls. There is also, typically, an effort to conceal the misstatement. Instances of management fraud may include omission of transactions or disclosures, fraudulent amounts, or misstatements of recorded amounts.

Audits cannot be expected to provide the same degree of assurance for the detection of material management fraud as is provided for an equally material error. Concealment by management makes fraud more difficult for auditors to find. The cost of providing equally high assurance for management fraud and for errors is economically impractical for both auditors and society.

Auditors do, however, have considerable responsibility for finding material management fraud. In recent years there has been increased emphasis on auditors' responsibility to evaluate factors that may indicate an increased likelihood that management fraud may be occurring. For example, assume that management is dominated by a president who makes most of the major operating and business decisions. She has a reputation in the business community for making optimistic projections about future earnings and then putting considerable pressure on operating and accounting staff to make sure those projections are met. She has also been associated with other companies in the past that have gone bankrupt. These factors, considered together, may cause the auditor to conclude that the likelihood of management fraud is fairly high. In such a circumstance, the auditor should put increased emphasis on searching for material management fraud.

The auditor may also uncover circumstances during the audit that may cause suspicions of management fraud. For example, the auditor may find that management has lied about the age of certain inventory items. When such circumstances are uncovered, the auditor must evaluate their implications and consider the need to modify the amount of audit evidence gathered.

Employee fraud The profession has also been emphatic that the auditor has less responsibility for the discovery of employee fraud than for errors. If auditors were responsible for the discovery of all employee fraud, auditing tests would have to be greatly expanded, because many types of employee fraud are extremely difficult if not impossible to detect. The procedures that would be necessary to uncover all cases of fraud would certainly be more expensive than the benefits would justify. For example, if there is fraud involving the collusion of several employees that includes the falsification of documents, it is unlikely that such a fraud would be uncovered in a normal audit.

Similar to what is done for assessing the likelihood of material management fraud, the auditor should also evaluate the likelihood of material employee fraud. That is normally done initially as a part of understanding the entity's internal control and assessing control risk. Audit evidence should be expanded when the auditor finds an absence of adequate controls or failure to follow prescribed procedures, if he or she believes material employee fraud could exist.

Illegal acts A topic related to fraud and error is illegal acts that have been committed by the client. While there are no Recommendations dealing with illegal acts presently in the CICA *Handbook*, an Exposure Draft (ED) proposing a new *Handbook* section 5136, "Illegal Acts," was issued by the Auditing Standards Board of the CICA in August, 1991. The ED defines an illegal act as "a violation of statutory law or government regulation attributable to the entity under audit, or to management or employees acting on the entity's behalf." Section 5136.05 points out that an auditor's responsibility is to comply with GAAS and, as a result, that the auditor may not detect an illegal act or become aware that an illegal act has occurred.

The performance of an illegal act by management or an employee of a company may affect the company (and the financial statements) in a variety of ways. For example, the payment of a bribe by a subsidiary in a foreign country could lead to expulsion of the company and/or expropriation of the company's assets; the balance sheet could be affected. Failing to dispose properly of untreated waste products could make the company liable for fines and penalties; the income statement could be affected. Even if the magnitude of the illegal act itself is not material, the consequences could well be so. As such, the auditor must be interested in illegal acts so that their potential impact may be properly evaluated.

When an illegal act is discovered, the auditor must consider whether such an act is a reflection of the company's corporate culture. Are such acts condoned or encouraged by management? If management does not promote ethical behavior, the auditor should question management's good faith and consider whether continued association with the client is desirable.

The ED in Section 5136 suggests that the auditor should inquire of management about its policies designed to prevent illegal acts and "obtain written representations from management [that there are no] violations or possible violations of laws and government regulations" that would affect the financial statements or notes thereto. Proposed Section 5136 goes on to say that, other than inquiry of management, the auditor should not search for illegal acts unless there is reason to believe they may exist.

If the auditor finds evidence that leads him or her to believe that an illegal act may have occurred, as was indicated above with respect to error and fraud, "the auditor should perform procedures to confirm or dispel [his or her] suspicion." The auditor may find indications of possible illegal acts in a variety of ways. For example, the minutes may indicate that an investigation by a government agency is in process, or the auditor may identify unusually large payments to consultants or government officials.

When the auditor believes an illegal act may have occurred, it is necessary to take several actions. First, the auditor should inquire of management at a level above those likely to be involved in the potential illegal act. Second, the auditor should consult with the client's lawyers or another specialist who is knowledgeable about the potential illegal act. Third, the auditor should consider accumulating additional evidence to determine if there actually is an illegal act. All three of these actions are intended to provide the auditor information about whether the suspected illegal act actually exists.

The first course of action when an illegal act has been identified is to consider the effects on the financial statements, including the adequacy of disclosures. These effects may be complex and difficult to resolve. For example, a violation of equal opportunity laws could involve significant fines, but it could also result in the loss of customers or key employees that could materially affect future revenues and expenses. If the auditor concludes that the disclosures relative to an illegal act are inadequate, the auditor should modify the auditor's report accordingly.

The auditor should communicate with a sufficiently senior level of management and the audit committee to make sure they know of the illegal act. If the client either refuses to accept the auditor's modified report or fails to take appropriate remedial action concerning the illegal act, the auditor may find it necessary to withdraw from the engagement. Such decisions are complex and normally involve consultation by the auditor with the auditor's lawyers.

Financial Statement Cycles

OBJECTIVE 4

Describe the financial-statement-cycles approach to segmenting the audit, and use this approach as a basis for further study.

Audits are performed by dividing the financial statements into smaller segments or components. The division makes the audit more manageable and aids in the assignment of tasks to different members of the audit team. For example, most auditors treat fixed assets and notes payable as different segments. Each segment is audited separately but not completely independently. (For example, the audit of fixed assets may reveal an unrecorded note payable.) After the audit of each segment is completed, including interrelationships with other segments, the results are combined. A conclusion can then be reached about the financial statements taken as a whole.

There are different ways of segmenting an audit. Looking at the financial statements in Figure 5–2, one obvious approach would be to treat every account balance on the statements as a separate segment. Segmenting that way is usually inefficient. It would result in the independent audit of such closely related accounts as inventory and cost of goods sold.

FIGURE 5–5

Information Flow from
Journals to Financial
Statements

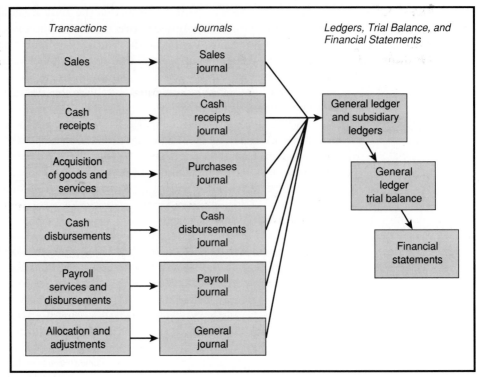

*The Cycle
Approach to
Segmenting
an Audit*

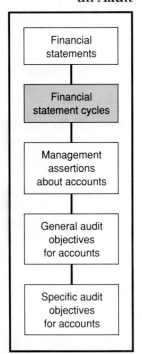

A more common way to divide an audit is to keep closely related types of transactions and account balances in the same segment. This is called the *cycle approach*. For example, sales, sales returns, and cash receipts transactions and the accounts receivable balance are all a part of the sales and collection cycle. Similarly, payroll transactions and accrued payroll are a part of the payroll and personnel cycle.

The logic of using the cycle approach can be seen by thinking about the way transactions are recorded in journals and summarized in the general ledger and financial statements. Figure 5–5 shows that flow. To the extent it is practical, the cycle approach combines transactions recorded in different journals with the general ledger balances that result from those transactions.

The cycles used in this text are shown in Table 5–1. The journals associated with each cycle for Hillsburg Hardware Ltd., as well as the 19X8 financial statement accounts are included.

The following observations expand the information contained in Table 5–1.

- All general ledger accounts and journals for Hillsburg Hardware Ltd. are included at least once. For a different company, the number and titles of journals and general ledger accounts would differ, but all would be included.
- Some journals and general ledger accounts are included in more than one cycle. When that occurs, it means the journal is used to record transactions from more than one cycle and indicates a tie-in between the cycles. The most important general ledger account included in and affecting several cycles is the general cash (cash in bank). General cash connects most cycles.
- The capital acquisition and repayment cycle is closely related to the acquisition of goods and services and payment cycle. The same three journals are used to record

TABLE 5–1

Cycles Applied to Hillsburg Hardware Ltd.

CYCLE	JOURNALS INCLUDED IN THE CYCLE (SEE FIGURE 5–5)	GENERAL LEDGER ACCOUNT INCLUDED IN THE CYCLE (SEE FIGURE 5–3)	
		Balance Sheet	*Income Statement*
Sales and collection	Sales journal Cash receipts journal General journal	Cash in bank Trade accounts receivable Other accounts receivable Allowance for uncollectible accounts	Sales Sales returns and allowances Bad debt expense
Acquisition and payment	Purchase journal Cash disbursements journal General journal	Cash in bank Inventories Prepaid expenses Land Buildings Delivery equipment Furniture and fixtures Accumulated depreciation Trade accounts payable Other accrued payables Income tax payable Deferred tax Goods and services tax payable	Advertising[S] Travel and entertainment[S] Sales meetings and training[S] Sales and promotional literature[S] Miscellaneous sales expense[S] Travel and entertainment[A] Stationery and supplies[A] Postage[A] Telephone and telegraph[A] Dues and memberships[A] Taxes[A] Depreciation – office building and equipment[A] Rent[A] Legal fees and retainers[A] Auditing[A] Insurance[A] Office repairs and maintenance expense[A] Miscellaneous office expense[A] Miscellaneous general expense[A] Gain on sale of assets Income taxes
Payroll and personnel	Payroll journal General journal	Cash in bank Accrued payroll Accrued payroll benefits	Salaries and commissions[S] Sales payroll benefits[S] Executive and office salaries[A] Administrative payroll benefits[A]
Inventory and warehousing	Purchase journal Sales journal General journal	Inventories	Cost of goods sold
Capital acquisition and repayment	Purchase journal Cash disbursements journal General journal	Cash in bank Notes payable Long-term notes payable Accrued interest Capital stock Retained earnings Dividends Dividends payable	Interest expense

S = Selling expense.
A = General and administrative expense.

FIGURE 5–6

Relationships Among
Transaction Cycles

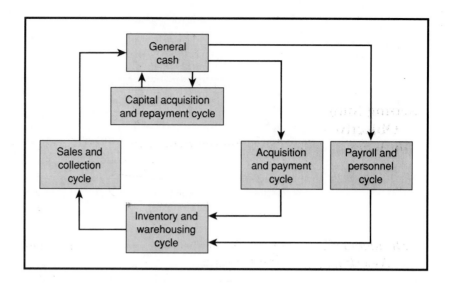

transactions for both cycles and the transactions are similar. There are two reasons for
treating capital acquisition and repayment separately from the acquisition of goods and
services. First, the transactions are related to financing a company rather than to its
operations. Second, most capital acquisition and repayment cycle accounts involve few
transactions, but each is often highly material and therefore should be audited extensively. Considering both reasons, it is more convenient to separate the two cycles.

■ The inventory and warehousing cycle is closely related to all other cycles, especially for
a manufacturing company. The cost of inventory includes raw materials (acquisition
and payment cycle), direct labor (payroll and personnel cycle), and manufacturing
overhead (acquisition and payment and payroll and personnel cycles). The sale of
finished goods involves the sales and collection cycle. Because inventory is material for
most manufacturing companies, it is common to borrow money using inventory as
security. In those cases, the capital acquisition and repayment cycle is also related to
inventory and warehousing.

Relationships Among Cycles

Figure 5–6 illustrates the relationship of the cycles to each other. In addition to the
five cycles, general cash is also shown. Each cycle is studied in detail in later
chapters.

Figure 5–6 shows that cycles have no beginning or end except at the origin
and final disposition of a company. A company begins by obtaining capital,
usually in the form of cash. In a manufacturing company, cash is used to acquire
raw materials, permanent assets, and related goods and services to produce inventory (acquisition and payment cycle). Cash is also used to acquire labor for the
same reason (payroll and personnel cycle). Acquisition and payment and payroll
and personnel are similar in nature, but the functions are sufficiently different to
justify separate cycles. The combined result of these two cycles is inventory
(inventory and warehousing cycle). At a subsequent point, the inventory is sold
and billings and collections result (sales and collection cycle). The cash thus
generated is used to pay dividends and interest and to start the cycles again. The
cycles interrelate in much the same way in a service company, but of course there
is no inventory.

Transaction cycles are of major importance in the conduct of the audit. For the most part, auditors treat each cycle separately as the audit is being performed. Although care should be taken to interrelate different cycles at different times, the auditor must treat the cycles somewhat independently in order to manage complex audits effectively.

Setting Audit Objectives for Accounts

Dividing the audit into components using the cycle approach helps the auditor to manage the audit, but further subdivision is required. For any given account balance within a cycle, there are several specific audit objectives that must be met. Knowledge of those objectives is essential to the study of auditing. They will be referred to repeatedly throughout the text. The framework used to develop specific audit objectives consists of management assertions and general audit objectives. These are studied next.

Management Assertions

Test

Assertions are implied or expressed representations by management about the accounts in the financial statements. As an illustration, the management of Hillsburg Hardware Ltd. asserts that cash of $41,000 (see Figure 5–2) was present in the company's bank accounts or on the premises as of the balance sheet date. Unless otherwise disclosed in the financial statements, management also asserts that the cash was unrestricted and available for normal use. Similar assertions exist for each asset, liability, shareholders' equity, revenue, expense, gain and loss item in the financial statements.

> **OBJECTIVE 5**
>
> Discuss the five categories of management assertions about financial information.

Management assertions are directly related to generally accepted accounting principles. These assertions are part of the *criteria management uses to record and disclose accounting information in financial statements*. Return to the definition of auditing in Chapter 1, on page 2. It states, in part, that auditing is a comparison of quantifiable information (financial statements) to established criteria (assertions established according to generally accepted accounting principles). Auditors must therefore understand the assertions to do adequate audits.

Section 5300.17 of the *CICA Handbook* lists and describes seven assertions that management makes with respect to items in the financial statements. We have combined these seven assertions into five as noted below; subsequent references in the text will be to the five assertions.

Financial statements

Financial statement cycles

Management assertions about accounts

General audit objectives for accounts

Specific audit objectives for accounts

ASSERTIONS LISTED IN THE *CICA HANDBOOK*	FIVE CATEGORIES OF ASSERTION
Existence	Existence or occurrence
Occurrence	
Completeness	Completeness
Ownership	Rights and obligations
Valuation	Valuation or allocation
Measurement	
Statement presentation	Presentation and disclosure

Know Them!

Assertions about existence or occurrence   These assertions deal with whether assets, obligations, and equities included in the balance sheet actually existed on the balance sheet date and whether revenues and expenses included on the income statement reflect transactions pertaining to the enterprise that actually occurred during the accounting period. For example, management asserts that merchandise inventory included in the balance sheet exists and is available for sale at the balance sheet date. Similarly, management asserts that sales in the income statement represent exchanges of goods or services that actually took place.

Assertions about completeness These management assertions state that all transactions and accounts that should be presented in the financial statements are included, that there are no unrecorded assets, liabilities or transactions. For example, management asserts that all sales of goods and services are recorded and included in the financial statements. Similarly, management asserts that notes payable in the balance sheet include all such obligations of the entity.

The completeness assertion deals with matters opposite from those of the existence or occurrence assertion. The completeness assertion is concerned with the possibility of omitting items from the financial statements that should have been included, whereas the existence or occurrence assertion is concerned with inclusion of amounts that should not have been.

Thus, recording a sale that did not take place would be a violation of the occurrence assertion, whereas the failure to record a sale that did occur would be a violation of the completeness assertion.

Assertions about rights and obligations These management assertions deal with whether assets are the rights of the entity and liabilities are the obligations of the entity at a given date. For example, management asserts that assets are owned by the company or amounts capitalized for leases in the balance sheet represent the cost of the entity's rights to leased property and that the corresponding lease liability represents an obligation of the entity.

Assertions about valuation or allocation These assertions deal with whether asset, liability, equity, revenue, expense, and gain and loss accounts have been included in the financial statements at appropriate amounts and in the proper period. For example, management asserts that property is recorded at historical cost and that such cost is systematically allocated to appropriate accounting periods through depreciation. Similarly, management asserts that trade accounts receivable included in the balance sheet are stated at net realizable value.

Assertions about presentation and disclosure These assertions deal with whether components of the financial statements are properly classified, described, and disclosed in accordance with generally accepted accounting principles, or if appropriate, with another appropriate disclosed basis of accounting. For example, management asserts that obligations classified as long-term liabilities in the balance sheet will not mature within one year. Similarly, management asserts that amounts presented as extraordinary items in the income statement are properly classified and described.

General and Specific Audit Objectives for Accounts

The auditor's objectives follow and are closely related to management assertions. That is not surprising, since the auditor's primary responsibility is to determine whether management assertions about financial statements are justified.

Audit objectives are intended to provide a *framework* to help the auditor obtain sufficient appropriate audit evidence required by the third examination standard and decide the proper evidence to accumulate given the circumstances of the engagement. The objectives remain the same from audit to audit, but the evidence varies, depending on the circumstances.

A distinction must be made between *general audit objectives* and *specific audit objectives* for each account balance. The general audit objectives discussed here are applicable to every account balance but are stated in broad terms. Specific audit objectives are also applied to each account balance on the financial statements but are stated in terms tailored to the engagement. Once you know the general audit objectives, they can be used to develop specific objectives for each account balance in the financial statements being audited.

Validity – amounts included are valid   This objective deals with whether the amounts included in the financial statements should actually be included. Inclusion of a sale in the sales journal and general ledger when no sale occurred violates the validity objective. This objective is the auditor's counterpart to the management assertion of existence or occurrence.

Completeness – existing amounts are included   This objective deals with whether all amounts that should be included have actually been included. Failure to include a sale in the sales journal and general ledger when a sale occurred violates the completeness objective. This objective is the counterpart to the management assertion of completeness.

The validity and completeness objectives emphasize opposite audit concerns; validity deals with potential overstatement and completeness with unrecorded transactions and amounts (understatement).

Ownership – amounts included are owned   In addition to existing, most assets must be owned before it is acceptable to include them in the financial statements. Similarly, liabilities must be owed by the entity (that is, the liability must be that of the entity and not that of some other entity). This objective is the auditor's counterpart to the management assertion of rights and obligations.

Valuation – amounts included are properly valued   The correct valuation of the individual balances making up the total account balance, including the arithmetic accuracy of all calculations and recognition of declines in net realizable value, is the concern of this objective. Valuation, as used in audit objectives, is less broad than when it is used as a management assertion, as shown in Table 5–2 on page 147.

Classification – amounts included are properly classified   Classification involves determining whether items are included in the correct accounts and accounts are properly displayed on the financial statements. For example, assets must be properly separated into short term and long term, and amounts due from affiliates, officers, and directors must be separated from amounts due from customers. The client's chart of accounts is the primary tool the auditor uses to determine whether the client has followed proper account classification.

Cutoff – transactions near the balance sheet date are recorded in the proper period   In testing for cutoff, the objective is to determine whether transactions are recorded in the proper period. The transactions that are most likely to be misstated are those recorded near the end of the accounting period. It is proper to think of cutoff tests as a part of verifying either the balance sheet accounts or the related

---

OBJECTIVE 6

Describe how the auditor develops general and specific audit objectives from management's assertions.

Financial statements

Financial statement cycles

Management assertions about accounts

General audit objectives for accounts

Specific audit objectives for accounts

income statement accounts, but for convenience auditors usually perform them as a part of auditing balance sheet accounts.

Mechanical accuracy – details in the account balance agree with related subsidiary ledger amounts, foot to the total in the account balance, and agree with the total in the general ledger Account balances on financial statements arise from and are supported by details in subsidiary ledgers, transactions listed in journals, and schedules prepared by clients. The mechanical accuracy objective is concerned that the details on lists are accurately prepared, correctly added, and agree with the general ledger. For example, individual accounts receivable on a listing of accounts receivable should be the same in the accounts receivable subsidiary ledger and the total should equal the general ledger control account.

Disclosure – account balance and related disclosure requirements are properly presented on the financial statements In fulfilling the disclosure objective, the auditor tests to make certain that all balance sheet and income statement accounts and related information are correctly set forth in the financial statements and properly described in the body and footnotes of the statements. This objective has its counterpart in the management assertion of presentation and disclosure.

After the general objective is understood, specific objectives for each account balance on the financial statements can be developed. There should be at least one specific objective for each general objective unless the auditor believes that objective is not relevant or is unimportant in the circumstances. There may be more than one specific objective for a general objective. For example, specific objectives for the ownership objective relating to the inventory of Hillsburg Hardware Ltd. could include (1) the company has title to all inventory items listed and (2) inventories are not pledged as collateral unless that fact is disclosed.

Relationships Among Management Assertions and Audit Objectives

The reason there are more general audit objectives than management assertions is to provide additional guidance to auditors in deciding what evidence to accumulate. Table 5–2 illustrates this by showing the relationships among management assertions, the general objectives, and specific objectives as applied to inventory for Hillsburg Hardware Ltd.

How Audit Objectives Are Met

OBJECTIVE 7

Describe the process by which audit objectives are met, and use it as a basis for further study.

Once the auditor has determined the specific audit objectives for each component in the financial statements, the evidence accumulation process can begin. The auditor determines the appropriate evidence to accumulate by following an audit process. An audit process is a well-defined methodology for organizing an audit to help the auditor accumulate sufficient appropriate audit evidence. There are four phases in the audit process. These are shown in Figure 5–7. An expanded summary of the four phases in the audit process is presented in Figure 10-10 on page 338. The remainder of this chapter provides a brief introduction to the four phases in the audit process shown in Figure 5–7.

Plan and Design an Audit Approach (Phase I)

For any given audit, there are many ways an auditor can accumulate evidence to meet the overall audit objectives. Two overriding considerations affect the approach the auditor selects: *sufficient appropriate audit evidence must be accumulated to meet the auditor's professional responsibility,* and *the cost of accumulating the evidence should be minimized.* The first consideration is the more

TABLE 5–2

Hillsburg
Hardware Ltd.:
Assertions and
Objectives Applied
to Inventory

MANAGEMENT ASSERTION	GENERAL AUDIT OBJECTIVE	SPECIFIC AUDIT OBJECTIVE APPLIED TO INVENTORY
Existence or occurrence	Validity	All recorded inventory exists at the balance sheet date.
Completeness	Completeness	All existing inventory has been counted and included in inventory summary.
Rights and obligations	Ownership	The company has title to all inventory items listed. Inventories are not pledged as collateral.
Valuation or allocation	Valuation	Inventory quantities agree with items physically on hand. Prices used to value inventories are materially correct. Extensions of price times quantity are correct and details are correctly added. Inventories have been written down where net realizable value is less than book value.
	Classification	Inventory items are properly classified as raw materials, work in process, or finished goods.
	Cutoff	Purchase cutoff at year-end is proper. Sales cutoff at year-end is proper.
	Mechanical accuracy	Total of inventory items agrees with general ledger.
Presentation and disclosure	Disclosure	Major categories of inventories and their bases of valuation are disclosed. The pledge or assignment of any inventories is disclosed.

FIGURE 5–7

Four Phases of an Audit

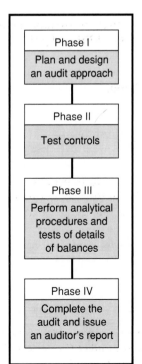

important, but cost minimization is necessary if public accounting firms are to be competitive and profitable. If there were no concern for controlling costs, decision making about the types and amounts of evidence to select would be easy. Auditors would keep adding evidence, without concern for efficiency, until they were sufficiently certain there were no material errors.

Concern for sufficient appropriate audit evidence and cost control necessitates planning the engagement. The plan should result in an effective audit approach at reasonable cost. Planning and designing an audit approach can be broken down into several parts. Two are addressed briefly here. Others are discussed in later chapters.

Obtaining knowledge of the client's business To interpret adequately the meaning of information obtained throughout the audit, an *understanding of the client's business and industry* is essential. Unique aspects of different businesses are reflected in the financial statements. An audit of a life insurance company could not be performed with due care without an understanding of the unique characteristics of that business. Imagine attempting to audit a client in the bridge construction industry without understanding the construction business and the percentage-of-completion method of accounting. A reasonable understanding of the client's business and industry is required by Section 5140 of the *CICA Handbook*.

Understanding the client's internal control and assessing control risk It was pointed out in Chapter 1 that the ability of the client's internal control to generate reliable financial information and safeguard assets and records is one of the most important and widely accepted concepts in the theory and practice of auditing. If the client has excellent internal control, *control risk* will be low and the amount of audit evidence to be accumulated can be significantly less than for internal control that is not adequate.

Examination Standard (ii) of generally accepted auditing standards in Section 5100.2 *requires* the auditor gain a sufficient understanding of internal control to plan the audit. This understanding is obtained by reviewing organization charts and procedural manuals, by discussions with client personnel, by completing internal control questionnaires and flowcharts, and by observing client activities.

After the auditor gains an understanding of internal control, he or she is in a position to evaluate how effective it should be in preventing and detecting errors and fraud and other irregularities. This evaluation involves identifying specific controls that reduce the likelihood that errors and fraud will occur and not be detected and corrected on a timely basis. This process is referred to as *assessing control risk*.

Test Controls (Phase II) Where the auditor has assessed control risk at a level below the maximum based on the identification of controls, he or she may then reduce the extent to which the accuracy of the financial statement information related directly to those controls must be validated through the accumulation of evidence. However, to justify using a control risk assessment below the maximum, the auditor must test the effectiveness of the controls. The procedures involved in this type of testing are commonly referred to as *tests of controls*.

tion. Inquiry includes asking questions of management and employees; observation includes watching an employee perform a certain task to determine the task is being performed (for example, watching a security guard check that doors are locked); reperformance includes redoing an employee's work to ensure it was done properly (for example, checking the price on an invoice to ensure the right price was used when the invoice was prepared); inspection includes examination of documents supporting transactions. It should be noted that a considerable amount of the evidence accumulated in support of financial statement amounts also involves transaction documentation. Whenever transaction documentation is examined for either or both of these purposes the tests are commonly referred to as *tests of transactions*.

Do Analytical Procedures and Tests of Details of Balances (Phase III)

Phase III procedures may be described as substantive procedures; there are two general categories or components of phase III procedures: analytical procedures and tests of details of balances. Analytical procedures are those that assess the overall reasonableness of transactions and balances. An example is to compare the current year's balance in each account to the prior year's and assess whether the change is reasonable considering the changes in the client's business. Tests of details of balances are specific procedures intended to test for monetary errors in the balances in the financial statements. Examples include direct written communication with customers for accounts receivable, observation of actual inventory, and examination of vendors' statements for accounts payable. These tests of ending balances are essential to the conduct of the audit because most of the evidence is obtained from a source independent of the client and therefore considered of high quality.

There is a close relationship among the general review of the client's circumstances, results of understanding internal control and assessing control risk, analytical procedures, and the tests of details of the financial statement account balances. If the auditor has obtained a reasonable level of assurance about the fair presentation of the financial statements through understanding internal control, assessing control risk, testing controls and analytical procedures, the tests of details can be significantly reduced. In most instances, however, some tests of details of significant financial statement account balances are necessary.

Complete the Audit and Issue an Auditor's Report (Phase IV)

After the auditor has completed all the procedures, it is necessary to combine the information obtained to reach an *overall conclusion* as to whether the financial statements are fairly presented. This is a highly subjective process that relies heavily on the auditor's professional judgment. In practice, the auditor continuously combines the information obtained as he or she proceeds through the audit. The final combination is simply a summation at the completion of the engagement. When the audit is completed, the public accountant must issue an auditor's report to accompany the client's published financial statements. The report must meet well-defined technical requirements that are affected by the scope of the audit and the nature of the findings. These reports have already been studied in Chapter 2.

Summary

This chapter discusses the objectives of the audit and the way the auditor subdivides an audit to result in specific audit objectives. The auditor then accumulates evidence to obtain assurance that each objective has been satisfied. Figure 5–8 summarizes the way that subdivision is done in this book.

FIGURE 5–8 Developing Specific Audit Objectives for Audits of Financial Statements

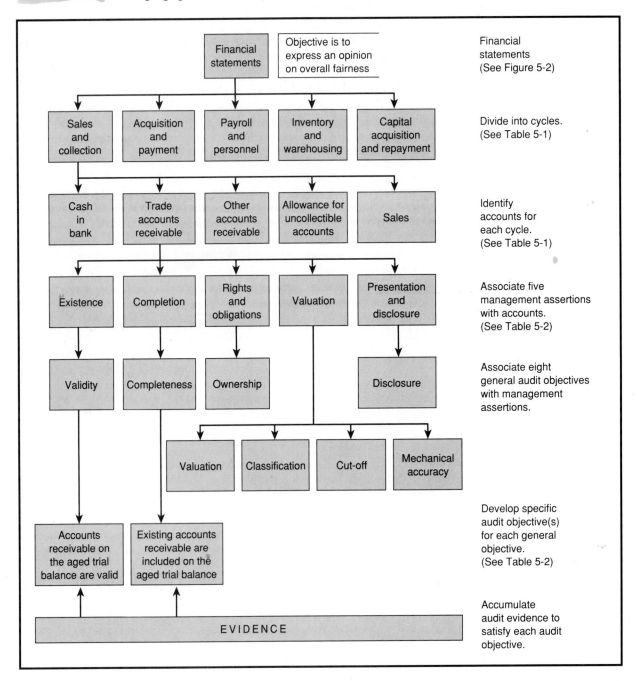

REVIEW QUESTIONS

5–1 State the objective of the ordinary audit of financial statements. In general terms, how do auditors meet that objective?

5–2 Distinguish between management's and the auditor's responsibility for the financial statements being audited.

5–3   Distinguish between the terms *errors* and *fraud and other irregularities*. What is the auditor's responsibility for finding each?

5–4   Distinguish between management fraud and employee fraud. Discuss the likely difference between these two types of fraud on the fair presentation of financial statements.

5–5   "It is well accepted in auditing that throughout the conduct of the ordinary examination, it is essential to obtain large amounts of information from management and to rely heavily on management's judgments. After all, the financial statements are management's representations, and the primary responsibility for their fair presentation rests with management, not the auditor. For example, it is extremely difficult, if not impossible, for the auditor to evaluate the obsolescence of inventory as well as management can in a highly complex business. Similarly, the collectibility of accounts receivable and the continued usefulness of machinery and equipment is heavily dependent on management's willingness to provide truthful responses to questions." Reconcile the auditor's responsibility for discovering material misrepresentations by management with these comments.

5–6   List three major considerations that are useful in predicting the likelihood of management fraud in an audit. For each of the considerations, state two actions the auditor can take to evaluate its significance in the engagement.

5–7   Describe what is meant by the cycle approach to auditing. What are the advantages of dividing the audit into different cycles?

5–8   Identify the cycle to which each of the following general ledger accounts would ordinarily be assigned: sales, accounts payable, retained earnings, accounts receivable, inventory, and repairs and maintenance.

5–9   Why are sales, sales returns and allowances, bad debts, cash discounts, accounts receivable, and allowance for uncollectible accounts all included in the same cycle?

5–10   Define what is meant by a management assertion about financial statements. Identify the five broad categories of management assertions.

5–11   Distinguish between the general audit objectives and management assertions. Why are the general audit objectives more useful to auditors?

5–12   An acquisition of equipment repairs by a construction company is recorded in the wrong accounting period. Which audit objective has been violated? Which objective has been violated if the acquisition had been capitalized as a fixed asset rather than expensed?

5–13   Distinguish between the validity and completeness audit objectives. State the effect on the financial statements (overstatement or understatement) of a violation of each in the audit of accounts receivable.

5–14   What are specific audit objectives? Explain their relationship to the general audit objectives.

5–15   Identify the management assertion and general audit objective for the specific audit objective: All recorded fixed assets exist at the balance sheet date.

5–16   Explain how management assertions, general audit objectives, and specific audit objectives are developed for an account balance such as accounts receivable.

5–17   Identify the four phases of the audit. What is the relationship of the four phases to the objective of the audit of financial statements?

MULTIPLE CHOICE QUESTIONS

5-18 The following questions concern the reasons auditors do audits. Choose the best response.

    a. Which of the following *best* describes the reason why an independent auditor reports on financial statements?

        (1) A management fraud may exist, and it is more likely to be detected by independent auditors.

        (2) Different interests may exist between the company preparing the statements and the persons using the statements.

        (3) A misstatement of account balances may exist and is generally corrected as the result of the independent auditor's work.

        (4) Poorly designed internal control may be in existence.

    b. An independent audit aids in the communication of economic data because the audit

        (1) confirms the accuracy of management's financial representations.

        (2) lends credibility to the financial statements.

        (3) guarantees that financial data are fairly presented.

        (4) assures the readers of financial statements that any fraudulent activity has been corrected.

    c. The major reason an independent auditor gathers audit evidence is to

        (1) form an opinion on the financial statements.

        (2) detect fraud.

        (3) evaluate management.

        (4) assess control risk.   (AICPA adapted)

5-19 The following questions deal with errors and fraud. Choose the best response.

    a. An independent auditor has the responsibility to design the audit examination to provide reasonable assurance of detecting errors and fraud and other irregularities that might have a material effect on the financial statements. Which of the following, if material, would be a *fraud* as defined in the *CICA Handbook*?

        (1) Misappropriation of an asset or groups of assets.

        (2) Clerical mistakes in the accounting data underlying the financial statements.

        (3) Mistakes in the application of accounting principles.

        (4) Misinterpretation of facts that existed when the financial statements were prepared.

    b. Although the discovery of employee fraud is not the objective of the public accountant's ordinary audit engagement, the public accountant would be responsible for the detection of fraud if it is material and the public accountant failed to detect it due to

        (1) management's failure to disclose an unrecorded transaction. The documents pertaining to the transaction are kept in a confidential file.

        (2) management's description of internal control.

        (3) management's misstatement of the value of an inventory of precious gems.

        (4) the amount of fidelity bond coverage for certain employees not being compatible with the amount of potential defalcation that might be committed.

    c. If an independent auditor's examination leading to an opinion on financial statements causes the auditor to believe that *material* errors or fraud exist the auditor should

        (1) consider the implications and discuss the matter with appropriate levels of management.

(2) make the investigation necessary to determine whether the errors or fraud have in fact occurred.

(3) request that management investigate to determine whether the errors or fraud have in fact occurred.

(4) consider whether the errors or fraud were the result of a failure by employees to comply with existing internal control procedures.

(AICPA adapted)

5–20 The following are miscellaneous questions relating to Chapter 5. Choose the best response.

a. To emphasize auditor independence from management, many corporations follow the practice of

(1) appointing a partner of the public accounting firm conducting the examination to the corporation's audit committee.

(2) establishing a policy of discouraging social contact between employees of the corporation and the staff of the independent auditor.

(3) requesting that a representative of the independent auditor be on hand at the annual shareholders' meeting.

(4) having the independent auditor report to an audit committee of outside members of the board of directors.

b. The audit client's board of directors and audit committee refused to take any action with respect to an immaterial illegal act that was brought to their attention by the auditor. Because of their failure to act, the auditor withdrew from the engagement. The auditor's decision to withdraw was primarily due to doubts concerning

(1) inadequate financial statement disclosures.

(2) compliance with the *Canada Securities Act* of 1985.

(3) scope limitations resulting from their inaction.

(4) reliance on management's representations.

c. The primary responsibility for the adequacy of disclosure in the financial statements and footnotes rests with the

(1) partner assigned to the engagement.

(2) auditor in charge of field work.

(3) staff member who drafts the statements and footnotes.

(4) client.   (AICPA adapted)

DISCUSSION QUESTIONS AND PROBLEMS

5–21 The report on page 136 (Figure 5–4) and the report below are taken from the same page of a published annual report.

AUDITORS' REPORT TO THE SHAREHOLDERS

We have audited the consolidated balance sheets of Schneider Corporation as at October 27, 1990 and October 28, 1989 and the consolidated statements of earnings, retained earnings and changes in financial position for the years then ended. These financial statements are the responsibility of the Company's management. Our responsibility is to express an opinion on these financial statements based on our audits.

We conducted our audits in accordance with generally accepted auditing standards. Those standards require that we plan and perform an audit to obtain reasonable assurance whether the financial statements are free of material mis-statement. An audit includes examining, on a test basis, evidence supporting the amounts and disclosures in the financial statements. An audit also includes assessing the accounting principles used and significant estimates made by management, as well as evaluating the overall financial statement presentation.

In our opinion, these consolidated financial statements present fairly, in all material respects, the financial position of the Company as at October 27, 1990 and October 28, 1989 and the results of its operations and the changes in its financial position for the years then ended in accordance with generally accepted accounting principles.

Chartered Accountants
Kitchener, Canada
December 3, 1990

Required:

a. What are the purposes of the two reports and who was responsible for writing each?

b. What information does the management's report provide to users of financial statements?

c. Explain the purpose of the audit committee as described in the third paragraph of management's report. What is the relevance of the phrase "composed of a majority of outside directors"?

d. Is the auditor's report a standard, unqualified report or is it different? Explain your answer.

e. How long after the balance sheet date did the CA firm complete the audit field work?

5–22 Frequently, questions have been raised "regarding the responsibility of the independent auditor for the discovery of fraud (including defalcations and other similar irregularities), and concerning the proper course of conduct of the independent auditor when his or her examination discloses specific circumstances that arouse suspicion as to the existence of fraud."

Required:

a. What are (1) the function and (2) the responsibilities of the independent auditor in the examination of financial statements? Discuss fully, but in this part do not include fraud in the discussion.

b. What are the responsibilities of the independent auditor for the detection of fraud? Discuss fully.

c. What is the independent auditor's proper course of conduct when his or her examination discloses specific circumstances that arouse his or her suspicion as to the existence of fraud? (AICPA adapted)

5–23 A competent auditor has done a conscientious job of conducting an audit, but because of a clever fraud by management, a material error is included in the financial statements. The fraud, which is an overstatement of inventory, took place over several years, and it covered up the fact that the company's financial position was rapidly declining. The fraud was accidentally discovered in the latest audit by an unusually capable audit senior, and the audit committee was immediately informed. Subsequent investigation indicated the company was actually near bankruptcy, and the value of the stock dropped from $26 per share to $1 in less than one month. Among the losing shareholders were pension funds, university endowment funds, retired couples, and widows. The individuals responsible for perpetrating the fraud were also bankrupt.

After making an extensive investigation of the audit performance in previous years, the audit committee was satisfied that the auditor had done a high-quality audit and had followed generally accepted auditing standards in every respect. The audit committee concluded that it would be unreasonable to expect auditors to uncover this type of fraud.

Required: State your opinion as to who should bear the loss of the management fraud. Include in your discussion a list of potential bearers of the loss, and state why you believe they should or should not bear the loss.

5–24   The following are the classes of transactions and the titles of the journals used for Phillips Equipment Rental Co. Ltd.

CLASSES OF TRANSACTIONS	TITLES OF JOURNALS
Purchase returns	Cash receipts register
Rental revenue	Disbursements register
Charge-off of uncollectible accounts	Purchase journal
Purchases of goods and services (except payroll)	Revenue journal
Collection of Goods and Services Tax	Payroll register
Adjusting entries (for payroll)	Adjustments journal
Payroll service and payments	
Cash disbursements (except payroll)	
Cash receipts	

Required:
   a. Identify one financial statement balance that is likely to be affected by each of the nine classes of transactions.
   b. For each class of transaction, identify the journal that is likely to be used to record the transactions.
   c. Identify the transaction cycle that is likely to be affected by each of the nine classes of transactions.
   d. Explain how total rental revenue, as cited on the financial statements of Phillips Equipment Rental Co. Ltd., is accumulated in journals and is summarized on the financial statements. Assume there are several adjusting entries for rental revenue at the balance sheet date.

5–25   The following general ledger accounts are included in the trial balance for an audit client, Jones Wholesale Stationery Store Inc.

Income tax expense	Sales salaries expense	Sales
Income tax payable	Accumulated amortization of furniture and equipment	Salaries, office and general
Accounts receivable		Telephone and telegraph expense
Advertising expense	Notes payable	Bad-debt expense
Traveling expense	Allowance for doubtful accounts	Insurance expense
Accounts payable		Property tax payable
Bonds payable	Inventory	Interest receivable
Goods and services tax payable	Property tax expense	Interest income
Common stock	Interest expense	Accrued sales salaries
Unexpired insurance	Amortization expense – furniture and equipment	Rent expense
Furniture and equipment		Prepaid interest expense
Cash	ment	
Notes receivable – trade	Retained earnings	
Purchases		

Required:
   a. Identify the accounts in the trial balance that are likely to be included in each transaction cycle. Some accounts will be included in more than one cycle. Use the format shown below.

CYCLE	BALANCE SHEET ACCOUNTS	INCOME STATEMENT ACCOUNTS
Sales and collection		
Acquisition and payment		
Payroll and personnel		
Inventory and warehousing		
Capital acquisition and repayment		

b. How would the general ledger accounts in the trial balance probably differ if the company were a retail store rather than a wholesale company? How would they differ for a hospital or a government unit?

5–26 The following is the detailed chart of accounts for Atlantic Metal Specialties Ltd.

BALANCE SHEET ACCOUNTS (100-299)

Assets (100-199)

Current Assets (100-129)

101	Cash in bank
102	Payroll cash
103	Petty cash
106	Notes receivable – trade
109	Accounts receivable
109.1	Allowance for doubtful accounts
115	Finished goods
116	Work in process
117	Materials
120	Prepaid property tax
121	Prepaid insurance
122	Miscellaneous prepaid items

Property, Plant, and Equipment (130-159)

130	Land
132	Buildings
132.1	Accumulated amortization – buildings
135	Machinery and equipment – factory
135.1	Accumulated amortization – machinery and equipment – factory
143	Automobiles
143.1	Accumulated amortization – automobiles
146	Office furniture and fixtures
146.1	Accumulated amortization – office furniture and fixtures

Intangible Assets (170-179)

170	Goodwill
171	Patents
172	Franchises, licenses, and other privileges

Liabilities and Capital (200-299)

Current Liabilities (200-219)

201	Notes payable
203	Accounts payable
206	Accrued payroll
207	Accrued interest payable
208	Accrued sales tax
209	Other accrued liabilities
210	Goods and services tax payable
211	Employees income tax payable
212	Employee benefits payable
214	Estimated federal income tax payable
216	Long-term debt (due within one year)
218	Dividends payable

Long-Term Liabilities (220-229)

220	Bonds payable
222	Mortgage payable
224	Other long-term debt
226	Deferred income tax payable

Capital (250-299)

250	Common stock
260	Retained earnings

INCOME STATEMENT ACCOUNTS (300-899)

Sales (300-349)

301	Sales
301.1	Sales returns
301.2	Sales allowances
301.3	Sales discounts
301.4	Goods and services tax

Cost of Goods Sold (350-399)

351	Cost of goods sold
353	Purchases
353.1	Purchase returns
353.2	Purchase allowances
356	Materials price variance
357	Materials quantity variance
358	Purchases discounts
366	Labor rate variance
367	Labor efficiency variance

372	Applied factory overhead
376	Factory overhead spending variance
377	Factory overhead idle capacity variance
378	Factory overhead efficiency variance
379	Over-or underapplied factory overhead

Factory Overhead (400-499)

400	Factory overhead control
401	Salaries – factory
411	Indirect materials
412	Indirect labor
414	Freight in
417	Training

420	Overtime premium
422	Employee benefits
425	Vacation pay
427	Worker's compensation
434	Fuel – factory
436	Light and power
438	Telephone and telegraph
440	Tools
442	Defective work
450	Insurance expense
460	Amortization expense – buildings
461	Amortization expense – machinery and equipment
462	Repairs and maintenance of buildings
463	Repairs and maintenance of roads
464	Repairs and maintenance of transportation facilities
465	Repairs and maintenance of machinery and equipment
480	Rent of equipment
485	Property tax
486	Amortization of patents

Marketing Expenses (500-599)

500	Marketing expenses control
501	Salaries – sales supervision
503	Salaries – salespeople
504	Salaries – clerical help
507	Sales commissions
515	Freight out
522	Employee benefits
530	Supplies
534	Fuel
536	Light and power
538	Telephone and telegraph
546	Postage
548	Travel expenses
550	Insurance expense
560	Amortization expense – buildings
561	Amortization expense – automobiles
562	Repairs and maintenance of buildings

565	Advertising
567	Display materials
568	Conventions and exhibits
580	Rent of equipment
585	Property tax

Administrative Expenses (600-699)

600	Administrative expenses control
601	Salaries – administrative
604	Salaries – administrative clerical help
620	Overtime premium
622	Employee benefits
630	Supplies
634	Fuel
636	Light and power
638	Telephone and telegraph
646	Postage
648	Travel expenses
650	Insurance expense
660	Amortization expense – buildings
661	Amortization expense – furniture and fixtures
662	Repairs and maintenance of buildings
670	Legal and accounting fees
680	Rent of equipment
685	Property tax
691	Donations
693	Uncollectible accounts expense

Other Expenses (700-749)

701	Interest paid on notes payable
703	Interest paid on mortgage
707	Interest paid on bonds

Other Income (800-849)

801	Income from investments
816	Interest earned
817	Rental income
818	Miscellaneous income

Income Deductions (890-899)

890	Federal income tax expense

Required:

a. Explain the differences among a chart of accounts, a general ledger trial balance, and financial statements. What are the relationships among them?

b. What are the reasons for and benefits of associating general ledger trial balance accounts with transaction cycles?

c. For each account in the chart of accounts, identify the transaction cycle to which the account pertains. Some accounts belong to more than one cycle.

5–27 Following are the detailed financial statements titles for Podilchak Electronics Ltd. Their business includes primary repairing and selling parts for televisions, VCRs, CD players and video games.

PODILCHAK ELECTRONICS
BALANCE SHEET
December 31, 19X8

Assets
Current assets
    Cash
    Accounts receivable
    Less: Allowance for doubtful
        accounts
    Notes receivable
    Inventories – at average cost
    Supplies on hand
    Prepaid expenses
        Total current assets

Long-term investments
    Securities at cost (market value
        $62,000)

Property, plant, and equipment
    Land – at cost
    Buildings – at cost

    Less: Accumulated amortization
        Total property, plant, and
        equipment

Intangible assets
    Goodwill
        Total assets

Liabilities and Shareholders' Equity
Current liabilities
    Notes payable to banks
    Accounts payable
    Goods and services tax payable
    Accrued interest on notes payable
    Accrued federal income taxes
    Accrued salaries, wages, and other
    expenses
    Deposits received from customers
        Total current liabilities

Long-term debt
    Twenty-year 8 percent debentures,
    due January 1, 19X9
        Total liabilities

Shareholders' equity
    Preferred stock, $1.80, cumulative
    Authorized and outstanding, 10,000
        shares
    Common
    Authorized, 200,000 shares; issued
        and outstanding, 100,000 shares
    Earnings retained in the business
        Appropriated
        Unappropriated
            Total shareholders' equity
            Total liabilities and
                shareholders' equity

PODILCHAK ELECTRONICS
INCOME STATEMENT
for the year ended December 31, 19X8

Sales
    Revenues
        Less: Sales discounts
            Sales returns and
            allowances
            Goods and services tax
    Net sales

Cost of goods sold
    Parts inventory, January 1, 19X8
    Purchases of parts
    Less: Purchase discounts
        Net purchases

    Freight and transportation-in
    Total parts available for sale
    Less: Merchandise inventory,
        December 31, 19X8
    Cost of goods sold
    Gross profit on sales

Operating expenses
    Selling expenses
        Sales salaries and commissions
        Sales office salaries
        Travel and entertainment
        Advertising expense
        Freight and transportation-out
        Shipping supplies and expense
        Postage and stationery
        Amortization of sales equipment
        Telephone and telegraph
    Administrative expenses
        Officers' salaries
        Office salaries
        Legal and professional services
        Utilities expense
        Insurance expense
        Amortization of building
        Amortization of office equipment
        Stationery, supplies, and postage
        Miscellaneous office expenses
            Income from operations

Other income
    Rental income

Other expense
    Interest on bonds and notes
        Income before taxes
Income taxes
        Net income for the year
        Earnings per share

Required: Identify the accounts in the detailed financial statements that are likely to be included in each transaction cycle. Some accounts will be included in more than one cycle. Use the format shown below.

CYCLE	BALANCE SHEET ACCOUNTS	INCOME STATEMENT ACCOUNTS
Sales and collection Acquisition and payment Payroll and personnel Inventory and warehousing Capital acquisition and repayment		

5–28 The following are specific audit objectives applied to the audit of accounts receivable (a through h) and management assertions (1 through 5). The list referred to in the specific audit objectives is the list of the accounts receivable from each customer at the balance sheet date.

SPECIFIC AUDIT OBJECTIVE

a. There are no unrecorded receivables.
b. Receivables have not been sold or discounted.
c. Uncollectible accounts have been provided for.
d. Receivables that have become uncollectible have been written off.
e. All accounts on the list are expected to be collected within one year.
f. Any agreement or condition that restricts the nature of trade receivables is known and disclosed.
g. All accounts on the list arose from the normal course of business and are not due from related parties.
h. Sales cutoff at year-end is proper.

MANAGEMENT ASSERTION

1. Existence or occurrence
2. Completeness
3. Rights and obligations
4. Valuation and allocation
5. Presentation and disclosure

Required: For each specific audit objective, identify the appropriate management assertion.

5–29 The following are specific audit objectives applied to the audit of accounts payable (a through g), management assertions (1 through 5), and general audit objectives (6 through 13).

SPECIFIC AUDIT OBJECTIVE

a. Accounts in the acquisition and payment cycle are properly disclosed.
b. Acquisition transactions in the acquisition and payment cycle are recorded in the proper period.
c. Accounts payable in the accounts payable list agree with related master file amounts, and the total is correctly added and agrees with the general ledger.

MANAGEMENT ASSERTION

1. Existence or occurrence
2. Completeness
3. Rights and obligation
4. Valuation or allocation
5. Presentation and disclosure

GENERAL AUDIT OBJECTIVE

6. Validity
7. Completeness
8. Ownership
9. Valuation
10. Classification
11. Cutoff
12. Mechanical accuracy
13. Disclosure

d. Accounts payable in the accounts payable list are properly classified.

e. Accounts payable in the accounts payable list are valid.

f. Existing accounts payable are in the accounts payable list.

g. Accounts payable in the accounts payable list are valued at the correct amount.

Required:

a. Explain the differences between management assertions, general audit objectives, and specific audit objectives and their relationships to each other.

b. For each specific audit objective, identify the appropriate management assertion.

c. For each specific audit objective, identify the appropriate general audit objective.

5–30 The following are two specific objectives in the audit of accounts payable. The list referred to in the objectives is the list of accounts payable taken from the accounts payable master file. The total of the list equals the accounts payable balance on the general ledger.

1. All accounts payable included on the list represent amounts due to valid vendors.

2. There are no unrecorded accounts payable.

Required:

a. Explain the difference between these two specific audit objectives.

b. Which of these two objectives applies to the general audit objective, validity, and which one applies to completeness?

c. For the audit of accounts payable, which of these two audit objectives would usually be more important? Explain.

5–31 The following are eight general objectives for the audit of any balance sheet account (1 through 8) and ten specific objectives for the audit of property, plant, and equipment (a through j).

GENERAL AUDIT OBJECTIVE

1. Validity
2. Completeness
3. Ownership
4. Valuation
5. Classification
6. Cutoff
7. Mechanical accuracy
8. Disclosure

SPECIFIC AUDIT OBJECTIVE

a. There are no unrecorded fixed assets in use.

b. The company has valid title to the assets owned.

c. Details of property, plant, and equipment agree with the general ledger.

d. Fixed assets physically exist and are being used for the purpose intended.

e. Property, plant, and equipment are recorded at the correct amount.

f. The company has a contractual right for use of assets leased.

g. Liens or other encumbrances on property, plant, and equipment items are known and disclosed.

    h. Cash disbursements and/or accrual cutoff for property, plant, and equipment items are proper.

    i. Expense accounts do not contain amounts that should have been capitalized.

    j. Amortization is determined in accordance with an acceptable method and is materially correct as computed.

Required:

    a. What are the purposes of the general audit objectives and the specific audit objectives? Explain the relationship between these two sets of objectives.

    b. For each general objective, identify one or more specific audit objectives. No letter can be used for more than one general objective.

6

TYPES OF EVIDENCE AND DOCUMENTATION

LEARNING OBJECTIVES

THOROUGH STUDY OF THIS CHAPTER WILL ENABLE YOU TO:

1. Explain the nature of audit evidence

2. Describe the four decisions on evidence gathering that the auditor must make in order to create an audit program

3. Define the third examination standard and discuss its relationship to the three determinants of the persuasiveness of evidence

4. List and describe the seven types of evidence used in auditing

5. Integrate the concepts of audit evidence, audit objectives, and evidence-gathering decisions

6. Explain the purposes of audit working papers

7. Discuss and apply the concepts behind the preparation and organization of audit working papers

8. Define terms commonly used in auditing

☐ This chapter begins by describing audit evidence and the four major evidence decisions. It also discusses the meaning of *sufficient appropriate audit evidence*. The seven types of evidence available to satisfy the third examination standard are then defined and discussed. The chapter ends with an examination of auditors' working papers.

Nature of Evidence

Evidence was defined in Chapter 1 as any *information used by the auditor* to determine whether the quantitative information being audited is stated in accordance with the established criterion. The information varies widely in the extent to which it persuades the auditor whether financial statements are stated in accordance with generally accepted accounting principles. Evidence includes persuasive information such as the auditor's count of marketable securities, and less persuasive information such as responses to questions by client employees.

Audit Evidence Contrasted with Legal and Scientific Evidence

The use of evidence is not unique to auditors. Evidence is also used extensively by scientists, lawyers, and historians.

Through television, most people are familiar with the use of evidence in legal cases dealing with the guilt or innocence of a party charged with a crime such as robbery. In legal cases, there are well-defined rules of evidence enforced by a judge for the protection of the innocent. It is common, for example, for legal evidence to be judged inadmissible on the grounds that it is irrelevant, prejudicial, or based on hearsay.

Similarly, in scientific experiments the scientist obtains evidence to draw conclusions about a theory. Assume, for example, a medical scientist is evaluating a new medicine that may provide relief for asthma sufferers. The scientist will gather evidence from a large number of controlled experiments over an extended period of time to determine the effectiveness of the medicine and whether there are any undesirable side-effects.

The auditor also gathers evidence to draw conclusions. Different evidence is used by auditors than by scientists and in cases of law, and it is used in different ways; but in all three cases evidence is used to reach conclusions. Table 6–1 illustrates key characteristics of evidence from the perspective of a scientist doing an experiment, a legal case involving an accused thief, and an auditor of financial

TABLE 6–1

Characteristics of Evidence for a Scientific Experiment, Legal Case, and Audit of Financial Statements

BASIS OF COMPARISON	SCIENTIFIC EXPERIMENT INVOLVING TESTING A MEDICINE	LEGAL CASE INVOLVING AN ACCUSED THIEF	AUDIT OF FINANCIAL STATEMENTS
Use of the evidence	Determine effects of using the medicine	Decide guilt or innocence of accused	Determine if statements are fairly presented
Nature of evidence	Results of repeated experiments	Testimony by witnesses and party involved	Various types of audit evidence
Party or parties evaluating evidence	Scientist	Jury and judge	Auditor
Certainty of conclusions from evidence	Vary from uncertain to near certainty	Requires guilt beyond a reasonable doubt	High level of assurance
Nature of conclusions	Recommend or not recommend use of medicine	Innocence or guilt of party	Issue one of several alternative types of auditor's reports
Typical consequences of incorrect conclusions from evidence	Society uses ineffective or harmful medicine	Guilty party is not penalized or innocent party found guilty	Statement users make incorrect decisions

statements. There are six bases of comparison. Note the similarities and differences among the three professions.

Audit Evidence Decisions

A major decision facing every auditor is determining the appropriate *amount of evidence* to accumulate to be satisfied that the components of the client's financial statements and the overall statements are fairly stated. This judgment is important because of the prohibitive cost of examining and evaluating all available evidence. For example, in an audit of financial statements of most organizations, it is impossible for the public accountant to examine all canceled cheques, vendors' invoices, documents evidencing the receipt of goods, sales invoices, shipping documents, customer orders, payroll time cards, and the many other types of documents and records.

> **OBJECTIVE 2**
>
> Describe the four decisions on evidence gathering that the auditor must make in order to create an audit program.

The auditor's *decisions* on evidence accumulation can be broken into the following four:

1. Which audit procedures to use
2. What sample size to select for a given procedure
3. Which particular items to select from the population
4. When to perform the procedures

Audit Procedures

Audit procedures are the detailed instructions for the collection of a particular type of audit evidence that is to be obtained at some time during the audit. For example, evidence such as physical inventory counts, comparisons of canceled cheques with cash disbursements, journal entries, and shipping document details is collected using audit procedures.

In designing audit procedures, it is common to spell them out in sufficiently specific terms to permit their use as instructions during the audit. For example, the following is an audit procedure for the verification of cash disbursements:

- Obtain the cash disbursements journal and compare the payee name, amount, and date on the canceled cheque with the cash disbursements journal.

Several commonly used audit procedure terms are defined and illustrated with examples in Appendix A to this chapter.

Sample Size

Once an audit procedure is selected, it is possible to vary the sample size from one to all the items in the population being tested. In the audit procedure above, suppose there are 6,600 cheques recorded in the cash disbursements journal. The auditor might select a sample size of 200 cheques for comparison with the cash disbursements journal. The decision of how many items to test must be made by the auditor for each audit procedure. The sample size for any given procedure is likely to vary from audit to audit.

Items to Select

After the sample size has been determined for a particular audit procedure, it is still necessary to decide the particular items to examine. If the auditor decides, for example, to select 200 canceled cheques from a population of 6,600 for comparison with the cash disbursements journal, several different methods can be used to select the specific cheques to be examined. The auditor could (1) select a week and examine the first 200 cheques, (2) select the 200 cheques with the largest amounts,

(3) select the cheques randomly, or (4) select those cheques the auditor thinks are most likely to be in error. Or a combination of these methods could be used.

Timing

An audit of financial statements usually covers a period such as a year, and an audit is usually not completed until several weeks or months after the end of the period. The timing of audit procedures can therefore vary from early in the accounting period to long after it has ended. In the audit of financial statements, the client normally wants the audit completed one to three months after year-end.

Audit Program

The detailed description of the results of the four evidence decisions for a specific audit is called an *audit program*. The audit program always includes a list of the audit procedures. It usually also states the sample sizes, particular items to select, and the timing of the tests. Normally, there is an audit program section for each component of the audit. Therefore, there will be an audit program section for accounts receivable, for sales, and so on. An example of an audit program that includes audit procedures, sample size, items to select, and timing is given on page 336 in Table 10–3. The right side of the audit program also includes the audit objectives for each procedure, as studied in Chapter 5.

Persuasiveness of Evidence

> **OBJECTIVE 3**
>
> Define the third examination standard and discuss its relationship to the three determinants of the persuasiveness of evidence.

The third examination standard requires the auditor to accumulate *sufficient appropriate evidence to support the opinion issued*. Because of the nature of audit evidence and the cost considerations of doing an audit, it is unlikely the auditor will be completely convinced that the opinion is correct. However, the auditor must be persuaded that his or her opinion is correct with a high level of assurance. By combining all evidence from the entire audit, the auditor is able to decide when he or she is sufficiently persuaded to issue an auditor's report.

The three determinants of the persuasiveness of evidence are sufficiency, appropriateness and timeliness. Notice that the first two are taken directly from the third examination standard; they are related. The determination of the sufficiency of particular audit evidence is directly related to the quality of that evidence; the more appropriate the evidence, the less that is required.

Sufficiency

The *quantity* of evidence obtained determines its sufficiency. Quantity is measured primarily by the sample size the auditor selects. For a given audit procedure, the evidence obtained from a sample of 200 would ordinarily be more sufficient than from a sample of 100.

An auditor normally examines only part of the information available; this concept is known as testing or sampling. As you will learn in Chapters 12 and 14, auditors use methodologies that allow them to make inferences about all the information available about an assertion or the population from which the sample is chosen.

There are several factors that determine the appropriate sample size in audits. The two most important ones are the auditor's expectation of errors and the effectiveness of the client's internal control. To illustrate, assume in the audit of Jones Computer Parts Inc. that the auditor concludes there is a high likelihood of obsolete inventory due to the nature of the client's industry. The auditor would sample more inventory items for obsolescence in an audit such as this than one where the likelihood of obsolescence was low. Similarly, if the auditor concludes that a client has effective rather than ineffective internal controls over recording fixed assets, a smaller sample size in the audit of purchases of fixed assets is warranted. Expectation of errors and internal control and their effect on sample size are critical topics in this book and are studied in depth in subsequent chapters, starting with Chapter 8.

In addition to sample size, the particular items tested affect the sufficiency of evidence. Samples containing population items with large dollar values, items with a high likelihood of error, and items that are representative of the population are usually considered sufficient. In contrast, most auditors would usually consider samples insufficient that contain only the largest dollar items from the population.

Appropriateness

Appropriateness or *competence* refers to the quality of evidence, to the degree to which the evidence can be considered believable or worthy of trust. If an auditor counted inventory, that evidence would be more competent than inventory figures given to the auditor by management. Generally, the more competent the evidence, the less evidence is needed. Many auditors, as well as the authors of this text, also use the term *reliability* of evidence as a synonym for appropriateness.

Appropriateness of evidence deals only with the audit procedures selected. Appropriateness cannot be improved by selecting a larger sample size or different population items. It can only be improved by selecting audit procedures that contain a higher quality of one or more of the following six characteristics of appropriate evidence.

Relevance Evidence must *pertain to or be relevant to the objective* the auditor is testing before it can be persuasive. For example, assume the auditor is concerned that a client is failing to bill customers for shipments (completeness objective). If the auditor selected a sample of duplicate sales invoices and traced each to related shipping documents, the evidence would *not be relevant* for the completeness objective. A relevant procedure would be to compare a sample of shipping documents with related duplicate sales invoices to determine if each had been billed.

Relevance can only be considered in terms of specific audit objectives. Evidence may be relevant to one objective but not to a different one. In the previous example, when the auditor traced from the duplicate sales invoices to related shipping documents, the evidence was relevant to the validity objective. Most evidence is relevant to more than one, but not all, objectives.

Auditor's direct knowledge Evidence obtained directly by the auditor through physical examination, observation, computation, and inspection is more competent than information obtained indirectly from either the client or a third party. For example, if the auditor calculates the gross margin as a percentage of sales and compares it with previous periods, the evidence would be more reliable than if the auditor relied on the calculations of the controller. Security counts made by the auditor are more reliable evidence than a confirmation of securities held by a third party.

Independence of provider Evidence obtained from a source outside the entity is more reliable than that obtained within. For example, external evidence such as communications from banks, lawyers, or customers is generally regarded as more reliable than answers obtained from inquiries of the client. Similarly, documents that originate from outside the client's organization are considered more reliable than are those that originate within the company and have never left the client's organization. An example of the former is an insurance policy and the latter a purchase requisition.

Effectiveness of client's internal control   When a client's internal control is effective, evidence obtained therefrom is more reliable than when it is weak. For example, if internal controls over sales and billing are effective, the auditor could obtain more appropriate evidence from sales invoices and shipping documents than if the controls were inadequate.

Qualifications of individuals providing the information   Although the source of information is independent, the evidence will not be reliable unless the individual providing it is qualified to do so. For this reason, confirmations from law firms and banks are typically more highly regarded than accounts receivable confirmations from persons not familiar with the business world. Also, evidence obtained directly by the auditor may not be reliable if he or she lacks the qualifications to evaluate the evidence. For example, examination of an inventory of diamonds by an auditor not trained to distinguish between diamonds and glass would not provide reliable evidence of the existence of diamonds.

Degree of objectivity   Objective evidence is more reliable than evidence that requires considerable judgment to determine whether it is correct. Examples of objective evidence include confirmation of accounts receivable and bank balances, the physical count of securities and cash, and adding (footing) a list of accounts payable to determine if it is the same as the balance in the general ledger. Examples of subjective evidence include confirmation by a client's lawyers of the likely outcome of outstanding lawsuits against the client, observation of obsolescence of inventory during physical examination, and inquiries of the credit manager about the collectibility of noncurrent accounts receivable. In evaluating the reliability of subjective evidence, the qualifications of the person providing the evidence is important.

Timeliness   The timeliness of audit evidence can refer either to when it was accumulated or to the period covered by the audit. Evidence is usually more persuasive for balance sheet accounts when it is obtained as close to the balance sheet date as possible. For example, the auditor's count of marketable securities on the balance sheet date would be more persuasive than a count two months earlier. For income statement accounts, evidence is more persuasive if there is a sample from the entire period under audit rather than from only a part of the period. For example, a random sample of sales transactions for the entire year would be more persuasive than a sample from only the first six months.

Combined Effect   The persuasiveness of evidence can be evaluated only after considering the combination of sufficiency, appropriateness, and timeliness. A large sample of evidence is not persuasive unless it is relevant to the objective being tested, that is, unless it is appropriate. A large sample of evidence that is neither appropriate nor timely is also not persuasive. Similarly, a small sample of only one or two pieces of

TABLE 6–2

Relationships Among
Evidence Decisions
and Persuasiveness

AUDIT EVIDENCE DECISIONS	QUALITIES AFFECTING PERSUASIVENESS OF EVIDENCE

Audit procedures	Appropriateness
	  Relevance
	  Auditor's direct knowledge
	  Independence of provider
	  Effectiveness of internal control
	  Qualifications of provider
	  Objectivity of evidence

Sample size and items to select	Sufficiency
	  Adequate sample size
	  Selecting appropriate population items

Timing	Timeliness
	  When procedures are performed
	  Portion of period audited

appropriate and timely evidence also lacks persuasiveness. The auditor must evaluate the degree to which all three qualities have been met in deciding persuasiveness.

There are direct relationships among the four evidence decisions and the three qualities that determine the persuasiveness of evidence. Table 6–2 shows those relationships.

To illustrate the relationships shown in Table 6–2 assume an auditor is verifying inventory that is a major item in the financial statements. Generally accepted auditing standards require that the auditor be reasonably persuaded that inventory is not materially misstated. The auditor must therefore obtain a sufficient amount of appropriate and timely evidence about inventory. This means deciding which procedures to use for auditing inventory to satisfy the appropriateness requirement, as well as determining the proper sample size and items to select from the population to satisfy the sufficiency requirement. Finally, the auditor must determine timing of these procedures. The combination of these four evidence decisions must result in sufficiently persuasive evidence to satisfy the auditor that inventory is materially correct. The audit program section for inventory will reflect these decisions. In practice, the auditor applies the four evidence decisions to specific audit objectives in deciding sufficient appropriate evidence.

Persuasiveness and Cost

In making decisions about evidence for a given audit, both persuasiveness and cost must be considered. It is rare when only one type of evidence is available for verifying information. The persuasiveness and cost of all alternatives should be considered before selecting the best type or types. The auditor's goal is to obtain a sufficient amount of timely, reliable evidence that is relevant to the information being verified, and to do so at the lowest possible total cost.

Types of Audit Evidence

The *CICA Handbook,* in the third examination standard, specifies that audit evidence may be obtained through the methods of inspection, observation, inquiry, confirmation, computation and analysis and then defines and explains the terms in Section 5300. These methods can be combined, divided and renamed into seven broad categories or *types of evidence* as follows:

EVIDENCE METHODS IN *CICA HANDBOOK*	SEVEN TYPES OF EVIDENCE
■ Inspection	■ Physical examination
	■ Documentation
■ Observation	■ Observation
■ Inquiry	■ Inquiries of the client
■ Confirmation	■ Confirmation
■ Computation	■ Mechanical accuracy
■ Analysis	■ Analytical procedures

6.9

The seven broad categories are defined and discussed below. The order in which the categories are listed and discussed should not be interpreted as signifying the relative strengths of the types or categories of evidence. In other words, the fact that "physical examination" appears at the top of the list does not mean that any evidence belonging to that category is automatically stronger than evidence belonging to another category. The quality of each piece of evidence, regardless of type, must be evaluated according to the criteria of its type.

Physical examination

Physical examination is the inspection or count by the auditor of a *tangible asset*. This type of evidence is most often associated with inventory and cash, but it is also applicable to the verification of securities, notes receivable, and tangible fixed assets. The distinction between the physical examination of assets, such as marketable securities and cash, and the examination of documents, such as canceled cheques and sales documents, is important for auditing purposes. If the object being examined, such as a sales invoice, has no inherent value, the evidence is called *documentation*. For example, before a cheque is signed, it is a document; after it is signed, it becomes an asset; and when it is canceled, it becomes a document again. Technically, physical examination of the cheque can only occur while the cheque is an asset.

Physical examination, which is a direct means of verifying that an asset actually exists, is regarded as one of the most reliable and useful types of audit evidence. Generally, physical examination is an objective means of ascertaining both the quantity and the description of the asset. In some cases, it is also a useful method for evaluating an asset's condition or quality. However, physical examination is not sufficient evidence to verify that existing assets are owned by the client, and in many cases the auditor is not qualified to judge such qualitative factors as obsolescence or authenticity. Proper valuation for financial statement purposes also usually cannot be determined by physical examination.

Documentation

Documentation, commonly referred to as *vouching,* is the auditor's examination of the *client's documents and records* to substantiate the information that is or should be included in the financial statements. The documents examined by the auditor are the records used by the client to provide information for conducting its business in an organized manner. Since each transaction in the client's organization is normally supported by at least one document, there is a large volume of this type of evidence available. For example, the client normally retains a customer order, a shipping document, and a duplicate sales invoice for each sales transaction. These same documents are useful evidence for verification by the auditor of the accuracy of the client's records for sales transactions. Documentation is a form of evidence widely used in every audit because it is usually readily available to the auditor at a relatively low cost. Sometimes it is the only reasonable type of evidence available.

6.11

Documents can be conveniently classified as internal and external. An *internal document* is one that has been prepared and used within the client's organization and is retained without ever going to an outside party such as a customer or a vendor. Examples of internal documents include duplicate sales invoices, employees' time reports, and inventory receiving reports. An *external document* is one that has been in the hands of someone outside the client's organization who is a party to the transaction being documented, but which is either currently in the hands of the client or readily accessible. In some cases, external documents originate outside the client's organization and end up in the hands of the client. Examples of this type of external document are vendors' invoices, canceled notes payable, and insurance policies. Other documents, such as canceled cheques, originate with the client, go to an outsider, and are finally returned to the client. The primary determinant of the auditor's willingness to accept a document as reliable evidence is whether it is internal or external, and when internal, whether it was created and processed under conditions of good internal control. Internal documents created and processed under conditions of weak internal control may not constitute reliable evidence.

Since external documents have been in the hands of both the client and another party to the transaction, there is some indication that both members are in agreement about the information and the conditions stated on the document. Therefore, external documents are regarded as more reliable evidence than internal ones.

Observation

Observation is the use of the senses to assess certain activities. Throughout the audit there are many opportunities to exercise sight, hearing, touch, and smell to evaluate a wide range of things. For example, the auditor may tour the plant to obtain a general impression of the client's facilities, observe whether equipment is rusty to evaluate whether it is obsolete, and watch individuals perform accounting tasks to determine whether the person assigned a responsibility is performing it. Observation is rarely sufficient by itself. It is necessary to follow up initial impressions with other kinds of corroborative evidence. Nevertheless, observation is useful in most parts of the audit.

Inquiries of the Client

Inquiry is the obtaining of *written* or *oral* information from the client in response to questions from the auditor. Although considerable evidence is obtained from the client through inquiry, it usually cannot be regarded as conclusive because it is not from an independent source and may be biased in the client's favor. Therefore, when the auditor obtains evidence through inquiry, it is normally necessary to obtain further corroborating evidence through other procedures. As an illustration, when the auditor wants to obtain information about the client's method of recording and controlling accounting transactions, he or she usually begins by asking the client how internal control operates. Later, the auditor performs tests of controls to determine if the transactions are recorded and authorized in the manner stated.

Confirmation

6.10

Confirmation describes the *receipt* of a *written or oral response* from an *independent third party* verifying the accuracy of information that was *requested by the auditor*. Since confirmations come from sources independent of the client, they are a highly regarded and often used type of evidence. However, confirmations are relatively costly to obtain and may cause some inconvenience to those asked to supply them. Therefore, they are not used in every instance in which they are applicable. Because of the high reliability of confirmations, auditors typically obtain written responses rather than oral ones whenever it is practical. Written confirmations are easier for supervisors to review and provide more support if it is necessary to demonstrate that a confirmation was received.

Whether or not confirmations should be used depends on the reliability needs of the situation as well as the alternative evidence available. Traditionally, confirmations are not used to verify individual transactions between organizations, such as sales transactions, because the auditor can use documents for that purpose. Similarly, confirmations are seldom used in the audit of fixed-asset additions because these can be verified adequately by documentation and physical examination. While confirmations are generally a very reliable form of evidence, the auditor must be aware that the third party providing the confirmation may be careless or may not have the correct information; the auditor should not automatically assume the confirmation is correct, especially if the response is unexpected or contradicts other evidence.

Unless impracticable or deemed to be harmful to the client's business, the confirmation of a sample of accounts receivable is *required* by the *CICA Handbook*. This requirement exists because accounts receivable usually represent a significant balance on the financial statements, and confirmations are a highly reliable type of evidence about them.

Although confirmation is not required for any account other than accounts receivable, this type of evidence is useful in verifying many types of information. The major types of information that are frequently confirmed, along with the source of the confirmation, are indicated in Table 6–3.

TABLE 6–3

Information Frequently Confirmed

INFORMATION	SOURCE
Assets	
Cash in bank	Bank
Accounts receivable	Debtor
Notes receivable	Maker
Owned inventory out on consignment	Consignee
Inventory held in public warehouses	Public warehouse
Cash surrender value to life insurance	Insurance company
Liabilities	
Accounts payable	Creditor
Notes payable	Lender
Advances from customers	Customer
Mortgages payable	Mortgagor
Bonds payable	Bondholder
Owners' Equity	
Shares outstanding	Registrar and transfer agent
Other Information	
Insurance coverage	Insurance company
Contingent liabilities	Company law firm(s), bank, and so forth
Bond indenture agreements	Bondholder
Collateral held by creditors	Creditor

To be considered reliable evidence, confirmations must be controlled by the auditor from the time their preparation is completed until they are returned. If the client controls the preparation of the confirmation, performs the mailing, or receives the responses, the auditor has lost control and with it independence; thus the reliability of the evidence is reduced.

Mechanical Accuracy

Testing of *mechanical accuracy* involves rechecking a sample of the computations and transfers of information made by the client during the period under audit. Rechecking of computations consists of testing the client's arithmetical accuracy. It includes such procedures as extending sales invoices and inventory, adding journals and subsidiary ledgers, and checking the calculation of depreciation expense and prepaid expenses. Rechecking of transfers of information consists of tracing amounts to be confident that when the same information is included in more than one place, it is recorded at the same amount each time. For example, the auditor normally makes limited tests to ascertain that the information in the sales journal has been included for the proper customer and at the correct amount in the subsidiary accounts receivable ledger and is accurately summarized in the general ledger. Many auditors refer to these types of tests as reperformance procedures.

Analytical Procedures

Analytical procedures use comparisons and relationships between financial and non-financial information to determine whether account balances appear reasonable. An example is comparing the gross margin percent in the current year with the preceding year's. For certain immaterial accounts, analytical procedures may be the only evidence needed. For other accounts, other types of evidence may be reduced when analytical procedures indicate that an account balance appears reasonable. In some cases, analytical procedures are also used to isolate accounts or transactions that should be investigated more extensively to help in deciding whether additional verification is needed. An example is comparison of the current period's total repair expense with previous years' and investigation of the difference, if it is significant, to determine the cause of the increase or decrease.

The auditor's own calculations generally constitute the information used for analytical procedures. Analytical procedures should be performed early in the audit to aid in deciding which accounts need no further verification, where other evidence can be reduced, and which audit areas should be more thoroughly investigated. Analytical procedures are examined in greater depth in Chapter 7.

Integration of Evidence Concepts

To understand the application of evidence to audits, it is important that the evidence concepts and ideas discussed in this chapter be integrated with concepts studied earlier. Four relationships are discussed in the remainder of this section. They demonstrate the integration of concepts and serve as summaries of Chapters 5 and 6.

Relationships Among Auditing Standards, Types of Evidence, and Audit Procedures

There are close relationships among auditing standards, which were studied in Chapter 1, types of evidence, and audit procedures. These relationships are shown in Figure 6–1. Notice that the standards are general, whereas audit procedures are specific. Types of evidence are broader than procedures and narrower than the standards.

FIGURE 6–1

Relationships Among
Auditing Standards,
Audit Evidence, and
Audit Procedures

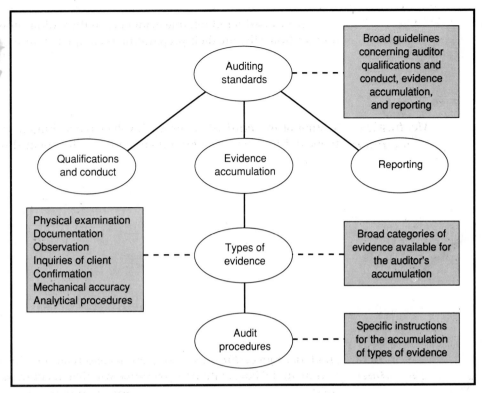

Relationship of Types of Evidence to Audit Objectives

OBJECTIVE 5

Integrate the concepts of audit evidence, audit objectives, and evidence-gathering decisions.

It is also important to understand the relationship of the type of evidence to audit objectives. The seven types of evidence available can be used to accomplish different audit objectives. For a given account and related accounts in a cycle, the auditor selects evidence to accomplish all the objectives at minimum cost. The relationship between types of evidence and audit objectives is shown in Table 6–4. Notice, for example, that almost all types of evidence provide evidence for the valuation objective, but only three are useful for ownership, classification, and disclosure. Similarly, documentation and inquiries of client provide evidence for all objectives but one, whereas mechanical accuracy satisfies only one objective.

Reliability of Types of Evidence

The criteria discussed earlier in the chapter for determining the reliability of evidence are related to the seven types of evidence in Table 6–5. Several observations are apparent from a study of Tables 6–4 and 6–5.

First, the effectiveness of the client's internal control has a significant effect on the reliability of most types of evidence. For example, internal documentation from a company with effective internal control is more reliable because the documents are more likely to be accurate. Similarly, analytical procedures will not be competent evidence if internal control permits the accounting system to produce data that are inaccurate.

Second, both physical examination and mechanical accuracy are likely to be highly reliable if internal control is effective, but their use differs considerably. These two types of evidence effectively illustrate that equally reliable evidence may be completely different. Table 6–4 shows physical examination is used pri-

TABLE 6–4

Types of Evidence and Audit Objectives

TYPE OF EVIDENCE	AUDIT OBJECTIVE							
	Validity	Completeness	Ownership	Valuation	Classification	Cutoff	Mechanical accuracy	Disclosure
Physical examination	✓	✓		✓	✓	✓		
Documentation	✓	✓	✓	✓	✓	✓		✓
Observation	✓	✓		✓				
Inquiries of client	✓	✓	✓	✓	✓	✓		✓
Confirmation	✓	✓	✓	✓		✓		✓
Mechanical accuracy							✓	
Analytical procedures	✓	✓		✓	✓	✓	✓	

marily to satisfy the validity, completeness, valuation, and cutoff objectives, whereas mechanical accuracy is likely to satisfy only the mechanical accuracy objective.

Third, a specific type of evidence is rarely sufficient by itself to provide competent evidence to satisfy any objective. It is apparent from examining Table 6–5 that observation, inquiries of client, and analytical procedures are examples of this.

Application of Types of Evidence to Evidence Decisions

Finally, an application of three types of evidence to the four evidence decisions for one audit objective is shown in Table 6–6. First, examine column 3 in Table 5–2 on page 147. These are the specific objectives of the audit of inventory for Hillsburg Hardware Ltd. The overall objective is to obtain persuasive evidence (sufficient, appropriate, and timely), at minimum cost, that inventory is materially correct. The auditor must therefore decide which audit procedures to use to satisfy each objective, what the sample size should be for each procedure, which items from the population to include in the sample, and when to perform each procedure.

One objective from Table 5–2 is selected for further study: inventory quantities agree with items physically on hand. Several types of evidence are available to satisfy this objective. Table 6–6 lists three types of evidence and gives examples of the four evidence decisions for each type.

Working Papers

The *CICA Handbook* states in Section 5145.02 that "Working papers are the [written] records kept by the auditor of procedures he [or she] applied and the results thereof, information he [or she] obtained and conclusions he [or she] reached in performing his [or her] examination [in accordance with GAAS] and preparing his [or her] report." In other words, the working papers document the evidence accumulated by the auditor. Working papers should include all the information the auditor considers necessary to conduct the examination adequately and to provide support for the auditor's report.

TABLE 6–5   Reliability of Types of Evidence

TYPE OF EVIDENCE	CRITERIA TO DETERMINE RELIABILITY / INDEPENDENCE OF PROVIDER	EFFECTIVENESS OF CLIENT'S INTERNAL CONTROL	AUDITOR'S DIRECT KNOWLEDGE	QUALIFICATIONS OF PROVIDER	OBJECTIVITY OF EVIDENCE
Physical Examination	Low	Varies	Yes	Normally high (auditor does)	High
Documentation	Varies – external more independent than internal	Varies	No	Varies	High
Observation	Low	Varies	Yes	Not applicable	Medium
Inquiries of Client	Low	Not applicable	No	Varies	Varies – low to high
Confirmation	High	Not applicable	No	Varies – usually high	High
Mechanical Accuracy	Low	Varies	Yes	High (auditor does)	High
Analytical Procedures	Low	Varies	Yes	Not applicable	Low

TABLE 6–6

Types of Evidence and Decisions for a Specific Audit Objective*

TYPE OF EVIDENCE	EVIDENCE DECISIONS / Audit Procedure	Sample Size	Items to Select	Timing
Observation	Observe client's personnel counting inventory to determine whether they are properly following instructions	All count teams	Not applicable	Balance sheet date
Physical examination	Recount inventory and compare quality and description to client's counts	120 items	40 items with large dollar value, plus 80 randomly selected	Balance sheet date
Documentation	Compare quantity on client's perpetual records to quantity on client's counts	70 items	30 items with large dollar value, plus 40 randomly selected	Balance sheet date

* Audit objective: Inventory quantities agree with items physically on hand.

Te͜sͬ

Purposes of Working Papers

The overall objective of working papers is to aid the auditor in providing reasonable assurance that an adequate audit was conducted in accordance with generally accepted auditing standards. More specifically, the working papers, as they pertain to the current year's audit, provide a basis for planning the audit, a record of the evidence accumulated and the results of the tests, data for determining the proper type of auditor's report, and a basis for review by managers and partners.

Basis for planning the audit If the auditor is to plan the current year's audit adequately, the necessary reference information must be available in the working papers. The papers include such diverse planning information as descriptive information about internal control, a time budget for individual audit areas, the audit program, and the results of the preceding year's audit.

Record of the evidence accumulated and the results of the tests The working papers are the primary means of documenting that an adequate audit was conducted in accordance with GAAS. If the need arises, the auditor must be able to demonstrate to regulatory agencies, such as the British Columbia Securities Commission, and to the courts that the audit was well planned and adequately supervised, the evidence accumulated was competent, sufficient, and timely, and the auditor's report was proper considering the results of the examination.

Data for determining the proper type of auditor's report The working papers provide an important source of information to assist the auditor in deciding the appropriate auditor's report to issue in a given set of circumstances. The data in the papers are useful for evaluating the adequacy of audit scope and the fairness of the financial statements. In addition, the working papers contain information needed for the preparation of the financial statements.

Basis for review by managers and partners The working papers are the primary frame of reference used by supervisory personnel to evaluate whether sufficient appropriate evidence was accumulated to justify the auditor's report. In addition to the purposes directly related to the auditor's report, the working papers can also serve as the basis for preparing tax returns, filings with the provincial securities commissions, and other reports; a source of information for issuing communications to the audit committee and management concerning various matters either required by generally accepted auditing standards or that the auditor believes could assist the client in improving operations; a frame of reference for training personnel; and an aid in planning and coordinating subsequent audits.

Contents and Organization

Each public accounting firm establishes its own approach to preparing and organizing working papers, and the beginning auditor must adopt his or her firm's approach. The emphasis in this text is on the general concepts common to all working papers.

Figure 6–2 illustrates the contents and organization of a typical set of papers. They contain virtually everything involved in the examination. There is a definite logic to the type of working papers prepared for an audit and the way they are arranged in the files, even though different firms may follow somewhat different approaches. In the figure, the working papers start with more general information, such as corporate data in the permanent files, and end with the financial statements and auditor's report. In between are the working papers supporting the auditor's tests.

FIGURE 6–2

Working Paper
Contents and
Organization

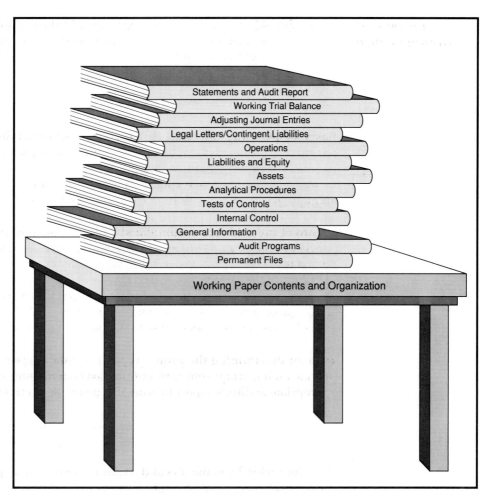

Working Paper Contents and Organization

Permanent Files   Permanent files are intended to contain data of a *historical or continuing nature* pertinent to the current examination. These files provide a convenient source of information about the audit that is of continuing interest from year to year. The permanent files typically include the following:

- *Extracts or copies of such company documents of continuing importance as the articles of incorporation, bylaws, bond indentures, and contracts.* The contracts are pension plans, leases, stock options, and so on. Each of these documents is of significance to the auditor for as many years as it is in effect.

- *Analyses, from previous years, of accounts that have continuing importance to the auditor.* These include accounts such as long-term debt, shareholders' equity accounts, goodwill, and fixed assets. Having this information in the permanent files enables the auditor to concentrate on analyzing only the changes in the current year's balance while retaining the results of previous years' audits in a form accessible for review.

- *Information related to the understanding of internal control and assessment of control risk.* This includes organization charts, flowcharts, questionnaires, and other internal control information, including enumeration of controls and weaknesses in the system.

■ *The results of analytical procedures from previous years' audits.* Among these data are ratios and percentages computed by the auditor, and the total balance or the balance by month for selected accounts. This information is useful in helping the auditor decide whether there are unusual changes in the current year's account balances that should be investigated more extensively.

Analytical procedures and the understanding of internal control and assessment of control risk are included in the current period working papers rather than in the permanent file by many public accounting firms.

Current Files   The current files include all working papers applicable to the year under audit. There is one set of permanent files for the client and a set of current files for each year's audit. The types of information included in the current file are briefly discussed in the sections that follow.

Audit program   The *audit program* is ordinarily maintained in a separate file to improve the coordination and integration of all parts of the audit, although some firms also include a copy of each section with that section's working papers. As the audit progresses, each auditor initials the program for the audit procedures performed and indicates the date of completion. The inclusion in the working papers of a well-designed audit program completed in a conscientious manner is evidence of a high-quality audit.

General information   Some working papers include current period information that is of a general nature rather than designed to support specific financial statement amounts. This includes such items as audit planning memos, abstracts or copies of minutes of the board of directors' meetings, abstracts of contracts or agreements not included in the permanent files, notes on discussions with the client, working paper review comments, and general conclusions. Documentation of the assessment of control risk may also be included.

Working trial balance   Since the basis for preparing the financial statements is the general ledger, the amounts included in that record are the focal point of the examination. As early as possible after the balance sheet date, the auditor obtains or prepares a listing of the general ledger accounts and their year-end balances. This schedule is the working trial balance.

The technique used by many firms is to have the auditor's working trial balance in the same format as the financial statements. Each line item on the trial balance is supported by a *lead schedule*, containing the detailed accounts from the general ledger making up the line item total. Each detailed account on the lead schedule is, in turn, supported by appropriate schedules evidencing the audit work performed and the conclusions reached. As an example, the relationship between cash as it is stated on the financial statements, the working trial balance, the lead schedule for cash, and the supporting working papers is presented in Figure 6–3. As the figure indicates, cash on the financial statements is the same as on the working trial balance and the total of the detail on the cash lead schedule. Initially, figures for the lead schedule were taken from the general ledger. The audit work performed resulted in an adjustment to cash that would be evidenced in the detail schedules and reflected on the lead schedule, the working trial balance, and the financial statements.

FIGURE 6–3

Relationship of
Working Papers to
Financial Statements

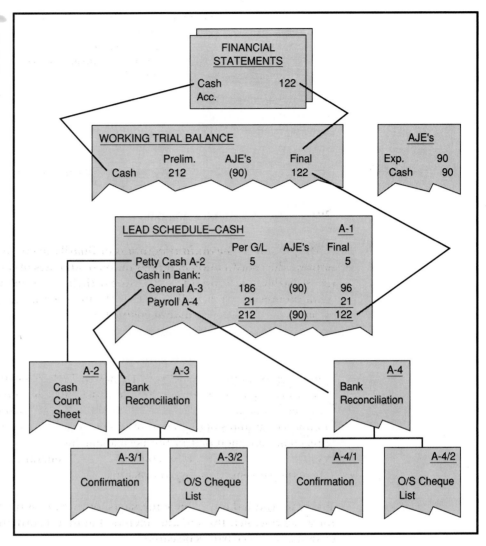

Adjusting and reclassification entries When the auditor discovers material errors in the accounting records, the financial statements must be corrected. For example, if the client failed to properly reduce inventory for obsolete raw materials, an adjusting entry can be suggested by the auditor to reflect the realizable value of the inventory. Even though adjusting entries discovered in the audit are typically prepared by the auditor, they must be approved and made by the client because the books and records are the client's and management has primary responsibility for the fair presentation of the statements. It is therefore important to remember that when the auditor believes that an adjusting or reclassification is required, the auditor must ask management to make the entry. Figure 6–3 illustrates an adjustment of the general cash account for $90.

Reclassification entries are frequently made in the statements to present accounting information properly, even when the general ledger balances are correct. A common example is the reclassification for financial statement purposes of material credit balances in accounts receivable to accounts payable. Because the balance in accounts receivable on the general ledger reflects the accounts receivable properly from the point of view of operating the company on a day-to-day basis, the reclassification entry is not included in the client's general ledger.

Only those adjusting and reclassification entries that significantly affect the fair presentation of financial statements must be made. The determination of when an error should be adjusted is based on *materiality*. The auditor should keep in mind that several immaterial errors that are not adjusted could result in a material overall misstatement when the errors are combined. It is common for auditors to summarize on a separate working paper all adjusting and reclassification entries that have not been recorded or posted to the accounts in the books or the working papers as a means of determining their cumulative effect.

Supporting schedules The largest portion of working papers includes the detailed schedules prepared by auditors in support of specific amounts on the financial statements. Many different types of schedules are used. Use of the appropriate type for a given aspect of the audit is necessary to document the adequacy of the audit and to fulfil the other objectives of work papers. Following are the major types of supporting schedules:

- *Analysis*. An analysis is designed to show the *activity in a balance sheet account* during the entire period under examination, tying together the beginning and ending balances. This type of schedule is normally used for accounts such as marketable securities, notes receivable, allowance for doubtful accounts, property plant, and equipment, long-term debt, and for all equity accounts. The common characteristic of these accounts is the significance of the activity in the account during the year. In most cases, the working papers for analysis have cross-references to other working papers.

- *Trial balance or list*. This type of schedule consists of the *details making up a year-end balance* of either a balance sheet or an income statement account. It differs from an analysis in that it includes only those items constituting the end-of-the-period balance. Common examples include trial balances or lists in support of trade accounts receivable, trade accounts payable, repair and maintenance expense, legal expense, and miscellaneous income. An example is included in Figure 6–4, page 182.

- *Reconciliation of amounts*. A reconciliation *supports a specific amount* and is normally expected to tie the amount recorded in the client's records to another source of information. Examples include the reconciliation of bank balances with bank statements, the reconciliation of subsidiary accounts receivable balances with confirmations for customers, and the reconciliation of accounts payable balances with vendors' statements. Figure 21–4 on page 707 is an example.

- *Tests of reasonableness*. A test of reasonableness schedule, as the name implies, contains information that enables the auditor to evaluate whether the client's balance appears to include an error considering the circumstances in the engagement. Frequently, auditors test depreciation expense, the provision for income taxes, and the allowance for doubtful accounts by tests of reasonableness. These tests are primarily analytical procedures.

- *Summary of procedures*. Another type of schedule *summarizes the results* of a specific audit procedure performed. Examples are the summary of the results of accounts receivable confirmation and the summary of inventory observations.

- *Examination of supporting documents*. A number of special-purpose schedules are designed to *show detailed tests performed*, such as examination of documents during tests of transactions or cutoffs. These schedules show no totals, and they do not tie in to the general ledger because they document only the tests performed and the results found. The schedules must, however, state a definite positive or negative conclusion about the objective of the test.

- *Informational*. This type of schedule contains information as opposed to audit evidence. These schedules include information for tax returns, and data such as time budgets and the client's working hours, which are helpful in administration of the engagement.

- *Outside documentation*. Much of the content of the working papers consists of the outside documentation gathered by auditors, such as confirmation replies and copies of client agreements. Although not "schedules" in the real sense, these are indexed and interfiled and procedures are indicated on them in the same manner as on the other schedules.

Preparation of Working Papers

The proper preparation of schedules to document the audit evidence accumulated, the results found, and the conclusions reached is an important part of the audit. The auditor must recognize the circumstances requiring the need for a schedule and the appropriate design of schedules to be included in the files. Although the design depends on the objectives involved, working papers should possess certain characteristics:

- Each working paper should be properly identified with such information as the client's name, the period covered, a description of the contents, the initial of the preparer, the date of preparation, and an index code.

- Working papers should be indexed and cross-referenced to aid in organizing and filing. One type of indexing is illustrated in Figure 6–3. The lead schedule for cash has been indexed as A-1, and the individual general ledger accounts making up the total cash on the financial statements are indexed as A-2 through A-4. The final indexing is for the schedules supporting A-3 and A-4.

- Completed working papers must clearly indicate the audit work performed. This is accomplished in three ways: by a written statement in the form of a memorandum, by initialing the audit procedures in the audit program, and by notations directly on the working paper schedules. Notations on working papers are accomplished by the use of *tick marks*, which are *symbols* written adjacent to the detail on the body of the schedule. These notations must be clearly explained at the bottom of the working paper.

- Each working paper should include sufficient information to fulfil the objectives for which it was designed. If the auditor is to prepare working papers properly, the auditor must be aware of his or her goals. For example, if a working paper is designed to list the detail and show the verification of support of a balance sheet account, such as prepaid insurance, it is essential that the detail on the working paper reconcile with the trial balance.

- The conclusions that were reached about the segment of the audit under consideration should be plainly stated.

The common characteristics of proper working paper preparation are indicated in Figure 6–4.

Ownership of Working Papers

The working papers prepared during the engagement, including those prepared by the client for the auditor, are the *property of the auditor*. The only time anyone else, including the client, has a legal right to examine the papers is when they are subpoenaed by a court as legal evidence or when they are required by the public accountant's professional organization in connection with disciplinary proceedings or practice inspection. At the completion of the engagement, working papers

FIGURE 6–4

Common
Characteristics of
Proper Working Papers

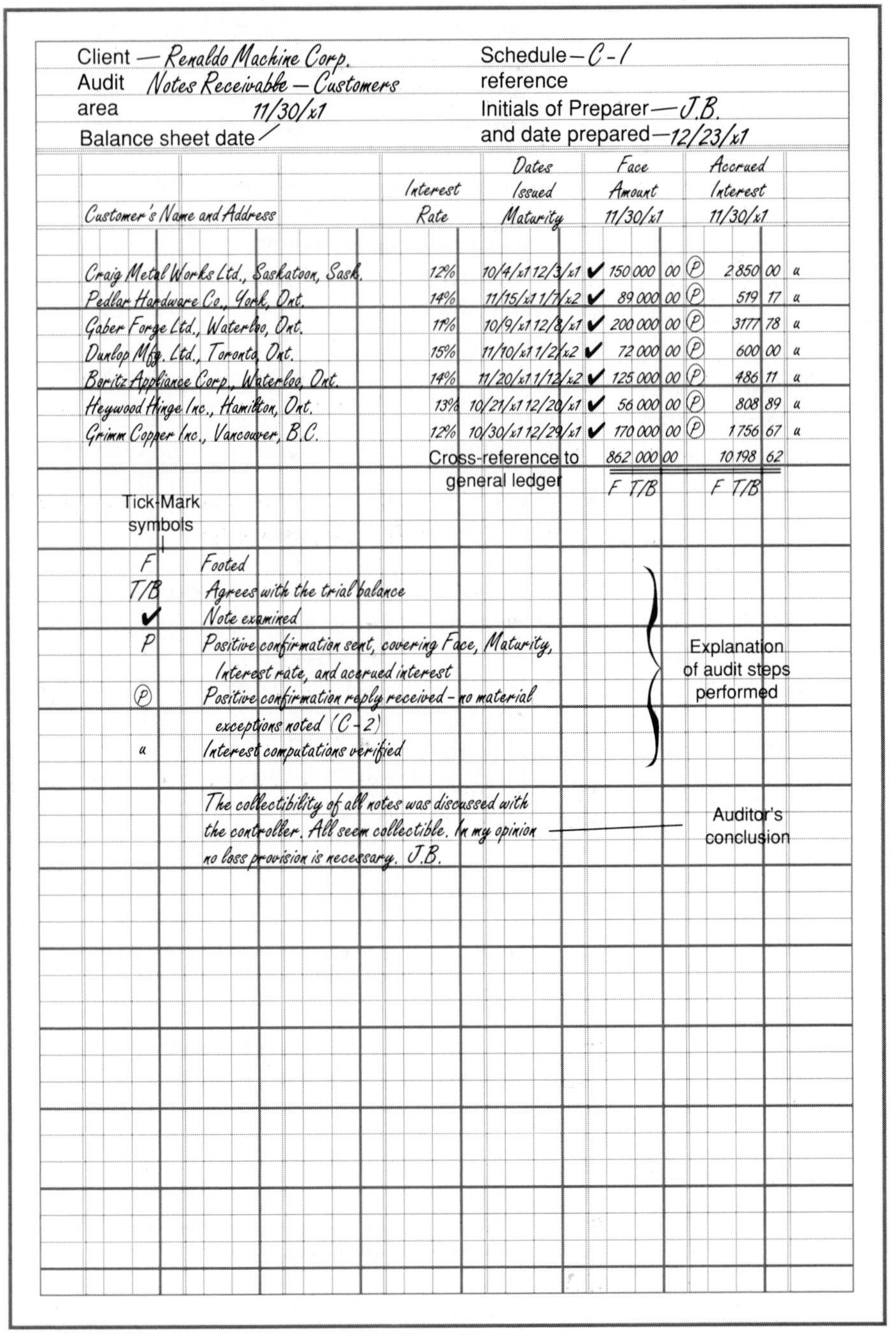

Client — *Renaldo Machine Corp.*							Schedule — *C-1*		
Audit *Notes Receivable — Customers*							reference		
area *11/30/x1*							Initials of Preparer — *J.B.*		
Balance sheet date							and date prepared — *12/23/x1*		

Customer's Name and Address	Interest Rate	Dates Issued Maturity	Face Amount 11/30/x1			Accrued Interest 11/30/x1	
Craig Metal Works Ltd., Saskatoon, Sask.	12%	10/4/x1 12/3/x1 ✔	150 000	00	Ⓟ	2 850	00	ɑ
Pedlar Hardware Co., York, Ont.	14%	11/15/x1 1/7/x2 ✔	89 000	00	Ⓟ	519	17	ɑ
Gaber Forge Ltd., Waterloo, Ont.	11%	10/9/x1 12/8/x1 ✔	200 000	00	Ⓟ	3177	78	ɑ
Dunlop Mfg. Ltd., Toronto, Ont.	15%	11/10/x1 1/2/x2 ✔	72 000	00	Ⓟ	600	00	ɑ
Baritz Appliance Corp., Waterloo, Ont.	14%	11/20/x1 1/12/x2 ✔	125 000	00	Ⓟ	486	11	ɑ
Heywood Hinge Inc., Hamilton, Ont.	13%	10/21/x1 12/20/x1 ✔	56 000	00	Ⓟ	808	89	ɑ
Grimm Copper Inc., Vancouver, B.C.	12%	10/30/x1 12/29/x1 ✔	170 000	00	Ⓟ	1 756	67	ɑ
Cross-reference to general ledger			862 000	00		10 198	62	
			F T/B			F T/B		

Tick-Mark symbols

F	Footed
T/B	Agrees with the trial balance
✔	Note examined
P	Positive confirmation sent, covering Face, Maturity, Interest rate, and accrued interest
Ⓟ	Positive confirmation reply received – no material exceptions noted (C-2)
ɑ	Interest computations verified

Explanation of audit steps performed

The collectibility of all notes was discussed with
the controller. All seem collectible. In my opinion
no loss provision is necessary. J.B.

Auditor's conclusion

are retained on the public accounting firm's premises for future reference. Many firms follow the practice of microfilming the working papers after several years to reduce storage costs.

Confidentiality of Working Papers

The need to maintain a confidential relationship with the client was discussed in Chapter 3. It was noted that the rules of conduct of the professional accounting bodies require their members not to disclose any confidential information obtained in the course of a professional engagement except with the consent of the client, or, as was noted above, when required by the courts or by the professional accounting associations.

During the course of the examination, auditors obtain a considerable amount of information of a confidential nature, including officer salaries, product pricing and advertising plans, and product cost data. If auditors divulged this information to outsiders or to client employees who have been denied access, their relationship with management would be seriously strained. Furthermore, having access to the working papers would give employees an opportunity to alter information on them. For these reasons, care must be taken to protect the working papers at all times.

Ordinarily, the working papers can be provided to someone else only with the express permission of the client. This is the case even if a public accountant sells his or her practice to another public accounting firm. Permission is not required from the client, however, if the working papers are subpoenaed by a court or are used in connection with disciplinary hearings or practice inspection conducted by the auditor's professional body.

APPENDIX A
Special Terms

Audit procedures are the detailed steps, usually written in the form of instructions, for the accumulation of the seven types of audit evidence. They should be sufficiently clear to enable members of the audit team to understand what is to be done.

Several different terms are commonly used to describe audit procedures. These are presented and defined in Table 6–7. To help you understand the terms, an illustrative audit procedure and type of evidence it is associated with are shown.

OBJECTIVE 8

Define terms commonly used in auditing.

REVIEW QUESTIONS

6–1 List the four major evidence decisions that must be made on every audit.

6–2 Describe what is meant by an audit procedure. Why is it important for audit procedures to be carefully worded?

6–3 Describe what is meant by an audit program section for accounts receivable. What four things should be included in an audit program?

6–4 State the third examination standard. Explain the meaning of each of the major phrases of the standard.

6–5 Explain why the auditor can only be persuaded beyond a reasonable doubt, rather than convinced, that the financial statements are correct.

6–6 Identify the three factors that determine the persuasiveness of evidence. How are these three factors related to audit procedures, sample size, items to select, and timing?

6–7 Distinguish between sufficiency and competence of evidence.

6–8 Identify the six characteristics that determine the appropriateness of evidence. For each characteristic, provide one example of a type of evidence that is likely to be appropriate.

Test Question

TABLE 6–7 Terms, Audit Procedures, and Types of Evidence	TERM AND DEFINITION	ILLUSTRATIVE AUDIT PROCEDURE	TYPE OF EVIDENCE
	Examine – A reasonably detailed study of a document or record to determine specific facts about it.	*Examine* a sample of vendors' invoices to determine whether the goods or services received are reasonable and of the type normally used by the client's business.	Documentation
	Scan – A less detailed examination of a document or record to determine if there is something unusual warranting further investigation.	*Scan* the sales journal, looking for large and unusual transactions.	Analytical procedures
	Read – An examination of written information to determine facts pertinent to the audit and the recording of those facts in a working paper.	*Read* the minutes of a board of directors' meeting and summarize all information that is pertinent to the financial statements in a working paper.	Documentation
	Compute – A calculation done by the auditor independent of the client.	*Compute* the inventory turnover ratios and compare to previous years as a test of inventory.	Analytical procedures
	Recompute – A calculation done to determine whether a client's calculation is correct.	*Recompute* the unit sales price times the number of units for a sample of duplicate sales invoices and compare the totals to the client's calculations.	Mechanical accuracy
	Foot – Addition of a column of numbers to determine if the total is the same as the client's.	*Foot* the sales journal for a one-month period and compare all totals to the general ledger.	Mechanical accuracy
	Trace – An instruction normally associated with documentation or mechanical accuracy. The instruction should state what the auditor is tracing and where it is being traced from and to. Frequently, an audit procedure that includes the term *trace* will also include a second instruction, such as *compare* or *recalculate*.	*Trace* a sample of sales transactions from the sales journal to sales invoices and *compare* customer name, date, and the total dollar value of the sale. *Trace* postings from the sales journal to the general ledger accounts.	Documentation Mechanical accuracy
	Compare – A comparison of information in two different locations. The instruction should state which information is being compared in as much detail as practical.	Select a sample of sales invoices and *compare* the unit selling price as stated on the invoice to the list of unit selling prices authorized by management.	Documentation
	Count – A determination of assets on hand at a given time. This term should only be associated with the type of evidence defined as physical examination.	*Count* petty cash on hand at the balance sheet.	Physical examination
	Observe – The act of observation should be associated with the type of evidence defined as observation.	*Observe* whether the two inventory count teams independently count and record inventory quantities.	Observation
	Inquire – The act of inquiry should be associated with the type of evidence defined as inquiry.	*Inquire* of management whether there is an obsolete inventory on hand at the balance sheet date.	Inquiries of client

6–9   List the seven types of audit evidence included in this chapter and give two examples of each.

6–10   What are the four characteristics of the definition of a confirmation? Distinguish between a confirmation and external documentation.

6–11   Distinguish between internal documentation and external documentation as audit evidence and give three examples of each.

6–12   Explain the importance of analytical procedures as evidence in determining the fair presentation of the financial statements.

6–13   List the purposes of working papers and explain why each purpose is important.

6–14   Explain why it is important for working papers to include each of the following: identification of the name of the client, description of the contents, period covered, initials of the preparer, date of the preparation, and an index code.

6–15   Define what is meant by a permanent file of working papers, and list several types of information typically included. Why does the auditor not include the contents of the permanent file with the current year's working papers?

6–16   Distinguish between the following types of current-period supporting schedules and state the purpose of each: analysis, trial balance, and overall reasonableness.

6–17   Why is it essential that the auditor not leave questions or exceptions in the working papers without an adequate explanation?

6–18   What type of working papers can be prepared by the client and used by the auditor as a part of the working paper file? When client assistance is obtained in preparing working papers, describe the proper precautions the auditor should take.

6–19   Who owns the working papers? Under what circumstances can they be used by other people?

6–20   A public accountant sells his auditing practice to another public accounting firm and proposes to include all the working papers as a part of the purchase price. What rule(s) of professional conduct are violated by this proposed action? Is there anything the public accountant can do so as not to break the rule(s)?

6–21   Mary Vander Saar is a public accountant. When asked to explain her audit philosophy with respect to evidence, she stated that the appropriateness of evidence was a more important concern to her than sufficiency, although both are important. What does she mean? Is she correct?

MULTIPLE CHOICE QUESTIONS

6–22   The following questions concern the appropriateness and persuasiveness of evidence. Choose the best response.

a. Which of the following types of documentary evidence should the auditor consider to be the most reliable?

(1) A sales invoice issued by the client and supported by a delivery receipt from an outside trucker.

(2) Confirmation of an account payable balance mailed by and returned directly to the auditor.

(3) A cheque, issued by the company and bearing the payee's endorsement, that is included with the bank statements mailed directly to the auditor.

(4) A working paper prepared by the client's controller and reviewed by the client's treasurer.

b. The most reliable type of documentary audit evidence that an auditor can obtain is

(1) physical examination by the auditor.

(2) calculations by the auditor from company records.

(3) confirmations received directly from third parties.

(4) external documents.

c. Audit evidence can come in different forms with different degrees of persuasiveness. Which of the following is the *least* persuasive type of evidence?

(1) Vendor's invoice.

(2) Bank statement obtained from the client.

(3) Computations made by the auditor.

(4) Prenumbered sales invoices.

d. Which of the following is the *least* persuasive documentation in support of an auditor's opinion?

(1) Schedules of details of physical inventory counts conducted by the client.

(2) Notation of inferences drawn from ratios and trends.

(3) Notation of appraisers' conclusions documented in the auditor's working papers.

(4) Lists of negative confirmation requests for which no response was received by the auditor. (AICPA adapted)

6-23 The following questions concern working papers. Choose the best response.

a. Which of the following is *not* a primary purpose of audit working papers?

(1) To coordinate the examination.

(2) To assist in preparation of the auditor's report.

(3) To support the financial statements.

(4) To provide evidence of the audit work performed.

b. Audit working papers are used to record the results of the auditor's evidence-gathering procedures. When preparing working papers, the auditor should remember that working papers should be

(1) kept on the client's premises so that the client can have access to them for reference purposes.

(2) the primary support for the financial statements being examined.

(3) considered as a part of the client's accounting records that are retained by the auditor.

(4) designed to meet the circumstances and the auditor's needs on each engagement.

c. Which of the following eliminates voluminous details from the auditor's working trial balance by classifying and summarizing similar or related items?

(1) Account analyses

(2) Supporting schedules

(3) Control accounts

(4) Lead schedules

d. During an audit engagement, pertinent data are compiled and included in the audit working papers. The working papers primarily are considered to be

(1) a client-owned record of conclusions reached by the auditors who performed the engagement.

(2) evidence supporting financial statements.

(3) support for the auditor's representations as to compliance with generally accepted auditing standards.

(4) a record to be used as a basis for the following year's engagement.

e. Although the quantity, type, and content of working papers will vary with the circumstances, the working papers generally would include the

(1) copies of those client records examined by the auditor during the course of the engagement.

    (2) evaluation of the efficiency and competence of the audit staff assistants by the partner responsible for the audit.

    (3) auditor's comments concerning the efficiency and competence of client management personnel.

    (4) auditing procedures followed, and the testing performed in obtaining evidential matter.
            (AICPA adapted)

DISCUSSION QUESTIONS AND PROBLEMS

6–24 The following are examples of documentation typically obtained by auditors:

1. Vendors' invoices
2. General ledgers
3. Bank statements
4. Canceled payroll cheques
5. Payroll time cards
6. Purchase requisitions
7. Receiving reports (documents prepared when merchandise is received)
8. Minutes of the board of directors
9. Remittance advices
10. Signed TD-1s (Employees' Income Tax Withholding Exemption Certificate)
11. Signed lease agreements
12. Duplicate copies of bills of lading
13. Subsidiary accounts receivable records
14. Canceled notes payable
15. Duplicate sales invoices
16. Articles of incorporation
17. Notes receivable

Required:
    a. Classify each of the preceding items according to type of documentation: (1) internal or (2) external.
    b. Explain why external evidence is more reliable than internal evidence.

6–25 The following are examples of audit procedures:

1. Review the accounts receivable with the credit manager to evaluate their collectibility.
2. Stand by the payroll time clock to determine whether any employee "punches in" more than one time.
3. Count inventory items and record the amount in the audit working papers.
4. Obtain a letter from the client's law firm addressed to the public accounting firm stating the law firm is not aware of any existing lawsuits.
5. Extend the cost of inventory times the quantity on an inventory listing to test whether it is accurate.
6. Obtain a letter from an insurance company to the public accounting firm stating the amount of the fire insurance coverage on building and equipment.
7. Examine an insurance policy stating the amount of the fire insurance coverage on buildings and equipment.
8. Calculate the ratio of cost of goods sold to sales as a test of overall reasonableness of gross margin relative to the preceding year.
9. Obtain information about the system of internal control by requesting the client to fill out a questionnaire.

10. Trace the total on the cash disbursements journal to the general ledger.

11. Watch employees count inventory to determine whether company procedures are being followed.

12. Examine a piece of equipment to make sure a major acquisition was actually received and is in operation.

13. Calculate the ratio of sales commissions expense to sales as a test of sales commissions.

14. Examine corporate minutes of directors' meetings to determine the authorization of the issue of bonds.

15. Obtain a letter from management stating there are no unrecorded liabilities.

16. Review the total of repairs and maintenance for each month to determine whether any month's total was unusually large.

17. Compare a duplicate sales invoice with the sales journal for customer name and amount.

18. Add the sales journal entries to determine whether they were correctly totaled.

19. Make a petty cash count to make sure the amount of the petty cash fund is intact.

20. Obtain a written statement from a bank stating the client has $2,671 on deposit and liabilities of $10,000 on a demand note.

Required:
Classify each of the preceding items according to the seven types of audit evidence: (1) physical examination,(2) documentation, (3) observation, (4) inquiries of the client, (5) confirmation, (6) mechanical accuracy, and (7) analytical procedures.

6–26 List two examples of audit evidence the auditor can use in support of each of the following:

a. Recorded value of entries in the purchase journal

b. Physical existence of inventory

c. Valuation of accounts receivable

d. Ownership of permanent assets

e. Liability for accounts payable

f. Obsolescence of inventory

g. Existence of petty cash

6–27 Seven different types of evidence were discussed. The following questions concern the reliability of that evidence:

a. Explain why confirmations are normally more reliable evidence than inquiries of the client.

b. Describe a situation in which confirmation would be considered highly reliable and another in which it would not be reliable.

c. Under what circumstances is the physical observation of inventory considered relatively unreliable evidence?

d. Explain why mechanical accuracy tests are highly reliable, but of relatively limited use.

e. Give three examples of relatively reliable documentation and three examples of less reliable documentation. What characteristics distinguish the two?

f. Give several examples in which the qualifications of the respondent or the qualifications of the auditor affect the reliability of the evidence.

g. Explain why analytical procedures are important evidence even though they are relatively unreliable by themselves.

6–28 In an examination of financial statements, an auditor must judge the appropriateness of the audit evidence obtained.

Required:

a. In the course of his or her examination, the auditor asks many questions of client officers and employees.

   (1) Describe the factors the auditor should consider in evaluating oral evidence provided by client officers and employees.

   (2) Discuss the competence and limitations of oral evidence.

b. An auditor's examination may include computation of various balance sheet and operating ratios for comparison with previous years and industry averages. Discuss the competence and limitations of ratio analysis.   (AICPA adapted)

6-29 As auditor of the Star Manufacturing Corp., you have obtained

a. a trial balance taken from the books of Star one month prior to year-end:

	DR. (CR.)
Cash in bank	$ 87,000
Trade accounts receivable	345,000
Notes receivable	125,000
Inventories	317,000
Land	66,000
Buildings, net	350,000
Furniture, fixtures, and equipment, net	325,000
Trade accounts payable	(213,000)
Goods and services tax payable	(22,000)
Mortgages payable	(400,000)
Capital stock	(300,000)
Retained earnings	(510,000)
Sales (net)	(3,130,000)
Cost of sales	2,300,000
General and administrative expenses	622,000
Legal and professional fees	3,000
Interest expense	35,000

b. There are no inventories consigned either in or out.

c. All notes receivable are due from outsiders and held by Star.

Required:

Which accounts should be confirmed with outside sources? Briefly describe from whom they should be confirmed and the information that should be confirmed. Organize your answer in the following format:

ACCOUNT NAME	FROM WHOM CONFIRMED	INFORMATION TO BE CONFIRMED

(AICPA adapted)

6-30 The following audit procedures were performed in the audit of inventory to satisfy specific audit objectives as discussed in Chapter 5. The audit procedures assume the auditor has obtained the inventory count sheets that list the client's inventory. The general audit objectives from Chapter 5 are also included.

AUDIT PROCEDURES	GENERAL AUDIT OBJECTIVES
1. Test extend unit prices times quantity on the inventory list, test foot the list and compare the total to the general ledger.	Validity Completeness Ownership
2. Trace selected quantities from the inventory list to the physical inventory to make sure it exists and the quantities are the same.	Valuation Classification Cutoff

3. Question operating personnel about the possibility of obsolete or slow-moving inventory.

Mechanical accuracy
Disclosure

4. Select a sample of quantities of inventory in the factory warehouse and trace each item to the inventory count sheets to determine if it has been included and if the quantity and description are correct.

5. Compare the quantities on hand and unit prices on this year's inventory count sheets with those in the preceding year as a test for large differences.

6. Examine sales invoices and contracts with customers to determine if any goods are out on consignment with customers. Similarly, examine vendors' invoices and contracts with vendors to determine if any goods on the inventory listing are owned by vendors.

7. Send letters directly to third parties who hold the client's inventory and request they respond directly to us.

Required:

a. Identify the type of audit evidence used for each audit procedure.

b. Identify the general audit objective or objectives satisfied by each audit procedure.

6–31 Audit procedures differ from, but are related to, types of evidence. The following questions relate to types of evidence and audit procedures.

Required:

a. What is an audit procedure?

b. Why should audit procedures be specific and carefully written?

c. For each of the following types of evidence, carefully write one audit procedure for the audit of accounts receivable.

TYPE OF EVIDENCE	AUDIT PROCEDURE
(1) Confirmation (2) Analytical procedures (3) Mechanical accuracy (4) Inquiries of the client (5) Documentation	

6–32 The following are nine situations, each containing two means of accumulating evidence.

1. Confirm accounts receivable with business organizations versus confirming receivables with consumers.

2. Physically examine 3-inch steel plates versus examining electronic parts.

3. Examine duplicate sales invoices when several competent people are checking each other's work versus examining documents prepared by a competent person in a one-person staff.

4. Physically examine inventory of parts for the number of units on hand versus examining them for the likelihood of inventory being obsolete.

5. Discuss the likelihood and amount of loss in a lawsuit against the client with client's in-house legal counsel versus discussion with the public accounting firm's own legal counsel.

6. Confirm a bank balance versus confirming the oil and gas reserves with a geologist specializing in oil and gas.

7. Confirm a bank balance versus examining the client's bank statements.
8. Physically count the client's inventory held by an independent party versus confirming the count with an independent party.
9. Physically count the client's inventory versus obtaining a count from the company president.

Required:

    a. Identify the six factors that determine the appropriateness of evidence.

    b. (1) For each of the nine situations, state whether the first or second type of evidence is more reliable.

       (2) Explain why you chose the first or second type for each of the nine situations.

       (3) For each situation, state which of the six factors discussed in the chapter affected the reliability of the evidence.

6–33 Following are 10 audit procedures with words missing and a list of several terms commonly used in audit procedures.

AUDIT PROCEDURES	TERMS
	a. Examine
	b. Scan
	c. Read
	d. Compute
	e. Recompute
	f. Foot
	g. Trace
	h. Compare
	i. Count
	j. Observe
	k. Inquire
	l. Confirm

1. _____ whether the accounts receivable bookkeeper is prohibited from handling cash.
2. _____ ratio of cost of goods sold to sales and compare the ratio to previous years.
3. _____ the sales journal and _____ the total to the general ledger.
4. _____ the sales journal, looking for large and unusual transactions requiring investigation.
5. _____ of management whether all accounting employees are required to take annual vacations.
6. _____ the balance in the bank account directly with the Crowchild Bank.
7. _____ all marketable securities as of the balance sheet date to determine whether they equal the total on the client's list.
8. _____ a sample of duplicate sales invoices to determine if the controller's approval is included and _____ each duplicate sales invoice to the sales journal for comparison of name and amount.
9. _____ the unit selling price times quantity on the duplicate sales invoice and compare the total to the amount on the duplicate sales invoice.
10. _____ the agreement between Rimouski Wholesale Inc. and the client to determine if the shipment is a sale or a consignment.

Required:

    a. For each of the 12 blanks in procedures 1 through 10, identify the most appropriate term. No term can be used more than once.

    b. For each of procedures 1 through 10, identify the type of evidence that is being used.

6–34 The preparation of working papers is an integral part of a public accountant's examination of financial statements. On a recurring engagement, a public accountant reviews his audit programs and working papers from his prior examination while planning his current examination to determine their usefulness for the current engagement.

Required:

    a. What are the purposes or functions of audit working papers?

    b. What records may be included in audit working papers?

    c. What factors affect the public accountant's judgment of the type and content of the working papers for a particular engagement? (AICPA adapted)

6–35 Do the following with regard to the working paper for ABC Company, Inc. shown below.

    a. List the deficiencies in the working paper.

    b. For each deficiency, state how the working paper could be improved.

    c. Prepare a similar working paper using the microcomputer with an electronic spreadsheet software program. Include an indication of the audit work done as well as the analysis of the client data. (Instructor's option.)

Figure for Problem 6–35

ABC Company Inc.
Notes Receivable
12/31/x1

Schedule	Date
Prepared by JD	1/21/x2
Approved by PP	2/5/x2

Acct. 110   Maker

	Apex Co.	Ajax, Inc.	J.J. Co.	P. Smith	Martin-Peterson	Tent Co.
Date Made	6/15/x0	11/21/x0	11/1/x0	7/26/x1	5/12/x0	9/3/x1
Due	6/15/x2	Demand	$200/mo.	$1000/mo.	Demand	$400/mo.
Face amount	5000 <	3591 <	13 180 <	25 000 <	2100 <	12 000 <
Value of Security	none	none	24 000	50 000	none	10 000
Note:						
Beg. bal.	4000 PWP	3591 PWP	12 780 PWP	—	2100 PWP	—
Addition				25 000		12 000
Payments	<1 000>	<3 591>	<2 400>	<5 000>	<2 100>	<1 600>
End. bal. ① Current	3 000 ✓	—	2 400 ✓	12 000	—	4 800
② Long-term	—	—	7 980	8 000	—	5 600
③ Total	3 000 C	-0-	10 380 C	20 000 C	-0-	10 400 C
	И	И	И	И	И	И
Interest: Rate	5%	5%	5%	5%	5%	5%
Pd to date	none	paid	12/31/81	9/30/81	paid	11/30/81
Beg. bal.	104 PWP	-0- PWP	24 PWP	-0-	-0- PWP	-0-
④ Earned	175 ✓	102 ✓	577 ✓	468 ✓	105 ✓	162 ✓
Received	-0-	<102>	<601>	<200>	<105>	<108>
⑤ Accrued at 12/31/81	279	-0-	-0-	268	-0-	54
	И	И	И	И	И	И

< ✓ - Tested
PWP - Agrees with prior year's working papers
① Total of $22,200 agrees with working trial balance.
② Total of $21,580 agrees with working trial balance.
③ Total of $43,780 agrees with working trial balance.
④ Total of $ 1,589 agrees with miscellaneous income analysis in operations W/P.
① Total of $ 601 agrees with A/R lead schedule.

7

AUDIT PLANNING AND ANALYTICAL PROCEDURES

LEARNING OBJECTIVES

THOROUGH STUDY OF THIS CHAPTER WILL ENABLE YOU TO:

1. Discuss why adequate audit planning is essential

2. Apply the steps involved in preplanning the audit

3. Know appropriate background information to obtain about an audit client

4. Know appropriate information to obtain about an audit client's legal obligations

5. Discuss the purposes of analytical procedures

6. Select the most appropriate analytical procedure from among the five major types

7. Design and apply analytical procedures using a seven-step approach

8. Explain the benefits of using statistical techniques and computer software for analytical procedures

☐ This chapter introduces the topic of planning an audit and designing an audit approach, and discusses three major parts of the planning process. You can see how planning fits into the overall audit by examining Figure 5–7 on page 147. Analytical procedures were introduced in Chapter 5 and discussed in Chapter 6 as one of the seven types of audit evidence, and are discussed in greater detail here.

Planning

The first generally accepted auditing examination standard in Section 5100 requires adequate planning.

OBJECTIVE 1
Discuss why adequate audit planning is essential.

> The work is to be adequately planned and properly executed. If assistants are employed they should be properly supervised.

Section 5150 of the *CICA Handbook* defines audit planning as "developing a general strategy and a detailed approach for the expected nature, extent, and timing of the examination."

There are three main reasons why the auditor should properly plan engagements: to enable the auditor to obtain sufficient appropriate audit evidence for the circumstances, to help keep audit costs reasonable, and to avoid misunderstandings with the client. Obtaining sufficient appropriate evidence is essential if the public accounting firm is to minimize legal liability and maintain a good reputation in the professional community. Keeping costs reasonable helps the firm remain competitive and thereby retain its clients, assuming the firm has a reputation for doing quality work. Avoiding misunderstandings with the client is important for good client relations and for facilitating quality work at reasonable cost. For example, suppose the auditor informs the client that the audit will be com-

FIGURE 7–1

Planning an Audit and Designing an Audit Approach

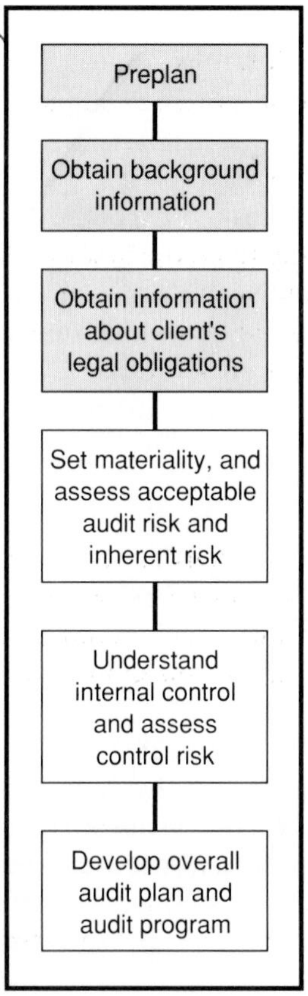

pleted before June 30 but is unable to finish it until August because of inadequate scheduling of staff. The client is likely to be upset with the public accounting firm and may even sue for breach of contract.

Figure 7–1 presents the six major parts of audit planning: preplanning, obtaining background information about the client, obtaining information about the client's legal obligations, assessing materiality and risk, understanding internal control and assessing control risk, and developing an overall audit plan and audit program. Each of the first five parts is intended to help the auditor develop the last part, an effective and efficient overall audit plan and audit program. The first three parts of the planning phase of an audit are studied in this chapter. The last three are studied separately in each of the next three chapters.

Preplan the Audit

Most preplanning takes place early in the engagement, frequently in the client's office, to the extent that this is practical. Preplanning involves deciding whether to accept or continue doing the audit for the client, evaluating the client's reasons for the audit, selecting staff for the engagement, and obtaining an engagement letter.

Client Acceptance and Continuance

Even though obtaining and retaining clients is not easy in a competitive profession such as public accounting, a public accounting firm must use care in deciding which clients are acceptable. The firm's legal and professional responsibilities are such that clients who lack integrity or argue constantly about the proper conduct of the audit and fees can cause more problems than they are worth.

New client investigation Before accepting a new client, most public accounting firms investigate the company to determine its acceptability. To the extent possible, the prospective client's standing in the business community, financial stability, and relations with its previous public accounting firm should be evaluated.

For prospective clients that have previously been audited by another public accounting firm, the new (successor) auditor is *required* by the rules of conduct of the institutes and *ordre* of chartered accountants and by the rules of conduct of CGA-Canada and by incorporating acts such as the *Canada Business Corporations Act* to communicate with the predecessor auditor. The purpose of the requirement is to help the successor auditor evaluate whether to accept the engagement. The communication may, for example, inform the successor auditor that the client lacks integrity or that there have been disputes over accounting principles, audit procedures, or fees.

The burden of initiating the communication rests with the successor auditor. Permission must be obtained from the client before the communication can be made because of the confidentiality requirement in the rules of conduct of the professional accounting bodies. Professional courtesy suggests the predecessor auditor is required to respond to the request for information. In the event there are legal problems or disputes between the client and the predecessor, the latter's response can be limited to stating that no information will be provided. The successor should seriously consider the desirability of accepting a prospective engagement, without considerable other investigation, if a client will not permit the communication or the predecessor will not provide a comprehensive response.

When a prospective client has not been audited by another public accounting firm, other investigations are needed. Sources of information include local lawyers, other public accountants, banks, and other businesses. In some cases,

---

OBJECTIVE 2

Apply the steps involved in preplanning the audit.

Preplan

Obtain background information

Obtain information about client's legal obligations

Set materiality, and assess acceptable audit risk and inherent risk

Understand internal control and assess control risk

Develop overall audit plan and audit program

the auditor may hire a professional investigator to obtain information about the reputation and background of the key members of management. The same approach can be followed when a predecessor auditor will not provide the desired information or if any indication of problems arises from the communication.

Continuing clients Considering whether or not to continue doing the audit of an existing client is as important a decision as deciding whether or not to accept a new client. For that reason many public accounting firms evaluate existing clients annually to determine whether there are reasons for not continuing to do the audit. Previous conflicts over such things as the appropriate scope of the audit, the type of opinion to issue, or fees may cause the auditor to discontinue association. The auditor may also determine that the client lacks basic integrity and therefore should no longer be a client. If there is a lawsuit against a public accounting firm by a client or a suit against the client by the public accounting firm, the firm probably should not do the audit because its independence could be questioned.

Identify Client's Reasons for Audit

Two major factors affecting the appropriate evidence to accumulate are the likely statement users and their intended uses of the statements. It will be shown in Chapter 8 that the auditor is likely to accumulate more evidence when the statements are to be used extensively. This is often the case for publicly held companies, those with extensive indebtedness, and companies that are to be sold in the near future.

The most likely uses of the statements can be determined from previous experience in the engagement and discussion with management. Throughout the engagement the auditor may get additional information as to why the client is having an audit and the likely uses of the financial statements.

Among the reasons for having an audit are that the audit is required by statute, the audit is required because the company seeks funds from the public through debt or equity financing, the audit is required by shareholder, partnership, or creditor agreements as a means of monitoring management, and to achieve the reduction in information risk that an audit provides.

Staff the Engagement

Assigning the appropriate staff to the engagement is important to meet the generally accepted auditing standards of Section 5100 and to promote audit efficiency. The general standard states:

> The examination should be performed and the report prepared by a person or persons having adequate technical training and proficiency in auditing.

Staff must, therefore, be assigned with that standard in mind. On larger engagements, there are likely to be one or more partners and staff at several experience levels doing the audit. Specialists in such technical areas as statistical sampling and computer auditing may also be assigned. On smaller audits there may be only one or two staff members.

A major consideration affecting staffing is the need for continuity from year to year. An inexperienced staff assistant is likely to become the most experienced nonpartner on the engagement within a few years. Continuity helps the public accounting firm maintain familiarity with the technical requirements and closer interpersonal relations with client personnel.

Another consideration is that the persons assigned be familiar with the client's industry. This is discussed shortly.

Obtain an Engagement Letter

A clear understanding of the terms of the engagement should exist between the client and the public accounting firm. The terms should be in writing to minimize misunderstandings. This is the purpose of an engagement letter.

The engagement letter is an agreement between the public accounting firm and the client for the conduct of the audit and related services. It should specify whether the auditor will perform an audit, a review, or a compilation, plus any other services such as tax returns or management services. It should also state any restrictions to be imposed on the auditor's work, deadlines for completing the audit, assistance to be provided by the client's personnel in obtaining records and documents, and schedules to be prepared for the auditor. It often includes an agreement on fees. The engagement letter is also a means of informing the client that the auditor is not responsible for the discovery of all acts of fraud or illegal acts.

The engagement letter does not affect the public accounting firm's responsibility to external users of audited financial statements, but it can affect legal responsibilities to the client. For example, if the client sued the public accounting firm for failing to find a fraud, one defence the public accounting firm could use would be a signed engagement letter stating that the audit would not include the detailed audit necessary to disclose a fraud.

Engagement letter information is important in planning the audit principally because it affects the timing of the tests and the total amount of time the audit and other services will take. If the deadline for submitting the audit report is soon after the balance sheet date, a significant portion of the audit must be done before the end of the year. When the auditor is preparing tax returns and a management letter, or if client assistance is not available, arrangements must be made to extend the amount of time for the engagement. Client-imposed restrictions on the audit could affect the procedures performed and possibly even the type of audit opinion issued. An example of an engagement letter for the audit of Hillsburg Hardware Ltd. is given in Figure 7–2. The financial statements for Hillsburg Hardware Ltd. are included on pages 133 and 134.

Obtain Background Information

An extensive understanding of the client's business and industry and knowledge about the company's operations are essential for doing an adequate audit. Most of this information is obtained at the client's premises, especially for a new client. Obtaining background information is accomplished in various ways, the most important of which are discussed as follows.

Obtain Knowledge of Client's Industry and Business

To interpret adequately the meaning of information obtained throughout the audit, it is essential to understand the *client's industry*. Unique aspects of different industries are reflected in the financial statements. For example, assume you are doing an audit of a mutual fund that is making significant investments in the oil and gas industry (as occurred in the *Fund of Funds* litigation discussed in Chapter 4). It would be important that you have an understanding of both mutual funds and the oil and gas industry to do an adequate audit. A reasonable understanding of the client's industry is required by Section 5140 of the *CICA Handbook*.

FIGURE 7–2

Engagement Letter

BORITZ, CARTER, KAO, SCOTT & CO., Chartered Accountants
Halifax, Nova Scotia B3M 3J5

Mr. Rick Chulick, President   June 14, 19X8
Hillsburg Hardware Ltd.
2146 Willow St.
Halifax, Nova Scotia B3H 3F9

Dear Mr. Chulick:

This letter confirms our arrangements for the audit of Hillsburg Hardware Ltd. for the year ended 12-31-X8.

The purpose of our engagement is to examine the company's financial statements for the year ended 12-31-X8 and evaluate the fairness of presentation of the statements in conformity with generally accepted accounting principles.

Our examination will be conducted in accordance with generally accepted auditing standards which will include a review of internal control and tests of controls to the extent we believe necessary. Accordingly, it will not include a detailed audit of transactions to the extent which would be required if the examination was intended to disclose defalcations or other irregularities that are not material to the financial statements, although their discovery may result.

We direct your attention to the fact that management has the responsibility for the proper recording of transactions in the books of account, for the safeguarding of assets, and for the substantial accuracy of the financial statements. Such statements are the responsibility of management.

The timing of our examination will be scheduled for performance and completion as follows:

	BEGIN	COMPLETE
Preliminary tests	9-11-X8	9-24-X8
Internal control letter		10-3-X8
Year-end closing	2-3-X9	2-18-X9
Delivery of report and tax return		3-10-X9

Assistance to be supplied by your personnel, including the preparation of schedules and analyses of accounts, is described on a separate attachment. Timely completion of this work will facilitate the conclusion of our examination.

Our fees are based on the amount of time required at various levels of responsibility, plus actual out-of-pocket expenses (travel, typing, telephone, etc.), payable upon presentation of our invoices. We will notify you immediately of any circumstances we encounter that could significantly affect our initial estimate of total fees of $16,000.

If the foregoing is in accordance with your understanding, please sign and return to us the duplicate copy of this letter.

Yours very truly,

Boritz

Boritz, Carter, Kao, Scott & Co.

Accepted By:
Date: 6-21-X8

OBJECTIVE 3

Know appropriate background information to obtain about an audit client.

Preplan

Obtain background information

Obtain information about client's legal obligations

Set materiality, and assess acceptable audit risk and inherent risk

Understand internal control and assess control risk

Develop overall audit plan and audit program

Knowledge of the client's industry can be obtained in different ways. These include discussions with the auditor in the firm who was responsible for the engagement in previous years and other auditors in the firm currently on similar engagements, as well as conferences with the client's personnel. Many of the larger public accounting firms have industry specialists who can be consulted for their expertise. Smaller firms that do not have the expertise can consult the practice advisory service of their professional body. There are often industry audit guides, textbooks, and technical magazines available for the auditor to study in most major industries. Some auditors follow the practice of subscribing to specialized journals for those industries to which they devote a large amount of time. Considerable knowledge can also be obtained by participating actively in industry associations and training programs.

A knowledge of those aspects of the client's business that differentiate it from other firms in its industry is needed to make industry comparisons. Similarly, information such as organizational structure, marketing and distribution practices, method of inventory valuation, and other unique characteristics of the client's business should be understood before the audit is started because such facts are used continuously in interpreting auditing information as it is obtained.

Companies filing their financial statements with a securities commission or whose securities are traded in a public market and all life insurance enterprises are required under Section 1700.07 of the *CICA Handbook* to disclose segment information by industry and by geographic area and the amount of export sales. Auditors must have sufficient knowledge of a company's business to enable them to evaluate whether segmented information should be disclosed and to determine whether the client's disclosure of segmented information is appropriate.

The auditor's *permanent files* frequently include the history of the company, a list of the major lines of business, and a record of the most important accounting policies in previous years. Study of this information and discussions with the client's personnel aid in understanding the business.

Tour the Plant and Offices

A tour of the client's facilities is helpful in obtaining a better understanding of the client's business and operations because it provides an opportunity to meet key personnel and observe operations firsthand. Discussions with nonaccounting employees during the tour and throughout the audit are useful in maintaining a broad perspective. The actual viewing of the physical facilities aids in understanding physical safeguards over assets and in interpreting accounting data by providing a frame of reference in which to visualize such assets as inventory in process and factory equipment. A knowledge of the physical layout also facilitates getting answers to questions later in the audit.

Review the Company's Policies

Many company policies and authorizations reflected in the financial statements are part of internal control but outside the scope of the accounting system. These include such things as authorization for disposal of a portion of the business, credit policies, loans to affiliates, and accounting policies for recording assets and recognizing revenue. Basic policy decisions must always be carefully evaluated as part of the audit to determine whether management has authorization from the board of directors to make certain decisions and to be sure the decisions of management are properly reflected in the statements.

A useful approach followed by many public accounting firms is to include a record in the permanent files of the most important policies followed by the client and the name of the person or group authorized to change the policy. The inclusion in the permanent files of the primary generally accepted accounting principles, such as the costs to be included in inventory valuation, is especially useful in helping the auditor determine whether the client has changed accounting principles. A periodic review of the information is important.

Identify Related Parties

Transactions with related parties are important to auditors because they must be *disclosed in the financial statements* if they are material. Generally accepted accounting principles require disclosure of the nature of the related-party relationship; a description of transactions, including dollar amounts; and amounts due from and to related parties.

A party is considered to be a *related party* in Section 3840 of the *CICA Handbook* when it "has the ability to exercise, directly or indirectly, control or significant influence over the operating and financial decisions of [another party]." A *related-party transaction* is any transaction between the client and a related party. Common examples include sales or purchase transactions between a parent company and its subsidiary, exchanges of equipment between two companies owned by the same person, and loans to officers. A less common example, described in Section 3840.17 as *economic dependence*, is the potential for exercise of significant influence on an audit client by its most important supplier or customer, lender or borrower, etc.

Because related-party transactions must be disclosed, it is important that all related parties be *identified and included in the permanent files* early in the engagement. Finding undisclosed related-party transactions is thereby enhanced. Common ways of identifying related parties include inquiry of management, review of filings with regulatory bodies such as securities commissions, and examination of shareholders' listings to identify principal shareholders.

Evaluate Need for Outside Specialists

When the auditor encounters situations requiring specialized knowledge, it may be necessary to consult a specialist. Section 5360 of the *CICA Handbook*, "Using the Work of a Specialist," establishes the requirements for selecting specialists and reviewing their work. Section 5365, "Communications with Actuaries," applies together with 5360 when the specialist is an actuary. Examples include using a diamond expert in evaluating the replacement cost of diamonds and an actuary for determining the appropriateness of the recorded value of insurance loss reserves. Another common use of specialists is consulting with lawyers on the legal interpretation of contracts and titles.

The auditor should have a sufficient understanding of the client's business to recognize the need for a specialist. Proper planning is necessary to make sure that a specialist is available when needed and that he or she is both competent and, if possible, independent of the client.

Obtain Information About Client's Legal Obligations

Three closely related types of legal documents and records should be examined early in the engagement: articles of incorporation and bylaws, minutes of board of directors' and shareholders' meetings, and contracts. Some information, such as contracts, must be disclosed in the financial statements. Other information, such as authorizations in the board of directors' minutes, is useful in other parts of the audit. Early knowledge of these legal documents and records enables auditors to interpret related evidence throughout the engagement and to make sure there is proper disclosure in the financial statements.

Articles of Incorporation and Bylaws

The *articles of incorporation* are granted by the federal government or by the province in which the company is incorporated and is the legal document necessary for recognizing a corporation as a separate entity. It includes the exact name of the corporation, the date of incorporation, the kinds and amounts of capital stock the corporation is authorized to issue, and the types of business activities the corporation is authorized to conduct. In specifying the kinds of capital stock, there is also included such information as the voting rights of each class of stock, preferences and conditions necessary for dividends, and prior rights in liquidation.

> **OBJECTIVE 4**
>
> Know appropriate information to obtain about an audit client's legal obligations.

The *bylaws* include the rules and procedures adopted by the shareholders of the corporation. They specify such things as the fiscal year of the corporation, the frequency of shareholder meetings, the method of voting for directors, and the duties and powers of the corporate officers.

The auditor must understand the requirements of the articles of incorporation and the bylaws in order to determine whether the financial statements are properly presented. The correct disclosure of the shareholders' equity, including the proper payment of dividends, depends heavily on these requirements.

Minutes of Directors' and Shareholders' Meetings

The *corporate minutes* are the official record of the meetings of the board of directors and shareholders. They include summaries of the most important topics discussed at these meetings and the decisions made by the directors and shareholders. If the auditor fails to examine the minutes, he or she may easily overlook information essential to determining whether the financial statements are materially correct. Information such as the following is usually included in the minutes:

- Declaration of dividends
- Authorization of compensation of officers
- Acceptance of contracts and agreements
- Authorization of the acquisition of property
- Approval of mergers
- Authorization of long-term loans
- Approval to pledge securities
- Authorization of individuals to sign cheques
- Reports on the progress of operations
- Appointment or re-appointment of auditors

While examining the corporate minutes, the auditor normally identifies information significant to the fair presentation of the financial statements. The auditor includes the information in the working papers by making an abstract of the minutes or by obtaining a copy and underlining significant portions. Some time before the audit is completed, there must be a follow-up of this information to be sure management has complied with actions taken by the shareholders and the board of directors. As an illustration, the authorized compensation of officers should be traced to each individual officer's payroll record as a test of whether the correct total compensation was paid. Similarly, the auditor should compare the authorizations for the acquisition of equipment in the minutes with the equipment records if the board of directors must approve all new acquisitions of equipment over a specified amount, such as $100,000.

Contracts

Clients become involved in different types of contracts that are of interest to the auditor. These can include such diverse items as long-term notes and bonds payable, stock options, pension plans, contracts with vendors for future delivery of supplies, government contracts for completion and delivery of manufactured products, royalty agreements, union contracts, and leases.

Most contracts are of primary interest in individual parts of the audit and, in practice, receive special attention during the different phases of the detailed tests. For example, the provisions of a pension plan would receive substantial emphasis as a part of the audit of the unfunded liability for pensions. The auditor should review and abstract the documents early in the engagement to gain a better perspective of the organization and to become familiar with potential problem areas. Later these documents can be examined more carefully as a part of the tests of individual audit areas.

In examining contracts, primary attention should focus on any aspect of the legal agreement affecting financial disclosure. Contracts can have an important effect on the statements when the subject of the contract must be directly included at a specific dollar value, as in the case of a mortgage or bond liability. The potential effect of a contract on the statements will naturally depend on its nature. A long-term note has a completely different disclosure requirement than a government contract for the delivery of finished goods.

Summary of the Purposes of Audit Planning

There are several purposes of the planning procedures discussed in this section. The primary purpose is to obtain information that requires follow-up during the audit. Doing so is the first step in obtaining sufficient appropriate evidence. Examples include identifying approvals in the minutes of such items as dividends and officers' salaries, and searching for the names of related parties to help the auditor determine if related party transactions exist. Other purposes include evaluating whether to accept a new audit client or continue auditing an existing one, staffing the engagement, and obtaining an engagement letter. Figure 7–3 summarizes the three major parts of audit planning discussed in this section and the key components of each part, with a brief illustration of how a public accounting firm applied each component to a continuing client, Hillsburg Hardware Ltd.

Analytical Procedures

Analytical procedures (analytical tests) are defined by Section 5300.30 of the *CICA Handbook* as "[techniques involving] studying and evaluating the interrelationships between elements of financial and other information." The CICA research study, *Analytical Review*, defines analytical review as

> **OBJECTIVE 5**
>
> Discuss the purposes of analytical procedures.

- "a generally recognized substantive audit procedure that encompasses the study and evaluation of relationships between elements of financial and nonfinancial information, the comparison of such relationships and recorded balances with the auditor's assessment of the expected relationships and balances, and the investigation of significant fluctuations or the lack of expected fluctuations identified as a result of such study, evaluation and comparison."[1]

---

1 Smith, D.G., *Analytical Review*, Toronto: CICA, 1983, p. 5.

FIGURE 7–3 Key subparts of preplanning, obtaining background information and obtaining information about client's legal obligations applied to Hillsburg Hardware Ltd.

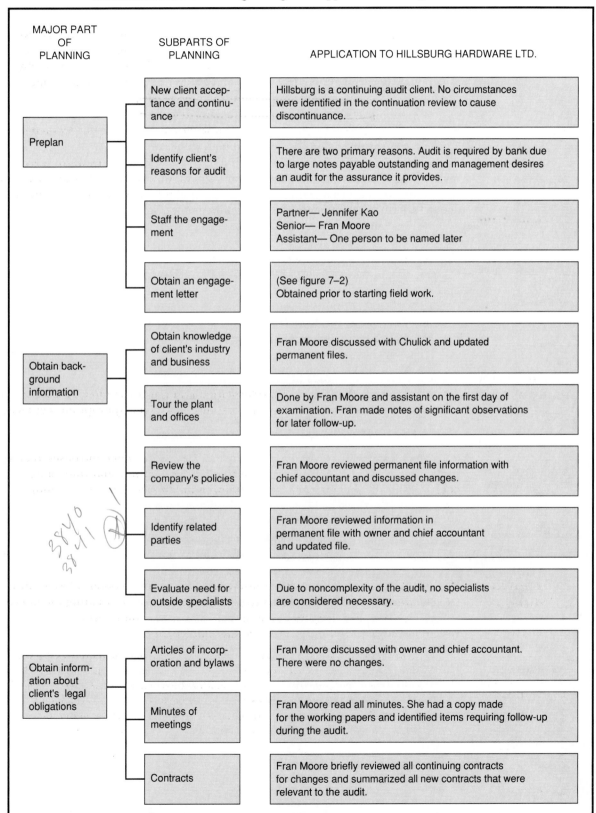

MAJOR PART OF PLANNING	SUBPARTS OF PLANNING	APPLICATION TO HILLSBURG HARDWARE LTD.
Preplan	New client acceptance and continuance	Hillsburg is a continuing audit client. No circumstances were identified in the continuation review to cause discontinuance.
	Identify client's reasons for audit	There are two primary reasons. Audit is required by bank due to large notes payable outstanding and management desires an audit for the assurance it provides.
	Staff the engagement	Partner— Jennifer Kao Senior— Fran Moore Assistant— One person to be named later
	Obtain an engagement letter	(See figure 7–2) Obtained prior to starting field work.
Obtain background information	Obtain knowledge of client's industry and business	Fran Moore discussed with Chulick and updated permanent files.
	Tour the plant and offices	Done by Fran Moore and assistant on the first day of examination. Fran made notes of significant observations for later follow-up.
	Review the company's policies	Fran Moore reviewed permanent file information with chief accountant and discussed changes.
	Identify related parties	Fran Moore reviewed information in permanent file with owner and chief accountant and updated file.
	Evaluate need for outside specialists	Due to noncomplexity of the audit, no specialists are considered necessary.
Obtain information about client's legal obligations	Articles of incorporation and bylaws	Fran Moore discussed with owner and chief accountant. There were no changes.
	Minutes of meetings	Fran Moore read all minutes. She had a copy made for the working papers and identified items requiring follow-up during the audit.
	Contracts	Fran Moore briefly reviewed all continuing contracts for changes and summarized all new contracts that were relevant to the audit.

The emphasis in this second definition is on expectations developed by the auditor. For example, the auditor might compare current year recorded commissions expense to total recorded sales multiplied by the average commission rate as a test of the overall reasonableness of recorded commissions. For this analytical procedure to be relevant, the auditor has likely concluded that recorded sales are correctly stated, all sales earn a commission, and there is an average actual commission rate that is readily determinable.

While the *CICA Handbook*, in Section 5300, encourages the use of analytical procedures, it does not require their use in an audit. As you will discover in Chapter 23, analytical procedures are an integral part of review engagements. In the United States, the Auditing Standards Board has concluded that analytical procedures are so important that they are required during the planning phase and overall review or completion phase of all audits.

Purposes and Timing of Analytical Procedures

The most important reasons for utilizing analytical procedures are discussed in this section. As a part of that discussion, the appropriate timing is also examined.

Understanding the Client's Business

Earlier in the chapter, there is a discussion of the need to obtain knowledge about the client's industry and business. Analytical procedures are one of the techniques commonly used in obtaining that knowledge.

Generally, an auditor considers knowledge and experience about a client company obtained in prior years as a starting point for planning the examination for the current year. By conducting analytical procedures wherein the current year's unaudited information is compared to prior years' audited information, changes are highlighted. These changes can represent important trends or specific events, all of which will influence audit planning. For example, a decline in gross margin percentages over time may indicate increasing competition in the company's market area, and the need to consider more carefully inventory pricing during the audit. Similarly, an increase in the balance in fixed assets may indicate a significant acquisition that must be reviewed.

Assessment of the Entity's Ability to Continue as a Going Concern

Analytical procedures are often useful as an indication that the client company is encountering severe financial difficulty. The likelihood of financial failure must be considered by the auditor in the assessment of audit-related risks (discussed further in Chapter 8) as well as in connection with management's use of the going concern assumption in preparing the financial statements.[2] Certain analytical procedures can be helpful in that regard. For example, if a higher than normal ratio of long-term debt to net worth is coupled with a lower than average ratio of profits to total assets, a relatively high risk of financial failure may be indicated. Not only would such conditions affect the audit plan, they may indicate that substantial doubt exists about the entity's ability to continue as a going concern, which would require disclosure in the notes to the financial statements.

---

2   For an interesting and thorough coverage of this topic, see Boritz, J.E., *The Going Concern Assumption: Accounting and Implications*, Toronto: CICA, 1991.

Indication of the Presence of Possible Misstatements in the Financial Statements

Significant unexpected differences between the current year's unaudited financial data and other data used in comparisons are commonly referred to as *unusual fluctuations*. Unusual fluctuations occur when significant differences are not expected but do exist, or when significant differences are expected but do not exist. In either case, one of the possible reasons for an unusual fluctuation is the presence of an accounting error, or fraud or other irregularity. Thus, if the unusual fluctuation is large, the auditor must determine the reason for it and satisfy himself or herself that the cause is a valid economic event and not an error or fraud. For example, in comparing the ratio of the allowance for uncollectible accounts receivable to gross accounts receivable with that of the previous year, suppose the ratio had decreased while, at the same time, accounts receivable turnover also decreased. The combination of these two pieces of information would indicate a possible understatement of the allowance. This aspect of analytical procedures is often referred to as *attention directing* because it results in the performance of more detailed procedures by the auditor in the specific audit areas where errors or fraud might be found.

Reduction of Detailed Audit Tests

When an analytical procedure reveals no unusual fluctuations, the implication is that the possibility of a material error or irregularity is minimized. In that case, the analytical procedure constitutes substantive evidence in support of the fair statement of the related account balances, and it is possible to perform fewer detailed tests in connection with those accounts. For example, if analytical procedures results of a small account balance such as unexpired insurance are favorable, no detailed tests may be necessary. In other cases, certain audit procedures can be eliminated, sample sizes can be reduced, or the timing of the procedures can be moved further away from the balance sheet date.

Analytical procedures are usually inexpensive compared with tests of details. Most auditors therefore prefer to reduce tests of details with analytical procedures whenever possible. To illustrate, it may be far less expensive to calculate and review sales and accounts receivable ratios than to age accounts receivable. If it is possible to reduce confirmations by doing analytical procedures, considerable cost savings could occur.

The extent to which analytical procedures provide useful substantive evidence depends on their reliability in the circumstances. For some audit objectives and in some circumstances, they may be the most effective procedure to apply. These objectives might include proper classification of transactions, completeness of recording transactions, and accuracy of management's judgments and estimates in certain areas, such as the allowance for uncollectible accounts. For other audit objectives and circumstances, analytical procedures may be considered attention directing at best, and not relied on for gathering substantive evidence. An example is determining the validity of sales transactions. The factors that determine when analytical procedures are effective are discussed in a later section of the chapter.

Timing

Analytical procedures are performed principally at any of three times during an engagement. Some analytical procedures are ideally performed in the *planning phase* to assist in determining the nature, extent, and timing of work to be performed. Performance of analytical procedures during planning helps the auditor identify significant matters requiring special consideration later in the engagement. For example, the calculation of inventory turnover before inventory price tests are done may indicate the need for special care during those tests.

Analytical procedures are often done *during the substantive testing phase* of the examination in conjunction with other audit procedures. For example, the prepaid portion of each insurance policy might be compared with the same policy for the previous year as a part of doing tests of unexpired insurance.

Analytical procedures should also be done *during the completion phase* of the audit. Such tests are useful at that point as a final review for material misstatements or financial problems, and to help the auditor take a final "objective look" at the financial statements that have been audited. It is common for a partner to do the analytical procedures during the final review of working papers and financial statements. Typically, a partner has a good understanding of the client and its business because of ongoing relationships. Knowledge about the client's business combined with effective analytical procedures is a way to identify possible oversights in an audit.

The purposes of analytical procedures for each of the three different times they are performed is shown in Figure 7–4. Notice that purposes vary for different timing. Analytical procedures are performed during the planning phase for all four purposes, whereas the other two phases are used primarily to determine appropriate audit evidence and to reach conclusions about the fair presentation of financial statements.

Five Types of Analytical Procedures

An important part of using analytical procedures is to select the most appropriate procedures. There are five major types of analytical procedures:

1. Compare client and industry data.
2. Compare client data with similar prior-period data.
3. Compare client data with client-determined expected results.
4. Compare client data with auditor-determined expected results.
5. Compare client data with expected results utilizing nonfinancial data.

FIGURE 7–4

Purpass and Timing of Analytical Procedures

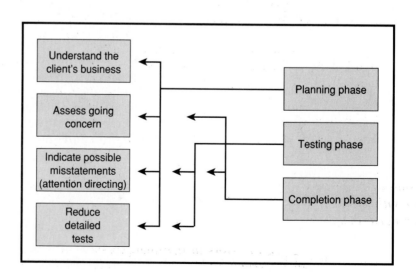

Compare Client and Industry Data

Suppose you are doing an audit and obtain the following information about the client and the average company in the client's industry:

	CLIENT		INDUSTRY	
	19X7	*19X6*	*19X7*	*19X6*
Inventory turnover	3.4	3.5	3.9	3.4
Gross margin percent	26.3%	26.4%	27.3%	26.2%

Looking only at client information for the two ratios shown, the company appears to be stable with no apparent indication of difficulties. However, compared with the industry, the client's position has worsened. In 19X6, the client did slightly better than the industry in both ratios. In 19X7, it did not do nearly as well. Although these two ratios by themselves may not indicate significant problems, the example illustrates how comparison of client data with industry data may provide useful information about the client's performance. For example, the company may have lost market share, its pricing may not be competitive, it may have incurred abnormal costs, or it may have obsolete items in inventory.

The Financial Post Company, Dun & Bradstreet Canada Limited, Robert Morris Associates, and other publishers accumulate financial information for thousands of larger companies and compile the data for different lines of business; local credit bureaus compile data for companies in their community. Many public accounting firms purchase these publications for use as a basis for industry comparisons in their audits.

The most important benefits of industry comparisons are as an aid to understanding the client's business and as an indication of the likelihood of financial failure. The ratios in Dun and Bradstreet, for example, are primarily of a type that bankers and other credit executives use in evaluating whether a company will be able to repay a loan. That same information is useful to auditors in assessing the relative strength of the client's capital structure, its borrowing capacity, and the likelihood of financial failure.

A major weakness in using industry ratios for auditing is the difference between the nature of the client's financial information and that of the firms making up the industry totals. Since the industry data are broad averages, the comparisons may not be meaningful. Frequently, the client's line of business is not the same as the industry standards. In addition, different companies follow different accounting methods, and this affects the comparability of data. If most companies in the industry use FIFO inventory valuation and straight-line depreciation, and the audit client uses LIFO and accelerated depreciation, comparisons may not be meaningful. This does not mean that industry comparisons should not be made. Rather, it is an indication of the need for care in interpreting the results.

Compare Client Data with Similar Prior-Period Data

Suppose the gross margin percent for a company has been between 26 and 27 percent for each of the past four years but is 23 percent in the current year. This decline in gross margin should be a concern to the auditor. The cause of the decline could be a change in economic conditions. However, it could also be caused by errors in the financial statements, such as sales or purchase cutoff errors, unrecorded sales, overstated accounts payable, or inventory costing

TABLE 7–1

Internal Comparisons and Relationships

RATIO OR COMPARISON	POSSIBLE MISSTATEMENT
Raw material turnover for a manufacturing company.	Misstatement of inventory or cost of goods sold or obsolescence of raw material inventory.
Sales commissions divided by net sales.	Misstatement of sales commissions including failure to accrue commissions owing.
Sales returns and allowances divided by gross sales.	Misclassified sales returns and allowances or unrecorded returns or allowances subsequent to year-end.
Goods and services tax payable (current year) divided by goods and services tax payable (preceding year).	Failure to accrue properly the goods and services tax owing at year end.
Each of the individual manufacturing expenses as a percentage of total manufacturing expense.	Significant misstatement of individual expenses within a total.

errors. The auditor should determine the cause of the decline in gross margin and consider the effect, if any, on evidence accumulation.

There are a wide variety of analytical procedures where client data are compared with similar data from one or more prior periods. The following are common examples.

Compare the current year's balance with that for the preceding year   One of the easiest ways to make this test is to include the preceding year's adjusted trial balance results in a separate column of the current year's trial balance worksheet. The auditor can easily compare the current year's and previous year's balance to decide early in the audit whether a particular account should receive more than the normal amount of attention because of a significant change in the balance. For example, if the auditor observes a substantial increase in supplies expense, the auditor should determine whether the cause was an increased use of supplies, a misstatement in the account due to a misclassification, or an error in supplies inventory.

Compare the detail of a total balance with similar detail for the preceding year   If there have been no significant changes in the client's operations in the current year, much of the detail making up the totals in the financial statements should also remain unchanged. By briefly comparing the detail of the current period with similar detail of the preceding period, it is often possible to isolate information that needs further examination. Comparison of details may take the form of details over time or details at a point in time. A common example of the former is comparing the monthly totals for the current and preceding year for sales, repairs, and other accounts. An example of the latter is comparing the details of loans payable at the end of the current year with those at the end of the preceding year.

Compute ratios and percentage relationships for comparison with previous years   The comparison of totals or details with previous years as described in the two preceding paragraphs has two shortcomings. First, it fails to consider growth or decline in business activity. Second, relationships of data to other data, such as sales to cost of goods sold, are ignored. Ratio and percentage relationships overcome both shortcomings. The example discussed earlier about the decline in gross margin is a common percentage relationship used by auditors.

A few types of ratios and internal comparisons are included in Table 7–1 to show the widespread use of ratio analysis. In all cases, the comparisons should be with calculations made in previous years for the same client. There are many potential ratios and comparisons available for use by an auditor. Subsequent chapters dealing with specific audit areas describe other examples.

Many of the ratios and percentages used for comparison with previous years are the same ones used for comparison with industry data. For example, it is useful to compare current year gross margin with industry averages and previous years. The same can be said for most of the ratios described in Appendix A.

There are also numerous potential comparisons of current- and prior-period data beyond those normally available from industry data. For example, the percent of each expense category to total sales can be compared with that of previous years. Similarly, in a multiunit operation (e.g., a retail chain), internal comparisons for each unit can be made with previous periods (for example, the revenue and expenses for individual Becker stores can be compared).

Compare Client Data with Client-Determined Expected Results

Most companies prepare *budgets* for various aspects of their operations and financial results. Since budgets represent the client's expectations for the period, an investigation of the most significant areas in which differences exist between budgeted and actual results may indicate potential errors. The absence of differences may also indicate that errors are unlikely. It is common, for example, in the audit of local, provincial, and federal governmental units to use this type of analytical procedure.

Whenever client data are compared with budgets, there are two special concerns. First, the auditor must evaluate whether the budgets were realistic plans. In some organizations, budgets are prepared with little thought or care and therefore are not realistic expectations. Using such information has little value as audit evidence. The second concern is the possibility that current financial information was changed by client personnel to conform to the budget. If that has occurred, the auditor will find no differences in comparing actual with budget even if there are errors in the financial statements. Discussing budget procedures with client personnel is used to satisfy the first concern. Assessment of control risk and detailed audit tests of actual data are usually done to minimize the likelihood of the latter concern.

Compare Client Data with Auditor-Determined Expected Results

A second common type of comparison of client data with expected results occurs when the *auditor calculates the expected balance for comparison with actual.* In this type of analytical procedure, the auditor makes an estimate of what an account balance should be by relating it to some other balance sheet or income statement account or accounts, or by making a projection based on some historical trend. An example of calculating an expected value based on relationships of accounts is the independent calculation of interest expense on long-term notes payable by multiplying the ending monthly balance in notes payable by the average monthly interest rate (see Figure 7–5). An example of using a historical trend would be where the moving average of the allowance for uncollectible accounts receivable as a percent of gross accounts receivable is applied to the balance of gross accounts receivable at the end of the audit year to determine an expected value for the current allowance.

FIGURE 7–5

Hillsburg Hardware
Overall Tests of
Interest Expense
December 31, 19X8

	Hillsburg Hardware Ltd.		Schedule *N-3* Date	
	Overall Test of Interest Expense		Prepared by *FM 3/6/x9*	
	12/31/x8		Approved by *JW 3/12/x9*	

Interest expense per general ledger   120,432 ①

Computation of estimate:

  Short-term loans

    Balance outstanding at month-end: ②
      Jan.   147 500
      Feb.   159 200
      Mar.   170 600
      Apr.   170 800
      May.   130 200
      June.   93 700
      July.   70 000
      Aug.   - 0 -
      Sept.   - 0 -
      Oct.   42 700
      Nov.   126 300
      Dec.   209 000
          Total   1,320 000

      Average (÷12) 110,000 @ 12.5% ③   13,750

  Long-term loans

    Beginning balance 1,326 000 ②
    Ending balance   1,206 000 ②
                      2,532 000
    Average (÷2) 1,266 000   @ 8.5% ④   107,610

          Estimated total interest expense   121,360

                    Differences   (928) ⑤

Legend and Comments
① *Agrees with general ledger and working trial balance.*
② *Obtained from general ledger.*
③ *Estimated, based on examination of several notes throughout the year with
   rates ranging from 12% to 13%.*
④ *Agrees with permanent file schedule of long-term debt.*
⑤ *Difference not significant. Indicates that interest expense per books is reasonable.*

*Compare Client
Data with
Expected Results
Utilizing
Nonfinancial Data*

Suppose that in auditing a hotel, you can determine the number of rooms, room rate for each room, and occupancy rate. Using those data, it is relatively easy to estimate total revenue from rooms to compare with recorded revenue. The same approach can sometimes be used to estimate such accounts as tuitions revenue at universities (average tuition times enrolment), factory payroll (total hours worked times wage rate), and cost of materials sold (units sold times materials cost per unit).

The major concern in using nonfinancial data is the accuracy of the data. In the previous illustration, it is appropriate to use an estimated calculation of hotel revenue as audit evidence unless the auditor is satisfied with the reasonableness of the count of the number of rooms, room rate, and occupancy rate. It would be more difficult for the auditor to evaluate the accuracy of the occupancy rate than the other two items.

*Approach to
Performing
Analytical
Procedures*

A seven-step approach is suggested for performing analytical procedures. They are summarized in Figure 7–6 and then discussed. These seven steps are applicable to all four purposes set forth in Figure 7–4, but they are especially relevant for the last two, indicating possible errors and reducing detailed tests.

Set Objectives

The first step in applying analytical procedures is to set the objectives, first broad ones and then more specific ones. The reason for specifying objectives is to aid in designing effective analytical procedures. The broad objectives involve deciding the basic purpose for performing the analytical procedure, such as to direct attention to areas for further testing during planning, to provide substantive evidence during the testing phase, or to assist in a final review of the audited financial statements. Often a combination of these broad objectives exists. For example, the auditor may plan for the analytical procedures to provide some substantive evidence, but if the results of an analytical procedure indicate an unusual fluctuation, it becomes attention directing.

> **OBJECTIVE 7**
>
> Design and apply analytical procedures using a seven-step approach.

The more specific objectives involve identifying the accounts and audit objectives within those accounts to which the procedures will be directed. For example, the specific objectives of analytical procedures might be gathering evidence in support of the completeness objective for sales transactions and the adequacy of the allowance for uncollectible accounts receivable.

*Design the
Analytical
Procedures*

The design of the specific analytical procedures depends upon the objectives the auditor sets. For example, if the objective is to gather evidence to support the adequacy of the allowance for uncollectible accounts, the auditor is likely to use ratios that relate sales to accounts receivable. One possible ratio is the calculation of the number of days' sales outstanding in accounts receivable for comparison to prior years. In designing analytical procedures, the auditor should consider the appropriateness of each of the five types discussed in the previous section.

The auditor should evaluate whether relationships are both *plausible and predictable* when analytical procedures are being designed. Relationships are plausible when there is a clear cause and effect relationship among them. For example, if selling expense is being tested by analyzing its trend as a percentage of sales, it must be assumed that a change in the level of sales will, in fact, produce a change in selling expense.

In some cases, the relationships among data are plausible, but not ade-

FIGURE 7–6 Seven-step approach to performing analytical procedures including an example

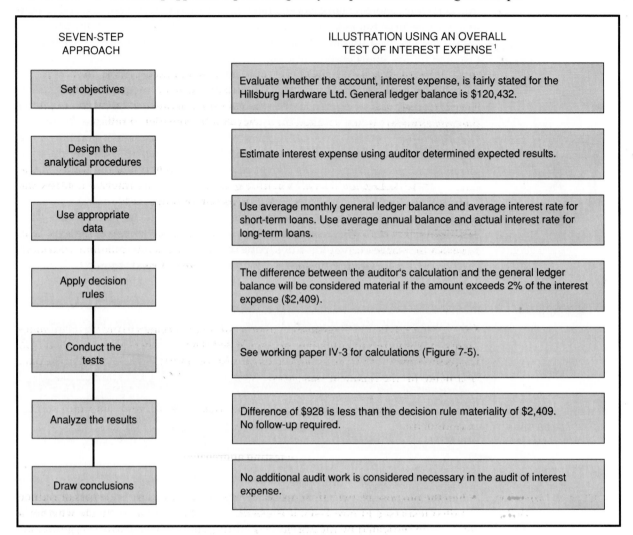

SEVEN-STEP APPROACH	ILLUSTRATION USING AN OVERALL TEST OF INTEREST EXPENSE[1]
Set objectives	Evaluate whether the account, interest expense, is fairly stated for the Hillsburg Hardware Ltd. General ledger balance is $120,432.
Design the analytical procedures	Estimate interest expense using auditor determined expected results.
Use appropriate data	Use average monthly general ledger balance and average interest rate for short-term loans. Use average annual balance and actual interest rate for long-term loans.
Apply decision rules	The difference between the auditor's calculation and the general ledger balance will be considered material if the amount exceeds 2% of the interest expense ($2,409).
Conduct the tests	See working paper IV-3 for calculations (Figure 7-5).
Analyze the results	Difference of $928 is less than the decision rule materiality of $2,409. No follow-up required.
Draw conclusions	No additional audit work is considered necessary in the audit of interest expense.

quately predictable to provide useful results. For example, accounts receivable may be expected to change in the direction of a change in the level of sales, but the magnitude of the change may vary greatly. As a result, using the ratio of accounts receivable to sales as substantive evidence in support of the accounts receivable balance would provide a low level of assurance.

As a general rule, relationships in a stable environment are more predictable than those in an unstable or dynamic environment. For example, the relationship of sales expense to sales is more stable, and thus more predictable, than the relationship of accounts receivable to sales, although both are plausible.

Use Appropriate Data   Four factors contribute heavily in selecting the appropriate data in designing analytical procedures.

1. **Relevance of data** For comparisons to be useful, the data used must be relevant to the objectives involved. For example, suppose the auditor is concerned with the

collectibility of accounts receivable and therefore plans to compute the trend in accounts receivable turnover as an analytical procedure to evaluate the adequacy of the allowance for doubtful accounts. If cash sales are significant, the sales figure used in the auditor's computation should be credit sales, not total sales.

Reliability of data If the data that current-year unaudited data are compared with are unreliable, the resulting comparisons will be of questionable value. Therefore, the auditor must consider the reliability of those data. Normally, if the data are previous years' audited data, they can be considered reliable. If they are from the current period, they can be considered reasonably reliable if they were developed under a good internal control structure or came from a source outside the accounting system that was considered reliable. Where the reliability of the data is questionable, such as information generated by weak internal control, the auditor should consider verifying the data as part of other audit tests.

Multiple-years data To determine trends that enable meaningful analysis, it is normally desirable to compare ratios, percentages, and absolute amounts with more periods than just the preceding one. Ideally, at least *four periods* should be included for each ratio and percentage used. To facilitate this, carry-forward schedules of ratio and trend calculations should be included in the permanent files.

Disaggregated data When analytical procedures are applied to the financial statements, it is referred to as testing the aggregated data. Disaggregation in analytical procedures means that the auditor does the tests on a further breakdown of the data that make up the financial statements. When done in a logical manner, analytical procedures for disaggregated data are more effective than for aggregated data. There are two primary ways to disaggregate data: into subunits and into shorter periods of time. For example, sales could be disaggregated by division, by month, or both. Disaggregation increases the likelihood of identifying offsetting errors and errors that might be overlooked in testing aggregated data.

Apply Decision Rules When the purpose of analytical procedures is to indicate possible errors or reduce detailed tests (see Figure 7–4), it is essential for the auditor to decide whether a fluctuation indicated by the application of an analytical procedure is significant. For example, if gross margin decreases from 26.2 percent to 25.7 percent, is that a significant or insignificant fluctuation? To decide whether a fluctuation is significant, some criterion, or *decision rule*, must be used. There is little in the professional literature to provide guidance in this area. However, the authors have observed the following two approaches used fairly extensively in practice.

Difference exceeds a stated dollar amount Where the difference exceeds an amount the auditor considers unacceptable the cause is investigated. For example, in the audit of commission expense for a given client, suppose the auditor considers a $5,000 error unacceptable. If a difference greater than that amount showed up in an analytical procedure concerning commission expense, the account balance would not be considered fairly stated. Additional detailed testing would therefore be performed.

Difference exceeds a fixed percentage In analytical procedures where it is difficult to frame a decision rule in terms of an absolute amount, a percent is often used. For example, the auditor may compare the current year's detailed expense account balances with the preceding year's and compute the percent change. Wherever the change exceeds 10 percent or some other percent the auditor believes appropriate, it is considered an unusual fluctuation.

Conduct the Tests, Analyze the Results and Draw Conclusions

Analytical procedures are conducted by making calculations based on the design of the test, classifying the results according to the decision rule, and performing follow-up procedures where unusual fluctuations are indicated or where there is no significant fluctuation when one is expected. Many auditors believe that the follow-up procedures are the most important aspect of analytical procedures because that is when there is the best opportunity to discover errors or fraud and other irregularities. For this reason, it would be regarded as a failure to fulfil the requirement of due care if an unusual fluctuation was indicated in an analytical procedure and the auditor did not properly investigate the cause.

Follow-up typically starts with discussions with management. Inquiries of appropriate management personnel are made about the possible causes of unusual fluctuations. Management's responses are considered by the auditor as to their information value and credibility. Where additional information is needed to obtain a satisfactory reason for the fluctuation, or where more reliable evidence is needed to support management's responses, detailed procedures, such as the examination of documents, will be performed. The proper application of follow-up procedures requires considerable judgment. The following factors affect the investigation:

- *Auditor's knowledge of the entity* The auditor is continually gathering information about the entity that provides a basis for judging the probable causes of unusual fluctuations and the credibility of management's responses to inquiries. For example, the auditor may know that there was a strike during the year and may conclude that the strike is a satisfactory explanation for a decline in sales volume.

- *Results of other audit procedures* A significant source of the auditor's knowledge is the results of audit procedures other than analytical procedures. Thus, if a fluctuation relates to a particular account that has been or will be subject to other audit procedures, that will affect the nature of the auditor's follow-up in an analytical procedure. For example, in auditing property accounts, the auditor will perform detailed procedures on major additions and retirements. Thus, the auditor will combine the follow-up investigation for an analytical procedure of the property accounts with the performance of those other procedures.

- *Inherent risk factors* Certain inherent risk factors, which will be discussed in Chapter 8, may indicate that management inquiries should not be relied on too extensively without obtaining significant corroborating evidence.

When effective analytical procedures result in no unusual fluctuations, the auditor has obtained substantive evidence in support of the accounts and objectives involved. On the other hand, where an unusual fluctuation is indicated and management is unable to offer a satisfactory explanation for its underlying cause, or the investigation beyond management's explanation fails to support it, the auditor must assume that there is high probability that an error or fraud exists. In this case, the auditor must design other appropriate audit procedures to determine whether such errors or fraud do, in fact, exist.

Using Statistical Techniques and Computer Software

The use of statistical techniques is desirable to make analytical procedures more relevant. Many auditors use computer software to make statistical and nonstatistical calculations easier. These two auditors' tools are discussed briefly.

Statistical Techniques

Several statistical techniques that aid in interpreting results can be applied to analytical procedures. The advantages of using statistical techniques are the ability to make more sophisticated calculations and their objectivity.

> **OBJECTIVE 8**
>
> Explain the benefits of using statistical techniques and computer software for analytical procedures.

The most common statistical technique for analytical procedures is regression analysis. Regression analysis is used to evaluate the reasonableness of a recorded balance by relating (regressing) the total to other relevant information. For example, the auditor might conclude that total selling expenses should be related to total sales, the previous year's selling expenses, and the number of salespeople. The auditor would then use regression analysis to statistically determine an estimated value of selling expenses for comparison with recorded values. Regression and other statistical methods commonly used for analytical procedures can be found in several advanced auditing texts dealing with statistical sampling techniques for auditing.

Auditor's Computer Software

Microcomputer-based audit software can be used to do extensive analytical procedures as a byproduct of other audit testing. In the past several years, many public accounting firms have begun to use computer software as a tool for doing more efficient and effective audits (see Chapter 15 for a more thorough study). One feature common to all such software is the ability to input the client's general ledger into the auditor's computer system. Adjusting entries and financial statements are thereby computerized to save time. The general ledger information for the client is saved and carried forward in the auditor's computerized data file year after year. The existence of current and previous years' general ledger information on the auditor's computer files permits extensive and inexpensive computerized analytical calculations. The analytical information can also be shown in different forms such as graphs and charts to help interpret the data.

A major benefit of computerized analytical procedures is the ease of updating the calculations when adjusting entries to the client's statements are made. If there are several adjusting entries to the clients' records, the analytical procedures calculations can be quickly revised. For example, a change in inventory and cost of goods sold affects a large number of ratios. All affected ratios would be revised at almost no cost with microcomputer software.

APPENDIX A Common Financial Ratios

Auditors' analytical procedures often include the use of general financial ratios during planning and final review of the audited financial statements. These are useful for understanding the most recent events and financial status of the business, and for viewing the statements from the perspective of a user. The general financial analysis may be effective for identifying possible problem areas for additional analysis and audit testing, as well as business problem areas for which the auditor can provide other assistance. This appendix presents a number of widely used general financial ratios.

**Short-Term
Debt-Paying
Ability**

$$\text{Current ratio} = \frac{\text{current assets}}{\text{current liabilities}}$$

$$\text{Quick ratio} = \frac{\text{cash + marketable securities + net accounts receivable}}{\text{current liabilities}}$$

$$\text{Cash ratio} = \frac{\text{cash + marketable securities}}{\text{current liabilities}}$$

Many companies follow an operating cycle whereby production inputs are obtained and converted into finished goods, and then sold and converted into cash. This requires an investment in working capital; that is, funds are needed to finance inventories and accounts receivable. A majority of these funds come from trade creditors and the balance will arise from initial capitalization, bank borrowings, and positive net cash flow from operations.

At any given time, the company will attain a net working capital position. This is the excess of current assets over current liabilities, and is also measured by the current ratio. Presumably, if net working capital is positive (that is, the current ratio is greater than 1.0), the company has sufficient available assets to pay its immediate debts; and the greater the excess (the larger the ratio), the better able the company is in this regard. Thus, companies with a comfortable net working capital position are considered preferred customers by their bankers and trade creditors and are given favorable treatment. Companies with inadequate net working capital will be in danger of not being able to obtain credit.

However, this is a somewhat simplistic view. The current assets of companies will differ in terms of both valuation and liquidity, and these aspects will affect a company's ability to meet its current obligations. One way to examine this problem is to restrict the analysis to the most available and objective current assets. Thus, the quick ratio eliminates inventories from the computation and the cash ratio further eliminates accounts receivable. Usually, if the cash ratio is greater than 1.0, the company has excellent short-term debt-paying ability. In some cases it is appropriate to state marketable securities at market value rather than cost in computing these ratios.

**Short-Term
Liquidity**

If a company does not have sufficient cash and cashlike items to meet its obligations, the key to its debt-paying ability will be the length of time it takes the company to convert less liquid current assets into cash. This is measured by the short-term liquidity ratios.

The two turnover ratios – accounts receivable and inventory – are very useful to auditors. Trends in the accounts receivable turnover ratio are frequently used in assessing the reasonableness of the allowance for uncollectible accounts. Trends in the inventory turnover ratio are used in identifying a potential inventory obsolescence problem.

$$\text{Average accounts receivable turnover} = \frac{\text{net sales}}{\text{average gross receivables}}$$

Average days to collect (or number of days' sales in accounts receivable) =

$$\frac{\text{average gross receivables} \times 365}{\text{net sales}}$$

$$\text{Average inventory turnover} = \frac{\text{cost of goods sold}}{\text{average inventory}}$$

$$\text{Average days to sell (or average day sales in inventory)} = \frac{\text{average inventory} \times 365}{\text{cost of goods sold}}$$

Average days to convert inventory to cash =
Average days to sell + average days to collect

When the short-term liquidity ratios (and the current ratio) are used to examine a company's performance over time or to compare performance among companies, differences in inventory accounting methods, fiscal year ends, and cash-credit sales mix can have a significant effect. With regard to inventories, a few companies have adopted the LIFO method. This can cause inventory values to differ significantly from FIFO values. When companies with different valuation methods are being compared, the company's LIFO value inventory can be adjusted to FIFO to obtain a better comparison.

When companies have different fiscal year ends, such that one is on a natural business year and the other is not, the simple average gross receivables and inventory figures for the former will be lower. This will tend to cause the natural business year company to appear more liquid than it really is. If this is a problem, an averaging computation with quarterly data can be used.

Finally, the use of net sales per the financial statements in the receivables liquidity ratios can be a problem when a significant portion of sales are for cash. This will be somewhat mitigated when the proportions are fairly constant among periods or companies for which comparisons are being made.

Ability to Meet Long-Term Debt Obligations and Preferred Dividends

$$\text{Debt to equity ratio} = \frac{\text{total liabilities}}{\text{total equity}}$$

$$\text{Tangible net assets to equity ratio} = \frac{\text{total equity} - \text{intangible assets}}{\text{total equity}}$$

$$\text{Times interest earned} = \frac{\text{operating income}}{\text{interest expense}}$$

Times interest and preferred dividends earned =

$$\frac{\text{operating income}}{\text{interest expense} + (\text{preferred dividends}/1 - \text{tax rate})}$$

A company's long-run solvency depends on the success of its operations and on its ability to raise capital for expansion or even survival over periods of temporary difficulty. From another point of view, common shareholders will benefit from the leverage obtained from borrowed capital that earns a positive net return.

A key measure in evaluating this long-term structure and capacity is the debt-to-equity ratio. If this ratio is too high, it may indicate the company has used up its borrowing capacity and has no cushion for future events. If it is too low, it may mean available leverage is not being used to the owner's benefit. If the ratio is trending up, it may mean earnings are too low to support the needs of the enterprise. And, if it is trending down, it may mean the company is doing well and setting the stage for future expansion.

The tangible net assets-to-equity ratio indicates the current quality of the company's equity by removing those assets whose realization is wholly dependent on future operations such as goodwill. This ratio can be used to interpret better the debt-to-equity ratio.

Lenders are generally concerned about a company's ability to meet interest payments as well as its ability to repay principal amounts. The latter will be appraised by evaluating the company's long-term prospects as well as its net asset position. The realizable value of assets will be important in this regard and may involve specific assets that collateralize the debt.

The ability to make interest payments is more a function of the company's ability to generate positive cash flows from operations in the short run, as well as over time. Thus, times interest earned shows how comfortably the company should be able to make interest (and preferred dividend) payments, assuming earnings trends are stable.

Operating and Performance Ratios

The key to remedying many financial ills is to improve operations. All creditors and investors, therefore, are interested in the results of operations of a business enterprise, and it is not surprising that a number of operating and performance ratios are in use. The most widely used operating and performance ratio is earnings per share, which is an integral part of the basic financial statements for most companies. Several additional ratios can be calculated and will give further insights into operations.

The first of these is the efficiency ratio. This shows the relative volume of business generated from the company's operating asset base. In other words, it shows whether sufficient revenues are being generated to justify the assets employed. When the efficiency ratio is low, there is an indication that additional volume should be sought before more assets are obtained. When the ratio is high, it may be an indication that assets are being fully utilized (that is, there is little excess capacity) and an investment in additional assets will soon be necessary.

The second ratio is the profit margin ratio. This shows the portion of sales that exceeds cost (both variable and fixed). When there is weakness in this ratio, it is generally an indication that either (1) gross margins (revenues in excess of variable costs) are too low or (2) volume is too low with respect to fixed costs.

$$\text{Earnings per share} = \frac{\text{earnings} - \text{preferred dividends}}{\text{number of common shares}}$$

$$\text{Efficiency ratio} = \frac{\text{net sales}}{\text{tangible operating assets}}$$

$$\text{Profit margin ratio} = \frac{\text{operating income}}{\text{net sales}}$$

$$\text{Profitability ratio} = \frac{\text{operating income}}{\text{tangible operating assets}}$$

$$\text{Return on total assets ratio} = \frac{\text{income before interest and taxes}}{\text{total assets}}$$

$$\text{Return on common equity ratio} =$$

$$\frac{\text{income before taxes} - (\text{preferred dividends}/1 - \text{tax rate})}{\text{common equity}}$$

Leverage ratios (computed separately for each source of capital other than common equity, for example, short-term debt, long-term debt, deferred taxes) =

$$\frac{(\text{return on total assets} \times \text{amount of source}) - \text{cost attributable to source}}{\text{common equity}}$$

$$\text{Book value per common share} = \frac{\text{common equity}}{\text{number of common shares}}$$

Two ratios that indicate the adequacy of earnings relative to the asset base are the profitability ratio and the return on total assets ratio. In effect, these ratios show the efficiency and profit margin ratios combined.

An important perspective on the earnings of the company is what kind of return is provided to the owners. This is reflected in the return (before taxes) on common equity. If this ratio is below prevailing long-term interest rates or returns on alternative investments, owners will perceive that they should convert the company's assets to some other use, or perhaps liquidate, unless return can be improved.

An interesting supplemental analysis is provided through leverage analysis. Here, the proportionate share of assets for each source of capital is multiplied times the company's return on total assets. This determines the return on each source of capital. The result is compared to the cost of each source of capital (for example, interest expense), and a net contribution by capital source is derived. If this amount is positive for a capital source, it may be an indication that additional capital should be sought. If the leverage is negative from a capital source, recapitalization alternatives and/or earnings improvements should be investigated. It is also helpful to use this leverage analysis when considering the debt-to-equity ratio.

The final operating and performance ratio is book value per common share. This shows the combined effect of equity transactions over time.

The use of operating and performance ratios is subject to the same accounting inconsistencies mentioned for the liquidity ratios previously identified. The usefulness of these ratios in making comparisons over time or among companies may be affected by the classification of operating versus nonoperating items, inventory methods, depreciation methods, amortization of goodwill, research and development costs, and off-balance-sheet financing.

Illustration Computation of the various ratios is illustrated using the financial statements of Hillsburg Hardware Ltd. introduced in Chapter 5 (pp. 133 – 134).

Simplifying assumptions:

1. Assumes average receivables and inventories for the year are not significantly different from the year-end balances.
2. Assumes there is no preferred stock and the tax rate is 48 percent.
3. Assumes all interest expense relates to long-term notes payable.
4. Assumes there are 250,000 common shares with a market value of $26 per share.
5. Assumes data taken from Figure 5–2.

$$\text{Earnings per share} = \frac{198 - 0}{250} = .79$$

$$\text{Current ratio} = \frac{2,550}{659} = 3.87$$

$$\text{Quick ratio} = \frac{41 + 948 + 47}{659} = 1.57$$

$$\text{Cash ratio} = \frac{41}{659} = .06$$

$$\text{Accounts receivable turnover} = \frac{7,154}{948} = 7.55$$

$$\text{Days to collect} = \frac{948 \times 365}{7,154} = 48.37 \text{ days}$$

$$\text{Inventory turnover} = \frac{5,162}{1,493} = 3.46$$

$$\text{Days to sell} = \frac{1,493 \times 365}{5,162} = 105.57 \text{ days}$$

$$\text{Days to convert to cash} = 48.37 + 105.57 = 153.94 \text{ days}$$

$$\text{Debt to equity} = \frac{(659 + 1,284)}{1,124} = 1.73$$

$$\text{Tangible net assets to equity} = \frac{1,124}{1,124} = 1.00$$

$$\text{Times interest earned} = \frac{369}{120} = 3.08$$

$$\text{Times interest and preferred dividends earned} = \frac{369}{(120 + (0/1 - .48)} = 3.08$$

$$\text{Efficiency ratio} = \frac{7,154}{3,067} = 2.33$$

$$\text{Profit margin ratio} = \frac{369}{7,154} = .05$$

$$\text{Profitability ratio} = \frac{369}{3,067} = .12$$

$$\text{Return on total assets} = \frac{369 + 36}{3,067} = .13$$

$$\text{Return on common equity} = \frac{285 - (0/1 - .48)}{1,124} = .25$$

Leverage ratios:

$$\text{Current liabilities} = \frac{(.13 \times 659) - 0}{1,124} = .08$$

$$\text{Long-term notes payable} = \frac{(.13 \times 1,206) - 120}{1,124} = .03$$

$$\text{Book value per common share} = \frac{1,124}{250} = 4.50$$

REVIEW QUESTIONS

7-1 What benefits does the auditor derive from planning audits?

7-2 Identify the six major steps in planning audits.

7-3 What are the responsibilities of the successor and predecessor auditors when a company is changing auditors?

7-4 What factors should an auditor consider prior to accepting an engagement? Explain.

7-5 What is the purpose of an engagement letter? What subjects should be covered in such a letter?

7-6 List the five types of information the auditor should obtain or review as a part of gaining background information for the audit, and provide one specific example of how the information will be useful in conducting an audit.

7-7 When a public accountant has accepted an engagement from a new client that is a manufacturer, it is customary for the public accountant to tour the client's plant facilities. Discuss the ways in which the public accountant's observations made during the course of the plant tour will be of help as he or she plans and conducts the audit.

7-8 An auditor often tries to acquire background knowledge of the client's industry as an aid to his or her audit work. How does the acquisition of this knowledge aid the auditor in distinguishing between obsolete and current inventory?

Test Ps 194

Test. /s 198

Test Pg 197-200

test Ps 194

No

7–9   Define what is meant by a related party. What are the auditor's responsibilities for related parties and related-party transactions?

7–10   Jennifer Bailey is an experienced senior auditor who is in charge of several important audits for a medium-sized firm. Her philosophy of conducting audits is to ignore all previous years' and permanent working papers until near the end of the audit as a means of keeping from prejudicing herself. She believes this enables her to perform the audit in a more independent manner because it eliminates the tendency of simply doing the same things in the current audit that were done on previous audits. Near the end of the audit Bailey reviews the working papers from the preceding year, evaluates the significance of any items she has overlooked, and modifies her evidence if she considers it necessary. Evaluate Bailey's approach to conducting an audit.

7–11   Your firm has performed the audit of Rogers Inc. for several years and you have been assigned the responsibility for the current audit. How would your review of the articles of incorporation and bylaws for this audit differ from that of the audit of a client that was audited by a different public accounting firm in the preceding year?

7–12   For the audit of Flin Flon Manufacturing Company Ltd., the audit partner asks you to read carefully the new mortgage contract with the Bank of Manitoba and abstract all pertinent information. List the information in a mortgage that is likely to be relevant to the auditor.

7–13   Identify four types of information in the client's minutes of the board of directors' meetings that are likely to be relevant to the auditor. Explain why it is important to read the minutes early in the engagement.

7–14   Identify the most important reasons for performing analytical procedures.

7–15   Your client, Harper Ltd., has a contractual commitment as a part of a bond indenture to maintain a current ratio of 2.0. If the ratio falls below that level on the balance sheet date, the entire bond becomes payable immediately. In the current year, the client's financial statements show that the ratio has dropped from 2.6:1 or 2.6 to 2.05:1 or 2.05 over the past year. How should this situation affect your audit plan?

7–16   Distinguish between attention-directing analytical procedures and those intended to reduce detailed substantive procedures.

7–17   Explain why the statement "Analytical procedures are essential in every part of an audit, but these tests are rarely sufficient by themselves for any audit area" is correct or incorrect.

7–18   Gail Gordon, a public accountant, has found ratio and trend analysis relatively useless as a tool in conducting audits. For several engagements she computed the industry ratios included in publications by The Financial Post Company and compared them with industry standards. For most engagements the client's business was significantly different from the industry data in the publication and the client would automatically explain away any discrepancies by attributing them to the unique nature of its operations. In cases in which the client had more than one branch in different industries, Gordon found the ratio analysis no help at all. How could Gordon improve the quality of her analytical procedures?

7–19   At the completion of every audit, Roger Morris, public accountant, calculates a large number of ratios and trends for comparison with industry averages and prior-year calculations. He believes the calculations are worth the relatively small cost of doing them because they provide him with an excellent overview of the client's operations. If the ratios are out of line, Morris discusses the reasons with the client and frequently makes suggestions on how to bring the ratio back in line in the future. In some cases, these discussions with management have been the basis for management services engagements. Discuss the major strengths and shortcomings in Morris's use of ratio and trend analysis.

7-5
210.

7-20 It is imperative that the auditor follow up on all material differences discovered through analytical procedures. What factors will affect such investigations?

MULTIPLE CHOICE QUESTIONS

7-21 The following questions concern the planning of the engagement. Select the best response.

    a. Which of the following is an effective audit planning and control procedure that helps prevent misunderstandings and inefficient use of audit personnel?

      (1) Arrange to make copies, for inclusion in the working papers, of those client-prepared documents examined by the auditor.

      (2) Arrange to provide the client with copies of the audit programs to be used during the audit.

      (3) Arrange a preliminary conference with the client to discuss audit objectives, fees, timing, and other information.

      (4) Arrange to have the auditor prepare and post any necessary adjusting or reclassification entries prior to final closing.

    b. An auditor is planning an audit engagement for a new client in a business with which he is unfamiliar. Which of the following would be the most useful source of information during the preliminary planning stage, when the auditor is trying to obtain a general understanding of audit problems that might be encountered?

      (1) Client manuals of accounts and charts of accounts.

      (2) Industry Audit Guides from professional accounting bodies.

      (3) Prior-year working papers of the predecessor auditor.

      (4) Latest annual and interim financial statements issued by the client.

    c. The independent auditor should acquire an understanding of a client's internal audit function to determine whether the work of internal auditors will be a factor in determining the nature, timing, and extent of the independent auditor's procedures. The work performed by internal auditors might be such a factor when the internal auditor's work includes

      (1) verification of the mathematical accuracy of invoices.

      (2) review of administrative practices to improve efficiency and achieve management objectives.

      (3) study and evaluation of internal control.

      (4) preparation of internal financial reports for management purposes.

        (AICPA adapted)

7-22 The following questions pertain to the predecessor/successor auditor relationship. Choose the best response.

    a. When approached to perform an audit for the first time, the public accountant should make inquiries of the predecessor auditor. This is a necessary procedure because the predecessor may be able to provide the successor with information that will assist the successor in determining

      (1) whether the predecessor's work should be used.

      (2) whether the company follows the policy of rotating its auditors.

      (3) whether in the predecessor's opinion internal control of the company has been satisfactory.

      (4) whether the engagement should be accepted.

    b. Hawkins requested permission to communicate with the predecessor auditor and review certain portions of the predecessor's working papers. The prospective client's refusal to permit this will bear directly on Hawkins' decision concerning the

      (1) adequacy of the preplanned audit program.

(2) ability to establish consistency in application of accounting principles between years.

(3) apparent scope limitation.

(4) integrity of management.

c. What is the responsibility of a successor auditor with respect to communicating with the predecessor auditor in connection with a prospective new audit client?

(1) The successor auditor has *no* responsibility to contact the predecessor auditor.

(2) The successor auditor should obtain permission from the prospective client to contact the predecessor auditor.

(3) The successor auditor should contact the predecessor regardless of whether the prospective client authorizes contact.

(4) The successor auditor need not contact the predecessor if the successor is aware of all available relevant facts.   (AICPA adapted)

7–23 The following questions deal with analytical procedures. Choose the best response.

a. Analytical procedures are

(1) statistical tests of financial information designed to identify areas requiring intensive investigation.

(2) analytical procedures of financial information made by a computer.

(3) substantive tests of financial information made by a study and comparison of relationships among data.

(4) diagnostic tests of financial information that may not be classified as evidential matter.

b. Significant unexpected fluctuations identified by analytical procedures will usually necessitate a(n)

(1) consistency qualification.

(2) understanding of the client's internal control structure.

(3) explanation in the representation letter.

(4) auditor investigation.

c. Which of the following situations has the best chance of being detected when a public accountant compares 19X8 revenues and expenses with the prior year and investigates all changes exceeding a fixed percentage?

(1) An increase in property tax rates has not been recognized in the company's 19X8 accrual.

(2) The cashier began lapping accounts receivable in 19X8.

(3) Because of worsening economic conditions, the 19X8 provision for uncollectible accounts was inadequate.

(4) The company changed its capitalization policy for small tools in 19X8.

d. Your analytical procedures and other tests of the Dey Corp. reveal that the firm's poor financial condition makes it unlikely that it will survive as a going concern. Assuming that the financial statements have otherwise been prepared in accordance with generally accepted accounting principles, what disclosure should you make of the company's precarious financial position?

(1) You should issue an unqualified opinion and, in a paragraph between the scope and opinion paragraphs of your report, direct the reader's attention to the poor financial condition of the company.

(2) You should insist that a note to the financial statements clearly indicates that the company appears to be on the verge of bankruptcy.

(3) You need not insist on any particular disclosure, since the company's poor financial condition is clearly indicated by the financial statements themselves.

(4) You should insist that the management report clearly indicate the problem. If that is done, no other disclosure is required.   (AICPA adapted)

DISCUSSION QUESTIONS AND PROBLEMS

7-24 Two public accountants were talking about their profession while golfing one day. One commented that she thought that the decision to continue as auditor for a client was as important as the decision whether to accept a company as a new client. Her golfing partner asked her what she meant.

Required: Explain to the second golfer what the first golfer meant.

7-25 Janet Chow, a senior manager in a public accounting firm, is explaining to a new manager, Reinhard Mueller, that planning is a very important part of every audit and that her planning includes a preliminary conference with the client to discuss audit objectives, fees, timing, and other topics. Reinhard replies that he thought the engagement letter covered those issues and that he thought the preliminary conference was a waste of time.

Required: Explain the value of the preliminary conference to Reinhard, including why both it and the engagement letter are important.

7-26 In late spring you are advised of a new assignment as in-charge accountant of your public accounting firm's recurring annual audit of a major client, Lancer Inc. You are given the engagement letter for the audit covering the current fiscal year and a list of personnel assigned to this engagement. It is your responsibility to plan and supervise the field work for the engagement.

Required: Discuss the necessary preparation and planning for the Lancer Inc. annual audit *prior* to beginning field work at the client's office. In your discussion include the sources you should consult, the type of information you should seek, the preliminary plans and preparation you should make for the field work, and any actions you should take relative to the staff assigned to the engagement.   (AICPA adapted)

7-27 Generally accepted accounting principles set certain requirements for disclosure of related parties and related-party transactions. There is also an Auditing Guideline that discusses related party transactions and economic dependence. For this problem you are expected to research appropriate *CICA Handbook* material.

Required: a. Define *related party* as used for generally accepted accounting principles and explain the disclosure requirements for related parties and related-party transactions.

b. Explain why disclosure of related-party transactions is relevant information for decision makers.

c. List the most important related parties who are likely to be involved in related-party transactions.

d. List several different types of related-party transactions that could take place in a company.

e. Discuss ways the auditor can determine the existence of related parties and related-party transactions.

f. For each type of related-party transaction, discuss different ways the auditor can evaluate whether they are recorded on an arm's-length basis assuming that the auditor knows the transactions exist.

g. Suppose you know that material related-party transactions had occurred and were transacted at significantly less favorable terms than ordinarily occur when business is done with independent parties. The client refuses to disclose these facts in the financial statements. What are your responsibilities?

h. Why is disclosure of information about economic dependence so important for decision makers?

7-28 The minutes of the board of directors of the Marygold Catalogue Company Ltd. for the year ended December 31, 19X6 were provided to you.

MEETING OF FEBRUARY 16, 19X6

Ruth Ho, chairman of the board, called the meeting to order at 4:00 P.M. The following directors were in attendance:

Margaret Aronson	Claude La Rose
Fred Brick	Lucille Renolds
Henri Chapdelaine	J. T. Schmidt
Ruth Ho	Marie Titard
Homer Jackson	Roald Asko

The minutes of the meeting of October 11, 19X5 were read and approved.

Marie Titard, president, discussed the new marketing plan for wider distribution of catalogues in the western market. She made a motion for approval of increased expenditures of approximately $50,000 for distribution costs that was seconded by Asko and unanimously passed.

The unresolved dispute with Revenue Canada over the tax treatment of leased office buildings was discussed with Harold Moss, the tax partner from Marygold's public accounting firm, Moss & Lawson. In Mr. Moss's opinion, the matter would not be resolved for several months and may result in an unfavorable settlement.

J.T. Schmidt moved that the computer equipment that was no longer being used in the Kingston office, because of new equipment acquired in 19X5, be donated to the Kingston Vocational School for use in their repair and training program. Margaret Aronson seconded the motion and it unanimously passed. Annual cash dividends were unanimously approved as being payable April 30, 19X6 for shareholders of record April 15, 19X6 as follows:

Class A common – $10 per share
Class B common – $5 per share

Officers' bonuses for the year ended December 31, 19X5 were approved for payment March 1, 19X6 as follows:

Marie Titard – President	$26,000
Lucille Renolds – Vice president	$12,000
Roald Asko – Controller	$12,000
Fred Brick – Secretary-treasurer	$ 9,000

Meeting adjourned 6:30 P.M.

Fred Brick, Secretary

MEETING OF SEPTEMBER 15, 19X6

Ruth Ho, chairman of the board, called the meeting to order at 4:00 P.M. The following directors were in attendance:

Margaret Aronson	Claude La Rose
Fred Brick	Lucille Renolds
Henri Chapdelaine	J. T. Schmidt
Ruth Ho	Marie Titard
Homer Jackson	Roald Asko

The minutes of the meeting of February 16, 19X6 were read and approved.

Marie Titard, president, discussed the improved sales and financial condition for 19X6. She was pleased with the results of the catalogue distribution and cost control for the company. No action was taken.

The nominations for officers were made as follows:

President — Marie Titard
Vice president — Lucille Renolds
Controller — Roald Asko
Secretary-treasurer — Fred Brick

The nominees were elected by unanimous voice vote.

Salary increases of 6 percent, exclusive of bonuses, were recommended for all officers for 19X7. Marie Titard moved that such salary increases be approved, seconded by J. T. Schmidt and unanimously approved.

	SALARY	
	19X6	19X7
Marie Titard, President	$90,000	$95,400
Lucille Renolds, Vice president	$60,000	$63,600
Roald Asko, Controller	$60,000	$63,600
Fred Brick, Secretary-treasurer	$40,000	$42,400

Roald Asko moved that the company consider adopting a pension/profit-sharing plan for all employees as a way to provide greater incentive for employees to stay with the company. Considerable discussion ensued. It was agreed without adoption that Asko should discuss the legal and tax implications with lawyer Cecil Makay and a public accounting firm reputed to be knowledgeable about pension and profit-sharing plans, Able and Bark.

Roald Asko discussed expenditure of $58,000 for acquisition of a new computer for the Kingston office to replace equipment that was purchased in 19X5 and has proven ineffective. A settlement has been tentatively reached to return the equipment for a refund of $21,000. Asko moved that both transactions be approved, seconded by Jackson and unanimously adopted. Fred Brick moved that a loan of $36,000, from the Kingston Bank, be approved. The interest is floating at 2 percent above prime. The collateral is to be the new computer equipment being installed in the Kingston office. A chequing account, with a minimum balance of $2,000 at all times until the loan is repaid, must be opened and maintained if the loan is granted. Seconded by La Rose and unanimously approved.

Lucille Renolds, chair of the audit committee, moved that the public accounting firm of Moss & Lawson be selected again for the company's annual audit and related tax work for the year ended December 31, 19X6. Seconded by Aronson and unanimously approved.

Meeting adjourned 6:40 P.M.

Fred Brick, Secretary

Required:

a. How do you, as the auditor, know that all minutes have been made available to you?

b. Read the minutes of the meetings of February 16 and September 15. Use the following format to list and explain information that is relevant for the 19X6 audit:

INFORMATION RELEVANT TO 19X6 AUDIT	AUDIT ACTION REQUIRED
1.	
2.	

    c. Read the minutes of the meeting of February 16, 19X6. Did any of that information pertain to the December 31, 19X5 audit? Explain what the auditor should have done during the December 31, 19X5 audit with respect to 19X6 minutes.

7–29 You are engaged in the annual audit of the financial statements of Maulack Corp., a medium-sized wholesale company that manufactures light fixtures. The company has 25 shareholders. During your review of the minutes you observe that the president's salary has been increased substantially over the preceding year by action of the board of directors. His present salary is much greater than salaries paid to presidents of companies of comparable size and is clearly excessive. You determine that the method of computing the president's salary was changed for the year under audit. In previous years, the president's salary was consistently based on sales. In the latest year, however, his salary was based on net income before income taxes. The Maulack Corp. is in a cyclical industry and would have had an extremely profitable year except that the increase in the president's salary siphoned off much of the income that would have accrued to the shareholders. The president is a substantial shareholder.

Required:
    a. What is the implication of this condition on the fair presentation of the financial statements?

    b. Discuss your responsibility for disclosing this situation.

    c. Discuss the effect, if any, that the situation has on your auditor's opinion as to

        (1) the fairness of the presentation of the financial statements.

        (2) the consistency of the application of accounting principles.

(AICPA adapted)

7–30 In auditing the financial statements of a manufacturing company that were prepared by electronic data-processing equipment, the public accountant has found that the traditional audit trail has been obscured. As a result, the public accountant may place increased emphasis on analytical procedures of the data under audit. These tests, which are also applied in auditing visibly posted accounting records, include the computation of ratios that are compared with prior-year ratios or with industrywide norms. Examples of analytical procedures are the computation of the rate of inventory turnover and the computation of the number of days in receivables.

Required:
    a. Discuss the advantages to the public accountant of the use of analytical procedures in an audit.

    b. In addition to the computations given above, list ratios that a public accountant may compute during an audit on balance sheet accounts and related income accounts. For each ratio listed, name the two (or more) accounts used in its computation.

    c. When a public accountant discovers that there has been a significant change in a ratio when compared with the preceding year's, he or she considers the possible reasons for the change. Give the possible reasons for the following significant changes in ratios:

        (1) The rate of inventory turnover (ratio of cost of sales and average inventory) has decreased from the preceding year's rate.

(2) The number of days' sales in receivables (ratio of average daily accounts receivable and sales) has increased over the prior year.

(AICPA adapted)

7–31 Your comparison of the gross margin percentage for Singh Drugs Ltd. for the years 19X3 through 19X6 indicates a significant decline. This is shown by the following information:

	19X6	19X5	19X4	19X3
Sales (thousands)	$14,211	$12,916	$11,462	$10,351
CGS (thousands)	9,223	8,266	7,313	6,573
Gross margin	$4,988	$4,650	$4,149	$3,778
Percentage	35.1	36.0	36.2	36.5

A discussion with Marilyn Adams, the controller, brings to light two possible explanations. She informs you that the industry gross profit percentage in the retail drug industry declined fairly steadily for three years, which accounts for part of the decline. A second factor was the declining percentage of the total volume resulting from the pharmacy part of the business. The pharmacy sales represent the most profitable portion of the business, yet the competition from discount drugstores prevents it from expanding as fast as the nondrug items such as magazines, candy, and many other items sold. Adams feels strongly that these two factors are the cause of the decline.

The following additional information is obtained from independent sources and the client's records as a means of investigating the controller's explanations:

	SINGH DRUGS				INDUSTRY GROSS PROFIT PERCENTAGE FOR RETAILERS OF DRUGS AND RELATED PRODUCTS
	Drug Sales	Non-drug Sales	Drug Cost of Goods Sold	Non-drug Cost of Goods Sold	
19X6	$5,126	$9,085	$3,045	$6,178	32.7
19X5	$5,051	$7,865	$2,919	$5,347	32.9
19X4	$4,821	$6,641	$2,791	$4,522	33.0
19X3	$4,619	$5,732	$2,665	$3,908	33.2

Required:

a. Evaluate the explanation provided by Adams. Show calculations to support your conclusions.

b. Which specific aspects of the client's financial statements require intensive investigation in this audit?

7–32 In the audit of the Worldwide Wholesale Inc., you performed extensive ratio and trend analysis. No material exceptions were discovered except for the following:

1. Commission expense as a percentage of sales has stayed constant for several years but has increased significantly in the current year. Commission rates have not changed.

2. The rate of inventory turnover has steadily decreased for four years.

3. Inventory as a percentage of current assets has steadily increased for four years.

4. The number of days' sales in accounts receivable has steadily increased for three years.

5. Allowance for uncollectible accounts as a percentage of accounts receivable has steadily decreased for three years.

6. The absolute amounts of depreciation expense and depreciation expense as a percentage of gross fixed assets are significantly smaller than in the preceding year.

Required:

a. Evaluate the potential significance of each of the exceptions above for the fair presentation of financial statements.

b. State the follow-up procedures you would use to determine the possibility of material errors.

7–33 As part of the analytical procedures of Mahogany Products, Inc., you perform calculations of the following ratios:

		INDUSTRY AVERAGES		MAHOGANY PRODUCTS, INC.	
RATIO		19X6	19X5	19X6	19X5
1. Current ratio		3.30	3.80	2.20	2.60
2. Days to collect receivables		87.00	93.00	67.00	60.00
3. Days to sell inventory		126.00	121.00	93.00	89.00
4. Purchases divided by accounts payable		11.70	11.60	8.50	8.60
5. Inventory divided by current assets		.56	.51	.49	.48
6. Operating earnings divided by tangible assets		.08	.06	.14	.12
7. Operating earnings divided by net sales		.06	.06	.04	.04
8. Gross margin percentage		.21	.27	.21	.19
9. Earnings per share		$14.27	$13.91	$2.09	$1.93

Required:

For each of the preceding ratios:

a. State whether there is a need to investigate the results further and, if so, the reason for further investigation.

b. State the approach you would use in the investigation.

c. Explain how the operations of Mahogany Products, Inc., appear to differ from those of the industry.

7–34 Following are the auditor's calculations of several key ratios for Cragston Star Products Ltd. The primary purpose of this information is to assess the risk of financial failure, but any other relevant conclusions are also desirable.

RATIO	19X6	19X5	19X4	19X3	19X2
Current ratio	2.08	2.26	2.51	2.43	2.50
Quick ratio	.97	1.34	1.82	1.76	1.64
Earnings before taxes divided by interest expense	3.50	3.20	4.10	5.30	7.10
Accounts receivable turnover	4.20	5.50	4.10	5.40	5.60
Days to collect receivables	108.20	83.10	105.20	80.60	71.60
Inventory turnover	2.03	1.84	2.68	3.34	3.36
Days to sell inventory	172.60	195.10	133.90	107.80	108.30
Net sales divided by tangible assets	.68	.64	.73	.69	.67
Operating earnings divided by net sales	.13	.14	.16	.15	.14

Operating earnings divided by tangible assets	.09	.09	.12	.10	.09
Net earnings divided by common equity	.05	.06	.10	.10	.11
Earnings per share	$4.30	$4.26	$4.49	$4.26	$4.14

Required:

a. What major conclusions can be drawn from this information about the company's future?

b. What additional information would be helpful in your assessment of this company's financial condition?

c. Based on the ratios above, which particular aspects of the company do you believe should receive special emphasis in the audit?

CASE

7–35 Solomon Corp. is a highly successful, closely held Moncton, New Brunswick, company that manufactures and assembles specialty parts for automobiles that are sold in auto parts stores in the East. Sales and profits have expanded rapidly in the past few years, and the prospects for future years are every bit as encouraging. In fact, the Solomon brothers are currently considering either selling out to a large company or going public to obtain additional capital.

The company originated in 1960 when Frank Solomon decided to manufacture tooled parts. In 1975 the company changed over to the auto parts business. Fortunately, it has never been necessary to expand the facilities, but space problems have recently become severe and expanded facilities will be necessary. Land and building costs in Moncton are currently extremely inflated.

Management has always relied on you for help in its problems inasmuch as the treasurer is sales oriented and has little background in the controllership function. Salaries of all officers have been fairly modest in order to reinvest earnings in future growth. In fact the company is oriented toward long-run wealth of the brothers more than toward short-run profit. The brothers have all of their personal wealth invested in the firm.

A major reason for the success of Solomon has been the small but excellent sales force. The sales policy is to sell to small auto shops at high prices. This policy is responsible for fairly high credit losses, but the profit margin is high and the results have been highly successful. The firm has every intention of continuing this policy in the future.

Your firm has been auditing Solomon Corp. since 1970, and you have been on the job for the past three years. The client has excellent internal control and has always been very cooperative. In recent years the client has attempted to keep net income at a high level because of borrowing needs and future sellout possibilities. Overall, the client has always been pleasant to deal with and willing to help in any way possible. There have never been any major audit adjustments, and an unqualified opinion has always been issued.

In the current year you have completed the tests of the sales and collection area. The tests of controls for sales and sales returns and allowances were excellent, and an extensive confirmation yielded no material errors. You have carefully reviewed the cutoff for sales and for sales returns and allowances and find these to be excellent. All recorded bad debts appear reasonable, and a review of the aged trial balance indicates that conditions seem about the same as in past years.

	12-31-X7 (CURRENT YEAR)	12-31-X6	12-31-X5	12-31-X4
Balance Sheet				
Cash	$ 49,615	$ 39,453	$ 51,811	$ 48,291
Accounts receivable	2,366,938	2,094,052	1,756,321	1,351,470
Allowance for doubtful accounts	(250,000)	(240,000)	(220,000)	(200,000)
Inventory	2,771,833	2,585,820	2,146,389	1,650,959
Current assets	$4,938,386	$4,479,325	$3,734,521	$2,850,720
Total assets	$8,698,917	$8,223,915	$7,233,451	$5,982,853
Current liabilities	$2,253,422	$2,286,433	$1,951,830	$1,625,811
Long-term liabilities	4,711,073	4,525,310	4,191,699	3,550,481
Owners' equity	1,734,422	1,412,172	1,089,922	806,561
Total liabilities and owners' equity	$8,698,917	$8,223,915	$7,233,451	$5,982,853
Income Statement				
Sales	$6,740,652	$6,165,411	$5,313,752	$4,251,837
Sales returns and allowances	(207,831)	(186,354)	(158,367)	(121,821)
Sales discounts allowed	(74,147)	(63,655)	(52,183)	(42,451)
Bad debts expense	(248,839)	(245,625)	(216,151)	(196,521)
Net sales	$6,209,835	$5,669,777	$4,887,051	$3,891,044
Gross margin	$1,415,926	$1,360,911	$1,230,640	$1,062,543
Net income after taxes	$ 335,166	$ 322,250	$ 283,361	$ 257,829
Aged Accounts Receivable				
0–30 days	$ 942,086	$ 881,232	$ 808,569	$ 674,014
31–60 days	792,742	697,308	561,429	407,271
61–120 days	452,258	368,929	280,962	202,634
> 120 days	179,852	146,583	105,361	67,551
Total	$2,366,938	$2,094,052	$1,756,321	$1,351,470

Required:

a. Evaluate the information in the case to provide assistance to management for improved operation of its business. Prepare the supporting analysis using the microcomputers and an electronic spreadsheet program. (Instructor's option).

b. Do you agree that sales, accounts receivable, and allowance for doubtful accounts are probably correctly stated? Show calculations to support your conclusion.

8

MATERIALITY AND RISK

5130
Avat Lisk mople

LEARNING	
OBJECTIVES	THOROUGH STUDY OF THIS CHAPTER WILL ENABLE YOU TO:

1. Apply the concept of materiality to the audit
2. Make a preliminary judgment about what amounts to consider material
3. Use materiality to evaluate audit findings
4. Define risk in auditing
5. Describe the audit risk model and its components
6. Consider the impact of business risk on audit risk

7. Consider the impact of several factors on the assessment of inherent risk
8. Discuss the relationships among the components of risk
9. Discuss risk for segments and measurement difficulties
10. Discuss how materiality and risk are related and integrated into the audit process

---

□ Materiality and risk are important to planning the audit and designing the audit approach. This chapter will show how these concepts fit into the planning phase of the audit.

The opinion paragraph in an auditor's report includes two important phrases that are directly related to materiality and risk. These phrases are emphasized in bold print in the following standard wording of an unqualified opinion.

■ **In our opinion,** these financial statements present fairly, **in all material respects,** the financial position of Watfor Corporation as at December 31, 19X9 and the results of its operations and the changes in its financial position for the year then ended in accordance with generally accepted accounting principles.

The phrase **in our opinion** is intended to inform users that auditors base their conclusions on professional judgment and do not guarantee or ensure the fair presentation of the financial statements. The phrase implies there is some *risk* that the financial statements are not fairly stated even when the opinion is unqualified.

The phrase **in all material respects** is intended to inform users that an expression of opinion in the auditor's report is limited to *material* financial information. Materiality is important because it is impractical for auditors to provide assurances that financial statements are accurate to the nearest dollar.

In addition to the wording of the opinion paragraph, both of these aspects comprise the primary thrust of the scope paragraph. That paragraph describes an audit as a process designed to obtain *reasonable assurance* (implying some level of risk) about whether the financial statements are free of *material* misstatement.

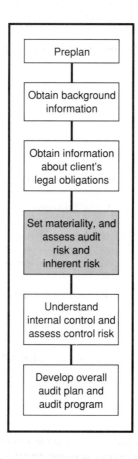

Materiality   Materiality was first discussed on pages 40-43 as a major consideration in determining the appropriate auditor's report to issue. The concepts of materiality discussed in this chapter are directly related to those in Chapter 2. We suggest you reread pages 40-43 before you study the following material.

Section 5130.05 of the *CICA Handbook* defines materiality in the following way:

A misstatement or the aggregate of all misstatements in financial statements is considered to be material if, in the light of the surrounding circumstances, it is probable that the decision of a person who is relying on the financial statements, and who has a reasonable knowledge of business and economic activities (the user), would be changed or influenced by such misstatement or the aggregate of all misstatements.

OBJECTIVE 1

Apply the concept of materiality to the audit.

The auditor's responsibility is to determine whether financial statements are materially misstated. If the auditor determines that there is a material misstatement, he or she will bring it to the client's attention so a correction can be made. If the client refuses to correct the statements, a qualified or an adverse opinion must be issued, depending on how material the misstatement is. Auditors must, therefore, have a thorough knowledge of the application of materiality.

A careful reading of the *CICA Handbook* definition reveals the difficulty auditors have in applying materiality in practice. The definition emphasizes the decisions of users who have a reasonable knowledge of business and economic activities and who rely on the statements to make decisions. Auditors, therefore, must have knowledge of the likely users of their clients' statements and the decisions that are being made. For example, if an auditor knows financial statements will be relied on in a buy-sell agreement for the entire business, the amount that the auditor considers material may be smaller than for an otherwise similar audit. In practice, auditors often do not know who the users are or what decisions will be made.

There are four closely related steps in applying materiality. They are shown in Figure 8–1 and discussed in this section. The steps start with setting a preliminary judgment about materiality. Estimation of the amount of errors in each segment takes place throughout the audit. The final two steps are done near the end of the audit during the engagement completion phase.

The CICA Auditing Guideline "Applying Materiality and Audit Risk Concepts in Conducting an Audit" suggests an auditor is concerned with three levels of misstatement in assessing whether or not there is a material misstatement:

1. Identified misstatement (IM) – the actual misstatement discovered in the sample tested; it has not been corrected by management.

2. Likely misstatement – the actual misstatement in the sample plus the projection of the actual misstatement in the sample to the population; the misstatement has not been corrected by management. The sum of the likely misstatements in the financial statements is called the likely aggregate misstatement (LAM).

3. Further possible misstatements – the misstatements over and above the likely aggregate misstatement that result from the imprecision in the sampling process. The sum of likely aggregate misstatement plus further possible misstatements is called the maximum possible misstatement (MPM).

The auditor is sure of an identified misstatement because it was determined to be the misstatement in the sample. The projection of that error to the population – the likely misstatement – is based on the assumption the sample is representative of the population. The auditor is fairly certain about the likely misstatement when he or she is talking to the client about making an adjustment; if the likely misstatement exceeds materiality, the auditor will require an adjustment.

Further possible misstatement is based on the imprecision in the sampling process; the sample may not be representative or the auditor may misinterpret

FIGURE 8–1

Steps in Applying
Materiality

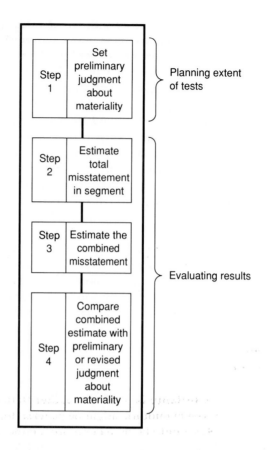

evidence.[1] The auditor recognizes that further possible misstatement is possible but not probable. It is more difficult to persuade the client to make an adjustment for further possible misstatement by virtue of its very definition. The auditor may or may not require an adjustment when the maximum possible misstatement, but not the likely aggregate misstatements, exceed materiality.[2]

**Set Preliminary
Judgment About
Materiality**

Ideally, an auditor decides early in the audit the combined amount of misstatements in the financial statements that would be considered material. Section 5130.30 states "The auditor should make preliminary decisions as to materiality . . . at the planning stage of the engagement"; this is the preliminary judgment about materiality in step 1 of Figure 8–1. This judgment need not be quantified but often is. It is called a preliminary judgment about materiality because it is a professional judgment and may change during the engagement if circumstances change.

The preliminary judgment about materiality is thus the maximum amount by which the auditor believes the statements could be misstated and still *not* affect the decisions of reasonable users. (Conceptually, this would be an amount that is

---

1 These two risks are called sampling risk and non-sampling risk respectively. They are discussed in detail in Chapter 12.

2 For a more extensive discussion of this topic see Leslie, Donald A., Teitlebaum, Albert D., and Anderson, Rodney J., *Dollar-Unit Sampling*, Toronto: Copp Clark Pitman, 1979, pp.19-23.

The lower $ ↑ Cost
The High $ ↓ Cost .

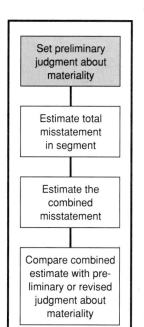

Set preliminary judgment about materiality

↓

Estimate total misstatement in segment

↓

Estimate the combined misstatement

↓

Compare combined estimate with preliminary or revised judgment about materiality

$1 less than materiality as defined in Section 5130. Preliminary materiality is defined in this manner as a convenience in application.) This judgment is one of the most important decisions the auditor makes. It requires considerable professional judgment.

The reason for setting a preliminary judgment about materiality is to help the auditor plan the appropriate evidence to accumulate. If the auditor sets a low dollar amount, more evidence is required than for a high amount. Examine again the financial statements of Hillsburg Hardware Ltd., on pages 133–134. What do you think is the combined amount of misstatements that would affect decisions of reasonable users? Do you believe a $100 misstatement would affect users' decisions? If so, the amount of evidence required for the audit is likely to be beyond that for which the management of Hillsburg Hardware can pay. Do you believe a $1 million misstatement would be material? Most experienced auditors would say that amount is far too large as a combined materiality amount.

The auditor may change the preliminary judgment about materiality during the audit. Whenever that is done, the new judgment is called a revised judgment about materiality. Reasons for using a revised judgment can include a change in one of the factors used to determine the preliminary judgment or a decision by the auditor that the preliminary judgment was too large or too small.

Factors Affecting Judgment

Several factors affect setting a preliminary judgment about materiality for a given set of financial statements. The most important of these are discussed below.

OBJECTIVE 2

Make a preliminary judgment about what amounts to consider material.

Materiality is a relative rather than an absolute concept A misstatement of a given magnitude might be material for a small company, whereas the same dollar error could be immaterial for a large one. For example, a total error of $1 million would be extremely material for Hillsburg Hardware Ltd., but it would be immaterial for a company such as Nova Corporation of Alberta. Hence, it is not possible to establish any dollar-value guidelines for a preliminary judgment about materiality applicable to all audit clients.

Bases are needed for evaluating materiality Since materiality is relative, it is necessary to have bases for establishing whether misstatements are material. The CICA Research Study *Materiality: The Concept and its Application to Auditing*[3] includes an extensive discussion of the methods auditors presently use to compute their preliminary judgments about materiality. The Auditing Guideline "Applying Materiality and Audit Risk Concepts in Conducting an Audit" also suggests bases. The suggested bases include:

1. 5 percent to 10 percent of net income before taxes. This number can be fairly volatile so most auditors use normalized net income (i.e., net income adjusted for unusual and non-recurring items such as a large inventory write-down) or average net income.
2. 1/2 percent to 5 percent of gross profit.
3. 1/2 percent to 1 percent of total assets.
4. 1/2 percent to 5 percent of shareholders' equity.
5. 1/2 percent to 1 percent of revenue.
6. The weighted average of methods 1 to 5.

---

3 Leslie, Donald A., *Materiality: The Concept and its Application to Auditing*, Toronto: CICA, 1985. pp.20-21.

7. A reducing percentage of the greater of revenue and assets.
8. 1/2 percent to 2 percent of expenses is suggested by the Guideline for non-profit entities.

[handwritten note in margin: Use 10% for small NI. 5% for large NI.]

Those methods that use a range of percentages generally require that the largest percentage be used for smaller dollar amounts and the smallest percentage be used for larger dollar amounts. For example, under method 1, 10 percent would be used if pre-tax net income was very small and 5 percent if it was very large; some percentage between 5 percent and 10 percent would be used for pre-tax net incomes between the two extremes.

Assume that for a given company, an auditor decided that a misstatement of income before taxes of $100,000 or more would be material, but a misstatement of $250,000 or more would be material for current assets. Section 5130.26 of the *CICA Handbook* suggests it would be inappropriate for the auditor to use a preliminary judgment about materiality of $250,000 for both income before taxes and current assets. The auditor must therefore plan to find all misstatements affecting income before taxes that exceed the preliminary judgment about materiality of $100,000. Since most errors affect both the income statement and balance sheet, the auditor will not be greatly concerned about the possibility of misstatement of current assets exceeding $250,000. However, some errors, such as misclassifying a long-term asset as a current one, affect only the balance sheet. The auditor will therefore also need to plan the audit with the $250,000 preliminary judgment about materiality for certain tests of current assets.

[handwritten note in margin: Reclassifying Notes Rec. To Boost Debt/Asset Ratio For Bank loan.]

Qualitative factors also affect materiality Certain types of misstatements are likely to be more important to users than others, even if the dollar amounts are the same. For example, amounts involving fraud and other irregularities are usually considered more important than unintentional errors of equal dollar amounts because fraud reflects on the honesty and reliability of the management or other personnel involved. To illustrate, most users would consider an intentional misstatement of inventory as being more important than clerical errors in inventory of the same dollar amount. In addition, while the amount of the fraud may be less than materiality, the impact of the fraud on the entity may be much in excess of materiality. For example, assume materiality for an entity with world-wide operations was $200,000. An illegal payment in another country of $25,000 would be less than materiality but could lead, if the illegal payment were to be discovered by the authorities in the other country, to fines or seizure of the entity's assets in that country that were many times the amount of the payment and much in excess of $200,000.

[handwritten note in margin: Higher Confidence level loss risk. ∴ more testing.]

Illustrative Guidelines

The CICA is currently unwilling to provide specific materiality guidelines to practitioners. The concern is that such guidelines might be applied without considering all the complexities that should affect the auditor's final decision. In addition, Leslie shows in *Materiality* that no single base works well in all situations.[4]

To show the application of materiality, illustrative guidelines are provided. They are intended only to help you better understand the concept of applying

---

4 See Leslie, Donald A., *Materiality: The Concept and its Application to Auditing*, Toronto: CICA, 1985, pp. 20-37.

FIGURE 8–2

Illustrative Materiality Guidelines

McCUTCHEON & WILKINSON,
CHARTERED ACCOUNTANTS
Edmonton, Alberta T6G 1N4
403/432-6900

POLICY STATEMENT   Sally J. Wilkinson
No. 32 IC   Karen McCutcheon
Title: Materiality Guidelines

Professional judgment is to be used at all times in setting and applying materiality guidelines. As a general guideline the following policies are to be applied:

1. The combined total of errors or fraud and other irregularities in the financial statements exceeding 10 percent is normally considered material. A combined total of less than 5 percent is presumed to be immaterial in the absence of qualitative factors. Combined errors or fraud between 5 percent and 10 percent require the greatest amount of professional judgment to determine their materiality.

2. The 5 percent to 10 percent must be measured in relation to the appropriate base. Many times there is more than one base to which errors should be compared. The following guides are recommended in selecting the appropriate base:
   a. *Income statement.* Combined misstatements in the income statement should ordinarily be measured at 5 percent to 10 percent of operating income before taxes. A guideline of 5 percent to 10 percent may be inappropriate in a year in which income is unusually large or small. When operating income in a given year is not considered representative, it is desirable to substitute as a base a more representative income measure. For example, average operating income for a three-year period may be used as the base.

      In the case of clients who operate in industries where operating income before taxes is not considered to be a useful base, $1/2$ percent to 1 percent of revenue will be used as a guideline.
   b. *Balance sheet.* Combined misstatements in the income statement should originally be evaluated for current assets, current liabilities, and total assets. For current assets and current liabilities, the guidelines should be between 3 percent and 6 percent, applied in the same way as for the income statement. For total assets the guideline should be between 1 percent and 2 percent, applied in the same way as for the income statement.

3. Qualitative factors should be carefully evaluated on all audits. In many instances they are more important than the guidelines applied to the income statement and balance sheet. The intended uses of the financial statements and the nature of the information on the statements, including footnotes, must be carefully evaluated.

4. If the guideline for the income statement is less than those selected for the balance sheet, the lesser amount should be used as a guideline for all misstatements that affect operating income before taxes. Misstatements such as misclassification errors would be evaluated using the greater amounts.

materiality in practice. The guidelines are stated in Figure 8–2 in the form of a policy guideline for a public accounting firm.

Application to Hillsburg Hardware Ltd.

Using the illustrative guidelines for McCutcheon & Wilkinson in Figure 8–2, it is now possible to decide on a preliminary judgment about materiality for Hillsburg Hardware Ltd. The guidelines are

	PRELIMINARY JUDGMENT ABOUT MATERIALITY			
	MINIMUM		MAXIMUM	
	Percentage	Dollar Amount	Percentage	Dollar Amount
Net revenue	$1/2$	36,000	1	72,000
Current assets	3	76,500	6	153,000
Total assets	1	31,000	2	61,000
Current liabilities	3	19,770	6	40,000

Assuming the auditor for Hillsburg Hardware decides the general guidelines are reasonable, the first step is to evaluate whether any qualitative factors significantly affect the materiality judgment. If not, the auditor must decide that if combined misstatements on the income statement were less than $36,000, the statements would be considered fairly stated. If the combined misstatements exceeded $72,000, the statements would not be considered fairly stated. If the misstatements were between $36,000 and $72,000, a more careful consideration of all facts would be required. The auditor then applies the same process to the other three bases. Given the suggested guidelines calculated above, the auditor would probably decide to use $31,000 to $61,000 as the preliminary judgment about materiality.

Dollar-unit Sampling[5] suggests that the preliminary judgment about materiality be adjusted for the effect of *net anticipated* misstatements to determine materiality available for unanticipated misstatements.

The illustration that follows is an example of adjusting for the effect of net anticipated misstatements:

Preliminary judgment about materiality		$150,000
Less		
Anticipated misstatements from specific tests	$20,000	
Carry forward misstatements from the previous year	30,000	
Anticipated client corrections	(15,000)	35,000
Materiality available for unanticipated misstatements		$115,000

The auditor, in the above example, is simply reducing the preliminary judgment of $150,000 for net anticipated misstatements of $35,000 to determine that $115,000 will be available for unanticipated misstatements. A useful analogy would be that of an individual going on a date who has $60.00 for dinner and a show, but needs $10.00 for cab fare at the end of the evening. The amount available for spending for the evening is $50.00, not $60.00. Similarly the amount available for unanticipated misstatements is really $115,000, not $150,000.

Some auditors allocate materiality to segments once they have determined materiality available for unanticipated misstatements. They use the amounts allo-

5 Leslie, Donald A., Teitlebaum, Albert D., and Anderson, Rodney J., *Dollar-unit Sampling*, Toronto: Copp Clark Pitman, 1979, pp. 178-179.

FIGURE 8–3

Illustration of Comparison of Maximum Possible Misstatement to Preliminary Judgment About Materiality

	MAXIMUM POSSIBLE MISSTATEMENT		
ACCOUNT	Likely Misstatement	Sampling Error	Total
Cash	0	NA	0
Accounts receivable	12,000	6,000	18,000
Inventory	31,500	15,750	47,250
Total estimated misstatement amount	$43,500	$16,800	$60,300
Preliminary judgment about materiality			$50,000

NA = Not applicable

cated to determine sample sizes and the amount of testing required. However, most auditors use materiality available for unanticipated misstatements in audit planning on the grounds that the auditor is concerned about the aggregate misstatement in the financial statements as a whole and not in the misstatement in a particular account balance.

Estimate Misstatement and Compare

The first step in applying materiality involves planning, whereas the last three (steps 2, 3, and 4 in Figure 8–1) result from performing audit tests. The last three steps are discussed in greater detail in later chapters; this section only shows their relationship to the first step.

When the auditor performs audit procedures for each segment of the audit, a worksheet is kept of all misstatements found. For example, assume the auditor finds six client errors in a sample of 200 in testing inventory costs (identified misstatement). These misstatements are used to estimate the *total* misstatements in inventory (step 2). The total is referred to as an estimate or often a "projection" because only a sample, rather than the entire population, was audited. The projected misstatement amounts (likely misstatements) for each account are combined on the worksheet (step 3), and then the combined misstatement (likely aggregate misstatement) is compared to materiality (step 4).

Figure 8–3 is used to illustrate the last three steps in applying materiality. For simplicity, only three accounts are included and the calculation of likely misstatements for accounts receivable and for inventory are shown. The preliminary judgment about materiality is $50,000. The likely misstatements are calculated based on actual audit tests. Assume, for example, that in auditing inventory, the auditor found $3,500 of net overstatement errors in a sample of $50,000 of the total population of $450,000. One way to calculate the estimate of the misstatements is to make a direct projection from the sample to the population and add an estimate for sampling error (further possible misstatements). The calculation of the direction projection is net errors in the sample ($3,500) ÷ total sampled ($50,000) × total recorded population value ($450,000) = direct projection estimate ($31,500). The estimate for sampling error results because the auditor has sampled only a portion of the population (this is discussed in detail in Chapters 12 and 14). In this simplified example, the estimate for sampling error is assumed to be 50 percent of the direct projection of the misstatement amounts for the accounts where sampling was used (accounts receivable and inventory).

Assume the error in the sample for accounts receivable (population $385,000) was $1,325; the total sampled was $42,500. The direct projection estimate or likely misstatement is [($1,325) ÷ ($42,500) × ($385,000)] $12,000.

OBJECTIVE 3

Use materiality to evaluate audit findings.

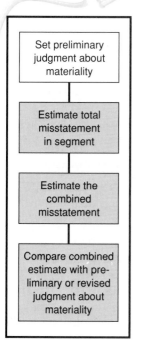

Set preliminary judgment about materiality

Estimate total misstatement in segment

Estimate the combined misstatement

Compare combined estimate with preliminary or revised judgment about materiality

In combining the errors in Figure 8–3, observe that the likely misstatements or direct projection errors for the three accounts add to $43,500. The total sampling error, however, is less than the sum of the individual sampling errors. This is because sampling error represents the maximum error in account details not audited. It is unlikely that this maximum error amount would exist in all accounts subjected to sampling. Thus, sampling methodology provides for determining a combined sampling error that takes this into consideration. Again, this is discussed in detail in Chapters 12 and 14.

Figure 8–3 shows that maximum possible misstatement for the three accounts of $60,300 exceeds the preliminary judgment about materiality of $50,000. Furthermore, the major area of difficulty is inventory, where the maximum possible misstatement is $47,250. Because the estimated maximum possible misstatement exceeds the preliminary judgment, the financial statements are not acceptable. The auditor can either determine whether the estimated aggregate misstatement actually exceeds $50,000 by performing additional audit procedures or require the client to make an adjustment for likely misstatements. Assuming additional audit procedures are performed, they would be concentrated in the inventory area.

If the estimated maximum possible misstatement for inventory had been $33,000 ($22,000 plus $11,000 sampling error), the auditor probably would not need to expand audit tests, since the total maximum possible misstatement was near the $50,000 preliminary judgement. It is likely that the auditor would have accepted the balances in the three amounts since the aggregate likely misstatement was only $34,000.

Risk

Risk in auditing means that the auditor accepts some level of uncertainty in performing the audit function. The auditor recognizes, for example, that there is uncertainty about the appropriateness of evidence, uncertainty about the effectiveness of a client's internal control, and uncertainty as to whether the financial statements are fairly stated when the audit is completed.

> **OBJECTIVE 4**
>
> Define risk in auditing.

An effective auditor recognizes that risks exist and deals with those risks in an appropriate manner. Most risks auditors encounter are difficult to measure and require careful thought to respond to appropriately. For example, assume the auditor determines that the client's industry is undergoing significant technological changes which affect both the client and the client's customers. This change may affect the obsolescence of the client's inventory, collectibility of accounts receivable, and perhaps even the ability of the client's business to continue. Responding to these risks properly is critical to achieving a quality audit.

The remainder of this chapter deals mostly with the risks that affect planning the engagement to determine the appropriate evidence to accumulate by applying the CICA's audit risk model. It concludes by showing the relationship between materiality and risk.

Illustration Concerning Risks and Evidence

Before discussing the audit risk model, an illustration, for a hypothetical company, is provided in Figure 8–4 as a frame of reference for the discussion. The illustration first shows that there are differences among cycles in the frequency and size of expected misstatements (A). For example, there are almost no misstatements expected in payroll and personnel, but many in inventory and warehous-

FIGURE 8—4   Illustration of Differing Evidence among Cycles

		SALES AND COLLECTION CYCLE	ACQUISITION AND PAYMENT CYCLE	PAYROLL AND PERSONNEL CYCLE	INVENTORY AND WAREHOUSING CYCLE	CAPITAL AND ACQUISITION REPAYMENT CYCLE
A	Auditor's assessment of expectation of material misstatement before considering internal control (inherent risk)	Expect some misstatements (medium)	Expect many misstatements (high)	Expect few misstatements (low)	Expect many misstatements (high)	Expect few misstatements (low)
B	Auditor's assessment of effectiveness of internal control to prevent or detect material misstatements (control risk)	Medium effectiveness (medium)	High effectiveness (low)	High effectiveness (low)	Low effectiveness (high)	Medium effectiveness (medium)
C	Auditor's willingness to permit material misstatements to exist after completing the audit (audit risk)	Low willingness (low)	Low willingness (low)	Low willingness (low)	Low willingness (low)	Low willingness (low)
D	Extent of evidence the auditor plans to accumulate (planned detection-risk)	Medium level (medium)	Medium level (medium)	Low level (high)	High level (low)	Medium level (medium)

ing. The reason may be that the payroll transactions are highly routine whereas there may be considerable complexities in recording inventory. Similarly, internal control is believed to differ in effectiveness among the five cycles (B). For example, internal controls in payroll and personnel are considered highly effective whereas those in inventory and warehousing are considered ineffective. Finally, the auditor has decided on a low willingness that material misstatements exist after the audit is complete for all five cycles (C). It is common for auditors to want an equally low likelihood of misstatements for each cycle after the audit is finished to permit the issuance of an unqualified opinion.

The previous considerations (A, B, C) affect the auditor's decision about the appropriate extent of evidence to accumulate (D). For example, because the auditor expects few misstatements in payroll and personnel (A) and internal control is effective (B), the auditor plans for less evidence (D) than for inventory and warehousing. Notice that the auditor has the same level of willingness to accept material misstatements after the audit is finished for all five cycles, but a different extent of evidence is needed for various cycles. The difference is caused by differences in the auditor's expectations of misstatements and assessment of internal control.

Audit Risk Model

The primary way that auditors deal with risk in planning audit evidence is through the application of the audit risk model. The source of the audit risk model is the professional literature in the *CICA Handbook* in Section 5130, "Materiality and Audit Risk in Conducting an Audit" and in the Auditing Guideline "Applying Materiality and Audit Risk Concepts in Conducting an Audit." A thorough understanding of the model is essential to effective auditing and to the study of the remaining chapters of this book.

The audit risk model is used primarily for planning purposes in deciding how much evidence to accumulate in each cycle. It is usually stated as follows:

OBJECTIVE 5

Describe the audit risk model and its components.

(handwritten top right): The lower PDR the more planned evidence needed. → How much the audit will uncover.

(handwritten left):
Plan Detection Risk. (PDR)
Audit risk — AR
Internal risk — IR
Control risk — CR

$$PDR = \frac{AR}{IR \times CR}$$

where

PDR = planned detection risk (also referred to as DR, detection risk)
AR = audit risk
IR = inherent risk
CR = control risk

A numerical example is provided for discussion, even though it is not practical in practice to measure as precisely as these numbers imply. The numbers used are for the inventory and warehousing cycle in Figure 8–4.

$$IR = 100\%$$
$$CR = 100\%$$
$$AR = 5\%$$
$$PDR = \frac{.05}{1.0 \times 1.0} = .05 = 5\%$$

(handwritten: Test)

Planned Detection Risk

(handwritten: Wee can use this? → Auditor controls)

(handwritten box: PDR ↓ PE↑ ; PDR ↑ PE↓)

Planned detection risk is a measure of the risk that audit evidence for a segment will fail to detect errors or fraud and other irregularities exceeding a tolerable amount, should such errors or fraud exist. There are two key points about planned detection risk: first, it is dependent on the other three factors in the model. Planned detection risk will change only if the auditor changes one of the other factors. Second, it determines the amount of evidence the auditor plans to accumulate, inversely with the size of planned detection risk. If planned detection risk is reduced, the auditor needs to accumulate more evidence to achieve the reduced planned risk. For example, in Figure 8–4 (D) planned detection risk is low for inventory and warehousing which causes planned evidence to be high. The opposite is true for payroll and personnel.

The planned detection risk of .05 in the numerical example above means the auditor plans to accumulate evidence until the risk of misstatements exceeding tolerable misstatement is reduced to 5 percent. If control risk had been .50 instead of 1.0, planned detection risk would be .10 and planned evidence could therefore be reduced.

Inherent Risk

(handwritten: → Client controls)

(handwritten: Risk an error will occur)

Inherent risk is a measure of the auditor's assessment of the likelihood that a material misstatement might occur in the first place, that is, before considering the effectiveness of internal accounting controls. Inherent risk is the susceptibility of the financial statements to material misstatement, assuming no internal controls. If the auditor concludes that there is a high likelihood of misstatement, ignoring internal controls, the auditor would conclude that inherent risk is high. Internal controls are ignored in setting inherent risk because they are considered separately in the audit risk model as control risk. In Figure 8–4 inherent risk (A) would be assessed high for inventory and lower for payroll and personnel and capital acquisitions and repayments. The assessment would likely be based on discussions with management, knowledge of the company, and results in prior year audits.

The relationship of detection risk and planned evidence to inherent risk is that detection risk is inversely related to inherent risk and thus evidence is

(handwritten margin: IR↑ PDR↑ ; Good PE↑ ; IR↓ PDR↓ PE↑ ; Who controls / Even risk)

directly related to inherent risk. Inherent risk for inventory in Figure 8–4 is high, and in the numerical example 1.0, which will result in a lower planned detection risk and more planned evidence than would be necessary had inherent risk been lower. Inherent risk is examined in greater detail later in the chapter.

→ Management function. (Client controls)

Control Risk

Control risk is a measure of the auditor's assessment of the likelihood that misstatements exceeding a tolerable amount in a segment will not be prevented or detected by the client's internal control. Control risk represents (1) an assessment of whether a client's internal control is effective for preventing or detecting errors or fraud and other irregularities, and (2) the auditor's intention to make that assessment at a level below the maximum (100 percent) as part of the audit plan. For example, assume the auditor concludes that internal control is completely ineffective to prevent or detect errors. That is the likely conclusion for inventory and warehousing in Figure 8–4 (B). The auditor would therefore assign a 100 percent risk factor to control risk. The more effective internal control, the lower the risk factor that *could* be assigned to control risk.

As with inherent risk, the relationship between control risk and detection risk is inverse, whereas the relationship between control risk and evidence is direct. For example, if the auditor concludes that internal controls are effective, planned detection risk can be increased and evidence therefore decreased. The auditor can increase planned detection risk when controls are effective because effective internal control reduces the likelihood of misstatements in the financial statements.

Before auditors can use a control risk of less than the maximum level of 100 percent, they must do three things: obtain an understanding of the client's internal control, evaluate how well it should function based on the understanding, and test internal control for effectiveness. The first of these is the *understanding* requirement that relates to all audits. The latter two are the *assessment of control risk* steps that are required when the auditor *chooses* to assess control risk at a level below the maximum.

Understanding internal control, assessing control risk, and their impact on evidence requirements are so important that the entire next chapter is devoted to that topic. However, it should be noted here that if the auditor elects not to assess control risk below the maximum level, control risk must be set at 100 percent regardless of the actual effectiveness of the underlying internal control. Use of the audit risk model in this circumstance then causes the auditor to control audit risk entirely through a low level of detection risk (assuming inherent risk is high).

Audit Risk

Audit risk is a measure of how willing the auditor is to accept that the financial statements may be materially misstated after the audit is completed and an unqualified opinion has been reached.[6] It is the subjectively determined risk that the auditor is willing to take that the *financial statements are not fairly stated after the audit is completed and an unqualified opinion has been reached.* When the auditor decides on a lower audit risk, it means the auditor wants to be more certain that the financial statements are *not* materially misstated. Zero risk would be certainty, and a 100 percent risk would be complete uncertainty (or a material

---

6 "The Parable of Bert and Ernie" by Stephen Aldersley in *CA Magazine* (March 1988), pp. 60-61, illustrates two different audit situations where the risk of misstatements occuring is similar but where the consequences of failing to detect the misstatements are quite different.

[handwritten notes at top: Only Accept 2% risk i.e. I Am 98% Sure they are correctly Stated.]

[handwritten notes in left margin: AR ↑ PDR ↑ PE ↓ ... CR ↓ PDR ↓ PE ↑]

misstatement with probability 1.0). Complete assurance (zero risk) of the accuracy of the financial statements is not economically practical. It has already been established in Chapter 5 that the auditor cannot guarantee the complete absence of material errors or fraud and other irregularities.

Frequently auditors refer to the terms *audit assurance, overall assurance,* or *level of assurance* instead of audit risk. Audit assurance or any of the equivalent terms is the complement of audit risk, that is, one minus audit risk. For example, audit risk of 2 percent is the same as audit assurance of 98 percent.

The concept of audit risk can be more easily understood by thinking in terms of a large number of audits, say, 10,000. What portion of these audits could include material errors without having an adverse effect on society? Certainly, the portion would be below 10 percent. It is probably much closer to one or one-half of 1 percent or perhaps even one-tenth of 1 percent. If an auditor believes the appropriate percentage for a given audit is 1 percent, then audit risk should be set at 1 percent.

Using the audit risk model, there is a <u>direct</u> relationship between audit risk and planned detection risk, and an inverse relationship between audit risk and planned evidence. For example, if the auditor decides to reduce audit risk, detection risk is thereby reduced and planned evidence must be increased.

Changing Audit Risk for Business Risk

OBJECTIVE 6

Consider the impact of business risk on audit risk.

Business risk is the risk that the auditor or audit firm will suffer harm, which Section 5130.15 describes as "risk of loss or injury to his or her professional practice from litigation, adverse publicity, or other events," because of a client relationship, even though the audit report rendered for the client was correct. For example, if a client declares bankruptcy after an audit is completed, there is a strong likelihood of a lawsuit against the public accounting firm even if the quality of the audit was good.

There is a difference of opinion among auditors as to whether business risk should be considered in planning the audit. Opponents of modifying the amount of evidence collected to account for business risk contend that auditors do not provide audit opinions with different levels of assurance and, therefore, should not provide more or less assurance because of business risk. Proponents contend that it is appropriate for auditors to accumulate additional evidence on audits where legal exposure is high as long as the assurance level is not decreased below a reasonably high level, even when there is low business risk.

When auditors modify evidence for business risk, it is done by control of audit risk. The authors believe a reasonably low audit risk is always desirable, but in some circumstances an even lower risk is needed because of business risk factors. Research has indicated several factors affect business risk and therefore audit risk. Only two of those are discussed here: the degree to which external users rely on the statements and the likelihood that a client will have financial difficulties after the audit report is issued.

The degree to which external users rely on the statements   When external users place heavy reliance on the financial statements, it is appropriate that audit risk be decreased. When the statements are heavily relied on, a great social harm could result if a material misstatement were to remain undetected in the financial statements. The cost of additional evidence can be more easily justified when the loss to users from material misstatements is substantial. Several factors are good indicators of the degree to which statements are relied on by external users:

- *Client's size*. Generally speaking, the larger a client's operations, the more widely used the statements will be. The client's size, measured by total assets or total revenues, will have an effect on audit risk.
- *Distribution of ownership*. The statements of publicly held corporations are normally relied on by many more users than those of private or closely held corporations. For these companies, the interested parties include the provincial securities administrators such as the Alberta Securities Commission, perhaps even the SEC, financial analysts, creditors, suppliers, the government, and the general public.
- *Nature and amount of liabilities*. When statements include a large amount of liabilities, they are more likely to be used extensively by actual and potential creditors than when there are few liabilities.

The likelihood that a client will have financial difficulties after the audit report is issued   If a client is forced to file for bankruptcy or suffers a significant loss after completion of the audit, there is a greater chance of the auditor being required to defend the quality of the audit than if the client were under no financial strain. There is a natural tendency for those who lose money in a bankruptcy or because of a stock price reversal to file suit against the auditor. This can result from the honest belief that the auditor failed to conduct an adequate audit or from the users' desire to recover part of their loss regardless of the adequacy of the audit work.

In situations in which the auditor believes the chance of financial failure or loss is high, and there is a corresponding increase in business risk for the auditor, the acceptable level of audit risk should be reduced. If a subsequent challenge does occur, the auditor will then be in a better position to defend the audit results successfully. The total audit evidence and costs will increase, but this is justifiable because of the additional risk of lawsuits the auditor faces.

It is difficult for an auditor to predict financial failure before it occurs, but certain factors are good indicators of its increased probability:

- *Liquidity position*. If a client is constantly short of cash and working capital, it indicates a future problem in paying bills. The auditor must assess the likelihood and significance of a weak liquidity position getting worse.
- *Profits (losses) in previous years*. When a company has rapidly declining profits or increasing losses for several years, the auditor should recognize the future solvency problems the client is likely to encounter. It is also important to consider the changing profits relative to the balance remaining in retained earnings.
- *Method of financing growth*. The more a client relies on debt as a means of financing, the greater the risk of financial difficulty if the client's operations become less successful. It is also important to evaluate whether permanent assets are being financed with short-term or long-term loans. Large amounts of required cash outflows during a short period of time can force a company into bankruptcy.
- *Nature of the client's operations*. Certain types of businesses are inherently riskier than others. For example, other things being equal, there is a much greater likelihood of bankruptcy of a stockbroker than of a utility.
- *Competence of management*. Competent management is constantly alert for potential financial difficulties and modifies its operating methods to minimize the effects of short-run problems. The ability of management must be assessed as a part of the evaluation of the likelihood of bankruptcy.

The auditor must investigate the client and assess the importance of each of the factors affecting the degree to which external users rely on the statements and the likelihood of the client's financial failure subsequent to the audit. Based on this investigation and assessment, the auditor should be able to set a tentative and highly subjective level of risk that the financial statements will include a material misstatement after the audit is completed. As the audit progresses, additional information about the client is obtained and the level of audit risk may be modified.

Inherent Risk

The inclusion of inherent risk in the audit risk model is one of the most important concepts in auditing. It implies that auditors should attempt to predict where misstatements are most and least likely in the financial statement segments. This information affects the total amount of evidence the auditor is required to accumulate and influences how the auditor's efforts to gather the evidence are allocated among the segments of the audit.

There is always some risk that the client has made misstatements that are individually or collectively large enough to make the financial statements misleading. The misstatements can be intentional or unintentional and they can affect the dollar balance in accounts or disclosure. Inherent risk can be low in some instances and extremely high in others.

The audit risk model shows the close relationship between inherent and control risks. For example, an inherent risk of 40 percent and a control risk of 60 percent affect detection risk and planned evidence the same as an inherent risk of 60 percent and a control risk of 40 percent. In both cases, multiplying IR by CR results in a denominator in the audit risk model of 24 percent. The combination of inherent risk and control risk can be thought of as the *expectation of misstatements after considering the effect of internal controls*. Inherent risk is the expectation of misstatements before considering the effect of internal controls.

At the start of the audit, there is not much that can be done about changing inherent risk. Instead, the auditor must *assess the factors* that make up the risk and *modify audit evidence* to take them into consideration. The auditor should consider several major factors when assessing inherent risk:

> **OBJECTIVE 7**
>
> Consider the impact of several factors on the assessment of inherent risk.

- Nature of the client's business including the nature of the client's products and services
- Integrity of management
- Client motivation
- Results of previous audits
- Initial versus repeat engagement
- Related parties
- Nonroutine transactions
- Judgment required to correctly record account balances and transactions
- Assets that are susceptible to misappropriation
- Makeup of the population

Nature of the Client's Business

Inherent risk for certain accounts is affected by the nature of the client's business. For example, there is a greater likelihood of obsolete inventory for an electronics manufacturer than for a steel fabricator. Similarly, loans receivable for a small loan company that makes unsecured loans are less likely to be collectible than those of a bank which makes only secured loans. Inherent risk is most likely to vary from business to business for accounts such as inventory, accounts and loans receivable, and property, plant, and equipment. The nature of the client's business should have little or no effect on inherent risk for accounts such as cash, notes, and mortgages payable.

Integrity of Management

When management is dominated by one or a few individuals who lack integrity, the likelihood of significantly misrepresented financial statements is greatly increased. For example, a lack of integrity of management has been found to exist in the great majority of significant accountants' liability cases. Auditors take substantial legal and professional risks when they do audits for clients lacking in integrity, and many public accounting firms will not do audits for such clients.

Frequently, management has a reasonable level of integrity but cannot be regarded as completely honest in all dealings. For example, management may deduct capital items as repairs and maintenance expense on tax returns, or a decision might be made not to inform a customer of a duplicate payment received. The public accounting firm should first evaluate whether it wants to do an audit for such a client. If the decision is made to do so, a high level of inherent risk may be necessary in *all* areas of the engagement to test for the possibility of intentional misstatements.

Client Motivation

In many situations, management may believe that it would be advantageous to misstate the financial statements. For example, if management receives a percentage of total profits as a bonus, there may be a tendency to overstate net income. Similarly, if a bond indenture requirement includes a specification that the current ratio must remain above a certain level, the client may be tempted to overstate current assets or to understate current liabilities by an amount sufficient to meet the requirement. Also, there may be considerable motivation for intentional understatement of income when management wants the company to pay less income taxes. If management lacks integrity, some specific type of motivation may then lead them to misstate financial reports.

Results of Previous Audits

Errors found in the previous year's audit have a high likelihood of occurring again in the current year's audit. This is because many types of errors are systemic in nature, and organizations are often slow in making changes to eliminate them. Therefore, an auditor would be negligent if the results of the preceding year's examination were ignored during the development of the current year's audit program. For example, if the auditor found a significant number of errors in pricing inventory, inherent risk would likely be high, and extensive testing would have to be done in the current audit as a means of determining whether the deficiency in the client's system had been corrected. If, however, the auditor has found no errors for the past several years in conducting tests of an audit area, the auditor is justified in reducing inherent risk, provided that changes in relevant circumstances have not occurred.

Initial Versus Repeat Engagement

Auditors gain experience and knowledge about the likelihood of misstatements after auditing a client for several years. The lack of previous years' audit results would cause most auditors to use a larger inherent risk for initial audits than for repeat engagements in which no material misstatements had been found. Most auditors set a high inherent risk in the first year of an audit and reduce it in subsequent years as they gain experience.

Related Parties Transactions between parent and subsidiary companies and those between management and the corporate entity are examples of related-party transactions as defined by the *CICA Handbook*'s Section 3840, "Related Party Transactions – Disclosure Considerations". These transactions do not occur between two independent parties dealing at "arm's length." Therefore, a greater likelihood exists of their misstatement, which should cause an increase in inherent risk.

Nonroutine Transactions Transactions that are unusual for the client are more likely to be incorrectly recorded by the client than routine transactions because the client lacks experience in recording them. Examples include fire losses, major property acquisitions, and lease agreements.

Judgment Required to Correctly Record Account Balances and Transactions Many account balances require estimates and a great deal of management judgment. Examples are allowance for uncollectible accounts receivable, obsolete inventory, liability for warranty payments, and bank loan loss reserves. Similarly, transactions for major repairs or partial replacement of assets are examples where considerable judgment is needed to correctly record the information.

Properly recording such items requires both knowledge and skill regarding the substance of the item and the related accounting theory. The inherent risk pertaining to material account balances and transactions involving a great deal of judgment is almost always high.

Assets that are Susceptible to Misappropriation The auditor should be concerned about the risk of possible defalcation in situations in which it is relatively easy to convert company assets to personal use. Such is the case when currency, marketable securities, or highly marketable inventory are not closely controlled. When the likelihood of defalcation is high, inherent risk is increased.

Makeup of the Population The individual items making up the total population also frequently affect the auditor's expectation of material misstatement. For example, most auditors would use a higher inherent risk for accounts receivable where most accounts are significantly overdue than when most accounts are current. Similarly, the potential for misstatements in inventory purchased several years ago would normally be greater than for inventory purchased in the past few months. Transactions with affiliated companies, amounts due from officers, cash disbursements made payable to cash, and accounts receivable outstanding for several months are examples of situations requiring a larger inherent risk and therefore greater investigation because there is usually a higher likelihood of misstatement than in more typical transactions.

Assessing Inherent Risk The auditor must evaluate the preceding factors and decide on an appropriate inherent risk factor for each cycle, account, and many times for each audit objective.[7] In doing this some factors, such as the integrity of management,

---

7 Recall from Chapter 5 that management makes assertions in recording and disclosing information in the financial statements and that the audit objectives follow and are closely linked to management's assertions. When the auditor talks about evaluating inherent risk at the audit objective level, he or she is also referring to the assertion level. For example, if the auditor assesses inherent risk as high for the completeness objective, he or she is also assessing it as high for the completion assertion.

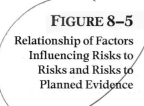

FIGURE 8–5

Relationship of Factors Influencing Risks to Risks and Risks to Planned Evidence

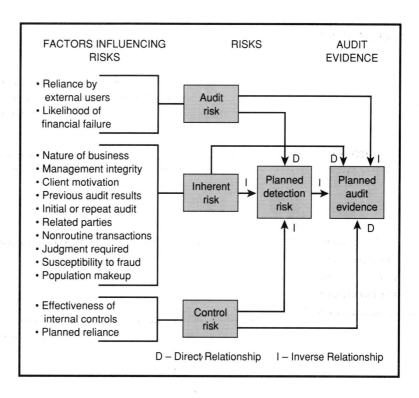

will affect many or perhaps all cycles, whereas others, such as nonroutine transactions, will affect only specific accounts or audit objectives. Although the profession has not established standards or guidelines for setting inherent risk, the authors believe auditors are generally conservative in making such assessments. Most auditors would probably set inherent risk at well above 50 percent, even in the best of circumstances, and at 100 percent when there is any reasonable possibility of significant misstatements. For example, assume that in the audit of inventory the auditor notes that (1) a large number of errors were found in the previous year and (2) inventory turnover has slowed in the current year. Many auditors would probably set inherent risk at a relatively high level (some would use 100 percent) for each audit objective for inventory in this situation.

Summary of Risks

OBJECTIVE 8

Discuss the relationships among the components of risk.

Figure 8–5 summarizes the factors that determine each of the risks, the relationship between the three component risks that determine detection risk to planned detection risk, and the relationship of all four risks to planned audit evidence. D in the figure indicates a direct relationship between a component risk and planned detection risk or planned evidence. I indicates an inverse relationship. For example, an increase in audit risk results in an increase in planned detection risk (D) and a decrease in planned audit evidence (I). Compare Figure 8–5 to Figure 8–4 on page 243 and observe that these two figures include the same concepts.

Other Materiality and Risk Considerations

Audit Risk for Segments

OBJECTIVE 9

Discuss risk for segments and measurement difficulties.

Both control risk and inherent risk are typically estimated for each cycle, each account and often even each audit objective (see footnote 7), not for the overall audit, and are likely to vary from cycle to cycle, account to account, and audit objective to audit objective on the same audit. Internal controls may be more effective for inventory-related accounts than those related to fixed assets. Control risk would therefore also be different for different accounts depending on the effectiveness of the controls. Factors affecting inherent risk, such as susceptibility to defalcation and routineness of the transactions, are also likely to differ from account to account. For that reason, it is normal to have inherent risk vary for different accounts in the same audit unless there is some strong overriding factor of concern, such as management integrity. The same considerations also apply with respect to audit objectives; the inherent or control risk could be different for the valuation objective for inventory than for the classification objective.

Audit risk is ordinarily set by the auditor for the entire audit and held constant for each major cycle and account. For example, assume the auditor sets audit risk at a medium level because of a limited number of users of the financial statements and previous normal operating profits. The auditor would likely use a medium audit risk for the audit of inventory, accounts receivable, fixed assets, and all other major accounts. Auditors normally use the same audit risk for each segment because the factors affecting audit risk are related to the entire audit, not individual accounts. For example, the extent financial statements are relied on for users' decisions are usually related to the overall financial statements, not just one or two accounts.

In some cases, however, a *lower* audit risk may be more appropriate for one account than for others. In the previous example, even though the auditor decided to use an audit risk of medium for the audit as a whole, the auditor might decide to reduce audit risk to low for inventory if inventory is used as collateral for a short-term loan.

Because control risk and inherent risk vary from cycle to cycle, account to account, or audit objective to audit objective, detection risk and required audit evidence will also vary. This conclusion should not be surprising. The circumstances of each engagement are different, and the extent of evidence needed will depend on the unique circumstances. For example, inventory might require extensive testing on an engagement due to weak internal controls and concern about obsolescence due to technological changes in the industry. On the same engagement, accounts receivable may require little testing because of effective internal controls, fast collection of receivables, excellent relationships between the client and customers, and good audit results in previous years. Similarly, for a given audit of inventory, an auditor may assess that there is a higher inherent risk of a valuation error because of the higher potential for obsolescence, but a low inherent risk of a classification error because there is only purchased inventory.

Relating Risks to Audit Objectives

It is common in practice to assess inherent and control risks for each objective. Auditors are able to effectively associate most risks with different objectives. It is reasonably easy to determine the relationship between a risk and one or two objectives. For example, obsolescence in inventory would be unlikely to affect any objective other than valuation.

TABLE 8–1

Relationships of Risk to Evidence

SITUATION	AUDIT RISK	INHERENT RISK	CONTROL RISK	DETECTION RISK	AMOUNT OF EVIDENCE REQUIRED
1	High	Low	Low	High	Low
2	Low	Low	Low	Medium	Medium
3	Low	High	High	Low	High
4	Medium	Medium	Medium	Medium	Medium
5	High	Low	Medium	Medium	Medium

Measurement Limitations

One major limitation in the application of the audit risk model is the difficulty of measuring the components of the model.[8] In spite of the auditor's best efforts in planning, the assessments of audit risk, inherent risk, and control risk and therefore planned detection risk are highly subjective and are approximations of reality at best. Imagine, for example, attempting to assess precisely inherent risk by determining the impact of factors such as the errors discovered in prior years' audits and technology changes in the client's industry.

To offset this measurement problem, many auditors use broad and subjective measurement terms, for example, "low," "medium," and "high." Table 8–1 shows how auditors can use the information to decide on the appropriate amount of evidence to accumulate. For example, in situation 1, the auditor has decided to accept a high audit risk for an account or objective. The auditor has concluded that there is a low risk of misstatement in the statements and that internal controls are effective. Therefore, a high detection risk is appropriate. As a result, a low level of evidence is needed. Situation 3 is at the opposite extreme. If both inherent and control risks are high, but the auditor wants a low audit risk, considerable evidence is required. The other three situations fall between the two extremes.

It is equally difficult to measure the amount of evidence implied by a given planned detection risk. A typical audit program that is intended to reduce detection risk to the planned level is a combination of several audit procedures, each using a different type of evidence which is applied to different audit objectives. Auditor's measurement methods are too imprecise to permit an accurate quantitative measure of the combined evidence. Instead, auditors subjectively evaluate whether sufficient evidence has been planned to satisfy a planned detection risk of low, medium, or high. Presumably, measurement methods are sufficient to permit an auditor to know that more evidence is needed to satisfy a low planned detection risk than for medium or high. Considerable professional judgment is needed to decide how much more.

In applying the audit risk model, auditors are concerned about both over- and underauditing, but most auditors are more concerned about the latter. Underauditing exposes the public accounting firm to legal liability and loss of professional reputation.

Because of the concern to avoid underauditing, auditors typically assess risks conservatively. For example, an auditor might not assess either control risk or inherent risk below .5 even when the likelihood of error is low. In these audits, a low risk might be .5, medium .8, and high 1.0, if the risks are quantified.

---

8 The interested reader is referred to Cushing, Barry E. and Loebbecke, James K., "Analytical Approaches to Audit Risk: A Survey and Analysis," *Auditing: A Journal of Practice and Theory* (Fall, 1983), P. 23-41.

Revising Risks and Evidence

The audit risk model is a *planning* model, and it is therefore of limited use in evaluating results. Great care must be used in revising the risk factors when the actual results are not as favorable as planned.

No difficulties occur when the auditor accumulates planned evidence and concludes that the assessment of each of the risks was reasonable or better than originally thought. The auditor will conclude that sufficient appropriate audit evidence has been collected for that account or cycle.

Special care must be exercised when the auditor decides, on the basis of accumulated evidence, that the original assessment of control risk or inherent risk was understated or audit risk was overstated. In such a circumstance, the auditor should follow a two-step approach. First, the auditor must revise the original assessment of the appropriate risk. It would violate due care to leave the original assessment unchanged if the auditor knows it is inappropriate. Second, the auditor should consider the effect of the revision on evidence requirements, *without the use of the audit risk model*. Research in auditing has shown that if a revised risk is used in the audit risk model to determine a revised planned detection risk, there is a danger of not increasing the evidence sufficiently. Instead, the auditor should carefully evaluate the implication of the revision of the risk and modify evidence appropriately, outside of the audit risk model. An example is used to illustrate revision of a factor in the audit risk model. Assume the auditor confirms accounts receivable and, based on the errors found, concludes that the original control risk assessment as low was inappropriate. The auditor should revise the estimate of control risk upward and carefully consider the effect of the revision on the additional evidence needed in the sales and collection cycle. That should be done without using the audit risk model to recalculate planned detection risk.

Relationship of Materiality and Risk and Audit Evidence

The concepts of materiality and risk in auditing are closely related and inseparable. Materiality is a measure of magnitude or size while risk is a measure of uncertainty. Taken together they measure the uncertainty of amounts of a given magnitude. For example, the statement that the auditor plans to accumulate evidence such that there is only a 5 percent risk (detection risk) of failing to uncover misstatements exceeding materiality of $25,000 (materiality), if such misstatements exist, is a precise and meaningful statement. If the statement eliminates either the risk or materiality portion, it would be meaningless. A 5 percent risk without a specific materiality measure could imply a $100 or $1 million misstatement is acceptable. A $25,000 overstatement without a specific risk could imply a 1 percent or 80 percent risk is acceptable.

As a general rule, there is a fixed relationship between materiality, risk and audit evidence that is reflected in Figure 8–6. If one of those components is changed, then one or both of the remaining components must also change. For example, if evidence is held constant and materiality is decreased, then the risk that a material but undiscovered misstatement could exist must increase. Similarly, if materiality were held constant and risk reduced, the required evidence would increase.

> **OBJECTIVE 10**
>
> Discuss how materiality and risk are related and integrated into the audit process.

Summary

This chapter discussed the effects of materiality and relevant risks on audit planning. The purpose of using materiality and risks is to help the auditor accumulate sufficient appropriate audit evidence in the most efficient way possible. Figure 8–7 shows the effect of materiality and the most important risks discussed in this chapter on the evidence decisions discussed in Chapter 6.

FIGURE 8–6

Relationship Between
Materiality, Risk, and
Audit Evidence

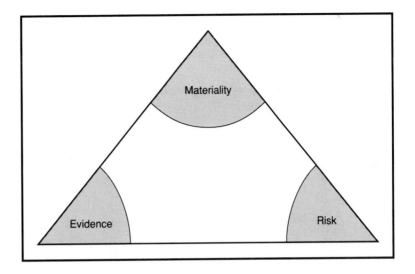

FIGURE 8–7

Relationship of
Materiality, Risks, and
Available Evidence to
Audit Planning

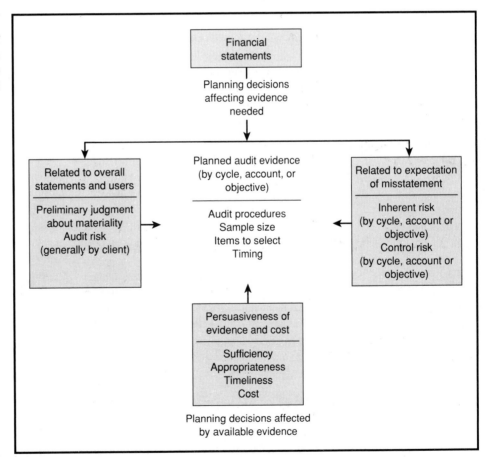

REVIEW QUESTIONS

8–1 Chapter 7 introduced the six parts of the planning phase of an audit. Which part is the evaluation of materiality and risk?

8–2 Define the meaning of the term *materiality* as it is used in accounting and auditing. What is the relationship between materiality and the term *present fairly* used in the auditor's report?

8–3 Explain why materiality is important but difficult to apply in practice.

8–4 What is meant by setting a preliminary judgment about materiality? Identify the most important factors affecting the preliminary judgment.

8–5 What is meant by using bases for setting a preliminary judgment about materiality? How would those bases differ for the audit of a manufacturing company and a government unit such as a school board?

8–6 Assume Rosanne Madden, a public accountant, is using 5 percent of net income before taxes as her major guideline for evaluating materiality. What qualitative factors should she also consider in deciding whether misstatements may be material?

8–7 Distinguish between the terms *materiality available for unanticipated misstatements* and *preliminary judgment about materiality*. How are they related to each other?

8–8 Differentiate between identified misstatements, likely misstatements and further possible misstatements. Explain why all three are important.

8–9 Explain why an auditor would adjust the preliminary judgment about materiality in calculating the materiality available for unanticipated misstatements.

8–10 How would the conduct of an audit of a medium-sized company be affected by the company's being a small part of a large conglomerate as compared with its being a separate entity?

8–11 Define the audit risk model and explain each term in the model.

8–12 What is meant by planned detection risk? What is the effect on the amount of evidence the auditor must accumulate when planned detection risk is increased from medium to high?

8–13 Explain the causes of an increased or decreased planned detection risk.

8–14 Define what is meant by inherent risk. Identify four factors that make for *high* inherent risk in audits.

8–15 Explain why inherent risk is estimated for cycles, account balances or even audit objectives rather than for the overall audit. What is the effect on the amount of evidence the auditor must accumulate when inherent risk is increased from medium to high for an account balance? Compare your answer with the one for 8–12.

8–16 Explain the effect of extensive errors found in the prior year's audit on inherent risk, planned detection risk, and planned audit evidence.

8–17 Explain what is meant by the term *audit risk*. What is its relevance to evidence accumulation?

8–18 Explain the relationship between audit risk and the legal liability of auditors.

8–19 State the two categories of circumstances that determine audit risk and list the factors that the auditor can use to indicate the degree to which each category exists.

8–20 Auditors have not been successful in measuring the components of the audit risk model. How is it possible to use the model in a meaningful way without a precise way of measuring the risk?

8–21 Explain the circumstances when the auditor should revise the components of the audit risk model and the effect of the revisions on planned detection risk and planned evidence.

MULTIPLE CHOICE QUESTIONS

8–22 The following questions deal with materiality. Choose the best response.

  a. Which one of the following statements is correct concerning the concept of materiality?

  (1) Materiality is determined by reference to guidelines established by the CICA.

  (2) Materiality depends only on the dollar amount of an item relative to other items in the financial statements.

  (3) Materiality depends on the nature of an item rather than the dollar amount.

  (4) Materiality is a matter of professional judgment.

  b. The concept of materiality will be least important to the public accountant in determining the

  (1) scope of his or her audit of specific accounts.

  (2) specific transactions that should be reviewed.

  (3) effects of audit exceptions upon the auditor's report.

  (4) effects of his or her direct financial interest in a client upon the public accountant's independence.   (AICPA adapted)

8–23 The following questions concern materiality and risk. Choose the best response.

  a. Edison Corporation has a few large accounts receivable that total $1,400,000. Victor Corporation has a great number of small accounts receivable that also total $1,400,000. The importance of an error in any one account is, therefore, greater for Edison than for Victor. This is an example of the auditor's concept of

  (1) materiality.

  (2) comparative analysis.

  (3) reasonable assurance.

  (4) relative risk.

  b. Which of the following elements ultimately determines the specific auditing procedures that are necessary in the circumstances to afford a reasonable basis for an opinion?

  (1) Auditor judgment

  (2) Materiality

  (3) Relative risk

  (4) Reasonable assurance

  c. Which of the following *best* describes the element of relative risk that underlies the application of generally accepted auditing standards, particularly the examination and reporting standards?

  (1) Cash audit work may have to be carried out in a more conclusive manner than inventory audit work.

  (2) Intercompany transactions are usually subject to less detailed scrutiny than arm's-length transactions with outside parties.

  (3) Inventories may require more attention by the auditor on an engagement for a merchandising enterprise than on an engagement for a public utility.

  (4) The scope of the examination need *not* be expanded if errors that arouse suspicion of fraud are of relatively insignificant amounts.   (AICPA adapted)

8–24 The following questions deal with materiality and risk, and their effect on audit reports. Choose the best response.

  a. A major customer of an audit client suffers a fire just prior to completion of year-end field work. The audit client believes that this event could have a *significant direct effect* on the financial statements. The auditor should

(1) advise management to disclose the event in notes to the financial statements.

(2) disclose the event in the auditor's report.

(3) withhold submission of the auditor's report until the extent of the direct effect on the financial statements is known.

(4) advise management to adjust the financial statements.

b. Late in December, Tech Products Ltd. sold its marketable securities that had appreciated in value and then repurchased them the same day. The sale and purchase transactions resulted in a *large gain*. Without the gain the company would have reported a loss for the year. Which of the following statements with respect to the auditor is correct?

(1) If the sale and repurchase are disclosed, an unqualified opinion should be rendered.

(2) The repurchase transaction is a sham and the auditor should insist upon a reversal or issue an adverse opinion.

(3) The auditor should withdraw from the engagement and refuse to be associated with the company.

(4) A denial of opinion should be issued.

c. A *material* change in an accounting estimate

(1) requires a modification in the auditor's report and disclosure in the financial statements.

(2) requires a modification in the auditor's report but does *not* require disclosure in the financial statements.

(3) affects comparability and may require disclosure in a note to the financial statements but does *not* require a modification in the auditor's report.

(4) involves the acceptability of the generally acceptable accounting principles used.

(AICPA adapted)

DISCUSSION QUESTIONS AND PROBLEMS

8–25 The following are different types of errors and fraud or other irregularities that can be encountered on an audit:

1. The use of a method of valuing inventory that is not in accordance with generally accepted accounting principles.

2. Accidental failure to disclose a lawsuit for patent infringement when the amount of the liability is unknown.

3. The recording as permanent assets expenditures that should have been recorded as repairs and maintenance.

4. The inclusion of invalid accounts in accounts receivable by preparing fictitious sales invoices to nonexisting customers.

Required:

a. Assuming the amounts are equally material, rank the types of errors and fraud listed above in terms of the difficulty of uncovering each one. (*Most difficult* is first.) Give reasons to support your answers.

b. Discuss whether auditors should have the same responsibility for uncovering the most difficult to find error or fraud as for discovering the least difficult one. Consider this from the point of view of the auditors and the users of financial statements.

8–26 Pages 259 and 260 include statements of earnings and financial position for Prairie Stores Corporation.

Statements of Earnings and Retained Earnings
Prairie Stores Corporation

		FOR THE 52 WEEKS ENDED	
	FOR THE 53 WEEKS ENDED MAY 3, 19X7	*April 28 19X6*	*April 29 19X5*
Revenues			
Net sales	$8,351,149	$6,601,255	$5,959,587
Other income	59,675	43,186	52,418
	8,410,824	6,644,441	6,012,005
Costs and expenses			
Cost of sales	5,197,375	4,005,548	3,675,369
Marketing, general and administrative expenses	2,590,080	2,119,590	1,828,169
Provision for loss on restructured operations	64,100	—	—
Interest expense	141,662	46,737	38,546
	7,993,217	6,171,875	5,542,084
Earnings from continuing operations before income taxes	417,607	472,566	469,921
Income taxes	196,700	217,200	214,100
Earnings from continuing operations	220,907	255,366	255,821
Provision for loss on discontinued operations, net of income taxes	$20,700	—	—
Net earnings	$200,207	$255,366	$255,821

Statements of Financial Position
Prairie Stores Corporation

ASSETS	*May 3, 19X7*	*April 28, 19X6*
Current assets		
Cash	$39,683	$37,566
Temporary investments (at cost, which approximates market)	123,421	271,639
Receivables, less allowances of $16,808 in 19x7 and $17,616 in 19x6	899,752	759,001
Inventories		
Finished product	680,974	550,407
Raw materials and supplies	443,175	353,795
	1,124,149	904,202
Deferred income tax benefits	9,633	10,468
Prepaid expenses	$57,468	$35,911
Current assets	2,254,106	2,018,787
Land, buildings, equipment, at cost, less accumulated depreciation	1,393,902	1,004,455
Investments in affiliated companies and sundry assets	112,938	83,455
Goodwill and other intangible assets	99,791	23,145
Total	$3,860,737	$3,129,842

LIABILITIES AND SHAREHOLDERS' EQUITY		
Current liabilities		
Notes payable	$280,238	$113,411
Current portion of long-term debt	64,594	12,336
Accounts and drafts payable	359,511	380,395
Accrued salaries, wages, and vacations	112,200	63,557
Accrued income taxes	76,479	89,151
Other accrued liabilities including goods and services tax	321,871	269,672
Current liabilities	**1,214,893**	**928,522**
Long-term debt	**730,987**	**390,687**
Other noncurrent liabilities	**146,687**	**80,586**
Deferred income taxes	**142,344**	**119,715**
Shareholders' equity		
Common stock issued, 51,017 shares in 19x7 and 50,992 in 19x6	200,195	199,576
Retained earnings	1,425,631	1,410,756
Shareholders' equity	**1,625,826**	**1,610,332**
Total	**$3,860,737**	**$3,129,842**

Required:

a. Use professional judgment in deciding on the preliminary judgment about materiality for earnings, current assets, current liabilities, and total assets. Your conclusions should be stated in terms of percentages and dollars.

b. Assume you complete the audit and conclude that your preliminary judgment about materiality for current assets, current liabilities, and total assets has been met. The actual estimate of misstatements in *earnings* exceeds your preliminary judgment. What should you do?

8–27 The following are terms discussed in Chapter 8:

1. Preliminary judgment about materiality
2. Estimate of the combined errors
3. Audit risk
4. Inherent risk
5. Estimated total error in a segment
6. Control risk
7. Detection risk

Required:

a. Identify which terms are *audit planning decisions* requiring professional judgment.

b. Identify which terms are *audit conclusions* resulting from application of audit procedures and requiring professional judgment.

c. Under what circumstances is it acceptable to change those items in part a, after the audit is started? Which items can be changed after the audit is 95 percent completed?

8–28 Describe what is meant by audit risk. Explain why each of the following statements is true:

a. A public accounting firm should attempt to achieve the same audit risk for all audit clients when circumstances are similar.

b. A public accounting firm should decrease audit risk for audit clients when external users rely heavily on the statements.

c. A public accounting firm should decrease audit risk for audit clients when there is a reasonably high likelihood of a client's filing bankruptcy.

d. Different public accounting firms should attempt to achieve reasonably similar audit risks for clients with similar circumstances.

8–29 State whether each of the following statements is true or false, and give your reasons:

a. The audit evidence accumulated for every client should be approximately the same, regardless of the circumstances.

b. If audit risk is the same for two different clients, the audit evidence for the two clients should be approximately the same.

c. If audit risk, inherent risk, and control risk are approximately the same for two different clients, the audit evidence for the two clients should be approximately the same.

8–30 The following questions deal with the use of the audit risk model.

a. Assume the auditor is doing a first-year municipal audit of Sackville, New Brunswick, and concludes that internal control is not likely to be effective.

  (1) Explain why the auditor is likely to set both inherent and control risks at 100 percent for most segments.

  (2) Assuming (1), explain the relationship of audit risk to planned detection risk.

  (3) Assuming (1), explain the effect of planned detection risk on evidence accumulation compared with its effect if planned detection risk were larger.

b. Assume the auditor is doing the third-year municipal audit of Sackville, New Brunswick, and concludes that internal controls are effective and inherent risk is low.

  (1) Explain why the auditor is likely to set inherent and control risks for material segments at a higher level than, say, 40 percent, even when the two risks are low.

  (2) For the audit of fixed asset accounts, assume inherent and control risks of 50 percent each, and an audit risk of 5 percent. Calculate planned detection risk.

  (3) For (2), explain the effect of planned detection risk on evidence accumulation compared with its effect if planned detection risk were smaller.

c. Assume the auditor is doing the fifth-year municipal audit of Sackville, New Brunswick, and concludes that audit risk can be set high, and inherent and control risks should be set low.

  (1) What circumstances would result in these conclusions?

  (2) For the audit of repairs and maintenance, inherent and control risk are set at 20 percent each. Audit risk is 5 percent. Calculate planned detection risk.

  (3) How much evidence should be accumulated in this situation?

8–31 Following are six situations that involve the audit risk model as it is used for planning audit evidence requirements. Numbers are used only to help you understand the relationships among factors in the risk model.

RISK	SITUATION					
	1	2	3	4	5	6
Audit risk	5%	5%	5%	5%	1%	1%
Inherent risk	100%	80%	40%	40%	80%	40%
Control risk	100%	40%	80%	50%	50%	50%
Planned detection risk	—	—	—	—	—	—

Required:

a. Explain what each of the four types of risk mean.

b. Calculate planned detection risk for each situation.

c. Using your knowledge of the relationships among the foregoing factors, state the effect on planned detection risk (increase or decrease) of changing each of the following factors while the other two remain constant.

(1) A decrease in audit risk

(2) A decrease in control risk

(3) A decrease in inherent risk

(4) An increase in control risk and a decrease in inherent risk of the same amount

d. Which situation requires the greatest amount of evidence and which requires the least?

8–32 Following are six situations that involve the audit risk model as it is used for planning audit evidence requirements in the audit of inventory.

		SITUATION					
RISK		1	2	3	4	5	6
Audit risk		High	High	Low	Low	High	Medium
Inherent risk		Low	High	High	Low	Medium	Medium
Control risk		Low	Low	High	High	Medium	Medium
Planned detection risk		—	—	—	—	—	—
Planned evidence		—	—	—	—	—	—

Required:

a. Explain what low, medium, and high mean for each of the four risks and planned evidence.

b. Fill in the blanks for planned detection risk and planned evidence using the terms *low, medium*, or *high*.

c. Using your knowledge of the relationships among the foregoing factors, state the effect on planned evidence (increase or decrease) of changing each of the following five factors, while the other three remain constant.

(1) An increase in audit risk

(2) An increase in control risk

(3) An increase in detection risk

(4) An increase in inherent risk

(5) An increase in inherent risk and a decrease in control risk of the same amount.

8–33 Using the audit risk model, state the effect on control risk, inherent risk, audit risk, and planned evidence for each of the following independent events. In each of the events a to j, circle one letter for each of the three independent variables and planned evidence: I = increase, D = decrease, N = no effect, and C = cannot determine from the information provided.

a. The client's management materially increased long-term contractual debt:
Control risk   I D Ⓝ C   Audit risk   Ⓘ D N C
Inherent risk   I DⓃ C   Planned evidence   I D N C

b. The company changed from a privately held company to a publicly held company:
Control risk   I D N C   Audit risk   I D N C
Inherent risk   I D N C   Planned evidence   I D N C

c. The auditor decided to assess control risk at a level below the maximum:
Control risk   I D N C   Audit risk   I D N C
Inherent risk   I D N C   Planned evidence   I D N C

d. The account balance increased materially from the preceding year without apparent reason:
Control risk   I D N C   Audit risk   I D N C

Inherent risk   I D N C   Planned evidence   I D N C

e. You determined through the planning phase that working capital, debt to equity ratio, and other indicators of financial health had improved during the past year:
Control risk   I D N C   Audit risk   I D N C
Inherent risk   I D N C   Planned evidence   I D N C

f. This is the second year of the engagement and there were few audit errors in the previous year. The auditor also decided to increase reliance on internal control:
Control risk   I D N C   Audit risk   I D N C
Inherent risk   I D N C   Planned evidence   I D N C

g. About halfway through the audit, you discover that the client is constructing its own building during idle periods, using factory personnel. This is the first time the client has done this and it is being done at your recommendation:
Control risk   I D N C   Audit risk   I D N C
Inherent risk   I D N C   Planned evidence   I D N C

h. In discussions with management, you conclude that management is planning to sell the business in the next few months. Because of the planned changes, several key accounting personnel quit several months ago for alternative employment. You also observe that the gross margin percent has significantly increased compared with that of the preceding year:
Control risk   I D N C   Audit risk   I D N C
Inherent risk   I D N C   Planned evidence   I D N C

i. There has been a change in several key management personnel. You believe that management is somewhat lacking in personal integrity, compared with the previous management. You believe it is still appropriate to do the audit:
Control risk   I D N C   Audit risk   I D N C
Inherent risk   I D N C   Planned evidence   I D N C

j. In auditing inventory, you obtain an understanding of internal control and perform tests of controls. You find it significantly improved compared with that of the preceding year. You also observe that due to technology changes in the industry, the client's inventory may be somewhat obsolete:
Control risk   I D N C   Audit risk   I D N C
Inherent risk   I D N C   Planned evidence   I D N C

8–34 In the audit of Whirland Chemical Corp., a large publicly traded company, you have been assigned the responsibility for obtaining background information for the audit. Your firm is auditing the client for the first time in the current year as a result of a dispute between Whirland and the previous auditor over the proper valuation of work-in-process inventory and the inclusion in sales of inventory that has not been delivered but has for practical purposes been completed and sold.

Whirland Chemical has been highly successful in its field in the past two decades, primarily because of many successful mergers negotiated by Lynn Randolph, the president and chairperson of the board. Even though the industry as a whole has suffered dramatic setbacks in recent years, Whirland continues to prosper, as evidenced by its constantly increasing earnings and growth. Only in the last two years have the company's profits turned downward. Lynn Randolph has a reputation for having been able to hire an aggressive group of young executives by the use of relatively low salaries combined with an unusually generous profit-sharing plan.

A major difficulty you face in the new audit is the lack of highly sophisticated accounting records for a company the size of Whirland. Lynn Randolph believes that profits come primarily from intelligent and aggressive action based on forecasts, not by relying on historical data that come after the fact. Most of the forecast data are generated by the sales and production department rather than by the accounting department. The personnel in the accounting department do seem competent but somewhat overworked and underpaid relative to other employees.

One of the recent changes that will potentially improve the record keeping is the installation of sophisticated computer equipment. All the accounting records are not computerized yet, but such major areas as inventory and sales are included in the new system. Most of the computer time is being reserved for production and marketing on the ground that these areas are more essential to operations than the record-keeping function.

The first six months' financial statements for the current year include a profit of approximately only 10 percent less than the first six months of the preceding year, which is somewhat surprising considering the reduced volume and the disposal of a segment of the business, Mercury Supply Inc. The disposal of this segment was considered necessary because it had become increasingly unprofitable over the past four years. At the time of its acquisition from Brian Randolph, who is a brother of Lynn Randolph, the company was highly profitable and it was considered a highly desirable purchase. The major customer of Mercury Supply Inc. was the Mercury Corporation, which is owned by Brian Randolph. Gradually the market for its products declined as the Mercury Corporation began diversifying and phasing out its primary products in favor of more profitable business. Even though Mercury Corporation is no longer buying from Mercury Supply Inc., it compensates for it by buying a large volume of other products from Whirland Chemical.

The only major difficulty Whirland faces right now, according to financial analysts, is underfinancing. There is an excessive amount of current debt and long-term debt because of the depressed capital markets. Management is reluctant to obtain equity capital at this point because the increased number of shares would decrease the earnings per share even more than 10 percent. At the present time, Lynn Randolph is negotiating with several cash-rich companies in the hope of being able to merge with them as a means of overcoming the capital problems.

Required:
a. List the major concerns you should have in the audit of Whirland Corp. and explain why they are potential problems.
b. State the appropriate approach to investigating the significance of each item you listed in a.

8–35 The existence of risk is implicit in the phrase "in my opinion" that appears in the auditor's report. The auditor is indicating that he or she is accepting some risk that the opinion rendered may be incorrect. In planning and executing an audit, the auditor strives to reduce this risk to a level that is acceptable to the client, the users and himself or herself.

Required:
Discuss what steps the auditor takes to reduce the risk to an acceptable level. What guidance do the professional standards provide to the auditor?

8–36 Some accountants have suggested that the auditor's report should include a statement of the materiality level and audit risk the auditor used in conducting the audit.

Required:
a. The proponents of such disclosure believe that the information would be useful to users of the financial statements being reported on. Explain fully why you think they have this view.
b. Some accountants oppose such disclosure. Explain why you think they are not in favor.
c. What is your position on the issue?

CASE

8–37 The purpose of this case is to give you practice in and an appreciation for the value of analytical procedures. This case involves preliminary analytical procedures of a publicly held company using information available from the annual report and information from partners. Data for several years' financial statements are presented for you to analyze; you are then asked to interpret the analyses from differing points of view. The data and supplemental information are presented in Exhibits I through V, which follow. The specific requirements for the case are as follows.

Background Information
ABC Corp. is a large retail chain. In recent years it has had as many as 110 stores and operated with 8,000 employees. Stores vary in size, but many are full-time department stores carrying both hard and soft goods.

ABC has financed its growth over the years with both equity capital and debt. The stock of ABC is listed on the Toronto and Montreal stock exchanges, is widely traded and of great interest to investors throughout Canada.

Exhibits I and II provide you with a comparative balance sheet and income statement for ABC for the most recent eight years. Exhibit III presents certain additional information that is important. Exhibit IV provides a limited awareness of industry information.

Required:
a. Identify any factors that would affect audit risk, inherent risk, or tolerable misstatement in the audit of ABC Corp.

b. Prepare a general financial analysis of the financial statements of ABC Corp. Use appropriate ratios and trends. These should focus on such methods as short-term debt-paying ability, liquidity, long-term debt-paying ability, and operating performance. Prepare the analysis using the microcomputer with appropriate financial analysis software (instructor option).

c. Interpret the analysis or analyses prepared from the viewpoint of each of the following:
   (1) Present auditor
   (2) Prospective auditor
   (3) Potential shareholder (securities analysts)
   (4) Shareholder
   (5) Banker
   (6) Supplier
   (7) Bondholder

d. Consider the various problems the company is having as developed in parts a and c. Indicate the appropriate ways an auditor might adjust his or her examination to deal with each problem identified.

The following are some additional miscellaneous facts about the company:

1. An agressive expansion program has been occurring. Well-managed chains normally take three to four years to generate a profit from new stores. In 19X8, 10 of ABC's stores were new.

2. There is a shift in credit policy from coupon-type credit to revolving charge accounts. Credit policies are somewhat lax.

3. High interest rates, because of the company's financial problems, are occurring at a time when borrowing needs are significant.

4. Retail sales generally are slumping; unemployment is high.

5. The company is having difficulties in carving out a place for itself in the retailing industry. It had been a blue-collar store for budget-minded value seekers. It has begun to buy better quality clothing, furnishings, and appliances to compete with Eaton's and Woodwards.

6. To decrease inventory levels, prices were slashed by 50 percent during the Christmas season.

EXHIBIT I ABC Corp. Balance Sheet (in thousands)

YEAR ENDED DECEMBER 31,

ASSETS	19X8	19X7	19X6	19X5	19X4	19X3	19X2	19X1
Cash	$ 45,951	$ 30,943	$ 49,851	$ 34,009	$ 32,977	$ 25,639	$ 25,141	$ 39,040
Accounts receivable, gross	597,382	547,323	481,446	424,178	381,757	324,358	282,647	237,068
Allowance for doubtful accounts	18,067	15,770	15,750	15,527	15,270	13,074	11,307	9,383
Accounts receivable, net	$ 579,315	$ 531,553	$ 465,696	$ 408,651	$ 366,487	$ 311,284	$ 271,340	$ 227,685
Inventories	450,637	399,533	298,676	260,492	222,128	208,623	183,722	174,631
Other current assets	26,782	17,846	17,006	16,031	11,546	9,844	7,462	7,967
Total current assets	$1,102,685	$ 979,875	$831,229	$719,183	$633,138	$555,390	$487,665	$449,323
Property, plant, and equipment, net	100,984	91,420	77,173	61,832	55,311	49,931	47,579	48,076
Noncurrent, nonoperating assets	49,313	39,402	36,268	26,613	24,121	21,629	19,986	17,847
TOTAL ASSETS	$1,252,982	$1,110,697	$944,670	$807,628	$712,570	$626,950	$555,230	$515,246
LIABILITIES AND SHAREHOLDERS' EQUITY								
Total current liabilities	$ 690,062	$ 633,067	$475,576	$459,000	$372,493	$290,118	$244,383	$225,403
Long-term debt	220,336	126,672	128,432	32,301	35,402	43,251	62,622	70,000
Other long-term liabilities	18,844	16,620	14,917	14,291	13,986	13,460	12,409	11,983
Preferred stock	7,465	8,600	9,053	9,600	11,450	13,250	14,750	15,000
Common equity	316,275	325,738	316,692	292,436	279,239	266,871	221,066	192,860
TOTAL LIABILITIES AND SHAREHOLDERS' EQUITY	$1,252,982	$1,110,697	$944,670	$807,628	$712,570	$626,950	$555,230	$515,246

EXHIBIT II ABC Corp. Income Statement (in thousands)

YEAR ENDED DECEMBER 31,

	19X8	19X7	19X6	19X5	19X4	19X3	19X2	19X1
Net sales	$1,853,773	$1,648,540	$1,378,251	$1,259,116	$1,214,666	$1,099,025	$982,244	$923,047
Cost of goods sold	1,181,711	1,036,140	856,259	780,669	762,975	696,031	627,860	588,405
Gross margin	$ 672,062	$ 612,400	$ 521,992	$ 478,447	$ 451,691	$ 402,994	$354,384	$334,642
Operating expenses, less depreciation	605,934	519,368	438,218	382,671	352,353	314,129	280,150	264,090
Depreciation expenses	13,579	12,004	10,577	9,619	8,972	8,388	8,203	7,524
Operating income (loss)	$ 52,549	$ 81,028	$ 73,197	$ 86,157	$ 90,366	$ 80,477	$ 66,031	$ 63,028
Other (income) expense	(6,679)	(5,702)	(4,034)	(4,313)	(3,556)	(2,918)	(4,069)	(2,404)
Interest expense	50,012	20,525	15,519	18,093	14,113	8,932	10,887	8,954
Income (loss) before special items	$ 9,216	$ 66,205	$ 61,712	$ 72,377	$ 79,809	$ 74,463	$ 59,213	$ 56,478
Taxes on income before extraordinary items	786	23,417	26,500	32,800	38,000	36,280	26,650	25,200
Net income (loss) before extraordinary items	$ 8,430	$ 42,788	$ 35,212	$ 39,577	$ 41,809	$ 38,183	$ 32,563	$ 31,278

EXHIBIT III ABC Corp. Additional Information (in thousands)

YEAR ENDED DECEMBER 31,

	19X8	19X7	19X6	19X5	19X4	19X3	19X2	19X1
Common dividends	$ 20,807	$ 20,829	$ 20,794	$ 20,426	$ 19,280	$ 17,160	$ 13,804	$ 13,528
Preferred dividends	335	293	346	395	457	526	563	563
Capital expenditures	23,143	26,251	25,918	16,141	14,357	10,626	7,763	15,257
Common shares outstanding at end of year	14,072	13,993	14,168	13,829	13,874	13,421	12,953	12,509
Market value excess, marketable securities	—	—	—	—	—	—	—	—
Amount of intangibles included in nonoperating assets	—	—	—	—	—	—	—	—
Present value of noncapitalized financing leases*	458,297	456,874	—	—	—	—	—	—
Lease payments for year#	103,367	90,243	74,628	62,138	53,054	—	—	—
Interest portion of lease payments not classified as interest expense	36,038	32,595	—	—	—	—	—	—
Interest attributable to debt in current liabilities	39,775	22,232	13,551	14,046	10,382	—	—	—

* The company does not capitalize financing leases despite the fact that the *CICA Handbook* requires that it do so.
# Operating leases only are included for 19X4 to 19X6; payments under both operating and financing leases are included for 19X7 and 19X8.

EXHIBIT IV

Industry Data 19X8

DUN & BRADSTREET	INDUSTRY AVERAGES:
Current assets/current debt	2.09 Times
Net profit/net sales	1.61 Percent
Net profit/tangible net worth	11.36 Percent
Net profit/net working capital	12.50 Percent
Net sales/tangible net worth	5.72 Times
Net sales/net working capital	6.88 Times
Net sales/Inventory	4.9 Times
Fixed assets/tangible net worth	32.3 Percent
Current debt/tangible net worth	77.5 Percent
Total debt/tangible net worth	129.7 Percent
Inventory/net working capital	139.8 Percent
Current debt/inventory	67.2 Percent
Funded debts/net working capital	39.2 Percent

EXHIBIT V

ABC Corp. Additional Facts and Opinions of Audit Partners

DATE	EVENTS
12/6/06	Arthur B. Carter opened a 25¢ store in Moncton, N.B. During the next two decades five similar stores were opened in the Maritimes.
1928	Stock offered to public
1940	Limitation of 25¢ merchandise removed and product line expanded.
1941	First stores opened in suburban areas. Had previously had only downtown stores.
1953	Chain had 20 stores.
1963	Chain expanded to 80 stores, one-half in the suburbs.
1966	Arthur B. Carter retired.
1969	Eleven stores opened in October, three in one day. During the next five years, the company opened 35 large stores, closed 27 smaller stores, and enlarged 8 successful stores.
19X8	
9/26	Nationwide group of banks agree to $600 million short-term loan despite significant earnings decline. Dividend omitted.
11/7	Agreement signed to accept Mastercard and Visa as alternatives to costly in-house financing.
12/9	Stock price at 2, down from 19X4 high of 70 5/8. Capitalization comprised of $600 million debt, $458 million present value of lease commitments, $202 million equity.
	Standard & Poor's downgrades ABC Corp. paper. Banks ease restrictive covenants (especially working capital and net worth requirements) in loan agreements and defer payment of amounts due.

9

THE STUDY OF THE
CLIENT'S INTERNAL
CONTROL AND
ASSESSMENT OF
CONTROL RISK

LEARNING OBJECTIVES

THOROUGH STUDY OF THIS CHAPTER WILL ENABLE YOU TO:

1. Discuss the nature of internal control and its importance to both management and the auditor

2. Describe the three concepts basic to the study of internal control

3. Identify the seven internal control objectives that must be applied to material transactions

4. Understand that internal control consists of the control environment and the control systems and discuss what these terms mean

5. Describe the requirements of understanding internal control and assessing control risk

6. Know how to obtain the necessary understanding of the client's internal control

7. Know how to assess control risk for each major type of transaction

8. Understand the process of designing and performing tests of controls, as a basis for further study

☐ Chapter 9 is the third chapter dealing with planning the audit and designing an audit approach. The shaded part of the chart included in the margin below shows where obtaining an understanding of the client's internal control and assessing control risk fit into planning the audit. The study of internal control, assessment of control risk, and related evidence gathering are a major component in the audit risk model studied in Chapter 8. Control risk is CR in the audit risk model. It was shown in Chapter 8 that the amount of evidence required can be reduced when there is effective internal control. This chapter shows why and how this can be done.

To understand how internal control is used in the risk model, knowledge of basic internal control concepts is needed. Accordingly, this chapter focuses on the meaning and objectives of internal control from both the client's and the auditor's point of view, the elements of internal control, and the auditor's methodology for fulfilling the requirements of the second examination standard.

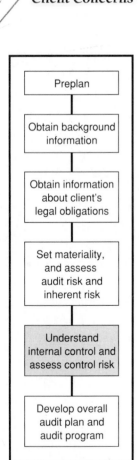

> **OBJECTIVE 1**
>
> Discuss the nature of internal control and its importance to both management and the auditor.

Client and Auditor Concerns

In designing a system for control, management is likely to have some of the same concerns auditors have in evaluating the system, as well as additional or different concerns. This section examines the concerns of both clients and auditors.

Client Concerns

The reason a company establishes a system for control is to help meet its own goals. Section 5200.03 of the *CICA Handbook* states:

> ■ Internal control consists of the policies and procedures established and maintained by management to assist in achieving its objective of ensuring, as far as practical, the orderly and efficient conduct of the entity's business.

The system consists of many specific *policies and procedures* designed to provide management with reasonable assurance that the goals and objectives it believes important to the entity will be met. These policies and procedures are often called *controls*, and collectively they comprise the entity's *internal control*.

Control systems must be *cost beneficial*. The controls adopted are selected by comparing the costs to the organization relative to the benefits expected. One benefit to management, but certainly not the most important, is the reduced cost of an audit when the auditor evaluates internal control as good or excellent and assesses control risk as well below maximum (that is, as low).

Management typically has the following five objectives in designing effective internal control.

Maintaining reliable systems Management must have reliable systems so that it will have accurate information for carrying out its operations. A wide variety of information is used for making critical business decisions. For example, the price to charge for products is based in part on information about the cost of making the products.

Ensuring timely preparation of reliable information Information must be reliable and timely if it is to be useful for management decision making.

Safeguarding assets The physical assets of a company can be stolen, misused, or accidentally destroyed unless they are protected by adequate controls. The same is true of nonphysical assets such as accounts receivable, important documents (confidential government contracts), and records (general ledger and journals). Safeguarding certain assets and records has become increasingly important since the advent of computer systems. Large amounts of information stored on computer media such as a disk or magnetic tape can be destroyed if care is not taken to protect them.

Optimizing the use of resources   The controls within an organization are meant to prevent unnecessary duplication of effort and waste in all aspects of the business, and to discourage other inefficient use of resources.

There may at times be a conflict between operational efficiency and safeguarding assets and records or providing reliable information. There is a cost attached to fulfilling these two objectives and, to the extent the cost exceeds the benefits, the results may be operationally inefficient.

Management institutes procedures and rules to meet the goals of the company. Internal control is meant to provide reasonable assurance that these are followed by company personnel.

Preventing and detecting error and fraud   The internal controls of a company play an important role in the prevention and detection of error and fraud or other irregularities. Management must weigh cost versus benefit when considering this objective. The cost of preventing a particular error should be balanced against the likelihood of the error occurring and the amount of the error that could occur.

Auditor Concerns   The study of the client's internal control and the resultant assessment of control risk are important to auditors and are specifically included as a generally accepted auditing standard. The second examination standard is:

- A sufficient understanding of internal control should be obtained to plan the audit. When control risk is assessed below maximum, sufficient appropriate audit evidence should be obtained through tests of controls to support the assessment.

Section 5200.05 points out that "Management's internal control objectives for the entity go beyond financial statement objectives." In other words, there are aspects of internal control that are of interest to management but not to the auditor; consequently, the auditor does not concern himself or herself with those aspects of internal control in planning the audit. An example would be internal controls that have been set up by management to ensure that accurate information about the company's market share is collected and provided to the company's marketing department.

The *CICA Handbook* in Section 5200.07 defines internal control that is relevant to the audit and the auditor as

- those policies and procedures established and maintained by management that affect the auditor's assessment of control risk relating to specific financial statement assertions at the account balance or class of transactions level.

Section 5200.08 explains that

- those policies and procedures pertain to the entity's ability to collect, record and process data and report financial information consistent with financial statement assertions, or other data the auditor uses in applying auditing procedures to verify financial statement assertions.

The two sections define those aspects of an entity's internal control in which the auditor is interested and explain why the auditor is interested.

Section 5200.07 states that internal control "in the context of the audit" is comprised of the entity's *control environment* and *control systems* installed by management. The auditor should consider both components together and not separately. Both of these components of internal control will be discussed under Objective 4 below.

<table>
<tr><td>

OBJECTIVE 2

Describe the three concepts basic to the study of internal control.

</td></tr>
</table>

The auditor should emphasize controls concerned with the reliability of data for *external reporting purposes*, but controls affecting internal management information, such as budgets and internal performance reports, should not be completely ignored. These types of information are often important sources of evidence in helping the auditor decide whether the financial statements are fairly presented. If the controls over these internal reports are considered inadequate, the value of the reports as evidence is diminished.

Basic Concepts

There are three basic concepts that underlie the study of internal control and assessment of control risk.

Management's Responsibility

Management, not the auditor, must establish and maintain the entity's controls. This concept is consistent with the requirement that management, not the auditor, is responsible for the preparation of financial statements in accordance with generally accepted accounting principles.

Reasonable Assurance

A company should develop internal control that provides reasonable but not absolute assurance that the financial statements are fairly stated. Internal control is developed by management after considering both the costs and benefits of the controls. Management is often unwilling to implement an ideal system because the costs may be too high. For example, it is unreasonable for auditors to expect management of a small company to hire several additional accounting personnel to bring about a small improvement in the reliability of accounting data. It is often less expensive to have auditors do more extensive auditing than to incur higher internal control costs.

Inherent Limitations

Internal control cannot be regarded as completely effective, regardless of the care followed in its design and implementation. Even if systems personnel could design an ideal system, its effectiveness depends on the competency and dependability of the people using it. For example, assume a procedure for counting inventory is carefully developed and requires two employees to count independently. If neither of the employees understands the instructions or if both are careless in doing the counts, the count of inventory is likely to be wrong. Even if the count is right, management might override the procedure and instruct an employee to increase the count of quantities in order to improve reported earnings. Similarly, the employees might decide to overstate the counts intentionally to cover up a theft of inventory by one or both of them. This is called collusion.

Because of these inherent limitations of controls and because auditors cannot have more than reasonable assurance of their effectiveness, there is almost always some level of control risk. Therefore, even with the most effectively designed internal control, the auditor must obtain audit evidence beyond testing the controls for most audit objectives for every material financial statement account. Stated differently, the control risk portion of the audit risk model must always be greater than zero.

Typical Accounting System

Regardless of the size of the organization, almost all accounting systems are now at least partially computerized. The extent of computerization varies widely from only recording manually prepared documents using a microcomputer to fully integrated systems in which the input is electronically entered, or even created by, the system. There is considerable variation among accounting systems used in business and government. Systems vary widely in technical complexity, often depending on the size and complexity of the business. Systems vary not only as to the extent to which they are computerized, but by type of electronic data processing (EDP) equipment and by the extent of hard copy information produced by the systems.

In discussing the elements of internal control, it is useful to identify those characteristics that accounting systems have in common, rather than their differences. Figure 9–1 identifies the four functions that are common to all accounting systems regardless of complexity. These functions apply to highly complex systems as well as to manual accounting systems. The flowchart in Figure 9–1 illustrates the four functions for a relatively simple computerized accounting system in which manually prepared documents are the source of input for each of the transaction cycles. In discussing the four functions in Figure 9–1, the frame of reference will be sales and accounts receivable. The same concepts apply to cash receipts and accounts receivable, purchases and accounts payable, cash disbursements and accounts payable, or to any other type of transaction and related transaction and master files.

Data preparation Preparation of accurate documents is the first step in the recording process in the flowchart in Figure 9–1. Most companies implement several control procedures to make sure that the source information to be entered into the computer is accurate. For sales, the preparing of accurate sales order and/or shipping documents is the first step in the recording process.

Data entry The conversion of information from the source document into a computer readable form is a mechanical process, such as through the use of a computer keyboard. Again, most companies have internal control to assure that data entry is accurate. For the example of sales transactions, the input from shipping documents might include the customer number, product number, and quantity shipped.

Transaction processing and master file update Besides accurate input, the accurate processing of transactions and updating of master files requires that the computer software is properly designed and reliable and the appropriate computer files are being used. For example, in processing sales transactions and updating the sales and accounts receivable master files, the sales maintenance update program and the accounts receivable master file must include all customers and have the correct unit selling price for each product and credit limits and payment terms for each customer. The master file must be properly updated to include accounts receivable outstanding for preparation of monthly statements and aging information for follow-up on slow paying customers. Most accounting

FIGURE 9–1 Typical Simple Computerized Accounting System

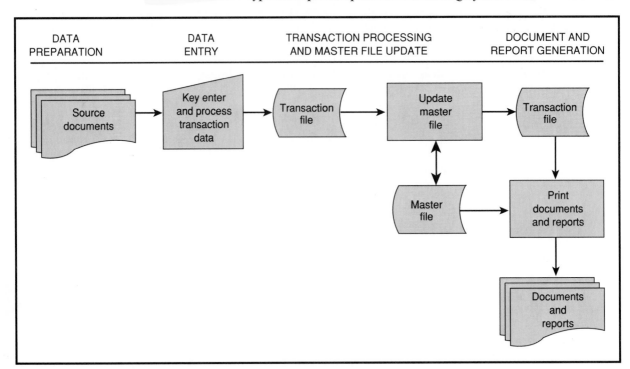

systems include many internal control to assure accurate transaction processing and master file updating.

Document and report generation The final step in the process is to generate documents and reports. For example, for sales, the most important document produced is the sales invoice. The reports are likely to include a sales journal, accounts receivable and sales general ledger balances, and an aged trial balance of accounts receivable. One of the documents commonly generated is an error correction report. Errors uncovered by the computer during any part of data entry or processing would be included on this report. For example, if a customer number was entered during key entry for which there was no customer on the accounts receivable master file, the system would indicate an error.

Method of Data Processing

The control concepts discussed in this chapter apply to all accounting systems regardless of complexity. There are major differences between a simple microcomputer-based accounting system using purchased software for a small service company and a complex EDP system for an international manufacturing business. Nevertheless, the control objectives are the same and the methodology discussed in this chapter is applicable to both.

For simplicity, most illustrations in this chapter apply to simple computerized systems. Unique considerations in more advanced EDP systems are studied in Chapter 15.

Detailed Internal Control Objectives

For any type of transaction in a client's system, several types of recording errors (misstatements) can occur. Payroll transactions, for example, can be in error if the wrong number of hours was charged on the time card or gross payroll was debited to the wrong account number in the payroll journal.

There are seven detailed objectives that internal control must meet to prevent misstatements in the journals and records. The client's internal control must be sufficient to provide reasonable assurance that

OBJECTIVE 3

Identify the seven internal control objectives that must be applied to material transactions.

---

1. *Recorded transactions are valid (validity).* Internal control cannot permit the inclusion of fictitious or nonexistent transactions in journals or other accounting records.
2. *Transactions are properly authorized (authorization).* If a transaction that is not authorized takes place, it could result in a fraudulent transaction, and it could also have the effect of wasting or destroying company assets.
3. *Existing transactions are recorded (completeness).* The client's procedures must prevent the omission of transactions from the records.
4. *Transactions are properly valued (valuation).* Adequate internal control includes procedures to avoid errors in calculating and recording transaction amounts at various stages in the recording process.
5. *Transactions are properly classified (classification).* The proper account classification according to the client's chart of accounts must be made in the journals if the financial statements are to be properly stated. Classification also includes such categories as division and product.
6. *Transactions are recorded at the proper time (timing).* The recording of transactions either before or after the time they took place increases the likelihood of failing to record transactions or of recording them at the improper amount. If early or late recording occurs at the end of the period, the financial statements will be misstated.
7. *Transactions are properly included in master files and correctly summarized (posting and summarization).* The accounting process involves capturing transactions, summarizing them by type in journal form and by affected account in the general ledger and master files. Regardless of the method used to enter transactions in the accounting system, adequate controls are needed to make sure classification and summarization is correct.

The seven detailed internal control objectives must be applied to each material type of transaction in the audit. Such transactions typically include sales, cash receipts, acquisitions of goods and services, payroll, and so on. Table 9–1 shows the internal control objectives applied to sales transactions.

Recall that Objective 5 in Chapter 5 focused on the assertions management makes in the financial statements. One of the objectives of internal control is to ensure that management can have confidence in making those assertions. It therefore seems logical that the internal control objectives just discussed parallel the audit objectives, and, by extension, the management assertions discussed in Chapter 5. For example, validity, completeness, valuation, classification, and timing (cut-off) are both internal control objectives and audit objectives. There are obvious links between the internal control objectives authorization and posting and summarization and the audit objectives ownership and disclosure.

Elements of Internal Control

A company's internal control includes two basic categories of policies and procedures that management designs and implements to provide reasonable assurance

TABLE 9–1	INTERNAL CONTROL OBJECTIVES – GENERAL FORM	INTERNAL CONTROL OBJECTIVES – SALES TRANSACTIONS
Internal Control Objectives for Sales Transactions	Recorded transactions are valid (validity)	Recorded sales are for shipments made to nonfictitious customers
	Transactions are properly authorized (authorization)	Sales transactions are properly authorized
	Existing transactions are recorded (completeness)	Existing sales transactions are recorded
	Transactions are properly valued (valuation)	Recorded sales are for the amount of goods shipped and are correctly billed and recorded
	Transactions are properly classified (classification)	Sales transactions are properly classified
	Transactions are recorded at the proper time (timing)	Sales are recorded on a timely basis
	Transactions are properly included in the master files and correctly summarized (posting and summarization)	Sales transactions are properly included in the master files and are correctly summarized

OBJECTIVE 4

Understand that internal
control consists of the
control environment and
control systems and
discuss what these
terms mean.

that its control objectives will be met. These are called the *elements of internal control* and are (1) the control environment and (2) control systems.

As discussed above, the elements contain many control-related policies and procedures. The auditor is concerned primarily with those relating to preventing or detecting material misstatements in the financial statements. Those aspects will be the focus of the remainder of the chapter.

The Control Environment

The essence of an effectively controlled organization lies in the attitude of its management. If top management believes control is important, others in the organization will sense that and respond by conscientiously observing the policies and procedures established. On the other hand, if it is clear to members of the organization that control is not an important concern to top management, and is given "lip service" rather than meaningful support, it is almost certain that control objectives will not be effectively achieved.

The *control environment* consists of the actions, policies and procedures that reflect the overall attitudes of top management, the directors, and the owners of an entity about control and its importance to the entity. For the purpose of understanding and assessing the control environment, the auditor should consider the nine factors taken from Section 5200 of the *CICA Handbook* and listed below. The nine factors, which individually and collectively enhance or diminish internal control in an entity, are:

- Management philosophy and operating style
- The functioning of the board of directors and its committees, particularly the audit committee
- Organizational structure
- Methods of assigning authority and responsibility
- Management control methods
- Systems development methodology
- Personnel policies and practices

- Management reaction to external influences
- Internal audit

Management Philosophy and Operating Style

Management should operate ethically and honestly and encourage like behavior among employees. "Actions speak louder than words" is a saying that most of us have heard since childhood. Management, through its activities, provides clear signals to employees about the importance of control. For example, does management take significant risks or are they risk averse? Are profit plans and budget data set as "best possible" plans or "most likely" targets? Can management be described as "fat and bureaucratic," "lean and mean," dominated by one or a few individuals, or is it "just right?" Does management use aggressive accounting to ensure budgets and goals are met? Understanding these and similar aspects of management's philosophy and operating style gives the auditor a sense of its attitude about control.

The Board of Directors and Audit Committee

The board and its committees should take an active role in running the company and not simply rubber-stamp management's activities. Does the audit committee meet with the auditors, both external and internal, and support them in their activities? Can the external or internal auditors go to the audit committee with concerns about the company's operations knowing they will be heard? By understanding how the board and its committees, and especially the audit committee, work, the auditor will be able to assess how active an oversight role they take with respect to the entity's accounting and financial reporting policies and practices.

Organization Structure

The entity's organizational structure defines the lines of responsibilities and authority that exist. Does the entity have an appropriate organizational structure for planning, directing and controlling operations? Are authority and responsibility assignments within the organization structure clear? By understanding the client's organizational structure, the auditor can learn the management and functional elements of the business and perceive how control-related policies and procedures can be carried out.

Methods of Assigning Authority and Responsibility

The methods of communicating assignment of authority and responsibility must take into account the reporting relationships and responsibilities existing within the entity and the entity's culture. Care must be taken that issues such as entity policy on ethical and social issues and organizational goals and objectives are considered. The communications might include such methods as memoranda from top management about the importance of control and control-related matters, formal organizational and operating plans, employee job descriptions and related policies, and policy documents covering employee behavior such as conflicts of interest and formal codes of conduct.

Management Control Methods

These are the methods that management uses to supervise the entity's activities. Management methods to monitor the activities of others enhance the effectiveness of internal control in two ways. First, the conduct of such methods sends a clear message about the importance of control. Second, the methods serve to detect misstatements that may have occurred.

An example that illustrates management control methods is an effective *budgeting system* including subsequent periodic reports of the results of operations compared to budgets. An organization that has effective planning identifies material differences between actual results and the plan, and takes appropriate corrective action at the proper management level.

Systems Development Methodology

Management has the responsibility for the development and implementation of the entity's systems and procedures. The auditor should know whether management has a methodology for developing and modifying systems and procedures or whether change occurs on an *ad hoc* basis.

Personnel Policies and Practices

An important aspect of any system of controls is personnel. If employees are competent and trustworthy, other controls can be absent and reliable financial statements will still result. Honest, efficient people are able to perform at a high level even when there are few other controls to support them. Even if there are numerous other controls, incompetent or dishonest people can reduce the system to a shambles. Even though personnel may be competent and trustworthy, people have certain innate shortcomings. They can, for example, become bored or dissatisfied, personal problems can disrupt their performance, or their goals may change.

Because of the importance of competent, trustworthy personnel in providing effective control, the methods by which persons are hired, evaluated and compensated are an important part of internal control.

Management Reaction to External Influences

While such influences are beyond management's control, management should be aware of external influences and be prepared to react appropriately. For example, management (and their tax advisers) should be so knowledgeable of the tax laws in filing corporate tax returns that an audit by Revenue Canada would not uncover any surprises.

Internal Audit

An effective, competent, independent, and well-trained internal audit department which reports to the audit committee of the board of directors can greatly enhance the operations of an entity by monitoring the effectiveness of other control-related policies and procedures and by performing operational audits (discussed further in Chapter 24).

In addition to its role in the entity's control environment, an adequate internal audit staff can contribute to reduced external audit costs by providing direct assistance to the external auditor. Section 5215 defines the way internal auditors affect the external auditor's evidence accumulation. If the external auditor obtains evidence that supports the competence, integrity and objectivity of internal auditors, the external auditor can rely on the internal auditor's work in a number of ways.

Summary

The auditor is interested in the control environment as a reflection of management's commitment to internal control for the entity. If the auditor concludes that management is actively, through some or all the nine factors listed above, attempting to develop strong internal control, the auditor will be able to conclude that it is likely that the entity's internal control can be relied on. On the other hand, if the auditor finds that management is not committed to a positive control environment, the information contained in the company's records is likely not to be very reliable.

Control Systems

Section 5200.13 of the *CICA Handbook* defines control systems as

> ■ those policies and procedures that collect, record and process data and report the resulting information, or [those policies and procedures] that enhance the reliability of such data and information.

The collecting, recording, processing and reporting pertains to the accounting system. Section 5200.15 states that enhancing the reliability of data and information is accomplished by such control procedures as

> ■ proper authorization of transactions and activities, appropriate segregation of duties, design and use of adequate documents and records, adequate safeguards over access to and use of assets and records, and computer-generated or manual verification of performance and accuracy of recorded amounts.

The ensuing discussion will divide control systems and procedures into two components or elements for ease of exposition; the two components are the *accounting system* and the *control procedures*. This division means that, for purposes of discussion in this text, there will be three elements of internal control: (1) the control environment; (2) the accounting system; and (3) the control procedures.

The Accounting System

An effective accounting system must satisfy all of the seven detailed internal control objectives identified earlier in the chapter (page 275). For example, the accounting system should be designed to assure that all shipments of goods by a company are correctly recorded as sales and reflected in the financial statements in the proper period. The system must also avoid duplicate recording of sales and recording a sale if a shipment did not occur.

For a small company with active involvement by the owner, a simple microcomputer accounting system involving primarily one honest competent accountant may provide an adequate accounting system. A larger company requires a more complex system which includes carefully defined responsibilities and written policies and procedures.

The Control Procedures

There are potentially many policies and procedures in any entity which could be classified as control procedures. Those enumerated above (from Section 5200.15) are discussed below.

Appropriate Segregation of Duties

Four general guidelines for separation of duties to prevent both intentional and unintentional misstatements are of special significance to auditors.

Separation of the custody of assets from accounting   The reason for not permitting the person who has temporary or permanent custody of an asset to account for that asset is to protect the firm against defalcation. When one person performs both functions, there is an excessive risk of that person's disposing of the asset for personal gain and adjusting the records to relieve himself or herself of responsibility. If the cashier, for example, receives cash and is responsible for data entry for cash receipts and sales, it is possible for the cashier to take the cash received from a customer and adjust the customer's account by failing to record a sale or by recording a fictitious credit to the account. Other examples of inadequate separation of the custodial function include the distribution of payroll cheques by the payroll data preparation clerk and the maintenance of inventory records by store-room personnel.

Separation of the authorization of transactions from the custody of related assets If possible, it is desirable to prevent persons who authorize transactions from having control over the related asset. For example, the same person should not authorize the payment of a vendor's invoice and also sign the cheque in payment of the bill. Similarly, the authority for adding new employees to or eliminating terminated employees from payroll should not be performed by the same person responsible for distributing payroll cheques. As illustrated, the authorization of a transaction and the handling of the related asset by the same person increases the possibility of defalcation within the organization.

Separation of operational responsibility from record-keeping responsibility If each department or division in an organization were responsible for preparing its own records and reports, there would be a tendency to bias the results to improve its reported performance. In order to ensure unbiased information, record keeping is typically included in a separate department under the controller.

Separation of duties within EDP To the extent practical, it is desirable to separate the major functions within EDP. Ideally, the following should all be separated.

- *Systems analyst* The systems analyst is responsible for the general design of the system. The analyst sets the objectives of the overall system and the specific design of particular applications.
- *Programmer* Based on the individual objectives specified by the systems analyst, the programmer develops special flowcharts for the application, prepares computer instructions, tests the program, and documents the results. It is important that the programmer not have access to input data or computer operation, since understanding of the program can easily be used for personal benefit.
- *Computer operator* The computer operator is responsible for running data through the system in conjunction with the computer program. The operator follows the instructions set forth in the *program run instructions* that have been developed by the programmer.
  Ideally, the operator should be prevented from having sufficient knowledge of the program to modify it immediately before or during its use. In several cases of recorded defalcation, the operator had covered an embezzlement by temporarily changing the original program.
- *Librarian* The librarian is responsible for maintaining the computer programs, transaction files, and other important computer records. The librarian provides a means of important physical control over these records and releases them only to authorized personnel.
- *Data control group* The function of the data control group is to test the effectiveness and efficiency of all aspects of the system. This includes the application of various controls, the quality of the input, and the reasonableness of the output.

Inasmuch as control group personnel perform internal verification, the importance of their independence is obvious.

Naturally, the extent of separation of duties depends heavily on the size of the organization. In many small companies it is not practical to segregate the duties to the extent suggested. In these cases, audit evidence may require modification.

Summary The overall organizational structure of a business must provide proper segregation of duties, yet still promote operational efficiency and effective communication. Segregation of duties varies widely across organizations, but four important ones of particular concern to the auditor are the following:

- Accounting is completely isolated under the controller, who has no custodial or operating responsibility.
- The custodianship of cash, including receipts and disbursements, is the responsibility of the secretary-treasurer.
- The internal auditor reports directly to the president or audit committee of the board of directors.
- Separation of duties within EDP is adequate considering the size of the organization.

Proper Authorization of Transactions and Activities

Every transaction must be properly authorized if controls are to be satisfactory. If any person in an organization could acquire or expend assets at will, complete chaos would result. Authorization can be either *general or specific*. General authorization means that management establishes policies for the organization to follow. Subordinates are instructed to implement these general authorizations by approving all transactions within the limits set by the policy. Examples of general authorization are the issuance of fixed price lists for the sale of products, credit limits for customers, and fixed reorder points for making purchases.

Specific authorization has to do with individual transactions. Management is often unwilling to establish a general policy of authorization for some transactions. Instead, it prefers to make authorizations on a case-by-case basis. An example is the authorization of a sales transaction by the sales manager for a used-car company.

The individual or group who can grant either specific or general authorization for transactions should hold a position commensurate with the nature and significance of the transactions. The policy for such authorizations should be established by top management. For example, a common policy is to have all acquisitions of capital assets over a set amount authorized by the board of directors.

There is also a distinction between authorization and approval. Authorization is a policy decision for either a general class of transactions or specific transactions. Approval is the implementation of management's general authorization decisions. For example, assume management sets a policy authorizing the ordering of inventory when there is less than a three-week supply on hand. That is a general authorization. When a department orders inventory, the clerk responsible for maintaining the perpetual record approves the order to indicate that the authorization policy has been met.

Design and Use of Adequate Documents and Records

Documents and *records* are the physical objects upon which transactions are entered and summarized. They include such diverse items as sales invoices, purchase orders, subsidiary ledgers, sales journals, and employee time cards. In a computerized accounting system, many of these documents and records are maintained in the form of computer files until they are printed out for specific purposes. Both documents of original entry and records upon which transactions are entered are important, but the inadequacy of documents normally causes greater control problems.

Documents perform the function of transmitting information throughout the client's organization and between different organizations. The documents must be adequate to provide reasonable assurance that all assets are properly controlled and all transactions correctly recorded. For example, if the receiving department fills out a receiving report when material is obtained, the accounts payable department can verify the quantity and description on the vendor's invoice by comparing it with the information on the receiving report.

Certain relevant principles dictate the proper design and use of documents and records. Documents and records should be

- Prenumbered consecutively to facilitate control over missing documents, and as an aid in locating documents when they are needed at a later date. (Significantly affects completeness objective.) The prenumbered documents should be stored in such a way that access to them is restricted so that employees can use the documents only in sequence.
- Prepared at the time a transaction takes place, or as soon thereafter as possible. When there is a longer time interval, records are less credible and the chance for error is increased. (Affects timing objective.)
- Sufficiently simple to ensure that they are clearly understood.
- Designed for multiple use whenever possible, to minimize the number of different forms. For example, a properly designed and used shipping document can be the basis for releasing goods from storage to the shipping department, informing billing of the quantity of goods to bill to the customer and the appropriate billing date, and updating the perpetual inventory records.
- Constructed in a manner that encourages correct preparation. This can be done by providing a degree of internal check within the form or record. For example, a document might include instructions for proper routing, blank spaces for authorizations and approvals, and designated column spaces for numerical data.

When data for the preparation of documents are entered into the computer, the effective design of the computer input screens is an important control mechanism.

Chart of accounts   A control closely related to documents and records is the *chart of accounts*, which classifies transactions into individual balance sheet and income statement accounts. The chart of accounts is an important control because it provides the framework for determining the information presented to management and other financial statement users. It must contain sufficient information to permit the presentation of financial statements in accordance with generally accepted accounting principles; but, in addition, the classification of the information should help management make decisions. Information by divisions, product lines, responsibility centers, and similar breakdowns should be provided for. The chart of accounts is helpful in preventing misclassification errors if it accurately and precisely describes which type of transactions should be in each account. It is especially important that the descriptions clearly distinguish between capital assets, inventories, and expense items, since these are the major categories of concern to external users of the financial statements. (Significantly affects the classification objective.)

Systems manuals The procedures for proper record keeping should be spelled out in systems manuals to encourage consistent application. The manuals should provide sufficient information to facilitate adequate record keeping and the maintenance of proper control over assets. For example, to ensure the proper recording of the purchase of raw materials, a copy of the purchase order for acquiring the merchandise and a copy of the receiving report when the raw materials are received should be sent to accounts payable. This procedure aids in properly recording purchases in the purchases journal, and it facilitates the determination of whether the vendor's invoice from the supplier should be paid.

Larger companies with reasonably complex computer systems will also maintain a standards manual pertaining to the EDP system. A standards manual typically includes four parts.

- *Systems requirements* This portion of the standards manual sets forth the broad objectives of any system, including the input and output of the system. For example, the objective for software in sales might include providing accounting information for the accounts receivable, master file and general ledger, calculating sales commissions, and providing information for the sales department. This portion of the standards manual also includes the requirements for reviewing and testing the software.

- *Programming documentation* As the name implies, this section is concerned with writing and testing the software programs. It therefore usually includes detailed flowcharts and specific requirements for developing or acquiring the program, as well as testing or changing it.

- *Program run instructions* These materials deal with operating the computer and therefore deal with operating schedules and instructions pertaining to various computer programs. Run books should require a description of the input, the detailed operating instructions (including all the steps to follow), possible error conditions, and a description of the output.

- *User instructions* User instructions concern who should receive output and the procedures to follow when the data is in error or the output is not in a usable form.

Documentation standards improve control over the development, maintenance, and use of computer programs. They provide the auditor with an understanding of the types of detailed information available about EDP systems that can be used as a source of evidence during the audit.

The protection of assets and records is essential to adequate internal control. If assets are left unprotected, they can be stolen. If records are not adequately protected, they can be stolen, damaged, or lost. In the event of such an occurrence, the accounting process as well as normal operations could be seriously disrupted. When a company is highly computerized, it is very important to protect its computer equipment, programs, and data files. The equipment and programs are very expensive and essential to operations. The data files are the records of the company, and if damaged, could be very costly, or even impossible, to reconstruct.

Adequate
Safeguards Over
Access to and Use
of Assets and
Records

The most important type of protective measure for safeguarding assets and records is the use of physical precautions. An example is the use of storerooms for inventory to guard against pilferage. When the storeroom is under the control of a competent and knowledgeable employee, he or she should be able to ensure that loss from obsolescence is minimized. Fireproof safes and safety deposit vaults for the protection of assets such as currency and securities are other important physical safeguards.

There are three categories of controls related to safeguarding EDP equipment, programs, and data files. As with other types of assets, *physical controls* are used to protect the computer facilities. Examples are locks on doors to the computer room and terminals, adequate storage space for software and data files to protect them from loss, and proper fire-extinguishing systems. *Access controls* deal with ensuring that only authorized people can use the equipment and have access to software and data files. One example is library procedures to guard against unauthorized use of programs and files. Another example is an on-line access password system. Under such a coding system, a password must be entered into a microcomputer or computer terminal before software programs will operate. *Backup* and *recovery procedures* are steps an organization can take in the event of a loss of equipment, programs, or data. For example, a backup copy of programs and critical data files stored in a safe remote location is a common backup control.

Computer-
generated or
Manual
Verification of
Performance and
the Accuracy of
Recorded Amounts

The last category of control procedures is the careful and continuous review of the other four, often referred to as *independent checks on performance* or internal verification. The need for independent checks arises because internal control tends to change over time unless there is a mechanism for frequent review. Personnel are likely to forget or intentionally fail to follow procedures, or become careless unless someone observes and evaluates their performance. In addition, both fraudulent and unintentional misstatements are possible, regardless of the quality of the controls.

An essential characteristic of the persons performing internal verification procedures is independence from the individuals originally responsible for preparing the data. A considerable portion of the value of checks on performance is lost when the individual doing the verification is a subordinate of the person responsible for preparing the data or lacks independence in some other way.

The least expensive means of internal verification is the separation of duties in the manner previously discussed. For example, when the bank reconciliation is performed by a person independent of the accounting records and handling of cash, there is an opportunity for verification without incurring significant additional costs. Some important types of verification can only be accomplished by a duplication of effort. For example, the counting of inventory by two different teams is costly, but frequently necessary.

Computerized accounting systems can be designed so that many internal verification procedures can be automated as part of the system. An illustration and discussion of these and other related control procedures are included in Appendix A.

Size of Business
and Controls

The size of a company does have a significant effect on the nature of internal control and the specific controls. Obviously, it is more difficult to establish adequate separation of duties in a small company.[1] It would also be unreasonable

---

1 A useful source of information about internal control and the small business is the CICA Audit Technique Study, *Audit of a Small Business*, Toronto: CICA, 1988.

FIGURE 9–2

Elements and
Subelements of Internal
Control

INTERNAL CONTROL		
Control Environment	*Accounting System*	*Control Procedures*
Subelements of control environment • management philosophy and operating style • organizational structure • audit committee • methods of assigning authority and responsibility • management control methods • internal audit function • personnel policies and procedures • external influences • systems development methodology	Objectives that must be satisfied • validity • authorization • completeness • valuation • classification • timing • posting and summarization	Categories of control procedures • adequate separation of duties • proper authorization of transactions and activities • adequate documents and records • physical control over assets and records • independent checks on performance

to expect a small firm to have internal auditors. However, if the various subelements of internal control are examined, it becomes apparent that most are applicable to both large and small companies. Even though it may not be common to formalize policies in manuals, it is certainly possible for a small company to have competent, trustworthy personnel with clear lines of authority; proper procedures for authorization, execution, and recording of transactions; adequate documents, records, and reports; physical controls over assets and records; and, to a limited degree, checks on performance.

A major control available in a small company is the knowledge and concern of the top operating person, who is frequently an owner-manager. A personal interest in the organization and a close relationship with the personnel makes possible careful evaluation of the competence of the employees and the effectiveness of the overall system. For example, internal control can be significantly strengthened if the owner conscientiously performs such duties as signing all cheques after carefully reviewing supporting documents, reviewing bank reconciliations, examining accounts receivable statements sent to customers, approving credit, examining all correspondence from customers and vendors, and approving bad debts.

Summary of
Internal Control

A summary of the three elements of internal control discussed in the preceding sections (control environment, accounting system, control procedures) is included in Figure 9–2.

Overview of
Understanding
Internal Control
for Audit
Planning
Purposes and
Assessing
Control Risk

The remainder of the chapter deals with obtaining information about internal control and using that information as a basis for audit planning. To help understand how the auditor accomplishes this, an overview of the relevant steps for obtaining an understanding of internal control, assessing control risk, and relating the results to tests of financial statement balances is shown in Figure 9–3. The process described by Figure 9–3 is discussed in this section, and then certain steps are elaborated upon in more detail in the remainder of the chapter.

FIGURE 9–3 Overview of the Study of a Client's Internal Control and Assessment of Control

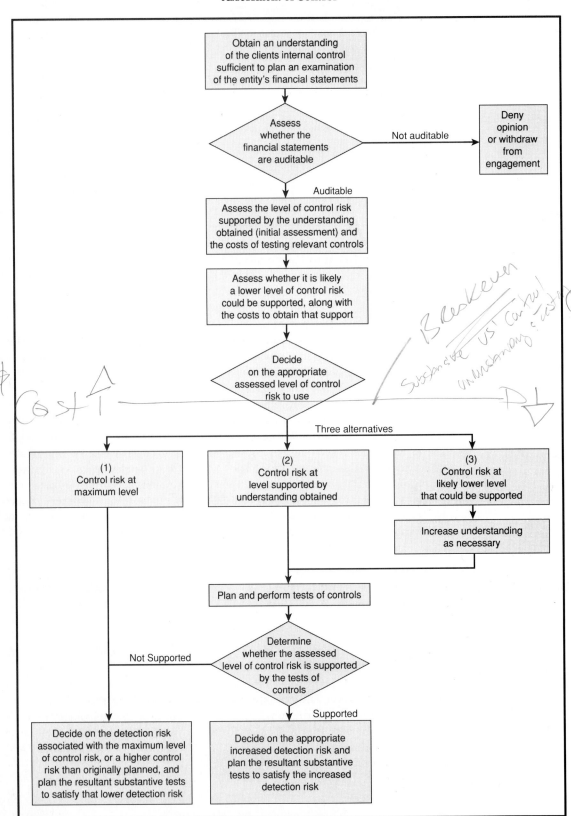

FIGURE 9–4

Understanding the
Internal Control for
Design and Operation

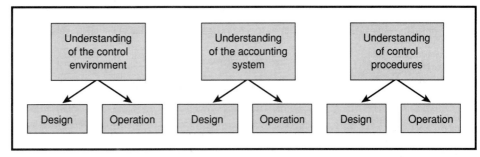

Reasons for
Understanding
Internal Control
Sufficient to Plan
the Examination

Section 5205.05 of the *CICA Handbook* requires the auditor to obtain sufficient understanding of the client's internal control for every audit. The extent of that understanding must, at a minimum, be sufficient to adequately plan the examination, in terms of four specific planning matters.

Auditability   The auditor must obtain information about the integrity of management and the nature and extent of the accounting records to be satisfied that sufficient appropriate audit evidence is available to support the financial statement balances and the auditor's report.

OBJECTIVE 5
Describe the requirements of understanding internal control and assessing control risk.

Potential material misstatements   The understanding should allow the auditor to identify the types of potential errors and fraud or other irregularities that might affect the financial statements, and to assess the risk that such errors and fraud might occur in amounts that are material to the financial statements.

Detection risk   Control risk in the planning form of the audit risk model directly affects detection risk for each audit objective [DR = AR ÷ (IR × CR)]. Information about internal control is used to assess control risk for each control objective, which in turn affects planned detection risk.

Design of tests   The information obtained should allow the auditor to design effective tests of the financial statement balances. Such tests include tests of details of balances, and analytical procedures, and are termed *substantive procedures*. These are discussed in more detail in Chapter 10.

Understanding
Internal Control
for Design and
Implementation

Each of the three elements of internal control must be studied and understood. In obtaining that understanding, the auditor should consider two aspects: (1) the *design* of the various policies and procedures within each control element and (2) whether they have been implemented or placed in *operation*. The need to consider the design and operation for each of the three elements is summarized in Figure 9–4.

Understanding the control environment   Information is obtained about the control environment for each of the subelements discussed earlier in the chapter. The auditor then uses the understanding as a basis for assessing management's and the directors' attitude and awareness about the importance of control. For example, the auditor might determine the nature of a client's budgeting system as a part of understanding the design of the control environment. The operation of the budgeting system might then be evaluated in part by inquiry of budgeting personnel to determine budgeting procedures and follow-up of differences between budget and actual. The auditor might also examine client schedules comparing actual results to budgets.

Understanding the accounting system   To understand the design of the accounting system, the auditor determines (1) the major classes of transactions of the entity; (2) how those transactions are initiated; (3) what accounting records exist and their nature; (4) how transactions are processed from initiation to completion, including the extent and nature of computer use; and (5) the nature and details of the financial reporting process followed. Typically, this is accomplished and documented by a *narrative description* of the system or by *flowcharting*. (These are described later in the chapter.) The operation of the accounting system is often determined by tracing one or a few transactions through the accounting system (called a *transaction walk-through*).

Understanding the control procedures   Auditors obtain an understanding of the control environment and accounting system in a similar manner for most audits, but obtaining an understanding of control procedures varies considerably. For smaller clients, it is common to identify few or even no control procedures because controls are often ineffective due to limited personnel. In that case, a high assessed level of control risk is used; that is, control risk is assessed at maximum. For clients with extensive controls where the auditor believes controls are likely to be excellent, it is often appropriate to identify many controls during the controls understanding phase. In still other audits, the auditor may identify a limited number of controls during this phase and then identify additional controls later in the process. The extent to which controls are identified is a matter of audit judgment. A methodology for identifying controls is studied later in the chapter.

Assessments and Decisions   Once an understanding of internal control that is sufficient for audit planning is obtained, two major assessments must be made. As shown in Figure 9–3, these also require the auditor to make certain decisions.

Assess whether the financial statements are auditable   The first assessment is whether the entity is auditable. Two primary factors determine auditability: the integrity of management and the adequacy of accounting records. Many audit procedures rely to some extent on the representations of management. For example, it is difficult for the auditor to evaluate whether inventory is obsolete without an honest assessment by management. If management lacks integrity, management may provide false representations causing the auditor to rely on unreliable evidence.

The accounting records serve as a direct source of audit evidence for most audit objectives. If the accounting records are deficient, necessary audit evidence may not be available. For example, if the client has not kept duplicate sales invoices and vendors' invoices it would normally not be possible to do an audit. Unless the auditor can identify an alternative source of reliable evidence, or unless appropriate records can be constructed for the auditor's use, the only recourse may be to consider the entity unauditable.

When it is concluded that the entity is not auditable, the auditor discusses the circumstances with the client (usually at the highest level) and either withdraws from the engagement or issues a denial form of auditor's report.

Assess the level of control risk supported by the understanding obtained   After obtaining an understanding of the design and operation of internal control, the auditor makes an assessment of control risk. Control risk is a measure of the auditor's expectation that internal control *will neither prevent material misstatements* from occurring, *nor detect and correct them* if they have occurred.

The assessment is made for each internal control objective for each major type of transaction. For example, the auditor makes an assessment of the validity objective for sales and a separate assessment for the completeness objective. There are different ways to express this expectation. Some auditors use a subjective expression such as high, moderate, or low. Others use numerical probabilities such as 1.0, .6, or .2.

The assessment usually starts with consideration of the control environment. If the attitude of management is that control is unimportant, it is doubtful that detailed control procedures will be reliable. The best course of action in that case is to assume that control risk for all objectives is at maximum (such as high or 1.0). On the other hand, if management's attitude is positive, the auditor then considers the specific policies and procedures within the subelements of the control environment, the accounting system, and control procedures. Those policies and procedures are used as a basis for an assessment below the maximum.

There are two important considerations about the assessment: First, the auditor does not have to make the assessment in a formal, detailed manner. In many audits, particularly of smaller companies, the auditor assumes that the control risk is at maximum whether or not it actually is. The auditor's reason for taking this approach is that he or she has concluded that it is more economical to more extensively audit the financial statement balances.

Second, even though the auditor believes control risk is low, the level of control risk *assessed* is limited to that level supported by the evidence obtained. For example, suppose the auditor believes that control risk for unrecorded sales is low, but has gathered little evidence in support of control procedures for the completeness objective. The auditor's assessment of control risk for unrecorded sales must either be moderate or high. It could be low only if additional evidence was obtained in support of the pertinent control procedures.

Tests of Controls   The assessment of control risk requires the auditor to consider the design of control policies and procedures to evaluate whether they should be effective in meeting specific control objectives. Some evidence will have been gathered in support of the design of the controls, as well as that they have been implemented, during the understanding phase. In order to use specific control policies and procedures as a basis for using control risk below maximum, however, specific evidence must be obtained about their *effectiveness* throughout the period under audit. The procedures to gather evidence about design and placement in operation during the understanding phase are termed *procedures to obtain an understanding*. The procedures to test effectiveness in support of assessing control risk below maximum are called *tests of controls*. Both are discussed in more detail later in the chapter.

Where the results of tests of controls support the design of the control policies and procedures as expected, the auditor proceeds to use the chosen assessed level of control risk as planned. If, however, the tests of controls indicate the policies and procedures did not operate effectively, the assessed level of control risk must be reconsidered. For example, the tests may indicate the application of a control was curtailed midway through the year, or that the person applying it made frequent errors. In such situations, a higher assessed level of control risk would be used, unless additional controls relating to the same objectives could be identified and found effective.

Detection Risk and Planned Tests of Financial Statements Balances

The result of the preceding steps is the assessed level of control risk, for each internal control objective, for each of the entity's major transaction types. Where the assessed level of control risk is below maximum, it will be supported by specific tests of controls. These assessments are then related to the specific audit objectives for the accounts affected by the major transaction types. The appropriate level of detection risk for each specific audit objective is then determined using the audit risk model. The relationship of control objectives to audit objectives and the selection and design of audit procedures for substantive tests of financial statement balances are discussed and illustrated in Chapter 10.

Procedures to Obtain the Necessary Understanding

In practice, the study of a client's internal control and assessment of control risk varies considerably from client to client. For smaller clients, many auditors obtain only a level of understanding sufficient to assess whether the statements are auditable, evaluate the control environment for management's attitude, and determine the adequacy of the client's accounting system. Often, for efficiency, control procedures are ignored, control risk is assumed to be maximum, and detection risk is therefore low.

For many larger clients, especially for repeat engagements, the auditor plans on a low assessed level of control risk for most parts of the audit before the audit starts. A common approach is to first obtain an understanding of the control environment and the accounting system at a fairly detailed level, next identify specific controls that will reduce control risk and make an assessment of control risk, and then test the controls for effectiveness. The auditor can conclude that control risk is low only after all three steps are completed. The three steps discussed above are now explained in more detail to illustrate further how the study of a client's internal control and assessment of control risk are done.

> **OBJECTIVE 6**
>
> Know how to obtain the necessary understanding of the client's internal control.

Procedures Relating to Design and Implementation

The auditor's task in obtaining an understanding of internal control is to find out about the elements of internal control, see that they have been implemented, and document the information obtained in a useful manner. The following are procedures relating to design and implementation.

Auditor's previous experience with the entity Most audits of a company are done annually by the same public accounting firm. Except for initial engagements, the auditor begins the audit with a great deal of information about the client's internal control developed in prior years. Because systems and procedures usually don't change frequently, this information can be updated and carried forward to the current year's audit.

Inquiries of client personnel A logical starting place for updating information carried forward from the previous audit, or for obtaining information initially, is with appropriate client personnel. Inquiries of client personnel at the management, supervisory, and staff level will usually be conducted as part of obtaining an understanding of the design of internal control. Care must be taken to document the information collected.

Client's policy and systems manuals To design, implement, and maintain its internal control, an entity must have extensive documentation of its own. This includes policy manuals and documents (such as a corporate code of conduct) and systems manuals and documents (such as an accounting manual and an organization chart). This information is studied by the auditor and discussed with company personnel to assure that they are properly interpreted and understood.

Inspection of documents and records The subelements of the control environment, the details of the accounting system, and the application of control procedures will all involve the creation of many documents and records. These will have been presented to some degree in the policy and systems manuals. By inspecting actual, completed documents and records, the auditor can bring the contents of the manuals to life and better understand them. Inspection also provides evidence that the control policies and procedures have been placed in operation.

Observation of entity activities and operations In addition to inspecting completed documents and records, the auditor can observe client personnel in the process of preparing them and carrying out their normal accounting and control activities. This further enhances understanding and knowledge that control policies and procedures have been placed in operation.Observation, inspection, and inquiry can be conveniently and effectively combined in the form of the transaction walk-through mentioned earlier. With that procedure, the auditor selects one or a few documents for the initiation of a transaction type and traces it (them) through the entire accounting process. At each stage of processing, inquiries are made and current activities are observed, in addition to inspecting completed documentation for the transaction or transactions selected.

Documentation of the Understanding Three commonly used methods of documenting the understanding of internal control are narratives, flowcharts, and internal control questionnaires. These may be used separately or in combination, as discussed below.

Narrative description A narrative is a written description of a client's internal control. An example of a narrative description of a portion of an accounting system is shown in problem 9-32 on page 314. Another example of a narrative description is included in the boxed material on page 306. A proper narrative of an accounting system and related control procedures includes four characteristics:

- The origin of every document and record in the system. For example, the description should state where customer orders come from and how sales invoices arise.
- All processing that takes place. For example, if sales amounts are determined by a computer program that multiplies quantities shipped by stored standard prices, that should be described.
- The disposition of every document and record in the system. The filing of documents, sending them to customers, or destroying them should be described.

- An indication of the control procedures relevant to the assessment of control risk. These typically include separation of duties (such as separating recording cash from handling cash); authorizations and approvals (such as credit approvals); and internal verification (such as comparison of unit selling price to sales contracts).

The use of narrative descriptions is common for internal control that is simple and easy to describe. Their disadvantage is the difficulty of describing the details of internal control in sufficiently clear and simple words to make it understandable and still provide enough information for effective analysis of controls and assessment of control risk.

Flowchart   An internal control flowchart is a symbolic, diagrammatic representation of the client's documents and their sequential flow in the organization. An adequate flowchart includes the same four characteristics identified above for narrative descriptions.

Flowcharting is advantageous primarily because it can provide a concise overview of the client's system which is useful to the auditor as an analytical tool in evaluation. A well-prepared flowchart aids in identifying inadequacies by facilitating a clear understanding of how the system operates. For most uses, it is superior to narrative descriptions as a method of communicating the characteristics of a system. It is easier to follow a diagram than to read a description. It is also usually easier to update a flowchart than a narrative description.

Techniques for proper flowchart preparation are included in Appendix B to this chapter for students who are not knowledgeable about flowcharting. An example of a flowchart is shown in Figure 9–11 on page 305.

It would be unusual to use both a narrative and a flowchart to describe the same system, since both are intended to describe the flow of documents and records in an accounting system. Sometimes a combination of a narrative and flowchart is used. The decision to use one or the other or a combination of the two is dependent on two factors: relative ease of understanding by current- and subsequent-year auditors and relative cost of preparation.

Internal control questionnaire   An internal control questionnaire asks a series of questions about the controls in each audit area, including the control environment, as a means of indicating to the auditor aspects of internal control that may be inadequate. In most instances, it is designed to require a "yes" or a "no" response, with "no" responses indicating potential internal control deficiencies.

The primary advantage of the questionnaire approach is the relative completeness of coverage of each audit area that a good instrument affords. Furthermore, a questionnaire can usually be prepared reasonably quickly at the beginning of the audit engagement. The primary disadvantage is that individual parts of the client's systems are examined without providing an overall view. In addition, a standard questionnaire is often inapplicable to some audit clients, especially smaller ones.

Figure 9–5 illustrates a part of an internal control questionnaire for the sales and collection cycle of Hillsburg Hardware Ltd. The questionnaire is also designed for use with the seven internal control objectives. Notice that each objective (A through G) is a detailed objective as it applies to sales transactions. The same is true for all other audit areas.

We believe the use of both questionnaires and flowcharts is highly desirable

FIGURE 9–5

Partial Internal Control
Questionnaire for Sales

Client _Hillsburg Hardware Ltd._   Audit Date _12/31/x8_
Auditor _MSW_   Date Completed _9/30/x8_   Reviewed by _F.R._   Date Completed _10/1/x8_

Objective (shaded) and Question	Yes	No	N/A	Remarks
Sales				
A. Recorded sales are for shipments actually made to nonficticious customers.				
1. Is the recording of sales supported by authorized shipping documents and approved customer orders?	✓			*Pam Dilley examines underlying documentation.*
B. Sales transactions are properly authorized.				
1. Is customers' credit approved by a reponsible official?	✓			*By Chulick, the president.*
2. Is a prenumbered written shipping order required for any merchandise to leave the premises?	✓			
3. Is an authorized price list used?	✓			
C. Existing sales transactions are recorded.				
1. Is a record of shipments maintained?	✓			
2. Is the shipping document controlled from the office in a manor that helps ensure that all shipments are billed?	✓			
3. Are shipping documents prenumbered and accounted for?	✓			
4. Are sales invoices prenumbered and accounted for?		✓		*Prenumbered but not accounted for. Additional substantive testing required.*
D. Recorded sales are for the amount of goods ordered and are correctly billed and recorded.				
1. Is there independent comparison of the quantity of the shipping document to sales invoices?	✓			*By Pam Dilley, controlled by Chulick.*
2. Are monthly statements sent to customers?	✓			
E. Sales transactions are properly classified.				*All sales are on account and there is only one sales account.*
1. Is there independent comparison of recorded sales to the chart of accounts?			✓	
F. Sales are recorded on a timely basis.				*There is a weakness in the system and additional substantive testing required.*
1. Is there independent comparison of dates on shipping documents to dates recorded?		✓		
G. Sales transactions are properly included in the subsidiary records and correctly summarized.				
1. Are journals independently footed and traced to the general ledger and printout of master file?		✓		*Examine for reasonableness by Chulick.*
2. Is there a comparison of customer names on shipping documents to posting in the printout of master file?	✓			*By Pam Dilley*

for understanding the client's system. Flowcharts provide an overview of the system, and questionnaires are useful checklists to remind the auditor of many different types of controls that should exist. When properly used, a combination of these two approaches should provide the auditor with an excellent description of the system.

It is often desirable to use the client's narratives or flowcharts and have the client fill out the internal control questionnaire. When understandable and reliable narratives, flowcharts, and questionnaires are not available from a client, which is frequently the case, the auditor must prepare them.

Assessing Control Risk

> **OBJECTIVE 7**
>
> Know how to assess control risk for each major type of transaction.

Once the auditor has obtained descriptive information and evidence in support of the design and operation of internal control, an assessment of control risk by detailed control objective can be made. This is normally done separately for each major type of transaction in each transaction cycle. For example, in the sales and collection cycle, the types of transactions usually involve sales, sales returns and allowances, cash receipts, and the provision for and write-off of uncollectible accounts.

Identify Control Objectives

The first step in the assessment is to identify the control objectives to which the assessment applies. This is done by applying the detailed internal control objectives introduced earlier, which are stated in general form, to each major type of transaction for the entity. Table 9–1 on page 276 illustrates the development of internal control objectives for sales transactions.

Identify Specific Controls

The next step is to identify the specific policies and procedures that contribute to accomplishing each objective. The auditor identifies pertinent controls by proceeding through the descriptive information about the client's internal control. Those policies and procedures that, in his or her judgment, provide control over the transaction involved are identified. In doing this, it is often helpful to refer back to the types of control procedures that *might* exist, and ask if they *do* exist. For example: Is there appropriate segregation of duties and how is it achieved? Are the documents used well designed? Are prenumbered documents properly accounted for?

In making this analysis, it is not necessary to consider *every* control. The auditor should identify and include those controls that are expected to have the greatest impact on meeting the control objectives. These are often termed *key controls*. The reason for including only key controls is that they will be sufficient to achieve the control objectives and should provide audit efficiency.

Identify and Evaluate Weaknesses

Weaknesses are defined as the *absence of adequate controls*, which increases the risk of misstatements existing in the financial statements. If, in the judgment of the auditor, there are inadequate controls to satisfy one of the objectives, expectation of such a misstatement occurring increases. For example, if no internal verification of the valuation of payroll transactions is taking place, the auditor may conclude there is a weakness in internal control.

A four-step approach can be used for identifying significant weaknesses.

FIGURE 9–6

Weaknesses in Internal
Control

Client *Airtight Machine Inc.*			Schedule *P-3*	
Weaknesses in Internal Control			Prepared by: *JR*	
Cycle *Sales and Collection*			Period *12/31/x8*	

Weaknesses	Compensating Control	Potenial Error	Materiality	Effect on Audit Evidence
1. The accounts receivable clerk approves credit memos and has access to cash.	The owner reviews all credit memos after they are recorded. He knows all customers.	N/A	N/A	N/A
2. There is no internal verification of the key entry of customer number, quantities and related information for sales invoices and credit memos. ª	None	Clerical errors in billings to customers, posting to master file and account classification.	Potenially material	Increase the substantive testing of sales transactions to 125 transactions.

ª Included in the control related matters letter.

Identify existing controls Because weaknesses are the absence of adequate controls, the auditor must first know which controls exist. The methods for identifying existing controls have already been discussed.

Identify the absence of key controls Internal control questionnaires, narratives, and flowcharts are useful to identify areas in which key controls are lacking and the likelihood of misstatements is thereby increased. Where control risk is assessed as moderate or high, there is usually an absence of controls.

Determine potential material misstatements that could result This step is intended to identify specific errors and fraud or other irregularities that are likely to result because of the absence of controls. The importance of a weakness is proportionate to the magnitude of the errors or fraud that are likely to result from it.

Consider the possibility of compensating controls A compensating control is one elsewhere in the system that offsets a weakness. A common example in a smaller company is active involvement of the owner. When a compensating control exists, the weakness is no longer a concern because the potential for misstatement has been sufficiently reduced.

Figure 9–6 shows the documentation of weaknesses for the sales and collection cycle. The effect on audit evidence column shows the effect of the weakness on the auditor's planned audit program.

FIGURE 9–7 Control Matrix for Sales – Airtight Machine Inc.

	Recorded sales are for shipments made to nonfictitious customers (validity)	Sales are properly authorized (authorization)	Existing sales transactions are recorded (completeness)	Recorded sales are for the amount of goods shipped and are correctly billed and recorded (valuation)	Recorded sales are properly classified (classification)	Sales are recorded on a timely basis (timing)	Sales transactions are properly included in the master files and correctly summarized (posting and summarization)
INTERNAL CONTROL							
Credit is approved before shipment occurs		C		C			
Sales are supported by authorized shipping documents and approved customer orders, which are attached to the duplicate sales invoice	C	C					
Separation of duties between billing, recording sales, and handling cash receipts	C		C				C
An approved price list is used to determine unit selling prices		C		C			
Shipping documents are forwarded to billing daily and billed the subsequent day			C			C	
Shipping documents and duplicate sales invoice numbers are accounted for weekly and traced to the sales journal			C			C	
Shipping documents are batched daily by quantity shipped	C		C	C		C	C
Statements are mailed to all customers each month	C			C			C
There is an adequate chart of accounts					C		
Sales journal is reviewed monthly for reasonableness of total and compared to the general ledger for sales and sales returns							C
Lack of internal verification of the key entry of customer number, quantities, and related information for sales invoices and credit memos				W	W		W
Assessment of control risk	low	low	low	mod	mod	low	mod

Left margin labels: INTERNAL CONTROL OBJECTIVES – SALES (top); ILLUSTRATIVE KEY CONTROLS, WEAKNESSES (left side)

C = The control partially or fully satisfies the control objective.
W = Weakness identified in Figure 9–6.

The Control Matrix Many auditors use a *control matrix* to assist in the control-risk-assessment process. Most control related procedures affect more than one control objective and often several different procedures affect a given control objective. These complexities make a control matrix a useful way to help assess control risk. The control matrix is used to assist in identifying both controls and weaknesses, and in assessing control risk.

Figure 9–7 illustrates the use of a control matrix for sales transactions of Airtight Machine Inc. In constructing the matrix, the internal control objectives for sales were listed as column headings, and pertinent controls that were identified were listed as headings for the rows. In addition, where significant weaknesses were identified, they were also entered as row headings below the listing of key controls. The body of the matrix was then used to show how the controls contribute to the accomplishment of the control objectives, and how weaknesses impact the objectives. In this illustration, a *C* was entered in each cell where a control partially or fully satisfied a control objective, and a *W* was entered to show the impact of the weaknesses.

Assess Control Risk
Once controls and weaknesses have been identified and related to control objectives, there can be an assessment of control risk. Again, the control matrix is a useful tool for that purpose. Referring to Figure 9–7, the auditor assessed control risk for Airtight's sales by reviewing each column for pertinent controls and weaknesses, and asking: "What is the likelihood that a material misstatement of the type to be controlled would not be prevented or detected and corrected by these controls, and what is the impact of the weaknesses?" If the likelihood is high, then control risk is high, and so forth.

Internal Control Letter and Related Matters
During the course of obtaining an understanding of the client's internal control and assessing control risk, auditors obtain information that is of interest to the audit committee in fulfilling its responsibilities. Generally, such information concerns significant deficiencies in the design or operation of internal control (weaknesses).

Audit committee communications Section 5220 suggests that the auditor communicate significant internal control weaknesses to an "appropriate representative of management." The most logical representative would be the audit committee and the communication should be done as a part of every audit examination. If the client does not have an audit committee, then the communication should go to the person or persons in the organization who have overall responsibility for internal control, such as the board of directors or the owner-manager. An illustrative internal-control-related-matters letter is shown in Figure 9–8.

Management letters In addition to significant weaknesses in internal control, auditors often observe less significant internal control related matters, as well as opportunities for the client to make operational improvements. These types of matters should also be communicated to the client. The form of communication is often a separate letter for that purpose, called a management letter.

Tests of Controls

The controls the auditor has identified in the assessment as reducing control risk (the key controls) must be supported by tests of controls to make sure they have been operating effectively throughout the audit period. For example, in Figure 9–7, each key control must be supported by sufficient tests of controls.

Procedures for Tests of Controls
Four types of procedures are used to support the operation of control-related policies and procedures. They are as follows:

FIGURE 9–8

Internal-Control-Related-Matters Letter

CHESLEY & BEDARD
Chartered Accountants
2016 Village Boulevard
Ottawa, Ontario K1S 5B6

February 12, 19X8

Audit Committee
Airtight Machine Inc.
1729 Athens Street
Ottawa, Ontario K1N 6N5

Dear Members of the Audit Committee:

In planning and performing our audit of the financial statements of Airtight Machine Inc. for the year ended December 31, 19X7, we considered its internal control in order to determine our auditing procedures for the purpose of expressing our opinion on the financial statements and not to provide assurance on internal control. However we noted certain matters involving internal control and its operation that we consider to be of such significance that we believe they should be reported to you. The matters being reported involve circumstances coming to our attention relating to significant deficiencies in the design or operation of internal control that, in our judgment, could adversely affect the organization's ability to record, process, summarize, and report financial data consistent with the assertions of management in the financial statements.

The matter noted is that there is a lack of independent verification of the key entry of the customer's name, product number, and quantity shipped on sales invoices and credit memos. As a consequence, errors in these activities could occur and remain uncorrected, adversely affecting both recorded net sales and accounts receivable. This deficiency is particularly significant because of the large size of the average sale of Airtight Machine Inc.

This report is intended solely for the information and use of the audit committee, board of directors, management, and others in Airtight Machine Inc.

Very truly yours,

Chesley & Bedard

Chesley & Bedard

OBJECTIVE 8

Understand the process of designing and performing tests of controls, as a basis for further study.

Inquiries of appropriate entity personnel Although inquiry is not generally a strong source of evidence about the effective operation of controls, it is an appropriate form of evidence. For example, the auditor may determine that unauthorized personnel are not allowed access to computer files by making inquiries of the person who controls the computer library.

Inspection of documents, records, and reports Many control-related activities and procedures leave a clear trail of documentary evidence. Suppose, for example, that when a customer order is received, it is used to create a customer sales order, which is approved for credit. (See the first and second key controls in Figure 9–7.)

The customer order is attached to the sales order as authorization for further processing. The auditor examines the documents to make sure they are complete and properly matched, and that required signatures or initials are present.

Observation Other types of control-related activities do *not* leave an evidential trail. For example, separation of duties relies on specific persons performing specific tasks and there is typically no documentation of the separate performance. (See the third key control in Figure 9–7.) For controls that leave no documentary evidence, the auditor generally observes them being applied.

Reperformance Reperformance is the process whereby the auditor applies policies and procedures from the control environment to a sample of transactions or balances. There are also control-related activities for which there are related documents and records, but their content is insufficient for the auditor's purpose of assessing whether controls are operating effectively. For example, assume prices on sales invoices are to be verified to a standard price list by client personnel as an internal verification procedure, but no indication of performance is entered on the sales invoices. (See the fourth key control in Figure 9–7.) In these cases, it is common for the auditor to actually reperform the control activity to see whether the proper results were obtained. For this example, the auditor can reperform the procedure by tracing the sales prices to the authorized price list in effect at the date of the transaction. If no errors are found, the auditor can conclude that the procedure is operating as intended. In Chapter 6 these procedures were referred to as tests of mechanical accuracy. The auditor may also reperform a procedure as a test of controls even is there is no indication of performance, if he or she feels reperformance is appropriate.

Extent of Procedures The extent to which tests of controls are applied depends on the intended assessed level of control risk. The lower the assessed level of control risk, the more extensive the tests of controls must be. For example, the auditor may look for additional key controls and increase the extent of testing of each control tested. For example, if the auditor wants to use a low assessed level of control risk, a larger sample size for inspections, observation, and reperformance procedures should be applied than for a higher assessed level of control risk.

Reliance on evidence from prior year's audit If evidence was obtained in the prior year's audit that indicates a key control was operating effectively, and the auditor determines that it is still in place, the extent of the tests of that control may be reduced to some extent in the current year. For example, in such circumstances, the auditor might use a reduced sample size in testing a control that leaves documentary evidence.

Testing less than the entire audit period Normally, tests of controls should be applied to transactions and controls for the entire period under audit. However, it is not always possible to do so. Where less than the entire period is tested, the auditor should consider the risk of relying on a control for the period not tested and determine whether substantive testing should be increased.

Relationship of Tests of Controls to Procedures to Obtain an Understanding

You will notice that there is a significant overlap between tests of controls and procedures to obtain an understanding. Both include inquiry, inspection, and observation. There are two primary differences in the application of these common procedures between phases. Section 5205 states: "The auditor needs to understand internal control only as it applies to the financial statements as a whole and to relevant assertions relating to significant account balances or classes of transactions." In other words, the procedures to gain an understanding are applied only to certain of all the control policies and procedures that have been instituted by the client. The auditor will obtain knowledge about the design of the relevant policies and procedures and determine whether or not they have been implemented. Tests of controls, on the other hand, are only applied when control risk has been assessed below maximum to establish whether the policies and procedures which have been determined to be key controls are operating effectively.

The second difference is that procedures to obtain an understanding are performed only on one or a few transactions or, in the case of observations, at a single point in time. Tests of controls are performed on larger samples of transactions (perhaps 20 to 100), and often observations are made at more than one point in time.

For key controls, tests of controls other than reperformance are essentially an *extension* of related procedures to obtain an understanding. For that reason, when auditors plan at the outset to obtain a low assessed level of control risk, they will combine both types of procedures and perform them simultaneously.

Figure 9–9 illustrates this concept in more detail. Where only the required minimum study of internal control is planned, the auditor will conduct a transaction walk-through. In so doing, the auditor determines that the audit documentation is complete and accurate, and observes that the control-related activities described are in operation.

When the control risk is assessed below the maximum level not only is a transaction walk-through performed, a larger sample of documents is inspected for indications of the effectiveness of the operation of controls. (The determination of appropriate sample size is discussed in Chapters 12 and 14.) Similarly, when observations are made, they will be more extensive and often at several points in time. Also, reperformance is an important tests of controls procedure.

APPENDIX A
Illustrative Internal Verification Procedures

To illustrate internal verification procedures, an example of the payroll for Smith Corp. is used. Assume there are 306 payroll transactions for one week. Each employee punches in daily using a time card machine which is *not on-line* to the computer system. The time cards are summarized by a payroll clerk and are the input for computer processing.

FIGURE 9–9

Relationship of Planned Assessed Level of Control Risk and Extent of Procedures

	PLANNED ASSESSED LEVEL OF CONTROL RISK	
Type of Procedure	*High Level:* *Obtaining an Understanding Only*	*Lower Level:* *Tests of Controls*
Inquiry	Yes – extensive	Yes – some
Inspection	Yes – with transaction walk-through	Yes – using sampling
Observation	Yes – with transaction walk-through	Yes – at multiple times
Reperformance	No	Yes – using sampling

Preprocessing Review

Input documents are typically the responsibility of a user department that transmits the documents to accounting before processing. Preprocessing review exists when someone from either the user department or accounting reviews the documents for such things as completeness and correctness. At Smith Corp. the assistant to the controller, Roy Lin, examines each time card for the name of the employee, the hours worked, and the wage rate. If he agrees with all the information, he initials a route slip accompanying the cards. He also counts the cards and writes the number 306 on the route slip, indicating there are 306 time cards.

Batching

When input documents are collected, controlled, and processed by discrete groups, it is referred to as *batching*. The 306 payroll transactions for Smith Corp. are a batch. Control techniques related to batching include use of batch numbers, transmittal documents, and control totals.

After transactions are batched, each batch is given a batch number that identifies it for further processing. Transmittal control forms and route slips are documents used in organizations to help ensure that all batches of data are entirely processed. The *transmittal control* form is used to log the receipt of data, the date they are processed, and the release of the data. This control device is useful both for determining which data have been received but not processed and for isolating where unprocessed data are located. The *route slip* is attached to the batch of data to inform the processing center of the proper path of processing and to provide a record of the actual processing performed. The route slip was prepared for payroll at Smith Corp. when Controller Fran West reviewed the data.

Control totals are used to determine whether all the data that were put into the system were processed. Generally, the purpose of a control total is to make certain that no data are lost in handling or processing, but in some cases it is used to verify that the dollar amount is correct. A count or summation of a batch of input must be completed before the input goes into the system. After the data are processed, the control total is compared with the final output. For example, the count of 306 payroll records for Smith Corp. is a control total called a *record count*. The record count of 306 is entered into the computer and will be compared by the computer with the actual number of transactions processed.

If gross payroll was known before the information was processed, it could have been used as a control total, called a *financial control total*. In payroll, gross payroll is usually not known until after the data are processed. Therefore, financial control totals are impractical.

A third type of control total, called a *hash total*, may be practical for Smith Corp.'s payroll. The total number of hours for all employees is manually added and entered as a control total. The computer can later compare hours actually worked with the control total. A hash total is a batch total based on some number not normally added. Examples are hours worked for payroll or units of different products sold for sales.

Conversion Verification

When data are put onto machine-readable media (such as disk or tape), there is a risk of key-entry errors. Four types of procedures are commonly used to detect those errors: key verification, check-digit verification, logic tests, and control total balancing.

Key verification involves having different operators (or the same operator) repeat the keying process for all or part of the entry data. If the results do not match, the transaction is not acceptable for further processing until the difference is corrected. Since the operators are generally instructed to key-enter the information exactly as it is stated on the original documents, this control is useful only for detecting key-entry errors.

A *check-digit* is a number that is part of an *identification number*. It is used as a means of determining whether a recorded identification number is correct. As a highly oversimplified example of check digits, assume that Smith Corp. personnel identification numbers for payroll range from 1 to 400. For the employee with the identification number 362, the number 11 (the summation of the three digits is the check digit in this example) could be added to the number for a new identification number of 36211. After this is done for each employee, the data entry equipment is programmed to determine whether the sum of the first three digits of each identification number equals the last two digits. This is a useful control for detecting key-entry errors. It is unnecessary to *key-verify* identification numbers if check digits are used.

Logic tests involve various types of computerized comparisons of input data with programmed criteria that determine the acceptability of the input data. If the data fail the logic test, they must be correctly reentered before they can be processed.

Examples of logic tests include the following:

- *Validity test.* Codes as entered, such as transaction codes, are compared with a table of valid codes. For example, employee numbers can be compared with a computerized file of employees.
- *Format test.* The content of a field is tested for a prescribed format. For example, the hours worked must contain only numbers and not letters.

Logic tests are often deferred until processing, which is discussed as a part of programmed controls. The advantage of including them at the input state is early correction. The disadvantage is the need for more expensive data-entry equipment.

Control total balancing was discussed as part of batching. Data entry equipment can be programmed to produce totals from data entered for use in balancing, or this step can be deferred until processing results are obtained. Most well-controlled systems reconcile control totals at several points.

Programmed Controls

Programmed controls are written into computer programs to detect erroneous input, processing, or output. They are similar to logic controls in conversion verification. They are somewhat expensive to implement because they often require extensive programming and storage of data. For example, in payroll, a complete list of employees, employee numbers, and department numbers for each employee must be stored in the computer.

Programmed controls are desirable because they enable the computer to check 100 percent of the data for certain types of exceptions. Where a programmed control indicates an error, the data are either rejected from further processing or printed after the processing has occurred. The following are common examples of programmed controls:

- *Validity test* – Compare identification number with an existing list to determine if it exists. (Is employee number included in a list of all employees?)
- *Completeness test* – Examine every field in a record to determine whether all are complete. (Is employee number, name, number of regular hours worked, number of overtime hours worked, and department number included and complete?)

- ■ *Matching test* – Compare two fields to determine if they match. (Is employee in the same department as the one to which he or she is assigned?)
- ■ *Reasonableness or limit test* – Compare contents to see if amounts are within defined limits. (Is employee's gross payroll less than or equal to 60 hours or $999 for the week?)

Postprocessing Review

Normally, either the user or the EDP control group, or both, review the output for errors. Frequently, someone compares the output with the original input. Fran West at Smith Corp. reviews a printout of payroll before cheques are issued. Employees, of course, also provide feedback for payroll errors, especially if no cheque is prepared or if there is any underpayment.

Master File Controls

Master file controls ensure the integrity of the master file at different times. Generally, they involve periodically printing out the contents of the master files for review of the data and printing out and reviewing changes made to the master files. Fran West at Smith Corp. also performs this responsibility.

Periodic Internal Audit

Because of the technical complexity of EDP and its effect on financial statements, it is important to have internal auditors review input, output, and programmed controls on an ongoing basis. It is also desirable to involve internal auditors during the systems development process for EDP applications to ensure there are adequate controls before applications are placed in service.

APPENDIX B Flowcharting Techniques

Auditors frequently prepare flowcharts of a client's accounting systems as a part of the study of internal control. At other times, auditors use client-prepared flowcharts. The material in this appendix is intended to provide guidance for proper flowcharting techniques to students who lack flowcharting knowledge or experience.

Types of Flowcharts

There are three common types of flowcharts: systems flowcharts, internal control flowcharts, and program flowcharts. Systems flowcharts are usually simple presentations of the flow of documents and records in the organization. Internal control flowcharts are more elaborate and show the segregation of duties and other controls present in the system. Program flowcharts are even more detailed, but they relate only to specific computer programs.

Auditors generally prefer internal control flowcharts for their purposes. Although they are more complex than systems flowcharts, the additional information is sufficiently important to justify their preparation and use. Program flowcharts are usually only used by auditors who are EDP audit specialists.

Symbols

Symbols are used to show predefined items, steps, and actions. No matter what symbols are used, the concept of flowcharting remains unchanged, but naturally the symbols must be defined. Different audit firms use different symbols, but most are similar in form. Figure 9–10 shows the basic symbols that have been adopted for this text and gives an example of each.

Illustration   A brief flowcharting illustration is useful at this point. Figure 9–11

FIGURE 9–10

Basic Flowcharting
Symbols

Document—paper documents and
   reports of all types.
Example: a sales invoice

Process symbol—any processing function;
   defined operation causing a change in value,
   form, or location of information[1].
Example: a billing clerk prepares a sales invoice.

Off-line storage—off-line storage of documents,
   records, and EDP files.
Example: a duplicate sales invoice is filed
   in numerical order.

Transmittal tape—a proof or adding machine tape
   used for control purposes.
Example: an adding machine tape of sales invoices.

Input/output symbol—used to indicate information
   entering or leaving system.
Example: a receipt of order from customer.

Decision—used to indicate a decision is made
   requiring different action for a "yes" or "no" answer
   (rarely used).
Example: is customer credit satisfactory?

No

Yes

Annotation—the addition of descriptive comments or
   explanatory notes as clarification.
Example: a billing clerk checks credit before
   preparing an invoice.

Directional flow lines—the direction of processing
   or data flow.

Connector—exit to, or entry from, another part of chart;
   keyed in by using numbers.
Example: a document transfer from one department
   into another department.

Symbols Unique to EDP Systems

Punched card	Punched tape	Magnetic tape	Disk or drum storage

---

[1] When the process is done manually it is common to use the symbol,

FIGURE 9–11   Flowchart

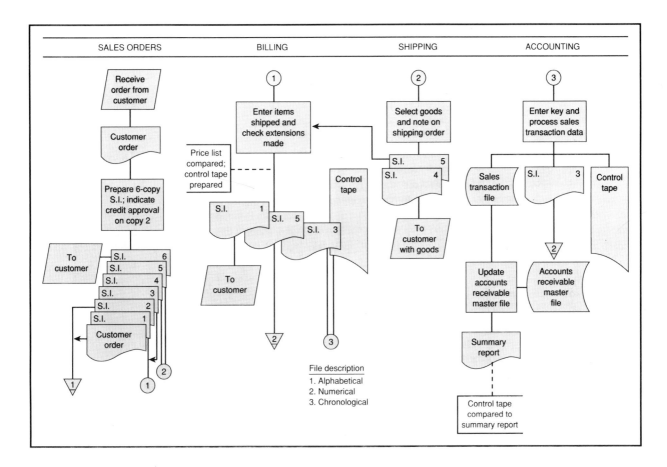

furnishes a flowchart for the narrative description that follows (see boxed material below) of the sales, billing, shipping, and accounting departments of a small wholesale company.

The sales department prepares a six-part invoice form from the customer's order. The customer order is filed alphabetically by customer after the sales invoice is prepared. Credit approval is indicated on copy 2, which is then filed with the customer order. Parts 1 (sales invoice) and 3 (ledger) are sent to billing, part 4 (packing slip) and part 5 (shipping order) are sent to shipping, and part 6 is sent to the customer as acknowledgment of the order.

    Shipping physically collects the items for shipment and notes on the shipping order that the goods were shipped. The packing slip is sent to the customer with the goods, and the shipping order is sent to billing.

    Billing enters the shipped items marked on the shipping order on the sales invoice and ledger copy, makes extensions and checks them, compares the prices with the price list, and runs a tape of the amounts on the ledger copy. The shipping order is then filed numerically. The sales invoice is sent to the customer, and the ledger copy and the tape are sent to accounting.

    In accounting, invoices are entered daily into a sales transaction file using the computer. The sales transaction files are then used to update the accounts receivable master file. A summary total of sales is printed daily and compared with the control tape received from billing. The control tape and sales invoices are filed daily. Journals, and ledgers, can be printed from the computer files on demand, but are typically printed monthly.

Techniques   Flowcharts communicate the flow of documents and records and several aspects of internal control. To help flowcharts communicate effectively:

- *Use specialized symbols*. These are shown in Figure 9–10.
- *Use flowlines*. Flowlines are used to indicate the direction of the flow. The flow-charting convention for arrowheads is that they should be used for all directions of flow except down and to the right. The authors recommend the use of arrow-heads whenever it adds clarity. In preparing flowcharts, flowlines should cross as infrequently as possible. When they must cross, use the following technique:

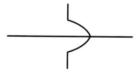

- *Show separation of duties*. Areas of responsibility are established on flowcharts as vertical columns or sections through which the flow of documents takes place horizontally (from left to right). This technique enables the reader to identify clearly changes in responsibility as the documents flow through the system. An example of separation by areas of responsibility is given in Figure 9–11.
- *Include relevant controls*. The inclusion of significant controls in a flowchart aids the auditor in understanding internal control and assessing control risks. Examples include authorizations, internal verification, and reconciliations. The flowchart in Figure 9–11 includes several controls.

- *Include written comments and clarification*. The use of comments and explanations is encouraged whenever it will help make a flowchart more complete or easier to understand. There are two types of written comments: annotations and footnotes. Annotations are included within the flowchart(- – -[ ). Footnotes are included at the bottom or on one side. Annotation is preferred when there is sufficient room on the flowchart. Frequently, control procedures can be identified most effectively by written comments. Annotations are shown in Figure 9–11.

- *Show the source of every document in the flowchart*. Every document must come from one of three sources: (1) a source outside the company, (2) a department not shown in the flowchart, or (3) a department being described in the flowchart.

- *Use a process symbol for every document or record prepared*. Every document must result from some type of action, such as preparing a payroll cheque. The action should be shown by use of a process symbol.

- Make sure that all documents that enter a process also leave that process. A process may change or use a document, but does not destroy it.

- *Show the disposition of every document in the flowchart*. Every document must go to one of three places: (1) a destination outside the company, (2) a department not shown in the flowchart, or (3) the files.

Notice in Figure 9–11 that the source and disposition of all documents are shown. Computer files such as the sales transaction file and master file exist within the function being flowcharted. Therefore, they do not flow anywhere and their source and disposition need not be shown.

Overall Approach   Incorporating the above flowcharting techniques should result in readable and relevant flowcharts. The following are the steps ordinarily followed in preparing flowcharts:

1. Decide which system or process is to be flowcharted (purchasing, sales, payroll).
2. Determine information about the documents, records and activities in the system through interviewing client personnel, observing their activities, and examining the documents and records including procedures manuals.
3. Develop a tentative organization for the flowchart, including separation of duties.
4. Draw a rough sketch of the system or process.
5. Draw the flowchart, including comments and annotations.
6. Trace the documents and records for one or two transactions through the flowchart to determine its accuracy. Questioning client personnel is also useful at this point.

REVIEW QUESTIONS

9–1   Chapter 7 introduced the six parts of the planning phase of audits. Which part is understanding internal control and assessing control risk? What parts precede and follow that understanding and assessing?

9–2   Identify the four functions that are common to all accounting systems. For each function, briefly explain what occurs in the payroll and personnel cycle.

9–3   Compare management's concerns about internal control with those of the auditor.

9–4   Frequently, management is more concerned about internal controls that promote operational efficiency than about those that result in reliable financial data. How can the independent auditor persuade management to devote more attention to controls affecting the reliability of accounting information when management has this attitude?

9–5 State the seven detailed internal control objectives.

9–6 What is meant by the control environment? What are the factors the auditor must evaluate to understand it?

9–7 What is the relationship between the control environment and control systems?

9–8 List the five internal control procedures and provide one specific illustration of a control in the sales area for each procedure.

9–9 The separation of operational responsibility from record keeping is meant to prevent different types of misstatements than the separation of the custody of assets from accounting. Explain the difference in the purposes of these two types of separation of duties.

9–10 Distinguish between general and specific authorization of transactions and give one example of each type.

9–11 For each of the following, give an example of a physical control the client can use to protect the asset or record:

1. Petty cash
2. Cash received by retail clerks
3. Accounts receivable records
4. Raw material inventory
5. Perishable tools
6. Manufacturing equipment
7. Marketable securities

9–12 Explain what is meant by internal checks on performance and give five specific examples of internal checks.

9–13 Distinguish between obtaining an understanding of internal control and assessing control risk. Also explain the methodology the auditor uses for each of them.

9–14 Define what is meant by a control and a weakness in internal control. Give two examples of each in the sales and collection cycle.

9–15 Frank James, a highly competent employee of Brinkwater Sales Corporation, had been responsible for accounting-related matters for two decades. His devotion to the firm and his duties had always been exceptional, and over the years he had been given increased responsibility. Both the president of Brinkwater and the partner of an independent public accounting firm in charge of the audit were shocked and dismayed to discover that James had embezzled more than $500,000 over a 10-year period by not recording billings in the sales journal and subsequently diverting the cash receipts. What major factors permitted the defalcation to take place?

9–16 Jeanne Maier, a public accountant, believes it is appropriate to obtain an understanding of internal control about halfway through the audit, after she is familiar with the client's operations and the way the system actually works. She has found through experience that filling out internal control questionnaires and flowcharts early in the engagement is not beneficial because the system rarely functions the way it is supposed to. Later in the engagement, it is feasible to prepare flowcharts and questionnaires with relative ease because of the knowledge already obtained on the audit. Evaluate her approach.

9–17 Distinguish between the objectives of an internal control questionnaire and the objectives of a flowchart for documenting information about a client's internal control. State the advantages and disadvantages of each of these two methods.

9–18 Explain what is meant by "significant deficiencies" as it relates to internal control. What should the auditor do when he or she has discovered significant deficiencies in internal control?

9–19   Examine the control matrix in Figure 9–7, page 296. Explain the purpose of the matrix. Also explain the meaning and effect of an assessment of control risk of low compared to one of medium.

9–20   Explain what is meant by tests of controls. Write one inspection of documents test of control and one reperformance test of controls for the following internal control: hours on time cards are re-added by an independent payroll clerk and initialed to indicate performance.

MULTIPLE CHOICE QUESTIONS

9–21   The following are general questions about internal control. Choose the best response.

    a.   When considering internal control, an auditor must be aware of the concept of reasonable assurance which recognizes that the

        (1)   employment of competent personnel provides assurance that the objectives of internal control will be achieved.

        (2)   establishment and maintenance of internal control is an important responsibility of the management and *not* of the auditor.

        (3)   cost of internal control should *not* exceed the benefits expected to be derived therefrom.

        (4)   separation of incompatible functions is necessary to ascertain that the internal control is effective.

    b.   When an auditor issues an unqualified opinion, it is implied that the

        (1)   entity has *not* violated provisions of the *Canada Business Corporations Act*.

        (2)   likelihood of management fraud is minimal.

        (3)   financial records are sufficiently reliable to permit the preparation of financial statements.

        (4)   entity's internal control is in conformity with criteria established by its audit committee.

    c.   Taylor Sales Corp. maintains a large full-time internal audit staff that reports directly to the chief accountant. Audit reports prepared by the internal auditors indicate that the system is functioning as it should and that the accounting records are reliable. The public accountant will probably

        (1)   eliminate tests of controls.

        (2)   increase the depth and study and evaluation of controls related to achievement of Taylor Sales Corp.'s corporate policies.

        (3)   avoid duplicating the work of the internal audit staff.

        (4)   place limited reliance on the work of the internal audit staff.

    d.   What is the independent auditor's principal purpose for obtaining an understanding of existing internal control and assessing control risk?

        (1)   To comply with generally accepted accounting principles.

        (2)   To obtain a measure of assurance of management's efficiency.

        (3)   To maintain a state of independence in mental attitude in all matters relating to the audit.

        (4)   To determine the nature, timing, and extent of subsequent audit work.

(AICPA adapted)

9–22   The following questions deal with weaknesses of internal control. Choose the best response.

    a.   In general, a material internal control weakness may be defined as a condition under which material errors or fraud would ordinarily *not* be detected within a timely period by

(1) an auditor during the normal obtaining of an understanding of internal control and assessment of control risk.
(2) a controller when reconciling accounts in the general ledger.
(3) employees in the normal course of performing their assigned functions.
(4) the chief financial officer when reviewing interim financial statements.

b. Which of the following statements with respect to suggested auditor communication of significant weaknesses in internal control is correct?

(1) Such communication is required to be in writing.
(2) Such communication must include a description of all weaknesses.
(3) Such communication is the principal reason for testing and evaluating internal controls.
(4) Such communication is incidental to the auditor's understanding of internal control and assessment of control risk.

c. Section 5220 suggests that the auditor who becomes aware of significant internal control weaknesses communicate this information to the

(1) person in charge of the area where the weakness was found.
(2) shareholders.
(3) internal auditors.
(4) audit committee and senior management. (AICPA adapted)

9–23 The following questions deal with internal controls in specific transaction cycles. Choose the best response.

a. Proper internal control over the payroll function would mandate which of the following?

(1) The payroll clerk should fill the envelopes with the cheques and a computation of the net wages.
(2) Unclaimed pay envelopes should be held by the payroll clerk.
(3) Each employee should be asked to sign a receipt.
(4) A separate chequeing account for payroll should be maintained.

b. To avoid potential errors and fraud well-designed internal control in the accounts payable area should include a separation of which of the following functions?

(1) Invoice verification and data entry into the computer.
(2) Invoice verification and merchandise ordering.
(3) Physical handling of merchandise received and preparation of receiving reports.
(4) Cheque signing and cancellation of payment documentation.

c. Which of the following is a standard internal control for cash disbursements?

(1) Cheques should be signed by the controller and at least one other employee of the company.
(2) Cheques should be sequentially numbered and the numerical sequence should be accounted for by the person preparing bank reconciliations.
(3) Cheques and supporting documents should be marked "paid" immediately after the cheque is returned with the bank statement.
(4) Cheques should be sent directly to the payee by the employee who prepares documents that authorize cheque preparation.

d. Which of the following policies is an internal control weakness related to the acquisition of factory equipment?

(1) Acquisitions are to be made through and approved by the department in need of the equipment.
(2) Advance executive approvals are required for equipment acquisitions.

(3) Variances between authorized equipment expenditures and actual costs are to be immediately reported to management.

(4) Depreciation policies are reviewed only once a year.   (AICPA adapted)

DISCUSSION QUESTIONS AND PROBLEMS

9–24 Each of the following internal control procedures has been taken from a standard internal control questionnaire used by a public accounting firm for assessing control risk in the payroll and personnel cycle.

1. Approval of department head or foreman on time cards is required prior to preparing payroll.

2. All prenumbered time cards are accounted for before beginning data entry for preparation of cheques.

3. Persons preparing the payroll do not perform other payroll duties (time-keeping, distribution of cheques) or have access to other payroll data or cash.

4. All clerical operations in payroll are double-checked before payment is made.

5. All voided and spoiled payroll cheques are properly mutilated and retained.

6. Personnel requires an investigation of an employment application from new employees. Investigation includes checking employee's background, former employers, and references.

7. Written termination notices, with properly documented reasons for termination, and approval of an appropriate official are required.

8. All cheques not distributed to employees are returned to the treasurer for safe-keeping.

Required:

a. For each internal control procedure, identify the type(s) of control procedures to which it applies (such as adequate documents and records or physical control over assets and records).

b. For each internal control procedure, identify the internal control objective(s) to which it applies.

c. For each internal control procedure, identify a specific error or fraud or other irregularity that is likely to be prevented if the procedure exists and is effective.

d. For each procedure, identify one audit test the auditor could use to uncover error or fraud resulting from the absence of the control.

9–25 The following are errors or fraud that have occurred in Fresh Foods Grocery Store Ltd., a wholesale and retail grocery company.

1. The incorrect price was used on sales invoices for billing shipments to customers because the wrong price was entered into the computer file.

2. A vendor's invoice was paid twice for the same shipment. The second payment arose because the vendor sent a duplicate copy of the original two weeks after the payment was due.

3. Employees in the receiving department took sides of beef for their personal use. When a shipment of meat was received, the receiving department filled out a receiving report and forwarded it to the accounting department for the amount of goods actually received. At that time, two sides of beef were put in an employee's pickup truck rather than in the storage freezer.

4. During the physical count of inventory of the retail grocery, one counter wrote down the wrong description of several products and miscounted the quantity.

5. A salesperson sold an entire carload of lamb at a price below cost because she did not know the cost of lamb had increased in the past week.

6. On the last day of the year, a truckload of beef was set aside for shipment but was not shipped. Because it was still on hand the inventory was counted. The shipping document was dated the last day of the year so it was also included as a current-year sale.

Required:

a. For each error or fraud, identify one or more types of controls that were absent.

b. For each error or fraud, identify the internal control objectives that have not been met.

c. For each error or fraud, suggest a control procedure to correct the deficiency.

9–26 The division of the following duties is meant to provide the best possible controls for the Meridian Paint Company Ltd., a small wholesale store.

*1. Assemble supporting documents for general and payroll disbursement.

*2. Sign general disbursement cheques.

*3. Input information to prepare cheques for signature, record cheques in the cash disbursements journal, and update the appropriate master files.

*4. Mail disbursement cheques to suppliers and deliver cheques to employees.

5. Cancel supporting documents to prevent their reuse.

*6. Approve credit for customers.

*7. Input shipping and billing information to bill customers, record invoices in the sales journal, and update the accounts receivable master file.

*8. Open the mail and prepare a prelisting of cash receipts.

*9. Enter cash receipts data to prepare the cash receipts journal and update the accounts receivable master file.

*10. Prepare daily cash deposits.

*11. Deliver daily cash deposits to the bank.

*12. Assemble the payroll time cards and input the data to prepare payroll cheques and update the payroll journal and payroll master files.

*13. Sign payroll cheques.

14. Update the general ledger at the end of each month and review all accounts for unexpected balances.

15. Reconcile the accounts receivable master file with the control account and review accounts outstanding more than 90 days.

16. Prepare monthly statements for customers by printing the accounts receivable master file; then mail the statements to customers.

17. Reconcile the monthly statements from vendors with the accounts payable master file.

18. Reconcile the bank account.

Required:

You are to divide the accounting-related duties 1 through 18 among Robert Smith, Karen Wong, and Barbara Chiu. All of the responsibilities marked with an asterisk are assumed to take about the same amount of time and must be divided equally between Smith and Wong. Both employees are equally competent. Chiu, who is president of the company, is not willing to perform any functions designated by an asterisk and a maximum of two of the other functions. (AICPA adapted)

9–27 Recently, while eating lunch with some friends at a cafeteria at your university, you observe a practice that is somewhat unusual. As you reach the end of the cafeteria line, an adding machine operator asks how many persons are in your party. He then totals the food purchases on the trays for all of your family and writes the number of persons included in the group on the adding machine tape. He hands you the tape and asks you to pay when you finish eating. Near the end of the meal, you decide you want a piece of pie and coffee so you return to the line, select your food, and again go through the line. The adding machine operator goes through the same procedures, but this time he staples the second tape to the original and returns it to you.

When you leave the cafeteria, you hand the stapled adding machine tapes to the cash register operator, who totals the two tapes, takes your money, and puts the tapes on a spindle.

Required:

a. What internal controls has the cafeteria instituted for its operations?

b. How can the manager of the cafeteria evaluate the effectiveness of the control procedures?

c. How do these controls differ from those used by most cafeterias?

d. What are the costs and benefits of the cafeteria's system?

9–28   Lew Pherson and Marie Violette are friends who are employed by different public accounting firms. One day during lunch they are discussing the importance of internal control in determining the amount of audit evidence required for an engagement. Pherson expresses the view that internal control must be carefully evaluated in all companies, regardless of their size, in basically the same manner. His public accounting firm requires a standard internal control questionnaire on every audit as well as a flowchart of every transaction area. In addition, he says the firm requires a careful evaluation of the system and a modification in the evidence accumulated based on the controls and weaknesses in the system.

Violette responds by saying she believes internal control cannot be adequate in many of the small companies she audits although she recognizes that the *CICA Handbook* requires her to "obtain a sufficient understanding." She disagrees with the Recommendations and goes on to say, "Why should I spend a lot of time obtaining an understanding of internal control and assessing control risk when I know it has all kinds of weaknesses before I start? I would rather spend the time it takes to fill out all those forms in testing whether the statements are correct."

Required:

a. Express in general terms the most important difference between the nature of the potential controls available for large and small companies.

b. Criticize the positions taken by Pherson and Violette, and express your own opinion about the similarities and differences that should exist in understanding internal control and assessing control risk for different-sized companies.

9–29   The following are partial descriptions of internal control for companies engaged in the manufacturing business:

1. When Ms Tomins orders materials for her machine-rebuilding plant, she sends a duplicate purchase order to the receiving department. During the delivery of materials, Mr. Smith, the receiving clerk, records the receipt of shipment on this purchase order. After recording, Mr. Smith sends the purchase order to the accounting department, where it is used to record materials purchased and accounts payable. The materials are transported to the storage area by forklifts. The additional purchased quantities are recorded on storage records.

2. Every day hundreds of employees clock in using time cards at Generous Motors Corporation. The timekeepers collect these cards once a week and deliver them to the computer department. There the data on these time cards are entered into the computer. The information entered into the computer is used in the preparation of the labor cost distribution records, the payroll journal, and the payroll cheques. The treasurer, Mrs. Webber, compares the payroll journal with the payroll cheques, signs the cheques, and returns them to Mr. Strode, the supervisor of the computer department. The payroll cheques are distributed to the employees by Mr. Strode.

3. The smallest branch of Connor Cosmetics Inc. in Medicine Hat employs Mary Cooper, the branch manager, and her sales assistant, Janet Hendrix. The branch uses a bank account in Medicine Hat to pay expenses. The account is

kept in the name of "Connor Cosmetics Inc. – Special Account." To pay expenses, cheques must be signed by Mary Cooper or by the treasurer of Connor Cosmetics, John Winters. Cooper receives the canceled cheques and bank statements. She reconciles the branch account herself and files canceled cheques and bank statements in her records. She also periodically prepares reports of disbursements and sends them to the home office.

Required:

a. List the weaknesses in internal control for each of the above. To identify the weaknesses, use the methodology that was discussed in the chapter.

b. For each weakness, state the type of error(s) that is (are) likely to result. Be as specific as possible.

c. How would you improve internal controls for each of the three companies?

(AICPA adapted)

9–30 You are a manager with a public accounting firm. In the course of reviewing a file prepared by a new senior staff accountant you notice there is no letter to the client concerning weaknesses in internal control over purchases and payments. You also note that the senior commented in the file that she had obtained the necessary understanding of internal control over purchases and payments to plan the audit and found internal control to be so weak that she planned to use a control risk assessment at maximum.

When you asked her about the apparent lack of communication, she says no letter was sent because the *CICA Handbook* does not require such a letter.

Required:

Prepare a response to the senior explaining why you (and your firm) believe such a letter is required despite the *Handbook's* not requiring it.

9–31 Yvon Anthony, a public accountant, prepared the flowchart on page 315, which portrays the raw materials purchasing function of one of Anthony's clients, Medium-Sized Manufacturing Corp., from the preparation of initial documents through the vouching of invoices for payment in accounts payable. Assume all documents are prenumbered.

Required:

Identify the weaknesses of internal control that can be determined from the flowchart. Use the methodology discussed in the chapter. Include internal control weaknesses resulting from activities performed or not performed.

(AICPA adapted)

CASES

9–32 The following is the description of sales and cash receipts for Fashion Fair Inc., a retail store dealing in expensive women's clothing. Sales are for cash or credit, using the store's own billing rather than credit cards.

Each salesclerk has her own sales book with prenumbered, three-copy, multi-colored sales slips attached, but perforated. Only a central cash register is used. It is operated by the store supervisor, who has been employed for 10 years by Alice Olson, the store owner. The cash register is at the store entrance to control theft of clothes.

Salesclerks prepare the sales invoices in triplicate. The original and the second copy are given to the cashier. The third copy is retained by the salesclerk in the sales book. When the sale is for cash, the customer pays the salesclerk, who marks all three copies "paid" and presents the money to the cashier with the invoice copies.

All clothing is put into boxes or packages by the supervisor after comparing the clothing to the description on the invoice and the price on the sales tag. She also rechecks the clerk's calculations. Any corrections are approved by the salesclerk. The clerk changes her sales book at that time.

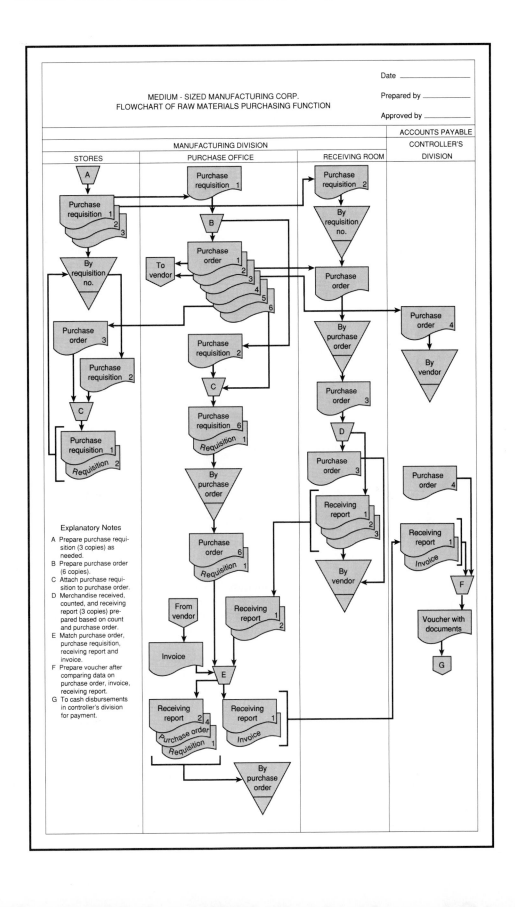

A credit sale is approved by the supervisor from an approved credit list after the salesclerk prepares the three-part invoice. Next, the supervisor enters the sale in her cash register as a credit or cash sale. The second copy of the invoice, which has been validated by the cash register, is given to the customer.

At the end of the day, the supervisor recaps the sales and cash and compares the totals to the cash register tape. The supervisor deposits the cash at the end of each day in the bank's lock box. The cashier's copies of the invoices are sent to the accounts receivable clerk along with a summary of the day's receipts. The bank mails the deposit slip directly to the accounts receivable clerk.

Each clerk summarizes her sales each day on a daily summary form, which is used in part to calculate employees' sales commissions. Marge Miske, the accountant, who is prohibited from handling cash, receives the supervisor's summary and the clerk's daily summary form. Daily, she puts all sales invoice information into the firm's microcomputer, which provides a complete printout of all input and summaries. The accounting summary includes sales by salesclerk, cash sales, credit sales, and total sales. Marge compares this output to the supervisor's and salesclerks' summaries and reconciles all differences.

The computer updates accounts receivable, inventory and general ledger master files. After the update procedure has been run on the computer, Marge's assistant files all sales invoices by customer number. A list of the invoice numbers in numerical sequence is included in the sales printout.

The mail is opened each morning by a secretary in the owner's office. All correspondence and complaints are given to the owner. The secretary prepares a prelist of cash receipts. He totals the list, prepares a deposit slip, and deposits the cash daily. A copy of the prelist, the deposit slip, and all remittances returned with the cash receipts are given to Marge. She uses this list and the remittances to record collections on receivables and update accounts receivable, again by computer. She reconciles the total receipts on the prelist to the deposit slip and to her printout. At the same time, she compares the deposit slip received from the bank for cash sales to the cash receipts journal.

Marge prepares a weekly aged trial balance of accounts receivable by use of the computer. A separate listing of all unpaid bills over 60 days is also automatically prepared. These are given to Alice Olson, who acts as her own credit collector. She also approves all charge-offs of uncollectible items and forwards the list to Marge, who writes them off.

Each month Marge prepares and mails statements to customers. Complaints and disagreements from customers are directed to Mrs. Olson, who resolves them and informs Marge in writing of any write-downs or errors that require correction.

The computer system also automatically totals the journals and posts the totals to the general ledger. A general ledger trial balance is printed out from which Marge prepares financial statements. Marge also prepares a monthly bank reconciliation and reconciles the general ledger to the aged accounts receivable trial balance.

Because of the importance of inventory control, Marge prints out the inventory perpetual totals monthly, on the last day of each month. Salesclerks count all inventory after store hours on the last day of each month for comparison to the perpetuals. An inventory shortages report is provided to Alice Olson. The perpetuals are adjusted by Marge after Alice Olson has approved the adjustments.

Required:

a. Flowchart the accounting system and related internal controls for sales and collections.

b. For each internal control objective for sales, identify one or more controls.

c. For each internal control objective for cash receipts, identify one or more controls.

d. Identify weaknesses of internal control in sales and cash receipts.

9-33 George Beemster, a public accountant, is examining the financial statements of the Chiliwack Sales Corporation, which recently installed an off-line electronic computer. The following comments have been extracted from Mr. Beemster's notes on computer operations and the processing and control of shipping notices and customer invoices:

- To minimize inconvenience Chiliwack converted without changing its existing data processing system, which used tabulating equipment. The computer company supervised the conversion and has provided training to all computer department employees (except data entry personnel) in systems design, operations, and programming.

- Each computer run is assigned to a specific employee who is responsible for making program changes, running the program, and answering questions. This procedure has the advantage of eliminating the need for records of computer operations because each employee is responsible for his or her own computer runs.

- At least one computer department employee remains in the computer room during office hours, and only computer department employees have keys to the computer room.

- System documentation consists of those materials furnished by the computer company – a set of record formats and program listings. These and the tape library are kept in a corner of the computer department.

- The company considered the desirability of programmed controls but decided to retain the manual controls from its existing system.

- Company products are shipped directly from public warehouses, which forward shipping notices to general accounting. There a billing clerk enters the price of the item and accounts for the numerical sequence of shipping notices from each warehouse. The billing clerk also prepares daily adding machine tapes (control tapes) of the units shipped and the unit prices.

- Shipping notices and control tapes are forwarded to the computer department for data entry and processing. Extensions are made on the computer. Output consists of invoices (in six copies) and the daily sales register. The daily sales register shows the aggregate totals of units shipped and unit prices that the computer operator compares with the control tapes.

- All copies of the invoice are returned to the billing clerk. The clerk mails three copies to the customer, forwards one copy to the warehouse, maintains one copy in a numerical file, and retains one copy in an open invoice file that serves as a detail accounts receivable record.

Required: Describe weaknesses in internal control over information and data flows and the procedures for processing shipping notices and customer invoices, and recommend improvements in these controls and processing procedures. (AICPA adapted)

Self-study for final [handwritten]

INTEGRATED CASE APPLICATION

9-34 ABC AUDIT – PART I

This case study of ABC Ltd. is presented in four parts. Each part deals with the material in the chapter in which that part appears. However, the parts are connected in such a way that in completing all four, you will gain a better understanding of how the parts of the audit are interrelated and integrated by the audit process. The parts appear in the following locations:

Part I – Understand internal control and assess control risk for acquisitions and cash disbursements, Chapter 9, page 318.

FIGURE 9–12

Information Relating to
Audit of Accounts
Payable – Previous Year

Accounts payable, 12-31-X4	
Number of accounts	52
Total accounts payable	$163,892.27
Range of individual balances	$27.83 – $14,819.62
Materiality for the audit	$45,000
Transactions, 19X4	
Acquisitions:	
Number of acquisitions	3,800
Total acquisitions	$2,933,812
Cash disbursements:	
Number of disbursements	2,600
Total cash disbursements	$3,017,112
Results of audit procedures – tests of controls for acquisitions (sample size of 100):	
Purchase order not approved	2
Purchase quantities, prices, and/or extensions not correct	1
Transactions charged to wrong general ledger account	1
Transactions recorded in wrong period	1
No other exceptions found	
Results of audit procedures – cash disbursements (sample size of 100):	
Cash disbursement recorded in wrong period	1
No other exceptions found	
Results of audit procedures – accounts payable	
20 percent of vendors' balances were verified; combined net understatement errors were projected to the population as follows:	
Three cutoff errors	$4,873.28
One difference in amounts due to disputes and discounts	$1,103.12
No adjustment was necessary, since the total projected error was not material.	

Part II – Design tests of controls, Chapter 11, page 390.

Part III – Determine sample sizes using attributes sampling and evaluate results, Chapter 12, page 432.

Part IV – Evaluation of the results of analytical procedures and tests of details of balances, Chapter 13, pages 464-469.

Background Information

ABC Ltd. is a medium-sized manufacturing company with a December 31 year-end. You have been assigned the responsibility of auditing acquisitions and payments and one related balance sheet account, accounts payable. The general approach to be taken will be to reduce assess control risk at a low level, if possible, for the two main types of transactions affecting accounts payable: purchases and cash disbursements. The following are furnished as background information:

Figure 9–12 – A summary of key information from the audit of acquisitions, cash disbursements and accounts payable in the prior year's audit.

Figure 9–13 – A flowchart description of the accounting system and internal controls for acquisitions and payments.

PART I

The purpose of Part I is to obtain an understanding of internal control and assess control risk for ABC Ltd.'s acquisition and cash disbursement transactions.

Required:

a. Study Figures 9-12 and 9-13 to gain an understanding of ABC's internal control.

b. Assess control risk as high, medium, or low on an objective-by-objective basis

FIGURE 9–13   ABC Ltd. – Acquisitions and Payment Cycle

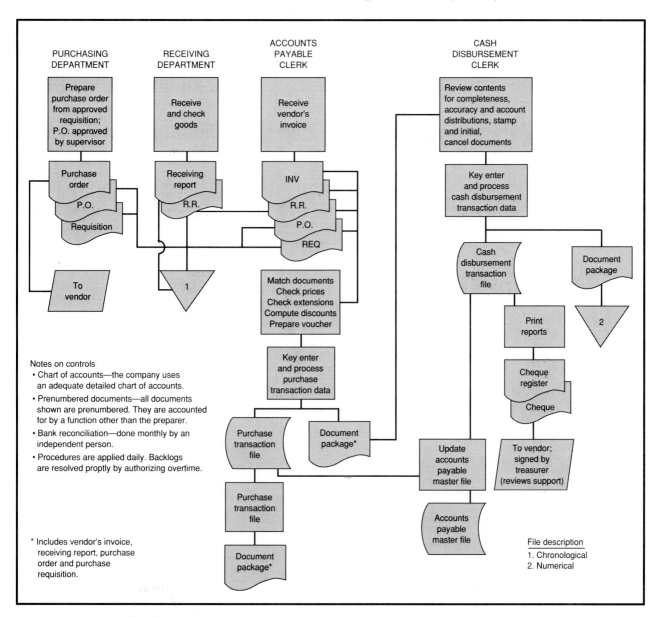

for the acquisitions and payments controls considering both internal controls and weaknesses. You should use a matrix similar to the one in Figure 9–7, page 296, for the assessment. There should be one matrix for acquisitions and a separate one for cash disbursements. The source of the internal controls and weaknesses is the information in Figure 9–13.

10

OVERALL AUDIT PLAN AND AUDIT PROGRAM

LEARNING OBJECTIVES

THOROUGH STUDY OF THIS CHAPTER WILL ENABLE YOU TO:

1. Describe the four types of audit tests used to determine the sufficiency and appropriateness of audit evidence

2. Discuss the relative costs of the audit tests, the relationships between types of tests and evidence, and among types of tests

3. Understand how the four types of tests should be emphasized in different circumstances

4. Know the methodology for the design of an audit program

5. Understand the relationship of specific internal control objectives to specific audit objectives

6. Integrate the four phases of the audit process

☐ The first five steps in the planning process shown in the margin are primarily for the purpose of helping the auditor develop an effective and efficient audit plan and audit program. As was indicated in Chapter 6, the audit program includes a listing of all of the audit procedures to be used to gather sufficient appropriate audit evidence. The related details for each procedure regarding sample size, the items to select, and the timing of the tests are also included.

321

The most important consideration in developing the audit plan and audit program is the planning form of the audit risk model:

$$PDR = \frac{AR}{IR \times CR}$$

where

PDR = planned detection risk
AR = audit risk
IR = inherent risk
CR = control risk

In previous chapters each of the independent variables (AR, IR, CR) has been discussed. In this chapter the relationship between these three variables, and the dependent variable (PDR) is studied.

In this chapter, the audit plan and audit program are discussed in terms of four basic types of audit tests. First, the nature of each type of test is defined and discussed. Next, the relative emphasis on the different types of tests that result from differing audit plans is studied. The chapter ends with a summary of the audit process as developed in this and the previous five chapters.

Types of Tests

There are four basic types of tests auditors use in determining whether financial statements are fairly stated: *procedures to obtain an understanding of internal control, tests of controls, analytical procedures,* and *tests of details of balances.* The last two types of test are included in the term "substantive procedures" by the *CICA Handbook.* Most audit procedures fall into one of these four categories.

Procedures to Obtain an Understanding of Internal Control

The methodology and procedures used to obtain an understanding of internal control were studied in Chapter 9. During that phase of an audit, the auditor must focus attention on both the *design* and the *operation* of aspects of internal control to the extent necessary to effectively plan the rest of the audit. A critical point made in Chapter 9 was the requirement to support the understanding obtained with evidence. The purpose of the procedures performed, then, is to provide both understanding and evidence to support it. Five types of audit procedures that relate to the auditor's understanding of internal control were identified in Chapter 9:

> **OBJECTIVE 1**
>
> Describe the four types of audit tests used to determine the sufficiency and appropriateness of audit evidence.

- Auditor's previous experience with the entity
- Inquiries of client personnel
- Examination of clients' policy and procedures manuals
- Inspection of documents and records
- Observation of entity activities and operations

These procedures are performed in combination to obtain an understanding of the design of particular control policies and procedures and to determine whether they have been placed in operation. For example, for the use of budgeting as a control procedure, the auditor would know that budgets are used based on prior experience, reaffirm their use and design by inquiry of management, and inspect recent budgets, variance and follow-up reports as a means of determining that they are currently being used.

Tests of Controls

A major use of the auditor's understanding of the client's internal control will be to assess control risk relative to the various internal control objectives that exist. Where the auditor believes control policies and procedures are effectively designed, and where it is efficient to do so, he or she will elect to assess control risk at a level that reflects that evaluation (i.e., at a level that would be described as moderate or low). In doing this, however, the assessed level of control risk must be limited to the level supported by evidence obtained. The procedures used to obtain such evidence are called tests of controls.

Tests of controls are directed toward the *effectiveness* of controls, both in terms of their design and their operation. These tests involve the following types of evidence:

- Inquiries of client personnel
- Inspection of documents and records
- Observation of the application of specific policies and procedures
- Reperformance of the application of specific policies and procedures by the auditor

The first three of these types of evidence are the same as types of evidence obtained in understanding internal control. Thus, the assessment of control risk and tests of controls can be thought of as a continuation of the audit procedures used to obtain the understanding of internal control. The main difference is that with tests of controls, the objective will be more specific and the tests will be more extensive. For example, if the client's budgeting process is to be used as a basis for assessing a low level of risk that expenditures are misclassified, in addition to the procedures described in the example given for obtaining an understanding, the auditor might also select a recent budget report, trace its contents to source records, prove its mathematical accuracy, examine all variance reports and memos that flow from it, talk to responsible personnel about the follow-up actions they took, and examine documentation in support of those actions. In effect, when the auditor decides to assess control risk below maximum level for any particular internal control objective, the procedures used to obtain an understanding of internal control are folded into the tests of controls. The amount of additional evidence required for tests of controls will depend on the amount and extensiveness of evidence obtained in gaining the understanding.

To illustrate typical tests of controls, it is useful to return to the controls matrix for Airtight Machine Inc. in Figure 9-7, page 296. For each of the ten controls included in Figure 9-7, Figure 10–1 identifies a test of controls that might be performed to test the effectiveness of each control. Notice that no control is performed for the weakness in Figure 9-7. It would make no sense to determine if the absence of a control procedure is being adequately performed.

Dual Purpose Tests

An auditor may perform auditing procedures which are both tests of controls and analytical procedures (described below) on the same sample of transactions or balances for efficiency; such procedures are known as *dual purpose tests*. Dual purpose tests provide evidence of whether or not the controls being tested were operating effectively during the period and about the validity of data produced by the accounting system. Reperformance always simultaneously provides evidence about both controls and monetary correctness.

Figure 10–2 illustrates a dual purpose test. For simplicity, two assumptions are made. First, only sales and cash receipts transactions and three general ledger balances make up the sales and collection cycle. Second, the beginning balances

FIGURE 10–1

Illustration of Tests of
Controls

ILLUSTRATIVE KEY CONTROLS	TYPICAL TESTS OF CONTROLS
Credit is approved before shipment occurs.	Examine a page of customer orders to determine the existence of authorized initials indicating credit approval (documentation).
Sales are supported by authorized shipping documents and approved customer orders, which are attached to the duplicate sales invoice.	Examine a sample of duplicate sales invoices to determine that each one is supported by an attached authorized shipping document and approved customer order (documentation).
Separation of duties between billing, recording sales, and handling cash receipts.	Observe whether personnel responsible for handling cash have no accounting responsibilities and inquire as to their duties (observation and inquiry).
An approved price list is used to determine unit selling prices.	Observe whether a price list is used when invoices are prepared and compare the price list with a list of current selling prices (observation and documentation).
Shipping documents are forwarded to billing daily and billed the subsequent day.	Observe whether shipping documents are forwarded daily to billing and observe when they are billed (observation).
Shipping documents and duplicate sales invoice numbers are accounted for weekly and traced to the sales journal.	Account for a sequence of duplicate sales invoice and shipping documents and trace each to the sales journal (documentation and reperformance).
Shipping documents are batched daily by quantity shipped.	Examine a sample of daily batches, re-add the shipping quantities, and trace totals to reconciliation with input reports (reperformance).
Statements are mailed to all customers each month.	Observe whether statements are mailed for a month and inquire about whose responsibility it is (observation and inquiry).
There is an adequate chart of accounts.	Examine a sample of sales invoices to determine whether each one has an account number and that the account number is correct (documentation and reperformance).
The sales journal is reviewed monthly for reasonableness of total and compared to the general ledger for sales and sales returns.	Re-add the sales journal for one month and trace the total to the general ledger (reperformance).

in cash ($47) and accounts receivable ($96) were audited in the previous year and are considered correct. If the auditor verifies that sales ($660) and collection ($590) transactions were correctly recorded in the journals and posted in the general ledger, he or she can conclude that the ending balance in accounts receivable ($166) and sales ($660) are correct. (Cash disbursements ($563) will have to be audited before the auditor can reach a conclusion about the balance in cash in bank.) The auditor verifies the recording and summarizing of transactions by the dual purpose test. In this example, there will be one set of procedures for sales and another for cash receipts.

Subsequent

③

Analytical Procedures
As discussed in Chapter 7, *analytical procedures* involve comparisons of recorded amounts to expectations developed by the auditor. They often involve the calculation of ratios by the auditor for comparison with the previous years' ratios and other

FIGURE 10–2

Relationship of
Transactions to
Journals and General
Ledger

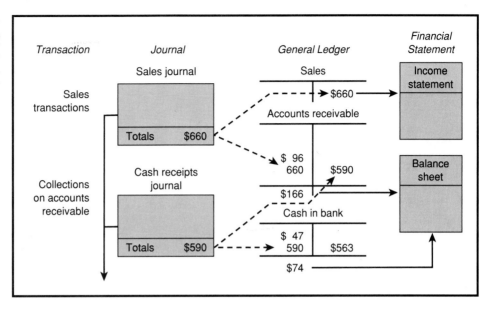

related data. For example, in Figure 10–2 the auditor could compare sales, collections, and accounts receivable in the current year to amounts in previous years and calculate the gross margin percentage for comparison to previous years.

4 Purposes for A.P.

There are four purposes of analytical procedures, all of which were discussed in Chapter 7: understanding the client's business, assessment of the entity's ability to continue as a going concern, indication of the presence of possible misstatements in the financial statements, and reduction of detailed audit tests. All of these help the auditor decide the extent of other audit tests. To illustrate, if analytical procedures indicate there may be misstatements, more extensive investigation may be needed. An example is an unexpected change in the current year's gross margin percentage compared to the previous year's. Other tests may be needed to determine if there is an error in sales or cost of goods sold that caused the change. On the other hand, if no material fluctuations are found using analytical procedures and the auditor concludes that fluctuations should not have occurred, other tests may be reduced. Section 5300, "Audit Evidence" and the third examination standard of GAAS indicate that analytical procedures are one of the procedures the auditor uses to gain "sufficient appropriate audit evidence," that is, analytical procedures are a substantive procedure.

Subsequent

(4)

Tests of Details of Balances

Section 5300 of the *CICA Handbook* includes analytical procedures, when used to reduce detailed audit tests, as a substantive procedure. Section 5300.04 states that "substantive procedures are used to gain evidence as to the validity of the data produced by the accounting system." In order to avoid confusion, this text will use the terms "analytical procedures" and "tests of details of balances" to describe the two components when they are considered as separate activities and the term substantive procedures to describe the testing for dollar errors or fraud directly affecting the correctness of financial statement balances.

Tests of details of balances focus on the ending general ledger balances for both balance sheet and income statement accounts, but the primary emphasis in most tests

FIGURE 10–3

Types of Audit Tests

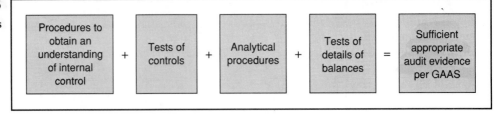

of details of balances is on the balance sheet. (Terms such as "detailed tests" and "direct tests of balances" may be used interchangeably with "tests of details of balances.") Examples include direct communication in writing with customers for accounts receivable, physical examination of inventory, and examination of vendors' statements for accounts payable. These tests of ending balances are essential to the conduct of the audit because, for the most part, the evidence is obtained from a source independent of the client and, thus, is considered to be of high quality.

Examine Figure 10–2 to see the role of tests of details of balances in the audit. There are three general ledger accounts in the figure: sales, accounts receivable, and cash in bank. Detailed tests of the balances in these accounts would be performed. These would include audit procedures such as confirmation of receivables balances, sales cutoff tests, and review of the bank account reconciliation. The extent of these tests depends on the results of tests of controls, and analytical procedures relating to these accounts.

Tests of details of balances have the objective of establishing the monetary correctness of the accounts they relate to and, therefore, are substantive tests. For example, confirmations test for monetary errors and are therefore substantive. Similarly, counts of inventory and cash on hand are also substantive tests.

Summary

Figure 10–3 summarizes the four types of tests. Procedures to obtain an understanding of internal control and tests of controls are concerned with evaluating whether controls are sufficiently effective to justify reducing control risk and thereby reducing substantive audit tests. Analytical procedures emphasize the overall reasonableness of transactions and the general ledger balances, and tests of details of balances emphasize the ending balances in the general ledger. Together the four types of audit tests enable the auditor to gather sufficient appropriate audit evidence to express an opinion on the financial statements.

Relationship Between Tests and Evidence

Only certain types of evidence (confirmation, documentation and so forth) are obtained through each of the four types of tests. Table 10–1 summarizes the relationship between types of tests and types of evidence. Several observations about Table 10–1 follow:

- Procedures to obtain an understanding of internal control and tests of controls involve only documentation, observation, inquiry and mechanical accuracy.
- More types of evidence are obtained using tests of details of balances than by using any other type of test. Only tests of details of balances involve confirmation and physical examination.
- Inquiries of clients are made with every type of test; documentation can be used for every type of test except analytical procedures.

TABLE 10–1

Relationship Between
Types of Tests and
Evidence

TYPE OF TEST	TYPE OF EVIDENCE						
	Physical Examination	Confirmation	Documentation	Observation	Inquiries of the Client	Mechanical Accuracy	Analytical Procedures
Procedures to obtain an understanding of internal control			✔	✔	✔		
Tests of controls			✔	✔	✔	✔	
Analytical procedures					✔		✔
Tests of details of balances	✔	✔	✔		✔	✔	

Relative Costs   The types of tests are listed in order of increasing cost as follows:

- Analytical procedures
- Procedures to obtain an understanding of internal control and tests of controls
- Tests of details of balances

The reason analytical procedures are least costly is the relative ease of making calculations and comparisons. Often, considerable information about potential errors can be obtained by simply comparing two or three numbers.

Tests of controls are also low in cost because the auditor is making inquiries and observations, examining such things as initials on documents and outward indications of other control procedures and performing reperformance which includes recalculations and tracings. Frequently, tests of controls can be done on a large number of items in a relatively short time.

Tests of details of balances are almost always considerably more costly than any of the other types of procedures. It is costly to send confirmations and to count assets. Because of the high cost of tests of details of balances, auditors usually try to plan the audit to minimize their use.

Naturally, the cost of each type of evidence varies in different situations. For example, the cost of an auditor's test counting inventory (a substantive test of the details of the inventory balance) frequently depends on the nature and dollar value of the inventory, its location, and the number of different items.

Relationship Between Tests of Controls and Substantive Procedures   To understand better the nature of tests of controls and substantive tests, an examination of how they differ is useful. An exception in a test of controls is only an *indication* of the likelihood of errors and fraud or other irregularities affecting the dollar value of the financial statements, whereas an exception in a substantive test *is* a financial statement misstatement. Exceptions in tests of controls are often referred to as control test deviations. Thus, control test deviations are significant only if they occur with sufficient frequency to cause the auditor to believe there may be material dollar misstatements in the statements. Substantive tests should then be performed to determine whether dollar misstatements have actually occurred.

As an illustration, assume the client's controls require an independent clerk to verify the quantity, price, and extension of each sales invoice, after which the clerk must initial the duplicate invoice to indicate performance. A test of controls audit procedure would be to examine a sample of duplicate sales invoices for the

FIGURE 10–4

Audit Assurance from
Control Risk
Assessment and Tests
of Controls and
Substantive Procedures

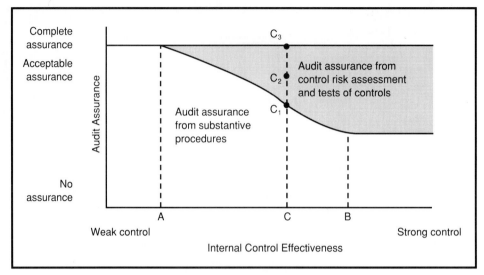

initials of the person who verified the quantitative data. If there are a significant number of documents without a signature, the auditor should follow up with tests to determine if there are any errors. This can be done by extending the tests of the duplicate sales invoices to include verifying prices, extensions, and footings (reperformance) or by increasing the sample size for the confirmation of accounts receivable (substantive test of details of balances). Of course, even though the control procedure is not operating effectively, the invoices may be correct. This will be the case if the person originally preparing the sales invoices did a conscientious and competent job. Similarly, even if there is an initial, there may be monetary errors due to initialing without performance or with careless performance of the internal control procedure. For these reasons, Section 5210.18 includes reperformance as one of the several auditing procedures performed as tests of controls. Some auditors prefer to reperform, to find evidence of monetary errors, only when there is indication of the need to do so.

As explained in Chapter 9, there is a trade-off between tests of controls and substantive tests. The auditor makes a decision during planning whether to assess control risk below maximum. Tests of controls must be performed to determine whether the assessed control risk is supported. If it is, planned detection risk in the audit risk model is increased and substantive procedures can therefore be reduced. Figure 10–4 shows the relationship between substantive tests and control risk assessment (including tests of controls) at differing levels of internal control effectiveness.

The shaded area in Figure 10–4 is the maximum assurance obtainable from control risk assessment and tests of controls. For example, any point to the left of point A, assessed control risk is 1.0 because the auditor evaluates internal control as ineffective. Any point to the right of point B results in no further reduction of control risk because the public accounting firm has established a minimum assessed control risk it will permit.

After the auditor decides the effectiveness of the client's internal control, it is appropriate to select any point within the shaded area of Figure 10–4 consistent with the level of control risk the auditor decides to support. To illustrate, assume

TABLE 10–2

Variations in Test Emphasis

	PROCEDURES TO OBTAIN AN UNDERSTANDING OF INTERNAL CONTROL	TESTS OF CONTROLS	ANALYTICAL PROCEDURES	TESTS OF DETAILS OF BALANCES
Audit 1	E	E	E	S
Audit 2	M	M	E	M
Audit 3	M	N	M	E
Audit 4	M	M	E	E

E = extensive amount of testing, M = medium amount of testing, S = small amount of testing, N = no testing.

the auditor contends that internal control effectiveness is at point C. Tests of controls at the C_1 level would provide the minimum control risk, given internal control. The auditor could choose to perform no tests of controls (point C_3) which would support a control risk of 1.0. Any point between the two, such as C_2, would also be appropriate. If C_2 is selected, the audit assurance from tests of controls is C_3-C_2 and from substantive tests is C-C_2. The auditor will likely select C_1, C_2, or C_3 based upon the relative cost of tests of controls and substantive tests.

Variation in Audit Plans

There are significant variations in the extent to which the four types of tests can be used in different audits for differing levels of internal control effectiveness. There can also be variations from cycle to cycle within a given audit, from account balance to account balance within a particular cycle and even between assertions for a particular account balance.[1] Table 10–2 shows the emphasis on different types of tests for four different audits. In each case, assume sufficient appropriate audit evidence was accumulated. An analysis of each audit follows.

> **OBJECTIVE 3**
>
> Understand how the four types of tests should be emphasized in different circumstances.

Analysis of audit 1 This client is a large company with sophisticated internal controls. The auditor, therefore, performs extensive tests of controls and relies heavily on the client's internal control to reduce substantive tests. Extensive analytical procedures are also performed to reduce tests of details of balances which are, therefore, minimized. Because of the emphasis on tests of controls and analytical procedures, this audit can be done inexpensively.

Analysis of audit 2 This company is medium sized, with some controls. The auditor has, therefore, decided to do a medium amount of testing for all types of tests except analytical procedures, which will be done extensively.

Analysis of audit 3 This company is medium sized, but has few effective controls. No tests of controls are done because reliance on internal control is inappropriate when controls are insufficient. The emphasis is on tests of details of balances, but some analytical procedures are also done. The reason for limiting analytical procedures is the auditor's expectations of errors in the account balances. The cost of the audit is likely to be relatively high because of the amount of detailed substantive testing.

---

1 The interested reader is referred to the audit planning worksheet for an account balance presented as Exhibit 3 in an article by Professor J. Efrim Boritz in *CA Magazine*, August, 1988. p.58. The exhibit shows how the auditor achieves assurance for the different accounts receivable assertions from different audit procedures.

Analysis of audit 4   The original plan on this audit was to follow the approach used in audit 2. However, the auditor found extensive control test deviations and significant errors using dual purpose tests and analytical procedures. The auditor, therefore, concluded that internal control was not effective. Extensive tests of details of balances are performed to offset the unacceptable results of the other tests. The costs of this audit are higher because tests of controls and dual purpose tests were performed but could not be used to reduce tests of details of balances.

It is essential to keep in mind that considerations other than internal control affect evidence accumulation. As discussed in Chapter 8, inherent risk and audit risk are also important determinants of the appropriate extent of substantive procedures, especially tests of details of balances.

Design of the Audit Program

A combined audit approach is appropriate for most audits; such an approach consists of tests of controls and substantive procedures. As you read above, substantive procedures include analytical procedures and tests of details of balances. Thus the audit program for most audits is designed in three parts: tests of controls, analytical procedures, and tests of details of balances. There will likely be a separate set of subaudit programs for each transaction cycle. An example in the sales and collection cycle might be tests of controls audit programs for sales and cash receipts; an analytical procedures audit program for the entire cycle; and tests of details of balances audit programs for cash, accounts receivable, bad-debt expense, allowance for uncollectible accounts, and miscellaneous accounts receivable.

> **OBJECTIVE 4**
>
> Know the methodology for the design of an audit program.

Tests of Controls

The tests of controls audit program normally includes a descriptive section documenting the understanding obtained about internal control. It is also likely to include a description of the procedures performed to obtain an understanding of internal control and the planned assessed level of control risk. Both the procedures performed and planned control risk affect the tests of controls audit program. The methodology to design tests of controls is shown in Figure 10–5. The first three steps in the figure were described in Chapter 9. When controls are effective and planned control risk is low, there will be heavy emphasis on tests of controls. Some dual purpose tests may also be included. If control risk is assessed at maximum, the auditor will use a substantive audit approach, that is, only substantive procedures will be used. The procedures already performed in obtaining an understanding of internal control may affect tests of controls.

 Audit Procedures   The approach to designing tests of controls emphasizes satisfying the internal control objectives developed in Chapter 9. A three-step approach is followed when control risk is assessed below maximum:

1. Apply the detailed internal control objectives to the class of transactions being tested, such as sales.
2. Identify specific control policies and procedures that should reduce control risk for each internal control objective.
3. For each internal control policy or procedure to which reduction in control risk is attributed (key controls), develop appropriate tests of controls.

This three-step approach to designing tests of controls is summarized in Figure 10–6. The approach is illustrated in several chapters in the text. For example, see

FIGURE 10–5

Methodology for
Designing Tests of
Controls

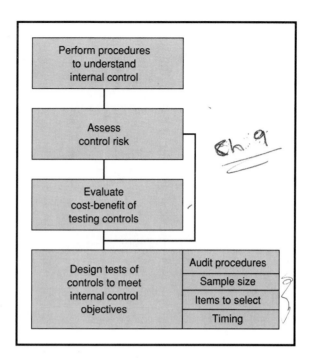

Table 11-1 on pages 359-360 for an application three-step procedure for the audit of sales transactions. Each of the steps corresponds to a column in Table 11-1.

Analytical Procedures

Because they are relatively inexpensive, many auditors perform extensive analytical procedures on all audits. As stated in Chapter 7, analytical procedures are performed at three different stages of the audit: in the planning stage to help the auditor decide the other evidence needed to meet the desired audit risk, during the audit in conjunction with tests of details of balances as part of substantive procedures, and near the end of the audit as a final test of reasonableness (required).

Choosing the appropriate analytical procedures requires the auditor to use professional judgment. The appropriate use of analytical procedures and illustrative ratios are included in Chapter 7. There are also examples in several subsequent chapters. For example, Table 13–1 on page 437 illustrates several analytical procedures for the audit of accounts receivable.

Tests of Details of Balances

The methodology for designing tests of details of balances is oriented to the audit objectives developed in Chapter 5 (pages 144-145). For example, if the auditor is verifying accounts receivable, the planned tests must be sufficient to satisfy each of the objectives. In planning tests of details of balances to satisfy those objectives, many auditors follow a methodology such as the one shown in Figure 10–7 for accounts receivable. The design of these tests is normally the most difficult part of the entire planning process. Designing such procedures is subjective and requires considerable professional judgment.

A discussion of the key decisions in designing tests of details of balances as shown in Figure 10–7 follows.

FIGURE 10–6

Three-Step Approach to Designing Tests of Controls

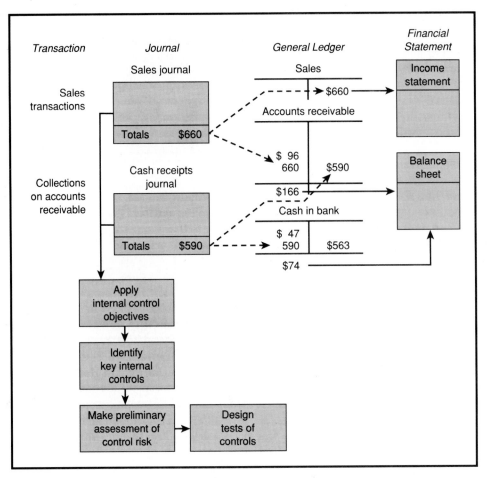

Assess audit risk and inherent risk for accounts receivable   As discussed in Chapter 8, audit risk is normally decided for the audit as a whole, rather than by cycle. An exception might be when the auditor believes that a misstatement of a specific account such as accounts receivable would negatively affect users more than the same size misstatement of any other account. For example, if accounts receivable is pledged to a bank as security on a loan, audit risk may be set lower for sales and collections than for other cycles.

Inherent risk is assessed by identifying any aspect of the client's history, environment, or operations that indicates a high likelihood of misstatement in the current year's financial statements. Considerations affecting inherent risk that were discussed in Chapter 8 applied to accounts receivable include make-up of accounts receivable, nature of the client's business, initial engagement, and so on. An account balance for which inherent risk has been assessed as high would result in more evidence accumulation than for an account with low inherent risk.

Inherent risk also can be extended to individual audit objectives. For example, because of adverse economic conditions in the client's industry, the auditor may conclude that there is a high risk of uncollectible accounts receivable (valuation objective). Inherent risk could still be low for all other objectives.

FIGURE 10–7

Methodology for
Designing Tests of
Details of Financial
Statement Balances –
Accounts Receivable

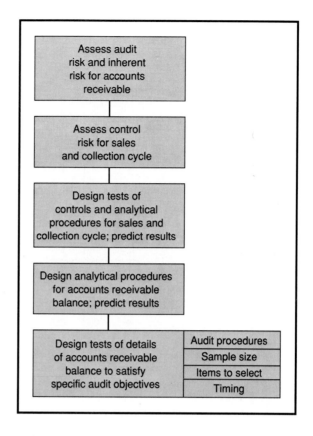

Assess control risk   Control risk is evaluated in the manner discussed in Chapter 9 and in earlier parts of this chapter. That methodology would be applied to both sales and collection in the audit of accounts receivable. Effective controls reduce control risk and therefore the evidence required for substantive procedures; inadequate controls increase the substantive evidence needed.

Design and predict tests of controls and analytical procedures results   The methodology for designing tests of controls and analytical procedures was discussed earlier in this section and will be illustrated in subsequent chapters. The tests are designed with the expectation that certain results will be obtained. These predicted results affect the design of tests of details of balances as discussed below.

Design tests of details of balances to satisfy specific audit objectives   The planned tests of details of balances include audit procedures, sample size, items to select, and timing. Procedures must be selected and designed for each account and each audit objective within each account. The specific audit objectives for accounts receivable are shown on pages 438 and 439.

A difficulty the auditor faces in designing tests of details of balances is the need to predict the outcome of the tests of controls and analytical procedures before they are performed. This is necessary because the auditor should design tests of details of balances during the planning phase, but the appropriate design

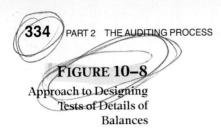

FIGURE 10–8

Approach to Designing Tests of Details of Balances

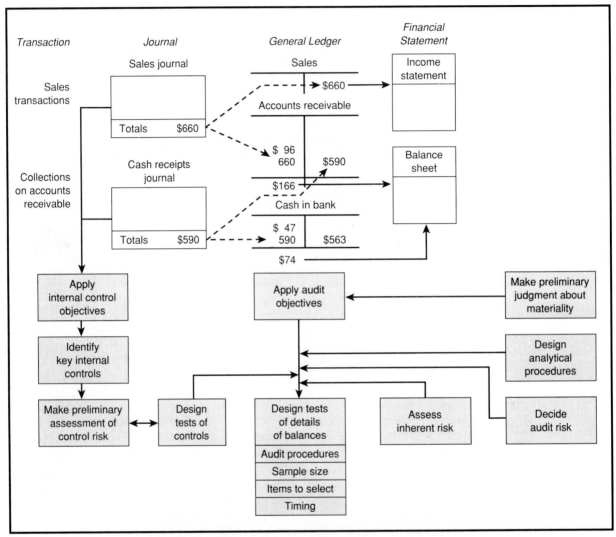

depends on the outcome of the other tests. In planning tests of details of balances, the auditor usually predicts that there will be few or no exceptions in tests of controls and analytical procedures, unless there are reasons to believe otherwise.

If the results of the tests of controls and analytical procedures are *not* consistent with the predictions, the tests of details of balances will need to be changed as the audit progresses.

The discussion about the approach to designing tests of details of balances applied to accounts receivable is summarized in Figure 10–8. The unshaded portion of the upper part of the figure is the financial information being audited. The light shading in the lower left is the design of tests of controls as discussed in Figure 10–7. The figure shows that the tests of controls affect the design of the tests of details of balances. The lower right portion shows the design of tests of details of balances and the factors affecting that decision.

FIGURE 10–9

Disaggregation Level to Which Planning Activities Are Applied

PLANNING ACTIVITY	Overall Audit	Cycle	Account	Internal Control Objective	Audit Objective
Preplan audit	P				
Obtain background information	P				
Obtain information about client's legal obligations	P				
Set preliminary judgment about materiality	P				
Assess audit risk	P				
Assess inherent risk			P		
Understand internal control					
Control environment	P				
Accounting system		P			
Control procedures		P			
Identify key internal controls				P	
Identify internal control weaknesses				P	
Design tests of controls					P
Assess control risk				P	
Design analytical procedures			P		
Design tests of details of balances					P

P = Primary level to which planning activity is applied.

One of the most difficult parts of auditing is properly applying the factors that affect tests of details of balances. Each of the factors is subjective, requiring considerable professional judgment. The impact of each factor on tests of details of balances is equally subjective. For example, if inherent risk is reduced from medium to low, there is agreement that tests of details of balances can be reduced. Deciding the specific effect on audit procedures, sample size, timing, and items to select is a difficult decision.

Level of Disaggregation of Planning Activities

The various planning activities discussed in Chapters 5 through 10 are applied at different levels of disaggregation, depending on the nature of the activity. Figure 10–9 shows the primary planning activities and the levels of disaggregation normally applied. These levels of disaggregation range from the overall audit to the audit objective for each account. For example, when the auditor obtains background information about the client's business and industry, it pertains to the overall audit. As the audit progresses, the information will first be used in assessing audit risk and assessing inherent risk and later is likely to affect tests of details of balances.

Illustrative Audit Program

Table 10–3 shows the tests of details of balances segment of an audit program for accounts receivable. The format used relates the audit procedures to the audit objectives. Notice that most procedures satisfy more than one objective. Also, more than one audit procedure is used for each objective. Audit procedures can be added or deleted as the auditor considers necessary. Sample size, items to select, and timing can also be changed for most procedures.

The audit program in Table 10–3 was developed after consideration of all the factors affecting tests of details of balances and is based on several assumptions about inherent risk, control risk, and the results of tests of controls and analytical proce-

TABLE 10–3 Tests of Details of Balances Audit Program for Accounts Receivable

							AUDIT OBJECTIVES				
SAMPLE SIZE	ITEMS TO SELECT	TIMING*	TESTS OF DETAILS OF BALANCES AUDIT PROCEDURES	Validity	Ownership	Completeness	Valuation	Classification	Cutoff	Mechanical Accuracy	Disclosure
Trace 20 items; foot 2 pages and all subtotals	Random	I	1. Obtain an aged list of receivables: trace accounts to the master file, foot schedule and trace to general ledger.							x	
All	All	Y	2. Obtain an analysis of the allowance for doubtful accounts and bad debt expense: test accuracy, examine authorization for write-offs, and trace to general ledger.	x		x	x				
100	30 largest 70 random	I	3. Obtain direct confirmation of accounts receivable and perform alternative procedures for nonresponses.	x	x	x	x	x	x		
NA	NA	Y	4. Review accounts receivable control account for the period. Investigate the nature of, and review support for, any large or unusual entries or any entries not arising from normal journal sources. Also investigate any significant increases or decreases in sales toward year end.	x	x		x	x	x		x
All	All	Y	5. Review receivables for any that have been assigned or discounted.		x						x
NA	NA	Y	6. Investigate collectibility of account balances.				x				
All	All	Y	7. Review lists of balances for amounts due from related parties or employees, credit balances, and unusual items, as well as notes receivable due after one year.	x				x			x
30 transactions for sales and cash receipts; 10 for credit memos	50% before and 50% after year-end	Y	8. Determine that proper cutoff procedures were applied at the balance sheet date to ensure that sales, cash receipts, and credit memos have been recorded in the correct period.						x		

*I = Interim.
Y = Year-end.
NA = Not applicable.

TABLE 10–4   Relationship of Internal Control Objectives to Audit Objectives

INTERNAL CONTROL OBJECTIVE	RELATED AUDIT OBJECTIVE	NATURE OF RELATIONSHIP	EXPLANATION
Validity	Validity or completeness	Direct	—
Authorization	Ownership	Indirect	Authorization may be required to acquire and dispose of assets, but the relationship is not strong.
Completeness	Completeness or validity	Direct	—
Valuation	Valuation	Partial	Valuation controls are strong in assuring the accuracy of transactions at the time of recording, but they are not strong with regard to recording subsequent declines in value.
Classification	Classification	Partial	Classifications of controls are strong in assuring the chart of accounts is followed, but they are not strong in assuring financial presentations are correct.
Timing	Cutoff	Direct	—
Posting and summarization	Mechanical accuracy	Direct	—
	Disclosure	None	Internal controls provide very little assurance that proper disclosures will be made.

dures. As indicated, if those assumptions are materially incorrect, the planned audit program will require revision. For example, analytical procedures could indicate potential errors for several objectives, tests of controls results could indicate weak internal controls, or new facts could cause the auditor to change inherent risk.

Relationship of Internal Control Objectives to Audit Objectives

Since tests of details of balances must be designed to satisfy specific objectives for each account and the extent of these tests can be reduced when internal control is adequate, it is important to understand how detailed internal control objectives relate to specific audit objectives. A general presentation of these relationships is shown in Table 10–4. The major implication of Table 10–4 is that even when all internal control objectives are being met, the auditor will still rely primarily on substantive procedures to meet the ownership and disclosure objectives, the valuation objective for declines in value, and the classification objective for financial statement presentation.

The relationship of internal control objectives to audit objectives is shown in greater detail in Figure 13-1, page 436. That figure shows how internal control objectives for sales, sales returns and allowances, and collections affect accounts receivable audit objectives. Notice that the validity internal control objective for sales affects the validity audit objective for accounts receivable whereas the validity internal control objective for sales returns and allowances and collections affects the completeness objective for accounts receivable.

OBJECTIVE 5

Understand the relationship of specific internal control objectives to specific audit objectives.

Summary of the Audit Process

The four phases of an audit were introduced at the end of Chapter 5. Considerable portions of Chapters 6 through 10 have discussed the different aspects of the process. Figure 10–10 shows the four phases for the entire audit process. Table 10–5 shows the timing of the tests in each phase for an audit with a December 31 balance sheet date.

OBJECTIVE 6

Integrate the four phases of the audit process.

FIGURE 10–10

Summary of the Audit Process

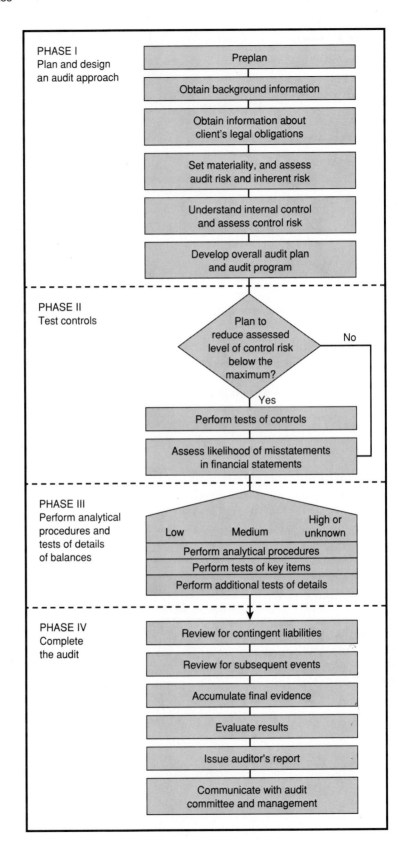

TABLE 10–5

Timing of Tests

Ch. 6

Phase I	Plan and design audit approach. Update understanding of internal control. Update audit program.	6-30-X4
Phase II	Perform tests of controls for first 9 months of the year.	9-30-X4
Phase III	Confirm accounts receivable. Observe inventory.	10–31-X4
	Count cash. Perform cutoff tests. Request various other confirmations.	12-31-X4
Balance sheet date	Do analytical procedures, complete tests of controls, and do most tests of details of balances.	1-7-X5
Books closed Phase IV	Summarize results, review for contingent liabilities, review for subsequent events, and finalize audit.	3-8-X5
Last date of field work	Issue auditor's report.	3-15-X5

Phase I: Plan and Design an Audit Approach

Chapters 6 through 10 have emphasized various aspects of planning the audit. At the end of phase I, the auditor should have a well-defined audit plan and a specific audit program for the entire audit.

Information obtained during preplanning, obtaining background information and obtaining information about the clients' legal obligation (first three boxes in Figure 10–10) is used primarily to assess audit risk and inherent risk. Assessments of materiality, audit risk, inherent risk, and control risk are used to develop an overall audit plan and audit program.

Phase II: Test Controls

Actual performance of the tests of controls occurs during this phase. The objectives of phase II are to (1) obtain evidence in support of the specific control policies and procedures that contribute to the auditor's assessed level of control risk (i.e., where it is reduced below maximum) and (2) when dual-purpose tests are used, to obtain evidence in support of the monetary correctness of transactions. The former objective is met by performing tests of controls, and the latter by performing substantive procedures. Many of both types of tests are conducted simultaneously on the same transactions. When controls are not considered effective, or when control deviations are discovered, substantive tests will be expanded in phase III.

Since the results of tests of controls are a major determinant of the extent of substantive procedures (analytical procedures and tests of details of balances), they are often performed two or three months before the balance sheet date. This helps the auditor plan for contingencies, revise the audit program for unexpected results, and complete the audit as soon after the balance sheet date as possible.

Phase III: Perform Analytical Procedures and Tests of Details of Balances

The objective of phase III is to obtain sufficient additional evidence to determine whether the ending balances and footnotes in financial statements are fairly stated. The nature and extent of the work will depend heavily on the findings of the two previous phases.

There are two general categories of phase III procedures: analytical procedures and tests of details of balances. Analytical procedures are those that assess the overall reasonableness of transactions and balances. Tests of details of balances are specific procedures intended to test for monetary errors in the balances in the financial statements. Certain key transactions and amounts are so important that each one must be audited. Other items can be sampled.

Table 10–5 shows most analytical procedures being done after the balance sheet date on the basis that there is not much benefit to calculating ratios and making comparisons before the client has finished preparing its financial statements. Ideally, analytical procedures are done before tests of details of balances. They can then be used to determine how extensively to test balances. However, analytical procedures are frequently done with preliminary data prior to year end as a means of planning and directing other audit tests to specific areas. Because of their low cost, it is common to use analytical procedures whenever they are relevant.

Table 10–5 also shows tests of details of balances are normally done last. On some audits, all are done after the balance sheet date. When clients want to issue statements soon after the balance sheet date, however, the more time-consuming tests of details of balances will be done at interim dates prior to year end with additional work being done to "roll forward" the audited interim-date balances to year end.

Phase IV: Complete the Audit

After the first three phases are completed, it is necessary to accumulate some additional evidence for the financial statements, summarize the results, issue the auditor's report and perform other forms of communication. This phase has several parts.

Review for contingent liabilities Contingent liabilities are potential liabilities that must be disclosed in the client's footnotes. Auditors must make sure the disclosure is adequate. A considerable portion of the search for contingent liabilities is done during the first three phases, but additional testing is done during phase IV. Contingent liabilities are studied in Chapter 22.

Review for subsequent events Occasionally, events occurring subsequent to the balance sheet date but before the issuance of the financial statements and auditor's report will have an effect on the information presented in the financial statements. Specific review procedures are designed to bring to the auditor's attention any subsequent events that may require recognition in the financial statements. Review for subsequent events is also studied in Chapter 22.

Accumulate final evidence In addition to the evidence obtained for each cycle during phases I and II and for each account during phase III, it is also necessary to gather evidence for the financial statements as a whole during the completion phase. This evidence includes performing final analytical procedures, evaluating the going concern assumption, obtaining a client representation letter, and reading the annual report to make sure that the financial statements and the auditor's report have been accurately reproduced in the annual report, that the annual report is consistent with the financial statements, and that there are no material misstatements of fact in the annual report.

Issue auditor's report The type of auditor's report issued depends on the evidence accumulated and the audit findings. The appropriate reports for differing circumstances were studied in Chapter 2.

Communicate with audit committee and management The auditor should communicate internal control related matters to and discuss any problems encountered on the audit with the audit committee or senior management. In addition, Sections 5135.18 and 5405.12 and proposed Section 5136.19 require the auditor to communicate certain other matters to the audit committee or management upon completion of the audit or sooner. Although not required, auditors often also make suggestions to management to improve business performance.

REVIEW QUESTIONS

10–1   What is the purpose of tests of controls? Identify specific accounts on the financial statements that are affected by performing tests of controls for acquisitions.

10–2   Distinguish between a test of controls and a substantive procedure. Give two examples of each.

10–3   Explain what is meant by reperformance. Give an example.

10–4   State a test of controls audit procedure to test the effectiveness of the following control: approved wage rates are used in calculating employees' earnings. State a test of controls audit procedure to determine whether approved wage rates are actually used in calculating employees' earnings.

10–5   An auditor may perform tests of controls and substantive procedures simultaneously as a matter of audit convenience. But the substantive procedures and sample size are, in part, dependent upon the results of the tests of controls. How can the auditor resolve this apparent inconsistency?

10–6   Evaluate the following statement: "Tests of sales and collection transactions are such an essential part of every audit that I like to perform them as near the end of the audit as possible. By that time I have a fairly good understanding of the client's business and its internal control because confirmations, cutoff tests, and other procedures have already been completed."

10–7   Explain how the calculation and comparison to previous years of the gross margin percentage and the ratio of accounts receivable to sales is related to the confirmation of accounts receivable and other tests of the accuracy of accounts receivable.

10–8   Distinguish between a combined audit approach and a substantive audit approach. Give one example of when each might be appropriate for the acquisition and payment cycle.

10–9   Assume that the client's internal controls over the recording and classifying of permanent asset additions are considered weak because the individual responsible for recording new acquisitions has inadequate technical training and limited experience in accounting. How would this situation affect the evidence you should accumulate in auditing permanent assets as compared with another audit in which the controls are excellent? Be as specific as possible.

10–10   For each of the seven types of evidence discussed in Chapter 6, identify whether it is applicable for procedures to obtain an understanding of internal control, tests of controls, analytical procedures, and tests of details of balances.

10–11   Rank the following types of tests in terms of cost, from most to least costly: analytical procedures, tests of details of balances, and tests of controls.

10–12   In Figure 10–4, explain the difference among C_3, C_2, and C_1. Explain the circumstances under which it would be a good decision to obtain audit assurance from substantive tests at part C_1. Do the same for parts C_2 and C_3.

10–13   The following are three decision factors related to the assessed level of control risk: effectiveness of internal controls, cost-effectiveness of a reduced assessed level of control risk, and results of tests of controls. Identify the combination of conditions for these three factors that is required before a reduction in substantive procedures is permitted.

10–14   Table 10–2 illustrates variations in the emphasis on different types of audit tests. What are the benefits to the auditor of identifying the best mix of tests?

10–15   State the three-step approach to designing tests of controls.

10–16 Explain the relationship between the methodology for designing tests of transactions in Figure 10–5 to the methodology for designing tests of details of balances in Figure 10–7.

10–17 Why is it desirable to design tests of details of balances before performing tests of controls? State the assumptions the auditor must make in doing that. What does the auditor do if the assumptions are wrong?

10–18 Explain the relationship between materiality available for unanticipated misstatements, inherent risk, and control risk to planned tests of details of balances.

10–19 List the eight detailed audit objectives in the verification of the ending balance in inventory, and provide one useful audit procedure for each of the objectives.

10–20 Why do auditors frequently consider it desirable to perform audit tests throughout the year rather than wait until year-end? List several examples of evidence that can be accumulated prior to the end of the year.

MULTIPLE CHOICE QUESTIONS

10–21 The following questions concern types of audit tests. Choose the best response.

a. The auditor looks for an indication on duplicate sales invoices to see if the invoices have been verified. This is an example of a

    (1) substantive procedure.
    (2) test of controls.
    (3) analytical procedure.
    (4) dual-purpose test.

b. Analytical procedures may be classified as being primarily

    (1) tests of controls.
    (2) substantive procedures.
    (3) tests of ratios.
    (4) tests of details of balances.

c. Failure to detect material dollar misstatements in the financial statements is a risk that the auditor mitigates primarily by

    (1) performing substantive procedures.
    (2) performing tests of controls.
    (3) evaluating internal control.
    (4) obtaining a client representation letter.

d. Before reducing assessed control risk, the auditor obtains a reasonable degree of assurance that internal control is operating as planned. The auditor obtains this assurance by performing

    (1) substantive procedures.
    (2) analytical procedures.
    (3) tests of controls.
    (4) tests of trends and ratios.

e. The auditor faces a risk that the examination will not detect material misstatements that occur in the accounting process. In regard to minimizing this risk, the auditor relies primarily on

    (1) substantive procedures.
    (2) tests of controls.
    (3) internal control.
    (4) statistical analysis.   (AICPA adapted)

10–22 The following questions deal with tests of controls. Choose the best response.

a. Which of the following statements relating to tests of controls is most accurate?

      (1) Auditing procedures cannot concurrently provide both evidence of the effectiveness of internal control and evidence required for substantive procedures.

      (2) Tests of controls include observations of the proper segregation of duties that ordinarily may be limited to the normal audit period.

      (3) Tests of controls should be based upon proper application of an appropriate statistical sampling plan.

      (4) Tests of controls ordinarily should be performed as of the balance sheet date or during the period subsequent to that date.

  b. Which of the following would be *least* likely to be included in an auditor's test of controls?

      (1) Inspection.

      (2) Observation.

      (3) Inquiry.

      (4) Confirmation.

  c. The two phases of the auditor's involvement with internal control are sometimes referred to as "understanding and assessment" and "tests of controls." In the tests of controls phase, the auditor attempts to

      (1) obtain a reasonable degree of assurance that the client's controls are in use and are operating as planned.

      (2) obtain sufficient appropriate audit evidence to afford a reasonable basis for the auditor's opinion.

      (3) obtain assurances that informative disclosures in the financial statements are reasonably adequate.

      (4) obtain knowledge and understanding of the client's prescribed procedures and methods.

  d. Which of the following is ordinarily considered a test of controls audit procedure?

      (1) Send confirmation letters to banks.

      (2) Count and list cash on hand.

      (3) Examine signatures on cheques.

      (4) Obtain or prepare reconciliations of bank accounts as of the balance sheet date.   (AICPA adapted)

10–23 The following questions concern the sequence and timing of audit tests. Choose the best response.

  a. A conceptually logical approach to the auditor's evaluation of internal control consists of the following four steps:

    I. Determine the internal control procedures that should prevent or detect errors and fraud or other irregularities.

    II. Identify weaknesses to determine their effect on the nature, timing, or extent of auditing procedures to be applied and suggestions to be made to the client.

    III. Determine whether the necessary procedures are prescribed and are being followed satisfactorily.

    IV. Consider the types of errors and fraud or other irregularities that could occur.

  What should be the order in which these four steps are performed?

      (1) I, II, III, and IV.

      (2) I, III, IV, and II.

      (3) III, IV, I, and II.

      (4) IV, I, III, and II.

  b. The sequence of steps in gathering evidence as the basis of the auditor's opinion is:

(1) substantive procedures, assessment of control risk, and tests of controls.

(2) assessment of control risk, substantive procedures, and tests of controls.

(3) assessment of control risk, tests of controls, and substantive procedures.

(4) tests of controls, assessment of control risk, and substantive procedures.

c. Which of the following procedures is *least* likely to be performed before the balance sheet date?

(1) Observation of inventory.

(2) Assessment of control risk for cash disbursements.

(3) Search for unrecorded liabilities.

(4) Confirmation of receivables. (AICPA adapted)

DISCUSSION QUESTIONS AND PROBLEMS

10–24 The following are 11 audit procedures taken from an audit program:

1. Foot the trial balance of accounts payable and compare the total with the general ledger.

2. Examine vendors' invoices to verify the ending balance in accounts payable.

3. Compare the balance in employee benefits expense with previous years. The comparison takes the increase in employee benefits rates into account.

4. Discuss the duties of the cash disbursements bookkeeper with him and observe whether he has responsibility for handling cash or preparing the bank reconciliation.

5. Confirm accounts payable balances directly with vendors.

6. Account for a sequence of cheques in the cash disbursements journal to determine whether any have been omitted.

7. Examine the internal auditor's initials on monthly bank reconciliations as an indication of whether they have been reviewed.

8. Examine vendors' invoices and other documentation in support of recorded transactions in the purchases journal.

9. Multiply the commission rate by total sales and compare the result with commission expense.

10. Examine vendors' invoices and other supporting documents to determine whether large amounts in the repair and maintenance account should be capitalized.

11. Examine the initials of vendors' invoices that indicate internal verification of pricing, extending, and footing by a clerk.

Required:

a. Indicate whether each procedure is a test of controls, analytical procedure, or a test of details of balances.

b. Identify the type of evidence for each procedure.

10–25 The following are audit procedures from different transaction cycles:

1. Foot and cross-foot the cash disbursements journal and trace the balance to the general ledger.

2. Select a sample of entries in the acquisitions journal and trace each one to a related vendor's invoice to determine if one exists.

3. Compute inventory turnover for each major product and compare with previous years.

4. Confirm a sample of notes payable balances, interest rates, and collateral with lenders.

5. Foot the accounts payable list and compare the balance with the general ledger.

6. Examine documentation for acquisition transactions before and after the balance sheet date to determine whether they are recorded in the appropriate period.

7. Observe whether cash is prelisted daily at the time it is received by the president's secretary.

8. Inquire of the credit manager whether each account receivable on the aged trial balance is collectible.

Required:

   a. For each audit procedure, identify the transaction cycle being audited.

   b. For each audit procedure, identify the type of evidence.

   c. For each audit procedure, identify whether it is a test of controls or a substantive procedure.

   d. For each substantive audit procedure, identify whether it is a test of details of balances or an analytical procedure.

   e. For each test of controls, identify the internal control objective or objectives being satisfied.

   f. For each test of details of balances procedure, identify the audit objective or objectives being satisfied.

10–26 For each of the following controls, identify whether the control leaves an audit trail, and a test of controls audit procedure the auditor can use to test the effectiveness of the control.

   a. An accounting clerk accounts for all shipping documents on a monthly basis.

   b. Bank reconciliations are prepared by the controller, who does not have access to cash receipts.

   c. As employees check in daily by using time clocks, a supervisor observes to make certain no individual "punches in" more than one time card.

   d. Vendors' invoices are approved by the controller after she examines the purchase order and receiving report attached to each invoice.

   e. The cashier, who has no access to accounting records, prepares the deposit slip and delivers the deposit directly to the bank on a daily basis.

   f. An accounting clerk verifies the price, extensions, and footings of all sales invoices in excess of $300 and initials the duplicate sales invoice when he has completed the procedure.

   g. All mail is opened and cash is prelisted daily by the president's secretary, who has no other responsibility for handling assets or recording accounting data.

10–27 The following are independent internal control procedures commonly found in the acquisition and payment cycle. Each control is to be considered independently.

   1. At the end of each month an accounting clerk accounts for all prenumbered receiving reports (documents evidencing the receipt of goods) issued during the month, and he traces each one to the related vendor's invoice and purchase journal entry. The clerk's tests do not include testing quantity or description of the merchandise received.

   2. The cash disbursements bookkeeper is prohibited from handling cash. The bank account is reconciled by another person even though the bookkeeper has sufficient expertise and time to do it.

   3. Before a cheque is prepared to pay for purchases by the accounts payable department, the related purchase order and receiving report are attached to the vendor's invoice being paid. A clerk compares the quantity on the invoice with the receiving report and purchase order, compares the price with the purchase order, recomputes the extensions, re-adds the total, and examines the account number indicated on the invoice to determine whether it is prop-

erly classified. He indicates his performance of these procedures by initialing the invoice.

4. Before a cheque is signed by the controller, she examines the supporting documentation accompanying the cheque. At that time she initials each vendor's invoice to indicate her approval.

5. After the controller signs the cheques, her secretary writes the cheque number and the date the cheque was issued on each of the supporting documents to prevent their reuse.

Required:

a. For each of the internal control procedures, state the internal control objective(s) the control is meant to fulfill.

b. List one test of controls audit procedure for each control procedure the auditor could perform to test the effectiveness of the control.

c. List one test of controls involving reperformance for each control the auditor could perform to determine whether financial errors are actually taking place.

10–28 The following internal control procedures for the acquisition and payment cycle were selected from a standard internal control questionnaire.

1. Vendors' invoices are recalculated prior to payment.

2. Approved price lists are in use for acquisitions.

3. Prenumbered receiving reports are prepared as support for purchases and are numerically accounted for.

4. Dates on receiving reports are compared with vendors' invoices before entry into the acquisitions journal.

5. The accounts payable master file is updated, balanced, and reconciled to the general ledger monthly.

6. Account classifications are reviewed by someone other than the preparer.

7. All cheques are signed by the owner or manager.

8. The cheque signer compares data on supporting documents with cheques.

9. All supporting documents are canceled after cheque signing by the cheque signer or an independent person.

10. Cheques are mailed by the owner or manager or a person under his supervision after signing.

Required:

a. For each control, identify which element of the five categories of internal control procedures is applicable (segregation of duties, proper authorization of transactions and activities, adequate documents or records, safeguards over access to and use of assets and records, or computer-generated or manual verification of performance and the accuracy of recorded amounts).

b. For each control, state which internal control objective or objectives is applicable.

c. For each control, write an audit procedure that could be used to test the control for effectiveness.

d. For each control, identify a likely misstatement, assuming the control does not exist or is not functioning.

e. For each likely error, identify a substantive procedure to determine if the error exists.

10–29 Jennifer Schaefer, a public accountant, follows the philosophy of performing interim tests of controls on every December 31 audit as a means of keeping overtime to a minimum. Typically, the interim tests are performed some time between August and November.

Required:

a. Evaluate her decision to perform interim tests of controls.

b. Under what circumstances is it acceptable for her to perform *no additional* tests of controls work as a part of the year-end audit tests?

c. If she decides to perform no additional testing, what is the effect on other tests she performs during the remainder of the engagement?

10–30 Following are several decisions that the auditor must make in an audit. Letters indicate alternative conclusions that could be made:

DECISIONS	ALTERNATIVE CONCLUSIONS
1. Determine whether is it cost effective to perform tests of controls.	A. It is cost effective B. It is not cost effective
2. Perform tests of details of balances	C. Perform reduced tests D. Perform expanded tests
3. Assess internal control risk	E. Controls are effective F. Controls are not effective
4. Perform tests of controls	G. Controls are effective H. Controls are not effective

Required:

a. Identify the sequence the auditor should follow in making decisions 1 through 4.

b. For the audit of sales, collections, and accounts receivable, an auditor reached the following conclusions: A, D, E, H. Put the letters in the appropriate sequence and evaluate whether the auditor's logic was reasonable. Explain your answer.

c. For the audit of inventory and related inventory cost records, and auditor reached the following conclusions: B, C, E, G. Put the letters in the appropriate sequence and evaluate whether the auditor used good professional judgment. Explain your answer.

d. For the audit of property, plant, and equipment and related acquisition records, an auditor reached the following conclusions: A, C, F, G. Put the letters in the appropriate sequence and evaluate whether the auditor used good professional judgment. Explain your answer.

e. For the audit of payroll expenses and related liabilities, an auditor recorded the following conclusions: D, F. Put the letters in the appropriate sequence and evaluate whether the auditor used good professional judgment. Explain your answer.

10–31 The following are three situations in which the auditor is required to develop an audit strategy:

1. The client has inventory at approximately 50 locations in the three Maritime provinces. The inventory is difficult to count and can be observed only by traveling by automobile. The internal controls over acquisitions, payments, and perpetual records are considered effective. This is the fifth year that you have done the audit and audit results in past years have always been excellent.

2. This is the first year of an audit of a medium-sized company that is considering selling its business because of severe underfinancing. A review of the acquisition and payment cycle indicates that controls over disbursements are excellent, but controls over accounts payable cannot be considered effective. The client lacks receiving reports and a policy as to the proper timing to record acquisitions. When you review the general ledger, you observe that there are many adjusting entries to correct accounts payable.

3. You are doing the audit of a small loan company with extensive receivables from customers. Controls over granting loans, collections, and loans outstand-

ing are considered effective, and there is extensive followup of all outstanding loans weekly. You have recommended a computer system for the past two years, but management believes the cost is too great, given their low profitability. Collections are an ongoing problem because many of the customers have severe financial problems. Because of adverse economic conditions, loans receivable have significantly increased and collections are less than normal. In previous years, you have had relatively few adjusting entries.

Required:

Use a format like Table 10–2 to make your recommendations for the appropriate evidence mix for all three parts below.

a. For audit one, recommend an evidence mix for inventory and cost of goods sold. Justify your answer.

b. For audit two, recommend an evidence mix for the audit of acquisitions and accounts payable. Justify your answer.

c. for audit three, recommend an evidence mix for the audit of outstanding loans. Justify your answer.

10–32 Brad Jackson was assigned to the audit of a client that had not been audited by any public accounting firm in the preceding year. In conducting the audit, he did no testing of the beginning balance of accounts receivable, inventory, or accounts payable on the grounds that the auditor's report is being limited to the ending balance sheet, the income statement, and the statement of changes in financial position. No comparative financial statements are to be issued.

Required:

a. Explain the error in Jackson's reasoning.

b. Suggest an approach Jackson can follow in verifying the beginning balance in accounts receivable.

c. Why does the same problem not exist in the verification of beginning balances on continuing audit engagements?

10–33 Kim Bryan is confused by the inconsistency of the three audit partners she has been assigned to on her initial three audit engagements. On the first engagement, she spent a considerable amount of time in the audit of cash disbursements by examining canceled cheques and supporting documentation, but almost no testing was spent in the verification of permanent assets. On the second engagement, a different partner had her do less intensive tests in the cash disbursements area and take smaller sample sizes than in the first audit even though the company was much larger. On her most recent engagement under a third audit partner, there was a thorough test of cash disbursement transactions, far beyond that of the other two audits, and an extensive verification of permanent assets. In fact, this partner insisted on a complete physical examination of all permanent assets recorded on the books. The total audit time on the most recent audit was longer than that of either of the first two audits in spite of the smaller size of the company. Bryan's conclusion is that the amount of evidence to accumulate depends on the audit partner in charge of the engagement.

Required:

a. State several factors that could explain the difference in the amount of evidence accumulated in each of the three audit engagement as well as the total time spent.

b. What could the audit partners have done to help Bryan understand the difference in the audit emphasis on the three audits?

c. Explain how these three audits are useful in developing Bryan's professional judgment. How could the quality of her judgment have been improved on the audits?

10–34 The following are parts of a typical audit for a company with a fiscal year-end of July 31.

1. Confirm accounts payable.

    2. Do tests of controls for acquisitions and payroll.

    3. Do other tests of details of balances for accounts payable.

    4. Do tests for review of subsequent events.

    5. Preplan the audit.

    6. Issue the audit report.

    7. Understand internal control and assess control risk.

    8. Do analytical procedures for accounts payable.

    9. Set acceptable audit risk and decide preliminary judgment about materiality.

Required:

    a. Put parts 1 through 9 of the audit in the sequential order in which you would expect them to be performed in a typical audit.

    b. Identify those parts that would frequently be done before July 31.

CASE

10–35 Gale Brewer, a public accountant, has been the partner in charge of the Merkle Manufacturing Corp., a client listed on the Alberta Stock Exchange, for six years. Merkle has had excellent growth and profits in the past decade, primarily as a result of the excellent leadership provided by Sylvia Merkle and other competent executives. Brewer has always enjoyed a close relationship with the company and prides himself on having made several constructive comments over the years that have aided in the success of the firm. Several times in the past few years Brewer's public accounting firm has considered rotating a different audit team on the engagement, but this has been strongly resisted by both Brewer and Merkle.

    For the first few years of the audit, internal control was inadequate and the accounting personnel had inadequate qualifications for their responsibilities. Extensive audit evidence was required during the audit, and numerous adjusting entries were necessary. However, because of Brewer's constant prodding, the internal control improved gradually and competent personnel were hired. In recent years, there were normally no audit adjustments required, and the extent of the evidence accumulation was gradually reduced. During the past three years, Brewer was able to devote less time to the audit because of the relative ease of conducting the audit and the cooperation obtained throughout the engagement.

    In the current year's audit, Brewer decided the total time budget for the engagement should be kept approximately the same as in recent years. The senior in charge of the audit, Barbara Warren, was new on the job and highly competent, and she had the reputation of being able to cut time off the budget. The fact that Merkle had recently acquired a new division through merger would probably add to the time, but Warren's efficiency would probably compensate for it.

    The interim tests of internal control took somewhat longer than expected because of the use of several new assistants, a change in the accounting system to computerize the inventory and several other aspects of the accounting records, a change in accounting personnel, and the existence of a few more errors in the tests of the system. Neither Brewer nor Warren was concerned about the budget deficit, however, because they could easily make up the difference at year-end.

    At year-end, Warren assigned the responsibility for inventory to an assistant who also had not been on the audit before but was competent and extremely fast at his work. Even though the total value of inventory increased, he reduced the size of the sample from that of other years because there had been few errors the preceding year. He found several items in the sample that were overstated due to errors in pricing and obsolescence, but the combination of all of the errors in the sample was immaterial. He completed the tests in 25 percent less time than the preceding year. The entire audit was completed on schedule and in slightly less time than the preceding year. There were only a few adjusting entries for the year, and only two of them were material. Brewer was extremely pleased with the results and wrote a special letter to Warren and the inventory assistant complimenting them on the audit.

Six months later Brewer received a telephone call from Merkle and was informed that the company was in serious financial trouble. Subsequent investigation revealed that the inventory had been significantly overstated. The major cause of the misstatement was the inclusion of obsolete items in inventory (especially in the new division), errors in pricing due to the new computer system, and the inclusion of nonexistent inventory in the final inventory listing. The new controller had intentionally overstated the inventory to compensate for the reduction in sales volume from the preceding year.

Required:

a. List the major deficiencies in the audit and state why they took place.

b. What things should have been apparent to Brewer in the conduct of the audit?

c. If Brewer's firm is sued by shareholders or creditors, what is the likely outcome?

11

AUDIT OF THE SALES AND COLLECTION CYCLE

LEARNING OBJECTIVES

THOROUGH STUDY OF THIS CHAPTER WILL ENABLE YOU TO:

1. Describe the accounts, documents and records, and functions that comprise the sales and collection cycle

2. Determine the client's internal controls over sales transactions, design and perform tests of controls, and assess related control risk

3. Apply the methodology for controls over sales transactions to controls over sales returns and allowances

4. Determine the client's internal controls over cash receipts transactions, design and perform tests of controls, and assess related control risk

5. Apply the methodology for controls over the sales and collection cycle to write-offs of uncollectible accounts receivable

6. Develop an integrated audit plan for the sales and collection cycle

☐ This chapter presents information on the nature of the sales and collection cycle, primary internal control considerations for the cycle, and tests of controls procedures used for verifying sales, cash receipts, sales returns and allowances, and the charge-off of uncollectible accounts. Turn briefly to examine Figure 10–10 on page 338. This chapter assumes most aspects of phase I of the audit process

Chapter is on test of controls

have been completed. The chapter emphasizes the appropriate audit procedures for tests of controls in phase II for the sales and collection cycle. A case illustration for Hillsburg Hardware Ltd. of an audit program for sales and cash receipts and how it was developed is included at the end of the chapter. A discussion of proper sample sizes and items to select is deferred until Chapter 12. Audit procedures relating to tests of details of balances for accounts receivable, allowance for uncollectible accounts, and bad debt expense (phase III of Figure 10–10) are the subject of Chapter 13.

The overall objective in the audit of the sales and collection cycle is to evaluate whether the account balances affected by the cycle are fairly presented in accordance with generally accepted accounting principles. The following are typical accounts included in the sales and collection cycle:

- Sales
- Sales returns and allowances
- Bad-debt expense
- Cash discounts taken
- Trade accounts receivable
- Allowance for uncollectible accounts
- Cash in the bank (debits from cash receipts)

The goods and services tax is collected by an entity and remitted to the federal government; the entity merely acts as a conduit for the government. Accordingly, in Figure 5–3 on page 135, the Hillsburg Hardware trial balance shows *goods and services tax payable* (the liability) and *goods and services tax* (the contra account to sales) as being in the Acquisitions and Payment cycle, which is discussed in Chapter 17.

For example, look at the adjusted trial balance for Hillsburg Hardware Ltd. on page 135. Accounts on the trial balance affected by the sales and collection cycle are identified by the letter *S* in the left margin. Each of the above accounts is included, except cash discounts taken. For other audits the names and the nature of the accounts may vary, of course, depending on the industry and client involved. There are differences in account titles for a service company, a retail company, and an insurance company, but the basic concepts are the same. To provide a frame of reference for understanding the material in this chapter, a wholesale merchandising company is assumed.

A brief summary of the way accounting information flows through the various accounts in the sales and collection cycle is illustrated in Figure 11–1 by the use of T-accounts. This figure shows that with the exception of cash sales, every transaction and amount ultimately is included in the accounts receivable or allowance for uncollectible accounts balances. For simplicity, the assumption is made that the same internal control exists for both cash and credit sales.

For the most part, the audit of the sales and collection cycle can be performed independently of the audit of other cycles and subjectively combined with the other parts of the audit as the evidence accumulation process proceeds. Auditors must keep in mind that the concept of materiality requires them to consider the combination of misstatements in all parts of the audit before making a final judgment on the fair presentation of the financial statements. This is done by stopping at various times throughout the engagement and integrating the parts of the audit.

FIGURE 11–1

Accounts in the Sales
and Collection Cycle

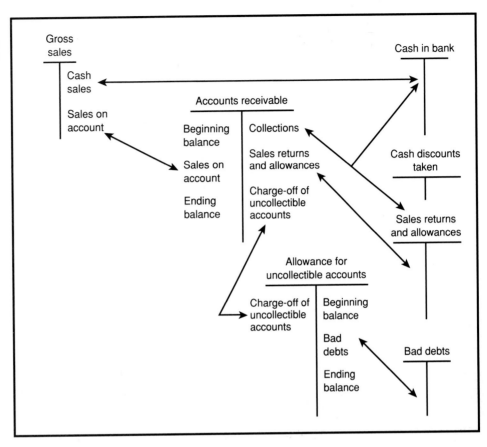

Nature of the Sales and Collection Cycle

The sales and collection cycle involves the decisions and processes necessary for the transfer of the ownership of goods and services to customers after they are made available for sale. It begins with a request by a customer and ends with the conversion of material or service into an account receivable, and ultimately into cash.

The sales and collection cycle for a typical wholesale company is illustrated in Figure 11–2 with an *overview flowchart*. This type of flowchart is meant to aid readers in understanding the sales and collection function rather than to serve as a means of understanding internal control. Therefore, it does not include all documents nor all internal controls. A detailed flowchart for obtaining an understanding of internal control is illustrated in Figure 11–5 on page 373.

Documents and Records

Several important documents and records are typically used in the sales and collection cycle.

Customer order   A request for merchandise by a customer. It may be received by telephone, letter, a printed form that has been sent to prospective and existing customers, through salespeople, or in other ways.

FIGURE 11–2 Flowchart of the Sales and Collection Cycle

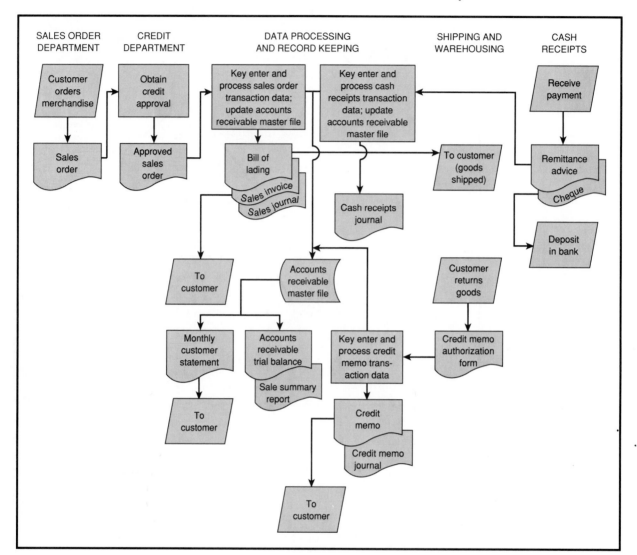

Sales order A document for recording the description, quantity, and related information for goods ordered by a customer. This is frequently used to show credit approval and authorization for shipment.

Shipping document A document prepared to initiate shipment of the goods, indicating the description of the merchandise, the quantity shipped, and other relevant data. The original is sent to the customer and one or more copies are retained. It is also used as a signal to bill the customer. One type of shipping document is a bill of lading, which is a written contract between the carrier and seller of the receipt and shipment of goods. Often bills of lading include only the number of boxes or kilograms shipped, rather than complete details of quantity and description. Throughout the text, we assume complete details are included on bills of lading. The computer operator informs the computer by a key entry that the goods described on the shipping document have been shipped.

Sales invoice   A document indicating the description and quantity of goods sold, the price including freight, insurance, terms, and other relevant data. Typically, it is automatically prepared by the computer after the customer number, quantity, and destination of goods shipped, and sales terms are entered. The sales invoice is the method of indicating to the customer the amount of a sale and due date of a payment. The original is sent to the customer and one or more copies are retained. The sales invoice information in the computer is the basis for recording sales transactions and updating the accounts receivable master file for those transactions.

Sales journal   A journal for recording sales transactions. A detailed sales journal includes each sales transaction. It usually indicates gross sales for different classifications, such as product lines, the entry to accounts receivable, and miscellaneous debits and credits such as goods and services tax collected. The sales journal can also include sales returns and allowances transactions. This journal is generated for any time period from the sales transactions included in the computer files. Details from the journal are posted to the accounts receivable master file and journal totals are posted to the general ledger by the computer.

Summary sales report   A computer generated document that summarizes sales for a period. The report typically includes information analyzed by key components such as sales person, product, and territory.

Credit memo   A document indicating a reduction in the amount due from a customer because of returned goods or an allowance granted. It often takes the same general form as a sales invoice, but it supports reductions in accounts receivable rather than increases.

Remittance advice   A document that accompanies the sales invoice mailed to the customer and can be returned to the seller with the cash payment. It is used to indicate the customer name, the sale invoice number, and the amount of the invoice when the payment is received. If the customer fails to include the remittance advice with his or her payment, it is common for the person opening the mail to prepare one at that time. A remittance advice is used to permit the immediate deposit of cash and to improve control over the custody of assets.

Cash receipts journal   A journal for recording cash receipts from collections, cash sales, and all other cash receipts. It indicates total cash received, the credit to accounts receivable at the gross amount of the original sale, trade discounts taken, and other debits and credits. The daily entries in the cash receipts journal are supported by remittance advices. The journal is generated for any time period from the cash receipts transactions included in the computer files.

Uncollectible account authorization form   A document used internally, indicating authority to write an account receivable off as uncollectible.

Accounts receivable master file   A file for recording individual sales, cash receipts, and sales returns allowances for each customer and maintaining customer account balances. The master file is updated from the sales, sales returns and allowances, and cash receipts computer transaction files. The total of the individual account balances in the master file equals the total balance of accounts receivable in the general ledger. A printout of the accounts receivable master file shows, by customer, the beginning balance in accounts receivable, each sales transaction, sales returns and allowances, collections, and the ending balance. Whenever the term master file is used in this book, it refers to either the computer file or a printout of that file.

Accounts receivable trial balance A listing of the amount owed by each customer at a point in time. This is prepared directly from the accounts receivable master file. It is most frequently an *aged* trial balance, showing how old the accounts receivable components of each customer's balance are as of the report date.

Monthly statement A document sent to each customer indicating the beginning balance of accounts receivable, the amount and date of each sale, cash payments received, credit memos issued, and the ending balance due. It is, in essence, a copy of the customer's portion of the accounts receivable master file.

Functions in the Cycle

An understanding of the functions that take place in a typical client's organization for the sales and collection cycle is useful for understanding how an audit of the cycle is conducted. Students often find it difficult to envision which documents exist in any given audit area and how they flow through the client's organization. It is unlikely for anyone to understand the audit process without an understanding of accounting systems. The following functions for the sales and collection cycle are examined briefly at this point:

- Processing customer orders
- Granting credit
- Shipping goods
- Billing customers and recording sales
- Processing and recording cash receipts
- Processing and recording sales returns and allowances
- Charging off uncollectible accounts receivable
- Providing for bad debts

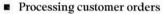

Processing customer orders The request for goods by a customer is the starting point for the entire cycle. Legally, it is an offer to buy goods under specified terms. The receipt of a customer order results in the fairly immediate creation of a sales order.

Granting credit Before goods are shipped, a properly authorized person must *approve credit* to the customer for sales on account. Weak practices in credit approval frequently result in excessive bad debts and accounts receivable that may be uncollectible. For most firms, an indication of credit approval on the sales order is the approval to ship the goods.

Shipping goods This critical function is the first point in the cycle where company assets are given up. Most companies recognize sales when goods are shipped. A shipping document is prepared at the time of shipment; this can be done automatically by the computer based on sales order information. The shipping document, which is frequently a multicopy bill of lading, is essential to the proper billing of shipments to customers. Companies that maintain perpetual inventory records also update them based on shipping information.

Billing customers and recording sales Since the billing of customers is the means by which the customer is informed of the amount due for the goods, it must be done correctly and on a timely basis. The most important aspects of billing are making sure that all shipments made have been billed, no shipment has been billed more than once, and each one is billed for the proper amount. Billing at the proper amount is dependent on charging the customer for the quantity shipped at the authorized price. The authorized price includes consideration for freight charges, insurance, and terms of payments.

In most systems, billing of the customer includes preparation of a multicopy sales invoice and simultaneous updating of the sales transactions file and the accounts receivable master file. This information is used to generate the sales journal and, along with cash receipts and miscellaneous credits, allows preparation of the accounts receivable trial balance. Errors in any part of the billing process can result in significant misstatements in the financial statements.

Processing and recording cash receipts The preceding four functions are necessary for getting the goods into the hands of customers, properly billing them, and reflecting the information in the accounting records. The remaining functions involve the collection and recording of cash and the other means of reducing accounts receivable.

In processing and recording cash receipts, the most important concern is the possibility of theft. Theft can occur before receipts are entered in the records or later. The most important consideration in the handling of cash receipts is that all cash must be deposited in the bank at the proper amount on a timely basis and recorded in the cash receipts transaction file, which is used to prepare the cash receipts journal and update the accounts receivable master file. Remittance advices are important for this purpose.

Processing and recording sales returns and allowances When a customer is dissatisfied with the goods, the seller frequently accepts the return of the goods or grants a reduction in the charges. Returns and allowances must be correctly and promptly recorded in the sales returns and allowances transaction file and the accounts receivable master file. *Credit memos* are normally issued for returns and allowances to aid in maintaining control and to facilitate record keeping.

Charging off uncollectible accounts receivable Regardless of the aggressiveness of credit departments, it is not unusual if some customers do not pay their bills. When the company concludes that an amount is no longer collectible, it must be charged off. Typically, this occurs after a customer files bankruptcy or the account is turned over to a collection agency. Proper accounting requires an adjustment for these uncollectible accounts.

Providing for bad debts The provision for bad debts must be sufficient to allow for the current period sales that the company will be unable to collect in the future. For most companies the provision represents a residual, resulting from management's end-of-period adjustment of the allowances for uncollected accounts.

FIGURE 11–3

Methodology for
Designing Tests of
Controls for Sales

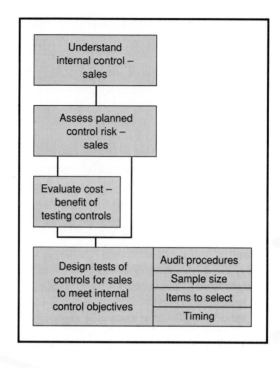

Internal Controls
and Tests of
Controls for
Sales

The methodology for obtaining an understanding of the client's internal control
and designing tests of controls for sales is shown in Figure 11–3. That methodology was studied in general terms in Chapters 9 and 10. It is applied specifically to
sales in this section with emphasis on designing tests of controls audit procedures. The tests are usually performed at an interim date if internal control is
effective, but they can also be done after the balance sheet date. Decisions on the
appropriate sample size and the items to select are studied in Chapter 12.

Objectives,
Controls, and Tests

Table 11–1 summarizes the application of the concepts discussed in previous
chapters to the audit of sales. This summary integrates internal control objectives
with key internal controls and tests of controls. A discussion of the table's most
important points is included here.

OBJECTIVE 2

Determine the client's
internal controls over
sales transactions,
design and perform
tests of controls and
assess related control
risk.

Internal control objectives The objectives included in the table are derived from
the framework developed in Chapter 9. Although certain internal controls satisfy
more than one objective, it is convenient to consider each objective separately to
facilitate a better understanding of the entire audit process.

Key controls The internal controls in sales are designed to achieve the seven
objectives discussed in Chapter 9. If the controls necessary to satisfy any one of
the objectives are inadequate, the likelihood of misstatements related to that
objective is increased, regardless of the controls for the other objectives. The
methodology for determining existing controls was studied in Chapter 9.

Tests of controls For each internal control there exists a related test of control to
verify its effectiveness. In most audits it is relatively easy to determine the nature
of the test of the control from the nature of the control itself. For example, if the

TABLE 11–1 Summary of Objectives, Controls, and Tests of Controls for Sales

INTERNAL CONTROL OBJECTIVE	KEY INTERNAL CONTROL	COMMON TESTS OF CONTROLS
Recorded sales are for shipments actually made to nonfictitious customers (validity).	Recording of sales is supported by authorized shipping documents and approved customer orders.	Examine copies of sales invoices for supporting bills of lading and customers' orders.
	Sales invoices are prenumbered and properly accounted for.	Account for integrity of numerical sequence of sales invoices.
	Only customer numbers included as valid in the computer data files are accepted when they are entered.	Examine printouts of transactions rejected by the computer as having invalid customer numbers.
	Monthly statements are sent to customers; complaints receive independent follow-up.	Observe whether statements are mailed and examine customer correspondence files.
Sales transactions are properly authorized (authorization).	Specific or general authorization must occur, through proper procedures, at three key points: Granting of credit before shipment takes place Shipment of goods Determination of prices and terms, freight, and discounts	Examine documents for proper approval at these three points.
Existing sales transactions are recorded (completeness).	Shipping documents (that is, bills of lading) are prenumbered and accounted for.	Account for integrity of numerical sequence of shipping documents.
	Sales invoices are prenumbered and accounted for.	Account for integrity of numerical sequence of sales invoices.

COMMON TESTS OF CONTROLS (continued column):

Review the sales journal, general ledger, and accounts receivable master file or trial balance for large or unusual items. *

Trace sales journal entries to copies of sales orders, sales invoices, and shipping documents.

Trace shipping documents to entry of shipments in perpetual inventory records.

Trace credit entries in accounts receivable master file to valid source.

Compare prices on sales invoices with authorized price lists or properly executed contracts.

Trace shipping documents to resultant sales invoices and entry into sales journal and accounts receivable master file.

TABLE 11–1 *(Continued)*

INTERNAL CONTROL OBJECTIVE	KEY INTERNAL CONTROL	COMMON TESTS OF CONTROLS	*[handwritten: evidence to support a specific Audit objective]*
Recorded sales are for the amount of goods shipped and are correctly billed and recorded (valuation).	Internal verification of invoice preparation. Approved unit selling prices are entered into the computer and used for all sales. Batch totals are compared with computer summary reports.	Examine indication of internal verification on affected documents. Examine approved computer printout of unit selling prices.† Examine file of batch totals for initials of data control clerk; compare totals to summary reports.†	Recompute information on sales invoices. Trace entries in sales journal to sales invoices. Trace details on sales invoices to shipping documents, price lists, and customers' orders.
Sales transactions are properly classified (classification).	Use of adequate chart of accounts. Internal review and verification.	Review chart of accounts for adequacy. Examine indication of internal verification on affected documents.	Examine documents supporting sales transactions for proper classification.
Sales are recorded on a timely basis (timeliness).	Procedures requiring billing and recording of sales on a daily basis as close to time of occurrence as possible. Internal verification.	Examine documents for unbilled shipments and unrecorded sales. Examine indication of internal verification on affected documents.	Compare dates of recorded sales transactions with dates on shipping records.
Sales transactions are properly included in the master files and are correctly summarized (posting and summarization).	Regular monthly statements to customers. Internal verification of accounts receivable master file contents. Comparison of accounts receivable master file or trial balance totals with general ledger balance.	Observe whether statements are mailed. Examine indication of internal verification. Examine initials on general ledger account indicating comparison.	Foot journals and trace postings to general ledger and accounts receivable master files.

* This analytical procedure can also apply to other objectives, including completeness, valuation, and timeliness.
† This control would be tested on many audits by using the computer.

internal control is to initial customer orders after they have been approved for credit, the test of control is to examine the customer order for a proper initial.

Several of the tests of controls in Table 11–1 can be performed using the computer. For example, one of the key internal controls to prevent invalid transactions is to include a list of valid customer numbers in the computer files. If an invalid customer number is entered into the computer, it is rejected as invalid. A test of control is for the auditor to attempt to enter invalid customer numbers into the computer to make sure the computer control is in operation. Tests of controls where the auditor uses the computer are studied in Chapter 15. For this chapter, all tests of controls are performed manually.

Observe that the tests of controls in Table 11–1 relate directly to the internal controls. For each control there should be at least one test of control.

Section 5210.21 of the *CICA Handbook* discusses auditing procedures which are called *dual-purpose* tests and which "satisfy the objectives of both tests of controls and substantive procedures." In addition, Section 5210.32 suggests that monetary misstatements may be discovered as a result of performing tests of controls. The tests of controls in the right-hand column of Table 11–1 include dual-purpose tests; they are classed for purposes of the text as tests of controls since their purpose is to assist the auditor in determining control risk. These tests of controls are related to the objectives in the first or left-hand column and are designed to determine whether any monetary errors of the type relating to that objective exist in the transaction. The audit procedures used are affected by the internal controls for that objective. Materiality, results of the prior year, and the other factors discussed in Chapter 8 also affect the procedures used. Some of the audit procedures employed when internal controls are inadequate are discussed in a later section.

It is essential to understand the relationships among the columns in Table 11–1. The first column includes the seven internal controls and tests of controls audit objectives. The general objectives are the same for any class of transactions, but the specific objectives vary for sales, cash receipts, or any other classes of transactions. Column two lists one or more illustrative internal controls *for each internal control objective*. It is essential that any given control be related to one or more specific objective(s). Next, the common tests of controls in column three relate *to a given internal control*. A test of control has no meaning unless it tests a particular control. The table contains at least one test of control in column three for each internal control in column two. Finally, the tests of controls in the table's last column are evidence to support *a specific audit objective* in column one. These tests of controls are not directly related to the key control or test of control columns, but the extent of these tests of controls depends, in part, on which key controls exist and on results of the tests of controls in the third column.

Design and Performance Formats

The information presented in Table 11–1 is intended to help auditors *design audit programs* that satisfy the audit objectives in a given set of circumstances. If certain objectives are important in a given audit or when the controls are different for different clients, the methodology helps the auditor design an effective and efficient audit program.

After the appropriate audit procedures for a given set of circumstances have been designed, they must be performed. It is likely to be inefficient to do the audit procedures as they are stated in the design format of Table 11–1. In converting from a design to a performance format, procedures are combined. This will

- Eliminate duplicate procedures.
- Make sure that when a given document is examined, all procedures to be performed on that document are done at that time.
- Enable the auditor to do the procedures in the most effective order. For example, by footing the journal and reviewing the journal for unusual items first, the auditor gains a better perspective in doing the detailed tests.

The process of converting from a design to a performance format is illustrated for the Hillsburg Hardware Ltd. case application at the end of this chapter. The design format is shown on pages 376-378. The performance format is shown on page 379.

Internal Controls and Tests of Controls In this section the key internal controls and related tests of controls included in Table 11–1 are discussed in greater detail. For convenience they are discussed in terms of individual internal controls rather than internal control objectives.

Adequate documents and records Since each company has a unique system of originating, processing, and recording transactions, it may be difficult to evaluate whether its procedures are designed for maximum control; nevertheless, adequate record-keeping procedures must exist before most of the internal control objectives can be met. Some companies, for example, automatically prepare a multicopy prenumbered sales invoice at the time a customer order is received. Copies of this document are used to approve credit, authorize shipment, record the number of units shipped, and bill customers. Under this system, there is almost no chance of the failure to bill a customer if all invoices are accounted for periodically. Under a different system, in which the sales invoice is prepared only after a shipment has been made, the likelihood of the failure to bill a customer is high unless some compensating control exists.

Proper tests of control procedures for testing record keeping, including the adequacy of documents and the timeliness of recording, depend on the nature of the control. For example, if the client requires that a duplicate sales invoice be attached to every sales order to prevent failing to bill a customer for shipped goods, a useful test of control is to account for a sequence of sales orders and examine each one to make sure a duplicate sales invoice is attached.

Prenumbered documents The use of prenumbered documents is meant to prevent both the *failure to bill* or record sales and the occurrence of *duplicate* billings and recordings. Of course, it does not do much good to have prenumbered documents unless they are properly accounted for. An example of the use of this control is the filing, by a billing clerk, of a copy of all shipping documents in sequential order after each shipment is billed, with someone else periodically accounting for all numbers and investigating the reason for any missing documents. Another example is to program the computer to prepare a listing of unused numbers at month's end with follow-up by appropriate personnel.

A common test for this control is to account for a sequence of various types of documents, such as duplicate sales invoices selected from the sales journal, watching for omitted and duplicate numbers or invoices outside the normal sequence. This test simultaneously provides evidence of both the validity and completeness objectives.

Mailing of monthly statements The mailing of monthly statements by someone who has no responsibility for handling cash or preparing the sales and accounts receivable records is a useful control because it encourages a response from customers if the balance is improperly stated. For maximum effectiveness, all disagreements about the balance in the account should be directed to a designated official who has no responsibility for handling cash or recording sales or accounts receivable.

The auditor's observations of the mailing of statements by a properly designated person and the examination of customer correspondence files are useful tests of controls to evaluate whether monthly statements have been sent to customers.

Proper authorization The auditor is concerned about authorization at *three key points:* credit must be properly authorized before a sale takes place; goods should be shipped only after proper authorization; and prices, including base terms, freight, and discounts, must be authorized. The first two controls are meant to prevent the loss of company assets by shipping to fictitious customers or those who will fail to pay for the goods. Price authorization is meant to make sure the sale is billed at the price set by company policy.

It is easy to test the effectiveness of internal controls for authorization by examining documents for proper approval at each of these three key points. In some systems, however, authorization for credit is automated by having the credit limit for each customer entered in the accounts receivable master file for reference at the time of sale. In these systems, the auditor must determine that the credit limits on file have been properly authorized and that the programmed limit checks are properly functioning.

Adequate separation of duties Proper separation of duties is useful to prevent various types of misstatements, both intentional and unintentional. To prevent fraud, it is important that anyone responsible for inputting sales and cash receipts transaction information into the computer be denied access to cash. It is also desirable to separate the credit-granting functions from the sales function, since credit checks are intended to offset the natural tendency of sales personnel to optimize volume even at the expense of high bad debt write-offs. It is equally desirable that personnel responsible for doing internal comparisons are independent of those entering the original data. For example, comparison of batch control totals to summary reports and comparison of accounts receivable master file totals to the general ledger balance should be done by someone independent of those who input sales and cash receipt transactions.

The appropriate tests of controls for separation of duties are ordinarily restricted to the auditor's observations of activities and discussions with personnel. For example, it is possible to observe whether the billing clerk has access to cash when opening incoming mail or depositing cash. It is usually also necessary to ask personnel what their responsibilities are and if there are any circumstances where their responsibilities are different from the normal policy. For example, the employee responsible for billing customers may state that she does not have access to cash. Further discussion may bring out that when the cashier is on vacation, she takes over the cashier's duties.

Internal verification procedures The use of independent persons for checking the processing and recording of sales transactions is essential for fulfilling each of the seven internal control objectives. Table 11–2 shows a typical internal verifica-

TABLE 11–2
Internal Verification
Procedures

INTERNAL CONTROL OBJECTIVE	EXAMPLE OF AN INTERNAL VERIFICATION PROCEDURE
Recorded sales are valid.	Account for a sequence of sales invoices and examine supporting documentation.
Sales are properly authorized.	Examine credit files for customers to determine if credit was approved in accordance with company policy.
Existing sales transactions are recorded.	Account for a sequence of bills of lading and trace them to the sales journal.
Recorded sales are properly valued.	Compare quantity on sales invoices with shipping document records.
Recorded sales are properly classified.	Compare supporting documents for recorded sales with the chart of accounts.
Sales are recorded on a timely basis.	Examine unbilled shipping documents in the possession of the billing clerk to determine whether shipments that should already have been billed are included.
Sales transactions are properly included in the subsidiary records and correctly summarized.	Review the accounts receivable master file for unusual or incorrect items.

tion procedure for each objective. Examining the initials of the person responsible for checking documents is one example of a test of control procedure the external auditor can use.

Other Tests of Control

The tests of controls listed in the right-hand column of Table 11–1 are of a type that are more specific than those listed in the third column; because they are more specific, their application varies considerably depending on the circumstances. In subsequent paragraphs, the procedures frequently *not* performed are emphasized, since they are the ones requiring an audit decision. The procedures are discussed in the same order in which they were included in Table 11–1. It should be noted that some procedures fulfill more than one objective.

Recorded sales are valid For this objective, the auditor is concerned with the possibility of *two types of misstatements:* sales being included in the journals for which no shipment was made and, alternatively, shipments being made to fictitious customers and recorded as sales. As might be imagined, the inclusion of invalid sales is rare, but the potential consequences are significant because they lead to an overstatement of assets and income.

The appropriate tests of contols for detecting invalid transactions depend on where the auditor believes the misstatements are likely to take place. Normally, the auditor tests for invalid sales only if he or she believes a control weakness exists; therefore, the nature of the tests depends on the nature of the weakness. To test for recorded sales for which there were no actual shipments, the auditor can trace from selected entries in the sales journal to make sure a related copy of the bill of lading and other supporting documents exist. If the auditor is also concerned about the possibility of a fictitious duplicate copy of a shipping document, it may be necessary to trace the amounts to the perpetual inventory records as a test of whether inventory was reduced. A test of the possibility of a shipment to a fictitious customer is to examine the sales orders corresponding to a sales transaction entry in the sales journal for the existence of credit approval and shipping authorization. Another effective approach to auditing for invalid sales transactions is to trace the *credit* for the accounts receivable in the master file to its source. If the receivable was actually collected in cash or the goods returned, there must originally have been a valid sale. If the credit was for a bad-debt charge-off or a credit memo, or if the account was still unpaid at the time of the audit, intensive follow-up by examining shipping and customer order documents is required, since each of these could indicate a fictitious sales transaction.

It should be kept in mind that *the ordinary audit is not primarily intended to detect fraud* unless the effect on the financial statements is material. The preceding tests should be necessary only if the auditor is particularly concerned about the occurrence of fraud due to inadequate controls.

Sales are properly authorized   It is normally necessary to test by reperformance whether the company's general credit, shipping, and pricing policies are being properly followed in the day-to-day operations. This is especially important with regard to the pricing of sales. Reperformance pricing tests are done by comparing the actual price charged for different products, including freight and terms, with the price list or file authorized by management. If product prices are negotiated on an individual sale basis, the tests usually involve determining that the proper authorization by the sales manager or other appropriate official has occurred. Also, existing contracts are examined, and in some cases even confirmed directly with the customer. Procedures to test pricing are normally necessary regardless of the quality of the controls, but the sample size can be reduced if the controls are adequate.

Existing sales transactions are recorded   In many audits, the auditor will not be as concerned about the completeness objective on the ground that overstatements of assets and income are a greater concern in the audit of sales transactions than their understatement. If there are inadequate controls, which is likely if the client does no independent internal tracing from shipping documents to the sales journal, substantive procedures will be necessary.

An effective procedure to test for unbilled shipments is to trace selected shipping documents from a file in the shipping department to related duplicate sales invoices and the sales journal. To conduct a meaningful test using this procedure, the auditor must be confident that all shipping documents are included in the file. This can be done by accounting for a numerical sequence of the documents.

It is important that auditors understand the difference between tracing from source documents to the journals and tracing from the journals back to supporting documents. The former is a test for *omitted transactions* (completeness objective), whereas the latter is a test for *invalid transactions* (validity objective).

In testing for the validity objective, the starting point is the journal. A sample of invoice numbers is selected *from* the journal and traced *to* duplicate sales invoices, shipping documents, and customer orders. In testing for the completeness objective, the likely starting point is the shipping document. A sample of shipping documents is selected and traced *to* duplicate sales invoices and the sales journal as a test of omissions.

When designing audit procedures for the validity and completeness objectives, the starting point for tracing the document is essential. This is referred to as the *direction of tests*. For example, if the auditor is concerned about the validity objective but traces in the wrong direction (from shipping documents to the journals), a serious audit deficiency exists.

When testing for the other five objectives, the direction of tests is usually not relevant. For example, the valuation of sales transactions can be tested by tracing from a duplicate sales invoice to a shipping document or vice versa.

Recorded sales are properly valued   The correct valuation of sales transactions concerns shipping the amount of goods ordered, correctly billing for the amount of goods shipped, and correctly recording the amount billed in the accounting records. Reperformance to make sure that each of these aspects of valuation is correct are ordinarily conducted in every audit.

Typical reperformance tests include recomputing information in the accounting records to verify whether it is proper. A common approach is to start with entries in the sales journal and compare the total of selected transactions with accounts receivable master file entries and duplicate sales invoices. Prices on the duplicate sales invoices are normally compared with an approved price list, extensions and footings are recomputed, and the details listed on the invoices are compared with shipping records for description, quantity, and customer identification. Frequently, customer orders and sales orders are also examined for the same information.

The comparison of tests of controls and substantive procedures for the valuation objective is a good example of how audit time can be saved when effective internal controls exist. It is obvious that the test of controls for this objective takes almost no time because it involves examining only an initial or other evidence of internal verification. Since the sample size for substantive procedures can be reduced if this control is effective, a significant saving will result from performing the test of controls due to its lower cost.

Recorded sales are properly classified   Charging the correct general ledger account is less of a problem in sales than in some other transaction cycles, but it is still of some concern. When there are cash and credit sales, it is important not to debit accounts receivable for a cash sale, or to credit sales for collection of a receivable. It is also important not to classify sales of operating assets, such as buildings, as sales. For those companies using more than one sales classification, such as companies issuing segmented earnings statements, proper classification is essential.

It is common to test sales for proper classification as part of testing for valuation. The auditor examines supporting documents to determine the proper classification of a given transaction and compares this with the actual account to which it is charged.

Sales are recorded on a timely basis   It is important that sales be billed and recorded as soon after shipment takes place as possible to prevent the unintentional omission of transactions from the records and to make sure sales are recorded in the proper period. At the same time that tests of controls with respect to the valuation objective are being performed, it is common to compare the date on selected bills of lading or other shipping documents with the date on related duplicate sales invoices, the sales journal, and the accounts receivable master file. Significant differences indicate a potential cutoff problem.

Sales transactions are properly included in the master file and correctly summarized   The proper inclusion of all sales transactions in the accounts receivable master file is essential because the accuracy of these records affects the client's

* Mechanical Accuracy *

ability to collect outstanding receivables. Similarly, the sales journal must be correctly totaled and posted to the general ledger if the financial statements are to be correct. In every audit, it is necessary to perform some clerical accuracy tests by footing the journals and tracing the totals and details to the general ledger and the master file to check whether there are intentional or unintentional misstatements in the computer program. Only the sample size is affected by the quality of the internal controls. Tracing from the sales journal to the master file is typically done as a part of fulfilling other objectives, but footing the sales journal and tracing the totals to the general ledger is done as a separate procedure.

The distinction between the summarization and other objectives is that summarization includes footing journals, master file records, and ledgers and tracing from one to the other among those three. Whenever footing and comparisons are restricted to these three records, the process is summarization. Valuation, for example, involves comparing documents with each other or with journals and master file records. To illustrate, comparing a duplicate sales invoice with either the sales journal or master file entry is a valuation objective procedure. Tracing an entry from the sales journal to the master file is a summarization procedure.

Sales Returns and Allowances

The audit objectives and the client's methods of controlling misstatements are essentially the same for processing credit memos as those described for sales, with two important differences. The first relates to *materiality*. In many instances sales returns and allowances are so immaterial that they can be ignored in the audit altogether. The second major difference relates to *emphasis on objectives*. For sales returns and allowances, the primary emphasis is normally on testing the validity of recorded transactions as a means of uncovering any diversion of cash from the collection of accounts receivable that has been covered up by a fictitious sales return or allowance.

Naturally, the other objectives should not be ignored. But because the objectives and methodology for auditing sales returns and allowances are essentially the same as for sales, we will not include a detailed study of the area. The reader should be able to apply the same logic to arrive at suitable controls and tests of controls to verify the amounts.

> **OBJECTIVE 3**
>
> Apply the methodology for controls over sales transactions to controls over sales returns and allowances.

11-29

Internal Controls and Tests of Controls for Cash Receipts

The same methodology used for designing tests of controls over sales transactions is used for designing tests of controls for cash receipts. Similarly, cash receipts tests of controls audit procedures are developed around the same framework used for sales; that is, given the internal control objectives, key internal controls for each objective are determined and tests of controls for each control related to each objective are developed. As in all other audit areas the tests of controls depend on the controls the auditor has identified to reduce the assessed level of control risk after consideration of the tests of controls and the other considerations in the audit.

Key internal controls and common tests of controls to satisfy each of the internal control objectives for cash receipts are listed in Table 11–3. Since this summary follows the same format as the previous one for sales, no further explanation of its meaning is necessary.

The detailed discussion of the internal controls and tests of controls that was

> **OBJECTIVE 4**
>
> Determine the client's internal controls over cash receipts transactions, design and perform tests of the controls, and assess related control risk.

included for the audit of sales is not included for cash receipts. Instead, the audit procedures that are most likely to be misunderstood are explained in more detail.

An essential part of the auditor's responsibility in auditing cash receipts is identification of weaknesses in internal control that increase the likelihood of fraud. In expanding on Table 11–3, the emphasis will be on those audit procedures that are designed primarily for the discovery of fraud. However, the reader should keep in mind throughout this discussion that the non-fraud procedures included in the table are the auditor's primary responsibility. Those procedures that are not discussed are omitted only because their purpose and the methodology for applying them should be apparent from their description.

Determining Whether Cash Received Was Recorded

The most difficult type of cash defalcation for the auditor to detect is that which occurs *before the cash is recorded* in the cash receipts journal or other cash listing. For example, if a grocery store clerk takes cash and intentionally fails to register the receipt of cash on the cash register, it is extremely difficult to discover the theft. To prevent this type of fraud, internal controls such as those included in the third objective in Table 11–3 are implemented by many companies. The type of control will, of course, depend on the type of business. For example, the controls for a retail store in which the cash is received by the same person who sells the merchandise and rings up the cash receipts should be different from the controls for a company in which all receipts are received through the mail several weeks after the sales have taken place.

It is normal practice to trace from *prenumbered remittance advices* or *prelists of cash receipts* to the cash receipts journal and subsidiary accounts receivable records as a test of the recording of actual cash received. This test will only be effective if the cash was listed on a cash register tape or some other prelisting at the time it was received.

If the auditor is particularly concerned about weaknesses in internal control that could lead to fraudulently omitted cash receipts, there is an effective but time-consuming approach that combines a part of the cash receipts tests with the audit of sales transactions. When the auditor traces a sales transaction to the debit in the customer's subsidiary ledger, the auditor can also trace the subsequent *credit* that reduces the account receivable to its source. The credit must arise from cash received, sales returns and allowances, or accounts charged off as uncollectible. In testing the credits to the sales transactions, the auditor traces the cash receipts to the cash receipts journal, the sales returns and allowances to a properly authorized credit memo and the sales returns and allowances journal, and the accounts charged off to proper authorization. Any sales transactions not credited are still a part of accounts receivable and are tested as a part of the confirmation of a sample of the outstanding balances in accounts receivable. In this approach the auditor is looking for sales *without a valid credit* in the accounts receivable master file, which would be an indication of a possible defalcation. Of course, if an employee is able to omit the recording of a sale and subsequently takes the cash receipt from the customer before it is recorded, the procedure described here would be ineffective.

Prepare Proof of Cash Receipts

A useful audit procedure to test whether all recorded cash receipts have been deposited in the bank account is a proof of cash receipts. In this test the total cash receipts recorded in the cash receipts journal for a given period, such as a month, are reconciled with the actual deposits made to the bank during the same period. There may be a difference in the two due to deposits in transit and other items, but

TABLE 11–3 Summary of Objectives, Controls, and Tests of Controls for Cash Receipts

INTERNAL CONTROL OBJECTIVE	KEY INTERNAL CONTROL		COMMON TESTS OF CONTROLS
Recorded cash receipts are for funds actually received by the company (validity).	Separation of duties between handling cash and record keeping.	Observation.	Review the cash receipts journal, general ledger, and accounts receivable master file or trial balance for large and unusual amounts.*
	Independent reconciliation of bank accounts.	Observation.	Trace from cash receipts journal to bank statements. Proof of cash receipts.
Cash discounts are authorized (authorization).	A policy on granting cash discounts must exist.	Discussion with management.	Examine remittance advices and sales invoices to determine whether discounts allowed are consistent with company policy.
	Approval of cash discounts.	Examine remittance advices for proper approval.	
Cash received is recorded in the cash receipts journal (completeness).	Separation of duties between handling cash and record keeping.	Discussion with personnel and observation.	Trace from remittances or prelisting to cash receipts journal.
	Use of remittance advices or a prelisting of cash.	Account for numerical sequence or examine prelisting.	
	Immediate endorsement of incoming cheques.	Observation.	
	Internal verification of the recording of cash receipts.	Examine indication of internal verification.	
	Regular monthly statements to customers.	Observation.	
Recorded cash receipts are deposited and recorded at the amount received (valuation).	Same as previous objective.	Same as previous objective.	Proof of cash receipts.
	Regular reconciliation of bank accounts.	Review monthly bank reconciliations.	
	Batch totals are compared with computer summary reports.	Examine file of batch totals for initials of data control clerk; compare totals to summary reports.	
Cash receipts are properly classified (classification).	Use of adequate chart of accounts.	Review chart of accounts.	Examine documents supporting cash receipts for proper classification.
	Internal review and verification.	Examine indication of internal verification.	
Cash receipts are recorded on a timely basis (timeliness).	Procedure requiring recording of cash receipts on a daily basis.	Observe unrecorded cash at any point of time.	Compare dates of deposits with dates in the cash receipts journal and prelisting of cash receipts.
	Internal verification.	Examine indication of internal verification.	
Cash receipts are properly included in the master file and are correctly summarized (posting and summarization).	Regular monthly statements to customers.	Observe whether statements are mailed.	Foot journals and trace postings to general ledger and accounts receivable master file.
	Internal verification of accounts receivable master file contents.	Examine indication of internal verification.	
	Comparison of accounts receivable master file or trial balance totals with general ledger balance.	Examine initials on general ledger account indicating comparison.	

* This analytical procedure can also apply to other objectives, including completeness, valuation, and timeliness.

the amounts can be reconciled and compared. The procedure is not useful in discovering cash receipts that have not been recorded in the journals or time lags in making deposits, but it can help uncover recorded cash receipts that have not been deposited, unrecorded deposits, unrecorded loans, bank loans deposited directly into the bank account, and similar errors. A proof of cash receipts and cash disbursements is illustrated in Chapter 21 on page 713. This somewhat time-consuming procedure is ordinarily used only when the controls are weak. In rare instances in which controls are extremely weak the period covered by the proof of cash receipts may be the entire year.

Test to Discover Lapping

Lapping, which is a common type of defalcation, is the postponement of entries for the collection of receivables to *conceal an existing cash shortage*. The defalcation is perpetrated by a person who handles cash receipts and then enters them into the computer system. He or she defers recording the cash receipts from one customer and covers the shortages with receipts of another. These in turn are covered from the receipts of a third customer a few days later. The employee must continue to cover the shortage through repeated lapping, replace the stolen money, or find another way to conceal the shortage.

This defalcation can be easily prevented by separation of duties. It can be detected by comparing the name, amount, and dates shown on remittance advices with cash receipts journal entries and related duplicate deposit slips. Since the procedure is relatively time consuming, it is ordinarily performed only when there is specific concern with defalcation because of a weakness in the internal control structure.

Audit Tests for Uncollectible Accounts

OBJECTIVE 5

Apply the methodology for controls over the sales and collection cycle to write-offs of uncollectible accounts receivable.

Validity and *proper authorization* are the most important considerations the auditor should keep in mind in the verification of the write-off of individual uncollectible accounts. A major concern in testing accounts charged off as uncollectible is the possibility of the client covering up a defalcation by charging off accounts receivable that have already been collected. The major control for preventing this type of fraud is proper authorization of the write-off of uncollectible accounts by a designated level of management only after a thorough investigation of the reason the customer has not paid.

Normally, verification of the accounts charged off takes relatively little time. A typical procedure is the examination of approvals by the appropriate persons. For a sample of accounts charged off, it is also usually necessary for the auditor to examine correspondence in the client's files establishing their uncollectibility. In some cases the auditor will also examine credit reports such as those provided by Dun & Bradstreet Canada Limited or Creditel. After the auditor has concluded that the accounts charged off by general journal entries are proper, selected items should be traced to the accounts receivable master file as a test of the records.

Effect of Results of Tests of Controls

The results of the tests of controls will have a significant effect on the remainder of the audit, especially on the tests of details of balances part of substantive procedures. The parts of the audit most affected by the tests of the sales and collection cycle transactions are the balances in *accounts receivable, cash, bad-debt expense,* and *allowance for doubtful accounts.* Furthermore, if the results of the tests are unsatisfactory, it is necessary to do additional substantive testing for the propriety of sales, sales returns and allowances, charge-off of uncollectible accounts, and processing of cash receipts.

At the completion of the tests of controls, it is essential to *analyze each control test exception* to determine its cause and the implication of the exception on the assessed level of control risk, which may affect the supported detection risk and thereby the substantive procedures. The methodology and implications of exceptions analysis are explained more fully in Chapter 12.

The most significant effect of the results of the tests of controls in the sales and collection cycle is on the confirmation of accounts receivable. The type of confirmation, the size of the sample, and the timing of the test are all affected by the results of tests of controls. The effect of the tests on accounts receivable, bad-debt expense, and allowance for uncollectible accounts is considered in Chapter 13.

Case Illustration – Hillsburg Hardware Ltd. – Part I

The concepts for testing the sales and collection cycle presented in this chapter are now illustrated for Hillsburg Hardware Ltd. The company's financial statements and the general ledger trial balance were shown in Chapter 5. Additional information was included in other chapters. A study of this case is intended to illustrate a methodology for designing audit procedures and integrating different parts of the audit.

Hillsburg Hardware Ltd. is a small wholesale distributor of hardware to independent, high-quality hardware stores in eastern Canada. This is the fourth year of the audit of this client, and there have never been any significant misstatements discovered in the tests. During the current year, a major change has occurred. The chief accountant left the firm and has been replaced by Erma Swanson. There has also been some turnover of other accounting personnel.

The overall assessment by management is that the accounting personnel are reasonably competent and highly trustworthy. The president, Rick Chulick, has been the chief operating officer for approximately ten years. He is regarded as a highly competent, honest individual who does a conscientious job. The following information is provided from the auditor's files:

> **OBJECTIVE 6**
>
> Develop an integrated audit plan for the sales and collection cycle.

- *The organization chart and flowchart of the internal control structure prepared for the audit.* This information is included in Figures 11–4 and 11–5. Sales returns and allowances for this client are too immaterial to include in the flowchart or to verify in the audit.

- *Internal controls and weaknesses, and assessment of control risk for sales and cash receipts.* An appropriate approach to identifying and documenting internal controls and weaknesses and assessing control risk is included for sales in Figure 11–6 and for cash receipts in Figure 11–7. There are several things the auditor, Francine Martel, did to complete each matrix. First she identified internal controls from flowcharts, internal control questionnaires, and discussions with client personnel. Only flowcharts are available in the Hillsburg case. Second, she identified weaknesses using the same sources. Third, she decided which internal control objectives are affected by the internal controls and weaknesses. Finally, she assessed control risk using the information obtained in the preceding three steps. The use of the objective-by-objective matrix in Figures 11–6 and 11–7 is primarily to help Francine Martel effectively assess control risk.

- *Tests of controls for each internal control.* The tests of controls for sales are included in the third column and fifth column of Table 11–4 and for cash receipts the same columns in Table 11–5. The source of the internal controls is Figure 11–6

FIGURE 11–4

Hillsburg Hardware
Organization Chart:
Personnel

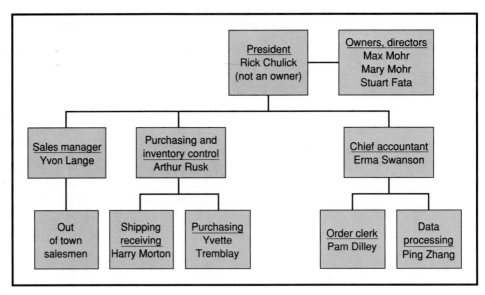

for sales and Figure 11–7 for cash receipts. Francine decided the appropriate tests for each control.

Notice that certain objectives in Tables 11–4 and 11–5 either have no controls (for example, classification and timing) or existing controls are such that there are weaknesses (for example, validity and completeness in Table 11–4; completeness in Table 11–5). The tests of controls listed in the right-hand column of Tables 11–4 and 11–5 are designed to determine if the client's accounting transactions have been properly authorized, correctly recorded and summarized in the journals and correctly posted to the appropriate ledger. Tests such as these were described in Chapter 10 as dual-purpose tests; they are both tests of controls and substantive procedures. As was suggested earlier in this chapter, the purpose of such tests is to assist the auditor in assessing control risk.

Francine decided on the tests of controls listed in the right-hand column for the different objectives after considering assessed control risk, the tests of controls listed in the third column, and weaknesses of internal control for that objective.

Notice that the use of the objective-by-objective format in Tables 11–4 and 11–5 is to help Francine more effectively decide the appropriate tests. She could have decided tests of controls as easily by selecting tests of controls for each internal control included in Figure 11–6 and 11–7.

■ *Tests of controls audit program in a performance format.* The tests of controls in Table 11–4 and Table 11–5 are combined into one audit program in Figure 11–8. The cross-referencing of the numbers in parentheses shows that no procedures have been added to or deleted from Figure 11–8 and the wording is unchanged. The reasons Francine prepared the performance format audit program were to eliminate audit procedures that were included more than once in Tables 11–4 and 11–5 and to include them in an order that permits audit assistants to complete the procedures as efficiently as possible. Sample size and the particular items for inclusion in the sample are not included here, but they are considered in an extension of the case in the Hillsburg Hardware case illustration at the end of Chapter 12.

After the tests of controls have been performed, it will be essential to *analyze each test of control exception* to determine its cause and the implication of the exception on the assessed level of control risk, which may affect the supported detection risk and thereby the substantive procedures. The methodology and implications of exceptions analysis are explained more fully in Chapter 12.

FIGURE 11–5   Hillsburg Hardware – Flowchart of Sales and Collections

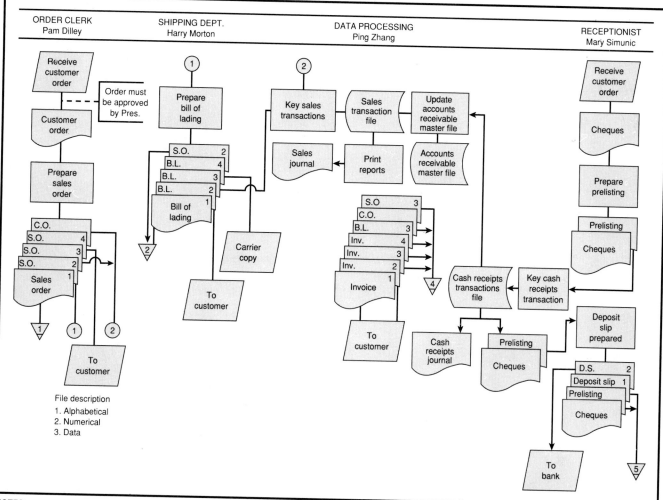

NOTES

1. All correspondence is sent to the president.
2. All sales order numbers are accounted for weekly by the chief accountant.
3. All bills of lading numbers are accounted for weekly by the chief accountant.
4. Sales amount recorded on sales invoice is based on standard price list. It is stored in a computer data file and can only be changed with authorization of the chief accountant.
5. Duplicate sales invoice is compared with bill of lading daily by Pam Dilley for descriptions and quantities and the sales invoice is reviewed for reasonableness of the extensions and footing. She initials a copy of the invoice before the original is mailed to the customer.
6. Sales are batched daily by Pam Dilley. The batch totals are compared to the sales journal weekly.
7. Statements are sent to customers monthly.
8. Accounts receivable master file total is compared with general ledger by the chief accountant on a monthly basis.

9. Unpaid invoices are filed separately from paid invoices.
10. The receptionist stamps incoming cheques with a restrictive endorsement immediately upon receipt.
11. There are no cash sales.
12. Deposits are made at least weekly.
13. Cash receipts are batched daily by the receptionist. The batch totals are compared to the cash receipts journal weekly.
14. The bank account is reconciled by the chief accountant on a monthly basis.
15. All bad debt expense and charge-off of bad debts are approved by the president after being initiated by the chief accountant.
16. Financial statements are printed monthly by the chief accountant and reviewed by the president.
17. All errors are reviewed daily by the chief accountant immediately after the updating run. Corrections are made the same day.

FIGURE 11–6 Assessment of Control Risk Matrix for Hillsburg Hardware Ltd. – Sales

	INTERNAL CONTROL	INTERNAL CONTROL OBJECTIVES – SALES						
		Recorded sales are for shipments made to nonfictitious customers (validity)	*Sales transactions are properly authorized (authorization)*	*Existing sales transactions are recorded (completeness)*	*Recorded sales are for the amount of goods shipped and are correctly billed and recorded (valuation)*	*Sales transactions are properly classified (classification)*	*Sales are recorded on a timely basis (timing)*	*Sales transactions are properly included in the accounts receivable master file and correctly summarized (posting and summarization)*
CONTROLS	Dilley examines documents before bill is sent to customer (C1)	C			C			
	Credit is approved by Chulik before shipment (C2)		C		C			
	Bills of lading are accounted for weekly by Swanson to make sure they are billed (C3)			C				
	Batch totals are compared with computer summary reports (C4)	C		C	C			
	Swanson compares accounts receivable master file total with general ledger account (C5)							C
	Monthly statements are sent to customers (C6)	C			C			C
WEAKNESSES	Lack of internal verification for the possibility of sales invoices being recorded more than once (W1)	W						
	Lack of control to test for timely recording (W2)						W	
	Lack of internal verification that sales invoices are included in the sales journal (W3)			W				
	Assessment of control risk	Medium	Low	Medium	Low	Low*	High	Low

* Since there are no cash sales, classification is not a problem.
C = Control.
W = Weakness.

FIGURE 11–7 Assessment of Control Risk Matrix for Hillsburg Hardware Ltd. – Cash Receipts

	INTERNAL CONTROL	INTERNAL CONTROL OBJECTIVES – CASH RECEIPTS: Recorded cash receipts are for funds actually received by the company (validity)	Cash discounts are authorized (authorization)	Cash received is recorded in the cash receipts journal (completeness)	Recorded cash receipts are deposited at the amount received (valuation)	Cash receipts are properly classified (classification)	Cash receipts are recorded on a timely basis (timing)	Cash receipts are properly included in the accounts receivable master file and are correctly summarized (posting and summarization)
CONTROLS	Swanson reconciles bank account (C1)	C			C			
	Cheques are stamped with a restrictive endorsement (C2)			C				
	Statements are sent to customers monthly (C3)			C	C			
	Batch totals are compared with computer summary reports (C4)	C		C	C			
	Swanson compares accounts receivable master file total with general ledger account (C5)							C
WEAKNESSES	Prelisting of cash is not used to verify recorded cash receipts (W1)			W				
	Receptionist handles cash after it is returned from cash receipts (W2)			W				
	Zhang has access to cash receipts and maintains accounts receivable records (W3)			W				
	Cash receipts are not deposited daily (W4)						W	
	Lack of internal verification of classification of cash receipts (W5)					W		
	Assessment of control risk	Low	NA	High	Low	High	High	Medium

NA = Not applicable.
C = Control.
W = Weakness.

TABLE 11–4 Internal Controls and Tests of Controls for Hillsburg Hardware Ltd. – Sales* (design format)

OBJECTIVE	EXISTING CONTROL†	TESTS OF CONTROLS	WEAKNESS	TESTS OF CONTROLS
Recorded sales are for shipments actually made to nonfictitious customers	Dilley examines documents before bill is sent to customer (C1)	Account for a sequence of sales invoices in the sales journal (11) Examine underlying documents for indication of internal verification by Pam Dilley (12b)	Lack of internal verification for the possibility of sales invoices being recorded more than once (W1)	Review journals and master file for unusual transactions and amounts (1) Trace recorded sales from the sales journal to the file of supporting documents which includes a duplicate sales invoice, bill of lading, sales order and customer order (13)
	Batch totals are compared with computer summary reports (C4)	Examine file of batch totals for initials of data control clerk (8)		
	Monthly statements are sent to customers (C6)	Observe whether monthly statements are mailed (6)		
Sales transactions are properly authorized	Credit is approved by Chulik before shipment (C2)	Examine customer order for credit approval by Chulick (12e)		
Existing sales transactions are recorded	Bills of lading are accounted for weekly by Swanson to make sure they are billed (C3)	Account for a sequence of shipping documents (9)	Lack of internal verification that sales invoices are included in the sales journal (W3)	Trace selected shipping documents to the sales journal to be sure each one has been included (10)
	Batch totals are compared with computer summary reports (C4)	Examine file of batch totals for initials of data control clerk (8)		
Recorded sales are for the amount of goods shipped and are correctly billed and recorded	Dilley examines documents before bill is sent to customer (C1) Credit is approved by Chulik before shipments (C2) Batch totals are compared with computer summary reports (C4) Monthly statements are sent to customers (C6)	Examine underlying documents for indication of internal verification by Dilley (12d) Examine customer order for credit approval by Chulick (12e) Examine file of batch totals for initials of data control clerk (8) Observe whether monthly statements are mailed (6)		Trace selected duplicate sales invoice numbers from the sales journal to: (12) a. Duplicate sales invoice, and check for the total amount recorded in journal, date, customer name and account classification. Check the pricing, extensions and footings (12b) b. Bill of lading and test for customer name, product description, quantity, and date (12c) c. Duplicate sales order and test for customer name, product description, quantity and date (12d) d. Customer order and test for customer name, product description, quantity and date (12e)

TABLE 11–4   *(Continued)*

OBJECTIVE	EXISTING CONTROL†	TESTS OF CONTROLS	WEAKNESS	TESTS OF CONTROLS
Sales transactions are properly classified	None			Examine duplicate sales invoice for proper account classification (12b)
Sales are recorded on a timely basis	None		Lack of control for test of timely recording (W2)	Compare dates on the bill of lading, duplicates sales invoice, and sales journal (14)
Sales transactions are properly included in the accounts receivable master file and are correctly summarized	Swanson compares accounts receivable master file total with general ledger account (C5) Monthly statements are sent to customers (6)	Observe whether Swanson compares master file total with general ledger account (7) Observe whether monthly statements are mailed (6)		Trace selected duplicate sales invoice numbers from the sales journal to the accounts receivable master file, and test for amount, date and invoice number (12a) Foot and crossfoot the sales journal and trace the totals to the general ledger (3)

* The procedures are summarized into a performance format in Figure 11–8. The number and letter in parentheses after the procedure refers to Figure 11–8.

† Only the primary (key) control(s) for each objective is shown. Most objectives are also affected by one or more additional controls.

TABLE 11–5   Internal Controls and Tests of Controls for Hillsburg Hardware Ltd. – Cash Receipts* (design format)

OBJECTIVE	EXISTING CONTROL†	TESTS OF CONTROLS	WEAKNESS	TESTS OF CONTROLS
Recorded cash receipts are for funds actually received by the company	Swanson reconciles bank account (C1) Batch totals are compared with computer summary reports (C4)	Observe whether Swanson reconciles the bank account (4) Examine file of batch totals for initials of data control clerk (8)		Review the journals and master file for unusual transactions and amounts (1) Review the master file for miscellaneous credits (2) Prepare a proof of cash receipts (18) Trace cash receipt entries from the cash receipts journal to the bank statement, testing for dates and amounts of deposits (19)
Cash discounts are authorized	Not applicable			

TABLE 11–5 *(Continued)*

OBJECTIVE	EXISTING CONTROL†	TESTS OF CONTROLS	WEAKNESS	TESTS OF CONTROLS
Cash received is recorded in the cash receipts journal	Cheques are stamped with a restrictive endorsement (C2) Statements are sent to customers monthly (C3) Batch totals are compared with computer summary reports (C4)	Observe whether a restrictive endorsement is used on cash receipts (5) Observe whether monthly statements are mailed (6) Examine file of batch totals for initials of data control clerk (8)	Prelisting of cash is not used to verify recorded cash receipts (W1) Receptionist handles cash after it is returned from cash receipts (W2) Zhang has access to cash receipts and maintains accounts receivable records (W3)	Obtain the prelisting of cash receipts, and trace amounts to the cash receipts journal, testing for names, amounts, and dates (15) Compare the prelisting of cash receipts with the duplicate deposit slip, testing for names, amounts, and dates (16)
Recorded cash receipts are deposited at the amount received	Swanson reconciles bank account (C1) Statements are sent to customers monthly (C3) Batch totals are compared with computer summary reports (C4)	Observe whether Swanson reconciles the bank account (4) Observe whether monthly statements are mailed (6) Examine file of batch totals for initials of data control clerk (8)		The procedures for the validity objective also fulfill this objective
Cash receipts are properly classified	None		Lack of internal verification of classification of cash receipts (W5)	Examine prelisting for proper account classification (17)
Cash receipts are recorded on a timely basis	None		Cash receipts are not deposited daily (W4)	Trace the total from the cash receipts journal to the bank statement, testing for a delay in deposit (16)
Cash receipts are properly included in the accounts receivable master file and are correctly summarized	Swanson compares accounts receivable master file total with general ledger account (C5)	Observe whether Swanson compares master file total with general ledger account (7)		Trace selected entries from the cash receipts journal to entries in the accounts receivable master file, and test for dates and amounts (20) Trace selected credits from the accounts receivable master file to the cash receipts journal and test for dates and amounts (21) Foot and crossfoot the cash receipts journal and trace totals to the general ledger (3)

* The procedures are summarized into a performance format in Figure 11–8. The number in parentheses after the procedure refers to Figure 11–8.
† Only the primary (key) control(s) for each objective is shown. Most objectives are also affected by one or more additional controls.

FIGURE 11–8

Audit Program for
Hillsburg Hardware
Ltd.: Performance
Format

HILLSBURG HARDWARE LTD.

Audit Procedures for Sales and Cash Receipts
(Sample Size and the Items in the Sample Are Not Included)

GENERAL
1. Review journals and master file for unusual transactions and amounts.
2. Review the master file for miscellaneous credits.
3. Foot and crossfoot the sales and cash receipts journals, and trace the totals to the general ledger.
4. Observe whether Erma Swanson reconciles the bank account.
5. Observe whether a restrictive endorsement is used on cash receipts.
6. Observe whether monthly statements are mailed.
7. Observe whether Erma Swanson compares master file total with general ledger account.
8. Examine file of batch totals for initials of data control clerk.

SHIPMENT OF GOODS
9. Account for a sequence of shipping documents.
10. Trace selected shipping documents to the sales journal to be sure that each one has been included.

BILLING OF CUSTOMERS AND RECORDING THE SALES IN THE RECORDS
11. Account for a sequence of sales invoices in the sales journal.
12. Trace selected duplicate sales invoice numbers from the sales journal to:
    a. accounts receivable master file and test for amount, date, and invoice number.
    b. duplicate sales invoice and check for the total amount recorded in the journal, date, customer name, and account classification. Check the pricing, extensions, and footings. Examine underlying documents for indication of internal verification by Pam Dilley.
    c. bill of lading and test for customer name, product description, quantity, and date.
    d. duplicate sales order and test for customer name, product description, quantity, and date and indication of internal verification by Pam Dilley.
    e. customer order and test for customer name, product description, quantity, date and credit approval of Rick Chulick.
13. Trace recorded sales from the sales journal to the file of supporting documents, which includes a duplicate sales invoice, bill of lading, sales order, and customer order.
14. Compare dates on the bill of lading, duplicate sales invoice, and sales journal.

PROCESSING CASH RECEIPTS AND RECORDING THE AMOUNTS
IN THE RECORDS
15. Obtain the prelisting of cash receipts, and trace amounts to the cash receipts journal, testing for names, amounts, and dates.
16. Compare the prelisting of cash receipts with the duplicate deposit slip, testing for names, amounts, and dates. Trace the total from the cash receipts journal to the bank statement, testing for a delay in deposit.
17. Examine prelisting for proper account classification.
18. Prepare a proof of cash receipts.
19. Trace cash receipt entries from the cash receipts journal to the bank statement, testing for dates and amounts of deposits.
20. Trace selected entries from the cash receipts journal to entries in the accounts receivable master file and test for dates and amounts.
21. Trace selected credits from the accounts receivable master file to the cash receipts journal and test for dates and amounts.

REVIEW QUESTIONS

11–1 Describe the nature of the following documents and records and explain their use in the sales and collection cycle: bill of lading, sales invoice, credit memo, remittance advice, monthly statement to customers.

11–2 Explain the importance of proper credit approval for sales. What effect do adequate controls in the credit function have on the auditor's evidence accumulation?

11–3 Distinguish between bad debt expense and the charge-off of uncollectible accounts. Explain why they are audited in completely different ways.

11–4 List the internal control objectives for the verification of sales transactions. For each objective, state one internal control the client can use to reduce the likelihood of errors.

11–5 State two tests of controls the auditor can use to verify the following sales objective: Recorded sales are stated at the proper amount.

11–6 List the most important duties that should be segregated in the sales and collection cycle. Explain why it is desirable that each duty be segregated.

11–7 Explain how prenumbered shipping documents and sales invoices can be useful controls for preventing errors in sales.

11–8 What three types of authorizations are commonly used in internal control for sales? For each authorization, state a test of controls the auditor could use to verify whether the control was effective in preventing errors.

11–9 Explain the purpose of footing and crossfooting the sales journal and tracing the totals to the general ledger.

11–10 What is the difference between the auditor's approach in verifying sales returns and allowances and that for sales? Explain the reasons for the difference.

11–11 Explain why auditors usually emphasize the detection of fraud in the audit of cash. Is this consistent or inconsistent with the auditor's responsibility in the audit? Explain.

11–12 List the internal control objectives for the verification of cash receipts. For each objective, state one internal control the client can use to reduce the likelihood of errors.

11–13 List several audit procedures the auditor can use to determine whether all cash received was recorded.

11–14 Explain what is meant by *proof of cash receipts* and state its purpose.

11–15 Explain what is meant by *lapping*, and discuss how the auditor can uncover it. Under what circumstances should the auditor make a special effort to uncover lapping?

11–16 What audit procedures are most likely to be used to verify accounts receivable charged off as uncollectible? State the purpose of each of these procedures.

11–17 State the relationship between the confirmation of accounts receivable and the results of the tests of controls.

11–18 Under what circumstances is it acceptable to perform tests of controls for sales and cash receipts at an interim date?

11–19 Deirdre Brandt, a public accountant, tested sales transactions for the month of March in an audit of the financial statements for the year ended December 31, 19X7. Based on the excellent results of the tests of controls, she decided to significantly reduce her substantive tests of details of balances at year-end. Evaluate this decision.

MULTIPLE CHOICE QUESTIONS

11–20 The following questions deal with internal controls in the sales and collection cycle. Choose the best response.

   a. For effective internal control, the EDP billing function should be performed by the

   (1) accounting department.
   (2) sales department.
   (3) shipping department.
   (4) credit and collection department.

   b. A company policy should clearly indicate that defective merchandise returned by customers is to be delivered to the

   (1) sales clerk.
   (2) receiving clerk.
   (3) inventory control clerk.
   (4) accounts receivable clerk.

   c. For good internal control, the credit manager should be responsible to the

   (1) sales manager.
   (2) customer service manager.
   (3) controller.
   (4) treasurer.

   d. For good internal control, the EDP billing department should be under the direction of the

   (1) controller.
   (2) credit manager.
   (3) sales manager.
   (4) treasurer.   (AICPA adapted)

11–21 For each of the following types of misstatements (parts a through d), select the control that should have prevented the misstatement:

   a. A manufacturing company received a substantial sales return in the last month of the year, but the credit memorandum for the return was not prepared until after the auditors had completed their field work. The returned merchandise was included in the physical inventory.

   (1) Aging schedules of accounts receivable are prepared periodically.
   (2) Credit memoranda are prenumbered and all numbers are accounted for.
   (3) A reconciliation of the trial balance of customers' accounts with the general ledger control is prepared periodically.
   (4) Receiving reports are prepared for all materials received and such reports are numerically controlled.

   b. The sales manager credited a salesman, Sean Boyle, with sales that were actually "house account" sales. Later, Boyle divided his excess sales commissions with the sales manager.

   (1) The summary sales entries are checked periodically by persons independent of sales functions.
   (2) Sales orders are reviewed and approved by persons independent of the sales department.
   (3) The internal auditor compares the sales commission statements with the cash disbursements record.
   (4) Sales orders are prenumbered, and all numbers are accounted for.

   c. A sales invoice for $5,200 was computed correctly but, in error, was key entered as $2,500 to the sales journal and to the accounts receivable master file. The customer remitted only $2,500, the amount on her monthly statement.

(1) Prelistings and predetermined totals are used to control postings.

(2) Sales invoice serial numbers, prices, discounts, extensions, and footings are independently checked.

(3) The customers' monthly statements are verified and mailed by a responsible person other than the bookkeeper who prepared them.

(4) Unauthorized remittance deductions made by customers or other matters in dispute are investigated promptly by a person independent of the accounts receivable function.

d. Copies of sales invoices show different unit prices for apparently identical items.

(1) All sales invoices are checked as to all details after their preparation.

(2) Differences reported by customers are satisfactorily investigated.

(3) Statistical sales data are compiled and reconciled with recorded sales.

(4) All sales invoices are compared with the customers' purchase orders.

(AICPA adapted)

11–22 The following questions deal with audit evidence for the sales and collection cycle. Choose the best response.

a. Auditors sometimes use comparison of ratios as audit evidence. For example, an unexplained decrease in the ratio of gross profit to sales may suggest which of the following possibilities?

(1) Unrecorded purchases.

(2) Unrecorded sales.

(3) Merchandise purchases being charged to selling and general expense.

(4) Fictitious sales.

b. An auditor is testing sales transactions. One step is to trace a sample of debit entries from the accounts receivable master file back to the supporting duplicate sales invoices. What would the auditor intend to establish by this step?

(1) Sales invoices represent valid sales.

(2) All sales have been recorded.

(3) All sales invoices have been properly posted to customer accounts.

(4) Debit entries in the accounts receivable master file are properly supported by sales invoices.

c. To verify that all sales transactions have been recorded, a test of controls should be completed on a representative sample drawn from

(1) entries in the sales journal.

(2) the billing clerk's file of sales orders.

(3) a file of duplicate copies of sales invoices for which all prenumbered forms in the series have been accounted.

(4) the shipping clerk's file of duplicate copies of bills of lading.

d. A public accountant is examining the financial statements of a small telephone company and wishes to test whether customers are being billed. One procedure that she might use is to

(1) check a sample of listings in the telephone directory to the billing control.

(2) trace a sample of postings from the billing control to the subsidiary accounts receivable master file.

(3) balance the accounts receivable master files to the general ledger control account.

(4) confirm a representative number of accounts receivable.

(AICPA adapted)

DISCUSSION QUESTIONS AND PROBLEMS

11–23 Items 1 through 8 are selected questions of the type generally found in internal control questionnaires used by auditors to obtain an understanding of internal control in the sales and collection cycle. In using the questionnaire for a particular client, a "yes" response to a question indicates a possible internal control, whereas a "no" indicates a potential weakness.

1. Are sales invoices independently compared with customers' orders for prices, quantities, extensions, and footings?

2. Are sales orders, invoices, and credit memoranda issued and filed in numerical sequence and are the sequences accounted for periodically?

3. Are the selling function and cash register functions independent of the cash receipts, shipping, delivery, and billing functions?

4. Are all C.O.D., scrap, equipment, and cash sales accounted for in the same manner as charge sales and is the record keeping independent of the collection procedure?

5. Is the collection function independent of, and does it constitute a check on billing and recording sales?

6. Are accounts receivable master files balanced regularly to control accounts by an employee independent of billing functions?

7. Are cash receipts entered in books of original entry by persons independent of the mail-opening and receipts-listing functions?

8. Are receipts deposited intact daily on a timely basis?

Required:
   a. For each of the questions above, state the internal control objectives being fulfilled if the control is in effect.

   b. For each control, list a test of controls procedure to test its effectiveness.

   c. For each of the questions above, identify the nature of the potential financial misstatements.

   d. For each of the potential misstatements in part c, list a substantive audit procedure to determine whether a material error exists.

11–24 The following errors or fraud are included in the accounting records of the Joyce Manufacturing Ltd.:

1. A sales invoice was misadded by $1,000.

2. A material sale was unintentionally recorded for the second time on the last day of the year. The sale had originally been recorded two days earlier.

3. Cash paid on accounts receivable was stolen by the mail clerk when the mail was opened.

4. Cash paid on accounts receivable that had been prelisted by a secretary was stolen by the bookkeeper who records cash receipts and accounts receivable. He failed to record the transactions.

5. A shipment to a customer was not billed because of the loss of the bill of lading.

6. Merchandise was shipped to a customer, but no bill of lading was prepared. Since billings are prepared from bills of lading, the customer was not billed.

7. A sale to a residential customer was unintentionally classified as a commercial sale.

Required:
   a. For each misstatement, state a control that should have prevented it from occurring on a continuing basis.

   b. For each misstatement, state a substantive audit procedure that could uncover it.

11–25 The following are commonly performed tests of controls audit procedures in the sales and collection cycle:

1. Examine sales returns for approval by an authorized official.
2. Account for a sequence of shipping documents and examine each one to make sure a duplicate sales invoice is attached.
3. Account for a sequence of sales invoices and examine each one to make sure a duplicate copy of the shipping copy is attached.
4. Compare the quantity and description of items on shipping documents with the related duplicate sales invoices.
5. Trace recorded sales in the sales journal to the related accounts receivable master file and compare the customer name, date, and amount for each one.
6. Review the prelisting in the cash receipts book to determine whether cash is prelisted on a daily basis.
7. Reconcile the recorded cash receipts on the prelisting of cash receipts with the cash receipts journal and the bank statement for a one-month period.

Required:
    a. State which of the seven internal control objectives each of the audit procedures fulfills.
    b. Identify the type of evidence used for each audit procedure, such as confirmation and observation.

11–26 The following are selected internal control objectives and audit procedures for sales transactions:

OBJECTIVES

1. Recorded sales are valid.
2. Existing sales are recorded.
3. Sales transactions are properly included in the accounts receivable master file and are correctly summarized.

PROCEDURES

1. Trace a sample of shipping documents to related duplicate sales invoices and the sales journal to make sure the shipment was billed.
2. Examine a sample of duplicate sales invoices to determine if each one has a shipping document attached.
3. Examine the sales journal for a sample of sales transactions to determine if each one has a tick mark in the margin indicating it has been compared to the accounts receivable master file for customer name, date, and amount.
4. Examine a sample of shipping documents to determine if each one has a duplicate sales invoice number written on the bottom left corner.
5. Trace a sample of debit entries in the accounts receivable master file to the sales journal to determine if the date, customer name, and amount are the same.
6. Trace a sample of duplicate sales invoices to related shipping documents filed in the shipping department to make sure a shipment was made.

Required:
    a. For each objective, identify at least one specific error that could occur.
    b. Describe the differences between the purposes of the first and second objectives.
    c. For each objective, identify one test of controls.
    d. For each test of control, state the internal control that is being tested. Also, identify or describe an error the client is trying to prevent by use of the control.

11–27 The following sales procedures were encountered during the regular annual audit of Marvel Wholesale Distributing Company Ltd.

Customer orders are received by the sales order department. A clerk computes the approximate dollar amount of the order and sends it to the credit department for approval. Credit approval is stamped on the order and sent to the accounting department. A microcomputer is then used to generate two copies of a sales invoice. The order is filed in the customer order file.

The customer copy of the sales invoice is held in a pending file awaiting notification that the order was shipped.

The shipping copy of the sales invoice is routed through the warehouse and the shipping department has authority for the respective departments to release and ship the merchandise. Shipping department personnel pack the order and manually prepare a three-copy bill of lading: the original copy is mailed to the customer, the second copy is sent with the shipment, and the other is filed in sequence in the bill of lading file. The sales invoice shipping copy is sent to the accounting department with any changes resulting from lack of available merchandise.

A clerk in accounting matches the received sales invoice shipping copy with the sales invoice customer copy from the pending file. Quantities on the two invoices are compared and prices are compared on an approved price list. The customer copy is then mailed to the customer, and the shipping copy is sent to the data processing department.

The data processing clerk enters the sales invoice data onto the computer which is used to prepare the sales journal and update the accounts receivable master file. She files the shipping copy in the sales invoice file in numerical sequence.

a. In order to gather audit evidence concerning the proper credit approval of sales, the auditor would select a sample of transaction documents from the population represented by the

    (1) customer order file.
    (2) bill of lading file.
    (3) customers' accounts receivable master file.
    (4) sales invoice file.

b. In order to determine whether the internal controls operated effectively to minimize errors of failure to post invoices to customers' accounts receivable master file, the auditor would select a sample of transactions from the population represented by the

    (1) customer order file.
    (2) bill of lading file.
    (3) customers' accounts receivable master file.
    (4) sales invoice file.

c. In order to determine whether the internal controls operated effectively to minimize errors of failure to invoice a shipment, the auditor would select a sample of transactions from the population represented by the

    (1) customer order file.
    (2) bill of lading file.
    (3) customers' accounts receivable master file.
    (4) sales invoice file.

d. In order to gather audit evidence that uncollected items in customers' accounts represented valid trade receivables, the auditor would select a sample of items from the population represented by the

    (1) customer order file.
    (2) bill of lading file.

(3) customers' accounts receivable master file.

(4) sales invoice file. (AICPA adapted)

11–28 The following are common audit procedures for tests of sales and cash receipts.

1. Comparing the quantity and description of items on duplicate sales invoices with related shipping documents.

2. Tracing recorded cash receipts in the accounts receivable master file to the cash receipts journal and compare the customer name, date, and amount of each one.

3. Examining duplicate sales invoices for an indication that unit selling prices were compared to the approved price list.

4. Examining duplicate sales invoices to determine whether the account classification for sales has been included on the document.

5. Examining the sales journal for related-party transactions, notes receivable, and other unusual items.

6. Selecting a sample of customer orders and tracing the document to related shipping documents, vendors' invoices, and accounts receivable records master file for comparison of name, date, and amount.

7. Doing a proof of cash receipts.

8. Examining a sample of remittance advices for approval of cash discounts.

9. Accounting for a numerical sequence of remittance advices and determining if there is a cross-reference mark for each one, indicating it has been recorded in the cash receipts journal.

Required:
a. State which of the internal control objectives each of the audit procedures fulfills.

b. For each test of controls, state a substantive test that could be used to determine whether there was a monetary error.

11–29 Appliances Repair and Service Corp. bills all customers rather than collecting in cash when services are provided. All mail is opened by Tom Gyders, treasurer. Gyders, an accountant, is the most qualified person in the company who is in the office daily. He can, therefore, solve problems and respond to customers' needs quickly. Upon receipt of cash, he immediately prepares a listing of the cash and a duplicate deposit slip. Cash is deposited daily. Gyders uses the listing to enter the financial transactions in the computerized accounting records. He also contacts customers about uncollected accounts receivable. Because he is so knowledgeable about the business and each customer, he grants credit, authorizes all sales allowances, and charges off uncollectible accounts. The owner is extremely pleased with the efficiency of the company. He can run the business without spending much time there because of Gyders' effectiveness.

Imagine the owner's surprise when he discovers that Gyders has committed a major theft of the company's collections. He did so by not recording sales, recording improper credits to recorded accounts receivable, and overstating receivables.

Required:
a. Given that cash was prelisted, went only to the treasurer, and was deposited daily, what internal control deficiency permitted the fraud?

b. What are the benefits of a prelisting of cash? Who should prepare the prelisting and what duties should that person *not* perform?

c. Assume an appropriate person, as discussed in part b, prepares a prelisting of cash. What is to prevent that person from taking the cash after it is prelisted, but before it is deposited?

d. Who should deposit the cash, given your answer to part b?

11–30 The receptionist at Cheng Supply Corp. prelists cash before making daily deposits. He gives the data processing clerk remittance advices, which she uses to enter the cash receipts transactions onto the computerized accounting records. Monthly, the controller prepares a proof of cash receipts, and prints out a copy of the cash receipts journal and compares it to the prelisting.

Required:

a. Define a proof of cash receipts and state its purpose.

b. For the following errors or fraud, state whether it is (1) likely to be uncovered by a proof of cash receipts, (2) likely to be uncovered by a comparison of the prelisting to the cash receipts journal, (3) likely to be uncovered by either (1) or (2), or (4) not likely to be uncovered by either (1) or (2).

   1. Cash was prelisted and correctly inputted to the computerized accounting records, but the bank credited the wrong amount to Cheng's bank account.

   2. The receptionist unintentionally failed to give the data processing clerk two remittance advices for which the cash had been prelisted.

   3. The receptionist unintentionally threw away an unopened envelope that included a cheque and remittance advice.

   4. The data processing clerk made a transposition error in entering the transaction into the computerized accounting records (she recorded a receipt as $4,621 rather than $6,421).

   5. The data processing clerk recorded the cash received at the correct amount, but credited the wrong customer's account.

   6. The receptionist listed the cash receipts, but afterward withheld a cheque for his own use and did not forward the remittance advice to the data processing clerk.

c. For those questions in part b that you answered (4), identify an audit procedure that is likely to uncover the error.

11–31 You were asked in September, 19X8 by the board of management of your church to review its accounting procedures. As part of this review you have prepared the following comments relating to the collections made at weekly services and record keeping for members' pledges and contributions:

   1. The finance committee is responsible for preparing an annual budget based on the anticipated needs of the various church committees and for the annual fall "pledge campaign" in which most members make a commitment to contribute a certain amount to the church over the following year.

   2. The financial records are maintained by the treasurer who has authority to sign cheques drawn on the church bank account.

   3. The ushers each Sunday take up the collection during the services and place it uncounted in a deposit bag in the church safe. The term "safe" is a misnomer: the lock does not work and the door is merely closed. This fact is well known to church members since most have ushered at one time. The board of management and finance committee are not concerned since they believe that the members, as good church-goers, can be trusted.

   4. The treasurer, who is retired, comes in Monday morning, counts the collection and deposits it into the church's bank account. Some members use predated numbered envelopes but most do not. The treasurer does not keep a record of members' givings.

   5. The treasurer would issue receipts to each member every January based on the amounts pledged for the preceding year by that member. The givings up to 19X6 had always exceeded the amounts pledged so the value of receipts given out was less than total givings; the excess was recorded as "loose" or "open" collection. In 19X7, the total of the receipts given out by the treasurer exceeded the total funds received by the church.

   6. The church is registered as a charity under the *Income Tax Act* and is required to file a return each year to comply with its rules. The chairperson of the

finance committe is upset because the church has received an angry letter from Revenue Canada in connection with the return for 19X7.

Required: Identify the weaknesses and recommend improvements in procedures for

a. collections made at weekly services

b. record keeping for members' pledges and contributions. Use the methodology for identifying weaknesses that was discussed in Chapter 9. Organize your answer sheets as follows:

WEAKNESS	RECOMMENDED IMPROVEMENT

(AICPA adapted)

11–32   The customer billing and collection functions of Rainbow Inc., a small paint manufacturer, are attended to by a receptionist, an accounts receivable clerk, and a cashier who also serves as a secretary. The company's paint products are sold to wholesalers and retail stores.

The following describes *all* the procedures performed by the employees of Rainbow Inc. pertaining to customer billings and collections:

1. The mail is opened by the receptionist, who gives the customers' purchase orders to the accounts receivable clerk. Fifteen to 20 orders are received each day. Under instructions to expedite the shipment of orders, the accounts receivable clerk at once prepares a five-copy sales invoice form that is distributed as follows:

   (a) Copy 1 is the customer billing copy and is held by the accounts receivable clerk until notice of shipment is received.

   (b) Copy 2 is the accounts receivable department copy and is held for the ultimate updating of the accounting records.

   (c) Copies 3 and 4 are sent to the shipping department.

   (d) Copy 5 is sent to the storeroom as authority for the release of goods to the shipping department.

2. After the paint order has been moved from the storeroom to the shipping department, the shipping department prepares the bills of lading and labels the cartons. Sales invoice copy 4 is inserted in a carton as a packing slip. After the trucker has picked up the shipment, the customer's copy of the bill of lading and copy 3, on which are noted any undershipments, are returned to the accounts receivable clerk. The company does not "back order" in the event of undershipments; customers are expected to reorder the merchandise. Rainbow's copy of the bill of lading is filed by the shipping department.

3. When copy 3 and the customer's copy of the bill of lading are received by the accounts receivable clerk, copies 1 and 2 are completed by numbering them and inserting quantities shipped, unit prices, extensions, discounts, and totals. Copies 2 and 3 are stapled together.

4. The accounts receivable clerk then enters the sales transactions into the computerized accounting records from copy 2. Only the quantities, prices, discounts, and accounts are entered, as the computer computes extensions and totals. These extensions and totals are then compared to copy 1. The accounts

receivable clerk then mails copy 1 and the copy of the bill of lading to the customer. Copy 2 is then filed, along with staple attached copy 3, in numerical order.

5. Since Rainbow Inc. is short of cash, the deposit of receipts is also expedited. The receptionist turns over all mail receipts and related correspondence to the accounts receivable clerk, who examines the cheques and determines that the accompanying vouchers or correspondence contain enough detail to permit the entering of the transactions onto the computer. The accounts receivable clerk then endorses the cheques and gives them to the cashier who prepares the daily deposit. No currency is received in the mail, and no paint is sold over the counter at the factory.

6. The accounts receivable clerk uses the vouchers or correspondence that accompanied the cheques to enter the transactions onto the computerized accounting records. The accounts receivable clerk is the one who corresponds with customers about unauthorized deductions for discounts, freight or advertising allowances, returns, and so forth, and prepares the appropriate credit memos. Disputed items of large amounts are turned over to the sales manager for settlement. Each month the accounts receivable clerk prints out a trial balance of accounts receivable and compares the total with the general ledger control accounts for accounts receivable.

Required:

a. Identify the internal control weaknesses in Rainbow Inc.'s procedures related to customer billings and remittances and the accounting for these transactions. Use the methodology for identifying weaknesses that was discussed in Chapter 9.

b. For each weakness, identify the error or fraud that could result.

c. For each weakness, list one substantive audit procedure for testing the significance of the potential error.   (AICPA adapted)

CASE

11–33   The Meyers Pharmaceutical Corp., a drug manufacturer, has the following internal controls for billing and recording accounts receivable:

1. An incoming customer's purchase order is received in the order department by a clerk who prepares a prenumbered company sales order form in which is inserted the pertinent information, such as the customer's name and address, customer's account number, quantity, and items ordered. After the sales order form has been prepared, the customer's purchase order is stapled to it.

2. The sales order form is then passed to the credit department for credit approval. Rough approximations of the billing values of the orders are made in the credit department for those accounts on which credit limitations are imposed. After investigation, approval of credit is noted on the form.

3. Next the sales order form is passed to the billing department where a clerk uses a microcomputer to generate the customer's invoice. It automatically cross-multiplies the number of items with the unit price, and adds the extended amounts for the total amount of the invoice. The billing clerk determines the unit prices for the items from a list of billing prices.

   The microcomputer automatically accumulates daily totals of customer account numbers and invoice amounts to provide "hash" totals and control amounts. These totals, which are inserted in a daily record book, serve as predetermined batch totals for verification of inputs into the computerized accounting records.

The billing is done on prenumbered, continuous, carbon-interleaved forms having the following designations:

(a) Customer's copy.

(b) Sales department copy, for information purposes.

(c) File copy.

(d) Shipping department copy, which serves as a shipping order. Bills of lading are also prepared as carbon copy byproducts of the invoicing procedure.

4. The shipping department copy of the invoice and the bills of lading are then sent to the shipping department. After the order has been shipped, copies of the bill of lading are returned to the billing department. The shipping department copy of the invoice is filed in the shipping department.

5. In the billing department one copy of the bill of lading is attached to the customer's copy of the invoice and both are mailed to the customer. The other copy of the bill of lading, together with the sales order form, is then stapled to the invoice file copy and filed in invoice numerical order.

6. As the microcomputer is generating invoices, it is also storing the transactions on disk. This disk is then used to update the computerized accounting records. This update procedure is run daily and a summary report is generated. Hard copy output of all journals and ledgers is prepared.

7. Periodically, an internal auditor traces a sample of sales orders all the way through internal control to the journals and ledgers, testing both the procedures and dollar amounts. The procedures include comparing control totals with output, recalculating invoices and refooting journals, and tracing totals to the master file and general ledger.

Required:

a. Flowchart the billing function as a means of understanding the system.

b. List the internal controls over sales for each of the seven internal control objectives.

c. For each control, list a useful test of control to verify the effectiveness of the control.

d. Describe your audit approach, combined or substantive, for the sales and collection cycle. Explain why you selected the approach you did.

INTEGRATED CASE APPLICATION

11–34 *ABC AUDIT – PART II*

In Part I of this case study (pages 317-320) you obtained an understanding of internal control and made an initial assessment of control risk for each internal control objective for acquisition and cash disbursement transactions. The purpose of Part II is to continue the assessment of the level of control risk by deciding the appropriate tests of controls.

Assume that in Part I, it was determined that the key internal controls are the following:

1. Segregation of the purchasing, receiving, and cash disbursement functions

2. Review of supportive documents and signing of cheques by an independent, authorized person

3. Use of prenumbered cheques, properly accounted for

4. Use of prenumbered purchase orders, properly accounted for

5. Use of prenumbered document package, properly accounted for

6. Internal verification of document package prior to preparation of cheques

7. Independent monthly reconciliation of bank statement.

For requirements a and b, you should follow a format similar to the one illustrated for sales in Table 11–1, pages 359 and 360. You should prepare one matrix for acquisitions and a separate one for cash disbursements. Observe that the first column in each matrix should include the same information as the top row in the worksheet you prepared for Problem 9-34. Also, the key internal controls include only those seven from above and the tests of controls include only those you developed in requirement a.

Required:

a. Design tests of control audit procedures that will provide appropriate evidence for each of these controls. Do not include more than two tests of controls for each internal control.

b. Although controls appear to be well designed and test of control deviations are not expected, last year's results indicate errors may still exist. Therefore, you decide to perform dual-purpose tests for acquisitions and cash disbursements. Design substantive procedures for each internal control objective. Do not include more than two substantive procedures for any internal control objective. Use Tables 11–4 on pages 376-77 and 11–5 on pages 377-78 as frames of reference.

c. Combine the test of controls and substantive procedures designed in requirements (a) and (b) into a performance format. Include both tests of acquisitions and cash disbursements in the same audit program. Use Figure 11–8 on page 379 as a frame of reference for preparing the performance format audit program.

12

AUDIT SAMPLING FOR TESTS OF CONTROLS

Two Types ① *Representative* ② *Specific Item.*

LEARNING OBJECTIVES	
	THOROUGH STUDY OF THIS CHAPTER WILL ENABLE YOU TO:

1. Explain the concept of representative sampling
2. Distinguish between statistical and nonstatistical sampling
3. Select representative samples
4. Define and describe attributes sampling
5. Use attributes sampling in tests of controls and for other audit purposes
6. Apply sampling concepts and methodology to the audit plan for the sales and collection cycle

☐ Once the auditor has decided which procedures to select and when they should be performed, it is still necessary to determine the appropriate *number* of items to sample from the population and *which ones* to choose. This chapter examines the process the auditor goes through in making these two decisions for tests of controls and the methodology followed after the decisions are made. The sales and collection cycle is used as a frame of reference for discussing these concepts. In the early part of the chapter, the selection of items from the population by the use of *nonstatistical* and *statistical methods* is examined. The remainder of the chapter deals with the use of *attributes sampling* as it is applied to tests of controls. The use of *variables sampling* is studied in Chapter 14.

Representative Samples

OBJECTIVE 1

Explain the concept of representative sampling.

Whenever auditors select a sample from a population, they may decide to select a representative sample or to select specific items from the population. An item may be a specific item by virtue of its size (high value item) or nature (key item). The CICA publication, *Extent of Audit Testing*, suggests that specific item testing is useful when the auditor is interested in examining transactions that are particularly large (high value) in relation to the other transactions or that are unusual (key item), for example, more risky than the other transactions. A *representative* sample is one in which the characteristics in the sample are the same as those of the population. For example, assume a client's internal control procedures require a clerk to attach a shipping document to every duplicate sales invoice, but the procedure is not followed exactly 3 percent of the time. If the auditor selects a sample of 100 duplicate sales invoices and finds three missing, the sample is representative. Both representative sampling and specific items testing have particular uses, although they may be used together. The auditor may, for instance, select specific items and then choose a representative sample from the balance of the population.

In practice, auditors do not know whether a sample is representative, even after all testing is completed. Auditors can, however, increase the likelihood of a sample being representative by using care in its design, selection, and evaluation.

Two things can cause a sample result to be nonrepresentative: nonsampling error and sampling error. The risk of these occurring is termed *nonsampling risk* and *sampling risk*; both can be controlled.

Nonsampling risk or nonsampling error occurs when audit tests do not uncover existing exceptions in the sample. In the previous example in which three shipping documents were not attached to duplicate sales invoices, if the auditor concluded that no exceptions existed, there is a nonsampling error.

The two causes of nonsampling error are the auditor's failure to recognize exceptions and inappropriate or ineffective audit procedures. An auditor might fail to recognize an exception because of exhaustion, boredom, or lack of understanding of what to look for. An ineffective audit procedure for the exceptions in question would be to examine a sample of shipping documents and determine if each is attached to a set of duplicate sales invoices, rather than to examine a sample of duplicate sales invoices. Careful design of audit procedures and proper supervision and instruction are ways to reduce nonsampling risk.

Sampling risk (sampling error) is an inherent part of sampling that results from testing less than the entire population. Even with zero nonsampling error, there is always a chance that a sample is not representative. For example, if a population has a 3 percent exception rate, the auditor could easily select a sample of 100 items containing fewer or greater than three exceptions.

There are two ways to reduce sampling risk: increase sample size and use an appropriate method of selecting sample items from the population. An example of an appropriate method of selecting a sample is random (probabilistic) selection.

---

1 *Extent of Audit Testing*, Toronto: CICA, 1980, pp.10–11.

Statistical versus Nonstatistical Sampling

It is acceptable for auditors to use either statistical or nonstatistical sampling methods. Statistical sampling is the use of mathematical measurement techniques to calculate formal statistical results. The primary benefit of statistical methods is the quantification of sampling risk. (You probably recall calculating a statistical result at a 95 percent confidence level in a statistics course. The 95 percent confidence level provides a 5 percent sampling risk.) In nonstatistical sampling, the auditor does not quantify sampling risk. Instead, conclusions are reached about populations on a more judgmental basis.

> **OBJECTIVE 2**
>
> Distinguish between statistical and nonstatistical sampling.

There are four parts of both statistical and nonstatistical methods: planning the sample, selecting the sample, performing the tests, and evaluating the results. The purposes of planning the sample are to make sure the audit tests are performed in a manner to provide the desired sampling risk and to minimize the likelihood of nonsampling error. Selecting the sample involves deciding how to select sample items from the population. Performing the tests is the examination of documents and doing other audit tests. Evaluating the results involves drawing conclusions based on the audit tests. To illustrate, assume an auditor selects a sample of 100 duplicate sales invoices from a population, tests each to determine if a shipping document is attached, and determines that there are 3 exceptions. Deciding that a sample size of 100 was needed is a part of planning the sample. Deciding which 100 items to select from the population is a sample selection problem. Doing the audit procedure for each of the 100 items and determining that there were three exceptions constitutes performing the tests. Reaching conclusions about the likely exception rate in the total population when there is a sample exception rate of 3 percent is an evaluation problem.

Nonstatistical Sampling

Most of the remainder of this chapter discusses doing tests of transactions using a statistical method called attributes sampling. It is the most common statistical method for performing tests of controls. The following discussion of attributes sampling should not be interpreted as a criticism of performing audit tests without using statistical sampling. First, many audit tests must be performed outside a statistical sampling context. This includes footing of journals, reviewing records, and having discussions with personnel. Second, in many instances the cost of performing random (probabilistic) selection or testing a sufficient number of items to warrant a statistical inference exceeds the benefits of that approach.

The primary reason for not criticizing nonstatistical sampling, however, is the fact that in most instances it *does not differ* substantially from statistical methods. A careful examination of the steps that will be applied using attributes sampling indicates that except for the degree of formality required, the methods are essentially the same for a nonstatistical or a statistical approach. The most important differences are in specifying planning decisions and conclusions in more precise ways for statistical sampling. In addition, there is a difference in the way the auditor generalizes from the sample to the population. Nevertheless, the decisions that are made when the auditor uses statistical sampling must also be made, on a more intuitive basis, for nonstatistical sampling.

Probabilistic and Nonprobabilistic Sample Selection

There are two methods of sample selection – probabilistic and non-probabilistic. In probabilistic selection every population item has a known chance of being selected. In nonprobabilistic selection (often called judgmental selection) the auditor decides which items to select. Both methods are acceptable and com-

TABLE 12–1

Relationship of
Methods of Selecting
Samples to Evaluating
Results

METHOD OF SELECTING SAMPLE	METHOD OF EVALUATING RESULTS	
	Statistical	*Nonstatistical*
Probabilistic	Preferable	Acceptable
Nonprobabilistic	Not acceptable	Mandatory

Note: The most common method of probabilistic sample selection used for tests of controls is random selection.

monly used. Probabilistic selection is required for all statistical sampling methods including attributes sampling. It is acceptable to make nonstatistical evaluations using probabilistic selection, but many practitioners prefer not to. A summary of the relationship of probabilistic and nonprobabilistic selection to statistical and nonstatistical evaluation is shown in Table 12–1.

Advantages of
Attributes
Sampling

The most important advantage of attributes sampling for tests of controls as compared with nonstatistical sampling is the requirement of *formally* specifying the auditor's judgments. We believe this encourages more careful and precise thinking about the *objectives* of the audit tests. We also believe the ability to determine the results achieved in terms of formally measured conclusions is a significant benefit of attributes sampling. A second advantage of attributes sampling is the requirement that a probabilistic selection method be used. We believe that probabilistic selection improves the likelihood of a representative sample.

**Random
Selection**

A randomly selected sample or *random sample* is one in which every possible combination of items in the population has an equal chance of constituting the sample. The only way the auditor can be confident a random sample has been obtained is by adopting a formal methodology that is designed to accomplish this. Three methods of random selection are discussed: *random number tables, computer terminals,* and *systematic sampling*. All three are commonly used.

OBJECTIVE 3

Select representative
samples.

Random Number
Tables

A *random number table* is a listing of independent random digits conveniently arranged in tabular form to facilitate the selection of random numbers with multiple digits. An example of such a table, taken from the Interstate Commerce Commission "Table of 105,000 Random Decimal Digits," is included as Table 12–2. This table has numbered lines and columns, with five digits in each column, as a convenience in reading the tables and documenting the portion of the table used.

The proper use of random number tables is important to ensure the selection of an unbiased sample. Four major steps are involved in the use of the tables.

Establish a numbering system for the population   Before a set of random numbers can be selected from the table, each item in the population must be identified with a *unique number*. This is usually not a problem, because many of the populations from which the auditor wants a random sample consist of prenumbered documents. When prenumbered documents are not used, some type of numbering system must be developed. In rare instances the entire population may have to be renumbered, but ordinarily a simple approach can be devised to meet the objective. An illustration is the selection of a random sample of accounts

TABLE 12–2

Random Number Table

ITEM	(1)	(2)	(3)	(4)	(5)	(6)	(7)	(8)
				COLUMN				
1000	37039	97547	64673	31546	99314	66854	97855	99965
1001	25145	84834	23009	51584	66754	77785	52357	25532
1002	98433	54725	18864	65866	76918	78825	58210	76835
1003	97965	68548	81545	82933	93545	85959	63282	61454
1004	78049	67830	14624	17563	25697	07734	48243	94318
1005	50203	25658	91478	08509	23308	48130	65047	77873
1006	40059	67825	18934	64998	49807	71126	77818	56893
1007	84350	67241	54031	34535	04093	35062	58163	14205
1008	30954	51637	91500	48722	60988	60029	60873	37423
1009	86723	36464	98305	08009	00666	29255	18514	49158
1010	50188	22554	86160	92250	14021	65859	16237	72296
1011	50014	00463	13906	35936	71761	95755	87002	71667
1012	66023	21428	14742	94874	23308	58533	26507	11208
1013	04458	61862	63119	09541	01715	87901	91260	03079
1014	57510	36314	30452	09712	37714	95482	30507	68475
1015	43373	58939	95848	28288	60341	52174	11879	18115
1016	61500	12763	64433	02268	57905	72347	49498	21871
1017	78938	71312	99705	71546	42274	23915	38405	18779
1018	64257	93218	35793	43671	64055	88729	11168	60260
1019	56864	21554	70445	24841	04779	56774	96129	73594
1020	35314	29631	06937	54545	04470	75463	77112	77126
1021	40704	48823	65963	39359	12717	56201	22811	24863
1022	07318	44623	02843	33299	59872	86774	06926	12672
1023	94550	23299	45557	07923	75126	00808	01312	46689
1024	34348	81191	21027	77087	10909	03676	97723	34469
1025	92277	57115	50789	68111	75305	53289	39751	45760
1026	56093	58302	52236	64756	50273	61566	61962	93280
1027	16623	17849	96701	94971	94758	08845	32260	59823
1028	50848	93982	66451	32143	05441	10399	17775	74169
1029	48006	58200	58367	66577	68583	21108	41361	20732
1030	56640	27890	28825	96509	21363	53657	60119	75385

receivable for confirmation from a trial balance that contains 40 pages with up to 90 lines per page. An item is a line on the listing with an outstanding balance. The combination of page numbers and line numbers provides a unique identifying number for every item in the population.

Establish correspondence between the random number table and the population Once the numbering system has been established for the population, correspondence is established by deciding the *number of digits* to use in the random number table and their *association with the population numbering system*. For example, assume the auditor is selecting a sample of 100 duplicate sales invoices from a file of prenumbered sales invoices beginning with document number 3272 and ending with 8825. Since the invoices contain a four-digit number, it is necessary to use four digits in the random number table. If the first four digits of each five-digit set are used and the starting point in the random number table in Table 12–2 is item 1000, column 1, the first invoice for inclusion in the sample is 3703. The next three numbers are *outside the range* of the population and are *discarded*. The next sample item is invoice 7804, and so forth.

Establish a route for using the table The route defines which digits the auditor uses in a column and the method of reading the table. For a three-digit number, it is, for example, acceptable to use the first three digits, the middle three, or the last three. It is also acceptable to select numbers by reading vertically down columns or horizontally along rows. The route is an *arbitrary decision*, but it needs to be *established in advance* and *followed consistently*.

Select a starting point   Selecting a random starting point in the table is necessary only to eliminate the predictability of the sample. If an employee of the client has a copy of the random number tables used in selecting the random numbers and knows the starting point for their selection, the employee can determine which items the auditor will be testing. It is acceptable to pick a starting point by simply using a "blind stab" into the table with a pencil. The number the pencil falls on is the first item included in the sample and the place from which the established route begins.

Special Considerations

Discards   A difficulty in the use of random number tables occurs when there are a large number of *discards*. Discards increase the time it takes to select the sample and enhance the likelihood of making errors in using the table. Certain shortcuts can be used to reduce the discards, but care must be taken to avoid unequal probability of selection. An example is the selection of a random sample from a population of prenumbered shipping documents numbered from 14067 to 16859. If a five-digit number is used in the tables, only about three numbers out of 100 are usable ($16,859 - 14,067 \div 100,000 = .028$). The discards can be greatly reduced by ignoring the first digit, which is common to all population items, and using a four-digit number in the table. The discards can be further reduced by carefully redefining the way the first digit in the four-digit random number is used. For example, 1 through 3 could be defined to produce a first digit 4, 4 through 6 a first digit 5, and 7 through 9 a first digit 6. Thus, the random number 7426 from the table would be shipping document number 16426 in the population. This method reduces the discards to only about 10 percent, but it is fairly complicated and difficult to use.

Documentation   Regardless of the method used in selecting a random sample, it is necessary to have *proper documentation*. This is beneficial as a means of rechecking and reviewing the selection of the numbers, expanding the sample if additional items are desired, and defending the methodology if the quality of the audit is questioned. *Minimum documentation* would include sufficient information in the working papers to permit the reproduction of the numbers at a later date. This includes the name and page number of the table, the correspondence between the population and the table used, the route, the starting point, and the sample size. Many auditors simply include in the working papers a copy of the table they used, with the random numbers identified. (For an example, see Figure 12–3.)

Replacement versus nonreplacement sampling   In selecting a random sample, there is a distinction between replacement and nonreplacement sampling. In *replacement sampling*, an element in the population can be included in the sample more than once if the random number corresponding to that element is selected from the table more than once; whereas in *nonreplacement sampling*, an element can be included only once. If the random number corresponding to an element is selected more than once in nonreplacement sampling, it is simply treated as a discard the second time. Although both selection approaches are consistent with sound statistical theory, auditors rarely use replacement sampling.

(2) **Computers**

Most public accounting firms now utilize microcomputers that include programs for the selection of random numbers. The advantages of this approach over random number tables are *time savings, reduced likelihood of auditor error* in selecting the numbers, and *automatic documentation.*

In using computers, it is still necessary for each population item to have a *unique identification number,* and *correspondence* must be established between the population numbers and the random numbers generated by the computer. There is no need for concern about discards in establishing correspondence because the computer can eliminate most types of discards.

For a typical computer program, it is necessary to input the smallest and largest numbers in the population sequence, the quantity of random numbers desired, and in some cases a random number to start the program. In addition, the auditor usually has the option of getting the list of random numbers in *selection order,* in *ascending numerical sequence,* or both. The input and output from a computer are illustrated in Figure 12–1. In this illustration the auditor is selecting a sample of 30 shipping documents from the same prenumbered population sequence discussed earlier in which the document numbers ranged from 14067 to 16859.

(3) **Systematic Selection**

In systematic selection, the auditor calculates an *interval* and then methodically selects the items for the sample based on the size of the interval. The interval is determined by dividing the population size by the number of sample items desired. For example, if a population of sales invoices ranges from 652 to 3151 and the desired sample size is 125, the interval is 20 [$(3,151 - 651) \div 125$]. The auditor must now select a random number between 0 and 19 to determine the starting point for the sample. If the randomly selected number is 9, the first item in the sample is invoice number 661 (652 + 9). The remaining 124 items are 681 (661 + 20), 701 (681 + 20), and so on through item 3141.

The advantage of systematic sampling is its *ease of use.* In most populations the systematic sample can be drawn quickly, the approach automatically puts the numbers in sequential order, and documentation is easy.

A major problem with the use of systematic sampling is the possibility of *bias.* Because of the way in which systematic samples are selected, once the first item in the sample is selected, all other items are chosen automatically. This causes no problem if the characteristic of interest, such as test of control deviations, are distributed randomly throughout the population; however, in many cases they are not. If test of control deviations occurred at a certain time of the month or with certain types of documents, a systematic sample would have a higher likelihood of failing to obtain a representative sample than would the two methods previously discussed. This shortcoming is sufficiently serious that some public accounting firms do not permit the use of systematic sampling. Other firms require a careful examination of the way the population is listed to evaluate the possibility of a systematic error. In the opinion of the authors, *the use of systematic sampling is not advisable* unless the two other approaches discussed in this section are impractical.

FIGURE 12–1

Random Selection by
Use of a Computer

```
__ RUN (TRC900) SAMGEN

THIS PROGRAM GENERATES UP TO 1,000 SINGLE
    OR SETTED RANDOM NUMBERS.

FILE OPTION-YES OR NO? NO
QUIK OPTION-YES OR NO? NO
```

* * * * * * * D A T A   I N P U T * * * * * * * *

(1) INPUT THE QUANTITY OF RANDOM NUMBERS
    TO BE GENERATED? 30
(2) ARE THE NUMBERS FORMATTED INTO SETS-
    YES OR NO? NO
(6) INPUT THE QUANTITY OF DIGITS IN THE
    LARGEST NUMBER? 5
(7) INPUT THE NUMBER OF RANGES OF VALUES
    TO BE GENERATED (MAX = 50)? 1
(8) FOR EACH OF THE 1 RANGES INPUT THE
    LOWER (L) AND UPPER (U) LIMITS.
    SEPARATE SETS, IF ANY, WITH A HYPHEN
    (12) (-).

    RANGE

    1 – L? 14067
        U? 16559

(9) PRINT SELECTION-INPUT 1 FOR
    NUMERICAL ORDER, 2 FOR
    SELECTION ORDER OR 3 FOR BOTH?
    3
(10) DO YOU WANT TO CHANGE ANY INPUTS-
    YES OR NO? NO
    ***INPUT COMPLETE-DATA CHECK
    WILL BEGIN**********
(11) DO YOU WANT A LISTING OF RANGES
    SELECTED BEFORE DATA CHECK
    CONTINUES-YES OR NO? NO
(12) TOTAL COUNTED ITEMS = 2493
    REASONABLE-YES OR NO? YES

    ****DATA CHECK COMPLETE****
    **RANDOM NUMBER GENERATION
        WILL BEGIN*************

    ****GENERATION COMPLETE****

    RANDOM NUMBERS – NUMERICAL ORDER

* * * * * * * * O U T P U T * * * * * * * *

RANDOM NUMBERS – SELECTION ORDER	SEQUENCE SELECTED	RANDOM NUMBERS
16258	14	14090
15472	30	14134
16159	17	14199
15223	21	14224
15390	11	14249
15470	18	14273
15592	9	14297
14916	25	14431
14297	23	14682
15063	19	14775
14249	8	14916
16241	10	15063
15701	15	15100
14090	4	15223
15100	22	15308
16473	5	15390
14199	6	15470
14273	2	15472
14775	7	15592
15608	20	15608
14224	29	15674
15308	13	15701
14682	24	15742
15742	28	15900
14431	26	16017
16017	3	16159
16225	27	16225
15900	12	16241
15674	1	16258
14134	16	16473

```
***SORTING*******                              RUN FINISHED****
                                   ANOTHER RUN-YES OR NO? NO
```

Nonprobabilistic Selection

Three common approaches to selecting nonprobabilistic samples from accounting populations are *block sampling, haphazard selection*, and *judgmental methods*.

Block Sampling

Block sampling is the selection of several items in sequence. Once the first item in the block is selected, the remainder of the block is chosen automatically. One example of a block sample is the selection of a *sequence* of 100 sales transactions from the sales journal for the third week of March. A total sample of 100 could also be selected by taking 5 blocks of 20 items each, 20 blocks of 10, or 50 blocks of 2.

It is acceptable to use block sampling for tests of transactions only if a reasonable number of blocks are used. If few blocks are used, the probability of obtaining a nonrepresentative sample is too great, considering the possibility of such things as employee turnover, changes in the accounting system, and the seasonal nature of many businesses. The exact number of blocks has not been specified by the profession, but a "reasonable number" for most situations is probably at least nine blocks from nine different months.

Haphazard Selection

When the auditor goes through a population and selects items for the sample without regard to their size, source, or other distinguishing characteristics, the auditor is attempting to select without bias. This is called *haphazard selection*.

The most serious shortcoming of haphazard selection is the difficulty of remaining completely unbiased in selecting sample items. Due to the auditor's training and cultural bias, certain population items are more likely to be included in the sample than others. For some auditors, sales to certain customers and sales journal entries at the top of the page are more likely to be included in a sample than sales to unknown customers and entries in the middle of the page. For other auditors, entries in the middle of the page or large amounts would be more likely to be selected.

Judgmental Methods

Many auditors believe it is desirable to use professional judgment in selecting sample items for tests of transactions. When sample sizes are small, a random sample is often unlikely to result in representative samples. To improve the likelihood of a judgmental method being representative for tests of transactions, the auditor should keep the following in mind:

- In selecting items for examination, *each major type of transaction* in the cycle should be included. For example, in testing purchases of goods and services, it is inappropriate to test only raw materials purchases if the auditor is also interested in transactions such as advertising, repairs, and donations.
- When different persons or groups are responsible for processing transactions during the accounting period, some *transactions prepared by each person or group* should be tested. If there is a change of accounting personnel during the year or if transactions at different locations are handled differently, the likelihood of a nonrepresentative sample is increased when the tests are restricted to the transactions prepared by only one of the employees.
- When the auditor is testing for errors in amounts, *population items with large balances* should be tested more heavily than those with small balances. In tests of controls the auditor is interested in the adequacy of the controls, but the emphasis should be on testing larger dollar balances, since they are normally more likely to contain material misstatements.

Haphazard, block, and judgmental methods of selection are often useful and should not be automatically discarded as audit tools. In many situations, the cost of unbiased or more complex selection methods outweighs the benefits obtained from using them. For example, assume the auditor wants to trace credits from the accounts receivable master file to the cash receipts journal and other authorized sources as a test for the possibility of fictitious credits in the subsidiary records. A haphazard or block approach is simpler and less costly than random selection in this situation and would be employed by most auditors. It is preferable to use probabilistic selection methods for selecting samples whenever it is practical, but it is also necessary to consider the relationship between cost and benefit.

It is improper and a serious breach of due care to use *statistical measurement techniques* if the sample is selected by the haphazard, block, or any other nonprobabilistic approach. Only *probabilistic selection* is acceptable when the auditor intends to evaluate a sample statistically.

Attributes Sampling

Attributes sampling is a statistical method used to estimate the *proportion* of items in a population containing a characteristic or attribute of interest. This proportion is called the *occurrence rate* and is the ratio of the items containing the specific attribute to the total number of population items. The occurrence rate is usually expressed as a percentage. Auditors are usually interested in the occurrence of exceptions in populations and refer to the occurrence rate as a deviation rate or an error rate. An exception in attributes sampling may be a test of control deviation or a monetary error.

> **OBJECTIVE 4**
>
> Define and describe attributes sampling.

Assume, for example, that the auditor wants to determine the percentage of duplicate sales invoices that do not have shipping documents attached. There is an actual, but unknown, percentage of unattached shipping documents. The deviation rate in the sample is used to estimate statistically the population deviation rate. The estimate is expressed as an *interval estimate* of the population deviation rate and includes a *statement of probability* (confidence level) that the interval contains the actual population deviation rate. Furthermore, the interval may be *one sided* or *two sided*. A two-sided interval gives upper and lower limits of probable population deviation rate, which are referred to as the *computed lower deviation rate* (CLDR) and *computed upper deviation rate* (CUDR). The auditor might conclude, for example, that the percentage of unattached invoices is between one percent (CLDR) and 4 percent (CUDR) at a 95 percent confidence level.

A one-sided interval specifies a CUDR only and represents the probable, highest deviation rate. This type of attributes estimate is the one most commonly used in tests of controls. One-sided intervals are the only type discussed in the remainder of this chapter.

Purpose

Auditors use attributes sampling in determining the appropriate assessed level of control risk. In Figure 10–10 on page 338, attributes sampling is used during phase II (tests of controls). Even though attributes sampling is used primarily for tests of controls, auditors also use attributes sampling for substantive procedures, particularly when performing both as dual-purpose tests.

Attributes sampling may be based on physical units or monetary units. In the case of the former, the occurrence or deviation rate would be a percentage; in the case of the latter, the deviation would be a monetary amount. While the balance of this chapter concentrates on physical attributes sampling, it is appropriate to briefly discuss monetary attributes sampling, also known as dollar unit sampling (DUS), and probability proportional to size sampling (PPS). Dollar unit sampling is dicussed in some detail in Chapter 14.

In physical attribute sampling, the sampling unit is usually a document, such as a cheque, or a transaction, such as a sale. In monetary attributes sampling, the sampling unit is the individual dollar. If sales for the year were made up of 15,000 transactions with a dollar value of $30,000,000, the sampling unit for physical attributes sampling would be an invoice, while the sampling unit for monetary attributes sampling would be each of the 30,000,000 dollars. In the case of the former, each of the 15,000 invoices would have an equal chance of selection; in the case of the latter, each of the 30,000,000 dollars would have an equal chance of selection.

Monetary attribute sampling allows the result of the testing to be stated in dollar terms. It also increases the probability that larger invoices, totaling larger dollar amounts than smaller invoices, will be selected. Monetary attribute sampling is appropriate for tests of controls. Its application is not dissimilar to that of the physical unit attribute sampling described in this chapter.

Auditors who use attributes sampling, rather than a nonstatistical approach, do so in order to measure the *sampling risk* inherent in every sampling process. If an auditor selects a sample of 100 items from a population and finds two exceptions without using a statistical method, the auditor can conclude the *sample deviation rate* is 2 percent. But the auditor is interested in the population deviation rate, not the sample deviation rate. The only objective way to obtain a measure of the highest population deviation rate (CUDR) at a specified confidence level is to use statistical methods.

Physical attributes sampling measures deviation rates, whereas monetary attributes sampling and *variables sampling*, which is studied in Chapter 14, measure the dollar value of the errors. Attributes sampling is typically used for tests of controls and variables sampling for tests of details of balances. Tests of details of balances deal mostly with monetary errors and therefore are suitable for variable sampling. Since tests of controls do not directly involve dollar errors, physical attributes sampling is generally used but monetary attributes sampling is also used.

Sampling Distribution   The determination of the CUDR at a specific confidence level for a given number of exceptions in a sample is based on the use of mathematically determined sampling distributions. Assume that a population of sales invoices exists, 5 percent of which have no shipping document attached. If the auditor takes a random sample of 50 invoices, how many will have missing shipping documents? The sample could contain no deviations or it might contain 6 or 7. The *probability* of each possible number of deviations that would exist in the sample forms the *sampling distribution*. The sampling distribution for the described sample population is shown in Table 12–3.

It can be seen in Table 12–3 that with a sample of 50 items from a population with a deviation rate of 5 percent, the likelihood of obtaining a sample with at least one deviation is 92.31 percent (1 – .0769).

There is a unique sampling distribution for each population deviation rate and sample size, which is mathematically determined. The distribution for a

TABLE 12–3

Probability of Each
Deviation Rate

NUMBER OF DEVIATIONS	PERCENTAGE OF DEVIATION*	PROBABILITY	CUMULATIVE PROBABILITY
0	0	.0769	.0769
1	2	.2025	.2794
2	4	.2611	.5405
3	6	.2199	.7604
4	8	.1360	.8964
5	10	.0656	.9620
6	12	.0260	.9880
7	14	.0120	1.0000

*The sample size is 50 so the percentage of deviations is two times the sample deviation rate.

sample size of 100 from a population with a 5 percent deviation rate is different from the previous one, as is the distribution for a sample of 60 from a population with a 3 percent deviation rate.

In actual audit situations, auditors do not take repeated samples from known populations. They take one sample from an unknown population and get a specific number of deviations in that sample. But knowledge about sampling distributions enables auditors to make statistical statements about the population. For example, if the auditor selected a sample of 50 sales invoices to test for attached shipping documents and found one exception, the auditor could examine the previous probability table and know there is a 20.25 percent probability that the sample came from a population with a 5 percent deviation rate, and a 79.75 percent (1 – .2025) probability that the sample was taken from a population having some other error rate. Since it is similarly possible to calculate the probability distributions for other population deviation rates, these can be examined in the aggregate to draw more specific statistical conclusions about the unknown population being sampled. These sampling distributions are the basis for the tables used by auditors for attributes sampling.

Use of Tables   Auditors use statistical tables to determine the statistical results of attributes sampling as a way of saving time. Tables that are prepared from the sampling distributions previously described are readily available and simple to use. The only difficulty is the occasional lack of availability of the information on the table in exactly the form the auditor wants it. Usually, this problem can be overcome by using interpolation, or the calculations underlying the tables can be made on a more refined basis using a computer program. The use of the tables is shown shortly.

Use of Attributes Sampling in Auditing   With this basic background about attributes sampling, it is now possible to examine its use in auditing. The CICA has not issued Recommendations or an Auditing Guideline on this subject, although it is discussed in *Extent of Audit Testing*. The most important processes in attributes sampling are how the auditor determines the sample size and evaluates the results.

This section includes terminology taken directly from SAS 39, "Audit Sampling," and knowledge of the following terms is essential.

OBJECTIVE 5	
Use attributes sampling in tests of controls and for other audit purposes.	

TERM	DEFINITION
Terms Related to Planning	
Attribute	The characteristic being tested in the application.
Acceptable risk of overreliance on internal control (ARO)	The risk the auditor is willing to take of accepting a control as effective, when the true population deviation rate is greater than the tolerable deviation rate.
Tolerable deviation rate (TDR)	Deviation rate the auditor will permit in the population and still be willing to accept control risk assessed below maximum.
Estimated population deviation rate (EPDR)	Deviation rate the auditor expects to find in the population, before testing begins.
Initial sample size	Sample size determined from attributes sampling tables considering the above factors in planning.
Finite correction factor	A factor reflecting the effect of small population sizes, used to reduce initial sample size.
Terms Related to Evaluating Results	
Deviation	Exception from the attribute in a sample item.
Sample deviation rate (SDR)	Number of deviations in the sample divided by the sample size.
Computed upper deviation rate (CUDR)	The highest deviation rate in the population at a given ARO. Determined from attributes sampling tables.
Computed precision interval	A measure of the inability to determine accurately the population deviation rate.

In studying attributes sampling for tests of transactions, it is useful to separate the main steps and to study each one. They are divided into steps related to planning the sample, selecting the sample and performing the tests, and evaluating the results. The following provides an outline of the methodology for using attributes sampling:

PLANNING THE SAMPLE

1. State the objectives of the audit test.
2. Define attributes and deviation conditions.
3. Define the population.
4. Define the sampling unit.
5. Specify tolerable deviation rate.
6. Specify acceptable risk of overreliance.
7. Estimate the population deviation rate.
8. Determine the initial sample size.

SELECTING THE SAMPLE AND PERFORMING THE TESTS

9. Randomly select the sample.
10. Perform the audit procedures.

EVALUATING THE RESULTS

11. Generalize from the sample to the population.
12. Analyze deviations.
13. Decide the acceptability of the population.

State the Objectives of the Audit Test

The overall objectives of the test must be stated in terms of the particular transaction cycle being tested. Generally, the overall objective of tests of controls is to test the controls in a particular cycle. In the test of the sales and collection cycle, the overall objective is usually to test the effectiveness of internal controls for sales or cash receipts. The objectives of the audit test are normally decided as a part of designing the audit program, which was discussed for sales and collections in Chapter 11.

Define Attributes and Deviation Conditions

The auditor must carefully define the characteristics (attributes) being tested and the deviation conditions whenever attributes sampling is used. Unless a precise statement of what constitutes an attribute is made in advance, the staff person who performs the audit procedure will have no guidelines for identifying deviations.

Attributes of interest and deviation conditions come directly from the audit program. Assume the following partial audit program for sales:

1. Review sales transactions for large and unusual amounts (substantive procedure).
2. Observe whether the duties of the accounts receivable clerk are separate from handling cash (test of control).
3. Examine a sample of duplicate sales invoices for
   a. credit approval by the credit manager (test of control).
   b. existence of an attached shipping document (test of control).
   c. inclusion of a chart of accounts number (test of control).
4. Select a sample of shipping documents and trace each to related duplicate sales invoices for existence (test of control).
5. Compare the quantity on each duplicate sales invoice with the quantity on related shipping documents (test of control).

Attributes sampling is inappropriate for the first two procedures in this audit program. The first is an analytical procedure for which sampling is inappropriate. The second is an observation procedure for which no documentation exists. Attributes sampling can be used for the remaining five procedures.

Table 12–4 shows the five attributes of interest and deviation conditions for those five audit procedures.

Each of these five attributes is verified for every item randomly selected for the sample. The absence of the attribute for any sample item is a deviation for that attribute.

Define the Population

The population represents the body of data about which the auditor wishes to generalize. The auditor can define the population to include whatever data are desired but he or she must *randomly sample from the entire population* as it has been defined. He or she may *generalize only about that population which has been sampled*. For example, in performing tests of recorded sales transactions, the auditor generally defines the population as all recorded sales for the year. If

TABLE 12–4	ATTRIBUTE	DEVIATION CONDITION
Attributes Defined	1. The duplicate sales invoice is approved for credit.	Lack of initials indicating credit approval.
	2. A copy of the shipping document is attached to duplicate sales invoice.	Shipping document not attached to duplicate sales invoice.
	3. The account number charged is included on the duplicate sales invoice.	Account number not included on duplicate sales invoice.
	4. A duplicate sales invoice exists for each shipping document.	Duplicate sales invoice does not exist for shipping document.
	5. The quantity on the sales invoice is the same as on the shipping document.	Quantity different on shipping document and duplicate sales invoice.

the auditor randomly samples from only one month's transactions, it is invalid to draw statistical conclusions about the invoices for the entire year.

It is important that the auditor carefully define the population in advance, consistent with the objectives of the audit tests. Furthermore, in some cases it may be necessary to define more than one population for a given set of audit procedures. For example, if the auditor intends to trace from sales invoices to shipping documents (attributes 1 through 3 in Table 12–4) and from shipping documents to duplicate sales invoices (attributes 4 and 5 in Table 12–4), there are two populations (one population of shipping documents and another of duplicate sales invoices).

Define the Sampling Unit

The major consideration in defining the sampling unit is to make it consistent with the objectives of the audit tests. Thus, the definition of the population and the planned audit procedures usually dictate the appropriate sampling unit. For example, if the auditor wants to determine how frequently the client fails to fill a customer's order, the sampling unit must be defined as the customer's order. If, however, the objective is to determine whether the proper quantity of the goods described on the customer's order is correctly shipped and billed, it is possible to define the sampling unit as the customer's order, the shipping document, or the duplicate sales invoice.

In Table 12–4, the appropriate sample unit for attributes 1 through 3 is the duplicate sales invoice. For attribute 4 the appropriate sampling unit is the shipping document. Either the duplicate sales invoice or the shipping document is appropriate for attribute 5.

Specify Tolerable Deviation Rate

Establishing the tolerable deviation rate (TDR) requires *professional judgment* on the part of the auditor. TDR represents the deviation rate the auditor will permit in the population and still be willing to assess control risk below maximum. For example, assume the auditor decides that TDR for attribute 1 in Table 12–4 is 6 percent. That means the auditor has decided that even if 6 percent of the duplicate sales invoices are not approved for credit, the credit approval control is still effective. TDR is the result of an auditor's judgment. The suitable TDR is a question of *materiality* and is therefore affected by both the definition and the *importance of the attribute.*

TDR has a significant effect on sample size. A larger sample size is needed for a small TDR than for a large one. For example, a larger sample is required for a TDR of 4 percent for attribute 1 in the previous paragraph than for a TDR of 6 percent.

Specify Acceptable Risk of Overreliance

Whenever a sample is taken, there is a risk that the quantitative conclusions about the population will be incorrect. This is always true unless 100 percent of the population is tested. As has already been stated, this is the case with both non-statistical and statistical sampling.

For attributes sampling in tests of controls, that risk is called *acceptable risk of overreliance on internal control (ARO)*. ARO is the risk the auditor is willing to take of accepting a control procedure as effective when the true population deviation rate is greater than TDR. Assume, for illustration purposes, that TDR is 6 percent, ARO is 10 percent, and the true population deviation rate is 8 percent. (The control procedure in this case is not acceptable because the true deviation rate of 8 percent exceeds TDR. The auditor does not know that because the true rate is unknown.) The ARO of 10 percent means that the auditor is willing to take a 10 percent risk of concluding that the control is effective after all testing is completed, even when it is ineffective. If the auditor finds the control effective in this illustration, the auditor will have overrelied on internal control (used a lower assessed level of control risk than what was justified); hence the term *acceptable risk of overreliance on internal control.*

Choosing the appropriate ARO in a particular situation is a decision in which the auditor must use his or her best judgment. Since the risk of overreliance on internal control is a measure of the level of risk that the auditor is willing to take, the main consideration is the extent to which the auditor plans to assess control risk below maximum. If the auditor plans to assess control risk below maximum as a basis for reducing substantive procedures, a lower ARO is desirable. Referring to Figure 9-3, the most common situation where attributes sampling would be used is when the auditor decides to assess control risk at a lower level than can be supported by understanding internal control (alternative 3). If the auditor decides to assess control risk at the maximum level (alternative 1), tests of controls are not performed. If control risk is assessed at the level supported by understanding internal control (alternative 2), tests of controls are often restricted to inquiry and transaction walk-through tests.

The auditor can establish different TDR and ARO levels for different attributes of a particular audit test. For example, it is common for auditors to use a higher tolerable deviation rate and acceptable risk of overreliance on internal controls for tests of credit approval than for tests of the existence of duplicate sales invoices and bills of lading.

Table 12–5 is an illustrative guideline for establishing tolerable deviation rates and acceptable risks of overreliance on internal control for tests of controls. They should not be interpreted as representing CICA recommendations. They illustrate guidelines a public accounting firm could issue to its staff.

Estimate the Population Deviation Rate

In attributes sampling, an *advance estimate* of the expected population deviation rate (EPDR) is necessary to plan the appropriate sample size. If the expected population deviation rate is low, a relatively small sample size will satisfy the auditor's tolerable deviation rate. It is common to use the *results of the preceding year's audit* to make this estimate; but if last year's results are not available, or if they are considered unreliable, the auditor can take a small *preliminary sample* of the current year's population for this purpose. It is not critical that the estimate be precise because the current year's sample deviation rate is ultimately used to estimate the population characteristics.

	FACTOR	JUDGMENT	GUIDELINE
TABLE 12–5 Statistical Sample Sizes: Tests of Controls	Planned assessed level of control risk. Consider: Nature, extent, and timing of substantive procedures; i.e., greater substantive procedures, higher planned assessed control risk and vice versa. Quality of evidence available for tests of controls; i.e., the lower the quality of evidence, the higher the assessed level of control risk.	Lowest level Moderate level Higher level	ARO of 5% ARO of 10% ARO of 20%
	Significance of the transactions and related account balances the internal controls are intended to affect.	Highly significant balances Significant balances Less significant balances	 TDR of 4% TDR of 5% TDR of 6%

Notes: Certain significant items may be nonstatistically selected in addition to the statistical sample. The guidelines should also recognize that there may be variations in AROs based on audit considerations. The guidelines above are the most conservative that should be followed.

Determine the Initial Sample Size

Four factors determine the initial sample size for attributes sampling: *population size, tolerable deviation rate, acceptable risk of overreliance on internal control,* and *expected population deviation rate.* Population size is not a major factor in the early part of the following discussion and is examined later. The initial sample size is so called because the deviations in the actual sample must be evaluated before it is possible to decide whether the sample is sufficiently large to achieve the audit objectives.

When the three major factors affecting sample size have been determined, it is possible to compute an initial sample by using tables.

The two tables that make up Table 12–6 are taken from the AICPA Audit Sampling Guide. They are the same except that the first one is for a 5 percent and the second one a 10 percent risk of overreliance. These tables are "one-sided tables," which means that they represent the *upper* deviation rate for a given acceptable risk of overreliance.

Use of the tables In using the tables to compute the initial sample size, four steps are required:

1. Select the table corresponding to the acceptable risk of overreliance.
2. Locate the tolerable deviation rate at the top of the table.
3. Locate the expected deviation rate in the far left column.
4. Read down the appropriate tolerable deviation rate column until it intersects with the appropriate expected population deviation rate row. The number at the intersection is the initial sample size.

To illustrate, assume an auditor is willing to assess control risk at a reduced level for credit approval if the rate of missing credit approvals in the population (attribute 1 in Table 12–4) does not exceed 6 percent (TDR), at a 5 percent ARO level. On the basis of past experience, EPDR has been about 2 percent. Use the 5 percent acceptable risk of overreliance table; locate the 6 percent tolerable deviation rate column; read down to where the column intersects with the 2 percent expected population deviation rate row. The initial sample size is determined to be 127.

Is 127 a large enough sample size for this audit? It is not possible to answer that question until after the tests have been performed. If the actual deviation rate

TABLE 12–6 Determining Sample Size for Attributes Sampling

EXPECTED POPULATION DEVIATION RATE (IN PERCENTAGE)	\multicolumn{11}{c}{TOLERABLE DEVIATION RATE (IN PERCENTAGE)}										
	2	3	4	5	6	7	8	9	10	15	20
\multicolumn{12}{c}{5 PERCENT RISK OF OVERRELIANCE}											
0.00	149	99	74	59	49	42	36	32	29	19	14
.25	236	157	117	93	78	66	58	51	46	30	22
.50	*	157	117	93	78	66	58	51	46	30	22
.75	*	208	117	93	78	66	58	51	46	30	22
1.00	*	*	156	93	78	66	58	51	46	30	22
1.25	*	*	156	124	78	66	58	51	46	30	22
1.50	*	*	192	124	103	66	58	51	46	30	22
1.75	*	*	227	153	103	88	77	51	46	30	22
2.00	*	*	*	181	127	88	77	68	46	30	22
2.25	*	*	*	208	127	88	77	68	61	30	22
2.50	*	*	*	*	150	109	77	68	61	30	22
2.75	*	*	*	*	173	109	95	68	61	30	22
3.00	*	*	*	*	195	129	95	84	61	30	22
3.25	*	*	*	*	*	148	112	84	61	30	22
3.50	*	*	*	*	*	167	112	84	76	40	22
3.75	*	*	*	*	*	185	129	100	76	40	22
4.00	*	*	*	*	*	*	146	100	89	40	22
5.00	*	*	*	*	*	*	*	158	116	40	30
6.00	*	*	*	*	*	*	*	*	179	50	30
7.00	*	*	*	*	*	*	*	*	*	68	37
\multicolumn{12}{c}{10 PERCENT RISK OF OVERRELIANCE}											
.00	114	76	57	45	38	32	28	25	22	15	11
.25	194	129	96	77	64	55	48	42	38	25	18
.50	194	129	96	77	64	55	48	42	38	25	18
.75	265	129	96	77	64	55	48	42	38	25	18
1.00	*	176	96	77	64	55	48	42	38	25	18
1.25	*	221	132	77	64	55	48	42	38	25	18
1.50	*	*	132	105	64	55	48	42	38	25	18
1.75	*	*	166	105	88	55	48	42	38	25	18
2.00	*	*	198	132	88	75	48	42	38	25	18
2.25	*	*	*	132	88	75	65	42	38	25	18
2.50	*	*	*	158	110	75	65	58	38	25	18
2.75	*	*	*	209	132	94	65	58	52	25	18
3.00	*	*	*	*	132	94	65	58	52	25	18
3.25	*	*	*	*	153	113	82	58	52	25	18
3.50	*	*	*	*	194	113	82	73	52	25	18
3.75	*	*	*	*	*	131	98	73	52	25	18
4.00	*	*	*	*	*	149	98	73	65	25	18
4.50	*	*	*	*	*	218	130	87	65	34	18
5.00	*	*	*	*	*	*	160	115	78	34	18
5.50	*	*	*	*	*	*	*	142	103	34	18
6.00	*	*	*	*	*	*	*	182	116	45	25
7.00	*	*	*	*	*	*	*	*	199	52	25
7.50	*	*	*	*	*	*	*	*	*	52	25
8.00	*	*	*	*	*	*	*	*	*	60	25
8.50	*	*	*	*	*	*	*	*	*	68	32

* Sample is too large to be cost-effective for most audit applications.

Notes:

1. This table assumes a large population.
2. Sample sizes are the same in certain columns even when expected population deviation rates differ, because of the method of constructing the tables. Sample sizes are calculated for attributes sampling using the expected number of deviations in the population, but auditors can deal more conveniently with expected population deviation rates. For example, in the 15 percent column for tolerable deviation rate, at an ARO of 5 percent, initial sample size for most EPDRs is 30. One deviation, divided by a sample size of 30, is 3.3 percent. Therefore, for all EPDRs greater than zero, but less than 3.3 percent, initial sample size is the same.

in the sample turns out to be greater than 2 percent, the auditor will be unsure of the effectiveness of the internal controls. This will become apparent as we proceed.

Effect of population size In the preceding discussion, the size of the population was ignored in determining the initial sample size. It may seem strange to some readers, but statistical theory proves that in most types of populations to which attributes sampling applies, the population size is a *minor* consideration in determining sample size. This is true because representativeness is ensured by the random selection process. Once a sample is obtained that includes a good cross-section of items, additional items are not needed.

The tables used by most auditors, including those in this text, are based on infinite population sizes. It is possible to take the population size into consideration in determining the initial sample size by making an adjustment called the *finite correction factor*. The finite correction factor has the effect of significantly reducing the sample size only when more than 10 percent of the population is included in the sample. The calculation is as follows:

$$n = \frac{n'}{1 + n'/N}$$

where

n' = sample size before considering the effect of the population size

N = population size

n = revised sample size after considering the effect of the population size

As an example, assume the size of the population of sales orders in the previous problem to be 1,000. The revised sample size is computed as follows:

$$n = \frac{127}{1 + (127/1,000)} = 113$$

If the population is 10,000 rather than 1,000, the revised sample size is 125, which is not much lower than the 127 shown in the table.

It is never improper to use the finite correction factor. What determines its use is whether the reduction in sample size is worth the additional calculation cost.

Effect of a change in the factors In order to understand properly the concepts underlying statistical sampling in auditing, the reader should understand the effect of changing any of the four factors that determine sample size when the other factors remain unchanged. Table 12–7 illustrates the effect of increasing each of the four factors; a decrease will have the opposite effect.

TABLE 12–7

Effect on Sample Size of Changing Factors

TYPE OF CHANGE	EFFECT ON INITIAL SAMPLE SIZE
Increase acceptable risk of overreliance	Decrease
Increase tolerable deviation rate	Decrease
Increase estimated population deviation rate	Increase
Increase population size	Increase (minor effect)

A combination of two factors has the greatest effect on sample size: TDR minus EPDR. A brief illustration using an ARO of 10 percent shows the effect. Using Table 12–6, if TDR is 7 percent and EPDR is 4.5 percent, the difference is 2.5 percent and the initial sample is 218. If TDR is 9 percent and EPDR is 2 percent, the difference is 7 percent and the initial sample size is 42.

Why the large difference in sample size? It is caused by sampling risk. If the auditor finds an actual sample deviation rate of 2 percent, there is little risk, even with small samples, of the population rate exceeding 9 percent. If the auditor finds an actual sample deviation rate of 4.5 percent, there is a much greater risk of the true rate exceeding 7 percent. A larger sample is therefore needed to reduce the risk. Examine Table 12–6. An asterisk indicates the intersection of TDR and EPDR, where sample sizes are not likely to be cost-effective. In all cases, TDR minus EPDR is 3 percent or less.

Randomly Select the Sample

After the initial sample size for the attributes sampling application has been computed, the auditor must choose the particular items in the population to be included in the sample. It is essential that the selection be random whenever statistical sampling is used. This can be done by the use of random number tables, computers, or systematic sampling as previously discussed.

Perform the Audit Procedures

The audit procedures are performed in the same manner in statistical sampling as in *nonstatistical* sampling. The auditor examines each item in the sample to determine whether it is consistent with the definition of the attribute and maintains a record of all the deviations found.When audit procedures have been completed for an attributes sampling application, there will be a sample size and number of deviations for each attribute. For example, using the example from Table 12–4 on page 406, there may be a sample size of 125 and two deviations for attribute 1, a sample size of 150 and three deviations for attribute 2, and so on.

Generalize from the Sample to the Population

The *sample deviation rate* (SDR) can easily be calculated from the actual sample results. SDR equals the actual number of deviations divided by the actual sample size. For example, continuing the example in the previous paragraph, attribute 1 from Table 12–4 has an SDR of 1.6 percent (2 ÷ 125) and attribute 2 has an SDR of 2 percent (3 ÷ 150). It would be wrong for the auditor to conclude that the population deviation rate is exactly the same as the sample deviation rate. Earlier in the chapter it was shown that sampling risk prevented the auditor from concluding that the population deviation rate is the same as the sample deviation rate.

The auditor must compute the upper deviation rate (CUDR) at the acceptable risk of overreliance on internal control (ARO). CUDR is the highest deviation rate in the population, given the risk of overreliance the auditor considers acceptable. CUDR is determined by using an attributes sampling table, such as the ones in Table 12–8. These are consistent with those used for determining the initial sample size.

Use of the tables In using tables to compute the upper deviation rate, four steps are required:

1. Select the table corresponding to the risk of overreliance. The risk of overreliance should be the same as ARO used for determining the initial sample size.
2. Locate the actual number of deviations found in the audit tests at the top of the table.

TABLE 12–8 Evaluating Sample Results Using Attributes Sampling

SAMPLE SIZE	ACTUAL NUMBER OF DEVIATIONS FOUND										
	0	1	2	3	4	5	6	7	8	9	10
				5 PERCENT RISK OF OVERRELIANCE							
25	11.3	17.6	*	*	*	*	*	*	*	*	*
30	9.5	14.9	19.5	*	*	*	*	*	*	*	*
35	8.2	12.9	16.9	*	*	*	*	*	*	*	*
40	7.2	11.3	14.9	18.3	*	*	*	*	*	*	*
45	6.4	10.1	13.3	16.3	19.2	*	*	*	*	*	*
50	5.8	9.1	12.1	14.8	17.4	19.9	*	*	*	*	*
55	5.3	8.3	11.0	13.5	15.9	18.1	*	*	*	*	*
60	4.9	7.7	10.1	12.4	14.6	16.7	18.8	*	*	*	*
65	4.5	7.1	9.4	11.5	13.5	15.5	17.4	19.3	*	*	*
70	4.2	6.6	8.7	10.7	12.6	14.4	16.2	18.0	19.7	*	*
75	3.9	6.2	8.2	10.0	11.8	13.5	15.2	16.9	18.4	20.0	*
80	3.7	5.8	7.7	9.4	11.1	12.7	14.3	15.8	17.3	18.8	*
90	3.3	5.2	6.8	8.4	9.9	11.3	12.7	14.1	15.5	16.8	18.1
100	3.0	4.7	6.2	7.6	8.9	10.2	11.5	12.7	14.0	15.2	16.4
125	2.4	3.7	4.9	6.1	7.2	8.2	9.3	10.3	11.3	12.2	13.2
150	2.0	3.1	4.1	5.1	6.0	6.9	7.7	8.6	9.4	10.2	11.0
200	1.5	2.3	3.1	3.8	4.5	5.2	5.8	6.5	7.1	7.7	8.3
				10 PERCENT RISK OF OVERRELIANCE							
20	10.9	18.1	*	*	*	*	*	*	*	**	
25	8.8	14.7	19.9	*	*	*	*	*	*	*	*
30	7.4	12.4	16.8	*	*	*	*	*	*	*	*
35	6.4	10.7	14.5	18.1	*	*	*	*	*	*	*
40	5.6	9.4	12.8	15.9	19.0	*	*	*	*	*	*
45	5.0	8.4	11.4	14.2	17.0	19.6	*	*	*	*	*
50	4.5	7.6	10.3	12.9	15.4	17.8	*	*	*	*	*
55	4.1	6.9	9.4	11.7	14.0	16.2	18.4	*	*	*	*
60	3.8	6.3	8.6	10.8	12.9	14.9	16.9	18.8	*	*	*
70	3.2	5.4	7.4	9.3	11.1	12.8	14.6	16.2	17.9	19.5	*
80	2.8	4.8	6.5	8.3	9.7	11.3	12.8	14.3	15.7	17.2	18.6
90	2.5	4.3	5.8	7.3	8.7	10.1	11.4	12.7	14.0	15.3	16.6
100	2.3	3.8	5.2	6.6	7.8	9.1	10.3	11.5	12.7	13.8	15.0
120	1.9	3.2	4.4	5.5	6.6	7.6	8.6	9.6	10.6	11.6	12.5
160	1.4	2.4	3.3	4.1	4.9	5.7	6.5	7.2	8.0	8.7	9.5
200	1.1	1.9	2.6	3.3	4.0	4.6	5.2	5.8	6.4	7.0	7.6

* Over 20 percent.
Note: This table presents computed upper deviation rates as percentages. Table assumes a large population.

3. Locate the actual sample size in the leftmost column.
4. Read down the appropriate actual number of deviations column until it intersects with the appropriate sample size row. The number at the intersection is the computed upper deviation rate.

To illustrate the use of the tables, assume an actual sample size of 125 and two deviations in attribute 1. Using a risk of overreliance of 5 percent, CUDR is 4.9 percent. Stated another way the result is: the computed upper deviation rate for attribute 1 is 4.9 percent at a 5 percent risk of overreliance. Does this result indicate that if 100 percent of the population were tested, the true deviation rate would be 4.9 percent? No, the true deviation rate is unknown, but there is a 5 percent risk that if the auditor concludes the true deviation rate does not exceed 4.9 percent, he or she will be wrong.

A useful way of looking at the statistical results is by combining the *sample deviation rate* and the *computed precision interval*. The sample deviation rate equals the number of deviations divided by sample size, in this case 1.6 percent. The computed precision interval is 3.3 percent (4.9 percent minus 1.6 percent). It represents a statistical measure of the inability to determine accurately the population deviation rate due to the restriction of the test to a sample. The combination of the two is the highest deviation rate, which is called the computed upper deviation rate at the risk level specified.

The *finite correction factor* can also be used to adjust the computed upper deviation rate. The revised CUDR is calculated as follows:

$$\text{Revised CUDR} = \left[\left(\text{CUDR} - \text{SDR} \right) \times \sqrt{\frac{N - n}{N}} \right] + \text{SDR}$$

where

$$
\begin{aligned}
\text{CUDR} &= \text{Original computed upper deviation rate} \\
\text{SDR} &= \text{Sample deviation rate} \\
N &= \text{Population size} \\
n &= \text{Sample size}
\end{aligned}
$$

In the previous example, the revised computed precision interval is approximately 3.1 percent assuming a population size of 1,000 [3.3 percent × $\sqrt{(1{,}000 - 125)} \div 1{,}000$]. This means the revised computed upper deviation rate is 4.7 percent (1.6 percent plus 3.1 percent). The reduction in the computed upper deviation rate is ordinarily not worth the effort to calculate it unless more than 10 percent of the population has been tested.

Analyze Deviations   In addition to determining the CUDR for each attribute, it is necessary to analyze *individual deviations* to determine the breakdown in internal control that caused them. Deviations could be caused by carelessness of employees, misunderstood instructions, intentional failure to perform procedures, or many other factors. The nature of a deviation and its cause have a significant effect on the qualitative evaluation of the system. For example, if all the deviations in the tests of internal verification of sales invoices occurred while the person normally responsible for performing the tests was on vacation, this would affect the auditor's evaluation of the internal control structure and the subsequent investigation.

Decide the Acceptability of the Population   It is important to distinguish between the TDR and ARO that were *chosen* by the auditor before the tests were performed and the CUDR and ARO that *resulted* from the sample. The former represent the *standards that were deemed necessary* by the auditor; the latter are the *results objectively computed* on the basis of the sample.

Before the population can be considered acceptable, the CUDR determined on the basis of the actual sample results must be *less than or equal to* TDR when both are based on ARO. In the example just given, in which the auditor has specified that he or she would accept a 6 percent population deviation rate at a 5 percent ARO and the computed upper deviation rate was 4.7 percent, the requirements of the sample have been met. In this case the control being tested can be used to reduce the assessed level of control risk as planned, provided a careful analysis of the cause of deviation does not indicate the possibility of a significant problem in an aspect of the control not previously considered.

When CUDR is greater than TDR it is necessary to take specific action. Four courses of action can be followed.

Revise TDR or ARO   This alternative should be followed only when the auditor has concluded that the original specifications were too conservative. Relaxing either TDR or ARO may be difficult to defend if the auditor is ever subject to review by a court, a securities commission, or a professional association disciplinary committee. If these requirements are changed, it should be done on the basis of careful thought.

Expand the sample size   An increase in the sample size has the effect of decreasing the CUDR if the actual sample deviation rate does not increase. This can be demonstrated in Table 12–8 by keeping the sample deviation rate constant and observing the decrease in the CUDR as sample size increases.

Table 12–9 shows the CUDR for four different sample sizes when the sample deviation rate is constant at 2 percent. The reason for the decrease in CUDR when sample size increases and SDR remains constant is a reduction of sampling error. Sampling error gets smaller as sample size increases. If the entire population were tested, it would be zero.

Revise assessed control risk   If the results of the tests of controls do not support the planned assessed control risk, the auditor should revise assessed control risk upward. The effect of the revision is likely to increase substantive procedures. For example, if tests of controls of internal verification procedures for verifying prices, extensions, and quantities on sales invoices indicate those procedures are not being followed, the auditor should increase substantive procedure tests of the pricing, extensions, and footings. An expansion of confirmations of accounts receivable may also help to discover whether there are material misstatements.

The decision whether to increase sample size until CUDR is less than TDR or to revise assessed control risk must be made on the basis of cost versus benefit. If the sample is not expanded, it is necessary to revise assessed control risk upward and therefore perform additional substantive procedures. The cost of additional tests of controls must be compared with that of additional substantive procedures. Of course, there is always a chance that an expanded attributes sample will continue to produce unacceptable results, in which case additional substantive tests will still be necessary.

Write a letter to management   This action is desirable, in combination with one of the other three above, regardless of the nature of the deviations. When the auditor determines that internal control is not operating effectively, management should be informed.

TABLE 12–9

Effect on CUDR of Increase in Sample Size

SAMPLE SIZE	NUMBER OF DEVIATIONS	SDR (IN PERCENTAGE)	CUDR (IN PERCENTAGE)
50	1	2	9.1
100	2	2	6.2
150	3	2	5.1
200	4	2	4.5

In some instances, it may be acceptable to limit the action to writing a letter to management when CUDR exceeds TDR. This occurs if the auditor has no intention of reducing the assessed control risk or has already carried out sufficient substantive procedures to his or her own satisfaction when conducting the tests of controls.

Summary of
Attribute Steps

Figure 12–2 summarizes the steps used in attributes sampling. It is apparent from the figure that planning is an essential part of using sampling. The purposes of that planning are to make sure the audit procedures are properly applied and the sample size is appropriate for the circumstances. Sample selection is also important and must be done with care to avoid nonsampling errors. The time-consuming part of attributes sampling is performing the audit procedures. Performance must be done carefully to correctly determine the number of deviations in the sample. Evaluating the results includes making the statistical calculations for comparison to the tolerable deviation rate, doing the judgmental analysis of the deviations and finally deciding the acceptability of the population.

Other
Considerations

For the sake of greater continuity, in the preceding discussion we bypassed several important considerations related to selecting the proper sample size and drawing conclusions about the results. We now turn to those topics.

FIGURE 12–2
Summary of Attributes
Steps

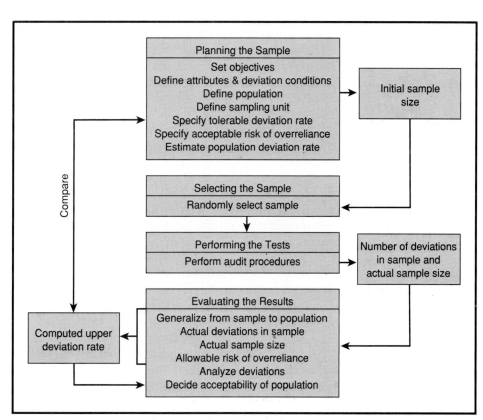

Random Selection versus Statistical Measurement

Auditors often do not understand the distinction between random (probabilistic) selection and statistical measurement. It should now be clear that random selection is a part of statistical sampling but is not, by itself, statistical measurement. To have statistical measurement, it is necessary to generalize mathematically from the sample to the population.

It is acceptable to use random selection procedures without drawing statistical conclusions, but this practice is questionable if a reasonably large sample size has been selected. Whenever the auditor takes a random sample, regardless of his or her basis for determining its size, there is a *statistical measurement inherent in the sample*. Since there is little or no cost involved in computing the upper deviation rate, we believe that should be done whenever possible. It would, of course, be inappropriate to draw a statistical conclusion unless the sample were randomly selected.

Adequate Documentation

It is important that the auditor retain adequate records of the procedures performed, the methods used to select the sample and perform the tests, the results found in the tests, and the conclusions drawn. This is necessary as a means of *evaluating the combined results* of all tests and as a basis for *defending the audit* if the need arises. An example of the type of documentation commonly found in practice is included in the case illustration for Hillsburg Hardware at the end of the chapter.

Need for Professional Judgment

A criticism occasionally leveled against statistical sampling is that it reduces the use of professional judgment. An examination of the 13 steps discussed above indicates how unwarranted this criticism is. For proper application of attributes sampling, it is necessary to use professional judgment in most of the steps. For example, selection of the initial sample size depends primarily on the TDR, ARO, and EPDR. Choosing the first two requires the exercise of high-level professional judgment; the latter requires a careful estimate. Similarly, the final evaluation of the adequacy of the entire application of attributes sampling, including the adequacy of the sample size, must also be based on high-level professional judgment.

Case Illustration – Hillsburg Hardware Ltd. – Part II

OBJECTIVE 6

Apply sampling concepts and methodology to the audit plan for the sales and collection cycle.

To illustrate the concepts discussed in this chapter, the Hillsburg Hardware Ltd. case from Chapter 11 is extended to include determination of sample size, the selection of items for testing, and the conclusions drawn on the basis of the results of the tests. The only parts of the tests of the sales and collection cycle included here are the tests of credit approval, the shipment of goods, the billing of customers, and recording the amounts in the records. It should be kept in mind that the procedures for Hillsburg Hardware Ltd. were developed specifically for that client and would probably not be applicable for a different audit. The audit procedures for these tests are repeated in Table 12–10 along with comments to indicate the relationship of each procedure to attributes sampling.

In applying attributes sampling to the procedures for Hillsburg Hardware Ltd., there are only two functions for which statistical sampling is being used: the shipment of goods and the billing of customers. Emphasis is placed on the billing of customers in the illustration because the duplicate sales invoice is the sampling unit for most of the audit procedures. In order to concentrate on the attributes sampling applications for the billing function, comments about the shipping

TABLE 12–10

Audit Procedures

PROCEDURE	COMMENT
Shipment of Goods	
9. Account for a sequence of shipping documents.	It is possible to do this by selecting a random sample and accounting for all customer orders selected. This requires a separate set of random numbers, since the sampling unit is different than for the other tests.
10. Trace selected shipping documents to the sales journal to be sure that each one has been included.	No deviations are expected, and a 6 percent TDR is considered acceptable at an ARO of 10 percent. A sample size of 38 is selected. The shipping documents are traced to the sales journal. This is done for all 38 items. There are no exceptions for either test. The results are considered acceptable. There is no further information about this portion of the tests in this illustration.
Billing of Customers and Recording the Sales in the Records	
11. Account for a sequence of sales invoices in the sales journal.	The audit procedures for billing and recording sales (procedures 11 to 14) are the only ones tested using attributes sampling for this case illustration. The attributes sampling data sheet includes each of these procedures as attributes.
12. Trace selected duplicate sales invoice numbers from the sales journal to a. accounts receivable master file and test for amount, date, and invoice number. b. duplicate sales invoice and check for the total amount recorded in the journal, date, customer name, and account classification. Check the pricing, extensions, and footings. Examine underlying documents for indication of internal verification by Pam Dilley. c. bill of lading and test for customer name, product description, quantity, and date. d. duplicate sales order and test for customer name, product description, quantity, and date and indication of internal verification by Pam Dilley. e. Customer order and test for customer name, product description, quantity, date, and credit approval by Rick Chulick.	
13. Trace recorded sales from the sales journal to the file of supporting documents, which includes a duplicate sales invoice, bill of lading, sales order, and customer order.	
14. Compare dates on the bill of lading, duplicate sales invoice, and sales journal.	

Note: Random selection and statistical sampling are not applicable for the 8 general audit procedures in Figure 11–8. Advanced statistical techniques, such as regression analysis, could be applicable for analysis of the results of analytical procedures. Random selection could be used for procedure 3.

function are restricted to those shown adjacent to the list of audit procedures in the table. The reader should recognize, however, that the attributes sampling methodology followed for the shipping function would be essentially the same as the methodology illustrated for the billing function in the remainder of the case.

Objectives, Population, and Sampling Unit

Most auditors use some type of preprinted form to document each attributes sampling application. An example of a commonly used form is given in Figure 12–3. The top part of the form includes a definition of the objective, the population, and the sampling unit.

Define the Attributes of Interest

The attributes used in this application are taken directly from the audit program. The procedures that can be used as attributes for a particular application of attributes sampling depend on the definition of the sampling unit. In this case, all the procedures in the billing function can be included. The nine attributes used for this case are listed in Figure 12–3. The definition of the attribute is a critical part of attributes sampling. The decision as to which attributes to combine and which ones to keep separate is the most important aspect of the definition. If all possible types of attributes, such as customer name, date, price, and quantity, are separated for each procedure, the large number of attributes makes the problem unmanageable. However, if all the procedures are combined into one or two attributes, greatly dissimilar misstatements are evaluated together. Somewhere in between is a reasonable compromise.

Establish TDR, ARO, EPDR and Determine Initial Sample Size

The TDR for each attribute is decided on the basis of the auditor's judgment of what deviation rate is material. The failure to record a sales invoice would be highly significant, especially considering this particular system; therefore, as indicated in Figure 12–3, the lowest TDR (3 percent) is chosen for attribute 1. The incorrect billing of the customer represents potentially significant errors, but no error is likely to be for the full amount of the invoice. As a result, a 4 percent TDR is chosen for each of the attributes directly related to the billing of shipments and recording the amounts in the records. The last four attributes have higher TDRs, since they are of less importance for the audit.

An ARO of 10 percent is decided on because the potential for reducing assessed control risk is limited even if the internal controls tested are proven effective, due to several internal control weaknesses.

The expected population deviation rate is based on previous years' results, modified upward slightly due to the change in personnel. Initial sample size for each attribute is determined from Table 12–6 on the basis of the above considerations. This information is summarized for all attributes in Figure 12–3. For convenience in selection and evaluation, the auditor decided to select a sample of 75 for attribute 1, 100 for attributes 2 through 5, 65 for attributes 6 and 9, and 50 for the other 2.

Random Selection

The random selection for the case is straightforward except for the need for different sample sizes for different attributes. This problem can be overcome by selecting a random sample of 50 for use on all 9 attributes followed by another sample of 15 for all attributes except 7 or 8, an additional 10 for all except 6 through 9, and 25 more for attributes 2 through 5. The documentation for the selection of the first 50 numbers is illustrated in Figure 12–4.

FIGURE 12–3

Statistical Sampling
Data Sheet: Attributes

Client *Hillsburg Hardware*   Year end *12/31/x8*
Audit Area *Tests of Controls-Billing Function*   Pop. size *5,853*

Define the objective(s) *Examine duplicate sales invoices and related documents to determine if the system has functioned as intended and as described in the audit program.*

Define the population precisely (including stratification, if any) *Sales invoices for the period 1/1/x8 to 12/31/x8. First invoice number= 3 600. Last invoice number= 9 452.*

Define the sampling unit, organization of population items, and random selection procedures *Sales invoice number, recorded in the sales journal sequentially; random number table.*

Description of attributes	Planned Audit					Actual Results		
	EPDR	TDR	ARO	Initial sample size	Sample size	Number of deviations	Sample deviation rate	CUDR
1. Existence of the sales invoice number in the sales journal.	0	3	10	76	75	0	0	3.0
2. Amount and other data in the master file agree with sales journal entry.	1	4	10	96	100	2	2	5.2
3. Amount and other data in the sales invoice agree with sales journal entry.	1	4	10	96	100	0	0	2.3
4. Evidence that pricing, extensions, and footings are checked (initials and correct amount).	1	4	10	96	100	10	10	15.0
5. Quantity and other data on the bill of lading agree with the duplicate sales invoice.	1	4	10	96	100	4	4	7.8
6. Quantity and other data on the sales order agree with the duplicate sales invoice.	1	6	10	64	65	1	1.5	5.9
7. Quantity and other data on the customer order agree with the duplicate sales invoice.	2	8	10	48	50	0	0	4.5
8. Credit is approved by Rick Chulick.	2	8	10	48	50	12	24	>20
9. The file of supporting documents includes a duplicate sales invoice, bill of lading, sales order and customer order.	1	6	10	64	65	0	0	3.5

Intended use of sampling results:

1. Effect on Audit Plan: *Controls tested through attributes 1,3,6,7 and 9 can be relied upon as illustrated on working paper 7-6. Additional emphasis is needed in confirmation, allowance for uncollectible accounts, cut-off tests, and price tests due to results of tests for attributes 2,4,5 and 8.*

2. Recommendations to Management: *Each of the exceptions should be discussed with management. Specific recommendations are needed to correct the internal verification of sales invoices and to improve the approach to credit approvals.*

Perform the Procedures and Generalize to the Population

The audit procedures that are included in the audit program and summarized in the attributes sampling data sheet must be carefully performed for every item in the sample. As a means of documenting the tests and providing information for review, it is common to include a worksheet of the results. Some auditors prefer to include a worksheet containing a listing of all items in the sample; others prefer to limit the documentation to identifying the deviations. This latter approach is followed in the example (Figure 12–5).

FIGURE 12–4

Random Sample for
Testing Sales

Hillsburg Hardware
Random Sample for Testing Sales

	(1)	(2)	(3)	(4)	(5)	(6)
1086	77339	64605	*4* 82583	*18* 85011	00955	*50* 84348
1087	61714	57933	*5* 37342	26000	*33* 93611	93346
1088	15232	48027	15832	*19* 62924	11509	*End* 95853
1089	41447	34275	10779	*20* 83515	*34* 63899	30932
1090	23244	43524	16382	*21* 36340	*35* 73581	76780
1091	53460	83542	25224	*22* 70378	*36* 49604	14609
1092	53442	16897	*6* 61578	05032	*37* 81825	76822
1093	55543	19096	04130	23104	*38* 60534	44842
1094	18185	63329	02340	*23* 63111	*39* 41768	74409
1095	02372	45690	*7* 38595	23121	*40* 73818	74454
1096	51715	35492	*8* 61371	*24* 87132	*41* 81585	55439
1097	24717	16785	*9* 42786	*25* 86585	21858	39489
1098	78002	32604	*10* 87295	*26* 93702	99438	68184
1099	35995	08275	*11* 62405	*27* 43313	03249	74135
1100	29152	*Start* 86922	31508	*28* 42703	*42* 59638	31226
1101	84192	90150	02904	26835	17174	42301
1102	21791	24764	*12* 53674	30093	*43* 45134	24073
1103	63501	05040	*13* 71881	17759	*44* 91881	69614
1104	07149	*1* 69285	*14* 55481	24889	*45* 67061	06631
1105	59443	98962	*15* 74778	*29* 36920	*46* 65620	36794
1106	39059	*2* 58021	28485	*30* 43052	99001	44400
1107	73176	*3* 58913	22638	*31* 69769	21102	72292
1108	11851	09065	96033	02752	*47* 58232	56504
1109	37515	25668	*16* 55785	*32* 66463	*48* 52758	67588
1110	45324	00016	*17* 46818	04373	*49* 75360	87519

Population = 3600 to 9452
Correspondence – First 4 digits in table.
Route – Read down to end of column; start at top of next column.
Sample size – 50, represented by sequential numbers 1 to 50.

At the completion of the testing, the deviations are tabulated to determine the number of deviations in the sample for each attribute. This enables the auditor to compute the sample deviation rate and determine the CUDR from the tables. This information is summarized in Figures 12–6 and 12–7.

Deviation Analysis The final part of the application consists of analyzing the deviations to determine their cause and drawing conclusions about each attribute tested. For every attribute for which CUDR exceeds TDR, it is essential that some conclusion concerning follow-up action be drawn and documented. The deviation analysis and conclusions reached are illustrated in Figure 12–7 and summarized at the bottom of the data sheet in Figure 12–6.

FIGURE 12–5

Inspection of Sample
Items for Attributes

Hillsburg Hardware
INSPECTION OF SAMPLE ITEMS FOR ATTRIBUTES
DECEMBER 31, 19X8

Prepared by _MSW_
Date _2/3/x9_

Identity of item selected	Deviations										
Invoice no.	(1)	(2)	(3)	(4)	(5)	(6)	(7)	(8)	(9)	(10)	(11)
3634					X						
3859				X				X			
3990				X							
4071		X		X							
4222					X						
4270								X			
4331								X			
4513				X	X						
4681						X		X			
4859				X							
5367								X			
5578								X			
5802								X			
5823								X			
5963								X			
6157		X		X							
6229				X							
6311								X			
7188					X						
7536				X							
8351								X			
8517				X							
8713								X			
9445				X							
No. Errors	0	2	0	10	4	1	0	12	0		
Sample size	75	100	100	100	100	65	50	50	65		

FIGURE 12–6

Statistical Sampling
Data Sheet: Attributes

Client *Hillsburg Hardware* Year end *12/31/x8*
Audit Area *Tests of Controls-Billing Function* Pop. size *5,853*

Define the objective(s) *Examine duplicate sales invoices and related documents to determine if the system has functioned as intended and as described in the audit program.*

Define the population precisely (including stratification, if any) *Sales invoices for the period 1/1/x8 to 12/31/x8. First invoice number= 3 600. Last invoice number= 9 452.*

Define the sampling unit, organization of population items, and random selection procedures *Sales invoice number, recorded in the sales journal sequentially; random number table.*

Description of attributes	Planned Audit				Actual Results			
	EPDR	TDR	ARO	Initial sample size	Sample size	Number of deviations	Sample deviation rate	CUDR
1. Existence of the sales invoice number in the sales journal.	0	3	10	76				
2. Amount and other data in the master file agree with sales journal entry.	1	4	10	96				
3. Amount and other data in the sales invoice agree with sales journal entry.	1	4	10	96				
4. Evidence that pricing, extensions, and footings are checked (initials and correct amount).	1	4	10	96				
5. Quantity and other data on the bill of lading agree with the duplicate sales invoice.	1	4	10	96				
6. Quantity and other data on the sales order agree with the duplicate sales invoice.	1	6	10	64				
7. Quantity and other data on the customer order agree with the duplicate sales invoice.	2	8	10	48				
8. Credit is approved by Rick Chulick.	2	8	10	48				
9. The file of supporting documents includes a duplicate sales invoice, bill of lading, sales order and customer order.	1	6	10	64				

Intended use of sampling results:

1. Effect on Audit Plan:

2. Recommendations to Management:

FIGURE 12–7

Analysis of Exceptions

Hillsburg Hardware
ANALYSIS OF EXCEPTIONS
December 31, 19x8

Prepared by *MSW*
Date *2/3/x9*

Attribute	Number of exceptions	Nature of exceptions	Effect on the audit and other comments
2	2	Both errors were posted to the wrong account and were still outstanding after several months. The amounts were for $125.00 and $393.00.	Because the upper deviation rate is greater than TDR, additional substantive work is needed. Perform expanded confirmation procedures and review older uncollected balances thoroughly.
4	10	In 6 cases there were no initials for internal verification. In 2 cases the wrong price was used but the errors were under $10 in each case. In 1 case there was a pricing error of $1000. In 1 case freight was not charged. (Three of the last 4 exceptions had initials for internal verification.)	As a result, have independent client personnel recheck a random sample of 500 duplicate sales invoices under our control. Also, expand the confirmation of accounts receivable.
5	4	In each case the date on the duplicate sales invoice was several days later than the shipping date.	Do extensive tests of the sales cut-off by comparing recorded sales to the shipping documents.
6	1	Just 106 items were shipped and billed though the sales order was for 112 items. The reason for the difference was an error in the perpetual inventory master file. The perpetuals indicated that 112 items were on hand, when there were actually 106. The system does not backorder for undershipments smaller than 25%.	No expansion of tests of controls or substantive tests. The system appears to be working effectively.
8	12	Credit was not approved. Four of these were for new customers. Discussed with Chulick, who stated his busy schedule did not permit approving all sales.	Expand the year-end procedures extensively in evaluating allowance for uncollectible accounts. This includes scheduling of cash receipts subsequent to year end and for all outstanding accounts receivable.

REVIEW QUESTIONS

12–1 State what is meant by a representative sample and explain its importance in sampling audit populations.

12–2 Explain the major difference between statistical and nonstatistical sampling. What are the four main parts of statistical and nonstatistical methods?

12–3 Compared with nonprobabilistic selection, what are the major advantages of probabilistic selection?

12–4 Explain the difference between "sampling with replacement" and "sampling without replacement." Which method do auditors usually follow? Why?

12–5 Explain what is meant by a random number table. Describe how an auditor would select 35 random numbers from a population of 1,750 items by using a random number table.

12–6 Describe systematic sampling and explain how an auditor would select 35 numbers from a population of 1,750 items using this approach. What are the advantages and disadvantages of systematic sampling?

12–7 What is the purpose of using attributes sampling in auditing?

12–8 Explain what is meant by block sampling and describe how an auditor could obtain five blocks of 20 sales invoices from a sales journal.

12–9 Define each of the following terms:
   a. Acceptable risk of overreliance on internal control
   b. Computed upper deviation rate
   c. Estimated population deviation rate
   d. Sample deviation rate
   e. Tolerable deviation rate

12–10 Describe what is meant by a sampling unit. Explain why the sampling unit for verifying the validity of recorded sales differs from the sampling unit for testing for the possibility of omitted sales.

12–11 Distinguish between the tolerable deviation rate and the computed upper deviation rate. How is each determined?

12–12 Distinguish between a sampling error and a nonsampling error. How can each be reduced?

12–13 What is meant by an attribute in attributes sampling? What is the source of the attributes that the auditor selects?

12–14 Explain the difference between an attribute and a deviation condition. State the deviation condition for the audit procedure: the duplicate sales invoice has been initialed indicating the performance of internal verification.

12–15 Identify the factors an auditor uses to decide the appropriate tolerable deviation rate. Compare the sample size for a tolerable deviation rate of 6 percent with that of 3 percent, all other factors being equal.

12–16 Identify the factors an auditor uses to decide the appropriate acceptable risk of overreliance on internal control. Compare the sample size for an acceptable risk of overreliance of 10 percent with that of 5 percent, all other factors being equal.

12–17 State the relationship between the following:
   a. Acceptable risk of overreliance and sample size
   b. Population size and sample size
   c. Tolerable deviation rate and sample size
   d. Estimated population deviation rate and sample size

12–18   Assume the auditor has selected 100 sales invoices from a population of 100,000 to test for an indication of internal verification of pricing and extensions. Determine the upper deviation rate at a 5 percent risk of overreliance if three deviations existed in the sample. Explain the meaning of the statistical results in auditing terms.

12–19   Explain what is meant by analysis of deviations and discuss its importance.

12–20   When the computed upper deviation rate exceeds the tolerable deviation rate, what courses of action are available to the auditor? Under what circumstances should each of these be followed?

12–21   Distinguish between random selection and statistical measurement. State the circumstances under which one can be used without the other.

12–22   List the major decisions the auditor must make in using attributes sampling. State the most important considerations involved in making each decision.

MULTIPLE CHOICE QUESTIONS

12–23   The following items apply to random sampling from large populations for attributes sampling. Select the most appropriate response for each question.

a.   A public accountant wishes to determine the percentage of items in a client's inventory with annual sales of less than 50 percent of the units on hand at the inventory date. Which of the following exhibits the characteristic the public accountant is measuring?

ITEM	UNITS IN INVENTORY	UNITS SOLD THIS YEAR
(1) Firs	251	525
(2) Furs	243	124
(3) Friezes	198	98
(4) Furzes	144	92

b.   If all other factors specified in a sampling plan remain constant, changing the acceptable risk of overreliance from 10 percent to 5 percent would cause the required sample size to

(1) increase.
(2) remain the same.
(3) decrease.
(4) become indeterminate.

c.   If all other factors specified in a sampling plan remain constant, changing the tolerable deviation rate from 8 percent to 12 percent would cause the required sample size to

(1) increase.
(2) remain the same.
(3) decrease.
(4) become indeterminate.   (AICPA adapted)

12–24   The following items apply to random sampling from large populations using attributes sampling. Select the best response.

a.   In a random sample of 1,000 records, a public accountant determines that the rate of occurrence of deviations is 2 percent. The accountant can state that the deviation rate in the population is

(1) not more than 3 percent.
(2) not less than 2 percent.

(3) probably about 2 percent.

(4) not less than one percent.

b. From a random sample of items listed from a client's inventory count, a public accountant estimates with a 10 percent acceptable risk of overreliance that the computed deviation rate is between 4 percent and 6 percent. The accountant's major concern is that there is 1 chance in 20 that the true deviation rate in the population is

(1) more than 6 percent

(2) less than 6 percent.

(3) more than 4 percent.

(4) less than 4 percent.

c. If, from a particular random sample, a public accountant can state with a 5 percent acceptable risk of overreliance that the deviation rate in the population does not exceed 20 percent, the accountant can state that the deviation rate does not exceed 25 percent with

(1) 5 percent risk.

(2) risk greater than 5 percent.

(3) risk less than 5 percent.

(4) cannot determine from the information provided.

d. If a public accountant wishes to select a random sample that must have a 10 percent acceptable risk of overreliance and a tolerable deviation rate of 10 percent, the size of the sample to be selected will decrease as the estimate of the

(1) occurrence rate increases.

(2) occurrence rate decreases.

(3) population size increases.

(4) risk of overreliance increases. (AICPA adapted)

12–25 The following questions relate to physical unit attributes sampling and monetary unit attributes sampling. Select the most appropriate response.

(a) In a dollar-unit sampling plan, the probability that any given account balance will be included in the sample is proportionate to

(1) the confidence level chosen for the sample.

(2) the size of the account balance.

(3) the number of accounts in the population.

(4) the tolerable deviation rate chosen by the auditor.

(b) Populations of accounting data often contain many small value items and some large value items. Such a population is described in statistical terms as

(1) highly discrete

(2) highly homogeneous

(3) highly heterogeneous

(4) highly skewed.

(c) The standard deviation of a population of data is a statistical measure of

(1) the average value of data items.

(2) the correlation of data.

(3) the dispersion of data.

(4) the skewness of data.

(d) Attribute sampling plans would be most appropriate in auditing situations where the auditor is performing

(1) tests of controls.

(2) analytical review procedures.

(3) tests of details of balances.

(4) none of the above. (CICA adapted)

DISCUSSION QUESTIONS AND PROBLEMS

12–26 a. In each of the following independent problems, design an unbiased random sampling plan using the random number table in Table 12–2. The plan should include defining the sampling unit, establishing a numbering system for the population, and establishing a correspondence between the random number table and the population. After the plan has been designed, select the first five sample items from the random number table for each problem. Use a starting point of item 1009, column 1, for each problem. Read down the table using the leftmost digits in the column. When you reach the last item in a column, start at the top of the next column.

    1. Prenumbered sales invoices in a sales journal where the lowest invoice number is one and the highest is 6211.

    2. Prenumbered bills of lading where the lowest document number is 21926 and the highest is 28511.

    3. Accounts receivable on 10 pages with 60 lines per page except the last page, which has only 36 full lines. Each line has a customer name and an amount receivable.

    4. Prenumbered invoices in a sales journal where each month starts over with number one. (Invoices for each month are designated by the month and document number.) There are a maximum of 20 pages per month with a total of 185 pages for the year. All pages have 75 invoices except for the last page for each month.

b. Write a computer program in BASIC, or use an available random number generator, to obtain the above samples with the microcomputer (instructor option).

12–27 You desire a random sample of 80 sales invoices for the examination of supporting documents. The invoices range from numbers one to 9500 for the period January 1 through December 31. There are 128 pages of sales invoices numbered one through 128. Each page has 75 lines, but the last page in each month sometimes has a few less.

Required:

a. Design four different methods of selecting random numbers from the above population using a random number table or systematic sampling.

b. Which method do you consider the most desirable? Why?

12–28 Lenter Supply Corp. is a medium-sized distributor of wholesale hardware supplies in southern Manitoba. It has been a client of yours for several years and has instituted excellent internal control for the control of sales at your recommendation.

    In providing control over shipments, the client has prenumbered "warehouse removal slips" that are used for every sale. It is company policy never to remove goods from the warehouse without an authorized warehouse removal slip. After shipment, two copies of the warehouse removal slip are sent to billing for the computerized preparation of a sales invoice. One copy is stapled to the duplicate copy of a prenumbered sales invoice, and the other copy is filed numerically. In some cases more than one warehouse removal slip is used for billing one sales invoice. The smallest warehouse removal slip number for the year is 14682 and the largest is 37521. The smallest sales invoice number is 47821 and the largest is 68507.

    In the audit of sales, one of the major concerns is the effectiveness of the controls in making sure all shipments are billed. The auditor has decided to use attributes sampling in testing internal control.

Required:

a. State an effective audit procedure for testing whether shipments have been billed. What is the sampling unit for the audit procedure?

b. Assuming that the auditor expects no deviations in the sample but is willing to accept a tolerable deviation rate of 3 percent, at a 10 percent risk of overreliance, what is the appropriate sample size for the audit test?

c. Design a random selection plan for selecting the sample from the population using the random number table. Select the first ten sample items from Table 12–2. Use a starting point of item 1013, column 3.

d. Your supervisor suggests the possibility of performing other sales tests with the same sample as a means of efficiently using your audit time. List two other audit procedures that could conveniently be performed using the same sample and state the purpose of each of the procedures.

e. Is it desirable to test the validity of sales with the random sample you have designed in part c? Why?

12–29 The following is a partial audit program for the audit of cash receipts.

1. Review the cash receipts journal for large and unusual transactions.
2. Trace entries from the prelisting of cash receipts to the cash receipts journal to determine if each is recorded.
3. Compare customer name, date, and amount on the prelisting with the cash receipts journal.
4. Examine the related remittance advice for entries selected from the prelisting to determine if cash discounts were approved.
5. Trace entries from the prelisting to the deposit slip to determine if each has been deposited.

Required:

a. Identify which audit procedures could be tested using attributes sampling.

b. What is the appropriate sampling unit for the tests in part a?

c. List the attributes for testing in part a.

d. Assume an acceptable risk of overreliance of 5 percent and a tolerable deviation rate of 8 percent for tests of controls. The estimated population deviation rate for tests of controls is 2 percent. Calculate the initial sample size for each attribute.

12–30 The following questions concern the determination of the proper sample size in attributes sampling using the following table:

	1	2	3	4	5	6	7
Acceptable risk of overreliance (in percentage)	10	5	5	5	10	10	5
Tolerable deviation rate (in percentage)	6	6	5	6	20	20	2
Estimated population deviation rate (in percentage)	2	2	2	2	5	2	0
Population size	1,000	100,000	6,000	1,000	500	500	1,000,000

Required:

a. For each of the columns numbered 1 through 7, determine the initial sample size needed to satisfy the auditor's requirements from the appropriate part of Table 12–6. Whenever the sample size is more than 10 percent of the population, adjust it with the finite correction factor.

b. Using your understanding of the relationship between the foregoing factors and sample size, state the effect on the initial sample size (increase or decrease) of changing each of the following factors while the other three are held constant:

(1) An increase in acceptable risk of overreliance

(2) An increase in the tolerable deviation rate

(3) An increase in the estimated population deviation rate

(4) An increase in the population size

c. Explain why there is such a large difference in the sample sizes for columns 3 and 6.

d. Compare your answers in part b with the results you determined in part a. Which of the four factors appears to have the greatest effect on the initial sample size? Which one appears to have the least effect?

e. Why is the sample size referred to as the initial sample size?

12–31 The questions below relate to determining the computed upper deviation rate in attributes sampling using the following table:

	1	2	3	4	5	6	7	8
Acceptable risk of overreliance (in percentage)	10	5	5	5	5	5	5	5
Population size	5,000	5,000	5,000	50,000	500	900	5,000	500
Sample size	200	200	50	200	100	100	100	25
Number of deviations	4	4	1	4	2	10	0	0

Required:

a. For each of the columns 1 through 8, determine the computed upper deviation rate from the appropriate table. Adjust the computed upper deviation rate with the finite correction factor if the sample size exceeds 10 percent of the population.

b. Using your understanding of the relationship between the four factors above and the computed upper deviation rate, state the effect on the computed upper deviation rate (increase or decrease) of changing each of the following factors while the other three are held constant:

(1) A decrease in the acceptable risk of overreliance

(2) A decrease in the population size

(3) A decrease in the sample size

(4) A decrease in the number of deviations in the sample

c. Compare your answers in part b with the results you determined in part a. Which of the factors appears to have the greatest effect on the computed upper deviation rate? Which one appears to have the least effect?

d. Why is it necessary to compare the computed upper deviation rate with the tolerable deviation rate?

12–32 The following are auditor judgments and audit sampling results for six populations. Assume large population sizes.

	1	2	3	4	5	6
Estimated population deviation rate (in percentage)	2	0	3	1	1	8
Tolerable deviation rate (in percentage)	6	3	8	5	20	15
Acceptable risk of overreliance on internal control (in percentage)	5	5	10	5	10	10
Actual sample size	100	100	60	100	20	60
Actual number of deviations in the sample	2	0	1	4	1	8

Required:

a. For each population, did the auditor select a smaller sample size than is indicated by using the tables for determining sample size? Evaluate selecting either a larger or smaller size than those determined in the tables.

b. Calculate the sample deviation rate and computed upper deviation rate for each population.

c. For which of the six populations should the sample results be considered unacceptable? What options are available to the auditor?

d. Why is analysis of the deviations necessary even when the populations are considered acceptable?

e. For the following terms, identify which is an audit decision, a nonstatistical estimate made by the auditor, a sample result, and a statistical conclusion about the population:

(1) Estimated population deviation rate
(2) Tolerable deviation rate
(3) Acceptable risk of overreliance on internal control
(4) Actual sample size
(5) Actual number of deviations in the sample
(6) Sample deviation rate
(7) Computed upper deviation rate

12–33 For the examination of the financial statements of Scotia Inc., Rosa Schellenberg, a public accountant, has decided to apply attributes sampling in the tests of sales transactions. Based on her knowledge of Scotia's operations in the area of sales, she decides that the estimated population deviation rate is likely to be 3 percent and that she is willing to accept a 5 percent risk that the true deviation rate is not greater than 6 percent. Given this information, Schellenberg selects a random sample of 150 sales invoices from the 5,000 written during the year and examines them for exceptions. She notes the following exceptions in her work papers. There is no other documentation.

INVOICE NO.	COMMENT
5028	Sales invoice was originally footed incorrectly but was corrected by client before the bill was sent out.
6791	Voided sales invoice examined by auditor.
6810	Shipping document for a sale of merchandise could not be located.
7364	Sales invoice for $2,875 has not been collected and is six months past due.
7625	Client unable to locate the duplicate sales invoice.
8431	Invoice was dated three days later than the date entered in the sales journal.
8528	Customer order is not attached to the duplicate sales invoice.
8566	Billing is for $100 less than it should be due to a pricing error. No indication of internal verification is included on the invoice.
8780	Client unable to locate the duplicate sales invoice.
9169	Credit not authorized, but the sale was for only $7.65.
9974	Lack of indication of internal verification of price extensions and postings of sales invoice.

Required:

a. Which of the preceding should be defined as an exception?

b. Explain why it is inappropriate to set a single acceptable tolerable deviation rate and estimated population deviation rate for the combined errors.

c. For each attribute in the population that is tested, determine the computed upper deviation rate assuming a 5 percent acceptable risk of overreliance for each attribute. (You must decide which attributes should be combined, which should be kept separate, and which exceptions are actual exceptions before you can determine the computed upper deviation rate.)

d. State the appropriate analysis of deviations for each of the exceptions in the sample.

12–34 In performing tests of controls over sales transactions for Verdun Ltee., a hardware retailer, Claude Armand, a public accountant, is concerned with the internal verification of pricing, extensions, and footings of sales invoices and the accuracy of the calculations. In testing sales using attributes sampling, he is using separate attributes to test the existence of internal verification and the accuracy of calculation. Since internal controls are considered good, Armand uses a 10 percent acceptable risk of overreliance, a zero estimated population deviation rate, and a 5 percent tolerable deviation rate for both attributes; therefore, the initial sample size is 45 items which he rounded up to 50.

In conducting the tests, Armand finds three sample items for which there was no indication of internal verification on the sales invoice, but no sales invoices tested in the sample had a financial error.

Required:
a. Determine the computed upper deviation rate for both the attributes, assuming a population of 5,000 sales invoices.

b. Compare the computed upper deviation rate with the tolerable deviation rate.

c. Discuss the most desirable course of action the auditor should follow in deciding the effect of the computed upper deviation rate exceeding the tolerable deviation rate.

d. Which type of deviation analysis is appropriate in this case?

CASE

12–35 For the audit of St. John's Supply Corp., Carole Wever, a public accountant, is conducting a test of sales for nine months of the year ended December 31, 19X8. Included among her audit procedures are the following:

1. Foot and crossfoot the sales journal and trace the balance to the general ledger.

2. Review all sales transactions for reasonableness.

3. Select a sample of recorded sales from the sales journal and trace the customer name and amounts to duplicate sales invoices and the related shipping document.

4. Select a sample of shipping document numbers and perform the following tests:

   (a) Trace the shipping document to the related duplicate sales invoice.
   (b) Examine the duplicate sales invoice to determine whether a copy of the shipping document, shipping order, and customer order are attached.
   (c) Examine the shipping order for an authorized credit approval.
   (d) Examine the duplicate sales invoice for an indication of internal verification of quantity, price, extensions, footings, and tracing the balance to the accounts receivable master file.
   (e) Compare the price on the duplicate sales invoice with the approved price list and the quantity with the shipping document.
   (f) Trace the balance in the duplicate sales invoice to the sales journal and accounts receivable master file for customer name, amount, and date.

Required:
a. For which of these procedures could attributes sampling be conveniently used?

b. Considering the audit procedures Wever has developed, what is the most appropriate sampling unit for conducting most of the attributes sampling tests?

c. Set up an attributes sampling data sheet. For each test of controls, assume a tolerable deviation rate of 5 percent and an estimated population deviation rate of one percent. Use a 10 percent acceptable risk of overreliance.

    d. For the audit procedures not included in the attributes sampling test in part c, describe appropriate nonstatistical sampling procedures to determine the items to include in the sample.

INTEGRATED CASE APPLICATION

12–36 *ABC AUDIT – PART III*

    In Part II of the ABC Integrated Application Case audit application, a tests of controls audit program was designed for acquisitions and cash disbursements. In Part III, sample sizes will be determined using attributes sampling and the results of the tests will be evaluated.

    a. Use the performance format audit program you prepared for acquisitions and cash disbursements from Problem 11–34 to prepare an attributes sampling data sheet. Use Figure 12–3 as a frame of reference for preparing the data sheet. Complete all parts of the data sheet except those parts that are blank in Figure 12–3. Use the following additional information to complete this requirement:

        1. Prepare only one attributes sampling data sheet.

        2. Decide the appropriate sampling unit and select all audit procedures that are appropriate for that sampling unit from the performance format audit program you prepared in Problem 11–34.

        3. Use judgment in deciding EPDR, TDR and ARO for each attribute. Assume planned assessed control risk is low for each procedure.

    b. Design a random sample plan using a table of random numbers for the attribute with the largest sample size in requirement a. Select the first ten random numbers using Table 12–2. Document the design and ten numbers selected using documentation similar to that in Figure 12–4.

    c. Assume you performed all audit procedures included in Problem 11–34 using the sample sizes in Problem 12–36. The only exceptions found when you performed the tests were one missing indication of internal verification on a vendor's invoice, one acquisition of inventory transaction recorded for $200.00 more than the amount stated in the vendor's invoice (the vendor was also overpaid by $200), and one vendor invoice recorded as an acquisition eighteen days after the receipt of the goods. Complete the attributes sample data sheet prepared in part a. Use Figure 12–6 as a frame of reference for completing the data sheet.

13

COMPLETING THE TESTS IN THE SALES AND COLLECTION CYCLE: ACCOUNTS RECEIVABLE

LEARNING OBJECTIVES

THOROUGH STUDY OF THIS CHAPTER WILL ENABLE YOU TO:

1. Relate results of tests of controls for sales to tests of details of balances for accounts receivable

2. Describe the relationship between control objectives and audit objectives in the sales and collection cycle

3. Design and perform analytical procedures for accounts in the sales and collection cycle

4. Design and perform tests of details of accounts receivable

5. Obtain and evaluate accounts receivable confirmations

6. Integrate into the audit plan all evidence obtained regarding controls, transactions, and accounts in the sales and collection cycle

☐ Chapter 13 is concerned with the analytical procedures and tests of details of balances for the accounts in the sales and collection cycle and the relationship of those tests to the assessment of control risk and tests of controls. The primary account covered is accounts receivable. There is also a discussion of auditing allowance for uncollectible accounts and the income statement accounts in the cycle. The specific objectives for tests of details of balances presented in Chapter 10 are the frame of reference used to discuss the audit tests for accounts receivable. Confirmation of accounts receivable, which is the most important test of details of balances for accounts receivable, receives particular emphasis.

Before examining a methodology for completing the audit of the sales and collection cycle, a brief review of the tests of the cycle that were discussed in previous chapters is appropriate. These tests have a direct effect on the evidence needed to complete the audit of the cycle.

To help the reader maintain perspective, refer again to Figure 10–10 on page 338. Tests of controls for the sales and collection cycle, which were studied in Chapters 11 and 12, are phase II in Figure 10–10. Tests of details of balances for the sales and collection cycle, which are studied here, are phase III.

Tests of Controls

OBJECTIVE 1

Relate results of tests of controls for sales to tests of details of balances for accounts receivable.

The overall objective in auditing the sales and collection cycle is to evaluate whether sales, sales returns and allowances, bad-debt expense, accounts receivable, allowance for uncollectible accounts, and cash receipts are properly reflected in the financial records in accordance with the tests of controls and tests of details of balances objectives discussed in earlier chapters. The emphasis in Chapters 11 and 12 was on obtaining an understanding of the client's internal control and assessing control risk, primarily through tests of controls. Examine Figure 11–3 on page 358. The last two chapters dealt primarily with the methodology for designing tests of controls for sales and cash receipts. The understanding of the client's internal control comes about through flowcharting the client's sales and collection cycle, completing an internal control questionnaire, and tracing one or two transactions through the system from the customer's order to the collection of cash. The initial assessment of control risk is normally accomplished by relating the seven objectives of internal control to the flowchart and internal control questionnaire, and to the internal control procedures in order to identify controls and weaknesses in the system. The tests of controls for the cycle enable the auditor to decide on the appropriate assessed level of control risk and to evaluate the correctness of the dollar amounts in the records.

In accumulating evidence for tests of controls, the importance of modifying the evidence for the circumstances of the audit cannot be overemphasized. The determination of the proper audit procedures, timing of the tests, sample size, and particular items to include in the sample can only be made after a careful analysis of internal control and the other relevant factors in the engagement. The decision making involved in this process is one of the most important aspects of auditing.

Audit Procedures

Tests of controls procedures for testing internal control effectiveness need to be performed when the auditor intends to assess control risk below maximum and thereby reduce planned substantive procedures. Whether or not to perform tests of controls is a cost-benefit question and should be decided on the basis of a comparison of the cost of testing internal controls with the savings if substantive procedures are reduced.

The auditor may wish to perform substantive procedures at the time tests of controls are performed; that is, to perform dual-purpose tests that were discussed in Chapter 9. The purpose of the substantive procedure would be to determine the magnitude of any misstatements in the recording of transactions and balances.

Sample Size

Three major factors affect the number of sample items for tests of controls: the deviation rate the auditor is willing to accept in the population, the deviation rate expected in the population, and the risk the auditor is willing to take that the sample will not be representative of the population.[1] The first factor concerns materiality. The second is based primarily on previous years' experience with the client. The risk factor is affected by the extent to which the auditor plans to assess control risk below maximum and the overall audit risk the auditor considers appropriate. Population size has some effect on sample size, but it is generally not significant in transactions testing.

When internal control is believed to be of high quality, the auditor should ordinarily use a low risk of overreliance for tests of controls. The result is an increased sample size for tests of controls.

Items to Select

In tests of controls, it is essential to obtain a representative sample. Therefore, random selection is generally desirable and is required when statistical methods are used. However, if the auditor observes unusual transactions or amounts, they should be investigated even if they are not included in the random sample. In addition, many auditors believe it is important to review all large transactions.

Timing

The auditor can decide to do tests of controls at an interim date or wait until after year-end. Interim tests are performed to aid in finishing the audit soon after the balance sheet date because of client preferences and to help the public accounting firm spread its work load throughout the year.

Interim testing is always acceptable, but it may be necessary to do extensive testing of transactions occurring between the interim and balance sheet dates. Factors reducing the amount of the additional evidence required include satisfactory test results in the interim tests, a short interval between the interim and balance sheet dates, and no changes in internal control after the interim date.

Relationship Between Internal Control and Audit Objectives

Several previous chapters have illustrated the difference between internal control objectives and audit objectives. Auditors use internal control objectives to determine internal controls and weaknesses, decide tests of controls, and evaluate the results of those tests. Audit objectives are used to decide analytical procedures and tests of details of balances for accounts such as accounts receivable and to evaluate the results of those tests.

When the auditor makes evidence decisions using audit objectives for analytical procedures and tests of details of balances, the results of the tests of controls must be thought of in terms of audit objectives, not internal control objectives. Figure 13–1 shows one way auditors use the results of internal control objectives to satisfy audit objectives. Three classes of transactions are shown to

---

OBJECTIVE 2
Describe the relationship between control objectives and audit objectives in the sales and collection cycle.

---

1 For attributes sampling, these are referred to as tolerable deviation rate, expected population deviation rate, and acceptable risk of overreliance on internal control.

FIGURE 13–1

Relationship Between Internal Control and Audit Objectives for the Sales and Collection Cycle

CLASS OF TRANSACTION	INTERNAL CONTROL OBJECTIVES	ACCOUNTS RECEIVABLE AUDIT OBJECTIVES							
		Validity	Ownership	Completeness	Valuation	Classification	Cutoff	Mechanical Accuracy	Disclosure
Sales	Validity	X	X						
	Authorization	X	X		X				
	Completeness			X					
	Valuation				X				
	Classification					X			X
	Timing						X		
	Posting and summarization							X	
Sales Returns and Allowances	Validity			X					
	Authorization				X				
	Completeness	X							
	Valuation				X				
	Classification					X			
	Timing						X		
	Posting and summarization							X	
Collections	Validity			X					
	Authorization				X				
	Completeness	X							
	Valuation				X				
	Classification					X			
	Timing						X		
	Posting and summarization							X	

affect accounts receivable in Figure 13–1. For many audits sales returns and allowances are immaterial and can be ignored. Several observations follow:

- It is evident from Figure 13–1 that whereas most internal control objectives relate to only one accounts receivable audit objective, that is not always the case. For example, the authorization internal control objective for sales affects three audit objectives.

TABLE 13–1

Analytical Procedures for Sales and Collections

ANALYTICAL PROCEDURE	POSSIBLE MISSTATEMENT
Compare gross margin percentage with previous years (by product line).	Overstatement or understatement of sales.
Compare sales by month (by product line) over time.	Overstatement or understatement of sales.
Compare sales returns and allowances as a percentage of gross sales with previous years (by product line).	Overstatement or understatement of sales returns and allowances.
Compare individual customer balances over a stated amount with previous years.	Misstatements in accounts receivable.
Compare bad debt expense as a percentage of gross sales with previous years.	Uncollectible accounts receivable that have not been provided for.
Compare number of days accounts receivable outstanding with previous years.	Overstatement or understatement of allowance for uncollectible accounts.
Compare aging categories as a percentage of accounts receivable with previous years.	Overstatement or understatement of allowance for uncollectible accounts.
Compare allowance for uncollectible accounts as a percentage of accounts receivable with previous years.	Overstatement or understatement of allowance for uncollectible accounts.

■ For sales, the validity internal control objective affects the validity audit objective, but for sales returns and allowances and collections the validity internal control objective affects the completeness audit objective. A similar relationship exists for the completeness internal control objective. The reason for this somewhat surprising conclusion is that an increase of sales increases accounts receivable, but an increase of sales returns and allowances or collections decreases accounts receivable. For example, recording a sale that did not occur violates the validity internal control objective and validity audit objective (both overstatements). Recording a cash receipt that did not occur violates the validity internal control objective, but it violates the completeness audit objective for accounts receivable, because a receivable that is still outstanding is no longer included in the records.

■ The measurement of audit assurance for audit objectives in accounts receivable obtained through the tests of controls is highly subjective. For example, assume the auditor did extensive tests of controls for the sales valuation objective, but almost none for the valuation objective for collections and sales returns and allowances. The auditor would need to subjectively determine the affect of the tests of control in all three areas on the valuation objective for accounts receivable.

Analytical Procedures

After the auditor has completed the study of the client's internal control, assessed control risk, and performed tests of controls, it is appropriate to design and perform *analytical procedures*. Analytical procedures are normally performed after the balance sheet date but before the tests of details of balances audit procedures are finalized or performed. Typical accounts that concern the auditor in performing analytical procedures for the sales and collection cycle are shown in Figure 11–1 on page 353. Income statement and balance sheet accounts are examined concurrently for reasonableness using analytical procedures and receive equal attention.

Table 13–1 presents examples of the major types of ratios and comparisons for the sales and collection cycle and potential misstatements that may be indi-

OBJECTIVE 3

Design and perform analytical procedures for accounts in sales and collection cycle.

cated by the analytical procedures. The results of the analytical procedures should affect the auditor's decisions about the extent of tests of details of balances needed for accounts receivable.

In addition to the analytical procedure in Table 13–1, there should also be a review of accounts receivable for large and unusual amounts. Individual receivables that deserve special attention are large balances, accounts that have been outstanding for a long time, receivables from affiliated companies, officers, directors, and other related parties, and credit balances. The auditor should review the listing of accounts (aged trial balance) at the balance sheet date to determine which accounts should be investigated further.

Tests of Details of Balances

OBJECTIVE 4

Design and perform tests of details of accounts receivable.

Tests of details of balances for all cycles emphasize balance sheet accounts. Income statement accounts are not ignored, but they are verified more as a byproduct of the balance sheet tests than by detailed testing. For the sales and collection cycle the most important account is accounts receivable, but the allowance for uncollectible accounts is also tested.

The methodology for deciding which tests of details of balances to perform was discussed in Chapter 10. Figure 13–2 summarizes the methodology for accounts receivable, which is usually the major balance sheet account in the sales and collection cycle. The purpose of the methodology is to help the auditor decide on the appropriate audit procedures, sample size, items to select, and timing of the tests of accounts receivable. Some auditors allocate materiality to segments once they have determined materiality available for unanticipated misstatements; this is done at the same time that audit risk and inherent risk are assessed (first box in Figure 13–2). They use the amounts allocated to determine sample sizes and the amount of testing required. However, *most* auditors use the entire amount of materiality available for unanticipated misstatements in audit planning on the grounds that the auditor is concerned about the aggregate misstatement in the financial statements as a whole and not in the misstatement in a particular account balance.

Figure 13–2 is slightly different from Figure 10–7 on page 333 because of differences in assumptions about when the tests of details of balances were designed. In Figure 10–7, the tests of details were designed before tests of controls and analytical procedures were performed. In Figure 13–2, the tests of details were designed after the other tests were completed. Figure 13–2 stresses that the design of tests of details for accounts receivable is done only after all of the preceding items have been completed.

The section that follows discusses tests of details of balances for accounts receivable and the allowance for uncollectible accounts. The tests of details are discussed by reference to the eight audit objectives introduced in Chapter 5. These objectives for accounts receivable are[2]

- Accounts receivable are mechanically accurate.
- Accounts receivable are valid.
- Existing accounts receivable are included.
- Accounts receivable are owned.
- Accounts receivable are properly valued.

2 "Accounts receivable are mechanically accurate" is included as the first objective here, compared with being included as objective seven in chapter 5, because tests for mechanical accuracy are normally done first.

FIGURE 13–2

Methodology for
Designing Tests of
Details of Balances for
Accounts Receivable

(handwritten: ① Analytical Proces)
(handwritten: ② Test of Retail of Bal)

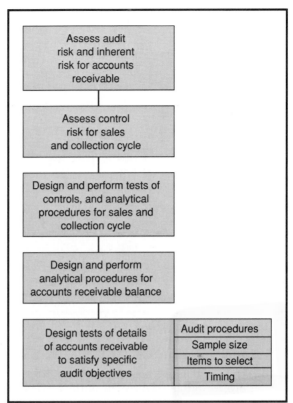

- Accounts receivable are properly classified.
- Transactions are recorded in the proper period. *(handwritten: — Cut off)*
- Accounts receivable disclosures are proper.

Confirmation of accounts receivable is the most important test of details of accounts receivable. Confirmation is discussed briefly in studying the appropriate tests for each of the audit objectives, then separately in more detail.

Accounts Receivable Are Mechanically Accurate

Most tests of accounts receivable and the allowance for uncollectible accounts are based on the *aged trial balance*. An aged trial balance is a listing of the balances in the accounts receivable master file at the balance sheet date. It includes the individual total balances outstanding and a breakdown of each balance by the time passed between the date of sale and the balance sheet date. An illustration of a typical aged trial balance, in this case for Hillsburg Hardware Ltd., is given in Figure 13–3. Notice that the total is the same as accounts receivable on the general ledger trial balance on page 135.

Testing the information on the aged trial balance for mechanical accuracy is a necessary audit procedure. It is ordinarily done before any other tests to assure the auditor that the population being tested agrees with the general and subsidiary ledgers. The total column and the columns depicting the aging must be test footed, and the total on the trial balance compared to the general ledger. In

FIGURE 13–3 Aged Trial Balance for Hillsburg Hardware Ltd.

			Aging, Based on Invoice Date				
	Hillsburg Hardware Ltd. Accounts Receivable Aged Trial Balance 12/31/X8		Schedule Prepared by Client Approved by	Date 1/5/X9			
Account Number	Customer	Balance 12/31/X8	0-30 days	31-60 days	61-90 days	91-120 days	over 120
01011	Adams Supply Ltd.	7,329	4,511	2,818			
01044	Argonaut, Inc.	1,542	1,542				
01100	Atwater Brothers	10,519	10,519				
01191	Beekman Bearings Corp.	4,176	3,676		500		
01270	Brown and Phillips	3,000				3,000	
01301	Christopher Plumbing Ltd.	789					789
09733	Travelers Equipment Ltd.	2,976	2,976				
09742	Underhill Parts and Maintenance	8,963	8,963				
09810	UJW Co. Ltd.	5,111	1,811	1,700	1,600		
09907	Zephyr Plastics Corp.	14,300	9,300	5,000			
		1,009,800	785,856	128,466	55,432	34,446	5,600

addition, a sample of individual balances should be traced to supporting documents such as duplicate sales invoices to verify the customer name, balance, and proper aging. The extent of the testing for mechanical accuracy depends on the number of accounts involved and the degree to which the master file has been tested as a part of tests of controls and the extent to which the schedule has been verified by an internal auditor or other independent person before it is given to the auditor.

Accounts Receivable Are Valid

The most important test of details of balances for determining the validity of recorded accounts receivable is the confirmation of customers' balances. When customers do not respond to confirmations, auditors also examine supporting documents to verify the shipment of goods and evidence of subsequent cash receipts to determine whether the accounts were collected. Normally, auditors do not examine shipping documents or evidence of subsequent cash receipts for any account in the sample that is confirmed, but these documents are used extensively as alternative evidence for nonresponses.

Existing Accounts Receivable Are Included

It is difficult to test for account balances omitted from the aged trial balance except by relying on the self-balancing nature of the accounts receivable master file. For example, if the client decided to exclude an account receivable from the trial balance to deceive the auditor, the only likely way it would be discovered is by footing the accounts receivable trial balance and reconciling the balance with the control account in the general ledger.

If all sales to a customer are omitted from the sales journal, the understatement of accounts receivable is almost impossible to uncover by tests of details of balances. The understatement of sales and accounts receivable is best uncovered by tests of controls for shipments made but not recorded (completeness objective for tests of controls) and by analytical procedures.

Accounts Receivable Are Owned

The ownership of accounts receivable ordinarily causes no audit problems because the receivables usually belong to the client, but in some cases a portion of the receivables may have been factored or sold at discount. Generally, the client's customers are not aware of the existence of discounting; therefore, the confirmation of receivables will not bring it to light. A review of the minutes, discussions with the client, confirmation with banks, and the examination of correspondence files are usually sufficient to uncover instances in which the receivables are not owned.

Accounts Receivable Are Properly Valued

Confirmation of the gross value of accounts selected from the trial balance is the most common test of details of balances for valuation of accounts receivable. When customers do not respond to confirmation requests, auditors examine supporting documents, in the same way as described for the validity objective. Tests of the debits and credits to particular customers' balances are done by examining supporting documentation for shipments and collections.

Allowance for uncollectible accounts   A second part of the valuation objective for accounts receivable is determining the *realizable value* of the outstanding balances; that is, the amount that will ultimately be collected. The client's estimate of the total amount that is uncollectible is represented by the allowance for uncollectible accounts. Although it is not possible to predict the future precisely, it is necessary for the auditor to evaluate whether the allowance is reasonable considering all available facts.

The starting point for the evaluation of the allowance for uncollectible accounts is to review the results of the tests of internal control that are concerned with the client's credit policy. If the client's credit policy has remained unchanged and the results of the tests of credit policy and credit approval are consistent with those of the preceding year, the change in the balance in the allowance for uncollectible accounts should reflect only changes in economic conditions and sales volume. However, if the client's credit policy or the degree to which it correctly functions has significantly changed, great care must be taken to consider the effects of these changes as well.

A common way to evaluate the adequacy of the allowance is to examine carefully the noncurrent accounts on the aged trial balance to determine which ones have not been paid subsequent to the balance sheet date. The size and age of unpaid balances can then be compared with similar information from previous years to evaluate whether the amount of noncurrent receivables is increasing or decreasing over time. The examination of credit files, discussions with the credit manager, and review of the client's correspondence file may also provide insights into the collectibility of the accounts. These procedures are especially important if a few large balances are noncurrent and are not being paid on a regular basis.

There are two pitfalls in evaluating the allowance by reviewing individual noncurrent balances on the aged trial balance. First, the current accounts are ignored in establishing the adequacy of the allowance even though some of these amounts will undoubtedly become uncollectible. Second, it is difficult to compare the results of the current year with those of previous years on such an unstructured basis. If the accounts are becoming progressively uncollectible over a period of several years, this fact could be overlooked. A way to avoid these difficulties is to establish the history of bad debt charge-offs over a period of time as a frame of reference for evaluating the current year's allowance. As an example, if historically a certain percentage of the total of each age category becomes uncollectible, it is relatively easy to compute whether the allowance is properly stated. If 2 percent of current accounts, 10 percent of 30-to 90-day accounts, and 35 percent of all balances over 90 days ultimately become uncollectible, these percentages can easily be applied to the current year's aged trial balance totals and the result compared with the balance in the allowance account. Of course, the auditor has to be careful to modify the calculations for changed conditions.

Bad debt expense After the auditor is satisfied with the allowance for uncollectible accounts, it is easy to verify bad debt expense. Assume that (1) the beginning balance was verified as a part of the previous audit, (2) the uncollectible accounts charged off were verified as a part of the tests of controls, and (3) the ending balance in the allowance account has been verified by various means. Then bad debt expense is simply a residual balance that can be verified by a mechanical test.

Accounts Receivable Are Properly Classified

It is normally relatively easy to evaluate the classification of accounts receivable by reviewing the aged trial balance for material receivables from affiliates, officers, directors, or other related parties. If notes receivable or accounts that should not be classified as a current asset are included with the regular accounts these should also be segregated. Finally, if the credit balances in accounts receivable are significant, it is appropriate to reclassify them as accounts payable.

There is a close relationship between the classification objective as discussed here and the disclosure objective. Classification concerns determining whether the client has correctly separated different classifications of accounts receivable. Disclosure concerns making sure the classifications are properly presented. For example, under the classification objective, the auditor determines if receivables from related parties have been separated on the aged trial balance. Under the disclosure objective, the auditor determines if related-party transactions are correctly shown in the financial statements.

Transactions Are Recorded in the Proper Period

Cutoff errors can occur for *sales, sales returns and allowances,* and *cash receipts.* They take place when current period transactions are recorded in the subsequent period or subsequent period transactions are recorded in the current period.

The objective of cutoff tests is the same regardless of the type of transaction, but the procedures vary. The objective is to verify whether transactions near the end of the accounting period are recorded in the proper period. The cutoff objective is one of the most important in the cycle because errors in cutoff can significantly affect current period income. For example, the intentional or unintentional inclusion of several large, subsequent period sales in the current period or the exclusion of several current-period sales returns and allowances can materially overstate net earnings.

In determining the reasonableness of cutoff, a threefold approach is needed: first, decide on the appropriate *criteria for cutoff*; second, evaluate whether the client has established *adequate procedures* to ensure a reasonable cutoff; and third, *test* whether a reasonable cutoff was obtained.

Sales cutoff The criterion used by most clients for determining when a sale takes place is the *shipment of goods*, but some companies record invoices at the time title passes. The passage of title can take place before shipment (as in the case of custom-manufactured goods), at the time of shipment, or subsequent to shipment. For the correct measurement of current-period income, the method must be in accordance with generally accepted accounting principles and consistently applied.

The most important part of evaluating the client's method of obtaining a reliable cutoff is to determine the procedures in use. When a client issues prenumbered shipping documents sequentially, it is usually a simple matter to evaluate and test cutoff. Moreover, the segregation of duties between the shipping and the billing function also enhances the likelihood of recording transactions in the proper period. However, if shipments are made by company truck, the shipping records are not numbered, and shipping and billing department personnel are not independent of each other, it may be difficult, if not impossible, to be assured of an accurate cutoff.

When the client's internal control is adequate, the cutoff can usually be verified by obtaining the shipping document number for the last shipment made at the end of the period and comparing this number with current and subsequent period recorded sales. As an illustration, assume the shipping document number for the last shipment in the current period is 1489. All recorded sales before the end of the period should bear a shipping document number preceding number 1490. There should also be no sales recorded in the subsequent period for a shipment with a bill of lading numbered 1489 or lower. This can easily be tested by comparing recorded sales with the related shipping document for the last few days of the current period and the first few days of the subsequent period.

If internal control is unusual or inadequate, it is necessary to understand it thoroughly before cutoff tests are determined. In extreme circumstances, the auditor may need to physically observe shipments and control documents near the end of the period.

Sales returns and allowances cutoff Generally accepted accounting principles require that sales returns and allowances be *matched with related sales* if the amounts are material. For example, if current period shipments are returned in the subsequent period, the proper treatment of the transactions is the inclusion of the sales return in the current period. (The returned goods would be treated as current period inventory.) For most companies, however, sales returns and allowances are recorded in the *accounting period in which they occur,* under the assumption of approximately equal, offsetting errors at the beginning and end of each accounting period. This is acceptable as long as the amounts are not significant.

When the auditor is confident that the client records all sales returns and allowances promptly, the cutoff tests are simple and straightforward. The auditor can examine supporting documentation for a sample of sales returns and allowances recorded during several weeks subsequent to the closing date to determine the date of the original sale. If the amounts recorded in the subsequent period are significantly different from unrecorded returns and allowances at the beginning of the period under audit, an adjustment must be considered. If internal control for recording sales returns and allowances is evaluated as ineffective, a larger sample is needed to verify cutoff.

Cash receipts cutoff For most audits a proper cash receipts cutoff is *less important* than either the sales or the sales returns and allowances cutoff because the improper cutoff of cash affects only the cash and the accounts receivable balances, not earnings. Nevertheless, if the misstatement is material, it could affect the fair presentation of these accounts, particularly when cash is a small or negative balance.

It is easy to test for a cash receipts cutoff error (frequently referred to as *holding the cash receipts book open*) by tracing recorded cash receipts to subsequent period bank deposits on the bank statement. If there is a delay of several days, this could indicate a cutoff error.

The confirmation of accounts receivable may also be relied on to some degree to uncover cutoff errors for sales, sales returns and allowances, and cash receipts, especially when there is a long interval between the date the transaction took place and the recording date. However, when the interval is only a few days, mail delivery delays may cause confusion of cutoff errors with normal reconciliation differences. For example, if a customer mails and records a cheque to a client for payment of an unpaid account on December 30 and the client receives and records the amount on January 2, the records of the two organizations will be different on December 31. This is not a cutoff error, but a *reconcilable difference* due to the delivery time; it will be difficult for the auditor to evaluate whether a cutoff error or a normal reconciling item occurred when a confirmation reply is the source of information.

Accounts Receivable Disclosures Are Proper

In addition to testing for the proper statement of the dollar amount in the general ledger, the auditor must also determine that information about the account balance resulting from the sales and collection cycle is properly disclosed in the financial statements. The auditor must decide whether the client has properly combined amounts and disclosed related-party information in the statements. To evaluate the adequacy of the disclosure, the auditor must have a thorough understanding of generally accepted accounting principles and disclosure requirements.

An important part of the evaluation involves deciding whether material amounts requiring separate disclosure have actually been separated in the statements. For example, Sections 3020.01 and 3840 of the *CICA Handbook* require that receivables from officers and affiliated companies be segregated from accounts receivable from customers if the amounts are material. Similarly, under Section 1700, it is necessary for companies over a certain size to disclose information about revenues, operations, and assets for different segments of the business as well as information about export sales.

The proper aggregation of general ledger balances in the financial statements also requires combining account balances that are not relevant for external users of the statements. If all accounts included in the general ledger were disclosed separately on the statements, most statement users would be more confused than enlightened.

As a part of proper disclosure, the auditor is also required to evaluate the adequacy of the *footnotes*. One of the major lawsuits in the history of the profession, the *Continental Vending* case, discussed in Chapter 4, revolved primarily around the adequacy of the footnote disclosure of a major receivable from an affiliated company. The required footnote disclosure includes information about the pledging, discounting, factoring, and assignment of accounts receivable. Of course, in order to evaluate the adequacy of these disclosures, it is first necessary to know of their existence and to have complete information about their nature. This is generally obtained in other parts of the audit by such procedures as examining the minutes, reviewing contracts and agreements, confirming the bank accounts, and discussing the existence of information requiring disclosure with management.

Confirmation of Accounts Receivable

One of the most important audit procedures is the *confirmation of accounts receivable*. The primary purpose of accounts receivable confirmation is to satisfy the *validity, valuation,* and *cutoff* objectives.

CICA Handbook Requirements

Two major audit procedures are formally required by the *CICA Handbook*: the *confirmation of accounts receivable* and the *physical examination of inventory*. These requirements are probably a result of the 1938 landmark U.S. legal case, *McKesson and Robbins*, in which a massive fraud involving fictitious accounts receivable and inventory was not uncovered in the audit. There was ample support to demonstrate that the confirmation of receivables and the physical observation of inventory would have brought the fraud to light, but at that time neither of these procedures was normally performed. Both Canada and the U.S. now require confirmation and physical examination.

> **OBJECTIVE 5**
>
> Obtain and evaluate accounts receivable confirmations.

The direct confirmation of accounts receivable is part of generally accepted auditing standards. The auditor does not have the option of not confirming receivables and substituting other procedures unless such confirmation is not "practicable" or the auditor considers such confirmation would be harmful to the client's business. The onus is on the auditor to determine if alternative procedures can be substituted or whether the scope of the audit is so limited by a failure to send direct confirmations that a qualification of the auditor's report or a denial of opinion is appropriate.

Assumptions Underlying Confirmations

An auditor makes two assumptions when accepting a confirmation as evidence. The first is that the person returning the confirmation is independent of the company and thus will provide an unbiased response. If this assumption is invalid, as would be the case if the confirmation of a fraudulent accounts receivable was sent to a company owned by an associate of the person committing the fraud, the value of the returned confirmation becomes zero. The second assumption is that the person returning the confirmation has knowledge of the account and the intent of the confirmation, and has carefully checked the balance to his or her books and records to ensure that the confirmation is in agreement. However, this second assumption may also not always be valid. Research has shown that some people return confirmations without really checking the balance; such a confirmation would have no value.

In many cases the auditor is able to assess the independence of the person returning the confirmation, but sometimes a relationship may exist of which the auditor is not aware. Furthermore, it is almost always impossible for an auditor to know how much care was taken in checking the balance before the confirmation was signed and returned. Thus weaknesses may exist in the confirmation of receivables; however despite the possibility of weakness, confirmation is a procedure on which auditors rely.

Confirmation and Tests of Controls

The value of accounts receivable confirmation as evidence can be visualized more clearly by relating it to the tests of controls discussed in Chapters 10 and 11. If the beginning balance of accounts receivable can be assumed correct and careful tests of controls are conducted, the likelihood of material misstatements in the ending balance of accounts receivable is reduced. This conclusion assumes the internal controls being tested were considered effective, and tests of controls results verified the effectiveness of the controls.

For discovering certain types of misstatements, confirmations are typically more effective than tests of controls. Examples include invalid accounts, disputed amounts, and uncollected accounts where the debtor has moved and left no forwarding address. Although confirmations cannot ensure the discovery of any of these types of misstatements, they are more reliable than tests of controls because confirmations are evidence obtained from an independent source, whereas tests of controls rely on internally created documents.

Confirmations are less likely to uncover omitted transactions and accounts than tests of controls for two reasons. First, in order to send a confirmation it is necessary to have a list of accounts receivable from which to select. Naturally, an omitted account will not be included in the population from which the sample is selected. Second, if an account with an omitted transaction is circularized, customers may ignore the confirmation or, alternatively, state that the amount is correct.

Clerical errors in billing customers and recording the amounts in the accounts can be effectively discovered by confirmation and tests of controls. Confirmations are typically more effective in uncovering overstatements of accounts receivable than understatements, whereas tests of controls are effective for discovering both.

The important concept in this discussion is the *substitutability* of tests of sales transactions and confirmation. For a given level of audit risk, the auditor can choose to emphasize tests of controls and thereby reduce confirmations, or alternatively emphasize confirmations and thereby reduce tests of sales transactions. The extent to which the auditor should emphasize confirmations or tests of controls for any given audit should depend on the relative costs and benefits of each. For example, if internal control is excellent and there are a large number of accounts receivable, it is normally more cost effective to emphasize tests of controls and request fewer confirmations. However, it would be inappropriate to bypass confirmations altogether. On the other hand, if internal control is ineffective or if there are a small number of large accounts receivable, most auditors would confirm most of the receivables and do only a few tests of controls.

Although the remaining sections in this chapter refer specifically to the confirmation of accounts receivable from customers, the concepts apply equally to other receivables such as notes receivable, amounts due from officers, and employee advances.

Confirmation Decisions

In performing confirmation procedures, the auditor must decide the type of confirmation to use, timing of the procedures, sample size, and individual items to select. Each of these is discussed, along with the factors affecting the decision.

Type of confirmation Two common types of confirmations are used for confirming accounts receivable: *positive* and *negative*. A *positive* confirmation is a communication addressed to the debtor requesting him or her to confirm directly whether the balance as stated on the confirmation request is correct or incorrect. Figure 13–4 illustrates a positive confirmation in the audit of Island Hardware

FIGURE 13–4

Positive Confirmation

Best Always
A Reply
goes to
Auditor

Fox, Pedlar & Co.   Chartered Accountants

Cabot Bldg.
P.O. Box 123
3 King Street North
St. John's, Canada A1C 3R5

(709) 384-1205

Dear Sir(s):

Re: Island Hardware Ltd.
In connection with our audit of the accounts of the above company, we would appreciate receiving from you confirmation of your account. The company's records show an amount receivable from you of $175.00 on June 30, 19X8. *B/s Date*
Do you agree with this amount? If you do, would you please sign this letter in the space below. However, if you do not, would you please note at the foot of this letter or on the reverse side, the details of any differences.
Would you then be good enough to return the letter directly to us in the envelope enclosed for your convenience.

Yours faithfully,

Fox & Pedlar

FOX, PEDLAR & CO.
Per:

Please provide Fox, Pedlar & Co. with this information.

_____

The above amount was due by me (us) at the date mentioned.

_____

Validity
The Amt is
correct not
lower.

Ltd. A *negative* confirmation is also addressed to the debtor, but requests a response only when the debtor disagrees with the stated amount. Figure 13–5 illustrates a negative confirmation in the audit of Island Hardware Ltd. that is a gummed label and would be attached to a customer's monthly statement. Many auditors today use their own or the client's EDP system to print the complete positive or negative confirmation, thus saving time and effort.

A positive confirmation is *more reliable* evidence because the auditor can perform follow-up procedures if a response is not received from the debtor. With a negative confirmation, failure to reply can only be regarded as a correct response even though the debtor may have ignored the confirmation request.

Offsetting the reliability disadvantage, negative confirmations are *less expensive* to send than positive confirmations, and thus more can be distributed for the same total cost. The determination of which type of confirmation to use is an auditor's decision, and it should be based on the facts in the audit. Section 6020.09 of the *CICA Handbook* states a preference for the use of positive confirmations in the following circumstances:

Positive

FIGURE 13–5

Negative Confirmation

An jet lost in Post
And ya would Asume
The AMt is Correct.

AUDITOR'S ACCOUNT CONFIRMATION

Please examine this statement carefully. If it does NOT agree with your records, please report any exceptions directly to our auditors

FOX, PEDLAR & CO.
Cabot Bldg.
P.O. Box 123
3 King Street North
St. John's, Canada
A1C 3R5

who are making an examination of our financial statements. A stamped, addressed envelope is enclosed for your convenience in replying.

Do not send your remittance to our auditors.

- When there are individual balances of relatively large amounts
- When there are few debtors
- When there is evidence or suspicion of fraud or serious error

Often the auditor will use a combination of positive and negative confirmation.

Negative
When No you use pos
Yoo

When these conditions do not exist, it is acceptable to use negative confirmations. Typically, when negative confirmations are used, the auditor puts considerable emphasis on the effectiveness of internal control as evidence of the fairness of accounts receivable, and assumes the large majority of the recipients will provide a conscientious reading and response to the confirmation request. Negative confirmations are often used for audits of municipalities, retail stores, and other industries in which the receivables are due from the general public. In these cases more weight is placed on tests of controls than on confirmations, and it is also believed customers in these industries will provide a conscientious response.

It is also common to use a combination of negative and positive confirmations by sending the latter to accounts with large balances and the former to those with small balances.

Timing The most reliable evidence from confirmations is obtained when they are sent as close to the balance sheet date as possible, as opposed to confirming the accounts several months before year-end. This permits the auditor to test directly the accounts receivable balance on the financial statements without making any inferences about the transactions taking place between the confirmation date and the balance sheet date. However, as a means of completing the audit on a timely basis, it is frequently convenient to confirm the accounts at an interim date. This is permissible if internal control is adequate and can provide reasonable assurance that sales, cash receipts, and other credits are properly recorded between the date of the confirmation and the end of the accounting period. Other factors the auditor is likely to consider in making the decision are the materiality of accounts receivable and the auditor's exposure to lawsuits because of the possibility of client bankruptcy and similar risks.

If the decision is made to confirm accounts receivable prior to year-end, it may be necessary to test the transactions occurring between the confirmation date and the balance sheet date by examining such internal documents as duplicate sales invoices, shipping documents, and evidence of cash receipts, in addition to performing analytical procedures of the intervening period.

Sample size   The main considerations affecting the number of confirmations to send are as follows:

- The materiality of total accounts receivable. If accounts receivable is highly material relative to the other asset balances, a larger sample size is necessary than when it is immaterial.
- The number of accounts receivable.
- The distribution in the size of the accounts. If all the accounts are approximately the same size, fewer need to be confirmed than when their size is distributed over a wide range of values.
- The results of obtaining an understanding of the client's internal control and tests of controls.
- The results of the confirmation tests in previous years.
- The likelihood of client bankruptcy and similar factors that affect desired audit risk.
- The type of confirmation being used. More confirmations are usually required for negative than for positive confirmations.
- The results of related analytical procedures.

A discussion of these factors in the context of variables statistical sampling is given in Chapter 14.

Selection of the items for testing   Some type of *stratification is desirable* with most confirmations. A typical approach to stratification is to consider both the size of the outstanding balance and the length of time an account has been outstanding as a basis for selecting the balances for confirmation. In most audits, the emphasis should be on confirming larger and older balances, since these are most likely to include a significant misstatement. But it is also important to sample some items from every material stratum of the population. In many cases, the auditor selects all accounts above a certain dollar amount and selects a random sample from the remainder.

In selecting the items for confirmation, it is important that the auditor have complete *independence* in choosing the accounts to be confirmed. If the client dictates which accounts to select or refuses to grant permission to confirm certain accounts, the ability to operate independently is seriously threatened. However, clients do frequently request that certain accounts not be confirmed. Although this is undesirable and should be resisted, it is acceptable if the amounts are not material, the client's reasons appear valid, and it is possible to verify the balances in the accounts by other means. If the account balances that the client will not grant permission to confirm are material in relation to the financial statements as a whole, the standards of the profession do not permit the issuance of an unqualified opinion.

Maintaining Control

After the items for confirmation have been selected, the auditor must maintain control of the confirmations until they are returned from the customer. If the client's assistance is obtained in preparing the confirmations, enclosing them in envelopes, or putting stamps on the envelopes, close supervision by the auditor is required. A return address must be included on all envelopes to make sure that undelivered mail is received by the public accounting firm. Similarly, self-addressed return envelopes accompanying the confirmations must be addressed for delivery to the public accounting firm's office. It is even important to mail the confirmations *outside* the client's office. All these steps are necessary to ensure independent communication between the auditor and the customer.

When a confirmation request is returned as undelivered mail it is necessary to evaluate carefully the reason why the request was not delivered. In most cases it represents a customer who has moved without paying his or her bill, but there is always the possibility of it being a fraudulent account. Even if it is a valid receivable, the existence of a large number of these accounts could indicate a serious collectibility problem that must be reflected in the allowance for uncollectible accounts.

Follow-up on Nonresponses

When positive confirmations are used, SAS 1 (AU 331) requires follow-up procedures for confirmations not returned by the customer. It is common to send second and sometimes even third requests for confirmations. Even with these efforts, some customers do not return the confirmation, so it is necessary to follow up with *alternative procedures*. The objective of alternative procedures is to determine by a means other than confirmation whether the nonconfirmed account was valid and properly stated at the confirmation date. For any positive confirmation not returned, the following documentation can be examined to verify the validity and valuation of individual sales transactions making up the ending balance in accounts receivable.

1. **Subsequent cash receipts** Evidence of the receipt of cash subsequent to the confirmation date includes examining remittance advices, entries in the cash receipts records, or perhaps even subsequent credits in the accounts receivable subsidiary records. On the one hand, the examination of evidence of subsequent cash receipts is a highly useful alternative procedure because it is reasonable to assume that a customer would not make a payment unless it was a valid receivable. On the other hand, the fact of payment does not establish whether there was an obligation on the date of the confirmation. In addition, care should be taken to match specifically each unpaid sales transaction with evidence of its payment as a test for disputes or disagreements over individual outstanding invoices.

2. **Duplicate sales invoices** These are useful in verifying the actual issuance of a sales invoice and the actual date of the billing.

3. **Shipping documents** These are important in establishing whether the shipment was actually made and as a test of cutoff.

4. **Correspondence with the client** Usually, the auditor does not need to review correspondence as a part of alternative procedures, but correspondence can be used to disclose disputed and questionable receivables not uncovered by other means. The extent and nature of the alternative procedures depend primarily upon

the materiality of the nonresponses, the types of misstatements discovered in the confirmed responses, the subsequent cash receipts from the nonresponses, and the auditor's conclusions about internal control. It is normally desirable to account for all unconfirmed balances with alternative procedures even if the amounts are small, as a means of properly generalizing from the sample to the population.

Analysis of Differences   When the confirmation requests are returned by the customer, it is necessary to determine the reason for any reported differences. In many cases, they are caused by timing differences between the client's and the customer's records. It is important to distinguish between these and *exceptions*, which represent misstatements of the accounts receivable balance. The most commonly reported types of differences in confirmations follow.

Payment has already been made   Reported differences typically arise when the customer has made a payment prior to confirmation date, but the client has not received the payment in time for recording before the confirmation date. Such instances should be carefully investigated to determine the possibility of a cash receipts cutoff error, lapping, or a theft of cash.

Goods have not been received   These differences typically result because the client records the sale at the date of shipment and the customer records the purchase when the goods are received. The time the goods are in transit is frequently the cause of differences reported on confirmations. These should be investigated to determine the possibility of the customer not receiving the goods at all or the existence of a cutoff error on the client's records.

The goods have been returned   The client's failure to record a credit memo could result from timing differences or the improper recording of sales returns and allowances. Like other differences, these must be investigated.

Clerical errors and disputed amounts   The most likely case of reported differences in a client's records occurs when the customer states that there is an error in the price charged for the goods, the goods are damaged, the proper quantity of goods was not received, and so forth. These differences must be investigated to determine whether the client is in error and what the amount of the error is.

In most instances the auditor will ask the client to reconcile the difference and, if necessary, will communicate with the customer to resolve any disagreements. Naturally, the auditor must carefully verify the client's conclusions on each significant difference.

Drawing Conclusions   When all differences have been resolved, including those discovered in performing alternative procedures, it is important to *reevaluate internal control*. Each client misstatement must be analyzed to determine whether it was consistent or inconsistent with the original assessed level of control risk. If a significant number of misstatements take place that are inconsistent with the assessment of control risk, it is necessary to revise the assessment and consider the effect of the revision on the audit.

It is also necessary to generalize from the sample to the entire population of accounts receivable. Even though the sum of the errors in the sample may not significantly affect the financial statements, the auditor must consider whether

TABLE 13–2

Comparative Information for Hillsburg Hardware Ltd. – Sales and Collection Cycle

	AMOUNT (IN THOUSANDS)		
	12-31-X8	12-31-X7	12-31-X6
Sales	$7,216	$6,321	$5,937
Sales returns and allowances	62	57	50
Gross margin	1,992	1,738	1,621
Accounts receivable	1,010	898	825
Allowance for uncollectible accounts	62	77	69
Bad debt expense	166	164	142
Total current assets	2,550	2,239	2,099
Total assets	3,067	3,301	3,057
Net earnings before taxes	285	436	397
Number of accounts receivable	258	221	209
Number of accounts receivable with balances over $5,000	37	32	30

TABLE 13–3

Analytical Procedures for Hillsburg Hardware Ltd. – Sales and Collection Cycle

	12–31-X8	12–31-X7	12–31-X6
Gross margin percent	27.6%	27.5%	27.3%
Sales returns and allowances/gross sales	.8	.9	.8
Bad debt expense/net sales	2.3	2.6	2.4
Allowance for uncollectible accounts/accounts receivable	6.1	8.6	8.4
Number of days receivables outstanding	50.8	51.6	50.4
Net accounts receivable/total current assets	37.1	36.7	36.0

Comment: Allowance as a percentage of accounts receivable has declined from 8.6 to 6.1. Number of days receivable outstanding and economic conditions do not justify this change.

the population is likely to be materially misstated. This conclusion can be arrived at by using statistical sampling techniques or on a nonstatistical basis.

The final decision about accounts receivable and sales is whether sufficient evidence has been obtained through analytical procedures, tests of controls, cut-off procedures, confirmation and other substantive procedures to justify drawing conclusions about the correctness of the stated balance.

Case Illustration – Hillsburg Hardware – Part III

The Hillsburg Hardware Ltd. case illustration from Chapters 11 and 12 continues here to include the determination of the tests of details of balances audit procedures in the sales and collection cycle. Table 13–2 includes comparative trial balance information for the sales and collection cycle for Hillsburg Hardware Ltd. Some of that information is used to illustrate several analytical procedures in Table 13–3. None of the analytical procedures indicated potential errors except the ratio of the allowance of uncollectible accounts to accounts receivable. The explanation at the bottom of Table 13–3 comments on the potential error.

Fran Moore prepared the planning worksheet in Figure 13–6 as an aid to help her decide the extent of planned tests of details of balances. The source of each of the columns are as follows:

OBJECTIVE 6

Integrate into the audit plan all evidence obtained regarding controls, transactions, and accounts in the sales and collection cycle.

- *Audit risk.* Fran assessed audit risk as high because of the good financial condition of the company, its financial stability, and the relatively few users of the financial statements.
- *Inherent risk.* Fran assessed inherent risk as low for all objectives except valua-

TABLE 13–4

Tests of Details of Balances Objectives and Audit Program for Hillsburg Hardware Ltd. – Sales and Collection Cycle (Design Format)

OBJECTIVE	AUDIT PROCEDURE
Specific Objectives	
Accounts receivable in the aged trial balance agree with related master file amounts, and the total is correctly added and agrees with the general ledger.	Trace 10 accounts from the trial balance to accounts on master file. (5) Foot two pages of the trial balance, and total all pages. (6) Trace the balance to the general ledger. (7)
The accounts receivable on the aged trial balances are valid.	Confirm accounts receivable using positive confirmations. Confirm all amounts over $5,000 and a nonstatistical sample of the remainder. (9) Perform alternative procedures for all confirmations not returned on the first or second request. (10)
Existing accounts receivable are included in the aged trial balance.	Trace 5 accounts from the accounts receivable master file to the aged trial balance. (8)
Accounts receivable on the trial balance are owned.	Review the minutes of the board of directors for any indication of pledged or factored accounts receivable. (4) Inquire of management whether any receivables are pledged or factored. (4)
Accounts receivable in the trial balance are properly valued.	Confirm accounts receivable using positive confirmations. Confirm all amounts over $5,000 and a nonstatistical sample of the remainder. (9) Perform alternative procedures for all confirmations not returned on the first or second request. (10) Trace 10 accounts from the aging schedule to the accounts receivable master file to test for the correct aging on the trial balance. (5) Foot the aging columns on the trial balance and total the pages. (6) Crossfoot the aging columns. (6) Discuss with the credit manager the likelihood of collecting older accounts. Examine subsequent cash receipts and the credit file on all accounts over 90 days and evaluate whether the receivables are collectible. (11) Evaluate whether the allowance is adequate after performing other audit procedures relating to collectibility of receivables. (12)
Accounts receivable on the aged trial balances are properly classified.	Review the receivables listed on the aged trial balance for notes and related party receivables. (3) Inquire of management whether there are any related party notes or long-term receivables included in the trial balances. (4)
Transactions in the sales and collection cycle are recorded in the proper period.	Select the last 50 sales transactions from the current year's sales journal and the first 50 from the subsequent year's and trace each to the related shipping documents, checking for the date of actual shipment and the correct recording. (13) Review large sales returns and allowances after the balance sheet date to determine whether any should be included in the current period. (14)
Accounts in the sales and collection cycle and related information are properly disclosed.	Review the minutes of the board of directors' meetings for any indication of pledged or factored accounts receivable. (3) Inquire of management whether any receivables are pledged or factored. (4)

Note: The procedures are summarized into a performance format in Table 13–5. The number in parentheses after the procedure refers to Table 13–5.

FIGURE 13–6 Planning Worksheet to Decide Tests of Details of Balances for Hillsburg Hardware Ltd. – Accounts Receivable

AUDIT OBJECTIVES	ACCEPTABLE AUDIT RISK (1)	INHERENT RISK	CONTROL RISK		ANALYTICAL PROCEDURES	PLANNED DETECTION RISK FOR TESTS OF DETAILS OF BALANCES
			SALES	CASH RECEIPTS		
Validity	high	low	medium	high	good results	medium
Ownership	high	low	low	not applicable	not applicable	high
Completeness	high	low	medium	low	good results	high
Valuation	high	medium	high	low	unacceptable results	low
Classification	high	low	low	high	good results	high
Cutoff	high	low	high	high	good results	low
Mechanical Accuarcy	high	low	low	medium	good results	high
Disclosure	high	low	not applicable	not applicable	not applicable	high

1 High audit risk means there is a low exposure to the risk factors and therefore less planned evidence than for a low audit risk. It is assessed for the engagement as a whole.

TABLE 13–5

Tests of Details of Balances Audit Program for Hillsburg Hardware Ltd. – Sales and Collection Cycle (Performance Format)

1. Review accounts receivable trial balance for large and unusual receivables.
2. Calculate analytical procedures indicated in carry-forward working papers (not included) and follow up any significant changes from prior years.
3. Review the receivables listed on the aged trial balance for notes and related party receivables.
4. Inquire of management whether there are any related-party, notes, or long-term receivables included in the trial balance. Inquire as to whether any receivables are pledged or factored.
5. Trace 10 accounts from the trial balance to the accounts receivable master file for aging and the balance.
6. Foot 2 pages of the trial balance for aging columns and balance and total all pages and crossfoot the aging.
7. Trace the balance to the general ledger.
8. Trace 5 accounts from the accounts receivable master file to the aged trial balance.
9. Confirm accounts receivable using positive confirmations. Confirm all amounts over $5,000 and a nonstatistical sample of the remainder.
10. Perform alternative procedures for all confirmations not returned on the first or second request.
11. Discuss with the credit manager the likelihood of collecting older accounts. Examine subsequent cash receipts and the credit file on all larger accounts over 90 days and evaluate whether the receivables are collectible.
12. Evaluate whether the allowance is adequate after performing other audit procedures relating to collectibility of receivables.
13. Select the last 50 sales transactions from the current year's sales journal and the first 50 from the subsequent year's and trace each to the related shipping documents, checking for the date of actual shipment and the correct recording.
14. Review large sales returns and allowances after the balance sheet date to determine whether any should be included in the current period.

tion. In past years, there have been audit adjustments to the allowance for uncollectible accounts because it was found to be understated.

- *Control risk*. Assessed control risk for sales and collections is taken from the assessment of control risk matrix for sales and cash receipts, modified by the results of the tests of controls. The control risk matrix is shown in Figures 11–6 and 11–7 on pages 374 and 375. The results of the tests of controls in Chapter 12 were consistent with the assessments of control risk in Chapter 11, except for the valuation objective for sales. The initial assessment was low but tests of controls results changed the assessment to high. The results of tests of controls confirmed that the assessment of high control risk for cutoff was correct.
- *Analytical procedures*. See Table 13–3.

Table 13–4 shows the tests of details audit program for accounts receivable, by objective, and for the allowance for uncollectible accounts. The audit program reflects the conclusions recorded on the planning worksheet in Figure 13–6. Table 13–5 shows the audit program in a performance format. The audit procedures are identical to those in Table 13–4 except for procedures 1 and 2, which are analytical procedures. The numbers in parentheses are a cross-reference between the two tables.

REVIEW QUESTIONS

13–1   Distinguish between tests of details of balances and tests of controls for the sales and collection cycle. Explain how the tests of controls affect the tests of details.

13–2   Cynthia Roberts, a public accountant, expresses the following viewpoint: "I do not believe in performing tests of controls for the sales and collection cycle. As an alternative I send a lot of negative confirmations on every audit at an interim date. If I find a lot of errors I analyze them to determine their cause. If internal control is inadequate, I send positive confirmations at year-end to evaluate the amount of errors. If the negative confirmations result in minimal errors, which is often the case, I have found that internal control is effective without bothering to perform tests of controls, and the CICA's confirmation requirement has been satisfied at the same time. In my opinion the best test of internal control is to go directly to third parties." Evaluate her point of view.

13–3   List five analytical procedures for the sales and collection cycle. For each test, describe a misstatement that could be identified.

13–4   Identify the eight audit objectives for the audit for accounts receivable. For each objective, list one audit procedure.

13–5   Which of the eight audit objectives for the audit of accounts receivable can be partially satisfied by confirmations with customers?

13–6   State the purpose of footing the total column in the client's trial balance, tracing individual customer names and amounts to the accounts receivable master file, and tracing the total to the general ledger. Is it necessary to trace each amount to the master file? Why?

13–7   Distinguish between valuation tests of gross accounts receivable and tests of the realizable value of receivables.

13–8   Explain why you agree or disagree with the following statement: "In most audits it is more important to test carefully the cutoff for sales than for cash receipts." Describe how you perform each type of test assuming the existence of prenumbered documents.

13–9   Evaluate the following statement: "In many audits in which accounts receivable is material, the requirement of confirming customer balances is a waste of time and would not be performed by competent auditors if it were not required by the CICA. When internal control is excellent and there are a large number of small receivables from customers who do not recognize the function of confirmation, it is a meaningless procedure. Examples include well-run utilities and department stores. In these situations, tests of controls are far more effective than confirmations."

13–10 Distinguish between a positive and a negative confirmation and state the circumstances in which each should be used. Why do public accounting firms frequently use a combination of positive and negative confirmations on the same audit?

13–11 Under what circumstances is it acceptable to confirm accounts receivable prior to the balance sheet date?

13–12 State the most important factors affecting the sample size in confirmations of accounts receivable.

13–13 In Chapter 12, one of the points brought out was the need to obtain a representative sample of the population. How can this concept be reconciled with the statement in this chapter that the emphasis should be on confirming larger and older balances, since these are most likely to contain misstatements?

13–14 Define what is meant by "alternative procedures" and explain their purpose. Which alternative procedures are the most reliable? Why?

13–15 Explain why the analysis of exceptions is important in the confirmation of accounts receivable, even if the misstatements in the sample are not material.

13–16 State three types of differences that might be observed in the confirmation of accounts receivable that do not constitute misstatements. For each, state an audit procedure that would verify the difference.

13–17 What is the relationship of each of the following to the sales and collection cycle: flowcharts, assessing control risk, tests of controls, and tests of details of balances?

MULTIPLE CHOICE QUESTIONS

13–18 The following questions concern analytical procedures in the sales and collection cycle. Choose the best response.

a. As a result of analytical procedures, the independent auditor determines that the gross profit percentage has declined from 30 percent in the preceding year to 20 percent in the current year. The auditor should

  (1) investigate the credit manager's performance.
  (2) evaluate management's performance in causing this decline.
  (3) require footnote disclosure.
  (4) consider the possibility of a misstatement in the financial statements.

b. Once a public accountant has determined that accounts receivable have increased due to slow collections in a "tight money" environment, the public accountant would be likely to

  (1) increase the balance in the allowance for bad-debt account.
  (2) review the going concern ramifications.
  (3) review the credit and collection policy.
  (4) expand tests of collectibility.

c. In connection with his review of key ratios, the public accountant notes that Pyzi Inc. had accounts receivable equal to 30 days' sales at December 31, 19X0, and to 45 days' sales at December 31, 19X1. Assuming that there had been no changes in economic conditions, clientele, or sales mix, this change most likely would indicate

    (1) a steady increase in sales in 19X1.
    (2) an easing of credit policies in 19X1.
    (3) a decrease in accounts receivable relative to sales in 19X1.
    (4) a steady decrease in sales in 19X1.   (AICPA adapted)

13–19 The following questions deal with confirmation of accounts receivable. Choose the best response.

    a. In connection with her examination of the Beke Supply Corp. for the year ended August 31, 19X1, Sylvia Lowe, a public accountant, has mailed accounts receivable confirmations to three groups as follows:

GROUP NUMBER	TYPE OF CUSTOMER	TYPE OF CONFIRMATION
1	Wholesale	Positive
2	Current retail	Negative
3	Past-due retail	Positive

    The confirmation responses from each group vary from 10 percent to 90 percent. The most likely response percentages are

    (1) Group 1 – 90 percent, Group 2 – 50 percent, Group 3 – 10 percent
    (2) Group 1 – 90 percent, Group 2 – 10 percent, Group 3 – 50 percent
    (3) Group 1 – 50 percent, Group 2 – 90 percent, Group 3 – 10 percent
    (4) Group 1 – 10 percent, Group 2 – 50 percent, Group 3 – 90 percent

    b. The negative form of accounts receivable confirmation request is particularly useful *except* when

    (1) internal control surrounding accounts receivable is considered to be effective.
    (2) a large number of small balances are involved.
    (3) the auditor has reason to believe the persons receiving the requests are likely to give them consideration.
    (4) individual account balances are relatively large.

    c. Which of the following is the best argument against the use of negative confirmations of accounts receivable?

    (1) The cost per response is excessively high.
    (2) There is *no* way of knowing if the intended recipients received them.
    (3) Recipients are likely to feel that the confirmation is a subtle request for payment.
    (4) The inference drawn from receiving no reply may *not* be correct.

    d. The return of a positive confirmation of accounts receivable without an exception attests to the

    (1) collectibility of the receivable balance.
    (2) accuracy of the receivable balance.
    (3) accuracy of the aging of accounts receivable.
    (4) accuracy of the allowance for bad debts.   (AICPA adapted)

DISCUSSION QUESTIONS AND PROBLEMS

13–20 The following are common tests of details of balances for the audit of accounts receivable.

    1. Obtaining a list of aged accounts receivable, footing the list, and tracing the total to the general ledger.

2. Tracing 35 accounts to the accounts receivable master file for name, amount, and age categories.

3. Examining and documenting collections on accounts receivable for 20 days after the engagement date.

4. Requesting 25 positive and 65 negative confirmations of accounts receivable.

5. Performing alternative procedures on accounts not responding to second requests by examining subsequent collections documentation and shipping reports or sales invoices.

6. Testing the sales cutoff by tracing entries in the sales journal for 15 days before and after engagement date to shipping reports, if available, and/or sales invoices.

7. Determining and disclosing accounts pledged, discounted, sold, assigned, or guaranteed by others.

8. Evaluating the materiality of credit balances in the aged trial balance.

Required:
For each audit procedure, identify the audit objective or objectives it partially or fully satisfies.

13–21   The following misstatements are sometimes found in the sales and collection account balances:

1. Cash received from collections of accounts receivable in the subsequent period are recorded as current period receipts.

2. The allowance for uncollectible accounts is inadequate due to the client's failure to reflect depressed economic conditions in the allowance.

3. Several accounts receivable are in dispute due to claims of defective merchandise.

4. The pledging of accounts receivable to the bank for a loan is not disclosed in the financial statements.

5. Goods shipped and included in the current period sales were returned in the subsequent period.

6. Several accounts receivable in the accounts receivable master file are not included in the aged trial balance.

7. One account receivable in the accounts receivable master file is included on the aged trial balance twice.

8. Long-term interest-bearing notes receivable from affiliated companies are included in accounts receivable.

9. The trial balance total does not equal the amount in the general ledger.

Required:
a. For each misstatement, identify the audit objective to which it pertains.

b. For each misstatement, list an internal control that should prevent it.

c. For each misstatement, list one test of details of balances audit procedure that the auditor can use to detect it.

13–22   The following are audit procedures in the sales and collection cycle.

1. Examine a sample of shipping documents to determine if each has a sales invoice number included on it.

2. Discuss with the sales manager whether any sales allowances have been granted after the balance sheet date that may apply to the current period.

3. Add the columns on the aged trial balance and compare the total with the general ledger.

4. Observe whether the controller makes an independent comparison of the total on the general ledger with the trial balance of accounts receivable.

5. For the month of May, count the approximate number of shipping documents

filed in the shipping department, and compare the total with the number of sales invoices in the sales journal.

6. Compare the date on a sample of shipping documents throughout the year with related duplicate sales invoices and the accounts receivable master file.

7. Examine a sample of customer orders and see if each has a credit authorization.

8. Send letters directly to former customers whose accounts have been charged off as uncollectible to determine if any have actually been paid.

9. Examine the master file of accounts receivable to see if each has an indication of *C* for a regular customer, *N* for interest-bearing receivables, and *R* for related parties.

10. Compare the date on a sample of shipping documents a few days before and after the balance sheet date with related sales journal transactions.

11. Compute the ratio of allowance for uncollectible accounts divided by accounts receivable and compare with previous years.

12. Examine a sample of noncash credits in the accounts receivable master file to determine if the internal auditor has initialed each indicating internal verification.

Required:

a. For each procedure, identify the applicable type of audit evidence.

b. For each procedure, identify which of the following it is:
   (1) Test of controls
   (2) Analytical procedure
   (3) Test of details of balances

c. For those procedures you identified as a test of controls, what internal control objective or objectives are being satisfied?

d. For those procedures you identified as a test of details of balances, what audit objective or objectives are being satisfied?

13–23   The following are the eight audit objectives, eight tests of details of balances for accounts receivable, and seven tests of controls for sales and collections.

OBJECTIVE	TEST OF DETAILS OF BALANCES OR TEST OF CONTROLS AUDIT PROCEDURE
Validity	1. Confirm accounts receivable.
Ownership	2. Review sales returns after the balance sheet date to determine if any are applicable to the current year.
Completeness	
Valuation	3. Compare dates on shipping documents and the sales journal throughout the year.
Classification	
Cutoff	4. Perform alternative procedures for nonresponses to confirmation.
Disclosure	
Mechanical accuracy	5. Examine sales transactions for related-party or employee sales recorded as regular sales.
	6. Examine duplicate sales invoices for consignment sales and other shipments for which title has not passed.
	7. Trace a sample of accounts from the accounts receivable master file to the aged trial balance.
	8. Trace recorded sales transactions to shipping documents to determine if a document exists.
	9. Examine the financial statements to determine if all related parties, notes, and pledged receivables are properly presented.
	10. Examine duplicate sales invoices for initials that indicate internal verification of extensions and footings.
	11. Trace a sample of shipping documents to related sales invoice entries in the sales journal.

12. Compare amounts and dates on the aged trial balance and accounts receivable master file.
13. Trace from the sales journal to the accounts receivable master file to make sure the information is the same.
14. Trace a sample of accounts receivable from the accounts receivable master file to the aged trial balance.
15. Inquire of management whether there are notes from related parties included with trade receivables.

Required:

a. Identify which procedures are tests of details of balances and which are tests of controls.

b. Identify one test of details and one test of controls that will partially satisfy each objective. (Tests of controls are not used for disclosure.) Each procedure must be used at least once.

13–24 André Auto Parts Inc. sells new parts for foreign automobiles to auto dealers. Company policy requires that a prenumbered shipping document be issued for each sale. At the time of pickup or shipment, the shipping clerk writes the date on the shipping document. The last shipment made in the fiscal year ended August 31, 19X7, was recorded on document 2167. Shipments are billed in the order the billing clerk receives the shipping documents.

For late August and early September, shipping documents are billed on sales invoices as follows:

SHIPPING DOCUMENT NO.	SALES INVOICE NO.
2163	4332
2164	4326
2165	4327
2166	4330
2167	4331
2168	4328
2169	4329
2170	4333
2171	4335
2172	4334

The August and September sales journals have the following information included:

Sales Journal – August 19X7

DAY OF MONTH	SALES INVOICE NO.	AMOUNT OF SALE
30	4326	$ 726.11
30	4329	1,914.30
31	4327	419.83
31	4328	620.22
31	4330	47.74

Sales Journal – September 19X7

DAY OF MONTH	SALES INVOICE NO.	AMOUNT OF SALE
1	4332	$2,641.31
1	4331	106.39
1	4333	852.06
2	4335	1,250.50
2	4334	646.58

Required:

a. What are the generally accepted accounting principles requirements for a correct sales cutoff?

b. Which sales invoices, if any, are recorded in the wrong accounting period, assuming a periodic inventory? Prepare an adjusting entry to correct the financial statement for the year ended August 31, 19X7.

c. Assume the shipping clerk accidentally wrote August 31 on shipping documents 2168 through 2172. Explain how that would affect the correctness of the financial statements. How would you, as an auditor, discover that error?

d. Describe, in general terms, the audit procedures you would follow in making sure cutoff for sales is accurate at the balance sheet date.

e. Identify internal controls that would reduce the likelihood of cutoff errors. How would you test each control during tests of controls?

13–25 John Gossling, CA, is examining the financial statements of a manufacturing company with a significant amount of trade accounts receivable. Gossling is satisfied that the accounts are properly summarized and classified and that allocations, reclassifications, and valuations are made in accordance with generally accepted accounting principles. He is planning to use accounts receivable confirmation requests to satisfy the third examination standard as to trade accounts receivable.

Required:

a. Identify and describe the two forms of accounts receivable confirmation requests and indicate what factors Gossling will consider in determining when to use each.

b. Assume that Gossling has received a satisfactory response to the confirmation requests. Describe how he could evaluate collectibility of the trade accounts receivable.

c. What are the implications to a public accountant if during his or her examination of accounts receivable some of a client's trade customers do not respond to the request for positive confirmation of their accounts?

d. What auditing steps should a public accountant perform if there is no response to a second request for a positive confirmation?   (AICPA adapted)

13–26 You have been assigned to the confirmation of aged accounts receivable for the Blank Paper Company Ltd. audit. You have tested the trial balance and selected the accounts for confirming. Before the confirmation requests are mailed, the controller asks to look at the accounts you intend to confirm to determine whether she will permit you to send them.

She reviews the list and informs you that she does not want you to confirm six of the accounts on your list. Two of them are credit balances, one is a zero balance, two of the other three have a fairly small balance, and the remaining balance is highly material. The reason she gives is that she feels the confirmations will upset these customers, because "they are kind of hard to get along with." She does not want the credit balances confirmed because it may encourage the customer to ask for a refund.

In addition, the controller asks you to send an additional 20 confirmations to customers she has listed for you. She does this as a means of credit collection for "those stupid idiots who won't know the difference between a public accountant and a credit collection agency."

Required:

a. Is it acceptable for the controller to review the list of accounts you intend to confirm? Discuss.

b. Discuss the appropriateness of sending the 20 additional confirmations to the customers.

c. Assuming the auditor complies with all the controller's requests, what is the effect on the auditor's opinion?

13–27 You have been assigned to the first examination of the accounts of the North Battleford Corp. for the year ending March 31, 19X8. Accounts receivable were confirmed on December 31, 19X7, and at that date the receivables consisted of approximately two hundred accounts with balances totaling $956,750. Seventy-five of these accounts with balances totaling $650,725 were selected for confirmation. All but 20 of the confirmation requests have been returned; thirty were signed without comments, 14 had minor differences which have been cleared satisfactorily, while 11 confirmations had the following comments:

1. We are sorry but we cannot answer your request for confirmation of our account as Duck Lake Inc. uses an accounts payable voucher system.
2. The balance of $1,050 was paid on December 23, 19X7.
3. The balance of $7,750 was paid on January 5, 19X8.
4. The balance noted above has been paid.
5. We do not owe you anything at December 31, 19X7, as the goods, represented by your invoice dated December 30, 19X7, number 25,050, in the amount of $11,550, were received on January 5, 19X8, on FOB destination terms.
6. An advance payment of $2,500 made by us in November 19X7 should cover the two invoices totaling $1,350 shown on the statement attached.
7. We never received these goods.
8. We are contesting the propriety of this $12,525 charge. We think the charge is excessive.
9. Amount okay. As the goods have been shipped to us on consignment, we will remit payment upon selling the goods.
10. The $10,000, representing a deposit under a lease, will be applied against the rent due to us during 19X9, the last year of the lease.
11. Your credit memo dated December 5, 19X7, in the amount of $440 cancels the balance above.

Required:

What steps would you take to clear satisfactorily each of the above 11 comments? (AICPA adapted)

13–28 You have examined the financial statements of Boiestown Limited for several years. Internal control for accounts receivable is very satisfactory. Boiestown Limited is on a calendar-year basis. An interim audit, which included confirmation of the accounts receivable, was performed on August 31 and indicated that the accounting for cash, sales, sales returns and allowances, and receivables was very reliable.

The company's sales are principally to manufacturing concerns. There are about 1,500 active trade accounts receivable of which about 35 percent represent 65 percent of the total dollar amount. The accounts receivable are maintained alphabetically in a master file of accounts receivable.

Shipping document data are keyed into a computerized system that simultaneously produces a sales invoice, sales journal, and an updated accounts receivable master file.

All cash receipts are in the form of customers' cheques. Information for cash receipts is obtained from the remittance advice portions of the customers' cheques. The computer operator compares the remittance advices with the list of cheques that was prepared by another person when the mail was received. As for sales, a cash receipts journal and updated accounts receivable master file are simultaneously prepared after the cash receipts information is entered.

Summary totals are produced monthly by the computer operations department for updating the general ledger master file accounts such as cash, sales, and accounts receivable. An aged trial balance is prepared monthly.

Required:

Prepare the additional audit procedures necessary for testing the balances in the sales and collection cycle. (Ignore bad debts and allowance for uncollectible accounts.)

(AICPA adapted)

13–29   In the confirmation of accounts receivable for the Millbank Service Company Inc., 85 positive and no negative confirmations were mailed to customers. This represents 35 percent of the dollar balance of the total accounts receivable. For all nonresponses second requests were sent, but there were still 10 customers who did not respond. The decision was made to perform alternative procedures on the 10 unanswered confirmation requests. An assistant is requested to conduct the alternative procedures and report to the senior auditor after he has completed his tests on two accounts. He prepared the following information for the working papers:

1. Confirmation request no. 9
   Customer name – Jolene Milling Co.
   Balance – $3,621 at December 31, 19X7
   Subsequent cash receipts per the accounts
      receivable master file.

January 15, 19X8 – $1,837	
January 29, 19X8 – $1,263	
February 6, 19X8 – $1,429	

2. Confirmation request no. 26
   Customer name – Rosenthal Repair Service Ltd.
   Balance – $2,500 at December 31, 19X7
   Subsequent cash receipts per the accounts
      receivable master file

   February 9,   19X8 – $500

   Sales invoices per the accounts receivable
      master file (I examined the duplicate invoice)

   September 1, 19X7 – $4,200

Required:

a. If you were called upon to evaluate the adequacy of the sample size, the type of confirmation used, and the percentage of accounts confirmed, what additional information would you need?

b. Discuss the need to send second requests and perform alternative procedures for nonresponses.

c. Evaluate the adequacy of the alternative procedures used for verifying the two nonresponses.

CASE

13–30   You are auditing the sales and collection cycle for Maritime Cabinets Limited, a small manufacturer of high quality furniture in Nova Scotia. Maritime makes cabinets to order for local contractors and home renovators, and some stock items for local furniture stores and hardware stores. The company has a reputation for excellent cabinet work and weak record keeping. The cabinet makers have a reputation of doing all aspects of their job well, but due to a shortage of accounting personnel, there is not time for internal verification or careful performance. In previous years your public accounting firm has found quite a few errors in billings, collections, and accounts receivable. As was mentioned, most of the manufacturing is to order so the two largest assets are accounts receivable and property, plant, and equipment.

The company has several large loans payable to a local bank, and the bank has told management that they are reluctant to extend more credit, especially considering the declining market for high-quality furniture. In the past, loans from the owners have made up deficits, but in the past year, the owners simply have not been able to raise any more money personally.

In previous years, the response you have had to confirmation requests has been frustrating at best. The response rate has been extremely low and those who did respond did not know the purpose of the confirmations or their correct outstanding balance. You have had the same experience in confirming receivables at other businesses in the area.

You conclude that control over cash is excellent and the likelihood of fraud is extremely small. You are less confident about unintentional errors in billing, recording sales, cash receipts, accounts receivable, and bad debts.

Required:

a. Identify major audit risks in this audit.

b. What inherent risks are you concerned about?

c. In this audit of the sales and collection cycle, which types of tests are you likely to emphasize?

d. For each of the following, explain whether you plan to emphasize the test and give reasons.

  (1) Tests of controls
  (2) Analytical procedures
  (3) Test of details of balances

INTEGRATED CASE APPLICATION

13–31 *ABC AUDIT – PART IV*

Parts I (pp. 318–320), II (pp. 390–391), and III (p. 432) of this case study dealt with obtaining an understanding of internal control and assessing control risk for transactions affecting accounts payable of ABC Ltd. In Part IV, we begin the audit of the accounts payable balance itself by addressing analytical procedures.

You will assume that your understanding of internal control over purchases and cash disbursements and the related tests of controls supports an assessment of control risk of low. You will also assume that analytical procedures support the overall reasonableness of the balance. Accounts payable at December 31, 19X5 are included in Figure 13–7.

Required:

a. List those relationships, ratios, and trends that you believe will provide useful information about the overall reasonableness of accounts payable.

b. Prepare an audit program in a design format for tests of details of balances for accounts payable. Before preparing the audit program, you should review the Hillsburg Hardware Case Illustration starting on page 371. You should prepare a matrix similar to the one in Figure 13–6 page 454 for accounts payable. Assume assessed control risk is low for all internal control objectives and analytical procedures results were satisfactory for those audit objectives where analytical procedures are relevant. The design format audit program should include audit procedures for each procedure.

c. Prepare an audit program for accounts payable in a performance format, using the audit procedures for part (b).

d. Assume for requirement (b) that (1) assessed control risk had been high rather than low for each internal control objective, (2) inherent risk was high for each audit objective, and (3) analytical procedures indicated a high potential for error. What would the effect have been on the audit procedures and sample sizes for part (b).

e. Figure 13–8 presents six replies to the request for information from twenty vendors specified in Figure 13–9. These are the replies for which follow-up indicates a difference between the vendor's balance and the company's records. The auditor's follow-up findings are indicated on each reply. Calculate the estimated error in accounts payable based on the errors in accounts payable confirmation and other relevant information provided in Problem 13–31. Be sure to consider likely errors in accounts payable not confirmed and sampling error. Prepare a worksheet similar to the one illustrated in Figure 13–

FIGURE 13–7

ABC Ltd. Trial Balance of Trade Accounts Payable December 31, 19X5

Advent Sign Mfg. Co.Ltd.	$2,500.00	M & A Milling Ltd.	4,662.00
Alder Insurance Co.	660.00	Maritime Power	3,698.15
Bauer and Adamson	86.00	Midatlantic Gas Corp.	2,442.10
Bleyl & Sons Ltd.	1,500.00	Monsanto Chemical Canada Ltd.	14,622.15
Can-Amer Computing Service	1,211.00	Nielsen Enterprises	437.56
Central Steel, Inc.	8,753.00	Norris Industries, Inc.	9,120.00
Chelsea Development Corp.	1,800.00	Pare Tile Corp.	320.00
Commercial Supply Ltd.	3,250.00	Permaloy Manufacturing	3,290.00
Country Electric Ltd.	980.00	Petro-Canada.	11,480.00
Diamond Janitorial Service	750.00	Polein Drill and Bit Ltd.	2,870.16
Dictaphone Corp.	675.00	Propec Inc.	510.00
Douglas Equipment Ltd.	6,425.00	Rayno Sales and Service	1,917.80
Ellison, Robt. & Assoc.	346.10	Reames Construction, Inc.	4,500.00
FMC Corp.	15,819.00	Remington Supply Co. Ltd.	9,842.10
Fiberchem Inc.	6,315.80	Ritter Engineering Corp.	1,200.00
Fuller Travel	943.00	Roberts Bros. Service	189.73
GAFCO, Inc.	5,750.00	S & S Truck Painting	819.00
Glade Specialties	1,000.00	Sanders, Geo. A. & Co.	346.00
Granger Supply Corp.	4,250.00	Semco, Inc.	50.20
Hesco Services	719.62	Shell Oil	12,816.27
Innes, Brush & Co. CAs	1,500.00	Stationary Supply Ltd.	619.12
J & L Plastics Corp.	1,412.00	Thermal Tape Co. Ltd.	123.00
Judkins Co. Ltd.	2,500.00	Todd Machinery, Inc.	6,888.12
Kazco. Mfg. Corp.	1,627.30	Valco Sales Ltd.	1,429.00
Kedman Company	19.27	Vermax Corp.	284.00
Koch Plumbing Contractors	2,750.00	Waco Electronics, Inc.	126.33
Kohler Products Inc.	10,483.23	Western Maritimes Supply Ltd.	2,369.62
Lakeshore Inc.	1,850.00	Williams Controls, Inc.	1,915.00
Landscape Services Ltd.	420.00	Xerox Canada Inc.	3,250.00
Lundberg Coatings, Inc.	2,733.10	Yates Supply Co.	919.70
		Total	$192,085.53

Other related information:

■ The vendors with the greatest volume of transactions during the year are:

Central Steel, Inc.	Monsanto Chemical Canada Ltd.
Commercial Supply Ltd.	Norris Industries, Inc.
FMC Corp.	Petro-Canada
Fiberchem Inc.	Remington Supply Co. Ltd.
GAFCO, Inc.	Shell Oil

10 on page 469 to aid in your analysis. The exception for Fiberchem is analyzed as an illustration. Assume that ABC took a complete physical inventory at December 31, 19X5 and the auditor concluded that recorded inventory reflects all inventory on hand at the balance sheet date.

Use the microcomputer with appropriate software to prepare this worksheet and analysis (instructor option).

f. Based on the confirmation responses and your analysis in requirement (e), what are your conclusions about the fairness of the recorded balance in accounts payable for ABC Ltd. and your assessments of control risk as low for all internal control objectives?

STATEMENT FROM ADVENT SIGN MFG. CO. ITD.

ABC Ltd.
Halifax, N.S.

Amounts Due as of December 31, 19X5:

First progress billing per contract	$2,500.00(1)
Second progress billing per contract	1,500.00(2)
Total due	$4,000.00

Auditor's Notes:

(1) Agrees with accounts payable listing.

(2) Progress payment due as of December 31, 19X5 per contract for construction of new custom electric sign. Sign installed on January 15, 19X6.

STATEMENT FROM FIBERCHEM INC.

ABC Ltd.
Halifax, N.S.

Amounts Due as of December 31, 19X5:

INVOICE NO.	DATE	AMOUNT	BALANCE DUE
8312	11-22-X5	$2,217.92	$2,217.92
8469	12-02-X5	2,540.11	4,758.03
8819	12-18-X5	1,557.77	6,315.80(1)
9002	12-30-X5	2,403.42(2)	8,719.22

Auditor's Notes:

(1) Agrees with accounts payable listing.

(2) Goods received December 31, 19X5. Due to New Year's Eve shut-down, recorded on January 2, 19X6.

STATEMENT FROM FULLER TRAVEL

ABC Ltd.
Halifax, N.S.

Amounts Due as of December 31, 19X5:

TICKET NO.	DATE	AMOUNT	BALANCE DUE
843 601 102	12-04-X5	$280.00(2)	$ 280.00
843 601 819	12-12-X5	280.00(2)	560.00
843 602 222	12-21-X5	383.00(1)	943.00
843 602 919	12-26-X5	383.00(2)	1,326.00

Auditor's Notes:

(1) Ticket not used and returned for credit. Credit given on January 19X6 statement.

(2) The total of these items of $943.00 agrees with accounts payable listing.

FIGURE 13–8

Continued

STATEMENT FROM NORRIS INDUSTRIES, INC.

ABC Ltd.
Halifax, N.S.

Amounts Due as of December 31, 19X5:

INVOICE NO.	DATE	AMOUNT	BALANCE DUE
14896	12-27-X5	$9,120.00	$ 9,120.00(1)
15111	12-27-X5	4,300.00(2)	13,420.00

Auditor's Notes:

(1) Agrees with accounts payable listing.

(2) Goods shipped FOB Norris Industries' plant on December 21, 19X5, arrived at ABC Ltd. on January 4, 19X6.

STATEMENT FROM PETRO-CANADA

ABC Ltd.
Halifax, N.S.

Amounts Due as of December 31, 19X5:

INVOICE NO.	DATE	AMOUNT	BALANCE DUE
DX10037	12-02-X5	$2,870.00	$ 2,870.00
DX11926	12-09-X5	2,870.00	5,740.00
DX12619	12-16-X5	2,870.00	8,610.00
DX14777	12-23-X5	2,870.00	11,480.00(1)
DX16908	12-30-X5	2,870.00(2)	14,350.00

Auditor's Notes:

(1) Agrees with accounts payable listing.

(2) Goods shipped FOB ABC Ltd. Arrived on January 3, 19X6.

STATEMENT FROM REMINGTON SUPPLY CO. LTD.

ABC Ltd.
Halifax, N.S.

Amounts Due as of December 31, 19X5:

INVOICE NO.	DATE	AMOUNT	BALANCE DUE
141702	11-11-X5	$3,712.09(2)	$ 3,712.09
142619	11-19-X5	1,984.80(1)	5,696.89
142811	12-04-X5	2,320.00(2)	8,016.89
143600	12-21-X5	3,810.01(2)	11,826.90
143918	12-26-X5	3,707.00(3)	15,533.90

Auditor's Notes:

(1) Paid by ABC Ltd. on December 28, 19X5. Payment in transit at year-end.

(2) The total of these items of $9,842.10 agrees with accounts payable listing.

(3) Goods shipped FOB Remington Supply on December 26, 19X5, arrived at ABC Ltd. on January 3, 19X6.

HIGH-VOLUME ITEMS

1.	Central Steel, Inc.	$ 8,753.00
2.	Commercial Supply Ltd.	3,250.00
3.	FMC Corp.	15,819.00
4.	Fiberchem Inc.	6,315.80
5.	GAFCO, Inc.	5,750.00
6.	Monsanto Chemical Canada Ltd.	14,622.15
7.	Norris Industries, Inc.	9,120.00
8.	Petro-Canada	11,480.00
9.	Remington Supply Co. Ltd.	9,842.10
10.	Shell Oil	12,816.27

OTHER MATERIAL ITEMS

11.	Kohler Products Inc.	10,483.23

RANDOM SAMPLE OF ADDITIONAL ITEMS

12.	Advent Sign Mfg. Co. Ltd.	2,500.00
13.	Country Electric Ltd.	980.00
14.	Fuller Travel	943.00
15.	J & L Plastics Corp.	1,412.00
16.	M & A Milling Ltd.	4,662.00
17.	Permaloy Manufacturing	3,290.00
18.	S & S Truck Painting	819.00
19.	Todd Machinery, Inc.	6,888.12
20.	Western Maritime Supply Ltd.	2,369.62
	TOTAL TESTED	$132,115.29

FIGURE 13–10 ABC Ltd. Analysis of Trade Accounts Payable December 31, 19X5

VENDOR	BALANCE PER BOOKS	AMOUNT CONFRMED BY VENDOR	DIFFERENCE: BOOKS OVER (UNDER) AMOUNT CONFIRMED	RECONCILABLE DIFFERENCE NO ERROR	ERROR IN ACCOUNTS PAYABLE DR (CR)	ERROR IN RELATED ACCOUNTS Balance Sheet Error Dr (Cr)	Income Statement Error Dr (Cr)	BRIEF EXPLANATION
Fiberchem	$6,315.80	$8,719.22	$2,403.42		$(2,403.42)		$2,403.42	Unrecorded A/P Dr Purchases

14

AUDIT SAMPLING FOR TESTS OF DETAILS OF BALANCES

LEARNING OBJECTIVES

THOROUGH STUDY OF THIS CHAPTER WILL ENABLE YOU TO:

1. Distinguish between sampling of controls and sampling of details of account balances

2. Define and describe dollar unit sampling

3. Determine error bounds when no errors are found in a sample and when errors are found in a sample

4. Take appropriate actions when errors are found in the sample

5. Define and describe variables sampling

6. Apply difference estimation to tests of details of balances

☐ The primary topics in this chapter are determining sample size, selecting sample items, and reaching audit conclusions for tests of details of balances. Both nonstatistical and statistical methods are discussed, but the emphasis is on the latter. Chapter 14 is the last of four chapters in which evidence concepts are applied to the sales and collection cycle.

Comparison with Attributes Sampling for Tests of Controls

OBJECTIVE 1

Distinguish between sampling of controls and sampling of details of account balances.

Most of the sampling concepts discussed in Chapter 12 for tests of controls apply equally to sampling for tests of details of balances. In both cases, the auditor wants to make inferences about the entire population based on a sample. A method is needed that takes into account the imperfection of sampling as opposed to testing the entire population. Sampling and nonsampling risks are therefore important for both tests of controls and tests of details of balances. In dealing with sampling risk, it is acceptable to use either nonstatistical or statistical methods for both types of tests.

The most important difference between tests of controls and tests of details of balances is in what the auditor wants to measure. In tests of controls, the primary concern is testing the effectiveness of internal controls. When an auditor does tests of controls, the purpose is to determine if the deviation rate in the population is sufficiently low to justify assessing control risk below maximum to reduce substantive procedures. When statistical sampling is used for tests of controls, attributes sampling is ideal because it measures the frequency of occurrence (deviation rate). In tests of details of balances, the concern is determining whether the monetary amount of an account balance is materially misstated. Attributes sampling, therefore, is seldom useful for tests of details of balances. Instead, auditors use two types of statistical methods that provide results in *dollar* terms. These are *dollar unit sampling* and *variables sampling*. Dollar unit sampling, which is used widely in auditing, is illustrated in the body of this chapter. Variables sampling, which is used less extensively in auditing, is discussed in Appendix A.

Nature of the Problem for Tests of Details of Balances

When auditors sample for tests of details of balances, the objective is to determine whether the account balance being audited is fairly stated. There are three major decisions the auditor must make in the sampling process: determine the sample size, select the population items for auditing, and evaluate the sample results. These three decisions all result from the need to keep costs low by sampling, rather than auditing the entire population. They each require that the auditor obtain a *representative* sample.

To illustrate the nature of the sampling problem, a simple example is used. For Problem 14–27 on page 507, a listing of 40 accounts receivable totaling $207,295 is shown. Assume the auditor has decided to determine whether that balance is fairly stated by sending a sample of positive confirmations and performing alternative procedures for nonresponses.

Determine Sample Size

The auditor should plan to send a sufficiently large number of confirmations (sample size) to permit a correct decision about whether the population is fairly stated, but no more than is needed. Using the audit risk model (detection risk = audit risk/inherent risk × control risk), each factor in the model, plus materiality, will affect the appropriate sample size. Assume in this case that the auditor decides to select 15 sample items from the population of 40 for confirmation.

Select Population Items

It was shown in Chapter 12 that the auditor must select sample items to give reasonable assurance of a representative sample. In the receivables confirmation example, it would certainly be inappropriate to select the largest 15 items or the first 15 items on the list. It would also be inappropriate to select a random sample across all 40 items because the amounts constituting the accounts receivable population vary considerably. A better approach for sample selection is to use a stratified sample.

Stratified sampling is a method of sampling in which all the items in the population are divided into two or more subpopulations. Sampling is then done from each stratum. The purpose of stratification is to permit the auditor to emphasize certain population items and deemphasize others. In most audit sampling situations for confirming accounts receivable, auditors want to emphasize the larger recorded values; therefore, stratification is typically done on the basis of the size of recorded dollar values. In some cases the auditor may choose to emphasize receivables outstanding for a long time or receivables from certain locations. Stratification would be done on the basis of the number of days outstanding or location of the customer in those cases.

Examining the population in Problem 14–27, there are many different ways to stratify the population. Assume the auditor decided to stratify as follows:

STRATUM	STRATUM CRITERIA	NUMBER IN POPULATION	DOLLARS IN POPULATION
1	>$10,000	3	$ 88,955
2	$5,000 – $10,000	10	71,235
3	<$5,000	27	47,105
		40	$207,295

When selecting a stratified sample, the sample size is determined for each stratum and selected from that stratum. Any of the methods discussed in Chapter 12 – random, systematic, or haphazard – can be used to select the sample items. In the example, assume the auditor decides to select all three accounts from stratum 1 and six each from stratum 2 and stratum 3, for a total sample size of fifteen. Notice that a larger portion of the population items are selected from stratum 1 than 2 and from stratum 2 than 3. The auditor has thereby emphasized larger recorded values in confirming the accounts receivable, but no segment of the population has been ignored.

Evaluate Results Assume the auditor sends first and second requests for confirmations and performs alternative procedures. Assume also that the following conclusions are reached about the sample after reconciling all timing differences:

STRATUM	SAMPLE SIZE	DOLLARS AUDITED Recorded Value	Audited Value	CLIENT ERROR
1	3	$ 88,955	$ 91,695	$(2,740)
2	6	43,995	43,024	971
3	6	13,105	10,947	2,158
	15	$146,055	$145,666	$ 389

Does the auditor conclude that accounts receivable is overstated by $389? No, the auditor is interested in the *population* results, not those for the sample. It is therefore necessary to project from the sample to the population to estimate the population error. The first step is to make a *point estimate*. There are different ways to calculate the point estimate, but a common way to do it is to assume that errors in the unaudited population are proportional to the errors actually found in the sample. That calculation must be made by stratum and then totaled, rather than determined for the total errors. The point estimate is calculated as follows:

STRATUM	CLIENT ERROR ÷ RECORDED VALUE FROM SAMPLE	×	RECORDED BOOK VALUE FOR STRATUM	=	POINT ESTIMATE
1	$(2,740)/$88,955		$88,955		$(2,740)
2	971 / 43,995		71,235		1,572
3	2,158 / 13,105		47,105		7,757
Total					$6,589

The point estimate of the error in the population is $6,589, which means that the estimate of the errors is a $6,589 overstatement. The point estimate of $6,589 is larger than the sample error of $389 because to determine the point estimate, the auditor estimated the errors in the population items that were not audited. The calculation of the point estimate assumed, for each stratum, that the unaudited dollars had the same proportion of errors as those that were audited. In stratum 1, the point estimate, $2,740, is the same as the sample error because all population items were audited, whereas in stratum 3 the point estimate, $7,757, is nearly four times as large as the sample error, $2,158, because only about one-fourth of the population dollars were verified.

The point estimate, by itself, is not an adequate measure of the population error. The actual error will be more or less than the point estimate whenever the errors in the unaudited portion of a stratum are not proportional to those found in the audited portion. It is not appropriate for the auditor to assume the unaudited portion of a population has the same proportion of errors as the audited portion. *Sampling risk* must be considered.

As stated in Chapters 8 and 12, sampling risk (sampling error) is an inherent part of sampling that results from testing less than the entire population. In evaluating the results of a sample, the auditor should consider sampling risk. One of several statistical methods can be followed, or the auditor can use a nonstatistical approach. For the example in this section, the total sampling error is assumed to be $10,000, which could be either an overstatement or an understatement of the point estimate. For now, there is no discussion of how the sampling error is determined.

The estimated total population error can now be calculated as a combination of the point estimate and sampling error. The estimated range of the population error is $6,589 (point estimate) ± $10,000 (sampling error). The estimate of the largest likely overstatement error is $16,589 (6,589 + 10,000), and the largest likely understatement error is $3,411 (6,589 − 10,000). The auditor therefore concludes that the true error is likely to be between an overstatement of $16,589 and an understatement of $3,411.

To summarize, several steps were required to determine the estimated total error. First, the auditor determined the error in each sample item by performing the audit tests (identified misstatement); second, sample errors were summarized by stratum; third, a projection of the point estimate was made by stratum and in total (likely misstatement); and finally, sampling error was determined and used to calculate the estimated total population misstatement (further possible misstatements).

The final step is the evaluation of the audit results. In evaluation, the auditor must decide whether the population misstatement is sufficiently material to require further action or whether the population can be accepted as fairly stated. For the example being used, if either an overstatement error of $16,589 or an understatement error of $3,411 would materially affect the fair presentation of accounts receivable, the account could not be accepted. Even if the amounts are not considered material, the auditor must wait to make a final evaluation until the entire audit is completed. The estimated total misstatements in accounts receivable must then be combined with estimates of the misstatements in all other parts of the audit to evaluate the effect of all misstatements on the financial statement as a whole.

Dollar Unit Sampling

Dollar unit sampling (DUS)[1] is a recent innovation in sampling methodology that was developed specifically for use by auditors. It is now the most commonly used method of statistical sampling for tests of details of balances. This is because it has the statistical simplicity of attributes sampling yet provides a statistical result expressed in dollars. Dollar unit sampling is also referred to as *monetary unit sampling, cumulative monetary amount sampling,* and *sampling with probability proportional to size.* This method of statistical sampling is used to illustrate sample size determination, sample selection, and evaluation of results for tests of details of balances. The approach used for illustrating dollar unit sampling was also used for attributes sampling. The following steps are involved, with the steps for attributes included in the right column for comparison:

OBJECTIVE 2

Define and describe dollar unit sampling.

STEPS – DOLLAR UNIT SAMPLING	STEPS – ATTRIBUTES SAMPLING (see page 404)
Planning the Sample	**Planning the Sample**
1. State the objectives of the audit test.	1. State the objectives of the audit test.
2. Define error conditions.	2. Define attributes and deviation conditions.
3. Define the population.	3. Define the population.
4. Define the sampling unit.	4. Define the sampling unit.
5. Specify tolerable misstatement.	5. Specify tolerable deviation rate.
6. Specify acceptable risk of incorrect acceptance.	6. Specify acceptable risk of over-reliance.
7. Estimate the error rate in the population.	7. Estimate the population deviation rate.
8. Determine the initial sample size.	8. Determine the initial sample size.

[1] Perhaps the most authoritative source on dollar-unit sampling is Leslie, Donald A., Teitlebaum, Albert D. and Anderson, Rodney J., *Dollar-unit Sampling: A Practical Guide for Auditors*, Toronto: Copp Clark Pitman, 1979. The reader who wishes to pursue the subject in more depth is encouraged to read this work.

Selecting the Sample and Performing the Tests
9. Randomly select the sample.
10. Perform the audit procedures.

Evaluating the Results
11. Generalize from the sample to the population.
12. Analyze the errors.
13. Decide the acceptability of the population.

Selecting the Sample and Performing the Tests
9. Randomly select the sample.
10. Perform the audit procedures.

Evaluating the Results
11. Generalize from the sample to the population.
12. Analyze deviations.
13. Decide the acceptability of the population.

State the Objectives of the Audit Test

For dollar unit sampling, the objectives of the test are to determine the estimated errors in the population being audited and to decide whether the population is fairly stated. The values of the estimates of errors in dollar unit sampling are referred to as *error bounds*. If the estimates in the previous example had been determined using dollar unit sampling, the overstatement estimate of $16,589 would be called the *upper error bound* and the understatement estimate of $3,411 would be the *lower error bound*.

Define Error Conditions

Dollar unit sampling measures the dollar errors in the population. The major difference between dollar unit sampling and attributes sampling is that in dollar unit sampling, the measure is in dollars rather than the rate of occurrence. The reasons for the difference between dollar unit and attributes sampling are discussed in Chapter 12 and in the introduction to this chapter.

Define the Population

When using dollar unit sampling, the population is defined as the *recorded dollar population*. The auditor then evaluates whether the recorded population is overstated or understated. For example, the population of accounts receivable in Problem 14–27 on pages 507-508 consists of $207,295. Most audit sampling populations would, of course, contain far more items and would likely total a much larger dollar amount.

Because of the method of sample selection in dollar unit sampling, which is explained shortly, it is not possible to evaluate the likelihood of unrecorded items in the population. Assume, for example, that dollar unit sampling is used to evaluate whether inventory is fairly stated. It is not possible to use dollar unit sampling to evaluate whether certain inventory items exist but have not been counted. If the completion objective is important in the audit test, and it usually is, that objective must be satisfied separately from the dollar unit sampling tests.

Define the Sampling Unit

The most significant feature of dollar unit sampling is the definition of the sampling unit as *an individual dollar in an account balance*. The name of the statistical method, dollar unit sampling, results from this distinctive feature. For example, in the population on pages 507-508, the dollar unit is 1 dollar and the population size for dollar unit sampling is therefore $207,295, not the 40 physical units discussed earlier.

Another significant feature of dollar unit sampling is its *automatic* emphasis on physical units with the largest recorded dollar balances. Since the random sample is selected on the basis of individual dollars, an account with a large balance has a greater chance of being included than an account with a small one. For example, in accounts receivable confirmation, an account with a $5,000 balance has a 10 times greater probability of being included than one with a $500 balance, since it contains 10 times as many dollar units. As a result, there is no need to use stratified sampling in dollar unit sampling. It does stratification automatically.

Specify Tolerable Misstatement

Another unique aspect of dollar unit sampling is the use of the materiality available for unanticipated misstatements, as discussed in Chapter 8, to directly determine the tolerable misstatement amount for the audit of each account being audited using dollar unit sampling. Some sampling techniques, such as those discussed in Appendix A, require the auditor to specify a materiality amount for the account being audited. This is not required when dollar unit sampling is used. For example, assume the auditor decides the preliminary judgment about materiality should be $60,000 for the financial statements as a whole. That materiality amount of $60,000 or a derivative of it, as discussed below, would be used as tolerable misstatement in all applications of dollar unit sampling such as for inventory, accounts receivable, and accounts payable. Where other tests besides those using dollar unit sampling are expected to reveal errors, tolerable misstatement for dollar unit sampling must take those errors into consideration. In the above example, if total errors of $10,000 were expected in other tests, tolerable misstatement (materiality available for unanticipated misstatements) for all dollar unit sampling tests would be $50,000 (i.e., $60,000-$10,000).

There is an inverse relationship between the tolerable misstatement size and the required sample size. For example, if the auditor decides to reduce tolerable misstatement from $60,000 to $50,000, the sample size needed for dollar unit sampling would increase.

Specify Acceptable Risk of Incorrect Acceptance

As was indicated for attributes sampling, whenever a sample is taken, there is a risk that the quantitative conclusions about the population will be incorrect. This is always true unless 100 percent of the population is tested. This is the case with all nonstatistical and statistical sampling techniques.

Acceptable risk of incorrect acceptance (ARIA) is the risk the auditor is willing to take of accepting a balance as correct when the true error in the balance is equal to or greater than tolerable misstatement. To illustrate, assume tolerable misstatement is $60,000, ARIA is 10 percent, and the true error, which is unknown, is $65,000. The ARIA of 10 percent means the auditor is willing to take a 10 percent risk of concluding that the balance is correct after all testing is completed, even if it is misstated by $60,000 or more. ARIA is the equivalent term to acceptable risk of overreliance on internal control (ARO) for attributes sampling.

There is an inverse relationship between ARIA and required sample size. If, for example, the auditor decides to reduce ARIA from 10 to 5 percent, the required sample size would increase.

The primary factor affecting the auditor's decision about ARIA is control risk in the audit risk model, which is the extent to which the auditor relies on internal controls. When internal controls are effective, control risk can be reduced, which permits the auditor to increase ARIA, which in turn reduces the required sample size.

FIGURE 14–1

Effect of ARO and
ARIA on Required
Evidence

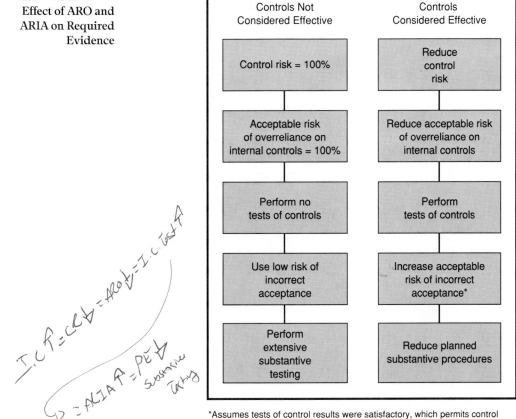

*Assumes tests of control results were satisfactory, which permits control risk to remain low.

A difficulty students often have is understanding how acceptable risk of overreliance on internal control (ARO) and acceptable risk of incorrect acceptance (ARIA) affect evidence. In Chapter 10 it was shown that substantive procedures can be reduced if tests of controls are performed and internal controls are found effective. The effects of ARO and ARIA are consistent with that conclusion. If the auditor concludes that internal controls may be effective, control risk can be reduced, which requires a lower ARO, *which requires more tests of controls.* If controls are found effective, control risk can remain low, which permits the auditor to increase ARIA, *which requires less substantive testing.* This conclusion is summarized in Figure 14–1.

Besides control risk, ARIA is also affected directly by audit risk and inversely by other substantive procedures already performed on the account balance, assuming effective results. For example, if audit risk is reduced, ARIA must also be reduced. If analytical procedures were performed and there is no indication of problem areas, there is a lower likelihood of misstatements in the account being tested, and ARIA can be increased. Stated differently, the analytical procedures are accumulated evidence in support of the account balance; therefore, less evidence from the detailed test using sampling is required to achieve acceptable audit risk. Figure 14–2 illustrates these relationships.

FIGURE 14–2 Relationship Between Factors Affecting ARIA, Effect on ARIA, and Required Sample Size for Dollar Unit Sampling

FACTOR AFFECTING ARIA	EXAMPLE	EFFECT ON ARIA	EFFECT ON SAMPLE SIZE IN DOLLAR UNIT SAMPLING
Effectiveness of internal controls (control risk)	Internal controls are effective (reduced control risk)	Increase	Decrease
Audit risk	Likelihood of bankruptcy is high (reduced audit risk)	Decrease	Increase
Analytical procedures	Analytical procedures performed with no indications of likely errors	Increase	Decrease

Estimate the Error Rate in the Population

Dollar unit sampling is normally used when the auditor believes there are likely to be no significant errors in the population. If an expected error rate of even 2 or 3 percent is likely, a different statistical sampling method than dollar unit sampling or alternately nonstatistical sampling would normally be used. This is because dollar unit sampling tends to be inefficient with moderate or large error rates. An estimated error rate of zero or one percent is therefore typical when dollar unit sampling is used.

Determine the Initial Sample Size

The appropriate sample size for dollar unit sampling is easy to calculate. However, it will be easier to explain after the methodology for calculating results is shown. How to determine sample size is therefore deferred until the end of the chapter.

Randomly Select the Sample

To select dollar unit samples it is first necessary to select a random sample of those dollar units. It is also necessary to identify the physical units associated with each dollar unit. The dollar units are needed to calculate the statistical results, but the physical units are needed to conduct the audit tests.

Random and systematic selection Dollar unit samples can be obtained using random sampling or systematic sampling techniques in a number of ways. An illustration of an accounts receivable population, including cumulative totals, is provided in Table 14–1 to demonstrate these methods.

1. *Random number table – cumulative amounts.* Assume that the auditor wants to select a random sample of four items for confirmation using dollar unit sampling. Since the sampling unit is defined as an individual dollar, the population size is 7,376 and four digits are needed from a random number table. Using the first four digits in the random number table, Table 12–2 on page 396, with a starting point of line 1002, column 4, the usable random numbers representing random dollars are 6,586, 1,756, 850, and 6,499. The population physical unit items that contain these random dollars are determined by reference to the cumulative total column. They are items 11 (containing dollars 6,577 through 6,980), 4 (dollars 1,699 through 2,271), 2 (dollars 358 through 1,638), and 10 (dollars 5,751 through 6,576). These will be audited, and the result for each physical unit will be applied to the random dollar it contains.

   The statistical methods used to evaluate dollar unit samples permit the inclusion of a physical unit in the sample more than once. That is, in the previous example, if the random numbers had been 6,586, 1,756, 856, and 6,599, the

TABLE 14–1

Accounts Receivable
Population

POPULATION ITEM (physical unit)	RECORDED AMOUNT	CUMULATIVE TOTAL (dollar unit)
1	$ 357	$ 357
2	1,281	1,638
3	60	1,698
4	573	2,271
5	691	2,962
6	143	3,105
7	1,425	4,530
8	278	4,808
9	942	5,750
10	826	6,576
11	404	6,980
12	396	7,376

sample items would be 11, 4, 2, and 11. Confirmations would be sent for population items 2, 4, and 11, but item 11 would be treated as two sample items statistically, and the sample total would be four items because four dollar units were involved.

2. *Systematic sampling.* The selection procedures followed for systematic sampling of dollar unit samples are closely related to those for random selection. As with random selection, the sampling unit is an individual dollar and the population is the recorded total. An interval is determined the same way as for any systematic plan, by dividing the population size by the desired sample size. In the previous example, the interval is 1,844 (7,376 ÷ 4). A starting point between zero and 1,843 is randomly selected by the use of a random number table (assume it is 921), and the interval is added. The random numbers are therefore 921; 2,765 (921 + 1,844); 4,609; and 6,453. The population items are 2, 5, 8, and 10.

Systematic sampling for dollar unit sampling has the same potential bias as previously discussed in Chapter 12, but the likelihood is less because random dollars are being selected rather than random physical units. It is unlikely that a company will intentionally or unintentionally arrange population items in a manner that affects the randomness of the distribution of the errors among different dollars. Some public accounting firms use only systematic sampling for dollar unit samples.

3. *Computer techniques.* Computer programs can easily be used to generate and order sample item numbers for use in the first two methods discussed. Also, many public accounting firms have special computer programs that select dollar unit samples when the population data are in machine-readable form.

Problems with dollar unit selection   Population items having a zero recorded balance have no chance of being selected with dollar unit sampling even though they may be misstated. Similarly, small balances that are significantly understated have little chance of being included in the sample. If the auditor is concerned about this problem, it can be overcome by doing specific audit tests for zero and small balances.

Another problem is the inability to include negative balances, such as credit balances in accounts receivable, in a dollar unit sample. It is possible to ignore negative balances for dollar unit sampling and test those amounts by some other means. An alternative is to treat them as positive balances and add them to the total being tested; however, this complicates the evaluation process.

Perform the Audit Procedures

To perform the audit procedures, the auditor first selects a sample on the basis of dollar units and identifies the physical units containing the dollar units by using one of the methods described above. The auditor then applies the appropriate audit procedures to determine whether each physical unit does or does not contain a misstatement.

For example, in the confirmation of accounts receivable the auditor would mail the sample of confirmations in the manner described in Chapter 13 and determine the amount of misstatement in each account confirmed. For nonresponses, alternative procedures would be used to determine the misstatement.

Generalize from the Sample to the Population

As discussed at the beginning of the chapter, the auditor must project errors from the sample results to the population and determine sampling error. There are four important aspects of generalizing from the sample to the population using dollar unit sampling:

OBJECTIVE 3

Determine error bounds when no errors are found in a sample and when errors are found in a sample.

- Attributes sampling tables are used to calculate the results. In using an attributes table, such as the one on page 412, the table becomes one for evaluating sample results using dollar unit sampling rather than attributes sampling. Risk of overreliance on the table is replaced with risk of incorrect acceptance, and actual number of deviations is replaced with actual number of errors.
- The attributes results must be converted to dollars. Dollar unit sampling concerns an estimate of the error in the population, not the percent of items in the population that contain an error.
- The auditor must make an assumption about the percentage of error for each population item that is in error. This assumption enables the auditor to use the attributes tables to estimate dollar errors.
- The statistical results when dollar unit sampling is used are referred to as error bounds. Both an upper error bound and lower error bound are calculated.

Generalizing When No Errors Are Found

Suppose the auditor is confirming a population of accounts receivable for monetary correctness. The population totals $1,200,000, and a sample of one hundred confirmations is obtained. Upon audit, no errors are uncovered in the sample. The auditor wants to determine the overstatement and understatement estimate of errors in accounts receivable, which are the *upper error bound* and *lower error bound*. Using the attributes sampling table on page 412, and assuming a risk of incorrect acceptance of 5 percent, both the upper and lower bounds are determined by locating the intersection of the sample size (100) and actual number of errors (0) in the same manner used for attributes sampling. The percent error is 3 percent; it is referred to as a percent error bound. The upper percent error bound and the lower percent error bound are therefore both 3 percent.

Based on the sample results and the error bounds from the attributes table, the auditor can conclude that not more than 3 percent of the dollar units are misstated. However, a major difference exists between attributes and dollar unit sampling results. For tests of controls, a deviation either exists or does not exist. For monetary tests, the error in each dollar could vary between one cent and the full dollar (for understatements the error can be more than a dollar).

The auditor must make an assumption of the *average percent of error for population items that contain an error; this is termed tainting in Dollar Unit*

Sampling: A Practical Guide for Auditors.[2] The assumption significantly affects the error bounds. To illustrate the concept of average percent of error or tainting assumption, three cases will be assumed: (1) overstatements and understatements both equal 100 percent errors; (2) overstatements and understatements both equal 10 percent errors; and (3) overstatements equal 20 percent errors and understatements equal 200 percent errors.

Assumption 1   Overstatement errors equal 100 percent; understatement errors equal 100 percent; error bounds at a 5 percent risk of incorrect acceptance are

$$\text{Upper error bound} = \$1,200,000 \times 3\% \times 1 = \$36,000$$

$$\text{Lower error bound} = \$1,200,000 \times 3\% \times 1 = \$36,000$$

The assumption is that, on the average, those population items in error will be misstated by the full dollar amount of the recorded value. Since the error bound is 3 percent, the dollar value of the error is not likely to exceed $36,000. If all the errors are overstated, there will be an overstatement of $36,000. If they are all understated, there will be an understatement of $36,000.

The assumption of 100 percent errors is extremely conservative, especially for overstatements. Assume that the actual population error rate is 3 percent. The following two conditions would both have to exist before the $36,000 properly reflected the upper error bound:

■ All errors would have to be overstatements. Offsetting errors would reduce the amount of the overstatement.

■ All population items in error would have to be 100 percent misstated. There could not, for example, be an error such as a cheque written for $262 that was recorded at $226.

In the calculation of the error bounds of $36,000 overstatement and understatement, the auditor did not calculate a point estimate and sampling error in the manner discussed earlier in the chapter. This is because tables were used that include both a point estimate and a sampling error to derive the upper error rate provided.

Thus, even though the point estimate and sampling unit are not calculated for dollar unit sampling, they are implicit in the determination of error bounds.

Assumption 2   Overstatement errors equal 10 percent; understatement errors equal 10 percent; error bounds at a 5 percent risk are

$$\text{Upper error bound} = \$1,200,000 \times 3\% \times .1 = \$3,600$$

$$\text{Lower error bound} = \$1,200,000 \times 3\% \times .1 = \$3,600$$

The assumption is that, on the average, those items in error will be misstated by no more than 10 percent. If all items were misstated in one direction, the error bounds would be +$3,600 and −$3,600. The change in assumption from 100 percent to 10 percent errors significantly affects the error bounds.

---

2 See Leslie, Teitlebaum and Anderson, op. cit., pp.122-123 and 390.

Assumption 3 Overstatement errors equal 20 percent; understatement errors equal 200 percent; error bounds at a 5 percent risk are

$$\text{Upper error bound} = \$1,200,000 \times 3\% \times \;.2 = \$\;7,200$$

$$\text{Lower error bound} = \$1,200,000 \times 3\% \times 2.0 = \$72,000$$

The justification for a larger percent for understatements is the larger potential percent error. For example, an accounts receivable recorded at $20 that should have been recorded at $200 is understated by 900 percent [(200 − 20)/20], whereas one that is recorded at $200 that should have been recorded at $20 is overstated by 90 percent [(200 − 20)/200].

Items containing large understatement errors may have a small recorded value, due to those errors. As a consequence, because of the mechanics of dollar unit sampling, few of them will have a chance of being selected in the sample. Because of this, some auditors select an additional sample of small items to supplement the dollar unit sample whenever understatement errors are an important audit concern.

Appropriate percent of error assumption The appropriate assumption to make regarding the overall percent of error in those population items containing an error is an auditor's decision. The auditor must set these percentages based on personal judgment in the circumstances. In the absence of convincing information to the contrary, most auditors believe it is desirable to assume a 100 percent error for both overstatements and understatements. This approach is considered highly conservative, but it is easier to justify than any other assumption. In fact, the reason upper and lower limits are referred to as error bounds when dollar unit sampling is used, rather than maximum likely error or the commonly used statistical term *confidence limit,* is because of widespread use of that very conservative assumption. Unless stated otherwise the 100 percent error assumption is used in the chapter and problem materials.

Generalizing When Errors Are Found This section presents the evaluation method when there are monetary errors in the sample. The same illustration is continued; the only change is the assumption about the errors. The sample size remains at one hundred and the recorded value is still $1,200,000, but now five errors in the sample are assumed. The errors are shown in Table 14–2.

The four aspects of generalizing from the sample to the population discussed earlier still apply, but their use is modified as follows:

TABLE 14–2
Errors

CUSTOMER NO.	RECORDED ACCOUNTS RECEIVABLE AMOUNT	AUDITED ACCOUNTS RECEIVABLE AMOUNT	ERROR	ERROR ÷ RECORDED AMOUNT
2073	$ 6,200	$ 6,100	$ 100	.016
5111	12,910	12,000	910	.0705
5206	4,322	4,450	(128)	(.0296)
7642	23,000	22,995	5	.0002
9816	8,947	2,947	6,000	.6706

TABLE 14–3

Percent Error Bounds

NUMBER OF ERRORS	UPPER PRECISION LIMIT FROM TABLE	INCREASE IN PRECISION LIMIT RESULTING FROM EACH ERROR (LAYERS)
0	.03	.03
1	.047	.017
2	.062	.015
3	.076	.014
4	.089	.013

- *Overstatement and understatement errors are dealt with separately, and then combined.* First, initial upper and lower error bounds are calculated separately for overstatement and understatement errors. Next, a point estimate of overstatements and understatements is calculated. The point estimate of understatements is used to reduce the initial upper error bound, and the point estimate of overstatements is used to reduce the initial lower error bound. The method and rationale for these calculations are illustrated using the four overstatement errors and one understatement error in Table 14–2.

- *A different error assumption is made for each error, including the zero errors.* When there were no errors in the sample, an assumption was required as to the average percent of error for the population items in error. The error bounds were calculated showing several different assumptions. Now that errors have been found, sample information is available to use in determining the error bounds. The error assumption is still required, but it can be modified.

- *The most conservative error assumption is 100 percent for all errors.* For overstatements, the upper error bound would be $106,800 (1,200,000 × 1.0 × .089). The .089 is determined from the 5 percent risk attributes sampling table on page 412 for a sample size of one hundred with four errors.

   Where errors are found, a 100 percent assumption for all errors is not only exceptionally conservative but also inconsistent with the error results. A common assumption in practice, and the one followed in this book, is to assume the actual sample errors are representative of the population errors. This assumption requires the auditor to calculate the average that each sample item was in error (error ÷ recorded accounts receivable amount), and apply that rate to the population. The calculation of the rate for each error is shown in the last column in Table 14–2. As will be explained shortly, an error assumption is still needed for the zero error portion of the computed results. For this example, a 100 percent error assumption is used for both overstatements and understatements.

- *The auditor must deal with layers of the computed upper deviation rate from the attributes table.* The reason for doing so is that there are different error assumptions for each error. Layers are calculated by first determining the computed upper deviation rate from the table for each error and then calculating each layer. Table 14–3 shows the layers.

- *Error assumptions must be associated with each layer.* The most common method of associating error assumptions is to be conservative by associating the largest dollar error percents with the largest layers. Table 14–4 shows the association. For example, the largest average error was .671 for customer 9816. That error is associated with the layer factor of .017, the largest layer where errors were found. The portion of the upper precision limit related to the zero error layer has an error assumption of 100 percent, which is still conservative. Table 14–4 shows the calculation of error bounds before consideration of offsetting errors. The upper error bound was calculated as if there were no understatement errors and the lower error bound was calculated as if there were no overstatement errors.

TABLE 14–4 Illustration of Determination of Initial Upper and Lower Error Bounds

NUMBER OF ERRORS	UPPER PRECISION LIMIT PORTION*	RECORDED VALUE	UNIT ERROR ASSUMPTION	ERROR BOUND PORTION (COLUMNS 2 × 3 × 4)
Overstatements				
0	.030	$1,200,000	1.0	$36,000
1	.017	1,200,000	.6706	13,680
2	.015	1,200,000	.0705	1,269
3	.014	1,200,000	.0161	270
4	.013	1,200,000	.0002	3
Upper precision limit	.089			
Initial error bound				$51,222
Understatements				
0	.030	$1,200,000	1.0	$36,000
1	.017	1,200,000	.0296	604
Lower precision limit	.047			
Initial error bound				$36,604

* Risk of incorrect acceptance of 5%. Sample size of 100.

Adjustment for offsetting errors Most dollar unit sampling users believe this approach just discussed is overly conservative when there are offsetting errors. If an understatement error is found, it is logical and reasonable that the bound for overstatement errors should be lower than it would be had no understatement errors been found, and vice versa. The adjustment of bounds for offsetting errors is made as follows: (1) a point estimate of errors is made for both understatement and overstatement errors and (2) each bound is reduced by the opposite point estimate.

The point estimate for overstatements is calculated by multiplying the average overstatement error in the dollar units audited times the recorded value. The same approach is used for calculating the point estimate for understatements. For example, for understatements there was one error of 3 cents per dollar unit in a sample of 100. The understatement point estimate is therefore $355 (.0296/100 × $1,200,000). Similarly, the overstatement point estimate is $9,089 [(.6706 + .0705 + .0161 + .0002) ÷ 100 × $1,200,000].

Table 14–5 shows the adjustment of the bounds that follow from this procedure. The initial upper bound of $51,222 is reduced by the estimated most likely understatement error of $355 to an adjusted bound of $50,867. The initial lower bound of $36,604 is reduced by the estimated most likely overstatement error of $9,089 to an adjusted bound of $27,515. Thus, given the methodology and assumptions followed, the auditor concludes that there is a 5 percent risk that accounts receivable is overstated by $50,867 or more, or understated by $27,515 or more. It should be noted that if the error assumptions were changed, the error bounds would also change. The reader should be advised that the method used to adjust the bounds for offsetting errors is but one of several in current use. The method illustrated here is taken from Leslie, Teitlebaum, and Anderson.[3] All the methods in current use are reliable and somewhat conservative.

The following seven steps summarize the calculation of the adjusted error bounds for dollar unit sampling when there are offsetting errors. The calculation of the adjusted upper error bound for the four overstatement errors in Table 14–2 is used to illustrate.

---

3 Op. cit.

TABLE 14–5   Illustration of Determination of Adjusted Error Bounds

NUMBER OF ERRORS	UNIT ERROR ASSUMPTION	SAMPLE SIZE	RECORDED POPULATION	POINT ESTIMATE	BOUNDS
Initial overstatement bound					$51,222
Understatement error 1	.0296	100	$1,200,000	$ 355	$ (355)
Adjusted overstatement bound					$50,867
Initial understatement bound					$36,604
Overstatement errors					
1	.6706				
2	.0705				
3	.0161				
4	.0002				
Sum	.7572	100	$1,200,000	$9,089	(9,089)
Adjusted understatement bound					$27,515

STEPS TO CALCULATE ADJUSTED ERROR BOUNDS	CALCULATION FOR OVERSTATEMENTS IN TABLE 14–2
1. Determine error for each sample item, keeping overstatements and understatements separate.	Table 14–2 Four overstatements
2. Calculate error per dollar unit in each sample item (error/recorded value).	Table 14–2 .0161, .0705, .0002, .6706
3. Layer errors per dollar unit from highest to lowest, including the percent error assumption for sample items not in error.	Table 14–4 1.0, .6706, .0705, .0161, .0002
4. Determine upper precision limit for attributes sampling table and determine the percent error bound for each error (layer).	Table 14–3 Total of 8.9% for four errors; calculate five layers
5. Calculate initial upper and lower error bounds for each layer and total.	Table 14–4 Total of $51,222
6. Calculate point estimate for overstatements and understatements.	Table 14–5 $355 for understatements $50,867 adjusted overstatement limit
7. Calculate adjusted upper and lower error bounds.	

Analyze the Errors

As for attributes sampling, an evaluation of the nature and cause of the errors is needed. For example, in confirming accounts receivable, suppose all errors resulted from the client's failure to record returned goods. The auditor should determine why that type of error occurred so often and whether it could affect the fair presentation of financial statements.

OBJECTIVE 4
Take appropriate actions when errors are found in the sample.

An important part of error analysis is deciding whether any modification of the audit risk model is needed. If the auditor concluded that the failure to record the returns discussed in the previous paragraph resulted from a breakdown of internal controls, it might be necessary to reassess control risk. That in turn would probably cause the auditor to reduce ARIA, which would increase the error bounds for the dollar unit sampling calculations.

Decide the Acceptability of the Population

Whenever a statistical method is used, a decision rule is needed to decide whether the population is acceptable. The decision rule for dollar unit sampling is:

> If *both* the lower error bound (LEB) and upper error bound (UEB) fall between the understatement and overstatement tolerable misstatement amounts, accept the conclusion that the book value is not misstated by a material amount; otherwise, conclude the book value is misstated by a material amount.

This decision rule is illustrated below: The auditor should conclude that both the LEB and UEB for situations 1, 2, and 3 fall completely within both the understatement and overstatement tolerable misstatements. Therefore, the conclusion that the population is not misstated by a tolerable misstatement amount is accepted. For situations 4, 5, 6, and 7, either LEB or UEB, or both, are outside tolerable misstatements. Therefore, the population book value is rejected.

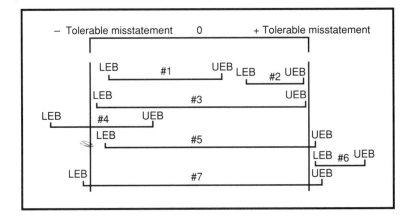

Assume in the example being used that the auditor had set a tolerable misstatement for the audit of $40,000 overstatement or understatement. That means the auditor will accept the recorded value if he or she concludes that accounts receivable is not overstated or understated by more than $40,000. As was previously shown, the auditor selected a sample of 100, found five errors, and calculated the lower bound to be $27,515 and the upper bound to be $50,867. Application of the decision rule leads the auditor to the conclusion that the population should not be accepted because the upper error bound is more than tolerable misstatement of $40,000.

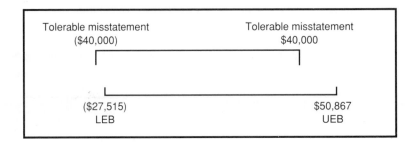

Action When a Population Is Rejected

When one or both of the error bounds lie outside the tolerable misstatement range and the population is not considered acceptable, there are several possible courses of action.

Perform expanded audit tests in specific areas   If an analysis of the errors indicates that most of the errors are of a particular type, it may be desirable to restrict the additional audit effort to the problem area. For example, if an analysis of the exceptions in confirmations indicates that most of the errors result from failure to record sales returns, an extended search could be made of returned goods to make sure they have been recorded. However, great care must be taken to evaluate the cause of all errors in the sample before a conclusion is drawn about the proper emphasis in the expanded tests; there may be more than one problem area.

Increase the sample size   When the auditor increases the sample size, both the upper and lower error bounds become smaller if the rate of errors in the expanded sample, their dollar amount, and their direction are similar in nature to those in the original sample. Increasing the sample size, therefore, may satisfy the auditor's tolerable misstatement requirements.

Increasing the sample size enough to satisfy the auditor's tolerable misstatement standards is often *costly,* especially when the error bounds are well beyond the auditor's tolerable misstatement standards. Even if the sample size is increased, there is no assurance of a satisfactory result. If the number, amount, and direction of the errors in the extended sample are proportionately greater or more variable than in the original sample, the results are still likely to be unacceptable. For accounts receivable confirmation, it is also difficult to increase the sample size because the requests should be sent out near the end of the month being confirmed. By the time the auditor discovers that the sample was not large enough, several weeks have usually passed. Despite all of these difficulties, in many instances the auditor must extend the sample to obtain more information about the population. It is much more common to increase sample size in other audit areas in which dollar unit sampling is used than in confirming receivables, but even for confirmations it is occasionally necessary.

Adjust the account balance   When one of the error bounds is larger than the auditor will accept, the client may be willing to adjust the book value. The amount of the adjustment is usually calculated using nonstatistical methods or more advanced dollar unit sampling techniques. In the previous example, if both the auditor and client were willing to decrease the book value of accounts receivable by $10,867 ($50,867 − $40,000), the population would be acceptable in terms of the upper bound. Since the lower bound would then be $(38,386), it would also be acceptable. A problem arises whenever the sampling error of the statistical interval is greater than the amount of tolerable misstatement (situation #7 in the chart on page 486). In such a case, no adjustment will solve the problem, as either the upper or lower bound will always exceed tolerable misstatement. The auditor will have to expand the tests or increase the sample size to obtain more complete and/or precise information.

*[handwritten annotation: Only when not both.
If so increase S.S.]*

Request the client to correct the population In some cases the client's records are so inadequate that a correction of the entire population is required before the audit can be completed. For example, in accounts receivable, the client may be asked to prepare the aging schedule again if the auditor concludes that it has significant errors. Whenever the client changes the valuation of some items in the population, it is of course necessary to audit the results again.

Refuse to give an unqualified opinion If the auditor believes the recorded amount in accounts receivable or any other account is not fairly stated, it is necessary to follow at least one of the above alternatives or *to qualify the audit opinion* in an appropriate manner. If the auditor believes there is a reasonable chance that the financial statements are materially misstated, it would be a serious breach of auditing standards to issue an unqualified audit report.

Determining Sample Size

The method used to determine sample size for dollar unit sampling is similar to that used for physical unit attributes sampling, applying the attributes sampling tables. The five things that must be known or specified have already been discussed in this chapter. An example is used to illustrate determining sample size.

Materiality The preliminary judgment about materiality is normally the basis for the tolerable misstatement amount used. If errors in nondollar-unit-sampling tests are expected, tolerable misstatement would be materiality less those amounts, that is, materiality available for unanticipated misstatements discussed in Chapter 8. Tolerable misstatement may be different for overstatements or understatements. For this example, tolerable misstatement for both overstatements and understatements is $100,000.

Assumption of the average percent of error for population items that contain an error Again there may be a separate assumption for the upper and lower bounds. This is also an auditor judgment. It should be based on auditors' knowledge of the client and past experience, and if less than 100 percent is used, the assumption must be clearly defensible. For this example, 50 percent is used for overstatements and 100 percent for understatements.

Acceptable risk of incorrect acceptance ARIA is an auditor judgment and is often reached with the aid of the audit risk model. It is 5 percent for this example.

Recorded population value The dollar value of the population is taken from the client's general ledger and other totals being audited. For this example, it is $5 million.

Estimate of the error rate in the population Normally the estimate of the error rate in the population for dollar unit sampling is zero. This is the case in the example.

These assumptions are summarized as follows:

Tolerable misstatement (same for upper and lower)	$100,000
Average percent of error assumption, overstatements	50%
Average percent of error assumption, understatements	100%
Risk of incorrect acceptance	5%
Accounts receivable per general ledger	$5 million
Estimate of the error rate in the population	0

The sample size is calculated as follows:

	UPPER BOUND	LOWER BOUND
Tolerable misstatement	100,000	100,000
Average percent of error assumption	÷ 0.50	÷ 1.00
	200,000	100,000
Recorded population value	÷ 5,000,000	÷ 5,000,000
Allowable percent error bound	4%	2%
Required sample size from the attributes table – 5 percent risk of incorrect acceptance	Not applicable*	149

*need S.S.
that meets
Both Criteria*

* The sample size from Table 12–6 (5 percent risk of overreliance) on page 409 is 74. It is smaller than the required sample size for the lower bound and is therefore not applicable.

If 149 sample items are selected and there are no errors in the sample, both the upper bound and lower bound requirements will be met. However, if there are any understatement errors, the lower tolerable misstatement bound will not be satisfied. Several overstatement errors could be found and still satisfy the upper tolerable misstatement bound because the upper bound is 4 percent compared with 2 percent for the lower bound. Where the auditor is concerned that this situation may occur, he or she can guard against it by arbitrarily increasing sample size above the amount determined by the tables. For example, in this illustration, the auditor might use a sample size of 200 instead of 149.

Audit Uses of Dollar Unit Sampling

Dollar unit sampling is particularly appealing to auditors for at least four reasons. First, it automatically increases the likelihood of selecting high dollar items from the population being audited. Auditors make a practice of concentrating on these items because they generally represent the greatest risk of material misstatements. Stratified sampling can also be used for this purpose, but dollar unit sampling is often easier to apply.

A second advantage of dollar unit sampling is that it frequently reduces the cost of doing the audit testing because several sample items could be tested at once. For example, if one large item makes up 10 percent of the total recorded dollar value of the population and the sample size is 100, the dollar unit sampling selection method is likely to result in approximately 10 percent of the sample items from that one large population item. Naturally, that item needs to be audited only once, but it counts as a sample of 10. If the item is in error, it is also counted as 10 errors. Larger population items may be eliminated from the sampled population by auditing them 100 percent and evaluating them separately if the auditor so desires.

Third, dollar unit sampling is appealing because of its ease of application. Dollar unit samples can be evaluated by the application of simple tables. It is easy to teach and to supervise the use of dollar unit techniques. Firms that use dollar unit sampling extensively utilize special tables that streamline sample size determination and evaluation even further than shown here.

Finally, dollar unit sampling always gives the statistical conclusion as a dollar amount. This provides a definite advantage over the use of attributes sampling, the result of which is stated in terms of frequency of the items in error.

The primary disadvantage of dollar unit sampling is twofold. First, the total error bounds resulting when errors are found may be too high to be useful to the auditor. This is because these evaluation methods are inherently conservative when errors are found and often produce bounds far in excess of materiality. To overcome this problem, large samples may be required. Second, it may be cumbersome to select dollar unit samples from large populations without computer assistance.

For all these reasons, dollar unit sampling is most commonly used when zero or very few errors are expected, a dollar result is desired, and the population data are maintained on computer files.

APPENDIX A
Variables
Sampling

There are several sampling techniques that constitute the general class of methods called variables sampling. Those studied in this appendix are difference estimation, ratio estimation, and mean-per-unit estimation. Before discussing the three methods and when it is most appropriate to use each, sampling distributions and statistical inference are discussed.

Sampling Distributions

Although auditors can assess the general nature of populations for the purpose of selecting the most appropriate sampling method, they do not know the mean value (average) or the distribution of the misstatement amounts or the audited values of the populations they are testing in audit engagements. The population characteristics must be estimated from samples. That, of course, is the purpose of the audit test. In this section there is a discussion of sampling distributions, which are essential to drawing conclusions about populations on the basis of samples using variables sampling methods.

> **OBJECTIVE 5**
>
> Define and describe variables sampling.

Assume that an auditor, as an experiment, took thousands of repeated samples of equal size from a population of accounting data having a mean value of $\overline{X}$. For each sample the auditor calculates the mean value of the items in the sample as follows:

$$\overline{x} = \frac{\Sigma x_j}{n}$$

where

$\overline{x}$ = mean value of the sample items
x_j = value of each individual sample item
n = sample size

After calculating $\overline{x}$ for each sample, the auditor plots them into a *frequency distribution*. The frequency distribution of the sample will likely be as shown in Figure 14–3.

A distribution of the sample means such as this is *always normal* and has all the characteristics of the *normal curve:* (1) the curve is symmetrical, and (2) the sample means fall within known portions of the sampling distribution around the average or mean of those means, measured by the distance along the horizontal axis in terms of *standard deviations*. Further, the mean of the sample means (the midpoint of the sampling distribution) is equal to the population mean and the standard deviation of the sampling distribution is equal to $SD/\sqrt{n}$. SD is the population standard deviation and n is the sample size.

To illustrate, assume a population with a mean of $40 and a standard deviation of $15 ($\overline{X}$ = $40 and SD = $15), from which we elected to take many random samples of one hundred items each. The standard deviation of our sampling

FIGURE 14–3

Frequency Distribution
of Sample Means

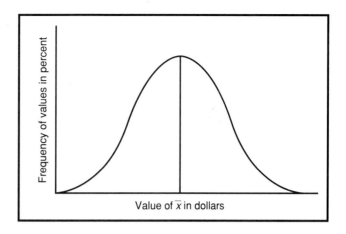

distribution would be $1.50 (SD/$\sqrt{n}$ = 15/$\sqrt{100}$ = 1.50). The reference to "standard deviation" of the population and to "standard deviation" of the sampling distribution often is confusing. To avoid the confusion the standard deviation of the distribution of the sample means is often called the *standard error of the mean* (SE). With this information, the tabulation of the sampling distribution can be made, as shown in Table 14–6.

To summarize, three things are important about the results of the experiment of taking a large number of samples from a known population:

■ The sample mean value ($\bar{x}$) with the highest frequency of occurrence is equal to the population mean ($\bar{X}$).

■ The shape of the frequency distribution is that of a normal curve if the sample is reasonably large, *regardless of the distribution of the population*. A graphic representation of this conclusion is shown in Figure 14–4.

■ The percentage of sample means between any two values of the sampling distribution is measurable. The percentage can be calculated by (1) determining the number of standard errors of the mean between any two values and (2) determining the percentage of sample means represented from a table for normal curves.

Statistical
Inference

Naturally when the auditor samples from a population in an actual audit situation, the auditor does not know the population's characteristics and there is ordinarily only one sample taken from the population. But the *knowledge of*

TABLE 14–6

Calculated Sampling
Distribution from a
Population with a
Known Mean and
Standard Deviation

(1) NUMBER OF STANDARD ERRORS OF THE MEAN (CONFIDENCE COEFFICIENT)	**(2)** VALUE [(1) × $1.50]	**(3)** RANGE AROUND $\bar{X}$ [$40 ± (2)]	**(4)** PERCENT OF SAMPLE MEANS INCLUDED IN RANGE
1	$1.50	$38.50–$41.50	68.2
2	$3.00	$37.00–$43.00	95.4
3	$4.50	$35.50–$44.50	99.7

(taken from table for normal curve)

FIGURE 14–4

Sampling Distribution
for a Population
Distribution

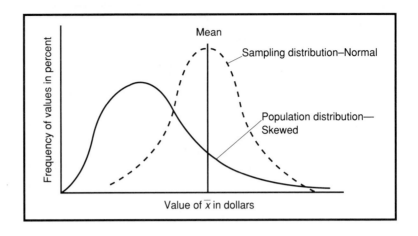

sampling distributions enables auditors to draw statistical conclusions (that is, to make statistical inferences) about the population. For example, assume that the auditor takes a sample from a population and calculates $\bar{x}$ as $46 and SE as $9 (the way to calculate SE will be shown later). We can now calculate a confidence interval of the population mean using the logic gained from the study of sampling distributions. It is

$$CI_{\bar{x}} = \hat{\bar{X}} \pm Z \cdot SE$$

where

$CI_{\bar{x}}$ = confidence interval for the population mean

$\hat{\bar{X}}$ = point estimate of the population mean

Z = confidence coefficient $\begin{cases} 1 = 68.2\% \text{ confidence level} \\ 2 = 95.4\% \text{ confidence level} \\ 3 = 99.7\% \text{ confidence level)} \end{cases}$

SE = standard error of the mean

For the example:

$$CI_{\bar{x}} = \$46 \pm 1(\$9) = \$46 \pm \$9 \quad \text{at a 68.2\% confidence level}$$

$$CI_{\bar{x}} = \$46 \pm 2(\$9) = \$46 \pm \$18 \text{ at a 95.4\% confidence level}$$

$$CI_{\bar{x}} = \$46 \pm 3(\$9) = \$46 \pm \$27 \text{ at a 99.7\% confidence level}$$

The results can also be stated in terms of confidence limits ($CL_{\bar{x}}$). The upper confidence limit ($UCL_{\bar{x}}$) is $\hat{\bar{X}} + Z \cdot SE$ ($46 + $18 = $64 at a 95 percent confidence level) and a lower confidence limit ($LCL_{\bar{x}}$) is $\hat{\bar{X}} - Z \cdot SE$ ($46 − $18 = $28 at 95 percent confidence level).

Graphically, the results are as follows:

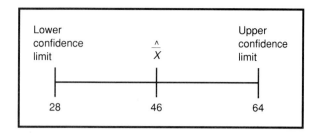

The conclusion about the confidence interval based on a sample from an unknown population can be stated in different ways, but care must be taken to avoid incorrect conclusions. In making statistical inferences the auditor should remember that the true population value is unknown. There is always a possibility that the sample is not representative of the true population value. The auditor can say, in the previous example, that the confidence interval for the true population mean value is $46 ± $18 at a 95 percent confidence level or that the true population mean value is between $28 and $64 at a 95 percent confidence level.

Variables Methods

The statistical inference process just discussed is used for all the variables sampling methods. The main difference among the various methods is in the characteristic of each sample item and thus in the population being measured. The three variables methods are now discussed individually.

Difference estimation *Difference estimation* is used to measure the estimated total error amount in a population when there is both a recorded value and an audited value for each item in the sample. An example is to confirm a sample of accounts receivable and determine the difference (error) between the client's recorded amount and the amount the auditor considers correct for each selected account. The auditor makes an estimate of the population error based on the number of errors, average error size, and individual error size in the sample. The result is stated as a point estimate plus or minus a computed precision interval at a stated confidence level. An illustration using difference estimation is shown later in the chapter.

Difference estimation frequently results in smaller sample sizes than any other method, and it is relatively easy to use. For that reason difference estimation is used frequently by auditors.

Ratio estimation *Ratio estimation* is similar to difference estimation except that the point estimate of the population error is determined by multiplying the portion of sample dollars in error times the total recorded population book value. The ratio estimate results in even smaller sample sizes than difference estimation *if the size of the errors in the population is proportionate to the recorded value of the population items*. If the size of the individual errors is independent of the recorded value, the difference estimate results in smaller sample sizes.

Mean-per-unit estimation In *mean-per-unit estimation,* the auditor is concerned with the *audited value* rather than the error amount of each item in the sample. Except for the definition of what is being measured, the mean-per-unit estimate is calculated in exactly the same manner as the difference estimate. The *point estimate* of the audited value is the average audited value of items in the sample times the population size. The *computed precision interval* is computed on the basis of the audited value of the sample items rather than the errors. When the auditor has computed the upper and lower confidence limits, a decision is made about the acceptability of the population by comparing these amounts with the recorded book value.

Stratification   As discussed earlier in the chapter, *stratified sampling* is a method of sampling in which all the elements in the total population are divided into two or more subpopulations. Each subpopulation is then independently tested and statistically measured. After the results of the individual parts have been computed, they are combined into one overall population estimate in terms of a confidence interval. Stratification is applicable to difference, ratio, and mean-per-unit estimation, but it is most commonly used with mean-per-unit estimation.

Subdividing or stratifying a population is not unique to statistical sampling, of course. Auditors have traditionally emphasized certain types of items when they are testing a population. For example, in confirming accounts receivable, it has been customary to place more emphasis on large accounts than on small ones. The major difference is that in statistical stratified sampling, the approach is more objective and better defined than it is under most traditional stratification methods. It was shown earlier that dollar unit sampling automatically emphasizes physical units with larger recorded balances.

Sampling Risks   Acceptable risk of incorrect acceptance was discussed earlier for dollar unit sampling. For variables sampling, acceptable risk of incorrect rejection (ARIR) is also used. The distinctions between and uses of the two risks must be understood.

ARIA   After an audit test is performed and statistical results calculated, the auditor must conclude either that the population is not materially misstated or that it is materially misstated. ARIA is the statistical risk that the auditor has accepted a population that is actually *materially misstated;* this risk is also called beta risk. ARIA is a serious concern to auditors because there are potential legal implications in concluding that an account balance is fairly stated when it is in error by a material amount.

An account balance can be either overstated or understated, but not both; therefore, ARIA is a one-tailed statistical test. The confidence coefficients for ARIA are therefore different from the confidence level. (Confidence level $= 1 - 2$ ARIA; for example, if ARIA is 10 percent, the confidence level is 80 percent.) The confidence coefficients for various ARIAs are shown in Table 14–7 together with confidence coefficients for the confidence level and ARIR.

ARIR   ARIR is the statistical risk that the auditor has concluded that a population is materially misstated when it is not; this risk is also called alpha risk. The only time ARIR affects the auditor's actions is when an auditor concludes that a population is not fairly stated. The most likely action when the auditor finds a balance not fairly stated is to increase the sample size or perform other tests. An increased sample size will usually lead the auditor to conclude that the balance was fairly stated if the account is not materially in error.

ARIR is important only when there is a high cost to increasing the sample size or performing other tests. ARIA is always important. Confidence coefficients for ARIR are also shown in Table 14–7.

TABLE 14–7

Confidence Coefficient for Confidence Levels, ARIAs and ARIRs

CONFIDENCE LEVEL (%)	ARIA (%)	ARIR (%)	CONFIDENCE COEFFICIENT
99	.5	1	2.58
95	2.5	5	1.96
90	5	10	1.64
80	10	20	1.28
75	12.5	25	1.15
70	15	30	1.04
60	20	40	.84
50	25	50	.67
40	30	60	.52
30	35	70	.39
20	40	80	.25
10	45	90	.13
0	50	100	.0

ARIA and ARIR are summarized in Table 14–8. It may seem from Table 14–8 that the auditor should attempt to minimize ARIA and ARIR. The way to accomplish that is by increasing the sample size, thus minimizing the risks. Since that is costly, having reasonable ARIA and ARIR is a more desirable goal.

Illustration Using Difference Estimation

OBJECTIVE 6

Apply difference estimation to tests of details of balances.

As previously discussed, there are several different types of variables sampling techniques that may be applicable to auditing in different circumstances. One of these, *difference estimation,* has been selected as a means of illustrating the concepts and methodology of variables sampling. The reason for using difference estimation is its relative simplicity and its use by practitioners. When the method is considered reliable in a given set of circumstances, it is preferred by most auditors.

In explaining difference estimation, the steps in determining whether the account balance in the audit of accounts receivable is correctly stated are illustrated. Positive confirmations in the audit of Hart Lumber Corp. are used as a frame of reference to illustrate the use of difference estimation. There are 4,000 accounts receivable listed on the aged trial balance with a recorded value of $600,000. Internal controls are considered somewhat weak and a large number of small errors in recorded amounts are expected in the audit. Total assets are $2,500,000 and net earnings before taxes are $400,000. Audit risk is reasonably high because of the limited users of the statements and the good financial health of Hart Lumber. Analytical procedures results indicated no significant problem.

The assumptions throughout are either that all confirmations were returned or that effective alternative procedures were carried out. Hence, the sample size is the number of positive confirmations mailed.

TABLE 14–8

ARIA and ARIR

ACTUAL AUDIT DECISION	ACTUAL STATE OF THE POPULATION	
	Materially Misstated	*Not Materially Misstated*
Conclude that the population is materially misstated	Correct conclusion – no risk	Incorrect conclusion – risk is ARIR
Conclude that the population is not materially misstated	Incorrect conclusion – risk is ARIA	Correct conclusion – no risk

Decisions Needed to Determine Sample Size   The auditor must make three decisions before the sample size can be determined for a test using difference estimation to evaluate whether an account balance is materially misstated. The first two were discussed as a part of dollar unit sampling.

Tolerable misstatement for the audit test   The amount of error the auditor is willing to accept is a *materiality* question. The auditor needs to set tolerable misstatement for accounts receivable (that is, to allocate part of the preliminary judgment about materiality for the audit of Hart Lumber to accounts receivable) and decides to accept a tolerable misstatement of $21,000 in the audit of accounts receivable.

ARIA   The risk of accepting accounts receivable as correct if it is actually misstated by more than $21,000 is affected by audit risk, results of the tests of controls, analytical procedures, and the relative significance of accounts receivable in the financial statements. In Hart Lumber, an ARIA of 10 percent is used.

After the auditor specifies the tolerable misstatement and ARIA, the hypothesis can be stated. The auditor's hypothesis for the audit of accounts receivable for Hart Lumber is: accounts receivable is not misstated by more than $21,000 at an ARIA of 10 percent.

ARIR   The risk of rejecting accounts receivable as incorrect if it is not actually misstated by a material amount is affected by the additional cost of resampling. Since it is fairly costly to confirm receivables a second time, an ARIR of 25 percent is used. For audit tests for which it is not costly to increase the sample size, a much higher ARIR is common.

Other Information   Three additional pieces of information are needed to determine sample size:

Population size   The population size is determined by count, as it was for attributes sampling. An accurate count is much more important in variables sampling because sample size and the computed precision limits are directly affected by population size. The population size for Hart Lumber's accounts receivable is 4,000.

Expected point estimate   An advance estimate of the population point estimate is needed for difference estimation, much as the expected error rate is needed for attributes sampling. The advance estimate is $1,500 (overstatement) for Hart Lumber, based on the previous year's audit tests.

Advance population standard deviation estimate – variability of the population   An advanced estimate of the variation in the errors in the population as measured by the population standard deviation is needed to determine the initial sample size. The calculation of the standard deviation is shown later. For Hart Lumber, it is estimated to be $20 based on the previous year's audit tests.

Calculate the Initial Sample Size   The initial sample size for Hart Lumber can be now calculated from the following formula:

$$n = \left[\frac{N(Z_A + Z_R)SD^*}{API^*} \right]^2$$

where

n = initial sample size

N = population size

Z_A = confidence coefficient for ARIA (see Table 14–7)

Z_R = confidence coefficient for ARIR (see Table 14–7)

SD^* = advance estimate of the standard deviation

API^* = allowable precision internal = $TM - E^*$

TM = tolerable misstatement for the population (materiality)

E^* = estimated point estimate of the population error

Applied to Hart Lumber, this equation yields

$$n = \left[\frac{4,000(1.28 + 1.15)20}{21,000 - 1,500} \right]^2 = (9.97)^2 = 100$$

Take a Random Sample   The *sampling unit* is defined as the individual balance on the accounts receivable aged trial balance. The random sample is selected in the same manner as for attributes sampling, probably on the basis of page number and line number. The number of confirmations mailed is the sample size. The number of confirmations that must be sent for Hart Lumber is 100.

Determine the Value of each Error in the Sample   For confirmations, the error is the *difference* between the confirmation response and the client's balance after the reconciliation of all timing differences and customer errors. For example, if a customer returns a confirmation and states the correct balance is $887.12, and the balance in the client's records is $997.12, the difference of $110 is an overstatement error if the auditor concludes that the client's records are incorrect. For *nonresponses,* the errors discovered by alternative procedures are treated identically to those discovered through confirmation. At the end of this step, there is an error value for each item in the sample, many of which are likely to be zero. The errors for Hart Lumber are shown in Table 14–9; the sum of the errors (termed *identified misstatement* in Chapter 8 and the Auditing Guideline "Applying Materiality and Audit Risk Concepts in Conducting an Audit") is $226.48.

Compute the Point Estimate of the Total Error   The *point estimate* is a direct extrapolation from the errors in the sample to the errors in the population (termed *likely misstatement* in Chapter 8). The calculation of the likely misstatement for Hart Lumber is shown in Table 14–9, step 3.

It is unlikely, of course, for the actual, but unknown, error to be *exactly* the same as the likely misstatement. It is more realistic to estimate the error in terms of a confidence interval determined by the likely misstatement plus and minus a computed precision interval. It should be apparent at this point that the calculation of the confidence interval is an essential part of variables sampling and that the process used to develop it depends on obtaining a *representative sample.*

Compute an Estimate of the Population Standard Deviation

The population *standard deviation* is a statistical measure of the *variability* in the values of the individual items in the population. If there is a large amount of variation in the values of population items, the standard deviation is larger than when the variation is small. For example, in the confirmation of accounts receivable, errors of $4, $14, and $26 have far less variation than the set $2, $275, and $812. Hence, the standard deviation is smaller in the first set.

The standard deviation has a significant effect on the computed precision interval. As might be expected, the ability to predict the value of a population is better when there is a small rather than a large amount of variation in the individual values of the population.

A reasonable estimate of the value of the population standard deviation is computed by the auditor using the standard statistical formula shown in Table 14–9, step 4. The size of the standard deviation estimate is determined solely by the characteristics of the auditor's sample results and is not affected by professional judgment.

Compute the Precision Interval

The *precision interval* is calculated by a statistical formula. The results are a dollar measure of the inability to predict the true population error because the test was based on a sample rather than on the entire population. In order for the computed precision interval to have any meaning, it must be associated with ARIA. The formula to calculate the precision interval is shown in Table 14–9, step 5.

An examination of the formula in step 5 of Table 14–9 indicates that the effect of changing each factor while the other factors remain constant is as follows:

TYPE OF CHANGE	EFFECT ON THE UPPER PRECISION LIMIT
Increase ARIA	Decrease
Increase the likely misstatement	Increase
Increase the standard deviation	Increase
Increase the sample size	Decrease

Calculating sample size The formula for determining the sample size (see page 497) is derived from the one for calculating the computed precision interval (Table 14–9, step 5), but there are important differences:

- The formula for sample size uses allowable precision interval (tolerable misstatement minus expected likely misstatement) instead of computed precision interval (CPI). The use of these two terms in the formulas is equivalent to the use of desired upper deviation rate and computed upper deviation rate for attributes sampling.
- The only confidence coefficient included in calculating CPI is for ARIA. The reason is that after the audit tests are performed, the auditor wants to find out if the population is acceptable. If it is, only ARIA is relevant because there can be no ARIR when the population is accepted.
- The actual standard deviation, based on the sample results, is used for calculating CPI instead of the advance estimate used for calculating sample size.
- The likely estimate, based on the sample result, is used for calculating the confidence limits instead of the advance estimate used for calculating sample size.

TABLE 14–9 Calculation of Confidence Limits

STEP	STATISTICAL FORMULA	ILLUSTRATION FOR HART LUMBER CORP.
1. Take a random sample of size n.	n = sample size	One hundred accounts receivable are selected randomly from the aged trial balance containing 4,000 accounts.
2. Determine the value of each error in the sample.		Seventy-five accounts are confirmed by customers, and 25 accounts are verified by alternative procedures. After reconciling timing differences and customer errors, the following twelve items were determined to be client errors (understatements):

$$
\begin{array}{ll}
1. \ 12.75 & 7. \ (.87) \\
2. \ (69.46) & 8. \ 24.32 \\
3. \ 85.28 & 9. \ 36.59 \\
4. \ 100.00 & 10. \ (102.16) \\
5. \ (27.30) & 11. \ 54.71 \\
6. \ 41.06 & 12. \ 71.56 \\
& \text{Sum} = 226.48
\end{array}
$$

STEP	STATISTICAL FORMULA	ILLUSTRATION FOR HART LUMBER CORP.
3. Compute the likely misstatement.	$\bar{e} = \dfrac{\Sigma e_i}{n}$ $\hat{E} = N\bar{e}$ or $N\dfrac{\Sigma e_i}{n}$	$\bar{e} = \dfrac{226.48}{100} = 2.26$ $\hat{E} = 4{,}000(2.26) = \$9{,}040$ or $\hat{E} = 4{,}000\left(\dfrac{226.48}{100}\right) = \$9{,}040$

where
$\bar{e}$ = average error in the sample
Σ = summation
e_i = an individual error in the sample
n = sample size
$\hat{E}$ = likely misstatement
N = population size

TABLE 14-9 *Continued*

STEP	STATISTICAL FORMULA	ILLUSTRATION FOR HART LUMBER CORP.
4. Compute the population standard deviation of the errors from the sample.	$$SD = \sqrt{\frac{\Sigma(e)^2 - n(\bar{e})^2}{n-1}}$$ where SD = standard deviation e = an individual error in the sample n = sample size $\bar{e}$ = average error in sample	(rounded to nearest dollar) e_i $(e_i)^2$ 1. 13 169 2. (69) 4,761 3. 85 7,225 4. 100 10,000 5. (27) 729 6. 41 1,681 7. (1) 1 8. 24 576 9. 36 1,296 10. (102) 10,404 11. 55 3,025 12. 72 5,184 227 45,051 $$SD = \sqrt{\frac{45,051 - 100(2.26)^2}{99}}$$ $$SD = 21.2$$
5. Compute the precision interval for the estimate of the population total error at the desired confidence level.	$$CPI = NZ_A \frac{SD}{\sqrt{n}} \sqrt{\frac{N-n}{N}}$$ where CPI = computed precision interval N = population size Z_A = confidence coefficient for ARIA (see Table 14–7) SD = population standard deviation n = sample size $\sqrt{\frac{N-n}{N}}$ = finite correction factor	$$CPI = 4,000 \cdot 1.28 \cdot \frac{21.2}{\sqrt{100}} \sqrt{\frac{4,000 - 100}{4,000}}$$ $$= 4,000 \cdot 1.28 \cdot \frac{21.2}{10} \cdot .99$$ $$= 4,000 \cdot 1.28 \cdot 2.10 = \$10,750$$
6. Compute the confidence limits at the CL desired.	$$UCL = \hat{E} + CPI$$ $$LCL = \hat{E} - CPI$$ where UCL = computed upper confidence limit LCL = computed lower confidence limit $\hat{E}$ = likely misstatement CPI = computed precision interval at desired CL	$$UCL = \$9,040 + \$10,750 = \$19,790$$ $$LCL = \$9,040 - \$10,750 = \$(1,710)$$

Compute the **The confidence limits, which define the confidence interval, are calculated by**
Confidence Limits combining the likely misstatement and the computed precision interval at the
desired confidence level (likely misstatement ± computed precision interval).
The formula to calculate the confidence limits is shown in Table 14–9, step 6.

The lower and upper confidence limits for Hart Lumber are ($1,710) and
$19,790, respectively. There is a 10 percent statistical risk that the population is
understated by more than $1,710, and the same risk that it is overstated by more
than $19,790. This is because an ARIA of 10 percent is equivalent to a confidence
level of 80 percent.

Application of the Essentially, the same decision rule used earlier in the chapter for dollar unit
Decision Rule sampling is applicable to difference estimation. The decision rule is:

> If the two-sided confidence interval for the errors is completely within the plus and minus
> tolerable errors, accept the hypothesis that the book value is not misstated by a material
> amount. Otherwise, accept the hypothesis that the book value is misstated by a material
> amount.

Application of the decision rule to Hart Lumber Corp. leads the auditor to the
conclusion that the population should be accepted, since both confidence limits
are within the tolerable misstatement range:

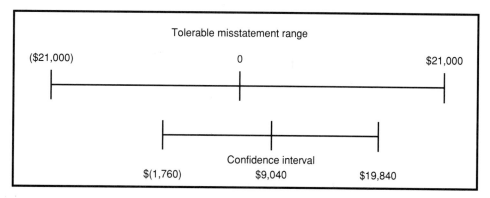

Analysis Given that the actual standard deviation (21.2) was larger than the
advance estimate (20), and the likely misstatement $9,040 was larger than the
advance estimate ($1,500), it may seem surprising that the population was
accepted. The reason is that the use of a reasonably small ARIR caused the sample
size to be larger than if ARIR had been 100 percent. If ARIR had been 100 percent,
which is common when the additional audit cost to increase the sample size is
small, the required sample size would have been only 28:

$$\left[\frac{4,000(1.28 + 0)20}{21,000 - 1,500} \right]^2 = 28$$

Assuming a sample size of 28 and the same likely misstatement and standard
deviation, the upper confidence limit would have been significantly higher than
$21,000, and, therefore, the population book value would have been rejected. One

reason that auditors use ARIR is to reduce the likelihood of needing to increase the sample size if the standard deviation or likely misstatement is larger than was expected.

Action When a Hypothesis is Rejected

When one or both of the confidence limits lie outside the tolerable error range, the population is not considered acceptable. The courses of action are the same as those discussed for dollar unit sampling (pages 487-488) except a better estimate of the population error is practical.

For example, in the Hart Lumber case, if the confidence level had been $9,040 ± $15,800, and the client is willing to reduce the book value by $9,040, the results are now 0 ± $15,800. The new computed lower confidence limit would be an understatement of $15,800, and the upper confidence limit a $15,800 overstatement, which are both acceptable. The minimum adjustment the auditor could make and still have the population acceptable is $3,840 [($9,040 + $15,800) − $21,000].

The client, however, may be unwilling to adjust the balance on the basis of a sample. Furthermore, if the computed precision interval exceeds the allowable error, an adjustment to the books cannot be made that will satisfy the auditor. This would be the case in the above example if the acceptable error were only $15,000.

APPENDIX B Formulas for Dollar Unit Sampling

Formulas for calculating error bounds for dollar unit sample evaluation follow. Each formula is illustrated with the example that has already been shown in the text.

The following symbols are used:

$D(i)$ = maximum total population error bound when i errors are found (D_o for overstatement errors and D_u for understatement errors)

Y = total population recorded dollars

$Pu(i)$ = upper precision limit from the one-sided attributes table for i errors

$E(i)$ = amount of a dollar unit error number $i [E_o(i)$ for overstatement error number i, and $E_u(i)$ for understatement error number i]

M = assumed maximum amount of error in any population dollar unit (M_o for overstatement error and M_u for understatement error)

MLE = estimated most likely error (MLE_o for overstatement error and MLE_u for understatement error)

$\sum$ = summation

n = sample size

No Errors Found

Formula where no errors are found

$$D(0) = Y \cdot Pu(0) \cdot M$$

Illustration   100 percent error assumption; 5 percent risk; sample size 100.

$$\text{Upper and lower bounds} = \$1{,}200{,}000 \times .03 \times 1 = \$36{,}000$$

Errors Found   **Formula where errors are found (before adjustment)**

$$D(i) = Y \cdot [Pu(0) \cdot M] + Y \cdot [Pu(1) - Pu(0)] \cdot E(1) + Y \cdot [Pu(2) - Pu(1)] \cdot E(2)$$
$$+ \cdots + Y \cdot [Pu(i) - Pu(i-1)] \cdot E(i)]$$

Illustration   100 percent error assumption; four overstatement errors and one understatement error; errors are ordered from the largest dollar unit error to the smallest; 5 percent risk; sample size 100. Therefore,

$$E_o(1) = .6706$$
$$E_o(2) = .0705$$
$$E_o(3) = .0161$$
$$E_o(4) = .0002$$
$$E_u(1) = .0296$$

The 5 percent risk bound for maximum total population overstatement error (before adjustment) is:

$$\begin{aligned}
D_o(4) &= [(1{,}200{,}000)(.03)(1.00)] + [(1{,}200{,}000)(.047 - .03)(.6706)] \\
&\quad + [(1{,}200{,}000)(.062 - .047)(.0705)] + [(1{,}200{,}000)(.076 - .062)(.0161)] \\
&\quad + [(1{,}200{,}000)(.089 - .076)(.0002)] \\
&= 36{,}000 + 13{,}680 + 1{,}269 + 270 + 3 \\
&= 51{,}222
\end{aligned}$$

and the 5 percent risk bound for maximum total population understatement error (before adjustment) is:

$$\begin{aligned}
D_u(1) &= [(1{,}200{,}000)(.03)(1.00)] + [(1{,}200{,}000)(.047 - .03)(.0296)] \\
&= 36{,}000 + 604 \\
&= 36{,}604
\end{aligned}$$

Formula for adjustment for offsetting errors

$$D_o \text{ adjusted} = D_o(i) - MLE_u$$
$$D_u \text{ adjusted} = D_u(i) - MLE_o$$

where

$$MLE = \sum E(i) \cdot \frac{Y}{n}$$

Illustration

$$MLE_o = (.6706 + .0705 + .0161 + .0002)(1{,}200{,}000/100)$$

$$= (.7574)(12{,}000)$$

$$= 9{,}089$$

$$MLE_u = (.0296)(1{,}200{,}000/100)$$

$$= (.0296)(12{,}000)$$

$$= 355$$

$$D_o \text{ adjusted} = 51{,}222 - 355$$

$$= 50{,}867$$

$$D_u \text{ adjusted} = 36{,}604 - 9{,}089$$

$$= 27{,}515$$

REVIEW QUESTIONS

14–1   What major difference between tests of controls and tests of details of balances makes attributes sampling inappropriate for tests of details of balances?

14–2   Define *stratified sampling* and explain its importance in auditing. How could an auditor obtain a stratified sample of 30 items from each of three strata in the confirmation of accounts receivable?

14–3   Distinguish between the point estimate (likely misstatement) of the total errors and the true value of the errors in the population. How can each be determined?

14–4   Evaluate the following statement made by an auditor: "On every aspect of the audit where it is possible, I calculate the likely misstatement and evaluate whether the amount is material. If it is, I investigate the cause and continue to test the population until I determine whether there is a serious problem. The use of statistical sampling in this manner is a valuable audit tool."

14–5   Define *dollar unit sampling* and explain its importance in auditing. How does it combine the features of attributes and variables sampling?

14–6   Define what is meant by sampling risk. Does sampling risk apply to dollar unit sampling, attributes sampling, and variables sampling? Explain.

14–7   What are the major differences in the steps used to do dollar unit sampling and attributes sampling?

14–8   The 2,620 inventory items described in question 14–14 are listed on 44 inventory pages with 60 lines per page. There is a total for each page. The client's data are not in machine-readable form, and the public accounting firm does not have a computer terminal available. Describe two ways in which a dollar unit sample can be selected in this situation. Explain which method is most likely to be followed here.

14–9   Explain how the auditor determines tolerable misstatement for dollar unit sampling.

14–10   Explain what is meant by acceptable risk of incorrect acceptance. What are the major audit factors affecting ARIA?

14–11   Evaluate the following statement made by an auditor: "I took a random sample and derived a 90 percent confidence interval of $800,000 to $900,000. That means that the true population value will be between $800,000 and $900,000, 90 percent of the time."

14–12 A sample size of 160 items is selected in a test of purchase transactions to determine whether the receiving report is attached to the related vendors' invoices. The population size is 5,000 items and the recorded purchases for the year are $1,800,000. All of the vendors' statements are found to have a receiving report attached. Calculate the statistical results for attributes sampling and for dollar unit sampling at a 10 percent risk.

14–13 What is meant by the "percent of error assumption" for dollar unit sampling in those population items that are in error? Why is it common to use a 100 percent error assumption when it is almost certain to be highly conservative?

14–14 An auditor is determining the appropriate sample size for testing inventory valuation using dollar unit sampling. The population has 2,620 inventory items valued at $12,625,000. The tolerable understatement or overstatement is $500,000 at a 10 percent risk of incorrect acceptance. No errors are expected in the population. Calculate the preliminary sample size using a 100 percent average error assumption.

14–15 Assume that a sample of 100 units was obtained in sampling the inventory in Question 14–14. Assume further that the following three errors were found:

ERROR	RECORDED VALUE	AUDITED VALUE
1	$ 897.16	$ 609.16
2	47.02	0
3	1621.68	1522.68

Calculate adjusted error bounds for the population. Draw audit conclusions based on the results.

14–16 Why is it difficult to determine the appropriate sample size for dollar unit sampling? How should the auditor determine the proper sample size?

14–17 What is meant by a decision rule using dollar unit sampling? State the decision rule.

14–18 What alternative courses of action are appropriate when a population is rejected using dollar unit sampling? When should each option be followed?

14–19 Define what is meant by the population standard deviation and explain its importance in variables sampling. What is the relationship between the population standard deviation and the required sample size?

14–20 In using difference estimation, an auditor took a random sample of one hundred inventory items from a large population to test for proper pricing. Several of the inventory items were in error, but the combined net amount of the sample error was not material. In addition, a review of the individual errors indicated that no error was by itself material. As a result, the auditor did not investigate the errors or make a statistical evaluation. Explain why this practice is improper.

14–21 Distinguish among difference estimation, ratio estimation, mean-per-unit estimation, and stratified mean-per-unit estimation. Give one example in which each could be used. When would dollar unit sampling be preferable to any of these?

14–22 An essential step in difference estimation is the comparison of each computed confidence limit with tolerable misstatement. Why is this step so important, and what should the auditor do if one of the confidence limits is larger than the tolerable misstatement?

14–23 Explain the circumstances in which difference estimation may not be a useful audit tool.

14–24 Give an example of the use of attributes sampling, dollar unit sampling, and variables sampling in the form of an audit conclusion.

MULTIPLE CHOICE QUESTIONS

14–25 The following questions refer to the use of stratified sampling in auditing. For each one, select the best response.

a. Felix Santos decides to use stratified sampling. The basic reason for using stratified sampling rather than unrestricted random sampling is to

(1) reduce as much as possible the degree of variability in the overall population.

(2) give every element in the population an equal chance of being included in the sample.

(3) allow the person selecting the sample to use his or her own judgment in deciding which elements should be included in the sample.

(4) reduce the required sample size from a nonhomogeneous population.

b. In an examination of financial statements, a public accountant will generally find stratified sampling techniques to be most applicable to

(1) recomputing net wage and salary payments to employees.

(2) tracing hours worked from the payroll summary back to the individual time cards.

(3) confirming accounts receivable for residential customers at a large electric utility.

(4) reviewing supporting documentation for additions to plant and equipment.

c. From prior experience, a public accountant is aware that cash disbursements contain a few unusually large disbursements. In using statistical sampling, the public accountant's best course of action is to

(1) eliminate any unusually large disbursements that appear in the sample.

(2) continue to draw new samples until no unusually large disbursements appear in the sample.

(3) stratify the cash disbursements population so that the unusually large disbursements are reviewed separately.

(4) increase the sample size to lessen the effect of the unusually large disbursements. (AICPA adapted)

14–26 The following apply to dollar unit sampling. For each one, select the best response.

a. The auditor's failure to recognize an error in an amount or an error in an internal control data processing procedure is described as a

(1) statistical error.

(2) sampling error.

(3) standard error of the mean.

(4) nonsampling error.

b. An auditor makes separate tests of controls and tests of details of balances in the accounts payable area, which has good internal control. If the auditor uses statistical sampling for both of these tests, the acceptable risk established for the test of details of balances is normally

(1) the same as that for tests of controls.

(2) greater than that for tests of controls.

(3) less than that for tests of controls.

(4) totally independent of that for tests of controls.

c. How should an auditor determine the tolerable misstatement required in establishing a statistical sampling plan?

(1) By the materiality of an allowable margin of error the auditor is willing to accept.

(2) By the amount of reliance the auditor will place on the results of the sample.

(3) By reliance on a table of random numbers.

(4) By the amount of risk the auditor is willing to take that material errors will occur in the accounting process.   (AICPA adapted)

DISCUSSION QUESTIONS AND PROBLEMS

14–27 The following is the entire extended inventory for Jake's Bookbinding Company Ltd. The population is smaller than would ordinarily be the case for statistical sampling, but an entire population is useful to show how to select samples by dollar unit sampling.

POPULATION ITEM	RECORDED AMOUNT	POPULATION ITEM	RECORDED AMOUNT
1	$ 1,410	21	$ 4,865
2	9,130	22	770
3	660	23	2,305
4	3,355	24	2,665
5	5,725	25	1,000
6	8,210	26	6,225
7	580	27	3,675
8	44,110	28	6,250
9	825	29	1,890
10	1,155	30	27,705
11	2,270	31	935
12	50	32	5,595
13	5,785	33	930
14	940	34	4,045
15	1,820	35	9,480
16	3,380	36	360
17	530	37	1,145
18	955	38	6,400
19	4,490	39	100
20	17,140	40	8,435
			$207,295

Required:

a. Select a random dollar unit sample of ten items using Table 12–2 (page 396). Use a starting point of item 1000, column 1. Take the first digit in the column to the right of the one being used to get six digits. Use only odd columns for the first five digits. Identify the physical units associated with the random numbers. (Hint: First digit translated as follows: $1-3 = 0$; $4-6 = 1$; $7-9 = 2$; $0 = $ discard.)

b. Select a random sample of ten items using systematic dollar unit sampling. Use a starting point of 1857. Identify the physical units associated with the random numbers.

c. Which sample items will always be included in the systematic dollar unit sample regardless of the starting point? Will that also be true of random number table dollar unit sampling?

    d. Which method is preferable in terms of ease of selection in this case?

    e. Why would an auditor use dollar unit sampling?

14–28 You are planning to use dollar unit sampling to evaluate the results of accounts receivable confirmation for the Meridian Corp. You have already performed tests of controls for sales, sales returns and allowances, and cash receipts, and they are considered excellent. Owing to the quality of the controls, you decide to use a risk of incorrect acceptance of 10 percent. There are 3,000 accounts receivable with a gross value of $6,800,000. An overstatement or understatement of more than $150,000 would be considered material.

Required:

    a. Calculate the required sample size.

    b. Explain the methodology of obtaining sample items for confirmation. Your explanation should include how to select the random numbers and the receivable items to be confirmed.

    c. Assume the sample size you selected for part a was 150 items. Twenty-five of the random numbers were for accounts that had already been selected by other random numbers. Calculate the error bounds, assuming no errors were found in the sample.

    d. What conclusion can you reach about the population?

14–29 In the audit of Price Seed Company Ltd. for the year ended September 30, the auditor set a tolerable misstatement of $50,000 at an ARIA of 10 percent. A dollar unit sample of one hundred was selected from an accounts receivable population that had a recorded balance of $1,975,000. The following differences were uncovered in the confirmation:

ACCOUNTS RECEIVABLE PER RECORDS	ACCOUNTS RECEIVABLE PER CONFIRMATION	FOLLOW-UP COMMENTS BY AUDITOR
1. $2,728.00	$2,498.00	Pricing errors on two invoices.
2. $5,125.00	-0-	Customer mailed cheque 9/26; company received cheque 10/3.
3. $3,890.00	$1,190.00	Merchandise returned 9/30 and counted in inventory; credit was issued 10/6.
4. $ 791.00	$ 815.00	Footing error on an invoice.
5. $ 548.00	$1,037.00	Goods were shipped 9/28; sale was recorded on 10/6.
6. $3,115.00	$3,190.00	Pricing error on a credit memorandum.
7. $1,540.00	-0-	Goods were shipped on 9/29; customer received goods 10/3; sale was recorded on 9/30.

Required:

    a. Calculate the upper and lower error bounds on the basis of the client errors in the sample.

    b. Is the population acceptable as stated? If not, what options are available to the auditor at this point? Which option should the auditor select? Explain.

14–30 You intend to use dollar unit sampling as a part of the audit of several accounts for Roynpower Manufacturing Inc. You have done the audit for the past several years, and there has rarely been an adjusting entry of any kind. Your audit tests of controls for all the transactions cycles were completed at an interim date, and control risk has been assessed as low. You therefore decide to use an ARIA of 10 percent for all tests of details of balances.

    You intend to use dollar unit sampling in the audit of the three most material asset balance sheet account balances: accounts receivable, inventory, and marketable securities. You feel justified in using the same risk of overreliance for each audit area because of the low assessed control risk.

The recorded balances and related information for the three accounts are as follows:

	RECORDED VALUE
Accounts receivable	$ 3,600,000
Inventory	4,800,000
Marketable securities	1,600,000
	$10,000,000

Net earnings before taxes for Roynpower are $2,000,000. You decide that materiality will be $100,000 for the client.

The audit approach to be followed will be to determine the total sample size needed for all three accounts. A sample will be selected from all $10 million, and the appropriate testing for a sample item will depend on whether the item is a receivable, inventory, or marketable security. The audit conclusions will pertain to the entire $10 million, and no conclusion will be made about the three individual accounts unless significant errors are found in the sample.

Required:

a. Evaluate the audit approach of testing all three account balances in one sample.

b. Calculate the required sample size for all three accounts.

c. Calculate the required sample size for each of the three accounts, assuming you decide that the tolerable misstatement in each account is $100,000. (Recall that tolerable misstatement equals preliminary judgment about materiality for dollar unit sampling.)

d. Assume you select the random sample using a seven-digit random number table. How would you identify which sample item in the population to audit for the number 4,627,871? What audit procedures would be performed?

e. Assume you select a sample of two hundred sample items for testing and you find one error in inventory. The recorded value is $987.12, and the audit value is $887.12. Calculate the error bounds for the three combined accounts and reach appropriate audit conclusions.

14-31 An audit partner is developing an office training program to familiarize his professional staff with statistical decision models applicable to the audit of dollar-value balances. He wishes to demonstrate the relationship of sample sizes to population size and variability and the auditor's specifications as to tolerable error and ARIA. The partner prepared the following table to show comparative population characteristics and audit specifications of the two populations.

	CHARACTERISTICS OF POPULATION 1 RELATIVE TO POPULATION 2		AUDIT SPECIFICATIONS AS TO A SAMPLE FROM POPULATION 1 RELATIVE TO A SAMPLE FROM POPULATION 2	
	Size	Variability	Tolerable Misstatement	ARIA
Case 1	Equal	Equal	Equal	Lower
Case 2	Equal	Larger	Larger	Equal
Case 3	Larger	Equal	Smaller	Higher
Case 4	Smaller	Smaller	Equal	Higher
Case 5	Larger	Equal	Equal	Lower

Required:

In items (1) through (5) below you are to indicate for the specific case from the table above the required sample size to be selected from population 1 relative to the sample from population 2.

(1) In case 1 the required sample size from population 1 is _____ .
(2) In case 2 the required sample size from population 1 is _____ .
(3) In case 3 the required sample size from population 1 is _____ .
(4) In case 4 the required sample size from population 1 is _____ .
(5) In case 5 the required sample size from population 1 is _____ .

Your answer should be selected from the following responses:

a. Larger than the required sample size from population 2.

b. Equal to the required sample size from population 2.

c. Smaller than the required sample size from population 2.

d. Indeterminate relative to the required sample size from population 2.

(AICPA adapted)

14–32 In auditing the valuation of inventory, the auditor, Claire Butler, decided to use difference estimation. She decided to select an unrestricted random sample of 80 inventory items from a population of 1,840 that had a book value of $175,820. Butler had decided in advance that she was willing to accept a maximum error in the population of $6,000 at an ARIA of 5 percent. There were eight errors in the sample which were as follows:

AUDIT VALUE	BOOK VALUE	SAMPLE ERRORS
$ 812.50	$ 740.50	$(72.00)
12.50	78.20	65.70
10.00	51.10	41.10
25.40	61.50	36.10
600.10	651.90	51.80
.12	0	(.12)
51.06	81.06	30.00
83.11	104.22	21.11
Total $1,594.79	$1,768.48	$173.69

Required:

a. Calculate the likely misstatement, the computed precision interval, the confidence interval, and the confidence limits for the population. Label each calculation. Use the microcomputer for this purpose (instructor option).

b. Should Butler accept the book value of the population? Explain.

c. What options are available to her at this point?

14–33 In confirming accounts receivable with a recorded value of $6,250,000 for the Blessman Wholesale Drug Corp., Gerald Bloomstad, a public accountant, has decided that if the total error in the account exceeds $60,000, he will consider the error material. He believes the likely misstatement will approximate $20,000. He has decided to use unrestricted random sampling for difference estimation, and he believes a 5 percent ARIA is appropriate considering the circumstances of the engagement. Although Bloomstad does not know the standard deviation, he decides to estimate it a little bit high to make sure he does not undersample. The standard deviation is estimated at $22. There are 14,300 total accounts receivable in the trial balance.

Required:

a. Calculate the number of accounts receivable Bloomstad should confirm.

b. Assuming only 100 confirmation responses are received in the first and second requests, what should the auditor do?

c. What would the sample size in part (a) have been if the estimated standard deviation were $32 instead of $22?

    d. What would the sample size in part (a) have been if tolerable misstatement was $80,000 and the likely misstatement was $20,000?

    e. What would the sample size in part (a) have been if the tolerable misstatement was $90,000 and the likely misstatement was $50,000? Explain the relationship between your answers in parts (a) and (e).

14–34 Marjorie Jorgenson, a public accountant, is verifying the accuracy of outstanding accounts payable for Marygold Hardware Ltd., a large single-location retail hardware store. There are 650 vendors listed on the outstanding accounts payable list. She has eliminated from the population 40 vendors that have large ending balances and will audit them separately. There are now 610 vendors.

    She plans to do one of three tests for each item in the sample: examine a vendor's statement in the client's hands, obtain a confirmation when no statement is on hand, or extensively search for invoices when neither of the first two are obtained. There are no accounts payable subsidiary records available, and a large number of errors is expected. Marjorie has obtained facts or made audit judgments as follows:

ARRIR	20 percent	ARIA	10 percent
Upper error limit	$45,000	Expected error	$20,000
Recorded book value	$600,000	Estimated standard deviation	$280

Required:

    a. Under what circumstances is it desirable to use unstratified difference estimation in the situation described? Under what circumstances would it be undesirable?

    b. Calculate the required sample size for the audit tests of accounts payable assuming that ARIR is ignored.

    c. Assume that the auditor selects exactly the sample size calculated in part b. The likely misstatement calculated from the sample results is $21,000 and the estimated population standard deviation is 267. Is the population fairly stated as defined by the decision rule? Explain what causes the result to be acceptable or unacceptable.

    d. Calculate the required sample size for the audit tests of accounts payable assuming the ARIR is considered.

    e. Explain the reason for the large increase of the sample size resulting from including ARIR in determining sample size.

    f. Fred Lehne, a member of Marjorie's staff, calculates the required sample size using the formula without consideration of ARIR. After the sample size is determined, he increases the sample size by 25 percent. Fred believes that this does the same thing as using ARIR without having to bother to make the calculation. Is this approach appropriate? Evaluate the desirability of the approach.

15

AUDITING COMPLEX EDP SYSTEMS

☐ Most organizations use electronic data processing (EDP), at least to some extent, in processing financial and accounting information. To this point, the text has described internal control in terms of simple or noncomplex computerized systems. In this chapter, we discuss complex EDP systems and their effect on internal control and on auditing.

The focus on noncomplex systems in the first part of the book had several purposes. First, it is important to understand noncomplex systems inasmuch as they are used extensively in business and government. Second, the authors have found that students understand basic internal control concepts that are common to both noncomplex and more complex systems when they are studied in the less abstract context of noncomplex systems. Finally, and most important, most complex EDP-based accounting systems rely extensively on the same type of procedures for control that are used in noncomplex systems.

There is no distinction between the audit concepts applicable to complex electronic data processing and those applicable to noncomplex systems. When computers or other aspects of EDP systems are introduced, generally accepted auditing standards, the rules of conduct, legal liability, and the basic concepts of evidence accumulation remain the same. However, some of the specific methods appropriate for implementing the basic auditing concepts do change as systems become more complex.

The Auditing Standards Board has issued a series of EDP Auditing Guidelines that are based on International Auditing Guidelines issued by the International Auditing Practices Committee (IAPC) of the International Federation of Accountants (IFAC). These Guidelines are included in a separate section of Volume II of the *CICA Handbook*.

This chapter is organized around the following topics:

- Complexity of EDP systems
- Effect of EDP on organizations
- EDP controls
- Obtaining an understanding of internal control in an EDP environment
- Auditing without relying on computer controls
- Auditing with the use of a computer
- Microcomputer-aided auditing
- Audit of a computer service bureau

Complexity of EDP Systems

Although most business and nonbusiness enterprises use EDP in some way, the extent of use and the characteristics of the EDP systems in use vary considerably. Before studying the effect of EDP on auditing, it is appropriate to consider the different types of EDP systems in terms of the characteristics that are significant to the auditor.

Technical Complexity

EDP systems can be defined by their technical complexity and the extent to which they are used in an organization. In the past, technical complexity was synonymous with size. Although large systems usually are more complex, there are also many complex small systems due to the miniaturization of computer circuitry. Systems can be made *complex* in one or a combination of the following ways.

> **OBJECTIVE 1**
>
> Explain how EDP systems affect business organizations.

Real-time processing A real-time system allows direct access into the computer. Transactions can be put directly into the system so that master files are updated at the time the entry is made, rather than on a delayed, batch basis. Similarly, output of the current status of data file contents is available as requested. Real-time systems use display terminals for both input and output purposes. These systems also allow programming and certain operator functions to be done immediately (that is, in "real-time"). Such systems are sometimes called on-line systems.

Communications systems Communications channels can connect the computer directly to users anywhere in the world. These users may have a variety of facilities for reception, including display terminals, intelligent terminals, microcomputers, card readers, line printers, and high-speed printers.

Distributed processing When the computing function is apportioned among central processing units spread geographically and connected by a communications system, it is called *distributed processing*.

Electronic Funds Transfer(EFT)[1] EFT payment systems tranfer funds by means of electronic impulses, rather than by conventional means such as cheques. References to the "cashless society" are to EFT.

One example of a cashless system involves the *debit card* that includes the customer's account number, and could include other information about the customer. The customer would present his or her card to a merchant when making a purchase. The merchant would input the customer's name, card number, and information about the purchase on a terminal; the total amount of the purchase would be debited to the customer's account and credited to the merchant's account by the issuing bank at the time of inputting the information, that is, at the time of the transaction.

Other examples of EFT are point-of-sale (POS) services that some stores now use as well as direct deposits and preauthorized payment (DD/PP) services. Point-of-sale services permit the store to charge a customer's account receivable and relieve inventory electronically when a sale is entered. Direct deposits and preauthorized payment services include deposits to employee bank accounts for payroll and prearranged payments from accounts, such as mortgage payments and life insurance premiums.

Data base management As the number of users and volume of data processed expands, the same data may be included on different files. The result is an inefficient use of file space and a need to update files continually. A data base management system solves this problem by storing each element of data in a central file and by permitting the sharing of data from that file among various users. Efficiency is gained because each element of data is stored only once and consistency is achieved because all users utilize the same data. When any given computer application is processed, the data are formatted into a desired file structure.

Multi-tasking The operating system manages the activities of the computer system. A simple operating system manages the application of one function at a time. Inefficiency often results when the central processing unit (CPU) and the various peripheral devices are idle while other functions are being carried out. Complex operating systems overcome this by a process known as multi-tasking; this process allows different functions to be carried out simultaneously.

Extent of Use The extent to which EDP is used in a system is also related to complexity. Usually, when more business and accounting functions are performed by computer, the

---

1 Jefim Efrim Boritz, *Computer Control & Audit Guide* (7th Edition), University of Waterloo Centre for Accounting Research and Education, 1989, pp. 1.30-1.31.

system must become more complex to accommodate processing needs. One way a system can become more complex is by increasing the number of transaction cycles that are computerized.

Complexity is also increased as the number of functions that are computerized in a given cycle is increased. For example, we know from Chapter 11 that the following are typical functions in the sales and collection cycle:

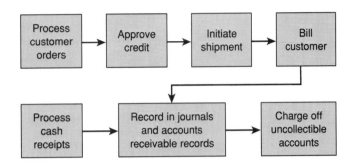

In a partially computerized system, EDP may begin with the preparation of the billing and include processing cash receipts and recording the cash receipts and sales journals and updating the accounts receivable master file. In a fully computerized system, customer orders might be received by telephone and entered into terminals by operators as they are received. Every aspect of processing from that point could be done by computer.

Effect of EDP on Organizations

Facilities An immediate and obvious change brought about by many EDP systems is in facilities. Physically large systems, called full-scale systems, require a separate computer room with special environmental controls (temperature, humidity, fire protection, locking devices, and so forth). Physically smaller systems, called microcomputer systems, can often be operated practically unnoticed in a normal office environment.

Staffing When small systems are acquired, hardware and software are often purchased together. Also, programs and equipment are often operated by regular employees. These smaller systems require some training of personnel, but no programming or other special EDP skills. As a result, large numbers of EDP specialists do not have to be hired to manage and operate small EDP systems. In large-scale systems, an entire function is often created to operate EDP. Many times the EDP function includes programmers, operators, a librarian, data-entry clerks, and data control clerks, as well as managers.

Implications of EDP for Internal Control[2]

Certain characteristics of EDP systems that are distinct from those of manual systems affect internal control. EDP may enhance internal control or it may increase the potential for material misstatement. An example of the former is the fact that an EDP system processes data consistently, however great the volume of transactions; a manual system, on the other hand, is prone to human error (i.e.,

2 See also Boritz, op. cit., pp. 2.2-2.10.

inconsistent application) and to breakdown if the volume of transactions increases significantly.

Centralization of data and segregation of duties

The use of EDP generally brings data gathering and accumulation activities of different parts of the organization into one department. This change has the advantage of *centralizing data* and permitting *higher-quality controls* over operations. It may also result in the elimination of the control provided by *division of duties* of independent persons who perform related functions and compare their results. As an illustration, in many manual systems different individuals prepare the sales journal and subsidiary records. The accuracy of their results is tested by comparing the subsidiary ledger with the total balance in the general ledger.

In a noncomplex computerized system, sales orders and perhaps even sales invoices may be prepared manually. The computer will likely prepare the sales journal and accounts receivable master file simultaneously. There is typically detailed output available for comparison to shipping documents and customer orders. In a complex system, clerks may enter customer orders with the use of keyboards from remote locations. Shipping documents, sales invoices, the sales journal and accounts receivable master file are usually prepared or updated simultaneously.

The organizational structure also frequently changes by taking the record-keeping function out of the hands of those who have custody of assets and putting it into the EDP center. This is a desirable change if it does not merely change the opportunity for defalcation from operating personnel to EDP personnel. The latter are in a position to take company assets for their own use if they also prepare or process documents that result in the disposal of the assets. For example, if EDP personnel have access to documents authorizing the shipment of goods, in essence they have indirect access to inventory. Auditors must use great care in evaluating effective segregation of duties in EDP systems.

Methods of authorization

It is common in more advanced EDP systems to have certain types of transactions initiated automatically by the computer. Examples are the calculation of interest on savings accounts and the ordering of inventory when prespecified order levels are reached. In these instances, authorization will not be made for each transaction, as occurs in a less complex system; it will be implicit in management's acceptance of the design of the computer system.

Visibility of Information

In noncomplex EDP systems, there are often source documents in support of each transaction, and most results of processing are printed out. Thus, input, output, and, to a great extent, processing are visible to the EDP user and auditor. This is no longer always true. With the use of real-time on-line systems, data are entered directly into the system at the point of transaction (e.g., point of sale) and various transactions are generated internally by the system.

Visibility of input data   In many systems, transactions may be entered directly into the computer through terminals. These entries may or may not be based on source documents. They may, for example, be based on telephone messages. Even if there are source documents, processing may cause retrieval to be difficult, or the documents may only exist for a short time. In these cases, the data put into the system may not be visible to the auditor. It would be in machine-readable form, accessible by computer, thus requiring the auditor to take special steps to retrieve it.

Visibility of processing   Most significant computer processes are internal and are not directly observable. Some transactions, as indicated above, may be initiated by a computer program and performed with no visible evidence. Internal controls, as discussed later in this chapter, may exist within a computer program; therefore, no visible evidence of their execution is available.

Visibility of transaction trail   A *transaction trail* (also called an *audit trail*) is the accumulation of source documents and records that allows the organization to trace accounting entries back to where they were initiated and vice-versa. As discussed above, when a system is computerized, source documents may be eliminated and data may be maintained only in machine-readable form. Furthermore, a computer has the ability to process transactions that accomplish several purposes simultaneously. For example, the production of a unit of finished goods inventory may be processed by a computer to update perpetual inventory records, develop standard cost variances, reorder raw materials, and develop production reports by location. Because of these characteristics, reports may be produced by a computer without a visible transaction trail that can be related to the individual transactions. In addition, this problem can be further complicated by the fact that the data may be in summary form and details may be omitted and thus eliminated.

A good transaction trail is important to follow-up on customer and management inquiries and for effective auditing. Since most companies keep only three generations (child, parent, and grandparent) of data, the timing of the audit is very important if the auditor wants to examine the transaction trail for the year. Generally, each generation represents transactions for a month; three generations might be June, July , and August.

Potential for Material Misstatement   In addition to those things already discussed, several factors increase the likelihood of material misstatements in the financial statements. They are therefore of great concern to the auditor.

Reduced human involvement   In noncomplex systems, extensive handling of transaction data and processing results provides opportunities for observing whether errors or fraud and other irregularities have occurred. These opportunities are reduced in more complex EDP systems. Often the personnel who deal with the initial processing of the transactions never see the final results. Even if they do, the results are highly summarized, so that it would be difficult to recognize misstatements or problems. On the other hand, reduced human involvement, as is pointed out above, may be a strength in that the data are processed consistently.

Uniformity of processing   An important characteristic of EDP is uniformity of processing. Once information is placed in the computer system, it will be processed consistently with previous and subsequent information as long as some aspect of the system itself is not changed. This is important from an audit point of view because it means the system will process a particular type of transaction correctly or incorrectly consistently. A risk, therefore, exists that erroneous processing can result in the accumulation of a great number of errors in a short period of time, especially if the transaction trail or segregation of duties is inadequate. As a result, the emphasis in auditing more complex EDP systems for accuracy of processing is likely to be on testing for unusual transactions and for changes in the system over time rather than on testing a large sample of similar transactions.

Unauthorized access Data-processing systems allow easy access to data and use of the data by those who have legitimate purposes. However, these facilities may also allow easy access for illegitimate purposes. Furthermore, transactions may be initiated through the computer, programs may be improperly changed, and confidential information may be obtained in an unauthorized manner. These are all significant risks, underlined by several sizable computer-related frauds disclosed in recent years.

Loss of data When great amounts of data are centralized, there is an increased risk that they could be lost or destroyed; for instance, a fire could destroy all the company's records and, thus, its ability to function. The ramifications of this could be severe. "[T]he potential loss of data and programs due to this centralization constitutes a new, and significant, source of risk."[3] Not only is there the potential for misstated financial statements, but the organization may need to cease operations for a significant period.[4]

Potential for Improved Control

Despite circumstances that may increase the potential for errors and fraud and other irregularities, well-controlled EDP systems have a greater potential for reducing errors and irregularities. This is due to the characteristic of uniformity of processing, as already discussed. At the present time, however, the potential for error and fraud reduction has not been realized principally because of a lack of commitment from management.

EDP systems need effective administration by virtue of their underlying technology and its demands. It is difficult to implement and maintain an EDP system successfully without being well-organized, having good procedures and documentation, and using effective administration. These in turn foster good control.

EDP systems are used to provide management with more information and more effective analysis of the information obtained than are manual systems; similarly, complex systems can provide more information and more effective analysis than noncomplex systems. This expansion of information, coupled with a wide variety of analytical tools that are practical with the computer, provides management with the ability to supervise the activities of the organization more effectively and to review and follow up on the results of these activities. This can significantly enhance overall control.

Other Characteristics Affecting Internal Control

Speed and Analysis Computers allow data to be processed quickly according to specified criteria. Since they are very fast, computers permit much more data to be processed in a given time than a manual system, and accounting control procedures may be programmed into an EDP system so that the processing is done in accordance with certain parameters. For example, the system could perform a credit check as part of invoice preparation; the amount of the order and the

---

3 Ibid., p. 2.9.

4 See Boritz, op. cit., pp.2.1 and 3.15–3.16.

customer's receivable balance could be automatically checked against a file of customers and their credit limits. If the credit limit for the customer is exceeded by the order, the order can be flagged.

Inflexibility EDP systems are less flexible than manual systems. Making changes to an EDP system that is in place is difficult and often expensive. Changes must be made with care because in many cases other parts of the system have to be changed at the same time.

EDP Controls

Internal controls were discussed in Chapter 9 and are therefore only summarized in this chapter.

In Chapter 9, a distinction was made between the control environment, accounting system and control procedures. The control environment in complex EDP systems is even more critical than for less complex ones because there is greater potential for errors and fraud. For example, an organization with divisions in several countries, each with complex EDP, requires a sound control environment to assure that accurate accounting information is provided. Similarly, control procedures in such a company must be more carefully designed and evaluated more frequently than in less complex systems. It is not surprising that almost all large companies with complex EDP have internal audit staffs with training in EDP.

The types of controls in an EDP system can be conveniently classified into *general controls* and *application controls*. A general control relates to all parts of the EDP system and would therefore be evaluated early in the audit. Application controls apply to a specific use of the system, such as the processing of sales or cash receipts, and must be evaluated specifically for every area which is to be audited and in which the client uses the computer. Figure 15–1 illustrates the difference between general controls and application controls.

When an EDP system is used, accounting controls – those discussed in Chapter 4 – which relate to the reliability of accounting records and safeguarding of assets, may be computerized and become parts of the general or application controls of the EDP system. Figure 15–2 shows the relationships of accounting controls to general and application controls that may occur.[5] Verifying selling prices is a procedure unique to the sales and collection cycle. If the procedure is done manually, it would be found in area B (of Figure 15–2), if it is done by the computer, it would be found in area F. If the general controls include a limit check on transactions, it would be found in area G since it also is an accounting control and an application control.

This section discusses internal controls in an EDP environment.[6] The material is drawn from the CICA publications, *Computer Control Guidelines*, Second Edition (*CCG II*) and *Computer Audit Guidelines*, as well as from *Computer Control & Audit Guide* by J.E. Boritz. *Computer Audit Guidelines* outlines a computer audit, explains in some depth the review of the system of controls along with the verification and evaluation of controls, suggests specific audit techniques

OBJECTIVE 2

Describe EDP-related internal controls and their impact on evidence accumulation.

5 Adapted from Boritz, op. cit., pp. 6.1-10.28.

6 For more extensive coverage of this topic the student is directed to three CICA research studies, *Controlling and Auditing Small Computer Systems* by S. J. Gaston, 1986, *Computer Control Guidelines* (2nd Edition), 1986, and *Computer Audit Guidelines*, 1975, and to Boritz, op. cit.

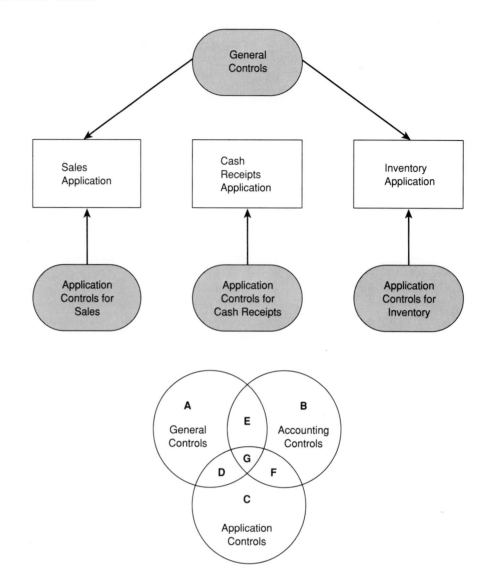

FIGURE 15–1

Relationship of Internal
Controls to Audit

FIGURE 15–2

Relationship of
Accounting Controls to
General and
Application Controls

the auditor of an EDP system might consider in planning the audit, and proposes guides for the evaluation of in-house computers and outside data centers. *Computer Control Guidelines* discusses controls in the context of the roles of the participants in the EDP system. The roles examined in *CCG II* are as follows:

- Senior management
- Users
- Information systems management
  - Development
  - Processing
  - Support[7]

---

7 *Computer Control Guidelines* (2nd Edition), Toronto: CICA, 1986, p.10. Reprinted with permission, © Canadian Institute of Chartered Accountants, Toronto, Ontario.

Senior management here refers to the senior management of the enterprise, or client; users are any users of the EDP or information system. Development, processing, and support may be in a central information systems department or in the user departments.

The discussion about EDP or information systems controls is in two parts:

1. Objectives relating to general controls.
2. Objectives relating to applications controls.

Objectives Relating to General Controls

There are four topics covered under this heading:

- Responsibility for controls (control objective A)
- Information systems development and acquisition (control objectives B to E)
- Information systems processing (control objectives F to H)
- Segregation of incompatible functions and security controls (control objectives I to M)

Each topic, which represents a chapter in *CCG II*, is discussed below. The control objectives A to M and the related control standards are taken from *CCG II*.

A. Responsibility for control *CCG II* observes that senior management has the responsibility for establishing control over the information produced by the enterprise and the information systems that produce that information. The standards that will lead to the establishment of control are listed below:

1. Senior management should establish policies governing the information systems of the entity. Established policies enable employees to know what the objectives of the enterprise are and how management expects them to be achieved.
2. Senior management should assign responsibilities for information, both its processing and its use. This may be accomplished by assigning responsibility for all information system activities to a central information systems department, by assigning responsibility for some information systems activities to a central information systems department and the other activities to user departments. There are advantages and disadvantages to all these arrangements. The main point is that responsibility be assigned in some manner.
3. User management should be responsible for providing information that supports the objectives and policies of the entity.
4. User management should be responsible for the completeness, accuracy, authorization, security, and timeliness of information.
5. Information systems management should be responsible for providing the information systems capabilities necessary for the achievement of the defined information systems objectives and policies of the entity.
6. Senior management should approve plans for the development and acquisition of information systems.
7. Senior management should monitor the extent to which the development, operation, and control of information systems complies with [the entity's] established policies and plans.

Note that user management and information systems management have certain responsibilities along with senior management.

B. To ensure that the information systems selected meet the needs of the entity There are a number of considerations that must be taken into account if a new system (either newly developed or acquired) is to be optimal. *Computer Control & Audit Guide* lists six causes of information systems failure:

1. Orientation of the system to the computer rather than to the user;
2. Incorrect definition of the system's prime users and their related priorities;
3. Vesting responsibility for the systems development and implementation with the incorrect management group;
4. Inadequate communication to company personnel of the nature and purpose of the system;
5. Failure to recognize and control the effects of company power politics; and
6. Underestimating the complexity of the design and implementation stages of the system development process.[8]

How can you tell when a conversion takes place?

CCG II suggests four control standards:

1. The decision to develop or acquire an information system should be made in accordance with the objectives and policies of the entity. A preliminary survey should be conducted to help determine if further research into a new system is warranted.
2. There should be procedures to determine costs, savings, and benefits before a decision is made to develop or acquire an information system. A feasibility study should be conducted and begin with the findings of the preliminary survey; estimated costs and benefits of alternative plans should be quantified.
3. Procedures should be established to ensure that the information system being developed or acquired meets user requirements. There are five sequential steps to this standard: analysis of user requirements; development of an initial design based on those requirements; development of detailed specifications for the system; conversion of the detailed design into programs and testing of them; development of a detailed user manual to train users.
4. Information systems and programs should be adequately tested prior to use. The developers and users should participate in the testing.

Behavioral considerations such as those listed below are also important and should not be ignored:[9]

- The effects of system change on humans
- The human costs and benefits of systems
- The political motives for system change that may be inconsistent with an organization's goal
- The cognitive limits of human problem-solving in information requirements analysis, calling for methods that can compensate for such limitations
- Ergonomic factors

C. To ensure the efficient implementation of information systems Implementation is a complex process that involves the interaction of users, the development team, and the information systems processing group in the conversion process. User satisfaction with the results of the system development tends to vary directly with the implementation effort. The key to successful implementation is planning

---

8 Boritz, op. cit., p. 7.2. Material taken from *Computer Control & Audit Guide* reprinted with permission.

9 See J.E. Boritz and E. Hirst, "The Human Issues in Systems Development," *CA Magazine* (September 1986), pp. 56-61.

and assigning responsibility.[10] *CCG II* lists seven control standards to follow in order to achieve an efficient and effective implementation:

1. Responsibility should be assigned for implementation of information systems.
2. Standards should be established and enforced to ensure the efficiency and effectiveness of the implementation of information systems.
3. There should be procedures to ensure that information systems are implemented in accordance with the established standards.
4. An approved implementation plan should be used to measure progress.
5. Effective control should be maintained over the conversion of information and the initial operation of the information system.
6. User management should participate in the conversion of data from the existing system to the new system.
7. Final approval should be obtained from user management prior to operation of the new information system.

The implementation of a new system or development involves the conversion or creation of master files. Care must be taken by those involved to make certain that the data are accurately converted to the new system. The risk of errors is quite high as is the cost, in terms of time and effort, of restoring data integrity. In addition, some errors may never be corrected.

D. To ensure the efficient and effective maintenance of information systems   Once the information system has been successfully implemented, it must be efficiently and effectively maintained so that it functions at the desired level (i.e., so that it does not degrade). Maintenance may require a modification of the system, and the same care should be taken in designing the modification as was taken with the original development.

The following six control standards are suggested by *CCG II*:

1. There should be procedures to document and schedule all planned changes to information systems.
2. There should be procedures to ensure that only authorized changes are made.
3. Only authorized, tested, and documented changes to information systems should be accepted into production.
4. There should be procedures to report planned information systems changes to information systems management and to the users affected.
5. There should be procedures to allow for and control emergency changes.
6. There should be procedures to ensure that controls are in place to prevent unauthorized changes to information systems.

E. To ensure that the development and acquisition of information systems are carried out in an efficient and effective manner   *CCG II* suggests the following control standards for this objective:

1. Standards should be established and enforced to ensure the efficiency and effectiveness of the systems development and acquisition processes.
2. There should be procedures to make certain that all systems are developed and acquired in accordance with the established standards.

---

10 Boritz, op. cit., p. 7.35.

3. An approved development and acquisition plan (project plan) should be used to measure progress.

4. All personnel involved in systems development and acquisition activities should receive adequate training and supervision.

The external auditor should be involved in the development and acquisition process from its early stages. Such participation is likely to occur only if the auditor makes senior management aware of the value of and need for his or her involvement. Areas in which the auditor could become involved include the following:

- Assessing the adequacy of internal controls in planned new systems
- Assessing the adequacy of management trails
- Assessing the appropriateness of accounting principles to be applied
- Providing a supplemental link between management and the EDP department or data center
- Monitoring the conversion to the new system[11]

F. To ensure that present and future requirements of users of information systems processing can be met There should be a clear understanding between the users and information systems processing personnel of what the former expect from the system and what the latter expect the system to provide. It is important that information systems processing management keep senior and user management aware of new technology that could affect the entity's systems; in this way the entity could take advantage of technological change where and when appropriate.

The control standards suggested by *CCG II* for this objective follow:

1. There should be a written agreement between users and information systems processing, defining the nature and level of services to be provided. The presence of a written agreement that has been agreed to by both users and information systems processing reduces the likelihood of later misunderstandings if the system does not meet user requirements.

2. There should be appropriate management reporting within information systems processing.

3. Information systems processing management should keep senior and user management informed of technical developments that could support the achievement of the objectives and policies of the entity.

4. There should be procedures to examine the adequacy of information systems processing resources to meet the objectives of the entity in the future.

5. There should be procedures for the approval, monitoring, and control of the acquisition and upgrading of hardware and systems software.

G. To ensure the efficient and effective use of resources within information systems processing *CCG II* suggests four control standards applicable to this end:

1. A budget for information systems processing activities should be prepared on a regular basis.

2. Standards should be established and enforced to ensure efficient and effective use of information systems processing resources.

---

11 Ibid., p. 7.42.

3. There should be procedure to ensure that information processing problems are detected and corrected on a timely basis.

4. Users of information systems processing facilities should be accountable for the resources used by them.

H. To ensure complete, accurate, and timely processing of authorized information systems *CCG II* suggests seven control standards for this objective, which is concerned with the ongoing activities of information systems processing. Of these control standards, 4 and 5 are stipulated to make certain that user needs are met. The following are all seven standards:

1. Standards should be established and enforced to ensure a complete, accurate, and timely processing of [the] authorized information systems.

2. There should be operating procedures for all functions of information systems processing.

3. Information systems processing activities should be recorded and reviewed for compliance with established operating standards and procedures.

4. There should be written agreements between users and information systems processing, defining the nature and level of services to be provided.

5. Information systems processing activities should be scheduled to guarantee that the established user service requirements can be met.

6. Appropriate maintenance should be applied to hardware, systems software, and storage media.

7. Only authorized, tested, and documented new and changed information systems should be accepted into production.

I. To ensure that there is an appropriate segregation of incompatible functions within the entity The segregation of duties was discussed in Chapter 9 as a necessary element of internal control; this concept applies under an EDP system as well as under a manual system. The control standard established in *CCG II* regarding this matter states, "The organization structure established by senior management should provide for an appropriate segregation of incompatible functions."

Boritz's *Computer Control & Audit Guide* suggests that the segregation of duties (control objective I) and security (control objectives J, K, L, and M) are related topics:[12]

- [The segregation of duties and security] both have a *pervasive influence* on the other controls discussed in *Computer Control Guidelines*; i.e., application controls depend extensively on security controls to prevent unauthorized access to those transactions during processing.

- The controls over security and segregation are *closely inter-linked*. Security controls are needed to ensure segregation of incompatible functions but are also of a much wider scope. It might be easiest to think of segregation as a subset of security as displayed in Figure [15–3].

- Controls over segregation and security are *both necessary* to ensure the effective operation of programmed control procedures and to ensure the integrity of the system and information generated from it.

---

12 Ibid., pp. 9.1-9.2.

FIGURE 15–3

Segregation of Duties
and Security

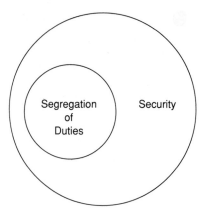

J. To ensure that all access to information and information systems is authorized *CCG II* suggests the following control standard: "There should be procedures to ensure that information systems are accessed in accordance with established policies and procedures."

K. To ensure that hardware facilities within information systems processing are physically protected from unauthorized access and from accidental or deliberate loss or damage *CCG II* suggests three control standards for this objective:

1. Hardware facilities within information systems processing should be physically separated from other departments in the entity.
2. Physical access to hardware facilities within information systems processing should be restricted to authorized personnel.
3. There should be procedures to ensure that environmental conditions (such as temperature and humidity) for hardware facilities are adequately controlled.

Security procedures, such as passwords, should also be utilized. Boritz's *Computer Control & Audit Guide* suggests the following are other measures for fulfilling this control objective:[13]

- *Safe storage* All files and programs should be stored in a safe location when not in use.
- *Separation/isolation of information processing facilities* Hardware facilities within information systems processing should be separated from other departments in the organization and should be physically protected from fire, flood or vandalism. This protection may include the location of the computer room in a remote area, the use of locks and the installation of fire detectors and automatic extinguishers.
- *Environment controls* Computer hardware and media are sensitive to excess humidity, power surges, temperature, or pollution, and the computer installation should accordingly be controlled to the manufacturer's specifications.

L. To ensure that information systems processing can be recovered and resumed after operations have been interrupted Interruption means that some

---

13 Ibid., pp. 9.22-9.23.

force external to the information system (e.g., a power outage, fire, or vandalism) has interrupted the data processing and prevented normal operation. The interruption may be temporary or permanent.

Because of the concentration of data in an EDP system the consequences of an interruption to the systems processing can be severe. Backup for and the recovery of the systems are very important. Control objectives L and M are specifically concerned with the ability of the entity to recover from interruptions. *CCG II* suggests three control standards for dealing with such events:

1. There should be procedures to allow information systems processing to resume operations in the event of an interruption.
2. Emergency, backup, and recovery plans should be documented and tested on a regular basis to ensure that they remain current and operational.
3. Personnel should receive adequate training and supervision in emergency backup and recovery procedures.

The greater the potential consequences of equipment failure, the more extensive the backup should be. For example, some financial institutions that have on-line real-time systems would need extensive backup; they could not function if they suffered an interruption in information systems processing. On the other hand, a small company that only had payroll on an EDP system could probably switch to manual processing until the problem causing the interruption was corrected.

Computer Control & Audit Guide lists four areas of concern with respect to back-up and recovery:[14]

- [Master] file back-up
- Program back-up
- Off-site storage
- Equipment back-up

In addition, contingency plans to continue operations in the event of an interruption and insurance against potential losses from the destruction of data, programs or equipment are important.

M. To ensure that critical user activities can be maintained and recovered following interruption to normal operations This objective indicates that user management also has a responsibility to minimize the effects of momentary or lengthy interruptions, and *CCG II* suggests three standards for fulfilling this responsibility:

1. There should be backup and recovery plans to allow users of information systems to resume operations in the event of an interruption.
2. All information and resources required by users to resume processing should be backed up appropriately.
3. User personnel should receive adequate training and supervision in the [conduct of] the recovery procedures.

---

14 Ibid., pp. 9.24–9.26.

Objectives Relating to Applications Controls

Application controls are of two types:

- User or manual controls. Examples would include test-checking payroll computations in a computerized payroll application, requiring two signatures on cheques in a computerized payment system, and scanning inventory listings prepared by a computer.
- Programmed controls. An example of a programmed control would be the performance by the system of a credit check against a master list of customers and all orders processed. These controls are usually dependent on general EDP controls. The general controls make certain that the programs, which incorporate the programmed control procedures, are
  - secure from unauthorized access and alterations
  - properly designed, developed, and tested
  - properly processed by the computer.[15]

Application controls may also be classified according to their source: controls over input and output are outside the computer; programmed controls are built into the software; and, finally, hardware controls, which affect the application, are an integral part of the equipment. None of these controls can be evaluated in isolation, since one can substitute for another. For instance, computer editing (a programmed control) can replace visual editing (an input control). *Computer Control & Audit Guide* states that what is important is whether taken together the controls fulfill certain essential objectives. The following factors can affect whether or not a specific technique is appropriate:

1. The nature of the application. Some systems are conducive to user controls and others requiring complex calculations and logic are best served by programmed control procedures.
2. The cost effectiveness of controls. The benefits from employing certain control techniques must outweigh the costs of expected loss from not employing those control techniques.
3. The strength of general EDP controls. The risk of programmed controls performing incorrectly is greatly reduced when adequate general EDP controls exist.
4. The effectiveness and availability of alternative application controls.
5. The timeliness of controls. Normally there is a time-usefulness tradeoff; if the control causes a delay in the processing of transactions or the availability of information, then its usefulness could be greatly diminished.[16]

CCG II lists three objectives that should be met in the area of application controls, identified below as N, O, and P.

N. To ensure that application controls are designed with due regard to the controls relating to segregation of incompatible functions, security, development, and processing of information systems This objective suggests that application controls should be designed to emphasize programmed controls; however, where programmed controls are weak, user controls become more important than otherwise they would be. The control standard states, "Application controls should be designed with regard to any weaknesses in segregation, security, development and processing controls which may affect the information system."

---

15 *Computer Control Guidelines* (2nd Edition), op. cit., p.132.

16 Boritz, op. cit., p. 10.4.

O. To ensure that information provided by the information systems is complete, authorized, and accurate The following seven control standards are intended to guarantee that information processed by the information system meets these three criteria:

1. There should be procedures to ensure that all transactions (including those used to change semi-permanent data and to correct errors) are initially recorded.
2. There should be procedures to ensure that all accepted transactions are authorized.
3. There should be procedures to ensure that all authorized transactions are recorded accurately.
4. There should be procedures to ensure that all authorized transactions are processed.
5. There should be procedures to ensure that all authorized transactions are processed accurately.
6. There should be procedures to ensure that output is reviewed by users for completeness, accuracy and consistency.
7. There should be some method of ensuring that control procedures relating to completeness, accuracy and authorization are enforced.

P. To ensure the existence of adequate management trails Management and audit trails are necessary to meet normal requests from management and others for further information than that provided in primary output reports. Trails enable one to trace the transactions involved in the processing of data. Having such trails is especially important for auditors, who need to be able to "trace summarized figures back to the specific transactions involved (or vice versa), to know which transactions trigger which other transactions, to understand the basis for complex computational outputs, and to identify the items making up a sum."[17] A transaction processing trail is also useful for answering the questions of customers, suppliers, employees, and government regulatory agencies.

To fulfill this objective *CCG II* suggests two control standards:

1. Policies and procedures for record retention should be established.
2. There should be some method of identifying and locating the component records involved in the processing of a transaction and in the production of information.

Computer Control & Audit Guide includes the following among techniques for making certain an adequate processing trail exists:

- The maintenance of detailed documents or file records that contain a total or summary amount in a form that facilitates their accessibility (e.g., printed reports, microfilm, machine-readable form).
- The unique identification of each document and file record to permit accessibility (e.g., document number, unique record keys, batch numbers, etc.).
- The maintenance of detailed documents that explain the computational logic that leads to the automatic generation of new amounts or the initiation of new transactions.
- The maintenance of adequate cross-reference lists at key points in transaction processing where transactions are generated or regrouped (e.g., batched).
- The maintenance of retention procedures for each type of record should indicate the storage medium used, labelling requirements, retention period, authorization

---

17 Ibid., p. 10–21.

required to access records and the persons charged with the responsibility of record retention.[18]

To understand how a transaction processing trail can be maintained it is necessary to become acquainted with the different types of transaction processing systems. There are two common types of transaction processing systems with which you should especially be familiar; these are *batch systems* and *on-line systems*.

Batch Systems A batch is a group of related transactions that are processed together as a group, or batch. For example, the time cards of the employees in a department could be a batch; the sales made by a branch office in a day could be a batch. In this system the user departments gather the documents to be processed into batches, record the details of the batch into a batch control log, and forward the batches to the EDP group for processing. Control totals are used to ensure that all the items in the batch are processed. Three methods of arriving at control totals follow:

- *Record counts* The number of items in the batch (e.g., payroll time cards) is entered into the computer and compared by it with the number of items in the batch.
- *Financial control total* The dollar value of the batch is compared to the dollar value processed by the computer.
- *Hash totals* Some number that is not normally added (e.g., the total of the employee numbers of the employees whose time cards were batched) is manually added as a control total and compared by the computer with the hash total of the numbers of the employees whose time cards were processed as part of the batch.

After the batch has been processed by the EDP group, the output is sent to the user groups and checked against the batch control log. With this system a transaction processing trail would be based on these batches.

On-line Systems In this type of processing system the user interacts directly with the computer by means of a terminal. Processing is usually instantaneous. The user performs many of the functions that the EDP group performs in batch processing, such as error correction and program scheduling. One person does the work of many in this situation and consequently a great reliance must be placed on programmed controls, such as passwords. Control totals may not be available and so ensuring completeness as well as the maintenance of trails will depend on programmed controls such as sequential numbering of transactions.

Understanding Internal Control in an EDP Environment

The objective of understanding internal control and assessing control risk is the same for a manual or for a noncomplex or complex EDP system: to aid in determining, on the basis of the adequacy of existing internal controls, the audit evidence that should be accumulated. Similarly, the techniques for all types of systems are to obtain information about the client's internal control, to identify controls and weaknesses, to initially assess control risk, and to ascertain that internal controls are actually operating in accordance with the plan.

A problem often arises in evaluating complex EDP systems because process-

---

18 Ibid., p. 10–21.

ing transactions usually involves more steps than in a noncomplex system, and thus opens up opportunities for errors and fraud. This means there is usually a need for a greater number of internal control procedures in a complex EDP system. Furthermore, many controls will deal with the invisible portions of the transaction trail. These will often be technical in nature. For that reason many public accounting firms use EDP specialists to evaluate internal control when the client has significant EDP.

In obtaining information about the client's internal control, the auditor is concerned with determining the existence of the EDP controls enumerated in Chapter 9, including Appendix A, and their adequacy in meeting internal control objectives. Of course, it is also necessary to evaluate the non-EDP controls discussed earlier in the book, such as use and control of prenumbered documents and separation of the custody over assets from the recording function.

It is common to begin the obtaining of an understanding of internal control of an EDP system by the development or examination of: *flowcharts and EDP questionnaires*, and a study of the *error listings* generated by the system. The flowcharts and questionnaires have counterparts in non-EDP systems, but an error listing is unique to EDP systems. In most cases it is desirable to use all three approaches in understanding internal control because they offer different types of information. The flowchart emphasizes the organization of the company and the flow of information throughout the system, whereas the internal control questionnaire emphasizes specific controls without relating individual controls to one another. The error listing supports both these approaches by showing the actual errors that were reported by the EDP system. Ultimately, the auditor must use the information obtained to determine the most important controls and weaknesses in internal control.

After the auditor obtains an understanding of EDP internal control, the auditor is in a position to decide the degree to which he or she plans to assess control risk below the maximum. In doing this, the auditor must consider the related non-EDP controls and the entire internal control affecting each application. When controls in one segment, such as the EDP controls, are weak, the auditor may determine that controls in the other segments are compensating, and vice versa. Whenever the auditor feels that control risk cannot be assessed below the maximum, he or she will of course expand the substantive procedures portion of the audit. This approach to control risk assessment is the same as that discussed in Chapters 9 through 13.

If the auditor decides internal control may be effective, it is necessary to proceed with the study by obtaining an in-depth understanding of internal control and by performing tests of controls. The procedures should include observing and interviewing personnel, performing tests of controls, and investigating exceptions to controls and procedures.

As in noncomplex systems, the auditor may decide not to assess control risk below maximum in complex systems even if internal controls are adequate. This approach is followed if the auditor believes the cost of a study and test of controls will exceed the reduction in the cost due to not needing to perform other procedures. When the auditor decides not to test the controls, control risk cannot be assessed below the maximum.

In April, 1989, the Steering Committee of the (then) Auditing Standards Committee set a new section of the *CICA Handbook* entitled "EDP Auditing Guidelines." The Guidelines in existence at the time of writing include "Auditing in an EDP Environment," "The Effects of an EDP Environment on the Study and

OBJECTIVE 3

Know the similarities and differences in obtaining an understanding of internal control in noncomplex and complex EDP systems.

Evaluation of the Accounting System and Related Internal Controls," and three guidelines based on supplements to the latter; the supplements deal with stand-alone microcomputers, on-line computer systems, and database systems. The guidelines are based on International Auditing Guidelines (IAG) 15 and 20 respectively, issued by the International Auditing Practices Committee (IAPC) of the International Federation of Accountants (IFAC). IAGs, the IAPC and the IFAC were discussed in Chapter 1.

Auditing in an EDP Environment Without Relying on Computer Controls

When an auditor uses only the user controls surrounding a system to assess control risk, he or she is commonly said to be *auditing around the computer* or *auditing without relying on computer controls*. Under this approach, the auditor obtains an understanding of internal control and performs tests of controls and account balance verification procedures in the same manner as in manual systems; there is no attempt to test the client's EDP controls (although the auditor may use the computer to perform audit procedures).

To audit around the computer, the auditor must have access to sufficient source documentation and a detailed listing of output in a readable form. This is possible only when all the following conditions are met:

> **OBJECTIVE 4**
>
> Decide when it is appropriate to audit only the non-EDP internal controls to assess control risk.

- The source documents are available in a nonmachine language.
- The documents are filed in a manner that makes it possible to locate them for auditing purposes.
- The output is listed in sufficient detail to enable the auditor to trace individual transactions from the source documents to the output and vice versa.

If any of these conditions does not exist, the auditor will have to rely on computer-oriented controls. Auditing around the computer is an acceptable and often desirable approach when the informational needs of the client's organization require it to maintain the necessary source documents and detailed output.

Complete dependence on manual controls and use of traditional techniques when conditions allow does not imply that the auditor ignores the EDP installation. The auditor continues to be responsible to obtain an understanding of internal control and to assess control risk as an aid in deciding on the appropriate audit procedures and the sample size necessary for each procedure. This includes both manual and EDP segments.

Auditing Through the Computer

Auditing through the computer means the auditor is relying on EDP controls. There are two ways in which the auditor uses the computer to perform audit procedures: (1) processing the auditor's test data on the client's computer system as a part of tests of controls, and (2) testing the records maintained by the computer as a means of verifying the client's financial statements. These procedures are accomplished by use of test data and generalized audit software. There is an EDP Auditing Guideline issued by the Steering Committee of the Auditing Standards Committee in 1989 entitled "Computer-assisted Audit Techniques"; it provides useful guidance on the use of computer-assisted audit techniques (CAATs) such as audit software and test data.

> **OBJECTIVE 5**
>
> Describe three ways to use the computer as an auditing tool.

Test Data Approach

The objective of the test data approach is to determine whether the client's computer programs can correctly handle valid and invalid transactions as they arise. To fulfill this objective, the auditor develops different types of transactions that are processed under his or her own control using the client's computer programs on the client's EDP equipment. The auditor's test data must include both *valid and invalid transactions* in order to determine whether the client's computer programs will react properly to different kinds of data. Since the auditor has complete knowledge of the errors that exist in the test data, it is possible for the auditor to check whether the client's system has properly processed the input. The auditor does this by examining the error listing and the details of the output resulting from the test data.

Figure 15–4 illustrates the use of the test data approach. As an illustration, assume an auditor is testing the effectiveness of a client's payroll internal controls that includes certain limit tests. The auditor prepares a payroll transaction with 140 hours for each week and processes it through the client's system in the manner shown in Figure 15–4. If the controls are effective, the client's system should not process that transaction. The error listing should therefore indicate that the number of hours exceeds the limit.

Test data are helpful in reviewing the client's system of processing data and its control over errors, but several difficulties must be overcome before this approach can be used. The major concerns follow.

Test data must include all relevant conditions the auditor desires to test The test data should test the adequacy of all the controls discussed previously that are applicable to the client's program under review. Because considerable competence is required in developing data to test for all the relevant types of errors that could occur, the assistance of an EDP specialist is generally required.

Program tested by the auditor's test data must be the same as that used throughout the year by the client One approach the auditor can take to ensure that this condition is met is to run the test data on a surprise basis, possibly at random times throughout the year. This approach is both costly and time consuming and may be impossible because it disrupts the client's processing. A more realistic method is to rely on the client's internal controls over making changes in the program.

In some cases, test data must be eliminated from the client's records The elimination of test data is necessary if the program being tested is for the updating of a master file such as the accounts receivable trial balance. It would not be proper to permit fictitious test transactions to remain permanently in a master file. There are feasible methods of eliminating test data, but they generally require the assistance of an EDP specialist. It should be noted that in circumstances in which elimination of test data is not feasible, it is common practice for auditors to enter only invalid data. These tests are incomplete. However, they are useful for testing certain edit commands, for example, the extent to which invalid transactions are rejected. They are also risky if the client's system has weaknesses which fail to reject the invalid data.

Auditor's Computer Program Approach The second approach to auditing with the computer is for the auditor to run his or her own program on a controlled basis in order to verify the client's data recorded in a machine language. Figure 15–5 illustrates the use of the computer program approach. For example, assume an auditor wants to add the client's schedule of accounts receivable, which is in machine-readable form. The client's master file is processed on either the auditor's or client's computer, using the auditor's com-

FIGURE 15-4

Test Data Approach

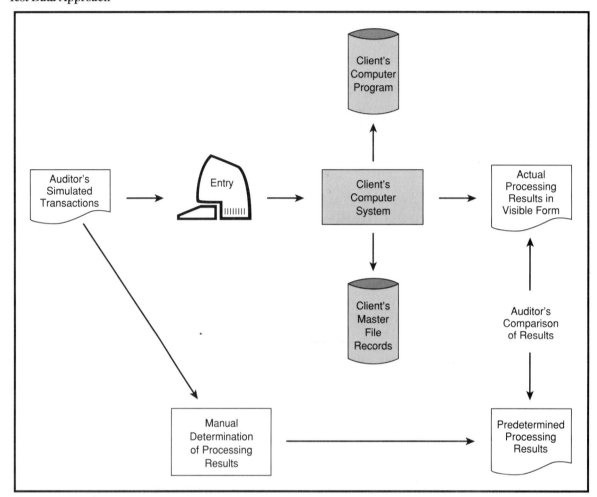

puter program. The auditor can compare the total generated by the computer with the general ledger total.

The auditor's computer program and the test data approach are complementary rather than mutually exclusive, in the same way that tests of controls and tests of details of balances verification are. In the test data approach, the auditor uses test data to evaluate the ability of the client's system to handle different types of transactions; in the auditor's computer program approach, the auditor tests the output of the system for correctness. A comparison of Figures 15-4 and 15-5 illustrates this difference.

The auditor can potentially perform many different kinds of tests and other functions with a computer program if the client's data are in a machine language. These include the following:

Verifying extensions and footings A computer program can be used to verify the accuracy of the client's computations by calculating the information independently. Examples include recalculating sales discounts taken and employees' net pay computations, footing an aging and totaling the client's accounts receivable trial balance.

FIGURE 15–5

Auditor's Computer
Program Approach

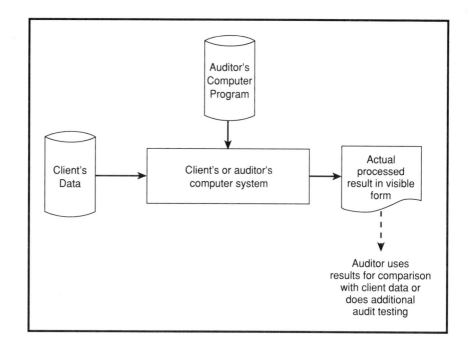

Examining records for quality, completeness, consistency, and correctness In auditing a manual system, the auditor routinely reexamines accounting records for propriety because they are visible and any inconsistencies or inaccuracies can be observed without difficulty. When auditing computerized records, the auditor's program can be instructed to scan all records for propriety in terms of specified criteria and to print out the exceptions. Examples include review of accounts receivable balances for amounts over the credit limit and review of payroll files for terminated employees.

Comparing data on separate files Where records on separate files should contain compatible information, a program can be used to determine if the information agrees or to make other comparisons. For instance, changes in accounts receivable balances between two dates can be compared with details of sales and cash receipts on transaction files, and payroll details can be compared with personnel records.

Summarizing or resequencing data and performing analyses Computer programs can be developed to change the format and aggregate data in a variety of ways. The ability to change the form of data allows the auditor to use the computer to prepare analyses used in audit procedures and to simulate the client's data processing systems to determine the reasonableness of recorded information. Examples include verifying accounts receivable aging, preparing general ledger trial balances, summarizing inventory turnover statistics for obsolescence analysis, and resequencing inventory items by location to facilitate physical observations.

Comparing data obtained through other audit procedures with company records Audit evidence gathered manually can be converted to machine-readable form (data entered) and compared with other machine-readable data.

Examples include comparing confirmation responses with the subsidiary records and comparing creditor statements with accounts payable files.

Selecting audit samples   The computer can be programmed to select samples from any machine-readable data in several different ways, including at random. It is also possible to use more than one criterion for sample selection, such as selection of 100 percent of high dollar accounts receivable and random sampling of all other receivables.

Printing confirmation requests   After a sample has been selected, the auditor can have the data printed on confirmation request forms. This is a useful time-saving device for the preparation of confirmations.

Generalized Audit Software   Although it is possible for auditors to write specific programs to perform the above functions, or to use existing client programs for that purpose, the most common approach is to use a generalized audit software (GAS) program.

A generalized audit software program is one developed by a public accounting firm or other organization and it can be used on different audits for most of the seven types of applications listed above. The generalized program consists of a series of computer programs that together perform various data processing functions. These, for the most part, can be described as data manipulations. Generalized programs are a development in auditing that has greatly increased the potential use of the computer for auditing tasks.

There are two important advantages to generalized programs. First, they are developed in such a manner that most of the audit staff can be quickly trained to use the program even if they have little formal EDP education. Second, with generalized programs, a single program can be applied to a wide range of tasks without having to incur the cost or inconvenience of developing individualized programs.

The decision whether or not to use audit software must be made by the auditor on the basis of his or her professional experience. Sometimes the auditor is forced to use the computer to perform procedures due to the inaccessibility of source documents and detailed listing of output. Even if records are accessible, it may be desirable to perform tests with the computer if sufficient appropriate audit evidence can be accumulated at a reduced cost.

Using Generalized Audit Software   Since generalized audit software programs are used extensively in public accounting firms, it is important that students of auditing understand them. An explanation of these programs in general terms is given below, followed by an illustration of how they could be used.

Figure 15–6 illustrates the GAS process for any application. The steps are as follows:

Objective setting   The purpose of the test must be carefully specified in advance to achieve the desired results. The objective can be to foot a data file, select a random sample, or perform one or more of the other tasks previously described.

Application design   The second step consists of three parts:

FIGURE 15–6

GAS Application
Process

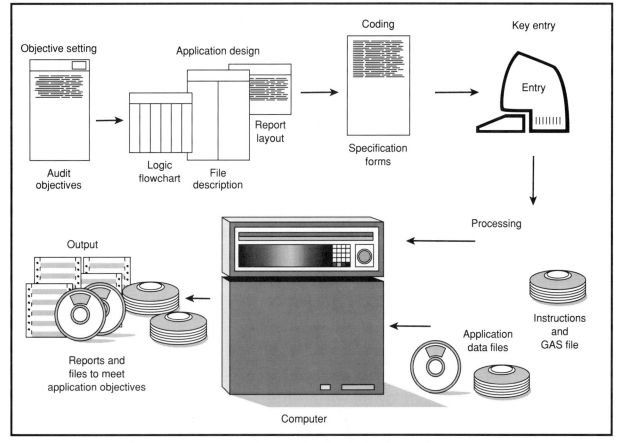

- Identify and describe the client's data files and the pertinent information to which access is desired. This is necessary to extract data from the client's files.
- Design the most useful format and contents of the auditor's GAS reports.
- Develop a logical approach to extract and manipulate the data obtained from the client's records. This is done by the auditor with the use of commands provided by GAS.

Coding   The results of the application design are then entered into the computer by the auditor using commands appearing on the monitor in the simple GAS language. These are instructions telling the GAS what to do with the client's files to meet the audit objectives specified.

Processing   The processing phase has two stages. In the first, the GAS directs the computer to read the data file and to extract pertinent information. It is important to understand that all further processing takes place on the extracted information. The client's data file is no longer used and is removed from the process, thus ensuring that it will not be inadvertently changed or destroyed. Should it be necessary for the GAS to produce an intermediate output file, it is referred to as a work file. The second stage involves the functions required to produce the GAS reports. At the completion of the processing, the client's data files are returned to the client and the GAS file is returned to the public accountant's office. Frequently, the GAS coding instructions are retained for possible use on subsequent audits. The GAS reports are used for their intended audit purpose and retained in the working papers as documentation.

Illustration for Accounts Receivable

The following is an illustration of a GAS application presented in terms of the steps given above.

Objective setting

1. Foot and crossfoot the accounts receivable master file and print the total and any crossfoot exceptions.
2. Determine if any balances are in excess of their credit limit and print a report of all exceptions.
3. Prepare and print an aging summary.
4. Randomly select accounts and print confirmations as follows:
   a. Positive confirmation of all accounts over $10,000 or over 90 days old.
   b. Positive confirmation of 25 percent of all accounts between $1,000 and $10,000 not over 90 days old.
   c. Negative confirmation of 5 percent of all others.
5. Print a control listing of accounts selected for confirmation.
6. Select 5 percent of all accounts to trace to source documents, for a test of aging.
7. Select and print a list of accounts for collectibility follow-up that are "for special handling."

Application design The client maintains accounts receivable on both a master file and a name and address file. Tables 15–1 and 15–2 list the file contents, noting whether the information was used in the application.

Coding The objectives of this application were met by coding the various GAS functions to process the client's data files as follows:

1. The accounts receivable master file was read and the designated information was extracted. This was followed by extracting the name, address, and risk information from the name and address file.
2. The extracted information was next subjected to the following selection criteria:
   a. Add the aging fields within each record and subtract total from balance due field. Place any difference in an aging overflow field and code the record for report no. 1.
   b. Foot aging and balance due fields for all records. The GAS prints such totals automatically.
   c. Compare the balance due field with the credit limit field. If the balance exceeds the limit, code the record for report no. 2.
   d. Compare balance due with $10,000. If greater than $10,000, code the record for positive confirmation and report no. 3.
   e. Compare aging fields ninety days, six months, and one year with zero. If greater than zero, code the record for positive confirmation and report no. 3.
   f. Compare balance due with $1,000. If greater than $1,000 and not previously coded for positive confirmation, select 25 percent at random and code for positive confirmation and report no. 3.
   g. Compare balance due with $1,000. If less than $1,000 and not coded for posi-

TABLE 15–1

Accounts Receivable Master File

ELEMENT NO.	DESCRIPTION OF CONTENTS	USED	NOT USED
1	Division	X	–
2	Customer number	X	–
3	Credit limit	X	–
4	Sales personnel code	–	X
5	Cash discount percent	–	X
6	Date of last payment	X	–
7	Date of last purchase	X	–
8	Balance due	X	–
	Aging of balance due:		
9	Current	X	–
10	30 days	X	–
11	60 days	X	–
12	90 days	X	–
13	6 months	X	–
14	1 year	X	–

Copyright © 1978, Touche Ross & Co. Reprinted with permission.

TABLE 15–2

Name and Address File

ELEMENT NO.	DESCRIPTION OF CONTENTS	USED	NOT USED
1	Division	X	–
2	Customer number	X	–
3	Customer name	X	–
4	Street address	X	–
5	City and province	X	–
6	Postal code	X	–
7	Shipping location code	–	X
8	Customer type	–	X
9	Risk-rating code	X	–
	1 = no risk		
	2 = normal handling		
	3 = approval required when balance over 60 days		
	4 = special handling required for each purchase		

Copyright © 1978, Touche Ross & Co. Reprinted with permission.

tive confirmation, select 5 percent at random and code for negative confirmation and report no. 4.

h. Select 5 percent of all accounts at random and code for report no. 5.

i. Code any records with a risk rating equal to 4 and not selected for confirmation to report no. 6.

Key entry and processing After the codes were entered and verified, they were processed with the GAS and the accounts receivable master file and the name and address file.

Reports The following reports were printed:

- Report no. 1 – all accounts in which aging does not crossfoot (if any)
- Report no. 2 – all accounts in which balance is in excess of credit limit (if any)
- Report no. 3 – accounts selected for positive confirmation and collectibility follow-up
- Report no. 4 – accounts selected for negative confirmation

- Report no. 5 – accounts for test of aging, showing all aging details, including dates of last payment and purchase
- Report no. 6 – additional high-risk accounts selected for collectibility follow-up

In addition, positive and negative confirmations were printed.

Microcomputer-Aided Auditing

A more recent development that complements the use of generalized audit software is the use of microcomputers to perform audit tasks. It is now common for auditors to take portable microcomputers to the client's office for use as an audit tool. Many audit tasks, such as analytical procedures and working paper preparation, can be performed. These are discussed shortly.

<table>
<tr><td>

OBJECTIVE 6

Know the types of software available for and uses of microcomputers in auditing.

</td></tr>
</table>

There is a difference between using generalized audit software and using the microcomputer as an audit tool. Recall that generalized audit software is a term used to describe programs written or purchased by the auditor for use on the client's EDP system. Using generalized audit software is a method of verifying the client's data that is recorded in a machine language. The microcomputer is hardware that the auditor takes to the audit; it can be used in conjunction with the client's EDP system, with data extracted from the client's EDP system or even with client's data that are not computerized or when the client's software is not compatible with the auditor's. The microcomputer may be plugged into the client's computer to act as a terminal or it may be used on its own as a "stand-alone" process. Often the microcomputer is also used with generalized audit software.

Auditors take both a microcomputer and software, such as that described below, to the client's office. Typically, input is entered into the microcomputer system by the auditor or a clerical assistant. That input is then used by the auditor for analysis or summarization. For instance, the client's trial balance is usually inputted into the microcomputer system and that is used to perform analytical procedures. Naturally, if the client's data is computerized and compatible with the auditor's software, input need not be put through the keyboard.

Types of Software

The specific tasks the auditor will perform by microcomputer depend, of course, on engagement circumstances, but a more important factor is the available software. Four types of software are frequently used by auditors: commercial general-use software, proprietary templates of commercial general-use software, special-use software, and custom programs written by the auditor.

Commercial general-use software A large number of software products are available for microcomputer use at low prices. Two of these, electronic spreadsheets and word processors, are particularly useful to auditors.

An *electronic spreadsheet* is a program that presents and manipulates data in the form of a matrix of interrelated values, with columns and rows, much like an accounting worksheet and many auditors' work papers. Labels (including extended narrative information) and values are entered in the cells of the matrix (that is, the intersection of each column and row), calculations can be performed with the values, and all or selected results can be displayed. The most popular electronic spreadsheet programs are Lotus 1-2-3, Excel, SuperCalc, and Quattro.

Word processors combine the capabilities of a typewriter with a microcomputer to allow the auditor to create and save text in almost any form. The text can be narrative but can also include numeric data in tabular form. WordPerfect and Word-Star are among the more popular word processing programs.

There are also generalized audit software packages such as IDEA and ACL that are used by some auditors.

Templates   Predesigned formats for such things as work papers and letters can be created and saved using both electronic spreadsheets and word processors. These are called *templates*. These templates are available for continuing use as standard formats for different engagements, or over time for the same engagement. Larger firms develop such templates centrally for distribution to each office.

Special-use software   The extensive use of microcomputers by auditors has created a market for special-use software. Some *auditor's software* is developed on a commercial basis by a number of organizations, including some large accounting firms. Most large public accounting firms have also developed this type of software for their internal use.

The degree of sophistication of this software varies considerably. The most popular use is for the development and maintenance of the working trial balance and lead sheets. However, some large firms are beginning to use programs that evaluate internal controls, assist in the evaluation of client judgments and estimates, and help plan evidence accumulation. The more advanced of these programs are sophisticated, and they incorporate *expert systems*.

Expert systems are part of the area known as artificial intelligence and are also called knowledge-based or rule-based systems. They are computer programs that emulate the problem-solving processes of human experts. An expert system has the knowledge of a human expert or experts built into it. The person using the system interacts with the program much the way a person might interact with an expert, calling on the knowledge of the expert in the program to solve the problem at hand.

Expert systems are in their infancy in the field of auditing. However, there are expert systems in other fields that are highly developed.[19] One such system, called *Mycin*, is used in the field of medicine to *assist* doctors in the diagnosis of infectious diseases. A doctor enters the information into the computer in response to questions the computer poses. Each question posed by the computer is based on answers the doctor has provided to previous questions; this is the sense in which the system is interactive. An expert system does not replace people; it only gives people access to an expert's knowledge. Each question is a question an expert in the area would ask, given the answers to the preceding questions. An expert system also permits the user to ask why any particular question was asked, for which it will provide a rationale (this is another aspect of the interactive nature of the expert systems). Finally, *Mycin* will tell the doctor how a patient, with all the symptoms the doctor has decribed in answer to *Mycin*'s questions, should be treated.

Researchers are working on developing expert systems in a number of areas in accounting and auditing. Several that are in use are *Auditor*, a program that assesses the adequacy of the client's allowance for doubtful accounts, *EDP Auditor*, a program that helps the auditor evaluate computer contols, and *Loan Probe*,

---

19   The interested reader is referred to Armitage, Howard M. and Boritz, J. Efrim, *Decision-Support and Expert Systems for Management Accountants*, Hamilton: The Society of Management Accountants of Canada, 1991, especially pages 1-36.

an expert system that aids the auditor in assessing a financial institution's loan loss provisions.[20]

Custom programs Some auditors are trained and skilled in writing computer programs on a microcomputer and use that skill in audit engagements. Such programs are usually costly to develop and less desirable than good commercial or special-use software. In some cases, however, software is not designed for a particular task the auditor wants done. It is appropriate to develop a special program in that situation.

Uses of
Microcomputers

Most microcomputer applications done in practice employ special-use software designed specifically for auditing or audit-related electronic spreadsheet and word processing templates. The other types of microcomputer software discussed in the previous section can also be used when special-use software is not available or is impractical.

Trial balances and lead schedule preparation The microcomputer can be used to develop a working trial balance and lead schedules for the various financial statement accounts. As adjusting and reclassification journal entries are being made, they are electronically posted and an updated trial balance is immediately available. When the audit work is done, the final trial balance accounts can be automatically aggregated for drafting the financial statements. If consolidated statements are needed, subtrial balances can also be combined.

Work paper preparation Microcomputer software is ideally suited for audit workpaper preparation. It is particularly helpful where standard formats are most applicable and where there are extensive calculations. Examples of these situations include proofs of cash bank balances, accounts receivable confirmation control and summarization, inventory price tests, fixed asset summaries and depreciation calculations, tax accruals, and interest computation tests.

Analytical procedures Analytical procedures (the comparison of amounts, development of ratios, and other analyses) are greatly facilitated by the microcomputer. Most special-use trial balance software programs offer an analytical procedures option as a by-product. Electronic spreadsheets are also ideal for such analysis and allow for tailoring. Figure 15–7 illustrates the use of an electronic spreadsheet for both analytical procedures and audit workpaper preparation.

Audit program preparation The simplest form of this application is to type the audit program on a word processor and save it from one year to the next to facilitate changes and updating. A more sophisticated use is to have a special-use program that will help the auditor think through the planning considerations of the audit and select appropriate procedures from an "audit procedures data base." These are then formulated into an audit program. The underlying logic would be the same as for the audit framework discussed in Chapters 10 through 13.

---

20 For further information see Boritz, op. cit., pp. 14.33-14.36 and J.E. Boritz, "The Race to Harness Brain Power," *CA Magazine* (August 1988), pp.52-59.

FIGURE 15–7 Ratio Analysis Using an Electronic Spreadsheet

ABC INC. RATIO ANALYSIS 12/31/X5 19X5 Financial Data (000's omitted)		Prepared by – Reviewed by – Ratios	19X5	19X4	19X3	19X2	19X1
Cash	8558	Short-Term Debt					
Accounts Rec. – gross	25164	Paying Ability:					
Allow. for D/a	−1400	Current ratio	2.07	2.29	2.24	2.50	1.91
Inventories	22172	Quick ratio	1.16	1.27	1.15	1.50	1.06
Other current assets	3468	Cash ratio	0.31	0.31	0.26	0.30	0.28
Fixed assets	115827						
Investments	16167	Short-Term					
		Liquidity:					
	189956	A/R turnover	6.01	5.88	5.24	5.91	5.81
		Days to collect	60	61	69	61	62
Current liabilities	27984	Inv. turnover	4.91	4.52	4.23	5.35	4.79
Long-term debt	50201	Days to sell	73	80	85	67	75
Deferred taxes	13889	Days to convert	133	141	154	128	137
Preferred stock	18009						
Common equity	79873	Long-Term					
		Liquidity:					
	189956	Debt to equity	0.94	0.98	0.88	0.82	0.78
		TNA to equity	0.96	0.96	0.96	0.96	0.96
Net sales	150559	Times int ernd	3.83	3.48	3.78	5.40	5.17
		Times int + PD Ed	2.03	1.70	1.66	2.28	2.01
Cost of sales	104903						
Depreciation	8183	Operating					
Other operating expenses	21177	Performance:					
Interest expense	4253	Efficiency	0.87	0.78	0.73	0.83	0.76
Other (income) expense	−905	Profit margin	0.11	0.09	0.10	0.12	0.11
Taxes on income	4290	Profitability	0.09	0.07	0.07	0.10	0.08
		Return on asset	0.09	0.07	0.06	0.09	0.08
	141901	Return on Equity:					
Net earnings	8658	Return Bef tax	0.12	0.08	0.08	0.12	0.10
Beg. retained earnings	76282	BV per share	13.15	12.56	12.17	12.11	11.90
Preferred dividends	−2029	Leverage from:					
Common dividends	−3038	S-T debt	0.03	0.02	0.02	0.02	0.03
		L-T debt	0.00	0.00	0.00	0.02	0.01
End. retained earnings	79873	Other Liab.	0.01	0.01	0.01	0.01	0.01
		Prd stock	−0.03	−0.03	−0.04	−0.03	−0.03
Capital expenditures	9553						
Common shares outstanding	6075						
Intan. assets in investment	4000						
Mkt. value of stock:							
Common	70000						
Preferred	20000						

Understand internal control There are several types of software that assist in this task. First, a word processor can be used to document internal control using a narrative description. Second, internal control questionnaires can be automated both to document descriptive information and perform some evaluative steps. And, third, special flowcharting software can be used for similar purposes.

Audit sampling Special-use software is available to design, select, and evaluate audit samples using a variety of statistical or nonstatistical techniques. It is also possible to use an electronic spreadsheet to do the evaluation, and to write a simple program when special-use software is not available.

Engagement management and time budgeting Spreadsheet software (particularly with the use of a template) is well suited to preparing time budgets and monitoring time spent in relation to budget. Word processors are extremely useful for the preparation of routine engagement correspondence, such as the engagement and management representation letters. Most special-use microcomputer software also includes these applications.

Generalized audit software preparation   Where GAS is to be used for client files, the microcomputer can facilitate development of the GAS specifications.

Quality Control Concerns

Special concerns about quality control arise when microcomputers are used. There are two primary reasons for these concerns: lack of visible data and unreliable software. First, much of the information about data and how it is manipulated may not be visible to the auditor or the auditor's supervisor. To check the work when it is performed, and to review it after completion, special effort must be taken to document input data and computational routines. Well-designed software can provide for such documentation. Second, the software used, or the use of the software, may not be reliable. Widely used commercial software should have been thoroughly tested and proved reliable by the developer. However, new software and specially created software may contain "bugs" that affect its reliability. Similarly, when commercial software is used by the auditor to create computational and logic routines, it is possible that mistakes will be made that cause the results to be in error. To protect against these situations, the auditor should always consider the need to test software and uses of it with test data and comparison with predetermined results.

The Future of Microcomputers in Auditing

As auditors gain more experience with microcomputers, their use will expand rapidly. As the power of microcomputers expands, these uses will become more sophisticated. The microcomputer will increasingly serve as a data and information communication tool and begin to assume many of the processing functions of full-scale computers. In summary, we foresee the day when the majority of the audit will involve use of the microcomputer and its descendants.

Audit of a Computer Service Bureau

Some clients now have their data processed at an independent computer service bureau rather than have their own computer. This is a logical approach for a business with an excessive volume of transactions for a manual system but inadequate volume to justify the cost of owning a computer.

In a computer service bureau operation, the client submits input data, which the service bureau processes for a fee and returns to the client along with the agreed-upon output. Generally, the service bureau is responsible for designing the computer system and providing adequate controls to ensure that the processing is reliable.

OBJECTIVE 7

Discuss the special concerns of the auditor when the client's information is processed by a computer service bureau.

The difficulty the independent auditor faces when a computer service bureau is used is in determining the adequacy of the service bureau's internal controls. The auditor cannot automatically assume the controls are adequate simply because it is an independent enterprise. If the client's service bureau application involves the processing of significant financial data, the auditor must consider the need to understand and test the service bureau's controls.

The extent of obtaining an understanding and testing of the service bureau should be based on the same criteria the auditor follows in evaluating a client's own internal control. The depth of the understanding depends on the complexity of the system, the locus of key controls and the extent to which the auditor intends to assess control risk below maximum to reduce other audit tests. If the auditor concludes that active involvement with the service bureau is the only feasible way to conduct the audit, it may be necessary to obtain an extensive understanding of the service bureau's internal control, test it by the use of test data and other tests of controls, and use the computer to perform tests of the type discussed in the preceding sections.

In recent years, it has become increasingly common to have *one* independent auditor obtain an understanding and test the service bureau's internal control for the use of *all* customers and their independent auditors. The purpose of these independent reviews is to provide customers with a reasonable level of assurance of the adequacy of the service center's internal control and to eliminate the need for redundant audits by customers' auditors. If the service bureau has many customers and each requires an understanding of the service bureau's internal control by its own independent auditor, the inconvenience to the service bureau can be substantial. When the service bureau's independent public accounting firm completes the audit of the controls and records, a special report under Section 5900, "Opinions on Control Procedures at a Service Organization," is issued indicating the scope of the audit and the conclusions. It is then the responsibility of the customer's auditor to decide the extent to which he or she wants to rely on the service bureau's auditor's report. Section 5310, "Audit Evidence Considerations when an Enterprise uses a Service Organization," is instructive in that regard.

Review Questions

15–1   What are the most important factors that characterize a simple or noncomplex EDP system? Identify the major technical factors that make EDP systems more complex.

15–2   Explain how the extent an EDP system is used affects its complexity.

15–3   Identify the major effects of EDP on organizations that use it.

15–4   Define what is meant by a transaction trail and explain how the client's introduction of EDP can alter it. How does this change affect the auditor?

15–5   Evaluate the following statement: "As EDP systems become more complex, the role of the traditional auditor declines. It is desirable that auditors involved with EDP systems either become competent in specialized computer concepts or use computer audit specialists on the engagement."

15–6   In what ways is the potential for fraud greater in an EDP system than in a manual system?

15–7   Discuss the advantages and disadvantages of the reduced involvement of client personnel in an EDP environment.

15–8   "An EDP system will greatly reduce the danger of error or fraud." Discuss the statement critically.

15–9   What is meant by application controls? Give several examples of the type of errors they are meant to prevent.

15–10   Explain where each of the following controls fits in Figure 15–2 and why. As an example, the verification of prices by computer would be in area F because it is an accounting control that uses the computer.

1. Changes to programs must be approved.
2. The treasurer reconciles the bank account monthly.
3. Customer purchases on account are flagged if they would increase the customer's account above the customer's credit limit.
4. File labels are checked by the operating system before the files are run.
5. There is a limit check on hours worked per pay period.
6. Only certain employees can change the prices on the master price list.
7. Cheques are prepared by the computer on instructions from the controller's department; they are signed by the treasurer's department.
8. The company maintains three generations of master tapes in off-site storage.

15–11 What group should bear the responsibility for establishing control over the information produced by an enterprise? How should that group establish that control?

15–12 What are the causes of information system failure? How does *Computer Control Guidelines* suggest an entity might reduce the likelihood of information systems failure?

15–13 How can the likelihood of a successful implementation of an information system be increased?

15–14 What concerns should an auditor have when a client converts to a new information system?

15–15 What should be the auditor's involvement in the development of a new information system by a client?

15–16 How can senior management ensure that the information systems needs of users are met?

15–17 What is the relationship between segregation of duties and security?

15–18 Discuss the controls that might be used to ensure security over information systems.

15–19 Why is recovery and resumption of operations after an interruption considered to be so important?

15–20 Differentiate between user and programmed controls.

15–21 Discuss the factors that affect decisions on what applications controls to employ.

15–22 Why does *Computer Control Guidelines* suggest that applications controls should emphasize programmed controls? When are user controls to be emphasized?

15–23 What are management trails? Why are they of interest to auditors?

15–24 What procedures and methods are suggested by *Computer Control Guidelines* for making certain output from information systems is correct?

15–25 Explain what is meant by auditing without relying on computer controls. Under what circumstances is it appropriate to follow this approach?

15–26 Explain what is meant by the test data approach to auditing through the computer. What are the major difficulties in using this approach?

15–27 List seven kinds of tests or other functions commonly performed by auditors' computer programs and give one specific example of each use.

15–28 Explain what is meant by generalized audit software and discuss its importance as an audit tool.

15–29 What is the role of microcomputers as an audit tool? Identify six tasks that can be done with the use of microcomputers.

15–30   Explain why it is unacceptable for an auditor to assume that an independent computer service bureau is providing reliable accounting information to an audit client. What can the auditor do to satisfy him- or herself that the service bureau's internal controls can be relied on for purposes of the audit?

Multiple Choice Questions

15–31   The following questions concern the characteristics of EDP systems. Choose the best response.

a. A management information system is designed to ensure that management possesses the information it needs to carry out its functions through the integrated actions of

(1)   data gathering, analysis, and reporting functions.
(2)   a computerized information retrieval and decision-making system.
(3)   statistical and analytical procedures functions.
(4)   production-budgeting and sales-forecasting activities.

b. The computer system *most* likely to be used by a large trust company for customers' accounts would be

(1)   an on-line, real-time system.
(2)   a batch processing system.
(3)   a generalized utility system.
(4)   a direct access data base system.

c. Which of the following conditions would *not* normally cause the auditor to question whether material errors or fraud or other irregularities exist?

(1)   Bookkeeping errors are listed on an EDP-generated exception report.
(2)   Differences exist between control accounts and supporting master files.
(3)   Transactions are *not* supported by proper documentation.
(4)   Differences are disclosed by confirmations.   (AICPA adapted)

15–32   The following questions concern auditing EDP systems. Choose the best response.

a. Which of the following client electronic data processing (EDP) systems generally can be audited without examining or directly testing the EDP computer programs of the system?

(1)   A system that performs relatively uncomplicated processes and produces detailed output.
(2)   A system that affects a number of essential master files and produces a limited output.
(3)   A system that updates a few essential master files and produces *no* printed output other than final balances.
(4)   A system that performs relatively complicated processing and produces very little detailed output.

b. Which of the following is true of generalized audit software programs?

(1)   They can be used only in auditing on-line computer systems.
(2)   They can be used on any computer without modification.
(3)   They each have their own characteristics that the auditor must carefully consider before using in a given audit situation.
(4)   They enable the auditor to perform all manual test of control procedures less expensively.

c. Assume that an auditor estimates that 10,000 cheques were issued during the accounting period. If an EDP application control that performs a limit check for each cheque request is to be subjected to the auditor's test data approach, the sample should include

(1) approximately 1,000 test items.

(2) a number of test items determined by the auditor to be sufficient under the circumstances.

(3) a number of test items determined by the auditor's reference to the appropriate sampling tables.

(4) at least three transactions.

d. An auditor will use the EDP test data method in order to gain certain assurances with respect to the

(1) input data.

(2) machine capacity.

(3) procedures contained within the program.

(4) degree of data entry accuracy   (AICPA adapted)

DISCUSSION QUESTIONS AND PROBLEMS

15–33   The following are errors that can occur in the sales and collection cycle.

1. A customer order was filled and shipped to a former customer that had already filed bankruptcy.

2. The price of goods ordered by a customer was approved by the sales manager, but the manager wrote down the price for the wrong amount.

3. The data entry clerk stopped for coffee and restarted data entry at the wrong place omitting several transactions.

4. A customer number on a sales invoice was transposed and, as a result, the invoice was charged to the wrong customer. By the time the error was found, the original customer was no longer in business.

5. A former computer operator, who is now a programmer, entered information for a fictitious sales return and ran it through the computer system at night. When the money came in, the operator took it.

6. A computer operator picked up a computerized data file for sales of the wrong week and processed them through the system a second time.

7. Making a data entry, a data entry clerk erroneously failed to enter the sales representative's district. As a result the salesman received no commission for that sale.

8. A nonexistent part number was included in the description of goods on a shipping document. Therefore, no charge was made for those goods.

Required:

a. Identify the internal control objective(s) to which the error pertains.

b. For each error, identify two computerized control procedures that would likely have prevented it.

15–34   You are doing the audit of Phelps College, a community college with approximately 2,500 students. With your firm's consultation, they have instituted an EDP system that separates the responsibilities of the computer operator, systems analyst, librarian, programmer, and data control group by having a different person do each function. Now, a budget reduction is necessary and one of the five people must be laid off. You are requested to give the college advice as to how the five functions could be performed with reduced personnel and minimal negative effects on internal control. The amount of time the functions take is not relevant, because all five people also perform nonaccounting functions.

Required:

a. Divide the five functions among four people in such a manner as to maintain the best possible control system.

b. Assume economic times become worse for Phelps College and they must terminate employment of another person. Divide the five functions among three people in such a manner as to maintain the best possible internal control structure. Again, the amount of time each function takes should not be a consideration in your decision.

   c. Assume economic times become so severe for Phelps that only two people can be employed to perform EDP functions. Divide the five functions between two people in such a manner as to maintain the best possible control system.

   d. If the five functions were performed by one person, would internal controls be so inadequate that an audit could not be performed? Discuss.

15–35 PH Inc., a pharmaceutical manufacturer, is projecting a period of continuous growth. At present, it is using a service bureau that is not meeting their needs.

Required:
   a. Outline the considerations to be addressed in a feasibility study on acquiring an in-house microcomputer.

   b. As the external auditor of PH Inc., which internal control problems arising from the proposed conversion to an in-house microcomputer would you address with your audit procedures?

   c. Assume that you have been satisfied with the internal controls at the service bureau in the past. When you look to the future when the proposed conversion to the in-house microcomputer will be complete, what changes, if any, do you foresee in your evaluation of internal controls and in your substantive audit procedures? (CICA adapted)

15–36 When auditing an EDP accounting system, the independent auditor should have a general familiarity with the effects of the use of EDP on the various characteristics of accounting control and on the auditor's study and evaluation of such control. The independent auditor must be aware of those control procedures that are commonly referred to as general controls and those that are commonly referred to as application controls. General controls relate to all EDP activities and application controls relate to specific accounting tasks.

Required:
   a. What are the general controls that should exist in EDP-based accounting systems?

   b. What are the purposes of each of the following categories of application controls?
     (1) Input controls
     (2) Processing controls
     (3) Output controls. (AICPA adapted)

15–37 The following are audit procedures taken from a public accounting firm's audit program for acquisitions and payments:

   1. Foot the list of accounts payable and trace the balance to the general ledger.

   2. Select a sample of accounts payable for confirmation emphasizing vendors with a large balance and those that the client transacts with frequently, but include several with small and zero balances.

   3. Compare all transactions recorded for four days before and after the balance sheet date with related receiving reports and vendors' invoices to determine the appropriate recording period.

   4. Examine a random sample of 100 acquisition transactions to determine if each was authorized by an appropriate official and paid within the discount period to obtain the maximum cash discount.

   5. Compare the total of each account payable outstanding, including zero balances, with those in the preceding year and examine vendors' statements for any total with a difference in excess of $500.

   6. Compare the unit cost on a random sample of 100 vendors' invoices with catalogs or other price lists and investigate any with a difference of more than 3 percent.

Required:

a. For each audit procedure, identify whether it is a test of controls or a test of details of balances.

b. Explain how generalized audit software could be used, at least in part, to perform some or all of each audit procedure. Assume all information is in both machine- and nonmachine-readable form. Also, identify audit procedures or parts of procedures to which the generalized audit software is not likely to be applicable. Use the following format:

PROCEDURE	DATA FILE OR FILES NEEDED	KIND OF TEST OR TESTS THE AUDITOR CAN PERFORM USING GAS	PROCEDURE FOR WHICH GAS IS LIKELY TO BE INAPPROPRIATE

15–38 You are conducting an audit of sales for the James Department Store Inc., a retail chain store located in Alberta with a computerized sales system in which computerized cash registers are integrated directly with accounts receivable, sales, perpetual inventory records, and sales commission expense. At the time of sale the salesclerks key-enter the following information directly into the cash register:

- Product number
- Quantity sold
- Unit selling price
- Store code number
- Salesclerk number
- Date of sale
- Cash sale or credit sale
- Customer account number for all credit sales

The total amount of the sale, including goods and services tax, is automatically computed by the system and indicated on the cash register's visual display. The only printed information for cash sales is the cash register receipt, which is given to the customer. For credit sales a credit slip is prepared and one copy is retained by the clerk and submitted daily to the accounting department.

A summary of sales is printed out daily in the accounting department. The summary includes daily and monthly totals by salesclerks for each store as well as totals for each of 93 categories of merchandise by store. Perpetual inventory and accounts receivable records are updated daily on magnetic tape, but supporting records are limited primarily to machine-readable records.

Required:

a. What major problems does the auditor face in verifying sales and accounts receivable?

b. How can the concept of test data be employed in the audit? Explain the difficulties the auditor would have to overcome in using test data.

c. How can generalized audit software be employed in this audit? List several tests that can be conducted using this approach.

d. The client is interested in installing several controls to signal cash register operators automatically when they have made an error. List four programmed controls the auditor could recommend to reduce the likelihood of these types of errors.

e. The client would also like to reduce the time it takes to key-enter the information into the cash register. Suggest several ways this could be accomplished, considering the information now being key-entered manually.

15–39 In the audit of Greenline Manufacturing Corp. for the year ended December 31,

19X8, Roberta Bondar, a public accountant, concluded that the lack of an audit trail for the property, plant, and equipment accounts precluded auditing that area in the traditional manner. As a result, the decision was made to use generalized audit software in the verification of certain aspects of the accounts. The GAS application includes the following specific objectives:

1. Foot the file and print totals by major property category for cost of all assets, cost of current additions, and accumulated and current depreciation for both book and tax purposes.

2. Prepare a listing of all additions over $5,000 for vouching and inspection.

3. Prepare a listing of all disposals for detailed verification.

4. Verify the calculations of depreciation expense for both book and tax purposes.

The permanent asset master file for December 31, 19X7 was saved by the client and includes the same information as the December 31, 19X8 file. Its contents are as follows:

ELEMENT NO.	DESCRIPTION OF CONTENTS
1	Asset number
2	Description
3	Type code
4	Location code
5	Year of acquisition
6	Cost
7	Accumulated depreciation – beginning book
8	Depreciation – YTD book
9	Useful life
10	Tax depreciation method – Capital cost allowance
11	Accumulated depreciation – beginning tax
12	Depreciation – YTD tax

Note: All fixed assets use the straight-line method for book depreciation. Tax depreciation is based on maximum capital cost allowance available.

Required:

a. Explain in detail how the information on the December 31, 19X7 and December 31, 19X8 master files should be used to fulfill the four audit objectives.

b. List the reports that will be generated by the GAS.

c. Explain what additional verification is necessary on each of these reports to satisfy the auditor that property, plant, and equipment is fairly stated.

15–40 A public accounting firm's client, Boos & Baumkirchner, Inc., is a medium-sized manufacturer of products for the leisure time activities market (camping equipment, scuba gear, bows and arrows, and so forth). During the past year, a computer system was installed, and inventory records of finished goods and parts were converted to computer processing. The inventory master file is maintained on a disk. Each record of the file contains the following information:

- Item or part number
- Description
- Size
- Unit-of-measure code
- Quantity on hand
- Cost per unit
- Total value of inventory on hand at cost
- Date of last sale or usage
- Quantity used or sold this year

- Economic order quantity
- Code number of major vendor
- Code number of secondary vendor

In preparation for year-end inventory, the client has two identical sets of preprinted inventory count cards. One set is for the client's inventory counts and the other is for the public accounting firm's use to make audit test counts. The following information has been recorded on the face of the cards:

- Item or part number
- Description
- Size
- Unit-of-measure code

In taking the year-end inventory, the client's personnel will write the actual counted quantity on the face of each card. When all counts are complete, the counted quantity will be entered into the computer using an optical scanner. The data on the cards will be processed against the disk file, and quantity-on-hand figures will be adjusted to reflect the actual count. A computer listing will be prepared to show any missing inventory count cards and all quantity adjustments of more than $100 in value. These items will be investigated by client personnel, and all required adjustments will be made. When adjustments have been completed, the final year-end balances will be computed and posted to the general ledger.

The public accounting firm has available generalized audit software that will run on the client's computer and can process the disk files; the public accounting firm has access to an optical scanner.

Required:

a. In general and without regard to the facts in this case, discuss the nature of generalized audit software and list the various types and uses.

b. List and describe at least five ways generalized audit software can be used to assist in all aspects of the audit of the inventory of Boos & Baumkirchner, Inc. (For example, the software can be used to read the disk inventory master file and list items and parts with a high unit cost or total value. Such items can be included in the test counts to increase the dollar coverage of the audit verification.) (AICPA adapted)

15–41 Mary Novakowski, a public accountant, is the auditor of Great Records Ltd., the largest retailer of CDs and cassettes in Edmonton. The company is a wholly-owned subsidiary of a nation-wide wholesale distributor of records. The ownership of the retail operation enables the parent company's management to keep abreast of changes in consumer buying patterns and tastes, thereby making the distributorship more quickly responsive to changes in demand than otherwise would be the case.

The merchandise inventory of Great Records Ltd. averages about 140,000 records of 15,000 different titles, 90 percent of which are cassettes and CDs. The remainder are LPs. In addition, there is a relatively small stock of peripheral items such as jewel boxes, CD and cassette racks, and tape and CD cleaners.

In order to provide current information on which CDs and cassettes are selling, and to provide accurate inventory information for stock control, re-ordering, and financial statement preparation, Great Records Ltd. recently began using point-of-sale computer terminals operating on-line with the parent company's computer. All records are identifiable by the manufacturer's alphanumeric code which identifies the manufacturer as well as the title. For the perpetual inventory system, they convert the alphanumeric code for each CD or tape to a strictly numeric code. This code, which is fixed in length, is printed on labels by the stock clerks and affixed to each CD or tape jacket when they are received and put into stock. The jewel boxes, racks and other sundry items are not included in the perpetual inventory system.

When a customer makes a purchase or returns merchandise, the sales clerk keys the following into the terminal:

1. a four-digit sales clerk identifier code,
2. ENTER,
3. one-digit transaction code (sale or return),
4. record stock number of first record sold or returned, if a CD or cassette; a one-digit code if a sundry item,
5. ENTER,
6. quantity of the specific items being purchased or returned,
7. x (multiplication symbol),
8. unit price,
9. ENTER,
10. repeats steps (4) through (9) for each item,
11. TOTAL (terminal displays the merchandise total, adds the automatically computer goods and services tax and displays the amount due or refundable),
12. amount tendered,
13. ENTER (causing the computer to calculate and display the change due), and
14. OFF.

The transaction is held by the computer without processing until the transaction is terminated by pressing the OFF key. This delay permits the clerk to void the transactions if an error has been made during entry. When the OFF key is depressed the inventory information (items (3), (4), and (6) above) is used to update the inventory master file, which is on disk. While the transaction is being entered, the terminal prints a sales slip. The sales slip is not released by the terminal until the transaction is completed. Voided sales slips must be approved by the store manager or assistant manager.

As part of her internal control review, Mary Novakowski has undertaken to assess the controls embodied in Great Records Ltd.'s inventory system. As part of this internal control review, she proposed to use test transactions to determine what controls were operating in the computerized sale entry portion of the system, as described above.

Required:

(a) List the controls that should be programmed into the sales entry system described above. List only those programmed controls that relate to the processing of individual sale and return transactions.

(b) Describe the transactions that you would include in a test deck in this case, and state which controls each transaction would test.

(c) Explain a procedure Novakowski may follow in conducting the above tests in order to protect the integrity of the Great Records Ltd. inventory master file.

(CICA adapted)

CASE

15–42   Your audit client, Quality Furniture Ltd., which employs 250 people and manufactures furniture, has recently acquired a minicomputer to replace its two mechanical bookkeeping machines. The bookkeeping machines are being used for all accounting operations, including the preparation of journals and ledgers and documents such as sales invoices, purchase orders, cheques, and customer statements. Quality has also contracted with a local programming firm to provide a complete set of standardized accounting programs designed for small manufacturing firms. This set of computer programs performs the following functions:

1. Customer order entry.
2. Customer shipments and invoicing.
3. Accounts receivable and customer remittances.
4. Sales analysis.
5. Purchase order entry.
6. Receipts from vendors and vendor invoice processing.
7. Accounts payable and cash disbursements.
8. Inventory control.
9. Production scheduling and reporting.
10. Cost accounting.
11. Payroll.
12. Fixed assets.
13. General ledger and financial statements.
14. Generalized information retrieval and report writing.

The minicomputer has just been delivered and the programming firm's representatives are working on the installation of the set of standardized accounting programs. The minicomputer hardware consists of three visual display terminals with attached keyboards, a 150 line/minute printer, a 50 million byte disc drive, a 10 million byte magnetic tape cassette drive, and 64,000 byte central processing unit. The minicomputer vendor's system software resides in 32,000 bytes of primary storage in the central processing unit and consists of a real-time program scheduler, an input/output control program, a BUSINESS BASIC language interpreter, and various utility programs for common data processing purposes (sort, merge, and copy data files, list programs, etc.).

The minicomputer hardware and the programming firm's software are designed so that all data input will be submitted through the keyboards attached to the visual display terminals. These terminals will also be used to call for information to be displayed on the terminal screen, to initiate the execution of computer programs that produce reports based on the data in the computer files, and to enter new programs or changes to existing programs. Data submitted to the minicomputer will either be processed immediately against master file records maintained on the magnetic disc drive or stored temporarily on the magnetic disc drive for subsequent batch processing against master file data.

The magnetic disc drive, which contains a fixed disc pack, will also contain the accounting programs being supplied by the programming firm. The magnetic tape cassette drive will serve as the means of providing backup copies of the data and programs stored on the fixed magnetic disc pack.

The set of accounting programs are "standardized modules" and must be tailored to each specific user firm's requirements. The tailoring process consists of modifying the programs.

1. to print outputs in a format desired by the user,
2. to insert various terms and tax rates applicable to the user (e.g. sales on a 2 percent-10, net-30),
3. to insert the user's account codings and additional custom programs desired by the user.

These programs are written in BUSINESS BASIC, a high-level computer programming language noted for its simplicity. The generalized information retrieval and report-writing feature allows a non-programmer to enter simple English-like commands through a visual display terminal to extract information and print exception reports based on any selection parameters specified by the user.

The only office staff at Quality are five clerical and bookkeeping personnel. There is no qualified accountant as Quality has relied on your firm for assistance in all accounting matters. Management consists of the owner/manager, a production manager, and several production supervisors. Your firm has provided monthly accounting services leading to the preparation of monthly financial statements. The bookkeeping machine operator is being trained to be the senior data entry operator and to handle the relatively simple operations of turning on the minicomputer, setting up forms on the printer, and backing up data files and programs on the magnetic disc to magnetic tape cassette. Quality's owner/manager hopes that the use of a minicomputer will allow the firm to reduce the office staff to three: a senior data entry operator, a junior clerk, and a secretary/receptionist.

One of the main reasons why Quality's owner/manager decided to buy this minicomputer was that its operation would not require the hiring of any full-time computer people. Both she and the senior bookkeeping machine operator have attended a five-day course on programming and on operating the equipment which she believes will be sufficient for either she or the operator to make any simple program changes that may be required at a future date. She plans to rely on the programming services firm for any major program changes that may be required in the future.

Required:

(a) Identify any significant control problems that may be created by the introduction of the minicomputer at Quality, and recommend to the owner/manager steps to reduce their significance.

(b) Discuss the impact that the installation of the minicomputer and the implementation of the related accounting systems could have on your audit work in the areas of analytical review, compliance tests and substantive tests.

(CICA adapted)

16

AUDIT OF THE PAYROLL AND PERSONNEL CYCLE

□ The payroll and personnel cycle involves the employment and payment of all employees, regardless of classification or method of determining compensation. The employees include executives on straight salary plus bonus, office workers on monthly salary with or without overtime, salespeople on a commission basis, and factory and unionized personnel paid on an hourly basis. The cycle is important for several reasons. First, the salaries, wages, employee benefits (e.g. Canada Pension, unemployment insurance, health and dental care, etc.) and other employer costs (e.g. workers' compensation), are a major expense in all companies. Second, labor is such an important consideration in the valuation of inventory in manufacturing and construction companies that the improper classification and allocation of labor can result in a material misstatement of net income.

Finally, payroll is an area in which large amounts of company resources are wasted because of inefficiency or are stolen through fraud.

The Hillsburg Hardware Ltd. trial balance on page 135 includes typical general ledger accounts affected by the payroll and personnel cycle. They are identified as payroll and personnel accounts by the letter *P* in the left column. In larger companies, many general ledger accounts are often affected by payroll. It is common, for example, for large companies to have fifty or more payroll expense accounts. Payroll also affects work-in-process and finished goods inventory accounts for manufacturing companies.

As with the sales and collection cycle, the audit of the payroll and personnel cycle includes obtaining an understanding of internal control, assessment of control risk, tests of controls, analytical procedures, and tests of details of balances. Accordingly, the first part of this chapter deals with the nature of the cycle, including documents and records, its primary functions and internal controls. The second part includes tests of controls for the cycle related to key internal controls. The third part discusses analytical procedures. Finally, the fourth part of the chapter focuses on verification by tests of details of balances of the related liability and expense accounts. These accounts include all salaries and wage expense accounts, employee benefits, and the liability for accrued wages, employee withholdings, employee benefits, and similar items connected with payroll.

The way in which accounting information flows through the various accounts in the payroll and personnel cycle is illustrated by T-accounts in Figure 16–1. In most systems, the accrued wages and salaries account is used only at the end of an accounting period. Throughout the period, expenses are charged when the employees are actually paid rather than when the labor costs are incurred. The accruals for labor are recorded by adjusting entries at the end of the period for any earned but unpaid labor costs.

Nature of the Cycle

The payroll and personnel cycle begins with the hiring of personnel and ends with payment to the employees for the services performed and to the government and other institutions for employee withholdings (that is, income tax, Canada (or Quebec) Pension Plan, unemployment insurance) and employee benefits (that is, required contributions by the employer for the Canada (or Quebec) Pension Plan, unemployment insurance, workers' compensation, hospital insurance plans, and voluntary or negotiated employer contributions to company pension, medical, or dental plans). In between, the cycle involves obtaining services from the employees consistent with the objectives of the company and accounting for the services in a proper manner. An overview flowchart of the payroll and personnel cycle for a typical small manufacturing company is shown in Figure 16–2.

> **OBJECTIVE 1**
>
> Describe the payroll and personnel cycle and the pertinent documents and records, functions, and internal controls.

Documents and Records

Various documents and records are of major importance in supporting the record flow used in the cycle. Among them are the following:

Personnel records Records that include such data as the date of employment, personnel investigations, rates of pay, authorized deductions, performance evaluations, and termination of employment.

Deduction authorization forms Forms authorizing payroll deductions, including the number of exemptions for withholding of income taxes (TD-1), Canada

FIGURE 16–1

Accounts in the Payroll
and Personnel Cycle

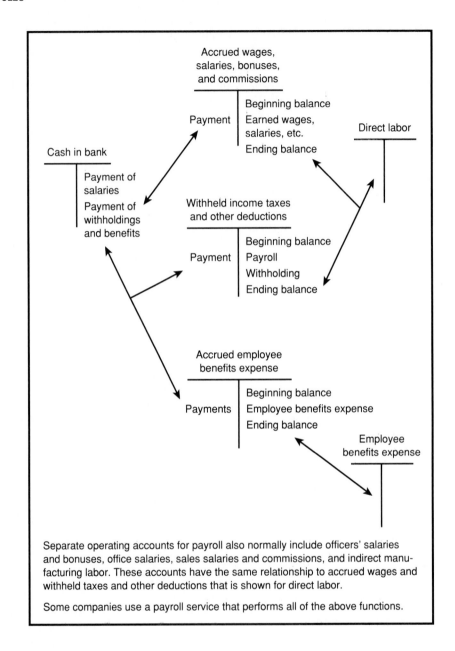

Separate operating accounts for payroll also normally include officers' salaries and bonuses, office salaries, sales salaries and commissions, and indirect manufacturing labor. These accounts have the same relationship to accrued wages and withheld taxes and other deductions that is shown for direct labor.

Some companies use a payroll service that performs all of the above functions.

Savings Bonds, charitable contributions, union dues, government or private insurance, and pension, medical or dental plans.

Rate authorization form A form authorizing the rate of pay. The source of the information is a labor contract, authorization by management, or, in the case of officers, authorization from the board of directors.

Time card A document indicating the time the employee started and stopped working each day and the number of hours the employee worked. For many

FIGURE 16–2

Flowchart of the Payroll
and Personnel Cycle

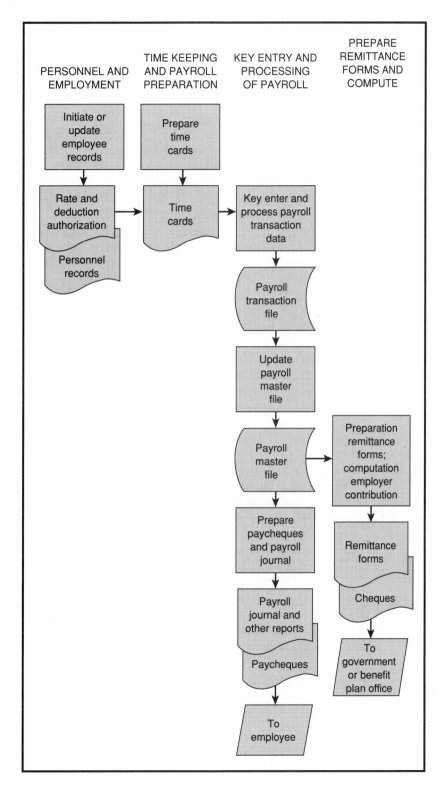

employees, the time card is prepared automatically by time clocks. Time cards are usually submitted weekly.

Job time ticket A document indicating particular jobs on which a factory employee worked during a given time period. This form is used only when an employee works on different jobs or in different departments.

Payroll cheque A cheque written to the employee for services performed. The amount of the cheque is the gross pay less taxes and other deductions withheld. After the cheque is cashed and returned to the company from the bank, it is referred to as a canceled cheque.

Payroll journal A journal for recording payroll cheques. It typically indicates gross pay, withholdings, and net pay. The payroll journal is generated for any time period from the payroll transactions included in the computer files. The details in the journal are also included in the payroll master file. Journal totals are posted to the general ledger by the computer.

Summary payroll report A computer generated document that summarizes payroll for a period in various forms. One summary is the totals debited to each general ledger account for payroll charges. These will equal gross payroll for the period. Another common summary for a manufacturing company is the totals charged to various jobs in a job cost accounting system. Similarly, commissions earned by each salesperson may be summarized.

Payroll master file A file for recording each payroll transaction for each employee and maintaining total employee wages paid for the year to date. The record for each employee includes gross pay for each payroll period, deductions from gross pay, net pay, cheque number and date. The master file is updated from payroll computer transaction files. The total of the individual employee earnings in the master file equals the total balance of gross payroll in various general ledger accounts.

T-4 form A form issued for each employee summarizing the earnings record for the calendar year. The information includes gross pay, income taxes withheld, and other withholdings, and taxable benefits such as employer contributions to government- or privately sponsored medical plans. The same information is also submitted to Revenue Canada and, if appropriate, provincial tax authorities. This information is prepared from the payroll master file and is normally prepared by the computer.

Employee withholdings and benefits remittance forms Forms submitted to the federal government and to other organizations for the payment of withholdings and employee benefits. The nature and due date of the forms vary depending on the type of withholding or benefit. For example, federal income tax withholding, Canada (or Quebec) Pension Plan withholding, and unemployment insurance withholding are due monthly, and workers' compensation is due quarterly. These forms are prepared from information on the payroll master file and are often prepared by the computer.

Cycle Functions
and Internal
Controls

Typically, four functions are accomplished through the payroll and personnel cycle. They are:

- Personnel and employment
- Timekeeping and payroll preparation
- Payment of payroll
- Preparation of payroll withholding and benefit remittance forms and payment thereof

These functions are now examined in detail for a typical manufacturing company in which employees are required to maintain a record of the job on which they are working. The emphasis in this discussion is on the use of certain internal controls to prevent errors in providing data and to ensure the safety of assets.

Personnel and employment   The personnel department provides an independent source for interviewing and hiring qualified personnel. The department is also an independent source of records for the internal verification of wage information.

From an audit point of view, the most important internal controls in personnel involve formal methods of informing the timekeeping and payroll preparation personnel of new employees, the authorization of initial and periodic changes in pay rates, and the termination date of employees no longer working for the company. As a part of these controls, segregation of duties is particularly important. No individual with access to time cards, payroll records, or cheques should also be permitted access to personnel records. A second important control is the adequate investigation of the competence and trustworthiness of new employees.

Timekeeping and payroll preparation   This function is of major importance in the audit payroll because it directly affects payroll expense for the period. It includes the preparation of time cards by employees; the summarization and calculation of gross pay, deductions, and net pay; the preparation of payroll cheques; and the preparation of payroll records. There must be adequate controls to prevent errors in each of these activities.

Adequate control over the time on the time cards includes the use of a time clock or other method of making certain that employees are paid for the number of hours they worked. There should also be controls to prevent anyone from checking in for several employees or submitting a fictitious time card.

The summarization and calculation of the payroll can be controlled by well-defined policies for the payroll department, separation of duties to provide automatic cross-checks, reconciliation of payroll hours with independent production records, and independent internal verification of all important data. For example, payroll policies should require a competent, independent person to recalculate actual hours worked, review for the proper approval of all overtime, and examine time cards for erasures and alterations. Similarly, batch control totals over hours worked can be calculated from payroll time cards and compared to the actual hours processed by the computer. Finally, a printout of wage and withholding rates included in the computer files can be printed and compared to authorized rates in the personnel files.

Controls over the preparation of payroll cheques include preventing those responsible for preparing the cheques from having access to time cards, signing or distributing cheques, or independently verifying payroll output. In addition, the cheques should be prenumbered and verified through independent bank reconciliation procedures.

When manufacturing labor affects inventory valuation, special emphasis should be put on controls to make sure labor is distributed to proper account classifications. There must also be adequate internal controls for recording job time tickets and other relevant payroll information in the cost accounting records. Independent internal verification of this information is an essential control.

Payment of payroll The actual signing and distribution of the cheques must be properly handled to prevent their theft. The controls should include limiting the authorization for signing the cheques to a responsible employee who does not have access to timekeeping or the preparation of the payroll, the distribution of payroll by someone who is not involved in the other payroll functions, and the immediate return of unclaimed cheques for redeposit. If a cheque-signing machine is used to replace a manual signature, the same controls are required; in addition, the cheque-signing machine must be carefully controlled.

Most companies use an *imprest payroll account* to prevent the payment of unauthorized payroll transactions. An imprest payroll account is a separate payroll account in which a small balance is maintained. A cheque for the exact amount of each net payroll is transferred from the general account to the imprest account immediately before the distribution of the payroll. The advantages of an imprest account are that it limits the client's exposure to payroll fraud, allows the delegation of payroll cheque-signing duties, separates routine payroll expenditures from irregular expenditures, and facilitates cash management. It also simplifies the reconciliation of the payroll bank account if it is done at the low point in the payment cycle.

An increasingly popular way of paying payroll is the use of electronic funds transfer (EFT). The company's bank or banks looks after the paying of employees electronically. The company provides the bank with a magnetic tape listing the employees' names, bank accounts and net wages each payroll period. The bank makes sure that each employee has the correct amount credited to his or her account on the proper day. While the company must pay the bank a fee for this service, the company is spared the task of preparing and delivering payroll cheques for each employee each period. Another advantage is that payroll can be centralized; most of the multi-office public accounting firms have centralized payroll and use EFT for payroll. As a result of these advantages, many large and small companies use EFT.

Preparation of payroll withholdings and benefits remittance forms and payment thereof The careful and timely preparation of all employee withholding and benefits remittance forms is necessary to avoid penalties and possible criminal charges against the company. The most important control in the preparation of these returns is a well-defined set of policies that carefully indicate when each form must be filed. Most computerized payroll systems include the preparation of employee withholding and benefits remittance forms using the information on the payroll transaction and master files. The independent verification by a competent individual of the output is an important control to prevent errors and potential liability for penalties.

FIGURE 16–3

Methodology for
Designing Tests of
Controls for Payroll
and Personnel

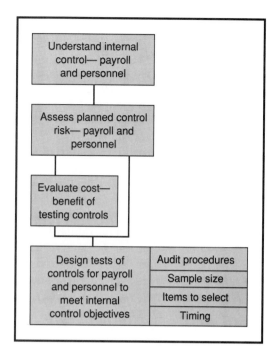

Tests of Controls

Figure 16–3 shows the methodology for designing tests of controls for the payroll and personnel cycle. It is the same methodology used in Chapter 11 for the sales and collection cycle.

OBJECTIVE 2

Design and perform
tests of controls for the
payroll and personnel
cycle.

Tests of controls procedures are the *most important* means of verifying account balances in the payroll and personnel cycle. The emphasis on tests of controls is due to the lack of independent third-party evidence, such as confirmation, for verifying accrued wages, withholdings, accrued benefits payable, and other balance sheet accounts. Furthermore, in most audits the amounts in the balance sheet accounts are small and can be verified with relative ease if the auditor is confident that payroll transactions are correctly entered into the computer and withholding and benefit remittance forms are properly prepared.

Even though the tests of controls are the most important part of testing payroll, many auditors spend little time in this area. In many audits, there is a minimal risk of material misstatements even though payroll is frequently a significant part of total expenses. There are three reasons for this: employees are likely to complain to management if they are underpaid, all payroll transactions are typically uniform and uncomplicated, and payroll transactions are extensively audited by federal and provincial governments for income tax withholding and for Canada Pension, unemployment insurance, and health care payments.

Auditors often extend their procedures considerably in the audit of payroll under the following circumstances: (1) when payroll significantly affects the valuation of inventory and (2) when the auditor is concerned about the possibility of material fraudulent payroll transactions because of weak internal control.

*Relationship
Between Payroll
and Inventory
Valuation*

In audits in which payroll is a significant portion of inventory, such as frequently occurs for manufacturing and construction companies, the improper account classification of payroll can significantly affect asset valuation for accounts such as work in process, finished goods, or construction in process.

For example, the overhead charged to inventory at the balance sheet date can be overstated if the salaries of administrative personnel are inadvertently or intentionally charged to indirect manufacturing overhead. Similarly, the valuation of inventory is affected if the direct labor cost of individual employees is improperly charged to the wrong job or process. When some jobs are billed on a cost-plus basis, revenue and the valuation of inventory are both affected by charging labor to incorrect jobs.

When labor is a material factor in inventory valuation, there should be special emphasis on testing the internal controls over proper classification of payroll transactions. Consistency from period to period, which is essential for classification, can be tested by reviewing the chart of accounts and procedures manuals. It is also desirable to trace job tickets or other evidence of an employee's having worked on a particular job or process to the accounting records that affect inventory valuation. For example, if each employee must account for all of his or her time on a weekly basis by assigning it to individual job numbers, a useful test is to trace the recorded hours of several employees for a week to the related job-cost records to make sure each has been properly recorded. It may also be desirable to trace from the job-cost records to employee summaries as a test for nonexistent payroll charges being included in inventory.

Tests for Fictitious Payroll

Although auditors are not primarily responsible for the detection of fraud, they must extend audit procedures when internal controls over payroll are inadequate. There are several ways employees can significantly defraud a company in the payroll area. This discussion is limited to tests for the two most common types: fictitious employees and fraudulent hours.

Fictitious employees The issuance of payroll cheques to individuals who do not work for the company frequently results from the continuance of an employee's cheque after his or her employment has been terminated. Usually, the person committing this type of defalcation is a payroll clerk, foreman, fellow employee, or perhaps the former employee. For example, under some internal controls a foreman could clock in daily for an employee and approve the time card at the end of the time period. If the foreman also distributes paycheques, considerable opportunity for defalcation exists.

Certain procedures can be performed on canceled cheques as a means of detecting defalcation. A procedure used on payroll audits is to compare the names on canceled cheques with time cards and other records for authorized signatures and reasonableness of the endorsements. It is also common to scan endorsements on canceled cheques for unusual or recurring second endorsements as an indication of a possible fictitious cheque. The examination of cheques that are recorded as voided is also desirable to make sure they have not been fraudulently used.

A test for invalid employees is to trace selected transactions recorded in the payroll journal to the personnel department to determine whether the employees were actually employed during the payroll period. The endorsement on the canceled cheque written out to an employee can be compared with the authorized signature on the employee's withholding authorization forms.

A procedure that tests for proper handling of terminated employees is to select several files from the personnel records for employees who were terminated in the current year to determine whether each received his or her termination pay in accordance with company policy. Continuing payments to terminated employees is tested by examining the payroll records in the subsequent period to ascertain that the employee is no longer being paid. Naturally, this procedure is not effective if the personnel department is not informed of terminations.

In some cases, the auditor may request a surprise payroll payoff. This is a procedure in which each employee must pick up and sign for his or her cheque in the presence of a supervisor and the auditor. Any cheques that have not been claimed must be subject to an extensive investigation to determine whether an unclaimed cheque is fraudulent. Surprise payoff is frequently expensive and in some cases may even cause problems with a labor union, but it may be the only likely means of detecting a defalcation.

Fraudulent hours   Because of the lack of available evidence, it is usually difficult for an auditor to discover if an employee records more time on his or her time card than actually worked. One procedure is to reconcile the total hours paid according to the payroll records with an independent record of the hours worked, such as those often maintained by production control. Similarly, it may be possible to observe an employee clocking in more than one time card under a buddy approach. However, it is ordinarily easier for the client to prevent this type of defalcation by adequate controls than for the auditor to detect it.

Internal Controls and Tests of Controls

Following the same approach used in Chapter 11 for tests of sales and cash receipts transactions, the internal controls and tests of controls for each internal control objective and related monetary errors are summarized in Table 16–1. Again, the reader should recognize that

- The internal controls will vary from company to company; therefore, the auditor must identify the controls and weaknesses for each organization.
- Controls the auditor intends to use for reducing assessed control risk must be tested with tests of control.
- The tests of controls will vary depending on the assessed control risk and the other considerations of the audit, such as the effect of payroll on inventory.
- The tests of controls are not actually performed in the order given in Table 16–1. The tests of controls are performed in as convenient a manner as possible, using a performance format audit program.

The purposes of the internal controls and the meaning and methodology of audit tests that can be used for payroll should be apparent from the description in Table 16–1. An extended discussion of these procedures is therefore not necessary.

Other Considerations

Three aspects of the payroll and personnel cycle and the related tests of controls that were not included in the preceding summary also require consideration: preparation of payroll withholdings and benefits remittance forms, timely payment of the taxes withheld and other withholdings and benefits, and reimbursement of payroll imprest account.

Preparation of payroll withholdings and benefits remittance forms   As a part of understanding the internal control structure, the auditor should review the preparation of at least one of each type of employee withholding and benefits remittance form the client is responsible for filing. There is a potential liability for unpaid balances and penalty and interest if the client fails to properly prepare the forms.

TABLE 16–1   Summary of Objectives, Controls, and Tests of Controls for Payroll

INTERNAL CONTROL OBJECTIVE	KEY INTERNAL CONTROL	COMMON TESTS OF CONTROLS	COMMON TESTS OF CONTROLS
Recorded payroll payments are for work actually performed by non-fictitious employees (validity).	Time cards are approved by foremen. Time clock is used to record time. Adequate personnel file. Separation of duties between personnel, timekeeping, and payroll disbursements. Only employees included as valid in the computer data files are accepted when they are entered.	Examine the cards for indication of approvals. Examine time cards. Review personnel policies. Review organization chart, discuss with employees, and observe duties being performed. Examine printouts of transactions rejected by the computer as having invalid employee numbers.†	Review the payroll journal, general ledger, and payroll earnings records for large or unusual amounts.* Compare canceled cheques with payroll journal for name, amount, and date. Examine canceled cheques for proper endorsement. Compare canceled cheques with personnel records.
Payroll transactions are properly authorized (authorization).	Specific or general authorization and approval is important at five points: Authorization to work. Hours worked, especially overtime. Wage rate, salary, or commission rate. Withholdings, including amounts for insurance and payroll savings. Issuance of cheque.	Examine personnel files. Examine time cards for indication of approval. Examine payroll records for indication of internal verification. Examine authorizations in personnel file. Examine payroll records for indication of approval.	Compare time cards with independent record of hours worked.
Existing payroll transactions are recorded (completeness).	Payroll cheques are prenumbered and accounted for. Independent preparation of bank reconciliation.	Account for a sequence of payroll cheques. Discuss with employees and observe reconciliation.	Reconcile the disbursements in the payroll journal with the disbursements on the payroll bank statement. Prove the bank reconciliation.
Recorded payroll transactions are for the amount of time actually worked and at the proper pay rate; withholdings are properly calculated (valuation).	Internal verification of calculations and amounts. Batch totals are compared with computer summary reports.	Examine indication of internal verification. Examine file of batch totals for initials of data control clerk; compare totals to summary reports.†	Recompute hours worked from time cards. Compare pay rates with union contract, approval by board of directors, or other source. Recompute gross pay. Check withholdings by reference to appropriate tables and authorization forms in personnel file.Recompute net pay. Compare canceled cheque with payroll journal for amount.
Payroll transactions are properly classified (classification).	Adequate chart of accounts. Internal verification of classification.	Review chart of accounts. Examine indication of internal verification.	Compare classification with chart of accounts or procedures manual. Review time card for employee department and job ticket for job assignment, and trace through to labor distribution.

TABLE 16–1   *(Continued)*

INTERNAL CONTROL OBJECTIVE	KEY INTERNAL CONTROL	COMMON TESTS OF CONTROLS	COMMON TESTS OF CONTROLS
Payroll transactions are recorded on a timely basis (timeliness).	Procedures require recording transactions as soon as possible after the payroll is paid. Internal verification.	Examine procedures manual and observe when recording takes place. Examine indication of internal verification.	Compare date of recorded cheque in the payroll journal with date on canceled cheques and time cards. Compare date on cheque with date the cheque cleared the bank.
Payroll transactions are properly included in the payroll master file; they are properly summarized (posting and summarization).	Internal verification of payroll master file contents. Comparison of payroll master file with payroll general ledger totals.	Examine indication of internal verification. Examine initialed summary total reports indicating comparisons have been made.	Test clerical accuracy by footing the payroll journal and tracing postings to general ledger and the payroll master file earnings.

* This analytical procedure can also apply to other objectives, including completeness, valuation, and timeliness.
† This control would be tested on many audits by using the computer.

A detailed reconciliation of the information on the remittance forms and the payroll records may be necessary when the auditor believes that there is a reasonable chance the remittance forms may be improperly prepared. Indications of potential errors in the forms include the payment of penalties and interest in the past for improper payments, new personnel in the payroll department who are responsible for the preparation of the remittance forms, the lack of internal verification of the information, and the existence of serious liquidity problems for the client.

Payment of the taxes withheld and other withholdings and benefits on a timely basis   It is desirable to test whether the client has fulfilled its legal obligation in submitting payments for all payroll withholdings and benefits as a part of the payroll tests even though the payments are usually made from general cash disbursements. The withholdings of concern in these tests are such items as taxes, Canada (or Quebec) Pension Plan, unemployment insurance, union dues, insurance, and Canada Savings Bonds. The auditor must first determine the client's requirements for submitting the payments. The requirements are determined by reference to such sources as tax laws, Canada Pension Plan rules, unemployment insurance rules, union contracts, and agreements with employees. After the auditor knows the requirements, it is easy to determine whether the client has paid the proper amount on a timely basis by comparing the subsequent payment with the payroll records.

Reimbursement of the payroll imprest account   If the client uses an imprest payroll bank account, the periodic payment from the general cash account to the payroll account for net payroll is usually such a large amount that it should be tested for at least one payroll period. The major audit concern is the adequacy of the internal controls for making sure the cheque is prepared for the proper amount and deposited before payroll cheques are handed out. The auditor should ascertain whether the amount of the canceled cheque paid from the general cash account equals the net payroll for the payroll period.

Analysis of Exceptions and Conclusions

Most internal controls for payroll are highly structured and well controlled in order to control cash disbursed and to minimize employee complaints and dissatisfaction. It is common to use electronic data processing techniques to prepare all journals and payroll cheques. In-house systems are often used, as are outside service centre systems and electronic funds transfers. It is usually not difficult to establish good control in payroll. For factory and office employees, there are usually a large number of relatively homogeneous, small amount transactions. There are fewer executive payroll transactions, but they are ordinarily consistent in timing, content, and amount. Because of relatively consistent payroll concerns from company to company, high-quality computer systems are available. Consequently, auditors seldom expect to find exceptions in testing payroll transactions. Occasionally control test deviations occur, but most monetary errors are corrected by internal verification controls or in response to employee complaints. There are, however, specific types of errors that give the auditor particular concern in auditing payroll transactions:

OBJECTIVE 3
Assess control risk for payroll.

- Classification errors in charging labor to inventory and job cost accounts. As previously indicated, these can result in misstated earnings.
- Computational errors when a computerized system is used. Recall that one of the primary characteristics of the computer is processing consistency. If a calculation error is made for one item, it is probably made on every other similar item.
- Any errors that indicate possible fraud, particularly relating to the executive payroll.

Generally, the tests of controls performed in the payroll cycle will use *attributes sampling* under a plan that assumes a zero deviation rate. Sampling size should be large enough to give the auditor a reasonable chance of finding at least one deviation if an intolerable quantity of deviations exists.

If classification errors are found through this procedure, the sample selected for attributes will often then be used to make a *variables estimate* of the total monetary error involved. Sample expansion is usually necessary, however, to achieve a precise enough estimate to conclude whether the total error is material in amount.

If a computational error or one indicating possible fraud is found, specific investigation will be required to determine what allowed such an error to occur. Generally, further sampling and estimation are not done; rather, a nonstatistical approach based on the circumstances is taken.

If no exceptions are found, or if those found are not alarming or unexpected, the auditor will conclude that assessed control risk can be reduced as planned and he or she will proceed with the tests of details of balances of the affected accounts without modification.

Analytical Procedures

The use of analytical procedures is as important in the payroll and personnel cycle as it is in every other cycle. Table 16–2 illustrates analytical procedures for the balance sheet and income statement accounts in the payroll and personnel cycle that are useful for uncovering areas in which additional investigation is desirable.

OBJECTIVE 4
Design and perform analytical procedures for the payroll and personnel cycle.

TABLE 16–2 Analytical Procedures for Payroll and Personnel	ANALYTICAL PROCEDURE	POSSIBLE MISSTATEMENT
	Compare payroll expense account balance with previous years (adjusted for pay rate increases and increases in volume).	Misstatement of payroll expense accounts
	Compare direct labor as a percentage of sales with previous years.	Misstatement of direct labor
	Compare commission expense as a percentage of sales with previous years.	Misstatement of commission expense
	Compare payroll benefits expense as a percentage of salaries and wages with previous years (adjusted for changes in the benefits rates)	Misstatement of payroll benefits expense
	Compare accrued payroll benefits accounts with previous years.	Misstatement of accrued payroll benefits

Tests of Details of Balances for Liability and Expense Accounts

Figure 16–4 summarizes the methodology for deciding the appropriate tests of details of balances for payroll liability accounts. The methodology is the same as that followed in Chapter 13 for accounts receivable. Normally, however, payroll-related liabilities are less material than accounts receivable; therefore, there is less inherent risk. Some auditors allocate materiality to segments once they have determined materiality available for unanticipated misstatements. They use the amounts allocated to determine sample sizes and the amount of testing required. However, most auditors use materiality available for unanticipated misstatements in audit planning on the grounds that the auditor is concerned about the aggregate misstatement in the financial statements as a whole, and not in the misstatement in a particular account balance.

The verification of the liability accounts associated with payroll, often termed *accrued payroll expenses*, ordinarily is straightforward if internal control is operating effectively. When the auditor is satisfied that payroll transactions are being properly recorded in the payroll journal and the related employee withholding and benefits remittance forms are being accurately prepared and promptly paid, the tests of details of balances should not be time consuming.

The two major objectives in testing payroll-related liabilities are: accruals in the trial balance are properly valued and transactions in the payroll and personnel cycle are recorded in the proper period. The primary concern in both objectives is to make sure there are no understated or omitted accruals. The major liability accounts in the payroll and personnel cycle are now discussed.

Amounts Withheld from Employees' Pay

Income taxes withheld, but not yet disbursed, can be tested by comparing the balance with the payroll journal, the withholding remittance form prepared in the subsequent period, and the subsequent period cash disbursements. Other withheld items such as the Canada (or Quebec) Pension Plan, unemployment insurance, union dues, Canada Savings Bonds, and insurance can be verified in the same manner. If internal control is operating effectively, cutoff and valuation can easily be tested at the same time by these procedures.

Accrued Salaries and Wages

The accrual for salaries and wages arises whenever employees are not paid for the last few days or hours of earned wages until the subsequent period. Salaried personnel usually receive all of their pay except overtime on the last day of the

FIGURE 16–4

Methodology for
Designing Tests of
Details of Balances for
Payroll Liabilities

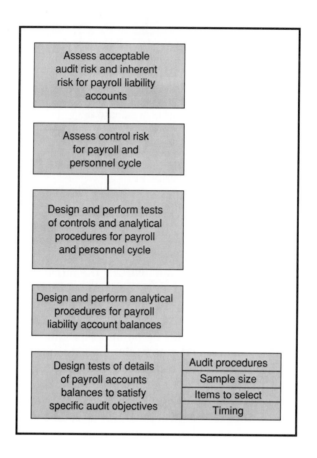

month, but frequently several days of wages for hourly employees are unpaid at the end of the year.

The correct cutoff and valuation of accrued salaries and wages depends on company policy, which should be followed consistently from year to year. Some companies calculate the exact hours of pay that were earned in the current period and paid in the subsequent period, whereas others compute an approximate proportion. For example, if the subsequent payroll results from three days' employment during the current year and two days' employment during the subsequent year, the use of 60 percent of the subsequent period's gross pay as the accrual is an example of an approximation.

Once the auditor has determined the company's policy for accruing wages and knows it is consistent with that of previous years, the appropriate audit procedure to test for cutoff and valuation is to recalculate the client's accrual. The most likely error of any significance in the balance is the failure to include the proper number of days of earned but unpaid wages.

Accrued
Commissions

The same concepts used in verifying accrued salaries and wages are applicable to accrued commissions, but the accrual is often more difficult to verify because companies frequently have several different types of agreements with salespeople and other commission employees. For example, some salespeople might be paid a commission every month and earn no salary, while others will get a monthly salary plus a commission paid quarterly. In some cases the commission varies for different products and may not be paid until several months after the end of the year. In verifying accrued commissions, it is necessary first to determine the nature of the commission agreement and then test the calculations based on the agreement. It is important to compare the method of accruing commissions with previous years for purposes of consistency. If the amounts are material, it is also common to confirm the amount that is due directly with the employees.

Accrued Bonuses In many companies, the year-end unpaid bonuses to officers and employees are such a major item that the failure to record them would result in a material misstatement. The verification of the recorded accrual can usually be accomplished by comparing it with the amount authorized in the minutes of the board of directors.

Accrued Vacation Pay, Sick Pay, or Other Benefits The consistent accrual of these liabilities relative to those of the preceding year is the most important consideration in evaluating the fairness of the amounts. The company policy for recording the liability must first be determined, followed by the recalculation of the recorded amounts.

Accrued Benefits This account will include the employer's share of Canada (or Quebec) Pension Plan payments and unemployment insurance payments as well as workers' compensation. The employer's share can be verified by examining remittance forms prepared in the subsequent period to determine the amount that should have been recorded as a liability at the balance sheet date.

Tests of Details of Balances for Expense Accounts Several accounts in the income statement are affected by payroll transactions. The most important are officers' salaries and bonuses, office salaries, sales salaries and commissions, and direct manufacturing labor. There is frequently a further breakdown of costs by division, product, or branch. Fringe benefits such as medical insurance may also be included in the expenses.

There should be relatively little additional testing of the income statement accounts in most audits beyond the analytical procedures, tests of controls, and related tests of liability accounts, which have already been discussed. Extensive additional testing should only be necessary when there are weaknesses in internal control, significant errors are discovered in the liability tests, or major unexplained variances are found in the analytical procedures. Nevertheless, some income statement accounts are often tested in the personnel and payroll cycle. These include officers' compensation, commissions, and total payroll.

Officers' compensation It is common to verify whether the total compensation of officers is the amount authorized by the board of directors, because some individuals may be in a position to pay themselves more than the authorized amount. The usual audit test is to obtain the authorized salary of each officer from the minutes of the board of directors meetings and compare it with the related earnings record.

Commissions Commission expense can be verified with relative ease if the commission rate is the same for each type of sale and the necessary sales information is available in the accounting records. The total commission expense can be verified by multiplying the commission rate for each type of sale by the amount of sales in that category. If the desired information is not available, it may be necessary to test the annual or monthly commission payments for selected salespeople and trace those to the total commission payments. When the auditor believes it is necessary to perform these tests, they are normally done in conjunction with tests of accrued liabilities.

Total payroll   This test involves the reconciliation of total payroll expense in the general ledger with the T-4 Summary the company must send in to Revenue Canada by the end of February each year. The objectives of the test are to determine whether payroll transactions were charged to a nonpayroll account or not recorded in the payroll journal at all. The audit objectives are certainly relevant, but it is questionable whether the procedure is useful in uncovering the type of error for which it was intended. Since the T-4 Summary and the payroll are both usually prepared directly from the payroll master file, the errors, if any, are likely to be in both records. The procedure may be worthwhile in rare situations, but it is usually not necessary to perform it. Tests of controls are a better means of uncovering these two types of errors in most audits.

REVIEW QUESTIONS

16–1   Identify five ledger accounts that are likely to be affected by the payroll and personnel cycle in most audits.

16–2   Explain the relationship between the payroll and personnel cycle and inventory valuation.

16–3   List five tests of controls that can be performed for the payroll cycle and state the purpose of each control being tested.

16–4   Explain why the percentage of total audit time in the cycle devoted to performing tests of controls is usually far greater for the payroll and personnel cycle than for the sales and collection cycle.

16–5   Evaluate the following comment by an auditor: "My job is to determine whether the payroll records are fairly stated in accordance with generally accepted accounting principles, not to find out whether they are following proper hiring and termination procedures. When I conduct an audit of payroll I keep out of the personnel department and stick to the time cards, journals, and payroll cheques. I don't care whom they hire and whom they fire, as long as they properly pay the ones they have."

16–6   Distinguish between the following payroll audit procedures and state the purpose of each: (1) Trace a random sample of prenumbered time cards to the related payroll cheques in the payroll register and compare the hours worked with the hours paid, and (2) trace a random sample of payroll cheques from the payroll register to the related time cards and compare the hours worked with the hours paid. Which of these two procedures is typically more important in the audit of payroll? Why?

16–7   In auditing payroll withholding and payroll benefits expense, explain why emphasis should normally be on evaluating the adequacy of the employee withholding and benefits remittance forms preparation procedures rather than the employee withholding and benefits liability. If the preparation procedures are inadequate, explain the effect this will have on the remainder of the audit.

16–8   List several analytical procedures for the payroll and personnel cycle and explain the type of error that might be indicated when there is a significant difference in the comparison of the current year with previous years' results for each of the tests.

16–9 Explain the circumstances under which an auditor should perform audit tests primarily designed to uncover fraud in the payroll and personnel cycle. List five audit procedures that are primarily for the detection of fraud and state the type of fraud the procedure is meant to uncover.

16–10 Distinguish between a payroll master file, a T-4 form, and an employee benefits remittance form. Explain the purpose of each.

16–11 List the supporting documents and records the auditor will examine in a typical payroll audit in which the primary objective is to detect fraud.

16–12 List the five types of authorizations in the payroll and personnel cycle and state the type of misstatement that is enhanced when each authorization is lacking.

16–13 Explain why it is common to verify total officers' compensation even when the tests of controls results in payroll are excellent. What audit procedures can be used to verify officers' compensation?

16–14 Explain what is meant by an imprest payroll account. What is its purpose as a control over payroll?

16–15 List several audit procedures the auditor can use to determine whether recorded payroll transactions are recorded at the proper amount.

16–16 Explain how attributes sampling can be used to test the payroll and personnel cycle.

MULTIPLE CHOICE QUESTIONS

16–17 The following questions concern internal controls in the payroll and personnel cycle. Choose the best response.

a. A factory supervisor at Steblecki Corporation discharged an hourly worker but did *not* notify the payroll department. The supervisor then forged the worker's signature on time cards and work tickets and, when giving out the cheques, diverted the payroll cheques drawn from the discharged worker to his own use. The most effective procedure for preventing this activity is to

(1) require written authorization for all employees added to or removed from the payroll.

(2) have a paymaster who has *no* other payroll responsibility distribute the payroll cheques.

(3) have someone other than persons who prepare or distribute the payroll obtain custody of unclaimed payroll cheques.

(4) from time to time, rotate persons distributing the payroll.

b. A public accountant reviews Hearst Ltd.'s payroll procedures. An example of an internal control weakness is to assign to a department supervisor the responsibility for

(1) distributing payroll cheques to subordinate employees.

(2) reviewing and approving time reports for subordinates.

(3) interviewing applicants for subordinate positions prior to hiring by the personnel department.

(4) initiating requests for salary adjustments for subordinate employees.

c. From the standpoint of good procedural control, distributing payroll cheques to employees is best handled by the

(1) accounting department.

(2) personnel department.

(3) treasurer's department.

(4) employee's departmental supervisor. (AICPA adapted)

16–18 The following questions concern audit testing of the payroll and personnel cycle. Choose the best response.

a. A computer operator perpetrated a theft by preparing erroneous T-4 forms. The operator's income tax withheld was overstated by $500 and the income tax withheld from all other employees was understated. Which of the following audit procedures would detect such a fraud?

   (1) Multiplication of the applicable rate by the individual's gross taxable earnings.

   (2) Using employees' TD-1 forms and withholding tables to determine whether deductions authorized per pay period agree with amounts deducted per pay period.

   (3) Footing and crossfooting of the payroll register followed by tracing postings to the general ledger.

   (4) Vouching canceled cheques to income tax withholding remittance forms.

b. In the audit of which of the following types of profit-oriented enterprises would the auditor be most likely to place special emphasis on tests of controls for proper classifications of payroll transactions?

   (1) A manufacturing organization

   (2) A retailing organization

   (3) A wholesaling organization

   (4) A service organization

c. A common audit procedure in the audit of payroll transactions involves tracing selected items from the payroll journal to employee time cards that have been approved by supervisory personnel. This procedure is designed to provide evidence in support of the audit proposition that

   (1) only proper employees worked and their pay was properly computed.

   (2) jobs on which employees worked were charged with the appropriate labor cost.

   (3) internal controls relating to payroll disbursements are operating effectively.

   (4) all employees worked the number of hours for which their pay was computed.

                                                                   (AICPA adapted)

DISCUSSION QUESTIONS AND PROBLEMS

16–19 Items 1 through 9 are selected questions typically found in internal control questionnaires used by auditors to obtain an understanding of the internal control structure in the payroll and personnel cycle. In using the questionnaire for a particular client, a "yes" response to a question indicates a possible internal control, whereas a "no" indicates a potential weakness.

1. Does an appropriate official authorize initial rates of pay and any subsequent change in rate?

2. Are written notices required documenting reasons for termination?

3. Are formal records such as time cards used for keeping time?

4. Is approval by a department head or supervisor required for all time cards before they are submitted for payment?

5. Does anyone verify pay rates, overtime hours, and computations of gross payroll before payroll cheques are prepared?

6. Does an adequate means exist for identifying jobs or products, such as work orders, job numbers, or some similar identification provided to employees to ensure proper coding of time records?

7. Are employees paid by cheques prepared by persons independent of timekeeping?

8. Are employees required to show identification to receive paycheques?

9. Is a continuing record maintained of all unclaimed wages?

Required:

   a. For each of the questions, state the internal control objective(s) being fulfilled if the control is in effect.

   b. For each control, list a test of control procedure to test its effectiveness.

   c. For each of the questions, identify the nature of the potential financial error(s) if the control is not in effect.

   d. For each of the potential errors in part (c), list a test of control audit procedure for determining whether a material error exists.

16–20 Following are some of the tests of controls procedures frequently performed in the payroll and personnel cycle. (Each procedure is to be done on a sample basis.)

1. Reconcile the monthly payroll total for directing manufacturing labor with the labor cost distribution.

2. Examine the time card for the approval of a foreman.

3. Recompute hours on the time card and compare the total with the total hours for which the employee has been paid.

4. Compare the employee name, date, cheque number, and amounts on canceled cheques with the payroll journal.

5. Trace the hours from the employee time cards to job tickets to make sure the total reconciles, and trace each job ticket to the job-cost record.

6. Account for a sequence of payroll cheques in the payroll journal.

7. Select employees from the personnel file who have been terminated and determine whether their termination pay was in accordance with the union contract. As part of this procedure, examine two subsequent periods to determine whether the terminated employee is still being paid.

Required: Identify the objective(s) of each of the procedures.

16–21 The following errors or omissions are included in the accounting records of Lathen Manufacturing Ltd.

1. Direct labor was unintentionally charged to job 620 instead of job 602 by the payroll clerk when he key entered the labor distribution sheets. Job 602 was completed and the costs were expensed in the current year, whereas job 620 was included in work-in-process.

2. Jane Block and Frank Demery take turns "punching in" for each other every few days. The absent employee comes in at noon and tells the supervisor that he or she had car trouble or some other problem. The supervisor does not know the employee is getting paid for the time.

3. The supervisor submits a fictitious time card for a former employee each week and delivers the related payroll cheque to the employee's house on the way home from work. They split the amount of the paycheque.

4. Employees frequently overlook recording their hours worked on job-cost tickets as required by the system. Many of the client's contracts are on a cost-plus basis.

5. The payroll clerk prepares a cheque to the same fictitious person every week when key entering payroll transactions in the microcomputer system, which also records the amount in the payroll journal. The clerk submits it along with all other payroll cheques for signature. When the cheques are returned to the clerk for distribution, the clerk takes the cheque and deposits it in a special bank account bearing that person's name.

6. In withholding income taxes from employees, the computer operator with-

holds $.50 extra from several employees each week and credits the amount to the operator's own employee earnings record.

7. The payroll clerk manually prepares payroll cheques, but frequently forgets to record one or two cheques in the microcomputer prepared payroll journal.

Required:

    a. For each error, state a control that should have prevented it from occurring on a continuing basis.

    b. For each error, state a test of control audit procedure that could uncover it.

16–22 The following audit procedures are typical of those found in auditing the payroll and personnel cycle.

1. Examining evidence of double-checking payroll wage rates and calculations by an independent person.

2. Obtaining a schedule of all accrued expenses and other liabilities and tracing to the general ledger.

3. Selecting a sample of 20 canceled payroll cheques and accounting for the numerical sequence.

4. Footing and crossfooting the payroll journal for two periods and tracing totals to the general ledger.

5. For accrued expenses, examining subsequent payments and supporting documents such as employee benefits remittance forms and receipts received.

6. Selecting a sample of 20 canceled payroll cheques and tracing to payroll journal entries for name, date, and amounts.

7. Computing direct labor, indirect labor, and commissions as a percentage of net sales and comparing with prior years.

8. Examining owner approval of rates of pay and withholdings.

9. Computing unemployment insurance expense as a percentage of total wages, salaries, and commissions.

10. Discussing with management any accrued payroll expenses or liabilities at the last engagement date that are not provided for currently.

11. Scanning journals for all periods for unusual transactions to determine if they are recorded properly.

12. Selecting a sample of 40 entries in the payroll journal and tracing each to an approved time card.

Required:

    a. Select the best type of test for each audit procedure from the following:

       (1) Test of controls

       (2) Analytical procedure

       (3) Test of details of balances

    b. For each test of control identify the applicable internal control objective(s).

    c. For each test of details of balances, identify the applicable audit objective(s).

16–23 The following are steps in the methodology for designing tests of controls and tests of details of balances for the payroll and personnel cycle:

1. Design tests of details of balances for payroll and personnel.

2. Evaluate risk for payroll expense and liability accounts.

3. Evaluate cost-benefit of assessing control risk as low for payroll.

4. Design and perform payroll- and personnel-related analytical procedures.

5. Identify controls and weaknesses in internal control for the payroll and personnel cycle.

6. Obtain an understanding of payroll and personnel cycle internal control.

7. Evaluate tests of controls results.

8. Design payroll and personnel tests of controls.

9. Assess inherent risk for payroll-related accounts.

Required:

    a. Identify those steps that are tests of controls and those that are tests of details of balances.

    b. Put steps that are tests of controls in the order of their performance in most audits.

    c. Put the tests of details of balances in their proper order.

16–24 In comparing total employee benefits expense with the preceding year, Marilyn Brendin, public accountant, observed a significant increase, even though the total number of employees had only increased from 175 to 195. To investigate the difference, she selected a large sample of payroll disbursement transactions and carefully tested the withholdings for each employee in the sample by referring to Canada Pension Plan and unemployment insurance and other benefits withholding tables. In her test she found no exceptions; therefore, she concluded that employee benefits expense was fairly stated.

Required:

    a. Evaluate Brendin's approach to testing employee benefits expense.

    b. Discuss a more suitable approach for determining whether employee benefits expense was properly stated in the current year.

16–25 As part of the audit of McGree Plumbing and Heating Ltd., you have responsibility for testing the payroll and personnel cycle. Payroll is the largest single expense in the client's trial balance, and hourly wages make up most of the payroll total. A unique aspect of its business is the extensive overtime incurred by employees on some days. It is common for employees to work only three or four days during the week but to work long hours while they are on the job. McGree's management has found that this actually saves money, in spite of the large amount of overtime, because the union contract requires payment for all travel time. Since many of the employees' jobs require long travel times and extensive startup costs, this policy is supported by both McGree and the employees.

    You have already carefully evaluated and tested payroll internal control and concluded that it contains no significant weaknesses. Your tests included tests of the time cards, withholdings, pay rates, the filing of all required employee withholding and benefits remittance forms, payroll cheques, and all other aspects of payroll.

    As part of the year-end tests of payroll, you are responsible for verifying all accrued payroll as well as the company's liability for withholdings and accrued benefits. The accrued factory payroll includes the last six working days of the current year. The client has calculated accrued wages by taking 60 percent of the subsequent period's gross payroll and has recorded it as an adjusting entry to be reversed in the subsequent period.

Required:

    List all audit procedures you would follow in verifying accrued payroll and the liability for withholdings and accrued employee benefits.

16–26 In the audit of Larnet Manufacturing Corp., the auditor concluded that internal controls were inadequate because of the lack of segregation of duties. As a result, the decision was made to have a surprise payroll payoff one month before the client's balance sheet date. Since the auditor had never been involved in a payroll payoff, she did not know how to proceed.

Required:

    a. What is the purpose of a surprise payroll payoff?

    b. What other audit procedures can the auditor perform that may fulfil the same objectives?

    c. Discuss the procedures the auditor should require the client to observe when the surprise payroll payoff is taking place.

d. At the completion of the payroll payoff, there are frequently several unclaimed cheques. What procedures should be followed for these?

16–27 Kowal Manufacturing Corp. employs about 50 production workers and has the following payroll procedures:

The factory supervisor interviews applicants and on the basis of the interview either hires or rejects them. When the applicant is hired, he or she prepares a TD1 form (Personal Tax Credit Return) and gives it to the supervisor. The supervisor writes the hourly rate of pay for the new employee in the corner of the TD1 form and then gives the form to a payroll clerk as notice that the worker has been employed. The supervisor verbally advises the payroll department of rate adjustments.

A supply of blank time cards is kept in a box near the entrance to the factory. Each worker takes a time card on Monday morning, fills in his or her name, and notes in pencil his or her daily arrival and departure times. At the end of the week the workers drop the time cards in a box near the door to the factory.

On Monday morning, the completed time cards are taken from the box by a payroll clerk. One of the payroll clerks then records the payroll transactions using a microcomputer system, which records all information for the payroll journal that was calculated by the clerk and automatically updates the employees' earnings records and general ledger. Employees are automatically removed from the payroll when they fail to turn in a time card.

The payroll cheques are manually signed by the chief accountant and given to the supervisor. The foreman distributes the cheques to the workers in the factory and arranges for the delivery of the cheques to the workers who are absent. The payroll bank account is reconciled by the chief accountant, who also prepares the various employee withholdings and benefits remittance forms.

Required:

a. List the most serious weaknesses in internal control and state the misstatements that are likely to result from the weaknesses. In your audit of Kowal's payroll, what will you emphasize in your audit tests? Explain.

b. List your suggestions for improving the Kowal Manufacturing Corp.'s internal controls for the factory hiring practices and payroll procedures.

(AICPA adapted)

16–28 During the first-year audit of Omato Wholesale Stationery Ltd. you observe that commissions amount to almost 25 percent of total sales, which is somewhat higher than in previous years. Further investigation reveals that the industry typically has larger sales commissions than Omato and that there is significant variation in rates depending on the product sold.

At the time a sale is made, the salesperson records his or her commission rate and the total amount of the commissions on the office copy of the sales invoice. When sales are entered into the microcomputer system for the recording of sales, the debit to sales commission expense and credit to accrued sales commission are also recorded. As part of recording the sales and sales commission expense, the accounts receivable clerk verifies the prices, quantities, commission rates, and all calculations on the sales invoices. Both the accounts receivable and the salespersons' commission master files are updated when the sale and sales commission are recorded. On the fifteenth day after the end of the month, the salesperson is paid for the preceding month's sales commissions.

Required:

a. Develop an audit program to verify sales commission expense, assuming that no audit tests have been conducted in any audit area to this point.

b. Develop an audit program to verify accrued sales commissions at the end of the year, assuming that the tests you designed in part (a) resulted in no significant errors.

16–29 Dunlop Ltd., a property management company, has a subsidiary, Riber Ltd., that is constructing an office building to be operated as a rental property by Dunlop.

The building is being constructed by an independent contractor on the basis of direct costs plus 20 percent. Direct costs are defined as material used and labor costs incurred in the construction. The 20 percent is intended to cover overhead and profit.

At August 31, 19X7 the degree of completion is estimated at 75 percent. Brett Dunlop, president of Dunlop has just asked you as Dunlop's and Riber's auditor to conduct an investigation of the labor costs which are about $1,000,000 over estimates. Dunlop has some concerns about the contractor's honesty. He says that he is satisfied with the material costs, however.

A review of the contract between Riber and the contractor reveals the following:

1. Wage rates, specified in the contract, are based on union contracts. The rates vary with the trade and worker's experience.

2. Employees are paid by the contractor. The payroll records are kept by an independent computer service bureau. The contractor sends a monthly payroll summary by employee to Riber to support her invoice.

3. Dunlop explained that construction workers' mobility made it very difficult to verify that employees listed on the monthly summary actually worked on the site. He added that he had no confidence in the timekeeping system used on the site.

4. The contract provides Riber with the right to examine the books of the contractor.

Required:
List the procedures you would perform to carry out the investigation requested by Dunlop. State why you would perform each procedure.

(CICA adapted)

16–30 In many companies, labor costs represent a substantial percentage of total dollars expended in any one accounting period. One of the auditor's primary means of verifying payroll transactions is by a detailed payroll test.

You are making an annual examination of Lethbridge Inc., a medium-sized manufacturing company. You have selected a number of hourly employees for a detailed payroll test. The following worksheet outline has been prepared.

COLUMN NUMBER	HEADING
1	Employee number
2	Employee name
3	Job classification
	Hours worked:
4	Straight time
5	Premium time
6	Hourly rate
7	Gross earnings
	Deductions:
8	Income tax withheld
9	Canada Pension Plan withheld
10	Unemployment insurance withheld
11	Union dues
12	Amount of cheque
13	Cheque number
14	Account number charged
15	Description of account

Required:
a. What factors should the auditor consider in selecting his or her sample of employees to be included in any payroll test?

    b. Using the column numbers above as a reference, state the principal way(s) that the information for each heading would be verified.

    c. In addition to the payroll test, the auditor employs a number of other audit procedures in the verification of payroll transactions. List five additional procedures that may be employed.   (AICPA adapted)

CASE

16–31 Roost and Briley, public accountants, are doing the audit of Leggert Lumber Inc., an international wholesale lumber broker. Due to the nature of their business, payroll and telephone expense are the two largest expenses.

    You are the in-charge auditor on the engagement responsible for writing the audit program for the payroll and personnel cycle. Leggert Lumber uses a computer service company to prepare weekly payroll cheques, update earnings records, and prepare the weekly payroll journal for their 30 employees. The president maintains all personnel files, knows every employee extremely well, and is a full-time participant in the business.

    All employees, except the president, check into the company building daily using a time clock. The president's secretary, Mary Clark, hands out the time cards daily, observes employees clocking in, collects the cards, and immediately returns them to the file. She goes through the same process when employees clock out on their way home.

    At the end of each week, employees calculate their own hours. Clark rechecks those hours, and the president approves all time cards. Each Tuesday, Clark prepares a *payroll input form* for delivery to the computer service centre. She files a copy of the form. The form has the following information for each employee:

INFORMATION	SOURCE
Employee name	Time card
Social insurance number	Employee list
Hourly labor rate*	Wage rate list (approved by president)
Regular hours	Time card
Overtime hours	Time card
Special deductions*	Special form (prepared by employee)
TD-1 information*	TD-1 form
Termination of employment*	President

* Included on input form only for new employees, terminations, and changes.

    The service center key enters the information from the payroll input form into its computer, updates master files, and prints out payroll cheques and a payroll register. The payroll register has the following headings:

Employee name	Employee benefits withheld
Social insurance number	Income taxes withheld
Regular hours	Other withholdings
Overtime hours	Other deductions
Regular payroll dollars	Net pay
Overtime payroll dollars	Cheque number
Gross payroll	

A line is prepared for each employee and the journal is totaled.

    Payroll cheques and the journal are delivered to Clark, who compares the information on the journal with her payroll input form and initials the journal. She gives the cheques to the president, who signs them and personally delivers them to employees.

Clark re-adds the journal and posts the totals to the ledger. Canceled cheques are mailed to the president, and he prepares a monthly bank reconciliation.

Required:

a. Is there any loss of documentation because of the computer service centre? Explain.

b. For each internal control objective for payroll, write appropriate tests of controls audit procedures. Consider both controls and weaknesses in writing your program.

c. Rearrange your design format audit program in part (b) into a performance format audit program.

d. Prepare an attributes sampling data sheet, such as the ones shown in Chapter 12, for the audit program in part (b). Set acceptable risk of overreliance and other factors required for attributes sampling as you consider appropriate. Do not assume you actually performed any tests.

17

AUDIT OF THE ACQUISITION AND PAYMENT CYCLE

LEARNING OBJECTIVES

THOROUGH STUDY OF THIS CHAPTER WILL ENABLE YOU TO:

1. Describe the acquisition and payment cycle, and the pertinent documents and records, functions, and internal controls

2. Design and perform tests of controls for the acquisition and payment cycle, and assess related control risk

3. Discuss the nature of accounts payable, and describe the related controls

4. Design and perform analytical procedures for accounts payable

5. Design and perform tests of details for accounts payable

☐ The third major transaction cycle discussed in this text is the acquisition of and payment for goods and services from outsiders. The acquisition of goods and services includes such items as the purchase of raw materials, equipment, supplies, utilities, repairs and maintenance, and research and development. The cycle does not include the acquisition and payment of employees' services or the internal transfers and allocations of costs within the organization. The former are a part of the payroll and personnel function, and the latter are audited as part of the verification of individual assets or liabilities. The acquisition and payment cycle also excludes the acquisition and repayment of capital (interest-bearing debt and owners' equity), which are considered separately in Chapter 20.

The audit of the acquisition and payment cycle is studied in Chapters 17 and 18. In this chapter, the basic format for discussing internal control introduced in earlier chapters is repeated. The first part of the chapter deals with the nature of the acquisition and payment cycle, including documents and records, and its primary functions and internal controls. The second part discusses tests of controls for the cycle related to key internal controls. The final part covers tests of details of accounts payable, the major balance sheet account in the cycle. It emphasizes the relationship between tests of controls and tests of details of balances. In Chapter 18, several other important balance sheet accounts that are a part of the acquisition and payment cycle are examined. These are manufacturing equipment, prepaid insurance, and accrued property taxes. The chapter also takes up tests of details of income statement accounts included in the acquisition and payment cycle.

The large number and different types of accounts included in the acquisition and payment cycle distinguish it from the other two cycles that we have studied.

Examine the trial balance for Hillsburg Hardware Ltd. on page 135. Accounts affected by the acquisition and payment cycle are identified by the letter "A" in the left column. Notice first that accounts affected by the cycle include asset, liability, expense, and miscellaneous income accounts, and second that more accounts are affected by acquisitions and payments than for all other cycles combined. This is true for most companies. It is not surprising, therefore, that it usually takes more time to audit the acquisition and payment cycle than any other.

The way the accounting information flows through the various accounts in the acquisition and payment cycle is illustrated by T-accounts in Figure 17–1. To keep the illustration manageable, only the control accounts are shown for the three major categories of expenses used by most companies. For each control account, examples of the subsidiary expense accounts are also given.

Figure 17–1 shows that every transaction is either debited or credited to accounts payable. Because many companies make some purchases directly by cheque or through petty cash, the figure is an oversimplification. We assume that cash transactions are processed in the same manner as all others.

Nature of the Cycle

The acquisition and payment cycle involves the decisions and processes necessary for obtaining the goods and services for operating a business. The cycle typically begins with the initiation of a purchase requisition by an authorized employee who needs the goods or services and ends with payment for the benefits received. Although the discussion that follows deals with a small manufacturing company that makes tangible products for sale to third parties, the same principles apply to a service company, a government unit, or any other type of organization.

The *functions* and *flow of documents* for the acquisition and payment cycle of a typical manufacturing company are illustrated in Figure 17–2. The overview flowchart is meant to show how the information in Figure 17–1 is generated. Many of the controls ordinarily integrated into internal control are not included at this point.

OBJECTIVE 1

Describe the acquisition and payment cycle, and the pertinent documents and records, functions, and internal controls.

FIGURE 17–1

Accounts in the
Acquisition and
Payment Cycle

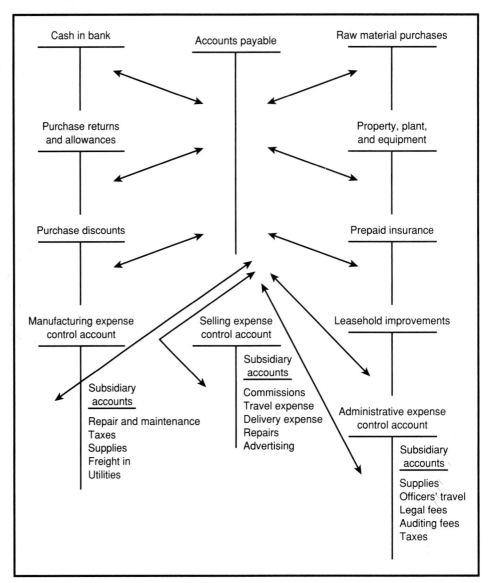

Documents and
Records

To support the record flow in the acquisition and payment cycle, several important documents and records are used. Among them are the following:

- **Purchase requisition** A request for goods and services by an authorized employee. It may take the form of a request for such acquisitions as materials by a shop supervisor or the storeroom supervisor, outside repairs by office or factory personnel, or insurance by the vice president in charge of property and equipment.

- **Purchase order** A document recording the description, quantity, and related information for goods and services the company intends to purchase. This document is frequently used to indicate authorization to procure goods and services.

- **Receiving report** A document prepared at the time tangible goods are received that indicates the description of goods, the quantity received, the date received, and other relevant data. The receipt of goods and services in the normal course of business represents the date clients normally recognize the liability for an acquisition.

- **Acquisition transactions file** A computer file used to record acquisitions of goods and services. The computer operator enters the vendor name or number and the additional information needed to record accounts payable, update accounts payable and inventory master files and prepare the cheque for the vendor when payment is due. For a purchase of inventory, the operator would enter each product's number and cost, the total amount of the purchase, account number of vendor, date when payment is due, and cash discount terms.

- **Acquisitions journal** A journal for recording acquisition transactions. A detailed acquisitions journal includes each acquisition transaction. It usually includes several classifications for the most significant types of acquisitions, such as the purchase of inventory, repairs and maintenance, supplies, the entry to accounts payable, and miscellaneous debits and credits. The acquisitions journal can also include acquisition returns and allowances transactions if a separate journal is not used. The acquisitions journal is generated for any time period from the acquisition transactions included in the computer files. Details from the journal are posted to the accounts payable master file and journal totals are posted to the general ledger by the computer.

- **Summary acquisitions report** A computer-generated document that summarizes acquisitions for a period. The report typically includes information analyzed by key components such as account classification, type of inventory, and division.

- **Vendor's invoice** A document that indicates such things as the description and quantity of goods and services received, price including freight, cash discount terms, and date of the billing. It is an essential document because it specifies the amount of money owed to the vendor for an acquisition.

- **Debit memo** A document indicating a reduction in the amount owed to a vendor because of returned goods or an allowance granted. It often takes the same general form as a vendor's invoice, but it supports reductions in accounts payable rather than increases.

- **Voucher** A document frequently used by organizations to establish a formal means of recording and controlling acquisitions. Vouchers include a cover sheet or folder for containing documents and a package of relevant documents such as the purchase order, copy of the packing slip, receiving report, and vendor's invoice. After payment, a copy of the cheque is added to the voucher package.

- **Cheque** The means of paying for the acquisition when payment is due. After the cheque is signed by an authorized person, it is an asset. It is normally prepared and printed by the computer on the basis of the information included in the acquisition transactions file. When cashed by the vendor and cleared by the client's bank, it is referred to as a canceled cheque.

- **Cash disbursements transaction file** A file for recording the individual payments made by cheque. It contains the total cash paid, the debit to accounts payable at the amount the transaction was recorded in the acquisition transaction file, discounts taken, and other debits and credits. The cheque amounts are accompanied by vendor identification number, cheque number, and date. The primary outputs generated from the file are the printed cheques and the cash disbursements journal, which shows the details contained in the file.

- **Accounts payable master file** A file for recording individual acquisitions, cash disbursements, and acquisition returns and allowances for each vendor. The master file is updated from the acquisition, returns and allowances, and cash disbursements computer transaction files. The total of the individual account balances in the master file equals the total balance of accounts payable in the general ledger. A printout of the accounts payable master file shows, by vendor, the beginning balance in accounts payable, each acquisition, acquisition returns and allowances, cash disbursements, and the ending balance. Many companies do not maintain an accounts payable master file by vendor. These companies pay on the basis of individual vendors' invoices. Therefore, the total of unpaid vendors' invoices in the master file equals total accounts payable.

- **Accounts payable trial balance** A listing of the amount owed by each vendor at a point in time. It is prepared directly from the accounts payable master file.

- **Vendor's statement** A statement prepared monthly by the vendor indicating the beginning balance, acquisitions, returns and allowances, payments to the vendor, and ending balance. These balances and activities are the vendor's representations of the transactions for the period and not the client's. Except for disputed amounts and timing differences, the client's accounts payable master file should be the same as the vendor's statement.

Functions in the Cycle and Internal Controls

A discussion of the primary functions in the acquisition and payment cycle will clarify what the auditor is trying to accomplish in the audit of the cycle. Four functions are involved:

1. Processing purchase orders
2. Receiving goods and services
3. Recognizing the liability
4. Processing and recording cash disbursements

These functions are discussed in the order of their occurrence in a typical transaction cycle (see Figure 17–2). The emphasis is on the most important controls used to prevent errors in processing data and to ensure safety of assets.

Processing purchase orders The request for goods or services by the client's personnel is the starting point for the cycle. The exact form of the request and the required approval depends on the nature of the goods and services and the company policy.

Proper *authorization* for acquisitions is an essential part of this function because it ensures that the goods and services purchased are for authorized company purposes and it avoids the purchase of excessive or unnecessary items. Most companies permit general authorization for the purchase of regular operating needs such as inventory at one level and acquisitions of capital assets or similar items at another. For example, purchases of permanent assets in excess of a specified dollar limit may require board of director action; items purchased relatively infrequently, such as insurance policies and long-term service contracts, are approved by certain officers; supplies and services costing less than a designated amount are approved by supervisors and department heads; and some types of raw materials and supplies are reordered automatically whenever they fall to a predetermined level. After the acquisition has been approved, there must be an *initiation of an order* to purchase the goods or services. An order is issued to a vendor for a specified item at a certain price to be delivered at or by a designated time. The order is usually in writing and is a legal document that is an offer to buy. For most routine items, a purchase order is used to indicate the offer.

It is common for companies to establish purchasing departments to ensure an adequate quality of goods and services at a minimum price. For good internal control, the purchasing department should not be responsible for authorizing the acquisition or receiving of the goods. All purchase orders should be prenumbered and should include sufficient columns and spaces to minimize the likelihood of unintentional omissions on the form when goods are ordered.

FIGURE 17–2

Flowchart of the
Acquisition and
Payment Cycle

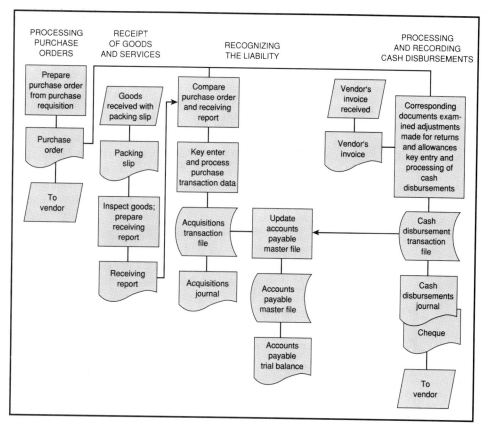

Receiving goods and services   The receipt by the company of goods or services from the vendor is a critical point in the cycle because it is the point at which most companies first recognize the associated liability on their records. When goods are received, adequate control requires examination for description, quantity, timely arrival, and condition.

Most companies have the receiving department initiate a receiving report as evidence of the receipt and examination of goods. One copy is normally sent to the storeroom and another to the accounts payable department for their information needs. To prevent theft and misuse, it is important that the goods be *physically controlled* from the time of their receipt until they are disposed of. The personnel in the receiving department should be independent of the storeroom personnel and the accounting department. Finally, the accounting records should transfer responsibility for the goods as they are transferred from receiving to storage and from storage to manufacturing.

Recognizing the liability The proper recognition of the liability for the receipt of goods and services requires *accurate and prompt* recording. The initial recording has a significant effect on the recorded financial statements and the actual cash disbursement; therefore, great care must be taken to include only valid company acquisitions at the correct amount.

In some companies, the recording of the liability for acquisitions is made on the basis of receipt of goods and services, and in other companies, it is deferred until the vendor's invoice is received. In either case, the accounts payable department typically has responsibility for verifying the propriety of acquisitions. This is done by comparing the details on the purchase order, the receiving report and the vendor's invoice to determine that the descriptions, prices, quantities, terms, and freight on the vendor's invoice are correct. Typically, extensions, footings and account distribution are also verified.

The acquisition transaction is entered in the computer where it is recorded as a liability and an expense or asset through the acquisition transaction file. The information is also used to update the accounts payable master file.

An important control in the accounts payable and EDP departments is to require that those personnel who record acquisitions *do not have access* to cash, marketable securities, and other assets. Adequate documents and records, proper procedures for record keeping, and independent checks on performance are also necessary controls in the accounts payable function.

Processing and recording cash disbursements For most companies, payment is made by computer-prepared cheques from information included in the acquisition transactions file at the time goods and services are received. Cheques are typically prepared in a multicopy format, with the original going to the payee, one copy filed with the vendor's invoice and other supporting documents, and another filed alphabetically by payee. In most cases individual cheques are recorded in a cash disbursements transactions file.

The most important controls in the cash disbursements function include the signing of cheques by an individual with proper authority, separation of responsibilities for signing the cheques and performing the accounts payable function, and careful examination of the supporting documents by the cheque signer at the time the cheque is signed.

The cheques should be prenumbered and printed on special paper that makes it difficult to alter the payee or amount. Care should be taken to provide physical control over blank, voided, and signed cheques. It is also important to have a method of canceling the supporting documents to prevent their reuse as support for another cheque at a later time. A common method is to write the cheque number on the supporting documents.

Tests of Controls In a typical audit, the most time-consuming accounts to verify by tests of details of balances are accounts receivable, inventory, permanent assets, accounts payable, and expense accounts. Of these five, four are directly related to the acquisition and payment cycle. The net time saved can be dramatic if the auditor can reduce the tests of details of the accounts by using tests of controls to verify the effectiveness of acquisition and payment internal control. It should not be surprising, therefore, that tests of controls for the acquisition and payment cycle receive a considerable amount of attention in well-conducted audits, especially when the client has effective internal control.

FIGURE 17–3

Methodology for
Designing Tests of
Controls for
Acquisitions and
Payments

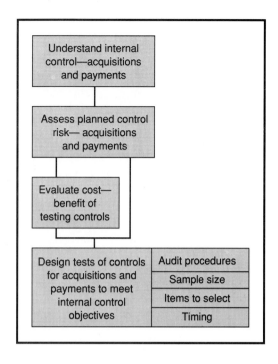

OBJECTIVE 2

Design and perform
tests of controls for the
acquisition and payment
cycle, and assess
related control risk.

Tests of controls for the acquisition and payment cycle are divided into two broad areas: *tests of acquisitions* and *tests of payments*. Acquisition tests concern three of the four functions discussed earlier in the chapter: processing purchase orders, receiving goods and services, and recognizing the liability. Tests of payments concern the fourth function, processing and recording cash disbursements.

The seven detailed internal control objectives developed in Chapter 9 are again used as the frame of reference for designing tests of acquisition and payment controls. For each objective, the auditor must go through the same logical process that has been discussed in previous chapters. First, the auditor must understand internal control to determine which controls exist. After the auditor has identified existing controls and weaknesses for each objective, an initial assessment of control risk can be made for each objective. At this point, the auditor must decide which controls he or she plans to test for control to satisfy the initial assessment of control risk. The substantive tests for monetary errors related to the objectives can be determined largely on the basis of this assessment and planned testing. After the auditor has developed the audit procedures for each objective, the procedures can be combined into an audit program that can be efficiently performed. Figure 17–3 summarizes that methodology. It is the same one used in Chapter 11 for sales and cash receipts. Again, the emphasis in the methodology is on determining the appropriate audit procedures, sample size, items to select, and timing.

*Verifying
Acquisitions*

Key internal controls and common tests of controls for each internal control objective are summarized in Table 17–1. An assumption underlying the internal controls and audit procedures is the existence of a separate acquisitions journal for recording all acquisitions.

TABLE 17–1 Summary of Objectives, Controls, and Tests of Controls for Acquisitions

INTERNAL CONTROL OBJECTIVE	KEY INTERNAL CONTROL	COMMON TESTS OF CONTROLS	
Recorded acquisitions are for goods and services received, consistent with the best interests of the client (validity).	Existence of purchase requisition, purchase order, receiving report, and vendor's invoice attached to the voucher.†	Examine documents in voucher for existence.	Review the acquisitions journal, general ledger, and accounts payable master file for large or unusual amounts.*
	Approval of acquisitions at the proper level.	Examine indication of approval.	Examine underlying documents for reasonableness and authenticity (vendors' invoices, receiving reports, purchase orders, and requisitions).
	Cancelation of documents to prevent their reuse.	Examine indication of cancelation.	
	Internal verification of vendors' invoices, receiving reports, purchase orders, and purchase requisitions.†	Examine indication of internal verification.	Trace inventory purchases to inventory master file. Examine permanent assets acquired.
Acquisition transactions are authorized (authorization).	Approval of acquisitions at the proper level.	Examine indication of approval.	Examine supporting documentation for propriety.
Existing acquisition transactions are recorded (completeness).	Purchase orders are prenumbered and accounted for.	Account for a sequence of purchase orders.	Trace from a file of receiving reports to the acquisitions journal.†
	Receiving reports are prenumbered and accounted for.†	Account for a sequence of receiving reports.	
	Vouchers are prenumbered and accounted for.	Account for a sequence of vouchers.	Trace from a file of vendor's invoices to the acquisitions journal.
Recorded acquisition transactions are correctly valued (valuation).	Internal verification of calculations and amounts.	Examine indication of internal verification.	Compare recorded transactions in the acquisitions journal with the vendor's invoice, receiving report, and other supporting documentation.†
	Batch totals are compared with computer summary reports.	Examine file of batch totals for initials of data control clerk; compare totals to summary reports.‡	Recompute the clerical accuracy on the vendors' invoices, including discounts and freight.
Acquisition transactions are properly classified (classification).	Adequate chart of accounts.	Examine procedures manual and chart of accounts.	Compare classification with chart of accounts by reference to vendors' invoices.
	Internal verification of classification.	Examine indication of internal verification.	
Acquisition transactions are recorded on a timely basis (timeliness).	Procedures require recording transactions as soon as possible after the goods and services have been received.	Examine procedures manual and observe whether unrecorded vendors' invoices exist.	Compare dates of receiving reports and vendors' invoices with dates in the acquisitions journal.†
	Internal verification.	Examine indication of internal verification.	
Acquisition transactions are properly included in the accounts payable and inventory master files, and are properly summarized (posting and summarization).	Internal verification of accounts payable master file contents.	Examine indication of internal verification.	Test clerical accuracy by footing the journals and tracing postings to general ledger and accounts payable and inventory master files.
	Comparison of accounts payable master file or trial balance totals with general ledger balance.	Examine initials on general ledger accounts indicating comparison.	

* This analytical procedure can also apply to other objectives including completeness, valuation, and timeliness.

† Receiving reports are used only for tangible goods and are therefore not available for services, such as utilities and repairs and maintenance. Frequently, vendors' invoices are the only documentation available.

‡ This control would be tested on many audits by using the computer.

In studying Table 17–1, it is important to relate internal controls to control objectives and to relate tests of controls to both internal controls and to monetary errors that would be absent or present due to controls and weaknesses in the system. It should be kept in mind that a set of procedures for a particular audit engagement will vary with the internal controls and other circumstances.

Four of the seven audit objectives for acquisitions deserve special attention. A discussion of each of these objectives follows.

Recorded acquisitions are for goods and services received, consistent with the best interests of the client (validity) If the auditor is satisfied that the controls are adequate for this objective, tests for improper and invalid transactions can be greatly reduced. Adequate controls are likely to prevent the client from including as a business expense or asset those transactions that primarily benefit management or other employees rather than the entity being audited. In some instances improper transactions are obvious, such as the acquisition of unauthorized personal items by employees or the actual embezzlement of cash by recording a fraudulent purchase in the voucher register. In other instances the propriety of a transaction is more difficult to evaluate, such as the payment of officers' memberships to country clubs, expense-paid vacations to foreign countries for members of management and their families, and management-approved illegal payments to officials of foreign countries. If the controls over improper or invalid transactions are inadequate, extensive examination of supporting documentation is necessary.

Existing acquisitions are recorded (completeness) Failure to record the acquisition of goods and services received directly affects the balance in accounts payable. The auditor can understand and test internal control to reduce assessed control risk and thereby reduce the tests of details of accounts payable if he or she is confident that all acquisitions are recorded on a timely and accurate basis. Since the audit of accounts payable generally takes a considerable amount of audit time, effective internal control, properly tested, can significantly reduce audit costs.

Acquisitions are correctly valued (valuation) Since the valuation of many asset, liability, and expense accounts depends on the correct recording of transactions in the acquisitions journal, the extent of tests of details of many balance sheet and expense accounts depends on the auditor's evaluation of the effectiveness of the internal controls over the correct valuation of acquisitions transactions. For example, if the auditor believes the permanent assets are correctly valued in the books of original entry, it is acceptable to vouch fewer current period acquisitions than if the controls are inadequate.

When a client uses perpetual inventory records, the tests of details of inventory can also be significantly reduced if the auditor believes the perpetuals are accurate. The controls over the acquisitions included in the perpetuals are normally tested as a part of the tests of controls for acquisitions, and the controls over this objective play a key role in the audit. The inclusion of both quantity and unit costs in the inventory perpetual records permits a reduction in the tests of the physical count and the unit costs of inventory if the controls are operating effectively.

Acquisitions are correctly classified (classification) The auditor can reduce the tests of details of certain individual accounts if he or she believes internal control is adequate to provide reasonable assurance of correct classification in the acquisitions journal. Although all accounts are affected to some degree by effective controls over classification, the two areas most affected are current period acquisitions of permanent assets and all expense accounts, such as repairs and maintenance, utilities, and advertising. Since vouching of current period permanent asset acquisitions for valuation and classification and verifying the classification of expense accounts are relatively time-consuming audit procedures, the saving in audit time can be significant.

Verifying Cash Disbursements

The basic format used for acquisitions is also used in Table 17–2 for the internal controls and tests of controls procedures for cash disbursements. The assumption underlying these controls and audit procedures is the existence of a separate cash disbursements and acquisitions journal. The comments made about the methodology and process for developing audit procedures for acquisitions apply equally to cash disbursements.

Once the auditor has decided on procedures, the acquisitions and cash disbursements tests are typically performed concurrently. For example, for a transaction selected for examination from the acquisitions journal, the vendor's invoice and the receiving report are examined at the same time as the related canceled cheque. Thus, the verification is speeded up without reducing the effectiveness of the tests.

Attributes Sampling for Tests of Controls

Because of the importance of tests of controls for acquisitions and payments, the use of attributes sampling is common in this audit area. The approach is basically the same as for the tests of sales transactions discussed in Chapter 12. It should be noted, however, with particular reference to the most essential objectives presented earlier, that most of the important attributes in the acquisition and payment cycle have a direct monetary effect on the accounts. Further, many of the types of errors that may be found represent a misstatement of earnings and are of significant concern to the auditor. For example, there may be inventory cutoff errors or an incorrect recording of an expense amount. Because of this, the tolerable deviation rate selected by the auditor in tests of many of the attributes in this cycle is relatively low. Since the dollar amounts of individual transactions in the cycle cover a wide range, it is also common to segregate very large and unusual items and to test them on a 100 percent basis.

 **Accounts Payable**

Accounts payable are *unpaid obligations* for goods and services received in the ordinary course of business. It is sometimes difficult to distinguish between accounts payable and accrued liabilities, but it is useful to define a liability as an account payable if the total amount of the obligation is *known and owed at the balance sheet date*. The accounts payable account therefore includes obligations for the acquisition of raw materials, equipment, utilities, repairs, and many other types of goods and services that were received before the end of the year. The great majority of accounts payable can also be recognized by the existence of vendors' invoices for the obligation. Accounts payable should also be distinguished from interest-bearing obligations. If an obligation includes the payment of interest, it should be recorded properly as a note payable, contract payable, mortgage payable, or bond.

TABLE 17–2   Summary of Objectives, Controls, and Tests of Controls for Cash Disbursements

INTERNAL CONTROL OBJECTIVE	KEY INTERNAL CONTROL	COMMON TESTS OF CONTROLS	
Recorded cash disbursements are for goods and services actually received (validity).	Adequate segregation of duties between accounts payable and custody of signed cheques.	Discuss with personnel and observe activities.	Review the cash disbursements journal, general ledger, and accounts payable master file for large or unusual amounts.*
	Examination of supporting documentation before signing of cheques by an authorized person.	Discuss with personnel and observe activities.	Trace the canceled cheque to the related acquisitions journal entry and examine for payee name and amount.
	Internal verification.	Examine indication of internal verification.	Examine canceled cheque for authorized signature, proper endorsement, and cancelation by the bank.
Recorded cash disbursement transactions are properly authorized (authorization).	Approval of payment on supporting documents at the time cheques are signed.	Examine indication of approval.	Examine supporting documents as a part of the tests of acquisitions.
Existing cash disbursement transactions are recorded (completeness).	Cheques are prenumbered and accounted for. A bank reconciliation is prepared monthly by an employee independent of recording cash disbursements or custody of assets.	Account for a sequence of cheques. Examine bank reconciliations and observe their preparation.	Reconcile recorded cash disbursements with the cash disbursements on the bank statement (proof of cash disbursements).
Recorded cash disbursement transactions are properly valued (valuation).	Internal verification of calculations and amounts. Monthly preparation of a bank reconciliation by an independent person.	Examine indication of internal verification. Examine bank reconciliations and observe their preparation.	Compare canceled cheques with the related acquisitions journal and cash disbursements journal entries. Recompute cash discounts. Prepare a proof of cash disbursements.
Cash disbursement transactions are properly classified (classification).	Adequate chart of accounts. Internal verification of classification.	Examine procedures manual and chart of accounts. Examine indication of internal verification.	Compare classification with chart of accounts by reference to vendors' invoices and acquisitions journal.
Cash disbursement transactions are recorded on a timely basis (timeliness).	Procedures require recording of transactions as soon as possible after the cheque has been signed. Internal verification.	Examine procedures manual and observe whether unrecorded cheques exist. Examine indication of internal verification.	Compare dates on canceled cheques with the cash disbursements journal. Compare dates on canceled cheques with the bank cancelation date.
Cash disbursement transactions are properly included in the accounts payable master file and are properly summarized (posting and summarization).	Internal verification of accounts payable master file contents. Comparison of accounts payable master file or trial balance totals with general ledger balance.	Examine indication of internal verification. Examine initials on general ledger accounts indicating comparison.	Test clerical accuracy by footing journals and tracing postings to general ledger and accounts payable master file.

* This analytical procedure can also apply to other objectives including completeness, evaluation, and timeliness.

FIGURE 17–4

Methodology for
Designing Tests of
Details of Balances for
Accounts Payable

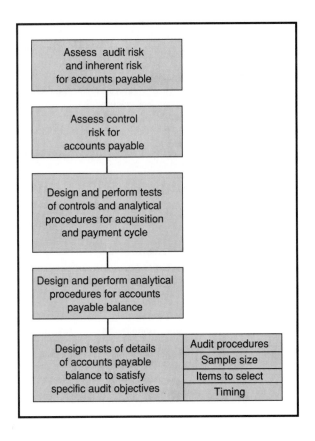

The methodology for designing tests of details for accounts payable is summarized in Figure 17–4. This methodology is the same as that used for accounts receivable in Chapter 13. It is common for accounts payable to be material and thus there may be several inherent risks. Internal controls are often ineffective for accounts payable because many companies depend on the vendors to bill them and remind them of unpaid bills. Tests of details for accounts payable, therefore, often need to be extensive.

OBJECTIVE 3

Discuss the nature of
accounts payable, and
describe the related
controls.

Internal Controls

The effects of the client's internal controls on accounts payable tests can be illustrated by two examples. In the first, assume the client has highly effective internal control of recording and paying for acquisitions. The receipt of goods is promptly documented by prenumbered receiving reports; prenumbered vouchers are promptly and efficiently prepared and recorded in the acquisition transactions file and the accounts payable master file. Payments are also made promptly when due, and the disbursements are immediately recorded in the cash disbursements transactions file and the accounts payable master file. On a monthly basis, individual accounts payable balances or the master file are reconciled with vendors' statements, and the total is compared with the general ledger by an independent person. Under these circumstances, the verification of accounts payable should require little audit effort once the auditor concludes that internal control is operating effectively.

TABLE 17–3

Analytical Procedures for Acquisition and Payments

ANALYTICAL PROCEDURE	POSSIBLE MISSTATEMENT
Compare related expense account balances with prior years.	Misstatement of accounts payable and expenses.
Review list of accounts payable for unusual, nonvendor, and interest-bearing payables.	Classification error for nontrade liabilities.
Compare individual accounts payable with previous years.	Unrecorded or invalid accounts, or misstatements.
Calculate ratio such as purchases divided by accounts payable, and accounts payable divided by current liabilities.	Unrecorded or invalid accounts, or misstatements.

In the second example, assume receiving reports are not used, the client defers recording acquisitions until cash disbursements are made, and, because of a weak cash position, bills are frequently paid several months after their due date. When an auditor faces such a situation, there is a high likelihood of an understatement of accounts payable; therefore, under these circumstances, extensive tests of details of accounts payable are necessary to determine whether accounts payable is properly stated at the balance sheet date.

The most important controls over accounts payable have already been discussed as part of the control and recording of acquisitions and cash disbursements. In addition to those controls, it is important to have a monthly reconciliation of vendors' statements with recorded liabilities and the accounts payable master file with the general ledger. This should be done by an independent person.

Analytical Procedures

The use of analytical procedures is as important in the acquisition and payment cycle as it is in every other cycle. Table 17–3 illustrates analytical procedures for the balance sheet and income statement accounts in the acquisition and payment cycle that are useful for uncovering areas in which additional investigation is desirable.

One of the most important analytical procedures for uncovering misstatements of accounts payable is comparing current-year expense totals to prior years. For example, by comparing utilities expense to the prior year, the auditor may determine that the last utilities bill for the year was not recorded. Comparing expenses to prior years is an effective analytical procedure for accounts payable because expenses from year to year are relatively stable.

OBJECTIVE 4

Design and perform analytical procedures for accounts payable.

Audit Objectives for Tests of Details

The overall objective in the audit of accounts payable is to determine whether accounts payable is fairly stated and properly disclosed. Seven of the eight specific audit objectives discussed in Chapter 5 are applicable to accounts payable. Although technically liabilities can be owned, that objective is ignored by most auditors.

The auditor should recognize the difference in emphasis between the audit of liabilities and the audit of assets. When assets are being verified, attention is focused on making certain that the balance in the account is not overstated. The validity of recorded assets is constantly questioned and verified by confirmation, physical examination, and examination of supporting documents. The auditor should certainly not ignore the possibility of assets being understated, but the fact remains that the auditor is more concerned about the possibility of overstatement

OBJECTIVE 5

Design and perform tests of details for accounts payable.

than understatement. The opposite approach is taken in verifying liability balances; that is, the main focus is on the discovery of understated or omitted liabilities.

The difference in emphasis in auditing assets and liabilities results directly from the *legal liability of public accountants*. If equity investors, creditors, and other users determine subsequent to the issuance of the audited financial statements that owners' equity was materially overstated, a lawsuit against the public accounting firm is fairly likely. Since an overstatement of owners' equity can arise either from an overstatement of assets or from an understatement of liabilities, it is natural for public accountants to emphasize those two types of misstatements. The probability of a successful lawsuit against a public accountant for failing to discover an understatement of owners' equity is far less likely.

Nevertheless, the auditing profession must avoid too much emphasis on protecting users from overstatements of owners' equity at the expense of ignoring understatements. If assets are consistently understated and liabilities are consistently overstated for large numbers of audited companies, the decision-making value of financial statement information is likely to decline. Therefore, even though it is natural for auditors to emphasize the possibility of overstating assets and understating liabilities, uncovering the opposite types of misstatements is also a significant responsibility.

Tests of Details of Accounts Payable

The same specific audit objectives, with minor modifications, that were used as a frame of reference for verifying accounts receivable in Chapter 13 are also applicable to liabilities. The most obvious difference in verifying liabilities is the nonapplicability of the ownership objective. Ownership is an important part of verifying assets but not liabilities. The second difference was discussed above: In auditing liabilities, the emphasis is on the search for understatements rather than for overstatements.

Table 17–4 includes the detailed objectives and common tests of details of balances procedures for accounts payable. The actual audit procedures will vary considerably depending on the materiality of accounts payable, the nature and effectiveness of internal control, and such things as acceptable audit risk and results of prior-year tests.

Out-of-Period Liabilities Tests

Because of the emphasis on understatements in liability accounts, out-of-period liability tests are important for accounts payable. The extent of tests to uncover unrecorded accounts payable, frequently referred to as the *search for unrecorded accounts payable*, depends heavily on assessed control risk and the materiality of the potential balance in the account. The same audit procedures to uncover unrecorded payables are applicable to the valuation objective. The audit procedures that follow are typical tests.

Examine underlying documentation for subsequent cash disbursements The purpose of this audit procedure is to uncover payments made in the subsequent accounting period that represent liabilities at the balance sheet date. The supporting documentation is examined to determine whether a payment was for a current period obligation. For example, if inventory was received prior to the balance sheet date, it will be so indicated on the receiving report. Frequently, documentation for payments made in the subsequent period are examined for several weeks, especially when the client does not pay its bills on a timely basis. Any payment

SPECIFIC AUDIT OBJECTIVE	COMMON TESTS OF DETAILS OF BALANCES PROCEDURES	COMMENTS
Accounts payable in the accounts payable list agree with related master file, and the total is correctly added and agrees with the general ledger (mechanical accuracy).	Foot the accounts payable list. Trace the total to the general ledger. Trace individual vendor's invoices to master file for names and amounts.	All pages need not ordinarily be footed. Unless controls are weak, tracing to master file should be limited.
Accounts payable in the accounts payable list are valid (validity).	Trace from accounts payable list to vendors' invoices and statements. Confirm accounts payable, emphasizing large and unusual amounts.	Ordinarily receives little attention because the primary concern is with understatements.
Existing accounts payable are in the accounts payable list (completeness).	Perform out-of-period liability tests (see discussion).	These are essential audit tests for accounts payable.
Accounts payable in the accounts payable list are properly valued (valuation).	Perform same procedures as those used for validity and out-of-period liability tests.	Ordinarily, the auditor is more concerned with understatements than with overstatements. The emphasis in these procedures for valuation is understatement rather than omission.
Accounts payable in the accounts payable list are properly classified (classification).	Review the list and master file for related parties, notes or other interest-bearing liabilities, long-term payables, and debit balances.	Knowledge of the client's business is essential for these tests.
Transactions in the acquisition and payment cycle are recorded in the proper period (cutoff).	Perform out-of-period liability tests (see discussion). Perform detailed tests as a part of physical observation of inventory (see discussion). Test for inventory in transit (see discussion).	These are essential audit tests for accounts payable. These are referred to as cutoff tests.
Accounts in the acquisition and payment cycle are properly disclosed (disclosure).	Review statements to make sure material related party, long-term, and interest-bearing liabilities are segregated.	Ordinarily not a problem.

that is for a current period obligation should be traced to the accounts payable trial balance to make sure it has been included as a liability.

Examine underlying documentation for bills not paid several weeks after the year-end This procedure is carried out in the same manner as the preceding one and serves the same purpose. The only difference is that it is done for unpaid obligations near the end of the examination rather than for obligations that have already been paid. For example, in an audit with a March 31 year-end, if the auditor examines the supporting documentation for cheques paid until June 28, bills that are still unpaid at that date should be examined to determine whether they are obligations of the year ended March 31.

Trace receiving reports issued before year-end to related vendors' invoices All merchandise received before the year end of the accounting period, indicated by the issuance of a receiving report, should be included as accounts payable. By tracing receiving reports issued at and before year-end to vendors' invoices and making sure they are included in accounts payable, the auditor is testing for unrecorded obligations.

Trace vendors' statements that show a balance due to the accounts payable trial balance If the client maintains a file of vendors' statements, any statement indicating a balance due can be traced to the listing to make sure it is included as an account payable.

Send confirmations to vendors with which the client does business Although the use of confirmations for accounts payable is less common than for accounts receivable, it is often used to test for vendors omitted from the accounts payable list, omitted transactions, and misstated account balances. Sending confirmations to active vendors for which a balance has not been included in the accounts payable list is a useful means of searching for omitted amounts. This type of confirmation is commonly referred to as *zero balance confirmation*. Additional discussion of confirmation of accounts payable is deferred until the end of the chapter.

Cutoff Tests   Cutoff tests for accounts payable are intended to determine whether transactions recorded a few days before and after the balance sheet date are included in the correct period. The five audit procedures discussed in the preceding section are directly related to cutoff for acquisitions, but they emphasize understatements. For the first three procedures, it is also appropriate to examine supporting documentation as a test of overstatement of accounts payable. For example, the third procedure is to trace receiving reports issued before year-end to related vendors' invoices in order to test for unrecorded accounts payable. To test for overstatement cutoff errors, the auditor should trace receiving reports issued *after* year-end to related invoices to make sure they are not recorded as accounts payable (unless they are inventory in transit, which will be discussed shortly). As has been previously stated, auditors are usually more concerned about understatements of liabilities than overstatements.

Since most cutoff tests have already been discussed, only two aspects are enlarged upon here: the examination of receiving reports and the determination of the amount of inventory in transit.

Relationship of cutoff to physical observation of inventory In determining that the accounts payable cutoff is correct, *it is essential that the cutoff tests be coordinated with the physical observation of inventory*. For example, assume that an inventory acquisition for $40,000 is received late in the afternoon of December 31, after the physical inventory is completed. If the acquisition is included in accounts payable and purchases, but excluded from inventory, the result is an understatement of net earnings of $40,000. Conversely, if the acquisition is excluded from both inventory and accounts payable, there is an error in the balance sheet, but the income statement is correct. The only way the auditor will know which type of error has occurred is to coordinate cutoff tests with the observation of inventory.

The cutoff information for purchases should be obtained *during the physical observation* of the inventory. At this time the auditor should review the procedures in the receiving department to determine that all inventory received was counted, and the auditor should record in his or her working papers the last receiving report number of inventory included in the physical count. During the year-end field work, the auditor should then test the accounting records for cutoff. The auditor should trace receiving report numbers to the accounts payable records to verify that they are correctly included or excluded.

For example, assume that the last receiving report number representing inventory included in the physical count was 3167. The auditor should record this document number and subsequently trace it and several preceding numbers to their related vendor's invoice and to the accounts payable list or the accounts payable master file to determine that they are all included. Similarly, accounts payable for purchases recorded on receiving reports with numbers larger than 3167 should be excluded from accounts payable.

When the client's physical inventory takes place before the last day of the year, it is still necessary to perform an accounts payable cutoff at the time of the physical count in the manner described in the preceding paragraph. In addition, the auditor must verify whether all acquisitions taking place between the physical count and the end of the year were added to the physical inventory and accounts payable. For example, if the client takes the physical count on December 27 for a December 31 year-end, the cutoff information is taken as of December 27. During the year-end field work, the auditor must first test to determine whether the cutoff was accurate as of December 27. After determining that the December 27 cutoff is accurate, the auditor must test whether all inventory received subsequent to the physical count, but before the balance sheet date, was added to inventory and accounts payable by the client.

Inventory in transit A distinction in accounts payable must be made between acquisitions of inventory that are on an *FOB destination* basis and those that are made *FOB origin* (or FOB shipping point). With the former, title passes to the buyer when it is received for inventory. Therefore, only inventory received prior to the balance sheet date should be included in inventory and accounts payable at year-end. When a purchase is on an FOB origin basis, the inventory and related accounts payable must be recorded in the current period if shipment occurred before the balance sheet date.

Determining whether inventory has been purchased on an FOB destination or origin basis is done by examining vendors' invoices. The auditor should examine invoices for merchandise received shortly after year-end to determine if they were on an FOB origin basis. For those that were, and when the shipment dates were prior to the balance sheet date, the inventory and related accounts payable must be recorded in the current period if the amounts are material.

Reliability of Evidence In deciding upon the appropriate evidence to accumulate for verifying accounts payable, it is essential that the auditor understand the relative reliability of the three primary types of evidence ordinarily used: vendors' invoices, vendors' statements, and confirmations.

Distinction between vendors' invoices and vendors' statements In verifying the valuation of an account balance, the auditor should make a major distinction between vendors' invoices and vendors' statements. In examining vendors' invoices and related supporting documents, such as receiving reports and purchase orders, the auditor gets highly reliable *evidence of the valuation of individual transactions*. A vendor's statement is not as desirable as invoices for verifying individual transactions because a statement only includes the total amount of the transaction. The units acquired, price, freight, and other data are not included. However, a statement has the advantage of including the ending balance according to the vendor's records. Which of these two documents is better for verifying the correct balance in accounts payable? *The vendor's statement is superior for verifying accounts payable* because it includes the ending balance. The auditor could compare existing vendors' invoices with the client's list and still not uncover missing ones, which is the primary concern in accounts payable. Which of these two documents is better for testing acquisitions in tests of controls? *The vendor's invoice is superior for verifying transactions* because the auditor is verifying individual transactions and the invoice shows the details of the acquisitions.

Difference between vendors' statements and confirmations The most important distinction between a vendor's statement and a confirmation of accounts payable is the source of the information. A vendor's statement has been prepared by an independent third party, but it is in the hands of the client at the time the auditor examines it. This provides the client with an opportunity to alter a vendor's statement or not make particular statements available to the auditor. A confirmation of accounts payable, which normally is a request for an itemized statement sent directly to the public accountant's office, provides the same information but can be regarded as more reliable. In addition, confirmations of accounts payable frequently include a request for information about notes and acceptances payable as well as consigned inventory that is owned by the vendor but stored on the client's premises. An illustration of a typical accounts payable confirmation request is given in Figure 17–5.

Because of the availability of vendors' statements and vendors' invoices, which are both relatively reliable evidence because they originate from a third party, the confirmation of accounts payable is less common than confirmation of accounts receivable. If the client has adequate internal control and vendors' statements are available for examination, confirmations are normally not sent. However, when the client's internal control is weak, when statements are not available, or when the auditor questions the client's integrity, it is desirable to send confirmation requests to vendors. Because of the emphasis on understatements of liability accounts, the accounts confirmed should include large accounts, active accounts, accounts with a zero balance, and a representative sample of all others.

In most instances in which accounts payable are confirmed, it is done shortly after the balance sheet date. However, if assessed control risk is low, it may be possible to confirm accounts payable at an interim date as a test of the effectiveness of internal control. Then if the confirmation indicates that the internal controls are ineffective, it is possible to design other audit procedures to test accounts payable at year-end.

When vendors' statements are examined or confirmations are received, there must be a *reconciliation* of the statement or confirmation with the accounts payable list. Frequently, differences are caused by inventory in transit, cheques mailed by the

FIGURE 17–5

Accounts Payable
Confirmation Request

Roger Mead Ltd.
1600 Westmount Ave. N.
Kenora, Ontario
P9N 1X7

January 15, 19X8

Szabo Sales Co. Ltd.
2116 King Street
Kenora, Ontario
P9N 1G3

To whom it may concern:

Our auditors, Adams and Lelik, CAs, are making an examination of our financial statements. For this purpose, please furnish directly to them, at their address noted below, the
following information as of December 31, 19X7.

   (1) Itemized statements of our accounts payable to you showing all unpaid items.

   (2) A complete list of any notes and acceptances payable to you (including any
which have been discounted) showing the original date, dates due, original
amount, unpaid balance, collateral and endorsers; and

   (3) An itemized list of your merchandise consigned to us.

Your prompt attention to this request will be appreciated. A stamped, addressed envelope is enclosed for your reply.

Yours truly,

Adams & Lelik

Adams and Lelik
Chartered Accountants
215 Tecumseh Crescent
Kenora, Ontario
P9N 2K5

client but not received by the vendor at the statement date, and delays in processing
the accounting records. The reconciliation is of the same general nature as that
discussed in Chapter 13 for accounts receivable. The documents typically used to
reconcile the balances on the accounts payable list with the confirmation or vendor's
statement include receiving reports, vendors' invoices, and canceled cheques.

Sample Size Sample sizes for accounts payable tests vary considerably depending on such
factors as the materiality of accounts payable, number of accounts outstanding,
assessed control risk, and results of the prior year. When a client's internal control
is weak, which is not uncommon for accounts payable, almost all population items
must be verified. In other situations, minimal testing is needed.

    Statistical sampling is less commonly used for the audit of accounts payable
than for accounts receivable. It is more difficult to define the population and
determine the population size in accounts payable. Since the emphasis is on
omitted accounts payable, it is essential that the population include all potential
payables. Defining the population to include all potential payables often makes

the population size unmanageable. Two examples in which variables sampling could practically be used to test accounts payable are:

- The auditor is satisfied that all vendors' names are included in the accounts payable list even though some may be at the wrong amount. The population is defined as all vendors on the list. The emphases on the tests are validity, valuation, and classification.
- The auditor is satisfied that all accounts payable at the balance sheet date have been paid subsequent to year-end. The population is defined as all disbursements subsequent to year-end.

REVIEW QUESTIONS

17–1   List five asset accounts, three liability accounts, and five expense accounts included in the acquisition and payment cycle for a typical manufacturing company.

17–2   List one possible internal control for each of the seven internal control objectives for cash disbursements. For each control, list a test of control procedure to test its effectiveness.

17–3   List one possible control for each of the seven internal control objectives for acquisitions. For each control, list a test of control procedure to test its effectiveness.

17–4   Evaluate the following statement by an auditor concerning tests of acquisitions and payments: "In selecting the acquisitions and disbursements sample for testing, the best approach is to select a random month and test every transaction for the period. Using this approach enables me to thoroughly understand internal control because I have examined everything that happened during the period. As a part of the monthly test, I also test the beginning and ending bank reconciliations and prepare a proof of cash for the month. At the completion of these tests I feel I can evaluate the effectiveness of internal control."

17–5   What is the importance of cash discounts to the client and how can the auditor verify whether they are being taken in accordance with company policy?

17–6   What are the similarities and differences in the objectives of the following two procedures: (1) select a random sample of receiving reports and trace them to related vendors' invoices and acquisitions journal entries, comparing the vendor's name, type of material and quantity purchased, and total amount of the acquisition, and (2) select a random sample of acquisitions journal entries and trace them to related vendors' invoices and receiving reports, comparing the vendor's name, type of material and quantity purchased, and total amount of the acquisition.

17–7   If an audit client does not have prenumbered cheques, what type of misstatement has a greater chance of occurring? Under the circumstances, what audit procedure can the auditor use to compensate for the weakness?

17–8   What is meant by a voucher and a voucher register? Explain how their use can improve an organization's internal controls.

17–9   Explain why most auditors consider the receipt of goods and services the most important point in the acquisition and payment cycle.

17–10 Explain the relationship between tests of the acquisition and payment cycle and tests of inventory. Give specific examples of how these two types of tests affect each other.

17–11 Explain the relationship between tests of the acquisition and payment cycle and tests of accounts payable. Give specific examples of how these two types of tests affect each other.

17–12   A common audit procedure is to review payments made by the client subsequent to the year end. What is the reason for this procedure and what does it prove?

17–13   Explain why it is common for auditors to send confirmation requests to vendors with "zero balances" on the client's accounts payable listing, but uncommon to follow the same approach in verifying accounts receivable.

17–14   Distinguish between a vendor's invoice and a vendor's statement. Which document should ideally be used as evidence in auditing acquisition transactions and which for directly verifying accounts payable balances? Why?

17–15   It is less common to confirm accounts payable at an interim date than accounts receivable. Explain why.

17–16   In testing the cutoff of accounts payable at the balance sheet date, explain why it is important that auditors coordinate their tests with the physical observation of inventory. What can the auditor do during the physical inventory to enhance the likelihood of an accurate cutoff?

17–17   Distinguish between FOB destination and FOB origin. What procedures should the auditor follow concerning acquisitions of inventory on an FOB origin basis near year-end?

MULTIPLE CHOICE QUESTIONS

17–18   The following questions concern internal controls in the acquisition and payment cycle. Choose the best response.

a. Effective internal control over the purchasing of raw materials should usually include all of the following procedures *except*

(1)   systematic reporting of product changes that will affect raw materials.

(2)   determining the need for the raw materials prior to preparing the purchase order.

(3)   obtaining third-party, written quality and quantity reports prior to payment for the raw materials.

(4)   obtaining financial approval prior to making a commitment.

b. Budd, the purchasing agent of Lake Hardware Wholesalers Ltd., has a relative who owns a retail hardware store. Budd arranged for hardware to be delivered by manufacturers to the retail store on a COD basis, thereby enabling his relative to buy at Lake's wholesale prices. Budd was probably able to accomplish this because of Lake's poor internal control over

(1)   purchase requisitions.

(2)   cash receipts.

(3)   perpetual inventory records.

(4)   purchase orders.

c. Which of the following is an internal control procedure that would prevent paid disbursement documents from being presented for payment a second time?

(1)   Unsigned cheques should be prepared by individuals who are responsible for signing disbursement cheques.

(2)   Disbursement documents should be approved by at least two responsible management officials.

(3)   The date on disbursement documents should be within a few days of the date the document is presented for payment.

(4)   The official signing the cheque should compare the cheque with the documents and should deface the documents.

d. The public accountant examines all unrecorded invoices on hand as of February 29, 19X8, the last day of field work. Which of the following errors is most likely to be uncovered by this procedure?

(1) Accounts payable are overstated at December 31, 19X7.

(2) Accounts payable are understated at December 31, 19X7.

(3) Operating expenses are overstated for the twelve months ended December 31, 19X7.

(4) Operating expenses are overstated for the two months ended February 29, 19X8. (AICPA adapted)

17–19 The following questions concern accumulating evidence in the acquisition and payment cycle. Choose the best response.

a. In comparing the confirmation of accounts payable with suppliers and confirmation of accounts receivable with debtors, the true statement is that

(1) confirmation of accounts payable with suppliers is a more widely accepted auditing procedure than is confirmation of accounts receivable with debtors.

(2) statistical sampling techniques are more widely accepted in the confirmation of accounts payable than in the confirmation of accounts receivable.

(3) as compared with the confirmation of accounts payable, the confirmation of accounts receivable will tend to emphasize accounts with zero balances at the balance sheet date.

(4) it is less likely that the confirmation request sent to the supplier will show the amount owed her than that the request sent to the debtor will show the amount due from him.

b. As part of her search for unrecorded liabilities, a public accountant examines invoices and account payable vouchers. In general this examination may be limited to

(1) unpaid accounts payable vouchers and unvouchered invoices on hand at the balance sheet date.

(2) accounts payable vouchers prepared during the subsequent period and unvouchered invoices received through the last day of field work, the dollar values of which exceed reasonable amounts.

(3) invoices received through the last day of field work (whether or not accounts payable vouchers have been prepared) but must include all invoices of any amount received during this period.

(4) a reasonable period following the balance sheet date, normally the same period used for the cutoff bank statement.

c. In order to efficiently establish the correctness of the accounts payable cutoff, an auditor will be *most* likely to

(1) coordinate cutoff tests with physical inventory observation.

(2) compare cutoff reports with purchase orders.

(3) compare vendors' invoices with vendors' statements.

(4) coordinate mailing of confirmations with cutoff tests.

(AICPA adapted)

DISCUSSION QUESTIONS AND PROBLEMS

17–20 Questions 1 through 8 are typically found in questionnaires used by auditors to obtain an understanding of internal control in the acquisition and payment cycle. In using the questionnaire for a particular client, a "yes" response to a question indicates a possible internal control, whereas a "no" indicates a potential weakness.

1. Is the purchasing function performed by personnel who are independent of the receiving and shipping functions and the payables and disbursing functions?
2. Are all vendors' invoices routed directly to accounting from the mailroom?
3. Are all receiving reports prenumbered and the numerical sequence checked by a person independent of receiving?
4. Are all extensions, footings, discounts, and freight terms on vendors' invoices checked for accuracy?
5. Does a responsible employee review and approve the invoice account distribution before it is recorded in the purchases journal?
6. Are cheques recorded in the cash disbursements journal as they are prepared?
7. Are all supporting documents properly canceled at the time the cheques are signed?
8. Is the custody of cheques after signature and before mailing handled by an employee independent of all payable, disbursing, cash, and general ledger functions?

Required:

    a. For each of the preceding questions, state the internal control objective(s) being fulfilled if the control is in effect.
    b. For each internal control, list a test of control procedure to test its effectiveness.
    c. For each of the preceding questions, identify the nature of the potential financial error(s) if the control is not in effect.
    d. For each of the potential errors in part (c), list a substantive audit procedure that can be used to determine whether a material error exists.

17–21 Following are some of the tests of controls procedures frequently performed in the acquisition and payment cycle. Each is to be done on a sample basis.

1. Trace transactions recorded in the purchase journal to supporting documentation, comparing the vendor's name, total dollar amounts, and authorization for purchase.
2. Account for a sequence of receiving reports and trace selected ones to related vendors' invoices and purchases journal entries.
3. Review supporting documents for clerical accuracy, propriety of account distribution, and reasonableness of expenditure in relation to the nature of the client's operations.
4. Examine documents in support of acquisition transactions to make sure each transaction has an approved vendor's invoice, receiving report, and purchase order included.
5. Foot the cash disbursements journal, trace postings of the total to the general ledger, and trace postings of individual payments to the accounts payable master file.
6. Account for a numerical sequence of cheques in the cash disbursements journal and examine all voided or spoiled cheques for proper cancelation.
7. Prepare a proof of cash disbursements for an interim month.
8. Compare dates on canceled cheques with dates on the cash disbursements journal and the bank cancelation date.

Required: State the purpose(s) of each procedure.

17–22 The following misstatements or omissions are included in the accounting records of Westgate Manufacturing Corp.

1. Telephone expense (account 2112) was unintentionally charged to repairs and maintenance (account 2121).
2. Purchases of raw materials are frequently not recorded until several weeks

after the goods are received due to the failure of the receiving personnel to forward receiving reports to accounting. When pressure from a vendor's credit department is put on Westgate's accounting department, it searches for the receiving report, records the transactions in the acquisitions journal, and pays the bill.

3. The accounts payable clerk prepares a monthly cheque to Story Supply Company for the amount of an invoice owed and submits the unsigned cheque to the treasurer for payment along with related supporting documents that have already been approved. When she receives the signed cheque from the treasurer, she records it as a debit to accounts payable and deposits the cheque in a personal bank account for a company named Story Company. A few days later she records the invoice in the acquisitions journal again, resubmits the documents and a new cheque to the treasurer, and sends the cheque to the vendor after it has been signed.

4. The amount of a cheque in the cash disbursements journal is recorded as $4,612.87 instead of $6,412.87.

5. The accounts payable clerk intentionally excluded from the cash disbursements journal seven larger cheques written and mailed on December 26 to prevent cash in the bank from having a negative balance on the general ledger. They were recorded on January 2 of the subsequent year.

6. Each month a fictitious receiving report is submitted to accounting by an employee in the receiving department. A few days later he sends Westgate an invoice for the quantity of goods ordered from a small company he owns and operates in the evening. A cheque is prepared, and the amount is paid when the receiving report and the vendor's invoice are matched by the accounts payable clerk.

Required:

    a. For each misstatement, identify the internal control objective that was not met.

    b. For each misstatement, state a control that should have prevented it from occurring on a continuing basis.

    c. For each misstatement, state a substantive audit procedure that could uncover it.

17–23 The following auditing procedures were performed in the audit of accounts payable:

1. Examine supporting documents for cash disbursements several days before and after year-end.

2. Examine the acquisition and payment journals for the last few days of the current period and first few days of the succeeding period, looking for large or unusual transactions.

3. Trace from the general ledger trial balance and supporting working papers to determine if accounts payable, related parties, and other related assets and liabilities are properly included on the financial statements.

4. For liabilities that are payable in a foreign currency, determine the exchange rate and check calculations.

5. Discuss with the bookkeeper whether any amounts included on the accounts payable list are due to related parties, debit balances, or notes payable.

6. Obtain vendors' statements from the controller and reconcile to a listing of accounts payable.

7. Obtain vendors' statements directly from vendors and reconcile to the listing of accounts payable.

8. Obtain a list of accounts payable. Re-add and compare with the general ledger.

Required:

    a. For each procedure, identify the type of audit evidence used.

AUDIT PROCEDURE	AUDIT OBJECTIVE						
	Validity	Completeness	Valuation	Classification	Cutoff	Mechanical Accuracy	Disclosure
1		X		X			
2							
3							
4							
5							
6							
7							
8							

    b. For each procedure, use the accompanying matrix to identify which audit objective(s) were satisfied. (Procedure 1 is completed as an illustration.)

    c. Evaluate the need to have certain objectives satisfied by more than one audit procedure.

17–24 In testing cash disbursements for Immanuel Klein Ltd., you have obtained an understanding of internal control. The controls are reasonably good, and no unusual audit problems have arisen in previous years.

    Although there are not many personnel in the accounting department, there is a reasonable separation of duties in the organization. There is a separate purchasing agent who has responsibility for ordering goods and a separate receiving department for counting the goods when they are received and for preparing receiving reports. There is a separation of duties between recording acquisitions and cash disbursements, and all information is recorded in the two journals independently. The controller reviews all supporting documents before signing the cheques and immediately mailing each cheque to respective vendor. Cheque copies are used for subsequent recording.

    All aspects of internal control seem satisfactory to you, and you perform minimum tests of 75 transactions as a means of assessing control risk. In your tests you discover the following exceptions:

1. Two items in the acquisitions journal have been misclassified.

2. Three invoices had not been initialed by the controller, but there were no dollar misstatements evident in the transactions.

3. Five receiving reports were recorded in the acquisitions journal at least two weeks later than their date on the receiving report.

4. One invoice had been paid twice. The second payment was supported by a duplicate copy of the invoice. Both copies of the invoice had been marked "paid."

5. One cheque amount in the cash disbursements journal was for $100 less than the amount stated on the vendor's invoice.

6. One voided cheque was missing.

7. Two receiving reports for vendor's invoices were missing from the transaction packet. One vendor's invoice had an extension error, and the invoice had been initialed that the amount had been checked.

Required:

a. Identify whether each of 1 through 7 was a control test deviation, a monetary error, or both.

b. For each deviation or error, identify which internal control objective was not met.

c. What is the audit importance of each of these exceptions?

d. What follow-up procedures would you use to determine more about the nature of each deviation or error?

e. How would each of these deviations or errors affect the balance of your audit? Be specific.

f. Identify internal controls that should have prevented each error.

17–25 You are the staff accountant testing the combined purchase and cash disbursements journal for a small audit client. Internal control is regarded as reasonably effective, considering the number of personnel.

The in-charge auditor has decided that a sample of 80 items should be sufficient for this audit because of the excellent controls and gives you the following instructions:

1. All transactions selected must exceed $100.

2. At least 50 of the transactions must be for purchases of raw material because these transactions are typically material.

3. It is not acceptable to include the same vendor in the sample more than once.

4. All vendors' invoices that cannot be located must be replaced with a new sample item.

5. Both cheques and supporting documents are to be examined for the same transactions.

6. The sample must be random, after modifications for instructions 1 through 5.

Required:

a. Evaluate each of these instructions for testing acquisition and cash disbursements transactions.

b. Explain the difficulties of applying each of these instructions to attributes sampling.

17–26 Each year near the balance sheet date when the president of Bargon Construction, Inc., takes a three-week vacation to Bermuda, she signs several cheques to pay major bills during the period she is absent. Jack Morgan, head bookkeeper for the company, uses this practice to his advantage. Morgan makes out a cheque to himself for the amount of a large vendor's invoice, and since there is no acquisitions journal, he records the amount in the cash disbursements journal as a purchase to the supplier listed on the invoice. He holds the cheque until several weeks into the subsequent period to make sure the auditors do not get an opportunity to examine the canceled cheque. Shortly after the first of the year when the president returns, Morgan resubmits the invoice for payment and again records the cheque in the cash disbursements journal. At that point, he marks the invoice "paid" and files it with all other paid invoices. Morgan has been following this practice successfully for several years and feels confident that he has developed a foolproof method.

Required:

a. What is the auditor's responsibility for discovering this type of embezzlement?

b. What weaknesses exist in the client's internal control?

c. What audit procedures are likely to uncover the fraud?

17–27 You were in the final stages of your examination of the financial statements of Ozine Corporation for the year ended December 31, 19X7, when you were consulted by the corporation's president who believes there is no point to your examining the 19X8 purchases journal and testing data in support of 19X8 entries. He stated that (a) bills pertaining to 19X7 that were received too late to be included in the December purchases journal were recorded as of the year-end by the corporation by journal entry, (b) the internal auditor made tests after the year-end, and (c) he would furnish you with a letter certifying that there were no unrecorded liabilities.

Required:

a. Should a public accountant's test for unrecorded liabilities be affected by the fact that the client made a journal entry to record 19X7 bills that were received late? Explain.

b. Should a public accountant's test for unrecorded liabilities be affected by the fact that a letter is obtained in which a responsible management official certifies that to the best of his knowledge all liabilities have been recorded? Explain.

c. Should a public accountant's test for unrecorded liabilities be eliminated or reduced because of the internal audit tests? Explain.

d. Assume that the corporation, which handled some government contracts, had no internal auditor but that an auditor from the Auditor General's office spent three weeks auditing the records and was just completing his work at this time. How would the public accountant's unrecorded liability test be affected by the work of the auditor from the Auditor General's office?

e. What sources in addition to the 19X8 purchases journal should the public accountant consider to locate possible unrecorded liabilities?

(AICPA adapted)

17–28 Because of the small size of the company and the limited number of accounting personnel, the Dry Goods Wholesale Company Ltd. initially records all acquisitions of goods and services at the time cash disbursements are made. At the end of each quarter when financial statements for internal purposes are prepared, accounts payable are recorded by adjusting journal entries. The entries are reversed at the beginning of the subsequent period. Except for the lack of an acquisitions journal, the controls over acquisitions are excellent for a small company. (There are adequate prenumbered documents for all acquisitions, proper approvals, and adequate internal verification wherever possible.)

Before the auditor arrives for the year-end audit, the bookkeeper prepares adjusting entries to record the accounts payable as of the balance sheet date. A list of all outstanding balances is prepared, by vendor, on an accounts payable listing and is given to the auditor. All vendors' invoices supporting the list are retained in a separate file for the auditor's use.

In the current year, the accounts payable balance has increased dramatically because of a severe cash shortage. (The cash shortage apparently arose from expansion of inventory and facilities rather than lack of sales.) Many accounts have remained unpaid for several months and the client is getting pressure from several vendors to pay the bills. Since the company had a relatively profitable year, management is anxious to complete the audit as early as possible so that the audited statements can be used to obtain a large bank loan.

Required:

a. Explain how the lack of an acquisitions journal will affect the auditor's tests of controls for acquisitions and payments.

b. What should the auditor use as a sampling unit in performing tests of acquisitions?

c. Assuming no misstatements are discovered in the auditor's tests of controls for acquisitions and payments, how will that result affect the verification of accounts payable?

d. Discuss the reasonableness of the client's request for an early completion of the audit and the implications of the request from the auditor's point of view.

e. List the audit procedures that should be performed in the year-end audit of accounts payable to meet the cutoff objective.

f. State your opinion as to whether it is possible to conduct an adequate audit in these circumstances.

17–29 Mincin, a public accountant, is the auditor of the Raleigh Corporation. Mincin is considering the audit work to be performed in the accounts payable area for the current year's engagement.

The prior year's working papers show that confirmation requests were mailed to 100 of Raleigh's 1,000 suppliers. The selected suppliers were based on Mincin's sample that was designed to select accounts with large dollar balances. A substantial number of hours were spent by Raleigh and Mincin resolving relatively minor differences between the confirmation replies and Raleigh's accounting records. Alternative audit procedures were used for those suppliers who did not respond to the confirmation requests.

Required:

a. Identify the accounts payable audit objectives that Mincin must consider in determining the audit procedures to be followed.

b. Identify situations in which Mincin should use accounts payable confirmations and discuss whether Mincin is required to use them.

c. Discuss why the use of large dollar balances as the basis for selecting accounts payable for confirmation might not be the most effective approach and indicate what more effective procedures could be followed when selecting accounts payable for confirmation.

(AICPA adapted)

17–30 As part of the June 30, 19X8 audit of accounts payable of Milner Products Ltd., the auditor sent 22 confirmations of accounts payable to vendors in the form of requests for statements. Four of the statements were not returned by the vendors, and five vendors reported balances different from the amounts recorded on Milner's accounts payable master file. The auditor made duplicate copies of the five vendors' statements to maintain control of the independent information and turned the originals over to the client's accounts payable clerk to reconcile the differences. Two days later the clerk returned the five statements to the auditor with the information on the working paper as follows:

Statement 1	Balance per vendor's statement	$ 6,618.01
	Payment by Milner June 30, 19X8	(4,601.01)
	Balance per master file	$ 2,017.00
Statement 2	Balance per vendor's statement	$ 9,618.93
	Invoices not received by Milner	(2,733.18)
	Payment by Milner June 15, 19X8	(1,000.00)
	Balance per master file	$ 5,885.75
Statement 3	Balance per vendor's statement	$26,251.80
	Balance per master file	20,516.11
	Difference cannot be located due to the vendor's	
	failure to provide details of its account balance	$ 5,735.69
Statement 4	Balance per vendor's statement	$ 6,170.15
	Credit memo issued by vendor on July 15, 19X8	(2,360.15)
	Balance per master file	$ 3,810.00

Statement 5	Balance per vendor's statement	$ 8,619.21
	Payment by Milner July 3, 19X8	(3,000.00)
	Unlocated difference not followed up due to minor amount	215.06
	Balance per master file	$ 5,834.27

Required:

a. Evaluate the acceptability of having the client perform the reconciliations, assuming the auditor intends to perform adequate additional tests.

b. Describe the additional tests that should be performed for each of the five statements that included differences.

c. What audit procedures should be performed for the nonresponses to the confirmation requests?

17–31 You have instructed Jasmine Singh, the audit senior on the Kao Corp. audit, to confirm accounts payable at December 31, 19X8. Kao Corp. has excellent internal control and a history of prompt payment of all current liabilities. The following procedures are suggested by Jasmine.

1. Obtain a list of accounts payable at December 31, 19X8, from Kao Corp. and
   (a) foot the list.
   (b) compare the total with balance shown in the general ledger.
   (c) compare the amounts shown on the list with the balances in the accounts payable master file.

2. Select accounts to confirm.
   (a) Select each account with a balance payable in excess of $2,000.
   (b) Select a random sample of 50 other accounts over $100.
   (c) Indicate the accounts to be confirmed on the accounts payable list, make a copy of the list, and give it to the accounts payable clerk along with instructions to type the vendor's name, address, and balance due on confirmations.

3. Compare the confirmations with the accounts payable master file.

4. Have Kao Corp.'s controller sign each confirmation.

5. Have the accounts payable clerk insert the confirmations and return envelopes addressed to your public accounting firm in Kao Corp.'s envelopes. The envelopes are also to be stamped and sealed by the clerk. This should all be done under the auditor's control.

6. Mail the confirmations.

Required: Evaluate the procedures for confirming accounts payable.

17–32 The physical inventory for Ajak Manufacturing Ltd. was taken on December 30, 19X8, rather than December 31 because the client had to operate the plant for a special order the last day of the year. At the time of the client's physical count, you observed that purchases represented by receiving report number 2631 and all preceding ones were included in the physical count, whereas inventory represented by succeeding numbers was excluded. On the evening of December 31, you stopped by the plant and noted that inventory represented by receiving report numbers 2632 through 2634 was received subsequent to the physical count, but prior to the end of the year. You later noted that the final inventory on the financial statements contained only those items included in the physical count. In testing accounts payable at December 31, 19X8, you obtain a schedule from the client to aid you in testing the adequacy of the cutoff. The schedule includes the following information that you have not yet resolved.

RECEIVING REPORT NUMBER	AMOUNT OF VENDOR'S INVOICE	AMOUNT PRESENTLY INCLUDED IN OR EXCLUDED FROM ACCOUNTS PAYABLE*	INFORMATION ON THE VENDOR'S INVOICE		
			Invoice Date	*Shipping Date*	*FOB Origin or Destination*
2631	$2,619.26	Included	12-30-X8	12-30-X8	Origin
2632	3,709.16	Excluded	12-26-X8	12-15-X8	Destination
2633	5,182.31	Included	12-31-X8	12-26-X8	Origin
2634	6,403.00	Excluded	12-16-X8	12-27-X8	Destination
2635	8,484.91	Included	12-28-X8	12-31-X8	Origin
2636	5,916.20	Excluded	1-3-X9	12-31-X8	Destination
2637	7,515.50	Excluded	1-5-X9	12-26-X8	Origin
2638	2,407.87	Excluded	12-31-X8	1-3-X9	Origin

* All entries to record inventory purchases are recorded by the client as a debit to purchases and a credit to accounts payable.

Required:

a. Explain the relationship between inventory and accounts payable cutoff.

b. For each of the receiving reports, state the error in inventory or accounts payable, if any exists, and prepare an adjusting entry to correct the financial statements, if an error exists.

c. Which of the errors in part b are most important? Explain.

17–33 You are provided with the following information about internal control relating to materials purchases for the Oonark Machinery Corp., a medium-sized firm that builds special machinery to order.

Materials purchase requisitions are first approved by the plant supervisor, who then sends them to the purchasing department. A prenumbered purchase order is prepared in triplicate by one of several department employees. Employees account for all purchase order numbers. The original copy is sent to the vendor. The receiving department is sent the second copy to use for a receiving report. The third copy is kept on file in the purchasing department along with the requisition.

Delivered materials are immediately sent to the storeroom. The receiving report, which is a copy of the purchase order, is sent to the purchasing department. A copy of the receiving report is sent to the storeroom. Materials are issued to factory employees subsequent to a verbal request by one of the supervisors.

When the mailroom clerk receives vendors' invoices, the clerk forwards them to the purchasing department employee who placed the order. The invoice is compared with the purchase order on file for price and terms by the employee. The invoice quantity is compared with the receiving department's report. After checking footings, extensions, and discounts, the employee indicates approval for payment by initialing the invoice. The invoice is then forwarded to the accounting department. Vendor name, date, gross and net invoice amounts, and account distribution are key-entered into the computer system for updating the acquisitions journal and accounts payable master file, and filed by payment date due. The vendor's invoice is filed in the accounting department. The purchase order and receiving report are filed in the purchasing department.

The accounting department requisitions prenumbered cheques from the cashier. They are manually prepared and then returned to the cashier, who puts them through the cheque-signing machine. After accounting for the sequence of numbers, the cashier sends the cheques to the accounting department where they are key entered to record cash disbursements and update accounts payable. The cheques are placed in envelopes and sent to the mailroom. At the end of each month a listing of the accounts payable master file is printed and the total is compared with the general ledger balance. Any differences disclosed are investigated.

Required:

a. Prepare a flowchart for the acquisition and payment cycle for Oonark Machinery Corp.

b. List the controls in existence for each of the seven internal control objectives for acquisitions.

c. For each control in part b, list one control test audit procedure to verify its effectiveness.

d. List the most important internal control weaknesses for acquisitions and payments.

e. Design an audit program to test internal control. The program should include, but not be limited to, the tests of controls from part c and procedures to compensate for the weaknesses in part d.

CASE

17–34 *PART 1*

The following tests of controls audit procedures for acquisitions and payments are to be used in the audit of Ward Publishing Company Ltd. You have concluded that internal control appears effective and a reduced assessed control risk is likely to be cost beneficial. Ward's active involvement in the business, good separation of duties, and a competent controller and other employees are factors affecting your opinion.

TESTS OF CONTROLS AUDIT PROCEDURES FOR ACQUISITIONS AND PAYMENTS

1. Foot and crossfoot the acquisitions and cash disbursements journals for two months and trace totals to postings in the general ledger.

2. Scan the acquisitions and cash disbursements journals for all months and investigate any unusual entries.

3. Reconcile disbursements per books to disbursements per bank statement for one month.

4. Examine evidence that the bank reconciliation is prepared by the controller.

5. Determine by observation that a cheque protector is in use.

6. Inquire and observe whether the accounts payable master file balances are periodically reconciled to vendors' statements by the controller.

7. Examine the log book as evidence that the numerical sequence of cheques is accounted for by someone independent of the preparation function.

8. Inquire and observe that cheques are mailed by D. Ward or someone under his supervision after he signs cheques.

9. Examine initials indicating the controller balances the accounts payable master file to the general ledger monthly.

10. Select a sample of entries in the cash disbursements journal, and

   a. obtain related canceled cheques and compare with entry for payee, date, and amount, and examine signature endorsement.

   b. obtain vendors' invoices, receiving reports, and purchase orders and

      (1) examine vendor's invoice to determine that all supporting documents are attached.

      (2) determine that documents agree with the disbursement.

      (3) compare vendor's name, amount, and date to entry.

      (4) determine if a discount was taken when appropriate.

      (5) examine vendors' invoices for initials indicating an independent review of chart of account codings.

(6) examine reasonableness of disbursement and account codings.

(7) review invoices for approval of purchases by Ward.

(8) review purchase order and/or purchase requisitions for proper approval.

(9) verify prices and recalculate footings and extensions on invoices.

(10) compare quantities and descriptions on purchase order, receiving report, and vendors' invoices to the extent applicable.

(11) examine vendor's invoice and receiving report to determine that the cheque number is included and the documents are marked "paid" at the time of cheque signing.

 c. Trace postings to the accounts payable master file for name, amount, and date.

  11. Select a sample of receiving reports issued during the year and trace to vendors' invoices and entries in the purchase journal.

 a. Compare type of merchandise, name of vendor, date received, quantities, and amounts.

 b. If the transaction is indicated in the acquisitions journal as paid, trace cheque number to entry in cash disbursements journal. If unpaid, investigate reasons.

 c. Trace transactions to accounts payable subsidiary record, comparing name, amount, and date.

Required:

Prepare all parts of an attributes sampling data sheet through the planned sample size for the above audit program, assuming a line item in the cash disbursements journal is used for the sampling unit. For all procedures for which the line item in the cash disbursements journal is not an appropriate sampling unit, assume audit procedures were performed on a nonstatistical basis. For all tests of controls performed mid-way in the audit use a tolerable deviation rate of 5 percent, and for all tests of controls performed at the end of the audit use a rate of 6 percent. Use an acceptable risk of overreliance of 10 percent. Plan for an estimated population deviation rate of one percent for tests of controls performed mid-way and zero percent for tests of controls performed at the end of the audit. Prepare the data sheet using the microcomputer (instructor option – also applies to Part 2).

PART 2

Assume a sample size of 50 for all procedures in Part 1, regardless of your answers in Part 1. For other procedures, assume an adequate sample size for the circumstance was selected. The only exceptions in your audit tests for all tests of controls audit procedures are as follows:

1. Procedure 2 – Two large transactions were identified as being unusual. Investigation determined that they were authorized acquisitions of fixed assets. They were both correctly recorded.

2. Procedure 10b(1) – A purchase order had not been attached to a vendor's invoice. The purchase order was found in a separate file and determined to be approved and appropriate.

3. Procedure 10b(5) – Six vendors' invoices were not initialed as being internally verified. Three actual misclassifications existed. The controller explained that she frequently did not review codings because of the competence of the accounting clerk doing the coding, and was surprised at the mistakes.

Required:

a. Complete the attributes sampling data sheet from Part 1.

b. Explain the effect of the exceptions on tests of details of accounts payable. Which objective or objectives are affected, and how do those objectives, in turn, affect the audit of accounts payable?

c. Given your tests of controls results, write an audit program for tests of details of balances for accounts payable. Assume:

   (1) The client provided a list of accounts payable, prepared from the master file.

   (2) Audit risk for accounts payable is high.

   (3) Inherent risk for accounts payable is low.

   (4) Analytical procedure results were excellent.

18

THE ACQUISITION AND PAYMENT CYCLE: VERIFICATION OF SELECTED ACCOUNTS

LEARNING OBJECTIVES

THOROUGH STUDY OF THIS CHAPTER WILL ENABLE YOU TO:

1. Recognize the many accounts besides accounts payable that are part of the acquisition and payment cycle

2. Design and perform the audit tests of manufacturing equipment and related accounts

3. Design and perform the audit tests of prepaid expenses

4. Design and perform the audit tests of accrued liabilities

5. Design and perform the audit tests of income and expense accounts

☐ An important characteristic of the acquisition and payment cycle is the large number of accounts involved. These include the following:

- Cash in the bank
- Inventory

- Rent payable
- Accrued professional fees

OBJECTIVE 1

Recognize the many accounts besides accounts payable that are part of the acquisition and payment cycle.

- Supplies
- Leases and leasehold improvements
- Land
- Buildings
- Manufacturing equipment
- Organization costs
- Patents, trademarks, and copyrights
- Commercial franchises
- Prepaid rent
- Prepaid taxes
- Prepaid insurance
- Accounts payable

- Accrued property taxes
- Income taxes payable
- Rent expense
- Goods and Services Tax payable
- Income tax expense
- Professional fees
- Cost of goods sold
- Property taxes
- Insurance expense
- Travel expense
- Utilities

Since the audit procedures for many of these accounts are similar, an understanding of the appropriate methodology for each can be obtained by studying the following selected account balances:

- Cash in the bank – affected by all transaction cycles (Chapter 21)
- Inventory – represents tangible assets and is typically used up in one year (Chapter 19)
- Prepaid insurance – represents prepaid expenses (Chapter 18)
- Manufacturing equipment – represents long-lived tangible assets (Chapter 18)
- Accounts payable – represents specific liabilities for which the amount and the date of the future payment are known (Chapter 17)
- Accrued property taxes – represents estimated liabilities (Chapter 18)
- Operations accounts – include several methods of verifying all accounts in this category (Chapter 18).

The methodology for designing tests of details of balances for the above accounts is the same as that shown in Figure 17–4 on page 594 for accounts payable. Each account is a part of the acquisition and payment cycle. Therefore, the only change required in the figure is to replace accounts payable with the account being audited. For example, if the account being discussed is accrued property taxes, simply substitute accrued property taxes for accounts payable in the first, second, and last boxes in the figure.

Property, plant, and equipment are assets that have expected lives of more than one year, are used in the business, and are not acquired for resale. The intention to use the assets as a part of the operation of the client's business and their expected life of more than one year are the significant characteristics that distinguish these assets from inventory, prepaid expenses, and investments.

Property, plant, and equipment can be classified as follows:

- Land and land improvements
- Buildings and building improvements
- Manufacturing equipment
- Furniture and fixtures
- Autos and trucks
- Leasehold improvements
- Construction of property, plant, and equipment in process

Audit of Manufacturing Equipment

In this section the audit of *manufacturing equipment* is discussed as an illustration of an appropriate approach to the audit of all property, plant, and equipment accounts. When there are significant differences in the verification of other types of property, plant, or equipment, they are briefly examined.

Overview of the Accounts

The accounts commonly used for manufacturing equipment are illustrated in Figure 18–1. The relationship of manufacturing equipment to the acquisition and the payment cycle is apparent by examining the debits to the asset account. Since the source of debits in the asset account is the acquisitions journal, the current period's additions to manufacturing equipment have already been partially verified as part of the tests of the acquisition and payment cycle.

OBJECTIVE 2

Design and perform the audit tests of manufacturing equipment and related accounts.

The primary accounting record for manufacturing equipment and other property, plant, and equipment accounts is generally a property, or fixed asset master file. The contents of the property master file must be understood for a meaningful study of the audit of manufacturing equipment. The master file will be composed of a set of records, one for each piece of equipment and other types of property owned. In turn, each record will include descriptive information, date of acquisition, original cost, current-year depreciation, and accumulated depreciation for the property. The totals for all records in the master file will equal the general ledger balances for the related accounts.

The master file will also contain information about property acquired and disposed of during the year. For disposals, proceeds, gains and losses will be included.

Audit Objectives

When auditing manufacturing equipment and the related depreciation and accumulated depreciation accounts, the objectives are to determine whether

FIGURE 18–1
Manufacturing Equipment and Related Accounts

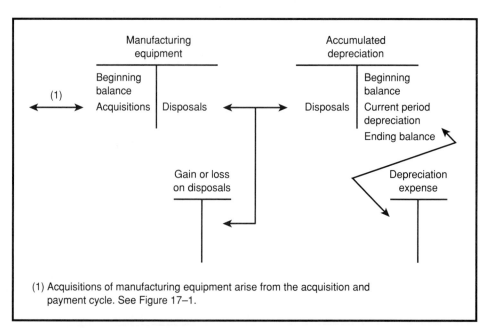

(1) Acquisitions of manufacturing equipment arise from the acquisition and payment cycle. See Figure 17–1.

- additions represent actual property installed or constructed that has been properly capitalized.
- costs and related depreciation for all significant retirements, abandonments, and disposals of property have been properly recorded.
- the balances in the property accounts, including the amounts carried forward from the preceding year, are properly stated.
- depreciation has been accurately computed using a method that is acceptable and consistent with previous periods.
- the balances in accumulated depreciation accounts are reasonable, considering expected useful lives of property units and possible net salvage values.
- government grants have been properly accounted for in records.
- the cost of additions and the proceeds from disposal have been properly accounted for in capital cost section of the tax file.

Auditing Manufacturing Equipment

Manufacturing equipment is normally audited differently from current asset accounts for three reasons: (1) there are usually fewer current period acquisitions of manufacturing equipment, (2) the amount of any given acquisition is often material, and (3) the equipment is likely to be kept and maintained in the accounting records for several years. Because of these differences, the emphasis in auditing manufacturing equipment is on the verification of current period acquisitions rather than on the balance in the account carried forward from the preceding year. In addition, the expected life of assets over one year requires depreciation and accumulated depreciation accounts, which are verified as a part of the audit of the assets. Additions should be traced to the capital cost section of the tax working papers.

Although the approach to verifying manufacturing equipment is dissimilar from that used for current assets, several other accounts are verified in much the same manner. These include patents, copyrights, catalogue costs, and all property, plant, and equipment accounts.

In the audit of manufacturing equipment, it is helpful to separate the tests into the following categories:

- Analytical procedures
- Verification of current-year acquisitions
- Verification of current-year disposals
- Verification of the ending balance in the asset account
- Verification of depreciation expense
- Verification of the ending balance in accumulated depreciation

Analytical Procedures

As in all audit areas, the nature of the analytical procedures depends on the nature of the client's operations. Table 18–1 illustrates the type of ratio and trend analysis frequently performed for manufacturing equipment.

Verification of Current-Year Acquisitions

The proper recording of current-year additions is important because of the long-term effect the assets have on the financial statements. The failure to capitalize a permanent asset, or the recording of an acquisition at the improper amount, affects the balance sheet until the firm disposes of the asset. The income statement is affected until the asset is fully depreciated.

Because of the importance of current-period acquisitions in the audit of manufacturing equipment, seven of the eight objectives for tests of details of

TABLE 18–1

Analytical Procedures
for Manufacturing
Equipment

ANALYTICAL PROCEDURE	POSSIBLE MISSTATEMENT
Compare depreciation expense divided by gross manufacturing equipment cost with previous years.	Error in computing depreciation.
Compare accumulated depreciation divided by gross manufacturing equipment cost with previous years.	Error in recording accumulated depreciation.
Compare monthly or annual repairs and maintenance, supplies expense, small tools expense, and similar accounts with previous years.	Expensing amounts that should be capital items.
Compare gross manufacturing cost divided by some measure of production with previous years.	Idle equipment or equipment that has been disposed of, but not written off.

balances are used as a frame of reference. (Disclosure is discussed on page 624 in connection with the verification of ending balances.)

The audit objectives and common audit tests are shown in Table 18–2. As in all other audit areas, the actual audit tests and sample size depend heavily on materiality, assessed control risk, and the results of prior-year tests. Materiality is of special importance for verifying current-year additions. They vary from immaterial amounts in some years to a large number of significant acquisitions in others. Valuation and classification are usually the major objectives for this part of the audit.

The starting point for the verification of current-year acquisitions is normally a schedule obtained from the client of all purchases recorded in the general ledger during the year. A typical schedule lists each addition separately and includes the date of the acquisition, vendor, description, notation of new or used, life of the asset for depreciation purposes, depreciation method, cost, and any relevant income tax information such as capital cost allowance rates and the investment tax credit if applicable. The client obtains this information from the property master file.

In studying Table 18–2, one should recognize the importance of examining vendors' invoices and related documents in verifying acquisitions of manufacturing equipment. That subject is discussed in the next section.

Examination of
Supporting
Documentation

The most common audit test to verify additions is examination of vendors' invoices and receiving reports (vouching). Additional vouching besides that which is done as a part of the tests of controls is frequently considered necessary to verify the current-period additions because of the complexity of many equipment transactions and the materiality of the amounts. It should ordinarily be unnecessary to examine supporting documentation for each addition, but it is normal to verify large and unusual transactions for the entire year as well as a representative sample of typical additions. The extent of the verification depends on the auditor's assessed control risk for acquisitions and the materiality of the additions.

Tests for acquisitions are accomplished by comparing the charges on vendors' invoices with recorded amounts. The auditor must be aware of the client's capitalization policies to determine whether acquisitions are valued in accordance with generally accepted accounting principles and are treated consistently

TABLE 18–2

Objectives and Tests of
Details of Balances for
Manufacturing
Equipment Additions

SPECIFIC AUDIT OBJECTIVE	COMMON TESTS OF DETAILS OF BALANCES PROCEDURES	COMMENTS
Current-year acquisitions as listed are valid (validity).	Examine vendors' invoices and receiving reports. Physically examine assets.	It is uncommon to physically examine additions unless controls are weak or amounts are material.
Existing acquisitions are listed (completeness).	Examine vendors' invoices of closely related accounts such as repairs and maintenance to uncover items that should be manufacturing equipment. Review lease and rental agreements.	This objective is one of the most important ones for manufacturing equipment.
Current-year acquisitions as listed are owned (ownership).	Examine vendors' invoices.	Ordinarily no problem for equipment. Property deeds, abstracts, and tax bills are frequently examined for land or major buildings.
Current-year acquisitions as listed are properly valued (valuation).	Examine vendors' invoices. Recalculation of investment tax credit if applicable.	Extent depends on effectiveness of internal controls.
Current-year acquisitions as listed are properly classified (classification).	Examine vendors' invoices in manufacturing equipment account to uncover items that should be classified as office equipment, part of the buildings, or repairs. Examine vendors' invoices of closely related accounts such as repairs to uncover items that should be manufacturing equipment. Examine rent and lease expense for capitalizable leases.	The objective is closely related to tests for omissions. It is done in conjunction with that objective and tests for valuation.
Current-year acquisitions in the acquisitions schedule agree with related master file amounts, and the total agrees with the general ledger (mechanical accuracy).	Foot the acquisitions schedule. Trace the total to the general ledger. Trace the individual acquisitions to the master file for amounts and descriptions.	These tests should be limited unless controls are weak. All increases in the general ledger balance for the year should reconcile to the schedule.
Current-year acquisitions are recorded in the proper period (cutoff).	Review transactions near the balance sheet date for proper period.	Usually done as a part of accounts payable cutoff tests.
Accounts in the acquisition and payment cycle are properly disclosed (disclosure).	None.	Done as a part of tests of year-end balances.

with those of the preceding year. For example, many clients automatically expense items that are less than a certain amount, such as $100. The auditor should be alert for the possibility of material transportation and installation costs, as well as the trade-in of existing equipment.

As a part of the valuation objective, the auditor must also test, by recalculation, the client's calculations of the investment tax credit taken on qualified additions. The proper credit against income taxes owing by the company for an acquisition depends on the tax laws governing the investment tax credit for the particular year under audit, the nature of the asset, and its location.

The auditor should also ensure that government grants for fixed assets are properly accounted for as required by Section 3800 of the *CICA Handbook*, "Accounting for Government Assistance."

In conjunction with testing current-period additions for existence and valuation, the auditor should also review recorded transactions for proper classification. In some cases, amounts recorded as manufacturing equipment should be classified as office equipment or as a part of the building. There is also the possibility that the client has improperly capitalized repairs, rents, or similar expenses.

The inclusion of transactions that should properly be recorded as assets in repairs and maintenance expense, lease expense, supplies, small tools, and similar accounts is a common client error. The error results from lack of understanding of generally accepted accounting principles and some clients' desire to avoid income taxes. The likelihood of these types of misclassifications should be evaluated in conjunction with obtaining an understanding of the internal control structure in the acquisition and payment cycle. If the auditor concludes that material errors are likely, it may be necessary to vouch the larger amounts debited to the expense accounts. It is a common practice to do this as a regular part of the audit of the property, plant, and equipment accounts.

Verification of Current-Year Disposals

Internal controls   The most important internal control over the disposal of manufacturing equipment is the existence of a formal method to inform management of the sale, trade-in, abandonment, or theft of recorded machinery and equipment. If the client fails to record disposals, the original cost of the manufacturing equipment account will be overstated indefinitely, and the net book value will be overstated until the asset is fully depreciated. Another important control to protect assets from unauthorized disposal is a provision for authorization for the sale or other disposal of manufacturing equipment. Finally, there should be adequate internal verification of recorded disposals to make sure assets are correctly removed from the accounting records.

Audit tests   The two major objectives in the verification of the sale, trade-in, or abandonment of manufacturing equipment are *existing disposals are recorded* and *recorded disposals are properly valued*.

The starting point for verifying disposals is the client's schedule of recorded disposals. The schedule typically includes the date the asset was disposed of, the name of the person or firm acquiring the asset, the selling price, the original cost of the asset, the acquisition date, the accumulated depreciation of the asset, and the capital cost allowance recapture, if any. Mechanical accuracy tests of the schedule are necessary, including footing the schedule, tracing the totals on the schedule to the recorded disposals in the general ledger, and tracing the cost and accumulated depreciation of the disposals to the property master file. The proceeds from disposal should be traced to the capital cost section of the tax working papers.

Because the failure to record disposals of manufacturing equipment no longer used in the business can significantly affect the financial statements, *the search for unrecorded disposals is essential.* The nature and adequacy of the controls over disposals affect the extent of the search. The following procedures are frequently used for verifying disposals:

- Review whether newly acquired assets replace existing assets.
- Analyze gains on the disposal of assets and miscellaneous income for receipts from the disposal of assets.
- Review plant modifications and changes in product line, taxes, or insurance coverage for indications of deletions of equipment.
- Make inquiries of management and production personnel about the possibility of the disposal of assets.

When an asset is sold or disposed of without having been traded in for a replacement asset, the *valuation* of the transaction can be verified by examining the related sales invoice and property master file. The auditor should compare the cost and accumulated depreciation in the master file with the recorded entry in the general journal and recompute the gain or loss on the disposal of the asset for comparison with the accounting records.

Two areas deserve special attention in the valuation objective. The first is the *trade-in of an asset for a replacement.* When trade-ins occur, the auditor should be sure the new asset is properly capitalized and the replaced asset properly eliminated from the records, considering the book value of the asset traded in and the additional cost of the new asset. The second area of special concern is the disposal of assets affected by *capital cost allowance recapture.* Since the recapture affects the current year's income tax expense and liability, the auditor must evaluate its significance. While discussion of the tax implications is beyond the scope of this text, the auditor should ensure that the proceeds on disposal are properly recorded in the tax working papers.

Verification of Asset Balance

Internal controls   The nature of the internal controls over existing assets determines whether it is necessary to verify manufacturing equipment acquired in prior years. Important controls include the use of a master file for individual fixed assets, adequate physical controls over assets that are easily movable (such as tools and vehicles), assignment of identification numbers to each plant asset, and periodic physical count of fixed assets and their reconciliation by accounting personnel. A formal method of informing the accounting department of all disposals of permanent assets is also an important control over the balance of assets carried forward into the current year.

Audit tests   Usually, the auditor does not obtain a list from the client of all assets included in the ending balance of manufacturing equipment. Instead, audit tests are determined on the basis of the master file.

Typically, the first audit step concerns the mechanical accuracy objective: manufacturing equipment as listed in the master file agrees with the general ledger. Examining a printout of the master file that totals to the general ledger balance is ordinarily sufficient. The auditor may choose to test foot a few pages.

After assessing control risk for the validity objective, the auditor must decide whether it is necessary to verify the existence (validity) of individual items of manufacturing equipment included in the master file. If the auditor believes there is a high likelihood of significant missing permanent assets that are still recorded in the accounting records, an appropriate procedure is to select a sample from the master file and examine the actual assets. In rare cases, the auditor may believe it is necessary that the client take a complete physical inventory of fixed assets to make sure they actually exist. If a physical inventory is taken, the auditor normally observes the count.

Ordinarily, it is unnecessary to test the valuation of fixed assets recorded in prior periods because presumably they were verified in previous audits at the time they were acquired. But the auditor should be aware that companies may occasionally have on hand manufacturing equipment that is no longer used in operations. If the amounts are material, the auditor should evaluate whether they should be written down to net realizable value or at least be disclosed separately as "nonoperating equipment."

A major consideration in verifying the ending balance in permanent assets is the possibility of existing *legal encumbrances* (disclosure objective). A number of methods are available to determine if manufacturing equipment is encumbered. These include reading the terms of loan and credit agreements and mailing loan confirmation requests to banks and other lending institutions. Information with respect to encumbered assets may also be obtained through discussions with the client or confirmations with legal counsel. In addition, it is desirable to obtain information on possible liens by checking with the sheriff in the locale where the company operates. In Ontario, for a small fee, the auditor may request information from the Department of Corporate and Consumer Affairs about the existence of encumbrances under the *Personal Property Security Act*. Other provinces have similar procedures for checking on liens and encumbrances.

The *proper disclosure* of manufacturing equipment in the financial statements must be carefully evaluated to make sure generally accepted accounting principles are followed. Manufacturing equipment should include the gross cost and should ordinarily be separated from other permanent assets. Leased property should also be disclosed separately, and all liens on property must be included in the footnotes.

Verification of Depreciation Expense

Depreciation expense is one of the few expense accounts that is not verified as a part of tests of controls. The recorded amounts are determined by *internal allocations* rather than by exchange transactions with outside parties. When depreciation expense is material, more tests of details of depreciation expense are required than for an account that has already been verified through tests of controls.

The most important objective for depreciation expense is proper valuation. Two major concerns are involved in the valuation objective: Determining whether the client is following *a consistent depreciation policy* from period to period and whether the client's *calculations are accurate*. In determining the former, there are four considerations: the useful life of current period acquisitions, the method of depreciation, the estimated salvage value, and the policy of depreciating assets in the year of acquisition and disposition. The client's policies can be determined by having discussions with the client and comparing the responses with the information in the auditor's permanent files.

In deciding on the reasonableness of the useful lives assigned to newly acquired assets, the auditor must consider a number of factors: the actual physical life of the asset, the expected useful life (taking into account obsolescence and the company's normal policy of upgrading equipment), and established company policies on trading in equipment. Occasionally, changing circumstances may necessitate a re-evaluation of the useful life of an asset. When this occurs, a change in accounting estimate rather than a change in accounting principle is involved. The effect of this on depreciation must be carefully evaluated.

A useful method of testing depreciation is to make a calculation of its overall reasonableness. The calculation is made by multiplying the undepreciated fixed assets by the depreciation rate for the year. In making these calculations, the auditor must of course make adjustments for current-year additions and disposals, assets with different lengths of life, and assets with different methods of depreciation. The calculations can be made fairly easily if the public accounting firm includes in the permanent file a breakdown of the fixed assets by method of depreciation and length of life. If the overall calculations are reasonably close to the client's totals and if assessed control risk for depreciation expense is low, tests of details for depreciation can be minimized.

In many audits, it is also desirable to check the mechanical accuracy of depreciation calculations. This is done by recomputing depreciation expense for selected assets to determine whether the client is following a proper and consistent depreciation policy. To be relevant, the detailed calculations should be tied in to the total depreciation calculations by footing the depreciation expense on the property master file and reconciling the total with the general ledger. Assuming the client maintains computerized depreciation and amortization records, it may be desirable to consider using the computer in testing the calculations.

Verification of Accumulated Depreciation

The debits to accumulated depreciation are normally tested as a part of the audit of disposals of assets, whereas the credits are verified as a part of depreciation expense. If the auditor traces selected transactions to the accumulated depreciation records in the property master file as a part of these tests, little additional testing should be required.

Two objectives are usually emphasized in the audit of accumulated depreciation:

- Accumulated depreciation as stated in the property master file agrees with the general ledger. This objective can be satisfied by test footing the accumulated depreciation on the property master file and tracing the total to the general ledger.
- Accumulated depreciation in the master file is properly valued.

In some cases, the life of manufacturing equipment may be significantly reduced because of such changes as reductions in customer demands for products, unexpected physical deterioration, or a modification in operations. Because of these possibilities, it is necessary to evaluate the adequacy of the allowances for accumulated depreciation each year to make sure the realizable value of the assets exceeds their net book value.

Audit of Prepaid Expenses

Prepaid expenses, deferred charges, and intangibles are assets that vary in life from several months to several years. Their inclusion as assets results more from the concept of matching expenses with revenues than from their resale or liquidation value. The following are examples:

- Prepaid rent
- Organization costs
- Prepaid taxes
- Patents

- Prepaid insurance
- Trademarks
- Deferred charges
- Copyrights

Audit Objectives

The objectives in the verification of the prepaid expenses, deferred charges, and intangibles are much the same as for other asset accounts. The eight detailed audit objectives are also applicable to these accounts.

One typical difference between these assets and others, such as accounts receivable and inventory, is the immateriality of the former in many audits. Frequently, analytical procedures are sufficient for prepaid expenses, deferred charges, and intangibles.

In this section the audit of prepaid insurance is discussed as an account representative of this group because (1) it is found in most audits – virtually every company has some type of insurance; (2) it is typical of the problems frequently encountered in the audit of this class of accounts; and (3) the auditor's responsibility for the review of insurance coverage is an additional consideration not encountered in the other accounts in this category.

Overview of Prepaid Insurance

The accounts typically used for prepaid insurance are illustrated in Figure 18–2. The relationship between prepaid insurance and the acquisition and payment cycle is apparent in examining the debits to the asset account. Since the source of the debits in the asset account is the purchase journal, the payments of insurance premiums have already been partially tested by means of the tests of the acquisition and payment transactions.

Internal Controls

The internal controls for prepaid insurance and insurance expense can be conveniently divided into three categories: controls over the acquisition and recording of insurance, controls over the insurance register, and controls over the charge-off of insurance expense.

FIGURE 18–2

Prepaid Insurance and Related Accounts

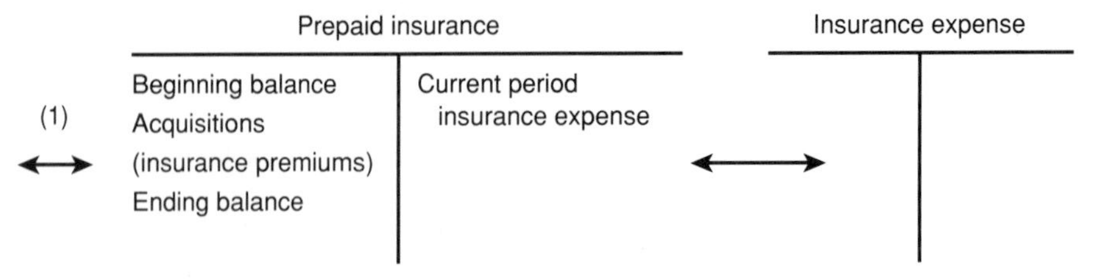

	Prepaid insurance		Insurance expense
(1) ←→	Beginning balance Acquisitions (insurance premiums) Ending balance	Current period insurance expense	←→

(1) Acquisitions of insurance premiums arise from the acquisition and payment cycle. This can be observed by examining Figure 17–1.

Controls over the acquisition and recording of insurance are a part of the acquisition and payment cycle. These should include proper authorization for new insurance policies and payment of insurance premiums consistent with the procedures discussed in that cycle.

A record of insurance policies in force and the due date of each policy *(insurance register)* is an essential control to make sure the company has adequate insurance at all times. The control should include a provision for periodic review of the adequacy of the insurance coverage by an independent qualified person.

After they have been completed, the detailed records of the information in the prepaid insurance register should be verified by someone independent of the person preparing them. A closely related control is the use of monthly "standard journal entries" for insurance expense. If a significant entry is required to adjust the balance in prepaid insurance at the end of the year, it indicates a potential error in the recording of the acquisition of insurance throughout the year or in the calculation of the year-end balance in prepaid insurance.

Audit Tests   Throughout the audit of prepaid insurance and insurance expense, the auditor should keep in mind that the amount in insurance expense is a residual based on the beginning balance in prepaid insurance, the payment of premiums during the year, and the ending balance. The only verification of the balance in the expense account that is ordinarily necessary are analytical procedures and a brief test to be sure the charges to insurance expense arose from credits to prepaid insurance. Since the payments of premiums are tested as part of the tests of controls and analytical procedures, the emphasis in the tests of details of balances is on prepaid insurance.

In the audit of prepaid insurance, a schedule is obtained from the client or prepared by the auditor that includes each insurance policy in force, policy number, insurance coverage for each policy, premium amount, premium period, insurance expense for the year, and prepaid insurance at the end of the year. An example of a schedule obtained from the client for the auditor's working papers is given in Figure 18–3. The auditor's tests of prepaid insurance are normally indicated on the schedule.

Analytical procedures   A major consideration the auditor should keep in mind throughout the audit of prepaid insurance is the frequent *immateriality* of the beginning and ending balances. Furthermore, few transactions are debited and credited to the balance during the year, most of which are small and simple to understand. Therefore, the auditor can generally spend very little time verifying the balance. When the auditor plans not to verify the balance in detail, analytical procedures become increasingly important as a means of identifying potentially significant errors. The following are commonly performed analytical procedures of prepaid insurance and insurance expense:

- Compare total prepaid insurance and insurance expense with previous years as a test of reasonableness.
- Compute the ratio of prepaid insurance to insurance expense and compare it with previous years.
- Compare the individual insurance policy coverage on the schedule obtained from the client with the preceding year's schedule as a test of the elimination of certain policies or a change in insurance coverage.

FIGURE 18–3

Schedule of Prepaid Insurance

ABC Company, Inc.
Prepaid Insurance
12/31/x4

Schedule: F-2
Prepared by Chan-IL 1/20/x5
Approved by QQ 1/25/x5

Insurer	Policy Number	Coverage	Term	Annual Premium	Unexpired Premium 1/1/x4	Additions	Expense	Unexpired Premium 12/31/x4
Ever-ready Casualty Co.	IBB-7906 ②	Auto liability, collision, comprehensive, uninsured motorist—covers all autos owned and leased by the company.	6/1/x3-x4	6 300	2 625 ₁₄		2 625	— ₁₄
			6/1/x3-x5 ①	7 000	—	7 000	4 083	C 2 917 ₁₄
Interprovincial Insurance Co.	74-88-914 ②	Multi-peril—Headquarters and plant, including contents.	3/15/x3-x4 ①	12 600	2 625 ₁₄	1 800 ③	4 425	— ₁₄
			3/15/x3-x5 ①	15 100	—	15 000	11 954	C 3 046 ₁₄
Standard Surety Co.	193016 ②	Blanket Position Bond - $25,000	7/1/x3-x4	1 200	600 ₁₄	—	600	— ₁₄
Commercial Bonding Co.	717-639 ②	Commercial Blanket Bond $100,000	7/1/x4-x5	800	—	800	400	C 400 ₁₄
					5 850 ₁₄	24 600 ₁₄	24 087	6 363 ₁₄
Reconciliation to Insurance Expense (General Account):								
Dependable Insurance	DIC-9161	Personal property–Sales offices	1/1/x4-12/31/x4	500			500	
Insurance Expense							24 587 ₁₄	

① Policy term is 3 years, expiring 3/14/x6; premium shown is annual portion. Annual premium is estimated, subject to annual review and adjustment. Premium is payable in monthly installments under terms of contract. (See work paper section CC, Contracts Payable.)

② Reviewed and briefed policies; details of coverage in permanent file.

③ Blanket Position Bond replaced by Commercial Blanket Bond on expiration.

₁₄ Agreed to last year's schedule of prepaid insurance in work papers.
M Verified calculation/footing/cross-footing.
GL Agreed to general ledger.
C Unexpired premium confirmed by broker; confirmation filed at F-2/1.

Annual premium adjustment; traced to invoice and voucher.

- Compare the computed prepaid insurance balance for the current year on a policy-by-policy basis with that of the preceding year as a test of an error in calculation.

- Review the *insurance coverage* listed on the prepaid insurance schedule with an appropriate client official or insurance broker for adequacy of coverage. The auditor cannot be an expert on insurance matters, but his or her understanding of accounting and the valuation of assets is important in making certain a company is not underinsured.

For many audits, no additional tests need be performed beyond the review for overall reasonableness unless the tests indicate a high likelihood of a significant error or assessed control risk is high. The remaining audit procedures should be performed only when there is a special reason for doing so. The discussion of these tests is organized around the audit objectives for performing tests of details of asset balances. For convenience, certain objectives are combined and the order in which they are discussed is different from that previously used.

Insurance policies in the prepaid schedule are valid and all existing policies are listed (validity and completeness) The verification of validity and tests for omissions of the insurance policies in force can be tested in one of two ways: by referring to supporting documentation or by obtaining a confirmation of insurance information from the company's insurance agent. The first approach entails examining insurance invoices and policies in force. If these tests are performed, they should be done on a limited test basis. Sending a confirmation to the client's insurance agent is preferable because it is usually less time consuming than vouching tests, and it provides 100 percent verification. The use of confirmations for this purpose has grown rapidly in the past few years.

Insurance policies in the prepaid schedule are owned (ownership) The party who will receive the benefit if an insurance claim is filed is considered the owner. Ordinarily, the recipient named in the policy is the client, but when there are mortgages or other liens, the insurance claim may be payable to a creditor. The review of insurance policies for claimants other than the client is an excellent test of unrecorded liabilities and pledged assets.

Prepaid amounts on the schedule are properly valued and the total is correctly added and agrees with the general ledger (valuation and mechanical accuracy) The valuation of prepaid insurance involves verifying the total amount of the insurance premium, the length of the policy period, and the allocation of the premium to unexpired insurance. The amount of the premium for a given policy and its time period can be verified simultaneously by examining the premium invoice or the confirmation from an insurance agent. Once these two have been verified, the client's calculations of unexpired insurance can be tested by recalculation. The schedule of prepaid insurance can then be footed and the totals traced to the general ledger to complete the mechanical accuracy tests.

The related expense to prepaid insurance is properly classified (classification) The proper classification of debits to different insurance expense accounts should be reviewed as a test of the income statement. In some cases the appropriate expense account is obvious because of the type of insurance (such as insurance on a piece of equipment), but in other cases allocations are necessary. For example, fire insurance on the building may require allocation to several accounts, including manufacturing overhead. Consistency with previous years is the major consideration in evaluating classification.

Insurance transactions are recorded in the proper period (cutoff) Cutoff for insurance expense is normally not a significant problem because of the small number of policies and the immateriality of the amount. If the cutoff is checked at all, it is reviewed as a part of accounts payable cutoff tests.

Prepaid insurance is properly disclosed (disclosure) In most audits, prepaid insurance is combined with other prepaid expenses and included as a current asset. The amount is usually small and not a significant consideration to statement users.

Audit of Accrued Liabilities

Accrued liabilities are estimated unpaid obligations for services or benefits that have been received prior to the balance sheet date. Many accrued liabilities represent future obligations for unpaid services resulting from the passage of time but are not payable at the balance sheet date. For example, the benefits of property rental accrue throughout the year; therefore, at the balance sheet date a certain portion of the total rent cost that has not been paid should be accrued. If the balance sheet date and the date of the termination of the rent agreement are the same, any unpaid rent is more appropriately called rent payable than an accrued liability.

> **OBJECTIVE 4**
>
> Design and perform the audit tests of accrued liabilities.

A second type of accrual is one in which the amount of the obligation must be estimated due to the uncertainty of the amount due. An illustration is accrued warranty costs with respect to a new or modified product: the company would have difficulty estimating the warranty expense since experience with established products would only be of very limited assistance. The following are common accrued liabilities, including payroll-related accruals discussed as a part of Chapter 16.

- Accrued officers' bonuses
- Accrued commissions
- Accrued income taxes
- Accrued interest
- Accrued payroll

- Accrued payroll taxes
- Accrued pension costs
- Accrued professional fees
- Accrued rent
- Accrued warranty costs

The verification of accrued expenses varies depending on the nature of the accrual and the circumstances of the client. For most audits, accruals take little audit time, but in some instances accounts such as accrued income taxes, warranty costs, and pension costs are material and require considerable audit effort. To illustrate, the audit of accrued property taxes is discussed in the next section.

Auditing Accrued Property Taxes

The accounts typically used by companies for accrued property taxes are illustrated in Figure 18–4. The relationship between accrued property taxes and the acquisition and payment cycle is the same as for prepaid insurance and is apparent from examining the debits to the liability account. Since the source of the debits is the cash disbursement journal, the payments of property taxes have already been partially tested by means of the tests of the acquisition and payment cycle.

As for insurance expense, the balance in property tax expense is a residual

FIGURE 18–4

Accrued Property
Taxes and Related
Accounts

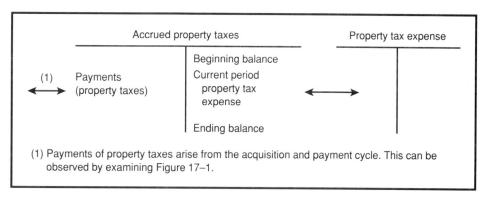

(1) Payments of property taxes arise from the acquisition and payment cycle. This can be
observed by examining Figure 17–1.

amount that results from the beginning and ending balances in accrued property taxes and the payments of property taxes. Therefore, the emphasis in the tests should be on the ending property tax liability and payments. In verifying accrued property taxes, all eight audit objectives except ownership are relevant. But two are of special significance:

1. Existing properties for which accrual of taxes is appropriate are on the accrual schedule. The failure to include properties for which taxes should be accrued would understate the liability (completeness). A material error could occur, for example, if taxes on property were not paid before the balance sheet date and were not included as accrued property taxes.

2. Accrued property taxes are properly valued. The greatest concern in valuation is the consistent treatment of the accrual from year to year (valuation).

The primary methods of testing for the inclusion of all accruals are (1) to perform the accrual tests in conjunction with the audit of current-year property tax payments and (2) to compare the accruals with those of previous years. In most audits there are few property tax payments, but each payment is often material and therefore it is common to verify each one.

First, the auditor should obtain a schedule of property tax payments from the client and compare each payment with the preceding year's schedule to determine whether all payments have been included in the client-prepared schedule. It is also necessary to examine the permanent asset working papers for major additions and disposals of assets that may affect the property taxes accrual. If the client is expanding its operations, all property affected by local property tax regulations should be included in the schedule even if the first tax payment has not yet been made.

After the auditor is satisfied that all taxable property has been included in the client-prepared schedule, it is necessary to evaluate the reasonableness of the total amount of property taxes on each property being used as a basis to estimate the accrual. In some instances the total amount has already been set by the taxing authority, and it is possible to verify the total by comparing the amount on the schedule with the tax bill in the client's possession. In other instances the preceding year's total payments must be adjusted for the expected increase in property tax rates.

The auditor can verify the accrued property tax by recomputing the portion of the total tax applicable to the current year for each piece of property. The most important consideration in making this calculation is to use the same portion of each tax payment as the accrual that was used in the preceding year unless justifiable conditions exist for a change. After the accrual and property tax expense for each piece of property have been recomputed, the totals should be added and compared with the general ledger. In many cases, property taxes are charged to more than one expense account. When this happens, the auditor should test for proper classification by evaluating whether the proper amount was charged to each account.

A typical working paper showing the property tax expense, the accrued property taxes, and the audit procedures used to verify the balances is illustrated in Figure 18–5.

Audit of Operations

The audit of operations is meant to determine whether the income and expense accounts in the financial statements are fairly presented in accordance with generally accepted accounting principles. The auditor must be satisfied that each of the income and expense totals included in the income statement as well as net earnings is not materially misstated.

In conducting audit tests of the financial statements, the auditor must always be aware of the importance of the income statement to users of the statements. It is clear that many users rely more heavily on the income statement than on the balance sheet for making decisions. Equity investors, long-term creditors, union representatives, and frequently even short-term creditors are more interested in the ability of a firm to generate profit than in the liquidity value or book value of the individual assets.

Considering the purposes of the statement of earnings, the following two concepts are essential in the audit of operations:

1. The matching of periodic expense to periodic income is necessary for a proper determination of operating results.
2. The consistent application of accounting principles for different periods is necessary for comparability.

These concepts must be applied to the recording of individual transactions and to the combining of accounts in the general ledger for statement presentation.

> **OBJECTIVE 5**
> Design and perform the audit tests of income and expense accounts.

Approach to Auditing Operations

The audit of operations cannot be regarded as a separate part of the total audit process. A misstatement of an income statement account will most often equally affect a balance sheet account, and vice versa. The audit of operations is so intertwined with the other parts of the audit that it is necessary to interrelate different aspects of testing operations with the different types of tests previously discussed. A brief description of these tests serves as a review of material covered in other chapters; but more important, it shows the interrelationship of different parts of the audit with operations testing. The parts of the audit directly affecting operations are

- Analytical procedures
- Tests of controls
- Analysis of account balances
- Tests of details of balance sheet accounts
- Tests of allocations

FIGURE 18–5

Schedule for Property
Taxes

Burnaby Company Inc.
Property Tax Worksheet
10/31/x4

Schedule *I-6*   Date
Prepared by PR 11/15/x5
Approved by GS 11/20/x5

Tax Bill No.	Area Assessing Code Authority	Property	Assessed Value (1)	Total Tax (2)	Period Covered (3)	Prepaid Beginning Balance	Prepaid Additions	Prepaid Expense	Prepaid Ending Balance	Accrued Beginning Balance	Accrued Additions	Accrued Expense	Accrued Ending Balance
		West Coast Facilities											
526391	51	*Fraser County Westside Warehouse*	400 000	16 000	19x4	2 500	16 000 ✓ T	15 833	2 667 x				
526392	51	*Fraser County Headquarters Bldg.*	250 000	10 000	19x4	1 563	10 000 ✓ T	9 896	1 667 x				
179.23	A	*Manitoba Facility Flin Flon County Manufacturing Plant*	2 000 000	23 000	19x4					3 667	23 000 ✓	22 834	38.33 x
						4 063 ×L⁴	26 000 ×L⁴	25 729 ×	4 334 ×	3 667 ×L⁴	23 000 ×	22 834 ×	3 833 ×

(1) Assessed valuation is defined by the laws of both provinces as 50%
    of "true and fair value."

(2) Mill rates:
    Fraser County .0400 ($40 per $1,000)
    Portage County .0115 ($11.50 per $1,000) for 19x4.

(3) Taxes are payable as follows:
    West Coast site — one half no later than April 30
        and the balance no later than October 31,
        for the current calendar year.

    Manitoba site — payable in full not later than December 31
        following assessment date, which is June 30.

L⁴ Agreed to last year's workpapers.
✓ Agreed to county tax due notice (identified in left column).
T Traced to cancelled cheque and validated receipt.
× Footed, cross-footed.

The emphasis in this section is on the operations accounts directly related to the acquisition and payment cycle, but the same basic concepts apply to the operations accounts in all other cycles.

Analytical Procedures

Analytical procedures were first discussed in Chapter 7 as a general concept and have been referred to in subsequent chapters as a part of particular audit areas. Analytical procedures should be thought of as a part of the test of the fairness of the presentation of both balance sheet and income statement accounts. A few analytical procedures and their effect on operations in the acquisition and payment cycle are shown in Table 18–3 below.

Tests of Controls

Tests of controls have the effect of simultaneously verifying balance sheet and operations accounts. For example, when an auditor concludes that internal controls are adequate to provide reasonable assurance that transactions in the acquisitions journal are valid, properly valued, correctly classified, and recorded in a timely manner, evidence exists as to the correctness of individual balance sheet accounts such as accounts payable and fixed assets, and income statement accounts such as advertising and repairs. Conversely, inadequate controls and errors discovered through tests of controls are an indication of the likelihood of misstatements in both the income statement and the balance sheet.

Understanding internal control and the related tests of controls to determine the appropriate assessed control risk are the most important means of verifying many of the operations accounts in each of the transaction cycles. For example, if the auditor concludes after adequate tests that assessed control risk can be reduced to a low level, the only additional verification of operating accounts such as utilities, advertising, and purchases should be analytical procedures and cut-off tests. However, certain income and expense accounts are not verified at all by tests of controls and others must be tested more extensively by other means. These are discussed as we proceed.

TABLE 18–3
Analytical Procedures
for Operations

ANALYTICAL PROCEDURE	POSSIBLE MISSTATEMENT
Compare individual expenses with previous years.	Overstatement or understatement of a balance in an expense account.
Compare individual asset and liability balances with previous years.	Overstatement or understatement of a balance sheet account that would also affect an income statement account (that is, a misstatement of inventory affects cost of goods sold).
Compare individual expenses with budgets.	Misstatement of expenses.
Compare gross margin percentage with previous years.	Misstatement of cost of goods sold.
Compare inventory turnover ratio with previous years.	Misstatement of cost of goods sold.
Compare prepaid insurance expense with previous years.	Misstatement of insurance expense.
Compare commission expense divided by sales with previous years.	Misstatement of commission expense.
Compare individual manufacturing expenses divided by total manufacturing expenses with previous years.	Misstatement of individual manufacturing expenses.

Analysis of Account Balances

For some accounts, the amounts included in the operations accounts must be analyzed even though the two previously mentioned tests have been performed. The meaning and methodology of analysis of accounts will be described first, followed by a discussion of when expense account analysis is appropriate.

Expense account analysis is the examination of underlying documentation of the individual transactions and amounts making up the total of a particular expense account. The underlying documents are of the same nature as those used for examining transactions as a part of tests of acquisitions controls and include

FIGURE 18–6

Expense Analysis for Legal Expense

Fundy Corp.
General and Administrative Expenses
6/30/x6

Schedule V-10   Date
Prepared by CG 7/21/x6
Approved by SW 7/28/x6

Acct. 913—Legal Expense

Paid to	For	Date	Amount	
② Alexander J. Schweppe Retainer —12 months @ $500		Monthly	① 6 000	✓
	Fundy vs Carson — patent infringement suit	Apr. 14 / Aug. 9	2 800 / 3 109	✓ ✓
② Smith, Tom & Ball	Consultation re: inquiry from Health and Welfare Canada	June 6 / July 10	200 / 200	✓ ✓
③ L. Marvin Hall	Assistance in collecting overdue receivable from Starr Mfg. Ltd.	Nov. 10	105	✓
			12 414 GL	

① Per minutes of meeting of Board of Directors 1/10/x5 Schweppe reappointed general counsel with retainer.
② Lawyer's letters requested { Received 7/23/x5, all matters listed are covered therein; letters filed in General Section of workpapers.
③ Lawyers letters not requested. Per phone conversation with Mr. Hall, 7/21/x5, he rarely represents the company, and and his services have been limited to collection problems. The Starr Mfg. matter was closed in October 19x5, and he has not been involved in any other matters related to the company since that time.

✓ Examined statement and vouchers.
и Footed
GL Agreed to general ledger

invoices, receiving reports, purchase orders, and contracts. Figure 18–6 illustrates a typical working paper showing expense analysis for legal expenses.

Thus, expense accounts analysis is closely related to tests of controls. The major difference is the degree of concentration on an individual account. Since the test of controls is meant to assess the appropriate level of control risk, it constitutes a general review that usually includes the verification of many different accounts. The analysis of expense and other operations accounts consists of the examination of the transactions in particular accounts to determine the propriety, classification, valuation, and other specific information about each account analyzed.

Cutoff tests, which are typically thought of as tests of details of balance sheet accounts, simultaneously affect both the income statement and the balance sheet. An example is when the auditor verifies the cutoff of sales as a part of the audit of accounts receivable. It does not matter whether cutoff tests are regarded as tests of operations or tests of the balance sheet – they affect both. The only reason for performing cutoff tests as a part of verifying balance sheet accounts is convenience.

Also, in many instances the expense account analysis as discussed above takes place as a part of the verification of the related asset. For example, it is common to analyze repairs and maintenance as a part of verifying fixed assets, rent expense as a part of verifying prepaid or accrued rent, and insurance expense as a part of testing prepaid insurance.

Tests of Allocations

Several expense accounts that have not yet been discussed arise from the internal allocation of accounting data. These include expenses such as depreciation, depletion, and the amortization of copyrights and catalogue costs. The allocation of manufacturing overhead between inventory and cost of goods sold is an example of a different type of allocation that affects the expenses. Naturally, these accounts must be tested in some way during the course of the audit.

Allocations are important because they determine whether a particular expenditure is an asset or a current-period expense. If the client fails to follow generally accepted accounting principles or fails to calculate the allocation properly, the financial statements can be materially misstated. The allocation of many expenses such as the depreciation of fixed assets and the amortization of copyrights is required because the life of the asset is greater than one year. The original cost of the asset is verified at the time of acquisition, but the charge-off takes place over several years. Other types of allocations directly affecting the financial statements arise because the life of a short-lived asset does not expire on the balance sheet date. Examples include prepaid rent and insurance. Finally, the allocation of costs between current-period manufacturing expenses and inventory is required by generally accepted accounting principles as a means of reflecting all the costs of making a product.

In testing the allocation of expenditures such as prepaid insurance and manufacturing overhead, the two most important considerations are adherence to generally accepted accounting principles and consistency with the preceding period. The two most important audit procedures for allocations are tests for overall reasonableness and recalculation of the client's results. The most common way to perform these tests is as a part of the audit of the related asset or liability accounts. For example, depreciation expense is usually verified as part of the audit of property, plant, and equipment; the amortization of patents is tested as part of verifying new patents or the disposal of existing ones; and the allocations between inventory and cost of goods sold are verified as part of the audit of inventory.

Review of Related Party Transactions

While the examination of underlying documents in the tests of controls is designed primarily to verify transactions with third parties, related transactions with affiliates and subdivisions within the client's organization are also included in the examination. The possibility of improper recording and disclosing of transactions between interdependent entities was discussed in Chapter 7 in the section dealing with related party transactions. The auditing of related party transactions is discussed in an Auditing Guideline in the *CICA Handbook*, entitled "Related Party Transactions and Economic Dependence."

When a client deals with related parties, Section 3840 of the *Handbook* requires the nature of the relationship, the nature and extent of transactions, and amounts due to and from the related parties, and the terms of settlement be properly disclosed if the financial statements are to be in conformity with GAAP. Often intercompany transactions must be eliminated from the accounts to avoid double counting. Services and inventory acquired from related parties must be properly valued, and other exchange transactions must be carefully evaluated for propriety and reasonableness. Obviously, related party transactions must be audited more extensively than those with third parties.

REVIEW QUESTIONS

18–1   Explain the relationship between tests of controls for the acquisition and payment cycle and tests of details of balances for the verification of property, plant, and equipment. Which aspects of property, plant, and equipment are directly affected by the tests of controls and which are not?

18–2   Explain why the emphasis in auditing property, plant, and equipment is on the current-period acquisitions and disposals rather than on the balances in the account carried forward from the preceding year. Under what circumstances will the emphasis be on the balances carried forward?

18–3   What is the relationship between the audit of property accounts and the audit of repair and maintenance accounts? Explain how the auditor organizes the audit to take this relationship into consideration.

18–4   List and briefly state the purpose of all audit procedures that might reasonably be applied by an auditor to determine that all property, plant, and equipment retirements have been recorded on the books.

18–5   In auditing depreciation expense, what major considerations should the auditor keep in mind? Explain how each can be verified.

18–6   Explain the relationship between the tests of controls for the acquisition and payment cycle and tests of details of balances for the verification of prepaid insurance.

18–7   Explain why the audit of prepaid insurance should ordinarily take a relatively small amount of audit time if the client's assessed control risk for acquisitions is low.

18–8   Distinguish between the evaluation of the adequacy of insurance coverage and the verification of prepaid insurance. Explain which is more important in a typical audit.

18–9   What are the similarities and differences in verifying prepaid insurance and patents?

18–10   Explain the relationship between rent payable and the tests of controls for the acquisition and payment cycle. Which aspects of rent payable are not verified as a part of the tests of controls?

18–11   How should the emphasis differ in verifying income taxes payable and accrued warranty expense?

18–12   In verifying accounts payable it is common to restrict the audit sample to a small portion of the population items, whereas in auditing accrued property taxes it is common to verify all transactions for the year. Explain the reason for the difference.

18–13   Which documents will be used to verify prepaid property taxes and the related expense accounts?

18–14   List three expense accounts that are tested as part of the acquisition and payment cycle or the payroll and personnel cycle. List three expense accounts that are not directly verified as a part of either of these cycles.

18–15   What is meant by the analysis of expense accounts? Explain how expense account analysis relates to the tests of controls that the auditor has already completed for the acquisition and payment cycle.

18–16   How would the approach for verifying repair expense differ from that used to audit depreciation expense? Why would the approach be different?

18–17   List the factors that should affect the auditor's decision whether or not to analyze a particular account balance. Considering these factors, list four expense accounts that are commonly analyzed in audit engagements.

18–18   Explain how costs of goods sold for a wholesale company could in part be verified by each of the following types of tests:
   a. Analytical procedures
   b. Tests of controls
   c. Analysis of account balances
   d. Tests of details of balance sheet accounts
   e. Tests of allocations

MULTIPLE CHOICE QUESTIONS

18–19   The following questions concern internal controls in the acquisition and payment cycle. Choose the best response.
   a. If preparation of a periodic scrap report is essential in order to maintain adequate control over the manufacturing process, the data for this report should be accumulated in the
      (1) accounting department.
      (2) production department.
      (3) warehousing department.
      (4) budget department.
   b. Which of the following is an internal control weakness related to factory equipment?
      (1) Cheques issued in payment of purchases of equipment are *not* signed by the controller.

(2) All purchases of factory equipment are required to be made by the department in need of the equipment.

(3) Factory equipment replacements are generally made when estimated useful lives, as indicated in depreciation schedules, have expired.

(4) Proceeds from sales of fully depreciated equipment are credited to other income.

c. With respect to an internal control measure that will assure accountability for fixed asset retirements, management should implement controls that include

(1) continuous analysis of miscellaneous revenue to locate any cash proceeds from sale of plant assets.

(2) periodic inquiry of plant executives by internal auditors as to whether any plant assets have been retired.

(3) continuous use of serially numbered retirement work orders.

(4) periodic observation of plant assets by the internal auditors.

(AICPA adapted)

18–20 The following questions concern analytical procedures in the acquisition and payment cycle. Choose the best response.

a. Which of the following is the most reliable analytical procedure approach to verification of the year-end financial statement balances of a wholesale business?

(1) Verify depreciation expense by multiplying the depreciable asset balances by one divided by the depreciation rate.

(2) Verify commission expense by multiplying sales revenue by the company's standard commission rate.

(3) Verify interest expense, which includes imputed interest, by multiplying long-term debt balances by the year-end prevailing interest rate.

(4) Verify the workers' compensation liability by multiplying total payroll costs by the workers' compensation contribution rate in effect during the year.

b. The controller of Eigram Manufacturing, Inc., wants to use ratio analysis to identify the possible existence of idle equipment or the possibility that equipment has been disposed of without having been written off. Which of the following ratios would best accomplish this objective?

(1) Depreciation expense/book value of manufacturing equipment.

(2) Accumulated depreciation/book value of manufacturing equipment.

(3) Repairs and maintenance cost/direct labor costs.

(4) Gross manufacturing equipment cost/units produced.

c. Which of the following analytical procedures should be applied to the income statement?

(1) Select sales and expense items and trace amounts to related supporting documents.

(2) Ascertain that the net income amount in the statement of changes in financial position agrees with the net income amount in the income statement.

(3) Obtain from the proper client representatives, the beginning and ending inventory amounts that were used to determine costs of sales.

(4) Compare the actual revenues and expenses with the corresponding figures of the previous year and investigate significant differences.

(AICPA adapted)

18–21 The following questions concern the audit of asset accounts in the acquisition and payment cycle. Choose the best response.

a. Patentex Inc. developed a new secret formula that is of great value because it resulted in a virtual monopoly. Patentex has capitalized all research and development costs associated with this formula. Greene, public accountant, who is examining the research and development account, will probably

(1) confer with management regarding transfer of the research component of the total from the balance sheet to the income statement.

(2) confirm that the secret formula is registered and on file with the county clerk's office.

(3) confer with management regarding a change in the title of the account to "goodwill."

(4) confer with management regarding ownership of the secret formula.

b. Which of the following is the *best* evidence of real estate ownership at the balance sheet date?

(1) Insurance policy

(2) Original deed held in the client's safe

(3) Paid real estate tax bills

(4) Lawyer's statement on closing

(AICPA **adapted**)

18–22 The following questions concern the audit of liabilities or operations. Choose the best response.

a. Which of the following audit procedures is *least* likely to detect an unrecorded liability?

(1) Analysis and recomputation of interest expense

(2) Analysis and recomputation of depreciation expense

(3) Mailing of standard bank confirmation forms

(4) Reading of the minutes of meetings of the board of directors

b. Which of the following *best* describes the independent auditor's approach to obtaining satisfaction concerning depreciation expense in the income statement?

(1) Verify the mathematical accuracy of the amounts charged to income as a result of depreciation expense.

(2) Determine the method for computing depreciation expense and ascertain that it is in accordance with generally accepted accounting principles.

(3) Reconcile the amount of depreciation expense to those amounts credited to accumulated depreciation accounts.

(4) Establish the basis for depreciable assets and verify the depreciation expense.

c. Before expressing an opinion concerning the results of operations, the auditor would *best* proceed with the examination of the income statement by

(1) applying a rigid measurement standard designed to test for understatement of net income.

(2) analyzing the beginning and ending balance sheet inventory amounts.

(3) making net income comparisons to published industry trends and ratios.

(4) examining income statement accounts concurrently with the related balance sheet accounts.

(AICPA **adapted**)

DISCUSSION QUESTIONS AND PROBLEMS

18–23 The following three questions explore different problems related to the audit of fixed assets.

(a) During your year-end audit of Beechwood, Inc., you learn the company developed a new type of heat pump and has capitalized all costs associated with the research on and development of it. Explain fully what action you would take and what you would say to management in your discussion about this issue.

      (b) Explain how an auditor determines real estate ownership by a client.

      (c) Briefly discuss why an auditor would be interested in the payee(s) of a client's property insurance policies.

18–24 For each of the following errors in property, plant, and equipment accounts, state an internal control the client could install to prevent the error from occurring and a substantive audit procedure the auditor could use to discover the error.

1. The asset lives used to depreciate equipment are less than reasonable, expected useful lives.

2. Capitalizable assets are routinely expensed as repairs and maintenance, perishable tools, or supplies expense.

3. Construction equipment that is abandoned or traded for replacement equipment is not removed from the accounting records.

4. Depreciation expense for manufacturing operations is charged to administrative expenses.

5. Tools necessary for the maintenance of equipment are stolen by company employees for their personal use.

6. Acquisitions of property are recorded at an improper amount.

7. A loan against existing equipment is not recorded in the accounting records. The cash receipts from the loan never reached the company because they were used for the down payment on a piece of equipment now being used as an operating asset. The equipment is also not recorded in the records.

18–25 The following types of internal controls are commonly employed by organizations for property, plant, and equipment:

1. A fixed asset master file is maintained with a separate record for each fixed asset.

2. Written policies exist and are known by accounting personnel to differentiate between capitalizable additions, freight, installation costs, replacements, and maintenance expenditures.

3. Purchases of permanent assets in excess of $20,000 are approved by the board of directors.

4. Whenever practical, equipment is labeled with metal tags and is inventoried on a systematic basis.

5. Depreciation charges for individual assets are calculated for each asset; recorded in a fixed asset master file that includes cost, depreciation, and accumulated depreciation for each asset; and verified periodically by an independent clerk.

Required:

    a. State the purpose of each of the internal controls listed above. Your answer should refer to the type of error that is likely to be reduced because of the control.

    b. For each internal control, list one test of controls the auditor can use to test for its existence.

    c. List one test of controls for testing whether the control is actually preventing errors in property, plant, and equipment.

18–26 The following audit procedures were planned by Marissa Tomasetti, a public accountant, in the audit of the acquisition and payment cycle for Cooley Products, Inc.

1. Review the acquisitions journal for large and unusual transactions.

2. Send letters to several vendors, including a few for which the recorded accounts payable balance is zero, requesting them to inform us of their balance due from Cooley. Ask the controller to sign the letter.

3. Examine a sample of receiving report numbers and determine whether each one has an initial indicating that it was recorded as an account payable.

4. Select a sample of equipment listed on fixed asset master files and inspect the asset to determine that it exists and what condition it is in.

5. Refoot the acquisitions journal for one month and trace all totals to the general journal.

6. Calculate the ratio of equipment repairs and maintenance to total equipment, and compare with previous years.

7. Obtain from the client a written statement that all fixed assets accounts payable have been included in the current period financial statements and have been correctly valued.

8. Select a sample of canceled cheques and trace each one to the cash disbursements journal, comparing the name, date, and amount.

9. For 20 nontangible acquisitions, select a sample of line items from the acquisitions journal and trace each to related vendors' invoices. Examine whether each transaction appears to be an appropriate expenditure for the client and whether each was approved and recorded at the correct amount and date in the journal and charged to the correct account per the chart of accounts.

10. Examine invoices included in the client's unpaid invoice file at the audit report date to determine if they were recorded in the appropriate accounting period.

11. Recalculate the portion of insurance premiums on the client's unexpired insurance schedule that is applicable to future periods.

12. When the cheque signer's assistant writes "paid" on supporting documents, watch whether she does it after the documents are reviewed and the cheques are signed.

Required:

a. For each procedure, identify the type of evidence being used.

b. For each procedure, identify whether it is an analytical procedure, test of controls, or test of details of balances.

c. For each test of controls, identify the internal control objectives being met.

d. For each test of details of balances, identify the audit objectives being met.

18–27 Hardware Manufacturing Company Limited, a closely held corporation, has operated since 19X4 but has not had its financial statements audited. The company now plans to issue additional capital stock to be sold to outsiders and wishes to engage you to examine its 19X8 transactions and render an opinion on the financial statements for the year ended December 31, 19X8.

The company has expanded from one plant to three and has frequently acquired, modified, and disposed of all types of equipment. Fixed assets have a net book value of 70 percent of total assets and consist of land and buildings, diversified machinery and equipment, and furniture and fixtures. Some property was acquired by donation from shareholders. Depreciation was recorded by several methods using various estimated lives.

Required:

a. May you confine your examination solely to 19X8 transactions as requested by this prospective client whose financial statements have not previously been examined? Why?

b. Prepare an audit program for the January 1, 19X8, opening balances of the land, building, and equipment and accumulated depreciation accounts of Hardware Manufacturing Company Limited. You need not include tests of 19X8 transactions in your program.

(AICPA adapted)

18–28 The following program has been prepared for the audit of prepaid real estate taxes of a client that pays taxes on twenty-five different pieces of property, some of which have been acquired in the current year.

1. Obtain a schedule of prepaid taxes from the client and tie the total to the general ledger.
2. Compare the charges for annual tax payments with property tax assessment bills.
3. Recompute prepaid amounts for all payments on the basis of the portion of the year expired.

Required:
    a. State the purpose of each procedure.
    b. Evaluate the adequacy of the audit program.

18–29 As part of the audit of different audit areas, it is important to be alert for the possibility of unrecorded liabilities. For each of the following audit areas or accounts, describe a liability that could be uncovered and the audit procedures that could uncover it.
    a. Minutes of the board of directors' meetings
    b. Land and buildings
    c. Rent expense
    d. Interest expense
    e. Cash surrender value of life insurance
    f. Cash in the bank
    g. Officers' travel and entertainment expense

18–30 While you are having lunch with a banker friend, you become involved in explaining to him how your firm conducts an audit in a typical engagement. Much to your surprise, your friend is interested and is able to converse intelligently in discussing your philosophy of emphasizing the study of internal control, analytical procedures, tests of controls, and tests of details of balance sheet accounts. At the completion of your discussion, he says, "That all sounds great except for a couple of things. The point of view we take these days at our bank is the importance of a continuous earnings stream. You seem to be emphasizing fraud detection and a fairly stated balance sheet. We would rather see you put more emphasis than you apparently do on the income statement."

Required:
How would you respond to your friend's comments?

18–31 Eugene Fikursky, a staff assistant, has been asked to analyze interest and legal expense as a part of the first-year audit of Chinook Manufacturing Corp. In searching for a model to follow, Fikursky looked at other completed working papers in the current audit file and concluded that the closest thing to what he was looking for was a working paper for repair and maintenance expense account analysis. Following the approach used in analyzing repairs and maintenance, all interest and legal expenses in excess of $500 were scheduled and verified by examining supporting documentation.

Required:
    a. Evaluate Fikursky's approach to verifying interest and legal expense.
    b. Suggest a better approach to verifying these two account balances.

18–32 In performing tests of the acquisition and payment cycle for Oakville Manufacturing, Inc., the staff assistant did a careful and complete job. Since internal control was evaluated as excellent before tests of controls were performed and was determined to be operating effectively on the basis of the lack of exceptions in the tests of controls, the decision was made to reduce significantly the tests of expense account analysis. The in-charge auditor decided to reduce but not eliminate the acquisition-related expense account analysis for repair expense, legal and other professional expense, miscellaneous expense, and utilities expense on the ground that they should always be verified more extensively than normal accounts. The decision was also made to eliminate any account analysis for the purchase of raw materials, depreciation expense, supplies expense, insurance expense, and the current period additions to fixed assets.

Required:
a. List other considerations in the audit besides the quality of internal control that should affect the auditor's decision as to which accounts to analyze.

b. Assuming no significant problems were identified on the basis of the other considerations in part a, evaluate the auditor's decision to reduce but not to eliminate expense account analysis for each account involved. Justify your conclusions.

c. Assuming no significant problems were identified on the basis of the other considerations in part a, evaluate the auditor's decision to eliminate expense account analysis for each account involved. Justify your conclusions.

CASES

18–33 Examine the tests of controls results, including the attributes sampling application in Case 17–34 for Ward Publishing Company Ltd. Assume you have already reached several conclusions.

1. Your tests of details of balances for accounts payable are completed and you found no exceptions.

2. Audit risk for property, plant, and equipment and all expenses is high.

3. Inherent risk for property, plant, and equipment is high because in the current year the client has purchased a material amount of new and used printing equipment and traded in older equipment. Some of the new equipment was ineffective and returned; an allowance was received on others. Inherent risk for expense accounts is low.

4. New computer equipment and some printing equipment is being leased. The client has never leased equipment before.

5. Analytical procedures for property, plant, and equipment are inconclusive because of the large increases in acquisition and disposal activity.

6. Analytical procedures show that repairs, maintenance, and small tools expenses have increased materially, both in absolute terms and as a percentage of sales. Two other expenses have also materially increased and one has materially decreased.

7. In examining the attributes sample for tests of controls, you observe that no sample items included any property, plant, and equipment or lease transactions.

Required:
a. Explain the relationship between the tests of controls results in Case 17–34 and the audit of property, plant, and equipment and leases.

b. How would the tests of controls results and your conclusions (1 through 7) affect your planned tests of details for property, plant, and equipment and leases? State your conclusions for each audit objective. Do not write an audit program.

c. Explain the relationship between the tests of controls results in Case 17–34 and the audit of expenses.

d. How would the tests of controls results and your conclusions (1 through 7) affect your planned tests of details of balances for expenses? Do not write an audit program.

18–34 You are doing the audit of the Ute Corporation, for the year ended December 31, 19X6. The schedule on page 645 for the property, plant, and equipment and related allowance for depreciation accounts has been prepared by the client. You have compared the opening balances with your prior year's audit work papers.

**UTE CORPORATION ANALYSIS OF PROPERTY, PLANT, AND EQUIPMENT
AND RELATED ALLOWANCE FOR DEPRECIATION ACCOUNTS
Year Ended December 31, 19X6**

DESCRIPTION	FINAL 12/31/X5	ADDITIONS	RETIREMENTS	PER BOOKS 12/31/X6
Assets				
Land	$ 22,500	$ 5,000		$ 27,500
Buildings	120,000	17,500		137,500
Machinery and equipment	385,000	40,400	$26,000	399,400
	$527,500	$62,900	$26,000	$564,400
Allowance for Depreciation				
Building	$ 60,000	$ 5,150		$ 65,150
Machinery and equipment	173,250	39,220		212,470
	$233,250	$ 44,370		$277,620

The following information is found during your audit:

1. All equipment is depreciated on the straight-line basis (no salvage value taken into consideration) based on the following estimated lives: buildings, 25 years; all other items, 10 years. The corporation's policy is to take one-half-year's depreciation on all asset acquisitions and disposals during the year.

2. On April 1, the corporation entered into a 10-year lease contract for a die-casting machine with annual rentals of $5,000, payable in advance every April 1. The lease is cancelable by either party (60 days' written notice is required), and there is no option to renew the lease or buy the equipment at the end of the lease. The estimated useful life of the machine is ten years with no salvage value. The corporation recorded the die-casting machine in the machinery and equipment account at $40,400, the present value at the date of the lease, and $2,020, applicable to the machine, has been included in depreciation expense for the year.

3. The corporation completed the construction of a wing on the plant building on June 30. The useful life of the building was not extended by this addition. The lowest construction bid received was $17,500, the amount recorded in the buildings account. Company personnel were used to construct the addition at a cost of $16,000 (materials, $7,500; labor, $5,500; and overhead, $3,000).

4. On August 18, $5,000 was paid for paving and fencing a portion of land owned by the corporation and used as a parking lot for employees. The expenditure was charged to the land account.

5. The amount shown in the machinery and equipment asset retirement column represents cash received on September 5, upon disposal of a machine purchased in July 19X2 for $48,000. The bookkeeper recorded depreciation expense of $3,500 on this machine in 19X6.

6. Crux City donated land and building appraised at $10,000 and $40,000, respectively, to the Ute Corporation for a plant. On September 1, the corporation began operating the plant. Since no costs were involved, the bookkeeper made no entry for the foregoing transaction.

Required:

a. In addition to inquiry of the client, explain how you found each of the given six items during the audit.

b. Prepare the adjusting journal entries with supporting computations that you would suggest at December 31, 19X6, to adjust the accounts for the above transactions. Disregard income tax implications.   (AICPA adapted)

19

AUDIT OF THE INVENTORY AND WAREHOUSING CYCLE

LEARNING OBJECTIVES

THOROUGH STUDY OF THIS CHAPTER WILL ENABLE YOU TO:

1. Describe the inventory and warehousing cycle and the pertinent functions, documents and records, and internal controls

2. Explain the significance of the five parts of the inventory and warehousing cycle to the auditor

3. Design and perform audit tests of cost accounting

4. Design and perform analytical procedures for the accounts in the inventory and warehousing cycle

5. Design and perform physical observation audit tests for inventory

6. Design and perform audit tests of pricing and compilation for inventory

7. Explain how the various parts of the audit of the inventory and warehousing cycle are integrated

☐ Inventory takes many different forms, depending on the nature of the business. For retail or wholesale businesses, the most important inventory is merchandise on hand, available for sale. For hospitals, it includes food, drugs, and medical supplies. A manufacturing company has raw materials, purchased parts, and supplies for use in production, goods in the process of being manufactured, and finished goods available for sale. We have selected manufacturing company inventories for presentation in this text. However, most of the principles discussed apply to other types of businesses as well.

For the reasons that follow, the audit of inventories is often the most complex and time-consuming part of the audit:

- Inventory is generally a major item on the balance sheet, and it is often the largest item making up the accounts included in working capital.
- The inventory is in different locations, which makes physical control and counting difficult. Companies must have their inventory accessible for the efficient manufacture and sale of the product, but this dispersal creates significant audit problems.
- The diversity of the items in inventories creates difficulties for the auditor. Such items as jewels, chemicals, and electronic parts present problems of observation and valuation.
- The valuation of inventory is also difficult due to such factors as obsolescence and the need to allocate manufacturing costs to inventory.
- There are several acceptable inventory valuation methods, but any given client must apply a method consistently from year to year. Moreover, an organization may prefer to use different valuation methods for different parts of the inventory.

The trial balance for Hillsburg Hardware Ltd. on page 135 shows that only two accounts are affected by inventories and warehousing: inventory and cost of goods sold. However, both accounts are highly material. For a manufacturing company, far more accounts are affected because labor, acquisitions of raw materials, and all indirect manufacturing costs affect inventory.

The physical flow of goods and the flow of costs in the inventory and warehousing cycle for a manufacturing company are shown in Figure 19–1. The direct tie-in of the inventory and warehousing cycle to the acquisition and payment cycle and the payroll and personnel cycle can be seen by examining the debits to the raw materials, direct labor, and manufacturing overhead T-accounts. The direct tie-in to the sales and collection cycle occurs at the point where finished goods are relieved (credited) and a charge is made to cost of goods sold. This close relationship to other transaction cycles in the organization is a basic characteristic of the audit of the inventory and warehousing cycle for a manufacturing company.

OBJECTIVE 1

Describe the inventory and warehousing cycle and the pertinent functions, documents and records, and internal controls.

Functions in the Cycle and Internal Controls

The inventory and warehousing cycle can be thought of as comprising two separate but closely related systems, one involving the actual *physical flow of goods*, and the other the *related costs*. As inventories move through the company, there must be adequate controls over both their physical movement and their related costs. A brief examination of the six functions making up the inventory and warehousing cycle will help students understand these controls and the audit evidence needed to test their effectiveness.

Process Purchase Orders

Purchase requisitions are used to request the purchasing department to place orders for inventory items. Requisitions may be initiated by stockroom personnel when inventory reaches a predetermined level, orders may be placed for the materials required to produce a particular customer order, or orders may be initiated on the basis of a periodic inventory count by a responsible person. Regardless of the method followed, the controls over purchase requisitions and the related purchase orders are evaluated and tested as part of the acquisition and payment cycle.

FIGURE 19–1

Flow of Inventory and
Costs

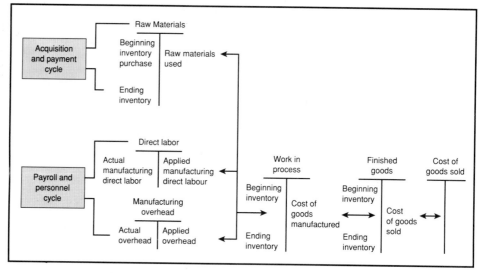

Receive New Materials
Receipt of the ordered materials is also part of the acquisition and payment cycle. Material received should be inspected for quantity and quality. The receiving department produces a *receiving report* that becomes a part of the necessary documentation before payment is made. After inspection, the material is sent to the storeroom and the receiving documents are typically sent to purchasing, the storeroom, and accounts payable.

Store Raw Materials
When materials are received, they are stored in the stockroom until needed for production. Materials are issued out of stock to production upon presentation of a properly approved materials requisition, work order, or similar document that indicates the type and quantity of materials needed. This requisition document is used to update the perpetual inventory master files and to make book transfers from the raw materials to work-in-process accounts.

Process the Goods
The processing portion of the inventory and warehousing cycle varies greatly from company to company. The determination of the items and quantities to be produced is generally based on specific orders from customers, sales forecasts, predetermined finished goods inventory levels, and economic production runs. Frequently, a separate production control department is responsible for the determination of the type and quantities of items to be produced. Within the various production departments, provision must be made to account for the quantities produced, control of scrap, quality controls, and physical protection of the material in process. The production department must generate production and scrap

reports so that accounting can reflect the movement of materials in the books and determine accurate costs of production.

In any company involved in manufacturing, adequate *cost accounting internal control* is an important part of the processing of goods function. Internal control is necessary to indicate the relative profitability of the various products for management planning and control and to value inventories for financial statement purposes. There are basically two types of cost systems, although many variations and combinations of these systems are employed: *job cost* and *process cost*. The main difference is whether costs are accumulated by individual jobs when material is issued and labor costs incurred (job cost), or whether they are accumulated by particular processes, with unit costs for each process assigned to the products passing through the process (process cost).

Cost accounting records consist of master files, worksheets, and reports that accumulate material, labor, and overhead costs by job or process as the costs are incurred. When jobs or products are completed, the related costs are transferred from work-in-process to finished goods on the basis of production department reports.

Store Finished Goods

As finished goods are completed by the production department, they are placed in the stockroom awaiting shipment. In companies with good internal controls, finished goods are kept under physical control in a separate limited access area. The control of finished goods is often considered part of the sales and collection cycle.

Ship Finished Goods

Shipping of completed goods is an integral part of the sales and collection cycle. Any shipment or transfer of finished goods must be authorized by a properly approved shipping document. The controls for shipment have already been studied in previous chapters.

Perpetual Inventory Master Files

One of the records used for inventory that has not been previously discussed is a perpetual inventory master file. Separate perpetual records are normally kept for raw materials and finished goods. Most companies do not use perpetuals for work-in-process.

Perpetual inventory master files can include only information about the units of inventory purchased, sold and on hand, or they can also include information about unit costs. The latter is more typical of well-designed computerized systems.

For purchases of raw materials, the perpetual inventory master file is updated automatically when purchases of inventory are processed as a part of recording acquisitions. For example, when the computer system enters the number of units and unit cost for each raw material purchase, this information is used to update perpetual inventory master files along with the acquisitions journal and accounts payable master file. Chapter 17 described the recording of purchase transactions.

Transfers of raw material from the storeroom must be separately entered into the computer to update the perpetual records. Typically, only the units transferred need to be entered because the computer can determine the unit costs from the master file. Raw material perpetual inventory master files that have unit costs include, for each raw material, beginning and ending units on hand and unit

FIGURE 19–2

Functions in the
Inventory and
Warehousing Cycle

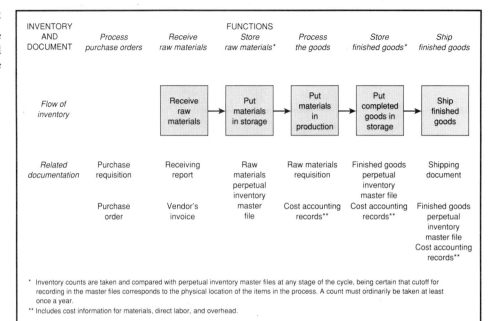

* Inventory counts are taken and compared with perpetual inventory master files at any stage of the cycle, being certain that cutoff for recording in the master files corresponds to the physical location of the items in the process. A count must ordinarily be taken at least once a year.
** Includes cost information for materials, direct labor, and overhead.

costs, units and unit cost of each purchase and units and unit cost of each transfer into production.

Finished goods perpetual inventory master files include the same type of information as raw materials perpetuals, but are considerably more complex if costs are included along with units. Finished goods costs include raw materials, direct labor, and manufacturing overhead, which often requires allocations and detailed record keeping. When finished goods perpetuals include unit costs, the cost accounting records must be integrated into the computer system.

*Summary of
Inventory
Documentation*

The physical movement and related documentation in a basic inventory and warehousing cycle is shown in Figure 19–2. The figure reemphasizes the important point that the recording of costs and movement of inventory as shown in the books must correspond to the physical movements and processes.

**Parts of the Audit
of Inventory**

The overall objective in the audit of the inventory and warehousing cycle is to determine that raw materials, work-in-process, finished goods inventory, and cost of goods sold are fairly stated on the financial statements. The basic inventory and warehousing cycle can be divided into five distinct parts.

Acquire and Record Raw Materials, Labor, and Overhead

This part of the inventory and warehousing cycle includes the first three functions in Figure 19–2: processing of purchase orders, receipt of raw materials, and storage of raw materials. The internal controls over these three functions are first understood, then tested as a part of performing tests of controls in the acquisition and payment cycle and the payroll and personnel cycle. At the completion of the acquisition and payment cycle, the auditor should be satisfied that acquisitions of raw materials and manufacturing costs are correctly stated. Similarly, when labor is a significant part of inventory, the payroll and personnel cycle tests should verify the proper accounting for these costs.

Transfer Assets and Costs

Internal transfers include the fourth and fifth functions in Figure 19–2: processing the goods and storing finished goods. These two activities are not related to any other transaction cycles and therefore must be studied and tested as part of the inventory and warehousing cycle. The accounting records concerned with these functions are referred to as the *cost accounting records*.

Ship Goods and Record Revenue and Costs

The recording of shipments and related costs, the last function in Figure 19–2, is part of the sales and collection cycle. Thus, the internal controls over the function are understood and tested as a part of auditing the sales and collection cycle. The tests of controls should include procedures to verify the accuracy of the perpetual inventory master files.

Physically Observe Inventory

Observing the client taking a physical inventory count is necessary to determine whether recorded inventory actually exists at the balance sheet date and is properly counted by the client. Inventory is the first audit area for which physical examination is an essential type of evidence used to verify the balance in an account. Physical observation is studied in this chapter.

Price and Compile Inventory

The costs used to value the physical inventory must be tested to determine whether the client has correctly followed an inventory method that is in accordance with generally accepted accounting principles and is consistent with previous years. The audit procedures used to verify these costs are referred to as *price tests*. In addition, the auditor must verify whether the physical counts were correctly summarized, the inventory quantities and prices were correctly extended, and the extended inventory was correctly footed. These tests are called *compilation tests*.

Figure 19–3 summarizes the five parts of the audit of the inventory and warehousing cycle and shows the cycle in which each is audited. The first and third parts of the audit of the inventory and warehousing cycle have already been studied in connection with the other cycles. The importance of the tests of these other cycles should be kept in mind throughout the remaining sections of this chapter.

FIGURE 19–3

Audit of Inventory

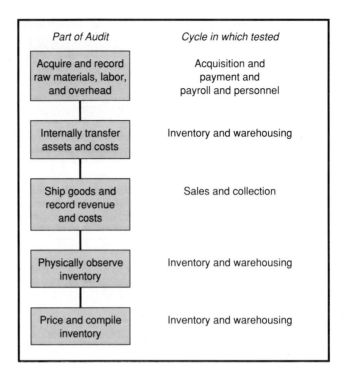

Part of Audit	Cycle in which tested
Acquire and record raw materials, labor, and overhead	Acquisition and payment and payroll and personnel
Internally transfer assets and costs	Inventory and warehousing
Ship goods and record revenue and costs	Sales and collection
Physically observe inventory	Inventory and warehousing
Price and compile inventory	Inventory and warehousing

Audit of Cost Accounting

OBJECTIVE 3

Design and perform audit tests of cost accounting.

The cost accounting internal controls of different companies vary more than most other internal controls because of the wide variety of items of inventory and the level of sophistication desired by management. For example, a company that manufactures an entire line of farm machines will have a completely different kind of cost records and internal controls than a steel fabricating shop that makes and instals custom-made metal cabinets. It should also not be surprising that small companies whose owners are actively involved in the manufacturing process will need less sophisticated records than will large multiproduct companies.

Cost Accounting Controls

Cost accounting controls are those related to the physical inventory and the consequent costs from the point at which raw materials are requisitioned to the point at which the manufactured product is completed and transferred to storage. It is convenient to divide these controls into two broad categories: physical controls over raw materials, work-in-process, and finished goods inventory, on the one hand, and controls over the related costs, on the other.

Almost all companies need physical controls over their assets to prevent loss from misuse and theft. The use of physically segregated, limited access storage areas for raw material, work-in-process, and finished goods is one major control to protect assets. In some instances the assignment of custody of inventory to specific responsible individuals may be necessary to protect the assets. Approved prenumbered documents for authorizing movement of inventory also protect the assets from improper use. Copies of these documents should be sent directly to accounting by the persons issuing them, bypassing people with custodial responsibilities. An example of an effective document of this type is an approved materials requisition for obtaining raw materials from the storeroom.

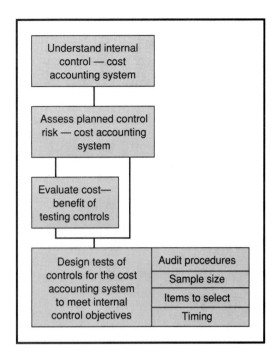

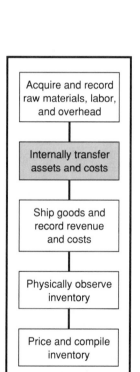

Perpetual inventory master files maintained by persons who do not have custody of or access to assets are another useful cost accounting control. Perpetual inventory master files are important for a number of reasons: they provide a record of items on hand, which is used to initiate production or purchase of additional materials or goods; they provide a record of the use of raw materials and the sale of finished goods, which can be reviewed for obsolete or slow-moving items; and they provide a record that can be used to pinpoint responsibility for custody as a part of the investigation of differences between physical counts and the amount shown on the records.

Another important consideration in cost accounting is the existence of adequate internal control that integrates production and accounting records for the purpose of obtaining accurate costs for all products. The existence of adequate cost records is important to management as an aid in pricing, controlling costs, and costing inventory.

Tests of Cost Accounting   The concepts in auditing cost accounting are no different from those discussed for any other transaction cycle. Figure 19–4 shows the methodology the auditor should follow in deciding which tests to perform. In auditing cost accounting, the auditor is concerned with four aspects: physical controls over inventory, documents and records for transferring inventory, perpetual inventory master files, and unit cost records.

Physical controls   The auditor's tests of the adequacy of the physical controls over raw materials, work-in-process, and finished goods must be restricted to observation and inquiry. For example, the auditor can examine the raw materials storage area to determine whether the inventory is protected from theft and misuse by the existence of a locked storeroom. The existence of an adequate storeroom with a competent custodian in charge also ordinarily results in the orderly storage of inventory. If the auditor concludes that the physical controls are so inadequate that the inventory will be difficult to count, the auditor should expand his or her observation of physical inventory tests to make sure that an adequate count is carried out.

Documents and records for transferring inventory   The auditor's primary concerns in verifying the transfer of inventory from one location to another are that the recorded transfers are valid, the transfers that have actually taken place are recorded, and the quantity, description, and date of all recorded transfers are accurate. First, it is necessary to understand the client's internal control for recording transfers before relevant tests can be performed. Once internal control is understood, the tests can easily be performed by examining documents and records. For example, a procedure to test the validity and accuracy of the transfer of goods from the raw material storeroom to the manufacturing assembly line is to account for a sequence of raw material requisitions, examine the requisitions for proper approval, and compare the quantity, description, and date with the information on the raw material perpetual inventory master files. Similarly, completed production records can be compared with perpetual inventory master files to be sure all manufactured goods were physically delivered to the finished goods storeroom.

Perpetual inventory master files   The existence of adequate perpetual inventory master files has a major effect on the *timing and extent* of the auditor's physical examination of inventory. For one thing, when there are accurate perpetual inventory master files it is frequently possible to test the physical inventory prior to the balance sheet date. An interim physical inventory can result in significant cost savings for both the client and the auditor, and enables the client to receive the audited statements earlier. Perpetual inventory master files also enable the auditor to reduce the extent of the tests of physical inventory when the assessed level of control risk related to physical observation of inventory is low.

Tests of the perpetual inventory master files for the purpose of reducing the tests of physical inventory or changing their timing are done through the use of documentation. Documents to verify the purchase of raw materials can be examined when the auditor is verifying acquisitions as part of the tests of the acquisition and payment cycle. Documents supporting the reduction of raw material inventory for use in production and the increase in the quantity of finished goods inventory when goods have been manufactured are examined as part of the tests of the cost accounting documents and records in the manner discussed in the preceding section. Support for the reduction in the finished goods inventory through the sale of goods to customers is ordinarily tested as part of the sales and collection cycle. Usually, it is relatively easy to test the accuracy of the perpetuals after the auditor determines how internal control is designed and decides to what degree assessed control risk should be reduced.

Unit cost records   Obtaining accurate cost data for raw materials, direct labor, and manufacturing overhead is an essential part of cost accounting. Adequate cost accounting records must be integrated with production and other accounting records in order to produce accurate costs of all products. Cost accounting records are pertinent to the auditor in that the valuation of ending inventory depends on the proper design and use of these records.

In testing the inventory cost records, the auditor must first develop an understanding of internal control. This is frequently somewhat time-consuming because the flow of costs is usually integrated with other accounting records, and it may not be obvious how internal control provides for the internal transfers of raw materials and for direct labor and manufacturing overhead as production is carried out.

Once the auditor understands internal control, the approach to internal verification involves the same concepts that were discussed in the verification of sales and purchase transactions. Whenever possible, it is desirable to test the cost accounting records as a part of the acquisition, payroll, and sales tests to avoid testing the records more than once. For example, when the auditor is testing purchase transactions as a part of the acquisition and payment cycle, it is desirable to trace the units and unit costs of raw materials to the perpetual inventory master files and the total cost to the cost accounting records. Similarly, when payroll costs data are maintained for different jobs, it is desirable to trace data from the payroll summary directly to the job cost record as a part of testing the payroll and personnel cycle.

A major difficulty in the verification of inventory cost records is determining the reasonableness of cost allocations. For example, the assignment of manufacturing overhead costs to individual products entails certain assumptions that can significantly affect the unit costs of inventory and therefore the fairness of the inventory valuation. In evaluating these allocations, the auditor must consider the reasonableness of both the numerator and the denominator that result in the unit costs. For example, in testing overhead applied to inventory on the basis of direct labor dollars, the overhead rate should approximate total actual manufacturing overhead divided by total actual direct labor dollars. Since total manufacturing overhead is tested as part of the tests of the acquisition and payment cycle and direct labor is tested as part of the payroll and personnel cycle, determining the reasonableness of the rate is not difficult. However, if manufacturing overhead is applied on the basis of machine hours, the auditor must verify the reasonableness of the machine hours by separate tests of the client's machine records. A major consideration in evaluating the reasonableness of all cost allocations, including manufacturing overhead, is consistency with previous years.

Analytical Procedures

Analytical procedures are as important in auditing inventory and warehousing as any other cycle. Table 19–1 includes several common analytical procedures and possible errors that may be indicated when fluctuations exist. Several of those analytical procedures have also been included in other cycles. An example is the gross margin percent.

Tests of Details for Inventory

The methodology for deciding which tests of details of balances to do for inventory and warehousing is essentially the same as that discussed for accounts receivable, accounts payable, and all other balance sheet accounts. It is shown in Figure 19–5. Notice that test results of several other cycles besides inventory and warehousing affect tests of details of balances for inventory.

TABLE 19-1

Analytical Procedures for Inventory and Warehousing

<table>
<tr><th>ANALYTICAL PROCEDURE</th><th>POSSIBLE MISSTATEMENT</th></tr>
<tr><td>Compare gross margin percentage with previous years.</td><td>Overstatement or understatement of inventory.</td></tr>
<tr><td>Compare inventory turnover (costs of goods sold divided by average inventory) with previous years.</td><td>Obsolete inventory</td></tr>
<tr><td>Compare unit costs of inventory with previous years.</td><td>Overstatement or understatement of unit costs.</td></tr>
<tr><td>Compare extended inventory value with previous years.</td><td>Errors in compilation, unit costs, or extensions.</td></tr>
<tr><td>Compare current-year manufacturing costs with previous years (variable costs should be adjusted for changes in volume).</td><td>Misstatement of unit costs of inventory, especially direct labor and manufacturing overhead.</td></tr>
</table>

OBJECTIVE 4

Design and perform analytical procedures for the accounts in the inventory and warehousing cycle.

FIGURE 19-5

Methodology for Designing Tests of Details of Balances for Inventory

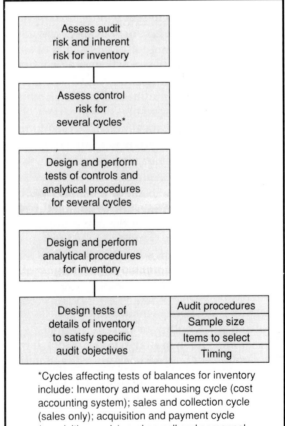

Because of the complexity of auditing inventory, two aspects of tests of details of balances are discussed separately: (1) physical observation and (2) pricing and compilation. These topics are studied in the next two sections.

Physical Observation of Inventory

OBJECTIVE 5

Design and perform physical observation audit tests for inventory.

Prior to the late 1930s, auditors generally avoided responsibility for determining either the physical existence or the accuracy of the count of inventory. Audit evidence for inventory quantities was usually restricted to obtaining a certification from management as to the correctness of the stated amount. In 1938, the discovery of major fraud in the McKesson & Robbins Company in the United States caused a reappraisal by the accounting profession of its responsibilities relating to inventory. In brief, the financial statements for McKesson & Robbins at December 31, 1937, which were "certified to" by a major accounting firm, reported total consolidated assets of $87 million. Of this amount, approximately $19 million was subsequently determined to be fictitious: $10 million in inventory and $9 million in receivables. Due primarily to their adherence to generally accepted auditing practice of that period, the auditing firm was not held directly at fault in the inventory area. However, it was noted that if certain procedures, such as observation of the physical inventory, had been carried out, the fraud would probably have been detected.

Section 6030.05 of the *CICA Handbook* states:

- Observation of the client's physical stocktaking, whether this is done at the end of the financial period or at some other date, is considered a most useful auditing procedure in assessing the degree of care which management exercises in establishing the existence and condition of inventories.

This notion of physical attendance is reinforced by Section 6030.09:

- *Generally accepted auditing procedures in respect of inventories should include: (b) attendance by the auditors at the stocktaking, whether this is at the end of the financial period or at other times. . . .*

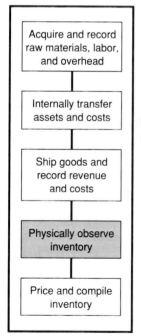

Acquire and record raw materials, labor, and overhead

Internally transfer assets and costs

Ship goods and record revenue and costs

Physically observe inventory

Price and compile inventory

"If attendance at stocktaking is not practicable in the circumstances," Section 6030.10 permits the auditor to apply *"other satisfactory procedures."* The phrase "not practicable" is taken to mean not feasible in the circumstances and not merely inconvenient or difficult. For example, an auditor who was appointed after a company's year end would find it not practicable to count inventory; driving 100 kilometres to attend an inventory count at a remote location may not be practical or convenient. If precluded, for any reason, from attending the physical stocktaking, the auditor must exercise judgment in deciding whether or not attendance was "practicable."

An essential point in the Section 6030 requirements is the distinction between the observation of the physical count and the responsibility for taking the count. The client has responsibility for setting up the procedures for taking an accurate physical inventory and actually making and recording the counts. The auditor's responsibility is to evaluate and observe the client's physical procedures and draw conclusions about the adequacy of those procedures and about the quantity and condition of the physical inventory.

Section 6030.07 does permit the auditor to count the inventory at a time other than the client's stocktaking "if the accounting system provides a good internal control over the inventories."

Controls   Regardless of the client's inventory record-keeping method, there must be a periodic physical count of the inventory items on hand. The client can take the physical count at or near the balance sheet date, at a preliminary date, or on a cycle basis throughout the year. The last two approaches are appropriate only if there are adequate perpetual inventory master files.

In connection with the client's physical count of inventory, adequate control procedures include proper instructions for the physical count, supervision by responsible personnel, independent internal verification of the counts, independent reconciliations of the physical counts with perpetual inventory master files, and adequate control over count tags or sheets.

An important aspect of the auditor's understanding of the client's physical inventory control procedures is complete familiarity with them before the inventory begins. This is obviously necessary to evaluate the effectiveness of the client's procedures, but it also enables the auditor to make constructive suggestions beforehand. If the inventory instructions do not provide adequate controls, the auditor must spend more time making sure the physical count is accurate.

Audit Decisions   The auditor's decisions in the physical observation of inventory are of the same general nature as in any other audit area: selection of audit procedures, timing, determination of sample size, and selection of the items for testing. The selection of the audit procedures is discussed throughout the section; the other three decisions are discussed briefly at this time.

Timing   The auditor decides whether the physical count can be taken prior to year-end primarily on the basis of the accuracy of the perpetual inventory master files. When an interim physical count is permitted, the auditor observes it at that time and also tests the perpetuals for transactions from the date of the count to year-end. When the perpetuals are accurate, it may be unnecessary for the client to count the inventory every year. Instead, the auditor can compare the perpetuals with the actual inventory on a sample basis at a convenient time. When there are no perpetuals and the inventory is material, a complete physical inventory must be taken by the client near the end of the accounting period and tested by the auditor at the same time.

Sample size   Sample size in physical observation is usually impossible to specify in terms of the number of items because the emphasis during the tests is on observing the client's procedures rather than on selecting particular items for testing. A convenient way to think of sample size in physical observation is in terms of the total number of hours spent rather than the number of inventory items counted. The most important determinants of the amount of time needed to test the inventory are the adequacy of the internal controls over the physical counts, the accuracy of the perpetual inventory master files, the total dollar amount and the type of inventory, the number of different significant inventory locations, and the nature and extent of errors discovered in previous years. In some situations inventory is such a significant item that dozens of auditors are necessary to observe the physical count, whereas in other situations one person can complete the observation in a short time.

Selection of items   The selection of the particular items for testing is an important part of the audit decision in inventory observation. Care should be taken to observe the counting of the most significant items and a representative sample of typical inventory items, to inquire about items that are likely to be obsolete or damaged, and to discuss with management the reasons for excluding any material items.

Physical Observation Tests

The same specific objectives that have been used in previous sections for tests of details of balances provide the frame of reference for discussing the physical observation tests. However, before the specific objectives are discussed, some comments that apply to all the objectives are appropriate.

The most important part of the observation of inventory is determining whether the physical count is being taken in accordance with the client's instructions. To do this effectively, *it is essential that the auditor be present* while the physical count is taking place. When the client's employees are not following the inventory instructions, the auditor must either contact the supervisor to correct the problem or modify the physical observation procedures. For example, if the procedures require one team to count the inventory and a second team to recount it as a test of accuracy, the auditor should inform management if he or she observes both teams counting together.

Obtaining an adequate understanding of the client's business is even more important in physical observation of inventory than for most aspects of the audit because inventory varies so significantly for different companies. A proper understanding of the client's business and its industry enables the auditor to ask about and discuss such problems as inventory valuation, potential obsolescence, and existence of consignment inventory intermingled with owned inventory. A useful starting point for becoming familiar with the client's inventory is for the auditor to tour the client's facilities, including receiving, storage, production, planning, and record-keeping areas. The tour should be led by a supervisor who can answer questions about production, especially about any changes in the past year.

Common tests of details audit procedures for physical inventory observation are shown in Table 19–2. For convenience, the order of the objectives is changed from that in previous chapters. The assumption throughout is that the client records inventory on prenumbered tags on the balance sheet date.

In addition to the detailed procedures included in Table 19–2, the auditor should walk through all areas where inventory is warehoused to make sure that all inventory has been counted and properly tagged. It is desirable to compare high dollar value inventory to counts in the previous year and inventory master files as a test of reasonableness. These two procedures should not be done until the client has completed its physical counts.

Audit of Pricing and Compilation

An important part of the audit of inventory is to perform all the procedures necessary to make certain the physical counts were properly priced and compiled. *Pricing* includes all the tests of the client's unit prices to determine whether they are correct. *Compilation* includes all the tests of the summarization of the physical counts, the extension of price times quantity, footing the inventory summary, and tracing the totals to the general ledger.

TABLE 19–2

Objectives and Tests of Details of Balances for Physical Inventory Observation

SPECIFIC AUDIT OBJECTIVE	COMMON INVENTORY OBSERVATION PROCEDURES	COMMENTS
Inventory as recorded on tags is valid. (validity)	Select a random sample of tag numbers and identify the tag with that number attached to the actual inventory. Observe whether movement of inventory takes place during the count.	The purpose is to uncover the inclusion of nonexistent items as inventory.
Existing inventory is counted and tagged (completeness).	Examine inventory to make sure it is tagged. Observe whether movement of inventory takes place during the count. Inquire as to inventory in other locations.	Special concern should be directed to omission of large sections of inventory.
Inventory as recorded on tags is owned (ownership).	Inquire as to consignment or customer inventory included on client's premises. Be alert for inventory that is set aside or specially marked as indications of nonownership.	
Inventory is counted accurately and excludes unusable items (valuation).	Recount client's counts to make sure the recorded counts are accurate on the tags (also check descriptions and unit of count, such as dozen or gross). Compare physical counts with perpetual inventory master file. Record client's counts for subsequent testing. Test for obsolete inventory by inquiry of factory employees and management, and alertness for items that are damaged, rust-or dust-covered, or located in inappropriate places.	Recording client counts in the working papers on *inventory count sheets* is done for two reasons: to obtain documentation that an adequate physical examination was made, and to test for the possibility that the client might change the recorded counts after the auditor leaves the premises.
Inventory is classified correctly on the tags (classification).	Examine inventory descriptions on the tags and compare with the actual inventory for raw material, work in process, and finished goods. Evaluate whether the percent of completion recorded on the tags for work in process is reasonable.	These tests would be done as a part of the first procedure in the valuation objective.
Information is obtained to make sure sales and inventory purchases are recorded in the proper period (cut-off).	Record in the working papers for subsequent follow-up the last shipping document number used at year-end. Make sure the inventory for that item was excluded from the physical count. Review shipping area for inventory set aside for shipment, but not counted. Record in the working papers for subsequent follow-up the last receiving report number used at year-end. Make sure the inventory for that item was included in the physical count. Review receiving area for inventory that should be included in the physical count.	Obtaining proper cutoff information for sales and purchases is an essential part of inventory observation. The appropriate tests during the field work were discussed for sales in Chapter 11 and for purchases in Chapter 17.

TABLE 19–2
(Continued)

SPECIFIC AUDIT OBJECTIVE	COMMON INVENTORY OBSERVATION PROCEDURES	COMMENTS
Tags are accounted for to make sure none are missing (mechanical accuracy).	Account for all used and unused tags to make sure none are lost or intentionally omitted. Record the tag numbers for those used and unused for subsequent follow-up.	These tests should be done at the completion of the physical count.
Inventory is adequately disclosed (disclosure).		Disclosure tests cannot be done until the inventory is compiled, priced, extended, and totaled.

OBJECTIVE 6

Design and perform audit tests of pricing and compilation for inventory.

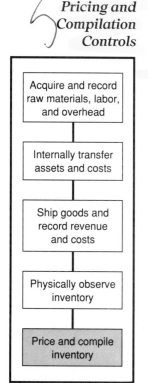

Pricing and Compilation Controls

The existence of adequate internal control for unit costs that is integrated with production and other accounting records is important to ensure that reasonable costs are used for valuing ending inventory. One important internal control is the use of *standard cost records* that indicate variances in material, labor, and overhead costs and can be used to evaluate production. When standard costs are used, procedures must be designed to keep the standards updated for changes in production processes and costs. The review of unit costs for reasonableness by someone independent of the department responsible for developing the costs is also a useful control over valuation.

An internal control designed to prevent the overstatement of inventory through the inclusion of obsolete inventory is a formal review and reporting of obsolete, slow-moving, damaged, and overstated inventory items. The review should be done by a competent employee by reviewing perpetual inventory master files for inventory turnover and holding discussions with engineering or production personnel.

Compilation internal controls are needed to provide a means of ensuring that the physical counts are properly summarized, priced at the same amount as the unit records, correctly extended and totaled, and included in the general ledger at the proper amount. Important compilation internal controls are adequate documents and records for taking the physical count and proper internal verification. If the physical inventory is taken on prenumbered tags and carefully reviewed before the personnel are released from the physical examination of inventory, there should be little risk of error in summarizing the tags. The most important internal control over accurate determination of prices, extensions, and footings is internal verification by a competent, independent person.

Pricing and Compilation Procedures

The specific objectives for tests of details of balances are also useful in discussing pricing and compilation procedures. The objectives and related tests are shown in Table 19–3 on page 662, except for the cutoff objective. The order followed is again changed for convenience. Physical observation, which was previously discussed, is a major source of cutoff information for sales and purchases. The tests of the accounting records for cutoff are done as a part of sales (sales and collection cycle) and purchases (acquisition and payment cycle).

The frame of reference for applying the objectives is a listing of inventory obtained from the client that includes each inventory item's description, quantity, unit price, and extended value. The inventory listing is in inventory item description order with raw material, work-in-process, and finished goods separated. The total equals the general ledger balance.

TABLE 19–3

Objectives and Tests of Details of Balances for Inventory Pricing and Compilation

SPECIFIC AUDIT OBJECTIVE	COMMON TESTS OF DETAILS OF BALANCES PROCEDURES	COMMENTS
Inventory items in the inventory listing schedule are valid (validity).	Trace inventory listed in the schedule to inventory tags and auditor's recorded counts for existence and description.	The following objectives (except mechanical accuracy) are affected by the results of the physical inventory observation. The tag numbers and counts verified as a part of physical inventory observation are traced to the inventory listing schedule as a part of these tests.
Existing inventory items are included in the inventory listing schedule (completeness).	Account for unused tag numbers shown in the auditor's working papers to make sure no tags have been added. Trace from inventory tags to the inventory listing schedules and make sure inventory on tags are included. Account for unused tag numbers to make sure none have been deleted.	
Inventory items in the inventory listing schedule are owned (ownership).	Trace inventory tags identified as nonowned during the physical observation to the inventory listing schedule to make sure these have not been included. Review contracts with suppliers and customers and inquire of management for the possibility of the inclusion of consigned or other nonowned inventory, or the exclusion of owned inventory that is not included.	
Inventory items in the inventory listing schedule are properly valued (valuation).	Trace inventory listed in the schedule to inventory tags and auditor's recorded counts for quantity and description. Perform price tests of inventory. For a discussion of price tests, see text material on pages 659-664.	
Inventory items in the inventory listing schedule are properly classified (classification).	Compare the classification into raw materials, work in process, and finished goods by comparing the descriptions on inventory tags and auditor's recorded test counts with the inventory listing schedule.	
Inventory in the inventory listing schedule agrees with the physical inventory counts, the extensions are correct, and the total is correctly added and agrees with the general ledger (mechanical accuracy).	Perform compilation tests (see validity, existence, and valuation objectives). Extend the quantity times the price on selected items. Foot the inventory listing schedules for raw materials, work in process, and finished goods. Trace the totals to the general ledger.	Unless controls are weak, extending and footing tests should be limited.
Inventory and related accounts in the inventory and warehousing cycle are properly disclosed (disclosure).	Examine financial statements for proper disclosure, including: Separate disclosure of raw materials, work in process, and finished goods. Proper description of the inventory costing method. Description of pledged inventory. Inclusion of significant sales and purchase commitments.	Pledging of inventory and sales and purchase commitments are usually uncovered as a part of other audit tests.

Valuation of Inventory

The proper valuation (pricing) of inventory is often one of the most important and time-consuming parts of the audit. In performing pricing tests, three things about the client's method of pricing are extremely important: the method must be in accordance with generally accepted accounting principles, the application of the method must be consistent from year to year, and replacement cost versus market value must be considered. Because the method of verifying the pricing of inventory depends on whether items are purchased or manufactured, these two categories are discussed separately.

Pricing purchased inventory   The primary types of inventory included in this category are raw materials, purchased parts, and supplies. As a first step in verifying the valuation of purchased inventory, it is necessary to establish clearly whether FIFO, LIFO, weighted average, or some other valuation method is being used. It is also necessary to determine which costs should be included in the valuation of a particular item of inventory. For example, the auditor must find out whether freight, storage, discounts, and other costs are included and compare the findings with the preceding year's audit working papers to make sure the methods are consistent.

In selecting specific inventory items for pricing, emphasis should be put on the larger dollar amounts and on products that are known to have wide fluctuations in price, but a representative sample of all types of inventory and departments should be included as well. Stratified variables or dollar unit sampling is commonly used in these tests.

The auditor should list the inventory items he or she intends to verify for pricing and request the client to locate the appropriate vendors' invoices. It is important that sufficient invoices be examined to account for the entire quantity of inventory for the particular item being tested, especially for the FIFO valuation method. Examining a sufficient number of invoices is useful to uncover situations in which clients value their inventory on the basis of the most recent invoice only and, in some cases, to discover obsolete inventory. As an illustration, assume that the client's valuation of a particular inventory item is $12.00 per unit for 1,000 units, using FIFO. The auditor should examine the most recent invoices for acquisitions of that inventory item made in the year under audit until the valuation of all of the 1,000 units is accounted for. If the most recent acquisition of the inventory item was for 700 units at $12.00 per unit and the immediately preceding acquisition was for 600 units at $11.30 per unit, the inventory item in question is overstated by $210.00 (300 × $.70).

When the client has perpetual inventory master files that include unit costs of acquisitions, it is usually desirable to test the pricing by tracing the unit costs to the perpetuals rather than to vendors' invoices. In most cases the effect is to reduce the cost of verifying inventory valuation significantly. Naturally, when the perpetuals are used to verify unit costs, it is essentially to test the unit costs on the perpetuals to vendors' invoices as a part of the tests of the acquisition and payment cycle.

In pricing inventory, it is necessary to consider whether historical or replacement cost is lower. The most recent cost of an inventory item as indicated on a vendor's invoice of the subsequent period is a useful way to test for replacement cost, but it is also necessary to consider the sales value of the inventory item and the possible effect of rapid fluctuation of prices. Finally, it is necessary to consider the possibility of obsolescence in the evaluation process.

Pricing manufactured inventory The auditor must consider the cost of raw materials, direct labor, and manufacturing overhead in pricing work-in-process and finished goods. The need to verify each of these has the effect of making the audit of work-in-process and finished goods inventory more complex than the audit of purchased inventory. Nevertheless, such considerations as selecting the items to be tested, testing for whether cost or market value is lower, and evaluating the possibility of obsolescence also apply.

In pricing raw materials in manufactured products, it is necessary to consider both the unit cost of the raw materials and the number of units required to manufacture a unit of output. The unit cost can be verified in the same manner as that used for other purchased inventory – by examining vendors' invoices or perpetual inventory master files. Then it is necessary to examine engineering specifications, inspect the finished product, or find a similar method to determine the number of units it takes to manufacture a particular product.

Similarly, the hourly costs of direct labor and the number of hours it takes to manufacture a unit of output must be verified while testing direct labor. Hourly labor costs can be verified by comparison with labor payroll or union contracts. The number of hours needed to manufacture the product can be determined from engineering specifications or similar sources.

The proper manufacturing overhead in work-in-process and finished goods is dependent on the approach being used by the client. It is necessary to evaluate the method being used for consistency and reasonableness and to recompute the costs to determine whether the overhead is correct. For example, if the rate is based on direct labor dollars, the auditor can divide the total manufacturing overhead by the total direct labor dollars to determine the actual overhead rate. This rate can then be compared with the overhead rate used by the client to determine unit costs.

When the client has *standard costs records*, an efficient and useful method of determining valuation is by the review and analysis of variances. If the variances in material, labor, and manufacturing overhead are small, it is evidence of reliable cost records.

Integration of the Tests

The most difficult part of understanding the audit of the inventory and warehousing cycle is grasping the interrelationship of the many different tests the auditor makes to evaluate whether inventory and cost of goods sold are fairly stated. Figure 19–6 and the discussions that follow are designed to aid the reader in perceiving the audit of the inventory and warehousing cycle as a series of integrated tests.

OBJECTIVE 7

Explain how the various parts of the audit of the inventory and warehousing cycle are integrated.

Tests of the acquisition and payment cycle Whenever the auditor verifies acquisitions as part of the tests of the acquisition and payment cycle, evidence is being obtained about the accuracy of raw materials purchased and all manufacturing overhead costs except labor. These acquisition costs either flow directly into cost of goods sold or become the most significant part of the ending inventory of raw material, work-in-process, and finished goods. In audits involving perpetual inventory master files, it is common to test these as a part of tests of controls procedures in the acquisition and payment cycle. Similarly, if manufacturing costs are assigned to individual jobs or processes, they are usually tested as a part of the same cycle.

FIGURE 19–6

Interrelationship of
Various Audit Tests

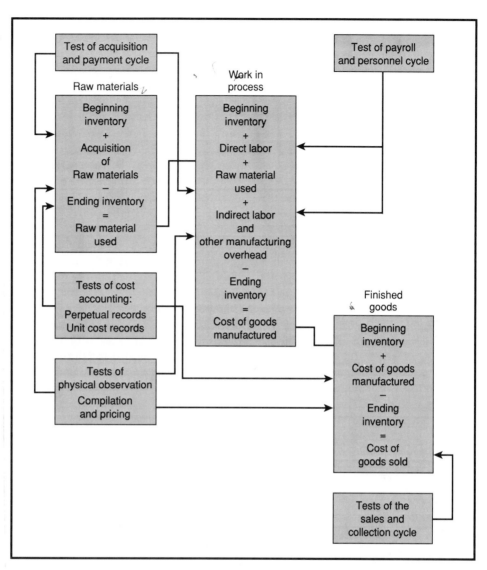

Tests of the payroll and personnel cycle   When the auditor verifies labor costs, the same comments apply as for acquisitions. In most cases, the cost accounting records for direct and indirect labor costs can be tested as part of the audit of the payroll and personnel cycle if there is adequate advance planning.

Tests of the sales and collection cycle   Although the relationship is less close between the sales and collection cycle and the inventory and warehousing cycle than between the two previously discussed, it is still important. Most of the audit testing in the storage of finished goods as well as the shipment and recording of sales takes place when the sales and collection cycle is tested. In addition, if standard cost records are used, it may be possible to test the standard cost of goods sold at the same time that sales tests are performed.

Tests of cost accounting   Tests of cost accounting are meant to verify the controls affecting inventory that were not verified as part of the three previously discussed cycles. Tests are made of the physical controls, transfers of raw material costs to work-in-process, transfers of costs of completed goods to finished goods, perpetual inventory master files, and unit cost records.

Physical inventory, compilation, and pricing   In most audits the underlying assumption in testing the inventory and warehousing cycle is that cost of goods sold is a residual of beginning inventory plus acquisitions of raw materials, direct labor, and other manufacturing costs minus ending inventory. When the audit of inventory and cost of goods sold is approached with this idea in mind, the importance of ending inventory becomes obvious. Physical inventory, compilation, and pricing are each equally important in the audit because an error in any one results in misstated inventory and cost of goods sold.

In testing the physical inventory, it is possible to rely heavily on the perpetual inventory master files if they have been tested as a part of one or more of the previously discussed tests. In fact, if the perpetual inventory master files are considered reliable, the auditor can observe and test the physical count at some time during the year and rely on the perpetuals to keep adequate records of the quantities.

When testing the unit costs, it is also possible to rely, to some degree, on the tests of the cost records made during the tests of transactions cycles. The existence of standard cost records is also useful for the purpose of comparison with the actual unit costs. If the standard costs are used to represent historical cost, they must be tested for reliability.

REVIEW QUESTIONS

19–1   Give the reasons why inventory is often the most difficult and time-consuming part of many audit engagements.

19–2   Explain the relationship between the acquisition and payment cycle and the inventory and warehousing cycle in the audit of a manufacturing company. List several audit procedures in the acquisition and payment cycle that support your explanation.

19–3   State what is meant by cost accounting records and explain their importance in the conduct of an audit.

19–4   Many auditors assert that certain audit tests can be significantly reduced for clients with adequate perpetual records that include both unit and cost data. What are the most important tests of the perpetual records the auditor must make before he or she can reduce the assessed level of control risk? Assuming the perpetuals are determined to be accurate, which tests can be reduced?

19–5   Before the physical examination, the auditor obtains a copy of the client's inventory instructions and reviews them with the controller. In obtaining an understanding of inventory procedures for a small manufacturing company, these deficiencies are identified: shipping operations will not be completely halted during the physical examination, and there will be no independent verification of the original inventory count by a second counting team. Evaluate the importance of each of these deficiencies and state its effect on the auditor's observation of inventory.

19–6   At the completion of an inventory observation, the controller requested a copy of all recorded test counts from the auditor to facilitate the correction of all discrepancies between the client's and the auditor's counts. Should the auditor comply with the request? Why?

19–7   What major audit procedures are involved in testing for the ownership of inventory during the observation of the physical counts and as a part of subsequent valuation tests?

19–8   In the verification of the amount of the inventory, one of the auditor's concerns is that slow-moving and obsolete items be identified. List the auditing procedures that could be employed to determine whether slow-moving or obsolete items have been included in inventory.

19–9   During the taking of physical inventory, the controller intentionally withheld several inventory tags from the employees responsible for the physical count. After the auditor left the client's premises at the completion of the inventory observation, the controller recorded nonexistent inventory on the tags and thereby significantly overstated earnings. How could the auditor have uncovered the misstatement, assuming there are no perpetual records?

19–10   Explain why a proper cutoff of purchases and sales is heavily dependent on the physical inventory observation. What information should be obtained during the physical count to make sure cutoff is accurate?

19–11   Define what is meant by compilation tests. List several examples of audit procedures to verify compilation.

19–12   List the major analytical procedures for testing the overall reasonableness of inventory. For each test, explain the type of misstatement that could be identified.

19–13   Included in the December 31, 19X7 inventory of the Kupitz Supply Ltd. are 2,600 deluxe ring binders in the amount of $5,902. An examination of the most recent purchases of binders showed the following costs: January 26, 19X8, 2,300 at $2.42 each; December 6, 19X7, 1,900 at $2.28 each; November 26, 19X7, 2,400 at $2.07 each. What is the error in valuation of the December 31, 19X7 inventory for deluxe ring binders assuming FIFO inventory valuation? What would your answer be if the January 26, 19X8 purchase was for 2,300 binders at $2.12 each?

19–14   Ruswell Manufacturing Ltd. applied manufacturing overhead to inventory at December 31, 19X7 on the basis of $3.47 per direct labor hour. Explain how you would evaluate the reasonableness of total direct labor hours and manufacturing overhead in the ending inventory of finished goods.

19–15   Each employee for the Gedding Manufacturing Co., a firm using a job-cost inventory costing method, must reconcile his or her total hours worked with the hours worked on individual jobs using a job time sheet at the time weekly payroll time cards are prepared. The job time sheet is then stapled to the time card. Explain how you could test the direct labor dollars included in inventory as a part of the payroll and personnel tests.

19–16   Assuming that the auditor properly documents receiving report numbers as a part of the physical inventory observation procedures, explain how he or she should verify the proper cutoff of purchases, including tests for the possibility of raw materials in transit, later in the audit.

MULTIPLE CHOICE QUESTIONS

19–17   The following questions concern internal controls in inventory and warehousing. Choose the best response.

   a. In a company whose materials and supplies include a great number of items, a fundamental deficiency in control requirements would be indicated if

   (1) a perpetual inventory master file is not maintained for items of small value.
   (2) the storekeeping function were to be combined with production and record keeping.
   (3) the cycle basis for physical inventory taking was to be used.
   (4) minor supply items were to be expensed when purchased.

b. For control purposes, the quantities of materials ordered may be omitted from the copy of the purchase order that is
   (1) forwarded to the accounting department.
   (2) retained in the purchasing department's files.
   (3) returned to the requisitioner.
   (4) forwarded to the receiving department.

c. Which of the following procedures would *best* detect the theft of valuable items from an inventory that consists of hundreds of different items selling for $1 to $10 and a few items selling for hundreds of dollars?
   (1) Maintain a perpetual inventory master file of only the more valuable items with frequent periodic verification of the validity of the perpetuals.
   (2) Have an independent public accounting firm prepare an internal control report on the effectiveness of the administrative and accounting controls over inventory.
   (3) Have separate warehouse space for the more valuable items with sequentially numbered tags.
   (4) Require an authorized officer's signature on all requisitions for the more valuable items.   (AICPA adapted)

19–18 The following questions concern testing the client's internal control for inventory and warehousing. Choose the best response.

a. When an auditor tests a client's cost accounting records, the auditor's tests are *primarily* designed to determine that
   (1) quantities on hand have been computed based on acceptable cost accounting techniques that reasonably approximate actual quantities on hand.
   (2) physical inventories are in substantial agreement with book inventories.
   (3) internal control is in accordance with generally accepted accounting principles and is functioning as planned.
   (4) costs have been properly assigned to finished goods, work-in-process, and cost of goods sold.

b. The accuracy of perpetual inventory master files may be established, in part, by comparing perpetual inventory records with
   (1) purchase requisitions.
   (2) receiving reports.
   (3) purchase orders.
   (4) vendor payments.

c. When evaluating inventory controls with respect to segregation of duties, a public accountant would be *least* likely to
   (1) inspect documents.
   (2) make inquiries.
   (3) observe procedures.
   (4) consider policy and procedure manuals.   (AICPA adapted)

19–19 The following questions deal with tests of details of balances and analytical procedures for inventory. Choose the best response.

a. An auditor would be *most* likely to learn of slow-moving inventory through
   (1) inquiry of sales personnel.
   (2) inquiry of stores personnel.
   (3) physical observation of inventory.

(4) review of perpetual inventory master files.

b. An inventory turnover analysis is useful to the auditor because it may detect

(1) inadequacies in inventory pricing.

(2) methods of avoiding cyclical holding costs.

(3) the optimum automatic reorder points.

(4) the existence of obsolete merchandise.

c. A public accountant examining inventory may appropriately apply sampling for attributes in order to estimate the

(1) average price of inventory items.

(2) percentage of slow-moving inventory items.

(3) dollar value of inventory.

(4) physical quantity of inventory items.   (AICPA adapted)

DISCUSSION QUESTIONS AND PROBLEMS

19–20 Items 1 through 8 are selected questions typically found in questionnaires used by auditors to obtain an understanding of internal control in the inventory and warehousing cycle. In using the questionnaire for a particular client, a "yes" response to a question indicates a possible internal control, whereas a "no" indicates a potential weakness.

1. Does the receiving department prepare prenumbered receiving reports and account for the numbers periodically for all inventory received, showing the description and quantity of materials?

2. Is all inventory stored under the control of a custodian in areas where access is limited?

3. Are all shipments to customers authorized by prenumbered shipping orders?

4. Is a detailed perpetual inventory master file maintained for raw materials inventory?

5. Are physical inventory counts made by someone other than storekeepers and those responsible for maintaining the perpetual inventory master file?

6. Are standard cost records used for raw materials, direct labor, and manufacturing overhead?

7. Is there a stated policy with specific criteria for writing off obsolete or slow-moving goods?

8. Is the clerical accuracy of the final inventory compilation checked by a person independent of those responsible for preparing it?

Required:

a. For each of the preceding questions, state the purpose of the internal control.

b. For each internal control, list a test of controls procedure to test its effectiveness.

c. For each of the preceding questions, identify the nature of the potential financial misstatement(s) if the control is not in effect.

d. For each of the potential misstatements in part (c), list a substantive audit procedure to determine whether a material error exists.

19–21 The cost accounting records are often an essential area to audit in a manufacturing or construction company.

Required:

a. Why is it important to review the cost accounting records and test their accuracy?

b. For the audit of standard cost accounting records in which 35 parts are manufactured, explain how you would determine whether each of the following were reasonable for part no. 21.

(1) Standard direct labor hours
(2) Standard direct overhead rate
(3) Standard overhead rate
(4) Standard units of raw materials
(5) Standard cost of a unit of raw materials
(6) Total standard cost

19-22 Following are audit procedures frequently performed in the inventory and warehousing cycle for a manufacturing company.

1. Compare the client's count of physical inventory at an interim date with the perpetual inventory master file.
2. Trace the auditor's test counts recorded in the working papers to the final inventory compilation and compare the tag number, description, and quantity.
3. Compare the unit price on the final inventory summary with vendors' invoices.
4. Read the client's physical inventory instructions and observe whether they are being followed by those responsible for counting the inventory.
5. Account for a sequence of raw material requisitions and examine each requisition for an authorized approval.
6. Trace the recorded additions on the finished goods perpetual inventory master file to the records for completed production.
7. Account for a sequence of inventory tags and trace each tag to the physical inventory to make sure it actually exists.

Required: State the purpose(s) of each of the procedures.

19-23 The following errors or omissions are included in the inventory and related records of Westbox Manufacturing Company Ltd.

1. An inventory item was priced at $12 each instead of at the correct cost of $12 per dozen.
2. In taking the physical inventory, the last shipments for the day were excluded from inventory and were not included as a sale until the subsequent year.
3. The clerk in charge of the perpetual inventory master file altered the quantity on an inventory tag to cover up the shortage of inventory caused by its theft during the year.
4. After the auditor left the premises, several inventory tags were lost and were not included in the final inventory summary.
5. In recording raw material purchases, the improper unit price was included in the perpetual inventory master file. Therefore, the inventory valuation was misstated because the physical inventory was priced by referring to the perpetual records.
6. During the physical count, several obsolete inventory items were included.
7. Because of a significant increase in volume during the current year and excellent control over manufacturing overhead costs, the manufacturing overhead rate applied to inventory was far greater than actual cost.

Required:
a. For each misstatement, state an internal control that should have prevented it from occurring.
b. For each misstatement, state a substantive audit procedure that could be used to uncover it.

19-24 Often an important aspect of a public accountant's examination of financial statements is his or her observation of the taking of physical inventory.

Required:
a. What are the general objectives or purposes of the public accountant's obser-

vation of the taking of the physical inventory? (Do not discuss the procedures or techniques involved in making the observation.)

b. For what purposes does the public accountant make and record test counts of inventory quantities during his or her observation of the taking of the physical inventory? Discuss.

c. A number of companies employ outside service companies that specialize in counting, pricing, extending, and footing inventories. These service companies usually furnish a certificate attesting to the value of the inventory.

Assuming that the service company took the inventory on the balance sheet date:

(1) How much reliance, if any, can the public accountant place on the inventory certificate of outside specialists? Discuss.

(2) What effect, if any, would the inventory certificate of outside specialists have upon the type of report the public accountant would render? Discuss.

(3) What reference, if any, would the public accountant make to the certificate of outside specialists in the auditor's report?   (AICPA adapted)

19–25 You encountered the following situations during the December 31, 19X7, physical inventory of Latner Shoe Distributor Corp.

a. Latner maintains a large portion of the shoe merchandise in 10 warehouses throughout eastern and central Canada. This ensures swift delivery service for its chain of stores. You are assigned alone to the Halifax warehouse to observe the physical inventory process. During the inventory count, several express trucks pulled in for loading. Although infrequent, express shipments must be attended to immediately. As a result, the employees who were counting the inventory stopped to assist in loading the express trucks. What should you do?

b. (1) In one storeroom of 10,000 items, you have test counted about 200 items of high value and a few items of low value. You found no errors. You also note that the employees are diligently following the inventory instructions. Do you think you have tested enough items? Explain.

(2) What would you do if you counted 150 items and found a substantial number of counting errors?

c. In observing an inventory of liquid shoe polish, you note that a particular lot is five years old. From inspection of some bottles in an open box, you find that the liquid has solidified in most of the bottles. What action should you take?

d. During your observation of the inventory count in the main warehouse, you found that most of the prenumbered tags that had been incorrectly filled out are being destroyed and thrown away. What is the significance of this procedure and what action should you take?

19–26 In connection with her examination of the financial statements of Knutson Products Co. Ltd., an assembler of home appliances, for the year ended May 31, 19X7, Raymonde Mathieu, public accountant, is reviewing with Knutson's controller the plans for a physical inventory at the company warehouse on May 31, 19X7. Finished appliances, unassembled parts, and supplies are stored in the warehouse, which is attached to Knutson's assembly plant. The plant will operate during the count. On May 30, the warehouse will deliver to the plant the estimated quantities of unassembled parts and supplies required for May 31 production, but there may be emergency requisitions on May 31. During the count, the warehouse will continue to receive parts and supplies and to ship finished appliances. However, appliances completed on May 31 will be held in the plant until after the physical inventory.

Required: What procedures should the company establish to ensure that the inventory count includes all items that should be included and that nothing is counted twice?

(AICPA adapted)

19–27 You are assigned to the December 31, 19X6 audit of Sea Gull Airframes, Inc. The company designs and manufactures aircraft superstructures and airframe components. You observed the physical inventory at December 31 and are satisfied it was properly taken. The inventory at December 31, 19X6, has been priced, extended, and totaled by the client and is made up of about 5,000 inventory items with a total valuation of $8,275,000. In performing inventory price tests you have decided to stratify your tests, and you conclude that you should have two strata: items with a total value over $5,000 and those with a value of less than $5,000. The book values are as follows:

	NO. OF ITEMS	TOTAL VALUE
More than $5,000	500	$4,150,000
Less than $5,000	4,500	4,125,000
	5,000	$8,275,000

In performing your pricing and extension tests, you have decided to test about 50 inventory items in detail. You selected 40 of the over $5,000 items and ten of those under $5,000 at random from the population. You find all items to be correct except for some of the following items A through G, which you believe may be in error. You have tested the following items, to this point, exclusive of A through G.

	NO. OF ITEMS	TOTAL VALUE
More than $5,000	36	$360,000
Less than $5,000	7	2,600

Sea Gull Airframes uses a periodic inventory system and values its inventory at the lower of FIFO cost or market. You were able to locate all invoices needed for your examination. The seven inventory items in the sample you believe may be in error, along with the relevant data for determining the proper valuation, are shown as follows.

INVENTORY ITEMS POSSIBLY IN ERROR

DESCRIPTION	QUANTITY	PRICE	TOTAL
A. L37 spars	3,000 metres	$8.00/metre	$24,000
B. B68 metal formers	3000 centimetres	4.00/metre	12,000
C. R01 metal ribs	1,500 metres	10.00/metre	15,000
D. St26 struts	1,000 metres	8.00/metre	8,000
E. Industrial hand drills	45 units	20.00 each	900
F. L803 steel leaf springs	40 pairs	69.00 each	276
G. V16 fasteners	5.50 dozen	10.00/dozen	55

Note: Amounts are as stated on client's inventory.

INFORMATION FOR PRICING FROM INVOICES

VOUCHER NUMBER	VOUCHER DATE	DATE PAID	TERMS	RECEIVING REPORT DATE	INVOICE DESCRIPTION
7-68	8-01-X1	8-21-X1	Net FOB destination	8-01-X1	77 V16 fasteners at $10 per dozen
11-81	10-16-X6	11-15-X6	Net FOB destination	10-18-X6	1,100 metres R01 metal ribs at $9.50 per metre; 2,000 metres St26 struts at $8.20 per metre
12-06	12-08-X6	12-30-X6	2/10, n/30 FOB S.P.	12-10-X6	180 L803 steel leaf springs at $69 each
12-09	12-10-X6	12-18-X6	Net FOB destination	12-11-X6	45 industrial hand drills at $20 each; guaranteed for four years
12-18	12-27-X6	12-27-X6	2/10, n/30 FOB S.P.	12-21-X6	4,200 metres L37 spars at $8 per metre
12-23	12-24-X6	1-03-X7	2/10, n/30 FOB destination	12-26-X6	1280 centimetres B68 metal formers at $4 per metre
12-61	12-29-X6	1-08-X7	Net FOB destination	12-29-X6	1,000 metres R01 metal ribs at $10 per metre; 800 metres St26 struts at $8 per metre
12-81	12-31-X6	1-20-X7	Net FOB destination	1-06-X7	2,000 metres L37 spars at $7.50 per metre; 2,000 metres R01 metal ribs at $10 per metre

In addition, you noted a freight bill for voucher 12-23 in the amount of $200. This bill was entered in the freight-in account. Virtually all freight was for the metal formers.

This is the first time Sea Gull Airframes has been audited by your firm.

Required:

a. Review all information and determine the inventory errors of the seven items in question. State any assumptions you consider necessary to determine the amount of the errors.

b. Prepare a work paper schedule to summarize your findings. Use the microcomputer to prepare the schedule (instructor option).

19–28 The following calculations were made as of December 31, 19X7 from the records of the Aladdin Products Supply Corp., a wholesale distributor of cleaning supplies.

	19X7	19X6	19X5	19X4
Gross margin as percentage of sales	26.4%	22.8%	22.7%	22.4%
Inventory turnover	56.1 days	47.9 days	48.3 days	47.1 days

Required: List several logical causes of the changes in the two ratios. What should the auditor do to determine the actual cause of the changes?

19–29 In an annual audit at December 31, 19X7, you find the following transactions near the closing date:

1. Merchandise costing $1,822 was received on January 3, 19X8, and the related purchase invoice recorded January 5. The invoice showed the shipment was made on December 29, 19X7, FOB destination.

2. Merchandise costing $625 was received on December 28, 19X7, and the invoice was not recorded. You located it in the hands of the purchasing agent; it was marked "on consignment."

3. A packing case containing products costing $816 was standing in the shipping room when the physical inventory was taken. It was not included in the inventory because it was marked "Hold for shipping instructions." Your investigation revealed that the customer's order was dated December 18, 19X7, but that the case was shipped and the customer billed on January 10, 19X8. The product was a stock item of your client.

4. Merchandise received on January 6, 19X8, costing $720 was entered in the purchase register on January 7, 19X8. The invoice showed shipment was made FOB supplier's warehouse on December 31, 19X7. Since it was not on hand at December 31, it was not included in inventory.

5. A special machine, fabricated to order for a customer, was finished and in the shipping room on December 31, 19X7. The customer was billed on that date and the machine excluded from inventory, although it was shipped on January 4, 19X8.

Assume that each of the amounts is material.

Required:

a. State whether or not the merchandise should be included in the client's inventory.

b. Give your reason for your decision on each item. (AICPA adapted)

19–30 As a part of your clerical tests of inventory for Alouette Manufacturing Ltd., you have tested about 20 percent of the dollar items and have found the following exceptions:

1. Extension errors:

DESCRIPTION	QUANTITY	PRICE	EXTENSION AS RECORDED
Wood	465 board metres	$ 2.00/board metre	$ 93.00
Metal-cutting tools	29 units	30.00 each	670.00
Cutting fluid	16 barrels	40.00/barrel	529.00
Sandpaper	300 sheets	.95/hundred	258.00

2. Differences located in comparing last year's costs with the current year's costs on the client's inventory lists:

DESCRIPTION	QUANTITY	THIS YEAR'S COST	PRECEDING YEAR'S COST
TA-114 precision-cutting torches	12 units	$500.00 each	Unable to locate
Aluminum scrap	4,500 kg	.005/kg	$.065/kg
Lubricating oil	400 litres	1.60/litre	1.05/litre

3. Test counts that you were unable to find when tracing from the test counts to the final inventory compilation:

TAG NO.	QUANTITY	CURRENT-YEAR COST	DESCRIPTION
2958	15 tonnes	$75/tonnes	Cold-rolled bars
0026	2,000 metres	2.25/metre	4″ aluminum stripping

4. Page total, footing errors:

PAGE NO.	CLIENT TOTAL	CORRECT TOTAL
14	$1,375.12	$1,375.08
82	8,721.18	8,521.18

Required:

a. State the amount of the actual error in each of the four tests. For any item for which amount of the error cannot be determined from the information given, state the considerations that would affect your estimate of the error.

b. As a result of your findings, what would you do about clerical accuracy tests of the inventory in the current year?

c. What changes, if any, would you suggest in internal controls and procedures for Alouette Manufacturing during the compilation of next year's inventory to prevent each type of error?

19–31 You have been engaged for the audit of Saskatoon Chemicals Ltd. for the year ended December 31, 19X7. Saskatoon Chemicals is engaged in the wholesale chemical business and makes all sales at 25 percent over cost.

Following are portions of the client's sales and purchases accounts for the calendar year 19X7.

SALES

Date	Reference	Amount		BALANCE FORWARD	
			Date	Reference	Amount
12-31	Closing entry	$699,860			$658,320
			12-27	*SI#965	5,195
			12-28	SI#966	19,270
			12-28	SI#967	1,302
			12-31	SI#969	5,841
			12-31	SI#970	7,922
			12-31	SI#971	2,010
		$699,860			$699,860

PURCHASES

	BALANCE FORWARD		Date	Reference	Amount
Date	Reference	Amount			
		$360,300	12-31	Closing entry	$385,346
12-28	†RR#1059	3,100			
12-30	RR#1061	8,965			
12-31	RR#1062	4,861			
12-31	RR#1063	8,120			
		$385,346			$385,346

* SI, sales invoice.
† RR, receiving report.

You observed the physical inventory of goods in the warehouse on December 31, 19X7 and were satisfied that it was properly taken.

When performing a sales and purchases cutoff test, you found that at December 31, 19X7, the last receiving report that had been used was no. 1063 and that no shipments have been made on any sales invoices with numbers larger than no. 968. You also obtained the following additional information.

1. Included in the warehouse physical inventory at December 31, 19X7, were chemicals that had been purchased and received on receiving report no. 1060 but for which an invoice was not received until 19X8. Cost was $2,183.

2. In the warehouse at December 31, 19X7, were goods that had been sold and paid for by the customer but which were not shipped out until 19X8. They were all sold on sales invoice no. 965 and were not inventoried.

3. On the evening of December 31, 19X7, there were two cars on the Saskatoon Chemicals company siding:

   (a) Car AR38162 was unloaded on January 2, 19X8, and received on receiving report no. 1063. The freight was paid by the vendor.

   (b) Car BAE74123 was loaded and sealed on December 31, 19X7, and was switched off the company's siding on January 2, 19X8. The sales price was $12,700 and the freight was paid by the customer. This order was sold on sales invoice no. 968.

4. Temporarily stranded at December 31, 19X7, on a railroad siding were two cars of chemicals en route to the Sask-Man Pulp and Paper Co. Ltd. They were sold on sales invoice no. 966 and the terms were FOB destination.

5. En route to Saskatoon Chemicals on December 31, 19X7, was a truckload of material that was received on receiving report no. 1064. The material was shipped FOB destination and freight of $75 was paid by Saskatoon Chemicals. However, the freight was deducted from the purchase price of $975.

6. Included in the physical inventory were chemicals exposed to rain in transit and deemed unsalable. Their invoice cost was $1,250, and freight charges of $350 had been paid on the chemicals.

Required:

a. Compute the adjustments that should be made to the client's physical inventory at December 31, 19X7.

b. Prepare the auditor's worksheet adjusting entries that are required as of December 31, 19X7.   (AICPA adapted)

19–32 You are testing the summarization and cost of raw materials and purchased part inventories as a part of the audit of Rubber Products and Supply Corp. There are 2,000 inventory items with a total recorded value of $648,500.

Your audit tests are to compare recorded descriptions and counts with the final inventory listing, compare unit costs with vendors' invoices, and extend unit costs times quantity. An error in any of those is defined as a difference. You plan to use dollar unit sampling.

You make the following decisions about the audit of inventory:

Tolerable misstatement (same for upper as for lower)	$16,000
Average percent of error assumption-overstatements	50%
Average percent of error assumption-understatements	100%
Acceptable risk of incorrect acceptance	5%
Estimated error rate in the population	.5%

Required:

a. What are the advantages of using dollar unit sampling in this situation?

b. What is the sample size necessary to achieve your audit objectives using dollar unit sampling?

c. Without regard to your answer to part (b), assume that a sample of 60 items is selected and the following differences between book and audited values are identified (understatements are in parentheses); the book or recorded amounts are also shown.

ITEM NO.	DIFFERENCE	BOOK AMOUNT
1	$19	$ 700.
2	11	136.
3	(19)	820.
4	40	250.
5	90	300.
6	38	210.
7	(90)	2,150.
8	70	300.
9	(85)	950.
Total	$74	

For each of the other 116 items in the sample, there was no difference between the book and the audited values.

Based on this sample, calculate the adjusted overstatement and understatement error bounds.

d. Is the book value misstated?

CASE

19–33 You are observing inventory as a part of the August 31 year-end audit of Fortin Engine Supply Ltd., a wholesale and retail engine parts company. Inventory includes a large number of diverse parts varying from small bolts to large engines for earth-moving equipment.

The company has ceased operation during the physical count except for receiving goods from suppliers and making shipments to essential wholesale customers. On the morning of the physical count, which is Saturday, September 2, you record in your working papers the last shipping document and receiving report number issued the previous day. They are 109,314 and 41,682, respectively.

You observe the client's counting procedures and test count selected inventory yourself. You conclude the counts and descriptions are accurate. Before you leave the warehouse at the end of the day, after all counting is completed, you do several things:

1. Examine the receiving report book. The last number used was 41,685. The receiving clerk informs you all goods received on September 2 were kept in the receiving department with other goods received during the past two or three days.

2. Examine the shipping document book. The last number used was 109,317. The shipping department informs you that three shipments were made before noon, two were made after noon, and one was still in the shipping department.

3. Ask the receiving department to identify all goods received September 1. The receiver identifies receiving reports 41,680 through 41,682 as having been received September 1.

4. Ask the shipping department to identify all goods shipped or sold over the counter September 1. The shipper informs you goods on shipping documents 109,311 to 109,313 were shipped September 1, and shows you approximately 300 duplicate sales slips for September 1 over-the-counter sales. September 1 retail sales totaled $12,690, but they were not included in August sales.

5. Examine the client's inventory counts in the receiving department. Inventory had been counted only for receiving reports 41,674 to 41,684.

6. Examine the client's inventory counts in the shipping department. Inventory had been counted only for shipping documents 109,316 and 109,317. Further examination shows that inventory for all shipments made September 2 were included in the counts in the department from which the inventory was taken.

During the year-end audit work you obtain selling prices, costs, terms, and recording data for each receipt and shipment. They are as follows:

ACQUISITIONS OF INVENTORY

RECEIVING REPORT NO.	DATE SHIPPED	DATE RECEIVED	DOLLAR AMOUNT OF ACQUISITION	INCLUDED IN OR EXCLUDED FROM AUGUST ACQUISITIONS JOURNAL	FOB ORIGIN OR DESTINATION
41,679	8-29	8-31	$ 860	I	Destination
41,680	8-27	9-01	1,211	I	Origin
41,681	8-20	9-01	193	I	Origin
41,682	8-27	9-01	4,674	I	Destination
41,683	8-30	9-02	450	E	Destination
41,684	8-30	9-02	106	E	Origin
41,685	9-02	9-02	2,800	E	Origin
41,686	8-30	9-02	686	E	Destination

SHIPMENTS OF INVENTORY

SHIPPING DOCUMENT NO.	DATE SHIPPED	DOLLAR AMOUNT OF SALE	INCLUDED IN OR EXCLUDED FROM AUGUST SALES JOURNAL
109,310	8-31	$ 780	I
109,311	9-01	56	I
109,312	9-01	3,194	I
109,313	9-01	635	I
109,314	9-01	193	I
109,315	9-02	1,621	E
109,316	9-02	945	E
109,317	9-02	78	E
109,318	9-02	3,611	E

Required:

Assume the information you have obtained from the receiving and shipping departments about the September 1 receipts and shipments is accurate.

a. Prepare all adjustments for cutoff errors in accounts payable, assuming no acquisitions are made for cash.

b. Prepare all adjustments for errors in sales.

c. What is the amount of the client's error in inventory assuming a periodic inventory method, and no adjustments in part (a) or (b) affected inventory? For retail sales, assume the gross margin percentage is approximately 30 percent.

d. How would you determine whether the receiving and shipping departments have given you accurate information about the September 1 receipts and shipments of goods?

20

AUDIT OF THE CAPITAL ACQUISITION AND REPAYMENT CYCLE

LEARNING OBJECTIVES

THOROUGH STUDY OF THIS CHAPTER WILL ENABLE YOU TO:

1. Identify the accounts and the unique characteristics of the capital acquisition and repayment cycle

2. Design and perform the audit tests of notes payable and related accounts and transactions

3. Describe the primary concerns in the design and performance of the audit of owners' equity transactions

4. Design and perform the audit tests of transactions and balances for capital stock and retained earnings

---

OBJECTIVE 1

Identify the accounts and the unique characteristics of the capital acquisition and repayment cycle.

□ The final transaction cycle discussed in this text relates to the acquisition of capital resources in the form of interest-bearing debt and owner's equity and the repayment of the capital. The capital acquisition and repayment cycle also includes the payment of interest and dividends. The following are the major accounts in the cycle:

- Notes payable
- Contracts payable
- Mortgages payable
- Capital stock-preferred
- Capital stock-common
- Retained earnings

- Bonds payable
- Interest expense
- Accrued interest
- Cash in the bank

- Dividends declared
- Dividends payable
- Proprietorship-capital account
- Partnership-capital account

Four characteristics of the capital acquisition and repayment cycle significantly influence the audit of these accounts:

1. *Relatively few transactions affect the account balances, but each transaction is often highly material in amount.* For example, bonds are infrequently issued by most companies, but the amount of a bond issue is normally large. Due to their size, it is common to verify each transaction taking place in the cycle for the entire year as a part of verifying the balance sheet accounts. It is not unusual to see audit working papers that include the beginning balance of every account in the capital acquisition and repayment cycle and documentation of every transaction that occurred during the year.

2. *The exclusion of a single transaction could be material in itself.* Considering the effect of understatements of liabilities and owners' equity, which was discussed in Chapter 17, omission is a major audit concern.

3. *There is a legal relationship between the client entity and the holder of the stock, bond, or similar ownership document.* In the audit of the transactions and amounts in the cycle, the auditor must take great care in making sure that the significant legal requirements affecting the financial statements have been properly fulfilled and adequately disclosed in the statements.

4. *There is a direct relationship between the interest and dividends accounts and debt and equity.* In the audit of interest-bearing debt, it is desirable to simultaneously verify the related interest expense and interest payable. This holds true for owners' equity, dividends declared, and dividends payable.

The audit procedures for many of the accounts in the capital acquisition and repayment cycle can best be understood by selecting representative accounts for study. Therefore, this chapter discusses (1) the audit of notes payable and the related interest expense and interest payable to illustrate interest-bearing capital and (2) common stock, retained earnings, and dividends.

The methodology for determining tests of details of balances for owners' equity accounts is the same as that followed for all other accounts. For example, the methodology for notes payable is shown in Figure 20–1.

Notes Payable

OBJECTIVE 2

Design and perform the audit tests of notes payable and related accounts and transactions.

A *note payable* is a legal obligation to a creditor, which may be unsecured or secured by assets. Typically, a note is issued for a period somewhere between one month and one year, but there are also long-term notes of over a year. Notes are issued for many different purposes, and the pledged property includes a wide variety of assets, such as securities, inventory, and permanent assets. The principal and interest payments on the notes must be made in accordance with the terms of the loan agreement. For short-term loans, a principal and interest payment is usually required only when the loan becomes due; but for loans over 90 days, the note usually calls for monthly or quarterly interest payments.

Overview of Accounts

The accounts used for notes payable and related interest are shown in Figure 20–2. It is common to include tests of principal and interest payments as a part of the audit of the acquisition and payment cycle because the payments are recorded in the cash disbursements journal. But due to their relative infrequency, in many

FIGURE 20–1

Methodology for
Designing Tests of
Balances for Notes
Payable

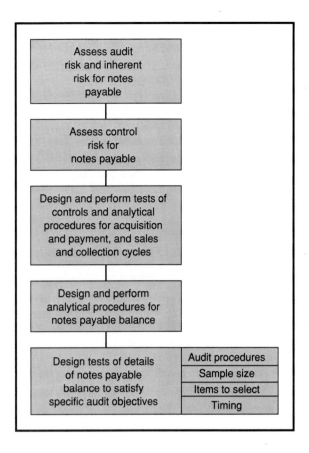

cases no capital transactions are included in the tests of controls sample. Therefore, it is also normal to test these transactions as a part of the capital acquisition
and repayment cycle.

Audit Objectives   The objectives of the auditor's examination of notes payable are to determine
whether

- Internal control over notes payable is adequate.
- Transactions for principal and interest involving notes are properly authorized
  and recorded as defined by the seven detailed tests of controls objectives.
- The liability for notes payable and the related interest expense and accrued liability are properly stated as defined by seven of the eight tests of details of balances
  objectives. (Ownership is applicable to notes payable, but it is usually not an
  important concern in the audit.)

Internal Controls   There are four important controls over notes payable:

- *Proper authorization for the issue of new notes.* Responsibility for the issuance of
  new notes should be vested in the board of directors or high-level management
  personnel. Generally, two signatures of properly authorized officials are required
  for all loan agreements. The amount of the loan, the interest rate, the repayment

FIGURE 20–2

Notes Payable and the Related Interest Accounts

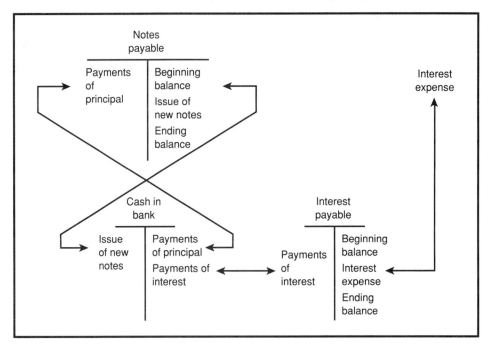

terms, and the particular assets pledged are all part of the approved agreement. Whenever notes are renewed, it is important that they be subject to the same authorization procedures as those for the issuance of new notes.

■ *Adequate controls over the repayment of principal and interest.* The periodic payments of interest and principal should be controlled as a part of the acquisition and payment cycle. At the time the note was issued, the accounting department should have received a copy in the same manner in which it receives vendors' invoices and receiving reports. The accounts payable department should automatically issue cheques for the notes when they become due, again in the same manner in which it prepares cheques for acquisitions of goods and services. The copy of the note is the supporting documentation for payment.

■ *Proper documents and records.* These include the maintenance of subsidiary records and control over blank and paid notes by a responsible person. Paid notes should be canceled and retained under the custody of an authorized official.

■ *Periodic independent verification.* Periodically, the detailed note records should be reconciled with the general ledger and compared with the note holders' records by an employee who is not responsible for maintaining the detailed records. At the same time, an independent person should recompute the interest expense on notes to test the accuracy and propriety of the recordkeeping.

Tests of Controls

Tests of notes payable transactions involve the issue of notes and the repayment of principal and interest. The audit tests are a part of tests of controls for cash receipts (Chapter 11) and cash disbursements (Chapter 17). Additional tests of controls are often performed as a part of tests of details of balances because of the materiality of individual transactions.

Notes payable and related interest tests of controls should emphasize testing

TABLE 20–1

Analytical Procedures
for Notes Payable

ANALYTICAL PROCEDURE	POSSIBLE MISSTATEMENT
Recalculate approximate interest expense on the basis of average interest rates and overall monthly notes payable.	Misstatement of interest expense or accrued interest, or omission of an outstanding note payable.
Compare individual notes outstanding with the prior year.	Omission or misstatement of a note payable.
Compare total balance in notes payable, interest expense, and accrued interest with prior year.	Misstatement of interest expense, accrued interest or notes payable.

the four important internal controls discussed in the previous section. In addition, the receipt and payment of proper amounts (valuation) is emphasized.

Analytical
Procedures

Analytical procedures are essential for notes payable because tests of details for interest expense and accrued interest can frequently be eliminated when results are favorable. Table 20–1 illustrates typical analytical procedures for notes payable and related interest accounts.

The auditor's independent estimate of interest expense, using average notes payable outstanding and average interest rates, tests the reasonableness of interest expense, but also tests for omitted notes payable. An illustration of an auditor's working paper where such an analytical procedure has been performed is illustrated in Figure 7-5, page 210. If actual interest expense had been materially larger than the auditor's estimate, one possible cause would be interest payments on unrecorded notes payable.

Tests of Details of
Balances

The normal starting point for the audit of notes payable is a *schedule of notes payable and accrued interest* obtained from the client. A typical schedule is shown in Figure 20–3. The usual schedule includes detailed information of all transactions that took place during the entire year for principal and interest, the beginning and ending balances for notes and interest payable, and descriptive information about the notes, such as the due date, the interest rate, and the assets pledged as collateral.

When there are numerous transactions involving notes during the year, it may not be practical to obtain a schedule of the type shown in Figure 20–3. In that situation, the auditor is likely to request that the client prepare a schedule of only those notes with unpaid balances at the end of the year. This would show a description of each note, its ending balance, and the interest payable at the end of the year, including the collateral and interest rate.

The objectives and common audit procedures are summarized in Table 20–2. The schedule of notes payable is the frame of reference for the procedures. The amount of testing depends heavily on materiality of notes payable and the effectiveness of internal control.

The three most important objectives in notes payable are

- Existing notes payable are included (completeness).
- Notes payable in the schedule are properly valued (valuation).
- Notes payable are properly disclosed (disclosure).

The first two objectives are important because an error could be material if even one note is omitted or misstated. Disclosure is important because generally

FIGURE 20–3 Schedule of Notes Payable and Accrued Interest

Farron Corp.
Notes Payable
12/31/x5

Schedule AA-4
Prepared by DB Date 1/12/x6
Approved by JL 1/16/x6

Payee	Date Made	Date Due	Face Amount of Note	Description	Security	Valuation	Notes Balance at Beginning of Period	Notes Additions	Notes Payments	Notes Balance at End of Period	Rate Paid to	Interest Accrued at Beginning of Period	Interest Expense	Interest Paid	Interest Accrued at End of Period
Bank of New Westminster	9/30/x4	9/30/x5	10 000	Investments		15 000	10 000		10 000 ③	–0– ④	9.5% Maturity ④	238	712 ⑥	950 ③	–0– ⑦
Fraser Trust Co.	9/30/x5	9/30/x6	10 000	Investments		16 000		10 000 ②		10 000 ④	10% Maturity ④		250 ⑥		250 ⑦
Fraser Trust Co.	10/31/x5	10/31/x6	10 000	Fixed Assets		22 000		10 000 ②		10 000 ④	10% Maturity ④		167 ⑥		167 ⑦
			30 000			53 000	10 000 ⑦ ⑧	20 000 ⑧	10 000 ⑧	20 000 ⑤ ⑦ ⑧		238 ⑦ ⑧	1129 ⑧	950 ⑧	417 ⑧

① –Traced to prior year audit workpapers.
② –Obtained copy of note included in permanent file.
③ –Examined cancelled note and cheque.
④ –Agreed to confirmation received from bank.
⑤ –Traced to general ledger.
⑥ –Recomputed expense; no differences noted.
⑦ –Cross-footed
⑧ –Footed

accepted accounting principles require that the footnotes adequately describe the terms of notes payable outstanding and the assets pledged as collateral for the loans. If there are significant restrictions on the activities of the company required by the loans, such as compensating balance provisions or restrictions on the payment of dividends, these must also be disclosed in the footnotes.

Owners' Equity

OBJECTIVE 3

Describe the primary concerns in the design and performance of an audit of owners' equity transactions.

A major distinction must be made in the audit of owners' equity between *publicly* and *closely held corporations*. While both may be *public companies* (that is, they are permitted by their articles of incorporation to issue shares to the public), closely held companies tend to be private companies whose share ownership is restricted. In most closely held corporations there are few if any transactions during the year for capital stock accounts, and there are typically only a few shareholders. The only transactions entered in the owners' equity section are likely to be the change in owners' equity for the annual earnings or loss and the declaration of dividends. The amount of time spent verifying owners' equity is frequently minimal for closely held corporations even though the auditor must test the existing corporate records.

For publicly held corporations, the verification of owners' equity is more complex due to the larger numbers of shareholders and frequent changes in the individuals holding the stock. In this section the appropriate tests for verifying the major accounts – capital stock, retained earnings, and the related dividends – in a publicly held corporation are discussed. The other accounts in owners' equity are verified in much the same way as these.

Overview of Accounts

An overview of the specific owners' equity accounts discussed in this section is given in Figure 20–4.

Audit Objectives

The objectives of the auditor's examination of owners' equity are to determine whether

- Internal control over capital stock and related dividends is adequate.
- Owners' equity transactions are recorded properly as defined by the seven internal control objectives.
- Owners' equity balances are properly stated and disclosed as defined by the tests of details of balances objectives (ownership is not applicable).

Internal Controls

Several important internal controls are of concern to the independent auditor in owners' equity: proper authorization of transactions, proper recordkeeping, adequate segregation of duties between maintaining owners' equity records and handling cash and stock certificates, and the use of an independent registrar and stock transfer agent.

Proper authorization of transactions Since each owners' equity transaction is typically material, many of these transactions must be approved by the board of directors. The following types of owners' equity transactions usually require specific authorization.

Issuance of Capital Stock The authorization includes the type of the equity to issue (such as preferred or common stock), number of shares to issue, issue price

FIGURE 20–4

Owners' Equity and
Dividends Accounts

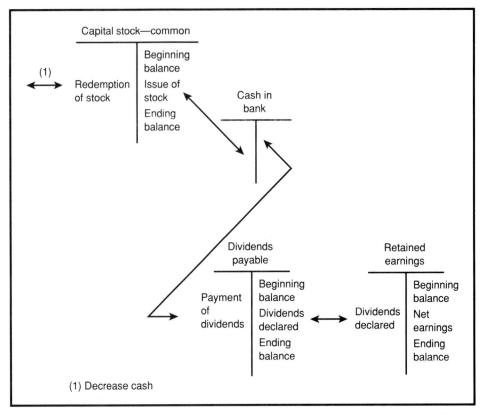

(also known as the *stated value*), privileges or conditions that attach to the stock, and date of the issue.

Repurchase or Redemption of Capital Stock   The repurchase or redemption of common or preferred shares, the timing of the repurchase (redemption), and the amount to pay for the shares should all be approved by the board of directors.

Declaration of Dividends   The board of directors should authorize the form of the dividends (such as cash or stock), the amount of the dividend per share, and the record and payment dates of the dividends.

Proper record keeping and segregation of duties   When a company maintains its own records of stock transactions and outstanding stock, internal control must be adequate to ensure that the actual owners of the stock are recognized in the corporate records, the correct amount of dividends is paid to the shareholders owning the stock as of the dividend record date, and the potential for employee fraud is minimized. The proper assignment of personnel and adequate record-keeping procedures are useful controls for these purposes.

The most important procedures for preventing errors in owners' equity are (1) well-defined policies for preparing stock certificates and recording capital stock transactions and (2) independent internal verification of information in the records. The client must be certain when issuing and recording capital stock that the relevant federal (for federally incorporated companies) or provincial (for provincially incorporated companies) laws governing corporations and the requirements in the articles of incorporation are being complied with. For example, the classes of shares and the number of shares the company is authorized to issue affect issuance and recording.

A control over capital stock used by most companies is the maintenance of stock certificate books and a shareholders' capital stock master file. A *capital stock certificate book* is a record of the issuance and repurchase of capital stock for the life of the corporation. There would normally be a book for each type (preferred or common) and each class (common, class A; common class B, etc.). The record for a particular capital stock transaction includes such information as the certificate number, the number of shares issued, the name of the person to whom it was issued, and the issue date. When shares are repurchased, the capital stock certificate book should include the canceled certificates and the date of their cancelation. A *shareholders' capital stock master file* is the record of the outstanding shares at any given time. The master file acts as a check on the accuracy of the capital stock certificate book and the preferred and common stock balances in the general ledger. It is also used as the basis for the payment of dividends.

The disbursement of cash for the payment of dividends should be controlled in much the same manner as has been described in Chapter 16 for the preparation and payment of payroll. Dividend cheques should be prepared from the capital stock certificate book by someone who is not responsible for maintaining the capital stock records. After the cheques are prepared, it is desirable to have an independent verification of the shareholders' names and the amount of the cheques and a reconciliation of the total amount of the dividend cheques with the total dividends authorized in the minutes. The use of a separate *imprest dividend account* is desirable to prevent the payment of a larger amount of dividends than was authorized.

Independent registrar and stock transfer agent Some companies engage an *independent registrar and stock transfer agent* (usually one organization such as a trust company performs both tasks but the job may be split between two such organizations) as a control to prevent the improper issue of stock certificates and to maintain shareholder records. The function of an independent registrar is to make sure that stock is issued by a corporation in accordance with the capital stock provisions in the articles of incorporation and the authorization of the board of directors. The registrar is responsible for signing all newly issued stock certificates and making sure old certificates are received and canceled before a replacement certificate is issued when there is a change in the ownership of the stock.

Most large corporations also employ the services of a *stock transfer agent* for the purpose of maintaining the shareholder records, including those documenting transfers of share ownership. The employment of a transfer agent not only serves as a control over the share records by putting them in the hands of an independent organization but reduces the cost of record keeping by the use of a specialist. Many companies also have the transfer agent disburse cash dividends to shareholders, thereby further improving internal control.

TABLE 20–2

Objectives and Tests of Details of Balances for Notes Payable and Interest

SPECIFIC AUDIT OBJECTIVE	COMMON TESTS OF DETAILS OF BALANCES PROCEDURES	COMMENTS
Notes payable in the schedule are valid (validity).	Confirm notes payable. Examine duplicate copy of notes for authorization. Examine corporate minutes for loan approval.	The validity objective is not as important as completeness or valuation.
Existing notes payable are included in the notes payable schedule (completeness).	Examine notes paid after year-end to determine whether they were liabilities at the balance sheet date. Obtain a *standard bank confirmation* that includes specific reference to the existence of notes payable from all financial institutions with which the client does business. (Bank confirmations are discussed more fully in Chapter 21.) Review the *bank reconciliation* for new notes credited directly to the bank account by the bank. On the bank reconciliation such a note should be indicated as a "reconciling item." Bank reconciliations are also discussed more fully in Chapter 21. Obtain confirmations from creditors who have held notes from the client in the past and are not currently included in the notes payable schedule. This is the same concept as a "zero balance" confirmation in accounts payable. Analyze interest expense to uncover a payment to a creditor who is not included in the notes payable schedule. This procedure is automatically done if the schedule is similar to the one in Figure 20–3 because all interest payments are reconciled with the general ledger. Examine paid notes for cancellation to make sure they are not still outstanding. They should be maintained in the client's files. Review the minutes of the board of directors for authorized but unrecorded notes.	This objective is important for uncovering both errors and irregularities. The first three of these procedures are done on most audits. The others are frequently done only when internal controls are weak.
Notes payable and accrued interest on the schedule are properly valued (valuation).	Examine duplicate copies of notes for principal and interest rates. Confirm notes payable, interest rates, and last date for which interest has been paid with holders of notes. Recalculate accrued interest.	In some cases it may be necessary to calculate, using present-value techniques, the imputed interest rates, or the principal amount of the note. An example is when equipment is purchased for a note.
Notes payable in the schedule are properly classified (classification).	Examine due dates on duplicate copies of notes to determine whether all or part of the notes are a noncurrent liability. Review notes to determine whether any are related party notes or accounts payable.	

TABLE 20–2
(Continued)

SPECIFIC AUDIT OBJECTIVE	COMMON TESTS OF DETAILS OF BALANCES PROCEDURES	COMMENTS
Notes payable are included in the proper period (cutoff).	Examine duplicate copies of notes to determine whether notes were dated on or before the balance sheet date.	Notes should be included as current-period liabilities when dated on or before the balance sheet date.
Notes payable in the notes payable schedule agree with the client's notes payable register or master file (mechanical accuracy).	Foot the notes payable list for notes payable and accrued interest. Trace the totals to the general ledger. Trace the individual notes payable to the master file.	Frequently, these are done on a 100 percent basis because of the small population size.
Notes payable, interest expense, and accrued interest are properly disclosed (disclosure).	Examine duplicate copies of notes. Confirm notes payable. Examine notes, minutes, and bank confirmations for restrictions. Examine balance sheet for proper disclosure of noncurrent portions, related parties, assets pledged as security for notes, and restrictions resulting from notes payable.	Proper statement presentation, including footnote disclosure, is an important consideration for notes payable.

Audit of Capital Stock

There are four main concerns in auditing capital stock:

- Existing capital stock transactions are recorded.
- Recorded capital stock transactions are authorized and properly valued.
- Capital stock is properly valued.
- Capital stock is properly disclosed.

OBJECTIVE 4

Design and perform the audit tests of transactions and balances for capital stock and retained earnings.

The first two concerns involve tests of controls, and the last two, tests of details of balances.

Existing capital stock transactions are recorded This objective is easily satisfied when a registrar or transfer agent is used. The auditor can confirm with them whether any capital stock transactions occurred and the valuation of existing transactions. Review of the minutes of the board of directors' meetings, especially near the balance sheet date, and examination of client-held stock record books are also useful to uncover issuances and repurchases of capital stock.

Recorded capital stock transactions are authorized and properly valued The issuance of new capital stock for cash, the merger with another company through an exchange of stock, the donation of shares, and the purchase of treasury shares each require extensive auditing. Regardless of the controls in existence, it is normal practice to verify all capital stock transactions because of their materiality and permanence in the records. Authorization can ordinarily be tested by examining the minutes of the board of directors' meetings.

The correct valuation of capital stock transactions for cash can be readily verified by confirming the amount with the transfer agent and tracing the amount of the recorded capital stock transactions to cash receipts. (In the case of treasury stock, the amounts are traced to the cash disbursements journal.) In addition, the auditor must verify whether the correct amounts were credited to capital stock by referring to the articles of incorporation to determine the stated value of the capital stock.

When capital stock transactions involve stock dividends, acquisition of property for stock, mergers, or similar noncash transfers, the verification of valuation may be considerably more difficult. For these types of transactions, the auditor must be certain that the client has correctly computed the amount of the capital stock issue in accordance with generally accepted accounting principles. For example, in the audit of a major merger transaction, the auditor has to evaluate whether the transaction is a purchase or, in very rare instances, a pooling of interests. Frequently, considerable research is necessary to determine which accounting treatment is correct for the existing circumstances. After the auditor reaches a conclusion as to the appropriate method, it is necessary to verify that the amounts were correctly computed.

Capital stock is properly valued The ending balance in the capital stock account is verified by first determining the number of shares outstanding at the balance sheet date. A confirmation from the transfer agent is the simplest way to obtain this information. When no transfer agent exists, the auditor must rely on examining the stock records and accounting for all shares outstanding in the stock certificate books, examining all canceled certificates, and accounting for blank certificates. After the auditor is satisfied that the number of shares outstanding is correct, the recorded value in the capital account can be verified by multiplying the number of shares by the stated value of the stock. It is audited by verifying the amount of recorded transactions during the year and adding them to or subtracting them from the beginning balance in the account.

A major consideration in the valuation of capital stock is verifying whether the number of shares used in the calculation of earnings per share is accurate. It is easy to determine the correct number of shares to use in the calculation when there is only one class of stock and a small number of capital stock transactions. The problem becomes much more complex when there are convertible securities, stock options, or stock warrants outstanding. A thorough understanding of Section 3500 of the *CICA Handbook* is important before the number of basic and fully diluted shares can be verified.

Capital stock is properly disclosed The most important sources of information for determining proper disclosure are the articles of incorporation, the minutes of board of directors' meetings, and the auditor's analysis of capital stock transactions. The auditor should determine that there is a proper description of each class of stock, including such information as the number of shares issued and outstanding and any special rights of an individual class. The proper disclosure of stock options, stock warrants, and convertible securities should also be verified by examining legal documents or other evidence of the provisions of these agreements.

Audit of Dividends   The emphasis in the audit of dividends is on the transactions rather than the ending balance. The exception is when there are dividends payable.

The seven internal control objectives for transactions are relevant for dividends. But typically dividends are audited on a 100 percent basis and cause few problems. The following are the most important objectives, including those concerning dividends payable:

- Recorded dividends are authorized.
- Existing dividends are recorded.

- Dividends are properly valued.
- Dividends as paid to shareholders are valid.
- Dividends payable are recorded.
- Dividends payable are properly valued.

Authorization can be checked by examining the minutes of board of directors' meetings for the amount of the dividend per share and the dividend date. When the auditor examines the board of directors' minutes for dividends declared, the auditor should be alert to the possibility of unrecorded dividends declared, particularly shortly before the balance sheet date. A closely related audit procedure is to review the permanent audit working paper file to determine if there are restrictions on the payment of dividends in bond indenture agreements or preferred stock provisions.

Valuation of a dividend declaration can be audited by recomputing the amount on the basis of the dividend per share and the number of shares outstanding. If the client uses a transfer agent to disburse dividends, the total can be traced to a cash disbursement entry to the agent and also confirmed.

When a client keeps its own dividend records and pays the dividends itself, the auditor can verify the total amount of the dividend by recalculation and reference to cash disbursed. In addition, it is necessary to verify whether the payment was made to the shareholders who owned the stock as of the dividend record date. The auditor can test this by selecting a sample of recorded dividend payments and tracing the payee's name on the canceled cheque to the dividend records to make sure the payee was entitled to the dividend. At the same time, the amount and the authenticity of the dividend cheque can be verified.

Tests of dividends payable should be done in conjunction with declared dividends. Any unpaid dividend should be included as a liability.

Audit of Retained Earnings

For most companies, the only transactions involving retained earnings are net earnings for the year and dividends declared. But there may also be corrections of prior-period earnings, prior-period adjustments charged or credited directly to retained earnings, and the setting up or elimination of appropriations of retained earnings.

The starting point for the audit of retained earnings is an analysis of retained earnings for the entire year. The audit schedule showing the analysis, which is usually a part of the permanent file, includes a description of every transaction affecting the account.

The audit of the credit to retained earnings for net income for the year (or the debit for a loss) is accomplished by simply tracing the entry in retained earnings to the net earnings figure on the income statement. The performance of this procedure must, of course, take place fairly late in the audit after all adjusting entries affecting net earnings have been completed.

An important consideration in auditing debits and credits to retained earnings other than net earnings and dividends is determining whether the transactions should have been included. For example, prior-period adjustments can be included in retained earnings only if they satisfy all four characteristics detailed in Section 3600.03 of the *CICA Handbook*. If there is a debit or credit to retained earnings because of a change in accounting principle or an error, the auditor should ensure the accounting is in accordance with "Accounting Changes," Section 1506 of the *CICA Handbook*.

After the auditor is satisfied that the recorded transactions are appropriately classified as retained earnings transactions, the next step is to decide whether they are properly valued. The audit evidence necessary to determine proper valuation depends on the nature of the transactions. If there is a requirement for an appropriation of retained earnings for a bond sinking fund, the correct amount of the appropriation can be determined by examining the bond indenture agreement.

Another important consideration in the audit of retained earnings is evaluating whether there are any transactions that should have been included but were not. If a stock dividend was declared, for instance, the market value of the securities issued should be capitalized by a debit to retained earnings and a credit to capital stock. Similarly, if the financial statements include appropriations of retained earnings, the auditor should evaluate whether it is still necessary to have the appropriation as of the balance sheet date. As an example, an appropriation of retained earnings for a bond sinking fund should be eliminated by crediting retained earnings after the bond has been paid off.

Primary concern in determining whether retained earnings is correctly disclosed on the balance sheet is the existence of any restrictions on the payment of dividends. Frequently, agreements with bankers, shareholders and other creditors prohibit or limit the amount of dividends the client can pay. These restrictions must be disclosed in the footnotes to the financial statements.

REVIEW QUESTIONS

20–1 List four examples of interest-bearing liability accounts commonly found in balance sheets. What characteristics do these liabilities have in common? How do they differ?

20–2 Why are liability accounts included in the capital acquisition and repayment cycle audited differently from accounts payable?

20–3 It is common practice to audit the balance in notes payable in conjunction with the audit of interest expense and interest payable. Explain the advantages of this approach.

20–4 Which internal controls should the auditor be most concerned about in the audit of notes payable? Explain the importance of each.

20–5 Which test of the reasonableness of notes payable in the financial statements is the most important in verifying notes payable? Which types of errors can the auditor uncover by the use of this test?

20–6 Why is it more important to search for unrecorded notes payable than for unrecorded notes receivable? List several audit procedures the auditor can use to uncover unrecorded notes payable.

20–7 What is the primary purpose of analyzing interest expense? Given this purpose, what primary considerations should the auditor keep in mind when doing the analysis?

20–8 Distinguish between the tests of controls and tests of details of balances for liability accounts in the capital acquisition and repayment cycle.

20–9 List four types of restrictions long-term creditors often put on companies when granting them a loan. How can the auditor find out about each of these restrictions?

20–10 Describe what is meant by an imputed interest rate. How does an auditor determine whether the client's imputed rate is reasonable? What should be done in the audit of notes payable after the auditor is satisfied that the rate is reasonable?

20–11 What are the primary objectives in the audit of owners' equity accounts?

20–12 Evaluate the following statement: "The articles of incorporation and the bylaws of a company are legal documents; therefore, they should not be examined by the auditors. If the auditor wants information about these documents, a lawyer should be consulted."

20–13 What are the major internal controls over owners' equity?

20–14 How does the audit of owners' equity for a closely held corporation differ from that for a publicly held corporation? In what respects are there no significant differences?

20–15 Describe the duties of a stock registrar and a transfer agent. How does the use of their services affect the client's internal controls?

20–16 What kinds of information can be confirmed with a transfer agent?

20–17 Evaluate the following statement: "The most important audit procedure to verify dividends for the year is a comparison of a random sample of canceled dividend cheques with a dividend list that has been prepared by management as of the dividend record date."

20–18 If a transfer agent disburses dividends for a client, explain how the audit of dividends declared and paid is affected. What audit procedures are necessary to verify dividends paid when a transfer agent is used?

20–19 What should be the major emphasis in auditing the retained earnings account? Explain your answer.

20–20 Explain the relationship between the audit of owners' equity and the calculations of earnings per share. What are the main auditing considerations in verifying the earnings per share figure?

MULTIPLE CHOICE QUESTIONS

20–21 The following multiple-choice questions concern interest-bearing liabilities. Choose the best response.

a. The auditor's program for the examination of long-term debt should include steps that require the

   (1) verification of the existence of the bondholders.
   (2) examination of any bond trust indenture.
   (3) inspection of the accounts payable master file.
   (4) investigation of credits to the bond interest income account.

b. During the year under audit, a company has completed a private placement of a substantial amount of bonds. Which of the following is the *most* important step in the auditor's program for the examination of bonds payable?

   (1) Confirming the amount issued with the bond trustee.
   (2) Tracing the cash received from the issue to the accounting records.
   (3) Examining the bond records maintained by the transfer agent.
   (4) Recomputing the annual interest cost and the effective yield.

c. Several years ago, Conway, Inc., secured a conventional real estate mortgage loan. Which of the following audit procedures would be *least* likely to be performed by an auditor examining the mortgage balance?

   (1) Examine the current year's canceled cheques.
   (2) Review the mortgage amortization schedule.

      (3) Inspect public records of registered mortgages.

      (4) Recompute mortgage interest expense.

20-22 The following questions concern the audit of owners' equity. Choose the best response.

  a. During an examination of a public company, the auditor should obtain written confirmation regarding debenture transactions from the

    (1) debenture holders.

    (2) client's lawyer.

    (3) internal auditors.

    (4) trustee.

  b. An audit program for the examination of the retained earnings account should include a step that requires verification of

    (1) market value used to charge retained earnings to account for a 2-for-1 stock split.

    (2) approval of the adjustment to the beginning balance as a result of a write-down of an account receivable.

    (3) authorization for both cash and stock dividends.

    (4) approval of the adjustment to the beginning balance as a result of a change in the estimated life of certain fixed assets.

  c. Where *no* independent stock transfer agents are employed and the corporation issues its own shares and maintains share records, canceled stock certificates should

    (1) be defaced to prevent reissuance and attached to their corresponding stubs.

    (2) *not* be defaced, but segregated from other stock certificates and retained in a canceled certificates file.

    (3) be destroyed to prevent fraudulent reissuance.

    (4) be defaced and sent to the Ministry of Corporate and Consumer Affairs.

(AICPA adapted)

DISCUSSION QUESTIONS AND PROBLEMS

20–23 Items 1 through 6 are questions typically found in a standard internal control questionnaire used by auditors to obtain an understanding of internal control for notes payable. In using the questionnaire for a particular client, a "yes" response indicates a possible internal control, whereas a "no" indicates a potential weakness.

  1. Are liabilities for notes payable incurred only after written authorization by a proper company official?

  2. Is a notes payable master file maintained?

  3. Is the individual who maintains the notes payable master file someone other than the person who approves the issue of new notes or handles cash?

  4. Are paid notes canceled and retained in the company files?

  5. Is a periodic reconciliation made of the notes payable master file with the actual notes outstanding by an individual who does not maintain the master file?

  6. Are interest expense and accrued interest recomputed periodically by an individual who does not record interest transactions?

Required:

  a. For each of the preceding questions, state the purpose of the control.

  b. For each of the preceding questions, identify the type of financial statement misstatement that could occur if the control were not in effect.

    c. For each of the potential misstatements in part (b), list an audit procedure that can be used to determine whether a material error exists.

20–24 The following are frequently performed audit procedures for the verification of bonds payable issued in previous years.

    1. Obtain a copy of the bond indenture agreement and review its important provisions.

    2. Determine that each of the bond indenture provisions has been met.

    3. Analyze the general ledger account for bonds payable, interest expense, and unamortized bond discount or premium.

    4. Test the client's calculations of interest expense, unamortized bond discount or premium, accrued interest, and bonds payable.

    5. Obtain a confirmation from the bondholder.

Required:

    a. State the purpose of each of the five audit procedures listed.

    b. List the provisions for which the auditor should be alert in examining the bond indenture agreement.

    c. For each provision listed in part b, explain how the auditor can determine whether its terms have been met.

    d. Explain how the auditor should verify the unamortized bond discount or premium.

    e. List the information that should be requested in the confirmation of bonds payable with the bondholder.

20–25 In making an audit of a corporation that has a bond issue outstanding, the trust indenture is reviewed and a confirmation as to the issue is obtained from the trustee.

Required:

List eight matters of importance to the auditor that might be found either in the indenture or in the confirmation obtained from the trustee. Explain briefly the reason for the auditor's interest in each of the items. (AICPA adapted)

20–26 Fox Corp. is a medium-sized industrial client that has been audited by your public accounting firm for several years. The only interest-bearing debt owed by Fox Corp. is $200,000 in long-term notes payable held by the bank. The notes were issued three years previously and will mature in six more years. Fox Corp. is highly profitable, has no pressing needs for additional financing, and has excellent internal controls over the recording of loan transactions and related interest costs.

Required:

    a. Describe the auditing that you think would be necessary for notes payable and related interest accounts in these circumstances.

    b. How would your answer differ if Fox Corp. were unprofitable, had a need for additional financing, and had weak internal controls?

20–27 The ending general ledger balance of $186,000 in notes payable for the Sterling Manufacturing Inc. is made up of 20 notes to 8 different payees. The notes vary in duration anywhere from 30 days to 2 years, and in amount from $1,000 to $10,000. In some cases the notes were issued for cash loans; in other cases the notes were issued directly to vendors for the purchase of inventory or equipment. The use of relatively short-term financing is necessary because all existing properties are pledged for mortgages. Nevertheless, there is still a serious cash shortage.

    Record-keeping procedures for notes payable are not good, considering the large number of loan transactions. There is no notes payable master file or independent verification of ending balances; however, the notes payable records are maintained by a secretary who does not have access to cash.

    The audit has been done by the same public accounting firm for several years. In the current year, the following procedures were performed to verify notes payable:

1. Obtain a list of notes payable from the client, foot the notes payable balances on the list, and trace the total to the general ledger.

2. Examine duplicate copies of notes for all outstanding notes included on the listing. Compare the name of the lender, amount, and due date on the duplicate copy with the list.

3. Obtain a confirmation from lenders for all listed notes payable. The confirmation should include the due date of the loan, the amount, and interest payable at the balance sheet date.

4. Recompute accrued interest on the list for all notes. The information for determining the correct accrued interest is to be obtained from the duplicate copy of the note. Foot the accrued interest amounts and trace the balance to the general ledger.

Required:
a. What should be the emphasis in the verification of notes payable in this situation? Explain.
b. State the purpose of each of the four audit procedures listed.
c. Evaluate whether each of the four audit procedures was necessary. Evaluate the sample size for each procedure.
d. List other audit procedures that should be performed in the audit of notes payable in these circumstances.

20–28 The following convenants are extracted from the indenture of a bond issue outstanding from McMullen Corp. The indenture provides that failure to comply with its terms in any respect automatically advances the due date of the loan to the date of noncompliance (the regular date is 20 years hence). Give any audit steps or reporting requirements you feel should be taken or recognized in connection with each one of the following with respect to your audit of McMullen Corp.

a. The debtor company shall endeavor to maintain a working capital ratio of 2 to 1 at all times, and, in any fiscal year following a failure to maintain said ratio, the company shall restrict compensation of officers to a total of $100,000. Officers for this purpose shall include chairman of the board of directors, president, all vice presidents, secretary, and treasurer.

b. The debtor company shall keep all property that is security for this debt insured against loss by fire to the extent of 100 percent of its actual value. Policies of insurance comprising this protection shall be filed with the trustee.

c. The debtor company shall pay all taxes legally assessed against property that is security for this debt within the time provided by law for payment without penalty, and shall deposit receipted tax bills or equally acceptable evidence of payment of same with the trustee.

d. A sinking fund shall be deposited with the trustee by semiannual payments of $300,000, from which the trustee shall, in his discretion, purchase bonds of this issue.   (AICPA adapted)

20–29 Evangeline Ltd. took out a 20-year mortgage on June 15, 19X8, for $2,600,000 and pledged its only manufacturing building and the land on which the building stands as collateral. Each month subsequent to the issue of the mortgage a monthly payment of $20,000 was paid to the mortgagor. You are in charge of the current-year audit for Evangeline, which has a balance sheet date of December 31, 19X8. The client has been audited previously by your public accounting firm, but this is the first time Evangeline Ltd. has had a mortgage.

Required:
a. Explain why it is desirable to prepare a working paper for the permanent file for the mortgage. What type of information should be included in the working paper?
b. Explain why the audit of mortgage payable, interest expense, and interest payable should all be done together.

    c. List the audit procedures that should ordinarily be performed to verify the issue of the mortgage, the balance in the mortgage and interest payable accounts at December 31, 19X8, and the balance in interest expense for the year 19X8.

20–30 Items 1 through 6 are common questions found in internal control questionnaires used by auditors to obtain an understanding of internal control for owners' equity. In using the questionnaire for a particular client, a "yes" response indicates a possible internal control, whereas a "no" indicates a potential weakness.

    1. Does the company use the services of an independent registrar or transfer agent?

    2. Are issues and retirements of stock authorized by the board of directors?

    3. If an independent registrar and transfer agent are not used:
       (a) Are unissued certificates properly controlled?
       (b) Are canceled certificates mutilated to prevent their reuse?

    4. Are common stock master files and stock certificate books periodically reconciled with the general ledger by an independent person?

    5. Is an independent transfer agent used for disbursing dividends? If not, is an imprest dividend account maintained?

    6. Are all entries in the owners' equity accounts authorized at the proper level in the organization?

Required:

    a. For each of the preceding questions, state the purpose of the control.

    b. For each of the preceding questions, identify the type of potential financial statement misstatements if the control is not in effect.

    c. For each of the potential misstatements in part b, list an audit procedure the auditor can use to determine whether a material error exists.

20–31 The following audit procedures are frequently performed by auditors in the verification of owners' equity:

    1. Review the articles of incorporation and bylaws for provisions relating to owners' equity.

    2. Review the minutes of the board of directors' meetings for the year for approvals related to owners' equity.

    3. Analyze all owners' equity accounts for the year and document the nature of any recorded change in each account.

    4. Account for all certificate numbers in the capital stock book for all shares outstanding.

    5. Examine the stock certificate book for any stock that was canceled.

    6. Recompute earnings per share.

    7. Review debt provisions and senior securities with respect to liquidation preferences, dividends in arrears, and restrictions on the payment of dividends or the issue of stock.

Required:

    a. State the purpose of each of these seven audit procedures.

    b. List the type of errors the auditors could uncover by the use of each audit procedure.

20–32 You are engaged in the audit of a corporation whose records have not previously been audited by you. The corporation has both an independent transfer agent and a registrar for its capital stock. The transfer agent maintains the record of shareholders and the registrar checks that there is no overissue of stock. Signatures of both are required to validate certificates.

    It has been proposed that confirmations be obtained from both the transfer agent and the registrar as to the stock outstanding at the balance sheet date. If such confirmations agree with the books, no additional work is to be performed as to capital stock.

Required:

If you agree that obtaining the confirmations as suggested would be sufficient in this case, give the justification for your position. If you do not agree, state specifically all additional steps you would take and explain your reasons for taking them.   (AICPA adapted)

20–33 The Bergonzi Corporation is a medium-sized wholesaler of grocery products with 4,000 shares of stock outstanding to approximately 25 shareholders. Because of the age of several retired shareholders and the success of the company, management has decided to pay dividends six times a year. The amount of the bimonthly dividend per share varies depending on the profits, but it is ordinarily between $5 and $7 per share. The chief accountant, who is also a shareholder, prepares the dividend cheques, records the cheques in the dividend journal, and reconciles the bank account. Important controls include manual cheque signing by the president and the use of an imprest dividend bank account.

The auditor verifies the dividends by maintaining a schedule of the total shares of stock issued and outstanding in the permanent working papers. The total amount of stock outstanding is multiplied by the dividends per share authorized in the minutes to arrive at the current total dividend. This total is compared with the deposit that has been made to the imprest dividend account. Since the transfer of stock is infrequent, it is possible to verify dividends paid for the entire year in a comparatively short time.

Required:

a. Evaluate the usefulness of the approach followed by the auditor in verifying dividends in this situation. Your evaluation should include both the strengths and the weaknesses of the approach.

b. List other audit procedures that should be performed in verifying dividends in this situation. Explain the purpose of each procedure.

20–34 In 1956 Claudette André and her brothers took over a small manufacturing company started by their father as a sideline to their regular occupations. What began as a small informal partnership eventually became a successful business, and when the sons of two of the original partners entered the firm, the need to formalize the relationship became obvious to everyone concerned. After lengthy discussions among themselves and with their lawyers and public accountants, the decision was made to enter into a clearly defined partnership agreement rather than to incorporate. The partnership agreement was completed in 1971.

The firm has continued to operate successfully without internal difficulties since that time. Great care has been taken by the firm to keep the affairs of the partnership entity and those of the individual partners completely separate. For example, if a personal transaction is paid by the partnership, the partner's capital account is charged.

Your firm has audited and provided accounting and tax advice to the partnership since the 1960s. The individuals involved in the audit over the years have concluded that the system of internal control is excellent. No unusual difficulties have been encountered in any year.

Required:

a. How much does the fact that the business is a partnership rather than a corporation affect the audit of the capital and repayment cycle? Be specific.

b. How do the tests of controls for each of the cycles other than the capital acquisition and repayment cycle differ when the client is a partnership rather than a corporation?

c. How do the tests of details of balances for each of the cycles other than the capital acquisition and repayment cycle differ when the client is a partnership rather than a corporation?

21

AUDIT OF CASH BALANCES

LEARNING OBJECTIVES

THOROUGH STUDY OF THIS CHAPTER WILL ENABLE YOU TO:

1. Describe the major types of cash accounts maintained by business entities

2. Describe the relationship of cash in the bank to the various transaction cycles

3. Design and perform the audit tests of the general cash account

4. Recognize when to extend the audit tests of the general cash account to test further for material fraud

5. Design and perform the audit tests of the payroll bank account

6. Design and perform the audit tests of petty cash

OBJECTIVE 1

Describe the major types of cash accounts maintained by business entities.

☐ The audit of cash balances is the last audit area studied in this text because the evidence accumulated for cash balances depends heavily on the results of the tests in all the various transactions cycles. For example, if the understanding of internal control and audit tests of controls of the acquisition and payment cycle lead the auditor to believe that it is appropriate to reduce assessed control risk to a low level, the auditor can reduce the detailed tests of the ending balance in cash. If, however, the auditor concludes that assessed control risk should be higher, extensive year-end testing may be necessary.

Types of Cash Accounts

It is important to understand the different types of cash accounts because the auditing approach to each varies. The following are the major types of cash accounts.

General Cash Account

The general account is the focal point of cash for most organizations because virtually all cash receipts and disbursements flow through this account at some time. The disbursements for the acquisition and payment cycle are normally paid from this account, and the receipts of cash in the sales and collection cycle are deposited in the account. In addition, the deposits and disbursements for all other cash accounts are normally made through the general account. Most small companies have only one bank account – the general cash account.

Imprest Payroll Account

As a means of improving internal control, many companies establish a separate imprest bank account for making payroll payments to employees. In an imprest payroll account, a fixed balance, such as $1,000, is maintained in a separate bank account. Immediately before each pay period, one cheque is drawn on the general cash account to deposit the total amount of the net payroll in the payroll account. After all payroll cheques have cleared the imprest payroll account, the bank account should have a $1,000 balance. The only deposits into the account are of the periodic weekly (e.g., semimonthly) payroll, and the only disbursements are paycheques to employees. For companies with many employees, the use of an imprest payroll account can improve internal control and reduce the time needed to reconcile bank accounts.

Branch Bank Account

For a company operating in multiple locations, it is frequently desirable to have a separate bank balance at each location. Branch bank accounts are useful for building public relations in local communities and permitting the centralization of operations at the branch level.

In some companies, the deposits and disbursements for each branch are made to a particular bank account, and the excess cash is periodically sent to the main office general bank account. The branch account in this instance is much like a general account, but at the branch level.

A somewhat different type of branch account consists of one bank account for receipts and a separate one for disbursements. All receipts are deposited in the branch bank, and the total is transferred to the general account periodically. The disbursement account is set up on an *imprest basis*, but in a different manner than an imprest payroll account. A fixed balance is maintained in the imprest account, and the authorized branch personnel use these funds for disbursements at their own discretion as long as the payments are consistent with company policy. When the cash balance has been depleted, an accounting is made to the home office and a reimbursement is made to the branch account from the general account *after* the expenditures have been approved. The use of an imprest branch bank account improves controls over receipts and disbursements.

Imprest Petty Cash Fund

A petty cash fund is actually not a bank account, but it is sufficiently similar to cash on deposit to merit inclusion. It is used for small cash purchases that can be paid more conveniently and quickly by cash than by cheque, or for the convenience of employees in cashing personal or payroll cheques. An imprest cash

FIGURE 21–1

Relationship of General
Cash to Other Cash
Accounts

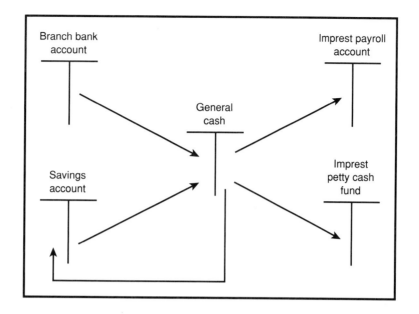

account is set up on the same basis as an imprest branch bank account, but the expenditures are normally for a much smaller amount. Typical expenses include minor office supplies, stamps, and small contributions to local charities. Usually a petty cash account does not exceed a few hundred dollars and may not be reimbursed more than once or twice each month.

Savings Accounts Excess cash accumulated during certain parts of the operating cycle that will be needed in the reasonably near future is usually invested in certificates of deposit or deposited in interest-bearing savings accounts. This money is not meant for use in the business until it is transferred back to the general cash account.

Figure 21–1 shows the relationship of general cash to the other cash accounts. All cash either originates from or is deposited in general cash. This chapter focuses on three types of accounts: the general cash account, the imprest payroll bank account, and the imprest petty cash fund. The others are similar to these and need not be discussed.

Cash in the Bank and Transaction Cycles

A brief discussion of the relationship between cash in the bank and the other transaction cycles serves a dual function: it clearly shows the importance of the tests of various transaction cycles to the audit of cash, and it aids in further understanding the integration of the different transaction cycles. Figure 21–2 illustrates the relationships of the various transaction cycles, the focal point being the general cash account.

An examination of Figure 21–2 indicates why the general cash account is considered significant in almost all audits even when the ending balance is immaterial. The amount of cash *flowing* into and out of the cash account is frequently larger than for any other account in the financial statements. Furthermore, the susceptibility of cash to defalcation is greater than for other types of assets because most other assets must be converted to cash to make them usable.

OBJECTIVE 2

Describe the relationship of cash in the bank to the various transaction cycles.

FIGURE 21–2

Relationships of Cash
in the Bank and
Transaction Cycles

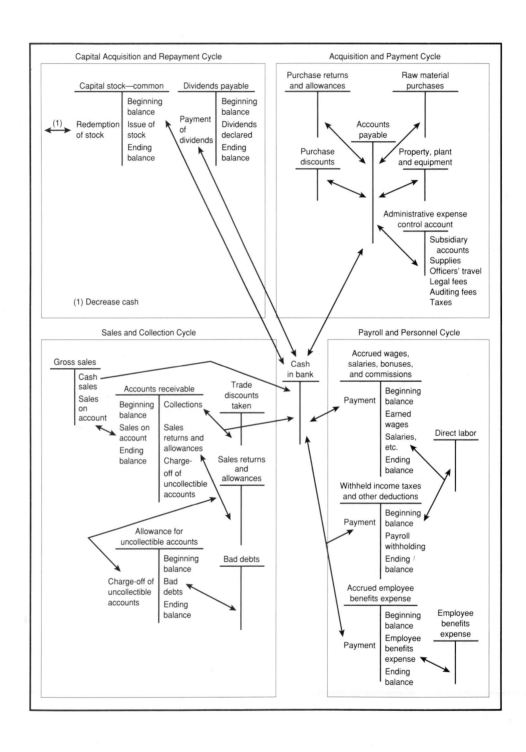

In the audit of cash, an important distinction should be made between verifying the client's reconciliation of the balance on the bank statement to the balance in the general ledger and verifying whether recorded cash in the general ledger correctly reflects all cash transactions that took place during the year. It is relatively easy to verify the client's reconciliation of the balance in the bank account to the general ledger, which is the primary subject of this chapter, but a significant part of the total audit of a company involves verifying whether cash transactions are properly recorded. For example, the following misstatements will each ultimately result in the improper payment of or the failure to receive cash, but none will normally be discovered as a part of the audit of the bank reconciliation:

- Failure to bill a customer
- Billing a customer at a lower price than called for by company policy
- A defalcation of cash by interception of collections from customers before they are recorded. The account is charged off as a bad debt.
- Duplicate payment of a vendor's invoice
- Improper payments of officers' personal expenditures
- Payment for raw materials that were not received
- Payment to an employee for more hours than he or she worked
- Payment of interest to a related party for an amount in excess of the going rate

If these misstatements are to be uncovered in the audit, their discovery must come about through the tests of controls that were discussed in the preceding chapters. The first three misstatements should be discovered as part of the audit of the sales and collection cycle, the next three in the audit of the acquisition and payment cycle, and the last two in the tests of the payroll and personnel cycle and the capital acquisition and repayment cycle, respectively.

Entirely different types of misstatements are normally discovered as a part of the tests of a bank reconciliation. For example,

- Failure to include a cheque that has not cleared the bank on the outstanding cheque list, even though it has been recorded in the cash disbursements journal
- Cash received by the client subsequent to the balance sheet date but recorded as cash receipts in the current year
- Deposits recorded in the cash book near the end of the year, deposited in the bank, and included in the bank reconciliation as a deposit in transit
- The existence of payments on notes payable that were debited directly to the bank balance by the bank but were not entered in the client's records

The appropriate methods for discovering the preceding misstatements by testing the client's bank reconciliation will become apparent as we proceed. At this point it is important only that the reader distinguish between tests of controls that are related to the cash account and tests that determine whether the book balance reconciles to the bank balance.

Audit of the General Cash Account

On the trial balance of Hillsburg Hardware Ltd., on page 135, there is only one cash account. Notice, however, that all cycles, except inventory and warehousing, affect cash in the bank.

The methodology for auditing year-end cash is essentially the same as for all other balance sheet accounts. The methodology is shown in Figure 21–3.

FIGURE 21–3

Methodology for
Designing Tests of
Details of Balances for
Cash in the Bank

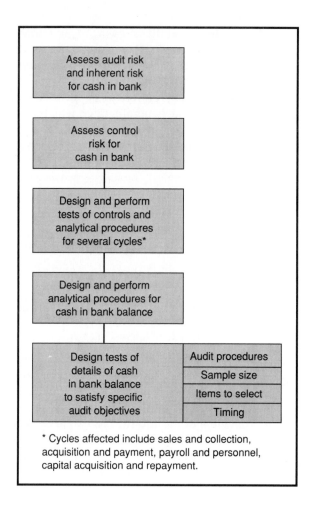

* Cycles affected include sales and collection,
acquisition and payment, payroll and personnel,
capital acquisition and repayment.

OBJECTIVE 3

Design and perform the
audit tests of the
general cash account.

The following factors, included in the figure, significantly influence the audit of
year-end cash:

- Cash is affected by most other cycles, which means there are many opportunities
  for error (evaluate tests of controls results).
- Although the cash balance itself is usually not large, the dollar amount of debits
  and credits affecting the balance normally is greater than for any other account
  (materiality).
- Cash is the most desirable asset for people to steal (inherent risk).

*Auditor's
Objectives*

In testing the year-end balance in the general cash account, the auditor must
accumulate sufficient evidence to evaluate whether cash, as stated on the balance
sheet, is fairly stated and properly disclosed in accordance with six of the eight
specific objectives used for all tests of details of balances. Ownership of general
cash and its classification on the balance sheet are not a problem.

Internal Controls

The internal controls over the year-end cash balances in the general account can be
divided into two categories: *controls over the transaction cycles* affecting the recording of cash receipts and disbursements and *independent bank reconciliations*.

The controls affecting the recording of cash transactions have been discussed in preceding chapters. For example, in the acquisition and payment cycle, major controls include the adequate segregation of duties between cheque signing and the accounts payable function, the signing of cheques only by a properly authorized person, the use of prenumbered cheques that are printed on special paper, adequate control of blank and voided cheques, careful review of supporting documentation by the cheque signer before cheques are signed, and adequate internal verification. If the controls affecting cash-related transactions are adequate, it is possible to reduce the audit tests of the year-end bank reconciliation.

Monthly reconciliation of the general bank account on a timely basis by someone independent of the handling or recording of cash receipts and disbursements is an essential control over the cash balance. The reconciliation is important to make sure the books reflect the same cash balance as the actual amount of cash in the bank after consideration of reconciling items, but even more important, the *independent* reconciliation provides a unique opportunity for an internal verification of cash receipts and disbursements transactions. If the bank statements are received unopened by the reconciler and physical control is maintained over the statements until the reconciliations are complete, the canceled cheques, duplicate deposit slips, and other documents included in the statement can be examined without concern for the possibility of alteration, deletions, or additions. A careful bank reconciliation by competent client personnel includes the following:

- Comparison of canceled cheques with the cash disbursements journal for date, payee, and amount
- Examination of canceled cheques for signature, endorsement, and cancelation
- Comparison of deposits in the bank with recorded cash receipts for date, customer, and amount
- Accounting for the numerical sequence of cheques, and the investigation of missing ones
- Reconciliation of all items causing a difference between the book and bank balance and the verification of their propriety
- Reconciliation of total debits on the bank statement with the totals in the cash disbursements journal
- Reconciliation of total credits on the bank statement with the totals in the cash receipts journal
- Review of month-end interbank transfers for propriety and proper recording
- Periodic follow-up on outstanding cheques and stop-payment notices

The first four of these internal procedures are directly related to the tests of controls that were discussed in previous chapters. The last five are directly related to the reconciliation of the book and bank balance and are discussed in greater detail later.

Because of the importance of monthly reconciliation of bank accounts, another common control for many companies is to have a responsible employee review the monthly reconciliation as soon as possible after its completion.

Analytical Procedures

In many audits, the year-end bank reconciliation is verified on a 100 percent basis. Testing the reasonableness of the cash balance is therefore less important than for most other audit areas.

It is common for auditors to compare the ending balance on the bank reconciliation, deposits in transit, outstanding cheques, and other reconciling items with the prior-year reconciliation. Similarly, auditors normally compare the ending balance in cash with previous months. These analytical procedures may uncover misstatements in cash.

Audit Procedures for Year-End Cash

A major consideration in the audit of the general cash balance is the possibility of fraud. The auditor must extend his or her procedures in the audit of year-end cash to determine the possibility of a material fraud when there are inadequate internal controls, especially the improper segregation of duties between the handling of cash and the recording of cash transactions in the journals. The study of cash in the following section assumes the existence of adequate controls over cash; therefore, fraud detection is not emphasized. At the completion of the study of typical audit procedures for the verification of year-end cash, procedures designed primarily for the detection of fraud are examined. The starting point for the verification of the balance in the general bank account is to obtain a bank reconciliation from the client for inclusion in the auditor's working papers. Figure 21–4 shows a bank reconciliation after adjustments. Notice that the bottom figure in the working paper is the adjusted balance in the general ledger.

In discussing the verification of year-end cash, six of the eight specific objectives that have been used in studying the audit of other asset balances are again used. There is no discussion of the ownership and classification objectives, since they are not significant for cash in the bank.

The frame of reference for the audit tests is the bank reconciliation. The objectives and common tests of details of balances are shown in Table 21–1. As in all other audit areas, the actual audit procedures depend on the considerations discussed in previous chapters. Also, because of their close relationship in the audit of year-end cash, the validity of recorded cash in the bank, valuation, and inclusion of existing cash (completeness) are combined. These three objectives are the most important ones for cash and therefore receive the greatest attention.

The following three procedures are discussed thoroughly because of their importance and complexity.

Receipt of a bank confirmation The direct receipt of a confirmation from every bank or other financial institution with which the client does business is necessary for every audit except when there are an unusually large number of inactive accounts. If the bank does not respond to a confirmation request, the auditor must send a second request or ask the client to telephone the bank. As a convenience to CAs as well as to bankers who are requested to fill out bank confirmations, the CICA has approved the use of a *standard bank confirmation* form. Figure 21–5 is an illustration of such a completed standard bank confirmation. As shown in Figure 21–5, it is referred to as a *bank confirmation*. This standard form has been agreed upon by the CICA and the Canadian Bankers' Association. Similarly, CGAAC and the Canadian Bankers Association have approved a similar bank confirmation form for use by CGAs. The importance of bank confirmations in the audit extends beyond the verification of the actual cash balance. It is typical for the bank to confirm loan information and bank balances on the same form. The confirmation in Figure 21–5 includes three outstanding loans and a contingent liability. Information on liabilities to the bank for notes, mortgages, or other debt typically includes the amount of the loan, the date of the loan, its due date, interest rate, and the existence of collateral.

FIGURE 21–4

Working Paper for a
Bank Reconciliation

Kao Corp.	Schedule *A-2*	Date	
Bank Reconciliation	Prepared by *DED*	*1/10/x5*	
	Approved by *SW*	*1/18/x5*	

12/31/x4

Acct. 101-General account, Bank of Waterloo

Balance per bank		109713	A-2/1
Add:			
Deposits in transit ①			
12/30	10 017		
12/31	11 100	21 117	
Deduct:			
Outstanding cheques ①			
# 7993 12/16	3 068		
8007 12/16	9 763		
8012 12/23	11 916		
8013 12/23	14 717		
8029 12/24	37 998		
8038 12/30	10 000	<87 462>	
Other reconciling items: Bank error			
Deposit to payroll account credited			
to General account by bank, in error		<15 200>	A-3
Balance per books, adjusted		28 168	T/B
Balance per books before adjustments		32 584	A-1
Adjustments:			
Unrecorded bank service charge	216		A-3
Non-sufficient funds cheque			
returned by bank, not			
collectible from customer	4 200	4 416	A-3
Balance per books, adjusted			

① Cutoff bank statement-procedures completed by   1/10/x5
                   DED   1/10/x5
② Cutoff bank statement enclosures returned to
     client, acknowledged by   M. Smith   1/12/x5

TABLE 21–1

Objectives and Tests of Details of Balances for General Cash in the Bank

SPECIFIC AUDIT OBJECTIVE	COMMON TESTS OF DETAILS OF BALANCES PROCEDURES	COMMENTS
Cash in the bank as stated on the reconciliation is valid (validity). Cash in the bank as stated on the reconciliation is correctly valued (valuation). Existing cash in the bank is included (completeness).	*(See extended discussion for each of these.)* Receipt and tests of a bank reconciliation. Receipt and test of a cutoff bank statement. Tests of the bank reconciliation. Extended tests of the bank reconciliation. Proof of cash. Tests for kiting.	These are the three most important objectives for cash in the bank. The procedures are combined because of their close interdependence. The last three procedures should be done only when there are internal control weaknesses.
Cash receipts and cash disbursements transactions are recorded in the proper period (cutoff).	Cash receipts: Count the cash on hand on the first day of the year and subsequently trace to deposits in transit and the cash receipts journal. Trace deposits in transit to subsequent period bank statement (cutoff bank statement). Cash disbursements: Record the last cheque number used on the last day of the year and subsequently trace to the outstanding cheques and the cash disbursements journal. Trace outstanding cheques to subsequent period bank statement.	When cash receipts received after year-end are included in the journal, a better cash position than actually exists is shown. It is called "holding open" the cash receipts journal. Holding open the cash disbursements journal reduces accounts payable and usually overstates the current ratio. The first procedure listed for receipts and disbursement cutoff tests requires the auditor's presence on the client's premises at the end of the last day of the year.
Cash in the bank as stated on the reconciliation foots correctly and agrees with the general ledger (mechanical accuracy).	Foot the outstanding cheque list and deposits in transit. Prove the bank reconciliation as to additions and subtractions, including all reconciling items. Trace the book balance on the reconciliation to the general ledger.	These tests are done entirely on the bank reconciliation, with no reference to documents or other records except the general ledger.
Cash in the bank is properly disclosed (disclosure).	Examine minutes, loan agreements, and obtain confirmation for restrictions on the use of cash and compensating balances. Review financial statements to make sure (a) material savings accounts and certificates of deposit are disclosed separately from cash in the bank, (b) cash restricted to certain uses and compensating balances are adequately disclosed, and (c) bank overdrafts are included as current liabilities.	An example of a restriction on the use of cash is cash deposited with a trustee for the payment of mortgage interest and taxes on the proceeds of a construction mortgage. A compensating balance is the client's agreement with a bank to maintain a specified minimum in its chequing account.

FIGURE 21–5

Standard Confirmation
of Financial Institution
Account Balance
Information

Use With No. 9
Window Envelope

BANK CONFIRMATION

CLIENT	CLIENT AUTHORIZED SIGNATURE	CHARTERED ACCOUNTANT
Kao Foods Inc. St. Jacobs Ontario N0L 1K0	J. Kao	Brown, Solomon + Co. P.O. Box 1939 Waterloo, Ontario N2L 1G1

BANK		Confirmation Date
NAME, BRANCH AND FULL MAILING ADDRESS Bank of Columbia West mount and old Post Road Waterloo, Ontario N2L 5M1	If at all possible, this Confirmation Request should arrive at the branch at least one week before Confirmation Date.	12 /31 /X2 All information to be provided as at this date
	BRANCH CONTACT NAME D. Armstrong	TELEPHONE NO. 787-1234
	AUTHORIZED SIGNATURE D. Armstrong	

ROUTE TO

Notes To Bank

- Please complete this confirmation as at Confirmation Date noted above, include name, telephone number and sign in the space provided above. Mail original in the enclosed envelope to the chartered accountant.
- Use the ROUTING SHEET provided by your Bank to collect data from your departments, then transfer the information to this form. In the absence of a Routing Sheet, use the ROUTE TO box to ensure the Bank confirmation is circulated to the appropriate departments in your branch.
- If the space provided is inadequate, please enter totals on this form and attach a statement giving full details as called for by the headings.
- For COMPLETION INSTRUCTIONS, see the reverse of this form.

① DEPOSITS/OVERDRAFTS   If none, so state

AMOUNT (Brackets if Overdraft)	If applicable		ACCOUNT NUMBER	TYPE OF ACCOUNT AND CURRENCY	INTEREST RATE
	ISSUE DATE	MATURITY DATE			
$109,371			654 22	General Account	
4,000			654 32	Payroll Account	

② LOANS/OTHER DIRECT LIABILITIES AND COLLATERAL SECURITY   Exclude overdrafts listed in Section ①   Include bankers' acceptances. If no items, so state

AMOUNT AND CURRENCY	NATURE OF LIABILITY	DUE DATE	NATURE OF COLLATERAL LODGED BY CUSTOMER TO SUPPORT THE LIABILITIES (If none, so state)	INTEREST RATES	DATE PAID TO
$90,000	Loan	Demand	General assignment of book debts	10%	12/31/X2
120,000	Loan	5/30/X5	Personal guarantee of J. Kao	12%	11/30/X2
40,000	Loan	Demand	Personal guarantee of B. Scott	11%	12/31/X2

③ CONTINGENT LIABILITIES   If none, so state. Exclude bankers' acceptances.

AMOUNT AND CURRENCY	DATE OF NOTE	DUE DATE	PAYABLE BY
$8,000	3/27/X1	3/27/X4	Kao Food Processing Ltd.

④ SECURITIES IN SAFE KEEPING: OTHER INFORMATION REQUESTED BY CHARTERED ACCOUNTANT   If none, so state. Exclude items already listed in Section ②

⑤ GUARANTEES COMFORT LETTERS

Were the customer's direct liabilities guaranteed or supported by comfort letters by third parties   ☐ Yes,   ☑ No

308
APPROVED 1986   The Canadian Bankers' Association and the Canadian Institute of Chartered Accountants

The auditor completes the boxes labeled "client," "chartered accountant," "bank," and "confirmation date"; a signing officer from the client signs in the "client" box authorizing the bank to provide the information; and the auditor sends the confirmation to the bank. While the bank should exercise due care in completing the confirmation, errors can occur. The auditor may wish to communicate with the bank if there is any information on the returned confirmation about which he or she is dubious or if any information that was expected is not reported.

After the bank confirmation has been received, the balance in the bank account confirmed by the bank should be traced to the amount stated on the bank reconciliation. Similarly, all other information on the reconciliation should be traced to the relevant audit working papers. In any case, if the information is not in agreement, an investigation must be made of the difference.

Receipt of a cutoff bank statement   A cutoff bank statement includes a partial-period bank statement and the related canceled cheques, duplicate deposit slips, and other documents included with bank statements, mailed by the bank directly to the public accounting firm's office. The purpose of the cutoff bank statement is to verify the reconciling items on the client's year-end bank reconciliation with evidence that is inaccessible to the client. To fulfil this purpose, the auditor requests the client to have the bank send directly to the auditor the statement for 7 to 10 days subsequent to the balance sheet date.

Many auditors prove the subsequent period bank statement if a cutoff statement is not received directly from the bank. They perform the proof in the month subsequent to the balance sheet date by (1) footing all the canceled cheques, debit memos, deposits, and credit memos; (2) checking to see that the bank statement balances when the footed totals are used; and (3) reviewing the items included in the footings to make sure they were canceled by the bank in the proper period and do not include any erasures or alterations. The purpose of this proof is to test whether the client's employees have omitted, added, or altered any of the documents accompanying the statement. It is obviously a test for intentional misstatements.

Tests of the bank reconciliation   The reason for testing the bank reconciliation is to verify whether the client's recorded bank balance is the same amount as the actual cash in the bank except for deposits in transit, outstanding cheques, and other reconciling items. In testing the reconciliation, the cutoff bank statement provides the information for conducting the tests. Several major procedures are involved:

- Trace the balance on the cutoff statement to the balance per bank on the bank reconciliation; a reconciliation cannot take place until these two are the same.
- Trace cheques included with the cutoff bank statement to the list of outstanding cheques on the bank reconciliation and to the cash disbursements journal. All cheques that cleared the bank after the balance sheet date and were included in the cash disbursements journal should also be included on the outstanding cheque list. If a cheque was included in the cash disbursements journal, it should be included as an outstanding cheque if it did not clear before the balance sheet date. Similarly, if a cheque cleared the bank prior to the balance sheet date, it should not be on the bank reconciliation.
- Investigate all significant cheques included on the outstanding cheque list that have not cleared the bank on the cutoff statement. The first step in the investigation should be to trace the amount of any items not clearing to the cash disburse-

ments journal. The reason for the cheque not being cashed should be discussed with the client, and if the auditor is concerned about the possibility of fraud, the vendor's accounts payable balance should be confirmed to determine whether the vendor has recognized the receipt of the cash in its records. In addition, the canceled cheque should be examined prior to the last day of the audit if it becomes available.

- Trace the deposits in transit to the subsequent bank statement. All cash receipts not deposited in the bank at the end of the year should be traced to the cutoff bank statement to make sure they were deposited shortly after the beginning of the new year.

- Account for other reconciling items on the bank statement and bank reconciliation. These include such items as bank service charges, bank errors and corrections, and unrecorded note transactions debited or credited directly to the bank account by the bank. These reconciling items should be carefully investigated to be sure they have been treated properly by the client.

Fraud-Oriented Procedures

It is frequently necessary for auditors to extend their year-end audit procedures to test more extensively for the possibility of material fraud when there are material internal control weaknesses. Many fraudulent activities are difficult if not impossible to uncover; nevertheless, auditors are responsible for making a reasonable effort to detect fraud when they have reason to believe it may exist. The following procedures for uncovering fraud are discussed in this section: extended tests of the bank reconciliation, proofs of cash, and tests for kiting.

> **OBJECTIVE 4**
>
> Recognize when to extend the audit tests of the general cash account to test further for material fraud.

Extended tests of the bank reconciliation   When the auditor believes the year-end bank reconciliation may be intentionally misstated, it is appropriate to perform extended tests of the year-end bank reconciliation. The purpose of the extended procedures is to verify whether all transactions included in the journals for the last month of the year were correctly included in or excluded from the bank reconciliation and to verify whether all items in the bank reconciliation were correctly included. Let us assume that there are material internal control weaknesses and the client's year-end is December 31. A common approach is to start with the bank reconciliation for November and compare all reconciling items with canceled cheques and other documents in the December bank statement. In addition, all remaining canceled cheques and deposit slips in the December bank statement should be compared with the December cash disbursements and receipts journals. All uncleared items in the November bank reconciliation and the December cash disbursements and receipts journals should be included in the client's December 31 bank reconciliation. Similarly, all reconciling items in the December 31 bank reconciliation should be items from the November bank reconciliation and December's journals that have not yet cleared the bank.

In addition to the tests just described, the auditor must also carry out procedures subsequent to the end of the year with the use of the bank cutoff statement. These tests would be performed in the same manner as previously discussed.

Proof of cash   Auditors frequently prepare a proof of cash when the client has material internal control weaknesses in cash. A proof of cash includes the following:

- A reconciliation of the balance on the bank statement with the general ledger balance at the beginning of the proof-of-cash period

- A reconciliation of cash receipts deposited with the cash receipts journal for a given period
- A reconciliation of canceled cheques clearing the bank with the cash disbursements journal for a given period
- A reconciliation of the balance on the bank statement with the general ledger balance at the end of the proof-of-cash period

A proof of cash of this nature is commonly referred to as a four-column proof of cash – one column is used for each of the types of information listed above. A proof of cash can be performed for one or more interim months, the entire year, or the last month of the year. Figure 21–6 shows a four-column proof of cash for an interim month.

The auditor uses a proof of cash to determine whether

- All recorded cash receipts were deposited.
- All deposits in the bank were recorded in the accounting records.
- All recorded cash disbursements were paid by the bank.
- All amounts that were paid by the bank were recorded.

The concern in an interim-month proof of cash is not with adjusting account balances, but rather with reconciling the amounts per books and bank.

When the auditor does a proof of cash, he or she is combining tests of controls and tests of details of balances. For example, the proof of the cash receipts is a test of recorded transactions, whereas the bank reconciliation is a test of the balance in cash at a particular time. The proof of cash is an excellent method of comparing recorded cash receipts and disbursements with the bank account and with the bank reconciliation. However, the auditor must recognize that the proof of cash disbursements is not for discovering cheques written for an improper amount, invalid cheques, or other errors in which the dollar amount appearing on the cash disbursements records is incorrect. Similarly, the proof-of-cash receipts is not useful for uncovering the theft of cash receipts or the recording and deposit of an improper amount of cash.

Tests for kiting   Embezzlers occasionally cover a defalcation of cash by a practice known as *kiting*: transferring money from one bank to another and improperly recording the transaction. Near the balance sheet date a cheque is drawn on one bank account and immediately deposited in a second account for credit before the end of the accounting period. In making this transfer, the embezzler is careful to make sure the cheque is deposited at a late enough date so that it does not clear the first bank until after the end of the period. Assuming the bank transfer is not recorded until after the balance sheet date, the amount of the transfer is recorded as an asset in both banks. Although there are other ways of perpetrating this fraud, each involves the basic device of increasing the bank balance to cover a shortage by the use of bank transfers.

A useful approach to test for kiting, as well as for unintentional errors in recording bank transfers, is to list all bank transfers made a few days before and after the balance sheet date and to trace each to the accounting records for proper recording. For example, if a bank transfer is recorded in the current period as a disbursement, the auditor should examine the bank cancelation date on the cheque to see when it cleared. If the cheque cleared after the balance sheet date, it should be included as an outstanding cheque. Similarly, transfers deposited in the bank near the end of the year or included as deposits in transit can be traced to

FIGURE 21–6

Interim Proof of Cash

	Schedule	Date
R. Mathieu, Inc. Interim Proof of Cash		
	Prepared by D.J.	7/15/x4
	Approved by MT	7/17/x4

12/31/x4

Acct. 101–General account, Bank of Waterloo

		5/31/x4	Receipts	Disbursements	6/30/x4
Balance per bank	①	121 782 12	627 895 20	631 111 96	118 565 36
Deposits in transit					
5/31	②	21 720 00	<21 720 00>		
6/30	②		16 592 36		16 592 36
Outstanding cheques					
5/31	③	36 396 50		<36 396 50>	
6/30	③			14 800 10	<14 800 10>
NSF cheques	④		<4 560 00>		<4 560 00>
To allow for effect of a cash disbursement recorded as a credit item in Cash Receipts Journal			8 500 00	8 500 00	
Balance per books, adjusted		107 105 62	626 707 56	613 455 56	120 357 62
Balance per books, unadjusted		107 105 62	626 707 56	614 957 04	118 856 14
Bank debit memos	⑤			120 00	<120 00>
Payroll cheques erroneously entered in General Disbursements Journal	⑥			<1 621 48>	1 621 48
Balance per books, adjusted		107 105 62	626 707 56	613 455 56	120 357 62

① Per 6/30/x4 bank statement.
② Detailed listing file below; traced to subsequent bank statements.
③ Outstanding cheque list filed below; examined cancelled cheques.
④ Detailed listing filed below; all NSF items were deposited and had cleared as of 7/15/x4.
⑤ Safety deposit rentals; traced to recording via journal entry. Requested list of contents of safety deposit boxes.
⑥ Traced to journal entry correcting error.

the cash receipts or disbursements journal to make sure they have been recorded in the journals in the proper period. For example, if a transfer was received by the bank and included as a deposit in transit on the bank reconciliation, kiting has probably occurred.

Even though audit tests of bank transfers are usually fraud oriented, they are often performed on audits in which there are numerous bank transfers, regardless of internal control. When there are numerous intercompany transfers, it is difficult to be sure each is correctly handled unless a schedule of transfers near the end of the year is prepared and each transfer is traced to the accounting records and bank statements. In addition to the possibility of kiting, inaccurate handling of transfers could result in a misclassification between cash and accounts payable. The materiality of transfers and the relative ease of performing the tests make many auditors believe they should always be performed.

Summary of fraud-oriented procedures In designing audit procedures for uncovering fraud, careful consideration should be given to the nature of the weaknesses in internal control, the type of fraud that is likely to result from the weaknesses, the potential materiality of the fraud, and the audit procedures that are most effective in uncovering the misstatement. When auditors are specifically testing for fraud, they should keep in mind that audit procedures other than tests of details of cash balances can also be useful. Examples of procedures that may uncover fraud in the cash receipts area include the confirmation of accounts receivable, tests for lapping, reviewing the general ledger entries in the cash account for unusual items, tracing from customer orders to sales and subsequent cash receipts, and examining approvals and supporting documentation for bad debts and sales returns and allowances. Similar tests can be used for testing for the possibility of fraudulent cash disbursements.

Audit of the Payroll Bank Account

Tests of the payroll bank reconciliation should take only a few minutes if there is an imprest payroll account and an independent reconciliation of the bank account such as that described for the general account. Typically, the only reconciling items are outstanding cheques, and for most audits the great majority clear shortly after the cheques are issued. In testing the payroll bank account balances, it is necessary to obtain a bank reconciliation, a bank confirmation, and a cutoff bank statement. The reconciliation procedures are performed in the same manner as those described for general cash. Naturally, extended procedures are necessary if the controls are inadequate or if the bank account does not reconcile with the general ledger imprest cash balance.

The discussion in the preceding paragraph should not be interpreted as implying that the audit of payroll is unimportant. A review of Chapter 16 should remind the reader that the most important audit procedures for verifying payroll are tests of controls. The most likely payroll errors will be discovered by those procedures rather than by checking the imprest bank account balance.

> **OBJECTIVE 5**
>
> Design and perform the audit tests of the payroll bank account.

Audit of Petty Cash

Petty cash is a unique account because it is frequently immaterial in amount, yet it is verified on most audits. The account is verified primarily because of the potential for defalcation and the client's expectation of an audit review even when the amount is immaterial.

Internal Controls over Petty Cash

The most important internal control for petty cash is the use of an imprest fund that is the responsibility of *one individual*. In addition, petty cash funds should not be mingled with other receipts, and the fund should be kept separate from all other activities. There should also be limits on the amount of any expenditure from petty cash, as well as on the total amount of the fund. The type of expenditure that can be made from petty cash transactions should be well defined by company policy.

OBJECTIVE 6

Design and perform the audit tests of petty cash.

Whenever a disbursement is made from petty cash, adequate internal controls require a responsible official's approval on a prenumbered petty cash form. The total of the actual cash and cheques in the fund plus the total unreimbursed petty cash forms that represent actual expenditures should equal the total amount of the petty cash fund stated in the general ledger. Periodically, surprise counts and a reconciliation of the petty cash fund should be made by the internal auditor or other responsible official.

When the petty cash balance runs low, a cheque payable to the petty cash custodian should be written on the general cash account for the reimbursement of petty cash. The cheque should be for the exact amount of the prenumbered vouchers that are submitted as evidence of actual expenditures. These vouchers should be verified by the accounts payable clerk and canceled to prevent their reuse.

Audit Tests for Petty Cash

The emphasis in verifying petty cash should be on testing petty cash transactions rather than the ending balance in the account. Even if the amount of the petty cash fund is small, there is potential for numerous improper transactions if the fund is frequently reimbursed.

An important part of testing petty cash is first to determine the client's procedures for handling the fund by discussing internal control with the custodian and examining the documentation of a few transactions. As a part of obtaining an understanding of internal control, it is necessary to identify internal controls and weaknesses. Even though most petty cash systems are not complex, it is often desirable to use a flowchart and an internal control questionnaire, primarily for documentation in subsequent audits. The tests of controls depend on the number and size of the petty cash reimbursements and the auditor's assessed level of control risk. When control risk is assessed at a low level and there are few reimbursement payments during the year, it is common for auditors not to test any further for reasons of immateriality. When the auditor decides to test petty cash, the two most common procedures are to count the petty cash balance and to carry out detailed tests of one or two reimbursement transactions. In such a case, the primary procedures should include footing the petty cash vouchers supporting the amount of the reimbursement, accounting for a sequence of petty cash vouchers, examining the petty cash vouchers for authorization and cancellation, and examining the attached documentation for reasonableness. Typical supporting documentation includes cash register tapes, invoices, and receipts.

The petty cash tests can ordinarily be performed at any time during the year, but as a matter of convenience they are typically done on an interim date. If the balance in the petty cash fund is considered material, which is rarely the case, it should be counted at the end of the year. Unreimbursed expenditures should be examined as a part of the count to determine whether the amount of unrecorded expenses is material.

REVIEW QUESTIONS

21–1   Explain the relationship between the initial assessed level of control risk, tests of controls for cash receipts, and the tests of details of cash balances.

21–2   Explain the relationship between the initial assessed level of control risk, tests of controls for cash disbursements, and the tests of details of cash balances. Give one example in which the conclusions reached about internal controls in cash disbursements would affect the tests of cash balances.

21–3   Why is the monthly reconciliation of bank accounts by an independent person an important internal control over cash balances? Which individuals would generally not be considered independent for this responsibility?

21–4   Evaluate the effectiveness and state the shortcomings of the preparation of a bank reconciliation by the controller in the manner described in the following statement: "When I reconcile the bank account the first thing I do is to sort the cheques in numerical order and find which numbers are missing. Next I determine the amount of the uncleared cheques by referring to the cash disbursements journal. If the bank account reconciles at that point, I am all finished with the reconciliation. If it does not, I search for deposits in transit, cheques from the beginning outstanding cheque list that still have not cleared, other reconciling items, and bank errors until it reconciles. In most instances, I can do the reconciliation in twenty minutes."

21–5   How do bank confirmations differ from positive confirmations of accounts receivable? Distinguish between them in terms of the nature of the information confirmed, the sample size, and the appropriate action when the confirmation is not returned after the second request. Explain the rationale for the differences between these two types of confirmations.

21–6   Evaluate the necessity of following the practice described by an auditor: "In confirming bank accounts I insist upon a response from every bank the client has done business with in the past two years, even though the account may be closed at the balance sheet date."

21–7   Describe what is meant by a cutoff bank statement and state its purpose.

21–8   Why are auditors usually less concerned about the client's cash receipts cutoff than the cutoff for sales? Explain the procedure involved in testing for the cutoff for cash receipts.

21–9   What is meant by an imprest bank account for a branch operation? Explain the purpose of using this type of bank account.

21–10   Explain the purpose of a four-column proof of cash. List two types of misstatements it is meant to uncover.

21–11   When the auditor fails to obtain a cutoff bank statement, it is common to "prove" the entire statement for the month subsequent to the balance sheet date. How is this done and what is its purpose?

21–12   Distinguish between *lapping* and *kiting*. Describe audit procedures that can be used to uncover each.

21–13   Assume that a client with excellent internal control uses an imprest payroll bank account. Explain why the verification of the payroll bank reconciliation ordinarily takes less time than the tests of the general bank account even if the number of cheques exceeds those written on the general account.

21–14   Distinguish between the verification of petty cash reimbursements and the verification of the balance in the fund. Explain how each is done. Which is more important?

21–15 Why is there a greater emphasis on the detection of fraud in tests of details of cash balances than for other balance sheet accounts? Give two specific examples that demonstrate how this emphasis affects the auditor's evidence accumulation in auditing year-end cash.

21–16 Explain why, in verifying bank reconciliations, most auditors emphasize the possibility of a nonexistent deposit in transit being included in the reconciliation and an outstanding cheque being omitted rather than the omission of a deposit in transit and the inclusion of a nonexistent outstanding cheque.

MULTIPLE CHOICE QUESTIONS

21–17 The following questions deal with auditing year-end cash. Choose the best response.

    a. A public accountant obtains a January 10 cutoff bank statement for a client directly from the bank. Very few of the outstanding cheques listed on the client's December 31 bank reconciliation cleared during the cutoff period. A probable cause for this is that the client

        (1) is engaged in kiting.

        (2) is engaged in lapping.

        (3) transmitted the cheques to the payees after year-end.

        (4) has overstated its year-end bank balance.

    b. The auditor should ordinarily mail confirmation requests to all banks with which the client has conducted any business during the year, regardless of the year-end balance, since

        (1) the confirmation form also seeks information about indebtedness to the bank.

        (2) this procedure will detect kiting activities that would otherwise not be detected.

        (3) the mailing of confirmation forms to all such banks is required by generally accepted auditing standards.

        (4) this procedure relieves the auditor of any responsibility with respect to nondetection of forged cheques.

    c. On December 31, 19X7, a company erroneously prepared an accounts payable transaction (debit cash, credit accounts payable) for a transfer of funds between banks. A cheque for the transfer was drawn January 3, 19X8. This error resulted in overstatements of cash and accounts payable at December 31, 19X7. Of the following procedures, the *least* effective in disclosing this error is review of the

        (1) December 31, 19X7, bank reconciliation for the two banks.

        (2) December 19X7 cheque register.

        (3) support for accounts payable at December 31, 19X7.

        (4) schedule of interbank transfers.   (AICPA adapted)

21–18 The following questions deal with discovering fraud in auditing year-end cash. Choose the best response.

    a. Which of the following is one of the better auditing techniques to detect kiting?

        (1) Review composition of authenticated deposit slips.

        (2) Review subsequent bank statements and canceled cheques received directly from the banks.

        (3) Prepare a schedule of bank transfers from the client's books.

        (4) Prepare year-end bank reconciliations.

    b. The cashier of Baker Company Ltd. in Yorkton, Saskatchewan, covered a shortage in the cash working fund with cash obtained on December 31 from a bank in Yorkton by cashing an unrecorded cheque drawn on the Regina branch of another bank used by the company. The auditor would discover this manipulation by

(1) preparing independent bank reconciliations as of December 31.

(2) counting the cash working fund at the close of business on December 31.

(3) investigating items returned with the bank cutoff statements.

(4) confirming the December 31 bank balances.

c. A cash shortage may be concealed by transporting funds from one location to another or by converting negotiable assets to cash. Because of this, which of the following is vital?

(1) Simultaneous confirmations

(2) Simultaneous bank reconciliations

(3) Simultaneous verification

(4) Simultaneous surprise cash count (AICPA adapted)

DISCUSSION QUESTIONS AND PROBLEMS

21–19 The following are fraud and other irregularities that might be found in the client's year-end cash balance (assume the balance sheet date is June 30).

1. A cheque was omitted from the outstanding cheque list on the June 30 bank reconciliation. It cleared the bank July 7.

2. A cheque was omitted from the outstanding cheque list on the bank reconciliation. It cleared the bank September 6.

3. Cash receipts collected on accounts receivable from July 2 to July 5 were included as June 29 and 30 cash receipts.

4. A loan from the bank on June 26 was credited directly to the client's bank account. The loan was not entered as of June 30.

5. A cheque that was dated June 26 and disbursed in June was not recorded in the cash disbursements journal, but it was included as an outstanding cheque on June 30.

6. A bank transfer recorded in the accounting records on July 2 was included as a deposit in transit on June 30.

7. The outstanding cheques on the June 30 bank reconciliation were underfooted by $2,000.

Required:

a. Assuming that each of these items are fraud and other irregularities, state the most likely motivation of the person responsible.

b. What internal control procedure could be instituted for each fraud and other irregularity to reduce the likelihood of occurrence?

c. List an audit procedure that could be used to discover each example of fraud and other irregularities.

21–20 Following are misstatements an auditor might find through tests of controls or by tests of details of cash balances:

1. The bookkeeper failed to record cheques in the cash disbursements journal that were written and mailed during the first month of the year.

2. The bookkeeper failed to record or deposit a material amount of cash receipts during the last month of the year. Cash is prelisted by the president's secretary.

3. The cash disbursements journal was held open for two days after the end of the year.

4. A cheque was paid to a vendor for a carload of raw materials that was never received by the client.

5. A discount on a purchase was not taken even though the cheque was mailed before the discount period had expired.

6. Cash receipts for the last two days of the year were recorded in the cash receipts journal for the subsequent period and listed as deposits in transit on the bank reconciliation.

7. A cheque written to a vendor during the last month of the year was recorded in the cash disbursements journal twice to cover an existing fraud. The cheque cleared the bank and did not appear on the bank reconciliation.

Required:

   a. List a substantive audit procedure to uncover each of the preceding misstatements.

   b. For each procedure in part (a), state whether it is a test of details of cash balances or a test of controls.

21–21 The following audit procedures are concerned with tests of details of general cash balances.

1. Compare the bank cancelation date with the date on the canceled cheque for cheques dated on or shortly before the balance sheet date.

2. Trace deposits in transit on the bank reconciliation to the cutoff bank statement and the current year cash receipts journal.

3. Obtain a standard bank confirmation from each bank with which the client does business.

4. Compare the balance on the bank reconciliation obtained from the client with the bank confirmation.

5. Compare the cheques returned along with the cutoff bank statement with the list of outstanding cheques on the bank reconciliation.

6. List the cheque number, payee, and amount of all material cheques not returned with the cutoff bank statement.

7. Review minutes of the board of directors' meetings, loan agreements, and bank confirmation for interest-bearing deposits, restrictions on the withdrawal of cash, and compensating balance agreements.

8. Prepare a four-column proof of cash.

Required: Explain the objective of each.

21–22 The following are two independent situations auditors might encounter in auditing cash.

1. The December 31 year-end bank reconciliation for Vanduzen Ltd. includes deposits in transit of $24,611, and an ending cash balance of $11,847. In tracing deposits in transit to a subsequent period bank reconciliation you determine that deposits for January 2 listed in the bank statement total $3,496 and deposits for January 3 total $2,961 and that the balance of the deposits in transit were deposited over the period January 4 to January 10. Additional investigation shows that average daily deposits are normally $3,000 and that company policy requires daily deposits.

2. The February year-end bank reconciliation for the interest-bearing chequing account from McCardle Sales Corp. includes outstanding cheques of more than $45,000 and an ending cash balance of $32,653. You observe that the total of outstanding cheques is typically closer to $10,000 to $15,000. In tracing the outstanding cheques to the cutoff bank statement, you determine that none of the larger cheques had cleared the bank even though most of them are written to vendors in the same city as the client. You also observe that the client's total current assets are $365,200 while total current liabilities are $174,800.

Required:
    a. Identify the nature of the probable fraud and other irregularity in each situation, and state the effect on the financial statements.

    b. State the probable motivation for each of the misstatements.

    c. Recommend the appropriate adjusting entry, if any, for each situation.

    d. Indicate what audit steps you carried out to determine that a fraud or other irregularity had been perpetrated.

21–23 Patrick Yip-Chuk Inc. had weak internal control over its cash transactions. Facts about its cash position at November 30, 19X8 were as follows:

The cash books showed a balance of $18,901.62, which included undeposited receipts. A credit of $100 on the bank's records did not appear on the books of the company. The balance per bank statement was $15,550. Outstanding cheques were no. 62 for $116.25, no. 183 for $150.00, no. 284 for $253.25, no. 8621 for $190.71, no. 8623 for $206.80, and no. 8632 for $145.28.

The cashier, Khalid Nasser, embezzled all undeposited receipts in excess of $3,794.41 and prepared the following reconciliation:

Balance, per books, November 30, 19X8		$18,901.62
Add: Outstanding cheques		
8621	$190.71	
8623	206.80	
8632	$145.28	442.79
		19,344,41
Less: Undeposited receipts		3,794.41
Balance per bank, November 30, 19X8		15,550.00
Deduct: Unrecorded credit		100.00
True cash, November 30, 19X8		$15,450.00

Required:
    a. Prepare a supporting schedule showing how much Khalid embezzled.

    b. How did he attempt to conceal his theft?

    c. Taking only the information given, name two specific features of internal control that were apparently missing.   (AICPA adapted)

21–24 You are auditing general cash for Trail Supply Corp. for the fiscal year ended July 31, 19X4. The client has not prepared the July 31 bank reconciliation. After a brief discussion with the owner you agree to prepare the reconciliation, with assistance from one of Trail Supply's clerks. You obtain the following information:

	GENERAL LEDGER	BANK STATEMENT
Beginning balance	$ 4,611	$ 5,753
Deposits		25,056
Cash receipts journal	25,456	
Cheques cleared		23,615
Cash disbursements journal	21,811	
July bank service charge		87
Note paid directly		6,100
NSF cheque		311
Ending balance	$ 8,256	$ 696

June 30 Bank Reconciliation

INFORMATION IN
GENERAL LEDGER
AND BANK STATEMENT

Balance per bank	$5,753
Deposits in transit	600
Outstanding cheques	1,742
Balance per books	4,611

Additional information obtained is:

1. Cheques clearing that were outstanding on June 30 totaled $1,692.

2. Cheques clearing that were recorded in the July disbursements journal totaled $20,467.

3. A cheque for $1,060 cleared the bank, but had not been recorded in the cash disbursements journal. It was for a purchase of inventory.

4. A cheque for $396 was charged to Trail Supply but had been written on a different company's bank account.

5. Deposits included $600 from June and $24,456 for July.

6. The bank charged Trail Supply's account for a nonsufficient funds (N.S.F.) cheque totaling $311. The credit manager concluded that the customer intentionally closed its account and the owner left the city. The cheque was turned over to a collection agency.

7. The bank deducted $5,800 plus interest from Trail's account for a loan made by the bank under an agreement signed four months ago. The note payable was recorded at $5,800 on Trail Supply's books.

Required:

   a. Prepare a bank reconciliation that shows both the unadjusted and adjusted balance per books.

   b. Prepare all adjusting entries.

   c. What audit procedures would you use to verify each item in the bank reconciliation?

21–25 Van Weelden Transport Ltd.'s head office is located in Winnipeg. It has a large branch in Brandon that maintains its own bank account. Cash is periodically transferred to the central account in Winnipeg. On the branch account's records, bank transfers are recorded as a debit to the home office clearing account and a credit to the branch bank account. Similarly, the home office account is recorded as a debit to the central bank account and a credit to the branch office clearing account. Gordon Whitefish is the head bookkeeper for both the home office and the branch bank accounts. Since he also reconciles the bank account, the senior auditor, Cindy Marintette, is concerned about the internal control weakness.

   As a part of the year-end audit of bank transfers, Marintette asks you to schedule the transfers for the last few days in 19X7 and the first few days of 19X8. You prepare the following list:

	DATE RECORDED IN THE HOME OFFICE CASH	DATE RECORDED IN THE BRANCH OFFICE CASH	DATE DEPOSITED IN THE HOME	
AMOUNT OF TRANSFER	RECEIPTS JOURNAL	DISBURSEMENTS JOURNAL	OFFICE BANK ACCOUNT	DATE CLEARED THE BRANCH BANK ACCOUNT
$12,000	12-27-X7	12-29-X7	12-26-X7	12-27-X7
26,000	12-28-X7	1- 2-X8	12-28-X7	12-29-X7
14,000	1- 2-X8	12-30-X7	12-28-X7	12-29-X7
11,000	12-26-X7	12-26-X7	12-28-X7	1- 3-X8
15,000	1- 2-X8	1- 2-X8	12-28-X7	12-31-X7
28,000	1- 7-X8	1- 5-X8	12-28-X7	1- 3-X8
37,000	1- 4-X8	1- 6-X8	1- 3-X8	1- 5-X8

Required:

a. In verifying each bank transfer, state the appropriate audit procedures you should perform.

b. Prepare any adjusting entries required in the home office records.

c. Prepare any adjusting entries required in the branch bank records.

d. State how each bank transfer should be included in the December 31, 19X7, bank reconciliation of the home office account after your adjustments in part (b).

e. State how each bank transfer should be included in the December 31, 19X7 bank reconciliation of the branch bank account after your adjustments in part (c).

21–26 Toyco Inc., a retail toy chain, honors two bank credit cards and makes daily deposits of credit card sales in two credit card bank accounts (Bank A and Bank B). Each day Toyco batches its credit card sales slips, bank deposit slips, and authorized sales return documents; data entry clerks enter the batched data on their terminals. The data are then processed by Toyco's electronic data processing department. Each week detailed computer printouts of the general ledger credit card cash accounts are prepared. Credit card banks have been instructed to make an automatic weekly transfer of cash to Toyco's general bank account. The credit card banks charge back deposits that include sales to holders of stolen or expired cards.

The auditor conducting the examination of the 19X8 Toyco financial statements has obtained the following copies of the detailed general ledger cash account printouts, the manually prepared bank reconciliations, and a summary of the bank statements, all for the week ended December 31, 19X8.

Toyco – Detailed General Ledger Credit Card Cash Account Printouts		
	BANK A DR. OR (CR.)	BANK B DR. OR (CR.)
Beginning balance, December 24, 19X8	$12,100	$ 4,200
Deposits		
December 27, 19X8	2,500	5,000
December 28, 19X8	3,000	7,000
December 29, 19X8	0	5,400
December 30, 19X8	1,900	4,000
December 31, 19X8	2,200	6,000
Cash transfer, December 27, 19X8	(10,700)	0
Chargebacks, expired cards	(300)	(1,600)
Invalid deposits (physically deposited in wrong account)	(1,400)	(1,000)
Redeposit of invalid deposits	1,000	1,400
Sales returns for week ending December 31, 19X8	(600)	(1,200)
Ending balance, December 31, 19X8	$ 9,700	$29,200

Toyco – Summary of the Bank Statements

	(CHARGES) OR CREDITS	
	BANK A	BANK B
Beginning balance, December 24, 19X8	$10,000	$ 0
Deposits dated		
December 24, 19X8	2,100	4,200
December 27, 19X8	2,500	5,000
December 28, 19X8	3,000	7,000
December 29, 19X8	2,000	5,500
December 30, 19X8	1,900	4,000
Cash transfers to general bank account		
December 27, 19X8	(10,700)	0
December 31, 19X8	0	(22,600)
Chargebacks		
Stolen cards	(100)	0
Expired cards	(300)	(1,600)
Invalid deposits	(1,400)	(1,000)
Bank service charges	0	(500)
Bank charge (unexplained)	(400)	$ 0
Ending balance, December 31, 19X8	$ 8,600	$ 0

Toyco – Bank Reconciliations

CODE NO.	ADD OR (DEDUCT)	
	BANK A	BANK B
1. Balance per bank statement, December 31, 19X8	$8,600	$ 0
2. Deposits in transit, December 31, 19X8	2,200	6,000
3. Redeposit of invalid deposits, physically deposited in wrong account	1,000	1,400
4. Difference in deposits of December 29, 19X8	(2,000)	(100)
5. Unexplained bank charge	400	0
6. Bank cash transfer not yet recorded	0	22,600
7. Bank service charges	0	500
8. Chargebacks not recorded, stolen cards	100	0
9. Sales returns recorded-but not reported to the bank	(600)	(1,200)
10. Balance per general ledger, December 31, 19X8	$9,700	$29,200

Required:

Based on a review of the December 31, 19X8, bank reconciliations and the related information available in the printouts and the summary of bank statements, describe what action(s) the auditor should take to obtain audit satisfaction *for each item* on the bank reconciliations. Assume that all amounts are material and all computations are accurate. Organize your answer sheet as follows, using the appropriate code number *for each item* on the bank reconciliations:

CODE NO.	ACTION(S) TO BE TAKEN BY THE AUDITOR TO OBTAIN AUDIT SATISFACTION
1.	

(AICPA adapted)

21–27   In connection with an audit you are given the following worksheet:

BANK RECONCILIATION, DECEMBER 31, 19X7

Balance per ledger December 31, 19X7		$17,174.86
Add:		
Collections received on the last day of December and charged to "cash in bank" on books but not deposited		2,662.25
Debit memo for customer's cheque returned unpaid (cheque is on hand but no entry has been made on the books)		200.00
Debit memo for bank service charge for December		5.50
		$20,142.61
Deduct:		
Cheques drawn but not paid by bank (see detailed list below)	$2,267.75	
Credit memo for proceeds of a note receivable which had been left at the bank for collection but which has not been recorded as collected	400.00	
Cheque for an account payable entered on books as $240.90 but drawn and paid by bank as $419.00	178.10	2,945.85
Computed balance		17,196.76
Unlocated difference		200.00
Balance per bank (checked to confirmation)		$16,996.76

CHEQUES DRAWN BUT NOT PAID BY BANK

NO.	AMOUNT
573	$ 67.27
724	9.90
903	456.67
907	305.50
911	482.75
913	550.00
914	366.76
916	10.00
917	218.90
	$2,267.75

Required:

a. Prepare a corrected reconciliation.

b. Prepare journal entries for items that should be adjusted prior to closing the books.

(AICPA adapted)

21–28   You are doing the first-year audit of Saint John School Supplies Ltd. and have been assigned responsibility for doing a four-column proof of cash for the month of October 19X4. You obtain the following information:

1.	Balance per books	September 30	$8,106
		October 31	3,850
2.	Balance per bank	September 30	5,411
		October 31	6,730
3.	Outstanding cheques	September 30	916
		October 31	1,278

4. Cash receipts for October

	per bank	26,536
	per books	19,711

5. Deposits in transit

	September 30	3,611
	October 31	693

6. Interest on a bank loan for the month of October, charged by the bank but not recorded, was $596.

7. Proceeds on a note of Jones Company Ltd. were collected by the bank on October 28, but were not entered on the books:

Principal	$3,300
Interest	307
	$3,607

8. On October 26, a $407 cheque of the Billings Corp. was charged to Saint John School Supplies' account by the bank in error.

9. Dishonored cheques are not recorded on the books unless they permanently fail to clear the bank. The bank treats them as disbursements when they are dishonored and deposits when they are redeposited. Cheques totaling $609 were dishonored in October; $300 was redeposited in October and $309 in November.

Required:

    a. Prepare a four-column proof of cash for the month ended October 31. It should show both adjusted and unadjusted cash.

    b. Prepare all adjusting entries.

21–29 The partner to whom you report has asked you to discuss the audit of cash balances for the benefit of new juniors who have just joined your public accounting firm. You have decided to build your talk around three questions.

    1. Why do we as auditors spend so much time worrying about cash when, comparatively, the cash balance on the balance sheet is quite small?

    2. Does it make any difference whether an independent person reconciles the bank accounts or merely checks the bank reconciliations?

    3. Why are we, as auditors, concerned about fraud in the cash balances when it is management's job to worry about employee fraud?

Required:

    Develop answers to the three questions posed above.

CASE

21–30 The following information was obtained in an audit of the cash account of Tuck Co. Ltd. as of December 31, 19X7. Assume that the public accountant is satisfied as to the validity of the cash book, the bank statements, and the returned cheques, except as noted.

    1. The bookkeeper's bank reconciliation at November 30, 19X7.

Balance per bank statement			$19,400
Add: Deposit in transit			1,100
Total			$20,500
Less: Outstanding cheques			
	#2540	$140	
	#1501	750	
	#1503	480	
	#1504	800	
	#1505	30	2,300
Balance per books			$18,200

2. A summary of the bank statement for December 19X7.

Balance brought forward	$ 19,400
Deposits	$148,700
	168,100
Charges	$132,500
Balance, December 31, 19X7	$ 35,600

3. A summary of the cash book for December 19X7 before adjustments.

Balance brought forward	$ 18,200
Receipts	$149,690
	167,890
Disbursements	$124,885
Balance, December 31, 19X7	$ 43,005

4. Included with canceled cheques returned with the December bank statement were the cheques listed below.

NUMBER	DATE OF CHEQUE	AMOUNT OF CHEQUE	COMMENT
1501	November 28, 19X7	$ 75	This cheque was in payment of an invoice for $750 and was recorded in the cash book as $750.
1503	November 28, 19X7	$ 580	This cheque was in payment of an invoice for $580 and was recorded in the cash book as $580.
1523	December 5, 19X7	$ 150	Examination of this cheque revealed that it was unsigned. A discussion with the client disclosed that it had been mailed inadvertently before it was signed. The cheque was endorsed and deposited by the payee and processed by the bank even though it was a legal nullity. The cheque was recorded in the cash disbursements.
1528	December 12, 19X7	$ 800	This cheque replaced 1504 that was returned by the payee because it was mutilated. Cheque 1504 was not canceled on the books.
_____	December 19, 19X7	$ 200	This was a counter cheque drawn at the bank by the president of the company as a cash advance for travel expense. The president overlooked informing the bookkeeper about the cheque.

____	December 20, 19X7	$ 300	The drawer of this cheque was the Tucker Company.
1535	December 20, 19X7	$ 350	This cheque had been labeled N.S.F. and returned to the payee because the bank had erroneously believed that the cheque was drawn by the Luck Company. Subsequently, the payee was advised to redeposit the cheque.
1575	January 5, 19X8	$10,000	This cheque was given to the payee on December 30, 19X7, as a postdated cheque with the understanding that it would not be deposited until January 5. The cheque was not recorded on the books in December.

5. Tuck Co. discounted its own 60-day note for $9,000 with the bank on December 1, 19X7. The discount rate was 6 percent. The accountant recorded the proceeds as a cash receipt at the face value of the note.

6. The accountant records customers' dishonored cheques as a reduction of cash receipts. When the dishonored cheques are redeposited they are recorded as a regular cash receipt. Two N.S.F. cheques for $180 and $220 were returned by the bank during December. The $180 cheque was redeposited, but the $220 cheque was still on hand at December 31.

   Cancellations of Tuck Co. Ltd. cheques are recorded by a reduction of cash disbursements.

7. December bank charges were $20. In addition, a $10 service charge was made in December for the collection of a foreign draft in November. These charges were not recorded on the books.

8. Cheque 2540 listed in the November outstanding cheques was drawn in 19X5. Since the payee cannot be located, the president of Tuck Co. agreed to the public accountant's suggestion that the cheque be written back into the accounts by a journal entry.

9. Outstanding cheques at December 31, 19X7, totaled $4,000, excluding cheques 2540 and 1504.

10. The cutoff bank statement disclosed that the bank had recorded a deposit of $2,400 on January 2, 19X8. The accountant had recorded this deposit on the books on December 31, 19X7, and then mailed the deposit to the bank.

Required: Prepare a four-column proof of cash of the cash receipts and cash disbursements recorded on the bank statement and on the company's books for the month of December 19X7. The reconciliation should agree with the cash figure that will appear in the company's financial statements.

(AICPA adapted)

22

COMPLETING THE AUDIT

☐ After the auditor has completed the tests in specific audit areas, it is necessary to summarize the results and perform additional testing of a more general nature. This is the fourth and last phase of the audit, as shown in Figure 10–10. The first four procedures for completing this audit phase are the major topics of this chapter. They are review for contingent liabilities, review for subsequent events, accumulate final evidence, and evaluate results. In addition, communications with the audit committee and management and subsequent discovery of facts existing at the date of the auditor's report are discussed.

Review for Contingent Liabilities

Section 3290.02, of the *CICA Handbook* defines a contingency as

> . . . an existing condition or situation involving uncertainty as to possible gain or loss to an enterprise that will ultimately be resolved when one or more future events occur or fail to occur.

The auditor is concerned both with the nature of the future event and with the amount involved. Just as he or she is concerned with recognizing a contingent liability, the auditor must also be able to recognize a recorded asset that is really a contingent asset and that has the effect of overstating the net worth of the business.

Three conditions indicate the existence of a *contingent liability*: (1) there is a potential future payment to an outside party that resulted from an existing condition, (2) there is uncertainty about the amount of the future payment, and (3) the outcome will be resolved by some future event or events. For example, contingencies include lawsuits that have been filed but not yet resolved.

This uncertainty of the future payment can vary from extremely likely to highly unlikely. Section 3290.06 of the *CICA Handbook* describes three levels of likelihood:

- *likely* – the chance of the occurrence (or non-occurrence) of the future event(s) is high;
- *unlikely* – the chance of the occurrence (or non-occurrence) of the future event(s) is slight;
- *not determinable* – the chance of the occurrence (or non-occurrence) of the future event(s) cannot be determined.

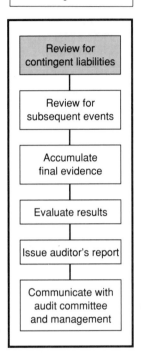

OBJECTIVE 1

Conduct a review for contingent liabilities.

- Review for contingent liabilities
- Review for subsequent events
- Accumulate final evidence
- Evaluate results
- Issue auditor's report
- Communicate with audit committee and management

If a potential loss is likely and the amount of the loss can be reasonably estimated, the loss should be accrued and indicated in the body of the financial statements. Disclosure in footnotes, but no accrual, is required if the amount of a likely loss cannot be reasonably estimated, or if the likelihood of the loss is not determinable. When the potential loss is unlikely, neither accrual nor disclosure is necessary. The decision as to the appropriate treatment requires considerable professional judgment. (A contingent gain should never be accrued but rather, if its future confirmation is very likely, it should be disclosed in the notes.)

When the proper disclosure in the financial statements of material contingencies is through footnotes, the footnote should describe the nature of the contingency to the extent it is known, an estimate of the amount or a statement that the amount cannot be estimated. The footnote should also state whether any settlement will be accounted for as a prior period adjustment or as a charge to income in the period in which the settlement occurs. The following is an illustration of a footnote related to pending litigation:

- The Company is a defendant in a legal action instituted in the Alberta Court of the Queen's Bench by Mountain Supply Ltd. for alleged product defect. The amount claimed is $792,000 and the Company is vigorously contesting the claim.

  The Company's legal counsel is unable, at the present time, to give any opinion with respect to the merits of this action. Settlement, if any, that may be made with respect to these actions, is expected to be accounted for as a charge against income for the period in which settlement is made.

Certain contingent liabilities are of considerable concern to the auditor:

- Pending litigation for patent infringement, product liability or other actions
- Income tax disputes
- Product warranties

- Notes receivable discounted
- Guarantees of obligations of others
- Unused balances in outstanding letters of credit
- Threat of expropriation of assets

Many of these potential obligations are ordinarily verified as an integral part of various segments of the engagement rather than as a separate activity near the end of the audit. For example, unused balances in outstanding letters of credit may be tested as a part of confirming bank balances and loans from banks. Similarly, income tax disputes can be checked as a part of analyzing income tax expense, reviewing the general correspondence file, and examining Revenue Canada reports and statements. Even if the contingencies are verified separately, it is common to perform the tests well before the last few days of completing the engagement to ensure their proper verification. The tests of contingent liabilities near the end of the engagement are more a review than an initial search.

General Audit Procedures   The appropriate audit procedures for testing contingencies are less well defined than those already discussed in other audit areas because the primary objective at the initial stage of the tests is to determine the *existence* of contingencies. As the reader knows from the study of other audit areas, it is more difficult to discover unrecorded transactions or events than to verify recorded information. Contingencies are often discovered as a byproduct of other auditing procedures as well as a result of specific steps designed to discover them. For instance, a confirmation received from a major supplier might reveal a purchase commitment. Once the auditor is aware that contingencies exist, the evaluation of their materiality and the disclosure required can ordinarily be satisfactorily resolved.

The following are some audit procedures commonly used to search for contingent liabilities. The list is not all inclusive, and each procedure is not necessarily performed on every audit.

- Inquire of management (orally and in writing) regarding the possibility of unrecorded contingencies. In these inquiries, the auditor must be specific in describing the different kinds of contingencies that may require disclosure. Naturally, inquiries of management are not useful in uncovering the intentional failure to disclose existing contingencies, but if management has overlooked a particular type of contingency or does not fully comprehend accounting disclosure requirements, the inquiry can be fruitful. At the completion of the audit, management is typically asked to make a written statement as a part of the letter of representation that it is aware of no undisclosed contingent liabilities.
- Review current and previous years' Revenue Canada notices of assessment. The reports may indicate areas in which disagreement over unsettled years is likely to arise. If an audit by Revenue Canada has been in progress for a long time, there is an increased likelihood of an existing tax dispute.
- Review the minutes of directors' and shareholders' meetings for indications of lawsuits or other contingencies.
- Analyze legal expense for the period under audit and review invoices and statements from the client's law firms for indications of contingent liabilities, especially lawsuits and pending tax assessments.
- Obtain a confirmation from all major law firms performing legal services for the client as to the status of pending litigation or other contingent liabilities. This procedure is discussed in more depth shortly.
- Review existing working papers for any information that may indicate a potential

contingency. For example, bank confirmations may indicate notes receivable discounted or guarantees of loans.

- Obtain letters of credit in force as of the balance sheet date and obtain a confirmation of the used and unused balance.
- Read contracts, agreements and related correspondence and documents.

Confirmation from
Client's Law Firms

A major procedure auditors rely on for discovering contingencies is sending a *letter of inquiry to the client's law firms* requesting they inform the auditor of pending litigation or any other information involving law firms that is relevant to financial statement disclosure. There are two categories of lawsuits: an *outstanding* or *asserted claim* exists when a suit has been brought or when the client has been notified that a suit will be brought; a *possible* or *unasserted claim* exists when no suit has been filed but is possible. An example of the latter is a situation where the lawyer is aware of a violation of a patent agreement that could be damaging to the client.

If an outstanding lawsuit is a contingent liability, the auditor should also obtain the professional opinion of the client's lawyer on the expected outcome of the lawsuit and the likely amount of the liability, including court costs.

As a matter of tradition, many public accounting firms analyze legal expense for the entire year and have the client send a standard lawyer's letter to every law firm the client has been involved with in the current or preceding year, plus any law firm the client occasionally engages. In some cases, this involves a large number of law firms, including some who deal in aspects of law that are far removed from potential lawsuits.

Law firms in recent years have become reluctant to provide certain information to auditors because of their own exposure to legal liability for providing incorrect or confidential information. The nature of the refusal of law firms to provide auditors with complete information about contingent liabilities falls into two categories: the refusal to respond due to a lack of knowledge about matters involving contingent liabilities; and the refusal to disclose information that the lawyer regards as confidential. As an example of the latter, the lawyer might be aware of a violation of a patent agreement that could result in a significant loss to the client if it were known (unasserted claim). The inclusion of the information in a footnote could actually cause the lawsuit and, therefore, be damaging to the client.

When the nature of the lawyer's legal practice does not involve contingent liabilities, the lawyer's refusal to respond causes no audit problems. It is certainly reasonable for lawyers to refuse to make statements about contingent liabilities when they are not involved with lawsuits or similar aspects of the practice of law that directly affect the financial statements.

A serious audit problem does arise, however, when a lawyer refuses to provide information that is within the lawyer's jurisdiction and may directly affect the fair presentation of financial statements. If a lawyer refuses to provide the auditor with information about material existing lawsuits (outstanding claims) or possible claims, *the audit report would have to be modified to reflect the lack of available evidence.* The "Joint Policy Statement concerning communications with law firms regarding claims and possible claims in connection with the preparation and audit of financial statements," an appendix to Section 6560 of the *CICA Handbook*, has the effect of encouraging lawyers to cooperate with auditors in obtaining information about contingencies, as the law firm's confidential relationship with its clients will not be violated. The Joint Policy Statement was approved by the Canadian Bar Association, the Council of the Bermuda Bar Association and the Auditing Standards Committee of the CICA.

The standard letter of confirmation to the client's law firm, which should be prepared on the client's letterhead and signed by one of the company's officials, should include the following:

- A list, prepared by management, of outstanding and possible claims with which the lawyer has had significant involvement.
- A description of the nature and the current status of each claim and possible claim.
- An indication of management's evaluation of the amount and likelihood of loss or gain for each claim and possible claim.
- A request that the lawyer reply to the client, with a signed copy going to the public accounting firm, advising whether management's descriptions and evaluations of the outstanding and possible claims are reasonable.

    Lawyers are not required to, and do not mention any omission of, possible claims in their response to the inquiry letter, and thus do not directly notify the auditor of them. Instead, lawyers discuss these possible claims with the client separately and inform management of its responsibility to inform the auditor. Whether management does so or not is its decision; Section 6560.19 requires the auditor to obtain a letter of representation from management that it has disclosed *all* outstanding and possible claims. In short, unless management discloses the existence of possible claims to the auditor, the auditor has no means of discovering whether or not any such claims exist.

    Any differences between management's identification and assessment of outstanding and possible claims and the law firm's would be resolved, if possible, in a meeting of the law firm, the auditor and management. Failure to resolve the differences would force the auditor to consider a reservation of opinion in the auditor's report.

- A request for information regarding any unlisted outstanding or potential legal actions or a statement that the client's list was complete.
- A statement that the inquiry letter is submitted in accordance with the Joint Policy Statement.

An example of a typical standard inquiry letter sent to a lawyer's office is shown in Figure 22–1. Notice in the first paragraph that the lawyer is requested to communicate about contingencies up to approximately *the date of the auditor's report*.

Evaluation of Known Contingent Liabilities
If the auditor concludes that there are contingent liabilities, he or she must evaluate the significance of the potential liability and the nature of the disclosure that is necessary in the financial statements. The potential liability is sufficiently well known in some instances to be included in the statements as an actual liability. In other instances, disclosure may be unnecessary if the contingency is highly remote or immaterial. Frequently, the public accounting firm obtains a separate evaluation of the potential liability from its own law firm rather than relying on management or management's lawyers. The client's law firm is an advocate for the client and frequently loses perspective in evaluating the likelihood of losing the case and the amount of the potential judgment.

FIGURE 22–1

Typical Inquiry of Lawyer

PEPPERTREE PRODUCE INC.
293 Rue Crécy
Montreal, Quebec

January 26, 19X8

Rowan and Gunz
Barristers and Solicitors,
412 Côte des Neiges,
Montréal, Quebec
H3C 1J7

To whom it may concern:

In connection with the preparation and audit of our financial statements for the fiscal period ended December 31, 19X7, we have made the following evaluations of claims and possible claims with respect to which your firm's advice or representation has been sought:

Description	*Evaluation*
Calvert Growers vs *Peppertree Produce Inc.*, non-payment of debt in the amount of $16,000, trial date not set.	Peppertree Produce Inc. disputes this billing on the grounds that the produce was spoiled, and expects to successfully defend this action.
Desjardins, Inc. vs *Peppertree Produce Inc.*, damages for breach of contract in the amount of $40,000, trial date not set.	It is probable that this action will be successfully defended.
Foodex Ltd. has a possible claim in connection with apples sold to them by Peppertree Produce Inc. The apples apparently had not been properly washed by the growers to remove insect spray, and a number of Foodex Ltd.'s customers became ill after eating said apples.	No claim has yet been made and we are unable to estimate possible ultimate loss.

Would you please advise us, as of February 28, 19X8 on the following points:
a. Are the claims and possible claims properly described?
b. Do you consider that our evaluations are reasonable?
c. Are you aware of any claims not listed above which are outstanding? If so, please include in your response letter the names of the parties and the amount claimed.

This enquiry is made in accordance with the Joint Policy Statement of January, 1978 approved by the Canadian Bar Association and the Auditing Standards Committee of the Canadian Institute of Chartered Accountants.

Please address your reply, marked "Privileged and Confidential," to this company and send a signed copy of the reply directly to our auditors, Jeannerette & Cie, Chartered Accountants, 1133 Rue Sherbrooke, Montreal, Quebec H3G 1M8.

Yours truly,
Charles D. Peppertree, President

Charles D. Peppertree

c.c. Jeannerette & Cie

Commitments

Closely related to contingent liabilities are commitments to purchase raw materials or to lease facilities at a certain price, agreements to sell merchandise at a fixed price, bonus plans, profit-sharing and pension plans, royalty agreements, and similar items. For a commitment, the most important characteristic is the *agreement to commit the firm to a set of fixed conditions* in the future regardless of what happens to profits or the economy as a whole. In a free economy, presumably the entity agrees to commitments as a means of bettering its own interests, but they may turn out to be less or more advantageous than originally anticipated.

Section 3280.01 of the *CICA Handbook* requires disclosure of the details of any contractual obligation that is significant to a client's current financial position or future operations. Examples include the following:

- Commitments involving a high degree of speculative risk not typical of the client's operations
- Commitments to make abnormal expenditures
- Commitments that require expenditures to be made for a considerable period of time

All commitments are ordinarily either described together in a separate footnote or combined in a footnote related to contingencies.

The search for unknown commitments is usually performed as a part of the audit of each audit area. For example, in verifying sales transactions the auditor should be alert for sales commitments. Similarly, commitments for the purchase of raw materials or equipment can be identified as a part of the audit of each of these accounts. The auditor should also be aware of the possibility of commitments as he or she is reading contracts and correspondence files, and inquiries should be made of management.

Review for Subsequent Events

The auditor has a responsibility to review transactions and events occurring after the balance sheet date to determine whether anything occurred that might affect the valuation or disclosure of the statements being audited. The auditing procedures employed to verify these transactions and events are commonly referred to as the *review for subsequent events* or *post-balance sheet review*.

The auditor's responsibility for reviewing for subsequent events is normally limited to the period beginning with the balance sheet date and ending with the date of the auditor's report. Since the date of the auditor's report corresponds to the completion of the important auditing procedures in the client's office, the subsequent events review should be completed near the end of the engagement. Figure 22–2 shows the period covered by a subsequent events review and the timing of that review.

> **OBJECTIVE 2**
>
> Conduct a post-balance sheet review for subsequent events.

Types of Subsequent Events

Two types of subsequent events require consideration by management and evaluation by the auditor: those that have a direct effect on the financial statements and require adjustment and those that have no direct effect on the financial statements but for which disclosure is advisable.

Those that have a direct effect on the financial statements and require adjustment These events or transactions provide additional information to management in determining the valuation of account balances as of the balance sheet date and to auditors in verifying the balances. For example, if the auditor is having difficulty

FIGURE 22–2

Period Covered by
Subsequent Events
Review

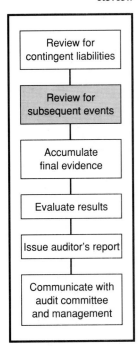

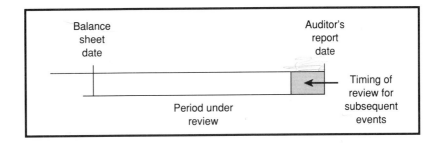

determining the correct valuation of inventory because of obsolescence, the sale of raw material inventory as scrap in the subsequent period should be used as a means of determining the correct valuation of the inventory as of the balance sheet date. The scrap value of the inventory would be entered in the accounting records as the carrying value of the inventory at the balance sheet date.

Such subsequent period events as the following require an adjustment of account balances in the current year's financial statements if the amounts are material:

- The declaration of bankruptcy due to deteriorating financial condition of a customer with an outstanding accounts receivable balance
- The settlement of litigation at an amount different from the amount recorded on the books
- The disposal of equipment not being used in operations at a price below the current book value
- The sale of investments at a price below recorded cost

Whenever subsequent events are used to evaluate the amounts included in the statements, care must be taken to distinguish between conditions that existed at the balance sheet date and those that came into being after the end of the year. The subsequent information should not be incorporated directly into the statements if the conditions causing the change in valuation did not take place until after year end. For example, the sale of scrap in the subsequent period would not be relevant in the valuation of inventory for obsolescence if the obsolescence took place after the end of the year. Also, an amount outstanding from a customer who declared bankruptcy after year-end due to uninsured fire damage to its premises, should not be removed from the accounts receivable balance until the year the damage took place.

Those that have no direct effect on the financial statements but for which disclosure is advisable   Subsequent events of this type provide evidence of conditions that did not exist at the date of the balance sheet being reported on but are so significant that they require disclosure even though they do not require adjustment. Ordinarily, these events can be adequately disclosed by the use of footnotes, but occasionally one may be so significant as to require *supplementing the historical statements* with statements that include the effect of the event as if it had occurred on the balance sheet date (i.e., *pro forma* statements).

Following are examples of events or transactions occurring in the subsequent period that may require disclosure rather than an adjustment in the financial statements:

- A decline in market value of investments
- The issuance of bonds or shares
- A decline in market value of inventory as a consequence of government action barring further sale of a product
- An uninsured loss of inventories as a result of fire or other disaster
- Purchase of a business or trademark
- The settlement of litigation where the event that caused the lawsuit took place subsequent to the balance sheet date

Audit Tests   The audit procedures for the subsequent events review can be conveniently divided into two categories: procedures normally integrated as a part of the verification of year-end account balances and those performed specifically for the purpose of discovering events or transactions that must be recognized as subsequent events.

The first category includes cutoff and valuation tests that are done as a part of the tests of details of balances. For example, subsequent period sales and purchases transactions are examined to determine whether the cutoff is accurate. Similarly, many valuation tests involving subsequent events are also performed as a part of the verification of account balances. As an example, it is common to test the collectibility of accounts receivable by reviewing subsequent period cash receipts. It is also a normal audit procedure to compare the subsequent period purchase price of inventory with the recorded cost as a test of lower of cost or market valuation. The procedures for cutoff and valuation have been discussed sufficiently in preceding chapters and are not repeated here.

The second category of tests is performed specifically for the purpose of obtaining information that must be incorporated into the current year's account balances or disclosed by a footnote. These tests include the following:

Inquire of management   The inquiries vary from client to client, but normally are about the existence of potential contingent liabilities or commitments, significant changes in the assets or capital structure of the company, the current status of items that were not completely resolved at the balance sheet date, and the existence of unusual adjustments made subsequent to the balance sheet date.

Inquiries of management about subsequent events must be held with the proper client personnel to obtain meaningful answers. For example, discussing tax or union matters with the accounts receivable supervisor would not be appropriate. Most inquiries should be made of the controller, the vice presidents and the president, depending on the information desired.

Correspond with law firms   Correspondence with law firms, which was previously discussed, takes place as a part of the search for contingent liabilities. In obtaining confirmation letters from law firms, the auditor must remember his or her responsibility for testing for subsequent events up to the date of the auditor's report. A common approach is to request the law firm to date and mail the letter as of the expected completion date for field work.

Review internal statements prepared subsequent to the balance sheet date   The emphasis in the review should be on (1) changes in the business relative to results for the same period in the year under audit and (2) changes across year end. The auditor should pay particular attention to major changes in the business or environment in which the client is operating. The statements should be discussed with management to determine whether they are prepared on the same basis as the current period statements, and there should be inquiries about significant changes in operating results.

Review records prepared subsequent to the balance sheet date   Journals and ledgers should be reviewed to determine the existence and nature of any transaction related to the current year. If the journals are not kept up to date, the documents relating to the journals should be reviewed.

Examine minutes prepared subsequent to the balance sheet date   The minutes of shareholders' and directors' meetings subsequent to the balance sheet date must be examined for important subsequent events affecting the current period financial statements.

Obtain a letter of representation   The letter of representation written by the client to the auditor formalizes statements the client has made about different matters throughout the audit, including discussions about subsequent events.

Dual Dating   Chapter 2 discussed dating the auditor's report and introduced the notion of *dual dating*, or *double dating*, from Section 5405 of the *CICA Handbook*. We will continue the discussion of double dating in the context of subsequent events. Occasionally, the auditor determines that an important subsequent event occurred after the field work was completed, but *before the auditor's report was issued*. The source of such information is typically management or the press. An example is the acquisition of another company by the audit client on April 23, when the last day of field work was April 11. In such a situation, Section 6550.06 of the *CICA Handbook* requires the auditor to extend audit tests for the newly discovered subsequent event to make sure the client has correctly accounted for it (i.e., either adjusted the statements or disclosed the event). The auditor has two equally acceptable options for expanding subsequent events tests: expand the period of all subsequent events tests to the date at which the auditor is satisfied that the newly determined subsequent event is correctly stated, or restrict the review to matters related to the new subsequent events. For the first option, the auditor's report date would be changed, whereas for the second, the auditor's report would be *dual dated*. In the previous example of the acquisition, assume the auditor returned to the client's premises and completed audit tests on April 30 pertaining only to the acquisition. The auditor's report would be dual dated as follows: April 11, 19X8 except for note 17, as to which the date is April 30.

Final Evidence Accumulation   The auditor has a few final accumulation responsibilities that apply to all cycles besides the search for contingent liabilities and the review for subsequent events. The three most important ones are discussed in this section, being final analytical procedures, evaluation of going concern assumption and obtaining a client representation letter. All three are done late in the engagement.

Final Analytical Procedures

Analytical procedures were introduced in Chapter 7 and applied to specific cycles in several other chapters. As discussed in Chapter 7, analytical procedures are normally used as a part of planning the audit, during the performance of detailed tests in each cycle as part of substantive procedures, and at the completion of the audit.

Analytical procedures done during the completion of the audit are useful as a final review for material misstatements or financial problems, and to help the auditor take a final "objective look" at the financial statements. It is common for a partner to do the analytical procedures during the final review of working papers and financial statements. Typically, a partner has a good understanding of the client and its business because of ongoing relationships. Knowledge of the client's business combined with effective analytical procedures help identify possible oversights in an audit.

> **OBJECTIVE 3**
>
> Design and perform the final steps in the evidence-accumulation segment of the audit.

Evaluate Going Concern Assumption

The Commission to Study the Public's Expectation of Audits (Macdonald Commission) suggested in Recommendation 10 that management should disclose in the financial statements if "there is significant danger that [the company] may not be able to continue as [a going concern] throughout the foreseeable future."[1] Recommendation 11 suggests that if there is "a serious risk of failure" the auditor should qualify his or her report only if management fails to adequately disclose the problem. The recommendation goes on to suggest that the *CICA Handbook* should be changed to require the auditor to highlight the risk in an additional paragraph in the auditor's report.[2] The implication of both recommendations is that the auditor should pay particular attention to the going concern assumption during the audit but especially when performing the final review of the disclosures in the financial statements.

U.S. standards (SAS 59) require the auditor to evaluate whether there is a substantial doubt about a client's ability to continue as a going concern for at least one year beyond the balance sheet date. If the auditor concludes that there is substantial doubt, the auditor's report should include an explanatory paragraph following the opinion paragraph to descibe that conclusion. International Auditing Guideline 23, "Going Concern," also requires the auditor to consider the appropriateness of the going concern assumption.

Canadian standards do not presently require the auditor to evaluate whether there is doubt about the client's ability to continue as a going concern for the foreseeable future. Section 5510 suggests what the auditor should do on becoming aware of conditions which may lead to going concern problems.

J.E. Boritz, in the CICA research study *The "Going Concern" Assumption: Accounting and Auditing Assumptions* suggests that "auditors, as part of every audit, should independently examine the support for management's implicit or explicit assertion about the validity of the "going concern" assumption."[3] He also suggests that the auditor should modify the auditor's report to reflect his or her

---

1 "50 Ways to Change our Ways," *CAmagazine*, July, 1988, page 42. The July issue of *CAmagazine* includes several articles dealing with the report of the Commission to Study the Public's Expectations of Audits (Macdonald Commission).

2 *Ibid.*, page 43.

3 Boritz, J.E., *The "Going Concern" Assumption: Accounting and Auditing Implications*, Toronto: Canadian Institute of Chartered Accountants, 1991, pages xiv and 102 to 104.

concern about the client's ability to operate when the "degree of doubt" about the validity of the going concern assumption exceeds 50 percent.[4]

It is the conclusion of the authors that the auditor should follow the suggestions with respect to the going concern assumption proposed by Boritz and the other sources described above.

Client Representation Letter

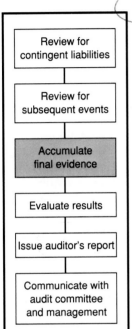

Review for contingent liabilities

Review for subsequent events

Accumulate final evidence

Evaluate results

Issue auditor's report

Communicate with audit committee and management

The *CICA Handbook* does not specifically require a letter of representation from a client, except in connection with communications with law firms (Section 6560.19). Such letters are, however, suggested in connection with prospectuses (Section 7100.14) and with review engagements (Auditing Guideline). However, many public accounting firms in Canada do require a letter of representation covering many of the aspects of the audit. For that reason, the requirements of the AICPA in SAS 19 are instructive.

SAS 19 (AU 333) *requires the auditor to obtain a letter of representation* that documents management's most important oral representations during the audit. The client representation letter is prepared on the client's letterhead, addressed to the public accounting firm, and signed by high-level corporate officials, usually the president and chief financial officer.

The letter should be dated as of the auditor's report date to make sure there are representations related to the subsequent events review. The letter implies that it has originated with the client, but it is common practice for the auditor to prepare the letter and request the client to type it on the company's letterhead and sign it. Refusal by a client to prepare and sign the letter would probably require a qualified opinion or denial of opinion.

There are two purposes of the client letter of representation:

- *To impress upon management its responsibility for the assertions in the financial statements.* For example, if the letter of representation includes a reference to pledged assets and contingent liabilities, honest management may be reminded of its unintentional failure to disclose the information adequately. To fulfil this objective, the letter of representation should be sufficiently detailed to act as a reminder to management.

- *To document the responses from management to inquiries about various aspects of the audit.* This provides written documentation of client representations in the event of disagreement or a lawsuit between the auditor and client.

    SAS 19 suggests many specific matters that should be included, when applicable, in a client representation letter. A few of these are:

- Management's acknowledgment of its responsibility for the fair presentation in the statements . . . in conformity with generally accepted accounting principles or [an appropriate disclosed] basis of accounting.

- Availability of all financial records and related data.

- Completeness and availability of all minutes of meetings of shareholders, directors and committees of directors.

- Information concerning related-party transactions and related amounts receivable or payable.

- Plans or intentions that may affect the carrying value or classification of assets or liabilities.

- Disclosure of compensating balances or other arrangements involving restrictions on cash balances, and disclosure of lines of credit or similar arrangements.

---

4 *Ibid.*, pages xiv to xv and 104 to 106.

A client representation letter is a written statement from a nonindependent source and therefore *cannot be regarded as reliable evidence*. The letter does provide minimal evidence that management has been asked certain questions, but its primary purpose is psychological and to protect the auditor from potential claims by management that it was unaware of its responsibilities.

Other Information in Annual Reports

Section 7500 of the *CICA Handbook* details the auditor's responsibilities for information in the annual report of a company. The primary responsibility is to ensure that the financial statements and auditor's report are accurately reproduced in the annual report. If the company's annual report has not been issued, correcting any misstatement is relatively easy; the auditor can simply ask management to correct the misstatement in the report. On the other hand, if the financial statements and annual report have already been issued when the misstatement is discovered, the auditor must be satisfied that management will take "reasonable steps" to notify users about the misstatement. If the auditor is not so satisfied, notice should be given to the board of directors and consideration should be given to what further action should be taken.

The auditor should also read the entire annual report to ascertain if any of the other information in the annual report is inconsistent with the financial statements. For example, assume the president's letter in the annual report refers to an increase in earnings per share from $2.60 to $2.93. The auditor is required to compare that information to the financial statements to make sure it corresponds. If the error is in the financial statements and they have not been issued, the auditor should have them corrected or issue a qualified report; if they have been issued, the auditor should treat the error as a subsequent discovery of an error (Section 5405) and notify management. If it is the annual report that requires revision, the auditor should notify management. If the auditor cannot gain satisfaction from management, including the audit committee and the board of directors, the auditor should consider what further action is warranted.

The auditor has responsibilities beyond searching for misstatements in the financial statements in the annual report or for inconsistencies between the financial statements and the other material in the annual report; Section 7500.20 requires the auditor to advise management of any material misstatements of fact that are contained in the annual report. The annual report may include, for instance, information about a fictitious lucrative contract with the company, which would affect the following years' business and profits significantly. If management refuses to correct the misstatements, the auditor should advise the audit committee and the board of directors. If satisfaction is still not obtained by the auditor, further action should be considered.

Management Discussion and Analysis

The academic and professional literature includes descriptions of research and articles that indicate that users of financial statements and annual reports are interested in an entity's future as well as in its past and present. While an entity's financial statements, including the notes to those statements, present information about the entity's financial position and financial history, until recently, there was little information to tell users what management of the entity expected to occur in the foreseeable future. In addition, there was a belief that it would be helpful to users if management were to provide a narrative expressing their interpretation of the entity's financial position and operations.

Section 4250, Future-oriented Financial Information (FOFI), was added to the *CICA Handbook* in 1989 to provide guidance on how such information would be prepared with the financial statements, but did not require that FOFI be provided. To date, few companies are providing information under Section 4250. There is an Auditing Guideline "Examination of a Financial Forecast or Projection Included in a Prospectus or Other Public Offering Document" that provides guidance on handling FOFI included in a prospectus but does not deal with the auditor's involvement when such information is included in an annual report.

In Canada and the United States, securities regulators, recognizing that there is a limit to the amount of information that can be communicated by the financial statements, including the notes, are requiring that companies that borrow money from or sell stock to the public provide a comment from management in the annual report; the comment would be supplementary to the financial statements and provide information about management's expectations. Such a report has come to be known as *management discussion and analysis* (MD&A).

MD&A is generally required by securities administrators in Canada. For example, the Ontario Securities Commission (OSC) requires most of its larger registrants to provide MD&A in their annual reports and suggests that MD&A also be provided with interim financial statements.[5] The description of MD&A in the Ontario Securities Commission's (OSC) Policy Statement 5.10[6] is helpful in understanding the concept.

> MD&A is supplemental analysis and explanation which accompanies but does not form part of the financial statements. MD&A provides management with the opportunity to explain in narrative form its current financial situation and future prospects. MD&A is intended to give the investor the ability to look at the [company issuing the financial statements] through the eyes of management by providing a historical and prospective analysis of the business of the [issuer]. MD&A requirements ask management to discuss the dynamics of the business and to analyze the financial statements. Coupled with the financial statements this information should allow investors to assess [the issuing company's] performance and future prospects.

The auditor's role with respect to MD&A is the same as the auditor's role with respect to the annual report as required by Section 7500.

Evaluate Results

At the completion of the application of all the specific audit procedures for each of the audit areas, it is necessary to integrate the results into *one overall conclusion*. Ultimately, the auditor must decide whether sufficient appropriate audit evidence has been accumulated to warrant the conclusion that the financial statements are stated in accordance with generally accepted accounting principles.

Figure 22–3 summarizes the parts of the audit that must be reviewed in the evaluation of results. The emphasis is on the conclusions reached through tests of controls, analytical procedures and tests of details of balances for each of the five cycles shown in the figure. Five aspects of evaluating the results are discussed.

OBJECTIVE 4

Integrate the audit evidence gathered, and evaluate the overall audit results.

---

5 The interested reader is referred to Ontario Securities Commision Policy Statement 5.10 "Annual Information Form and Management's Discussion and Analysis of Financial Condition and Results of Operations" or to the comparable release from the securities administrators in the reader's province. Appreciation is expressed to Ms. Brenda Eprile, Chief Accountant to the OSC for providing the authors with a copy of Policy Statement 5.10.

6 *Ibid.*, page 20.

FIGURE 22–3

Evaluating
Engagement Results

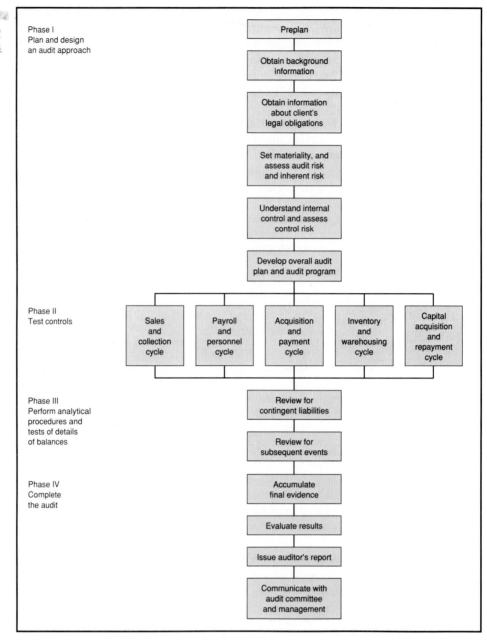

Sufficiency of Evidence

The final summarization of the adequacy of the evidence is a review by the auditor of the entire audit to determine whether all important aspects have been adequately tested considering the circumstances of the engagement. A major step in this process is review of the audit programs to make sure that all parts have been accurately completed and documented and that all audit objectives have been met. An important part of the review is to decide whether the audit program is adequate considering the problem areas that were discovered as the audit progressed. For example, if errors were discovered as a part of the tests of sales, the initial plans for the tests of details of accounts receivable balances may have been insufficient and should have been revised.

As an aid in drawing final conclusions about the adequacy of the audit evidence, auditors frequently use *completing the engagement checklists.* These are reminders of aspects of the audit that are frequently overlooked. An illustration of part of a completing the engagement checklist is given in Figure 22–4.

If the auditor concludes that he or she has *not* obtained sufficient evidence to draw a conclusion about the fairness of the client's representations, there are two choices: Additional evidence must be obtained, or either a qualified opinion or a denial of opinion must be issued. The former will be the more common choice as a client will not likely agree to have a qualified auditor's report because of the auditor's failure to do sufficient work.

Evidence Supports Auditor's Opinion

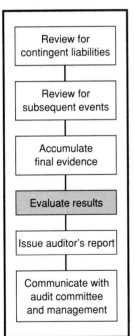

Review for contingent liabilities

Review for subsequent events

Accumulate final evidence

Evaluate results

Issue auditor's report

Communicate with audit committee and management

An important part of evaluating whether the financial statements are fairly stated is summarizing the misstatements uncovered in the audit. Whenever the auditor uncovers misstatements that are in themselves material, the trial balance should be adjusted to correct the statements. It may be difficult to determine the appropriate amount of adjustment because the true value of the misstatement is unknown; nevertheless, it is the auditor's responsibility to decide on the required adjustment. In addition to the material misstatements, there are often a large number of immaterial misstatements discovered that are not adjusted at the time they are found. It is necessary to combine individually immaterial misstatements to evaluate whether the combined amount is material. The auditor can keep track of the misstatements and combine them in several different ways, but many auditors use a convenient method known as an *unadjusted misstatement worksheet* or *summary of possible adjustments.* It is relatively easy to evaluate the overall significance of several immaterial misstatements with this type of working paper. An example of an unadjusted misstatement worksheet is given in Figure 22–5.

The auditor should consider carry-forward errors from the previous year in the analysis of errors and of the need for adjustment. For example, closing inventory was understated by $15,000 in 19X7 and overstated by $10,000 in 19x8, the effect on income in 19X8 would be $25,000. The individual errors may be immaterial, but the combined effect might well be material and require adjustment.

If the auditor believes that he or she *has* sufficient evidence, but it does not warrant a conclusion of fairly presented financial statements, the auditor again has two choices: the statements must be revised to the auditor's satisfaction, or either a qualified or an adverse opinion must be issued. Notice that the options here are different from those in the case of insufficient evidence obtained.

FIGURE 22–4

Completing the
Engagement Checklist

	YES	NO
1. *Examination of prior year's working papers*		
a. Were last year's working papers and review notes examined for areas of emphasis in the current-year audit?	____	____
b. Was the permanent file reviewed for items that affect the current year?	____	____
2. *Internal control*		
a. Has internal control been adequately understood and reviewed?	____	____
b. Is the scope of the audit adequate in light of the assessed level of control risk?	____	____
c. Have all major weaknesses been included in a management letter and material weakness in a letter to senior management?	____	____
3. *General documents*		
a. Were all current-year minutes and resolutions reviewed, abstracted and followed up?	____	____
b. Has the permanent file been updated?	____	____
c. Have all major contracts and agreements been reviewed and abstracted or copied to ascertain that the client complies with all existing legal requirements?	____	____

Financial Statement Disclosures

A major consideration in completing the audit is to determine whether the disclosures in the financial statements are adequate. Throughout the audit, the emphasis in most examinations is on verifying the accuracy of the balances in the general ledger by testing the most important accounts on the auditor's trial balance. Another important task is to make sure the account balances on the trial balance are correctly aggregated and disclosed on the financial statements. Naturally, adequate disclosure includes consideration of all of the statements including related footnotes.

Frequently, the auditor actually prepares the financial statements from the trial balance in small client audits and submits them to the client for approval. Performing this function may seem to imply that the client has been relieved of responsibility for the fair representation in the statements, but that is not the case. The auditor acts in the role of adviser when preparing the financial statements, but *management retains the final responsibility for approving the issuance of the statements.*

The review for adequate disclosure in the financial statements at the completion of the audit is not the only time the auditor is interested in proper disclosure. Unless the auditor is constantly alert for disclosure problems, it is impossible to perform the final disclosure review adequately. For example, as part of the examination of accounts receivable, the auditor must be aware of the need to separate accounts receivable, notes receivable and other amounts due from affiliates and those due from customers. Similarly, there must be a segregation of current from noncurrent receivables and a disclosure of the factoring or discounting of notes receivable if such is the case. An important part of verifying all account balances is determining whether generally accepted accounting principles were properly applied on a basis consistent with that of the preceding year. The auditor must carefully document this information in the working papers to facilitate the final review.

As part of the final review for financial statement disclosure, many public accounting firms require the completion of a *financial statement disclosure checklist* for every engagement. These questionnaires are designed to remind the

FIGURE 22–5

	Schedule A-3	Date
ABC Company Inc.	Prepared by PR	1/28
Summary of Possible Adjustments	Approved by GS	1/31

12/31/x4

Workpaper Source		Total Amount	Possible Adjustments –Dr <Cr>						
			Current Assets	Non-current Assets	Current Liabilities	Non-current Liabilities	Sales and Revenues	Costs and Expenses	Federal Income Tax
B-32 C-4	Unreimbursed petty cash vouchers	480	<480>		240			480	<240>
C-4	Possible underprovision in allowance for doubtful accounts	4000	<4000>		2000			4000	<2000>
C-8	Accounts receivable/Sales cutoff errors	600	600		<300>		<600>		300
D-2	Difference between physical inventory and books figures	5200	5200		<2600>			<5200>	2600
H-7/2	Unrecorded liabilities	4850	2000	1850	<4350>			1000	<500>
V-10	Repairs expense items which should be capitalized	900		900	<450>			<900>	450
	Totals		3320	2750	<5460>		<600>	<620>	610

Conclusions:

The net effects of the above items are as follows:

Working capital	$<2440>
Total assets	6070
Net income	<610>

None of these aggregate effects or of the individual items has a material effect on the financial statements in total or with respect to the components they pertain to. On this basis, adjustment of any or all of the items is passed.

Paul Roberts
1/28

auditor of common disclosure problems encountered on audits and also to facilitate the final review of the entire audit by an independent partner. An illustration of a partial financial statement disclosure checklist is given in Figure 22–6. Naturally, it is not sufficient to rely on a checklist to replace the auditor's own knowledge of generally accepted accounting principles. In any given audit, some aspects of the engagement require much greater expertise in accounting than can be obtained from such a checklist.

Working Paper Review

There are three main reasons why it is essential that the working papers be thoroughly reviewed by another member of the audit firm at the completion of the audit:

- *To evaluate the performance of inexperienced personnel.* A considerable portion of most audits is performed by audit personnel with less than four or five years of experience. These people may have sufficient technical training to conduct an

FIGURE 22–6

Financial Statement
Disclosure Checklist:
Property, Plant and
Equipment

	YES	NO
1. Are the following disclosures included in the financial statements or notes (Section 3060):		
a. Cost for each major category of capital assets?	___	___
b. The amount of amortization?	___	___
c. Accumulated amortization, including the amount of any write downs, for each major category of capital assets?	___	___
d. The amount of any write downs during the period?	___	___
e. The amortization method used, including the amortization period or rate, for each major category of capital assets including leased assets? (Section 3065.25 also)	___	___
f. The net carrying amount of a capital asset not being amortized because it is under construction or development, or has been removed from service for an extended period?	___	___
2. Are the nature, basis of measurement, amount, and related gains and losses of non-monetary transactions disclosed? (Section 3830.13)	___	___
3. Has consideration been given to disclosure of fully depreciated capital assets still in use?	___	___
4. Are carrying amounts of property mortgaged and encumbered by indebtedness disclosed? (Section 1500.12)	___	___
5. Is the carrying amount of property not a part of operations (i.e., idle, or held for investment or sale) segregated?	___	___
6. Are the following disclosures made for capital leases:		
a. The gross amount of assets under capital leases and the related accumulated amortization? (Section 3065.21)	___	___
b. Significant restrictions imposed on the lessee by the lease agreements? (Section 3065.22)	___	___
c. Future minimum lease payments for each of the next five years and in total? (Section 3065.24)	___	___
d. A separate deduction from the future minimum lease payments for executory costs and imputed interest? (Section 3065.24)	___	___
e. Interest expense, either separately or as part of interest on long-term debt? (Section 3065.26)	___	___
7. Are obligations and other details (e.g., interest rates, expiry dates) related to leased assets shown separately from other long-term liabilities? (Section 3065.22)	___	___
8. Is any portion of lease obligations due within one year classified as a current liability? (Section 3065.23)	___	___
9. Are the following disclosures made for operating leases:		
a. Future minimum lease payments for each of the next five years and in total? (Section 3065.32)	___	___
b. The nature of other commitments under operating leases? (Section 3065.32)	___	___

Note: Information in parentheses refers to authoritative professional literature.

adequate audit, but their lack of experience affects their ability to make sound professional judgments in complex situations.

- *To make sure that the audit meets the public accounting firm's standard of performance.* Within any organization, the performance quality of individuals varies considerably, but careful review by top-level personnel in the firm assists in maintaining a uniform quality of auditing.

- *To counteract the bias that frequently enters into the auditor's judgment.* Auditors may attempt to remain objective throughout the audit, but it is easy to lose proper perspective on a long audit when there are complex problems to solve.

Except for a final independent review, which is discussed shortly, the review of the working papers should be conducted by someone who is knowledgeable about the client and the unique circumstances in the audit. Therefore, the initial review of the working papers prepared by any given auditor is normally done by the auditor's immediate supervisor. For example, the least experienced auditor's work is ordinarily reviewed by the audit senior; the senior's immediate superior, who is normally a supervisor or manager, reviews the senior's work and also reviews less thoroughly the papers of the inexperienced auditor. Finally, the partner assigned to the audit must ultimately review all working papers, but the partner reviews those prepared by the supervisor or manager more thoroughly than the others.

Independent Review

At the completion of larger audits, it is common to have the financial statements and the entire set of working papers reviewed by a completely independent reviewer who has not participated in the engagement. This reviewer, usually a partner, frequently takes an adversary position to make sure the conduct of the audit was adequate. The audit team must be able to justify the evidence they have accumulated and the conclusions they reached on the basis of the unique circumstances of the engagement.

Summary of Evidence Evaluation

Figure 22–7 summarizes the evaluation of the sufficiency of the evidence and deciding whether the evidence supports the opinion. The top portion of the figure shows the planning decisions that determine the planned audit evidence.

Figure 22–7 summarizes how to evaluate the sufficiency of the evidence and decide whether the evidence supports the opinion. The top portion of the figure shows the planning decisions that determine the planned audit evidence. It was taken from Figure 8-7. The bottom portion shows how the auditor evaluates the sufficiency of the actual evidence by first evaluating whether the evidence gathered using substantive procedures was adequate to achieve the audit risk set for the audit given the auditor's assessment of inherent risk and control risk for the account and cycle and then making the same evaluation for the overall financial statements. The auditor also evaluates whether the evidence supports the audit opinion by first estimating misstatements in each account and then for the overall financial statements. In practice, both sets of evaluations are made at the same time. On the basis of these evaluations the auditor's report is issued for the financial statements.

Communicate with the Audit Committee and Management

After the audit is completed, there are several potential communications from the auditor to client personnel. Most of these are directed to the audit committee or senior management, but communications with operating management are also common.

Communicate Misstatements and Illegal Acts

Section 5135 of the *CICA Handbook* requires the auditor to ensure the appropriate level of management is informed of existing *misstatements* that are other than trivial. In addition, the auditor must ensure the audit committee or similarly designated group (e.g., board of directors, board of trustees) is informed of all significant misstatements, whether or not they are adjusted. Misstatements include intentional (fraud or other irregularities) or unintentional (errors) misstatements. The audit committee can be informed by either the auditor or management, and it should be done on a timely basis. This requirement indicates the increased concern over the auditor's responsibility for the detection and prevention of misstatements.

OBJECTIVE 5

Communicate effectively with the audit committee and management.

FIGURE 22–7   Evaluating Results and Reaching Conclusions on the Basis of Evidence

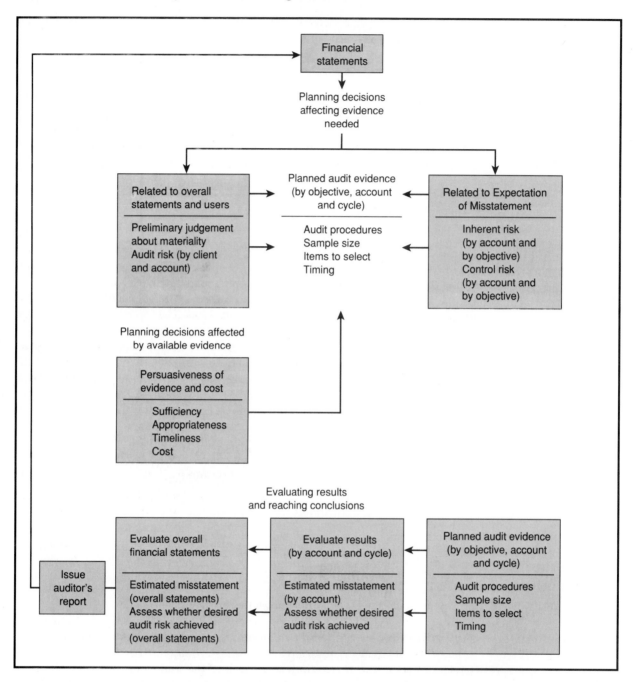

Illegal acts are violations of laws or government regulations. The auditor should communicate illegal acts other than fraud, such as noncompliance with waste disposal regulations, to the audit committee or equivalent group on a timely basis, although the *CICA Handbook* does not require this specifically. The audit committee may also expect the auditor to communicate such matters as unusual actions which increase the risk of loss to the company; actions that could cause serious embarrassment to the entity, such as breaches of the company's code of conduct; significant transactions that appear to be inconsistent with the ordinary course of business; or other matters. The audit committee's wishes should be discussed and clarified with the audit committee prior to undertaking the audit field work.

Communicate Reportable Internal Control Conditions

As discussed in Chapter 9, Section 5135 includes misstatements that indicate significant deficiencies in the design or operation of internal control in its definition of significant misstatements that must be reported to the audit committee. Although the auditor has no duty to report less significant internal control weaknesses identified during the audit to the client, he or she commonly does so as a client service. In addition, some auditors provide suggestions for improvements in internal control. In larger companies this communication is made to the audit committee and in smaller companies to the owners or senior management. The nature and form of that communication were discussed in Chapter 9.

Other Communication with Audit Committee

The auditor should communicate certain additional information obtained during the audit for audits where there is an audit committee or similarly designated body. Like all communications with the audit committee, the purpose is to keep the committee informed of auditing issues and findings that will assist them in performing their supervisory role for financial statements.

Audit committees were introduced in Chapter 3. It was pointed out there that their role as specified by the *Canada Business Corporations Act* was quite limited but that there were many useful functions the audit committee could perform. The following are issues that could be discussed with the audit committee, or a similarly designated body, by the auditor with the intent of keeping the audit committee informed:

- The auditor's responsibilities under generally accepted auditing standards, including responsibility for understanding and evaluating internal control and the concept of reasonable rather than absolute assurance.
- Planning of the current audit, including such matters as the general approach, areas of perceived high risk, materiality and risk levels selected, planned reliance on other auditors (including the internal audit department), and timing of the audit.
- The significant accounting principles and policies selected and applied to the financial statements, the existence of acceptable alternatives, and the acceptability of those selected by management.
- Management's judgments and estimates of sensitive accounting-related issues, and the auditor's conclusions about the reasonableness of them.
- Disagreements with management about the scope of the audit, applicability of accounting principles and wording of the audit report, whether or not satisfactorily resolved.
- Difficulties encountered in performing the audit, such as lack of availability of client personnel, failure to obtain necessary information and an unreasonable timetable in which to complete the audit.
- Any unresolved matters arising from review of the entire annual report and identification of misstatements in reproducing the financial statements or the auditor's report, or of inconsistencies between the statements and other information in the report.
- If the auditor becomes aware of any consultations with other accountants about

accounting or auditing matters, the auditor's opinions about the subjects of these consultations.

■ Any major issues discussed with management in connection with the appointment of the auditor, including those related to the application of accounting principles and auditing standards, and fees.

Communication with the audit committee normally takes place more than once during each audit and can be oral, written or both. For example, issues dealing with the auditor's responsibilities and significant accounting policies are usually discussed early in the audit, hopefully during the planning phase. Disagreements with management and difficulties encountered in performing the audit would be communicated after the audit is completed, or earlier if the problems hinder the auditor's ability to complete the audit. The most important matters are communicated in writing to minimize misunderstanding and to provide documentation in the event of subsequent disagreement.

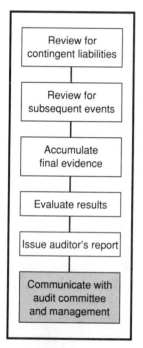

The purpose of a management letter (letter of recommendation) is to inform the client of the public accountant's recommendations for improving the client's business. The recommendations focus on suggestions for more efficient operations. The combination of the auditor's experience in various businesses and a thorough understanding gained in conducting the audit place the auditor in a unique position to provide management with assistance. Figure 22–8 shows a detailed example of a management letter.

A management letter is different from a required communication on internal control related matters discussed in Chapter 9. The latter is required whenever there are significant internal control weaknesses. A management letter is optional and is intended to help the client operate its business more effectively. Auditors write management letters for two reasons: to encourage a better relationship between the public accounting firm and management and to suggest additional tax and management services the public accounting firm can provide.

There is no standard format or approach for writing management letters. Each letter should be developed to meet the style of the auditor and the needs of the client, consistent with the public accounting firm's concept of management letters. It should be noted that many auditors combine the management letter with the required communication on internal control related matters. On smaller audits, it is common for the auditor to communicate operational suggestions orally rather than by letter.

Subsequent Discovery of Facts[7]

If the auditor becomes aware *after the audited financial statements have been released* that some information included in the statements is materially misleading, the auditor has an obligation under section 5405 of the *CICA Handbook* to make certain that users who are relying on the financial statements are informed about the misstatements.

---

7 The discussion in this section is more closely related to audit reports, which is the subject of Chapter 2, than it is to completing the audit. However, many students of auditing confuse the examination of subsequent period events as a part of post-balance sheet review with the subsequent discovery of facts existing at the balance sheet date. The latter is studied at this point to eliminate the confusion.

FIGURE 22–8

Management Letter

LINDSAY, BAXTER AND BRENNAN, CHARTERED ACCOUNTANTS
Duck Lake, Saskatchewan

March 3, 19X8

Board of Directors
SS Financial Industries Ltd. and Subsidiaries
92 Regent Street
Regina, Saskatchewan
S4S 0M4

In connection with our examination of the consolidated financial statements of SS Financial Industries Ltd. (SS Financial) for the year ending December 31, 19X7, we reviewed the companies' accounting procedures and internal control. While we believe the existing controls and procedures to be adequate in most respects, we noted the following areas in which we believe more effective internal control or increased efficiency is desirable.

General
SS Financial has reached a size and complexity that demands the full attention of a financially-oriented person. Therefore we recommend you consider employing an experienced person with a good background in accounting and finance.

Data Processing and Systems Integration
Systems design and program changes over the past two to three years have been made principally on a patchwork basis, with the result that newly implemented systems have not been fully integrated with existing systems, and program documentation has not been updated for all changes. Thus, it is possible for the same information to be processed differently through two systems, or for data to be processed through one part of a system and not another, with the result that general or control records are not in agreement with subsidiary records.

A thorough review of the data processing function should be undertaken, first, to define the systems and procedures as they now stand, including all reports produced and their distribution; second, to identify and set priorities for needed revisions to the existing systems; and third, to integrate the systems and procedures to provide accurate and complete data to the operations and production departments.

Contracts Receivable
A significant portion of the business of the corporations centers around the installment contracts receivable from customers. We believe there are several methods by which the contracts and related procedures could be improved.

The following points should be considered as a framework for providing strength in this area:

1. Complete centralization of contract responsibility in the finance subsidiary.
2. Use of prenumbered contract forms, all of which must be accounted for.
3. Use of prenumbered receipt forms, accounted for in the same manner as contract forms.
4. Establishment of a requirement that all contracts be recorded and ultimate disposition noted in the records. This should be accomplished by adoption of a policy defining follow-up procedures and standard disposition methods.
5. Design, implementation and enforcement of filing procedures that would provide adequate support of customer receivables.

FIGURE 22–8

(Continued)

Collection agencies

Contracts turned over to collection agencies during the past year are providing little return to the company and, in fact, may work to your detriment. Three customers against whom the collection agency has attempted to file suit or garnishment proceedings have been able to substantiate payment to a sales office for the alleged delinquency. Inasmuch as accounting procedures in effect at the time of processing these early contracts were somewhat lax, it would be difficult to defend against such claims. We recommend that you consider abandoning collection efforts on these contracts in light of the minimal return being received and the possibility that such action could result in unfavourable publicity.

Sales policies and techniques

Sales and collection data that we accumulated during our review indicated that the largest portion of uncollectible contracts arose from sales having one or more of the following characteristics:

1. Contract amount significantly larger than usual.
2. Contract payment period significantly longer than normal.
3. Downpayment significantly lower than normal.

We believe sales personnel should concentrate on "normal" sales, avoiding programs of excessive terms or nominal downpayments. The policy of encouraging accelerated cash payments should be continued.

The second major factor contributing to uncollectible contract balances is dissatisfaction on the part of the customer shortly after receipt of the merchandise. Collection personnel have encountered resistance from customers to whom sales people had apparently promised results other than those contained in the written agreement. We believe these problems could be minimized through the establishment and enforcement of sales guidelines to avoid implied guarantees beyond those in the service agreement.

To assist in achieving the goals outlined above, we recommend the present commission and bonus policies be modified to include collections to provide an incentive for obtaining acceptable credit risks and downpayments within established guidelines.

Operating Results, Reporting, and Planning

In light of the expansion of operations, we believe that consideration should be given to centralization of common procedures for increased control and efficiency. This would involve the centralization of the financing and contract handling functions in the finance subsidiary and the development of standardized accounting techniques and documents for submission to the central accounting office.

To provide meaningful management operating reports, corporate expenses should be identified and recorded as direct charges to the appropriate sales offices as costs of operations, or as general, administrative, and selling expenses. Sales and performance data should be accumulated, analyzed and applied in a comprehensive approach to management that includes cash forecasting and profit planning.

We suggest that a series of operating reports be designed and implemented to permit effective management control. The specific nature of the reports will be dictated by the requirements of management, but, at a minimum, should measure actual against planned performance.

We would be pleased to discuss the above comments and recommendations further with you and to assist in their implementation.

Lindsay, Baxter & Brennan

Lindsay, Baxter & Brennan
Chartered Accountants

OBJECTIVE 6

Identify the auditor's responsibilities when facts affecting the auditor's report are discovered after its issuance.

The *Handbook* requires the auditor first to discuss the matter with management and, if required or appropriate, with the board of directors or the audit committee. The auditor also has an obligation, under the *Canada Business Corporations Act* (Section 171(7)) to notify each of the directors. The directors are required to prepare and issue revised financial statements or otherwise inform the shareholders. The directors must also inform the director of the Corporations Branch of the Department of Consumer and Corporate Affairs and may have to inform other regulatory agencies.

If a director or officer discovers a misstatement of any size, he or she is required to notify the audit committee *and* the auditor. The responsibilities of the former are not specified, but presumably it would notify its fellow directors. The auditor would first decide if the misstatement is material and, if so, notify each director.

The most likely case in which the auditor is faced with this problem occurs when the financial statements are determined to include a material misstatement subsequent to the issuance of an unqualified report. Possible causes of misstatements are the inclusion of material fictitious sales, the failure to write off obsolete inventory, or the omission of an essential footnote. Regardless of whether the failure to discover the misstatement was the fault of the auditor or the client, the auditor's responsibility remains the same.

The most desirable approach to follow if the auditor discovers the statements are misleading is to request that the client issue an immediate revision of the financial statements containing an explanation of the reasons for the revision. The auditor may decide, after consideration of the misstatement, to revise the financial statements and issue a double dated auditor's report with respect to the misstatement. On the other hand, the auditor may decide that further work is required and a new auditor's report, with the current date, is necessary. The auditor's report, in any event, should clearly indicate that the previous statements were withdrawn and that they have been revised. This information would normally be in a paragraph following the opinion paragraph. If a subsequent period's financial statements were completed before the revised statements could be issued, it is acceptable to disclose the misstatements in the subsequent period's statements.

If the client refuses to cooperate in disclosing the misstated information, the auditor should inform the board of directors of this fact. In addition, the auditor should seek legal advice as to what he or she should do to discharge his or her responsibilities and consider resigning from the engagement.

It is important to understand that the subsequent discovery of facts requiring the recall or reissuance of financial statements *does not arise from developments occurring after the date of the auditor's report.* For example, if an account receiv-

FIGURE 22–9

Review for Subsequent Events and Subsequent Discovery of Facts

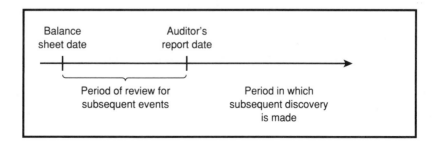

able is believed to be collectible after an adequate review of the facts at the date of the auditor's report, but the customer subsequently files bankruptcy, a revision of the financial statements is not required. The statements must be recalled or reissued only when information that would indicate that the statements were not fairly presented *already existed at the auditor's report date.*

In an earlier section, it was shown that the auditor's responsibility for subsequent events review begins as of the balance sheet date and ends on the date of the completion of the field work. Any pertinent information discovered as a part of the review can be incorporated in the financial statements before they are issued. Note that the auditor has no responsibility to search for subsequent facts of the nature discussed in this section, but if the auditor discovers that issued financial statements are improperly stated, he or she must take action to correct them. The auditor's responsibility for reporting on improperly issued financial statements does not start until the date of the auditor's report. Typically, an existing material misstatement is found as a part of the subsequent year's audit, or it may be reported to the auditor by the client.

Figure 22–9 shows the difference in the period covered by the review for subsequent events and that for the discovery of facts after the auditor's report date.

Review Questions

22–1   Distinguish between a contingent liability and an actual liability and give three examples of each.

22–2   In the audit of James Mobley Ltd., you are concerned about the possibility of contingent liabilities resulting in income tax disputes. Discuss the procedures you could use for an extensive investigation in this area.

22–3   Explain why the analysis of legal expense is an essential part of every audit engagement.

22–4   During the audit of the Merrill Manufacturing Corp., Ralph Pyson, a public accountant, has become aware of four lawsuits against the client through discussions with the client, reading corporate minutes and reviewing correspondence files. How should Pyson determine the materiality of the lawsuits and the proper disclosure in the financial statements?

22–5   Distinguish between an outstanding (asserted) and a possible (unasserted) claim. Explain why a client's law firm may not reveal a possible claim.

22–6   Describe the action that an auditor should take if a law firm refuses to provide information that is within its jurisdiction and may directly affect the fair presentation of the financial statements.

22–7   Distinguish between subsequent events requiring adjustment and those requiring disclosure. Give two examples of each type.

22–8   In obtaining confirmations from law firms, Betty Irwin's aim is to receive the confirmation letters as early as possible after the balance sheet date. This provides her with a signed letter from every law firm in time to investigate properly any exceptions. It also eliminates the problem of a lot of unresolved loose ends near the end of the audit. Evaluate Irwin's approach.

22–9   Explain why an auditor would be interested in a client's future commitments to purchase raw materials at a fixed price.

22–10   What major considerations should the auditor take into account in determining how extensive the review of subsequent events should be?

22-11 Identify five audit procedures normally done as a part of the review for subsequent events.

22-12 Distinguish between subsequent events occurring between the balance sheet date and the date of the auditor's report, and subsequent discovery of facts existing at the date of the auditor's report. Give two examples of each and explain the appropriate action by the auditor in each instance.

22-13 Miles Lawson, a public accountant, believes the final summarization is the easiest part of the audit if careful planning is followed throughout the engagement. He makes sure each segment of the audit is completed before he goes on to the next. When the last segment of the engagement is completed, he is finished with the audit. He believes this may cause each part of the audit to take a little longer, but he makes up for it by not having to do the final summarization. Evaluate Lawson's approach.

22-14 Compare and contrast the accumulation of audit evidence and the evaluation of the adequacy of the disclosures in the financial statements. Give two examples in which adequate disclosure could depend heavily on the accumulation of evidence and two others in which audit evidence does not normally significantly affect the adequacy of the disclosure.

22-15 Explain what the statement "The auditor should actively evaluate whether there is substantial doubt about the client's ability to continue as a going concern" means.

22-16 Distinguish between a client representation letter and a management letter, and state the primary purpose of each. List some items that might be included in each letter.

22-17 What is meant by reading other financial information in annual reports? Give an example of the type of information the auditor would examine.

22-18 Explain why you think securities regulators in certain jurisdictions require public companies to provide MD&A in their annual reports.

22-19 Distinguish between regular working paper review and independent review, and state the purpose of each. Give two examples of important potential findings in each of these two types of review.

MULTIPLE CHOICE QUESTIONS

22-20 The following questions deal with contingent liabilities. Choose the best response.

   a. The audit step most likely to reveal the existence of contingent liabilities is

      (1) a review of vouchers paid during the month following the year-end.
      (2) accounts payable confirmations.
      (3) an enquiry directed to law firms.
      (4) mortgage-note confirmation.

   b. When obtaining evidence regarding litigation against a client, the public accountant would be *least* interested in determining

      (1) an estimate of when the matter will be resolved.
      (2) the period in which the underlying cause of the litigation occurred.
      (3) the probability of an unfavorable outcome.
      (4) an estimate of the potential loss.

   c. The letter of audit enquiry addressed to the client's law firms will *not* ordinarily be

      (1) sent to a lawyer who was engaged by the audit client during the year and soon thereafter resigned from the engagement.

> (2) a source of corroboration of the information originally obtained from management concerning litigation, claims and assessments.
>
> (3) limited to references concerning only pending or threatened litigation with respect to which the lawyer has been engaged.
>
> (4) sent to a lawyer whose sole function was to process patent applications.

d. When a contingency is resolved immediately subsequent to the issuance of a report that included an appropriate note on the contingency, the auditor should

> (1) insist that the client issue revised financial statements.
>
> (2) inform the audit committee that the report *cannot* be relied upon.
>
> (3) take *no* action regarding the event.
>
> (4) inform the appropriate authorities that the report *cannot* be relied upon.

(AICPA adapted)

22–21 The following questions concern letters of representation. Choose the best response.

a. A principal purpose of a letter of representation from management is to

> (1) serve as an introduction to company personnel and an authorization to examine the records.
>
> (2) discharge the auditor from legal liability for his or her examination.
>
> (3) confirm in writing management's approval of limitations on the scope of the audit.
>
> (4) remind management of its primary responsibility for financial statements.

b. A representation letter issued by a client

> (1) is essential for the preparation of the audit program.
>
> (2) is a substitute for testing.
>
> (3) does *not* reduce the auditor's responsibility.
>
> (4) reduces the auditor's responsibility only to the extent that it is relied upon.

c. The date of the management representation letter should coincide with the

> (1) date of the auditor's report.
>
> (2) balance sheet date.
>
> (3) date of the latest subsequent event referred to in the notes to the financial statements.
>
> (4) date of the engagement agreement.

d. Management's refusal to furnish a written representation on a matter the auditor considers essential constitutes

> (1) *prima facie* evidence that the financial statements are *not* presented fairly.
>
> (2) a violation of the *Canada Business Corporations Act*.
>
> (3) a GAAP violation sufficient to preclude an unqualified opinion.
>
> (4) a scope limitation sufficient to preclude an unqualified opinion.

(AICPA adapted)

22–22 The following questions deal with review of subsequent events. Choose the best response.

a. Subsequent events for reporting purposes are defined as events that occur subsequent to the

> (1) balance sheet date.
>
> (2) date of the auditor's report.
>
> (3) balance sheet date but prior to the date of the auditor's report.
>
> (4) date of the auditor's report and concern contingencies that are not reflected in the financial statements.

b. A major customer of an audit client suffers a fire just prior to completion of year-end field work. The audit client believes that this event could have a significant direct effect on the financial statements. The auditor should

(1) advise management to disclose the event in notes to the financial statements.

(2) disclose the event in the auditor's report.

(3) withhold submission of the auditor's report until the extent of the direct effect on the financial statements is known.

(4) advise management to adjust the financial statements.

c. An example of an event occurring in the period of the auditor's field work subsequent to the end of the year being audited that normally would not require disclosure in the financial statements or the auditor's report would be

(1) decreased sales volume resulting from a general business recession.

(2) serious damage to the company's plant from a widespread flood.

(3) issuance of a widely advertised capital stock issue with restrictive covenants.

(4) settlement of a large liability for considerably less than the amount recorded.

d. With respect to issuance of an audit report that is dual dated for a subsequent event occurring after the completion of field work but before issuance of the auditor's report, the auditor's responsibility for events occurring subsequent to the completion of field work is

(1) extended to include all events occurring until the date of the last subsequent event referred to.

(2) limited to the specific event referred to.

(3) limited to all events occurring through the date of issuance of the report.

(4) extended to include all events occurring through the date of submission of the report to the client.

e. Karr has examined the financial statements of Lurch Corporation for the year ended December 31, 19X7. Although Karr's field work was completed on February 27, 19X8, Karr's auditor's report was dated February 28, 19X8 and was received by the management of Lurch on March 5, 19X8. On April 4, 19X8, the management of Lurch asked that Karr approve inclusion of this report in its annual report to shareholders, which will include unaudited financial statements for the first quarter ended March 31, 19X8. Karr approved the inclusion of this auditor's report in the annual report to shareholders. Under the circumstances Karr is responsible for inquiring as to subsequent events occurring through

(1) February 27, 19X8.

(2) February 28, 19X8.

(3) March 31, 19X8.

(4) April 4, 19X8.   (AICPA adapted)

DISCUSSION QUESTIONS AND PROBLEMS

22–23 Kathy Choi, a public accountant, has completed the audit of notes payable and other liabilities for Valley River Electrical Services Ltd. and now plans to audit contingent liabilities and commitments.

Required:

a. Distinguish between contingent liabilities and commitments and explain why both are important in an audit.

b. Identify three useful audit procedures for uncovering contingent liabilities that Choi would likely perform in the normal conduct of the audit, even if she had no responsibility for uncovering contingencies.

    c. Identify three other procedures Choi is likely to perform specifically for the purpose of identifying undisclosed contingencies.

22–24 In an examination of Marco Corporation as of December 31, 19X7, the following situations exist. No entries in respect thereto have been made in the accounting records.

1. Marco Corporation has guaranteed the payment of interest on the 10-year, first mortgage bonds of Chen Corp., an affiliate. Outstanding bonds of Chen Corp. amount to $150,000 with interest payable at 8 percent per annum, due June 1 and December 1 each year. The bonds were issued by Chen on December 31, 19X5, and all interest payments have been met by that company with the exception of the payment due December 1, 19X7. The Marco Corporation states that it will pay the defaulted interest to the bondholders on January 15, 19X8.

2. During the year 19X7, Marco Corporation was named as a defendant in a suit for damages by Dalton Inc. for breach of contract. An adverse decision to Marco Corporation was rendered and Dalton Inc. was awarded $40,000 damages. At the time of the audit, the case was under appeal to a higher court.

3. On December 23, 19X7, Marco Corporation declared a common share dividend of 1,000 shares with a stated value of $100,000 of its common stock, payable February 2, 19X8, to the common shareholders of record December 30, 19X7.

Required:

    a. Define *contingent liability*.

    b. Describe the audit procedures you would use to learn about each of the situations above.

    c. Describe the nature of the adjusting entries or disclosure, if any, you would make for each of these situations.

(AICPA adapted)

22–25 The field work for the June 30, 19X7 audit of Tracy Brewing Ltd. was finished August 19, 19X7, and the completed financial statements, accompanied by the signed auditor's reports, were mailed September 6, 19X7. In each of the highly material independent events (a through i), state the appropriate action (1 through 4) for the situation and justify your response. The alternative actions are as follows:

1. Adjust the June 30, 19X7 financial statements.

2. Disclose the information in a footnote in the June 30, 19X7 financial statements.

3. Request the client to recall the June 30, 19X7 statements for revision.

4. No action is required.

    The events are as follows:

    a. On December 14, 19X7, the auditor discovered that a debtor of Tracy Brewing went bankrupt on October 2, 19X7. The sale has taken place April 15, 19X7, but the amount appeared collectible at June 30, 19X7 and August 19, 19X7.

    b. On August 15, 19X7, the auditor discovered that a debtor of Tracy Brewing went bankrupt on August 1, 19X7. The most recent sale had taken place April 2, 19X6, and no cash receipts had been received since that date.

    c. On December 14, 19X7, the auditor discovered that a debtor of Tracy Brewing went bankrupt on July 15, 19X7 due to declining financial health. The sale had taken place January 15, 19X7.

    d. On August 6, 19X7, the auditor discovered that a debtor of Tracy Brewing went bankrupt on July 30, 19X7. The cause of the bankruptcy was an unexpected loss of a major lawsuit on July 15, 19X7 resulting from a product deficiency suit by a different customer.

  e. On August 6, 19X7, the auditor discovered that a debtor of Tracy Brewing went bankrupt on July 30, 19X7 for a sale that took place July 3, 19X7. The cause of the bankruptcy was a major uninsured fire on July 20, 19X7.

  f. On May 31, 19X7, the auditor discovered an uninsured lawsuit against Tracy Brewing that had originated on February 28, 19X7.

  g. On July 20, 19X7, Tracy Brewing settled a lawsuit out of court that had originated in 19X4 and is currently listed as a contingent liability.

  h. On September 14, 19X7, Tracy Brewing lost a court case that had originated in 19X6 for an amount equal to the lawsuit. The June 30, 19X7 footnotes state that in the opinion of legal counsel there will be a favorable settlement.

  i. On July 20, 19X7, a lawsuit was filed against Tracy Brewing for a patent infringement action that allegedly took place in early 19X7. In the opinion of legal counsel, there is a danger of a significant loss to the client.

22–26 In connection with his examination of Flowmeter Inc., for the year ended December 31, 19X7, Ira Hirsh, a public accountant, is aware that certain events and transactions that took place after December 31, 19X7 but before he issues his report dated February 28, 19X8, may affect the company's financial statements. The following material events or transactions have come to his attention:

  1. On January 3, 19X8, Flowmeter Inc., received a shipment of raw materials from Texas. The materials had been ordered in October 19X7 and shipped FOB shipping point in November 19X7.

  2. On January 15, 19X8, the company settled and paid a personal injury claim of a former employee as the result of an accident that occurred in March 19X7. The company had not previously recorded a liability for the claim.

  3. On January 25, 19X8, the company agreed to purchase for cash the outstanding shares of Porter Electrical Corp. The acquisition is likely to double the sales volume of Flowmeter Inc.

  4. On February 1, 19X8, a plant owned by Flowmeter Inc., was damaged by a flood resulting in an uninsured loss of inventory.

  5. On February 5, 19X8, Flowmeter Inc., issued and sold to the general public $2 million in convertible bonds.

Required:

For each of the events or transactions just described, indicate the audit procedures that should have brought the item to the attention of the auditor and the form of disclosure required in the financial statements, including the reasons for such disclosures.

Arrange your answers in the following format:

ITEM NO.	AUDIT PROCEDURES	REQUIRED DISCLOSURE AND REASONS

(AICPA adapted)

22–27 Melanie Adams is a partner in a medium-sized public accounting firm and takes an active part in the conduct of every audit she supervises. She follows the practice of reviewing all working papers of subordinates as soon as it is convenient, rather than waiting until the end of the audit. When the audit is nearly finished, Adams reviews the working papers again to make sure she has not missed anything significant. Since she makes most of the major decisions on the audit, there is rarely anything that requires further investigation. When she completes the review, she prepares a pencil draft of the financial statements, gets them approved by management, and has them typed and assembled in her firm's office. No other partner reviews the working papers because Adams is responsible for signing the auditor's reports.

Required:

a. Evaluate the practice of reviewing the working papers of subordinates on a continuing basis rather than when the audit is completed.

b. Is it acceptable for Adams to prepare the financial statements rather than make the client assume the responsibility?

c. Evaluate the practice of not having a review of the working papers by another partner in the firm.

22–28 Ruben Chavez, public accountant, has prepared a letter of representation for the president and controller to sign. It contains references to the following items:

1. Inventory is fairly stated at the lower of cost or market and includes no obsolete items.

2. All actual and contingent liabilities are properly included in the statements.

3. All subsequent events of relevance to the financial statements have been disclosed.

Required:

a. Why is it desirable to have a letter of representation from the client concerning the above matters when the audit evidence accumulated during the course of the engagement is meant to verify the same information?

b. To what extent is the letter of representation useful as audit evidence? Explain.

c. List several other types of information commonly included in a letter of representation.

22–29 In a management letter to the Cline Wholesale Company, Nora Bogdanovic, a public accountant, informed management of its weaknesses in the control of inventory. She elaborated on how the weaknesses could result in a significant misstatement of inventory by the failure to recognize the existence of obsolete items. In addition, Bogdanovic made specific recommendations on how to improve the internal control structure and save clerical time by installing a computer system for the company's perpetual records. Management accepted the recommendations and installed the system under Bogdanovic's direction. For several months, the system worked beautifully, but unforeseen problems developed when a master file was erased. The cost of reproducing and processing the inventory records to correct the error was significant, and management decided to scrap the entire project. The company sued Bogdanovic for failure to use adequate professional judgment in making the recommendations.

Required:

a. What is Bogdanovic's legal and professional responsibility in the issuance of management letters?

b. Discuss the major considerations that will determine whether she is liable in this situation.

22–30 In connection with your examination of the financial statements of Olars Mfg. Corporation for the year ended December 31, 19X6, your review of subsequent events disclosed the following items:

1. January 3, 19X7: The provincial government approved a plan for the construction of an express highway. The plan will result in the expropriation of a portion of the land owned by Olars Mfg. Corporation. Construction will begin in late 19X7. No estimate of the condemnation (expropriation) award is available.

2. January 4, 19X7: The funds for a $25,000 loan to the corporation made by Mr. Olars, the president, on July 15, 19X6 were obtained by him by a loan on his

personal life insurance policy. The loan was recorded in the account "loan from officers." Mr. Olars's source of the funds was not disclosed in the company records. The corporation pays the premiums on the life insurance policy, and Mrs. Olars, wife of the president, is the beneficiary.

3. January 7, 19X7: The mineral content of a shipment of ore enroute on December 31, 19X6 was determined to be 72 percent. The shipment was recorded at year-end at an estimated content of 50 percent by a debit to raw material inventory and a credit to accounts payable in the amount of $20,600. The final liability to the vendor is based on the actual mineral content of the shipment.

4. January 15, 19X7: Culminating a series of personal disagreements between Mr. Olars and his brother-in-law, the treasurer, the latter resigned, effective immediately, under an agreement whereby the corporation would purchase his 10% stock ownership at book value as of December 31, 19X6. Payment is to be made in two equal amounts in cash on April 1, 19X7 and October 1, 19X7. In December 19X6, the treasurer has obtained a divorce from his wife, who was Mr. Olars' sister.

5. January 31, 19X7: As a result of reduced sales, production was curtailed in mid-January and some workers were laid off. On February 5, 19X7, all the remaining workers went on strike. To date, the strike is unsettled.

6. February 10, 19X7: A contract was signed whereby Mammoth Enterprises purchases from Olars Mfg. Corporation all of the latter's fixed assets (including rights to receive the proceeds of any property condemnation), inventories and the right to conduct business under the name "Olars Mfg. Division." The effective date of the transfer will be March 1, 19X7. The sale price was $500,000 subject to adjustment following the taking of a physical inventory. Important factors contributing to the decision to enter into the contract were the policy of the board of directors of Mammoth Industries to diversify the firm's activities and the report of a survey conducted by an independent market appraisal firm that revealed a declining market for Olars products.

Required:

Assume that the items described above came to your attention prior to completion of your audit work on February 15, 19X7. For *each* item:

a. Give the audit procedures, if any, that would have brought the item to your attention. Indicate other sources of information that may have revealed the item.

b. Discuss the disclosure that you would recommend for the item, listing all details that you would suggest should be disclosed. Indicate those items or details, if any, that should not be disclosed. Give your reasons for recommending or not recommending disclosure of the items or details.

(AICPA adapted)

22–31 The following unrelated events occurred after the balance sheet date but before the auditor's report was prepared:

1. The granting of a retroactive pay increase.
2. Determination by Revenue Canada of additional income tax due for a prior year.
3. Charging the entity with restriction of trade by the federal government.
4. Declaration of a stock dividend.
5. Sale of a fixed asset at a substantial profit.

Required:

a. Explain how each of the items might have come to the auditor's attention.

b. Discuss the auditor's responsibility to recognize each of these in connection with his or her report. (AICPA adapted)

22–32 The philosophy of Barbara Hatton, public accountant, is to audit intensively transactions taking place during the current audit period, but to ignore subsequent transactions. She believes each year should stand on its own and be audited in the year in which the transactions take place. According to Hatton, "If a transaction recorded in the subsequent period is audited in the current period, it is verified twice – once this year and again in next year's audit. That is a duplication of effort and a waste of time."

Required:

a. Explain the fallacy in Hatton's argument.

b. Give six specific examples of information obtained by examining subsequent events that are essential to the current-period audit.

22–33 In analyzing legal expense for the Boastman Bottle Company, Bart Little, public accountant, observes that the company has paid legal fees to three different law firms during the current year. In accordance with his accounting firm's normal operating practice, Little requests standard confirmation letters as of the balance sheet date from each of the three law firms.

On the last day of field work, Little notes that one of the confirmations has not yet been received. The second confirmation request contains a statement to the effect that the law firm deals exclusively in registering patents and refuses to comment on any lawsuits or other legal affairs of the client. The third lawyer's letter states that there is an outstanding unpaid bill due from the client and recognizes the existence of a potentially material lawsuit against the client but refuses to comment further to protect the legal rights of the client.

Required:

a. Evaluate Little's approach to sending the confirmations and his follow-up on the responses.

b. What should Little do about each of the confirmations?

22–34 Betty Ann Jarrett, CA, was reading the annual report of Watgold Ltd. and noticed that the president's report contradicted several items in the audited financial statements included in the report. What are her responsibilities in this instance?

22–35 You are a partner in the public accounting firm of Lind and Hemming. One of your larger clients is Yukon Corp., a company incorporated under the *Canada Business Corporations Act*, which has a December 31 year end. Yukon's 19X7 audit was completed in January, 19X8; the auditor's report was dated January 28, 19X8.

It is now August, 19X8 and professional staff from your office are working at Yukon doing interim work on the December 31, 19X8 audit. Yesterday, the senior in charge of the audit gave you a memo dated August 4, 19X8 that reveals that the staff have discovered that several large blocks of inventory were materially overpriced at December 31, 19X7 and have since been written down to reflect their true value.

You have just finished reviewing the 19X7 working papers and have determined that the error was a sampling error; your firm does not appear to have been negligent.

Required:

What action would you take and why? Support your answer.

23

OTHER ENGAGEMENTS, SERVICES AND REPORTS

☐ In addition to being involved with audits of historical financial statements prepared in accordance with generally accepted accounting principles, public accounts commonly deal with situations involving other types of information, varying levels of assurance, and other types of reports. These are the subjects of this chapter and the following one. This chapter discusses eight specific types of engagements outside audits:

- Special reports where the auditor expresses an opinion on financial information other than financial statements, or on compliance with a contractual agreement, or where the public accountant applies certain auditing procedures to financial information
- Special engagements on internal control procedures at a service organization
- Review engagements and compilations
- Prospectuses
- Future-oriented financial information
- Reports on the application of accounting principles, auditing standards, or review standards
- Pension costs
- Pension fund financial statements

The chapter ends with an examination of the AICPA *Statement on Standards for Attestation Engagements*, a new area not yet codified in Canada.

Section 5020, "Association" was introduced in Chapter 2; recall that the section defines when a public accountant is associated with information and describes the accountant's responsibilities when he or she is associated.

This chapter describes the wide range of services that a public accountant can provide. It is very important that the accountant properly communicate to users of information with which the public accountant is associated the nature and extent of the association. There are a number of figures in this chapter which illustrate the various forms of communication the public accountant may issue. You should study them noting similarities to and differences between the auditor's report discussed in Chapter 2 and the communications in this chapter.

Engagement letters were discussed in Chapter 7; an illustration of an engagement letter appears in Figure 7–2. The various topics discussed below suggest the need for an engagement letter describing exactly what work the public accountant, acting as auditor or accountant, will do for the client and the proposed communication that will describe the work done (e.g., the Auditor's Report under Section 5805). The need for an engagement letter that is tailored to reflect the circumstances cannot be over-emphasized.

Special Reports

OBJECTIVE 1

Describe special engagements to examine financial statements, apply specified auditing procedures, and report on compliance.

Public accountants are also frequently asked to prepare special reports. In preparing these reports, they may be acting as *auditors,* as stipulated in Sections 5805 and 5815 of the *CICA Handbook,* or as *accountants,* as stipulated in Section 5810. Each of these sections will be covered in turn.

Because the nature of the engagement is different from that of a regular audit, an engagement letter in these cases is very important so that there are no misunderstandings as to what is wanted and what will be done.

It is important that the public accountant acting as auditor or accountant, when required to report in some specified form, ensure that his or her comments follow the form suggested in the *CICA Handbook*. At the same time, the public accountant must ensure that the communication indicates the accountant's involvement and the nature of the responsibility assumed. Successful communication may well be achieved by altering the wording of the communication from those in the *CICA Handbook*.

Reports
Expressing an
Audit Opinion on
Financial
Information other
than Financial
Statements
(Section 5805)

This section is concerned with an auditor's reporting on information such as employee bonuses, sales in a specified location where rent is based on sales, amounts calculated under a reporting insurance agreement or the costs of a capital project.

There are two primary differences between the report as discussed in Section 5805 and the auditor's report for a regular financial information audit.

- Materiality is defined in terms of the element, account or items involved rather than in relation to the overall statements. The effect ordinarily is to require more evidence than would be needed if the item being verified were just one of many parts of the statements, for example, if the sales account were being reported on as part of a regular audit.
- The auditor should comply with the general and examination standards i and iii but does not have to comply with the reporting standards.

The report required under Section 5805, like that required under Section 5400 for audited financial statements, will be entitled *Auditor's Report* and will include three paragraphs: an introductory paragraph, a scope paragraph, and an opinion paragraph. Each are discussed in turn below:

The introductory paragraph
- indicates that an audit was performed,
- identifies the relevant portions of any agreement, statute, or regulation under which the financial information was prepared and explains any significant interpretations of the agreement, statute, or regulation made by management in preparing the information,
- specifies the basis of accounting if other than GAAP,
- indicates any lack of consistent application of either accounting principles or of interpretation of the agreement, statute, or regulation by management from previous reports,
- states the respective responsibilities of management and the auditor.

The scope paragraph
- states that the audit was performed in accordance with GAAS,
- indicates that GAAS requires that the audit be planned and performed to obtain reasonable assurance that the financial information does not include any material misstatements.
- describes an audit indicating that the auditor examines evidence on a test basis, assesses management's estimates and the accounting principles used by management, and evaluates the overall presentation of the information reported on.

The opinion paragraph
- Includes the auditor's opinion on whether the financial information is presented fairly, in all material respects, in accordance with GAAP or with the basis of accounting described in the introductory paragraph, and in accordance with any interpretations of the agreement, statute, or regulation by management.

Figure 23–1 illustrates a report for royalties, which is a specified account.

AUDITOR'S REPORT ON SCHEDULE OF ROYALTIES

To the Directors of Ace Corp.

We have audited the schedule of royalties applicable to engine production of the Q Division of Ten Limited for the year ended December 31, 19X8 under the terms of a license agreement dated May 14, 19X3, between Ace Corp. and Ten Limited. We have been informed that, under Ten Limited's interpretation of the agreement referred to above, royalties were based on the number of engines produced after giving effect to a reduction for production retirements that were scrapped, but without a reduction for field returns that were scrapped, even though the field returns were replaced with new engines without charge to customers. The financial information is the responsibility of the management of Ten Limited. Our responsibility is to express an opinion on this financial information based on our audit.

We conducted our audit in accordance with generally accepted auditing standards. Those standards require that we plan and perform an audit to obtain reasonable assurance whether the financial information is free of material misstatement. An audit includes, on a test basis, evidence supporting the amounts and disclosures in the financial information. An audit also includes assessing the accounting principles used and significant estimates made by management, as well as evaluating the overall presentation of the financial information.

In our opinion, this schedule, when read together with the information set out in the introductory paragraph, presents fairly, in all material respects, the amount of royalties applicable to the number of engines produced by the Q Division of Ten Limited for the year ended December 31, 19X8, in accordance with the provision of the agreement referred to above and the interpretations thereof.

Val D'Or, Quebec
January 21, 19X9

Blagenko, Boyle & Kirzner
Chartered Accountants

---

*Reports on the
Results of
Applying Specified
Auditing
Procedures to
Financial
Information other
than Financial
Statements
(Section 5810)*

This section is concerned with an accountant's application of pre-specified auditing procedures to financial information in cases where an expression of an opinion is not expected. The client specifies what auditing procedures are to be applied and the form of report that is to be issued; therefore distribution of the report is normally restricted.

In this situation, the accountant should comply both with the general standard and the first examination standard. There should be an engagement letter between the client and the accountant specifying the nature of the engagement, the type of report to be issued, the proposed distribution of the report and, if possible, the procedures to be applied.

The report should specify

- The financial information to which the procedures were applied.
- The procedures applied.
- The factual results of the procedures; negative assurance should not be expressed.
- That an audit was not performed; there should be a disclaimer of opinion.
- Any restrictions on circulation of the report.

Figure 23–2 is an illustration of such a report. It was prepared in the situation where the financial statements are audited; gross sales were not audited on a store-by-store basis.

FIGURE 23–2

Example of a Report under Section 5810

ACCOUNTANTS' REPORT
IN CONNECTION WITH GROSS SALES

To Pedlar Limited

As requested by Okanagan Stores Limited, we report that the gross sales of the company's store at King Street, Kelowna, B.C. for the year ended June 30, 19X8 are recorded in the amount of $790,000 in the general ledger sales account of the company and form part of the company's gross sales in its financial statements for the year then ended, on which we reported on August 3, 19X8.

Our examination of the company's financial statements for the year ended June 30, 19X8 was not directed to the determination of gross sales or other financial information of individual stores. We have not performed an audit of and accordingly do not express an opinion on the amount of gross sales referred to in the preceding paragraph.

It is understood that this report is to be used solely for computing percentage rental and is not to be referred to or distributed to any person not a member of management of Pedlar Limited or Okanagan Stores Limited.

Kelowna, B.C.
August 8, 19X8

Carter & Wilhelm
Certified General Accountants

Reports on Compliance with Contractual Agreements, Statutes and Regulations (Section 5815)

This section is concerned with an auditor's report on a client's compliance with particular accounting and financial reporting requirements that have been included as terms of a contract or agreement, such as a loan agreement or a trust deed. For example, this report is often used to report to creditors on the client's compliance with restrictive covenants in a loan agreement or bond indenture, such as maintenance of a minimum current ratio or sinking fund payments. The auditor may in this situation express an opinion.

The auditor must comply with the general standard and the examination standards. An engagement letter setting out the terms of the engagement and the form of report is suggested.

The report required under Section 5810, like that required under Section 5400 for audited financial statements, will be entitled *Auditor's Report* and will include three paragraphs: an introductory paragraph, a scope paragraph, and an opinion paragraph. Each are discussed in turn below:

The introductory paragraph

- indicates that compliance with criteria established by provisions of the agreement, statute, or regulation was audited,
- identifies the relevant provisions of the agreement, statute, or regulation under which the financial information was prepared and explains any significant interpretations of the provisions of the agreement, statute, or regulation made by management in preparing the information,
- indicates any lack of consistent application of interpretation of the agreement, statute, or regulation by management from previous reports,
- states the respective responsibilities of management and the auditor.

The scope paragraph

- states that the audit was performed in accordance with GAAS,
- indicates that GAAS requires that the audit be planned and performed to obtain

reasonable assurance that the entity complied with criteria established by provisions of the agreement, statute, or regulation,

- describes an audit indicating that the auditor examines evidence on a test basis supporting compliance by the entity, evaluates overall compliance, and assesses management's estimates and, if applicable, the accounting principles used by management.

The opinion paragraph

- includes the auditor's opinion as to whether the entity has complied with, in all material respects, the criteria established by provisions of the agreement, statute, or regulation.

An illustration is provided by Figure 23–3.

Opinion on Control Procedures at a Service Organization

Some companies rely on a service organization to provide custodial services (for example, a public warehouse), provide data processing services (for example, process payroll and issue payroll cheques), or manage assets (for example, administer a company's pension plan). The auditor of such a company will require evidence that the service organization had internal controls in place to safeguard the company's assets and records and provide reliable and timely data to the company. The auditor could gather the necessary evidence at the service organization (who is not necessarily a client) or rely on an audit of the service organization's internal controls by another auditor. Section 5310 of the *CICA Handbook* describes how an auditor assesses the report of a service auditor.

An auditor may be engaged to report on a service organization's internal control. Section 5900 describes "matters that an auditor would consider when

FIGURE 23–3

Example of a Report under Section 5815

AUDITOR'S REPORT

To Georgian Trust Company

We have audited Victoria Limited's compliance with the accounting and financial reporting matters of Sections 1 to 3 of the Trust Deed dated February 28, 19X2, with Georgian Trust Company.

Compliance with the criteria established by the provisions of the Trust Deed is the responsibility of the management of Victoria Limited. Our responsibility is to express an opinion on this compliance based on our audit.

We conducted our audit in accordance with generally accepted auditing standards. Those standards require that we plan and perform an audit to obtain reasonable assurance whether Victoria Limited complied with the criteria established by the provisions of the Trust Deed referred to above. Such an audit includes examining, on a test basis, evidence supporting compliance, evaluating the overall compliance with the Trust Deed, and where applicable, assessing the accounting principles used and significant estimates made by management.

In our opinion, Victoria Limited is in compliance, in all material respects, with the accounting and financial reporting matters of Sections 1 to 3 of the Trust Deed dated February 28, 19X2, with Georgian Trust Company as at December 31, 19X8.

Lethbridge, Alberta
February 7, 19X9

Ally & Nanda
Chartered Accountants

<table>
<tr><td>

OBJECTIVE 2

Describe special engagements to examine control procedures.

</td></tr>
</table>

engaged to express an opinion on the design, effective operation and continuity of control procedures at a service organization."

There are two possible types of engagements:

- The auditor may be required to provide an opinion on the design and existence of control procedures at some date.
- He or she may be required to provide an opinion on the design, effective operation and continuity of control procedures during a period of time.

It is desirable that the auditor obtain a written engagement letter to clarify the scope and purpose of the engagement, as well as the opinion to be rendered.

Comparison to Requirements for Audits

When auditors perform an audit of financial statements, they obtain an understanding of internal control in accordance with the second examination standard. The scope of the study depends on the assessed level of control risk which will be used to determine the nature, timing and extent of related substantive tests. When control risk is assessed below maximum the auditor considers internal control, in effect for the entire audit period. Certain areas are *not* examined if control risk is assessed as maximum in those areas.

When the auditor is engaged to report on internal control, however, all areas of control will be included unless specifically excluded by agreement. Also, the time period covered will be a matter of agreement. The service auditor must comply with the general standard and the first and third examination standards.

Steps for Obtaining an Understanding and Testing Controls

Six steps, which are similar to those followed for a regular audit engagement, are followed when a public accountant is engaged to provide an opinion on internal control:

1. *Plan the scope of the engagement.* The auditor, client and others involved first agree on the areas to be covered and timing of the study.

2. *Review the design of internal control.* Next, the auditor obtains information about the internal control objectives of the system and the control procedures used to achieve control. A preliminary assessment is made to determine the apparent controls and weaknesses. The procedures for accomplishing this step are the same as those discussed in Chapter 9.

3. *Perform tests of controls to determine conformity with prescribed procedures.* Appropriate audit procedures using such means as observation, enquiry and tracing transactions through the system must be performed to determine whether the control procedures needed to meet the control objectives were being followed.

4. *Evaluate the results of the understanding and tests of controls.* A final evaluation is made of whether the design of the control procedures results in the meeting of internal control objectives.

5. *Obtain written representations from management.*

6. *Prepare the appropriate report.* The type of report prepared will depend on the purpose and scope of the engagement and the auditor's findings. Figure 23–4 shows a sample auditor's report prepared when the auditor makes a study and evaluation of the design and existence of control procedures. Figure 23–5 shows a sample auditor's report when the auditor examines the design, effective operation and continuity of control procedures.

FIGURE 23–4

Example of a Report on the Design and Existence of Control Procedures

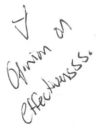

no opinion. Just test.

AUDITOR'S REPORT ON CONTROL PROCEDURES

To Normandy Trust Ltd.

We have examined the accompanying description of the stated internal control objectives of the Secur-Pension system of Normandy Trust Ltd. and the control procedures designed to achieve those objectives and have performed tests of the existence of those control procedures as at June 30, 19X1. Our examination was made in accordance with generally accepted auditing standards, and accordingly included such tests and other procedures as we considered necessary in the circumstances.

In our opinion, the control procedures included in the accompanying description were suitably designed to provide reasonable, but not absolute, assurance that the stated internal control objectives of the system described therein were achieved and the control procedures existed as at June 30, 19X1.

As we tested the existence of the control procedures only as at June 30, 19X1, we do not express an opinion on whether the control procedures existed at any other time.

Red Deer, Alberta
July 15, 19X1

MacKenzie & Chu
Certified General Accountants

Compilation and Review Services

OBJECTIVE 3

Understand compilation and review services that may be offered to clients.

Many public accountants are involved with nonpublic clients that do not have audits. A company may believe an audit is unnecessary due to the active involvement of the owners in the business, lack of significant debt or absence of regulations requiring the company to have one. Common examples are smaller companies and professional organizations such as partnerships of physicians and lawyers.

These organizations often engage a public accountant to provide tax services and to assist in the preparation of accurate financial information without an audit. Providing these services is a significant part of the practice of many smaller public accounting firms. When a public accountant provides any services involving

---

FIGURE 23–5

Example of a Report when the Design, Effectiveness and Continuity of Control Procedures Are Evaluated

Opinion on effectiveness.

AUDITOR'S REPORT ON CONTROL PROCEDURES

To Payroll Plus Ltd.

I have examined the accompanying description of the stated internal control objectives of P Pay system of Payroll Plus Ltd. and the control procedures designed to achieve those objectives and have performed tests of the effectiveness of those control procedures for the period from September 1, 19X4 to January 31, 19X5. My examination was made in accordance with generally accepted auditing standards, and accordingly included such tests and other procedures as I considered necessary in the circumstances.

In my opinion, the control procedures included in the accompanying description were suitably designed to provide reasonable, but not absolute, assurance that the stated internal control objectives of the system described therein were achieved, and the control procedures operated effectively from September 1, 19X4 to January 31, 19X5.

Halifax, Nova Scotia
February 28, 19X5

Don Masters
Chartered Accountant

financial statements, certain requirements exist. The requirements for review engagements are covered in *CICA Handbook* Sections 8100, 8200, 8500 and 8600. Requirements for compilation engagements appear in Section 9200.

Terms of Engagement

While the *Handbook* sections covering review and compilation engagements do not require an engagement letter, they do require that the public accountant and the client reach an understanding and agreement regarding the services to be provided. A *written* agreement as to the nature and extent of services is most appropriate. The *1136 Tenants* case examined in Chapter 4 is a good example of the problems that can arise if there is not a clear, written understanding between accountant and client. The engagement letter would include such items as follows:

- A description of the services to be provided.
- A discussion of the client's responsibility for providing complete and accurate information.
- A statement that an audit is not to be performed and that consequently, no opinion will be expressed. In the case of a compilation engagement, the fact that no assurance results should be stated.
- A note on any restrictions on the distribution of the statements.
- A statement that each page of the statements should be clearly marked "unaudited."
- The probable content of the communication to be appended by the accountant.
- The fact that the engagement cannot be relied on to detect fraud or error.
- It may also include a comment to the effect that the statements do not satisfy any statutory requirements.

Figure 23–6 provides an example of an engagement letter for a review of annual financial statements.

Review

Review is defined by CICA *Handbook* Section 8100.05 as consisting primarily of "enquiry, analytical procedures and discussion . . . . with the limited objective of assessing whether the information being reported on is plausible within the framework of appropriate criteria. (*Plausible* can be defined as worthy of belief, credible or justifiable.)"

General Review Standards

Section 8100, "General Review Standards," discusses the acceptance of an engagement and the standards applicable to review engagements. These include knowledge of the client's business, review procedures, documentation and reporting. Review engagements should be accepted by a public accountant only if the accountant believes that he or she has the necessary competence in the subject matter to be reported on.

Procedures suggested for reviews   Reviews imply a level of assurance somewhere between that of an audit and the absence of assurance provided by a compilation. A review does not include obtaining an understanding of internal control or tests of controls, independent confirmation or physical examination. The emphasis in reviews is in four broad areas:

- Obtain knowledge of the client's business. The information should be about the nature of the client's organization and business transactions, its accounting

FIGURE 23–6

Example of an
Engagement Letter for a
Review Engagement

JOSEPHINE LIMITED
677 PETER STREET
WINNIPEG, MANITOBA
R3Y 1Z6

Attention: Josephine Collins, President

Dear Ms. Collins:

The purpose of this letter is to outline the nature of my involvement with the financial statements of Josephine Limited for the year ending December 31, 19X2. As agreed, I will conduct a review, consisting primarily of inquiry, analytical procedures and discussion in accordance with generally accepted standards for review engagements.

Unless unanticipated difficulties are encountered, my report will be substantially in the following form:

I have reviewed the balance sheet of Client Limited as at December 31, 19X2 and the statements of income, retained eranings and changes in financial position for the year then ended. My review was made in accordance with generally accepted standards for review engagements and accordingly consisted primarily of enquiry, analytical procedures and discussion related to information supplied to me by the company.

A review does not constitute an audit and consequently I do not express an opinion on these financial statements.

Based on my review, nothing has come to my attention that causes me to believe that these financial statements are not, in all material respects, in accordance with generally accepted accounting principles.

This review does not constitute an audit. For example, it does not contemplate a study and evaluation of internal control, tests of accounting records and of responses to inquiries by obtaining audit evidence through inspection, observation or confirmation and other procedures ordinarily performed during an audit. Accordingly, this review is not intended to, and will not, result in the expression of an audit opinion nor the fulfilling of any statutory or other audit requirement. Since I am not accepting this engagement as auditor, I request that you do not record this as an auditing engagement in the minutes of your shareholder's meetings. You may wish to obtain legal advice concerning statutory auditing requirements.

It is understood that:

(a) you will provide the information required for me to complete this review;
(b) the responsibility for the accuracy and completeness of the representations in the financial statements remains with you;
(c) if my name is to be used in connection with the financial statements, you will attach my review engagement report when distributing the financial statements to third parties; and
(d) each page of the financial statements will be conspicuously marked "Unaudited."

This engagement cannot be relied upon to prevent or detect error and fraud and other irregularities. I wish to emphasize that control over and responsibility for the prevention and detection of error and fraud and other irregularities remains with management.

The arrangements outlined in this letter will continue in effect from year to year unless evidenced by a new engagement letter.

If you have any questions about the contents of this letter, please raise them with me. If the services outlined are in accordance with your requirements and if the above terms are acceptable to you, please sign the copy of this letter in the space provided and return it to me. I appreciate the opportunity of continuing to be of service to your company.

Yours very truly,

Friedman & Assoc.
Chartered Accountants

The services and terms set out are as agreed.
Josephine Limited
Per
(Name and title of the addressee)
(date)

records and employees, the basis, form and content of the financial statements, and accounting matters peculiar to the client's business and industry.

- Make inquiries of client personnel. The objective of these inquiries is to determine whether the financial statements are fairly presented, assuming that management does not intend to deceive the accountant. The CICA Auditing Guideline entitled "Performance of a Review of Financial Statements" lists illustrative inquiries. It has been reproduced in Table 23–1.
- Perform analytical procedures. These are meant to identify relationships and individual items that appear to be unusual. Analytical procedures performed during a review engagement would normally be less extensive than during an audit. The appropriate analytical procedures are not different from the ones already studied in Chapter 7 and in those chapters dealing with substantive procedures. Explanations for relationships and items that appear to be unusual would be obtained by inquiring of appropriate client personnel.
- Have discussions with management concerning information received and the information being reported on.

Generally accepted review standards The standards for review engagements are similar to generally accepted auditing standards, except that they deal with review and not audits. They are as follows:

General standard
The review should be performed and the review engagement report prepared by a person or persons having adequate technical training and proficiency in conducting reviews, and with due care and an objective state of mind.

Review standards
(i) The work should be adequately planned and properly executed. If assistants are employed, they should be properly supervised.
(ii) The public accountant should possess or acquire sufficient knowledge of the business carried on by the enterprise so that intelligent inquiry and assessment of information obtained can be made.
(iii) The public accountant should perform a review with the limited objective of assessing whether the information being reported on is plausible in the circumstances within the framework of an appropriate criteria. Such a review should consist of:
    (a) enquiry, analytical procedures and discussion; and
    (b) additional or more extensive procedures when the public accountant's knowledge of the business carried on by the enterprise and the results of the enquiry, and analytical procedures and discussion cause him or her to doubt the plausibility of such information.

Reporting standards
(i) The review engagement report should indicate the scope of the review. The nature of the review engagement should be made evident and be clearly distinguished from an audit.
(ii) The report should indicate, based on the review:
    (a) whether anything has come to the public accountant's attention that causes him or her to believe that the information is not, in all material respects, in accordance with appropriate criteria; or
    (b) that no assurance can be provided.
    The report should provide an explanation of the nature of any reservations contained therein and, if readily determinable, their effect.

TABLE 23–1 Example Enquiries for Review Engagements

PRELIMINARY CONSIDERATIONS

1. Are the services to be provided mutually agreed upon? Has the desirability of obtaining an engagement letter been considered?
2. Is it clear that an auditor has not been appointed with respect to financial statements which are the subject of this engagement?
3. Are generally accepted accounting principles being used? If not, is the basis of accounting being used appropriate in the circumstances?

KNOWLEDGE OF BUSINESS

1. Nature of business
   (a) What kind of business does the enterprise carry on?
   (b) Are there any unique or special characteristics of the industry in which the enterprise operates that require consideration?
   (c) What is the legal structure? (proprietorship, partnership, limited company, joint venture, etc.)
   (d) Where does the enterprise carry on business?
2. What are the major assets and liabilities, costs and expenses, and sources of revenue? Who are the major customers and suppliers.
3. Has a knowledge of the accounting system been obtained sufficient to understand the manner in which transactions are recorded, classified and summarized?
4. What books and records are kept:
   (a) general ledger?
   (b) books of original entry?
   (c) supporting records?
   (d) share records?
   (e) minutes?
   (f) other?
5. Has appropriate consideration been given to:
   (a) prior period financial statements?
   (b) prior period working paper and related files?
   (c) prior period accounting problems?
   (d) reservations in the previous report?

FINANCIAL STATEMENT ITEMS

1. Cash and banks
   (a) Has a reconciliation of balance per bank to balance per general ledger been prepared?
   (b) Have old or unusual outstanding items in the bank reconciliation been reviewed and adjusted when necessary?
   (c) How has the cut-off of cash transactions been effected?
2. Receivables
   (a) Is the trial balance total in agreement with the general ledger control account?
   (b) Is the method of determining allowance for doubtful accounts adequate?
   (c) How has the cut-off of sales transactions been effected?
   (d) Are receivables from employees, shareholders, affiliates, etc. separately disclosed?
   (e) Have receivables been pledged, discounted or factored?
3. Inventories
   (a) When was inventory counted?
   (b) Are procedures designed to arrive at a proper and consistent count?
   (c) Have inventory listings been reviewed as to quantities, prices, calculations, etc?
   (d) Have consignments in/out been considered?
   (e) What is the basis of valuation? Is such basis consistent?
   (f) Have write-downs for obsolescence been considered?
   (g) How has the cut-off of purchases/inventory, goods in transit, returned goods, etc. been effected?
4. Prepaid expenses
   When appropriate, has the prepaid portion of expenses been recorded?
5. Investments (loans, mortgages, intercorporate investments, etc.)
   (a) Have opening balances been reconciled to closing balances?
   (b) Have gains and losses on disposal been recorded?
   (c) Has investment income been accounted for?
   (d) Has current/non-current classification been made?
   (e) Has consolidation/equity accounting been considered?
   (f) Is there an indication of permanent impairment in value?
6. Property and equipment
   (a) Have opening balances of fixed assets and accumulated depreciation been reconciled to closing balances?
   (b) What significant changes have occurred in owned or leased fixed assets?
   (c) Have gains or losses on disposal been recorded?
   (d) Have capitalization criteria been applied consistently?
   (e) Has the repairs and maintenance account been reviewed for fixed asset additions?
   (f) Are fixed assets stated at cost?
   (g) What are the depreciation methods and rates? Are they consistent?
   (h) Is property mortgaged or otherwise encumbered?
   (i) Have capital leases been recorded properly?
7. Other assets
   (a) What is the nature and amount of other assets?
   (b) What is the amortization policy? Is it consistent?
   (c) Has current/non-current classification been made?
8. Accounts payable and accrued liabilities
   (a) Is the trial balance total in agreement with the general ledger control account?
   (b) What procedures were followed to determine that all major payables were recorded?
   (c) Are there any undisclosed bank or other short-term liabilities?
   (d) Have all significant accruals been set up?
   (e) Are secured liabilities appropriately described?
   (f) Are payables to employees, shareholders, affiliates, etc. separately disclosed?
9. Long-term liabilities
   (a) Are the terms and conditions disclosed?
   (b) Is interest expense recorded?
   (c) Has current/non-current classification been considered?
10. Income and other taxes
    (a) Has the relationship between the tax provision and pre-tax income been considered?
    (b) Have assessments or re-assessments been received?

TABLE 23–1   Example Enquiries for Review Engagements *(Continued)*

(c) Are there timing differences? If so, have deferred taxes been recorded?

(d) have sales and other taxes been considered?

11. Other liabilities

(a) What is the nature and amount of other liabilities?

(b) Has current/non-current classification been made?

(c) Have contingencies and commitments been considered?

12. Equity

(a) Are equity accounts and changes therein disclosed?

(b) Have share options, dividend restrictions, etc. been considered?

OVERALL REVIEW

1. Has appropriate consideration been given to:

(a) the inter-relationship of financial statement items?

(b) a comparison of significant components of the statement of income (in light of current operating and economic conditions) with budgets and figures for preceding periods?

(c) significant operating ratios?

(d) identification of related parties and related party transactions?

(e) whether or not the enterprise is economically dependent on anyone?

(f) the need to obtain bank confirmation of specific matters?

2. Have enquiries been made concerning matters discussed at meetings, if any, of shareholders and directors and committees thereof that may affect the financial statements?

3. Has there been communication with other public accountants who have reviewed or audited the financial statements of significant components of the reporting enterprise?

4. Have there been any changes in accounting principles and, if so, have these changes been adequately disclosed?

5. Are there any events which occurred after the end of the financial period which would have significant effect on the financial statements or would be significant to readers of the financial statements?

6. Have all matters that in your professional judgment are important to support the content of your report been documented?

7. Do the financial statements agree with the records of the enterprise?

FINAL CONSIDERATIONS

1. Have the financial statements and the review engagement report been discussed with the client?

2. Is the client satisfied that the financial statements are complete and accurate?

3. Has a letter of representation been obtained? Does it contain all representations by the client which should be documented?

4. Based on the review performed, do the financial statements appear to be plausible in the circumstances within the framework of generally accepted accounting principles.

5. Is the form and content of the review engagement report appropriate to this engagement and is it dated to correspond with the date of substantial completion of the review?

The requirement that the accountant have sufficient knowledge of the client's enterprise and type of business is made so that the accountant can assess whether the information to be reported on is plausible in the circumstances. The accountant would not be able to make the required inquiry and assessment of the information obtained without such knowledge. For instance, the accountant would not be able to assess the plausibility of manufactured inventory unless he or she had knowledge of the company's product and manufacturing processes.

The review standards should be appropriate to the particular engagement; for example, it is likely that procedures would differ between a review of financial statements and financial information. The review procedures do not preclude audit procedures if the accountant believes that more extensive procedures are required to assess plausibility. However, once the accountant decides to use more extensive procedures such as audit procedures, the particular procedure must be carried out to completion. The accountant may not carry out an audit procedure to partial completion simply because the engagement is a review.

Materiality would be measured in the same manner as with an audit.

Negative assurance should be expressed only when the standards applicable to a review engagement described above have been met.

In addition to the reporting standards listed above, the communication should identify the information presented, state that a review does not constitute

FIGURE 23–7

Example of a Report
Under Section 8200

REVIEW ENGAGEMENT REPORT

To R. Fortin

I have reviewed the balance sheet of Leger Inc. as at December 31, 19X7 and the statements of income, retained earnings and changes in financial position for the year then ended. My review was made in accordance with generally accepted standards established for review engagements and accordingly consisted primarily of inquiry, analytical procedures and discussion related to information supplied to me by the company.

A review does not constitute an audit and consequently I do not express an audit opinion on these financial statements.

Nothing has come to my attention as a result of my review that causes me to believe that these financial statements are not, in all material respects, in accordance with generally accepted accounting principles.

Montreal, Quebec
February 18, 19X8

A. Vachon
Chartered Accountant

an audit, and state that the review, which consisted primarily of inquiry, analytical procedures and discussion, was made in accordance with generally accepted standards for review engagements. The purpose of stating that a review does not constitute an audit is to ensure financial statement users are aware that a review provides a lower level of assurance than an audit. The accountant should also state, except when a reservation is required, that nothing has come to his or her attention as a result of his or her review that causes him or her to believe that the information is not, in all material respects, in accordance with an appropriate disclosed basis of accounting, which except in special circumstances should be generally accepted accounting principles, or in the case of non-financial information, other appropriate criteria. In addition, each page of information reported on should be marked "unaudited."

Reservations may be required in the accountant's report when the review cannot be completed, when there is a departure from the appropriate criteria or when the accountant concludes that the client's interpretation of an agreement or regulation is not reasonable. The reservation would be disclosed in a reservation paragraph in the review engagement report, which would appear immediately preceding the negative assurance paragraph. The reason for the reservation and the effect of the reservation on the information reported on should also be disclosed.

The discovery of an error after the release of the report by the accountant should be treated in the same way as the discovery of an error by an auditor after the release of audited financial statements.

Reviews of Financial Statements Section 8200 provides guidelines that apply in addition to those in Section 8100 when the accountant is reporting on interim or annual financial statements. An example of the report that the accountant would issue is shown in Figure 23–7.

Financial Information Other Than Financial Statements Section 8500 describes the sorts of financial information that might be included under this

FIGURE 23–8

Example of a Report
Under Section 8500

REVIEW ENGAGEMENT REPORT

To Kamloops Limited

At the request of Pacific Limited, I have reviewed the balance sheet of Pacific Limited as at March 31, 19X7 (calculated in accordance with the provisions of section X of the mortgage agreement with Kamloops Limited dated May 5, 19X1 and the interpretations set out in note 1). My review was made in accordance with generally accepted standards for review engagements and accordingly consisted primarily of inquiry, analytical procedures and discussion related to information supplied to me by the company.

A review does not constitute an audit and consequently I do not express an audit opinion on this matter.

Based on my review, nothing has come to my attention that causes me to believe that this balance sheet is not presented fairly in accordance with (the provisions of section X of the mortgage agreement with Kamloops Limited dated May 5, 19X1, and the interpretations set out in note 1).

Vancouver, B.C.
June 7, 19X8

L. Daryl
Chartered Accountant

---

grouping. It also refers the accountant to Section 5805 for further guidance in this matter. When the information is prepared in accordance with an agreement or regulation, and that agreement requires interpretations, the report should refer to such interpretations. Figure 23–8 shows the form a communication might take when reporting on financial information other than financial statements.

Reviews of Compliance with Agreements and Regulations Section 8600, besides describing what situations fall under this heading, lists what steps would be followed in these situations in addition to those listed in Section 8100. The accountant is referred to Section 5815, Audit Reports on Compliance. The accountant should read the relevant provisions of the agreement or regulation, inquire about how the client monitors its compliance with the provisions, and consider whether the provisions have been consistently applied. In the review engagement report, the public accountant is to identify the provisions of the agreement or regulation that establish the criteria on which his or her assessment of compliance is based. As well, any significant interpretations of the criteria made by the accountant when the criteria were unspecific and any significant changes in interpretations from the previous year are to be identified. Figure 23–9 presents an example of the report the accountant might issue.

Compilation   Compilation services are intended to enable a public accounting firm to compete with bookkeeping firms. It is common for smaller public accounting firms to own one or more microcomputers and provide bookkeeping services, monthly or quarterly financial statements, and tax services for smaller clients.

In such engagements, discussed in Section 9200, the public accountant provides assistance in compiling financial statements but is not required to provide any assurance about the statements. The statements may be complete (i.e., include balance sheet, income statement, and statement of changes in financial

FIGURE 23–9

Example of a Report
Under Section 8600

REVIEW ENGAGEMENT REPORT

To J. O'Sullivan

I have reviewed Separate Limited's compliance as at December 31, 19X8 with covenants to be complied with described in sections 8 to 10 inclusive of the agreement dated November 3, 19X1, with Waterloo Inc. My review was made in accordance with generally accepted standards for review engagements and accordingly consisted primarily of inquiry, analytical procedures and discussion related to information supplied to me by the company.

A review does not constitute an audit and consequently I do not express an audit opinion on this matter.

Nothing has come to my attention as a result of my review that causes me to believe that the company is not in compliance with covenants to be complied with described in sections 8 to 10 inclusive of this agreement.

Kingston, Ontario
January 18, 19X9

G. Orr
Chartered Accountant

---

position); they may be part of a complete set of financial statements; or they may be for the whole enterprise or for a part of the enterprise. The accountant assembles the information supplied by the client and ensures that it is arithmetically correct; the accountant is not concerned with whether the information is either accurate or complete nor whether the financial statements comply with GAAP. Although the accountant should not be associated with false or misleading financial statements, determining whether the statements are false or misleading can be difficult because of his or her limited involvement.

Section 9200 sets out criteria for accepting a compilation engagement:

    (a) the public accountant has no reason to believe that the information supplied to him or her for the purpose of compiling the financial statements is false or misleading; and

    (b) he or she believes that the client understands that:
        (i) such statements may not be appropriate for general purpose use; and
        (ii) uninformed readers could be misled unless they are aware of the possible limitations of the statements, and of the public accountant's very limited involvement.

Professional Standards There are standards that the public accountant must follow in performing a compilation engagement:

    (a) the services should be performed and the communication should be prepared by a person or persons having adequate technical training and proficiency in accounting, and with due care;

    (b) the work should be adequately planned and properly executed and if assistants are employed, they should be properly supervised; and

    (c) based on the knowledge he or she possesses of the client's affairs and information provided to him or her, the public accountant should compile financial statements which, so far as he or she knows, are not false or misleading.

If the public accountant ascertains that the financial statements may be false or

FIGURE 23–10

Example of Report
Under Section 9200

NOTICE TO READER

I have compiled the balance sheet of New B Ltd. as at March 31, 19X7 from information provided by management. I have not audited, reviewed or otherwise attempted to verify the accuracy or completeness of such information. Accordingly, readers are cautioned that this statement may not be appropriate for their purposes.

Halifax, N.S.
June 12, 19X8

R. Fundy
Chartered Accountant

---

misleading, he or she must obtain additional information and amend the statements or resign from the engagement.

Form of report   The communication from the public accountant in a compilation engagement is entitled "Notice to Reader." Each page of the statements should either include the "Notice to Reader" heading itself or the statement "Unaudited – See Notice to Reader." The communication should

(a) state that the public accountant compiled the statement from information provided by management;

(b) state that the public accountant did not audit, review or otherwise attempt to verify the accuracy or completeness of such information;

(c) caution readers that the statement may not be appropriate for their purposes; and

(d) not express any form of opinion or negative assurance.

An example of a Notice to Reader appears in Figure 23–10.

Departures from generally accepted accounting principles should not be referred to in the report as this may suggest that the public accountant has a responsibility to detect and report all such departures.

Interim Financial Information   Interim financial information may be audited, reviewed or compiled by a public accountant. The decision depends on how much assurance is desired from the accountant's involvement and how timely the information must be. Estimates are commonly made to prepare the information on a timely basis. Therefore, the information may not be as reliable as annual financial information. Since the objective of producing interim financial information is to provide up-to-date information to users of the statements, such information is usually not audited. Sections 8100, 8200, 8500 and 8600 should be consulted when interim financial information is reviewed. If it is compiled, Section 9200 is relevant. Figure 23–11 summarizes the important points of the above discussion.

Prospectuses   Section 7100, "The Auditor's Involvement with Prospectuses and Other Offering Documents," does not just apply to prospectuses but to all offering documents (such as takeover bid circulars, issuer bid circulars, information circulars and statements of material facts) to the extent that they are similar. That is, the requirements apply when the financial information being audited is similar to that found in a prospectus.

FIGURE 23-11 Comparison of Audit, Review and Compilation Engagements

Procedures	Amount of Evidence to be Collected	Used to Collect Evidence	Levels of Assurance Provided	Relative Cost of Engagement	Communication Title	Engagement Letter Desired	Proficiency Required in What?	Public Accountant Required to be Objective?	Knowledge of Business Required?	Understanding of Internal Control Required?	Documentation Required?
Audit	Extensive	Inspection, Observation, Enquiry, Confirmation, Computation, Analysis	High	High	Auditor's Report	Yes	Auditing	Yes	Yes	Yes	Yes
Review	Significant	Enquiry, Analysis, Discussion, Others if necessary	Moderate	Moderate	Review Engagement Report	Yes	Review	Yes	Yes	No, but may be required	Yes
Compilation	Minor	Computation	None	Low	Notice to Reader	Yes	Accounting	No	No	No	Not specifically stated, but desirable

OBJECTIVE 4

Understand the auditor's involvement with prospectuses and other offering documents.

The auditor comments on three aspects of a prospectus to securities regulatory authorities:

- The auditor consents to inclusion of his or her auditor's report in the prospectus.
- The auditor comments on any unaudited or pro-forma financial information that is included.
- The auditor advises the authorities that the entire prospectus has been read and that it contains no misrepresentations insofar as information taken from the financial statements is concerned.

The auditor must seek assurance that the financial information in the prospectus conforms with the requirements of the appropriate securities act and Section 4000, "Prospectuses," of the *CICA Handbook*. Securities legislation is a provincial jurisdiction and may vary from province to province. There is no federal securities legislation in Canada, in contrast to the United States, where securities are a federal, rather than a state, matter.

The auditor may also be requested to examine forecasts or projections included in the offering document. This involvement is discussed in a later section of this chapter.

Audited Financial Statements

The auditor normally has to report on comparative balance sheets and five year comparative statements of income, retained earnings and changes in financial position. Those statements should be reviewed to ensure that GAAP has been applied consistently over the five years and that any accounting changes and prior period adjustments have been accounted for correctly. When audited financial statements in the five year period have been audited by a predecessor auditor, he or she would have to consent to the inclusion of his or her auditor's report in the prospectus. The auditor's report would be similar to the standard report except that it would refer to the financial position at both year ends, and the results of operations and changes in financial position for the five years.

Unaudited Financial Statements

When the audited financial statements to be included in a prospectus are not current, unaudited interim financial information is included. The auditor normally provides a comfort letter to the securities regulatory authorities about the unaudited information. A *comfort letter* is a letter addressed to the authorities that provides negative assurance on the interim financial statements and indicates that they are unaudited. Figure 23–12 is an example of a comfort letter.

Review procedures consisting primarily of inquiry, analysis, and discussion (which are discussed earlier in the chapter) would be applied to determine whether the interim financial statements are plausible and in accordance with generally accepted accounting principles. The work done on the statements is subject to the general and first examination standard. The auditor must possess a reasonable knowledge of the client's business, of accounting and internal control systems, and of the industry.

Other Financial Information

As was mentioned previously, the auditor must be satisfied that other financial information derived from the financial statements is not misleading. If, for example, the prospectus contained a summary of the dollars spent on capital additions, the auditor would want to ensure that the summary was not misleading.

FIGURE 23–12

A Comfort Letter

APRIL 18, 19X9
ONTARIO SECURITIES COMMISSION

Dear Sirs:

Re: Mariposa Limited

We are the above company's auditors and on February 28, 19X9 we reported on the following financial statements included in the prospectus relating to the sale and issue of 1,000,000 common shares:

    Balance sheets as at December 31, 19X8 and 19X7;

    Statements of income, retained earnings and changes in financial position for each of the years in the five-year period ended December 31, 19X8.

The prospectus includes the following unaudited interim financial statements:

    Balance sheet as at March 31, 19X9;

    Statements of income, retained earnings and changes in financial position for the three months ended March 31, 19X9 and 19X8.

We have not examined any financial statements of the company as at any date or for any period subsequent to December 31, 19X8.

Although we have performed an examination for the year ended December 31, 19X8, the purpose and therefore the scope of the examination was to enable us to express our opinion on the financial statements as at December 31, 19X8 and for the year then ended, but not on the financial statements for any interim period within that year.

Therefore, we are unable to and do not express any opinion on the unaudited balance sheet as at March 31, 19X9 and the unaudited interim statements of income, retained earnings and changes in financial position for the three months ended March 31, 19X9 and 19X8 included in the prospectus or on the financial position, results of operations or changes in financial position as at any date or for any period subsequent to December 31, 19X8.

We have, however, performed procedures that meet the standards established by the Canadian Institute of Chartered Accountants relating to unaudited interim financial statements in prospectuses. On the basis of these procedures, nothing has come to our attention that would cause us to believe that the unaudited interim financial statements are not presented, in all material respects, in accordance with generally accepted accounting principles.

The procedures referred to in the preceding paragraph do not constitute an audit and would not necessarily reveal material adjustments that might be required to present fairly, in all material respects, the financial position of the company as at March 31, 19X9 and the results of its operations and the changes in its financial position for the three months ended March 31, 19X9 and 19X8 in accordance with generally accepted accounting principles.

This letter is provided solely for the purpose of assisting you in discharging your statutory responsibilities and should not be relied on for any other purpose.

Markdale
April 2X, 1989

                                 Bojovich & Company
                                 Chartered Accountants

      The auditor must also read the complete prospectus and be satisfied that the contents, insofar as they relate to matters on which the auditor might reasonably be expected to have knowledge as a result of his or her examination, are not misleading. If not satisfied, the auditor would consider withholding his or her consent letter and consulting legal counsel.

FIGURE 23–13

Example of a
Compilation Report on
Pro-forma Financial
Statements

COMPILATION REPORT

To the Directors of Adam Limited

We have reviewed, as to compilation only, the accompanying pro-forma combined balance sheet of Adam Limited and Alicia Limited as at December 31, 19X8 and the pro-forma combined statement of income for the year ended December 31, 19X8. These pro-forma combined financial statements have been prepared solely for inclusion in the prospectus relating to the sale and issue of 100,000 shares of common stock and are based on the audited financial statements of Adam Limited and Alicia Limited as at December 31, 19X8. The separate financial statements of Alicia Limited were examined and reported on by another auditor. In our opinion, these pro-forma combined financial statements have been properly compiled to give effect to the transactions and assumptions described in the notes thereto.

Calgary
February 14, 19X9

Kowalski & Butchart
Chartered Accountants

Pro-forma
Financial
Statements

Pro-forma financial statements are historical financial statements adjusted to give effect to a specific transaction. For instance, a company might be issuing a prospectus to raise $1,000,000 from the sale of bonds and planning to use the money to pay off short-term loans. The prospectus might include pro-forma financial statements that would show the new long-term debt and would not show the short-term that would be paid off.

The auditor should review pro-forma financial statements included in a prospectus to ensure that they have been properly compiled. Procedures could include:

- Obtaining evidence of completed transactions or firm commitments to proceed with transactions by inspection of agreements and correspondence.
- Ensuring adjustments to historical statements are made and disclosed.

A compilation report should be prepared by the auditor and included in the prospectus. An example of such a report, where the issuers propose to acquire another company, is shown in Figure 23–13.

Other Issues

Section 7100 defines a preliminary prospectus as " . . . a formal filing signed by officers of the [company] and the underwriters and is used to provide preliminary information to investors." The section also discusses the comfort letter to be sent to the securities regulatory authorities about the audited and unaudited financial statements included in the preliminary prospectus. The auditor should issue the comfort letter containing negative assurance only when satisfied that it can properly be issued. Figure 23–14 is an example of a comfort letter for a preliminary prospectus.

The auditor issues a letter termed a *consent letter* to the securities regulatory authorities consenting to the use of his or her auditor's report in the prospectus. The auditors must perform the appropriate review of the client's records for the period between the date of the audited statements and the date of the consent letter to ensure that all material subsequent events are properly disclosed. The auditor's consent letter should be issued and the auditor's report signed when the require-

FIGURE 23–14

Example of a Comfort
Letter for a Preliminary
Prospectus

MAY 10, 19X4
ALBERTA SECURITIES COMMISSION

Dear Sirs:

Re: Stuart Toys Limited

I refer to the preliminary prospectus of the above company dated May 10, 19X4 relating to the sale and issue of 1,000,000 Class "B" common shares.

I have reported to the shareholders on the following financial statements in the preliminary prospectus:

Balance sheets as at December 31, 19X3 and 19X2;

Statements of income, retained earnings and changes in financial position for each of the years in the five year period ended December 31, 19X3.

My report on the financial statements for 19X3 was dated February 28, 19X4.

I am withholding my signature from the draft report in the preliminary prospectus pending:

(a) reviewing events between the dates of the preliminary and final prospectuses;

(b) reviewing comments which may be issued by the Commission; and

(c) reading the final prospectus.

Based on the results of my audits of the financial statements referred to above and my limited inquiry and review procedures for the period from February 28, 19X4 to the date of this letter, I have no reason to believe that the financial statements do not present fairly, in all material respects, the financial position of the company as at December 31, 19X3 and 19X2, and the results of its operations and the changes in its financial position for each of the years in the five year period ended December 31, 19X3 in accordance with generally accepted accounting principles.

This letter is provided solely for the purpose of assisting the Alberta Securities Commission in discharging its responsibilities and should not be relied on for any other purpose.

Yours truly,

Pender & Assoc.
Chartered Accountants

ments of the *Handbook* have been met, when the underwriting agreement has been signed, and when the final prospectus and financial statements in the prospectus have been signed. The consent letter is normally dated concurrently with the final prospectus. Figure 23–15 is an example of a consent letter.

Assistance to Underwriters

The underwriters of an offering document may request the auditors to perform specific tasks, other than those required in connection with the financial statements relating to the offering document. The underwriters, for example, may want additional assurance about accounts receivable as at the date of the consent letter, which will probably be later than the date of either the auditor's report or the date of the comfort letter.

Before addressing other matters, the auditor must ensure they are within his or her expertise. If the additional work is performed, the auditor's letter to the underwriter should:

- Describe the financial information examined.
- State that an audit was not performed and no opinion is expressed.
- Describe the procedures performed and the results.

FIGURE 23–15

Example Consent Letter

JUNE 22, 19X4
ALBERTA SECURITIES COMMISSION

Dear Sirs:

Re: Stuart Toys Limited

We refer to the prospectus of the above company dated June 22, 19X4 relating to the sale and issue of 1,000,000 Class "B" common shares.

We consent to the use in the above mentioned prospectus of our report dated February 28, 19X4 to the directors of X Limited on the following financial statements:

Balance sheets as at December 31, 19X3 and 19X2;

Statements of income, retained earnings and changes in financial position for each of the years in the five year period ended December 31, 19X3.

We report that we have read the prospectus and have no reason to believe that there are any misrepresentations in the information contained therein that is derived from the financial statements upon which we have reported or that is within our knowledge as a result of our audit of such financial statements.

This letter is provided to the Alberta Securities Commission to which it is addressed pursuant to the requirements of its securities legislation and not for any other purpose.

Yours truly,

Pender & Assoc.
Chartered Accountants

- State that no assurance as to the sufficiency of the procedures for the underwriter's purposes is provided.
- Identify that the letter's distribution is restricted to the underwriter.

Future-oriented Financial Information

OBJECTIVE 5

Describe examinations of future-oriented financial information.

In September 1989, the CICA issued Section 4250, "Future-oriented Financial Information," which establishes accounting standards for such information, and the former Accounting Guideline was eliminated. The CICA also issued Auditing Guideline entitled "Examination of a Financial Forecast or Projection Included in a Prospectus or Other Public Offering Document." This Guideline is directed at prospective information included in offering documents. However, since no guidance exists for the auditor's involvement with other prospective information (e.g., that included in annual reports), public accountants use this Guideline as reference.

Chapter 1 points out that Accounting and Auditing Guidelines points out that they do not have the force of Recommendations. Their intent is to provide guidance in the absence of Recommendations.

Forecasts and Projections

Future-oriented financial information deals with the future, not with the past. Section 4250 describes two general types of future-oriented financial information: *forecasts* and *projections*. A forecast is prospective financial information prepared using assumptions reflecting management's judgment as to the most probable courses of action for the entity. The information is presented to the best of management's knowledge and belief. A projection is prepared using one or more assumptions (hypotheses) that do not necessarily reflect the most likely course of action in management's judgement.

Use of Prospective Financial Statements

Prospective financial statements are for either *general* use or *special* use. General use refers to use by any third party. An example of general use would be inclusion of a financial forecast in a prospectus for the sale of shares of a large public company. Special use refers to use by third parties with whom the responsible party is negotiating directly. An example of special purpose future-oriented financial information would be the inclusion of a financial projection in a takeover bid circular aimed at current shareholders of the company.

Acceptance of the Engagement

As with other types of engagements performed by the public accountant, it is important to ensure the nature and terms of involvement with future-oriented financial information are understood and agreed to by management, preferably in writing. Management should also acknowledge its responsibilities related to the financial information. The Guideline identifies a number of matters that should be agreed to by management and the public accountant:

- The anticipated form of the financial forecast.
- The period of time to be covered.
- The fact that management will prepare and present the forecast in accordance with accounting standards established by the CICA, and in accordance with any applicable securities requirements.
- The fact that management is responsible for the forecast: its presentation, the process of preparation, and the assumptions used.
- The fact that management is responsible for obtaining or developing appropriate support for the assumptions sufficient to enable the public accountant to report without reservation.
- The need for the public accountant to have access to outside specialists and third party reports obtained by management (for example, a feasibility study).
- The anticipated form and content of the public accountant's report.
- The fact that the public accountant has no responsibility to update his or her report for events and circumstances occurring after the date of that report.

Professional standards There are standards that the public accountant should follow in examining prospective information:

- The services should be performed by someone with adequate technical training and proficiency in auditing;
- The examination should be performed and the report prepared with due care and an objective state of mind
- The work should be adequately planned and any assistants should be supervised
- Sufficient evidence should be obtained to provide a reasonable basis for the report.
- Important matters should be documented to indicate that sufficient appropriate evidence has been obtained.

Before accepting such an engagement, the public accountant should ensure the following:

- There is adequate support for the assumptions used to prepare the financial information. For example, management of a new company may not be able to provide such support.
- Any hypotheses used do not significantly impair the quality of the financial information.

- Management is willing to disclose all significant assumptions.
- The period to be covered by the forecast or projection does not extend beyond the point where future results can be reasonably estimated.
- Any hypotheses are not false or misleading. If they are, the public accountant cannot be involved with the financial information.

Examination of Prospective Financial Statements

An examination of future-oriented financial information involves

- Evaluating the preparation of the future-oriented financial information.
- Evaluating the underlying assumptions and assessing the plausibility of hypotheses.
- Evaluating the presentation of the financial information for conformity with CICA presentation and disclosure guidelines (Section 4250). Accounting policies should be consistent with those used in the historical financial statements.
- Issuing an examination report.
- Obtaining a written letter of representation from management acknowledging its responsibility for preparing the forecast or projection and indicating that forecast figures are management's best estimate of the forecast results.

These evaluations are based primarily on accumulating evidence about the completeness and reasonableness of the underlying assumptions as disclosed in the prospective financial information. This requires the accountant to become familiar with the client's business and industry, to identify the significant matters on which the client's entity's future results are expected to depend ("key factors"), and to determine that appropriate assumptions have been included with respect to these.

In developing a knowledge of the industry and business, the public accountant should focus on areas such as:

- The availability and cost of resources the client needs for continuing operations.
- The nature and condition of markets in which the client operates.
- Specific industry factors such as competition, sensitivity to economic conditions, accounting principles and practices, regulatory requirements, and technology.
- Past performance by the client and its competitors.

Reporting

The accountant's report on an examination of financial statements should include

- An identification of the financial information presented.
- A description of the nature of the examination.
- A statement that the examination of the financial information was made in accordance with the Auditing Guideline issued by the CICA.
- A statement that the public accountant assumes no responsibility to update the report for events and circumstances occurring after the report date.
- The accountant's opinion as to whether the assumptions are suitably supported, consistent with the client's plans and provide a reasonable basis for the information; the forecast or projection reflects these assumptions; and the information is prepared in conformity with the CICA's presentation and disclosure standards.
- A caveat that the prospective results may not be achieved.
- A disclaimer of opinion as to the achievability of the forecast or projection.

For projections, the report would also:

- State that the assumptions used include an hypothesis.

FIGURE 23–16

Example Report on a
Financial Forecast

AUDITOR'S REPORT ON FINANCIAL FORECAST

To the Directors of Nomad Corp.

The accompanying financial forecast of Nomad Corp. consisting of a balance sheet as at June 30, 19X6 and the statements of income, retained earnings and changes in financial position for the period then ending has been prepared by management using assumptions with an effective date of June 30, 19X5. I have examined the support provided by management for the assumptions, and the preparation and presentation of this forecast. My examination was made in accordance with the applicable Auditing Guideline issued by The Canadian Institute of Chartered Accountants. I have no responsibility to update this report for events and circumstances occurring after the date of my report.

In my opinion: as at the date of this report, the assumptions developed by management are suitably supported and consistent with the plans of the Company, and provide a reasonable basis for the forecast; this forecast reflects such assumptions; and the financial forecast complies with the presentation and disclosure standards for forecasts established by the Canadian Institute of Chartered Accountants.

Since this forecast is based on assumptions regarding future events, actual results will vary from the information presented and the variations may be material. Accordingly, I express no opinion as to whether this forecast will be achieved.

Toronto
August 15, 19X5

McWhirter & Kedwell
Chartered Accountants

- State that since an hypothesis need not be supported, procedures were limited to ensuring it was consistent with the purpose of the projection.
- Provide an opinion regarding the consistency of the hypothesis with the purpose of the projection.

Figure 23–16 is an example of a report on a financial forecast. The date of the report would be the date of the completion of the field work by the public accountant.

Reports on the Application of Accounting Principles, Auditing Standards or Review Standards

Public accountants are being asked by clients of other public accountants to give opinions with respect to accounting issues, to the application of auditing or review standards, and provide generic opinions. This practice by clients has been described by the public accounting profession as "opinion shopping"; it occurs when the client of one public accounting firm disagrees with that accounting firm's opinion about a particular accounting treatment and goes to another public accounting firm (shops) for an opinion supporting the client's position. The client seeking the second opinion might intentionally or unintentionally not provide the second firm with *all* the facts the incumbent used, so that a potentially different opinion will be reached by the second firm. The Macdonald Commission and leaders of the profession have been critical of the practice because of its potential harmful impact on independence.

The Auditing Standards Board has issued a New *Handbook* section, Section 7600, to deal with the problem of opinion shopping. The new section does not attempt to stop the practice but rather sets some rules to be followed, so that the second public accounting firm provides its opinion using the same information as the incumbent.

The reporting accountant, the accountant asked for the second opinion, must

OBJECTIVE 6

Describe reports on the application of accounting principles, auditing standards or review standards come to agreement with the organization seeking the opinion on the nature of the engagement, the information to be provided by the organization, and the type of report wanted, plus any restrictions on its distribution. This agreement should be in the form of an engagement letter.

The reporting accountant should follow the general standard and examination standards (i) and (iii) of GAAS. If an entity requests the opinion, the reporting accountant should request permission from the entity to, and should, contact the entity's incumbent auditor. Sections 7600.09, 7600.12 and 7600.14 all stress that the reporting accountant should obtain "a written statement of all relevant facts and assumptions" from the party requesting the opinion. In the case of a request by the entity, Section 7600.09 states that the reporting accountant should "obtain a written statement from the entity [describing] the circumstances and nature of any relevant disagreements of the entity with its incumbent accountant or a third party."

The report should be in writing. Section 7600.18 specifies the content of the report so that users of it will fully understand the context and content of the report issued by the reporting accountant.

Audit of Pension Costs and Obligations

The Auditing Guideline entitled "Audit of Pension Costs and Obligations" is intended to provide guidance when auditing of defined benefit pension plans as described in Section 3460, "Pension Costs and Obligations," of the *CICA Handbook*. The Auditing Standards Board of the CICA and the Council of the Canadian Institute of Actuaries (CIA) issued a Joint Policy Statement in March 1991 to facilitate communications between the actuary and auditor. It describes when each can use the work of the other, how they should interact in carrying out their responsibilities, and how these responsibilities should be disclosed. The Statement is included in Section 5365, "Communication with Actuaries."

The auditor should consider the following factors in planning the audit of pension costs and obligations:

> **OBJECTIVE 7**
>
> Describe the auditor's involvement with pension costs and obligations.

- Materiality of the pension costs, assets, and obligations in relation to the sponsor's financial statements taken as a whole.
- Number and type of pension plans and the provisions of each plan.
- Extent to which the plan sponsor uses a service organization in the operation of the plan.
- Timing of the pension plan valuation, the need for extrapolations and the involvement of management and the actuary in determining the pension costs, assets, and obligations.
- Use of the work and report of the actuary.

In considering the use of the work and report of the actuary, Section 5365 would apply. Of particular concern is the assessment of the actuary's competence. The auditor would have to communicate with the actuary in order to ascertain whether the actuary's work is "appropriate for the purpose intended." Section 5365A lists a number of considerations for the auditor when he or she is using the actuary's work in connection with an audit of financial statements. The Guideline lists a number of considerations of which the auditor would seek confirmation from the actuary in the year of an actuarial valuation. It also lists what the concerns of the auditor would be in the years between actuarial valuations.

There are several matters regarding pension costs and obligations of which the auditor should be aware. The auditor should review the actuary's assumptions to assess whether they are reasonable and reflect the conditions that are likely to affect future events and whether they are internally and externally consistent. As a methodology for examining the appropriateness of the source data used by the actuary, the guideline suggests procedures from Section 5360, "Using the Work of a Specialist," that the auditor could apply.

The auditor must assess the actuary's work in a context of knowledge about the business and the actuary's methods, assumptions, and source data. The auditor should be reasonably assured that the source data is appropriate and that the financial statement assertions are in agreement with the actuary's findings. If the auditor reaches the conclusion that the actuary's work and report cannot be used, he or she should consider first consulting with the Review Committee of the CIA and have it review the work of the actuary. If the committee is also not satisfied with the work of the actuary, the auditor should consider appointing another actuary. As a final measure, he or she should contemplate qualifying the auditor's report.

The auditor must review management's extrapolation of pension costs and obligations. If the extrapolation was done by or with the assistance of an actuary, the auditor should communicate with the actuary to make certain that the extrapolation was accurate and properly done. If no actuary was involved, the auditor should look at consulting an actuary to review the extrapolation.

The auditor should also obtain a letter of representation from management that the pension costs, assets, and obligations were calculated and disclosed in accordance with Section 3460. The auditor should further think of getting management's representation on, among other details, source data, the completeness of the plans, the specific assumptions used, and the accuracy of the extrapolations.

The auditor should at the same time accumulate evidence to satisfy himself or herself about the existence, ownership, and valuation of the pension plan assets, considering their materiality relative to the total assets of the company. Section 3460 requires the basis of valuation of pension plan assets to be market value.

Finally, the auditor should ensure that contributions to and benefits paid by the pension plan are proper and that funding provisions and surplus withdrawals have been made with the approval of regulatory authority as well as having been accounted for properly in the sponsor's financial statements.

Audit of Pension Fund Financial Statements

OBJECTIVE 8

Describe an examination of pension fund financial statements.

The Auditing Guideline entitled "Auditor's Report on Pension Fund Financial Statements Filed with a Regulator" provides guidance for auditing pension fund statements of a defined benefit pension plan under a regulatory requirement. The suggested report format is similar to an audit report on compliance with regulations under Section 5815 except that a fourth paragraph is used to state that the pension fund financial statements and the auditor's report have been prepared for filing with the regulator and are not appropriate for any other purpose.

Attestation Standards

The CICA has not yet issued standards similar to the attestation standards issued by the AICPA. However, the unique nature of the standards makes it useful to include them. References are made to CPAs alone because the standards apply to CPAs.

During the past 10 to 15 years, CPAs have increasingly been asked to perform a variety of audit-like, or *attest*, services for different purposes. An example is a bank that requests a CPA to state in writing whether an audit client has adhered to all requirements of a loan agreement. As specific types of requests became common, specific standards were issued to give guidance on them. This guidance was usually in the form of an interpretation of generally accepted auditing standards. But since those standards relate primarily to historical financial statements prepared in accordance with generally accepted accounting principles, and the new services often dealt with other types of information, the guidance became difficult to formulate and communicate effectively without disrupting the cohesiveness of Statements of Auditing Standards.

OBJECTIVE 9

Understand the AICPA attestation standards, and the levels of assurance and types of engagements they provide.

This problem has been addressed by the profession through the issuance of the *Statement on Standards for Attestation Engagements*. The purpose of that statement is to provide a general framework for and set reasonable boundaries around the attest function. This is done by (1) providing guidance to AICPA standard-setting bodies in establishing detailed standards and interpretations of standards for specific types of services and (2) providing practitioners useful guidance in performing new and evolving attest services where no specific guidance exists.

The attestation standards, therefore, provide a *conceptual framework* for various types of services. They do not supersede or override any existing detailed standards relating to a specific type of service. However, the attestation standards will be considered in the development of any new detailed standards.

Table 23–2 compares the attestation standards with the eight Canadian generally accepted auditing standards discussed in Chapter 1. As would be expected, the attestation standards and the auditing standards are consistent, though the attestation standards are more general in nature.

Attest Engagement Defined

An attest engagement is defined by the statement on attestation standards as *"one in which a practitioner is engaged to issue or does issue a written communication that expresses a conclusion with respect to the reliability of a written assertion that is the responsibility of another party."* The practitioner might, for example, be a CPA doing an audit or a management consultant working for a CPA firm.

An *assertion* is "any declaration or set of related declarations taken as a whole, made by a party responsible for it." Thus, assertions are statements made by one party implicitly for use by another (third) party. Chapter 5 discusses the assertions made by management in historical financial statements.

As discussed in Chapter 1, having a competent, independent person render a conclusion about the reliability of the assertions increases their usefulness to a third party, by reducing the level of information risk.

The assertions that are made by a responsible party must be capable of evaluation against some reasonable and understandable criteria, and they must be capable of reasonably consistent estimation or measurement against those criteria. These requirements ensure that the assertions will contain useful information for third parties and that they will permit the practitioner to reach an effective and objective conclusion about them. If the criteria relating to an assertion were not clear and understandable to users, a practitioner's conclusion that they are reliable would serve no real purpose. Similarly, if measurement of data under the criteria was so subjective that a broad range of results could occur, little credibility would be added by practitioner involvement; in fact, such a situation might be misleading and therefore harmful.

Levels of Assurance

Assurance represents the degree of certainty the practitioner has attained, and wishes to convey, that the conclusions stated in his or her report are correct. As

TABLE 23–2 Comparison of Attestation Standards and Generally Accepted Auditing Standards	ATTESTATION STANDARDS	GENERALLY ACCEPTED AUDITING STANDARDS

	General standards
	1. The engagement shall be performed by a practitioner or practitioners having adequate technical training and proficiency in the attest function.
	
	2. The engagement shall be performed by a practitioner or practitioners having adequate knowledge in the subject matter of the assertion.
	
	3. The practitioner shall perform an engagement only if he or she has reason to believe that the following two conditions exist:
	  The assertion is capable of evaluation against reasonable criteria that either have been established by a recognized body or are stated in the presentation of the assertion in a sufficiently clear and comprehensive manner for a knowledgeable reader to be able to understand them.
	  The assertion is capable of reasonably consistent estimation or measurement using such criteria.
	
	4. In all matters relating to the engagement, an independence in mental attitude shall be maintained by the practitioner or practitioners.
	
	5. Due professional care shall be exercised in the performance of the engagement.
	
	Examination standards
	1. The work shall be adequately planned and assistants, if any, shall be properly supervised.
	
	2. Sufficient evidence shall be obtained to provide a reasonable basis for the conclusion that is expressed in the report.
		1. The examination should be performed and the report prepared by a person or persons having adequate technical training and proficiency in auditing, with due care and with an objective state of mind.
		
		1. The work should be adequately planned and properly executed. If assistants are employed they should be properly supervised.
		
		2. A sufficient understanding of internal control should be obtained to plan the audit. When control risk is assessed below maximum, sufficient appropriate audit evidence should be obtained through tests of controls to support the assessment.
		
		3. Sufficient appropriate audit evidence should be obtained, by such means as inspection, observation, inquiry, confirmation, computation, and analysis, to afford a reasonable basis to support the content of the report.

TABLE 23–2 *(Continued)*	ATTESTATION STANDARDS	GENERALLY ACCEPTED AUDITING STANDARDS
	Reporting standards	
	1. The report shall identify the assertion being reported on and state the character of the engagement.	1. The report should identify the financial statements and distinguish between the responsibilities of management and the responsibilities of the auditor.
	2. The report shall state the practitioner's conclusion about whether the assertion is presented in conformity with the established or stated criteria against which it was measured.	2. The report should describe the scope of the auditor's examination.
	3. The report shall state all of the practitioner's significant reservations about the engagement and the presentation of the assertion.	3. The report should contain either an expression of opinion on the financial statements or an assertion that an opinion cannot be expressed. In the latter case, the reasons therefor should be stated.
	4. The report on an engagement to evaluate an assertion that has been prepared in conformity with agreed-upon criteria or on an engagement to apply agreed-upon procedures should contain a statement limiting its use to the parties who have agreed upon such criteria or procedures.	4. Where an opinion is expressed, it should indicate whether the financial statements present fairly, in all material respects, the financial position, results of operations and changes in financial position in accordance with an appropriate disclosed basis of accounting, which except in special circumstances should be generally accepted accounting principles. The report should provide adequate explanation with respect to any reservation contained in such opinion.

discussed in the earlier chapters of this text, the level of assurance attained is the result of accumulating evidence. The greater the amount of competent, relevant evidence accumulated, the higher the level of assurance attained. The attestation standards define two levels of assurance: *high* and *moderate*. A third level of assurance – *no assurance* – is implied. Figure 23–17 summarizes these concepts.

Figure 23–17 indicates two matters of particular note. First, whenever a practitioner is *associated* with a set of assertions, he or she must perform some procedures and accumulate some evidence. When no assurance is given about the assertions, there will still be minimal evidence accumulated. For example, some evidence is gathered in a compilation engagement, although no assurance is given. Second, the amount of evidence gathered and the level of assurance attained are described in subjective terms. This is because they are subjective, and only a practitioner in the circumstances of an engagement can judge how much evidence is sufficient and what level of assurance has actually been attained.

Types of Engagements   The attest standards define three types of engagements and related forms of conclusions: examination, reviews, and agreed-upon procedures.

Audits of historical financial statements prepared in accordance with generally accepted accounting principles are one type of *examination*. They are governed by generally accepted auditing standards. Other types of examinations have been discussed earlier, including, for example, the examination of prospective financial information.

FIGURE 23–17

Relationship Between
Evidence
Accumulation and
Assurance Attained

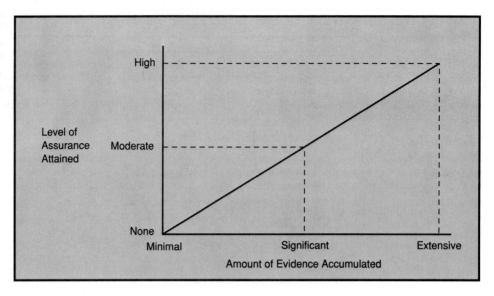

An examination results in a conclusion that is in a *positive* form. In this type of report, the practitioner makes a direct statement as to whether the presentation of the assertions, taken as a whole, conforms with the applicable criteria. An example of an examination report written under the general guidance of the attestation standards, rather than more detailed standards, is shown in Figure 23–18. This is for an engagement to determine that the rate of return on a hypothetical portfolio, based on a brokerage firm's buy-sell recommendations, is correct as represented in the firm's promotional materials. The example is illustrative of U.S. practice; remember that attestation standards do not presently exist in Canada.

FIGURE 23–18

Example of
Examination Report
Under the Attestation
Standards

TO MANAGEMENT
AKRON SECURITIES, INC.

We have examined the accompanying statement for investment performance statistics of the Akron Securities Model Portfolio for the year ended December 31, 19X5. Our examination was made in accordance with standards established by the American Institute of Certified Public Accountants, and accordingly, included such procedures as we considered necessary in the circumstances.

In our opinion, the statement of investment performance statistics referred to above presents the investment performance of the Akron Securities Model Portfolio for the year ended December 31, 19X5, in conformity with the actual results that would have been obtained if the buy and sell recommendations for the portfolio were followed as described in the buy-sell recommendations set forth in Note 1.

Farnsworth & Jackson, P.C.
Certified Public Accountants
Akron, Ohio
February 12, 19X6

A report on an examination is unrestricted as to distribution by the client after it is issued. This means that a client can provide the information being examined and the related report to anyone.

In a *review*, in the United States, the practitioner provides a conclusion in the form of a *negative assurance*. In this form, the practitioner's report states whether any information came to the practitioner's attention to indicate that the assertions are not presented in all material respects in conformity with the applicable criteria. A review report is also unrestricted in its distribution.

In an *agreed-upon procedures* engagement, the procedures to be performed are agreed upon by the practitioner, the responsible party making the assertions, and the specific persons who are the intended users of the practitioner's report. The degree of assurance being conveyed in such a report will vary with the specific procedures agreed to and performed. Accordingly, such reports are limited in their distribution to only the involved parties, who would have the requisite knowledge about those procedures and the level of assurance that would result from them. The form of the practitioner's conclusion in an agreed-upon procedures engagement is that of a negative assurance.

Figure 23–19 summarizes the foregoing discussion.

FIGURE 23–19

Types of Engagements and Related Reports

TYPE OF ENGAGEMENT	AMOUNT OF EVIDENCE	LEVEL OF ASSURANCE	FORM OF CONCLUSION	DISTRIBUTION
Examination	Extensive	High	Positive	General
Review	Significant	Moderate	Negative	General
Agreed-upon procedures	Varying	Varying	Negative	Limited

REVIEW QUESTIONS

23–1   Give three examples of the special reports that a public accountant may be asked to issue. Explain why these reports would be requested.

23–2   How does materiality differ in special reports from that in reports prepared as a part of any ordinary audit? Why?

23–3   Why is an engagement letter often considered more important in the case of special reports than in the case of a regular audit?

23–4   Why are reports expressing an opinion on financial information other than financial statements prepared by public accountants?

23–5   Why are reports on the results of applying specified auditing procedures to financial information other than financial statements prepared by public accountants?

23–6   Why are reports on compliance with contractual agreements prepared by public accountants?

23–7   What is an engagement to report on control procedures at a service organization? Describe the two types of engagement the auditor might undertake when issuing such a report.

23–8   List and discuss the standards applicable to review engagements.

23–9   How do the general standards applicable to review engagements differ from generally accepted auditing standards?

23–10 Contrast the level of assurance provided by negative assurance discussed in Sections

8100, 8200, 8500 and 8600 of the *CICA Handbook* with the level of assurance provided by the opinion given in the auditor's report.

23–11 What is the intent of Section 9200, "Compilation Engagements," of the *CICA Handbook*?

23–12 Discuss the standards for compilation engagements, and explain why they differ from those for review engagements and audits.

23–13 The financial statements prepared for a compilation engagement may not be complete according to GAAP. Why is this exception permitted? Provide examples of information that might be excluded.

23–14 What are the three aspects of an auditor's involvement with a prospectus?

23–15 What financial statements are included in a prospectus?

23–16 What is negative assurance in the context of a prospectus? What is a comfort letter?

23–17 What are the auditor's responsibilities with respect to financial information (other than financial statements) included in a prospectus?

23–18 What is opinion shopping? Describe what actions a public accountant should take if requested to give an opinion on specific circumstances or transactions of an entity.

23–19 On what does the auditor comment in his or her comments on financial forecasts? What does the auditor disclaim an opinion on and why?

23–20 What should the auditor's comments on financial forecasts include?

23–21 What significant factors should an auditor consider in deciding on the nature, timing, and extent of audit procedures in the audit of pension costs and obligations?

23–22 What factors must an auditor consider when relying on an actuary in the audit of pension costs and obligations?

23–23 Define what is meant by attestation standards. Distinguish between attestation standards and generally accepted auditing standards.

DISCUSSION QUESTIONS AND PROBLEMS

23–24 Prentice Manufacturing Limited is a Canadian-controlled public company that issued shares to the public for the first time in 1975. The shares are listed on both Canadian and U.S. stock exchanges. Al Prentice, the president of the company, approaches Don Migwam, a public accountant, who is currently performing the interim audit of the company. The company has decided to issue interim financial statements for the first time.

Mr. Prentice would like to publish the interim results following Migwam's review, and has asked him to do whatever is necessary to give his "certification" and suggest whatever changes are necessary to present these interim statements in accordance with generally accepted accounting principles. He informs Migwam that the three month statement of earnings will also be circulated to minority shareholders in the United States and will therefore likely have to conform to the American accounting pronouncements (AICPA, FASB) as well as Canadian ones.

Required: Assume the role of Don Migwam, a public accountant. Outline the following:

(a) the points you would include in a letter to Mr. Prentice on your responsibility with respect to the interim financial statements.

(b) the nature of any work you would have to perform in this regard.

(CICA adapted)

23–25 Three public accountants, Annette, Maureen, and Carlos, were discussing various problems they encountered in their practices. The subject of the requirements in the

CICA Handbook for consolidated financial statements arose, and the following conversation took place:

Annette: "One of the things that causes me a lot of problems is the requirement that any company having subsidiaries must consolidate. That means even small private companies. I don't think that's reasonable. Some of my clients don't want them, don't need them, don't understand them, and sure don't want to pay for them."

Maureen: "I agree. Several of our small clients refuse to present consolidated statements at all, claiming that they just don't need them. For our larger clients, we often report on a dual set of statements, one consolidated and the other prepared on a non-consolidated basis for corporation purposes. We approach both problems by qualifying our report whenever statements are not consolidated. Many of the clients don't really care if we qualify on a technical point like that and it saves a lot of trouble."

Carlos: "Well, I'm inclined to agree with the *Handbook*. We'll generally give an adverse opinion, where the statements are not consolidated in accordance with Section 1590. What we do for clients issuing a dual set of statements is address our report on the consolidated statements to the shareholders and our report on the non-consolidated statements to the directors. Then our report to the directors contains a clean opinion. After the opinion paragraph, we have a final paragraph saying that because the statements are not prepared for issuance to the shareholders, they are prepared on a non-consolidated basis and that the statements differ materially from the consolidated statements on which we reported to shareholders."

Annette: "Whenever we are reporting on non-consolidated financial statements, we change our opinion paragraph to say 'in accordance with the basis of accounting outlined in Note X' instead of 'in accordance with generally accepted accounting principles.' Note X then outlines the basis of accounting (non-consolidated) and the client's reasons for not consolidating the statements. This overcomes problems where a dual set of statements is issued or where the client simply refuses to consolidate."

Discuss the viewpoints of each accountant, Annette, Maureen, and Carlos. (CICA adapted)

23–26 Your firm has just accepted the audit appointment of Floss Ltd., a major confectionery retailer with more than 60 leased stores in shopping malls across Canada. Every lease calls for a base rent plus a percentage of the store's sales. The "sales escalation" clause in each lease requires Floss Ltd. to have its auditor issue a report to the lessor on the sales of the store covered by the lease. However, the leases do not specify the nature and extent of the audit effort or the form of report.

The audited financial statements show only the aggregate figure for sales at all stores, and the previous audits had involved visiting only some of the locations each year on a rotating basis. The former auditors had not extended their procedures for the purposes of reporting to lessors, but had simply reported to individual lessors the following:

> As requested by Floss Ltd., we report that the sales of the corporation's store in Penticton Plaza for the year ended September 30, 19X7 are recorded in the amount of $_____ in the general ledger sales account of the corporation.
>
> Our examination of the corporation's financial statements for the year ended June 30, 19X7 was not directed to the determination of sales of individuals stores, nor have we examined the corporation's financial statements for the three month period subsequent to June 30, 19X7. We have not performed an audit of, and accordingly do not express an opinion on, the amount of sales referred to in the preceding paragraph.

This year several lessors, including one that owns nine malls containing Floss Ltd. stores, have objected to this report, stating that it provides them with no assurance that sales at individual store locations are fairly stated. You, as a representative of your firm, have explained to the management of Floss Ltd. that it would cost considerably more in time and audit effort to provide an audit opinion on sales at each particular store location.

The management of Floss Ltd. is very unhappy with the prospect of paying the extra costs for an individual audit of sales at each location. The chief financial officer has observed that "it seems to us that your firm should be able to give some reasonable intermediate level of audit assurance between nothing, which is what the former auditors' reports seem to indicate, and a full scope audit opinion." In particular, the officer has asked why your firm cannot simply report, solely on the basis of your financial statement audit, as follows:

As requested by Floss Ltd., we report that in our opinion the sales of the corporation's store at Hilltop Plaza (Hamilton, Ontario) for the year ended September 30, 19X7 in the amount of $_____ are fairly stated in all respects material to the financial statements taken as a whole.

Required: Discuss the three reporting approaches identified by the chief financial officer of Floss Ltd. and any other reporting approaches that could satisfy both Floss Ltd. management and the lessors.

(CICA adapted)

23–27 Evaluate the following comments about financial statements prepared by an accountant as part of a review engagement:

When a public accountant associates his or her name with financial statements, prepared by the accountant as part of a review engagement, the accountant's only responsibility is to the client and that is limited to the proper summarization and presentation on the financial statements of information provided by the client. The review engagement report clearly states that an audit was not conducted and that negative assurance only is expressed. If a user relies on the financial statements, it is at the user's risk; the user should never be able to hold the public accountant responsible for inadequate performance. The user should interpret the financial statements as if they had been prepared by management.

23–28 You are doing a review engagement and the related tax work for Regency Tools, Inc., a tool and die company with $2,000,000 in sales. Inventory is recorded at $125,000. Prior year unaudited statements, prepared by the company without assistance from a public accounting firm, disclose that the inventory is based on "historical cost estimated by management." You determine four facts:

1. The company has been growing steadily for the past five years.
2. The unit cost of typical material used by Regency Tools has increased dramatically for several years.
3. The inventory cost has been approximately $125,000 for five years.
4. Management intends to use a value of $125,000 again for 19X7.

When you discuss with management the need to get a physical count and an accurate inventory, the response is negative. Management is concerned about the effects on income taxes of a more realistic inventory. The company has never been audited and has always estimated the historical cost of inventory. You are convinced, based upon inquiry and ratio analysis, that a conservative evaluation would be $500,000 at historical cost.

Required:
(a) What are the generally accepted accounting principle requirements for valuation and disclosure of inventory for unaudited financial statements?
(b) Identify the potential legal and professional problems that you face in this situation.
(c) What procedures would you normally follow for a review engagement when the inventory is a material amount? Be as specific as possible.
(d) How should you resolve the problem in this situation? Identify alternatives, and evaluate the costs and benefits to each.

23–29   Herbert Lewis, a public accountant, is in the process of completing two client engagements involving partnerships. One, U.K. Co., requires an audit for credit purposes whereas the other, Punch Co., involves the preparation of unaudited statements and schedules. Louis Geroux is a partner of both U.K. Co. and Punch Co. and, although the major owner, he holds less than 50 percent of the capital of each. Both businesses are new clients for Lewis.

Lewis informed Geroux that partners' salaries and interest on loans in each business must be reported separately in the financial statements and not hidden in the income statement expense figures. On hearing Lewis' comment, Geroux became very upset and said that he intended to check the matter out with another chartered accountant.

Approximately one week after Lewis' remark, Geroux met with Lewis and said that the other chartered accountant had told him that separate disclosure was not necessary. According to Geroux, the other chartered accountant gave the following arguments:

1. Separate disclosure is only necessary when salary and interest are not at fair values of services provided or at current interest rates.

2. The *CICA Handbook* does not require Lewis to approve of everything on financial statements he prepares under a review engagement.

3. Materiality should be considered. Lewis should merely expand his materiality limits and ignore the issue.

4. Separate disclosure would be required if both companies were incorporated. Geroux informed Lewis that he would consider inviting the other chartered accountant to take over the engagements, if some reasonable compromise could not be worked out with Lewis.

Required: Assume that you are Herbert Lewis, and give a reply to Louis Geroux concerning each of the arguments raised. If Geroux refuses to accept your point of view, what action would you take and why?   (CICA adapted)

23–30   As a part of the audit of Ren Gold Manufacturing Company Ltd., management has requested you to provide an opinion on additional information that would be provided only to management and the board of directors. Management informs you that the intent is to use the basic financial statements for bankers, other creditors, and the two owners who are not involved in management. The audited financial statements together with the additional information on which you have provided an opinion are to be used only by management and the board. Management requests the inclusion of specific information, but asks that no audit work be done beyond what is needed for the audited financial statements. The following is requested:

1. A schedule of insurance in force.

2. The auditor's feelings about the adequacy of the insurance coverage.

3. A five-year summary of the most important company ratios. The appropriate ratios are to be determined at the auditor's discretion.

4. A schedule of notes payable accompanied by interest rates, collateral, and a payment schedule.

5. An aged trial balance of accounts receivable and evaluation of the adequacy of the allowance for uncollectible accounts.

6. A summary of fixed asset additions and investment credit taken on each class of additions.

7. Material weaknesses in internal control and recommendations to improve internal control.

Required: (a) What is the difference between the basic audited financial statements and additional information?

(b) What are the purposes of additional information accompanying basic financial statements?

(c) For the previously listed items (1 through 7), state which ones you would be prepared to provide an opinion on and which ones you would exclude. Give reasons for your answer.

(d) Identify three other items that may appropriately be included as additional information.

23–31 Your public accounting firm is the auditor of Taylor Fruit Farms, Inc., a company located in Penticton, B.C., and incorporated under the laws of British Columbia. You have been requested by the management of Taylor to issue an opinion under Section 5815 of the *CICA Handbook* with respect to Taylor's compliance under the terms of a chattel mortgage issued by J.L. Lockwood Corp. as a part of your audit of Taylor Fruit Farms, Inc.. J.L. Lockwood Corp. is a supplier of irrigation equipment. Much of the equipment, including that supplied to Taylor, is sold on a secured contract basis. Taylor Fruit Farms is an audit client of yours, but Lockwood is not.

In addition to the present equipment, Taylor informs you that Lockwood is evaluating whether they should sell another $500,000 of equipment to Taylor Fruit Farms.

You have been requested to send them the report under Section 5815 concerning the following matters:

1. The current ratio has exceeded 2.0 in each quarter of the unaudited statements prepared by management and the annual audited statements.

2. Total owners' equity is more than $800,000.

3. The company has not violated any of the legal requirements of British Columbia fruit-growing regulations.

4. Management is competent and has made reasonable business decisions in the past three years.

5. Management owns an option to buy additional fruit land adjacent to their present property.

Required:

(a) Define the purpose of a report under Section 5815.

(b) Is it necessary to conduct an audit of a company before it is acceptable to issue a report on compliance under Section 5815?

(c) Would you include all five matters listed above in your report? Explain why you would exclude any from the report.

23–32 Carl Monson, the owner of Major Products Manufacturing Inc., a small successful longtime audit client of your firm, has requested you to work with them in preparing three-year forecasted information for the year ending December 31, 19X8 and two subsequent years. Monson informs you he intends to use the forecasts, together with the audited financial statements, to seek additional financing to expand the business. Monson has had little experience in formal forecast preparation and counts on you to assist him in any way possible. He wants the most supportive opinion possible from your firm to add to the credibility of the forecast. He informs you he is willing to do anything necessary to help you prepare the forecast.

First, he wants projections of sales and revenues and earnings from the existing business, which he believes could continue to be financed from existing capital.

Second, he intends to buy a company in a closely related business that is currently operating unsuccessfully. Monson states that he wants to sell some of the operating assets of the business and replace them with others. He believes that the company can then be made highly successful. He has made an offer on the new business, subject to obtaining proper financing. He also informs you he has received an offer on the assets he intends to sell.

Required:

    (a) Explain circumstances under which it would and would not be acceptable to undertake the engagement.

    (b) Why is it important that Monson understand the nature of your reporting requirements before the engagement proceeeds?

    (c) With what information will Monson have to provide you before you can complete the forecasted statements? Be as specific as possible.

    (b) Discuss, in as specific terms as possible, the nature of the report you will issue with the forecasts, assuming that you are able to properly complete them.

23–33 O'Sullivan, a public accountant, has completed the audit of Sarawak Lumber Supply Co. Ltd., and has issued a standard unqualified report. In addition to a report on the overall financial statements, the company needs a special audit report on three specific accounts: sales, net fixed assets and inventory valued at FIFO. The report is to be issued to Sarawak's lessor, who bases annual rentals on these three accounts. O'Sullivan was not aware of the need for the special report until after the overall audit was completed.

Required:

    (a) Explain why O'Sullivan is unlikely to be able to issue the special audit report without additional audit tests.

    (b) What additional tests are likely to be needed before the special report can be issued?

    (c) Assume that O'Sullivan is able to satisfy all the requirements needed to issue the special report, and write the report. Make any necessary assumptions.

CASE

23–34 On-line Computer Services Ltd. (OCS) is a computer data processing and systems design service company owned and managed by René Cyr. On June 1, 19X7, Cyr approached Carol Ogryzlo, a partner in a CA firm, in order to discuss two matters concerning OCS. Cyr stated that his bank required him to have a **CA** firm review or audit his company's financial statements as at December 31, 19X7 as a condition for granting a $1,000,000 line of credit to finance a proposed expansion of the company's operations. He requested that the CA firm submit a letter comparing the work required for a review with that required for an audit.

Secondly, Cyr requested that the CA firm provide him with a report to satisfy his customers' auditors that OCS processes their accounting data properly. He complained that he is getting more and more telephone calls from auditors asking to visit his offices to discuss data processing controls and that it is becoming a real nuisance to comply with their requests. He would like to be able to send any auditors asking for information about data processing controls a copy of this special report instead of having to have a meeting with them.

Ogryzlo made notes indicating that Cyr was a knowledgeable and aggressive individual. These notes also emphasized that Cyr had stressed that all of his accounting and income tax work has been handled by his controller, whom Cyr considered to be well qualified and very competent. Cyr also stressed that he did not expect to have to pay any significant amount for the firm's services because of his controller's good work and because he is confident that OCS's data processing controls are excellent.

Upon his return to the office, Ogryzlo outlined the above situation to John Green, a chartered accountant employed by the CA firm. John Green was instructed to attend the offices of OCS and, after visiting the offices for a few hours, he obtained the summarized financial statements of OCS (Exhibit I) and prepared the following notes from his observations and discussions with OCS's personnel.

A. *Organization*
   — OCS is organized into the following three departments, described in B, C and D, each with their own manager and staff as follows:
     (i) Systems Design and Programming-20 system analysts and programmers
     (ii) Computer and Data Entry-10 computer and data entry operators
     (iii) Administration and Accounting-8 administrative and accounting personnel.

B. *Systems Design and Programming*
   — Systems analysts and programmers provide
     (i) custom-design services for OCS service bureau customers
     (ii) in-house system design and maintenance, and
     (iii) custom-design and programming services on a contract basis to customers with their own in-house computer.

C. *Computer and Data Entry*
   — OCS operates a large computer installation providing timesharing, on-line, remote batch and local batch processing services.
   — Most customers use their own input/output terminals connected by telecommunication lines.
   — OCS also does some customer data entry.

D. *Administration and Accounting*
   — All OCS internal accounting systems are on computer.
   — Accounting clerks enter accounting data and call for accounting reports to be printed.
   — Updating of the accounting system is done daily on a batch processing basis.
   — Accounting reports produced are reviewed in detail by the controller, Cyr, and department managers.
   — Management bonuses are based on accounting reports produced.

E. *Revenue*
   (i) Data processing services
     — Services rendered are computed by a software package that records all computer use by each customer as usage takes place.
     — The package produces weekly and monthly analyses of usage as well as monthly billings to customers.
     — Charges to customers are a function of three factors:
       (1) volume of input and output through their terminals
       (2) size of their data files on OCS's magnetic disks and
       (3) the amount of central processing unit time required for processing.
   (ii) Systems design and programming
     — Services rendered are accounted for on an OCS developed time and expense software package.
     — Personnel prepare weekly time and expense reports that are entered by an accounting clerk.
     — The system maintains work-in-process records by customer and produces various reports to assist management in billing customers.
     — Management-determined customer billings are also entered into the system to reduce work-in-process and record accounts receivable.
     — The system also produces an aged listing of receivables and records customer collections and write-offs.

F. *Security and Documentation*
   — Systems design and programming are conducted with a strong emphasis on security.

- All system and program documentation is maintained in a locked file cabinet, under supervision of a librarian.
- Documentation is released to analysts or programmers only upon presentation of a signed request from the system design and programming manager.
- All systems documentation includes systems descriptions, narratives, input/output specifications and layouts, computer data file structures and layouts, program flowcharts and source statement listings, user and operator procedure manuals, and details of all system changes.
- Manuals are issued to all professional staff, and the systems design and programming manager conducts regular seminars and training sessions to ensure manuals are understood.
- All major changes must be approved by the manager of systems design and programming.
- Systems design and programming staff use on-line visual display terminals for program development and maintenance.
- The software package, which controls the on-line program changes, limits access only to the disk drive containing test programs.
- Only the manager of system design and programming can have access by a special password to "live" programs and files.
- All computer programs are written in COBOL and contain extensive edit and accuracy checks on all inputs, computations and outputs.
- Data processing service operations are located behind locked doors.
- Visitors are only allowed entry after being identified by senior staff and must be accompanied by staff at all times.
- Computer room access is only by special magnetic coded plastic cards.
- All files are stored in fireproof vaults when not in use.
- Backup copies of all important files and programs are created every second day and transported to a bank vault for safekeeping.

G. *Management Review*
- All internal accounting systems input is reviewed by the responsible accounting personnel prior to entry into systems.
- All output is reconciled with input and file totals.
- All cheques are reviewed by Cyr and the Controller prior to signature.

Required:

Assume the role of John Green, CA and

(a) Draft the letter requested by René Cyr, the owner-manager of On-line Computer Services Ltd., comparing the work required and explaining the different benefits provided by a review and an audit.

(b) Prepare a memo to Carol Ogryzlo, the partner, providing a general outline of
   (1) the procedures required to support a report to the customers' auditors.
   (2) the nature and content of the report that would then be issued if the results of your examination are satisfactory.

24

OPERATIONAL AND COMPREHENSIVE AUDITING

LEARNING OBJECTIVES	THOROUGH STUDY OF THIS CHAPTER WILL ENABLE YOU TO:

1. Distinguish operational auditing from financial auditing

2. Give an overview of operational audits and operational auditors

3. Plan and perform an operational audit

4. Describe the PSAAC Auditing Standards and Guidelines

5. Understand the PSAAC Recommendations relating to a value-for-money audit

6. Report on effectiveness

☐ Operational auditing and comprehensive auditing are two types of audit services that use financial statement audit-type procedures to accomplish special enagement objectives. In operational audits, the objectives relate to whether an organization's operating procedures and methods are efficient and effective. The term comprehensive audit was introduced in Chapter 1 under the heading "Types of Audits." It was described as having three components:

- A financial statement audit
- A compliance audit
- A value-for-money audit

Both types of engagements are in demand and represent a growing segment of public accountants' activities. They are also conducted by other professionals such as internal auditors and governmental auditors. Because of the emphasis on audits of historical financial statements throughout the book, the first part of this chapter stresses differences and similarities between financial and operational audits; comprehensive auditing is treated as a separate topic in the second half of the chapter.

While there are similarities between operational auditing and the value-for-money component of comprehensive auditing, for purposes of this text, operational auditing and comprehensive auditing will be treated a separate topics.

Operational Auditing

Although *operational auditing* is generally understood to deal with efficiency and effectiveness, there is less agreement on the use of that term than one might expect. Many people prefer to use the terms *management auditing* or *performance auditing* instead of operational auditing to describe the review of organizations for efficiency and effectiveness. Those people typically describe operational auditing broadly and include evaluating internal controls and even testing those controls for effectiveness (tests of controls) as a part of operational auditing. Others do not distinguish between the terms *performance auditing, management auditing,* and *operational auditing.*

> **OBJECTIVE 1**
>
> Distinguish operational auditing from financial auditing.

We prefer to use *operational auditing* broadly, as long as the purpose of the test is to determine the effectiveness or efficiency of any part of an organization. Testing the effectiveness of internal controls by an internal auditor is therefore a part of operational auditing if the purpose is to help an organization operate its business more effectively or efficiently. Similarly, the determination of whether a company has adequately trained assembly line personnel is also operational auditing if the purpose is to determine whether the company is effectively and efficiently producing products.

Differences Between Operational and Financial Auditing

Three major differences exist between operational and financial auditing: purpose of the audit, distribution of the reports, and inclusion of nonfinancial areas in operational auditing.

Purpose of the audit   The major distinction between financial and operational auditing is the purpose of the tests. Financial auditing emphasizes whether historical information was correctly recorded. Operational auditing emphasizes effectiveness and efficiency. The financial audit is oriented to the past, whereas an operational audit concerns operating performance for the future. An operational auditor, for example, may evaluate whether a type of new material is being purchased at the lowest cost to save money on future raw material purchases.

Distribution of the reports   For financial auditing, the report typically goes to many users of financial statements, such as shareholders and bankers; whereas operational audit reports are intended primarily for management. As indicated in Chapter 2, well-defined wording is needed for financial auditing reports as a result of the widespread distribution of the reports. Because of the limited distribution of operational reports and the diverse nature of audits for efficiency and effectiveness, operational auditing reports vary considerably from audit to audit.

Inclusion of nonfinancial areas Operational audits cover any aspect of efficiency and effectiveness in an organization and can therefore involve a wide variety of activities. For example, the effectiveness of an advertising program or efficiency of factory employees would be part of an operational audit. Financial audits are limited to matters that directly affect the fairness of financial statement presentations.

Effectiveness Versus Efficiency

Effectiveness refers to the accomplishment of objectives, whereas efficiency refers to the resources used to achieve those objectives. An example of effectiveness is the production of parts without defects. Efficiency concerns whether those parts are produced at minimum cost.

OBJECTIVE 2

Give an overview of operational audits and operational auditors.

Effectiveness Before an operational audit for effectiveness can be performed, there must be specific criteria for what is meant by effectiveness. An example of an operational audit for effectiveness would be to assess whether the elevator maintenance department of a hotel chain has met its assigned objective of achieving elevator safety in the chain's many hotels. Before the operational auditor can reach a conclusion about the department's effectiveness, criteria for elevator safety must be set. For example, is the objective to see that all elevators in the chain's hotels are inspected at least once a year? Is the objective to ensure that no fatalities occurred due to elevator breakdowns, or that no breakdowns occurred?

Efficiency Like effectiveness, there must be defined criteria for what is meant by doing things more efficiently before operational auditing can be meaningful. It is often easier to set efficiency than effectiveness criteria if *efficiency* is defined as reducing cost without reducing effectiveness. For example, if two different production processes manufacture a product of identical quality, the process with the lower cost is considered more efficient.

The following are several types of inefficiencies that frequently occur and often are uncovered through operational auditing.

TYPES OF INEFFICIENCY	EXAMPLE
■ Acquisition of goods and services is excessively costly.	■ Bids for purchases of materials are not required.
■ Raw materials are not available for production when needed.	■ An entire assembly line must be shut down because necessary materials were not ordered.
■ There is duplication of effort by employees.	■ Identical production records are kept by both the accounting and production departments because they are unaware of each other's activities.
■ Work is done that serves no purpose.	■ Copies of vendor's invoices and receiving reports are sent to the production department where they are filed without ever being used.
■ There are too many employees.	■ The office work could be done effectively with one less secretary.

Relationship Between Operational Auditing and Internal Controls

In Chapter 9, it was stated that management establishes internal control to help it meet its own goals. Certainly, two important goals of all organizations are efficiency and effectiveness. The following five concerns in setting up good internal control were identified and discussed in Chapter 9:

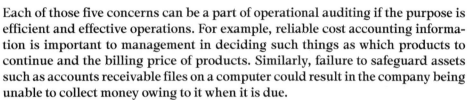

- To maintain reliable systems
- To ensure timely preparation of reliable information
- To safeguard assets including records
- To optimize the use of resources
- To prevent and detect error and fraud

Each of those five concerns can be a part of operational auditing if the purpose is efficient and effective operations. For example, reliable cost accounting information is important to management in deciding such things as which products to continue and the billing price of products. Similarly, failure to safeguard assets such as accounts receivable files on a computer could result in the company being unable to collect money owing to it when it is due.

There are two significant differences in internal control evaluation and testing for financial and operational auditing: the purpose of the evaluation and testing of internal controls, and the normal scope of internal control evaluation.

The primary purpose of internal control evaluation for financial auditing is to determine the extent of substantive audit testing required. The purpose of operational auditing is to evaluate efficiency and effectiveness of internal control and make recommendations to management. The control procedures might be evaluated in the same way for both financial and operational auditing, but the purpose is different. To illustrate, an operational auditor might determine if internal verification procedures for duplicate sales invoices are effective to ensure that the company does not offend customers but also receives all money owed. A financial auditor often does the same internal control evaluation, but the primary purpose is to reduce confirmation of accounts receivable or other substantive procedures. A secondary purpose, however, of many financial audits is to also make operational recommendations to management.

The scope of internal control evaluation for financial audits is restricted to matters affecting financial statement accuracy, whereas operational auditing concerns any control affecting efficiency or effectiveness. Therefore, for example, an operational audit could be concerned with policies and procedures established in the marketing department to determine the effectiveness of catalogues used to market products.

Types of Operational Audits

There are three broad categories of operational audits: functional, organizational, and special assignments. In each case, part of the audit is likely to concern evaluating internal controls for efficiency and effectiveness.

Functional

Functions are a means of categorizing the activities of a business, such as the billing function or production function. There are many different ways to categorize and subdivide functions. For example, there is an accounting function, but there are also cash disbursement, cash receipt, and payroll disbursement functions. There is a payroll function, but there are also hiring, timekeeping, and payroll disbursement functions.

As the name implies, a functional audit deals with one or more functions in an organization. It could concern, for example, the payroll function for a division or for the company as a whole.

A functional audit has the advantage of permitting specialization by auditors. Certain auditors within an internal audit staff can develop considerable expertise in an area, such as production engineering. They can more efficiently spend all their time auditing in that area. A disadvantage of functional auditing is the failure to evaluate interrelated functions. The production engineering function, for example, interacts with manufacturing and other functions in an organization.

Organizational

An operational audit of an organization deals with an entire organizational unit, such as a department, branch, or subsidiary. The emphasis in an organizational audit is on how efficiently and effectively functions interact. The plan of organization and the methods to coordinate activities are especially important in this type of audit.

Special Assignments

Special operational auditing assignments arise at the request of management. There are a wide variety of such audits. Examples include determining the cause of an ineffective EDP system, investigating the possibility of fraud or other irregularities in a division, and making recommendations for reducing the cost of a manufactured product.

Who Performs Operational Audits

Operational audits are usually performed by one of two groups: internal auditors or public accounting firms.

Internal Auditors

Internal auditors are in such a unique position to perform operational audits that some people use *internal auditing* and *operational auditing* interchangeably. It is, however, inappropriate to conclude that all operational auditing is done by internal auditors or that internal auditors do only operational auditing. Many internal audit departments do both operational and financial audits. Often, they are done simultaneously. An advantage that internal auditors have in doing operational audits is that they spend all their time working for the company they are auditing. They thereby develop considerable knowledge about the company and its business, which is essential to effective operational auditing.

To maximize their effectiveness, the internal audit department should report to the audit committee of the board of directors although in practice they often report to the president or a senior vice-president. In the latter case, they should also have access to and ongoing communications with the audit committee. This organizational structure helps internal auditors remain independent. For example, if internal auditors report to the controller, it is difficult for the internal auditor to evaluate independently and make recommendations to senior management about inefficiencies in the controller's operations.

In 1978, the Institute of Internal Auditors, an organization that functions for internal auditors much like the CICA does for CAs, the CGAAC for CGAs and the SMAC for CMAs, issued *Standards for the Practice of Internal Auditing* to provide practice guidelines to internal auditors. One important part of those standards is a section on the appropriate scope of internal auditors' work, which is described as follows:

- Internal auditors should review the reliability and integrity of financial and operating information and the means used to identify, measure, classify, and report such information.
- Internal auditors should review the internal control structure established to ensure compliance with those policies, plans, procedures, laws, and regulations which could have significant impact on operations and reports and should determine whether the organization is in compliance.
- Internal auditors should review the means of safeguarding assets and, as appropriate, verify the existence of such assets.
- Internal auditors should appraise the economy and efficiency with which resources are employed.
- Internal auditors should review operations or programs to ascertain whether results are consistent with established objectives and goals and whether the operations or programs are being carried out as planned.[1]

Notice that the last two items involve operational auditing.

Public Accounting Firms

When public accounting firms do an audit of historical financial statements, part of the audit usually consists of identifying operational problems and making recommendations that may benefit the audit client. The recommendations can be made orally, but they are typically made by use of a *management letter*. Management letters were discussed in Chapter 22.

The background knowledge about a client's business that an external auditor must obtain in doing an audit often provides useful information for giving operational recommendations. For example, suppose the auditor determined that inventory turnover for a client slowed considerably during the current year. The auditor is likely to determine the cause of the reduction to evaluate the possibility of obsolete inventory that would misstate the financial statements. In determining the cause of the reduced inventory turnover, the auditor may identify operational causes, such as ineffective inventory acquisition policies, that can be brought to the attention of management. An auditor who has a broad business background and experience with similar businesses is more likely to be effective at providing clients with relevant operational recommendations than a person who lacks those qualities.

It is also common for a client to engage a public accounting firm to do operational auditing for one or more specific parts of its business. Usually, such an engagement would occur only if the company does not have an internal audit staff or the internal audit staff lacks expertise in a certain area. In most cases, a management consulting staff of the public accounting firm, rather than the auditing staff, performs these services. For example, a company can ask the public accounting firm to evaluate the efficiency and effectiveness of its computer systems.

Independence and Competence of Operational Auditors

The two most important qualities for an operational auditor are *independence* and *competence*.

Whom the auditor reports to is important to ensure that investigation and recommendations are made without bias. Independence is seldom a problem for public accounting firm auditors because they are not employed by the company

---

1   *Standards for the Practice of Internal Auditing,* 1978 by the Institute of Internal Auditors, Inc. 249 Maitland Avenue, Altamonte Springs, FL 32701. Reprinted with permission.

being audited. As stated earlier, independence of internal auditors is enhanced by having the internal audit department report to the audit committee or president.

The responsibilities of operational auditors can also affect their independence. The auditor should not be responsible for performing operating functions in a company or for correcting deficiencies when ineffective or inefficient operations are found. For example, it would negatively affect auditors' independence if they were responsible for designing an EDP system for purchases or for correcting it if deficiencies were found during an audit of the purchasing system.

It is acceptable for auditors to recommend changes in operations, but operating personnel must have the authority to accept or reject the recommendations. If auditors had the authority to require implementation of their recommendations, the auditor would actually have the responsibility for auditing his or her own work the next time an audit was conducted. Independence would therefore be reduced.

The Institute of Internal Auditors considers independence of internal auditors critical. It has established in its *Statement of Responsibilities of Internal Auditing* a special requirement for independence, as follows:

- Internal auditors should be independent of the activities they audit. Internal auditors are independent when they can carry out their work freely and objectively. Independence permits internal auditors to render the impartial and unbiased judgments essential to the proper conduct of audits. It is achieved through organizational status and objectivity.

  Organizational status should be sufficient to assure a broad range of audit coverage, and adequate consideration of and effective action on audit findings and recommendations.

  Objectivity requires that internal auditors have an independent mental attitude, and an honest belief in their work product. Drafting procedures, designing, installing, and operating systems, are not audit functions. Performing such activities is presumed to impair audit objectivity.

Competence is, of course, necessary to determine the cause of operational problems and to make appropriate recommendations. Competence is a major problem when operational auditing deals with wide-ranging operating problems. For example, imagine the difficulties of finding qualified internal auditors who can evaluate both the effectiveness of an advertising program and the efficiency of a production assembly process. The internal audit staff doing that type of operational auditing would presumably have to include some personnel with backgrounds in marketing and others in production.

Criteria for Evaluating Efficiency and Effectiveness

A major difficulty found in operational auditing is in deciding on specific criteria for evaluating whether operations have been efficient and effective. In auditing historical financial statements, GAAP are the broad criteria for evaluating fair presentation. Audit objectives are used to set more specific criteria in deciding whether GAAP have been followed. In operational auditing, no such well-defined criteria exist.

One approach to setting criteria for operational auditing is to state that the objectives are to determine whether some aspect of the entity could be made more effective or efficient and to recommend improvements. This approach may be adequate for experienced and well-trained auditors, but it would be difficult for most auditors to follow such a poorly defined approach.

OBJECTIVE 3

Plan and perform an operational audit.

Specific Criteria   More specific criteria are usually desirable before operational auditing is started. For example, suppose you are doing an operational audit of the equipment layout in plants for a company. The following are some specific criteria, stated in the form of questions, that might be used to evaluate plant layouts:

- Were all plant layouts approved by home office engineering at the time of original design?
- Has home office engineering done a reevaluation study of plant layout in the past five years?
- Is each piece of equipment operating at 60 percent of capacity or more for at least three months each year?
- Does layout facilitate the movement of new materials to the production floor?
- Does layout facilitate the production of finished goods?
- Does layout facilitate the movement of finished goods to distribution centers?
- Does the plant layout effectively utilize existing equipment?
- Is the safety of employees endangered by plant layout?

Sources of Criteria   There are several sources that the operational auditor can utilize in developing specific evaluation criteria. These include the following:

- *Historical performance*. A simple set of criteria can be based on actual results from prior periods (or audits). The idea behind using these criteria is to determine whether things have become "better" or "worse" in comparison. The advantage of these criteria is that they are easy to derive; however, they may not provide much insight into how well or poorly the audited entity is really doing.
- *Comparable performance*. Most entities subject to an operational audit are not unique; there are many similar entities within the overall organization or outside it. In those cases, the performance data of comparable entities are an excellent source for developing criteria. For internal comparable entities, the data are usually readily available. Where the comparable entities are outside the organization, they will often be willing to make such information available. It is also often available through industry groups and governmental regulatory agencies.
- *Engineered standards*. In many types of operational auditing engagements, it may be possible and appropriate to develop criteria based on engineered standards – for example, time and motion studies to determine production output rates. These criteria are often time consuming and costly to develop, as they require considerable expertise; however, they may be very effective in solving a major operational problem and well worth the cost. It is also possible that some standards can be developed by industry groups for use by all their members, thereby spreading the cost and reducing it for each participant. These may be groups in the industry of the subject organization, or functional groups such as an EDP users' organization.
- *Discussion and agreement*. Sometimes objective criteria are difficult or costly to obtain, and criteria are developed through simple discussion and agreement. The parties involved in this process should include management of the entity to be audited, the operational auditor, and the entity or persons to whom the findings will be reported.

Phases in Operational Auditing   There are three phases in an operational audit: planning, evidence accumulation and evaluation, and reporting and follow-up.

Planning   The planning in an operational audit is similar to that discussed in earlier chapters for an audit of historical financial statements. Like audits of financial statements, the operational auditor must determine the scope of the engagement and communicate it to the organizational unit. It is also necessary to staff the engagement properly, obtain background information about the organizational unit, understand internal control, and decide on the appropriate evidence to accumulate.

The major difference between planning an operational audit and a financial audit is the extreme diversity in operational audits. Because of the diversity, it is often difficult to decide on specific objectives of an operational audit. The objectives will be based on the criteria developed for the engagement. As discussed in the preceding sections, these will depend on the specific circumstances at hand. For example, the objectives for an operational audit of the effectiveness of internal controls over petty cash would be dramatically different from those of an operational audit of the efficiency of a research and development department.

Another difference is that staffing is often more complicated in an operational audit than in a financial audit. This again is because of the breadth of the engagements. Not only are the areas diverse – for example, production control, advertising, and strategy planning – but the objectives within those areas often require special technical skills. For example, the auditor may need an engineering background to evaluate performance on a major construction project.

Finally, it is important to spend more time with the interested parties agreeing on the terms of the engagement and the criteria for evaluation in an operational audit than in a financial audit. This was alluded to in the preceding section for criteria developed through discussion. Regardless of the source of the criteria for evaluation, *it is essential that the auditee, the auditor, and the sponsor of the engagement be in clear and complete agreement on the objectives and criteria involved*. That agreement will facilitate effective and successful completion of the operational audit.

Evidence   The seven types of evidence studied in Chapter 6 and used throughout the book are
Accumulation and   equally applicable for operational auditing. Because internal controls and operat-
Evaluation   ing procedures are a critical part of operational auditing, it is common to extensively use documentation, client inquiry, and observation. Confirmation and mechanical accuracy are used less extensively for most operational audits than for financial audits because accuracy is not the purpose of most operational audits.

To illustrate evidence accumulation in operational auditing, we return to the example discussed earlier about evaluating the safety of elevators for a chain of hotels. Assume there is agreement that the objective is to determine whether the inspection is made annually of each elevator in every hotel in the chain by a competent inspector. To satisfy the completeness objective, the auditor would, for example, examine blueprints of the hotel buildings and elevator locations and trace them to the head office's master-list to ensure that all elevators are included in the population. Additional tests on newly constructed hotels would be appropriate to assess the timeliness with which the central listing is updated.

Assuming the head office list is determined to be complete, the auditor can select a sample of elevator locations and evidence can be collected as to the timing and frequency of inspections. The auditor may want to consider inherent risk by doing heavier sampling of older elevators or elevators with previous safety defects. The auditor may also want to examine evidence to determine whether the elevator inspectors were competent to evaluate elevator safety. The auditor may, for example, evaluate inspectors' qualifications by reviewing résumés, training programs, competency exams, and performance reports.

It is also likely that the auditor would want to reperform the inspection procedures for a sample of elevators to obtain evidence of inconsistencies in reported and actual conditions.

In the same manner as for financial audits, operational auditors must accumulate sufficient competent evidence to afford a reasonable basis for a conclusion about the objectives being tested. In the elevator example, the auditor must accumulate sufficient evidence about elevator safety inspections. After the evidence is accumulated, the auditor must decide whether it is reasonable to conclude that an inspection is made annually of each elevator in each hotel owned by the chain by a competent inspector.

Reporting and Follow-up

Two major differences between operational and financial auditing reports affect operational auditing reports. First, in operational audits, the report is usually sent only to management, with a copy to the unit being audited. The lack of third-party users reduces the need for standardized wording in operational auditing reports. Second, the diversity of operational audits requires a tailoring of each report to address the scope of the audit, findings, and recommendations.

The combination of these two factors results in major differences in operational auditing reports. Report writing often takes a significant amount of time to clearly communicate audit findings and recommendations.

Follow-up is common in operational auditing when recommendations are made to management. The purpose is to determine whether the recommended changes were made, and if not, why.

Examples of Operational Audit Findings

Each issue of the *Internal Auditor*, a bimonthly publication of the Institute of Internal Auditors, includes several internal operational audit findings submitted by practicing internal auditors. In reviewing a multitude of these reported findings, the authors concluded that almost all of them relate to efficiency rather than effectiveness. We believe the reason is that readers of the journal find efficiency findings more interesting reading than those related to effectiveness. If someone can state, for example, that an operational audit resulted in a savings of $68,000, it is likely to be more interesting than reporting on improved accuracy of financial reporting. The following examples from the *Internal Auditor* include two related to effectiveness and the rest to efficiency.

OUTSIDE JANITORIAL FIRM SAVES $160,000

- An internal auditor reviewed the efficiency and effectiveness of the janitorial services furnished by state employees for the buildings in the state capitol complex. The audit disclosed the costs of the janitorial services were excessive when compared to similar services performed by outside janitorial firms. In addition, the auditors found many janitorial tasks were not completed as required, resulting in unacceptable quality. A study of alternate janitorial services indicated equal or better service could be provided by an outside janitorial firm and at a saving of $137,000 a year. The auditor recommended the state seek competitive bids and contract with the janitorial firm submitting the lowest bid which meets the specifications. The resultant contract actually saved more than $160,000, and the quality of the cleaning improved noticeably.

MORE TIMELY CREDIT-MEMO PROCESSING

- A frequent complaint heard by the internal auditor concerned the inordinate amount of time required to process customers' credit memos. The auditor found the complaint was justified because an average of 14 working days elapsed between the receipt of the request and the actual issuance of the memo. In some cases, as many as 21 working days elapsed before the memo was issued.

  Using a time-phased flowchart, the auditor determined the requests were not moving in an efficient linear flow. As a matter of fact, the time-phased flowchart looked like a zigzag with a bad case of hiccups. The requests moved from the originator for removal of the supporting documents. The request then went back again to one of the approving departments for sorting, coding, and batching. Finally, the request was transmitted to the computer to issue the memo. Each step required from one to five working days, depending on the workload and complexity of the request.

  The auditor recommended each approving department perform all the required functions the first time it handled the request and substitute well-controlled procedures for after-the-fact approvals in place of the preapprovals. The recommendation was adopted, and credit memos are now being issued within five working days after the request is received. The auditor noted a higher degree of customers' satisfaction, and complaints have ceased.

ACQUISITION AUDITS SAVE $150,000

- Wanting to expand their share of the market, the company entered into agreements to acquire two smaller but similar companies. To help determine the fairness of the prices for the proposed purchases, the internal auditor performed several acquisition audits.

  The internal auditor found one company's net worth overstated by approximately $50,000 owing to obsolete inventory, idle assets, and unrecorded liabilities. The internal auditor also found the company was committed to irrevocable lease agreements totaling $700,000 as well as purchase agreements amounting to $500,000. The audit's results caused management to reduce the purchase price by $50,000 and also revise its postacquisition plans.

  During the audit of another company's books, the internal auditor found unrecorded travel and entertainment reports, salesperson's commissions, and purchase invoices. This finding alone reduced the net worth of the company by about $100,000. The auditor also found an improper sales cutoff for the period which would cause a future overstatement of the company's net worth.

  As a result of this audit, the purchase price was reduced for a savings of more than $100,000. The lack of controls which caused the overstatement of the company's net worth was corrected as a result of the internal auditor's recommendations.

USE THE RIGHT TOOL

- The company leased 25 heavy-duty trucks for use by service employees who installed and repaired about 20,000 vending machines in a large metropolitan area. All of the trucks were equipped with hydraulic lift-gates for loading and unloading vending machines.

  The internal auditor found that only a few of the trucks were actually delivering and picking up vending machines. The large majority of the trucks were used for service calls which consisted of on-the-scene repair of coin boxes or other simple adjustments not requiring the hydraulic lift-gates.

  The auditor recommended most of the heavy-duty trucks be phased out and replaced by conventional light vans. Management agreed and the savings in lease rates and operating expenses were estimated at $25,000 a year.

DOG-GONE REVENUES

■ During a review of the county agency responsible for collecting dog-licensing fees, the auditor wondered whether a lot of dogs did not live very long or the dog owners were not renewing the annual dog licenses as the law required. Fortunately for dog lovers, the auditor found the latter to be true. The auditor determined that the main reason for the nonrenewals was that no follow-up procedures existed. The county agency had never contacted owners about the nonrenewal of the dog licenses.

The auditor knew that another county's dog-licensing agency mailed a reminder letter to dog owners when the licence was not renewed and over a third of the owners who received the letter paid the fee. The auditor recommended such a procedure be instituted and, as a result, more than $40,000 in renewal fees were collected for an expenditure of less than $1,000.

COMPUTER PROGRAMS SAVE MANUAL LABOR

■ Employee profit-sharing legislation required an annual audit of profit-sharing plans. These internal auditors not only tested the finances, they also performed an operational review which provided a number of valuable recommendations to management.

The EDP auditors devised a number of computer-assisted audit programs to test control over enrollment in and termination from the company's profit-sharing plan. The computer assistance saved much manual labor and detected a number of findings such as employees on the plan with less than the required one year of service and terminated employees still on the plan. The computer portion of the audit program also detected conflicting data between the payroll and profit-sharing plan master files.

When shown the results of the audit, management corrected all the problems and instituted additional controls to prevent the problems in the future. And the additional controls were . . . well, guess. Yep, they wanted the EDP auditors to leave their computer programs in the machine. The profit-sharing-plan manager uses the programs periodically as a control to detect enrollment errors.

TIMELY DEPOSITING

■ During a cash review, the internal auditor found that bank deposits were not made until several days after the cash and cheques were received. The cause was a very complicated reconciliation/distribution process requiring 3 to 15 days to complete.

Management agreed to implement a direct-deposit or electronic-funds-transfer system and to perform the reconciliation/distribution process after the funds were deposited. The system's estimated additional interest is about $120,000 a year.

LAPPING OF ACCOUNTS RECEIVABLE

■ The company's treasurer saw the employee on a Saturday in Las Vegas and at work on Friday in New York and on Monday also. The employee worked late a few evenings each week and this was attributed to diligence. The employee never took a vacation, but claimed he needed extra money and took the vacation time as extra pay. The employee's duties were to open the mail, sort the cheques, count the cash, prepare the bank deposit, and post the accounts receivable ledger. Oh yes, the employee worked for a travel agency that received a great deal of cash from customers.

The perfect setup for lapping . . . as the auditor discovered.

After the Las Vegas incident, the company's treasurer thought it might be a good idea to have the auditor go over the books rather than wait for the year-end closing audit. Not that there was anything wrong, but seeing the employee in Las Vegas, well...

While reviewing deposit slips, the auditor found the details on 75 percent were different from what was recorded in cash receipts and posted to the accounts-receivable ledger. The auditor also determined from customers that cheques had not been credited on the recorded deposit date, but on a subsequent date. No doubt about it, the employee was manipulating the accounts receivable for personal gain, but by how much?

Fortunately for the auditor, the employee gave customers a receipt whenever cash was received and most of the customers had retained their receipts. The auditor secured some copies of these receipts and traced them to the deposit slips prepared on the same dates as the receipts. None of the slips agreed with the signed receipts. In fact, almost no cash was ever deposited. The amount of manipulation of the books was monumental – no wonder the employee worked nights and never had time for a vacation.

As we said, it was a perfect setup for lapping. No separation of duties, confirmation of accounts receivable, or internal controls. The auditor is still trying to determine the extent of loss.[2]

Comprehensive Auditing

The Public Sector Accounting and Auditing Committee (PSAAC) was introduced in Chapter 1 as one of the three Canadian Institute of Chartered Accountants' standard setting bodies; the other two are the Accounting Standards Board and the Auditing Standards Board. PSAAC has the responsibility for issuing accounting and auditing standards which contain *Recommendations* dealing with accounting and auditing issues in the public sector.

Paragraph .04 of the Introduction to the *PSAAC Handbook* indicates that the Accounting Recommendations apply to not-for-profit entities; the Accounting Recommendations in the *CICA Handbook* apply to profit-oriented entities partly- or wholly-owned by a federal, provincial or territorial government. An example of such a profit-oriented entity would be Manitoba Telephone System. paragraph .05 states that "the Auditing Recommendations of the Committee are intended to apply to all entities in the public sector."

As was pointed out in Chapter 1, under various legislation, the federal and provincial governments are required to have comprehensive audits of the many government departments for which they are responsible. In addition, as was also mentioned in Chapter 1, federal Crown corporations are required to have both annual financial audits and *special examinations* (essentially a value-for-money audit) performed on their operations and activities at least once every five years.

The Canadian Comprehensive Auditing Foundation was also introduced in Chapter 1.[3] It conducts research into, publishes material about, brings together people interested in, and provides courses dealing with comprehensive auditing. The theme that runs through the reports of the Auditor General of Canada, Denis Desautels, and the provincial auditors general, through material developed and

---

2 From *Round Table*, 1982 by The Institute of Internal Auditors, Inc., 249 Maitland Avenue, Altamonte Springs, FL 32701. Reprinted with permission.

3 The interested reader is directed to the Canadian Comprehensive Auditing Foundation (CCAF), whose offices are in Ottawa. The CCAF has published and continues to publish a wealth of material of interest. Much of the material in this part of Chapter 24 is drawn from CCAF material.

disseminated by the CCAF and through the PSAAC standards is accountability.[4] Comprehensive auditing, through its combination of a financial audit, a compliance audit, and a value-for-money audit(s) helps assess in a more complete way whether accountability has been served than does a financial audit alone.

PSAAC Auditing Standards and Guidelines

PSAAC Auditing Standard 1, "Auditing in the Public Sector," provides a setting for the Auditing Standards that followed it. As was pointed out above, a comprehensive audit has three components. PSAAC Auditing Standards 2, "Audit of Financial Statements in the Public Sector," 3, "Auditing for Compliance with Legislative and Related Authorities," and 4, "Value-for-Money Auditing Standards" were developed to provide guidance in the three kinds of audit respectively.

> **OBJECTIVE 4**
>
> Describe the PSAAC Auditing Standards and Guidelines.

Financial audits and compliance audits have a long history; auditors have been performing them for some time. Value-for-money audits are a newer concept and it is probably for that reason that PSAAC has issued two (and will shortly be issuing a third) Auditing Guidelines that pertain to value-for-money audits: 1, "Planning Value-for-Money Audits"; 2, "Knowledge of the Audit Entity in Planning Value-for-Money Audits"; and 3, "Engaging and Using Specialists in Value-for-Money Audits."

PSAAC Auditing Standards 2 and 3 are similar to the auditing standards in the *CICA Handbook* and will not be discussed further. Auditing Standard 4 will be dealt with in some detail since there are fairly significant differences between a financial audit and a value-for-money audit. At the same time there are many similarities between an operational audit, discussed in the first part of this chapter, and a value-for-money audit.

Value-for-Money Audits

There are two General Standards; the first is of particular interest because it recognizes the diversity of backgrounds that a value-for-money audit team will require. It states in paragraph .10:

- The person or persons carrying out the examination should possess or collectively possess the knowledge and competence necessary to fulfill the requirements of the particular audit.

> **OBJECTIVE 5**
>
> Understand the PSAAC Recommendations relating to a value-for-money audit.

Notice the similarity to the first two general standards relating to attestation engagements in Table 23-2. The knowledge and competence requirements are broader than for a financial audit.

The second General Standard for value-for-money audits appears in paragraph .14 and states the requirements with respect to due care and an objective state of mind.

There are three Examination Standards for value-for-money audits; the first and third are similar to the first and third examination standards of GAAS discussed in Chapter 1 of the text. The second Examination Standard is very different from the GAAS second examination standard but similar to the third general standard for attestation engagements listed in Table 23-2.

---

4 The CCAF publication *Comprehensive Auditing: Concepts, Components and Characteristics* (undated) states that accountability is "based on the assumption that those who confer responsibility should expect and should receive an appropriate accounting for the discharge of responsibilities conferred" (page 8). For example, voters confer responsibility to the elected members of parliament who should in turn be accountable to those voters; Parliament confers responsibility to the many departments and organizations that run the country such as Revenue Canada and National Defence – they should in turn be accountable to Parliament.

Earlier in this chapter, criteria for evaluating efficiency and effectiveness were discussed. Recall that the text stated that determining appropriate criteria to evaluate efficiency and effectiveness often proved difficult for operational auditors. As you might imagine, selecting appropriate criteria for a value-for-money audit is also difficult but necessary. Paragraph .24 states:

- Criteria for evaluating the matters subject to audit should be identified and the auditor should assess their suitability in the circumstances.

The following six paragraphs in the Standard expand on the Recommendation.

The Reporting Standards are not as specific as the reporting standards of GAAS for financial statement audits discussed in Chapter 2 because every value-for-money audit, like every operational audit, is different and the report must be tailored to the audit. Paragraph .37 suggests that the auditor's report should:

- Describe the objectives and the scope of the audit including any limitations therein.
- State that the examination was performed in accordance with the standards recommended in [Auditing Statement 4] and accordingly included such tests and other procedures as the auditor considered necesary in the circumstances.
- Identify the criteria [the auditor used] and describe the findings which form the basis for the auditor's conclusion.
- State the auditor's conclusions.

The report will vary depending on the auditor's mandate which is likely to vary from government department to government department and even within single departments. Like an operational audit report, the report may include the auditor's recommendations and management's response to those recommendations.

There are several other points worth noting in the Auditing Standard. Paragraphs .11 to .13 describe the different skills needed for a value-for-money audit and suggest an audit team might include persons with such diverse skills as engineering, statistical analysis, human resource management, and economics. The auditor in charge must be skilled in value-for-money auditing and also be able to coordinate the activities of these disparate specialists.

The auditor is concerned with the *significance* rather than the materiality of deviations or problems discovered; significance has more of a qualitative connotation and is therefore more appropriate than materiality, which has more of a quantitative connotation. For example, an auditor doing a value-for-money audit of the department of Employment & Immigration Canada that deals with refugees would probably assess the average processing time for an application and have to determine whether variances from departmental guidelines that he or she discovered were significant enough to report.

Effectiveness

OBJECTIVE 6
Report on effectiveness.

The reports the Auditor General of Canada and the provincial auditors general provide to their respective legislature are of a form called *direct reporting*. The form of report is similar to that provided to management on completion of a management audit. The report summarizes the auditor's findings with respect to an entity or portion of an entity that was audited. The report may or may not contain recommendations by the auditor and may or may not include comments from management responding to the auditor's findings and recommendations. The important point is that the report is prepared by the auditor and the contents are therefore the auditor's representations; remember, the representations in financial statements are those of management and the auditor's role is to provide an opinion on those representations.

The Canadian Comprehensive Auditing Foundation set an independent panel to study how effectiveness could best be audited and reported. The panel's report was published in 1987; it recommended that management issue a report in which they would make representations about effectiveness and that auditors opine on those representations. The panel suggested twelve attributes of effectiveness on which management would make the representations in its report.

The panel indicated that it believed the twelve attributes were a unit and suggested that all twelve attributes should be considered by management in making their representations. Management need not give all twelve attributes equal weight but all should be considered; an explanation should be provided by management with respect to any attribute that was not considered. The twelve attributes of effectiveness are:

- management direction
- relevance
- appropriateness
- acheivement of intended results
- acceptance
- secondary impacts
- costs and productivity
- responsiveness
- financial results
- working environment
- protection of assets
- monitoring and reporting[5]

Summary
The value-for-money component of comprehensive auditing is becoming increasingly important as federal, provincial, and municipal governments, school boards, hospitals, universities, and all other public sector organizations try to deal with declining revenues and increasing costs. Accountability to those who confer responsibility and funding must be provided.

REVIEW QUESTIONS

24–1 Describe what is meant by an operational audit.

24–2 Explain the differences in the terms *operational, performance,* and *management audits.*

24–3 Identify the three major differences between financial and operational auditing.

24–4 Distinguish between efficiency and effectiveness in operational audits. State one example of an operational audit explaining efficiency and another explaining effectiveness.

---

5 The source of the material on effectiveness is *Effectiveness: Reporting and Auditing in the Public Sector,* Ottawa: Canadian Comprehensive Auditing Foundation, 1987. The complete study and a summary report of it are available from the CCAF.

24–5   Identify the five concerns that management has in establishing internal control. Explain how each of those five concerns can be a part of operational auditing.

24–6   Distinguish among the following types of operational audits: functional, organizational, and special assignment. State an example of each for a hospital.

24–7   Explain why many people think of internal auditors as the primary group responsible for conducting operational audits.

24–8   What are the five parts of the scope of the internal auditor's work, according to the Institute of Internal Auditors' publication *Standards for the Practice of Internal Auditing*?

24–9   Explain the role of public accountants in operational auditing. How is this similar to and different from the role of internal auditors?

24–10 Under what circumstances are external auditors likely to be involved in operational auditing? Give one example of operational auditing by a public accounting firm.

24–11 Explain the difference in the independence of internal auditors and external auditors in the audit of historical financial statements. How is independence the same for operational auditing as it is for the audit of financial statements and how is it different? How can internal auditors best achieve independence for operational audits?

24–12 Expain what is meant by the criteria for evaluating efficiency and effectiveness. Provide five possible specific criteria for evaluating effectiveness of an EDP system for payroll.

24–13 Identify the three phases of an operational audit.

24–14 Explain how planning for operational auditing is similar to and different from financial auditing.

24–15 What are the major differences between reporting for operational and financial auditing?

24–16 Explain why the Auditor General of Canada performs comprehensive audits rather than simply performing financial audits of the various government departments.

24–17 Describe what the term "value-for-money audit" means.

24–18 What does the term "accountability" mean in the context of comprehensive auditing?

24–19 Why are criteria so important that they are mentioned specifically in PSAAC Auditing Standard 4. What does the term mean in this context. Provide an example of a criterion that might be used by an auditor in auditing the passenger service of Via Rail.

24–20 Explain the difference between direct reporting by the Auditor General and the method of reporting proposed under Objective 6.

MULTIPLE CHOICE QUESTIONS

The following questions are adapted from examinations given by the AICPA, the NAA (National Association of Accountants), and the IIA.

24–21 The following questions deal with operational auditing. Choose the best response.

a. Which of the following best describes the operational audit?

(1) It requires constant review by internal auditors of the administrative controls as they relate to the operations of the company.

(2) It concentrates on implementing financial and accounting controls in a newly organized company.

(3) It attempts and is designed to verify the fair presentation of a company's results of operations.

(4) It concentrates on seeking out aspects of operations in which waste would be reduced by the introduction of controls.

b. The evaluation of audit field work of an operating unit should answer the following questions:

1. What are the reasons for the results?
2. How can performance be improved?
3. What results are being achieved?

What is the chronological order in which these questions should be answered?

(1) 3 – 1 – 2.
(2) 1 – 3 – 2.
(3) 3 – 2 – 1.
(4) 1 – 2 – 3.
(5) 2 – 3 – 1.

c. The auditor is performing an operational audit of data processing's budgeting procedures. Which of the following procedures is least likely to be performed?

(1) Review the extent to which the budget identifies controllable expenditures.

(2) Review the total monetary budget and compare it with that of prior periods.

(3) Compare billing rates charged to users with those approved for the specified level of service.

(4) Reconcile depreciation on computer equipment to the property ledger.

d. Complaints from the public were received about processing automobile license applications in the provincial Ministry of Transportation. You were assigned by the provincial auditor general's office to review this operation. Which of the following should be your first audit step?

(1) Send out questionnaires to recent licensees.
(2) Test the system by licensing a vehicle.
(3) Discuss the nature of the complaints with the chief of the licensing office.
(4) Discuss the nature of the complaints with several licensing clerks.
(5) Discuss the nature of the complaints with the deputy minister in charge of motor vehicles licensing.

e. The first step an operational auditor should take in performing a management study to help the director of marketing determine the optimum allocation of the advertising budget to company products is to

(1) Analyze prior years' advertising costs.
(2) Hold discussions with media personnel.
(3) Establish and discuss with the director the key objectives of the study.
(4) Determine the amount of projected sales for the purpose of establishing the proposed sales budget.
(5) Both (1) and (2).

f. A preliminary survey of the human resources in a data processing function includes a review of personnel records and practices. When the audit objective is to ascertain the economy of operation of the data processing function, the internal auditor would seek evidence with respect to

(1) Procedures for rotation of job assignments.

    (2) Backup procedures relative to absenteeism, disability, and retirement.

    (3) Adequacy of the company's information dissemination procedures regarding personnel policies.

    (4) Assignment of personnel to tasks for which their education and training are appropriate.

    (5) Training programs that are in conformity with company policies and procedures.

24–22 The following questions deal with independence of auditors who do operational auditing. Choose the best response.

a. The operational auditor's independence is most likely to be compromised when the internal audit department is responsible directly to the

    (1) Vice president of finance.

    (2) President.

    (3) Controller.

    (4) Executive vice president.

    (5) Audit committee of the board of directors.

b. The independence of the internal audit department will most likely be assured if it reports to the

    (1) President.

    (2) Controller.

    (3) Treasurer.

    (4) Audit committee of the board of directors.

    (5) Vice president of finance.

c. Which of the following may compromise the independence of an internal auditor?

    (1) Reviewing EDP systems prior to implementation.

    (2) Performing an audit where the auditor recently had operating responsibilities.

    (3) Failing to review the audit report with the auditee prior to distribution.

    (4) Following up on corrective action in response to audit findings.

d. Which of the following would contribute least to the independence of the internal auditing department?

    (1) Having the director of internal auditing report directly to the chief operating officer of the organization.

    (2) Requiring the internal auditing staff to possess collectively the knowledge and skills essential to the practice of professional internal auditing within the organization.

    (3) Authorizing the director to meet directly and as needed with the audit committee of the board without the presence of management.

    (4) Having both management and the board of directors review and approve a formal written charter for the internal auditing department.

    (5) Requiring the director of internal auditing to submit to both management and the board periodic activity reports which highlight significant findings and recommendations as well as any significant deviations from approved audit schedules.

e. Operational auditors should be objective in performing audits. Which of the following situations violates standards concerning objectivity?

    (1) The auditor who reviews accounts receivable worked in that department for three months as a trainee two years ago.

    (2) The auditor reviews a department that continues to use procedures recommended by that auditor when the department was established.

    (3) The auditor reviews the same department for two years in succession.

(4) The auditor reviews a department in which the auditor has the responsibility for cosigning cheques.

24–23 The following questions deal with internal auditing departments and their responsibilities. Choose the best response.

a. Which of the following is generally considered to be a major reason for establishing an internal auditing function?

(1) To relieve overburdened management of the responsibility for establishing effective internal control.

(2) To ensure that operating activities comply with the policies, plans, and procedures established by management.

(3) To safeguard resources entrusted to the organization.

(4) To ensure the accuracy, reliability, and timeliness of financial and operating data used in management's decision making.

(5) To assist members of the organization in the measurement and evaluation of the effectiveness of established internal control.

b. Which of the following is generally considered to be the primary purpose of an internal auditor's evaluation of the adequacy of internal control?

(1) To determine if internal control is functioning as intended by management.

(2) To determie the extent of reliance the internal auditor can place on internal control in the process of evaluating the financial statements prepared by the organization.

(3) To determine if all risks and exposures of the enterprise have been reduced or eliminated by internal control.

(4) To determine if internal control provides reasonable assurance that the objectives and goals of the organization will be met in an efficient and economical manner.

c. With regard to corrective action on audit results, which of the following is not the internal auditor's responsibility?

(1) Soliciting auditees' suggestions for corrective actions.

(2) Recommending possible alternative corrective actions.

(3) Directing the particular corrective actions.

(4) Determining that the corrective actions are responsive to the audit results.

(5) Evaluating new policy statements to determine whether they address the unsatisfactory conditions disclosed in the audit results.

CASES

24–24 Mont Louis Hospital, which is affiliated with a leading university, has an extremely reputable research department that employs several renowned scientists. The research department operates on a project basis. The department consists of a pool of scientists and technicians who can be called upon to participate in a given project. Assignments are made for the duration of the project, and a project manager is given responsibility for the work.

All major projects undertaken by the research department must be approved by the hospital's administrative board. Approval is obtained by submitting a proposal to the board outlining the project, the expected amount of time required to complete the work, and the anticipated benefits. The board also must be informed of major projects that are terminated because of potential failure or technological changes which have occurred since the time of project approval. An overall review of the status of open projects is submitted to the board annually.

In many respects, profit-making techniques utilized by business firms are applied to the management of the research department. For example, the department performs preliminary research work on potential major projects it has selected prior to requesting the board to approve the project and commit large amounts of time and money. The department also assesses the potential for grants and future revenues of the project. Financial reports for the department and each project are prepared periodically and reviewed with the administrative board.

Over 75 percent of the cost of operating the department is for labor. The remaining costs are for materials utilized during research. Materials used for experimentation are purchased by the hospital's central purchasing department. Once delivered, the research department is held accountable for storage, utilization, and assignment of cost to the projects.

In order to protect the hospital's rights to discoveries made by the research department, staff members are required to sign waiver agreements at the time of hire, and at certain intervals thereafter. The agreements relinquish the employees' rights to patent and royalty fees relating to hospital work.

Mont Louis' excellent reputation is due in part to the success of the research department. The research department has produced quality research in the health care field and has always been able to generate revenues in excess of its costs. Mont Louis' administrative board believes that the hospital's continued reputation depends upon a strong research department, and therefore, the board has requested that the university's internal auditors perform an operational audit of the department. As a part of its request for the operational audit, the board presented the following set of objectives which the internal audit is to accomplish.

The operational audit to be conducted by the university's internal audit department should provide assurances that

- the research department has assessed the revenues and cost aspects of each project to confirm that the revenue potential is equal to or greater than estimated costs.
- appropriate controls exist to provide a means to measure how projects are progressing and to identify if corrective actions are required.
- financial reports prepared by the research department for presentation to the administrative board properly reflect all revenues (both endowment and royalty sources and appropriated funding) and all costs.

Required:

a. Evaluate the objectives presented by the administrative board to the university's internal audit department in terms of their appropriateness as objectives for an operational audit. Discuss fully

(1) the strengths of the objectives

(2) the modifications and/or additions needed to improve the set of objectives.

b. Outline, in general terms, the basic procedures that would be suitable for performing the audit of the research department.

c. Identify three documents that members of the university's internal auditing staff would be expected to review during the audit and describe the purpose that the review of each document serves in carrying out the audit.

(NAA adapted)

24–25   Lajod Ltd. has an internal audit department consisting of a manager and three staff auditors. The manager of internal audits, in turn, reports to the corporate controller. Copies of audit reports are routinely sent to the Audit Committee of the board of directors as well as the corporate controller and the individual responsible for the area or activity being audited.

The manager of internal audits is aware that the external auditors have relied on the internal audit function to a substantial degree in the past. However, in recent months, the external auditors have suggested there may be a problem related to the objectivity of the internal audit function. This objectivity problem may result in more extensive testing and analysis by the external auditors.

The external auditors are concerned about the amount of nonaudit work performed by the internal audit department. The percentage of nonaudit work performed by the internal auditors in recent years has increased to about 25 percent of their total hours worked. A sample of five recent nonaudit activities are as follows.

1. One of the internal auditors assisted in the preparation of policy statements on internal control. These statements included such things as policies regarding sensitive payments and standards of internal control.

2. The bank statements of the corporation are reconciled each month as a regular assignment for one of the internal auditors. The corporate controller believes this strengthens internal controls because the internal auditor is not involved in the receipt and disbursement of cash.

3. The internal auditors are asked to review the budget data in every area each year for relevance and reasonableness before the budget is approved. In addition, an internal auditor examines the variances each month, along with the associated explanations. These variance analyses are prepared by the corporate controller's staff after consultation with the individuals involved.

4. One of the internal auditors has recently been involved in the design, installation, and initial operation of a new computer system. The auditor was primarily concerned with the design and implementation of internal accounting controls and the computer application controls for the new system. The auditor also conducted the testing of the controls during the test runs.

5. The internal auditors are frequently asked to make accounting entries for complex transactions before the transactions are recorded. The employees in the accounting department are not adequately trained to handle such transactions. In addition, this serves as a means of maintaining internal control over complex transactions.

The manager of internal audits has always made an effort to remain independent of the corporate controller's office and believes the internal auditors are objective and independent in their audit and nonaudit activities.

Required:

a. Define *objectivity* as it relates to the internal audit function.

b. For each of the five situations outlined, explain whether the objectivity of Lajod Ltd.'s internal audit department has been materially impaired. Consider each situation independently.

c. The manager of audits reports to the corporate controller.
   (1) Does this reporting relationship result in a problem of objectivity? Explain your answer.
   (2) Would your answer to any of the five situations in requirement b above have changed if the manager of internal audits reported to the Audit Committee of the board of directors? Explain your answer.

(NAA adapted)

24–26 Van Staveren Corporation has an internal audit department operating out of the corporate headquarters. Various types of audit assignments are performed by the department for the eight divisions of the company.

The following findings resulted from recent audits of Van Staveren Corporation's Maritimes Division.

1. One of the departments in the division appeared to have an excessive turnover rate. Upon investigation, the personnel department seemed to be unable to find enough workers with the specified skills for this particular department. Some workers are trained on the job. The departmental supervisor is held accountable for labor efficiency variances but does not have qualified staff or

sufficient time to train the workers properly. The supervisor holds individual workers responsible for meeting predetermined standards from the day they report to work. This has resulted in a rapid turnover of workers who are trainable but not yet able to meet standards.

2. The internal audit department recently participated in a computer feasibility study for this division. It advised and concurred on the purchase and installation of a specific computer system. While the system is up and operating, the results are less than desirable. Although the software and hardware meet the specifications of the feasibility study, there are several functions unique to this division that the system has been unable to accomplish. Linking of files has been a particular problem. For example, several vendors have been paid for materials not meeting company specifications. A revision of the existing software is probably not possible, and a permanent solution probably requires replacing the existing computer system with a new one.

3. One of the products manufactured by this division was recently redesigned to eliminate a potential safety defect. This defect was discovered after several users were injured. At present, there are no pending lawsuits because none of the injured parties have identified a defect in the product as a cause of their injury. There is insufficient data to determine whether the defect was a contributing factor.

   The director of internal auditing and assistant controller is in charge of the Internal Audit Department and reports to the controller in corporate headquarters. Copies of internal audit reports are sent routinely to Van Staveren's board of directors.

Required:

a. Explain the additional steps in terms of field work, preparation of recommendations, and operating management review that ordinarily should be taken by Van Staveren Corporation's internal auditors as a consequence of the audit findings in the first situation (excessive turnover).

b. Discuss whether there are any objectivity problems with Van Staveren Corporation's internal audit department as revealed by the audit findings. Include in your discussion any recommendations to eliminate or reduce an objectivity problem, if one exists.

c. The internal audit department is part of the corporate controllership function and copies of the internal audit reports are sent to the board of directors.

   (1) Evaluate the appropriateness of the location of the internal audit department within Van Staveren's organizational structure.

   (2) Discuss who within Van Staveren Corporation should receive the reports of the internal audit department. (NAA adapted)

24–27 Haskin Inc. was founded 40 years ago and now has several manufacturing plants in central and western Canada. The evaluation of proposed capital expenditures became increasingly difficult for management as the company became geographically dispersed and diversified its product line. Thus, the Capital Budgeting Group was organized in 19X7 to review all capital expenditure proposals in excess of $50,000.

The Capital Budgeting Group conducts its annual planning and budget meeting each September for the upcoming calendar year. The group establishes a minimum return for investments (hurdle rate) and estimates a target level of capital expenditures for the next year based upon the expected available funds. The group then reviews the capital expenditure proposals that have been submitted by the various operating segments. Proposals that meet either the return on investment criterion or a critical need criterion are approved to the extent of available funds.

The Capital Budgeting Group also meets monthly, as necessary, to consider any projects of a critical nature that were not expected or requested in the annual budget review. These monthly meetings allow the Capital Budgeting Group to make adjustments during the year as new developments occur.

Haskin's profits have been decreasing slightly for the past two years in spite of a small but steady sales growth, a sales growth that is expected to continue through 19X9. As a result of the profit stagnation, top management is emphasizing cost control, and all aspects of Haskin's operations are being reviewed for cost reduction opportunities.

Haskin's internal audit department has become involved in the company-wide cost reduction effort. The department has already identified several areas where cost reductions could be realized and has made recommendations to implement the necessary procedures to effect the cost savings. Tom Watson, internal audit director, is now focusing on the activities of the Capital Budgeting Group in an attempt to determine the efficiency and effectiveness of the capital budgeting process.

In an attempt to gain a better understanding of the capital budgeting process, Watson decided to examine the history of one capital project in detail. A capital expenditure proposal of Haskin's Regina plant that was approved by the Capital Budgeting Group in 19X9 was selected randomly from a population of all proposals approved by the group at its 19X8 and 19X9 annual planning and budget meetings.

The Regina proposal consisted of a request for five new machines to replace equipment that was 20 years old and for which preventive maintenance had become very expensive. Four of the machines were for replacement purposes and the fifth was for planned growth in demand. Each of the four replacement machines was expected to result in annual maintenance cost savings of $10,000. The fifth machine was exactly like the other four and was expected to generate an annual contribution of $15,000 through increased output. Each machine cost $50,000 and had an estimated useful life of eight years.

Required:

a. Identify and discuss the issues that Haskin Inc.'s internal audit department must address in its examination and evaluation of Regina Plant's 19X9 capital expenditure project.

b. Recommend procedures to be used by Haskin's internal audit department in the audit review of Regina Plant's 19X9 capital expenditure project.

(NAA adapted)

24–28 Lecimore Limited has a centralized purchasing department which is managed by Joan Jones. Jones has established policies and procedures to guide the clerical staff and purchasing agents in the day-to-day operation of the department. She is satisfied that these policies and procedures are in conformity with company objectives and believes there are no major problems in the regular operations of the purchasing department.

Lecimore's internal audit department was assigned to perform an operational audit of the purchasing function. Their first task was to review the specific policies and procedures established by Jones. The policies and procedures are as follows:

- All significant purchases are made on a competitive bid basis. The probability of timely delivery, reliability of vendor, and so forth, are taken into consideration on a subjective basis.
- Detailed specifications of the minimum acceptable quality for all goods purchased are provided to vendors.
- Vendors' adherence to the quality specifications is the responsibility of the materials manager of the inventory control department and not the purchasing department. The materials manager inspects the goods as they arrive to be sure the quality meets the minimum standards and then sees that the goods are transferred from the receiving dock to the storeroom.

- All purchase requests are prepared by the materials manager based upon the production schedule for a four-month period.

The internal audit staff then observed the operations of the purchasing function and gathered the following findings:

- One vendor provides 90 percent of a critical raw material. This vendor has a good delivery record and is very reliable. Furthermore, this vendor has been the low bidder over the past few years.
- As production plans change, rush and expedite orders are made by production directly to the purchasing department. Materials ordered for canceled production runs are stored for future use. The costs of these special requests are borne by the purchasing department. Jones considers the additional costs associated with these special requests as "costs of being a good member of the corporate team."
- Materials to accomplish engineering changes are ordered by the purchasing department as soon as the changes are made by the engineering department. Jones is very proud of the quick response by the purchasing staff to product changes. Materials on hand are not reviewed before any orders are placed.
- Partial shipments and advance shipments (i.e., those received before the requested date of delivery) are accepted by the materials manager who notifies the purchasing department of the receipt. The purchasing department is responsible for follow-up on partial shipments. No action is taken to discourage advance shipments.

Required: Based upon the purchasing department's policies and procedures and the findings of Lecimore's internal audit staff

1. Identify weaknesses and/or inefficiencies in Lecimore Limited's purchasing function.

2. Make recommendations for those weaknesses/inefficiencies which you identify.

Use the following format in preparing your response.

WEAKNESSES/INEFFICIENCIES	RECOMMENDATIONS
1.	1.

(NAA adapted)

24–29 Superior Ltd. manufactures automobile parts for sale to the major Canadian automakers. Superior's internal audit staff is to review the internal controls over machinery and equipment and make recommendations for improvements where appropriate.

The internal auditors obtained the following information during the assignment.

- Requests for purchase of machinery and equipment are normally initiated by the supervisor in need of the asset. The supervisor discusses the proposed acquisition with the plant manager. A purchase requisition is submitted to the purchasing department when the plant manager is satisfied that the request is reasonable and if there is a remaining balance in the plant's share of the total corporate budget for capital acquisitions.
- Upon receiving a purchase requisition for machinery or equipment, the purchasing department manager looks through the records for an appropriate supplier. A formal purchase order is then completed and mailed.

When the machine or equipment is received, it is immediately sent to the user department for installation. This allows the economic benefits from the acquisition to be realized at the earliest possible date.

■ The property, plant, and equipment ledger control accounts are supported by lapsing schedules organized by year of acquisition. These lapsing schedules are used to compute depreciation as a unit for all assets of a given type which are acquired in the same year. Standard rates, depreciation methods, and salvage values are used for each major type of fixed asset. These rates, methods, and salvage values were set 10 years ago during the company's initial year of operation.

■ When machinery or equipment is retired, the plant manager notifies the accounting department so that the appropriate entries can be made in the accounting records.

■ There has been no reconciliation since the company began operations between the accounting records and the machinery and equipment on hand.

Required: Identify the internal control weaknesses and recommend improvements which the internal audit staff of Superior Ltd. should include in its report regarding the internal controls employed for fixed assets. Use the following format in preparing your answer.

WEAKNESSES	RECOMMENDATIONS
1.	1.

(NAA adapted)

24–30 Your public accounting firm has been asked by the chairperson of the local hospital to make a presentation to the board of the hospital about value-for-money auditing. The chairperson and several members of the Board attended a hospital convention recently and one of the speakers explained how beneficial a value-for-money audit had been for her hospital. She said it had helped improve efficiency, economy, and effectiveness at the hospital.

Required:
a. Describe how you would explain a value-for-money to the hospital board.
b. What benefits do you think the hospital would receive from a value-for-money audit?
c. Assume your firm was contracted to do a value-for-money audit for the hospital and you will be in charge of the audit. Describe the make-up of the audit team you would select for the audit.
d. Briefly describe how you would perform a value-for-money audit of the emergency department.

24–31 You have been asked by the president of your academic institution to explain how a value-for-money audit might improve the operations of the institution. The president is specifically concerned about the admissions area of the registrar's office.

Required:
a. Explain to the president what a value-for-money audit entails and why an academic institution such as yours might benefit from such an audit.
b. Outline the activities that might be examined in a value-for-money audit of the admissions area.
c. Select another area of your academic institution and outline the activities that might be examined in a value-for-money audit of that area.

ESSENTIAL TERMS

Absence of causal connection – a legal defense under which the professional claims that the damages claimed by the client were not brought about by any act of the professional (page 106)

Acceptable risk of incorrect acceptance (ARIA) – the statistical risk that the auditor has accepted a population that is actually materially misstated; also called Beta risk (page 494)

Acceptable risk of incorrect rejection (ARIR) – the statistical risk that the auditor has concluded that a population is materially misstated when it is not; also called Alpha risk (page 494)

Acceptable risk of overreliance on internal control (ARO) – the risk the auditor is willing to take of accepting a control as effective, when the true population deviation rate is greater than the tolerable deviation rate (page 404)

Access controls – safeguards against the use of a company's assets and records by unauthorized people (page 284)

Accounting – the process of recording, classifying, and summarizing economic events in a logical manner for the purpose of providing financial information for decision making (page 4)

Accounting system – the set of manual and/or computerized procedures and controls that provide for (1) identifying pertinent transactions and events, (2) accurate preparation of source documents, (3) accurate entry of data from the source documents; (4) accurate processing of transactions and updating of master files, and (5) generation of accurate documents and reports (page 273-274)

Accounts payable master file – a file for recording individual acquisitions, cash disbursements, and acquisition returns and allowances for each vendor, and maintaining vendor balances (page 585)

Accounts payable trial balance – a listing of the amount owed by each vendor at a point in time, which is prepared directly from the accounts payable master file (page 586)

Accounts receivable master file – a file for recording individual sales, cash receipts, and sales returns and allowances for each customer, and maintaining customer account balances (page 355)

Accounts receivable trial balance – a listing of the amount owed by each customer at a point in time (page 356)

Accrued liabilities – estimated unpaid obligations for services or benefits that have been received prior to the balance sheet date; common accrued liabilities include accrued commissions, accrued income taxes, accrued payroll, and accrued rent (pages 630)

Accrued payroll expenses – the liability accounts associated with payroll; these include accounts for accrued salaries and wages, accrued commissions, accrued bonuses, accrued benefits, and accrued payroll taxes (pages 569-571)

Acquisition and payment cycle – the transaction cycle that includes the acquisition of and payment for goods and services from suppliers outside the organization (page 582)

Acquisitions journal – a journal for recording acquisition transactions; the journal totals are automatically posted to the general ledger (page 585)

Acquisition transactions file – a computer file used to record acquisitions of goods and services; details from the transactions file are automatically posted to the accounts payable master file (page 585)

Adverse opinion – a report issued when the auditor believes the financial statements are so materially misstated or misleading as a whole that they do not present fairly the entity's financial position or the results of its operations and changes in financial position in conformity with generally accepted accounting principles (page 39)

Aged trial balance – a listing of the balances in the accounts receivable master file at the balance sheet date broken down according to the amount of time passed between the date of sale and the balance sheet date (page 439)

Allocation – the division of certain expenses, such as depreciation and manufacturing overhead, among several expense accounts (page 636)

Alpha risk – the statistical risk that the auditor has concluded that a population is materially misstated when it is not; also called acceptable risk of incorrect rejection (ARIR) (page 494)

Analysis – a supporting schedule that shows the activity in an income statement or balance sheet account during the entire period under examination tying together the beginning and ending balances (page 180)

Analytical procedures – techniques involving studying and evaluating the interrelationships between elements of financial and other information; assess the overall reasonableness of transactions and account balances; these methods involve comparisons of recorded amounts to expectations developed by the auditor (pages 149, 202, 324)

Application controls – controls that relate to a specific use of the EDP system, such as the processing of sales or cash receipts (page 519)

Appropriateness – the quality of audit evidence, the degree to which evidence can be considered believable or worthy of trust. Relevance, auditor's direct knowledge, effeciveness of client's internal control, qualifications of individuals providing the information and degree of objectivity are characteristics of appropriateness (page 166)

ARIA – see *acceptable risk of incorrect acceptance*

ARIR – see *acceptable risk of incorrect rejection*

ARO – see *acceptable risk of overreliance on internal control*

Articles of incorporation – granted by the federal government or by the province in which the company is incorporated; legal document for recognizing company as a separate entity; includes the name of the corporation, date of incorporation, kinds and amounts of capital stock the corporation is authorized to issue and the types of business activities the corporation is authorized to conduct (page 201)

Assertion – a statement made by one party implicitly for use by another (third) party (page 791)

Assurance – the practitioner's degree of certainty that the conclusions stated in his or her report are correct (page 791)

Attest engagement – one in which a practitioner is engaged to issue or does issue a written communication that expresses a conclusion with respect to the reliability of a written assertion that is the responsibility of another party (page 791)

Attestation – a written communication regarding the reliability of another party's written assertion (page 791)

Attribute – the characteristic being tested in the application (page 404)

Attributes sampling – a statistical, probabilistic method of sample evaluation which results in an estimate of the proportion of items in a population containing a characteristic or attribute of interest (page 401)

Audit assurance – a complement to *audit risk;* an audit risk of 2 percent is the same as an audit assurance of 98 percent; also called *overall assurance* and *level of assurance* (page 246)

Audit committee – selected members of a client's board of directors, whose responsibilities include helping auditors to remain independent of management (page 79-80)

Audit failure – a situation in which the auditor reaches or issues an erroneous opinion due to the failure to comply with the requirements of generally accepted auditing standards (page 98)

Audit program – a set of instructions for carrying out the audit plan; it contains a detailed description of the decisions the auditor has made regarding (1) the audit procedures to be used, (2) the size of each sample, (3) the methods chosen for selecting the items to examine, and (4) the proper timing of each audit procedure (page 165)

Auditor's report – the communication of audit findings to users (page 3)

Audit risk – a measure of the risk the auditor is willing to take that the financial statements may be materially misstated after the auditor has completed the report and rendered an unqualified opinion; see also *audit assurance* (page 98)

Audit risk model – a formal model reflecting the relationships between audit risk (AR), inherent risk (IR), control risk (CR), and planned detection risk (PDR); $PDR = AR \div IR \times CR$ (page 243-244)

Auditing – the process by which a competent, independent person accumulates and evaluates evidence about quantifiable information related to a specific economic entity for the purpose of determining and reporting on the degree of correspondence between the quantifiable information and established criteria (page 2)

Auditing Guidelines – interpretations of existing Recommendations or views of the Auditing Standards Board on particular matters of concern; less authoritative than Auditing Recommendations (page 16)

Auditing Recommendations – a framework for the auditor to use to assist him or her in the conduct of the audit engagement; the rules underlying the audits and related services activities carried on by the public accountants; the italicized portions of the *CICA Handbook*; issued by the Auditing Standards Board (page 16,17)

Auditing standards – general guidelines to aid auditors in fulfilling their professional responsibilities in the audit of historical financial statements (page 17)

Auditing Standards Board – a committee of the CICA that has the resposibility for issuing Auditing Recommendations and Auditing Guidelines (page 17)

Auditing without relying on computer controls – auditing without testing the client's EDP controls; this is acceptable if the auditor has access to source documents and a listing of output sufficient for tracing individual transactions (page 532)

Auditor General – responsible for auditing the ministries, departments and agencies reporting to the local, provincial and federal governments (page 6)

Backup and recovery procedures – safeguards against loss of computer programs and data; steps an organization can take in the event of a loss of equipment, programs or data (page 284)

Batching – in an EDP system, the collection, control, and processing of input documents in discrete groups (page 301)

Beta risk – the statistical risk that the auditor has accepted a population that is actually materially misstated; also called acceptable risk of incorrect acceptance (ARIA) (page 494)

Bill of lading – a shipping document that is a written contract between the seller of a shipment of goods and the carrier of the shipment (page 354)

Block sampling – a nonprobabilistic method of sample selection in which items are selected in measured sequences (page 400)

Branch bank account – a separate account that a branch of a company maintains at a local bank (page 700)

Breach of contract – failure of either or both parties to a contract to fulfill the requirements of the contract (page 101)

Budgets – written records of the client's expectations for the period; a comparison of budgets with actual results may indicate whether or not errors are likely (page 209)

Business failure – the inability of a business to meet its monetary obligations because of economic or business conditions (page 98)

Bylaws – the rules and procedures adopted by a corporation's shareholders, including the corporation's fiscal year and the duties and powers of its officers (page 201)

Canada Business Corporations Act – regulates companies incorporated under the Act (page 80)

Canadian Comprehensive Auditing Foundation (CCAF) – develops comprehensive auditing techniques to assist the work of the public sector auditor (page 7)

Canadian Institute of Chartered Accountants (CICA) – sets the accounting and auditing standards which must be followed by public accountants in Canada; regulates the CA profession (page 15)

Capital acquisition and repayment cycle – the transaction cycle that involves the acquisition of capital resources in the form of interest-bearing debt and owners' equity, and the repayment of the capital (page 679)

Capital stock certificate book – a record of the issuance and repurchase of capital stock for the life of the corporation (page 687)

Cash disbursements transaction file – a computer file for recording individual payments made by cheque, and printing out the cheques and the cash disbursements journal (page 585)

Cash receipts journal – the record of cash receipts from collections, cash sales, and all other sources (page 355)

Certified General Accountant (CGA) – one of the three professional designations in Canada relating to accounting/auditing (page 2)

Certified General Accountants Association of Canada (CGAAC) – one of the three major organizations in Canada providing a professional designation relating to accounting/auditing (page 2)

Certified Management Accountant (CMA) – one of the three professional designations in Canada relating to accounting and auditing (page 2)

Chartered Accountant (CA) – one of the three professional designations in Canada relating to accounting/auditing (page 2)

Chart of accounts – a listing of all the entity's accounts, which classifies transactions into individual balance-sheet and income-statement accounts (page 282)

Check digit – a number that is part of an identification number and is used to detect key-entry errors (page 302)

Checklist for completing the engagement – a reminder to the auditor of aspects of the audit that may have been overlooked (page 743)

Cheque – the means of paying for the acquisition when payment is due (page 585)

CLDR – see *computed lower deviation rate*

Client information – information communicated by a client to a professional (page 82)

Closely held corporations – corporations whose share ownership is restricted; typically, there are only a few shareholders and few if any transactions during the year for capital stock accounts; also called private corporations (page 685)

Collusion – a cooperative effort among employees to defraud a business of cash, inventory, or other assets (page 272)

Commitments – agreements that the entity will hold to a fixed set of conditions, such as the purchase or sale of merchandise at a stated price, at a future date, regardless of what happens to profits or to the economy as a whole (page 734)

Common law – laws developed through court decisions rather than through government statutes; also called judge-made law or case law (page 101)

Communications systems – channels connecting the computer directly to users who are geographically dispersed (page 514)

Competence – see Appropriateness

Compilation engagements – nonauditing engagements in which the public accountant provides assistance in compiling financial statements but is not required to provide assurance about the statements (page 777)

Compliance audit –   a review of an organization's financial records performed to determine whether the organization is following specific procedures or rules set down by some higher authority (page 5);

Comprehensive audit – audit in the public sector consisting of three components: (1) financial statement audit; (2) compliance audit; (3) value-for-money or operational audit considering economy, efficiency and effectiveness (page 6)

Computed lower deviation rate (CLDR) – the lower limit of probable population deviation rate (page 401)

Computed upper deviation rate (CUDR) – the upper limit of probable population deviation rate (page 401); the highest deviation rate in the population at a given ARO, as determined from attributes sampling tables (page 404)

Computer operator – person who feeds data into the EDP system according to the programmer's instructions (page 280)

Confidence level – statement of probability (page 401)

Confidential client information – client information which may not be disclosed without the specific consent of the client except under authoritative professional or legal investigation (page 82)

Confirmation – the auditor's receipt of a written or oral response from an independent third party verifying the accuracy of the information requested (page 171)

Constructive fraud – conduct that the law construes as fraud even though there was no intent to deceive; recklessness in the performance of an audit may be construed legally as fraud (page 101)

Contingent liability – a potential future obligation to an outside party for an unknown amount resulting from activities that have already taken place (page 729)

Contributory negligence – a legal defense under which the professional claims that the client failed to perform certain obligations to the professional, and that it is the client's failure to perform those obligations which brought about the damages claimed in the lawsuit (page 106)

Control environment – the actions, policies, and procedures that reflect the overall attitude of a company's owners, directors, and top managers toward internal control (page 276)

Control matrix – a list of control procedures against which the internal control objectives for a specific transaction cycle are matched; the control matrix helps the auditor identify strengths and weakness in internal control and assess control risk (page 296)

Control risk – a measure of the risk that misstatements exceeding a tolerable amount in a segment will not be prevented or detected by the client's internal control (page 245)

Control total – in an EDP system, a count or summation of a batch of input data to be compared with the final output after processing; the purpose is generally to make sure that no data were lost or misstated in handling or processing (page 301)

Conversion verification controls – EDP controls to detect errors in the keying-in of data (page 301)

Corporate minutes – the official record of the meetings of a corporation's board of directors and shareholders, in which corporate issues such as the declaration of dividends and the approval of contracts are documented (page 201)

Cost accounting controls – controls related to the physical inventory and the consequent costs from the point at which raw materials are requisitioned to the point at which the manufactured product is completed and transferred to storage (page 652)

Cost accounting internal control – the internal control structure is necessary to indicate the relative profitability of the company's various products for management planning and control and to value inventories for financial statement purposes (page 649)

Cost accounting records – the accounting records concerned with the manufacture and processing of the goods and storing finished goods (page 651)

Cost beneficial – providing a favourable relationship between the cost of an item and the benefit that the item is expected to deliver (page 270)

Credit memo – a document indicating a reduction in the amount due from a customer because of returned goods or an allowance granted (page 355)

Criminal liability – the possibility of being found guilty under criminal law; public accountants may be convicted of a criminal offense if they are found to have defrauded a person through knowing involvement with false financial statements (page 113-114)

CUDR – see *computed upper deviation rate*

Cumulative monetary amount sampling – see *dollar unit sampling*

Current files – all working papers applicable solely to the year under audit (page 178)

Customer order – the customer's written or oral request for merchandise (page 353)

Cutoff bank statement – a partial-period bank statement and the related cancelled cheques, duplicate deposit slips, and other documents included in bank statements, mailed by the bank directly to the auditor, in order to verify the reconciling items on the client's year-end bank reconciliation (page 710)

Cutoff errors – errors that take place as a result of current period transactions being recorded in a subsequent period, or subsequent period transactions being recorded in the current period (page 442)

Cycle approach – a method of segmenting an audit according to related transaction types (page 139)

Data base management – the formatting of data into a file structure such that each element of data is stored only once (page 514)

Data control group – people who test the effectiveness and efficiency of various aspects of the EDP system (page 280)

Debit memo – a document indicating a reduction in the amount owed to a vendor because of returned goods or an allowance granted (page 585)

Decision rules – criteria used to determine whether or not a fluctuation in an analytical procedure is significant; these criteria are often stated in terms of a dollar amount or a fixed percentage (page 213)

Deduction authorization form – a form with which the employee authorizes payroll deductions; the form includes the number of exemptions for withholding of income taxes, and deductions for Canada Savings Bonds, charitable funds, and the like (page 557-558)

Defalcation – theft of assets (page 368)

Denial of opinion – a report issued when the auditor

has not been able to become satisfied that the overall financial statements are fairly presented (page 39)

Deviation rate – the percentage of items in a population that exhibit evidence of error (page 401)

Difference estimation – a method of variables sampling in which the auditor makes an estimate of the population error based on the number of errors, average error size, and individual error size in the sample (page 493)

Direct projection method of estimating error – net errors in the sample, divided by the total sample, multiplied by the total recorded population value (page 241-242)

Disaggregated data – the complete (aggregated) data that make up the financial statements broken down into either subunits or shorter time-periods; disaggregation of data increases the likelihood of identifying errors (page 213)

Distributed processing – apportioning the computing function among central processing units spread geographically and connected by a communications system (page 514)

Documentation – the auditor's examination of the client's documents and records to substantiate the information that is or should be included in the financial statements; also known as vouching (page 169)

Documents – sales invoices, purchase orders, and similar items which substantiate the recording of transactions (page 282)

Dollar unit sampling – a variation on attributes sampling that provides a statistical result expressed in dollars; also referred to as monetary unit sampling, cumulative monetary amount sampling, and sampling with probability proportional to size (page 474)

Economic dependence – the potential for exercise of significant influence on an audit client by its most important supplier, customer, lender or borrower (page 200)

EDP – see *electronic data processing*

Effectiveness – the degree to which the organization's objectives are accomplished (page 806)

Efficiency – the degree to which costs are reduced without reducing effectiveness (page 806)

Electronic data processing (EDP) – computerized management and use of information (page 273, 512-513)

Electronic spreadsheet – a software program that presents and manipulates data in the form of a matrix of interrelated values, with columns and rows, much like an accounting worksheet (page 540)

Employee withholding and benefits remittance forms

– forms submitted to the federal government and other organizations for the payment of withholdings and employee benefits (page 560)

Engagement letter – an agreement between the public accounting firm and the client as to the conduct of the audit and related services (page 197)

Enquiry – the obtaining of written or oral information from the client in response to specific questions during the audit; also called inquiry (page 170)

EPDR – see *estimated population deviation rate*

Error – in accounting, an unintentional misstatement of the financial statements (page 137)

Error bounds – the values of the estimates of error limits in dollar unit sampling (page 480)

Error listing – a display of the actual errors that were reported by the EDP system (page 531)

Estimated population deviation rate (EPDR) – deviation rate the auditor expects to find in the population before testing begins (page 404)

Ethical dilemma – a situation in which a decision must be made about the appropriate action to take (page 68)

Ethics – a set of moral principles or values (page 65)

Evidence – any information used by the auditor to determine whether the quantifiable information being audited is stated in accordance with established criteria (page 3)

Examination – an attest engagement that results in a positive assurance as to whether or not the assertions under examination conform with the applicable criteria (page 794-794)

Examination of (schedule of) supporting documents – a supporting schedule that shows the detailed tests performed and the results found (page 180)

Expectation gap – the conflict between what some users expect from an audit report and what the audit report is designed to deliver; some users believe that an audit report is a guarantee as to the accuracy of the financial statements, although the report is in fact an opinion based on an audit conducted according to generally accepted auditing standards (page 99)

Expense account analysis – the examination of underlying documentation of the individual transactions and amounts making up the total of a particular expense account (page 635)

External document – a document, such as a vendor's invoice, that has been used by an outside party to the transaction being documented, and that the client now has or can easily obtain (page 170)

Financial interest – ownership of stock or any other direct investment by the public accountant in the client (page 78-79)

Financial statement disclosure checklist – a questionnaire that reminds the auditor of disclosure problems commonly encountered in audits, and that facilitates final review of the entire audit by an independent partner (page 744-745)

Finite correction factor – a factor reflecting the effect of small population sizes, which is used to reduce initial sample size (page 404)

Fixed asset master file – a computer file containing records for each piece of equipment and other types of property owned; the primary accounting record for manufacturing equipment and other property, plant, and equipment accounts (page 618)

Flowchart – a diagrammatic representation of the client's documents and records, and the sequence in which they are processed (page 292)

FOB destination – shipping contract in which title to the goods passes to the buyer when the goods are received (page 599)

FOB origin – shipping contract in which title to the goods passes to the buyer at the time that the goods are shipped (page 599)

Forecasts – prospective financial information prepared using assumptions reflecting management's judgment as to the most probable courses of action for the entity (page 785)

Fraud and other irregularities – a false assertion that has been made knowingly, or without belief in its truth, or recklessly without caring whether its true or not (page 101); in accounting, an intentional misstatement of the financial statements (page 137)

Functional audit – an operational audit that deals with one or more specific functions within an organization, such as the payroll function or the production engineering function (page 808)

Further possible misstatements – the misstatements over and above the likely aggregate misstatement that result from the imprecision in the sampling process (page 235)

GAS – see *generalized audit software*

General audit objectives – broadly stated audit goals aimed at establishing the validity, completeness, ownership, valuation, classification, proper period, accuracy, and proper disclosure of the accounts (pages 144-146)

General authorization – company-wide policies for the approval of all transactions within stated limits (page 281)

General cash account – the central bank account for most organizations; virtually all cash receipts and disbursements flow through this account at some time (page 700)

General controls – controls that relate to all parts of the EDP system (page 519)

Generalized audit software (GAS) – computer programs that can perform audit applications (page 536)

Generally accepted auditing standards (GAAS) – eight auditing standards, developed by the CICA consisting of the general standard, examination standards, and reporting standards (pages 17)

Haphazard selection – a nonprobabilistic method of sample -selection in which items are chosen without regard to their size, source, or other distinguishing characteristics (page 400)

Illegal acts – in accounting, violations of laws or government regulations, other than fraud (page 138)

Identified misstatement – the actual misstatement discovered in the sample tested; it has not been corrected by management (page 235)

Imprest branch bank account – a branch's local bank account for disbursements; when the fixed cash balance has been depleted, an accounting is made to the home office and a reimbursement is made to the branch account from the company's general cash account after the expenditures have been approved (page 700)

Imprest payroll account – a bank account to which the exact amount of payroll for the pay period is transferred by cheque from the employer's general cash account (page 562, 700)

Imprest petty cash fund – a fund of cash maintained within the company for small cash purchases or to cash employee's checks; the fund's fixed balance is comparatively small, and is usually reimbursed once a month (page 700-701)

Independence – the professional must take an unbiased viewpoint in the performance of audit tests, the evaluation of the results, and the issuance of the auditor's report; four facets: financial independence, independence of mental attitude, investigative independence, and reporting independence (page 77-79)

Independent auditor – a public accountant or accounting firm that performs audits of commercial and non-commercial financial entities (page 9)

Independent checks – procedures for continuous internal verification of other controls; separation of duties is the least expensive type of independent check because it involves no duplication of effort (page 284)

Independent registrar – outside person engaged by a corporation to make sure that its stock is issued in accordance with the capital stock provisions in the articles of incorporation and the authorization of the board of directors (page 687)

Independent review – a review of the financial statements and the entire set of working papers by a completely independent reviewer to whom the audit team must justify the evidence accumulated and the conclusions reached (page 747)

Information risk – reflects the possibility that the information upon which the business risk decision was made was inaccurate (page 10)

Informational schedule – a supporting schedule that contains nonaudit client information that will be helpful in administering the audit engagement (page 181)

Inherent risk – a measure of the risk that misstatements exceeding a tolerable amount would exist in a segment before consideration of internal controls (page 244)

Initial sample size – sample size determined from attributes sampling tables (page 404)

Input controls – controls such as proper authorization of documents, adequate documentation, and check digits, designed to assure that the information processed by the computer is valid, complete, and accurate (page 528)

Insurance register – a record of insurance policies in force and the due date of each policy (page 627)

Internal auditors – employed by individual companies to audit for management (page 8)

Internal control objectives – specific goals which an organization must meet in order to prevent misstatements in its journals and records; these goals are that each transaction be (1) valid, (2) authorized, (3) completely recorded, (4) properly valued, (5) properly classified, (6) recorded at the proper time, and (7) properly posted and summarized (page 275)

Internal control questionnaire – series of questions about the controls in each audit area (page 292)

Internal control – the set of policies and procedures designed to provide management with reasonable assurance that the goals of the business will be met (page 270)

Internal document – a document, such as an employee time report, that is prepared and used solely within the client's operation (page 170)

Internal verification – see *independent checks*

Interval – see *systematic selection*

Inventory and warehousing cycle – the transaction cycle that involves the physical flow of goods through the organization, as well as related costs (page 647)

Job cost system – the system of cost accounting in

which costs are accumulated by individual jobs when material is used and labour costs are incurred (page 649)

Job time ticket – a document indicating particular jobs on which a factory employee worked during a given time period (page 560)

Judgmental methods – use of professional judgment rather than statistical methods to select sample items for audit tests (page 400)

Key verification – a test for detecting operator errors in keying in entry data, in which all or part of the entry is repeated and the results are compared with the results of the original entry (page 301-302)

Kiting – the transfer of money from one bank account to another and improperly recording the transfer so that the amount is recorded as an asset in both accounts; this practice is used by embezzlers to cover a defalcation of cash (page 712)

Lack of duty to perform – a legal defense under which the professional claims that no contract existed with the client; therefore no duty existed to perform the disputed service for the client (page 103)

Lapping – a type of defalcation in which entries for the collection of receivables are postponed in order to conceal an existing cash shortage (page 370)

Lead schedule – the detailed general ledger accounts that make up each line item total on the balance sheet; lead schedules are drawn to support the working trial balance (page 178)

Legal liability – the professional's obligation under the law to provide all services promised and to perform those services with due care (page 97)

Letter of representation – a written communication from the client to the auditor formalizing statements the client has made about matters pertinent to the audit (page 737)

Level of assurance – see *audit assurance*

Liability account – an amount payable if the total amount of the obligation is known and owed at the balance sheet date (page 592)

Librarian – in an EDP system, the person who keeps and maintains the programs, transaction files, and other computer records (page 280)

Likely misstatement – the actual misstatement in the sample plus the projection of the actual misstatement in the sample to the population; the misstatement has not been corrected by management (page 235)

Liquidity – the ability of a company to convert current assets into cash (page 216)

Logic tests – computerized comparisons of input data with programmed criteria that determine the acceptability of the data (page 302)

Management assertions – implied or expressed representations by management about the accounts in the financial statements (page 143)

Management auditing – see *operational auditing*

Management discussion and analysis (MD&A) – supplemental analysis and explanation by management which accompanies but does not form part of the financial statements (page 741)

Management letters – the auditor's written communications to management to point out weaknesses in internal control and possibilities for operational improvements (page 297)

Master file controls – reviews of the master file for data content and any changes made to the master file (page 303)

Material misstatement – a misstatement in the financial statements, knowledge of which would affect a decision of a reasonable user of the statements (page 40)

Material uncertainties – significant matters whose outcome cannot be reasonably estimated when the financial statements are being issued (page 50)

Materiality – a misstatement or the aggregate of all misstatements in financial statements is considered to be material if, in light of the surrounding circumstances, it is probable that the decision of a person who is relying on the financial statements, and who has a reasonable knowledge of business and economic activities (the user), would be changed or influenced by such misstatement or the aggregate of all misstatements (page 235)

Mean-per-unit estimation – a method of variables sampling in which the auditor estimates the audited value of a population by multiplying the average audited value of the sample times the population size (page 493-494)

Mechanical accuracy test – the rechecking of a sample of the computations and transfers of information made by the client during the period under audit (page 172)

Microcomputers – portable computers that may be taken to a client's office for use as an audit tool (page 540)

Monetary unit sampling – see *dollar unit sampling*

Monthly statement – a document sent to each customer, which indicates the beginning balance of the customer's account receivable, the amount and date of each sale, cash payments received, credit memo issued, and the ending balance due (page 356)

Multi-tasking – computer operating systems that allow different functions to be carried out simultaneously (page 514)

Narrative – a written description of a client's internal control, including the origin, processing, and disposition of documents and records, and the relevant control procedures (page 291)

Negative confirmation – a letter, addressed to the debtor, requesting a response only if the debtor disagrees with the amount of the stated account balance (page 447)

Negligence – failure to exercise reasonable care in the performance of one's obligations to another (page 100)

Nonnegligent performance – a legal defense under which the professional claims that the disputed service was properly performed; an auditor or public accounting firm would claim that the audit was performed in accordance with generally accepted auditing standards (page 104)

Nonprobabilistic sample selection – a method of sample selection in which the auditor uses professional judgment to select items from the population (page 394)

Nonsampling risk – the chance of error when audit tests do not uncover existing exceptions in the sample; nonsampling error is caused by failure to recognize exceptions and by inappropriate or ineffective audit procedures (page 393)

Nonstatistical sampling – the auditor's use of professional judgment to select sample items, estimate the population values, and estimate sampling risk (page 394)

Note payable – a legal obligation to a creditor, which may be unsecured or secured by assets (page 680)

Observation – the use of the senses to assess certain activities (page 170)

Occurrence rate – the ratio of items in a population that contain a specific attribute to the total number of population items (page 401)

Operational auditing – a review of any part of an organization's operating procedures and methods for the purpose of evaluating efficiency and effectiveness; also referred to as management auditing and performance auditing (page 5)

Opinion shopping – when a public accountant is asked by a client of another public accountant to give an opinion with respect to accounting issues, to the application of accounting or review standards, or to provide a generic opinion (page 788)

Organizational audit – an operational audit that deals with an entire organizational unit, such as a department, branch, or subsidiary, to determine how efficiently and effectively functions interact (page 808)

Outside documentation – data outside the client's operation, such as copies of client agreements, that have been gathered by the auditor (page 181)

Overall assurance – see *audit assurance*

Payroll and personnel cycle – the transaction cycle that begins with the hiring of personnel, includes obtaining and accounting for services from the employees, and ends with payment to the employees for the services performed and to the government and other institutions for withholdings and employee benefits (page 557)

Payroll cheque – a cheque written to the employee for the authorized amount of pay for services performed, net of taxes and other deductions (page 560)

Payroll journal – a journal for recording payroll cheques; it typically indicates gross pay, withholdings, and net pay (page 560)

Payroll master file – a computer file for recording each payroll transaction for each employee, and maintaining total employee wages paid and related data for the year to date (page 560)

Performance auditing – see *operational auditing*

Permanent files – storehouses for client data of a historical or continuing nature pertinent to present and future audits (page 177)

Perpetual inventory master files – continuously updated computerized records of inventory items purchased and on hand, raw materials used, and the sale of finished goods (page 654)

Personnel records – records that include such data as the date of employment, personnel investigations, rates of pay, authorized deductions, performance evaluations, and termination of employment (page 557)

Persuasiveness – the convincing quality of evidence that is relevant, appropriate, sufficient, and timely (page 167,168)

Phases of the audit process – the four aspects of a complete audit: (1) planning and designing the audit, (2) testing controls, (3) performing analytical procedures and tests of details of balances, and (4) evaluating final results and communicating findings to the client (page 339-340)

Physical examination – the auditor's inspection or count of a tangible asset (page 169)

Planned detection risk (PDR) – a measure of the risk that audit evidence for a segment will fail to detect misstatements exceeding a tolerable amount, should such misstatements exist (page 244); audit risk (AR) divided by inherent risk (IR) times control risk (CR): $PDR = AR/(IR \times CR)$ (page 322)

Plausible relationships – logical cause-and-effect connections (page 211)

Point estimate – a method of projecting from the sample to the population to estimate the population error, commonly by assuming that errors in the unaudited population are proportional to the errors actually found in the sample; see also identified misstatement (page 473)

Positive confirmation – a letter, addressed to the debtor, requesting that the debtor indicate directly on the letter whether the stated account balance is correct or incorrect and, if incorrect, by what amount (page 446)

Postprocessing controls – reviews of output for errors (page 303)

Practice inspection – a review of a firm's quality control procedures over its auditing and accounting engagements and the unit's compliance with the *CICA Handbook* (page 21)

Preliminary judgment about materiality – the maximum amount by which the auditor believes the statements could be misstated and still *not* affect the decisions of reasonable users; used in audit planning (page 236)

Price tests – audit procedures used to verify the costs used to value physical inventory (page 651)

Pricing – testing of the client's unit prices to determine whether they are correct (page 659)

Privileged information – client information which the professional cannot be legally required to provide; information that an accountant obtains from a client is confidential but not privileged (page 82-83)

Privity of contract – relationship established within a contract between the parties to that contract (page 101)

Probabilistic sample selection – a method of sample selection in which every population item has a known chance of being selected (page 394)

Process cost system – the system of cost accounting in which costs are accumulated by particular processes, with unit costs for each process assigned to the products passing through the process (page 649)

Program controls – EDP controls written into computer programs for the purpose of detecting erroneous input, processing, or output of data (page 302)

Program run instructions – directions for operating a computer and software (page 283)

Programmer – person who develops EDP applications, prepares the instructions, tests the programs, and documents the results (page 280)

Programming documentation – a physical record of the requirements for, details of, and results of testing software programs (page 283)

Projections – prospective financial information prepared using assumptions reflecting management's judgment as to the most probable courses of action for the entity (same as forecast); as well, a projection is prepared using one or more assumptions (hypotheses) that do not necessarily reflect the most likely course of action in management's judgment (page 785)

Proof of cash – a four-column form that the auditor uses to reconcile the bank's record of the client's beginning balance, cash receipts deposited, cancelled cheques, and ending balance for the period, with the client's records (page 711-712)

Prospective financial statements – financial statements that deal with expected future data rather than with historical data (page 785)

Provincial securities commissions – provincial organizations with quasi-legal status which administer securities regulations within their jurisdiction (page 23)

Public Sector Accounting and Auditing Committee (PSAAC) – a committee of the CICA that has the responsibility for establishing accounting and auditing standards for entities in the public sector (page 16)

Publicly held corporations – corporations whose stock is publicly traded; typically, there are many shareholders and frequent changes in the ownership of the stock (page 685)

Purchase order – a document recording the description, quantity, and related information for goods and services that the company intends to purchase (page 584)

Purchase requisition – a request for goods and services by an authorized employee (page 584)

Qualified opinion – a report issued when the auditor believes that the overall financial statements are fairly stated but that either the scope of the audit was limited or the financial data indicated a failure to follow generally accepted accounting principles (page 39)

Random number table – a listing of independent random digits conveniently arranged in tabular form to facilitate the selection of random numbers with multiple digits (page 395)

Random sample – a sample in which every possible combination of items in the population has an equal chance of constituting the sample; a random sample may be obtained by using random number tables, computer programs, or systematic sampling (page 395)

Rate authorization form – a form authorizing the employee's rate of pay (page 558)

Ratio estimation – a method of variables sampling in

which the auditor makes an estimate of the population error by multiplying the portion of sample dollars in error by the total recorded population book value (page 493)

Realizable value (of accounts receivable) – the amount of the outstanding balances in accounts receivable that will ultimately be collected (page 441)

Real-time processing – an EDP system in which transactions can be entered directly into the computer for continuous, as opposed to batched, updating of the master files (page 513)

Reasonable assurance – the concept that the purpose of the auditor's report is to give the user a degree of confidence that any material misstatements in the financial statements will have been detected; the auditor's report does not guarantee the correctness of the financial statements (page 136-137)

Reasonable person concept – the idea that a person has a duty to exercise due care in the performance of his or her obligations to another (page 99-100)

Receiving report – a document prepared by the receiving department at the time tangible goods are received, indicating the description of the goods, the quantity received, the date received and other relevant data; it is part of the documentation necessary for payment to be made (pages 584, 648)

Reclassification entries – entries made in the financial statements to present accounting information properly, although the general ledger balances are correct (page 179)

Reconciliation of amounts – a supporting schedule that supports a specific amount; it normally ties the amount recorded in the client's records to another source of information, such as bank statements and customer confirmations (page 180)

Records – journals, ledgers, and similar items in which transactions are entered and accounts are maintained (page 282)

Regression analysis – a method of evaluating the reasonableness of a recorded balance, in which the analyst relates the total account balance to other relevant information using statistical means (page 215)

Related parties – a party is a related party when it has the ability to exercise, directly or indirectly, control or significant influence over the operating and financial decisions of another party (page 200)

Related-party transaction – any transaction between the client and a related party (page 200)

Relevance – the pertinence of the evidence to the objective being tested (page 166)

Reliability – see *Appropriateness*

Remittance advice – a document that indicates the cus-

tomer's name, the invoice number, and the amount of the invoice; the remittance advice is sent to the customer with the invoice, and should be returned to the seller with the cash payment (page 355)

Representative sample – a sample whose characteristics are the same as those of the population (page 393)

Review – consists primarily of enquiry, analytical procedures and discussion with the limited objectives of assessing whether the information being reported on is plausible within the framework of appropriate criteria (page 771)

Revised judgment about materiality – a change in the auditor's preliminary judgment made when the auditor determines that the preliminary judgment was too large or too small (page 237)

Risk – a measure of uncertainty (page 254)

Route slip – in an EDP system, the form attached to a batch of data to inform the processing centre of the proper path of processing and to provide a record of the actual processing performed (page 301)

Sales and collection cycle – involves the decisions and processes necessary for the transfer of the ownership of goods and services to customers after they are made available for sale; the transaction cycle that begins with sales; includes cash receipts, sales returns and allowances, and the charge-off of uncollectible accounts, and ends with cash in the bank (page 353)

Sales journal – the record of sales transactions (page 355)

Sales invoice – a document that identifies the customer and describes the goods sold, the quantity, price, terms, and other relevant data (page 355)

Sales order – a document that records the description of goods ordered by a customer, the quantity, and other related information (page 354)

Sample deviation rate (SDR) – number of deviations in the sample divided by the sample size (page 404)

Sampling distribution – the probability of each possible condition that would exist in a sample from a specified population (page 402)

Sampling risk – the chance of error inherent in tests of less than the entire population; sampling error may be reduced by using an increased sample size and using an appropriate method of selecting sample items from the population (page 393)

Sampling with probability proportional to size – see *dollar unit sampling*

SAS – see *Statements on Auditing Standards*

Savings account – bank account for holding excess cash accumulated during the operating cycle, which will be needed in the reasonably near future; the cash is not meant for use in the business until it is transferred to the general cash account (page 701)

SDR – see *sample deviation rate*

Securities and Exchange Commission (SEC) – a U.S. federal agency that oversees the orderly conduct of the securities markets in the United States; the SEC helps to provide investors in public corporations with reliable information upon which to make investment decisions (page 24)

Shipping document – a document prepared to initiate shipment of goods indicating the description of the merchandise, the quantity shipped, and other relevant data (page 354)

Simple operating systems – computer operating systems that allow only one function at a time to be carried out (page 514)

Society of Management Accountants of Canada (SMAC) – one of the three major organizations in Canada providing a professional designation relating to accounting/auditing (page 2)

Special assignments – management requests for an operational audit for a specific purpose, such as investigating the possibility of fraud in a division or making recommendations for reducing the cost of a manufactured product (page 808)

Specific audit objectives – individual goals, based on the general audit objectives, that the auditor develops for each account balance on the financial statements (page 145)

Specific authorization – case-by-case approval of transactions not covered by company-wide policies (page 281)

Special reports – engagements differing from regular audits in which the public accountant may be acting as either auditor or accountant (page 764)

Standard form to confirm bank account information – a form through which the bank responds to the auditor about bank balance and loan information provided on the confirmation (page 706)

Standard cost records – records that indicate variances between projected material, labour, and overhead costs, and the actual costs (page 661)

Standard unqualified auditor's report – the report a public accountant issues when all auditing conditions have been met, no significant misstatements have been discovered and left uncorrected, and it is the auditor's opinion that the financial statements are fairly stated in accordance with generally accepted accounting principles (page 35)

Standards for the Practice of Internal Auditing – guidelines issued by the Institute of Internal Auditors, covering the activities and conduct of internal auditors (page 808)

Standards manual – handbook maintained by companies with complex EDP systems, which specifies systems requirements, programming documentation, program run instructions, and user instructions (page 283)

Statement on Attestation Standards – a statement issued by the AICPA to provide a conceptual framework for various types of attest services (page 791)

Statements on Auditing Standards – pronouncements issued by the AICPA to interpret generally accepted auditing standards (page 17-18)

Statistical inferences – statistical conclusions that the auditor draws from knowledge of sampling distributions (page 491-492)

Statistical sampling – the use of mathematical measurement techniques to calculate formal statistical results and quantify sampling risk (page 394)

Stock transfer agent – outside person engaged by a corporation to maintain the shareholder records, and often to disburse cash dividends (page 687)

Stratification – a method of sampling in which all the elements in the total population are divided into two or more subpopulations which are independently tested and statistically measured (page 494)

Subsequent events – transactions and other pertinent events that occurred after the balance sheet date, which affect the valuation or disclosure of the statements being audited (page 734)

Sufficiency – the quantity of evidence; appropriate sample size (page 165)

Summary acquisitions report – a computer-generated document that summarizes acquisitions for a period (page 585)

Summary of procedures – a supporting schedule that summarizes the results of a specific audit procedure performed such as an accounts receivable confirmation (page 180)

Summary payroll report – a computer-generated document that summarizes payroll for a period in a variety of formats suited to company purposes (page 560)

Summary sales report – a computer-generated document that summarizes sales for a period (page 355)

Supporting schedules – detailed schedules prepared by auditors in support of specific amounts on the financial statements (page 180)

Systematic selection – a probabilistic method of sampling in which the auditor calculates an interval (the population size divided by the number of sample items desired), and selects the items for the sample based on the size of the interval and a randomly selected number between zero and the sample size (page 398)

Systems analyst – person who designs EDP systems (page 280)

Systems manual – handbook explaining the procedures for proper record keeping in an EDP system (page 283)

Systems requirements – the broad objectives of an EDP system, including the input and output of the system and the requirements for reviewing and testing the software (page 283)

TDR – see *tolerable deviation rate*

T-4 – a form issued for each employee summarizing the earnings record for the calendar year; same form is also submitted to Revenue Canada (page 560)

Templates – predesigned formats for work papers, letters, and the like, which can be created and saved using electronic spreadsheets and word processors (page 541)

Tests of acquisitions – tests of controls concerning the processing of purchase orders, the receipt of goods and services, and the recognition of liability (page 589)

Tests of controls – the auditor's methods for assessing the reliability of the client's internal controls; these methods include making inquiries of appropriate personnel, inspecting paperwork, observing how separation of duties and similar control-related activities are carried out, and personally reperforming selected control activities to verify the results (pages 148-149, 289, 297)

Tests of details of balances – tests for monetary misstatements in the balances of balance-sheet and income-statement accounts; these tests involve comparing inquiry and inspection of physical evidence, such as physical assets, documentation, and confirmation from independent sources such as customers and vendors (pages 149, 325-326)

Tests of (schedule of) reasonableness – a supporting schedule that contains information which enables the auditor to judge whether the client's balance appears to include a misstatement considering the circumstances of the engagement (page 180)

Third-party beneficiary – a party who does not have privity of contract but is intended by the contracting parties to have certain rights and benefits under the contract (page 101)

Time card – a document indicating the time that the employee started and stopped working each day and the number of hours worked (page 558)

Timeliness – the timing of the audit in relation to the period covered by the audit (page 167)

Tolerable deviation rate (TDR) – the maximum devia-

tion rate the auditor will permit in the population and still be willing to accept control risk assessed below maximum (page 404)

Tort action for negligence – a legal action taken by an injured party against the party whose failure to fulfill specified obligations resulted in the injury (page 101)

Transaction walk-through – the tracing of selected transactions through the accounting system (page 288)

Transmittal control form – in an EDP system, a log showing the dates of receipt, processing, and release of data (page 301)

Trial balance or list – a supporting schedule of the details that make up the year-end balance of either a balance sheet account or an income statement account (page 180)

Unadjusted misstatement worksheet – a summary of immaterial misstatements not adjusted at the time they were found, compiled in order to assess whether the combined amount is material; also known as a summary of possible adjustments (page 743)

Uncollectible account authorization form – an internal document authorizing the write-off of an account receivable (page 355)

Unusual fluctuations – significant unexpected differences between the current year's unaudited financial statements and other data used in comparisons (page 205)

User instructions – directions as to who should receive computer output and what to do if the output is not usable (page 283)

Value-for-money audit – an audit that considers the economy, efficiency and effectiveness with which operations are conducted (page 6)

Variables sampling – sampling techniques that use the statistical inference process (page 490)

Vendor's invoice – a document that indicates such things as the description and quantity of goods received, price including freight, cash discount terms and date of the billing (page 585)

Vendor's statement – a statement prepared monthly by the vendor, which indicates the customer's beginning balance, acquisitions, returns and allowances, payments, and ending balance (page 586)

Voucher – a document for formally recording and controlling acquisitions (page 585)

Vouching – see *documentation*

Word processors – software programs that combine the capabilities of a typewriter with a microcomputer to create and save text (page 540)

Working paper review – a thorough review of the completed audit by another member of the audit firm to ensure quality and counteract bias (page 745-746)

Working papers – document the evidence accumulated by the auditor; should include all the information the auditor considers necessary to conduct the examina-tion adequately and to provide support for the audi-tor's report (page 174)

Working trial balance – a schedule of the general ledger accounts and their year-end balances (page 178)

INDEX